America's
Top-Rated Cities:
A Statistical Handbook

Volume 4

2023
Thirtieth Edition

America's
Top-Rated Cities:
A Statistical Handbook

Volume 4: Eastern Region

Grey House
Publishing

Cover image: Boston, Massachusetts

PUBLISHER: Leslie Mackenzie
EDITORIAL DIRECTOR: Stuart Paterson
SENIOR EDITOR: David Garoogian

RESEARCHER & WRITER: Jael Bridgemahon; Laura Mars
MARKETING DIRECTOR: Jessica Moody

Grey House Publishing, Inc.
4919 Route 22
Amenia, NY 12501
518.789.8700 • Fax 845.373.6390
www.greyhouse.com
books@greyhouse.com

While every effort has been made to ensure the reliability of the information presented in this publication, Grey House Publishing neither guarantees the accuracy of the data contained herein nor assumes any responsibility for errors, omissions or discrepancies. Grey House accepts no payment for listing; inclusion in the publication of any organization, agency, institution, publication, service or individual does not imply endorsement of the editors or publisher.

Errors brought to the attention of the publisher and verified to the satisfaction of the publisher will be corrected in future editions.

Except by express prior written permission of the Copyright Proprietor no part of this work may be copied by any means of publication or communication now known or developed hereafter including, but not limited to, use in any directory or compilation or other print publication, in any information storage and retrieval system, in any other electronic device, or in any visual or audio-visual device or product.

This publication is an original and creative work, copyrighted by Grey House Publishing, Inc. and is fully protected by all applicable copyright laws, as well as by laws covering misappropriation, trade secrets and unfair competition.

Grey House has added value to the underlying factual material through one or more of the following efforts: unique and original selection; expression; arrangement; coordination; and classification.

Grey House Publishing, Inc. will defend its rights in this publication.

Copyright © 2023 Grey House Publishing, Inc.
All rights reserved

Thirtieth Edition
Printed in the U.S.A.

Publisher's Cataloging-in-Publication Data
(Prepared by The Donohue Group, Inc.)

America's top-rated cities. Vol. 4, Eastern region : a statistical handbook. — 1992-

   v. : ill. ; cm.
   Annual, 1995-
   Irregular, 1992-1993
   ISSN: 1082-7102

1. Cities and towns—Ratings—Eastern States—Statistics—Periodicals. 2. Cities and towns—Eastern States—Statistics—Periodicals. 3. Social indicators—Eastern States—Periodicals. 4. Quality of life—Eastern States—Statistics—Periodicals. 5. Eastern States—Social conditions—Statistics—Periodicals. I. Title: America's top rated cities. II. Title: Eastern region

HT123.5.S6 A44
307.76/0973/05   95644648

4-Volume Set	ISBN: 978-1-63700-534-7
Volume 1	ISBN: 978-1-63700-536-1
Volume 2	ISBN: 978-1-63700-537-8
Volume 3	ISBN: 978-1-63700-538-5
Volume 4	**ISBN: 978-1-63700-539-2**

Allentown, Pennsylvania

Background	1
Rankings	2
Business Environment	4
Demographics	4
Economy	6
Income	6
Employment	7
City Finances	9
Taxes	9
Transportation	10
Businesses	11
Living Environment	12
Cost of Living	12
Housing	12
Health	14
Education	15
Employers	17
Public Safety	17
Politics	18
Sports	18
Climate	18
Hazardous Waste	18
Air Quality	19

Boston, Massachusetts

Background	43
Rankings	44
Business Environment	49
Demographics	49
Economy	51
Income	51
Employment	52
City Finances	54
Taxes	54
Transportation	55
Businesses	56
Living Environment	58
Cost of Living	58
Housing	58
Health	60
Education	62
Employers	64
Public Safety	65
Politics	65
Sports	65
Climate	66
Hazardous Waste	66
Air Quality	66

Baltimore, Maryland

Background	21
Rankings	22
Business Environment	25
Demographics	25
Economy	27
Income	27
Employment	28
City Finances	30
Taxes	31
Transportation	32
Businesses	33
Living Environment	34
Cost of Living	34
Housing	34
Health	36
Education	38
Employers	39
Public Safety	40
Politics	41
Sports	41
Climate	41
Hazardous Waste	41
Air Quality	41

Charlotte, North Carolina

Background	69
Rankings	70
Business Environment	74
Demographics	74
Economy	76
Income	76
Employment	77
City Finances	79
Taxes	79
Transportation	80
Businesses	81
Living Environment	82
Cost of Living	82
Housing	82
Health	84
Education	86
Employers	87
Public Safety	88
Politics	88
Sports	88
Climate	89
Hazardous Waste	89
Air Quality	89

Cincinnati, Ohio

Background 91
Rankings 92
Business Environment 96
  Demographics 96
  Economy 98
  Income 98
  Employment 99
  City Finances 101
  Taxes 101
  Transportation 102
  Businesses 103
Living Environment 104
  Cost of Living 104
  Housing 104
  Health 106
  Education 108
  Employers 109
  Public Safety 110
  Politics 110
  Sports 110
  Climate 110
  Hazardous Waste 111
  Air Quality 111

Cleveland, Ohio

Background 113
Rankings 114
Business Environment 118
  Demographics 118
  Economy 120
  Income 120
  Employment 121
  City Finances 123
  Taxes 123
  Transportation 124
  Businesses 125
Living Environment 127
  Cost of Living 127
  Housing 127
  Health 129
  Education 131
  Employers 132
  Public Safety 133
  Politics 133
  Sports 133
  Climate 133
  Hazardous Waste 134
  Air Quality 134

Columbus, Ohio

Background 137
Rankings 138
Business Environment 141
  Demographics 141
  Economy 143
  Income 143
  Employment 144
  City Finances 146
  Taxes 146
  Transportation 147
  Businesses 148
Living Environment 149
  Cost of Living 149
  Housing 149
  Health 151
  Education 153
  Employers 155
  Public Safety 156
  Politics 156
  Sports 156
  Climate 157
  Hazardous Waste 157
  Air Quality 157

Durham, North Carolina

Background 159
Rankings 160
Business Environment 163
  Demographics 163
  Economy 165
  Income 165
  Employment 166
  City Finances 168
  Taxes 168
  Transportation 169
  Businesses 170
Living Environment 171
  Cost of Living 171
  Housing 171
  Health 173
  Education 175
  Employers 176
  Public Safety 177
  Politics 177
  Sports 177
  Climate 177
  Hazardous Waste 178
  Air Quality 178

Edison, New Jersey

Background 181
Rankings 182
Business Environment 185
  Demographics 185
  Economy 187
  Income 187
  Employment 188
  City Finances 190
  Taxes 191
  Transportation 192
  Businesses 193
Living Environment 194
  Cost of Living 194
  Housing 194
  Health 196
  Education 198
  Employers 200
  Public Safety 200
  Politics 201
  Sports 201
  Climate 201
  Hazardous Waste 201
  Air Quality 202

Greensboro, North Carolina

Background 205
Rankings 206
Business Environment 209
  Demographics 209
  Economy 211
  Income 211
  Employment 212
  City Finances 214
  Taxes 214
  Transportation 215
  Businesses 216
Living Environment 217
  Cost of Living 217
  Housing 217
  Health 219
  Education 220
  Employers 222
  Public Safety 222
  Politics 223
  Sports 223
  Climate 223
  Hazardous Waste 223
  Air Quality 223

Lexington, Kentucky

Background 225
Rankings 226
Business Environment 229
  Demographics 229
  Economy 231
  Income 231
  Employment 232
  City Finances 234
  Taxes 234
  Transportation 235
  Businesses 236
Living Environment 237
  Cost of Living 237
  Housing 237
  Health 239
  Education 241
  Employers 242
  Public Safety 242
  Politics 243
  Sports 243
  Climate 243
  Hazardous Waste 244
  Air Quality 244

Louisville, Kentucky

Background 247
Rankings 248
Business Environment 251
  Demographics 251
  Economy 253
  Income 253
  Employment 254
  City Finances 256
  Taxes 256
  Transportation 257
  Businesses 258
Living Environment 259
  Cost of Living 259
  Housing 259
  Health 261
  Education 263
  Employers 264
  Public Safety 264
  Politics 265
  Sports 265
  Climate 265
  Hazardous Waste 266
  Air Quality 266

Manchester, New Hampshire

Background 269
Rankings 270
Business Environment 272
  Demographics 272
  Economy 274
  Income 274
  Employment 275
  City Finances 277
  Taxes 277
  Transportation 278
  Businesses 279
Living Environment 280
  Cost of Living 280
  Housing 280
  Health 282
  Education 283
  Employers 284
  Public Safety 285
  Politics 285
  Sports 285
  Climate 285
  Hazardous Waste 286
  Air Quality 286

New York, New York

Background 309
Rankings 310
Business Environment 315
  Demographics 315
  Economy 317
  Income 318
  Employment 318
  City Finances 320
  Taxes 321
  Transportation 322
  Businesses 323
Living Environment 326
  Cost of Living 326
  Housing 326
  Health 328
  Education 333
  Employers 335
  Public Safety 336
  Politics 337
  Sports 337
  Climate 337
  Hazardous Waste 337
  Air Quality 338

New Haven, Connecticut

Background 289
Rankings 290
Business Environment 292
  Demographics 292
  Economy 294
  Income 294
  Employment 295
  City Finances 297
  Taxes 297
  Transportation 298
  Businesses 299
Living Environment 300
  Cost of Living 300
  Housing 300
  Health 302
  Education 304
  Employers 305
  Public Safety 305
  Politics 306
  Sports 306
  Climate 306
  Hazardous Waste 306
  Air Quality 307

Philadelphia, Pennsylvania

Background 341
Rankings 342
Business Environment 345
  Demographics 345
  Economy 347
  Income 347
  Employment 348
  City Finances 350
  Taxes 350
  Transportation 351
  Businesses 352
Living Environment 354
  Cost of Living 354
  Housing 354
  Health 356
  Education 358
  Employers 360
  Public Safety 361
  Politics 361
  Sports 361
  Climate 362
  Hazardous Waste 362
  Air Quality 362

Pittsburgh, Pennsylvania

Background	365
Rankings	366
Business Environment	370
Demographics	370
Economy	372
Income	372
Employment	373
City Finances	375
Taxes	375
Transportation	376
Businesses	377
Living Environment	378
Cost of Living	378
Housing	378
Health	380
Education	382
Employers	384
Public Safety	384
Politics	385
Sports	385
Climate	385
Hazardous Waste	385
Air Quality	386

Raleigh, North Carolina

Background	411
Rankings	412
Business Environment	416
Demographics	416
Economy	418
Income	418
Employment	419
City Finances	421
Taxes	421
Transportation	422
Businesses	423
Living Environment	424
Cost of Living	424
Housing	424
Health	426
Education	428
Employers	429
Public Safety	430
Politics	430
Sports	430
Climate	430
Hazardous Waste	431
Air Quality	431

Providence, Rhode Island

Background	389
Rankings	390
Business Environment	393
Demographics	393
Economy	395
Income	395
Employment	396
City Finances	398
Taxes	399
Transportation	400
Businesses	401
Living Environment	402
Cost of Living	402
Housing	402
Health	404
Education	405
Employers	407
Public Safety	407
Politics	408
Sports	408
Climate	408
Hazardous Waste	408
Air Quality	408

Richmond, Virginia

Background	433
Rankings	434
Business Environment	437
Demographics	437
Economy	439
Income	439
Employment	440
City Finances	442
Taxes	442
Transportation	443
Businesses	444
Living Environment	445
Cost of Living	445
Housing	445
Health	447
Education	449
Employers	450
Public Safety	451
Politics	451
Sports	451
Climate	451
Hazardous Waste	452
Air Quality	452

Virginia Beach, Virginia

Background.	455
Rankings.	456
Business Environment.	459
Demographics.	459
Economy.	461
Income.	461
Employment.	462
City Finances.	464
Taxes.	464
Transportation.	465
Businesses.	466
Living Environment.	467
Cost of Living.	467
Housing.	467
Health.	469
Education.	470
Employers.	472
Public Safety.	472
Politics.	473
Sports.	473
Climate.	473
Hazardous Waste.	473
Air Quality.	473

Washington, District of Columbia

Background.	475
Rankings.	476
Business Environment.	480
Demographics.	480
Economy.	482
Income.	482
Employment.	483
City Finances.	485
Taxes.	485
Transportation.	486
Businesses.	487
Living Environment.	489
Cost of Living.	489
Housing.	489
Health.	491
Education.	493
Employers.	495
Public Safety.	495
Politics.	496
Sports.	496
Climate.	496
Hazardous Waste.	496
Air Quality.	497

Wilmington, North Carolina

Background.	499
Rankings.	500
Business Environment.	502
Demographics.	502
Economy.	504
Income.	504
Employment.	505
City Finances.	507
Taxes.	507
Transportation.	508
Businesses.	509
Living Environment.	510
Cost of Living.	510
Housing.	510
Health.	512
Education.	513
Employers.	514
Public Safety.	515
Politics.	515
Sports.	515
Climate.	515
Hazardous Waste.	516
Air Quality.	516

Winston-Salem, North Carolina

Background.	519
Rankings.	520
Business Environment.	522
Demographics.	522
Economy.	524
Income.	524
Employment.	525
City Finances.	527
Taxes.	527
Transportation.	528
Businesses.	529
Living Environment.	530
Cost of Living.	530
Housing.	530
Health.	532
Education.	533
Employers.	535
Public Safety.	535
Politics.	535
Sports.	536
Climate.	536
Hazardous Waste.	536
Air Quality.	536

Worcester, Massachusetts

Background	539
Rankings	540
Business Environment	542
Demographics	542
Economy	544
Income	544
Employment	545
City Finances	547
Taxes	547
Transportation	548
Businesses	549
Living Environment	550
Cost of Living	550
Housing	550
Health	552
Education	553
Employers	555
Public Safety	555
Politics	556
Sports	556
Climate	556
Hazardous Waste	556
Air Quality	556

Appendixes

Appendix A: Comparative Statistics	A-3
Appendix B: Metropolitan Area Definitions	A-175
Appendix C: Government Type & Primary County	A-179
Appendix D: Chambers of Commerce	A-181
Appendix E: State Departments of Labor	A-187

Introduction

This thirtieth edition of *America's Top-Rated Cities* is a concise, statistical, 4-volume work identifying America's top-rated cities with estimated populations of approximately 100,000 or more. It profiles 100 cities that have received high marks for business and living from prominent sources such as *Forbes, Fortune, U.S. News & World Report, The Brookings Institution, U.S. Conference of Mayors, The Wall Street Journal,* and *CNNMoney*.

Each volume covers a different region of the country—Southern, Western, Central, Eastern—and includes a detailed Table of Contents, City Chapters, Appendices, and Maps. Each city chapter incorporates information from hundreds of resources to create the following major sections:

- **Background**—lively narrative of significant, up-to-date news for both businesses and residents. These combine historical facts with current developments, "known-for" annual events, and climate data.
- **Rankings**—fun-to-read, bulleted survey results from over 221 books, magazines, and online articles, ranging from general (Great Places to Live), to specific (Friendliest Cities), and everything in between.
- **Statistical Tables**—88 tables and detailed topics that offer an unparalleled view of each city's Business and Living Environments. They are carefully organized with data that is easy to read and understand.
- **Appendices**—five in all, appearing at the end of each volume. These range from listings of Metropolitan Statistical Areas to Comparative Statistics for all 100 cities.

This new edition of *America's Top-Rated Cities* includes cities that not only surveyed well, but ranked highest using our unique weighting system. We looked at violent crime, property crime, population growth, median household income, housing affordability, poverty, educational attainment, and unemployment. You'll find that we have included several American cities despite less-than-stellar numbers. New York, Los Angeles, and Miami remain world-class cities despite challenges faced by many large urban centers. Part of the criteria, in most cases, is that it be the "primary" city in a given metropolitan area. For example, if the metro area is Raleigh-Cary, NC, we would consider Raleigh, not Cary. This allows for a more equitable core city comparison. In general, the core city of a metro area is defined as having substantial influence on neighboring cities. A final consideration is location—we strive to include as many states in the country as possible.

New to this edition are:
Volume 1 - Brownsville, TX
Volume 2 - Greeley, CO; Salem, OR
Volume 4 - Greensboro, NC; Worcester, MA

Praise for previous editions:

> *"...[ATRC] has...proven its worth to a wide audience...from businesspeople and corporations planning to launch, relocate, or expand their operations to market researchers, real estate professionals, urban planners, job-seekers, students...interested in...reliable, attractively presented statistical information about larger U.S. cities."*
> —ARBA

> *"...For individuals or businesses looking to relocate, this resource conveniently reports rankings from more than 300 sources for the top 100 US cities. Recommended..."*
> —Choice

> *"...While patrons are becoming increasingly comfortable locating statistical data online, there is still something to be said for the ease associated with such a compendium of otherwise scattered data. A well-organized and appropriate update...*
> —Library Journal

BACKGROUND

Each city begins with an informative Background that combines history with current events. These narratives often reflect changes that have occurred during the past year, and touch on the city's environment, politics, employment, cultural offerings, and climate, and include interesting trivia. For example: Peregrine Falcons were rehabilitated and released into the wild from Boise City's World Center for Birds of Prey; Grand Rapids was the first city to introduce fluoride into its drinking water in 1945; and Thomas Alva Edison discovered the phonograph and the light bulb in the city whose name was changed in 1954 from Raritan Township to Edison in his honor.

RANKINGS

This section has rankings from a possible 221 books, articles, and reports. For easy reference, these Rankings are categorized into 16 topics including Business/Finance, Dating/Romance, and Health/Fitness.

The Rankings are presented in an easy-to-read, bulleted format and include results from both annual surveys and one-shot studies. **Fastest-Growing Economies . . . Best Drivers . . . Most Well-Read . . . Most Wired . . . Healthiest for Women . . . Best for Minority Entrepreneurs . . . Safest . . . Best to Retire . . . Most Polite . . . Best for Moviemakers . . . Most Frugal . . . Best for Bikes . . . Most Cultured . . . Least Stressful . . . Best for Families . . . Most Romantic . . . Most Charitable . . . Best for Telecommuters . . . Best for Singles . . . Nerdiest . . . Fittest . . . Best for Dogs . . . Most Tattooed . . . Best for Wheelchair Users**, and more.

Sources for these Rankings include both well-known magazines and other media, including *Forbes, Fortune, USA Today, Condé Nast Traveler, Gallup, Kiplinger's Personal Finance, Men's Journal,* and *Travel + Leisure,* as well as *Asthma & Allergy Foundation of America, American Lung Association, League of American Bicyclists, The Advocate, National Civic League, National Alliance to End Homelessness, MovieMaker Magazine, National Insurance Crime Bureau, Center for Digital Government, National Association of Home Builders,* and *Milken Institute.*

Rankings cover a variety of geographic areas; see Appendix B for full geographic definitions.

STATISTICAL TABLES

Each city chapter includes 88 tables and detailed topics—45 in Business and 43 in Living. Over 90% of statistical data has been updated. This edition also includes newly released data from the 2020 Census. A new table on household relationships has also be added, which includes information on same-sex spouses and unmarried partners.

Business Environment includes hard facts and figures on 8 major categories, including Demographics, Income, Economy, Employment, and Taxes. *Living Environment* includes 11 major categories, such as Cost of Living, Housing, Health, Education, Safety, and Climate.

To compile the Statistical Tables, editors have again turned to a wide range of sources, some well known, such as the *U.S. Census Bureau, U.S. Environmental Protection Agency, Bureau of Labor Statistics, Centers for Disease Control and Prevention,* and the *Federal Bureau of Investigation,* plus others like *The Council for Community and Economic Research, Texas A&M Transportation Institute,* and *Federation of Tax Administrators.*

APPENDIXES: Data for all cities appear in all volumes.
- **Appendix A**—*Comparative Statistics*
- **Appendix B**—*Metropolitan Area Definitions*
- **Appendix C**—*Government Type and County*
- **Appendix D**—*Chambers of Commerce and Economic Development Organizations*
- **Appendix E**—*State Departments of Labor and Employment*

Material provided by public and private agencies and organizations was supplemented by original research, numerous library sources and Internet sites. *America's Top-Rated Cities, 2023,* is designed for a wide range of readers: private individuals considering relocating a residence or business; professionals considering expanding their businesses or changing careers; corporations considering relocating, opening up additional offices or creating new divisions; government agencies; general and market researchers; real estate consultants; human resource personnel; urban planners; investors; and urban government students.

Customers who purchase the four-volume set receive free online access to *America's Top-Rated Cities* allowing them to download city reports and sort and rank by 50-plus data points.

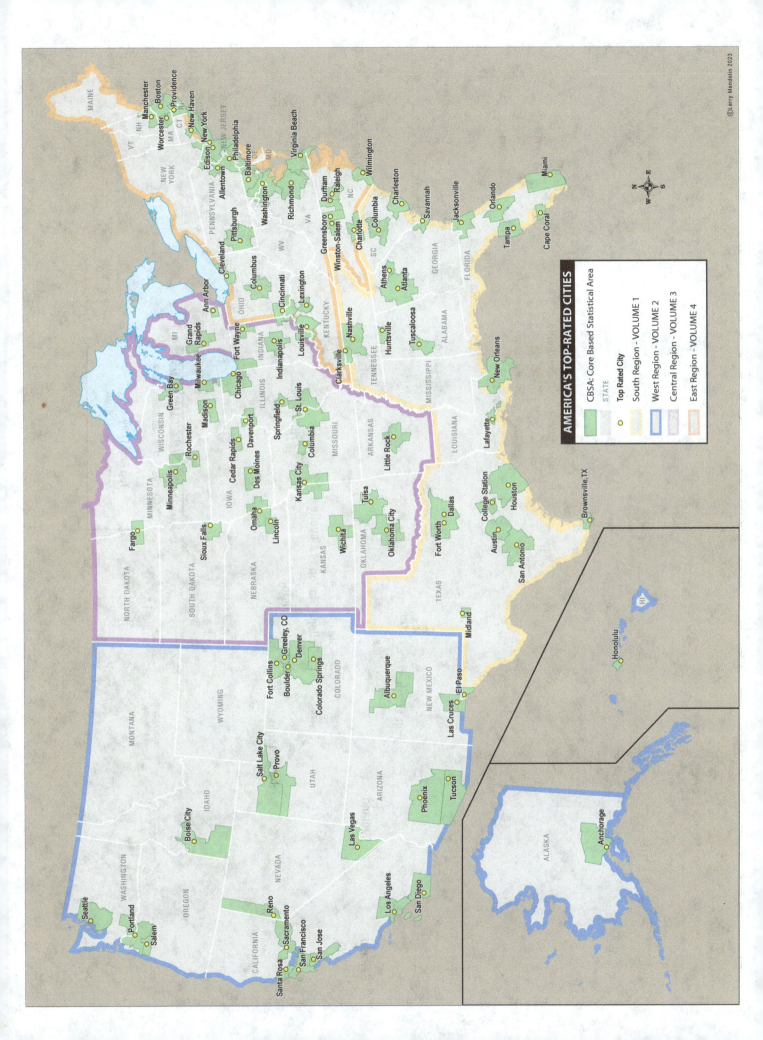

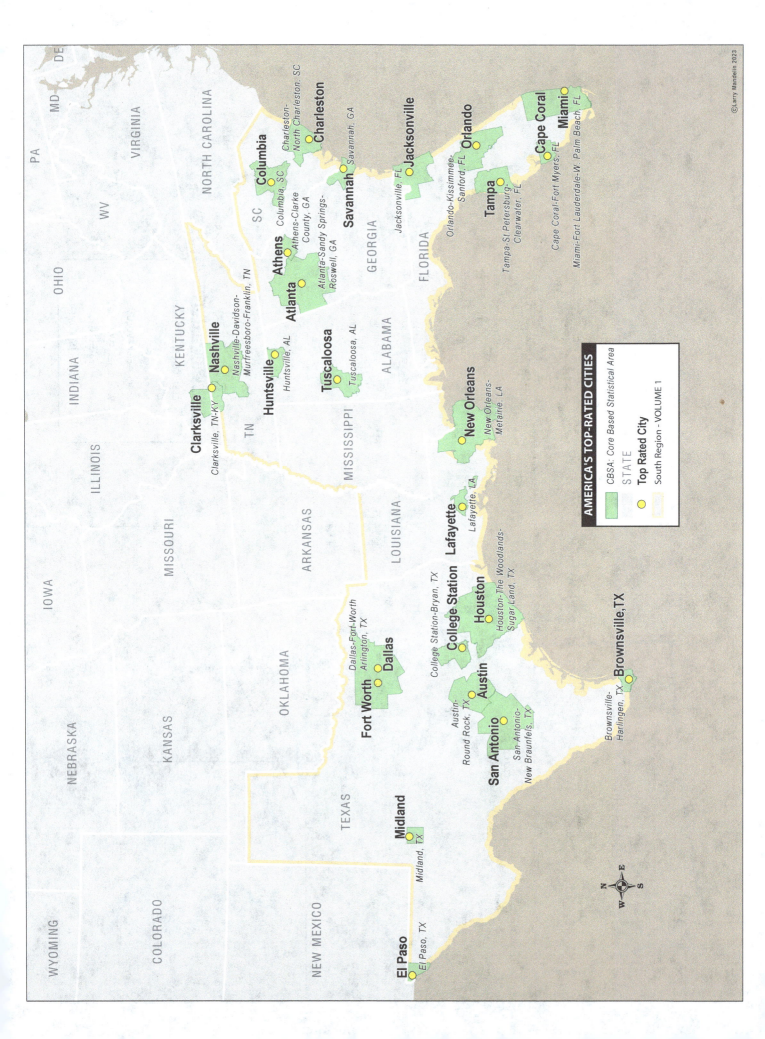

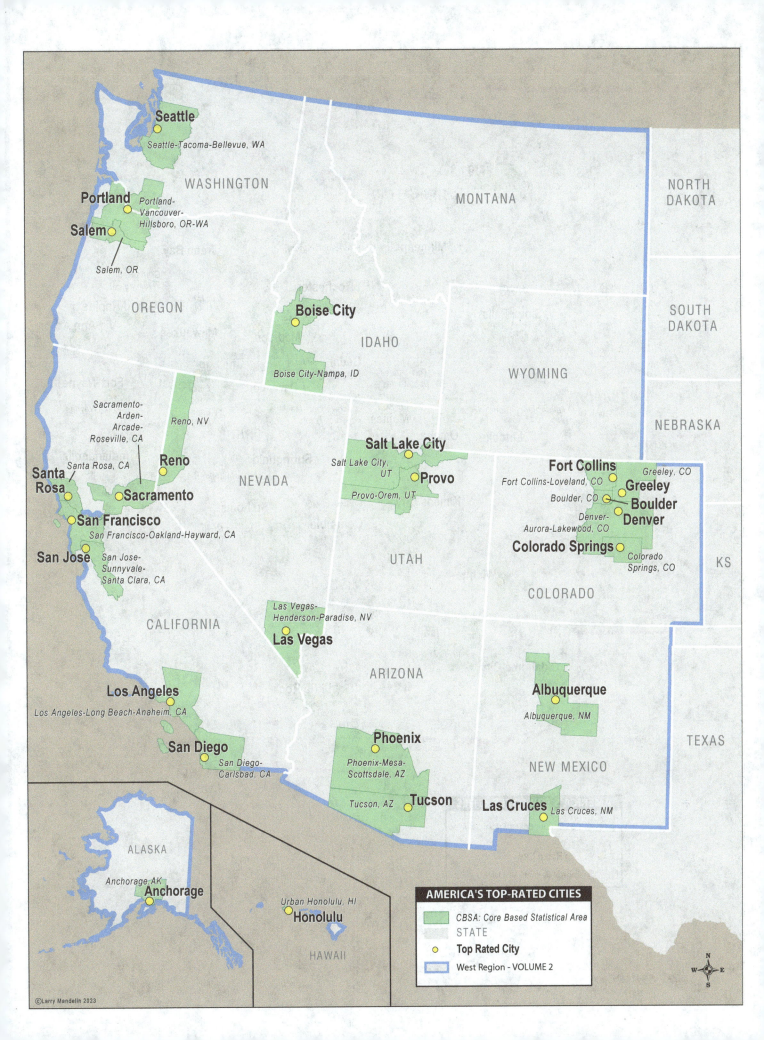

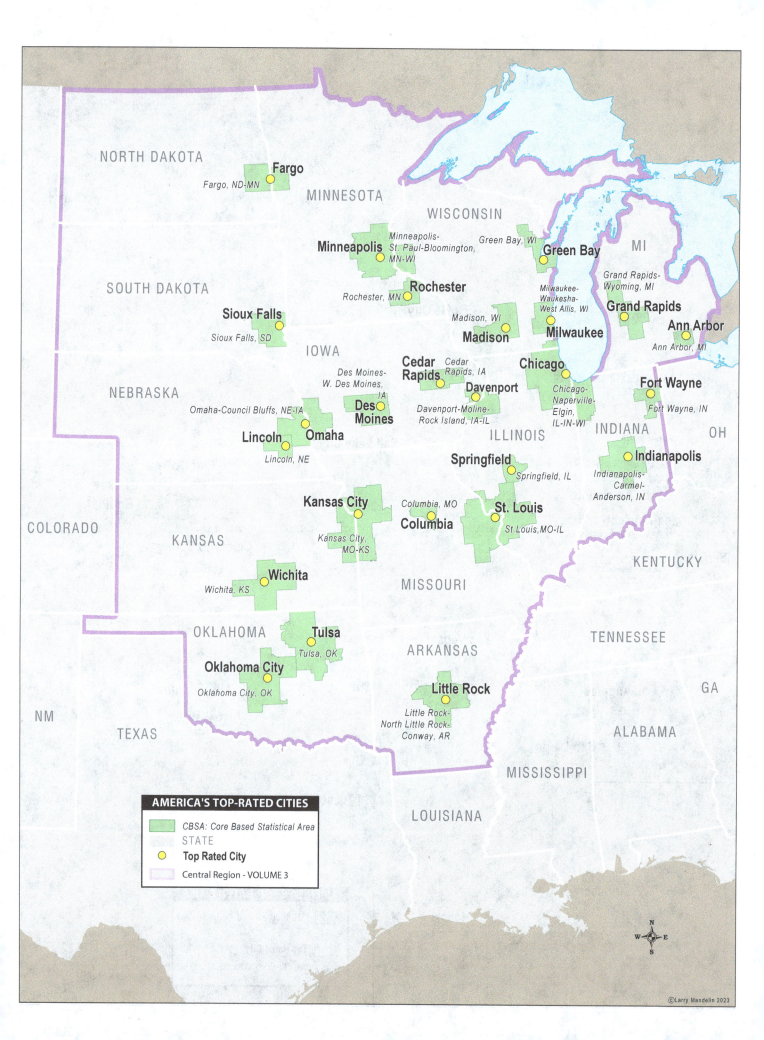

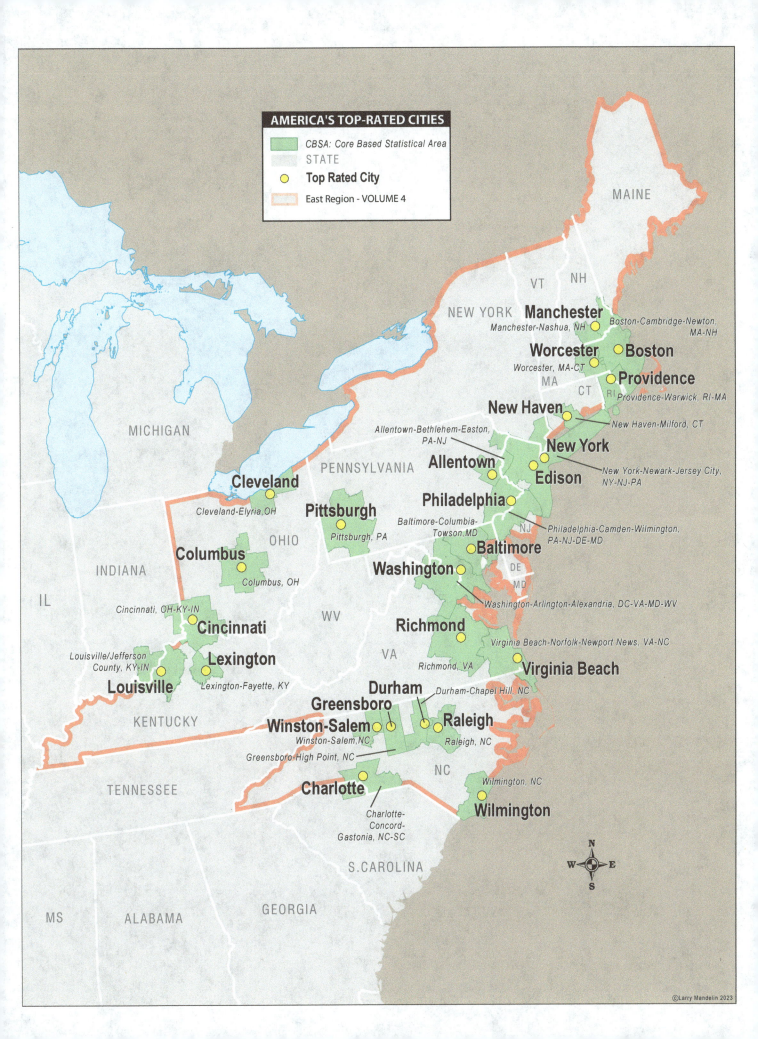

Allentown, Pennsylvania

Background

Allentown, the third-largest city in Pennsylvania, is located in Lehigh County along the Lehigh River in the eastern part of the state. The city has gone through periods of both economic prosperity and hard times at the hands of industry, but always managed to reinvent itself into a prosperous place for both businesses and residents. In recent years it was one of only six communities in the country to be named a "national success story."

The area was first settled in 1762 by wealthy shipping merchant William Allen, who was also the Chief Justice of the Province of Pennsylvania and the former Mayor of Philadelphia. He purchased 5,000 acres in the hopes of founding a commercial trading center, given the riverside location and proximity to Philadelphia. However, the river's low water level made trade impractical. Allen gave the property to his son in the 1770s. The settlement, originally called Northamptontown, hobbled along as a small agricultural community. In 1838, its name was officially changed to Allentown (affectionately called "Allen's town") and in 1867, the settlement was incorporated as a city.

In the mid-to-late nineteenth century, the construction of the Lehigh Canal and the Lehigh Valley Railroad enabled the transport of both raw materials and finished goods. The iron industry flourished. The Panic of 1873, followed by a depression, ended the railroad boom and iron furnaces closed.

By the beginning of the twentieth century, Allentown rebounded as silk manufacturing became central to the city. The city's economy also now included furniture, beer, and cigars. By 1928, over 140 silk and textile mills operated in the Lehigh Valley. Déjà vu set in however, when the popularity of synthetic materials sent the silk industry into a decline by the middle of the twentieth century. Though not as sudden as the iron industry's collapse, this downturn had a strong negative impact on Allentown's economy.

More recently, Allentown has been riding a wave of renovation and rehabilitation to its historic downtown, whose centerpiece is the PPL Center, a 8,500-seat entertainment venue and minor hockey league stadium home to the Lehigh Valley Phantoms. A hotel, restaurants, and 200,000-square foot office building accompany the Center complex. The city is also the home of a progressive, competency-based, experiential learning public high school, Building 21.

Allentown is home to several national companies and major regional employers including the Lehigh Valley Hospital and Health Network, St. Luke's Hospital and Health Network, Parkland School District, Victaulic Co., B. Braun Medical Inc., Phebe Ministries senior living, and the Pleasant Valley School District.

Major attractions in Allentown include Dorney Park & Wildwater Kingdom and Coca-Cola Park, the 8,278-seat minor league baseball home of the Lehigh Valley IronPigs. Cultural and historical venues include Miller Symphony Hall, Allentown Art Museum—known for American painting and sculpture—and Old Court House County Museum, exhibiting the history of Lehigh County. The city's two institutions of higher learning are Cedar Crest College and Muhlenberg College.

Allentown has a humid season that resembles a midwestern climate more than a northeastern one. Summers are hot and muggy. Winters are cold; spring and fall are generally mild. Rainfall is distributed evenly across the twelve months of the year. Allentown's climate is affected by the Blue Mountains, a 1,600-foot-high ridge located 12 miles north of the city that separates it somewhat from regional weather systems.

Rankings

Business/Finance Rankings

- The Brookings Institution ranked the nation's largest cities based on income inequality. Allentown was ranked #92 (#1 = greatest inequality). Criteria: the "95/20 ratio," a figure representing the income at which a household earns more than 95 percent of all other households, divided by the income at which a household earns more than only 20 percent of all other households. *Brookings Institution, "Household Income Inequality, Largest Cities of 97 Large U.S. Metro Areas, 2014-2016," February 5, 2018*

- The Brookings Institution ranked the 100 largest metro areas in the U.S. based on income inequality. Allentown was ranked #87 (#1 = greatest inequality). Criteria: the "95/20 ratio," a figure representing the income at which a household earns more than 95 percent of all other households, divided by the income at which a household earns more than only 20 percent of all other households. *Brookings Institution, "Household Income Inequality, 100 Largest U.S. Metro Areas, 2014-2016," February 5, 2018*

- Allentown was cited as one of America's top metros for total major capital investment facility projects in 2022. The area ranked #2 in the mid-sized metro area category (population 200,000 to 1 million). *Site Selection, "Top Metros of 2022," March 2023*

- The Allentown metro area appeared on the Milken Institute "2022 Best Performing Cities" list. Rank: #135 out of 200 large metro areas (population over 250,000). Criteria: job growth; wage and salary growth; high-tech output growth; housing affordability; household broadband access. *Milken Institute, "Best-Performing Cities 2022," March 28, 2022*

- *Forbes* ranked the 200 most populous metro areas to determine the nation's "Best Places for Business and Careers." The Allentown metro area was ranked #129. Criteria: costs (business and living); job growth (past and projected); income growth; quality of life; educational attainment (college and high school); projected economic growth; cultural and leisure opportunities; workplace tolerance laws; net migration patterns. *Forbes, "The Best Places for Business and Careers 2019: Seattle Still On Top," October 30, 2019*

Education Rankings

- Personal finance website *WalletHub* analyzed the 150 largest U.S. metropolitan statistical areas to determine where the most educated Americans are putting their degrees to work. Criteria: education levels; percentage of workers with degrees; education quality and attainment gap; public school quality rankings; quality and enrollment of each metro area's universities. Allentown was ranked #100 (#1 = most educated city). *www.WalletHub.com, "Most & Least Educated Cities in America," July 18, 2022*

Health/Fitness Rankings

- Allentown was identified as a "2022 Spring Allergy Capital." The area ranked #18 out of 100. Three groups of factors were used to identify the most challenging cities for people with allergies during the spring season: annual spring pollen scores; over the counter allergy medicine use; number of board-certified allergy specialists. *Asthma and Allergy Foundation of America, "Spring Allergy Capitals 2022," March 2, 2022*

- Allentown was identified as a "2022 Fall Allergy Capital." The area ranked #30 out of 100. Three groups of factors were used to identify the most challenging cities for people with allergies during the fall season: annual fall pollen scores; over the counter allergy medicine use; number of board-certified allergy specialists. *Asthma and Allergy Foundation of America, "Fall Allergy Capitals 2022," March 2, 2022*

- Allentown was identified as a "2022 Asthma Capital." The area ranked #3 out of the nation's 100 largest metropolitan areas. Criteria: estimated asthma prevalence; asthma-related mortality; and ER visits due to asthma. Risk factors analyzed but not factored in the rankings: annual pollen score; annual air quality; public smoking laws; access to board-certified asthma specialists; rescue and controller medication use; uninsured rate; poverty rate. *Asthma and Allergy Foundation of America, "Asthma Capitals 2022: The Most Challenging Places to Live With Asthma," September 14, 2022*

Real Estate Rankings

- The Allentown metro area was identified as one of the 20 best housing markets in the U.S. in 2022. The area ranked #19 out of 187 markets. Criteria: year-over-year change of median sales price of existing single-family homes between the 4th quarter of 2021 and the 4th quarter of 2022. *National Association of Realtors®, Median Sales Price of Existing Single-Family Homes for Metropolitan Areas, 4th Quarter 2022*

- Allentown was ranked #100 out of 235 metro areas in terms of housing affordability in 2022 by the National Association of Home Builders (#1 = most affordable). Criteria: the share of homes sold in that area affordable to a family earning the local median income, based on standard mortgage underwriting criteria. *National Association of Home Builders®, NAHB-Wells Fargo Housing Opportunity Index, 4th Quarter 2022*

Seniors/Retirement Rankings

- From its Best Cities for Successful Aging indexes, the Milken Institute generated rankings for metropolitan areas, weighing data in nine categories—health care, wellness, living arrangements, transportation and convenience, financial characteristics, education, employment, community engagement, and overall livability. The Allentown metro area was ranked #73 overall in the large metro area category. *Milken Institute, "Best Cities for Successful Aging, 2017" March 14, 2017*

Business Environment

DEMOGRAPHICS

Population Growth

Area	1990 Census	2000 Census	2010 Census	2020 Census	Population Growth (%)	
					1990-2020	2010-2020
City	105,066	106,632	118,032	125,845	19.8	6.6
MSA[1]	686,666	740,395	821,173	861,889	25.5	5.0
U.S.	248,709,873	281,421,906	308,745,538	331,449,281	33.3	7.4

Note: (1) Figures cover the Allentown-Bethlehem-Easton, PA-NJ Metropolitan Statistical Area
Source: U.S. Census Bureau, 1990 Census, 2000 Census, 2010 Census, 2020 Census

Race

Area	White Alone[2] (%)	Black Alone[2] (%)	Asian Alone[2] (%)	AIAN[3] Alone[2] (%)	NHOPI[4] Alone[2] (%)	Other Race Alone[2] (%)	Two or More Races (%)
City	38.3	13.2	2.1	0.8	0.1	30.1	15.5
MSA[1]	72.9	6.3	3.2	0.3	0.0	8.5	8.8
U.S.	61.6	12.4	6.0	1.1	0.2	8.4	10.2

Note: (1) Figures cover the Allentown-Bethlehem-Easton, PA-NJ Metropolitan Statistical Area; (2) Alone is defined as not being in combination with one or more other races; (3) American Indian and Alaska Native; (4) Native Hawaiian and Other Pacific Islander
Source: U.S. Census Bureau, 2020 Census

Hispanic or Latino Origin

Area	Total (%)	Mexican (%)	Puerto Rican (%)	Cuban (%)	Other (%)
City	54.5	2.6	27.6	0.8	23.5
MSA[1]	18.4	1.3	9.3	0.4	7.3
U.S.	18.4	11.2	1.8	0.7	4.7

Note: Persons of Hispanic or Latino origin can be of any race; (1) Figures cover the Allentown-Bethlehem-Easton, PA-NJ Metropolitan Statistical Area
Source: U.S. Census Bureau, 2017-2021 American Community Survey 5-Year Estimates

Age

Area	Percent of Population									Median Age
	Under Age 5	Age 5–19	Age 20–34	Age 35–44	Age 45–54	Age 55–64	Age 65–74	Age 75–84	Age 85+	
City	6.8	21.0	23.3	12.4	11.4	11.6	7.8	3.9	1.7	34.2
MSA[1]	5.0	18.5	18.2	11.8	12.9	14.6	11.0	5.6	2.5	41.9
U.S.	5.6	19.2	20.2	12.7	12.4	13.1	10.0	4.9	1.9	38.8

Note: (1) Figures cover the Allentown-Bethlehem-Easton, PA-NJ Metropolitan Statistical Area
Source: U.S. Census Bureau, 2020 Census

Disability by Age

Area	All Ages	Under 18 Years Old	18 to 64 Years Old	65 Years and Over
City	16.0	9.9	15.3	33.5
MSA[1]	12.7	5.5	10.2	30.3
U.S.	12.6	4.4	10.3	33.4

Note: Figures show percent of the civilian noninstitutionalized population that reported having a disability. Disability status is determined from six types of difficulty: vision, hearing, cognitive, ambulatory, self-care, and independent living. For children under 5 years old, hearing and vision difficulty are used to determine disability status. For children between the ages of 5 and 14, disability status is determined from hearing, vision, cognitive, ambulatory, and self-care difficulties. For people aged 15 years and older, they are considered to have a disability if they have difficulty with any one of the six difficulty types; Note: (1) Figures cover the Allentown-Bethlehem-Easton, PA-NJ Metropolitan Statistical Area
Source: U.S. Census Bureau, 2017-2021 American Community Survey 5-Year Estimates

Ancestry

Area	German	Irish	English	American	Italian	Polish	French[2]	Scottish	Dutch
City	9.8	4.7	2.0	2.7	4.2	1.8	0.7	0.4	0.8
MSA[1]	22.8	12.8	6.1	4.9	11.8	4.9	1.4	1.0	1.8
U.S.	12.8	9.6	8.1	5.7	5.0	2.7	2.2	1.6	1.1

Note: Figures are the percentage of the total population reporting a particular ancestry. The nine most commonly reported ancestries in the U.S. are shown. Figures include multiple ancestries (e.g. if a person reported being Irish and Italian, they were included in both columns); (1) Figures cover the Allentown-Bethlehem-Easton, PA-NJ Metropolitan Statistical Area; (2) Excludes Basque
Source: U.S. Census Bureau, 2017-2021 American Community Survey 5-Year Estimates

Foreign-born Population

Area				Percent of Population Born in					
	Any Foreign Country	Asia	Mexico	Europe	Caribbean	Central America[2]	South America	Africa	Canada
City	20.4	3.1	1.0	0.8	11.5	0.8	2.0	1.3	0.1
MSA[1]	9.7	2.7	0.4	1.4	2.8	0.5	1.1	0.6	0.1
U.S.	13.6	4.2	3.3	1.5	1.4	1.1	1.1	0.8	0.2

Note: (1) Figures cover the Allentown-Bethlehem-Easton, PA-NJ Metropolitan Statistical Area; (2) Excludes Mexico.
Source: U.S. Census Bureau, 2017-2021 American Community Survey 5-Year Estimates

Household Size

Area			Persons in Household (%)					Average Household Size
	One	Two	Three	Four	Five	Six	Seven or More	
City	29.5	29.5	14.0	14.3	7.4	3.1	2.1	2.70
MSA[1]	26.5	35.7	15.3	13.6	5.9	1.9	1.2	2.50
U.S.	28.1	33.8	15.5	12.9	6.0	2.3	1.4	2.60

Note: (1) Figures cover the Allentown-Bethlehem-Easton, PA-NJ Metropolitan Statistical Area
Source: U.S. Census Bureau, 2017-2021 American Community Survey 5-Year Estimates

Household Relationships

Area	House-holder	Opposite-sex Spouse	Same-sex Spouse	Opposite-sex Unmarried Partner	Same-sex Unmarried Partner	Child[2]	Grand-child	Other Relatives	Non-relatives
City	36.3	11.6	0.2	3.7	0.2	30.6	3.2	6.8	4.1
MSA[1]	38.8	18.7	0.2	2.9	0.1	28.2	2.0	4.1	2.5
U.S.	38.3	17.5	0.2	2.5	0.2	28.3	2.4	4.8	3.4

Note: Figures are percent of the total population; (1) Figures cover the Allentown-Bethlehem-Easton, PA-NJ Metropolitan Statistical Area; (2) Includes biological, adopted, and stepchildren of the householder
Source: U.S. Census Bureau, 2020 Census

Gender

Area	Males	Females	Males per 100 Females
City	60,577	65,268	92.8
MSA[1]	419,780	442,109	94.9
U.S.	162,685,811	168,763,470	96.4

Note: (1) Figures cover the Allentown-Bethlehem-Easton, PA-NJ Metropolitan Statistical Area
Source: U.S. Census Bureau, 2020 Census

Marital Status

Area	Never Married	Now Married[2]	Separated	Widowed	Divorced
City	46.7	34.6	3.9	5.0	9.8
MSA[1]	32.7	49.3	1.9	6.2	9.9
U.S.	33.8	48.0	1.8	5.6	10.8

Note: Figures are percentages and cover the population 15 years of age and older; (1) Figures cover the Allentown-Bethlehem-Easton, PA-NJ Metropolitan Statistical Area; (2) Excludes separated
Source: U.S. Census Bureau, 2017-2021 American Community Survey 5-Year Estimates

Religious Groups by Family

Area	Catholic	Baptist	Methodist	LDS[2]	Pentecostal	Lutheran	Islam	Adventist	Other
MSA[1]	18.6	0.4	2.3	0.4	0.6	5.4	0.7	1.2	11.0
U.S.	18.7	7.3	3.0	2.0	1.8	1.7	1.3	1.3	11.6

Note: Figures are the number of adherents as a percentage of the total population and cover the eight largest religious groups in the U.S; (1) Figures cover the Allentown-Bethlehem-Easton, PA-NJ Metropolitan Statistical Area; (2) Church of Jesus Christ of Latter-day Saints
Sources: 2020 U.S. Religion Census, Association of Statisticians of American Religious Bodies; The Association of Religion Data Archives (ARDA)

Religious Groups by Tradition

Area	Catholic	Evangelical Protestant	Mainline Protestant	Black Protestant	Islam	Judaism	Hinduism	Orthodox	Buddhism
MSA[1]	18.6	6.2	11.9	0.2	0.7	0.5	0.6	0.4	0.1
U.S.	18.7	16.5	5.2	2.3	1.3	0.6	0.4	0.4	0.3

Note: Figures are the number of adherents as a percentage of the total population; (1) Figures cover the Allentown-Bethlehem-Easton, PA-NJ Metropolitan Statistical Area
Sources: 2020 U.S. Religion Census, Association of Statisticians of American Religious Bodies; The Association of Religion Data Archives (ARDA)

6 Allentown, Pennsylvania

ECONOMY

Gross Metropolitan Product

Area	2020	2021	2022	2023	Rank[2]
MSA[1]	46.7	51.6	56.6	59.9	67

Note: Figures are in billions of dollars; (1) Figures cover the Allentown-Bethlehem-Easton, PA-NJ Metropolitan Statistical Area; (2) Rank is based on 2021 data and ranges from 1 to 381
Source: U.S. Conference of Mayors, U.S. Metro Economies: U.S. Metros Compared to Global and State Economies, June 2022

Economic Growth

Area	2018-20 (%)	2021 (%)	2022 (%)	2023 (%)	Rank[2]
MSA[1]	-0.3	5.9	3.6	2.6	159
U.S.	-0.6	5.7	3.1	2.9	–

Note: Figures are real gross metropolitan product (GMP) growth rates and represent average annual percent change; (1) Figures cover the Allentown-Bethlehem-Easton, PA-NJ Metropolitan Statistical Area; (2) Rank is based on 2020 2-year average annual percent change and ranges from 1 to 381
Source: U.S. Conference of Mayors, U.S. Metro Economies: U.S. Metros Compared to Global and State Economies, June 2022

Metropolitan Area Exports

Area	2016	2017	2018	2019	2020	2021	Rank[2]
MSA[1]	3,657.2	3,639.4	3,423.2	3,796.3	3,207.4	4,088.7	68

Note: Figures are in millions of dollars; (1) Figures cover the Allentown-Bethlehem-Easton, PA-NJ Metropolitan Statistical Area; (2) Rank is based on 2021 data and ranges from 1 to 388
Source: U.S. Department of Commerce, International Trade Administration, Office of Trade and Economic Analysis, Industry and Analysis, Exports by Metropolitan Area, data extracted March 16, 2023

Building Permits

Area	Single-Family			Multi-Family			Total		
	2021	2022	Pct. Chg.	2021	2022	Pct. Chg.	2021	2022	Pct. Chg.
City	0	27	–	0	0	0.0	0	27	–
MSA[1]	1,716	1,586	-7.6	890	723	-18.8	2,606	2,309	-11.4
U.S.	1,115,400	975,600	-12.5	621,600	689,500	10.9	1,737,000	1,665,100	-4.1

Note: (1) Figures cover the Allentown-Bethlehem-Easton, PA-NJ Metropolitan Statistical Area; Figures represent new, privately-owned housing units authorized (unadjusted data); All permit data are based on estimates with imputation
Source: U.S. Census Bureau, Manufacturing, Mining, and Construction Statistics, Building Permits, 2021, 2022

Bankruptcy Filings

Area	Business Filings			Nonbusiness Filings		
	2021	2022	% Chg.	2021	2022	% Chg.
Lehigh County	5	7	40.0	346	283	-18.2
U.S.	14,347	13,481	-6.0	399,269	374,240	-6.3

Note: Business filings include Chapter 7, Chapter 9, Chapter 11, Chapter 12, Chapter 13, Chapter 15, and Section 304; Nonbusiness filings include Chapter 7, Chapter 11, and Chapter 13
Source: Administrative Office of the U.S. Courts, Business and Nonbusiness Bankruptcy, County Cases Commenced by Chapter of the Bankruptcy Code, During the 12-Month Period Ending December 31, 2021 and Business and Nonbusiness Bankruptcy, County Cases Commenced by Chapter of the Bankruptcy Code, During the 12-Month Period Ending December 31, 2022

Housing Vacancy Rates

Area	Gross Vacancy Rate[2] (%)			Year-Round Vacancy Rate[3] (%)			Rental Vacancy Rate[4] (%)			Homeowner Vacancy Rate[5] (%)		
	2020	2021	2022	2020	2021	2022	2020	2021	2022	2020	2021	2022
MSA[1]	4.9	5.2	8.7	4.8	4.3	8.0	3.9	4.0	6.1	0.7	0.1	1.2
U.S.	10.6	10.8	10.5	8.2	8.4	8.2	6.3	6.1	5.8	1.0	0.9	0.8

Note: (1) Figures cover the Allentown-Bethlehem-Easton, PA-NJ Metropolitan Statistical Area; (2) The percentage of the total housing inventory that is vacant; (3) The percentage of the housing inventory (excluding seasonal units) that is year-round vacant; (4) The percentage of rental inventory that is vacant for rent; (5) The percentage of homeowner inventory that is vacant for sale
Source: U.S. Census Bureau, Housing Vacancies and Homeownership Annual Statistics: 2020, 2021, 2022

INCOME

Income

Area	Per Capita ($)	Median Household ($)	Average Household ($)
City	22,976	47,703	61,780
MSA[1]	37,945	73,091	96,205
U.S.	37,638	69,021	97,196

Note: (1) Figures cover the Allentown-Bethlehem-Easton, PA-NJ Metropolitan Statistical Area
Source: U.S. Census Bureau, 2017-2021 American Community Survey 5-Year Estimates

Household Income Distribution

Area	Percent of Households Earning							
	Under $15,000	$15,000 -$24,999	$25,000 -$34,999	$35,000 -$49,999	$50,000 -$74,999	$75,000 -$99,999	$100,000 -$149,999	$150,000 and up
City	13.0	12.4	10.9	16.1	19.7	11.2	10.9	5.7
MSA[1]	7.3	7.6	7.6	11.8	17.0	13.7	17.9	17.2
U.S.	9.4	7.8	8.2	11.4	16.8	12.8	16.3	17.3

Note: (1) Figures cover the Allentown-Bethlehem-Easton, PA-NJ Metropolitan Statistical Area
Source: U.S. Census Bureau, 2017-2021 American Community Survey 5-Year Estimates

Poverty Rate

Area	All Ages	Under 18 Years Old	18 to 64 Years Old	65 Years and Over
City	23.3	34.9	19.6	16.6
MSA[1]	10.4	15.9	9.4	7.3
U.S.	12.6	17.0	11.8	9.6

Note: Figures are percentage of people whose income during the past 12 months was below the poverty level;
(1) Figures cover the Allentown-Bethlehem-Easton, PA-NJ Metropolitan Statistical Area
Source: U.S. Census Bureau, 2017-2021 American Community Survey 5-Year Estimates

EMPLOYMENT

Labor Force and Employment

Area	Civilian Labor Force			Workers Employed		
	Dec. 2021	Dec. 2022	% Chg.	Dec. 2021	Dec. 2022	% Chg.
City	55,657	56,449	1.4	52,269	54,138	3.6
MSA[1]	447,351	458,516	2.5	428,287	443,287	3.5
U.S.	161,696,000	164,224,000	1.6	155,732,000	158,872,000	2.0

Note: Data is not seasonally adjusted and covers workers 16 years of age and older; (1) Figures cover the
Allentown-Bethlehem-Easton, PA-NJ Metropolitan Statistical Area
Source: Bureau of Labor Statistics, Local Area Unemployment Statistics

Unemployment Rate

Area	2022											
	Jan.	Feb.	Mar.	Apr.	May	Jun.	Jul.	Aug.	Sep.	Oct.	Nov.	Dec.
City	7.3	6.5	6.1	6.0	5.8	6.2	6.2	6.5	5.0	4.6	4.6	4.1
MSA[1]	5.5	4.8	4.5	4.1	3.9	4.4	4.5	4.5	3.3	3.2	3.3	3.3
U.S.	4.4	4.1	3.8	3.3	3.4	3.8	3.8	3.8	3.3	3.4	3.4	3.3

Note: Data is not seasonally adjusted and covers workers 16 years of age and older; (1) Figures cover the
Allentown-Bethlehem-Easton, PA-NJ Metropolitan Statistical Area
Source: Bureau of Labor Statistics, Local Area Unemployment Statistics

Average Wages

Occupation	$/Hr.	Occupation	$/Hr.
Accountants and Auditors	38.74	Maintenance and Repair Workers	24.13
Automotive Mechanics	23.90	Marketing Managers	66.34
Bookkeepers	21.73	Network and Computer Systems Admin.	41.40
Carpenters	26.50	Nurses, Licensed Practical	26.64
Cashiers	12.78	Nurses, Registered	39.14
Computer Programmers	48.46	Nursing Assistants	17.79
Computer Systems Analysts	45.52	Office Clerks, General	20.19
Computer User Support Specialists	29.17	Physical Therapists	48.05
Construction Laborers	23.73	Physicians	n/a
Cooks, Restaurant	15.53	Plumbers, Pipefitters and Steamfitters	32.16
Customer Service Representatives	19.08	Police and Sheriff's Patrol Officers	36.38
Dentists	76.30	Postal Service Mail Carriers	27.45
Electricians	35.65	Real Estate Sales Agents	27.37
Engineers, Electrical	52.01	Retail Salespersons	16.75
Fast Food and Counter Workers	12.66	Sales Representatives, Technical/Scientific	51.14
Financial Managers	74.84	Secretaries, Exc. Legal/Medical/Executive	20.39
First-Line Supervisors of Office Workers	31.48	Security Guards	17.28
General and Operations Managers	58.15	Surgeons	n/a
Hairdressers/Cosmetologists	16.54	Teacher Assistants, Exc. Postsecondary*	16.36
Home Health and Personal Care Aides	13.96	Teachers, Secondary School, Exc. Sp. Ed.*	35.24
Janitors and Cleaners	16.71	Telemarketers	14.10
Landscaping/Groundskeeping Workers	17.57	Truck Drivers, Heavy/Tractor-Trailer	27.04
Lawyers	64.68	Truck Drivers, Light/Delivery Services	22.74
Maids and Housekeeping Cleaners	14.89	Waiters and Waitresses	15.35

Note: Wage data covers the Allentown-Bethlehem-Easton, PA-NJ Metropolitan Statistical Area; (*) Hourly
wages were calculated from annual wage data based on a 40 hour work week; n/a not available.
Source: Bureau of Labor Statistics, Metro Area Occupational Employment & Wage Estimates, May 2022

Employment by Industry

Sector	MSA[1]		U.S.
	Number of Employees	Percent of Total	Percent of Total
Construction, Mining, and Logging	13,600	3.4	5.4
Private Education and Health Services	82,400	20.9	16.1
Financial Activities	12,900	3.3	5.9
Government	39,300	10.0	14.5
Information	5,300	1.3	2.0
Leisure and Hospitality	34,000	8.6	10.3
Manufacturing	41,400	10.5	8.4
Other Services	14,400	3.7	3.7
Professional and Business Services	52,000	13.2	14.7
Retail Trade	41,100	10.4	10.2
Transportation, Warehousing, and Utilities	43,200	11.0	4.9
Wholesale Trade	14,700	3.7	3.9

Note: Figures are non-farm employment as of December 2022. Figures are not seasonally adjusted and include workers 16 years of age and older; (1) Figures cover the Allentown-Bethlehem-Easton, PA-NJ Metropolitan Statistical Area
Source: Bureau of Labor Statistics, Current Employment Statistics, Employment, Hours, and Earnings

Employment by Occupation

Occupation Classification	City (%)	MSA[1] (%)	U.S. (%)
Management, Business, Science, and Arts	23.5	37.7	40.3
Natural Resources, Construction, and Maintenance	6.4	7.7	8.7
Production, Transportation, and Material Moving	28.9	17.0	13.1
Sales and Office	20.1	20.7	20.9
Service	21.1	16.8	17.0

Note: Figures cover employed civilians 16 years of age and older; (1) Figures cover the Allentown-Bethlehem-Easton, PA-NJ Metropolitan Statistical Area
Source: U.S. Census Bureau, 2017-2021 American Community Survey 5-Year Estimates

Occupations with Greatest Projected Employment Growth: 2022 – 2024

Occupation[1]	2022 Employment	2024 Projected Employment	Numeric Employment Change	Percent Employment Change
Home Health and Personal Care Aides	194,980	205,150	10,170	5.2
Laborers and Freight, Stock, and Material Movers, Hand	150,480	158,160	7,680	5.1
Stockers and Order Fillers	100,260	104,570	4,310	4.3
Industrial Truck and Tractor Operators	31,030	33,930	2,900	9.3
General and Operations Managers	114,430	116,380	1,950	1.7
Heavy and Tractor-Trailer Truck Drivers	88,610	90,560	1,950	2.2
Cooks, Restaurant	49,280	51,090	1,810	3.7
Registered Nurses	148,910	150,170	1,260	0.8
Market Research Analysts and Marketing Specialists	29,510	30,730	1,220	4.1
Light Truck or Delivery Services Drivers	44,200	45,390	1,190	2.7

Note: Projections cover Pennsylvania; (1) Sorted by numeric employment change
Source: www.projectionscentral.com, State Occupational Projections, 2022–2024 Short-Term Projections

Fastest-Growing Occupations: 2022 – 2024

Occupation[1]	2022 Employment	2024 Projected Employment	Numeric Employment Change	Percent Employment Change
Nurse Practitioners	8,090	8,990	900	11.1
Weighers, Measurers, Checkers, and Samplers, Recordkeeping	2,480	2,720	240	9.7
Machine Feeders and Offbearers	3,430	3,760	330	9.6
Industrial Truck and Tractor Operators	31,030	33,930	2,900	9.3
Occupational Therapy Assistants	2,740	2,940	200	7.3
Statisticians	2,840	3,040	200	7.0
Logisticians	8,310	8,880	570	6.9
Physical Therapist Assistants	5,700	6,090	390	6.8
Information Security Analysts (SOC 2018)	3,780	4,020	240	6.3
Physician Assistants	7,730	8,200	470	6.1

Note: Projections cover Pennsylvania; (1) Sorted by percent employment change and excludes occupations with numeric employment change less than 50
Source: www.projectionscentral.com, State Occupational Projections, 2022–2024 Short-Term Projections

CITY FINANCES

City Government Finances

Component	2020 ($000)	2020 ($ per capita)
Total Revenues	179,248	1,476
Total Expenditures	187,172	1,541
Debt Outstanding	92,812	764
Cash and Securities[1]	38,753	319

Note: (1) Cash and security holdings of a government at the close of its fiscal year, including those of its dependent agencies, utilities, and liquor stores.
Source: U.S. Census Bureau, State & Local Government Finances 2020

City Government Revenue by Source

Source	2020 ($000)	2020 ($ per capita)	2020 (%)
General Revenue			
From Federal Government	6,820	56	3.8
From State Government	18,131	149	10.1
From Local Governments	2,207	18	1.2
Taxes			
Property	38,381	316	21.4
Sales and Gross Receipts	0	0	0.0
Personal Income	35,754	294	19.9
Corporate Income	0	0	0.0
Motor Vehicle License	0	0	0.0
Other Taxes	19,575	161	10.9
Current Charges	56,613	466	31.6
Liquor Store	0	0	0.0
Utility	194	2	0.1

Source: U.S. Census Bureau, State & Local Government Finances 2020

City Government Expenditures by Function

Function	2020 ($000)	2020 ($ per capita)	2020 (%)
General Direct Expenditures			
Air Transportation	0	0	0.0
Corrections	0	0	0.0
Education	0	0	0.0
Employment Security Administration	0	0	0.0
Financial Administration	3,282	27	1.8
Fire Protection	20,305	167	10.8
General Public Buildings	5,880	48	3.1
Governmental Administration, Other	5,810	47	3.1
Health	8,500	70	4.5
Highways	17,770	146	9.5
Hospitals	0	0	0.0
Housing and Community Development	7,963	65	4.3
Interest on General Debt	2,523	20	1.3
Judicial and Legal	747	6	0.4
Libraries	0	0	0.0
Parking	0	0	0.0
Parks and Recreation	8,575	70	4.6
Police Protection	39,988	329	21.4
Public Welfare	0	0	0.0
Sewerage	0	0	0.0
Solid Waste Management	31,402	258	16.8
Veterans' Services	0	0	0.0
Liquor Store	0	0	0.0
Utility	0	0	0.0

Source: U.S. Census Bureau, State & Local Government Finances 2020

TAXES

State Corporate Income Tax Rates

State	Tax Rate (%)	Income Brackets ($)	Num. of Brackets	Financial Institution Tax Rate (%)[a]	Federal Income Tax Ded.
Pennsylvania	8.99	Flat rate	1	(a)	No

Note: Tax rates as of January 1, 2023; (a) Rates listed are the corporate income tax rate applied to financial institutions or excise taxes based on income. Some states have other taxes based upon the value of deposits or shares.
Source: Federation of Tax Administrators, State Corporate Income Tax Rates, January 1, 2023

State Individual Income Tax Rates

State	Tax Rate (%)	Income Brackets ($)	Personal Exemptions ($)			Standard Ded. ($)	
			Single	Married	Depend.	Single	Married
Pennsylvania	3.07	Flat rate	None	None	None	–	–

Note: Tax rates as of January 1, 2023; Local- and county-level taxes are not included; Federal income tax is not deductible on state income tax returns
Source: Federation of Tax Administrators, State Individual Income Tax Rates, January 1, 2023

Various State Sales and Excise Tax Rates

State	State Sales Tax (%)	Gasoline[1] ($/gal.)	Cigarette[2] ($/pack)	Spirits[3] ($/gal.)	Wine[4] ($/gal.)	Beer[5] ($/gal.)	Recreational Marijuana (%)
Pennsylvania	6	0.622	2.60	7.41	—	0.08	Not legal

Note: All tax rates as of January 1, 2023; (1) The American Petroleum Institute has developed a methodology for determining the average tax rate on a gallon of fuel. Rates may include any of the following: excise taxes, environmental fees, storage tank fees, other fees or taxes, general sales tax, and local taxes; (2) The federal excise tax of $1.0066 per pack and local taxes are not included; (3) Rates are those applicable to off-premise sales of 40% alcohol by volume (a.b.v.) distilled spirits in 750ml containers. Local excise taxes are excluded; (4) Rates are those applicable to off-premise sales of 11% a.b.v. non-carbonated wine in 750ml containers; (5) Rates are those applicable to off-premise sales of 4.7% a.b.v. beer in 12 ounce containers.
Source: Tax Foundation, 2023 Facts & Figures: How Does Your State Compare?

State Business Tax Climate Index Rankings

State	Overall Rank	Corporate Tax Rank	Individual Income Tax Rank	Sales Tax Rank	Property Tax Rank	Unemployment Insurance Tax Rank
Pennsylvania	33	42	20	16	16	22

Note: The index is a measure of how each state's tax laws affect economic performance. The lower the rank, the more favorable a state's tax system is for business. States without a given tax are given a ranking of 1. The scores/rankings for the District of Columbia do not affect other states. The 2023 index represents the tax climate as of July 1, 2022.
Source: Tax Foundation, State Business Tax Climate Index 2023

TRANSPORTATION

Means of Transportation to Work

Area	Car/Truck/Van		Public Transportation			Bicycle	Walked	Other Means	Worked at Home
	Drove Alone	Car-pooled	Bus	Subway	Railroad				
City	67.4	15.5	3.7	0.0	0.0	0.1	4.4	1.9	6.9
MSA[1]	78.4	7.9	1.2	0.1	0.1	0.1	2.3	1.2	8.7
U.S.	73.2	8.6	2.0	1.6	0.5	0.5	2.5	1.5	9.7

Note: Figures are percentages and cover workers 16 years of age and older; (1) Figures cover the Allentown-Bethlehem-Easton, PA-NJ Metropolitan Statistical Area
Source: U.S. Census Bureau, 2017-2021 American Community Survey 5-Year Estimates

Travel Time to Work

Area	Less Than 10 Minutes	10 to 19 Minutes	20 to 29 Minutes	30 to 44 Minutes	45 to 59 Minutes	60 to 89 Minutes	90 Minutes or More
City	10.6	33.2	30.0	15.2	4.3	4.6	2.1
MSA[1]	12.6	27.7	23.5	18.5	7.3	6.6	3.8
U.S.	12.4	28.5	21.0	20.9	8.2	6.2	2.9

Note: Note: Figures are percentages and include workers 16 years old and over; (1) Figures cover the Allentown-Bethlehem-Easton, PA-NJ Metropolitan Statistical Area
Source: U.S. Census Bureau, 2017-2021 American Community Survey 5-Year Estimates

Key Congestion Measures

Measure	1990	2000	2010	2015	2020
Annual Hours of Delay, Total (000)	4,679	12,248	12,630	14,186	7,535
Annual Hours of Delay, Per Auto Commuter	17	34	32	35	19
Annual Congestion Cost, Per Auto Commuter ($)	387	764	624	649	360

Note: Covers the Allentown PA-NJ urban area
Source: Texas A&M Transportation Institute, 2021 Urban Mobility Report

Freeway Travel Time Index

Measure	1985	1990	1995	2000	2005	2010	2015	2020
Urban Area Index[1]	1.06	1.06	1.12	1.14	1.14	1.14	1.15	1.09
Urban Area Rank[1,2]	53	85	57	62	73	71	67	40

Note: Freeway Travel Time Index—the ratio of travel time in the peak period to the travel time at free-flow conditions. For example, a value of 1.30 indicates a 20-minute free-flow trip takes 26 minutes in the peak (20 minutes x 1.30 = 26 minutes); (1) Covers the Allentown PA-NJ urban area; (2) Rank is based on 101 larger urban areas (#1 = highest travel time index)
Source: Texas A&M Transportation Institute, 2021 Urban Mobility Report

Public Transportation

Agency Name / Mode of Transportation	Vehicles Operated in Maximum Service[1]	Annual Unlinked Passenger Trips[2] (in thous.)	Annual Passenger Miles[3] (in thous.)
Lehigh and Northampton Transportation Authority (LANTA)			
Bus (directly operated)	65	2,636.0	14,137.9
Demand Response (purchased transportation)	52	151.4	1,394.9

Note: (1) Number of revenue vehicles operated by the given mode and type of service to meet the annual maximum service requirement. This is the revenue vehicle count during the peak season of the year; on the week and day that maximum service is provided. Vehicles operated in maximum service (VOMS) exclude atypical days and one-time special events; (2) Number of passengers who boarded public transportation vehicles. Passengers are counted each time they board a vehicle no matter how many vehicles they use to travel from their origin to their destination. (3) Sum of the distances ridden by all passengers during the entire fiscal year.
Source: Federal Transit Administration, National Transit Database, 2021

Air Transportation

Airport Name and Code / Type of Service	Passenger Airlines[1]	Passenger Enplanements	Freight Carriers[2]	Freight (lbs)
Lehigh Valley International (ABE)				
Domestic service (U.S. carriers - 2022)	13	419,741	8	115,403,057
International service (U.S. carriers - 2021)	0	0	0	0

Note: (1) Includes all U.S.-based major, minor and commuter airlines that carried at least one passenger during the year; (2) Includes all U.S.-based airlines and freight carriers that transported at least one pound of freight during the year.
Source: Bureau of Transportation Statistics, The Intermodal Transportation Database, Air Carriers: T-100 Domestic Market (U.S. Carriers), 2022; Bureau of Transportation Statistics, The Intermodal Transportation Database, Air Carriers: T-100 International Market (U.S. Carriers), 2021

BUSINESSES

Major Business Headquarters

Company Name	Industry	Rankings	
		Fortune[1]	Forbes[2]
Air Products & Chemicals	Chemicals	350	-
PPL	Utilities, gas and electric	469	-

Note: (1) Companies that produce a 10-K are ranked 1 to 500 based on 2021 revenue; (2) All private companies with at least $2 billion in annual revenue through the end of their most current fiscal year are ranked 1 to 246; companies listed are headquartered in the city; dashes indicate no ranking
Source: Fortune, "Fortune 500," 2022; Forbes, "America's Largest Private Companies," 2022

Living Environment

COST OF LIVING

Cost of Living Index

Composite Index	Groceries	Housing	Utilities	Trans-portation	Health Care	Misc. Goods/Services
105.5	98.0	112.5	102.2	104.4	98.6	105.2

Note: The Cost of Living Index measures regional differences in the cost of consumer goods and services, excluding taxes and non-consumer expenditures, for professional and managerial households in the top income quintile. It is based on more than 50,000 prices covering almost 60 different items for which prices are collected three times a year by chambers of commerce, economic development organizations or university applied economic centers in each participating urban area. The numbers shown should be read as a percentage above or below the national average of 100. For example, a value of 115.4 in the groceries column indicates that grocery prices are 15.4% higher than the national average. Small differences in the index numbers should not be interpreted as significant; Figures cover the Allentown PA urban area.
Source: The Council for Community and Economic Research, Cost of Living Index, 2022

Grocery Prices

Area[1]	T-Bone Steak ($/pound)	Frying Chicken ($/pound)	Whole Milk ($/half gal.)	Eggs ($/dozen)	Orange Juice ($/64 oz.)	Coffee ($/11.5 oz.)
City[2]	15.80	1.61	2.56	2.11	3.74	3.90
Avg.	13.81	1.59	2.43	2.25	3.85	4.95
Min.	10.17	0.90	1.51	1.30	2.90	3.46
Max.	19.35	3.30	4.32	4.32	5.31	8.59

*Note: (1) Values for the local area are compared with the average, minimum and maximum values for all 286 areas in the Cost of Living Index; (2) Figures cover the Allentown PA urban area; **T-Bone Steak** (price per pound); **Frying Chicken** (price per pound, whole fryer); **Whole Milk** (half gallon carton); **Eggs** (price per dozen, Grade A, large); **Orange Juice** (64 oz. Tropicana or Florida Natural); **Coffee** (11.5 oz. can, vacuum-packed, Maxwell House, Hills Bros, or Folgers).*
Source: The Council for Community and Economic Research, Cost of Living Index, 2022

Housing and Utility Costs

Area[1]	New Home Price ($)	Apartment Rent ($/month)	All Electric ($/month)	Part Electric ($/month)	Other Energy ($/month)	Telephone ($/month)
City[2]	485,339	1,679	-	99.25	82.35	193.11
Avg.	450,913	1,371	176.41	99.93	76.96	190.22
Min.	229,283	546	100.84	31.56	27.15	174.27
Max.	2,434,977	4,569	356.86	249.59	272.24	208.31

*Note: (1) Values for the local area are compared with the average, minimum and maximum values for all 286 areas in the Cost of Living Index; (2) Figures cover the Allentown PA urban area; **New Home Price** (2,400 sf living area, 8,000 sf lot, in urban area with full utilities); **Apartment Rent** (950 sf 2 bedroom/1.5 or 2 bath, unfurnished, excluding all utilities except water); **All Electric** (average monthly cost for an all-electric home); **Part Electric** (average monthly cost for a part-electric home); **Other Energy** (average monthly cost for natural gas, fuel oil, coal, wood, and any other forms of energy except electricity); **Telephone** (price includes the base monthly rate plus taxes and fees for three lines of mobile phone service).*
Source: The Council for Community and Economic Research, Cost of Living Index, 2022

Health Care, Transportation, and Other Costs

Area[1]	Doctor ($/visit)	Dentist ($/visit)	Optometrist ($/visit)	Gasoline ($/gallon)	Beauty Salon ($/visit)	Men's Shirt ($)
City[2]	107.20	115.92	108.43	4.12	53.07	35.54
Avg.	124.91	107.77	117.66	3.86	43.31	34.21
Min.	36.61	58.25	51.79	2.90	22.18	13.05
Max.	250.21	162.58	371.96	5.54	85.61	63.54

*Note: (1) Values for the local area are compared with the average, minimum and maximum values for all 286 areas in the Cost of Living Index; (2) Figures cover the Allentown PA urban area; **Doctor** (general practitioners routine exam of an established patient); **Dentist** (adult teeth cleaning and periodic oral examination); **Optometrist** (full vision eye exam for established adult patient); **Gasoline** (one gallon regular unleaded, national brand, including all taxes, cash price at self-service pump if available); **Beauty Salon** (woman's shampoo, trim, and blow-dry); **Men's Shirt** (cotton/polyester dress shirt, pinpoint weave, long sleeves).*
Source: The Council for Community and Economic Research, Cost of Living Index, 2022

HOUSING

Homeownership Rate

Area	2015 (%)	2016 (%)	2017 (%)	2018 (%)	2019 (%)	2020 (%)	2021 (%)	2022 (%)
MSA[1]	69.2	68.9	73.1	72.1	67.8	68.8	70.4	73.1
U.S.	63.7	63.4	63.9	64.4	64.6	66.6	65.5	65.8

Note: (1) Figures cover the Allentown-Bethlehem-Easton, PA-NJ Metropolitan Statistical Area
Source: U.S. Census Bureau, Housing Vacancies and Homeownership Annual Statistics: 2015-2022

Allentown, Pennsylvania 13

House Price Index (HPI)

Area	National Ranking[2]	Quarterly Change (%)	One-Year Change (%)	Five-Year Change (%)	Since 1991Q1 (%)
MSA[1]	104	-0.97	12.09	52.30	165.53
U.S.[3]	–	0.34	8.41	58.44	289.08

Note: The HPI is a weighted repeat sales index. It measures average price changes in repeat sales or refinancings on the same properties. This information is obtained by reviewing repeat mortgage transactions on single-family properties whose mortgages have been purchased or securitized by Fannie Mae or Freddie Mac since January 1975; (1) Figures cover the Allentown-Bethlehem-Easton, PA-NJ Metropolitan Statistical Area; (2) Rankings are based on annual percentage change for all metro areas containing at least 15,000 transactions over the last 10 years and ranges from 1 to 257; (3) figures based on a weighted average of Census Division estimates using a seasonally adjusted, purchase-only index; all figures are for the period ending December 31, 2022
Source: Federal Housing Finance Agency, Change in FHFA Metropolitan Area House Price Indexes, 2022Q4

Median Single-Family Home Prices

Area	2020	2021	2022p	Percent Change 2021 to 2022
MSA[1]	234.9	266.4	297.2	11.6
U.S. Average	300.2	357.1	392.6	9.9

Note: Figures are median sales prices of existing single-family homes in thousands of dollars; (p) preliminary; (1) Figures cover the Allentown-Bethlehem-Easton, PA-NJ Metropolitan Statistical Area
Source: National Association of Realtors, Median Sales Price of Existing Single-Family Homes for Metropolitan Areas, 4th Quarter 2022

Qualifying Income Based on Median Sales Price of Existing Single-Family Homes

Area	With 5% Down ($)	With 10% Down ($)	With 20% Down ($)
MSA[1]	89,695	84,975	75,533
U.S. Average	112,234	106,237	94,513

Note: Figures are preliminary; Qualifying income is based on a mortgage rate of 6.77%. Monthly principal and interest payment is limited to 25% of income; (1) Figures cover the Allentown-Bethlehem-Easton, PA-NJ Metropolitan Statistical Area
Source: National Association of Realtors, Qualifying Income Based on Median Sales Price of Existing Single-Family Homes for Metropolitan Areas, 4th Quarter 2022

Home Value

Area	Under $100,000	$100,000 -$199,999	$200,000 -$299,999	$300,000 -$399,999	$400,000 -$499,999	$500,000 -$999,999	$1,000,000 or more	Median ($)
City	19.9	58.7	14.0	3.6	1.8	1.4	0.5	145,700
MSA[1]	9.9	31.5	28.8	17.1	7.2	5.1	0.6	227,900
U.S.	16.2	24.2	20.1	13.6	8.3	13.6	4.1	244,900

Note: Figures are percentages except for median and cover owner-occupied housing units; (1) Figures cover the Allentown-Bethlehem-Easton, PA-NJ Metropolitan Statistical Area
Source: U.S. Census Bureau, 2017-2021 American Community Survey 5-Year Estimates

Year Housing Structure Built

Area	2020 or Later	2010 -2019	2000 -2009	1990 -1999	1980 -1989	1970 -1979	1960 -1969	1950 -1959	1940 -1949	Before 1940	Median Year
City	0.1	2.3	4.6	3.4	5.3	10.8	11.5	15.0	7.2	39.7	1952
MSA[1]	0.1	4.0	11.4	10.3	11.0	12.0	9.5	10.9	5.2	25.7	1969
U.S.	0.2	7.3	13.6	13.6	13.2	14.8	10.3	10.0	4.7	12.2	1979

Note: Figures are percentages except for Median Year; Note: (1) Figures cover the Allentown-Bethlehem-Easton, PA-NJ Metropolitan Statistical Area
Source: U.S. Census Bureau, 2017-2021 American Community Survey 5-Year Estimates

Gross Monthly Rent

Area	Under $500	$500 -$999	$1,000 -$1,499	$1,500 -$1,999	$2,000 -$2,499	$2,500 -$2,999	$3,000 and up	Median ($)
City	7.6	31.1	44.6	14.9	1.3	0.3	0.3	1,100
MSA[1]	8.9	28.4	39.4	17.7	3.9	0.9	0.9	1,141
U.S.	8.1	30.5	30.8	16.8	7.3	3.1	3.5	1,163

Note: Figures are percentages except for median; Gross rent is the contract rent plus the estimated average monthly cost of utilities (electricity, gas, and water and sewer) and fuels (oil, coal, kerosene, wood, etc.) if these are paid by the renter (or paid for the renter by someone else); (1) Figures cover the Allentown-Bethlehem-Easton, PA-NJ Metropolitan Statistical Area
Source: U.S. Census Bureau, 2017-2021 American Community Survey 5-Year Estimates

HEALTH

Health Risk Factors

Category	MSA[1] (%)	U.S. (%)
Adults aged 18–64 who have any kind of health care coverage	n/a	90.9
Adults who reported being in good or better health	n/a	85.2
Adults who have been told they have high blood cholesterol	n/a	35.7
Adults who have been told they have high blood pressure	n/a	32.4
Adults who are current smokers	n/a	14.4
Adults who currently use e-cigarettes	n/a	6.7
Adults who currently use chewing tobacco, snuff, or snus	n/a	3.5
Adults who are heavy drinkers[2]	n/a	6.3
Adults who are binge drinkers[3]	n/a	15.4
Adults who are overweight (BMI 25.0 - 29.9)	n/a	34.4
Adults who are obese (BMI 30.0 - 99.8)	n/a	33.9
Adults who participated in any physical activities in the past month	n/a	76.3

Note: (1) Figures for the Allentown-Bethlehem-Easton, PA-NJ Metropolitan Statistical Area were not available.
(2) Heavy drinkers are classified as adult men having more than 14 drinks per week and adult women having more than 7 drinks per week; (3) Binge drinkers are classified as males having five or more drinks on one occasion or females having four or more drinks on one occasion
Source: Centers for Disease Control and Prevention, Behaviorial Risk Factor Surveillance System, SMART: Selected Metropolitan Area Risk Trends, 2021

Acute and Chronic Health Conditions

Category	MSA[1] (%)	U.S. (%)
Adults who have ever been told they had a heart attack	n/a	4.0
Adults who have ever been told they have angina or coronary heart disease	n/a	3.8
Adults who have ever been told they had a stroke	n/a	3.0
Adults who have ever been told they have asthma	n/a	14.9
Adults who have ever been told they have arthritis	n/a	25.8
Adults who have ever been told they have diabetes[2]	n/a	10.9
Adults who have ever been told they had skin cancer	n/a	6.6
Adults who have ever been told they had any other types of cancer	n/a	7.5
Adults who have ever been told they have COPD	n/a	6.1
Adults who have ever been told they have kidney disease	n/a	3.0
Adults who have ever been told they have a form of depression	n/a	20.5

Note: (1) Figures for the Allentown-Bethlehem-Easton, PA-NJ Metropolitan Statistical Area were not available.
(2) Figures do not include pregnancy-related, borderline, or pre-diabetes
Source: Centers for Disease Control and Prevention, Behaviorial Risk Factor Surveillance System, SMART: Selected Metropolitan Area Risk Trends, 2021

Health Screening and Vaccination Rates

Category	MSA[1] (%)	U.S. (%)
Adults who have ever been tested for HIV	n/a	34.9
Adults who have had their blood cholesterol checked within the last five years	n/a	85.2
Adults aged 65+ who have had flu shot within the past year	n/a	68.6
Adults aged 65+ who have ever had a pneumonia vaccination	n/a	71.0

Note: (1) Figures for the Allentown-Bethlehem-Easton, PA-NJ Metropolitan Statistical Area were not available.
Source: Centers for Disease Control and Prevention, Behaviorial Risk Factor Surveillance System, SMART: Selected Metropolitan Area Risk Trends, 2021

Disability Status

Category	MSA[1] (%)	U.S. (%)
Adults who reported being deaf	n/a	7.2
Are you blind or have serious difficulty seeing, even when wearing glasses?	n/a	4.8
Are you limited in any way in any of your usual activities due to arthritis?	n/a	11.1
Do you have difficulty doing errands alone?	n/a	7.0
Do you have difficulty dressing or bathing?	n/a	3.6
Do you have serious difficulty concentrating/remembering/making decisions?	n/a	12.1
Do you have serious difficulty walking or climbing stairs?	n/a	12.8

Note: (1) Figures for the Allentown-Bethlehem-Easton, PA-NJ Metropolitan Statistical Area were not available.
Source: Centers for Disease Control and Prevention, Behaviorial Risk Factor Surveillance System, SMART: Selected Metropolitan Area Risk Trends, 2021

Mortality Rates for the Top 10 Causes of Death in the U.S.

ICD-10[a] Sub-Chapter	ICD-10[a] Code	Crude Mortality Rate[1] per 100,000 population	
		County[2]	U.S.
Malignant neoplasms	C00-C97	186.7	182.6
Ischaemic heart diseases	I20-I25	93.0	113.1
Other forms of heart disease	I30-I51	84.9	64.4
Other degenerative diseases of the nervous system	G30-G31	47.2	51.0
Cerebrovascular diseases	I60-I69	43.0	47.8
Other external causes of accidental injury	W00-X59	65.4	46.4
Chronic lower respiratory diseases	J40-J47	30.7	45.7
Organic, including symptomatic, mental disorders	F01-F09	77.8	35.9
Hypertensive diseases	I10-I15	22.4	35.0
Diabetes mellitus	E10-E14	26.8	29.6

Note: (a) ICD-10 = International Classification of Diseases 10th Revision; (1) Crude mortality rates are a three-year average covering 2019-2021; (2) Figures cover Lehigh County.
Source: Centers for Disease Control and Prevention, National Center for Health Statistics. National Vital Statistics System, Mortality 2018-2021 on CDC WONDER Online Database

Mortality Rates for Selected Causes of Death

ICD-10[a] Sub-Chapter	ICD-10[a] Code	Crude Mortality Rate[1] per 100,000 population	
		County[2]	U.S.
Assault	X85-Y09	3.5	7.0
Diseases of the liver	K70-K76	15.8	19.8
Human immunodeficiency virus (HIV) disease	B20-B24	Suppressed	1.5
Influenza and pneumonia	J09-J18	11.9	14.7
Intentional self-harm	X60-X84	12.6	14.3
Malnutrition	E40-E46	8.2	4.3
Obesity and other hyperalimentation	E65-E68	2.0	3.0
Renal failure	N17-N19	15.4	15.7
Transport accidents	V01-V99	9.1	13.6
Viral hepatitis	B15-B19	Unreliable	1.2

Note: (a) ICD-10 = International Classification of Diseases 10th Revision; (1) Crude mortality rates are a three-year average covering 2019-2021; (2) Figures cover Lehigh County; Data are suppressed when the data meet the criteria for confidentiality constraints; Crude mortality rates are flagged as unreliable when the rate would be calculated with a numerator of 20 or less.
Source: Centers for Disease Control and Prevention, National Center for Health Statistics. National Vital Statistics System, Mortality 2018-2021 on CDC WONDER Online Database

Health Insurance Coverage

Area	With Health Insurance	With Private Health Insurance	With Public Health Insurance	Without Health Insurance	Population Under Age 19 Without Health Insurance
City	88.6	46.4	50.2	11.4	4.7
MSA[1]	94.6	72.8	35.7	5.4	2.9
U.S.	91.2	67.8	35.4	8.8	5.3

Note: Figures are percentages that cover the civilian noninstitutionalized population; (1) Figures cover the Allentown-Bethlehem-Easton, PA-NJ Metropolitan Statistical Area
Source: U.S. Census Bureau, 2017-2021 American Community Survey 5-Year Estimates

Number of Medical Professionals

Area	MDs[3]	DOs[3,4]	Dentists	Podiatrists	Chiropractors	Optometrists
County[1] (number)	1,346	317	331	47	108	78
County[1] (rate[2])	359.4	84.6	88.1	12.5	28.8	20.8
U.S. (rate[2])	289.3	23.5	72.5	6.2	28.7	17.4

Note: Data as of 2021 unless noted; (1) Data covers Lehigh County; (2) Rate per 100,000 population; (3) Data as of 2020 and includes all active, non-federal physicians; (4) Doctor of Osteopathic Medicine
Source: U.S. Department of Health and Human Services, Health Resources and Services Administration, Bureau of Health Professions, Area Resource File (ARF) 2021-2022

EDUCATION

Public School District Statistics

District Name	Schls	Pupils	Pupil/ Teacher Ratio	Minority Pupils[1] (%)	LEP/ELL[2] (%)	IEP[3] (%)
Allentown City SD	21	16,189	16.4	92.5	17.0	21.3
Parkland SD	12	9,676	14.4	40.1	3.2	17.1

Note: Table includes school districts with 2,000 or more students; (1) Percentage of students that are not non-Hispanic white; (2) Percentage of students that are Limited English Proficient or English Language Learners (2018-19); (3) Percentage of students that have an Individualized Education Program (2019-20).
Source: U.S. Department of Education, National Center for Education Statistics, Common Core of Data, Local Education Agency (School District) Universe Survey: School Year 2021-2022

Highest Level of Education

Area	Less than H.S.	H.S. Diploma	Some College, No Deg.	Associate Degree	Bachelor's Degree	Master's Degree	Prof. School Degree	Doctorate Degree
City	19.4	36.5	19.3	7.5	11.5	3.8	1.1	0.8
MSA[1]	9.1	33.6	16.6	9.4	19.5	8.7	1.6	1.4
U.S.	11.1	26.5	20.0	8.7	20.6	9.3	2.2	1.5

Note: Figures cover persons age 25 and over; (1) Figures cover the Allentown-Bethlehem-Easton, PA-NJ Metropolitan Statistical Area
Source: U.S. Census Bureau, 2017-2021 American Community Survey 5-Year Estimates

Educational Attainment by Race

Area	High School Graduate or Higher (%)					Bachelor's Degree or Higher (%)				
	Total	White	Black	Asian	Hisp.[2]	Total	White	Black	Asian	Hisp.[2]
City	80.6	84.7	83.6	80.4	70.5	17.3	21.5	11.2	42.3	7.7
MSA[1]	90.9	92.5	87.6	89.0	77.5	31.2	32.2	21.7	61.7	15.7
U.S.	88.9	91.4	87.2	87.6	71.2	33.7	35.5	23.3	55.6	18.4

Note: Figures shown cover persons 25 years old and over; (1) Figures cover the Allentown-Bethlehem-Easton, PA-NJ Metropolitan Statistical Area; (2) People of Hispanic origin can be of any race
Source: U.S. Census Bureau, 2017-2021 American Community Survey 5-Year Estimates

School Enrollment by Grade and Control

Area	Preschool (%)		Kindergarten (%)		Grades 1 - 4 (%)		Grades 5 - 8 (%)		Grades 9 - 12 (%)	
	Public	Private	Public	Private	Public	Private	Public	Private	Public	Private
City	80.2	19.8	86.2	13.8	87.7	12.3	90.5	9.5	89.0	11.0
MSA[1]	52.6	47.4	86.9	13.1	89.7	10.3	91.2	8.8	91.3	8.7
U.S.	58.8	41.2	86.3	13.7	88.3	11.7	88.6	11.4	89.4	10.6

Note: Figures shown cover persons 3 years old and over; (1) Figures cover the Allentown-Bethlehem-Easton, PA-NJ Metropolitan Statistical Area
Source: U.S. Census Bureau, 2017-2021 American Community Survey 5-Year Estimates

Higher Education

Four-Year Colleges			Two-Year Colleges			Medical Schools[1]	Law Schools[2]	Voc/ Tech[3]
Public	Private Non-profit	Private For-profit	Public	Private Non-profit	Private For-profit			
0	8	0	3	0	3	0	0	7

Note: Figures cover institutions located within the Allentown-Bethlehem-Easton, PA-NJ Metropolitan Statistical Area and include main campuses only; (1) includes schools accredited by the Liaison Committee on Medical Education and the American Osteopathic Association's Commission on Osteopathic College Accreditation; (2) includes ABA-accredited schools, schools with provisional ABA accreditation, and state accredited schools; (3) includes all schools with programs that are less than 2 years.
Source: National Center for Education Statistics, Integrated Postsecondary Education System (IPEDS), 2021-22; Wikipedia, List of Medical Schools in the United States, accessed April 10, 2023; Wikipedia, List of Law Schools in the United States, accessed April 10, 2023

According to *U.S. News & World Report,* the Allentown-Bethlehem-Easton, PA-NJ metro area is home to one of the top 200 national universities in the U.S.: **Lehigh University** (#51 tie). The indicators used to capture academic quality fall into a number of categories: assessment by administrators at peer institutions; retention of students; faculty resources; student selectivity; financial resources; alumni giving; high school counselor ratings of colleges; and graduation rate. *U.S. News & World Report, "America's Best Colleges 2023"*

According to *U.S. News & World Report,* the Allentown-Bethlehem-Easton, PA-NJ metro area is home to two of the top 100 liberal arts colleges in the U.S.: **Lafayette College** (#39 tie); **Muhlenberg College** (#76 tie). The indicators used to capture academic quality fall into a number of categories: assessment by administrators at peer institutions; retention of students; faculty resources; student selectivity; financial resources; alumni giving; high school counselor ratings of colleges; and graduation rate. *U.S. News & World Report, "America's Best Colleges 2023"*

EMPLOYERS

Major Employers

Company Name	Industry
Air Products	Manufacturer
Amazon.com	Internet retailer
B. Braun Medical	Healthcare
Crayola	Electronics
Easton Hospital	Healthcare
Giant Food Stores	Grocery stores
Good Shepard Rehabilitation Network	Healthcare
Guardian Life Insurance Co.	Life insurance
HCR Manorcare	Healthcare
KidsPeace	Healthcare
Lehigh Carbon Community College	Education
Lehigh University	Education
Lehigh Valley Hospital and Health Network	Healthcare
Lutron Electronics Co.	Electronics
Mack Trucks	Trucking
Northampton Community College	Education
PPL	Utilities
Sacred Heart Healthcare System	Healthcare
Sands Casino Resort Bethlehem	Casino resort
Sodexo	Conglomerate
St. Luke's Hospital and Health Network	Healthcare
Wal-Mart Stores	Retail stores
Wegmans Food Market	Grocery stores
Weis Markets	Grocery stores
Wells Fargo	Banking and financial services

Note: Companies shown are located within the Allentown-Bethlehem-Easton, PA-NJ Metropolitan Statistical Area.
Source: Hoovers.com; Wikipedia

PUBLIC SAFETY

Crime Rate

Area	Total Crime	Violent Crime Rate				Property Crime Rate		
		Murder	Rape[3]	Robbery	Aggrav. Assault	Burglary	Larceny -Theft	Motor Vehicle Theft
City	2,669.6	5.7	52.5	139.5	188.7	427.6	1,656.1	199.4
Suburbs[1]	n/a	n/a	n/a	n/a	n/a	n/a	n/a	n/a
Metro[2]	n/a	n/a	n/a	n/a	n/a	n/a	n/a	n/a
U.S.	2,510.4	5.1	42.6	81.8	250.4	340.5	1,569.2	220.8

Note: Figures are crimes per 100,000 population; (1) All areas within the metro area that are located outside the city limits; (2) Figures cover the Allentown-Bethlehem-Easton, PA-NJ Metropolitan Statistical Area; n/a not available; (3) All figures shown were reported using the revised Uniform Crime Reporting (UCR) definition of rape; Due to the transition to the National Incident-Based Reporting System (NIBRS), limited city and metro area data was released for 2021.
Source: FBI Uniform Crime Reports, 2019 (data for 2020 was not available)

Hate Crimes

Area	Number of Quarters Reported	Number of Incidents per Bias Motivation					
		Race/Ethnicity/ Ancestry	Religion	Sexual Orientation	Disability	Gender	Gender Identity
City	4	0	0	0	0	0	0
U.S.	4	5,227	1,244	1,110	130	75	266

Note: Due to the transition to the National Incident-Based Reporting System (NIBRS), limited crime data was released for 2021.
Source: Federal Bureau of Investigation, Hate Crime Statistics 2020

Identity Theft Consumer Reports

Area	Reports	Reports per 100,000 Population	Rank[2]
MSA[1]	2,604	310	63
U.S.	1,108,609	339	-

Note: (1) Figures cover the Allentown-Bethlehem-Easton, PA-NJ Metropolitan Statistical Area; (2) Rank ranges from 1 to 391 where 1 indicates greatest number of identity theft reports per 100,000 population
Source: Federal Trade Commission, Consumer Sentinel Network Data Book 2022

Fraud and Other Consumer Reports

Area	Reports	Reports per 100,000 Population	Rank[2]
MSA[1]	8,101	963	113
U.S.	4,064,520	1,245	-

Note: (1) Figures cover the Allentown-Bethlehem-Easton, PA-NJ Metropolitan Statistical Area; (2) Rank ranges from 1 to 391 where 1 indicates greatest number of fraud and other consumer reports per 100,000 population
Source: Federal Trade Commission, Consumer Sentinel Network Data Book 2022

POLITICS

2020 Presidential Election Results

Area	Biden	Trump	Jorgensen	Hawkins	Other
Lehigh County	53.1	45.5	1.2	0.1	0.2
U.S.	51.3	46.8	1.2	0.3	0.5

Note: Results are percentages and may not add to 100% due to rounding
Source: Dave Leip's Atlas of U.S. Presidential Elections

SPORTS

Professional Sports Teams

Team Name	League	Year Established

No teams are located in the metro area
Source: Wikipedia, Major Professional Sports Teams of the United States and Canada, April 12, 2023

CLIMATE

Average and Extreme Temperatures

Temperature	Jan	Feb	Mar	Apr	May	Jun	Jul	Aug	Sep	Oct	Nov	Dec	Yr.
Extreme High (°F)	72	76	84	93	97	100	105	100	99	90	81	72	105
Average High (°F)	35	38	48	61	71	80	85	82	75	64	52	39	61
Average Temp. (°F)	28	30	39	50	60	70	74	72	65	54	43	32	52
Average Low (°F)	20	22	29	39	49	58	63	62	54	43	34	24	42
Extreme Low (°F)	-12	-7	-1	16	30	39	48	41	31	21	11	-8	-12

Note: Figures cover the years 1948-1990
Source: National Climatic Data Center, International Station Meteorological Climate Summary, 9/96

Average Precipitation/Snowfall/Humidity

Precip./Humidity	Jan	Feb	Mar	Apr	May	Jun	Jul	Aug	Sep	Oct	Nov	Dec	Yr.
Avg. Precip. (in.)	3.2	3.0	3.5	3.8	4.2	3.6	4.3	4.4	3.9	2.9	3.8	3.6	44.2
Avg. Snowfall (in.)	9	9	6	1	Tr	0	0	0	0	Tr	1	6	32
Avg. Rel. Hum. 7am (%)	77	76	75	75	78	79	82	86	88	86	82	79	80
Avg. Rel. Hum. 4pm (%)	62	57	51	48	52	52	52	55	57	56	60	64	55

Note: Figures cover the years 1948-1990; Tr = Trace amounts (<0.05 in. of rain; <0.5 in. of snow)
Source: National Climatic Data Center, International Station Meteorological Climate Summary, 9/96

Weather Conditions

Temperature			Daytime Sky			Precipitation		
5°F & below	32°F & below	90°F & above	Clear	Partly cloudy	Cloudy	0.01 inch or more precip.	0.1 inch or more snow/ice	Thunder-storms
6	123	15	77	148	140	123	20	31

Note: Figures are average number of days per year and cover the years 1948-1990
Source: National Climatic Data Center, International Station Meteorological Climate Summary, 9/96

HAZARDOUS WASTE

Superfund Sites

The Allentown-Bethlehem-Easton, PA-NJ metro area is home to seven sites on the EPA's Superfund National Priorities List: **Heleva Landfill** (final); **Hellertown Manufacturing Co.** (final); **Industrial Lane** (final); **Novak Sanitary Landfill** (final); **Palmerton Zinc Pile** (final); **Pohatcong Valley Ground Water Contamination** (final); **Rodale Manufacturing Co., Inc.** (final). There are a total of 1,165 Superfund sites with a status of proposed or final on the list in the U.S. *U.S. Environmental Protection Agency, National Priorities List, April 12, 2023*

AIR QUALITY

Air Quality Trends: Ozone

	1990	1995	2000	2005	2010	2015	2018	2019	2020	2021
MSA[1]	0.093	0.091	0.091	0.086	0.080	0.070	0.067	0.064	0.063	0.063
U.S.	0.087	0.089	0.081	0.080	0.072	0.067	0.069	0.065	0.065	0.067

Note: (1) Data covers the Allentown-Bethlehem-Easton, PA-NJ Metropolitan Statistical Area. The values shown are the composite ozone concentration averages among trend sites based on the highest fourth daily maximum 8-hour concentration in parts per million. These trends are based on sites having an adequate record of monitoring data during the trend period. Data from exceptional events are included.
Source: U.S. Environmental Protection Agency, Air Quality Monitoring Information, "Air Quality Trends by City, 1990-2021"

Air Quality Index

Area	Percent of Days when Air Quality was...[2]					AQI Statistics[2]	
	Good	Moderate	Unhealthy for Sensitive Groups	Unhealthy	Very Unhealthy	Maximum	Median
MSA[1]	69.9	29.0	0.8	0.3	0.0	153	43

Note: (1) Data covers the Allentown-Bethlehem-Easton, PA-NJ Metropolitan Statistical Area; (2) Based on 365 days with AQI data in 2021. Air Quality Index (AQI) is an index for reporting daily air quality. EPA calculates the AQI for five major air pollutants regulated by the Clean Air Act: ground-level ozone, particle pollution (aka particulate matter), carbon monoxide, sulfur dioxide, and nitrogen dioxide. The AQI runs from 0 to 500. The higher the AQI value, the greater the level of air pollution and the greater the health concern. There are six AQI categories: "Good" AQI is between 0 and 50. Air quality is considered satisfactory; "Moderate" AQI is between 51 and 100. Air quality is acceptable; "Unhealthy for Sensitive Groups" When AQI values are between 101 and 150, members of sensitive groups may experience health effects; "Unhealthy" When AQI values are between 151 and 200 everyone may begin to experience health effects; "Very Unhealthy" AQI values between 201 and 300 trigger a health alert; "Hazardous" AQI values over 300 trigger warnings of emergency conditions (not shown).
Source: U.S. Environmental Protection Agency, Air Quality Index Report, 2021

Air Quality Index Pollutants

Area	Percent of Days when AQI Pollutant was...[2]					
	Carbon Monoxide	Nitrogen Dioxide	Ozone	Sulfur Dioxide	Particulate Matter 2.5	Particulate Matter 10
MSA[1]	0.0	1.6	48.8	(3)	49.6	0.0

Note: (1) Data covers the Allentown-Bethlehem-Easton, PA-NJ Metropolitan Statistical Area; (2) Based on 365 days with AQI data in 2021. The Air Quality Index (AQI) is an index for reporting daily air quality. EPA calculates the AQI for five major air pollutants regulated by the Clean Air Act: ground-level ozone, particle pollution (also known as particulate matter), carbon monoxide, sulfur dioxide, and nitrogen dioxide. The AQI runs from 0 to 500. The higher the AQI value, the greater the level of air pollution and the greater the health concern; (3) Sulfur dioxide is no longer included in this table (as of December 8, 2021) because SO_2 concentrations tend to be very localized and not necessarily representative of broad geographical areas like counties and CBSAs.
Source: U.S. Environmental Protection Agency, Air Quality Index Report, 2021

Maximum Air Pollutant Concentrations: Particulate Matter, Ozone, CO and Lead

	Particulate Matter 10 (ug/m^3)	Particulate Matter 2.5 Wtd AM (ug/m^3)	Particulate Matter 2.5 24-Hr (ug/m^3)	Ozone (ppm)	Carbon Monoxide (ppm)	Lead (ug/m^3)
MSA[1] Level	44	9.9	27	0.069	n/a	0.06
NAAQS[2]	150	15	35	0.075	9	0.15
Met NAAQS[2]	Yes	Yes	Yes	Yes	n/a	Yes

Note: (1) Data covers the Allentown-Bethlehem-Easton, PA-NJ Metropolitan Statistical Area; Data from exceptional events are included; (2) National Ambient Air Quality Standards; ppm = parts per million; ug/m^3 = micrograms per cubic meter; n/a not available.
Concentrations: Particulate Matter 10 (coarse particulate)—highest second maximum 24-hour concentration; Particulate Matter 2.5 Wtd AM (fine particulate)—highest weighted annual mean concentration; Particulate Matter 2.5 24-Hour (fine particulate)—highest 98th percentile 24-hour concentration; Ozone—highest fourth daily maximum 8-hour concentration; Carbon Monoxide—highest second maximum non-overlapping 8-hour concentration; Lead—maximum running 3-month average
Source: U.S. Environmental Protection Agency, Air Quality Monitoring Information, "Air Quality Statistics by City, 2021"

Maximum Air Pollutant Concentrations: Nitrogen Dioxide and Sulfur Dioxide

	Nitrogen Dioxide AM (ppb)	Nitrogen Dioxide 1-Hr (ppb)	Sulfur Dioxide AM (ppb)	Sulfur Dioxide 1-Hr (ppb)	Sulfur Dioxide 24-Hr (ppb)
MSA[1] Level	10	42	n/a	6	n/a
NAAQS[2]	53	100	30	75	140
Met NAAQS[2]	Yes	Yes	n/a	Yes	n/a

Note: (1) Data covers the Allentown-Bethlehem-Easton, PA-NJ Metropolitan Statistical Area; Data from exceptional events are included; (2) National Ambient Air Quality Standards; ppm = parts per million; ug/m^3 = micrograms per cubic meter; n/a not available.
Concentrations: Nitrogen Dioxide AM—highest arithmetic mean concentration; Nitrogen Dioxide 1-Hr—highest 98th percentile 1-hour daily maximum concentration; Sulfur Dioxide AM—highest annual mean concentration; Sulfur Dioxide 1-Hr—highest 99th percentile 1-hour daily maximum concentration; Sulfur Dioxide 24-Hr—highest second maximum 24-hour concentration
Source: U.S. Environmental Protection Agency, Air Quality Monitoring Information, "Air Quality Statistics by City, 2021"

Baltimore, Maryland

Background

No one industry dominates Baltimore, but many of them have one thing in common: Baltimore's waterfront. The city's port facilities provide companies in Baltimore's municipal area with access to domestic and international markets. Not only that, but the port also has the advantage of being 150 miles closer to the Midwest than other eastern U.S. port cities.

With its easily accessible harbor, reached via a 42-foot-deep main channel from the Chesapeake Bay, Baltimore boasts strong roots in maritime commerce dating to the "Baltimore Clippers" built here that outran the British during wartime. In 2019, the Port of Baltimore handled $58.4 billion in foreign commerce (43.6 million tons), a record 11.1 million tons of general cargo, and a record 857,000 automobiles.

The city was founded in 1729 and named for the Lords Baltimore, Cecil and Charles Calvert, the first proprietors of colonial Maryland in the seventeenth century. In 1812, poet and attorney Francis Scott Key wrote "The Star-Spangled Banner" while watching from a warship the bombardment of the city by the British. Baltimore is the site of the first Roman Catholic cathedral in the country, the Basilica of the Assumption of the Blessed Virgin Mary, which was designed by Benjamin H. Latrobe. The first telegraph line in the United States was installed in Baltimore, and the nation's first gas streetlamp was lit here.

Despite the urban decay experienced from the 1950s through the 1970s, reconstruction of many of the city's old areas in the ensuing years has brought people back to Baltimore neighborhoods such as the Inner Harbor, Fells Point, Federal Hill, and Canton. The upscale Harbor East neighborhood extends the walkability and attraction of the waterside area between the Inner Harbor and Fells Point, with dining, hotels, and shopping.

Healthcare and higher education are the city's major employers, with Johns Hopkins University, Johns Hopkins Hospital and Health System, the University of Maryland-Baltimore, and the University of Maryland Medical System providing nearly 60,000 jobs.

The South Baltimore Gateway Partnership, formed in 2016, is currently working to use revenue from the Horseshoe Casino Baltimore, which opened in 2014, to revitalize neighborhoods around the casino.

Baltimore's light rail transportation services the Hunt Valley corporate, hotel, and shopping area north of the city, and passes through downtown on its way to Oriole Park and Anne Arundel County. There is also service to BWI Thurgood Marshall Airport and Amtrak's Baltimore Penn Station, as well as public subway and bus transportation. BWI is a major international airport, with over 36 airlines.

The Baltimore waterfront area is a retail and entertainment district, and includes the renovated Pier Four Power Plant, which is listed on the National Register of Historic Places and is has been repurposed as a mixed-use space that includes businesses, restaurants, and cultural venues. Baltimore boasts many museums, including Port Discovery children's museum, the Edgar Allen Poe House and Museum, the Baltimore Museum of Art and the American Visionary Art Museum, to name a few. Some other attractions include the Baltimore Symphony Orchestra, Fort McHenry, Maryland Science Center, and the National Aquarium in Baltimore. The Peabody Conservatory, founded in 1857, is located north of the harbor in picturesque Mount Vernon Square, while the Maryland Institute College of Art boasts alumnae such as Jeff Koons. Of MICA's BFA graduates who take jobs immediately after graduation, nearly 90 percent work in an art-related field.

The region is subject to frequent changes in weather, although the mountains to the west, and the Chesapeake Bay and ocean to the east produce a more equable climate compared with other locations farther inland at the same latitude. In the summer, the area is under the influence of the high-pressure system commonly known as the "Bermuda High" which brings warm, humid air. In winter, snow is frequently mixed with rain and sleet, but seldom remains on the ground for more than a few days. Severe thunderstorms are generally confined to summer and fall, and hurricanes during the same period are possible.

Rankings

Business/Finance Rankings

- According to *Business Insider*, the Baltimore metro area is a prime place to run a startup or move an existing business to. The area ranked #15. More than 300 metro areas were analyzed for factors that were of top concern to new business owners. Data was based on the 2019 U.S. Census Bureau American Community Survey, statistics from the CDC, Bureau of Labor Statistics employment report, and University of Chicago analysis. Criteria: business formations; percentage of vaccinated population; percentage of households with internet subscriptions; median household income; and share of work that can be done from home. *www.businessinsider.com, "The 20 Best Cities for Starting a Business in 2022 Include Baltimore, Boulder, and Boston," January 5, 2022*

- Based on metro area social media reviews, the employment opinion group Glassdoor surveyed 50 of the most populous U.S. metro areas and equally weighed cost of living, hiring opportunity, and job satisfaction to compose a list of "25 Best Cities for Jobs." Median pay and home value, and number of active job openings were also factored in. The Baltimore metro area was ranked #18 in overall job satisfaction. *www.glassdoor.com, "Best Cities for Jobs," February 25, 2020*

- The Brookings Institution ranked the nation's largest cities based on income inequality. Baltimore was ranked #16 (#1 = greatest inequality). Criteria: the "95/20 ratio," a figure representing the income at which a household earns more than 95 percent of all other households, divided by the income at which a household earns more than only 20 percent of all other households. *Brookings Institution, "Household Income Inequality, Largest Cities of 97 Large U.S. Metro Areas, 2014-2016," February 5, 2018*

- The Brookings Institution ranked the 100 largest metro areas in the U.S. based on income inequality. Baltimore was ranked #45 (#1 = greatest inequality). Criteria: the "95/20 ratio," a figure representing the income at which a household earns more than 95 percent of all other households, divided by the income at which a household earns more than only 20 percent of all other households. *Brookings Institution, "Household Income Inequality, 100 Largest U.S. Metro Areas, 2014-2016," February 5, 2018*

- Payscale.com ranked the 32 largest metro areas in terms of wage growth. The Baltimore metro area ranked #24. Criteria: quarterly changes in private industry employee and education professional wage growth from the previous year. *PayScale, "Wage Trends by Metro Area-1st Quarter," April 20, 2023*

- The Baltimore metro area was identified as one of the most debt-ridden places in America by the finance site Credit.com. The metro area was ranked #6. Criteria: residents' average credit card debt as well as median income. *Credit.com, "25 Cities With the Most Credit Card Debt," February 28, 2018*

- The Baltimore metro area appeared on the Milken Institute "2022 Best Performing Cities" list. Rank: #106 out of 200 large metro areas (population over 250,000). Criteria: job growth; wage and salary growth; high-tech output growth; housing affordability; household broadband access. *Milken Institute, "Best-Performing Cities 2022," March 28, 2022*

- *Forbes* ranked the 200 most populous metro areas to determine the nation's "Best Places for Business and Careers." The Baltimore metro area was ranked #87. Criteria: costs (business and living); job growth (past and projected); income growth; quality of life; educational attainment (college and high school); projected economic growth; cultural and leisure opportunities; workplace tolerance laws; net migration patterns. *Forbes, "The Best Places for Business and Careers 2019: Seattle Still On Top," October 30, 2019*

Children/Family Rankings

- Baltimore was selected as one of the most playful cities in the U.S. by KaBOOM! The organization's Playful City USA initiative honors cities and towns across the nation that have made their communities more playable. Criteria: pledging to integrate play as a solution to challenges in their communities; making it easy for children to get active and balanced play; creating more family-friendly and innovative communities as a result. *KaBOOM! National Campaign for Play, "2017 Playful City USA Communities"*

Culture/Performing Arts Rankings

- Baltimore was selected as one of the 25 best cities for moviemakers in North America. Great film cities are places where filmmaking dreams can come true, that offer more creative space, lower costs, and great outdoor locations. NYC & LA were intentionally excluded. Criteria: longstanding reputations as film-friendly communities; film community and culture; affordability; and quality of life. The city was ranked #14. *MovieMaker Magazine, "Best Places to Live and Work as a Moviemaker, 2023," January 18, 2023*

Education Rankings

- Personal finance website *WalletHub* analyzed the 150 largest U.S. metropolitan statistical areas to determine where the most educated Americans are putting their degrees to work. Criteria: education levels; percentage of workers with degrees; education quality and attainment gap; public school quality rankings; quality and enrollment of each metro area's universities. Baltimore was ranked #23 (#1 = most educated city). *www.WalletHub.com, "Most & Least Educated Cities in America," July 18, 2022*

- Baltimore was selected as one of the best cities for post grads by *Rent.com*. The city ranked among the top 10. Criteria: jobs per capita; unemployment rate; mean annual income; cost of living; rental inventory. *Rent.com, "Best Cities for College Grads," December 11, 2018*

- Baltimore was selected as one of America's most literate cities. The city ranked #23 out of the 84 largest U.S. cities. Criteria: number of booksellers; library resources; Internet resources; educational attainment; periodical publishing resources; newspaper circulation. *Central Connecticut State University, "America's Most Literate Cities, 2018," February 2019*

Health/Fitness Rankings

- For each of the 100 largest cities in the United States, the American Fitness Index®, compiled in partnership between the American College of Sports Medicine and the Elevance Health Foundation, evaluated community infrastructure and 34 health behaviors including preventive health, levels of chronic disease conditions, food insecurity, sleep quality, pedestrian safety, air quality, and community/environment resources that support physical activity. Baltimore ranked #67 for "community fitness." *americanfitnessindex.org, "2022 ACSM American Fitness Index Summary Report," July 12, 2022*

- The Baltimore metro area was identified as one of the worst cities for bed bugs in America by pest control company Orkin. The area ranked #8 out of 50 based on the number of bed bug treatments Orkin performed from December 2021 to November 2022. *Orkin, "The Windy City Can't Blow Bed Bugs Away: Chicago Ranks #1 For Third Consecutive Year On Orkin's Bed Bug Cities List," January 9, 2023*

- Baltimore was identified as a "2022 Spring Allergy Capital." The area ranked #77 out of 100. Three groups of factors were used to identify the most challenging cities for people with allergies during the spring season: annual spring pollen scores; over the counter allergy medicine use; number of board-certified allergy specialists. *Asthma and Allergy Foundation of America, "Spring Allergy Capitals 2022," March 2, 2022*

- Baltimore was identified as a "2022 Fall Allergy Capital." The area ranked #81 out of 100. Three groups of factors were used to identify the most challenging cities for people with allergies during the fall season: annual fall pollen scores; over the counter allergy medicine use; number of board-certified allergy specialists. *Asthma and Allergy Foundation of America, "Fall Allergy Capitals 2022," March 2, 2022*

- Baltimore was identified as a "2022 Asthma Capital." The area ranked #10 out of the nation's 100 largest metropolitan areas. Criteria: estimated asthma prevalence; asthma-related mortality; and ER visits due to asthma. Risk factors analyzed but not factored in the rankings: annual pollen score; annual air quality; public smoking laws; access to board-certified asthma specialists; rescue and controller medication use; uninsured rate; poverty rate. *Asthma and Allergy Foundation of America, "Asthma Capitals 2022: The Most Challenging Places to Live With Asthma," September 14, 2022*

Real Estate Rankings

- *WalletHub* compared the most populated U.S. cities to determine which had the best markets for real estate agents. Baltimore ranked #145 where demand was high and pay was the best. Criteria: sales per agent; annual median wage for real-estate agents; monthly average starting salary for real estate agents; real estate job density and competition; unemployment rate; home turnover rate; housing-market health index; and other relevant metrics. *www.WalletHub.com, "2021 Best Places to Be a Real Estate Agent," May 12, 2021*

- Baltimore was ranked #58 out of 235 metro areas in terms of housing affordability in 2022 by the National Association of Home Builders (#1 = most affordable). Criteria: the share of homes sold in that area affordable to a family earning the local median income, based on standard mortgage underwriting criteria. *National Association of Home Builders®, NAHB-Wells Fargo Housing Opportunity Index, 4th Quarter 2022*

Safety Rankings

- Allstate ranked the 200 largest cities in America in terms of driver safety. Baltimore ranked #200. Criteria: internal property damage claims over a two-year period from January 2016 to December 2017. The report helps increase the importance of safety and awareness behind the wheel. *Allstate, "Allstate America's Best Drivers Report, 2019" June 24, 2019*

- Baltimore was identified as one of the most dangerous cities in America by NeighborhoodScout. The city ranked #18 out of 100 (#1 = most dangerous). Criteria: number of violent crimes per 1,000 residents. The editors evaluated cities with 25,000 or more residents. *NeighborhoodScout.com, "2023 Top 100 Most Dangerous Cities in the U.S.," January 12, 2023*

- The National Insurance Crime Bureau ranked 390 metro areas in the U.S. in terms of per capita rates of vehicle theft. The Baltimore metro area ranked #156 (#1 = highest rate). Criteria: number of vehicle theft offenses per 100,000 inhabitants in 2021. *National Insurance Crime Bureau, "Hot Spots 2021," September 1, 2022*

Seniors/Retirement Rankings

- From its Best Cities for Successful Aging indexes, the Milken Institute generated rankings for metropolitan areas, weighing data in nine categories—health care, wellness, living arrangements, transportation and convenience, financial characteristics, education, employment, community engagement, and overall livability. The Baltimore metro area was ranked #67 overall in the large metro area category. *Milken Institute, "Best Cities for Successful Aging, 2017" March 14, 2017*

Transportation Rankings

- Business Insider presented an AllTransit Performance Score ranking of public transportation in major U.S. cities and towns, with populations over 250,000, in which Baltimore earned the #9-ranked "Transit Score," awarded for frequency of service, access to jobs, quality and number of stops, and affordability. *www.businessinsider.com, "The 17 Major U.S. Cities with the Best Public Transportation," April 17, 2018*

- The business website *24/7 Wall St.* reviewed U.S. Census data to identify the 25 cities where the largest share of households do not own a vehicle. Baltimore held the #9 position. *247wallst.com, "Cities Where No One Wants to Drive," January 12, 2020*

- According to the INRIX "2022 Global Traffic Scorecard," Baltimore was identified as one of the most congested metro areas in the U.S. The area ranked #15 out of 25. Criteria: average annual time spent in traffic and average cost of congestion per motorist. *Inrix.com, "Return to Work, Higher Gas Prices & Inflation Drove Americans to Spend Hundreds More in Time and Money Commuting," January 10, 2023*

Women/Minorities Rankings

- Personal finance website *WalletHub* compared more than 180 U.S. cities across two key dimensions, "Hispanic Business-Friendliness" and "Hispanic Purchasing Power," to arrive at the most favorable conditions for Hispanic entrepreneurs. Baltimore was ranked #116 out of 182. Criteria includes: share of Hispanic-Owned Businesses; Hispanic entrepreneurship rate to median annual income of Hispanics; Small Business-Friendliness score; cost of living; and number of Hispanics with at least a bachelor's degree. *WalletHub.com, "2019's Best Cities for Hispanic Entrepreneurs," May 1, 2019*

Miscellaneous Rankings

- The watchdog site, Charity Navigator, conducted a study of charities in major markets both to analyze statistical differences in their financial, accountability, and transparency practices and to track year-to-year variations in individual philanthropic communities. The Baltimore metro area was ranked #21 among the 30 metro markets in the rating category of Overall Score. *www.charitynavigator.org, "2017 Metro Market Study," May 1, 2017*

- *WalletHub* compared the 150 most populated U.S. cities to determine their operating efficiency. A "Quality of Services" score was constructed for each city and then divided by the total budget per capita to reveal which were managed the best. Baltimore ranked #130. Criteria: financial stability; economy; education; safety; health; infrastructure and pollution. *www.WalletHub.com, "2022's Best-& Worst-Run Cities in America," June 21, 2022*

- The National Alliance to End Homelessness listed the 25 most populous metro areas with the highest rate of homelessness. The Baltimore metro area had a high rate of homelessness. Criteria: number of homeless people per 10,000 population in 2016. *National Alliance to End Homelessness, "Homelessness in the 25 Most Populous U.S. Metro Areas," September 1, 2017*

Business Environment

DEMOGRAPHICS

Population Growth

Area	1990 Census	2000 Census	2010 Census	2020 Census	Population Growth (%) 1990-2020	Population Growth (%) 2010-2020
City	736,014	651,154	620,961	585,708	-20.4	-5.7
MSA[1]	2,382,172	2,552,994	2,710,489	2,844,510	19.4	4.9
U.S.	248,709,873	281,421,906	308,745,538	331,449,281	33.3	7.4

Note: (1) Figures cover the Baltimore-Columbia-Towson, MD Metropolitan Statistical Area
Source: U.S. Census Bureau, 1990 Census, 2000 Census, 2010 Census, 2020 Census

Race

Area	White Alone[2] (%)	Black Alone[2] (%)	Asian Alone[2] (%)	AIAN[3] Alone[2] (%)	NHOPI[4] Alone[2] (%)	Other Race Alone[2] (%)	Two or More Races (%)
City	27.8	57.8	3.6	0.4	0.0	4.8	5.5
MSA[1]	53.9	28.5	6.3	0.4	0.0	4.0	6.8
U.S.	61.6	12.4	6.0	1.1	0.2	8.4	10.2

Note: (1) Figures cover the Baltimore-Columbia-Towson, MD Metropolitan Statistical Area; (2) Alone is defined as not being in combination with one or more other races; (3) American Indian and Alaska Native; (4) Native Hawaiian and Other Pacific Islander
Source: U.S. Census Bureau, 2020 Census

Hispanic or Latino Origin

Area	Total (%)	Mexican (%)	Puerto Rican (%)	Cuban (%)	Other (%)
City	5.6	1.1	0.8	0.3	3.3
MSA[1]	6.2	1.4	1.0	0.2	3.6
U.S.	18.4	11.2	1.8	0.7	4.7

Note: Persons of Hispanic or Latino origin can be of any race; (1) Figures cover the Baltimore-Columbia-Towson, MD Metropolitan Statistical Area
Source: U.S. Census Bureau, 2017-2021 American Community Survey 5-Year Estimates

Age

Area	Under Age 5	Age 5–19	Age 20–34	Age 35–44	Age 45–54	Age 55–64	Age 65–74	Age 75–84	Age 85+	Median Age
City	5.5	16.6	27.0	13.1	10.7	12.6	8.9	4.0	1.6	35.5
MSA[1]	5.6	18.8	20.5	13.0	12.4	13.6	9.6	4.7	1.9	38.6
U.S.	5.6	19.2	20.2	12.7	12.4	13.1	10.0	4.9	1.9	38.8

Note: (1) Figures cover the Baltimore-Columbia-Towson, MD Metropolitan Statistical Area
Source: U.S. Census Bureau, 2020 Census

Disability by Age

Area	All Ages	Under 18 Years Old	18 to 64 Years Old	65 Years and Over
City	15.9	6.0	14.1	39.0
MSA[1]	11.8	4.6	9.7	30.8
U.S.	12.6	4.4	10.3	33.4

Note: Figures show percent of the civilian noninstitutionalized population that reported having a disability. Disability status is determined from six types of difficulty: vision, hearing, cognitive, ambulatory, self-care, and independent living. For children under 5 years old, hearing and vision difficulty are used to determine disability status. For children between the ages of 5 and 14, disability status is determined from hearing, vision, cognitive, ambulatory, and self-care difficulties. For people aged 15 years and older, they are considered to have a disability if they have difficulty with any one of the six difficulty types; Note: (1) Figures cover the Baltimore-Columbia-Towson, MD Metropolitan Statistical Area
Source: U.S. Census Bureau, 2017-2021 American Community Survey 5-Year Estimates

Ancestry

Area	German	Irish	English	American	Italian	Polish	French[2]	Scottish	Dutch
City	6.1	5.7	3.3	2.8	3.1	2.3	0.9	0.7	0.3
MSA[1]	14.3	11.3	8.0	4.6	5.9	3.8	1.4	1.5	0.6
U.S.	12.8	9.6	8.1	5.7	5.0	2.7	2.2	1.6	1.1

Note: Figures are the percentage of the total population reporting a particular ancestry. The nine most commonly reported ancestries in the U.S. are shown. Figures include multiple ancestries (e.g. if a person reported being Irish and Italian, they were included in both columns); (1) Figures cover the Baltimore-Columbia-Towson, MD Metropolitan Statistical Area; (2) Excludes Basque
Source: U.S. Census Bureau, 2017-2021 American Community Survey 5-Year Estimates

Foreign-born Population

Area	Any Foreign Country	Asia	Mexico	Europe	Caribbean	Central America[2]	South America	Africa	Canada
City	8.1	2.2	0.3	0.9	1.3	1.0	0.4	1.9	0.1
MSA[1]	10.5	4.3	0.4	1.3	0.8	1.1	0.5	1.9	0.1
U.S.	13.6	4.2	3.3	1.5	1.4	1.1	1.1	0.8	0.2

Note: (1) Figures cover the Baltimore-Columbia-Towson, MD Metropolitan Statistical Area; (2) Excludes Mexico.
Source: U.S. Census Bureau, 2017-2021 American Community Survey 5-Year Estimates

Household Size

Area	Persons in Household (%)							Average Household Size
	One	Two	Three	Four	Five	Six	Seven or More	
City	41.5	29.9	13.9	8.2	3.8	1.6	1.2	2.30
MSA[1]	29.2	32.7	16.2	13.0	5.7	2.1	1.2	2.60
U.S.	28.1	33.8	15.5	12.9	6.0	2.3	1.4	2.60

Note: (1) Figures cover the Baltimore-Columbia-Towson, MD Metropolitan Statistical Area
Source: U.S. Census Bureau, 2017-2021 American Community Survey 5-Year Estimates

Household Relationships

Area	House-holder	Opposite-sex Spouse	Same-sex Spouse	Opposite-sex Unmarried Partner	Same-sex Unmarried Partner	Child[2]	Grand-child	Other Relatives	Non-relatives
City	42.9	9.6	0.3	3.3	0.3	24.9	3.7	5.8	6.1
MSA[1]	38.7	16.8	0.2	2.4	0.2	28.7	2.5	4.8	3.5
U.S.	38.3	17.5	0.2	2.5	0.2	28.3	2.4	4.8	3.4

Note: Figures are percent of the total population; (1) Figures cover the Baltimore-Columbia-Towson, MD Metropolitan Statistical Area; (2) Includes biological, adopted, and stepchildren of the householder
Source: U.S. Census Bureau, 2020 Census

Gender

Area	Males	Females	Males per 100 Females
City	274,635	311,073	88.3
MSA[1]	1,365,439	1,479,071	92.3
U.S.	162,685,811	168,763,470	96.4

Note: (1) Figures cover the Baltimore-Columbia-Towson, MD Metropolitan Statistical Area
Source: U.S. Census Bureau, 2020 Census

Marital Status

Area	Never Married	Now Married[2]	Separated	Widowed	Divorced
City	52.3	27.2	3.1	6.0	11.4
MSA[1]	36.0	46.3	1.9	5.7	10.0
U.S.	33.8	48.0	1.8	5.6	10.8

Note: Figures are percentages and cover the population 15 years of age and older; (1) Figures cover the Baltimore-Columbia-Towson, MD Metropolitan Statistical Area; (2) Excludes separated
Source: U.S. Census Bureau, 2017-2021 American Community Survey 5-Year Estimates

Religious Groups by Family

Area	Catholic	Baptist	Methodist	LDS[2]	Pentecostal	Lutheran	Islam	Adventist	Other
MSA[1]	12.4	3.2	4.4	0.6	1.2	1.4	3.3	1.2	11.7
U.S.	18.7	7.3	3.0	2.0	1.8	1.7	1.3	1.3	11.6

Note: Figures are the number of adherents as a percentage of the total population and cover the eight largest religious groups in the U.S; (1) Figures cover the Baltimore-Columbia-Towson, MD Metropolitan Statistical Area; (2) Church of Jesus Christ of Latter-day Saints
Sources: 2020 U.S. Religion Census, Association of Statisticians of American Religious Bodies; The Association of Religion Data Archives (ARDA)

Religious Groups by Tradition

Area	Catholic	Evangelical Protestant	Mainline Protestant	Black Protestant	Islam	Judaism	Hinduism	Orthodox	Buddhism
MSA[1]	12.4	10.6	5.9	3.3	3.3	1.7	0.1	0.5	0.1
U.S.	18.7	16.5	5.2	2.3	1.3	0.6	0.4	0.4	0.3

Note: Figures are the number of adherents as a percentage of the total population; (1) Figures cover the Baltimore-Columbia-Towson, MD Metropolitan Statistical Area
Sources: 2020 U.S. Religion Census, Association of Statisticians of American Religious Bodies; The Association of Religion Data Archives (ARDA)

ECONOMY

Gross Metropolitan Product

Area	2020	2021	2022	2023	Rank[2]
MSA[1]	205.8	219.9	238.6	255.0	19

Note: Figures are in billions of dollars; (1) Figures cover the Baltimore-Columbia-Towson, MD Metropolitan Statistical Area; (2) Rank is based on 2021 data and ranges from 1 to 381
Source: U.S. Conference of Mayors, U.S. Metro Economies: U.S. Metros Compared to Global and State Economies, June 2022

Economic Growth

Area	2018-20 (%)	2021 (%)	2022 (%)	2023 (%)	Rank[2]
MSA[1]	-2.0	3.2	2.7	3.5	284
U.S.	-0.6	5.7	3.1	2.9	—

Note: Figures are real gross metropolitan product (GMP) growth rates and represent average annual percent change; (1) Figures cover the Baltimore-Columbia-Towson, MD Metropolitan Statistical Area; (2) Rank is based on 2020 2-year average annual percent change and ranges from 1 to 381
Source: U.S. Conference of Mayors, U.S. Metro Economies: U.S. Metros Compared to Global and State Economies, June 2022

Metropolitan Area Exports

Area	2016	2017	2018	2019	2020	2021	Rank[2]
MSA[1]	5,288.6	4,674.3	6,039.2	7,081.8	6,084.6	8,200.6	43

Note: Figures are in millions of dollars; (1) Figures cover the Baltimore-Columbia-Towson, MD Metropolitan Statistical Area; (2) Rank is based on 2021 data and ranges from 1 to 388
Source: U.S. Department of Commerce, International Trade Administration, Office of Trade and Economic Analysis, Industry and Analysis, Exports by Metropolitan Area, data extracted March 16, 2023

Building Permits

Area	Single-Family			Multi-Family			Total		
	2021	2022	Pct. Chg.	2021	2022	Pct. Chg.	2021	2022	Pct. Chg.
City	191	118	-38.2	1,366	1,539	12.7	1,557	1,657	6.4
MSA[1]	4,783	2,832	-40.8	3,051	3,756	23.1	7,834	6,588	-15.9
U.S.	1,115,400	975,600	-12.5	621,600	689,500	10.9	1,737,000	1,665,100	-4.1

Note: (1) Figures cover the Baltimore-Columbia-Towson, MD Metropolitan Statistical Area; Figures represent new, privately-owned housing units authorized (unadjusted data); All permit data are based on estimates with imputation
Source: U.S. Census Bureau, Manufacturing, Mining, and Construction Statistics, Building Permits, 2021, 2022

Bankruptcy Filings

Area	Business Filings			Nonbusiness Filings		
	2021	2022	% Chg.	2021	2022	% Chg.
Baltimore city County	18	17	-5.6	1,323	1,167	-11.8
U.S.	14,347	13,481	-6.0	399,269	374,240	-6.3

Note: Business filings include Chapter 7, Chapter 9, Chapter 11, Chapter 12, Chapter 13, Chapter 15, and Section 304; Nonbusiness filings include Chapter 7, Chapter 11, and Chapter 13
Source: Administrative Office of the U.S. Courts, Business and Nonbusiness Bankruptcy, County Cases Commenced by Chapter of the Bankruptcy Code, During the 12-Month Period Ending December 31, 2021 and Business and Nonbusiness Bankruptcy, County Cases Commenced by Chapter of the Bankruptcy Code, During the 12-Month Period Ending December 31, 2022

Housing Vacancy Rates

Area	Gross Vacancy Rate[2] (%)			Year-Round Vacancy Rate[3] (%)			Rental Vacancy Rate[4] (%)			Homeowner Vacancy Rate[5] (%)		
	2020	2021	2022	2020	2021	2022	2020	2021	2022	2020	2021	2022
MSA[1]	7.2	6.8	5.9	7.0	6.6	5.7	7.0	6.1	5.3	1.0	1.0	0.5
U.S.	10.6	10.8	10.5	8.2	8.4	8.2	6.3	6.1	5.8	1.0	0.9	0.8

Note: (1) Figures cover the Baltimore-Columbia-Towson, MD Metropolitan Statistical Area; (2) The percentage of the total housing inventory that is vacant; (3) The percentage of the housing inventory (excluding seasonal units) that is year-round vacant; (4) The percentage of rental inventory that is vacant for rent; (5) The percentage of homeowner inventory that is vacant for sale
Source: U.S. Census Bureau, Housing Vacancies and Homeownership Annual Statistics: 2020, 2021, 2022

INCOME

Income

Area	Per Capita ($)	Median Household ($)	Average Household ($)
City	34,378	54,124	79,399
MSA[1]	45,226	87,513	115,291
U.S.	37,638	69,021	97,196

Note: (1) Figures cover the Baltimore-Columbia-Towson, MD Metropolitan Statistical Area
Source: U.S. Census Bureau, 2017-2021 American Community Survey 5-Year Estimates

Household Income Distribution

Area	Percent of Households Earning							
	Under $15,000	$15,000 -$24,999	$25,000 -$34,999	$35,000 -$49,999	$50,000 -$74,999	$75,000 -$99,999	$100,000 -$149,999	$150,000 and up
City	16.6	9.1	8.9	12.2	17.1	10.8	12.7	12.8
MSA[1]	8.0	5.5	5.9	9.3	14.8	12.5	18.8	25.1
U.S.	9.4	7.8	8.2	11.4	16.8	12.8	16.3	17.3

Note: (1) Figures cover the Baltimore-Columbia-Towson, MD Metropolitan Statistical Area
Source: U.S. Census Bureau, 2017-2021 American Community Survey 5-Year Estimates

Poverty Rate

Area	All Ages	Under 18 Years Old	18 to 64 Years Old	65 Years and Over
City	20.3	27.9	18.2	18.6
MSA[1]	9.8	12.7	9.0	8.8
U.S.	12.6	17.0	11.8	9.6

Note: Figures are percentage of people whose income during the past 12 months was below the poverty level;
(1) Figures cover the Baltimore-Columbia-Towson, MD Metropolitan Statistical Area
Source: U.S. Census Bureau, 2017-2021 American Community Survey 5-Year Estimates

EMPLOYMENT

Labor Force and Employment

Area	Civilian Labor Force			Workers Employed		
	Dec. 2021	Dec. 2022	% Chg.	Dec. 2021	Dec. 2022	% Chg.
City	280,450	278,592	-0.7	262,676	266,256	1.4
MSA[1]	1,501,247	1,502,740	0.1	1,434,164	1,455,751	1.5
U.S.	161,696,000	164,224,000	1.6	155,732,000	158,872,000	2.0

Note: Data is not seasonally adjusted and covers workers 16 years of age and older; (1) Figures cover the Baltimore-Columbia-Towson, MD Metropolitan Statistical Area
Source: Bureau of Labor Statistics, Local Area Unemployment Statistics

Unemployment Rate

Area	2022											
	Jan.	Feb.	Mar.	Apr.	May	Jun.	Jul.	Aug.	Sep.	Oct.	Nov.	Dec.
City	6.3	6.1	5.8	4.9	5.1	6.1	5.6	5.9	5.1	5.6	5.0	4.4
MSA[1]	4.2	4.3	4.2	3.3	3.6	4.6	4.1	4.3	3.7	4.0	3.5	3.1
U.S.	4.4	4.1	3.8	3.3	3.4	3.8	3.8	3.8	3.3	3.4	3.4	3.3

Note: Data is not seasonally adjusted and covers workers 16 years of age and older; (1) Figures cover the Baltimore-Columbia-Towson, MD Metropolitan Statistical Area
Source: Bureau of Labor Statistics, Local Area Unemployment Statistics

Average Wages

Occupation	$/Hr.	Occupation	$/Hr.
Accountants and Auditors	42.20	Maintenance and Repair Workers	23.34
Automotive Mechanics	24.80	Marketing Managers	69.41
Bookkeepers	24.11	Network and Computer Systems Admin.	52.41
Carpenters	26.91	Nurses, Licensed Practical	28.83
Cashiers	14.41	Nurses, Registered	43.03
Computer Programmers	50.01	Nursing Assistants	17.71
Computer Systems Analysts	51.61	Office Clerks, General	19.28
Computer User Support Specialists	28.42	Physical Therapists	45.91
Construction Laborers	20.10	Physicians	120.21
Cooks, Restaurant	16.72	Plumbers, Pipefitters and Steamfitters	28.83
Customer Service Representatives	20.48	Police and Sheriff's Patrol Officers	34.65
Dentists	78.23	Postal Service Mail Carriers	27.22
Electricians	31.44	Real Estate Sales Agents	32.50
Engineers, Electrical	56.06	Retail Salespersons	15.99
Fast Food and Counter Workers	14.31	Sales Representatives, Technical/Scientific	50.13
Financial Managers	76.62	Secretaries, Exc. Legal/Medical/Executive	21.48
First-Line Supervisors of Office Workers	32.11	Security Guards	20.09
General and Operations Managers	55.22	Surgeons	162.71
Hairdressers/Cosmetologists	19.90	Teacher Assistants, Exc. Postsecondary*	19.37
Home Health and Personal Care Aides	15.32	Teachers, Secondary School, Exc. Sp. Ed.*	34.31
Janitors and Cleaners	16.24	Telemarketers	18.80
Landscaping/Groundskeeping Workers	18.68	Truck Drivers, Heavy/Tractor-Trailer	26.63
Lawyers	77.46	Truck Drivers, Light/Delivery Services	22.04
Maids and Housekeeping Cleaners	14.74	Waiters and Waitresses	17.63

Note: Wage data covers the Baltimore-Columbia-Towson, MD Metropolitan Statistical Area; (*) Hourly wages were calculated from annual wage data based on a 40 hour work week; n/a not available.
Source: Bureau of Labor Statistics, Metro Area Occupational Employment & Wage Estimates, May 2022

Employment by Industry

Sector	MSA[1]		U.S.
	Number of Employees	Percent of Total	Percent of Total
Construction, Mining, and Logging	84,700	6.0	5.4
Private Education and Health Services	269,400	19.1	16.1
Financial Activities	76,800	5.5	5.9
Government	225,000	16.0	14.5
Information	16,200	1.1	2.0
Leisure and Hospitality	121,300	8.6	10.3
Manufacturing	59,000	4.2	8.4
Other Services	48,400	3.4	3.7
Professional and Business Services	249,000	17.7	14.7
Retail Trade	126,400	9.0	10.2
Transportation, Warehousing, and Utilities	81,300	5.8	4.9
Wholesale Trade	51,500	3.7	3.9

Note: Figures are non-farm employment as of December 2022. Figures are not seasonally adjusted and include workers 16 years of age and older; (1) Figures cover the Baltimore-Columbia-Towson, MD Metropolitan Statistical Area
Source: Bureau of Labor Statistics, Current Employment Statistics, Employment, Hours, and Earnings

Employment by Occupation

Occupation Classification	City (%)	MSA[1] (%)	U.S. (%)
Management, Business, Science, and Arts	46.0	49.2	40.3
Natural Resources, Construction, and Maintenance	5.0	6.6	8.7
Production, Transportation, and Material Moving	11.4	9.3	13.1
Sales and Office	19.0	19.9	20.9
Service	18.6	15.0	17.0

Note: Figures cover employed civilians 16 years of age and older; (1) Figures cover the Baltimore-Columbia-Towson, MD Metropolitan Statistical Area
Source: U.S. Census Bureau, 2017-2021 American Community Survey 5-Year Estimates

Occupations with Greatest Projected Employment Growth: 2022 – 2024

Occupation[1]	2022 Employment	2024 Projected Employment	Numeric Employment Change	Percent Employment Change
Software Developers and Software Quality Assurance Analysts and Testers	58,780	61,600	2,820	4.8
Stockers and Order Fillers	48,230	50,540	2,310	4.8
Automotive Service Technicians and Mechanics	15,920	18,020	2,100	13.2
Heavy and Tractor-Trailer Truck Drivers	28,670	30,170	1,500	5.2
Cleaners of Vehicles and Equipment	8,600	10,010	1,410	16.4
Laborers and Freight, Stock, and Material Movers, Hand	34,790	36,120	1,330	3.8
Project Management Specialists and Business Operations Specialists, All Other	76,290	77,530	1,240	1.6
Maintenance and Repair Workers, General	24,540	25,510	970	4.0
Industrial Truck and Tractor Operators	11,690	12,650	960	8.2
First-Line Supervisors of Mechanics, Installers, and Repairers	11,680	12,580	900	7.7

Note: Projections cover Maryland; (1) Sorted by numeric employment change
Source: www.projectionscentral.com, State Occupational Projections, 2022–2024 Short-Term Projections

Fastest-Growing Occupations: 2022 – 2024

Occupation[1]	2022 Employment	2024 Projected Employment	Numeric Employment Change	Percent Employment Change
Upholsterers	200	260	60	30.0
Home Appliance Repairers	730	920	190	26.0
Automotive Glass Installers and Repairers	370	460	90	24.3
Automotive Body and Related Repairers	3,960	4,840	880	22.2
Coating, Painting, and Spraying Machine Setters, Operators, and Tenders (SOC 2018)	1,260	1,500	240	19.0
Automotive and Watercraft Service Attendants	2,770	3,290	520	18.8
Cleaners of Vehicles and Equipment	8,600	10,010	1,410	16.4
Motorboat Mechanics and Service Technicians	1,110	1,270	160	14.4
Automotive Service Technicians and Mechanics	15,920	18,020	2,100	13.2
Bus and Truck Mechanics and Diesel Engine Specialists	5,350	6,040	690	12.9

Note: Projections cover Maryland; (1) Sorted by percent employment change and excludes occupations with numeric employment change less than 50
Source: www.projectionscentral.com, State Occupational Projections, 2022–2024 Short-Term Projections

CITY FINANCES

City Government Finances

Component	2020 ($000)	2020 ($ per capita)
Total Revenues	3,941,794	6,642
Total Expenditures	4,463,406	7,521
Debt Outstanding	812,506	1,369
Cash and Securities[1]	44,217	75

Note: (1) Cash and security holdings of a government at the close of its fiscal year, including those of its dependent agencies, utilities, and liquor stores.
Source: U.S. Census Bureau, State & Local Government Finances 2020

City Government Revenue by Source

Source	2020 ($000)	2020 ($ per capita)	2020 (%)
General Revenue			
From Federal Government	29,232	49	0.7
From State Government	1,401,256	2,361	35.5
From Local Governments	20,064	34	0.5
Taxes			
Property	885,436	1,492	22.5
Sales and Gross Receipts	97,450	164	2.5
Personal Income	396,540	668	10.1
Corporate Income	0	0	0.0
Motor Vehicle License	0	0	0.0
Other Taxes	116,994	197	3.0
Current Charges	461,599	778	11.7
Liquor Store	0	0	0.0
Utility	216,396	365	5.5

Source: U.S. Census Bureau, State & Local Government Finances 2020

City Government Expenditures by Function

Function	2020 ($000)	2020 ($ per capita)	2020 (%)
General Direct Expenditures			
Air Transportation	0	0	0.0
Corrections	0	0	0.0
Education	1,549,330	2,610	34.7
Employment Security Administration	0	0	0.0
Financial Administration	28,363	47	0.6
Fire Protection	257,441	433	5.8
General Public Buildings	0	0	0.0
Governmental Administration, Other	229,924	387	5.2
Health	171,080	288	3.8
Highways	99,948	168	2.2
Hospitals	0	0	0.0
Housing and Community Development	67,316	113	1.5
Interest on General Debt	94,374	159	2.1
Judicial and Legal	61,596	103	1.4
Libraries	24,733	41	0.6
Parking	7,101	12	0.2
Parks and Recreation	49,080	82	1.1
Police Protection	536,087	903	12.0
Public Welfare	0	0	0.0
Sewerage	451,817	761	10.1
Solid Waste Management	81,719	137	1.8
Veterans' Services	0	0	0.0
Liquor Store	0	0	0.0
Utility	329,687	555	7.4

Source: U.S. Census Bureau, State & Local Government Finances 2020

TAXES

State Corporate Income Tax Rates

State	Tax Rate (%)	Income Brackets ($)	Num. of Brackets	Financial Institution Tax Rate (%)[a]	Federal Income Tax Ded.
Maryland	8.25	Flat rate	1	8.25	No

Note: Tax rates as of January 1, 2023; (a) Rates listed are the corporate income tax rate applied to financial institutions or excise taxes based on income. Some states have other taxes based upon the value of deposits or shares.
Source: Federation of Tax Administrators, State Corporate Income Tax Rates, January 1, 2023

State Individual Income Tax Rates

State	Tax Rate (%)	Income Brackets ($)	Personal Exemptions ($)			Standard Ded. ($)	
			Single	Married	Depend.	Single	Married
Maryland	2.0 - 5.75	1,000 - 250,000 (l)	3,200	6,400	3,200	2,350	4,700 (aa)

Note: Tax rates as of January 1, 2023; Local- and county-level taxes are not included; Federal income tax is not deductible on state income tax returns; (l) The income brackets reported for Maryland are for single individuals. For married couples filing jointly, the same tax rates apply to income brackets ranging from $1,000, to $300,000; (aa) Standard deduction amounts reported are maximums, Maryland standard deduction is 15% of AGI.
Source: Federation of Tax Administrators, State Individual Income Tax Rates, January 1, 2023

Various State Sales and Excise Tax Rates

State	State Sales Tax (%)	Gasoline[1] ($/gal.)	Cigarette[2] ($/pack)	Spirits[3] ($/gal.)	Wine[4] ($/gal.)	Beer[5] ($/gal.)	Recreational Marijuana (%)
Maryland	6	0.427	3.75	5.46	1.64	0.60	Not legal

Note: All tax rates as of January 1, 2023; (1) The American Petroleum Institute has developed a methodology for determining the average tax rate on a gallon of fuel. Rates may include any of the following: excise taxes, environmental fees, storage tank fees, other fees or taxes, general sales tax, and local taxes; (2) The federal excise tax of $1.0066 per pack and local taxes are not included; (3) Rates are those applicable to off-premise sales of 40% alcohol by volume (a.b.v.) distilled spirits in 750ml containers. Local excise taxes are excluded; (4) Rates are those applicable to off-premise sales of 11% a.b.v. non-carbonated wine in 750ml containers; (5) Rates are those applicable to off-premise sales of 4.7% a.b.v. beer in 12 ounce containers.
Source: Tax Foundation, 2023 Facts & Figures: How Does Your State Compare?

State Business Tax Climate Index Rankings

State	Overall Rank	Corporate Tax Rank	Individual Income Tax Rank	Sales Tax Rank	Property Tax Rank	Unemployment Insurance Tax Rank
Maryland	46	33	45	30	42	41

Note: The index is a measure of how each state's tax laws affect economic performance. The lower the rank, the more favorable a state's tax system is for business. States without a given tax are given a ranking of 1. The scores/rankings for the District of Columbia do not affect other states. The 2023 index represents the tax climate as of July 1, 2022.
Source: Tax Foundation, State Business Tax Climate Index 2023

TRANSPORTATION

Means of Transportation to Work

Area	Car/Truck/Van		Public Transportation			Bicycle	Walked	Other Means	Worked at Home
	Drove Alone	Car-pooled	Bus	Subway	Railroad				
City	58.2	7.8	11.8	1.2	1.1	0.8	5.9	2.7	10.8
MSA[1]	72.5	7.4	3.4	0.7	0.7	0.2	2.3	1.5	11.2
U.S.	73.2	8.6	2.0	1.6	0.5	0.5	2.5	1.5	9.7

Note: Figures are percentages and cover workers 16 years of age and older; (1) Figures cover the Baltimore-Columbia-Towson, MD Metropolitan Statistical Area
Source: U.S. Census Bureau, 2017-2021 American Community Survey 5-Year Estimates

Travel Time to Work

Area	Less Than 10 Minutes	10 to 19 Minutes	20 to 29 Minutes	30 to 44 Minutes	45 to 59 Minutes	60 to 89 Minutes	90 Minutes or More
City	6.7	23.6	23.3	25.6	8.7	7.4	4.7
MSA[1]	8.0	23.3	21.0	24.7	11.0	8.3	3.7
U.S.	12.4	28.5	21.0	20.9	8.2	6.2	2.9

Note: Note: Figures are percentages and include workers 16 years old and over; (1) Figures cover the Baltimore-Columbia-Towson, MD Metropolitan Statistical Area
Source: U.S. Census Bureau, 2017-2021 American Community Survey 5-Year Estimates

Key Congestion Measures

Measure	1990	2000	2010	2015	2020
Annual Hours of Delay, Total (000)	32,388	55,157	75,705	88,266	44,292
Annual Hours of Delay, Per Auto Commuter	30	41	47	55	27
Annual Congestion Cost, Per Auto Commuter ($)	674	861	940	1,013	549

Note: Covers the Baltimore MD urban area
Source: Texas A&M Transportation Institute, 2021 Urban Mobility Report

Freeway Travel Time Index

Measure	1985	1990	1995	2000	2005	2010	2015	2020
Urban Area Index[1]	1.12	1.17	1.20	1.23	1.26	1.24	1.25	1.07
Urban Area Rank[1,2]	21	17	21	22	22	24	24	57

Note: Freeway Travel Time Index—the ratio of travel time in the peak period to the travel time at free-flow conditions. For example, a value of 1.30 indicates a 20-minute free-flow trip takes 26 minutes in the peak (20 minutes x 1.30 = 26 minutes); (1) Covers the Baltimore MD urban area; (2) Rank is based on 101 larger urban areas (#1 = highest travel time index)
Source: Texas A&M Transportation Institute, 2021 Urban Mobility Report

Public Transportation

Agency Name / Mode of Transportation	Vehicles Operated in Maximum Service[1]	Annual Unlinked Passenger Trips[2] (in thous.)	Annual Passenger Miles[3] (in thous.)
Maryland Transit Administration (MTA)			
Bus (directly operated)	604	35,370.2	150,861.3
Commuter Bus (purchased transportation)	58	434.5	7,341.8
Commuter Rail (purchased transportation)	149	880.3	26,058.2
Demand Response (directly operated)	12	8.5	62.0
Demand Response (purchased transportation)	289	1,031.8	8,136.3
Demand Response - Taxi	162	537.6	2,367.1
Heavy Rail (directly operated)	42	1,615.6	7,624.8
Light Rail (directly operated)	17	2,458.7	12,135.9

Note: (1) Number of revenue vehicles operated by the given mode and type of service to meet the annual maximum service requirement. This is the revenue vehicle count during the peak season of the year; on the week and day that maximum service is provided. Vehicles operated in maximum service (VOMS) exclude atypical days and one-time special events; (2) Number of passengers who boarded public transportation vehicles. Passengers are counted each time they board a vehicle no matter how many vehicles they use to travel from their origin to their destination. (3) Sum of the distances ridden by all passengers during the entire fiscal year.
Source: Federal Transit Administration, National Transit Database, 2021

Air Transportation

Airport Name and Code / Type of Service	Passenger Airlines[1]	Passenger Enplanements	Freight Carriers[2]	Freight (lbs)
Baltimore-Washington International (BWI)				
Domestic service (U.S. carriers - 2022)	33	10,585,453	15	251,638,223
International service (U.S. carriers - 2021)	7	326,265	3	319,968

Note: (1) Includes all U.S.-based major, minor and commuter airlines that carried at least one passenger during the year; (2) Includes all U.S.-based airlines and freight carriers that transported at least one pound of freight during the year.
Source: Bureau of Transportation Statistics, The Intermodal Transportation Database, Air Carriers: T-100 Domestic Market (U.S. Carriers), 2022; Bureau of Transportation Statistics, The Intermodal Transportation Database, Air Carriers: T-100 International Market (U.S. Carriers), 2021

BUSINESSES

Major Business Headquarters

Company Name	Industry	Rankings	
		Fortune[1]	Forbes[2]
T. Rowe Price	Securities and asset management	443	-
Whiting-Turner Contracting	Construction	-	54

Note: (1) Companies that produce a 10-K are ranked 1 to 500 based on 2021 revenue; (2) All private companies with at least $2 billion in annual revenue through the end of their most current fiscal year are ranked 1 to 246; companies listed are headquartered in the city; dashes indicate no ranking
Source: Fortune, "Fortune 500," 2022; Forbes, "America's Largest Private Companies," 2022

Fastest-Growing Businesses

According to *Inc.*, Baltimore is home to one of America's 500 fastest-growing private companies: **Facet Wealth** (#46). Criteria: must be an independent, privately-held, for-profit, U.S. corporation, proprietorship or partnership as of December 31, 2021; revenues must be at least $100,000 in 2018 and $2 million in 2021; must have four-year operating/sales history. *Inc., "America's 500 Fastest-Growing Private Companies," 2022*

According to *Initiative for a Competitive Inner City (ICIC)*, Baltimore is home to five of America's 100 fastest-growing "inner city" companies: **Veltrust** (#24); **Nyla Technology Solutions** (#40); **Alpha Graphics** (#72); **Thg Companies** (#89); **Watkins Security Agency** (#96). Criteria for inclusion: company must be headquartered in or have 51 percent or more of its physical operations in an economically distressed urban area; must be an independent, for-profit corporation, partnership or proprietorship; must have 10 or more employees and have a five-year sales history that includes sales of at least $200,000 in the base year and at least $1 million in the current year with no decrease in sales over the two most recent years. Companies were ranked overall by revenue growth over the five-year period between 2017 and 2021. *Initiative for a Competitive Inner City (ICIC), "Inner City 100 Companies," 2022*

Living Environment

COST OF LIVING

Cost of Living Index

Composite Index	Groceries	Housing	Utilities	Trans- portation	Health Care	Misc. Goods/ Services
108.3	113.5	109.1	104.5	101.0	89.9	110.6

Note: The Cost of Living Index measures regional differences in the cost of consumer goods and services, excluding taxes and non-consumer expenditures, for professional and managerial households in the top income quintile. It is based on more than 50,000 prices covering almost 60 different items for which prices are collected three times a year by chambers of commerce, economic development organizations or university applied economic centers in each participating urban area. The numbers shown should be read as a percentage above or below the national average of 100. For example, a value of 115.4 in the groceries column indicates that grocery prices are 15.4% higher than the national average. Small differences in the index numbers should not be interpreted as significant; Figures cover the Baltimore MD urban area.
Source: The Council for Community and Economic Research, Cost of Living Index, 2022

Grocery Prices

Area[1]	T-Bone Steak ($/pound)	Frying Chicken ($/pound)	Whole Milk ($/half gal.)	Eggs ($/dozen)	Orange Juice ($/64 oz.)	Coffee ($/11.5 oz.)
City[2]	15.04	1.96	2.45	2.54	4.38	5.31
Avg.	13.81	1.59	2.43	2.25	3.85	4.95
Min.	10.17	0.90	1.51	1.30	2.90	3.46
Max.	19.35	3.30	4.32	4.32	5.31	8.59

Note: (1) Values for the local area are compared with the average, minimum and maximum values for all 286 areas in the Cost of Living Index; (2) Figures cover the Baltimore MD urban area; **T-Bone Steak** (price per pound); **Frying Chicken** (price per pound, whole fryer); **Whole Milk** (half gallon carton); **Eggs** (price per dozen, Grade A, large); **Orange Juice** (64 oz. Tropicana or Florida Natural); **Coffee** (11.5 oz. can, vacuum-packed, Maxwell House, Hills Bros, or Folgers).
Source: The Council for Community and Economic Research, Cost of Living Index, 2022

Housing and Utility Costs

Area[1]	New Home Price ($)	Apartment Rent ($/month)	All Electric ($/month)	Part Electric ($/month)	Other Energy ($/month)	Telephone ($/month)
City[2]	440,295	1,868	-	92.51	93.60	196.85
Avg.	450,913	1,371	176.41	99.93	76.96	190.22
Min.	229,283	546	100.84	31.56	27.15	174.27
Max.	2,434,977	4,569	356.86	249.59	272.24	208.31

Note: (1) Values for the local area are compared with the average, minimum and maximum values for all 286 areas in the Cost of Living Index; (2) Figures cover the Baltimore MD urban area; **New Home Price** (2,400 sf living area, 8,000 sf lot, in urban area with full utilities); **Apartment Rent** (950 sf 2 bedroom/1.5 or 2 bath, unfurnished, excluding all utilities except water); **All Electric** (average monthly cost for an all-electric home); **Part Electric** (average monthly cost for a part-electric home); **Other Energy** (average monthly cost for natural gas, fuel oil, coal, wood, and any other forms of energy except electricity); **Telephone** (price includes the base monthly rate plus taxes and fees for three lines of mobile phone service).
Source: The Council for Community and Economic Research, Cost of Living Index, 2022

Health Care, Transportation, and Other Costs

Area[1]	Doctor ($/visit)	Dentist ($/visit)	Optometrist ($/visit)	Gasoline ($/gallon)	Beauty Salon ($/visit)	Men's Shirt ($)
City[2]	80.00	115.58	87.78	3.67	56.91	27.22
Avg.	124.91	107.77	117.66	3.86	43.31	34.21
Min.	36.61	58.25	51.79	2.90	22.18	13.05
Max.	250.21	162.58	371.96	5.54	85.61	63.54

Note: (1) Values for the local area are compared with the average, minimum and maximum values for all 286 areas in the Cost of Living Index; (2) Figures cover the Baltimore MD urban area; **Doctor** (general practitioners routine exam of an established patient); **Dentist** (adult teeth cleaning and periodic oral examination); **Optometrist** (full vision eye exam for established adult patient); **Gasoline** (one gallon regular unleaded, national brand, including all taxes, cash price at self-service pump if available); **Beauty Salon** (woman's shampoo, trim, and blow-dry); **Men's Shirt** (cotton/polyester dress shirt, pinpoint weave, long sleeves).
Source: The Council for Community and Economic Research, Cost of Living Index, 2022

HOUSING

Homeownership Rate

Area	2015 (%)	2016 (%)	2017 (%)	2018 (%)	2019 (%)	2020 (%)	2021 (%)	2022 (%)
MSA[1]	65.3	68.5	67.5	63.5	66.5	70.7	67.5	70.4
U.S.	63.7	63.4	63.9	64.4	64.6	66.6	65.5	65.8

Note: (1) Figures cover the Baltimore-Columbia-Towson, MD Metropolitan Statistical Area
Source: U.S. Census Bureau, Housing Vacancies and Homeownership Annual Statistics: 2015-2022

House Price Index (HPI)

Area	National Ranking[2]	Quarterly Change (%)	One-Year Change (%)	Five-Year Change (%)	Since 1991Q1 (%)
MSA[1]	199	0.91	8.63	34.77	214.03
U.S.[3]	–	0.34	8.41	58.44	289.08

Note: The HPI is a weighted repeat sales index. It measures average price changes in repeat sales or refinancings on the same properties. This information is obtained by reviewing repeat mortgage transactions on single-family properties whose mortgages have been purchased or securitized by Fannie Mae or Freddie Mac since January 1975; (1) Figures cover the Baltimore-Columbia-Towson, MD Metropolitan Statistical Area; (2) Rankings are based on annual percentage change for all metro areas containing at least 15,000 transactions over the last 10 years and ranges from 1 to 257; (3) figures based on a weighted average of Census Division estimates using a seasonally adjusted, purchase-only index; all figures are for the period ending December 31, 2022
Source: Federal Housing Finance Agency, Change in FHFA Metropolitan Area House Price Indexes, 2022Q4

Median Single-Family Home Prices

Area	2020	2021	2022[p]	Percent Change 2021 to 2022
MSA[1]	328.5	358.1	378.2	5.6
U.S. Average	300.2	357.1	392.6	9.9

Note: Figures are median sales prices of existing single-family homes in thousands of dollars; (p) preliminary; (1) Figures cover the Baltimore-Columbia-Towson, MD Metropolitan Statistical Area
Source: National Association of Realtors, Median Sales Price of Existing Single-Family Homes for Metropolitan Areas, 4th Quarter 2022

Qualifying Income Based on Median Sales Price of Existing Single-Family Homes

Area	With 5% Down ($)	With 10% Down ($)	With 20% Down ($)
MSA[1]	108,753	103,029	91,582
U.S. Average	112,234	106,237	94,513

Note: Figures are preliminary; Qualifying income is based on a mortgage rate of 6.77%. Monthly principal and interest payment is limited to 25% of income; (1) Figures cover the Baltimore-Columbia-Towson, MD Metropolitan Statistical Area
Source: National Association of Realtors, Qualifying Income Based on Median Sales Price of Existing Single-Family Homes for Metropolitan Areas, 4th Quarter 2022

Home Value

Area	Under $100,000	$100,000 -$199,999	$200,000 -$299,999	$300,000 -$399,999	$400,000 -$499,999	$500,000 -$999,999	$1,000,000 or more	Median ($)
City	21.5	35.5	21.4	10.3	4.3	5.9	1.0	175,300
MSA[1]	6.7	15.8	23.5	20.6	12.8	18.2	2.4	319,500
U.S.	16.2	24.2	20.1	13.6	8.3	13.6	4.1	244,900

Note: Figures are percentages except for median and cover owner-occupied housing units; (1) Figures cover the Baltimore-Columbia-Towson, MD Metropolitan Statistical Area
Source: U.S. Census Bureau, 2017-2021 American Community Survey 5-Year Estimates

Year Housing Structure Built

Area	2020 or Later	2010 -2019	2000 -2009	1990 -1999	1980 -1989	1970 -1979	1960 -1969	1950 -1959	1940 -1949	Before 1940	Median Year
City	<0.1	3.4	3.6	3.9	4.3	5.7	8.6	15.8	11.9	42.8	1946
MSA[1]	0.1	6.0	9.4	13.4	13.4	12.9	10.4	12.8	6.2	15.4	1974
U.S.	0.2	7.3	13.6	13.6	13.2	14.8	10.3	10.0	4.7	12.2	1979

Note: Figures are percentages except for Median Year; Note: (1) Figures cover the Baltimore-Columbia-Towson, MD Metropolitan Statistical Area
Source: U.S. Census Bureau, 2017-2021 American Community Survey 5-Year Estimates

Gross Monthly Rent

Area	Under $500	$500 -$999	$1,000 -$1,499	$1,500 -$1,999	$2,000 -$2,499	$2,500 -$2,999	$3,000 and up	Median ($)
City	14.9	22.2	37.2	17.6	5.5	1.5	1.1	1,146
MSA[1]	8.2	14.4	35.1	26.4	11.0	3.0	2.0	1,387
U.S.	8.1	30.5	30.8	16.8	7.3	3.1	3.5	1,163

Note: Figures are percentages except for median; Gross rent is the contract rent plus the estimated average monthly cost of utilities (electricity, gas, and water and sewer) and fuels (oil, coal, kerosene, wood, etc.) if these are paid by the renter (or paid for the renter by someone else); (1) Figures cover the Baltimore-Columbia-Towson, MD Metropolitan Statistical Area
Source: U.S. Census Bureau, 2017-2021 American Community Survey 5-Year Estimates

HEALTH

Health Risk Factors

Category	MSA[1] (%)	U.S. (%)
Adults aged 18–64 who have any kind of health care coverage	92.9	90.9
Adults who reported being in good or better health	85.9	85.2
Adults who have been told they have high blood cholesterol	35.9	35.7
Adults who have been told they have high blood pressure	34.1	32.4
Adults who are current smokers	10.7	14.4
Adults who currently use e-cigarettes	5.0	6.7
Adults who currently use chewing tobacco, snuff, or snus	1.3	3.5
Adults who are heavy drinkers[2]	4.9	6.3
Adults who are binge drinkers[3]	14.6	15.4
Adults who are overweight (BMI 25.0 - 29.9)	31.9	34.4
Adults who are obese (BMI 30.0 - 99.8)	34.3	33.9
Adults who participated in any physical activities in the past month	78.0	76.3

Note: (1) Figures cover the Baltimore-Columbia-Towson, MD Metropolitan Statistical Area; (2) Heavy drinkers are classified as adult men having more than 14 drinks per week and adult women having more than 7 drinks per week; (3) Binge drinkers are classified as males having five or more drinks on one occasion or females having four or more drinks on one occasion
Source: Centers for Disease Control and Prevention, Behaviorial Risk Factor Surveillance System, SMART: Selected Metropolitan Area Risk Trends, 2021

Acute and Chronic Health Conditions

Category	MSA[1] (%)	U.S. (%)
Adults who have ever been told they had a heart attack	3.5	4.0
Adults who have ever been told they have angina or coronary heart disease	3.6	3.8
Adults who have ever been told they had a stroke	3.2	3.0
Adults who have ever been told they have asthma	15.3	14.9
Adults who have ever been told they have arthritis	24.9	25.8
Adults who have ever been told they have diabetes[2]	11.4	10.9
Adults who have ever been told they had skin cancer	5.9	6.6
Adults who have ever been told they had any other types of cancer	7.0	7.5
Adults who have ever been told they have COPD	5.3	6.1
Adults who have ever been told they have kidney disease	2.9	3.0
Adults who have ever been told they have a form of depression	18.8	20.5

Note: (1) Figures cover the Baltimore-Columbia-Towson, MD Metropolitan Statistical Area; (2) Figures do not include pregnancy-related, borderline, or pre-diabetes
Source: Centers for Disease Control and Prevention, Behaviorial Risk Factor Surveillance System, SMART: Selected Metropolitan Area Risk Trends, 2021

Health Screening and Vaccination Rates

Category	MSA[1] (%)	U.S. (%)
Adults who have ever been tested for HIV	43.8	34.9
Adults who have had their blood cholesterol checked within the last five years	89.0	85.2
Adults aged 65+ who have had flu shot within the past year	74.6	68.6
Adults aged 65+ who have ever had a pneumonia vaccination	76.4	71.0

Note: (1) Figures cover the Baltimore-Columbia-Towson, MD Metropolitan Statistical Area.
Source: Centers for Disease Control and Prevention, Behaviorial Risk Factor Surveillance System, SMART: Selected Metropolitan Area Risk Trends, 2021

Disability Status

Category	MSA[1] (%)	U.S. (%)
Adults who reported being deaf	5.7	7.2
Are you blind or have serious difficulty seeing, even when wearing glasses?	4.0	4.8
Are you limited in any way in any of your usual activities due to arthritis?	9.9	11.1
Do you have difficulty doing errands alone?	5.7	7.0
Do you have difficulty dressing or bathing?	2.8	3.6
Do you have serious difficulty concentrating/remembering/making decisions?	10.2	12.1
Do you have serious difficulty walking or climbing stairs?	10.9	12.8

Note: (1) Figures cover the Baltimore-Columbia-Towson, MD Metropolitan Statistical Area.
Source: Centers for Disease Control and Prevention, Behaviorial Risk Factor Surveillance System, SMART: Selected Metropolitan Area Risk Trends, 2021

Mortality Rates for the Top 10 Causes of Death in the U.S.

ICD-10[a] Sub-Chapter	ICD-10[a] Code	Crude Mortality Rate[1] per 100,000 population	
		County[2]	U.S.
Malignant neoplasms	C00-C97	209.3	182.6
Ischaemic heart diseases	I20-I25	136.1	113.1
Other forms of heart disease	I30-I51	71.0	64.4
Other degenerative diseases of the nervous system	G30-G31	18.1	51.0
Cerebrovascular diseases	I60-I69	64.2	47.8
Other external causes of accidental injury	W00-X59	69.6	46.4
Chronic lower respiratory diseases	J40-J47	37.1	45.7
Organic, including symptomatic, mental disorders	F01-F09	47.9	35.9
Hypertensive diseases	I10-I15	63.5	35.0
Diabetes mellitus	E10-E14	40.7	29.6

Note: (a) ICD-10 = International Classification of Diseases 10th Revision; (1) Crude mortality rates are a three-year average covering 2019-2021; (2) Figures cover Baltimore city.
Source: Centers for Disease Control and Prevention, National Center for Health Statistics. National Vital Statistics System, Mortality 2018-2021 on CDC WONDER Online Database

Mortality Rates for Selected Causes of Death

ICD-10[a] Sub-Chapter	ICD-10[a] Code	Crude Mortality Rate[1] per 100,000 population	
		County[2]	U.S.
Assault	X85-Y09	47.1	7.0
Diseases of the liver	K70-K76	19.1	19.8
Human immunodeficiency virus (HIV) disease	B20-B24	10.4	1.5
Influenza and pneumonia	J09-J18	15.7	14.7
Intentional self-harm	X60-X84	9.4	14.3
Malnutrition	E40-E46	Unreliable	4.3
Obesity and other hyperalimentation	E65-E68	3.5	3.0
Renal failure	N17-N19	16.1	15.7
Transport accidents	V01-V99	10.3	13.6
Viral hepatitis	B15-B19	2.8	1.2

Note: (a) ICD-10 = International Classification of Diseases 10th Revision; (1) Crude mortality rates are a three-year average covering 2019-2021; (2) Figures cover Baltimore city; Data are suppressed when the data meet the criteria for confidentiality constraints; Crude mortality rates are flagged as unreliable when the rate would be calculated with a numerator of 20 or less.
Source: Centers for Disease Control and Prevention, National Center for Health Statistics. National Vital Statistics System, Mortality 2018-2021 on CDC WONDER Online Database

Health Insurance Coverage

Area	With Health Insurance	With Private Health Insurance	With Public Health Insurance	Without Health Insurance	Population Under Age 19 Without Health Insurance
City	94.1	59.3	45.9	5.9	3.4
MSA[1]	95.2	75.1	33.7	4.8	3.2
U.S.	91.2	67.8	35.4	8.8	5.3

Note: Figures are percentages that cover the civilian noninstitutionalized population; (1) Figures cover the Baltimore-Columbia-Towson, MD Metropolitan Statistical Area
Source: U.S. Census Bureau, 2017-2021 American Community Survey 5-Year Estimates

Number of Medical Professionals

Area	MDs[3]	DOs[3,4]	Dentists	Podiatrists	Chiropractors	Optometrists
County[1] (number)	6,491	139	478	48	86	92
County[1] (rate[2])	1,113.1	23.8	82.9	8.3	14.9	16.0
U.S. (rate[2])	289.3	23.5	72.5	6.2	28.7	17.4

Note: Data as of 2021 unless noted; (1) Data covers Baltimore City County; (2) Rate per 100,000 population; (3) Data as of 2020 and includes all active, non-federal physicians; (4) Doctor of Osteopathic Medicine
Source: U.S. Department of Health and Human Services, Health Resources and Services Administration, Bureau of Health Professions, Area Resource File (ARF) 2021-2022

Best Hospitals

According to *U.S. News,* the Baltimore-Columbia-Towson, MD metro area is home to four of the best hospitals in the U.S.: **Johns Hopkins Hospital** (Honor Roll/15 adult specialties and 10 pediatric specialties); **Sheppard Pratt Hospital** (1 adult specialty); **University of Maryland Medical Center** (1 adult specialty and 1 pediatric specialty); **Wilmer Eye Institute at Johns Hopkins Hospital** (Honor Roll/15 adult specialties and 10 pediatric specialties). The hospitals listed were nationally ranked in at least one of 15 adult or 10 pediatric specialties. The number of specialties shown cover the parent hospital. Only 164 U.S. hospitals performed well enough to be nationally ranked in one or more specialties. Twenty hospitals in the U.S. made the Honor Roll. The Best Hospitals Honor Roll takes both the national rankings and the procedure and condition ratings into account. Hospitals received points if they were nationally ranked in one of the 15 adult specialties—the higher they ranked, the more points they got—and how many ratings of "high performing" they earned in the 17 procedures and conditions. *U.S. News Online, "America's Best Hospitals 2022-23"*

According to *U.S. News,* the Baltimore-Columbia-Towson, MD metro area is home to two of the best children's hospitals in the U.S.: **Johns Hopkins Children's Center** (10 pediatric specialties); **University of Maryland Children's Hospital** (1 pediatric specialty). The hospitals listed were highly ranked in at least one of 10 pediatric specialties. Eighty-six children's hospitals in the U.S. were nationally ranked in at least one specialty. Hospitals received points for being ranked in a specialty, and the 10 hospitals with the most points across the 10 specialties make up the Honor Roll. *U.S. News Online, "America's Best Children's Hospitals 2022-23"*

EDUCATION

Public School District Statistics

District Name	Schls	Pupils	Pupil/ Teacher Ratio	Minority Pupils[1] (%)	LEP/ELL[2] (%)	IEP[3] (%)
Baltimore City Public Schools	156	77,807	15.2	92.7	6.8	15.8
Baltimore County Public Schools	177	111,136	14.5	67.2	6.7	14.2

Note: Table includes school districts with 2,000 or more students; (1) Percentage of students that are not non-Hispanic white; (2) Percentage of students that are Limited English Proficient or English Language Learners (2018-19); (3) Percentage of students that have an Individualized Education Program (2019-20).
Source: U.S. Department of Education, National Center for Education Statistics, Common Core of Data, Local Education Agency (School District) Universe Survey: School Year 2021-2022

Best High Schools

According to *U.S. News,* Baltimore is home to two of the top 500 high schools in the U.S.: **Eastern Technical High School** (#224); **Western School of Technology and Env. Science** (#366). Nearly 18,000 public, magnet and charter schools were ranked based on their performance on state assessments and how well they prepare students for college. *U.S. News & World Report, "Best High Schools 2022"*

Highest Level of Education

Area	Less than H.S.	H.S. Diploma	Some College, No Deg.	Associate Degree	Bachelor's Degree	Master's Degree	Prof. School Degree	Doctorate Degree
City	13.7	28.1	18.8	5.2	17.2	11.3	3.2	2.5
MSA[1]	8.4	24.1	18.9	6.9	22.7	13.7	3.0	2.3
U.S.	11.1	26.5	20.0	8.7	20.6	9.3	2.2	1.5

Note: Figures cover persons age 25 and over; (1) Figures cover the Baltimore-Columbia-Towson, MD Metropolitan Statistical Area
Source: U.S. Census Bureau, 2017-2021 American Community Survey 5-Year Estimates

Educational Attainment by Race

Area	High School Graduate or Higher (%)					Bachelor's Degree or Higher (%)				
	Total	White	Black	Asian	Hisp.[2]	Total	White	Black	Asian	Hisp.[2]
City	86.3	91.5	84.1	90.2	72.2	34.2	59.7	18.7	71.6	32.9
MSA[1]	91.6	93.9	89.0	89.1	76.2	41.8	46.4	28.4	63.1	32.4
U.S.	88.9	91.4	87.2	87.6	71.2	33.7	35.5	23.3	55.6	18.4

Note: Figures shown cover persons 25 years old and over; (1) Figures cover the Baltimore-Columbia-Towson, MD Metropolitan Statistical Area; (2) People of Hispanic origin can be of any race
Source: U.S. Census Bureau, 2017-2021 American Community Survey 5-Year Estimates

School Enrollment by Grade and Control

Area	Preschool (%)		Kindergarten (%)		Grades 1 - 4 (%)		Grades 5 - 8 (%)		Grades 9 - 12 (%)	
	Public	Private	Public	Private	Public	Private	Public	Private	Public	Private
City	69.2	30.8	83.5	16.5	84.0	16.0	85.0	15.0	85.3	14.7
MSA[1]	47.8	52.2	82.9	17.1	85.3	14.7	84.6	15.4	83.2	16.8
U.S.	58.8	41.2	86.3	13.7	88.3	11.7	88.6	11.4	89.4	10.6

Note: Figures shown cover persons 3 years old and over; (1) Figures cover the Baltimore-Columbia-Towson, MD Metropolitan Statistical Area
Source: U.S. Census Bureau, 2017-2021 American Community Survey 5-Year Estimates

Higher Education

Four-Year Colleges			Two-Year Colleges			Medical Schools[1]	Law Schools[2]	Voc/ Tech[3]
Public	Private Non-profit	Private For-profit	Public	Private Non-profit	Private For-profit			
7	12	0	7	0	1	2	2	14

Note: Figures cover institutions located within the Baltimore-Columbia-Towson, MD Metropolitan Statistical Area and include main campuses only; (1) includes schools accredited by the Liaison Committee on Medical Education and the American Osteopathic Association's Commission on Osteopathic College Accreditation; (2) includes ABA-accredited schools, schools with provisional ABA accreditation, and state accredited schools; (3) includes all schools with programs that are less than 2 years.
Source: National Center for Education Statistics, Integrated Postsecondary Education System (IPEDS), 2021-22; Wikipedia, List of Medical Schools in the United States, accessed April 10, 2023; Wikipedia, List of Law Schools in the United States, accessed April 10, 2023

According to *U.S. News & World Report,* the Baltimore-Columbia-Towson, MD metro area is home to two of the top 200 national universities in the U.S.: **Johns Hopkins University** (#7 tie); **University of Maryland—Baltimore County** (#137 tie). The indicators used to capture academic quality fall into a number of categories: assessment by administrators at peer institutions; retention of students; faculty resources; student selectivity; financial resources; alumni giving; high school counselor ratings of colleges; and graduation rate. *U.S. News & World Report, "America's Best Colleges 2023"*

According to *U.S. News & World Report,* the Baltimore-Columbia-Towson, MD metro area is home to two of the top 100 liberal arts colleges in the U.S.: **United States Naval Academy** (#6 tie); **St. John's College (MD)** (#61 tie). The indicators used to capture academic quality fall into a number of categories: assessment by administrators at peer institutions; retention of students; faculty resources; student selectivity; financial resources; alumni giving; high school counselor ratings of colleges; and graduation rate. *U.S. News & World Report, "America's Best Colleges 2023"*

According to *U.S. News & World Report,* the Baltimore-Columbia-Towson, MD metro area is home to one of the top 100 law schools in the U.S.: **University of Maryland (Carey)** (#47 tie). The rankings are based on a weighted average of 12 measures of quality: peer assessment score; assessment score by lawyers/judges; median LSAT scores; median undergrad GPA; acceptance rate; employment rates for graduates; placement success; bar passage rate; faculty resources; expenditures per student; student/faculty ratio; and library resources. *U.S. News & World Report, "America's Best Graduate Schools, Law, 2023"*

According to *U.S. News & World Report,* the Baltimore-Columbia-Towson, MD metro area is home to two of the top 75 medical schools for research in the U.S.: **Johns Hopkins University** (#3 tie); **University of Maryland** (#29). The rankings are based on a weighted average of 11 measures of quality: quality assessment; peer assessment score; assessment score by residency directors; research activity; total research activity; average research activity per faculty member; student selectivity; median MCAT total score; median undergraduate GPA; acceptance rate; and faculty resources. *U.S. News & World Report, "America's Best Graduate Schools, Medical, 2023"*

EMPLOYERS

Major Employers

Company Name	Industry
Centers for Medicare and Medicaid Services	Federal government
Community College of Baltimore County	Educational services
Exelon	Energy products & services
Horseshoe Casino	Entertainment and recreation
Johns Hopkins Hospital & Health System	Healthcare
Johns Hopkins University	Educational services
Kennedy Krieger Institute	Healthcare
LifeBridge Health	Healthcare
Maryland Institute College of Art	Educational services
MedStar Health	Healthcare
Mercy Health Services	Healthcare
Social Security Administration	Federal government
St. Agnes HealthCare	Healthcare
T. Rowe Price	Financial services
University of Maryland Medical System	Healthcare
University System of Maryland	Educational services

Note: Companies shown are located within the Baltimore-Columbia-Towson, MD Metropolitan Statistical Area.
Source: Hoovers.com; Wikipedia

Best Companies to Work For

Brightview Senior Living, headquartered in Baltimore, is among "The 100 Best Companies to Work For." To pick the best companies, *Fortune* partnered with the Great Place to Work Institute. Two-thirds of a company's score is based on the results of the Institute's Trust Index survey, which is sent to a random sample of employees from each company. The questions related to attitudes about management's credibility, job satisfaction, and camaraderie. The other third of the scoring is based on the company's responses to the Institute's Culture Audit, which includes detailed questions about pay and benefit programs, and a series of open-ended questions about hiring practices, internal communication, training, recognition programs, and diversity efforts. Any company that is at least five years old with more than 1,000 U.S. employees is eligible. *Fortune, "The 100 Best Companies to Work For," 2023*

Brightview Senior Living, headquartered in Baltimore, is among "Fortune's Best Workplaces for Women." To pick the best companies, *Fortune* partnered with the Great Place to Work Institute. To be considered for the list, companies must be Great Place To Work-Certified. Companies must also employ at least 50 women, at least 20% of their non-executive managers must be female, and at least one executive must be female. To determine the Best Workplaces for Women, Great Place To Work measured the differences in women's survey responses to those of their peers and assesses the impact of demographics and roles on the quality and consistency of women's experiences. Great Place To Work also analyzed the gender balance of each workplace, how it compared to each company's industry, and patterns in representation as women rise from front-line positions to the board of directors. *Fortune, "Best Workplaces for Women," 2022*

IT@Johns Hopkins, headquartered in Baltimore, is among the "100 Best Places to Work in IT." To qualify, companies had to have a minimum of 100 total employees and five IT employees. The best places to work were selected based on DEI (diversity, equity, and inclusion) practices; IT turnover, promotions, and growth; IT retention and engagement programs; remote/hybrid working; benefits and perks (such as elder care and child care, flextime, and reimbursement for college tuition); and training and career development opportunities. *Computerworld, "Best Places to Work in IT," 2023*

PUBLIC SAFETY

Crime Rate

Area	Total Crime	Violent Crime Rate				Property Crime Rate		
		Murder	Rape[3]	Robbery	Aggrav. Assault	Burglary	Larceny -Theft	Motor Vehicle Theft
City	6,169.9	58.3	54.2	813.1	933.1	906.5	2,745.1	659.5
Suburbs[1]	2,213.3	3.9	31.8	88.1	260.3	217.8	1,485.2	126.1
Metro[2]	3,057.2	15.5	36.6	242.7	403.8	364.7	1,753.9	239.9
U.S.	2,510.4	5.1	42.6	81.8	250.4	340.5	1,569.2	220.8

Note: Figures are crimes per 100,000 population; (1) All areas within the metro area that are located outside the city limits; (2) Figures cover the Baltimore-Columbia-Towson, MD Metropolitan Statistical Area; (3) All figures shown were reported using the revised Uniform Crime Reporting (UCR) definition of rape; Due to the transition to the National Incident-Based Reporting System (NIBRS), limited city and metro area data was released for 2021.
Source: FBI Uniform Crime Reports, 2019 (data for 2020 was not available)

Hate Crimes

Area	Number of Quarters Reported	Number of Incidents per Bias Motivation					
		Race/Ethnicity/ Ancestry	Religion	Sexual Orientation	Disability	Gender	Gender Identity
City	3	3	0	2	0	0	0
U.S.	4	5,227	1,244	1,110	130	75	266

Note: Due to the transition to the National Incident-Based Reporting System (NIBRS), limited crime data was released for 2021.
Source: Federal Bureau of Investigation, Hate Crime Statistics 2020

Identity Theft Consumer Reports

Area	Reports	Reports per 100,000 Population	Rank[2]
MSA[1]	9,926	354	45
U.S.	1,108,609	339	-

Note: (1) Figures cover the Baltimore-Columbia-Towson, MD Metropolitan Statistical Area; (2) Rank ranges from 1 to 391 where 1 indicates greatest number of identity theft reports per 100,000 population
Source: Federal Trade Commission, Consumer Sentinel Network Data Book 2022

Fraud and Other Consumer Reports

Area	Reports	Reports per 100,000 Population	Rank[2]
MSA[1]	37,704	1,346	21
U.S.	4,064,520	1,245	-

Note: (1) Figures cover the Baltimore-Columbia-Towson, MD Metropolitan Statistical Area; (2) Rank ranges from 1 to 391 where 1 indicates greatest number of fraud and other consumer reports per 100,000 population
Source: Federal Trade Commission, Consumer Sentinel Network Data Book 2022

Baltimore, Maryland   41

POLITICS

2020 Presidential Election Results

Area	Biden	Trump	Jorgensen	Hawkins	Other
Baltimore City	87.3	10.7	0.7	0.6	0.7
U.S.	51.3	46.8	1.2	0.3	0.5

Note: Results are percentages and may not add to 100% due to rounding
Source: Dave Leip's Atlas of U.S. Presidential Elections

SPORTS

Professional Sports Teams

Team Name	League	Year Established
Baltimore Orioles	Major League Baseball (MLB)	1954
Baltimore Ravens	National Football League (NFL)	1996

Note: Includes teams located in the Baltimore-Columbia-Towson, MD Metropolitan Statistical Area.
Source: Wikipedia, Major Professional Sports Teams of the United States and Canada, April 12, 2023

CLIMATE

Average and Extreme Temperatures

Temperature	Jan	Feb	Mar	Apr	May	Jun	Jul	Aug	Sep	Oct	Nov	Dec	Yr.
Extreme High (°F)	75	79	87	94	98	100	104	105	100	92	86	77	105
Average High (°F)	41	44	53	65	74	83	87	85	79	68	56	45	65
Average Temp. (°F)	33	36	44	54	64	73	77	76	69	57	47	37	56
Average Low (°F)	24	26	34	43	53	62	67	66	58	46	37	28	45
Extreme Low (°F)	-7	-3	6	20	32	40	50	45	35	25	13	0	-7

Note: Figures cover the years 1950-1990
Source: National Climatic Data Center, International Station Meteorological Climate Summary, 9/96

Average Precipitation/Snowfall/Humidity

Precip./Humidity	Jan	Feb	Mar	Apr	May	Jun	Jul	Aug	Sep	Oct	Nov	Dec	Yr.
Avg. Precip. (in.)	2.9	3.0	3.5	3.3	3.7	3.7	3.9	4.2	3.4	3.0	3.2	3.3	41.2
Avg. Snowfall (in.)	6	7	4	Tr	Tr	0	0	0	0	Tr	1	4	21
Avg. Rel. Hum. 7am (%)	72	71	71	71	77	79	80	83	85	83	78	74	77
Avg. Rel. Hum. 4pm (%)	56	53	48	47	52	53	53	55	55	54	55	57	53

Note: Figures cover the years 1950-1990; Tr = Trace amounts (<0.05 in. of rain; <0.5 in. of snow)
Source: National Climatic Data Center, International Station Meteorological Climate Summary, 9/96

Weather Conditions

Temperature			Daytime Sky			Precipitation		
10°F & below	32°F & below	90°F & above	Clear	Partly cloudy	Cloudy	0.01 inch or more precip.	0.1 inch or more snow/ice	Thunder-storms
6	97	31	91	143	131	113	13	27

Note: Figures are average number of days per year and cover the years 1950-1990
Source: National Climatic Data Center, International Station Meteorological Climate Summary, 9/96

HAZARDOUS WASTE

Superfund Sites

The Baltimore-Columbia-Towson, MD metro area is home to nine sites on the EPA's Superfund National Priorities List: **68th Street Dump/Industrial Enterprises** (proposed); **Aberdeen Proving Ground (Edgewood Area)** (final); **Aberdeen Proving Ground (Michaelsville Landfill)** (final); **Bear Creek Sediments** (final); **Bush Valley Landfill** (final); **Curtis Bay Coast Guard Yard** (final); **Fort George G. Meade** (final); **Kane & Lombard Street Drums** (final); **Sauer Dump** (final). There are a total of 1,165 Superfund sites with a status of proposed or final on the list in the U.S. *U.S. Environmental Protection Agency, National Priorities List, April 12, 2023*

AIR QUALITY

Air Quality Trends: Ozone

	1990	1995	2000	2005	2010	2015	2018	2019	2020	2021
MSA[1]	0.100	0.103	0.088	0.089	0.084	0.073	0.071	0.070	0.064	0.071
U.S.	0.087	0.089	0.081	0.080	0.072	0.067	0.069	0.065	0.065	0.067

Note: (1) Data covers the Baltimore-Columbia-Towson, MD Metropolitan Statistical Area. The values shown are the composite ozone concentration averages among trend sites based on the highest fourth daily maximum 8-hour concentration in parts per million. These trends are based on sites having an adequate record of monitoring data during the trend period. Data from exceptional events are included.
Source: U.S. Environmental Protection Agency, Air Quality Monitoring Information, "Air Quality Trends by City, 1990-2021"

Air Quality Index

Area	Percent of Days when Air Quality was...[2]					AQI Statistics[2]	
	Good	Moderate	Unhealthy for Sensitive Groups	Unhealthy	Very Unhealthy	Maximum	Median
MSA[1]	68.8	27.1	4.1	0.0	0.0	140	45

Note: (1) Data covers the Baltimore-Columbia-Towson, MD Metropolitan Statistical Area; (2) Based on 365 days with AQI data in 2021. Air Quality Index (AQI) is an index for reporting daily air quality. EPA calculates the AQI for five major air pollutants regulated by the Clean Air Act: ground-level ozone, particle pollution (aka particulate matter), carbon monoxide, sulfur dioxide, and nitrogen dioxide. The AQI runs from 0 to 500. The higher the AQI value, the greater the level of air pollution and the greater the health concern. There are six AQI categories: "Good" AQI is between 0 and 50. Air quality is considered satisfactory; "Moderate" AQI is between 51 and 100. Air quality is acceptable; "Unhealthy for Sensitive Groups" When AQI values are between 101 and 150, members of sensitive groups may experience health effects; "Unhealthy" When AQI values are between 151 and 200 everyone may begin to experience health effects; "Very Unhealthy" AQI values between 201 and 300 trigger a health alert; "Hazardous" AQI values over 300 trigger warnings of emergency conditions (not shown).
Source: U.S. Environmental Protection Agency, Air Quality Index Report, 2021

Air Quality Index Pollutants

Area	Percent of Days when AQI Pollutant was...[2]					
	Carbon Monoxide	Nitrogen Dioxide	Ozone	Sulfur Dioxide	Particulate Matter 2.5	Particulate Matter 10
MSA[1]	0.0	7.4	60.5	(3)	32.1	0.0

Note: (1) Data covers the Baltimore-Columbia-Towson, MD Metropolitan Statistical Area; (2) Based on 365 days with AQI data in 2021. The Air Quality Index (AQI) is an index for reporting daily air quality. EPA calculates the AQI for five major air pollutants regulated by the Clean Air Act: ground-level ozone, particle pollution (also known as particulate matter), carbon monoxide, sulfur dioxide, and nitrogen dioxide. The AQI runs from 0 to 500. The higher the AQI value, the greater the level of air pollution and the greater the health concern; (3) Sulfur dioxide is no longer included in this table (as of December 8, 2021) because SO_2 concentrations tend to be very localized and not necessarily representative of broad geographical areas like counties and CBSAs.
Source: U.S. Environmental Protection Agency, Air Quality Index Report, 2021

Maximum Air Pollutant Concentrations: Particulate Matter, Ozone, CO and Lead

	Particulate Matter 10 (ug/m^3)	Particulate Matter 2.5 Wtd AM (ug/m^3)	Particulate Matter 2.5 24-Hr (ug/m^3)	Ozone (ppm)	Carbon Monoxide (ppm)	Lead (ug/m^3)
MSA[1] Level	27	8.9	21	0.075	1	n/a
NAAQS[2]	150	15	35	0.075	9	0.15
Met NAAQS[2]	Yes	Yes	Yes	Yes	Yes	n/a

Note: (1) Data covers the Baltimore-Columbia-Towson, MD Metropolitan Statistical Area; Data from exceptional events are included; (2) National Ambient Air Quality Standards; ppm = parts per million; ug/m^3 = micrograms per cubic meter; n/a not available.
Concentrations: Particulate Matter 10 (coarse particulate)—highest second maximum 24-hour concentration; Particulate Matter 2.5 Wtd AM (fine particulate)—highest weighted annual mean concentration; Particulate Matter 2.5 24-Hour (fine particulate)—highest 98th percentile 24-hour concentration; Ozone—highest fourth daily maximum 8-hour concentration; Carbon Monoxide—highest second maximum non-overlapping 8-hour concentration; Lead—maximum running 3-month average
Source: U.S. Environmental Protection Agency, Air Quality Monitoring Information, "Air Quality Statistics by City, 2021"

Maximum Air Pollutant Concentrations: Nitrogen Dioxide and Sulfur Dioxide

	Nitrogen Dioxide AM (ppb)	Nitrogen Dioxide 1-Hr (ppb)	Sulfur Dioxide AM (ppb)	Sulfur Dioxide 1-Hr (ppb)	Sulfur Dioxide 24-Hr (ppb)
MSA[1] Level	16	51	n/a	16	n/a
NAAQS[2]	53	100	30	75	140
Met NAAQS[2]	Yes	Yes	n/a	Yes	n/a

Note: (1) Data covers the Baltimore-Columbia-Towson, MD Metropolitan Statistical Area; Data from exceptional events are included; (2) National Ambient Air Quality Standards; ppm = parts per million; ug/m^3 = micrograms per cubic meter; n/a not available.
Concentrations: Nitrogen Dioxide AM—highest arithmetic mean concentration; Nitrogen Dioxide 1-Hr—highest 98th percentile 1-hour daily maximum concentration; Sulfur Dioxide AM—highest annual mean concentration; Sulfur Dioxide 1-Hr—highest 99th percentile 1-hour daily maximum concentration; Sulfur Dioxide 24-Hr—highest second maximum 24-hour concentration
Source: U.S. Environmental Protection Agency, Air Quality Monitoring Information, "Air Quality Statistics by City, 2021"

Boston, Massachusetts

Background

Who would think that Boston, a city founded upon the Puritan principles of hard work, plain living, sobriety, and unyielding religious conviction, would be known for such a radical act of throwing tea overboard from a ship? The answer lies in ship trading—the industry upon which Boston gained its wealth. Boston sea captains reaped more profits from West Indies molasses, mahogany from Honduras, and slaves from Guinea than did the English, who decided to impose additional taxes upon her colonial subjects. In defiance, Samuel Adams led the Sons of Liberty to throw a precious cargo of tea, so dear to the English, overboard. Events escalated, and the American Revolution began.

After the Revolution, Boston continued to grow into the Yankee capital—and educational center—that it is today. According to recent numbers, the greater Boston area hosts more than 118 colleges and universities. Boston's largest universities are Boston University, Northeastern University, University of Massachusetts/Boston, and Boston College. Cambridge, across the Charles River, is home to both the Massachusetts Institute of Technology (MIT) and Harvard University, which also has a presence in nearby Allston.

Boston's moniker is "The Hub." The largest city in the six-state New England region, it has been recognized not only as a city of historic importance in the American Revolution, but as a leading educational and medical center and as a site for historic architecture and world class cultural institutions.

Historic Faneuil Hall and the nearby Quincy Market have been renovated into a historical attraction and a festival marketplace of food and shopping. The Back Bay and fashionable Newbury Street offers art galleries, fashion boutiques, and open-air cafes, all of which draw tourists and residents alike. The Fenway neighborhood is home to the Boston Symphony Orchestra, Boston Pops, Berklee College of Music, Gardner Museum, and New England Conservatory. Along the city's downtown waterfront are the Museum of Science, New England Aquarium, and the Children's Museum.

Boston's historic buildings include Trinity Church, with its brilliant stained-glass windows, built in 1877. The African meeting house on Beacon Hill is the oldest surviving black church in North America. Christ Church (Old North Church) is the oldest church in Boston (1723) and was part of Paul Revere's ride. Modern architecture is represented by the John Hancock Tower by I.M. Pei and luxury hotels, including the Ritz Carlton Boston Common and the Four Seasons.

The TD Garden is home to the Boston Bruins and the Boston Celtics and a venue for concerts, shows and conventions. Gillette Stadium, a 68,000-seat outdoor coliseum hosts football, soccer, and other events in nearby Foxboro. Fenway Park, the oldest major league ballpark still in use, is home to the Boston Red Sox, 2018 World Series winners. Deep pride in their sports teams is a known characteristic of Bostonians. In addition to the Red Sox victory, the Celtics won the 2008 NBA championship, and the New England Patriots won the NFL Super Bowl in 2019, after which superstar quarterback Tom Brady left the team after 20 seasons.

The Boston Marathon is the world's oldest annual marathon and best-known road racing event. During the 2013 race, two explosions occurred close to the end of the course, halting the race, and preventing many from finishing. Three spectators were killed and more than 200 people were injured. Two brothers, allegedly motivated by extremist Islamist beliefs, planted the two bombs. One brother was killed by police and the other was sentenced to death.

Boston's colleges and universities have a major impact on the city's economy, attracting high-tech industries including computer hardware and software and biotech companies. Boston receives the largest amount of annual funding from the National Institutes of Health of all cities in the United States.

In 2021, Asian American Michelle Wu was the first women and first person of color elected to lead the city as mayor. It was the first time in history that Boston did not elect a white man.

Boston's weather is influenced by both tropical and polar air masses, proximity to several low-pressure storm tracks, and by its moderating East Coast location. Summer heat is relieved by sea breezes. Cold winters are often alleviated by the relatively warm ocean.

Rankings

General Rankings

- *US News & World Report* conducted a survey of more than 3,600 people and analyzed the 150 largest metropolitan areas to determine what matters most when selecting where to settle down. Boston ranked #18 out of the top 25 as having the best combination of desirable factors. Criteria: cost of living; quality of life and education; net migration; job market; desirability; and other factors. *money.usnews.com, "The 25 Best Places to Live in the U.S. in 2022-2023," May 17, 2022*

- The human resources consulting firm Mercer ranked 231 major cities worldwide in terms of overall quality of life. Boston ranked #36. Criteria: political, social, economic, and socio-cultural factors; medical and health considerations; schools and education; public services and transportation; recreation; consumer goods; housing; and natural environment. *Mercer, "Mercer 2019 Quality of Living Survey," March 13, 2019*

- Boston appeared on *Travel + Leisure's* list of "The 15 Best Cities in the United States." The city was ranked #10. Criteria: sights/landmarks; culture; food; friendliness; shopping; and overall value. *Travel + Leisure, "The World's Best Awards 2022" July 12, 2022*

- For its 35th annual "Readers' Choice Awards" survey, *Condé Nast Traveler* ranked its readers' favorite cities in the U.S. Whether it be a longed-for visit or a first on the list, these are the places that inspired a return to travel. The list was broken into large cities and cities under 250,000. Boston ranked #6 in the big city category. *Condé Nast Traveler, Readers' Choice Awards 2022, "Best Big Cities in the U.S." October 4, 2022*

Business/Finance Rankings

- According to *Business Insider*, the Boston metro area is a prime place to run a startup or move an existing business to. The area ranked #10. More than 300 metro areas were analyzed for factors that were of top concern to new business owners. Data was based on the 2019 U.S. Census Bureau American Community Survey, statistics from the CDC, Bureau of Labor Statistics employment report, and University of Chicago analysis. Criteria: business formations; percentage of vaccinated population; percentage of households with internet subscriptions; median household income; and share of work that can be done from home. *www.businessinsider.com, "The 20 Best Cities for Starting a Business in 2022 Include Baltimore, Boulder, and Boston," January 5, 2022*

- *24/7 Wall St.* used metro data from the Bureau of Labor Statistics' Occupational Employment database to identify the cities with the highest percentage of those employed in jobs requiring knowledge in the science, technology, engineering, and math (STEM) fields as well as average wages for STEM jobs. The Boston metro area was #10. *247wallst.com, "15 Cities with the Most High-Tech Jobs," January 11, 2020*

- Based on metro area social media reviews, the employment opinion group Glassdoor surveyed 50 of the most populous U.S. metro areas and equally weighed cost of living, hiring opportunity, and job satisfaction to compose a list of "25 Best Cities for Jobs." Median pay and home value, and number of active job openings were also factored in. The Boston metro area was ranked #20 in overall job satisfaction. *www.glassdoor.com, "Best Cities for Jobs," February 25, 2020*

- The Brookings Institution ranked the nation's largest cities based on income inequality. Boston was ranked #7 (#1 = greatest inequality). Criteria: the "95/20 ratio," a figure representing the income at which a household earns more than 95 percent of all other households, divided by the income at which a household earns more than only 20 percent of all other households. *Brookings Institution, "Household Income Inequality, Largest Cities of 97 Large U.S. Metro Areas, 2014-2016," February 5, 2018*

- The Brookings Institution ranked the 100 largest metro areas in the U.S. based on income inequality. Boston was ranked #10 (#1 = greatest inequality). Criteria: the "95/20 ratio," a figure representing the income at which a household earns more than 95 percent of all other households, divided by the income at which a household earns more than only 20 percent of all other households. *Brookings Institution, "Household Income Inequality, 100 Largest U.S. Metro Areas, 2014-2016," February 5, 2018*

- Payscale.com ranked the 32 largest metro areas in terms of wage growth. The Boston metro area ranked #28. Criteria: quarterly changes in private industry employee and education professional wage growth from the previous year. *PayScale, "Wage Trends by Metro Area-1st Quarter," April 20, 2023*

- The Boston metro area was identified as one of the most debt-ridden places in America by the finance site Credit.com. The metro area was ranked #16. Criteria: residents' average credit card debt as well as median income. *Credit.com, "25 Cities With the Most Credit Card Debt," February 28, 2018*

- For its annual survey of the "Most Expensive U.S. Cities to Live In," Kiplinger applied Cost of Living Index statistics developed by the Council for Community and Economic Research to U.S. Census Bureau population and median household income data for 265 urban areas. Boston ranked #9 among the most expensive in the country. *Kiplinger.com, "The 11 Most Expensive Cities to Live in the U.S.," April 15, 2023*

- Boston was identified as one of America's most frugal metro areas by *Coupons.com*. The city ranked #11 out of 25. Criteria: digital coupon usage. *Coupons.com, "America's Most Frugal Cities of 2017," March 22, 2018*

- Boston was cited as one of America's top metros for total corporate facility investment in 2022. The area ranked #8 in the large metro area category (population over 1 million). *Site Selection, "Top Metros of 2022," March 2023*

- Boston was identified as one of the happiest cities to work in by CareerBliss.com, an online community for career advancement. The city ranked #6 out of 10. Criteria: an employee's relationship with his or her boss and co-workers; daily tasks; general work environment; compensation; opportunities for advancement; company culture and job reputation; and resources. *Businesswire.com, "CareerBliss Happiest Cities to Work 2019," February 12, 2019*

- The Boston metro area appeared on the Milken Institute "2022 Best Performing Cities" list. Rank: #114 out of 200 large metro areas (population over 250,000). Criteria: job growth; wage and salary growth; high-tech output growth; housing affordability; household broadband access. *Milken Institute, "Best-Performing Cities 2022," March 28, 2022*

- *Forbes* ranked the 200 most populous metro areas to determine the nation's "Best Places for Business and Careers." The Boston metro area was ranked #41. Criteria: costs (business and living); job growth (past and projected); income growth; quality of life; educational attainment (college and high school); projected economic growth; cultural and leisure opportunities; workplace tolerance laws; net migration patterns. *Forbes, "The Best Places for Business and Careers 2019: Seattle Still On Top," October 30, 2019*

- Mercer Human Resources Consulting ranked 227 cities worldwide in terms of cost-of-living. Boston ranked #30 (the lower the ranking, the higher the cost-of-living). The survey measured the comparative cost of over 200 items (such as housing, food, clothing, domestic supplies, transportation, and recreation/entertainment) in each location. *Mercer, "2022 Cost of Living City Ranking," June 29, 2022*

Children/Family Rankings

- Boston was selected as one of the most playful cities in the U.S. by KaBOOM! The organization's Playful City USA initiative honors cities and towns across the nation that have made their communities more playable. Criteria: pledging to integrate play as a solution to challenges in their communities; making it easy for children to get active and balanced play; creating more family-friendly and innovative communities as a result. *KaBOOM! National Campaign for Play, "2017 Playful City USA Communities"*

Culture/Performing Arts Rankings

- Boston was selected as one of the 25 best cities for moviemakers in North America. Great film cities are places where filmmaking dreams can come true, that offer more creative space, lower costs, and great outdoor locations. NYC & LA were intentionally excluded. Criteria: longstanding reputations as film-friendly communities; film community and culture; affordability; and quality of life. The city was ranked #13. *MovieMaker Magazine, "Best Places to Live and Work as a Moviemaker, 2023," January 18, 2023*

Dating/Romance Rankings

- *Apartment List* conducted its Annual Renter Satisfaction Survey and asked renters "how satisfied are you with opportunities for dating in your current city." The cities were ranked from highest to lowest based on their satisfaction scores. Boston ranked #2 out of 85 cities. *Apartment List, "Best Cities for Dating 2022 with Local Dating Insights from Bumble," February 7, 2022*

Education Rankings

- Personal finance website *WalletHub* analyzed the 150 largest U.S. metropolitan statistical areas to determine where the most educated Americans are putting their degrees to work. Criteria: education levels; percentage of workers with degrees; education quality and attainment gap; public school quality rankings; quality and enrollment of each metro area's universities. Boston was ranked #6 (#1 = most educated city). *www.WalletHub.com, "Most & Least Educated Cities in America," July 18, 2022*

- Boston was selected as one of the best cities for post grads by *Rent.com*. The city ranked among the top 10. Criteria: jobs per capita; unemployment rate; mean annual income; cost of living; rental inventory. *Rent.com, "Best Cities for College Grads," December 11, 2018*

- Boston was selected as one of America's most literate cities. The city ranked #13 out of the 84 largest U.S. cities. Criteria: number of booksellers; library resources; Internet resources; educational attainment; periodical publishing resources; newspaper circulation. *Central Connecticut State University, "America's Most Literate Cities, 2018," February 2019*

Environmental Rankings

- The U.S. Environmental Protection Agency (EPA) released its list of U.S. metropolitan areas with the most ENERGY STAR certified buildings in 2022. The Boston metro area was ranked #10 out of 25. *U.S. Environmental Protection Agency, "2023 Energy Star Top Cities," April 26, 2023*

Food/Drink Rankings

- The U.S. Chamber of Commerce Foundation conducted an in-depth study on local food truck regulations, surveyed 288 food truck owners, and ranked 20 major American cities based on how friendly they are for operating a food truck. The compiled index assessed the following: procedures for obtaining permits and licenses; complying with restrictions; and financial obligations associated with operating a food truck. Boston ranked #20 overall (1 being the best). *www.foodtrucknation.us, "Food Truck Nation," March 20, 2018*

Health/Fitness Rankings

- For each of the 100 largest cities in the United States, the American Fitness Index®, compiled in partnership between the American College of Sports Medicine and the Elevance Health Foundation, evaluated community infrastructure and 34 health behaviors including preventive health, levels of chronic disease conditions, food insecurity, sleep quality, pedestrian safety, air quality, and community/environment resources that support physical activity. Boston ranked #13 for "community fitness." *americanfitnessindex.org, "2022 ACSM American Fitness Index Summary Report," July 12, 2022*

- Trulia analyzed the 100 largest U.S. metro areas to identify the nation's best cities for weight loss, based on the percentage of adults who bike or walk to work, sporting goods stores, grocery stores, access to outdoor activities, weight-loss centers, gyms, and average space reserved for parks. Boston ranked #8. *Trulia.com, "Where to Live to Get in Shape in the New Year," January 4, 2018*

- Boston was identified as one of the 10 most walkable cities in the U.S. by Walk Score. The city ranked #3. Walk Score measures walkability by analyzing hundreds of walking routes to nearby amenities, and also measures pedestrian friendliness by analyzing population density and road metrics such as block length and intersection density. *WalkScore.com, April 13, 2021*

- Boston was identified as a "2022 Spring Allergy Capital." The area ranked #68 out of 100. Three groups of factors were used to identify the most challenging cities for people with allergies during the spring season: annual spring pollen scores; over the counter allergy medicine use; number of board-certified allergy specialists. *Asthma and Allergy Foundation of America, "Spring Allergy Capitals 2022," March 2, 2022*

- Boston was identified as a "2022 Fall Allergy Capital." The area ranked #79 out of 100. Three groups of factors were used to identify the most challenging cities for people with allergies during the fall season: annual fall pollen scores; over the counter allergy medicine use; number of board-certified allergy specialists. *Asthma and Allergy Foundation of America, "Fall Allergy Capitals 2022," March 2, 2022*

- Boston was identified as a "2022 Asthma Capital." The area ranked #91 out of the nation's 100 largest metropolitan areas. Criteria: estimated asthma prevalence; asthma-related mortality; and ER visits due to asthma. Risk factors analyzed but not factored in the rankings: annual pollen score; annual air quality; public smoking laws; access to board-certified asthma specialists; rescue and controller medication use; uninsured rate; poverty rate. *Asthma and Allergy Foundation of America, "Asthma Capitals 2022: The Most Challenging Places to Live With Asthma," September 14, 2022*

- The Sharecare Community Well-Being Index evaluates 10 individual and social health factors in order to measure what matters to Americans in the communities in which they live. The Boston metro area ranked #4 in the top 10 across all 10 domains. Criteria: access to healthcare, food, and community resources; housng and transportation; economic security; feeling of purpose; physical, financial, social, and community well-being. *www.sharecare.com, "Community Well-Being Index: 2020 Metro Area & County Rankings Report," August 30, 2021*

Pet Rankings

- Boston appeared on *The Dogington Post* site as one of the top cities for dog lovers, ranking #7 out of 15. The real estate marketplace, Zillow®, and Rover, the largest pet sitter and dog walker network, introduced a new list of "Top Emerging Dog-Friendly Cities" for 2021. Criteria: number of new dog accounts on the Rover platform; and rentals and listings that mention features that attract dog owners (fenced-in yards, dog houses, dog door or proximity to a dog park). *www.dogingtonpost.com, "15 Cities Emerging as Dog-Friendliest in 2021," May 11, 2021*

Real Estate Rankings

- *WalletHub* compared the most populated U.S. cities to determine which had the best markets for real estate agents. Boston ranked #19 where demand was high and pay was the best. Criteria: sales per agent; annual median wage for real-estate agents; monthly average starting salary for real estate agents; real estate job density and competition; unemployment rate; home turnover rate; housing-market health index; and other relevant metrics. *www.WalletHub.com, "2021 Best Places to Be a Real Estate Agent," May 12, 2021*

- The Boston metro area was identified as one of the nations's 20 hottest housing markets in 2023. Criteria: listing views as an indicator of demand and number of days on the market as an indicator of pace. The area ranked #18. *Realtor.com, "January 2023 Top 20 Hottest Housing Markets," February 23, 2023*

- The Boston metro area was identified as one of the 20 least affordable housing markets in the U.S. in 2022. The area ranked #175 out of 186 markets. Criteria: qualification for a mortgage loan with a 10 percent down payment on a typical home. *National Association of Realtors®, Qualifying Income Based on Sales Price of Existing Single-Family Homes for Metropolitan Areas, 2022*

- Boston was ranked #169 out of 235 metro areas in terms of housing affordability in 2022 by the National Association of Home Builders (#1 = most affordable). Criteria: the share of homes sold in that area affordable to a family earning the local median income, based on standard mortgage underwriting criteria. *National Association of Home Builders®, NAHB-Wells Fargo Housing Opportunity Index, 4th Quarter 2022*

Safety Rankings

- Allstate ranked the 200 largest cities in America in terms of driver safety. Boston ranked #198. Criteria: internal property damage claims over a two-year period from January 2016 to December 2017. The report helps increase the importance of safety and awareness behind the wheel. *Allstate, "Allstate America's Best Drivers Report, 2019" June 24, 2019*

Seniors/Retirement Rankings

- From its Best Cities for Successful Aging indexes, the Milken Institute generated rankings for metropolitan areas, weighing data in nine categories—health care, wellness, living arrangements, transportation and convenience, financial characteristics, education, employment, community engagement, and overall livability. The Boston metro area was ranked #9 overall in the large metro area category. *Milken Institute, "Best Cities for Successful Aging, 2017" March 14, 2017*

Sports/Recreation Rankings

- Boston was chosen as one of America's best cities for bicycling. The city ranked #20 out of 50. Criteria: cycling infrastructure that is safe and friendly for all ages; energy and bike culture. The editors evaluated cities with populations of 100,000 or more. *Bicycling, "The 50 Best Bike Cities in America," October 10, 2018*

Transportation Rankings

- Business Insider presented an AllTransit Performance Score ranking of public transportation in major U.S. cities and towns, with populations over 250,000, in which Boston earned the #3-ranked "Transit Score," awarded for frequency of service, access to jobs, quality and number of stops, and affordability. *www.businessinsider.com, "The 17 Major U.S. Cities with the Best Public Transportation," April 17, 2018*

- The business website *24/7 Wall St.* reviewed U.S. Census data to identify the 25 cities where the largest share of households do not own a vehicle. Boston held the #4 position. *247wallst.com, "Cities Where No One Wants to Drive," January 12, 2020*

- According to the INRIX "2022 Global Traffic Scorecard," Boston was identified as one of the most congested metro areas in the U.S. The area ranked #2 out of 25. Criteria: average annual time spent in traffic and average cost of congestion per motorist. *Inrix.com, "Return to Work, Higher Gas Prices & Inflation Drove Americans to Spend Hundreds More in Time and Money Commuting," January 10, 2023*

Women/Minorities Rankings

- The *Houston Chronicle* listed the Boston metro area as #1 in top places for young Latinos to live in the U.S. Research was largely based on housing and occupational data from the largest metropolitan areas performed by *Forbes* and NBC Universo. Criteria: percentage of 18-34 year-olds; Latino college grad rates; and diversity. *blog.chron.com, "The 15 Best Big Cities for Latino Millenials," January 26, 2016*

- *24/7 Wall St.* compared median annual earnings for men and women who worked full-time, year-round, female employment in management roles, bachelor's degree attainment among women, female life expectancy, uninsured rates, and preschool enrollment to identify the best cities for women. The U.S. metropolitan area, Boston was ranked #9 in pay disparity and other gender gaps. *24/7 Wall St., "The Easiest (and Toughest) Cities to Be a Woman," January 11, 2020*

- Personal finance website *WalletHub* compared more than 180 U.S. cities across two key dimensions, "Hispanic Business-Friendliness" and "Hispanic Purchasing Power," to arrive at the most favorable conditions for Hispanic entrepreneurs. Boston was ranked #161 out of 182. Criteria includes: share of Hispanic-Owned Businesses; Hispanic entrepreneurship rate to median annual income of Hispanics; Small Business-Friendliness score; cost of living; and number of Hispanics with at least a bachelor's degree. *WalletHub.com, "2019's Best Cities for Hispanic Entrepreneurs," May 1, 2019*

Miscellaneous Rankings

- In its roundup of St. Patrick's Day parades "Gayot" listed the best festivals and parades of all things Irish. The festivities in Boston as among the best in North America. *www.gayot.com, "Best St. Patrick's Day Parades," March 2023*

- The watchdog site, Charity Navigator, conducted a study of charities in major markets both to analyze statistical differences in their financial, accountability, and transparency practices and to track year-to-year variations in individual philanthropic communities. The Boston metro area was ranked #23 among the 30 metro markets in the rating category of Overall Score. *www.charitynavigator.org, "2017 Metro Market Study," May 1, 2017*

- *WalletHub* compared the 150 most populated U.S. cities to determine their operating efficiency. A "Quality of Services" score was constructed for each city and then divided by the total budget per capita to reveal which were managed the best. Boston ranked #73. Criteria: financial stability; economy; education; safety; health; infrastructure and pollution. *www.WalletHub.com, "2022's Best- & Worst-Run Cities in America," June 21, 2022*

- The National Alliance to End Homelessness listed the 25 most populous metro areas with the highest rate of homelessness. The Boston metro area had a high rate of homelessness. Criteria: number of homeless people per 10,000 population in 2016. *National Alliance to End Homelessness, "Homelessness in the 25 Most Populous U.S. Metro Areas," September 1, 2017*

Business Environment

DEMOGRAPHICS

Population Growth

Area	1990 Census	2000 Census	2010 Census	2020 Census	Population Growth (%)	
					1990-2020	2010-2020
City	574,283	589,141	617,594	675,647	17.7	9.4
MSA[1]	4,133,895	4,391,344	4,552,402	4,941,632	19.5	8.5
U.S.	248,709,873	281,421,906	308,745,538	331,449,281	33.3	7.4

Note: (1) Figures cover the Boston-Cambridge-Newton, MA-NH Metropolitan Statistical Area
Source: U.S. Census Bureau, 1990 Census, 2000 Census, 2010 Census, 2020 Census

Race

Area	White Alone[2] (%)	Black Alone[2] (%)	Asian Alone[2] (%)	AIAN[3] Alone[2] (%)	NHOPI[4] Alone[2] (%)	Other Race Alone[2] (%)	Two or More Races (%)
City	47.1	20.6	11.3	0.4	0.1	10.1	10.5
MSA[1]	68.4	7.4	8.7	0.3	0.0	6.9	8.4
U.S.	61.6	12.4	6.0	1.1	0.2	8.4	10.2

Note: (1) Figures cover the Boston-Cambridge-Newton, MA-NH Metropolitan Statistical Area; (2) Alone is defined as not being in combination with one or more other races; (3) American Indian and Alaska Native; (4) Native Hawaiian and Other Pacific Islander
Source: U.S. Census Bureau, 2020 Census

Hispanic or Latino Origin

Area	Total (%)	Mexican (%)	Puerto Rican (%)	Cuban (%)	Other (%)
City	19.8	1.1	5.2	0.4	13.1
MSA[1]	11.6	0.7	2.8	0.3	7.8
U.S.	18.4	11.2	1.8	0.7	4.7

Note: Persons of Hispanic or Latino origin can be of any race; (1) Figures cover the Boston-Cambridge-Newton, MA-NH Metropolitan Statistical Area
Source: U.S. Census Bureau, 2017-2021 American Community Survey 5-Year Estimates

Age

Area	Percent of Population									Median Age
	Under Age 5	Age 5–19	Age 20–34	Age 35–44	Age 45–54	Age 55–64	Age 65–74	Age 75–84	Age 85+	
City	4.5	14.1	37.6	12.0	9.6	9.8	7.2	3.7	1.5	31.7
MSA[1]	4.9	17.2	22.6	12.5	12.6	13.5	9.8	4.8	2.1	39.0
U.S.	5.6	19.2	20.2	12.7	12.4	13.1	10.0	4.9	1.9	38.8

Note: (1) Figures cover the Boston-Cambridge-Newton, MA-NH Metropolitan Statistical Area
Source: U.S. Census Bureau, 2020 Census

Disability by Age

Area	All Ages	Under 18 Years Old	18 to 64 Years Old	65 Years and Over
City	11.8	6.3	8.7	38.3
MSA[1]	10.5	4.2	7.8	30.2
U.S.	12.6	4.4	10.3	33.4

Note: Figures show percent of the civilian noninstitutionalized population that reported having a disability. Disability status is determined from six types of difficulty: vision, hearing, cognitive, ambulatory, self-care, and independent living. For children under 5 years old, hearing and vision difficulty are used to determine disability status. For children between the ages of 5 and 14, disability status is determined from hearing, vision, cognitive, ambulatory, and self-care difficulties. For people aged 15 years and older, they are considered to have a disability if they have difficulty with any one of the six difficulty types; Note: (1) Figures cover the Boston-Cambridge-Newton, MA-NH Metropolitan Statistical Area
Source: U.S. Census Bureau, 2017-2021 American Community Survey 5-Year Estimates

Ancestry

Area	German	Irish	English	American	Italian	Polish	French[2]	Scottish	Dutch
City	4.8	13.1	4.9	2.2	7.2	2.1	1.8	1.1	0.4
MSA[1]	5.8	20.3	9.7	3.3	12.4	3.1	4.2	2.1	0.5
U.S.	12.8	9.6	8.1	5.7	5.0	2.7	2.2	1.6	1.1

Note: Figures are the percentage of the total population reporting a particular ancestry. The nine most commonly reported ancestries in the U.S. are shown. Figures include multiple ancestries (e.g. if a person reported being Irish and Italian, they were included in both columns); (1) Figures cover the Boston-Cambridge-Newton, MA-NH Metropolitan Statistical Area; (2) Excludes Basque
Source: U.S. Census Bureau, 2017-2021 American Community Survey 5-Year Estimates

Foreign-born Population

Area	Percent of Population Born in								
	Any Foreign Country	Asia	Mexico	Europe	Caribbean	Central America[2]	South America	Africa	Canada
City	28.1	7.6	0.4	3.1	8.6	2.5	2.3	3.0	0.4
MSA[1]	19.3	6.3	0.2	3.2	3.6	1.6	2.2	1.7	0.4
U.S.	13.6	4.2	3.3	1.5	1.4	1.1	1.1	0.8	0.2

Note: (1) Figures cover the Boston-Cambridge-Newton, MA-NH Metropolitan Statistical Area; (2) Excludes Mexico.
Source: U.S. Census Bureau, 2017-2021 American Community Survey 5-Year Estimates

Household Size

Area	Persons in Household (%)							Average Household Size
	One	Two	Three	Four	Five	Six	Seven or More	
City	36.2	32.7	15.1	9.4	3.9	1.6	0.9	2.30
MSA[1]	27.6	33.1	16.6	14.4	5.6	1.8	0.9	2.50
U.S.	28.1	33.8	15.5	12.9	6.0	2.3	1.4	2.60

Note: (1) Figures cover the Boston-Cambridge-Newton, MA-NH Metropolitan Statistical Area
Source: U.S. Census Bureau, 2017-2021 American Community Survey 5-Year Estimates

Household Relationships

Area	House-holder	Opposite-sex Spouse	Same-sex Spouse	Opposite-sex Unmarried Partner	Same-sex Unmarried Partner	Child[2]	Grand-child	Other Relatives	Non-relatives
City	41.4	10.4	0.5	3.1	0.4	20.6	1.7	5.3	9.7
MSA[1]	38.7	17.4	0.3	2.5	0.2	27.1	1.6	4.5	4.4
U.S.	38.3	17.5	0.2	2.5	0.2	28.3	2.4	4.8	3.4

Note: Figures are percent of the total population; (1) Figures cover the Boston-Cambridge-Newton, MA-NH Metropolitan Statistical Area; (2) Includes biological, adopted, and stepchildren of the householder
Source: U.S. Census Bureau, 2020 Census

Gender

Area	Males	Females	Males per 100 Females
City	319,326	356,321	89.6
MSA[1]	2,390,705	2,550,927	93.7
U.S.	162,685,811	168,763,470	96.4

Note: (1) Figures cover the Boston-Cambridge-Newton, MA-NH Metropolitan Statistical Area
Source: U.S. Census Bureau, 2020 Census

Marital Status

Area	Never Married	Now Married[2]	Separated	Widowed	Divorced
City	55.7	30.9	2.5	3.6	7.3
MSA[1]	37.3	47.6	1.6	4.9	8.7
U.S.	33.8	48.0	1.8	5.6	10.8

Note: Figures are percentages and cover the population 15 years of age and older; (1) Figures cover the Boston-Cambridge-Newton, MA-NH Metropolitan Statistical Area; (2) Excludes separated
Source: U.S. Census Bureau, 2017-2021 American Community Survey 5-Year Estimates

Religious Groups by Family

Area	Catholic	Baptist	Methodist	LDS[2]	Pentecostal	Lutheran	Islam	Adventist	Other
MSA[1]	37.0	1.0	0.7	0.5	0.7	0.2	2.2	0.9	7.1
U.S.	18.7	7.3	3.0	2.0	1.8	1.7	1.3	1.3	11.6

Note: Figures are the number of adherents as a percentage of the total population and cover the eight largest religious groups in the U.S; (1) Figures cover the Boston-Cambridge-Newton, MA-NH Metropolitan Statistical Area; (2) Church of Jesus Christ of Latter-day Saints
Sources: 2020 U.S. Religion Census, Association of Statisticians of American Religious Bodies; The Association of Religion Data Archives (ARDA)

Religious Groups by Tradition

Area	Catholic	Evangelical Protestant	Mainline Protestant	Black Protestant	Islam	Judaism	Hinduism	Orthodox	Buddhism
MSA[1]	37.0	3.4	3.2	0.3	2.2	1.1	0.3	0.9	0.4
U.S.	18.7	16.5	5.2	2.3	1.3	0.6	0.4	0.4	0.3

Note: Figures are the number of adherents as a percentage of the total population; (1) Figures cover the Boston-Cambridge-Newton, MA-NH Metropolitan Statistical Area
Sources: 2020 U.S. Religion Census, Association of Statisticians of American Religious Bodies; The Association of Religion Data Archives (ARDA)

ECONOMY

Gross Metropolitan Product

Area	2020	2021	2022	2023	Rank[2]
MSA[1]	480.3	526.5	569.8	601.7	8

Note: Figures are in billions of dollars; (1) Figures cover the Boston-Cambridge-Newton, MA-NH Metropolitan Statistical Area; (2) Rank is based on 2021 data and ranges from 1 to 381
Source: U.S. Conference of Mayors, U.S. Metro Economies: U.S. Metros Compared to Global and State Economies, June 2022

Economic Growth

Area	2018-20 (%)	2021 (%)	2022 (%)	2023 (%)	Rank[2]
MSA[1]	-0.1	6.7	3.2	2.4	146
U.S.	-0.6	5.7	3.1	2.9	–

Note: Figures are real gross metropolitan product (GMP) growth rates and represent average annual percent change; (1) Figures cover the Boston-Cambridge-Newton, MA-NH Metropolitan Statistical Area; (2) Rank is based on 2020 2-year average annual percent change and ranges from 1 to 381
Source: U.S. Conference of Mayors, U.S. Metro Economies: U.S. Metros Compared to Global and State Economies, June 2022

Metropolitan Area Exports

Area	2016	2017	2018	2019	2020	2021	Rank[2]
MSA[1]	21,168.0	23,116.2	24,450.1	23,505.8	23,233.8	32,084.2	12

Note: Figures are in millions of dollars; (1) Figures cover the Boston-Cambridge-Newton, MA-NH Metropolitan Statistical Area; (2) Rank is based on 2021 data and ranges from 1 to 388
Source: U.S. Department of Commerce, International Trade Administration, Office of Trade and Economic Analysis, Industry and Analysis, Exports by Metropolitan Area, data extracted March 16, 2023

Building Permits

Area	Single-Family			Multi-Family			Total		
	2021	2022	Pct. Chg.	2021	2022	Pct. Chg.	2021	2022	Pct. Chg.
City	53	53	0.0	3,459	3,882	12.2	3,512	3,935	12.0
MSA[1]	4,820	3,985	-17.3	11,782	10,469	-11.1	16,602	14,454	-12.9
U.S.	1,115,400	975,600	-12.5	621,600	689,500	10.9	1,737,000	1,665,100	-4.1

Note: (1) Figures cover the Boston-Cambridge-Newton, MA-NH Metropolitan Statistical Area; Figures represent new, privately-owned housing units authorized (unadjusted data); All permit data are based on estimates with imputation
Source: U.S. Census Bureau, Manufacturing, Mining, and Construction Statistics, Building Permits, 2021, 2022

Bankruptcy Filings

Area	Business Filings			Nonbusiness Filings		
	2021	2022	% Chg.	2021	2022	% Chg.
Suffolk County	23	42	82.6	224	221	-1.3
U.S.	14,347	13,481	-6.0	399,269	374,240	-6.3

Note: Business filings include Chapter 7, Chapter 9, Chapter 11, Chapter 12, Chapter 13, Chapter 15, and Section 304; Nonbusiness filings include Chapter 7, Chapter 11, and Chapter 13
Source: Administrative Office of the U.S. Courts, Business and Nonbusiness Bankruptcy, County Cases Commenced by Chapter of the Bankruptcy Code, During the 12-Month Period Ending December 31, 2021 and Business and Nonbusiness Bankruptcy, County Cases Commenced by Chapter of the Bankruptcy Code, During the 12-Month Period Ending December 31, 2022

Housing Vacancy Rates

Area	Gross Vacancy Rate[2] (%)			Year-Round Vacancy Rate[3] (%)			Rental Vacancy Rate[4] (%)			Homeowner Vacancy Rate[5] (%)		
	2020	2021	2022	2020	2021	2022	2020	2021	2022	2020	2021	2022
MSA[1]	6.8	7.4	6.2	5.6	6.2	5.4	4.7	4.5	2.5	0.4	0.5	0.7
U.S.	10.6	10.8	10.5	8.2	8.4	8.2	6.3	6.1	5.8	1.0	0.9	0.8

Note: (1) Figures cover the Boston-Cambridge-Newton, MA-NH Metropolitan Statistical Area; (2) The percentage of the total housing inventory that is vacant; (3) The percentage of the housing inventory (excluding seasonal units) that is year-round vacant; (4) The percentage of rental inventory that is vacant for rent; (5) The percentage of homeowner inventory that is vacant for sale
Source: U.S. Census Bureau, Housing Vacancies and Homeownership Annual Statistics: 2020, 2021, 2022

INCOME

Income

Area	Per Capita ($)	Median Household ($)	Average Household ($)
City	50,344	81,744	120,939
MSA[1]	53,033	99,039	135,411
U.S.	37,638	69,021	97,196

Note: (1) Figures cover the Boston-Cambridge-Newton, MA-NH Metropolitan Statistical Area
Source: U.S. Census Bureau, 2017-2021 American Community Survey 5-Year Estimates

52 Boston, Massachusetts

Household Income Distribution

Area	Percent of Households Earning							
	Under $15,000	$15,000 -$24,999	$25,000 -$34,999	$35,000 -$49,999	$50,000 -$74,999	$75,000 -$99,999	$100,000 -$149,999	$150,000 and up
City	14.9	7.2	5.5	7.7	11.9	10.5	16.1	26.2
MSA[1]	8.1	5.6	5.2	7.6	12.5	11.4	18.2	31.3
U.S.	9.4	7.8	8.2	11.4	16.8	12.8	16.3	17.3

Note: (1) Figures cover the Boston-Cambridge-Newton, MA-NH Metropolitan Statistical Area
Source: U.S. Census Bureau, 2017-2021 American Community Survey 5-Year Estimates

Poverty Rate

Area	All Ages	Under 18 Years Old	18 to 64 Years Old	65 Years and Over
City	17.6	23.7	15.6	21.0
MSA[1]	9.0	10.3	8.4	9.5
U.S.	12.6	17.0	11.8	9.6

Note: Figures are percentage of people whose income during the past 12 months was below the poverty level;
(1) Figures cover the Boston-Cambridge-Newton, MA-NH Metropolitan Statistical Area
Source: U.S. Census Bureau, 2017-2021 American Community Survey 5-Year Estimates

EMPLOYMENT

Labor Force and Employment

Area	Civilian Labor Force			Workers Employed		
	Dec. 2021	Dec. 2022	% Chg.	Dec. 2021	Dec. 2022	% Chg.
City	394,417	392,029	-0.6	379,015	380,790	0.5
NECTAD[1]	1,673,210	1,666,434	-0.4	1,614,446	1,622,005	0.5
U.S.	161,696,000	164,224,000	1.6	155,732,000	158,872,000	2.0

Note: Data is not seasonally adjusted and covers workers 16 years of age and older; (1) Figures cover the
Boston-Cambridge-Newton, MA New England City and Town Area Division
Source: Bureau of Labor Statistics, Local Area Unemployment Statistics

Unemployment Rate

Area	2022											
	Jan.	Feb.	Mar.	Apr.	May	Jun.	Jul.	Aug.	Sep.	Oct.	Nov.	Dec.
City	4.4	3.5	3.2	3.0	3.2	3.5	3.6	3.5	3.0	2.9	2.7	2.9
NECTAD[1]	4.2	3.4	3.1	2.8	2.9	3.1	3.0	3.0	2.7	2.7	2.5	2.7
U.S.	4.4	4.1	3.8	3.3	3.4	3.8	3.8	3.8	3.3	3.4	3.4	3.3

Note: Data is not seasonally adjusted and covers workers 16 years of age and older; (1) Figures cover the
Boston-Cambridge-Newton, MA New England City and Town Area Division
Source: Bureau of Labor Statistics, Local Area Unemployment Statistics

Average Wages

Occupation	$/Hr.	Occupation	$/Hr.
Accountants and Auditors	46.85	Maintenance and Repair Workers	27.11
Automotive Mechanics	25.85	Marketing Managers	80.96
Bookkeepers	27.28	Network and Computer Systems Admin.	52.37
Carpenters	34.31	Nurses, Licensed Practical	33.67
Cashiers	16.21	Nurses, Registered	51.44
Computer Programmers	55.26	Nursing Assistants	20.42
Computer Systems Analysts	57.55	Office Clerks, General	23.38
Computer User Support Specialists	35.38	Physical Therapists	46.36
Construction Laborers	31.95	Physicians	106.88
Cooks, Restaurant	19.78	Plumbers, Pipefitters and Steamfitters	39.70
Customer Service Representatives	24.00	Police and Sheriff's Patrol Officers	36.32
Dentists	89.08	Postal Service Mail Carriers	28.27
Electricians	39.81	Real Estate Sales Agents	38.33
Engineers, Electrical	61.23	Retail Salespersons	18.39
Fast Food and Counter Workers	16.22	Sales Representatives, Technical/Scientific	54.97
Financial Managers	88.25	Secretaries, Exc. Legal/Medical/Executive	25.44
First-Line Supervisors of Office Workers	36.88	Security Guards	19.80
General and Operations Managers	74.45	Surgeons	148.22
Hairdressers/Cosmetologists	23.51	Teacher Assistants, Exc. Postsecondary*	20.14
Home Health and Personal Care Aides	17.13	Teachers, Secondary School, Exc. Sp. Ed.*	40.58
Janitors and Cleaners	19.76	Telemarketers	19.82
Landscaping/Groundskeeping Workers	21.78	Truck Drivers, Heavy/Tractor-Trailer	27.78
Lawyers	97.55	Truck Drivers, Light/Delivery Services	23.55
Maids and Housekeeping Cleaners	19.01	Waiters and Waitresses	19.76

Note: Wage data covers the Boston-Cambridge-Nashua, MA-NH New England City and Town Area; (*) Hourly
wages were calculated from annual wage data based on a 40 hour work week; n/a not available.
Source: Bureau of Labor Statistics, Metro Area Occupational Employment & Wage Estimates, May 2022

Employment by Industry

Sector	NECTAD[1]		U.S.
	Number of Employees	Percent of Total	Percent of Total
Construction, Mining, and Logging	75,300	3.9	5.4
Private Education and Health Services	439,700	22.9	16.1
Financial Activities	160,000	8.3	5.9
Government	198,100	10.3	14.5
Information	69,000	3.6	2.0
Leisure and Hospitality	172,200	9.0	10.3
Manufacturing	77,100	4.0	8.4
Other Services	64,800	3.4	3.7
Professional and Business Services	419,800	21.9	14.7
Retail Trade	138,200	7.2	10.2
Transportation, Warehousing, and Utilities	48,200	2.5	4.9
Wholesale Trade	58,100	3.0	3.9

Note: Figures are non-farm employment as of December 2022. Figures are not seasonally adjusted and include workers 16 years of age and older; (1) Figures cover the Boston-Cambridge-Newton, MA New England City and Town Area Division
Source: Bureau of Labor Statistics, Current Employment Statistics, Employment, Hours, and Earnings

Employment by Occupation

Occupation Classification	City (%)	MSA[1] (%)	U.S. (%)
Management, Business, Science, and Arts	53.8	52.1	40.3
Natural Resources, Construction, and Maintenance	3.5	6.1	8.7
Production, Transportation, and Material Moving	6.4	8.2	13.1
Sales and Office	18.1	18.5	20.9
Service	18.2	15.2	17.0

Note: Figures cover employed civilians 16 years of age and older; (1) Figures cover the Boston-Cambridge-Newton, MA-NH Metropolitan Statistical Area
Source: U.S. Census Bureau, 2017-2021 American Community Survey 5-Year Estimates

Occupations with Greatest Projected Employment Growth: 2022 – 2024

Occupation[1]	2022 Employment	2024 Projected Employment	Numeric Employment Change	Percent Employment Change
Home Health and Personal Care Aides	116,330	122,940	6,610	5.7
Fast Food and Counter Workers	92,850	95,950	3,100	3.3
Cooks, Restaurant	32,200	34,940	2,740	8.5
General and Operations Managers	117,860	119,220	1,360	1.2
Waiters and Waitresses	43,720	45,070	1,350	3.1
Management Analysts	35,540	36,880	1,340	3.8
Heavy and Tractor-Trailer Truck Drivers	29,700	30,790	1,090	3.7
Light Truck or Delivery Services Drivers	25,360	26,390	1,030	4.1
Medical and Health Services Managers	19,250	20,190	940	4.9
First-Line Supervisors of Food Preparation and Serving Workers	21,360	22,230	870	4.1

Note: Projections cover Massachusetts; (1) Sorted by numeric employment change
Source: www.projectionscentral.com, State Occupational Projections, 2022–2024 Short-Term Projections

Fastest-Growing Occupations: 2022 – 2024

Occupation[1]	2022 Employment	2024 Projected Employment	Numeric Employment Change	Percent Employment Change
Farmworkers and Laborers, Crop, Nursery, and Greenhouse	6,040	6,610	570	9.4
Farmers, Ranchers, and Other Agricultural Managers	8,170	8,930	760	9.3
Cooks, Restaurant	32,200	34,940	2,740	8.5
Actuaries	880	950	70	8.0
Statisticians	2,110	2,270	160	7.6
Nurse Practitioners	7,530	8,050	520	6.9
Information Security Analysts (SOC 2018)	3,850	4,080	230	6.0
Home Health and Personal Care Aides	116,330	122,940	6,610	5.7
Logisticians	3,470	3,660	190	5.5
Operations Research Analysts	3,440	3,630	190	5.5

Note: Projections cover Massachusetts; (1) Sorted by percent employment change and excludes occupations with numeric employment change less than 50
Source: www.projectionscentral.com, State Occupational Projections, 2022–2024 Short-Term Projections

CITY FINANCES

City Government Finances

Component	2020 ($000)	2020 ($ per capita)
Total Revenues	4,574,172	6,604
Total Expenditures	4,384,023	6,330
Debt Outstanding	1,811,471	2,615
Cash and Securities[1]	2,697,426	3,895

Note: (1) Cash and security holdings of a government at the close of its fiscal year, including those of its dependent agencies, utilities, and liquor stores.
Source: U.S. Census Bureau, State & Local Government Finances 2020

City Government Revenue by Source

Source	2020 ($000)	2020 ($ per capita)	2020 (%)
General Revenue			
From Federal Government	87,860	127	1.9
From State Government	946,711	1,367	20.7
From Local Governments	1,353	2	0.0
Taxes			
Property	2,539,737	3,667	55.5
Sales and Gross Receipts	163,228	236	3.6
Personal Income	0	0	0.0
Corporate Income	0	0	0.0
Motor Vehicle License	0	0	0.0
Other Taxes	113,690	164	2.5
Current Charges	304,996	440	6.7
Liquor Store	0	0	0.0
Utility	161,156	233	3.5

Source: U.S. Census Bureau, State & Local Government Finances 2020

City Government Expenditures by Function

Function	2020 ($000)	2020 ($ per capita)	2020 (%)
General Direct Expenditures			
Air Transportation	0	0	0.0
Corrections	0	0	0.0
Education	1,603,191	2,314	36.6
Employment Security Administration	0	0	0.0
Financial Administration	82,269	118	1.9
Fire Protection	277,013	400	6.3
General Public Buildings	44,786	64	1.0
Governmental Administration, Other	20,704	29	0.5
Health	19,573	28	0.4
Highways	133,139	192	3.0
Hospitals	261,122	377	6.0
Housing and Community Development	91,423	132	2.1
Interest on General Debt	76,731	110	1.8
Judicial and Legal	7,697	11	0.2
Libraries	57,153	82	1.3
Parking	2,265	3	0.1
Parks and Recreation	107,282	154	2.4
Police Protection	439,588	634	10.0
Public Welfare	2,951	4	0.1
Sewerage	102,437	147	2.3
Solid Waste Management	64,793	93	1.5
Veterans' Services	0	0	0.0
Liquor Store	0	0	0.0
Utility	26,369	38	0.6

Source: U.S. Census Bureau, State & Local Government Finances 2020

TAXES

State Corporate Income Tax Rates

State	Tax Rate (%)	Income Brackets ($)	Num. of Brackets	Financial Institution Tax Rate (%)[a]	Federal Income Tax Ded.
Massachusetts	8.0 (k)	Flat rate	1	9.0 (k)	No

Note: Tax rates as of January 1, 2023; (a) Rates listed are the corporate income tax rate applied to financial institutions or excise taxes based on income. Some states have other taxes based upon the value of deposits or shares; (k) Business and manufacturing corporations pay an additional tax of $2.60 per $1,000 on either taxable Massachusetts tangible property or taxable net worth allocable to the state (for intangible property corporations). The minimum tax for both corporations and financial institutions is $456.
Source: Federation of Tax Administrators, State Corporate Income Tax Rates, January 1, 2023

State Individual Income Tax Rates

State	Tax Rate (%)	Income Brackets ($)	Personal Exemptions ($)			Standard Ded. ($)	
			Single	Married	Depend.	Single	Married
Massachusetts	5.0 (m)	Flat rate	4,400	8,800	1,000	–	–

Note: Tax rates as of January 1, 2023; Local- and county-level taxes are not included; Federal income tax is not deductible on state income tax returns; (m) Short-term capital gains in Massachusetts istaxed at 12% rate. An additional tax of 4% on income of $1 million.
Source: Federation of Tax Administrators, State Individual Income Tax Rates, January 1, 2023

Various State Sales and Excise Tax Rates

State	State Sales Tax (%)	Gasoline[1] ($/gal.)	Cigarette[2] ($/pack)	Spirits[3] ($/gal.)	Wine[4] ($/gal.)	Beer[5] ($/gal.)	Recreational Marijuana (%)
Massachusetts	6.25	0.2654	3.51	4.05	0.55	0.11	(h)

Note: All tax rates as of January 1, 2023; (1) The American Petroleum Institute has developed a methodology for determining the average tax rate on a gallon of fuel. Rates may include any of the following: excise taxes, environmental fees, storage tank fees, other fees or taxes, general sales tax, and local taxes; (2) The federal excise tax of $1.0066 per pack and local taxes are not included; (3) Rates are those applicable to off-premise sales of 40% alcohol by volume (a.b.v.) distilled spirits in 750ml containers. Local excise taxes are excluded; (4) Rates are those applicable to off-premise sales of 11% a.b.v. non-carbonated wine in 750ml containers; (5) Rates are those applicable to off-premise sales of 4.7% a.b.v. beer in 12 ounce containers; (h) 10.75% excise tax (retail price)
Source: Tax Foundation, 2023 Facts & Figures: How Does Your State Compare?

State Business Tax Climate Index Rankings

State	Overall Rank	Corporate Tax Rank	Individual Income Tax Rank	Sales Tax Rank	Property Tax Rank	Unemployment Insurance Tax Rank
Massachusetts	34	36	11	13	46	50

Note: The index is a measure of how each state's tax laws affect economic performance. The lower the rank, the more favorable a state's tax system is for business. States without a given tax are given a ranking of 1. The scores/rankings for the District of Columbia do not affect other states. The 2023 index represents the tax climate as of July 1, 2022.
Source: Tax Foundation, State Business Tax Climate Index 2023

TRANSPORTATION

Means of Transportation to Work

Area	Car/Truck/Van		Public Transportation			Bicycle	Walked	Other Means	Worked at Home
	Drove Alone	Car-pooled	Bus	Subway	Railroad				
City	36.1	5.5	10.6	15.5	1.1	2.0	14.4	2.6	12.3
MSA[1]	62.2	6.6	3.2	5.5	1.8	0.9	5.0	1.7	13.0
U.S.	73.2	8.6	2.0	1.6	0.5	0.5	2.5	1.5	9.7

Note: Figures are percentages and cover workers 16 years of age and older; (1) Figures cover the Boston-Cambridge-Newton, MA-NH Metropolitan Statistical Area
Source: U.S. Census Bureau, 2017-2021 American Community Survey 5-Year Estimates

Travel Time to Work

Area	Less Than 10 Minutes	10 to 19 Minutes	20 to 29 Minutes	30 to 44 Minutes	45 to 59 Minutes	60 to 89 Minutes	90 Minutes or More
City	6.9	20.4	19.6	29.8	12.1	9.1	2.1
MSA[1]	9.1	22.7	18.6	24.4	11.7	10.1	3.3
U.S.	12.4	28.5	21.0	20.9	8.2	6.2	2.9

Note: Note: Figures are percentages and include workers 16 years old and over; (1) Figures cover the Boston-Cambridge-Newton, MA-NH Metropolitan Statistical Area
Source: U.S. Census Bureau, 2017-2021 American Community Survey 5-Year Estimates

Key Congestion Measures

Measure	1990	2000	2010	2015	2020
Annual Hours of Delay, Total (000)	83,117	126,792	154,889	179,172	122,348
Annual Hours of Delay, Per Auto Commuter	44	61	65	75	50
Annual Congestion Cost, Per Auto Commuter ($)	1,327	1,520	1,478	1,578	1,103

Note: Covers the Boston MA-NH-RI urban area
Source: Texas A&M Transportation Institute, 2021 Urban Mobility Report

Freeway Travel Time Index

Measure	1985	1990	1995	2000	2005	2010	2015	2020
Urban Area Index[1]	1.15	1.19	1.21	1.26	1.27	1.26	1.28	1.12
Urban Area Rank[1,2]	15	12	16	13	18	19	19	10

Note: Freeway Travel Time Index—the ratio of travel time in the peak period to the travel time at free-flow conditions. For example, a value of 1.30 indicates a 20-minute free-flow trip takes 26 minutes in the peak (20 minutes x 1.30 = 26 minutes); (1) Covers the Boston MA-NH-RI urban area; (2) Rank is based on 101 larger urban areas (#1 = highest travel time index)
Source: Texas A&M Transportation Institute, 2021 Urban Mobility Report

Public Transportation

Agency Name / Mode of Transportation	Vehicles Operated in Maximum Service[1]	Annual Unlinked Passenger Trips[2] (in thous.)	Annual Passenger Miles[3] (in thous.)
Massachusetts Bay Transportation Authority (MBTA)			
Bus (directly operated)	775	47,350.4	124,526.9
Bus (purchased transportation)	69	461.9	1,076.3
Bus Rapid Transit (directly operated)	39	4,780.6	10,173.3
Commuter Rail (purchased transportation)	416	6,995.4	155,056.2
Demand Response (purchased transportation)	432	758.8	5,646.1
Ferryboat (purchased transportation)	8	173.6	1,382.1
Heavy Rail (directly operated)	336	44,823.2	146,795.5
Light Rail (directly operated)	155	14,774.0	36,878.7
Trolleybus (directly operated)	22	833.8	1,996.4

Note: (1) Number of revenue vehicles operated by the given mode and type of service to meet the annual maximum service requirement. This is the revenue vehicle count during the peak season of the year; on the week and day that maximum service is provided. Vehicles operated in maximum service (VOMS) exclude atypical days and one-time special events; (2) Number of passengers who boarded public transportation vehicles. Passengers are counted each time they board a vehicle no matter how many vehicles they use to travel from their origin to their destination. (3) Sum of the distances ridden by all passengers during the entire fiscal year.
Source: Federal Transit Administration, National Transit Database, 2021

Air Transportation

Airport Name and Code / Type of Service	Passenger Airlines[1]	Passenger Enplanements	Freight Carriers[2]	Freight (lbs)
Logan International (BOS)				
Domestic service (U.S. carriers - 2022)	30	14,486,034	16	193,066,841
International service (U.S. carriers - 2021)	7	441,953	5	5,757,968

Note: (1) Includes all U.S.-based major, minor and commuter airlines that carried at least one passenger during the year; (2) Includes all U.S.-based airlines and freight carriers that transported at least one pound of freight during the year.
Source: Bureau of Transportation Statistics, The Intermodal Transportation Database, Air Carriers: T-100 Domestic Market (U.S. Carriers), 2022; Bureau of Transportation Statistics, The Intermodal Transportation Database, Air Carriers: T-100 International Market (U.S. Carriers), 2021

BUSINESSES

Major Business Headquarters

Company Name	Industry	Rankings Fortune[1]	Rankings Forbes[2]
American Tower	Telecommunications	375	-
BCG (Boston Consulting Group)	Business services & supplies	-	41
Bain & Company	Business services & supplies	-	114
Fidelity Investments	Diversified financials	-	12
Fusion Worldwide	Technology hardware & equipment	-	217
Liberty Mutual Insurance Group	Insurance, property and casualty (stock)	78	-
New Balance	Retailing	-	130
Ropes & Gray	Services	-	206
State Street	Superregional banks	316	-
Suffolk	Construction	-	122
Vertex Pharmaceuticals	Pharmaceuticals	448	-
Wayfair	Internet services and retailing	275	-

Note: (1) Companies that produce a 10-K are ranked 1 to 500 based on 2021 revenue; (2) All private companies with at least $2 billion in annual revenue through the end of their most current fiscal year are ranked 1 to 246; companies listed are headquartered in the city; dashes indicate no ranking
Source: Fortune, "Fortune 500," 2022; Forbes, "America's Largest Private Companies," 2022

Fastest-Growing Businesses

According to *Inc.*, Boston is home to nine of America's 500 fastest-growing private companies: **Numerated** (#65); **HqO** (#75); **Accelevents** (#97); **OpenExchange** (#124); **Fairmarkit** (#159); **Notarize** (#167); **LinkSquares** (#379); **Caldwell IP** (#434); **Stynt** (#471). Criteria: must be an independent, privately-held, for-profit, U.S. corporation, proprietorship or partnership as of December 31, 2021; revenues must be at least $100,000 in 2018 and $2 million in 2021; must have four-year operating/sales history. *Inc., "America's 500 Fastest-Growing Private Companies," 2022*

According to *Initiative for a Competitive Inner City (ICIC)*, Boston is home to three of America's 100 fastest-growing "inner city" companies: **Proverb Agency** (#80); **Lindsey & Associates Realty** (#82); **Red's Best** (#99). Criteria for inclusion: company must be headquartered in or have 51 percent or more of its physical operations in an economically distressed urban area; must be an independent, for-profit corporation, partnership or proprietorship; must have 10 or more employees and have a five-year sales history that includes sales of at least $200,000 in the base year and at least $1 million in the current year with no decrease in sales over the two most recent years. Companies were ranked overall by revenue growth over the five-year period between 2017 and 2021. *Initiative for a Competitive Inner City (ICIC), "Inner City 100 Companies," 2022*

According to Deloitte, Boston is home to 12 of North America's 500 fastest-growing high-technology companies: **Corvus Insurance** (#8); **Numerated** (#29); **Wasabi Technologies** (#42); **Notarize** (#58); **LinkSquares** (#100); **Cue Biopharma** (#116); **Embark Veterinary** (#183); **Paratek Pharmaceuticals** (#252); **SmartLabs** (#340); **DataRobot** (#408); **Robin** (#474); **Salsify** (#492). Companies are ranked by percentage growth in revenue over a four-year period. Criteria for inclusion: company must be headquartered within North America; must own proprietary intellectual property or technology that is sold to customers in products that contributes to a significant portion of the company's operating revenue; must have been in business for a minumum of four years with 2018 operating revenues of at least $50,000 USD/CD and 2021 operating revenues of at least $5 million USD/CD. *Deloitte, 2022 Technology Fast 500*[TM]

58   Boston, Massachusetts

Living Environment

COST OF LIVING

Cost of Living Index

Composite Index	Groceries	Housing	Utilities	Trans-portation	Health Care	Misc. Goods/ Services
n/a	n/a	n/a	n/a	n/a	n/a	n/a

Note: The Cost of Living Index measures regional differences in the cost of consumer goods and services, excluding taxes and non-consumer expenditures, for professional and managerial households in the top income quintile. It is based on more than 50,000 prices covering almost 60 different items for which prices are collected three times a year by chambers of commerce, economic development organizations or university applied economic centers in each participating urban area. The numbers shown should be read as a percentage above or below the national average of 100. For example, a value of 115.4 in the groceries column indicates that grocery prices are 15.4% higher than the national average. Small differences in the index numbers should not be interpreted as significant; n/a not available.
Source: The Council for Community and Economic Research, Cost of Living Index, 2022

Grocery Prices

Area[1]	T-Bone Steak ($/pound)	Frying Chicken ($/pound)	Whole Milk ($/half gal.)	Eggs ($/dozen)	Orange Juice ($/64 oz.)	Coffee ($/11.5 oz.)
City[2]	n/a	n/a	n/a	n/a	n/a	n/a
Avg.	13.81	1.59	2.43	2.25	3.85	4.95
Min.	10.17	0.90	1.51	1.30	2.90	3.46
Max.	19.35	3.30	4.32	4.32	5.31	8.59

Note: (1) Values for the local area are compared with the average, minimum and maximum values for all 286 areas in the Cost of Living Index; (2) Figures cover the Boston MA urban area; n/a not available; **T-Bone Steak** (price per pound); **Frying Chicken** (price per pound, whole fryer); **Whole Milk** (half gallon carton); **Eggs** (price per dozen, Grade A, large); **Orange Juice** (64 oz. Tropicana or Florida Natural); **Coffee** (11.5 oz. can, vacuum-packed, Maxwell House, Hills Bros, or Folgers).
Source: The Council for Community and Economic Research, Cost of Living Index, 2022

Housing and Utility Costs

Area[1]	New Home Price ($)	Apartment Rent ($/month)	All Electric ($/month)	Part Electric ($/month)	Other Energy ($/month)	Telephone ($/month)
City[2]	n/a	n/a	n/a	n/a	n/a	n/a
Avg.	450,913	1,371	176.41	99.93	76.96	190.22
Min.	229,283	546	100.84	31.56	27.15	174.27
Max.	2,434,977	4,569	356.86	249.59	272.24	208.31

Note: (1) Values for the local area are compared with the average, minimum and maximum values for all 286 areas in the Cost of Living Index; (2) Figures cover the Boston MA urban area; n/a not available; **New Home Price** (2,400 sf living area, 8,000 sf lot, in urban area with full utilities); **Apartment Rent** (950 sf 2 bedroom/1.5 or 2 bath, unfurnished, excluding all utilities except water); **All Electric** (average monthly cost for an all-electric home); **Part Electric** (average monthly cost for a part-electric home); **Other Energy** (average monthly cost for natural gas, fuel oil, coal, wood, and any other forms of energy except electricity); **Telephone** (price includes the base monthly rate plus taxes and fees for three lines of mobile phone service).
Source: The Council for Community and Economic Research, Cost of Living Index, 2022

Health Care, Transportation, and Other Costs

Area[1]	Doctor ($/visit)	Dentist ($/visit)	Optometrist ($/visit)	Gasoline ($/gallon)	Beauty Salon ($/visit)	Men's Shirt ($)
City[2]	n/a	n/a	n/a	n/a	n/a	n/a
Avg.	124.91	107.77	117.66	3.86	43.31	34.21
Min.	36.61	58.25	51.79	2.90	22.18	13.05
Max.	250.21	162.58	371.96	5.54	85.61	63.54

Note: (1) Values for the local area are compared with the average, minimum and maximum values for all 286 areas in the Cost of Living Index; (2) Figures cover the Boston MA urban area; n/a not available; **Doctor** (general practitioners routine exam of an established patient); **Dentist** (adult teeth cleaning and periodic oral examination); **Optometrist** (full vision eye exam for established adult patient); **Gasoline** (one gallon regular unleaded, national brand, including all taxes, cash price at self-service pump if available); **Beauty Salon** (woman's shampoo, trim, and blow-dry); **Men's Shirt** (cotton/polyester dress shirt, pinpoint weave, long sleeves).
Source: The Council for Community and Economic Research, Cost of Living Index, 2022

HOUSING

Homeownership Rate

Area	2015 (%)	2016 (%)	2017 (%)	2018 (%)	2019 (%)	2020 (%)	2021 (%)	2022 (%)
MSA[1]	59.3	58.9	58.8	61.0	60.9	61.2	60.7	59.4
U.S.	63.7	63.4	63.9	64.4	64.6	66.6	65.5	65.8

Note: (1) Figures cover the Boston-Cambridge-Newton, MA-NH Metropolitan Statistical Area
Source: U.S. Census Bureau, Housing Vacancies and Homeownership Annual Statistics: 2015-2022

House Price Index (HPI)

Area	National Ranking[2]	Quarterly Change (%)	One-Year Change (%)	Five-Year Change (%)	Since 1991Q1 (%)
MD[1]	195	-1.14	8.90	44.63	310.81
U.S.[3]	–	0.34	8.41	58.44	289.08

Note: The HPI is a weighted repeat sales index. It measures average price changes in repeat sales or refinancings on the same properties. This information is obtained by reviewing repeat mortgage transactions on single-family properties whose mortgages have been purchased or securitized by Fannie Mae or Freddie Mac since January 1975; (1) Figures cover the Boston, MA Metropolitan Division; (2) Rankings are based on annual percentage change for all metro areas containing at least 15,000 transactions over the last 10 years and ranges from 1 to 257; (3) figures based on a weighted average of Census Division estimates using a seasonally adjusted, purchase-only index; all figures are for the period ending December 31, 2022
Source: Federal Housing Finance Agency, Change in FHFA Metropolitan Area House Price Indexes, 2022Q4

Median Single-Family Home Prices

Area	2020	2021	2022p	Percent Change 2021 to 2022
MSA[1]	563.7	642.2	685.6	6.8
U.S. Average	300.2	357.1	392.6	9.9

Note: Figures are median sales prices of existing single-family homes in thousands of dollars; (p) preliminary; (1) Figures cover the Boston-Cambridge-Newton, MA-NH Metropolitan Statistical Area
Source: National Association of Realtors, Median Sales Price of Existing Single-Family Homes for Metropolitan Areas, 4th Quarter 2022

Qualifying Income Based on Median Sales Price of Existing Single-Family Homes

Area	With 5% Down ($)	With 10% Down ($)	With 20% Down ($)
MSA[1]	196,833	186,473	165,754
U.S. Average	112,234	106,237	94,513

Note: Figures are preliminary; Qualifying income is based on a mortgage rate of 6.77%. Monthly principal and interest payment is limited to 25% of income; (1) Figures cover the Boston-Cambridge-Newton, MA-NH Metropolitan Statistical Area
Source: National Association of Realtors, Qualifying Income Based on Median Sales Price of Existing Single-Family Homes for Metropolitan Areas, 4th Quarter 2022

Home Value

Area	Under $100,000	$100,000 -$199,999	$200,000 -$299,999	$300,000 -$399,999	$400,000 -$499,999	$500,000 -$999,999	$1,000,000 or more	Median ($)
City	2.6	1.0	5.5	11.1	15.0	48.4	16.5	610,400
MSA[1]	2.5	3.6	10.6	18.0	17.3	38.5	9.4	487,600
U.S.	16.2	24.2	20.1	13.6	8.3	13.6	4.1	244,900

Note: Figures are percentages except for median and cover owner-occupied housing units; (1) Figures cover the Boston-Cambridge-Newton, MA-NH Metropolitan Statistical Area
Source: U.S. Census Bureau, 2017-2021 American Community Survey 5-Year Estimates

Year Housing Structure Built

Area	2020 or Later	2010 -2019	2000 -2009	1990 -1999	1980 -1989	1970 -1979	1960 -1969	1950 -1959	1940 -1949	Before 1940	Median Year
City	0.2	7.2	6.6	4.4	5.6	7.5	7.6	7.3	5.4	48.2	1943
MSA[1]	0.1	5.8	7.5	7.4	10.4	10.8	10.1	10.7	5.0	32.2	1962
U.S.	0.2	7.3	13.6	13.6	13.2	14.8	10.3	10.0	4.7	12.2	1979

Note: Figures are percentages except for Median Year; Note: (1) Figures cover the Boston-Cambridge-Newton, MA-NH Metropolitan Statistical Area
Source: U.S. Census Bureau, 2017-2021 American Community Survey 5-Year Estimates

Gross Monthly Rent

Area	Under $500	$500 -$999	$1,000 -$1,499	$1,500 -$1,999	$2,000 -$2,499	$2,500 -$2,999	$3,000 and up	Median ($)
City	14.1	10.7	13.3	20.9	17.7	9.6	13.6	1,783
MSA[1]	10.9	10.8	20.5	24.5	16.4	8.4	8.6	1,659
U.S.	8.1	30.5	30.8	16.8	7.3	3.1	3.5	1,163

Note: Figures are percentages except for median; Gross rent is the contract rent plus the estimated average monthly cost of utilities (electricity, gas, and water and sewer) and fuels (oil, coal, kerosene, wood, etc.) if these are paid by the renter (or paid for the renter by someone else); (1) Figures cover the Boston-Cambridge-Newton, MA-NH Metropolitan Statistical Area
Source: U.S. Census Bureau, 2017-2021 American Community Survey 5-Year Estimates

HEALTH

Health Risk Factors

Category	MD[1] (%)	U.S. (%)
Adults aged 18–64 who have any kind of health care coverage	96.2	90.9
Adults who reported being in good or better health	87.8	85.2
Adults who have been told they have high blood cholesterol	34.5	35.7
Adults who have been told they have high blood pressure	28.5	32.4
Adults who are current smokers	9.9	14.4
Adults who currently use e-cigarettes	5.1	6.7
Adults who currently use chewing tobacco, snuff, or snus	1.8	3.5
Adults who are heavy drinkers[2]	5.6	6.3
Adults who are binge drinkers[3]	17.9	15.4
Adults who are overweight (BMI 25.0 - 29.9)	33.4	34.4
Adults who are obese (BMI 30.0 - 99.8)	25.5	33.9
Adults who participated in any physical activities in the past month	79.8	76.3

Note: (1) Figures cover the Boston, MA Metropolitan Division; (2) Heavy drinkers are classified as adult men having more than 14 drinks per week and adult women having more than 7 drinks per week; (3) Binge drinkers are classified as males having five or more drinks on one occasion or females having four or more drinks on one occasion
Source: Centers for Disease Control and Prevention, Behaviorial Risk Factor Surveillance System, SMART: Selected Metropolitan Area Risk Trends, 2021

Acute and Chronic Health Conditions

Category	MD[1] (%)	U.S. (%)
Adults who have ever been told they had a heart attack	3.8	4.0
Adults who have ever been told they have angina or coronary heart disease	3.5	3.8
Adults who have ever been told they had a stroke	2.8	3.0
Adults who have ever been told they have asthma	14.4	14.9
Adults who have ever been told they have arthritis	21.7	25.8
Adults who have ever been told they have diabetes[2]	8.3	10.9
Adults who have ever been told they had skin cancer	7.0	6.6
Adults who have ever been told they had any other types of cancer	7.5	7.5
Adults who have ever been told they have COPD	5.2	6.1
Adults who have ever been told they have kidney disease	2.5	3.0
Adults who have ever been told they have a form of depression	17.8	20.5

Note: (1) Figures cover the Boston, MA Metropolitan Division; (2) Figures do not include pregnancy-related, borderline, or pre-diabetes
Source: Centers for Disease Control and Prevention, Behaviorial Risk Factor Surveillance System, SMART: Selected Metropolitan Area Risk Trends, 2021

Health Screening and Vaccination Rates

Category	MD[1] (%)	U.S. (%)
Adults who have ever been tested for HIV	37.2	34.9
Adults who have had their blood cholesterol checked within the last five years	89.0	85.2
Adults aged 65+ who have had flu shot within the past year	77.1	68.6
Adults aged 65+ who have ever had a pneumonia vaccination	69.2	71.0

Note: (1) Figures cover the Boston, MA Metropolitan Division.
Source: Centers for Disease Control and Prevention, Behaviorial Risk Factor Surveillance System, SMART: Selected Metropolitan Area Risk Trends, 2021

Disability Status

Category	MD[1] (%)	U.S. (%)
Adults who reported being deaf	4.3	7.2
Are you blind or have serious difficulty seeing, even when wearing glasses?	3.8	4.8
Are you limited in any way in any of your usual activities due to arthritis?	8.7	11.1
Do you have difficulty doing errands alone?	4.9	7.0
Do you have difficulty dressing or bathing?	3.1	3.6
Do you have serious difficulty concentrating/remembering/making decisions?	10.3	12.1
Do you have serious difficulty walking or climbing stairs?	9.5	12.8

Note: (1) Figures cover the Boston, MA Metropolitan Division.
Source: Centers for Disease Control and Prevention, Behaviorial Risk Factor Surveillance System, SMART: Selected Metropolitan Area Risk Trends, 2021

Mortality Rates for the Top 10 Causes of Death in the U.S.

ICD-10[a] Sub-Chapter	ICD-10[a] Code	Crude Mortality Rate[1] per 100,000 population	
		County[2]	U.S.
Malignant neoplasms	C00-C97	121.3	182.6
Ischaemic heart diseases	I20-I25	55.0	113.1
Other forms of heart disease	I30-I51	44.8	64.4
Other degenerative diseases of the nervous system	G30-G31	18.6	51.0
Cerebrovascular diseases	I60-I69	24.8	47.8
Other external causes of accidental injury	W00-X59	48.9	46.4
Chronic lower respiratory diseases	J40-J47	21.4	45.7
Organic, including symptomatic, mental disorders	F01-F09	44.9	35.9
Hypertensive diseases	I10-I15	20.4	35.0
Diabetes mellitus	E10-E14	20.3	29.6

Note: (a) ICD-10 = International Classification of Diseases 10th Revision; (1) Crude mortality rates are a three-year average covering 2019-2021; (2) Figures cover Suffolk County.
Source: Centers for Disease Control and Prevention, National Center for Health Statistics. National Vital Statistics System, Mortality 2018-2021 on CDC WONDER Online Database

Mortality Rates for Selected Causes of Death

ICD-10[a] Sub-Chapter	ICD-10[a] Code	Crude Mortality Rate[1] per 100,000 population	
		County[2]	U.S.
Assault	X85-Y09	5.8	7.0
Diseases of the liver	K70-K76	12.8	19.8
Human immunodeficiency virus (HIV) disease	B20-B24	1.5	1.5
Influenza and pneumonia	J09-J18	10.3	14.7
Intentional self-harm	X60-X84	6.4	14.3
Malnutrition	E40-E46	1.6	4.3
Obesity and other hyperalimentation	E65-E68	2.4	3.0
Renal failure	N17-N19	16.2	15.7
Transport accidents	V01-V99	4.9	13.6
Viral hepatitis	B15-B19	Unreliable	1.2

Note: (a) ICD-10 = International Classification of Diseases 10th Revision; (1) Crude mortality rates are a three-year average covering 2019-2021; (2) Figures cover Suffolk County; Data are suppressed when the data meet the criteria for confidentiality constraints; Crude mortality rates are flagged as unreliable when the rate would be calculated with a numerator of 20 or less.
Source: Centers for Disease Control and Prevention, National Center for Health Statistics. National Vital Statistics System, Mortality 2018-2021 on CDC WONDER Online Database

Health Insurance Coverage

Area	With Health Insurance	With Private Health Insurance	With Public Health Insurance	Without Health Insurance	Population Under Age 19 Without Health Insurance
City	96.6	68.6	35.9	3.4	1.7
MSA[1]	97.0	76.8	32.6	3.0	1.6
U.S.	91.2	67.8	35.4	8.8	5.3

Note: Figures are percentages that cover the civilian noninstitutionalized population; (1) Figures cover the Boston-Cambridge-Newton, MA-NH Metropolitan Statistical Area
Source: U.S. Census Bureau, 2017-2021 American Community Survey 5-Year Estimates

Number of Medical Professionals

Area	MDs[3]	DOs[3,4]	Dentists	Podiatrists	Chiropractors	Optometrists
County[1] (number)	12,539	137	1,819	76	121	284
County[1] (rate[2])	1,576.4	17.2	235.9	9.9	15.7	36.8
U.S. (rate[2])	289.3	23.5	72.5	6.2	28.7	17.4

Note: Data as of 2021 unless noted; (1) Data covers Suffolk County; (2) Rate per 100,000 population; (3) Data as of 2020 and includes all active, non-federal physicians; (4) Doctor of Osteopathic Medicine
Source: U.S. Department of Health and Human Services, Health Resources and Services Administration, Bureau of Health Professions, Area Resource File (ARF) 2021-2022

Best Hospitals

According to *U.S. News,* the Boston, MA metro area is home to seven of the best hospitals in the U.S.: **Beth Israel Deaconess Medical Center** (3 adult specialties); **Brigham and Women's Hospital** (Honor Roll/12 adult specialties); **Dana-Farber Brigham Cancer Center** (1 adult specialty and 1 pediatric specialty); **Mass Eye and Ear at Massachusetts General Hospital** (2 adult specialties); **Massachusetts General Hospital** (Honor Roll/12 adult specialties and 3 pediatric specialties); **New England Baptist Hospital** (1 adult specialty); **Spaulding Rehabilitation Hospital** (1 adult specialty). The hospitals listed were nationally ranked in at least one of 15 adult or 10 pediatric specialties. The number of specialties shown cover the parent hospital. Only 164 U.S. hospitals performed well enough to be nationally ranked in one or more specialties. Twenty hospitals in the U.S. made the

Honor Roll. The Best Hospitals Honor Roll takes both the national rankings and the procedure and condition ratings into account. Hospitals received points if they were nationally ranked in one of the 15 adult specialties—the higher they ranked, the more points they got—and how many ratings of "high performing" they earned in the 17 procedures and conditions. *U.S. News Online, "America's Best Hospitals 2022-23"*

According to *U.S. News*, the Boston, MA metro area is home to two of the best children's hospitals in the U.S.: **Boston Children's Hospital** (Honor Roll/10 pediatric specialties); **MassGeneral Hospital for Children** (3 pediatric specialties). The hospitals listed were highly ranked in at least one of 10 pediatric specialties. Eighty-six children's hospitals in the U.S. were nationally ranked in at least one specialty. Hospitals received points for being ranked in a specialty, and the 10 hospitals with the most points across the 10 specialties make up the Honor Roll. *U.S. News Online, "America's Best Children's Hospitals 2022-23"*

EDUCATION

Public School District Statistics

District Name	Schls	Pupils	Pupil/ Teacher Ratio	Minority Pupils[1] (%)	LEP/ELL[2] (%)	IEP[3] (%)
Boston	113	46,169	10.9	84.9	29.2	22.1

Note: Table includes school districts with 2,000 or more students; (1) Percentage of students that are not non-Hispanic white; (2) Percentage of students that are Limited English Proficient or English Language Learners (2018-19); (3) Percentage of students that have an Individualized Education Program (2019-20). Source: U.S. Department of Education, National Center for Education Statistics, Common Core of Data, Local Education Agency (School District) Universe Survey: School Year 2021-2022

Best High Schools

According to *U.S. News*, Boston is home to three of the top 500 high schools in the U.S.: **Boston Latin School** (#26); **John D. O'Bryant School of Mathematics and Science** (#230); **Boston Latin Academy** (#279). Nearly 18,000 public, magnet and charter schools were ranked based on their performance on state assessments and how well they prepare students for college. *U.S. News & World Report, "Best High Schools 2022"*

Highest Level of Education

Area	Less than H.S.	H.S. Diploma	Some College, No Deg.	Associate Degree	Bachelor's Degree	Master's Degree	Prof. School Degree	Doctorate Degree
City	11.8	18.5	12.9	4.7	27.8	15.7	5.1	3.6
MSA[1]	7.9	21.2	14.1	7.1	26.9	15.8	3.6	3.5
U.S.	11.1	26.5	20.0	8.7	20.6	9.3	2.2	1.5

Note: Figures cover persons age 25 and over; (1) Figures cover the Boston-Cambridge-Newton, MA-NH Metropolitan Statistical Area Source: U.S. Census Bureau, 2017-2021 American Community Survey 5-Year Estimates

Educational Attainment by Race

Area	High School Graduate or Higher (%)					Bachelor's Degree or Higher (%)				
	Total	White	Black	Asian	Hisp.[2]	Total	White	Black	Asian	Hisp.[2]
City	88.2	94.7	85.2	80.6	72.7	52.1	68.7	25.0	57.1	25.7
MSA[1]	92.1	95.1	86.2	86.6	73.7	49.7	52.5	29.6	64.1	24.9
U.S.	88.9	91.4	87.2	87.6	71.2	33.7	35.5	23.3	55.6	18.4

Note: Figures shown cover persons 25 years old and over; (1) Figures cover the Boston-Cambridge-Newton, MA-NH Metropolitan Statistical Area; (2) People of Hispanic origin can be of any race Source: U.S. Census Bureau, 2017-2021 American Community Survey 5-Year Estimates

School Enrollment by Grade and Control

Area	Preschool (%)		Kindergarten (%)		Grades 1 - 4 (%)		Grades 5 - 8 (%)		Grades 9 - 12 (%)	
	Public	Private	Public	Private	Public	Private	Public	Private	Public	Private
City	51.0	49.0	87.0	13.0	84.7	15.3	86.1	13.9	88.8	11.2
MSA[1]	45.1	54.9	88.5	11.5	91.0	9.0	89.6	10.4	86.5	13.5
U.S.	58.8	41.2	86.3	13.7	88.3	11.7	88.6	11.4	89.4	10.6

Note: Figures shown cover persons 3 years old and over; (1) Figures cover the Boston-Cambridge-Newton, MA-NH Metropolitan Statistical Area Source: U.S. Census Bureau, 2017-2021 American Community Survey 5-Year Estimates

Higher Education

Four-Year Colleges			Two-Year Colleges			Medical Schools[1]	Law Schools[2]	Voc/ Tech[3]
Public	Private Non-profit	Private For-profit	Public	Private Non-profit	Private For-profit			
7	51	1	9	4	2	3	7	21

Note: Figures cover institutions located within the Boston-Cambridge-Newton, MA-NH Metropolitan Statistical Area and include main campuses only; (1) includes schools accredited by the Liaison Committee on Medical Education and the American Osteopathic Association's Commission on Osteopathic College Accreditation; (2) includes ABA-accredited schools, schools with provisional ABA accreditation, and state accredited schools; (3) includes all schools with programs that are less than 2 years.
Source: National Center for Education Statistics, Integrated Postsecondary Education System (IPEDS), 2021-22; Wikipedia, List of Medical Schools in the United States, accessed April 10, 2023; Wikipedia, List of Law Schools in the United States, accessed April 10, 2023

According to *U.S. News & World Report*, the Boston, MA metro division is home to four of the top 200 national universities in the U.S.: **Boston College** (#36 tie); **Boston University** (#41 tie); **Northeastern University** (#44 tie); **Simmons University** (#151 tie). The indicators used to capture academic quality fall into a number of categories: assessment by administrators at peer institutions; retention of students; faculty resources; student selectivity; financial resources; alumni giving; high school counselor ratings of colleges; and graduation rate. *U.S. News & World Report, "America's Best Colleges 2023"*

According to *U.S. News & World Report*, the Boston, MA metro division is home to one of the top 100 liberal arts colleges in the U.S.: **Wellesley College** (#5). The indicators used to capture academic quality fall into a number of categories: assessment by administrators at peer institutions; retention of students; faculty resources; student selectivity; financial resources; alumni giving; high school counselor ratings of colleges; and graduation rate. *U.S. News & World Report, "America's Best Colleges 2023".*

According to *U.S. News & World Report*, the Boston, MA metro division is home to two of the top 100 law schools in the U.S.: **Boston University** (#17 tie); **Northeastern University** (#73 tie). The rankings are based on a weighted average of 12 measures of quality: peer assessment score; assessment score by lawyers/judges; median LSAT scores; median undergrad GPA; acceptance rate; employment rates for graduates; placement success; bar passage rate; faculty resources; expenditures per student; student/faculty ratio; and library resources. *U.S. News & World Report, "America's Best Graduate Schools, Law, 2023"*

According to *U.S. News & World Report*, the Boston, MA metro division is home to three of the top 75 medical schools for research in the U.S.: **Harvard University** (#1); **Boston University (Chobanian & Avedisian)** (#32 tie); **Tufts University** (#56 tie). The rankings are based on a weighted average of 11 measures of quality: quality assessment; peer assessment score; assessment score by residency directors; research activity; total research activity; average research activity per faculty member; student selectivity; median MCAT total score; median undergraduate GPA; acceptance rate; and faculty resources. *U.S. News & World Report, "America's Best Graduate Schools, Medical, 2023"*

According to *U.S. News & World Report*, the Boston, MA metro division is home to four of the top 75 business schools in the U.S.: **Harvard University** (#5 tie); **Boston College (Carroll)** (#41 tie); **Boston University (Questrom)** (#47 tie); **Babson College (Olin)** (#57 tie). The rankings are based on a weighted average of the following nine measures: quality assessment; peer assessment; recruiter assessment; placement success; mean starting salary and bonus; student selectivity; mean GMAT and GRE scores; mean undergraduate GPA; and acceptance rate. *U.S. News & World Report, "America's Best Graduate Schools, Business, 2023"*

64   Boston, Massachusetts

EMPLOYERS

Major Employers

Company Name	Industry
Beth Israel Deaconess Medical Center	General medical & surgical hospitals
BlueCross BlueShield of Massachusetts	Health insurance
Boston University	Colleges & universities
Children's Hospital Corporation	Specialty hospitals, except psychiatric
City of Lowell	Municipal government
EMC Corp.	Data management
Federal Deposit Insurance Corporation	Federal deposit insurance corporation (FDIC)
General Electric Company	Aircraft engines & engine parts
Harvard University	Colleges & universities
Internal Revenue Service	Taxation department, government
John Hancock Corp Tax Credit Fund I	Personal service agents, brokers, & bureaus
Lahey Clinic	General medical & surgical hospitals
Massachusetts General Hospital	Health care
Massachusetts Institute of Technology	Colleges & universities
MassMutual Financial Group	Life insurance, annuities, & retirement investment
Roche Bros. Supermarkets	Food/grocery
State Street Bank and Trust Company	State trust companies accepting deposits, commercial
Sun Healthcare Group	Accident & health insurance
The Admins of the Tulane Educational Fund	Hospital, medical school affiliation
Tufts Medical Center	Hospital management

Note: Companies shown are located within the Boston-Cambridge-Newton, MA-NH Metropolitan Statistical Area.
Source: Hoovers.com; Wikipedia

Best Companies to Work For

Bain & Company; Vertex Pharmaceuticals, headquartered in Boston, are among "The 100 Best Companies to Work For." To pick the best companies, *Fortune* partnered with the Great Place to Work Institute. Two-thirds of a company's score is based on the results of the Institute's Trust Index survey, which is sent to a random sample of employees from each company. The questions related to attitudes about management's credibility, job satisfaction, and camaraderie. The other third of the scoring is based on the company's responses to the Institute's Culture Audit, which includes detailed questions about pay and benefit programs, and a series of open-ended questions about hiring practices, internal communication, training, recognition programs, and diversity efforts. Any company that is at least five years old with more than 1,000 U.S. employees is eligible. *Fortune, "The 100 Best Companies to Work For," 2023*

Bain & Company; Toast; Vertex Pharmaceuticals, headquartered in Boston, are among "Fortune's Best Workplaces for Women." To pick the best companies, *Fortune* partnered with the Great Place to Work Institute. To be considered for the list, companies must be Great Place To Work-Certified. Companies must also employ at least 50 women, at least 20% of their non-executive managers must be female, and at least one executive must be female. To determine the Best Workplaces for Women, Great Place To Work measured the differences in women's survey responses to those of their peers and assesses the impact of demographics and roles on the quality and consistency of women's experiences. Great Place To Work also analyzed the gender balance of each workplace, how it compared to each company's industry, and patterns in representation as women rise from front-line positions to the board of directors. *Fortune, "Best Workplaces for Women," 2022*

Bain & Company; Toast; Vertex Pharmaceuticals, headquartered in Boston, are among "Fortune's Best Workplaces for Parents." To pick the best companies, *Fortune* partnered with the Great Place to Work Institute. To be considered for the list, companies must be Great Place To Work-Certified and have at least 50 responses from parents in the US. The survey enables employees to share confidential quantitative and qualitative feedback about their organization's culture by responding to 60 statements on a 5-point scale and answering two open-ended questions. Collectively, these statements describe a great employee experience, defined by high levels of trust, respect, credibility, fairness, pride, and camaraderie. In addition, companies provide organizational data like size, location, industry, demographics, roles, and levels; and provide information about parental leave, adoption, flexible schedule, childcare and dependent health care benefits. *Fortune, "Best Workplaces for Parents," 2022*

Liberty Mutual Insurance, headquartered in Boston, is among the "100 Best Places to Work in IT." To qualify, companies had to have a minimum of 100 total employees and five IT employees. The best places to work were selected based on DEI (diversity, equity, and inclusion) practices; IT turnover, promotions, and growth; IT retention and engagement programs; remote/hybrid working; benefits and perks (such as elder care and child care, flextime, and reimbursement for college tuition); and training and career development opportunities. *Computerworld, "Best Places to Work in IT," 2023*

Boston, Massachusetts 65

PUBLIC SAFETY

Crime Rate

Area	Total Crime	Violent Crime Rate				Property Crime Rate		
		Murder	Rape[3]	Robbery	Aggrav. Assault	Burglary	Larceny -Theft	Motor Vehicle Theft
City	2,490.8	8.3	26.4	131.8	457.9	243.5	1,439.4	183.6
Suburbs[1]	1,043.0	1.2	21.0	22.6	147.3	96.5	677.6	76.8
Metro[2]	1,249.7	2.2	21.8	38.2	191.6	117.5	786.3	92.1
U.S.	2,356.7	6.5	38.4	73.9	279.7	314.2	1,398.0	246.0

Note: Figures are crimes per 100,000 population; (1) All areas within the metro area that are located outside the city limits; (2) Figures cover the Boston, MA Metropolitan Division; (3) All figures shown were reported using the revised Uniform Crime Reporting (UCR) definition of rape; Due to the transition to the National Incident-Based Reporting System (NIBRS), limited city and metro area data was released for 2021.
Source: FBI Uniform Crime Reports, 2020

Hate Crimes

Area	Number of Quarters Reported	Number of Incidents per Bias Motivation					
		Race/Ethnicity/ Ancestry	Religion	Sexual Orientation	Disability	Gender	Gender Identity
City[1]	4	11	9	17	0	0	8
U.S.	4	5,227	1,244	1,110	130	75	266

Note: (1) Figures include one incident reported with more than one bias motivation; Due to the transition to the National Incident-Based Reporting System (NIBRS), limited crime data was released for 2021.
Source: Federal Bureau of Investigation, Hate Crime Statistics 2020

Identity Theft Consumer Reports

Area	Reports	Reports per 100,000 Population	Rank[2]
MSA[1]	11,719	241	115
U.S.	1,108,609	339	-

Note: (1) Figures cover the Boston-Cambridge-Newton, MA-NH Metropolitan Statistical Area; (2) Rank ranges from 1 to 391 where 1 indicates greatest number of identity theft reports per 100,000 population
Source: Federal Trade Commission, Consumer Sentinel Network Data Book 2022

Fraud and Other Consumer Reports

Area	Reports	Reports per 100,000 Population	Rank[2]
MSA[1]	43,727	901	148
U.S.	4,064,520	1,245	-

Note: (1) Figures cover the Boston-Cambridge-Newton, MA-NH Metropolitan Statistical Area; (2) Rank ranges from 1 to 391 where 1 indicates greatest number of fraud and other consumer reports per 100,000 population
Source: Federal Trade Commission, Consumer Sentinel Network Data Book 2022

POLITICS

2020 Presidential Election Results

Area	Biden	Trump	Jorgensen	Hawkins	Other
Suffolk County	80.6	17.5	0.9	0.5	0.5
U.S.	51.3	46.8	1.2	0.3	0.5

Note: Results are percentages and may not add to 100% due to rounding
Source: Dave Leip's Atlas of U.S. Presidential Elections

SPORTS

Professional Sports Teams

Team Name	League	Year Established
Boston Bruins	National Hockey League (NHL)	1924
Boston Celtics	National Basketball Association (NBA)	1946
Boston Red Sox	Major League Baseball (MLB)	1901
New England Patriots	National Football League (NFL)	1960
New England Revolution	Major League Soccer (MLS)	1996

Note: Includes teams located in the Boston-Cambridge-Newton, MA-NH Metropolitan Statistical Area.
Source: Wikipedia, Major Professional Sports Teams of the United States and Canada, April 12, 2023

66   Boston, Massachusetts

CLIMATE

Average and Extreme Temperatures

Temperature	Jan	Feb	Mar	Apr	May	Jun	Jul	Aug	Sep	Oct	Nov	Dec	Yr.
Extreme High (°F)	72	70	85	94	95	100	102	102	100	90	83	73	102
Average High (°F)	36	38	46	56	67	76	82	80	73	63	52	41	59
Average Temp. (°F)	30	31	39	48	58	68	74	72	65	55	45	34	52
Average Low (°F)	22	23	31	40	50	59	65	64	57	47	38	27	44
Extreme Low (°F)	-12	-4	1	16	34	45	50	47	37	28	15	-7	-12

Note: Figures cover the years 1945-1990
Source: National Climatic Data Center, International Station Meteorological Climate Summary, 9/96

Average Precipitation/Snowfall/Humidity

Precip./Humidity	Jan	Feb	Mar	Apr	May	Jun	Jul	Aug	Sep	Oct	Nov	Dec	Yr.
Avg. Precip. (in.)	3.8	3.6	3.8	3.7	3.5	3.1	2.9	3.6	3.1	3.3	4.4	4.1	42.9
Avg. Snowfall (in.)	12	12	8	1	Tr	0	0	0	0	Tr	1	8	41
Avg. Rel. Hum. 7am (%)	68	68	69	68	71	72	73	76	79	77	74	70	72
Avg. Rel. Hum. 4pm (%)	58	57	56	56	58	58	58	61	61	59	61	60	59

Note: Figures cover the years 1945-1990; Tr = Trace amounts (<0.05 in. of rain; <0.5 in. of snow)
Source: National Climatic Data Center, International Station Meteorological Climate Summary, 9/96

Weather Conditions

Temperature			Daytime Sky			Precipitation		
5°F & below	32°F & below	90°F & above	Clear	Partly cloudy	Cloudy	0.01 inch or more precip.	0.1 inch or more snow/ice	Thunder-storms
4	97	12	88	127	150	253	48	18

Note: Figures are average number of days per year and cover the years 1945-1990
Source: National Climatic Data Center, International Station Meteorological Climate Summary, 9/96

HAZARDOUS WASTE

Superfund Sites

The Boston, MA metro division is home to five sites on the EPA's Superfund National Priorities List: **Baird & McGuire** (final); **BJAT** (final); **Blackburn & Union Privileges** (final); **Lower Neponset River** (final); **South Weymouth Naval Air Station** (final). There are a total of 1,165 Superfund sites with a status of proposed or final on the list in the U.S. *U.S. Environmental Protection Agency, National Priorities List, April 12, 2023*

AIR QUALITY

Air Quality Trends: Ozone

	1990	1995	2000	2005	2010	2015	2018	2019	2020	2021
MSA[1]	0.078	0.085	0.067	0.075	0.066	0.065	0.061	0.052	0.053	0.059
U.S.	0.087	0.089	0.081	0.080	0.072	0.067	0.069	0.065	0.065	0.067

Note: (1) Data covers the Boston-Cambridge-Newton, MA-NH Metropolitan Statistical Area. The values shown are the composite ozone concentration averages among trend sites based on the highest fourth daily maximum 8-hour concentration in parts per million. These trends are based on sites having an adequate record of monitoring data during the trend period. Data from exceptional events are included.
Source: U.S. Environmental Protection Agency, Air Quality Monitoring Information, "Air Quality Trends by City, 1990-2021"

Air Quality Index

Area	Percent of Days when Air Quality was...[2]					AQI Statistics[2]	
	Good	Moderate	Unhealthy for Sensitive Groups	Unhealthy	Very Unhealthy	Maximum	Median
MSA[1]	77.0	21.6	1.1	0.3	0.0	153	40

Note: (1) Data covers the Boston-Cambridge-Newton, MA-NH Metropolitan Statistical Area; (2) Based on 365 days with AQI data in 2021. Air Quality Index (AQI) is an index for reporting daily air quality. EPA calculates the AQI for five major air pollutants regulated by the Clean Air Act: ground-level ozone, particle pollution (aka particulate matter), carbon monoxide, sulfur dioxide, and nitrogen dioxide. The AQI runs from 0 to 500. The higher the AQI value, the greater the level of air pollution and the greater the health concern. There are six AQI categories: "Good" AQI is between 0 and 50. Air quality is considered satisfactory; "Moderate" AQI is between 51 and 100. Air quality is acceptable; "Unhealthy for Sensitive Groups" When AQI values are between 101 and 150, members of sensitive groups may experience health effects; "Unhealthy" When AQI values are between 151 and 200 everyone may begin to experience health effects; "Very Unhealthy" AQI values between 201 and 300 trigger a health alert; "Hazardous" AQI values over 300 trigger warnings of emergency conditions (not shown).
Source: U.S. Environmental Protection Agency, Air Quality Index Report, 2021

Air Quality Index Pollutants

Area	Percent of Days when AQI Pollutant was...[2]					
	Carbon Monoxide	Nitrogen Dioxide	Ozone	Sulfur Dioxide	Particulate Matter 2.5	Particulate Matter 10
MSA[1]	0.0	3.3	53.4	(3)	43.0	0.3

Note: (1) Data covers the Boston-Cambridge-Newton, MA-NH Metropolitan Statistical Area; (2) Based on 365 days with AQI data in 2021. The Air Quality Index (AQI) is an index for reporting daily air quality. EPA calculates the AQI for five major air pollutants regulated by the Clean Air Act: ground-level ozone, particle pollution (also known as particulate matter), carbon monoxide, sulfur dioxide, and nitrogen dioxide. The AQI runs from 0 to 500. The higher the AQI value, the greater the level of air pollution and the greater the health concern; (3) Sulfur dioxide is no longer included in this table (as of December 8, 2021) because SO_2 concentrations tend to be very localized and not necessarily representative of broad geographical areas like counties and CBSAs.
Source: U.S. Environmental Protection Agency, Air Quality Index Report, 2021

Maximum Air Pollutant Concentrations: Particulate Matter, Ozone, CO and Lead

	Particulate Matter 10 (ug/m^3)	Particulate Matter 2.5 Wtd AM (ug/m^3)	Particulate Matter 2.5 24-Hr (ug/m^3)	Ozone (ppm)	Carbon Monoxide (ppm)	Lead (ug/m^3)
MSA[1] Level	50	8.3	18	0.067	1	n/a
NAAQS[2]	150	15	35	0.075	9	0.15
Met NAAQS[2]	Yes	Yes	Yes	Yes	Yes	n/a

Note: (1) Data covers the Boston-Cambridge-Newton, MA-NH Metropolitan Statistical Area; Data from exceptional events are included; (2) National Ambient Air Quality Standards; ppm = parts per million; ug/m^3 = micrograms per cubic meter; n/a not available.
Concentrations: Particulate Matter 10 (coarse particulate)—highest second maximum 24-hour concentration; Particulate Matter 2.5 Wtd AM (fine particulate)—highest weighted annual mean concentration; Particulate Matter 2.5 24-Hour (fine particulate)—highest 98th percentile 24-hour concentration; Ozone—highest fourth daily maximum 8-hour concentration; Carbon Monoxide—highest second maximum non-overlapping 8-hour concentration; Lead—maximum running 3-month average
Source: U.S. Environmental Protection Agency, Air Quality Monitoring Information, "Air Quality Statistics by City, 2021"

Maximum Air Pollutant Concentrations: Nitrogen Dioxide and Sulfur Dioxide

	Nitrogen Dioxide AM (ppb)	Nitrogen Dioxide 1-Hr (ppb)	Sulfur Dioxide AM (ppb)	Sulfur Dioxide 1-Hr (ppb)	Sulfur Dioxide 24-Hr (ppb)
MSA[1] Level	12	45	n/a	9	n/a
NAAQS[2]	53	100	30	75	140
Met NAAQS[2]	Yes	Yes	n/a	Yes	n/a

Note: (1) Data covers the Boston-Cambridge-Newton, MA-NH Metropolitan Statistical Area; Data from exceptional events are included; (2) National Ambient Air Quality Standards; ppm = parts per million; ug/m^3 = micrograms per cubic meter; n/a not available.
Concentrations: Nitrogen Dioxide AM—highest arithmetic mean concentration; Nitrogen Dioxide 1-Hr—highest 98th percentile 1-hour daily maximum concentration; Sulfur Dioxide AM—highest annual mean concentration; Sulfur Dioxide 1-Hr—highest 99th percentile 1-hour daily maximum concentration; Sulfur Dioxide 24-Hr—highest second maximum 24-hour concentration
Source: U.S. Environmental Protection Agency, Air Quality Monitoring Information, "Air Quality Statistics by City, 2021"

Charlotte, North Carolina

Background

Charlotte's relationship with England began amiably enough. Settled by Scotch-Irish and German migrants from Pennsylvania, New Jersey, and Virginia in 1750, the area was named for Charlotte Sophia of Mecklenburg-Strelitz, queen to England's King George III. The county in which Charlotte lies was named for Queen Charlotte Sophia's duchy of Mecklenburg.

Trouble started in 1775, however, when the citizens of Charlotte signed the Mecklenburg Resolves, a document invalidating the power of the king and the English Parliament over their lives. The British General Lord Cornwallis found subduing these "treasoners" so difficult, he called Charlotte a "hornet's nest of rebellion."

Today, a better-behaved Charlotte is a sophisticated metropolitan area, its thriving economy based in banking and finance, manufacturing, retail, education, government, health care, transportation, and telecommunications. Known as a center for the banking industry, Charlotte is the nucleus of the Carolinas crescent, an industrial arc extending from Raleigh, North Carolina, to Greenville, South Carolina. Thirteen Fortune 500 companies have a presence in the Charlotte area.

The Charlotte region is home to a significant number of energy-oriented organizations and is known as "Charlotte USA—The New Energy Capital." The region includes nearly 300 energy related companies, employing more than 30,000. The University of North Carolina at Charlotte has a reputation in energy education and research; its Energy Production and Infrastructure Center (EPIC) trains energy engineers and conducts research in the energy sector. Charlotte is also listed as a "gamma" global city by the Globalization and World Cities Research Network.

Charlotte offers exciting cultural and nightlife scenes, and scenes from the film "Talladega Nights" were filmed in and around Charlotte. Sports in the city include the NFL's Carolina Panthers and the NBA's Charlotte Hornets. Charlotte is also a center of NASCAR racing and the NASCAR Hall of Fame opened in Charlotte in 2010. In 2019, MLS awarded Charlotte its expansion team and the Charlotte FC began play in 2022 as the league's 28th franchise.

Charlotte was host to the Republican National Convention in 2020, the same year that CNN established a Charlotte bureau.

Attractions include the Blumenthal Performing Arts Center, which offers Broadway theater, ballet, and music productions; the U.S. National Whitewater Center, the world's largest artificial whitewater river; ImaginOn: The Joe & Joan Martin Educational Center; and the Mint Museum of Art and Discovery Place, one of America's top hands-on science museums with a planetarium and IMAX® Dome theater. The Levine Museum of the New South offers the nation's most comprehensive exhibits on post-Civil War southern society.

Significant institutions of higher education in the region include Queens University, the University of North Carolina at Charlotte, Davidson College and nearby Winthrop University.

Charlotte is located in the Piedmont of the Carolinas, a transitional area of rolling country between the mountains to the west and the Coastal Plain to the east. The city enjoys a moderate climate, characterized by cool winters and warm summers. Winter weather is changeable, with occasional cold periods, but extreme cold is rare. Snow is infrequent. Summer afternoons can be hot. Rainfall is evenly distributed throughout the year. The city took a direct hit from Hurricane Hugo in 1989, which caused massive damage. In 2002, Charlotte, and much of central North Carolina experienced an ice storm that resulted in 1.3 million people without power for weeks.

Rankings

General Rankings

- The Charlotte metro area was identified as one of America's fastest-growing areas in terms of population and business growth by *MagnifyMoney*. The area ranked #13 out of 35. The 100 most populous metro areas in the U.S. were evaluated on their change from 2011 to 2016 in the following categories: people and housing; workforce and employment opportunities; growing industry. *www.businessinsider.com, "The 35 Cities in the US with the Biggest Influx of People, the Most Work Opportunities, and the Hottest Business Growth," August 12, 2018*

- The Charlotte metro area was identified as one of America's fastest-growing areas in terms of population and economy by *Forbes*. The area ranked #19 out of 25. The 100 most populous metro areas in the U.S. were evaluated on the following criteria: estimated population growth; employment; economic output; wages; home values. *Forbes, "America's Fastest-Growing Cities 2018," February 28, 2018*

- Charlotte was selected as one of the best places to live in America by *Outside Magazine*. Criteria centered on diversity; sustainability; outdoor equity; and affordability. Local experts shared highlights from hands-on experience in each location. *Outside Magazine, "The 20 Most Livable Towns and Cities in America," October 15, 2021*

Business/Finance Rankings

- The Brookings Institution ranked the nation's largest cities based on income inequality. Charlotte was ranked #66 (#1 = greatest inequality). Criteria: the "95/20 ratio," a figure representing the income at which a household earns more than 95 percent of all other households, divided by the income at which a household earns more than only 20 percent of all other households. *Brookings Institution, "Household Income Inequality, Largest Cities of 97 Large U.S. Metro Areas, 2014-2016," February 5, 2018*

- The Brookings Institution ranked the 100 largest metro areas in the U.S. based on income inequality. Charlotte was ranked #53 (#1 = greatest inequality). Criteria: the "95/20 ratio," a figure representing the income at which a household earns more than 95 percent of all other households, divided by the income at which a household earns more than only 20 percent of all other households. *Brookings Institution, "Household Income Inequality, 100 Largest U.S. Metro Areas, 2014-2016," February 5, 2018*

- Payscale.com ranked the 32 largest metro areas in terms of wage growth. The Charlotte metro area ranked #8. Criteria: quarterly changes in private industry employee and education professional wage growth from the previous year. *PayScale, "Wage Trends by Metro Area-1st Quarter," April 20, 2023*

- The Charlotte metro area was identified as one of the most debt-ridden places in America by the finance site Credit.com. The metro area was ranked #18. Criteria: residents' average credit card debt as well as median income. *Credit.com, "25 Cities With the Most Credit Card Debt," February 28, 2018*

- Charlotte was identified as one of America's most frugal metro areas by *Coupons.com*. The city ranked #4 out of 25. Criteria: digital coupon usage. *Coupons.com, "America's Most Frugal Cities of 2017," March 22, 2018*

- Charlotte was identified as one of the happiest cities to work in by CareerBliss.com, an online community for career advancement. The city ranked #9 out of 10. Criteria: an employee's relationship with his or her boss and co-workers; daily tasks; general work environment; compensation; opportunities for advancement; company culture and job reputation; and resources. *Businesswire.com, "CareerBliss Happiest Cities to Work 2019," February 12, 2019*

- The Charlotte metro area appeared on the Milken Institute "2022 Best Performing Cities" list. Rank: #31 out of 200 large metro areas (population over 250,000). Criteria: job growth; wage and salary growth; high-tech output growth; housing affordability; household broadband access. *Milken Institute, "Best-Performing Cities 2022," March 28, 2022*

- *Forbes* ranked the 200 most populous metro areas to determine the nation's "Best Places for Business and Careers." The Charlotte metro area was ranked #7. Criteria: costs (business and living); job growth (past and projected); income growth; quality of life; educational attainment (college and high school); projected economic growth; cultural and leisure opportunities; workplace tolerance laws; net migration patterns. *Forbes, "The Best Places for Business and Careers 2019: Seattle Still On Top," October 30, 2019*

Children/Family Rankings

- Charlotte was selected as one of the most playful cities in the U.S. by KaBOOM! The organization's Playful City USA initiative honors cities and towns across the nation that have made their communities more playable. Criteria: pledging to integrate play as a solution to challenges in their communities; making it easy for children to get active and balanced play; creating more family-friendly and innovative communities as a result. *KaBOOM! National Campaign for Play, "2017 Playful City USA Communities"*

Education Rankings

- Personal finance website *WalletHub* analyzed the 150 largest U.S. metropolitan statistical areas to determine where the most educated Americans are putting their degrees to work. Criteria: education levels; percentage of workers with degrees; education quality and attainment gap; public school quality rankings; quality and enrollment of each metro area's universities. Charlotte was ranked #53 (#1 = most educated city). *www.WalletHub.com, "Most & Least Educated Cities in America," July 18, 2022*

- Charlotte was selected as one of America's most literate cities. The city ranked #57 out of the 84 largest U.S. cities. Criteria: number of booksellers; library resources; Internet resources; educational attainment; periodical publishing resources; newspaper circulation. *Central Connecticut State University, "America's Most Literate Cities, 2018," February 2019*

Environmental Rankings

- The U.S. Environmental Protection Agency (EPA) released its list of U.S. metropolitan areas with the most ENERGY STAR certified buildings in 2022. The Charlotte metro area was ranked #19 out of 25. *U.S. Environmental Protection Agency, "2023 Energy Star Top Cities," April 26, 2023*

- The U.S. Conference of Mayors and Walmart Stores sponsor the Mayors' Climate Protection Awards Program which recognize mayors for outstanding and innovative practices that address the climate crisis: increase energy efficiency in their cities, reduce carbon emissions and expand renewable energy. Charlotte received an Honorable Mention in the large city category. *U.S. Conference of Mayors, "2022 Mayors' Climate Protection Awards," June 3, 2022*

Health/Fitness Rankings

- For each of the 100 largest cities in the United States, the American Fitness Index®, compiled in partnership between the American College of Sports Medicine and the Elevance Health Foundation, evaluated community infrastructure and 34 health behaviors including preventive health, levels of chronic disease conditions, food insecurity, sleep quality, pedestrian safety, air quality, and community/environment resources that support physical activity. Charlotte ranked #54 for "community fitness." *americanfitnessindex.org, "2022 ACSM American Fitness Index Summary Report," July 12, 2022*

- The Charlotte metro area was identified as one of the worst cities for bed bugs in America by pest control company Orkin. The area ranked #14 out of 50 based on the number of bed bug treatments Orkin performed from December 2021 to November 2022. *Orkin, "The Windy City Can't Blow Bed Bugs Away: Chicago Ranks #1 For Third Consecutive Year On Orkin's Bed Bug Cities List," January 9, 2023*

- Charlotte was identified as a "2022 Spring Allergy Capital." The area ranked #57 out of 100. Three groups of factors were used to identify the most challenging cities for people with allergies during the spring season: annual spring pollen scores; over the counter allergy medicine use; number of board-certified allergy specialists. *Asthma and Allergy Foundation of America, "Spring Allergy Capitals 2022," March 2, 2022*

- Charlotte was identified as a "2022 Fall Allergy Capital." The area ranked #63 out of 100. Three groups of factors were used to identify the most challenging cities for people with allergies during the fall season: annual fall pollen scores; over the counter allergy medicine use; number of board-certified allergy specialists. *Asthma and Allergy Foundation of America, "Fall Allergy Capitals 2022," March 2, 2022*

- Charlotte was identified as a "2022 Asthma Capital." The area ranked #82 out of the nation's 100 largest metropolitan areas. Criteria: estimated asthma prevalence; asthma-related mortality; and ER visits due to asthma. Risk factors analyzed but not factored in the rankings: annual pollen score; annual air quality; public smoking laws; access to board-certified asthma specialists; rescue and controller medication use; uninsured rate; poverty rate. *Asthma and Allergy Foundation of America, "Asthma Capitals 2022: The Most Challenging Places to Live With Asthma," September 14, 2022*

Pet Rankings

- Charlotte appeared on *The Dogington Post* site as one of the top cities for dog lovers, ranking #4 out of 15. The real estate marketplace, Zillow®, and Rover, the largest pet sitter and dog walker network, introduced a new list of "Top Emerging Dog-Friendly Cities" for 2021. Criteria: number of new dog accounts on the Rover platform; and rentals and listings that mention features that attract dog owners (fenced-in yards, dog houses, dog door or proximity to a dog park). *www.dogingtonpost.com, "15 Cities Emerging as Dog-Friendliest in 2021," May 11, 2021*

Real Estate Rankings

- *WalletHub* compared the most populated U.S. cities to determine which had the best markets for real estate agents. Charlotte ranked #26 where demand was high and pay was the best. Criteria: sales per agent; annual median wage for real-estate agents; monthly average starting salary for real estate agents; real estate job density and competition; unemployment rate; home turnover rate; housing-market health index; and other relevant metrics. *www.WalletHub.com, "2021 Best Places to Be a Real Estate Agent," May 12, 2021*

- According to Penske Truck Rental, the Charlotte metro area was named the #6 moving destination in 2022, based on one-way consumer truck rental reservations made through Penske's website, rental locations, and reservations call center. *gopenske.com/blog, "Penske Truck Rental's 2022 Top Moving Destinations," April 27, 2023*

- Charlotte was ranked #12 in the top 20 out of the 100 largest metro areas in terms of house price appreciation in 2022 (#1 = highest rate). *Federal Housing Finance Agency, House Price Index, 4th Quarter 2022*

- Charlotte was ranked #140 out of 235 metro areas in terms of housing affordability in 2022 by the National Association of Home Builders (#1 = most affordable). Criteria: the share of homes sold in that area affordable to a family earning the local median income, based on standard mortgage underwriting criteria. *National Association of Home Builders®, NAHB-Wells Fargo Housing Opportunity Index, 4th Quarter 2022*

Safety Rankings

- Allstate ranked the 200 largest cities in America in terms of driver safety. Charlotte ranked #153. Criteria: internal property damage claims over a two-year period from January 2016 to December 2017. The report helps increase the importance of safety and awareness behind the wheel. *Allstate, "Allstate America's Best Drivers Report, 2019" June 24, 2019*

Seniors/Retirement Rankings

- From its Best Cities for Successful Aging indexes, the Milken Institute generated rankings for metropolitan areas, weighing data in nine categories—health care, wellness, living arrangements, transportation and convenience, financial characteristics, education, employment, community engagement, and overall livability. The Charlotte metro area was ranked #72 overall in the large metro area category. *Milken Institute, "Best Cities for Successful Aging, 2017" March 14, 2017*

- Charlotte made the 2022 *Forbes* list of "25 Best Places to Retire." Criteria, focused on overall affordability as well as quality of life indicators, include: housing/living costs compared to the national average and state taxes; air quality; crime rates; home price appreciation; risk associated with climate-change/natural hazards; availability of medical care; bikeability; walkability; healthy living. *Forbes.com, "The Best Places to Retire in 2022," May 13, 2022*

Women/Minorities Rankings

- Personal finance website *WalletHub* compared more than 180 U.S. cities across two key dimensions, "Hispanic Business-Friendliness" and "Hispanic Purchasing Power," to arrive at the most favorable conditions for Hispanic entrepreneurs. Charlotte was ranked #91 out of 182. Criteria includes: share of Hispanic-Owned Businesses; Hispanic entrepreneurship rate to median annual income of Hispanics; Small Business-Friendliness score; cost of living; and number of Hispanics with at least a bachelor's degree. *WalletHub.com, "2019's Best Cities for Hispanic Entrepreneurs," May 1, 2019*

Miscellaneous Rankings

- Charlotte was selected as a 2022 Digital Cities Survey winner. The city ranked #7 in the large city (500,000 or more population) category. The survey examined and assessed how city governments are utilizing technology to continue innovation, engage with residents, and persevere through the challenges of the pandemic. Survey questions focused on ten initiatives: cybersecurity; citizen experience; disaster recovery; business intelligence; IT personnel; data governance; business automation; IT governance; infrastructure modernization; and broadband connectivity. *Center for Digital Government, "2022 Digital Cities Survey," November 10, 2022*

- *WalletHub* compared the 150 most populated U.S. cities to determine their operating efficiency. A "Quality of Services" score was constructed for each city and then divided by the total budget per capita to reveal which were managed the best. Charlotte ranked #112. Criteria: financial stability; economy; education; safety; health; infrastructure and pollution. *www.WalletHub.com, "2022's Best- & Worst-Run Cities in America," June 21, 2022*

- The National Alliance to End Homelessness listed the 25 most populous metro areas with the highest rate of homelessness. The Charlotte metro area had a high rate of homelessness. Criteria: number of homeless people per 10,000 population in 2016. *National Alliance to End Homelessness, "Homelessness in the 25 Most Populous U.S. Metro Areas," September 1, 2017*

Business Environment

DEMOGRAPHICS

Population Growth

Area	1990 Census	2000 Census	2010 Census	2020 Census	Population Growth (%)	
					1990-2020	2010-2020
City	428,283	540,828	731,424	874,579	104.2	19.6
MSA[1]	1,024,331	1,330,448	1,758,038	2,660,329	159.7	51.3
U.S.	248,709,873	281,421,906	308,745,538	331,449,281	33.3	7.4

Note: (1) Figures cover the Charlotte-Concord-Gastonia, NC-SC Metropolitan Statistical Area
Source: U.S. Census Bureau, 1990 Census, 2000 Census, 2010 Census, 2020 Census

Race

Area	White Alone[2] (%)	Black Alone[2] (%)	Asian Alone[2] (%)	AIAN[3] Alone[2] (%)	NHOPI[4] Alone[2] (%)	Other Race Alone[2] (%)	Two or More Races (%)
City	41.7	33.1	7.1	0.6	0.1	9.6	7.9
MSA[1]	59.5	21.9	4.3	0.6	0.1	6.4	7.2
U.S.	61.6	12.4	6.0	1.1	0.2	8.4	10.2

Note: (1) Figures cover the Charlotte-Concord-Gastonia, NC-SC Metropolitan Statistical Area; (2) Alone is defined as not being in combination with one or more other races; (3) American Indian and Alaska Native; (4) Native Hawaiian and Other Pacific Islander
Source: U.S. Census Bureau, 2020 Census

Hispanic or Latino Origin

Area	Total (%)	Mexican (%)	Puerto Rican (%)	Cuban (%)	Other (%)
City	14.9	5.3	1.1	0.6	7.9
MSA[1]	10.6	4.6	1.1	0.4	4.6
U.S.	18.4	11.2	1.8	0.7	4.7

Note: Persons of Hispanic or Latino origin can be of any race; (1) Figures cover the Charlotte-Concord-Gastonia, NC-SC Metropolitan Statistical Area
Source: U.S. Census Bureau, 2017-2021 American Community Survey 5-Year Estimates

Age

Area	Percent of Population									Median Age
	Under Age 5	Age 5–19	Age 20–34	Age 35–44	Age 45–54	Age 55–64	Age 65–74	Age 75–84	Age 85+	
City	6.1	19.3	25.8	14.6	12.6	10.5	6.9	3.0	1.1	34.2
MSA[1]	5.8	20.2	20.0	13.6	13.7	12.3	8.8	4.2	1.4	37.8
U.S.	5.6	19.2	20.2	12.7	12.4	13.1	10.0	4.9	1.9	38.8

Note: (1) Figures cover the Charlotte-Concord-Gastonia, NC-SC Metropolitan Statistical Area
Source: U.S. Census Bureau, 2020 Census

Disability by Age

Area	All Ages	Under 18 Years Old	18 to 64 Years Old	65 Years and Over
City	7.8	2.6	6.5	27.9
MSA[1]	10.4	3.5	8.5	31.5
U.S.	12.6	4.4	10.3	33.4

Note: Figures show percent of the civilian noninstitutionalized population that reported having a disability. Disability status is determined from six types of difficulty: vision, hearing, cognitive, ambulatory, self-care, and independent living. For children under 5 years old, hearing and vision difficulty are used to determine disability status. For children between the ages of 5 and 14, disability status is determined from hearing, vision, cognitive, ambulatory, and self-care difficulties. For people aged 15 years and older, they are considered to have a disability if they have difficulty with any one of the six difficulty types; Note: (1) Figures cover the Charlotte-Concord-Gastonia, NC-SC Metropolitan Statistical Area
Source: U.S. Census Bureau, 2017-2021 American Community Survey 5-Year Estimates

Ancestry

Area	German	Irish	English	American	Italian	Polish	French[2]	Scottish	Dutch
City	8.0	6.9	7.0	4.8	3.4	1.5	1.3	1.7	0.5
MSA[1]	10.7	8.5	8.9	8.8	3.9	1.8	1.5	2.1	0.8
U.S.	12.8	9.6	8.1	5.7	5.0	2.7	2.2	1.6	1.1

Note: Figures are the percentage of the total population reporting a particular ancestry. The nine most commonly reported ancestries in the U.S. are shown. Figures include multiple ancestries (e.g. if a person reported being Irish and Italian, they were included in both columns); (1) Figures cover the Charlotte-Concord-Gastonia, NC-SC Metropolitan Statistical Area; (2) Excludes Basque
Source: U.S. Census Bureau, 2017-2021 American Community Survey 5-Year Estimates

Foreign-born Population

Area	Any Foreign Country	Asia	Mexico	Europe	Caribbean	Central America[2]	South America	Africa	Canada
City	17.3	5.3	2.5	1.3	1.2	3.1	1.5	2.1	0.2
MSA[1]	10.5	3.1	2.0	1.1	0.7	1.5	1.0	1.0	0.2
U.S.	13.6	4.2	3.3	1.5	1.4	1.1	1.1	0.8	0.2

Note: (1) Figures cover the Charlotte-Concord-Gastonia, NC-SC Metropolitan Statistical Area; (2) Excludes Mexico.
Source: U.S. Census Bureau, 2017-2021 American Community Survey 5-Year Estimates

Household Size

Area	Persons in Household (%)							Average Household Size
	One	Two	Three	Four	Five	Six	Seven or More	
City	34.1	31.7	15.1	12.0	4.7	1.5	1.0	2.50
MSA[1]	27.5	34.1	16.2	13.8	5.6	1.9	1.0	2.60
U.S.	28.1	33.8	15.5	12.9	6.0	2.3	1.4	2.60

Note: (1) Figures cover the Charlotte-Concord-Gastonia, NC-SC Metropolitan Statistical Area
Source: U.S. Census Bureau, 2017-2021 American Community Survey 5-Year Estimates

Household Relationships

Area	House-holder	Opposite-sex Spouse	Same-sex Spouse	Opposite-sex Unmarried Partner	Same-sex Unmarried Partner	Child[2]	Grand-child	Other Relatives	Non-relatives
City	40.6	15.2	0.2	2.8	0.2	28.0	2.1	4.9	4.2
MSA[1]	38.9	18.3	0.2	2.4	0.2	29.2	2.4	4.2	2.8
U.S.	38.3	17.5	0.2	2.5	0.2	28.3	2.4	4.8	3.4

Note: Figures are percent of the total population; (1) Figures cover the Charlotte-Concord-Gastonia, NC-SC Metropolitan Statistical Area; (2) Includes biological, adopted, and stepchildren of the householder
Source: U.S. Census Bureau, 2020 Census

Gender

Area	Males	Females	Males per 100 Females
City	421,316	453,263	93.0
MSA[1]	1,289,221	1,371,108	94.0
U.S.	162,685,811	168,763,470	96.4

Note: (1) Figures cover the Charlotte-Concord-Gastonia, NC-SC Metropolitan Statistical Area
Source: U.S. Census Bureau, 2020 Census

Marital Status

Area	Never Married	Now Married[2]	Separated	Widowed	Divorced
City	41.4	42.0	2.4	3.9	10.3
MSA[1]	33.1	49.3	2.3	5.0	10.3
U.S.	33.8	48.0	1.8	5.6	10.8

Note: Figures are percentages and cover the population 15 years of age and older; (1) Figures cover the Charlotte-Concord-Gastonia, NC-SC Metropolitan Statistical Area; (2) Excludes separated
Source: U.S. Census Bureau, 2017-2021 American Community Survey 5-Year Estimates

Religious Groups by Family

Area	Catholic	Baptist	Methodist	LDS[2]	Pentecostal	Lutheran	Islam	Adventist	Other
MSA[1]	12.1	13.9	7.0	0.7	2.2	1.1	1.7	1.4	15.9
U.S.	18.7	7.3	3.0	2.0	1.8	1.7	1.3	1.3	11.6

Note: Figures are the number of adherents as a percentage of the total population and cover the eight largest religious groups in the U.S; (1) Figures cover the Charlotte-Concord-Gastonia, NC-SC Metropolitan Statistical Area; (2) Church of Jesus Christ of Latter-day Saints
Sources: 2020 U.S. Religion Census, Association of Statisticians of American Religious Bodies; The Association of Religion Data Archives (ARDA)

Religious Groups by Tradition

Area	Catholic	Evangelical Protestant	Mainline Protestant	Black Protestant	Islam	Judaism	Hinduism	Orthodox	Buddhism
MSA[1]	12.1	26.4	9.5	3.4	1.7	0.2	0.2	0.4	0.1
U.S.	18.7	16.5	5.2	2.3	1.3	0.6	0.4	0.4	0.3

Note: Figures are the number of adherents as a percentage of the total population; (1) Figures cover the Charlotte-Concord-Gastonia, NC-SC Metropolitan Statistical Area
Sources: 2020 U.S. Religion Census, Association of Statisticians of American Religious Bodies; The Association of Religion Data Archives (ARDA)

ECONOMY

Gross Metropolitan Product

Area	2020	2021	2022	2023	Rank[2]
MSA[1]	184.0	204.1	222.9	238.2	21

Note: Figures are in billions of dollars; (1) Figures cover the Charlotte-Concord-Gastonia, NC-SC Metropolitan Statistical Area; (2) Rank is based on 2021 data and ranges from 1 to 381
Source: U.S. Conference of Mayors, U.S. Metro Economies: U.S. Metros Compared to Global and State Economies, June 2022

Economic Growth

Area	2018-20 (%)	2021 (%)	2022 (%)	2023 (%)	Rank[2]
MSA[1]	0.5	6.6	3.2	3.6	103
U.S.	-0.6	5.7	3.1	2.9	—

Note: Figures are real gross metropolitan product (GMP) growth rates and represent average annual percent change; (1) Figures cover the Charlotte-Concord-Gastonia, NC-SC Metropolitan Statistical Area; (2) Rank is based on 2020 2-year average annual percent change and ranges from 1 to 381
Source: U.S. Conference of Mayors, U.S. Metro Economies: U.S. Metros Compared to Global and State Economies, June 2022

Metropolitan Area Exports

Area	2016	2017	2018	2019	2020	2021	Rank[2]
MSA[1]	11,944.1	13,122.5	14,083.2	13,892.4	8,225.6	10,554.3	33

Note: Figures are in millions of dollars; (1) Figures cover the Charlotte-Concord-Gastonia, NC-SC Metropolitan Statistical Area; (2) Rank is based on 2021 data and ranges from 1 to 388
Source: U.S. Department of Commerce, International Trade Administration, Office of Trade and Economic Analysis, Industry and Analysis, Exports by Metropolitan Area, data extracted March 16, 2023

Building Permits

Area	Single-Family			Multi-Family			Total		
	2021	2022	Pct. Chg.	2021	2022	Pct. Chg.	2021	2022	Pct. Chg.
City	n/a	n/a	n/a	n/a	n/a	n/a	n/a	n/a	n/a
MSA[1]	20,830	19,029	-8.6	9,296	8,183	-12.0	30,126	27,212	-9.7
U.S.	1,115,400	975,600	-12.5	621,600	689,500	10.9	1,737,000	1,665,100	-4.1

Note: (1) Figures cover the Charlotte-Concord-Gastonia, NC-SC Metropolitan Statistical Area; Figures represent new, privately-owned housing units authorized (unadjusted data); All permit data are based on estimates with imputation
Source: U.S. Census Bureau, Manufacturing, Mining, and Construction Statistics, Building Permits, 2021, 2022

Bankruptcy Filings

Area	Business Filings			Nonbusiness Filings		
	2021	2022	% Chg.	2021	2022	% Chg.
Mecklenburg County	56	21	-62.5	460	459	-0.2
U.S.	14,347	13,481	-6.0	399,269	374,240	-6.3

Note: Business filings include Chapter 7, Chapter 9, Chapter 11, Chapter 12, Chapter 13, Chapter 15, and Section 304; Nonbusiness filings include Chapter 7, Chapter 11, and Chapter 13
Source: Administrative Office of the U.S. Courts, Business and Nonbusiness Bankruptcy, County Cases Commenced by Chapter of the Bankruptcy Code, During the 12-Month Period Ending December 31, 2021 and Business and Nonbusiness Bankruptcy, County Cases Commenced by Chapter of the Bankruptcy Code, During the 12-Month Period Ending December 31, 2022

Housing Vacancy Rates

Area	Gross Vacancy Rate[2] (%)			Year-Round Vacancy Rate[3] (%)			Rental Vacancy Rate[4] (%)			Homeowner Vacancy Rate[5] (%)		
	2020	2021	2022	2020	2021	2022	2020	2021	2022	2020	2021	2022
MSA[1]	6.6	7.7	7.4	6.3	7.4	7.0	5.6	6.8	5.9	1.0	1.3	0.7
U.S.	10.6	10.8	10.5	8.2	8.4	8.2	6.3	6.1	5.8	1.0	0.9	0.8

Note: (1) Figures cover the Charlotte-Concord-Gastonia, NC-SC Metropolitan Statistical Area; (2) The percentage of the total housing inventory that is vacant; (3) The percentage of the housing inventory (excluding seasonal units) that is year-round vacant; (4) The percentage of rental inventory that is vacant for rent; (5) The percentage of homeowner inventory that is vacant for sale
Source: U.S. Census Bureau, Housing Vacancies and Homeownership Annual Statistics: 2020, 2021, 2022

INCOME

Income

Area	Per Capita ($)	Median Household ($)	Average Household ($)
City	43,080	68,367	104,228
MSA[1]	38,783	69,559	98,559
U.S.	37,638	69,021	97,196

Note: (1) Figures cover the Charlotte-Concord-Gastonia, NC-SC Metropolitan Statistical Area
Source: U.S. Census Bureau, 2017-2021 American Community Survey 5-Year Estimates

Charlotte, North Carolina 77

Household Income Distribution

Area	Percent of Households Earning							
	Under $15,000	$15,000 -$24,999	$25,000 -$34,999	$35,000 -$49,999	$50,000 -$74,999	$75,000 -$99,999	$100,000 -$149,999	$150,000 and up
City	7.8	6.7	8.5	12.7	18.3	12.5	15.8	17.7
MSA[1]	7.9	7.3	8.3	12.1	17.7	13.1	16.4	17.2
U.S.	9.4	7.8	8.2	11.4	16.8	12.8	16.3	17.3

Note: (1) Figures cover the Charlotte-Concord-Gastonia, NC-SC Metropolitan Statistical Area
Source: U.S. Census Bureau, 2017-2021 American Community Survey 5-Year Estimates

Poverty Rate

Area	All Ages	Under 18 Years Old	18 to 64 Years Old	65 Years and Over
City	11.6	17.3	10.1	8.7
MSA[1]	10.7	14.9	9.7	8.4
U.S.	12.6	17.0	11.8	9.6

Note: Figures are percentage of people whose income during the past 12 months was below the poverty level;
(1) Figures cover the Charlotte-Concord-Gastonia, NC-SC Metropolitan Statistical Area
Source: U.S. Census Bureau, 2017-2021 American Community Survey 5-Year Estimates

EMPLOYMENT

Labor Force and Employment

Area	Civilian Labor Force			Workers Employed		
	Dec. 2021	Dec. 2022	% Chg.	Dec. 2021	Dec. 2022	% Chg.
City	498,644	513,354	3.0	481,757	496,911	3.1
MSA[1]	1,377,149	1,414,791	2.7	1,332,923	1,371,461	2.9
U.S.	161,696,000	164,224,000	1.6	155,732,000	158,872,000	2.0

Note: Data is not seasonally adjusted and covers workers 16 years of age and older; (1) Figures cover the
Charlotte-Concord-Gastonia, NC-SC Metropolitan Statistical Area
Source: Bureau of Labor Statistics, Local Area Unemployment Statistics

Unemployment Rate

Area	2022											
	Jan.	Feb.	Mar.	Apr.	May	Jun.	Jul.	Aug.	Sep.	Oct.	Nov.	Dec.
City	4.0	3.8	3.7	3.5	3.5	3.9	3.6	3.9	3.3	3.8	3.7	3.2
MSA[1]	3.7	3.7	3.5	3.2	3.4	3.8	3.4	3.6	3.1	3.7	3.5	3.1
U.S.	4.4	4.1	3.8	3.3	3.4	3.8	3.8	3.8	3.3	3.4	3.4	3.3

Note: Data is not seasonally adjusted and covers workers 16 years of age and older; (1) Figures cover the
Charlotte-Concord-Gastonia, NC-SC Metropolitan Statistical Area
Source: Bureau of Labor Statistics, Local Area Unemployment Statistics

Average Wages

Occupation	$/Hr.	Occupation	$/Hr.
Accountants and Auditors	45.21	Maintenance and Repair Workers	22.36
Automotive Mechanics	24.42	Marketing Managers	71.03
Bookkeepers	22.12	Network and Computer Systems Admin.	44.85
Carpenters	22.36	Nurses, Licensed Practical	26.52
Cashiers	12.80	Nurses, Registered	38.24
Computer Programmers	54.86	Nursing Assistants	15.93
Computer Systems Analysts	52.23	Office Clerks, General	18.96
Computer User Support Specialists	30.39	Physical Therapists	46.12
Construction Laborers	18.19	Physicians	133.48
Cooks, Restaurant	15.26	Plumbers, Pipefitters and Steamfitters	25.11
Customer Service Representatives	19.72	Police and Sheriff's Patrol Officers	28.24
Dentists	98.68	Postal Service Mail Carriers	27.50
Electricians	25.03	Real Estate Sales Agents	27.29
Engineers, Electrical	49.35	Retail Salespersons	15.72
Fast Food and Counter Workers	12.43	Sales Representatives, Technical/Scientific	54.96
Financial Managers	84.45	Secretaries, Exc. Legal/Medical/Executive	20.17
First-Line Supervisors of Office Workers	30.59	Security Guards	14.89
General and Operations Managers	64.62	Surgeons	276.15
Hairdressers/Cosmetologists	18.90	Teacher Assistants, Exc. Postsecondary*	13.20
Home Health and Personal Care Aides	12.92	Teachers, Secondary School, Exc. Sp. Ed.*	26.35
Janitors and Cleaners	14.10	Telemarketers	16.09
Landscaping/Groundskeeping Workers	17.24	Truck Drivers, Heavy/Tractor-Trailer	25.66
Lawyers	78.03	Truck Drivers, Light/Delivery Services	19.89
Maids and Housekeeping Cleaners	13.43	Waiters and Waitresses	13.70

Note: Wage data covers the Charlotte-Concord-Gastonia, NC-SC Metropolitan Statistical Area; (*) Hourly
wages were calculated from annual wage data based on a 40 hour work week; n/a not available.
Source: Bureau of Labor Statistics, Metro Area Occupational Employment & Wage Estimates, May 2022

Employment by Industry

Sector	MSA[1]		U.S.
	Number of Employees	Percent of Total	Percent of Total
Construction, Mining, and Logging	75,100	5.6	5.4
Private Education and Health Services	139,800	10.4	16.1
Financial Activities	121,600	9.1	5.9
Government	163,300	12.2	14.5
Information	26,400	2.0	2.0
Leisure and Hospitality	141,900	10.6	10.3
Manufacturing	111,000	8.3	8.4
Other Services	49,000	3.7	3.7
Professional and Business Services	226,700	16.9	14.7
Retail Trade	141,100	10.5	10.2
Transportation, Warehousing, and Utilities	80,200	6.0	4.9
Wholesale Trade	64,700	4.8	3.9

Note: Figures are non-farm employment as of December 2022. Figures are not seasonally adjusted and include workers 16 years of age and older; (1) Figures cover the Charlotte-Concord-Gastonia, NC-SC Metropolitan Statistical Area
Source: Bureau of Labor Statistics, Current Employment Statistics, Employment, Hours, and Earnings

Employment by Occupation

Occupation Classification	City (%)	MSA[1] (%)	U.S. (%)
Management, Business, Science, and Arts	45.0	41.9	40.3
Natural Resources, Construction, and Maintenance	6.9	8.3	8.7
Production, Transportation, and Material Moving	11.7	13.8	13.1
Sales and Office	21.7	21.6	20.9
Service	14.6	14.5	17.0

Note: Figures cover employed civilians 16 years of age and older; (1) Figures cover the Charlotte-Concord-Gastonia, NC-SC Metropolitan Statistical Area
Source: U.S. Census Bureau, 2017-2021 American Community Survey 5-Year Estimates

Occupations with Greatest Projected Employment Growth: 2022 – 2024

Occupation[1]	2022 Employment	2024 Projected Employment	Numeric Employment Change	Percent Employment Change
Cooks, Restaurant	45,830	53,440	7,610	16.6
Waiters and Waitresses	65,770	72,960	7,190	10.9
Software Developers	55,450	62,610	7,160	12.9
Cooks, Fast Food	82,470	88,860	6,390	7.7
Fast Food and Counter Workers	68,750	75,030	6,280	9.1
Laborers and Freight, Stock, and Material Movers, Hand	100,780	106,480	5,700	5.7
Retail Salespersons	125,490	130,210	4,720	3.8
General and Operations Managers	87,450	92,120	4,670	5.3
First-Line Supervisors of Food Preparation and Serving Workers	42,440	47,070	4,630	10.9
Stockers and Order Fillers	88,320	92,930	4,610	5.2

Note: Projections cover North Carolina; (1) Sorted by numeric employment change
Source: www.projectionscentral.com, State Occupational Projections, 2022–2024 Short-Term Projections

Fastest-Growing Occupations: 2022 – 2024

Occupation[1]	2022 Employment	2024 Projected Employment	Numeric Employment Change	Percent Employment Change
Cooks, Restaurant	45,830	53,440	7,610	16.6
Solar Photovoltaic Installers	390	450	60	15.4
Statisticians	1,710	1,960	250	14.6
Medical Scientists, Except Epidemiologists	3,630	4,160	530	14.6
Actuaries	950	1,080	130	13.7
Data Scientists	5,390	6,100	710	13.2
Soil and Plant Scientists	2,160	2,440	280	13.0
Software Developers	55,450	62,610	7,160	12.9
Software Quality Assurance Analysts and Testers	8,850	9,950	1,100	12.4
Bartenders	14,560	16,360	1,800	12.4

Note: Projections cover North Carolina; (1) Sorted by percent employment change and excludes occupations with numeric employment change less than 50
Source: www.projectionscentral.com, State Occupational Projections, 2022–2024 Short-Term Projections

CITY FINANCES

City Government Finances

Component	2020 ($000)	2020 ($ per capita)
Total Revenues	2,291,588	2,587
Total Expenditures	2,631,208	2,971
Debt Outstanding	4,230,808	4,777
Cash and Securities[1]	2,675,192	3,020

Note: (1) Cash and security holdings of a government at the close of its fiscal year, including those of its dependent agencies, utilities, and liquor stores.
Source: U.S. Census Bureau, State & Local Government Finances 2020

City Government Revenue by Source

Source	2020 ($000)	2020 ($ per capita)	2020 (%)
General Revenue			
From Federal Government	143,598	162	6.3
From State Government	161,866	183	7.1
From Local Governments	34,749	39	1.5
Taxes			
Property	505,521	571	22.1
Sales and Gross Receipts	323,673	365	14.1
Personal Income	0	0	0.0
Corporate Income	0	0	0.0
Motor Vehicle License	32,213	36	1.4
Other Taxes	60,902	69	2.7
Current Charges	700,707	791	30.6
Liquor Store	0	0	0.0
Utility	195,191	220	8.5

Source: U.S. Census Bureau, State & Local Government Finances 2020

City Government Expenditures by Function

Function	2020 ($000)	2020 ($ per capita)	2020 (%)
General Direct Expenditures			
Air Transportation	427,380	482	16.2
Corrections	0	0	0.0
Education	0	0	0.0
Employment Security Administration	0	0	0.0
Financial Administration	38,671	43	1.5
Fire Protection	138,466	156	5.3
General Public Buildings	10,844	12	0.4
Governmental Administration, Other	46,032	52	1.7
Health	0	0	0.0
Highways	137,621	155	5.2
Hospitals	0	0	0.0
Housing and Community Development	147,619	166	5.6
Interest on General Debt	171,232	193	6.5
Judicial and Legal	3,711	4	0.1
Libraries	0	0	0.0
Parking	486	< 1	< 0.1
Parks and Recreation	133,960	151	5.1
Police Protection	335,516	378	12.8
Public Welfare	493	< 1	< 0.1
Sewerage	309,997	350	11.8
Solid Waste Management	70,257	79	2.7
Veterans' Services	0	0	0.0
Liquor Store	0	0	0.0
Utility	579,654	654	22.0

Source: U.S. Census Bureau, State & Local Government Finances 2020

TAXES

State Corporate Income Tax Rates

State	Tax Rate (%)	Income Brackets ($)	Num. of Brackets	Financial Institution Tax Rate (%)[a]	Federal Income Tax Ded.
North Carolina	2.5	Flat rate	1	2.5	No

Note: Tax rates as of January 1, 2023; (a) Rates listed are the corporate income tax rate applied to financial institutions or excise taxes based on income. Some states have other taxes based upon the value of deposits or shares.
Source: Federation of Tax Administrators, State Corporate Income Tax Rates, January 1, 2023

State Individual Income Tax Rates

State	Tax Rate (%)	Income Brackets ($)	Personal Exemptions ($)			Standard Ded. ($)	
			Single	Married	Depend.	Single	Married
North Carolina	4.75	Flat rate	None	None	None	10,750	21,500

Note: Tax rates as of January 1, 2023; Local- and county-level taxes are not included; Federal income tax is not deductible on state income tax returns
Source: Federation of Tax Administrators, State Individual Income Tax Rates, January 1, 2023

Various State Sales and Excise Tax Rates

State	State Sales Tax (%)	Gasoline[1] ($/gal.)	Cigarette[2] ($/pack)	Spirits[3] ($/gal.)	Wine[4] ($/gal.)	Beer[5] ($/gal.)	Recreational Marijuana (%)
North Carolina	4.75	0.3875	0.45	16.40	1.00	0.62	Not legal

Note: All tax rates as of January 1, 2023; (1) The American Petroleum Institute has developed a methodology for determining the average tax rate on a gallon of fuel. Rates may include any of the following: excise taxes, environmental fees, storage tank fees, other fees or taxes, general sales tax, and local taxes; (2) The federal excise tax of $1.0066 per pack and local taxes are not included; (3) Rates are those applicable to off-premise sales of 40% alcohol by volume (a.b.v.) distilled spirits in 750ml containers. Local excise taxes are excluded; (4) Rates are those applicable to off-premise sales of 11% a.b.v. non-carbonated wine in 750ml containers; (5) Rates are those applicable to off-premise sales of 4.7% a.b.v. beer in 12 ounce containers.
Source: Tax Foundation, 2023 Facts & Figures: How Does Your State Compare?

State Business Tax Climate Index Rankings

State	Overall Rank	Corporate Tax Rank	Individual Income Tax Rank	Sales Tax Rank	Property Tax Rank	Unemployment Insurance Tax Rank
North Carolina	10	5	17	20	13	10

Note: The index is a measure of how each state's tax laws affect economic performance. The lower the rank, the more favorable a state's tax system is for business. States without a given tax are given a ranking of 1. The scores/rankings for the District of Columbia do not affect other states. The 2023 index represents the tax climate as of July 1, 2022.
Source: Tax Foundation, State Business Tax Climate Index 2023

TRANSPORTATION

Means of Transportation to Work

Area	Car/Truck/Van		Public Transportation			Bicycle	Walked	Other Means	Worked at Home
	Drove Alone	Car-pooled	Bus	Subway	Railroad				
City	68.8	8.6	1.9	0.3	0.1	0.1	1.8	1.8	16.7
MSA[1]	74.7	8.4	0.9	0.1	0.0	0.1	1.3	1.3	13.1
U.S.	73.2	8.6	2.0	1.6	0.5	0.5	2.5	1.5	9.7

Note: Figures are percentages and cover workers 16 years of age and older; (1) Figures cover the Charlotte-Concord-Gastonia, NC-SC Metropolitan Statistical Area
Source: U.S. Census Bureau, 2017-2021 American Community Survey 5-Year Estimates

Travel Time to Work

Area	Less Than 10 Minutes	10 to 19 Minutes	20 to 29 Minutes	30 to 44 Minutes	45 to 59 Minutes	60 to 89 Minutes	90 Minutes or More
City	8.6	29.6	26.7	23.2	6.5	3.3	2.1
MSA[1]	9.8	27.8	22.6	23.3	9.3	5.1	2.1
U.S.	12.4	28.5	21.0	20.9	8.2	6.2	2.9

Note: Note: Figures are percentages and include workers 16 years old and over; (1) Figures cover the Charlotte-Concord-Gastonia, NC-SC Metropolitan Statistical Area
Source: U.S. Census Bureau, 2017-2021 American Community Survey 5-Year Estimates

Key Congestion Measures

Measure	1990	2000	2010	2015	2020
Annual Hours of Delay, Total (000)	8,674	21,924	35,734	46,235	23,138
Annual Hours of Delay, Per Auto Commuter	26	38	45	52	24
Annual Congestion Cost, Per Auto Commuter ($)	416	789	1,024	1,224	585

Note: Covers the Charlotte NC-SC urban area
Source: Texas A&M Transportation Institute, 2021 Urban Mobility Report

Freeway Travel Time Index

Measure	1985	1990	1995	2000	2005	2010	2015	2020
Urban Area Index[1]	1.10	1.14	1.17	1.20	1.23	1.24	1.23	1.06
Urban Area Rank[1,2]	27	26	29	29	28	24	29	75

Note: Freeway Travel Time Index—the ratio of travel time in the peak period to the travel time at free-flow conditions. For example, a value of 1.30 indicates a 20-minute free-flow trip takes 26 minutes in the peak (20 minutes x 1.30 = 26 minutes); (1) Covers the Charlotte NC-SC urban area; (2) Rank is based on 101 larger urban areas (#1 = highest travel time index)
Source: Texas A&M Transportation Institute, 2021 Urban Mobility Report

Public Transportation

Agency Name / Mode of Transportation	Vehicles Operated in Maximum Service[1]	Annual Unlinked Passenger Trips[2] (in thous.)	Annual Passenger Miles[3] (in thous.)
Charlotte Area Transit System (CATS)			
Bus (purchased transportation)	159	5,906.0	24,555.0
Commuter Bus (purchased transportation)	22	38.8	575.6
Demand Response (directly operated)	71	142.4	1,293.0
Light Rail (directly operated)	28	2,599.6	13,053.7
Vanpool (directly operated)	24	36.8	1,709.8

Note: (1) Number of revenue vehicles operated by the given mode and type of service to meet the annual maximum service requirement. This is the revenue vehicle count during the peak season of the year; on the week and day that maximum service is provided. Vehicles operated in maximum service (VOMS) exclude atypical days and one-time special events; (2) Number of passengers who boarded public transportation vehicles. Passengers are counted each time they board a vehicle no matter how many vehicles they use to travel from their origin to their destination. (3) Sum of the distances ridden by all passengers during the entire fiscal year.
Source: Federal Transit Administration, National Transit Database, 2021

Air Transportation

Airport Name and Code / Type of Service	Passenger Airlines[1]	Passenger Enplanements	Freight Carriers[2]	Freight (lbs)
Charlotte-Douglas International (CLT)				
Domestic service (U.S. carriers - 2022)	30	21,374,765	13	146,705,186
International service (U.S. carriers - 2021)	6	973,745	4	6,980,434

Note: (1) Includes all U.S.-based major, minor and commuter airlines that carried at least one passenger during the year; (2) Includes all U.S.-based airlines and freight carriers that transported at least one pound of freight during the year.
Source: Bureau of Transportation Statistics, The Intermodal Transportation Database, Air Carriers: T-100 Domestic Market (U.S. Carriers), 2022; Bureau of Transportation Statistics, The Intermodal Transportation Database, Air Carriers: T-100 International Market (U.S. Carriers), 2021

BUSINESSES

Major Business Headquarters

Company Name	Industry	Rankings	
		Fortune[1]	Forbes[2]
Bank of America	Commercial banks	36	-
Belk	Retailing	-	163
Brighthouse Financial	Insurance, life and health (stock)	468	-
Duke Energy	Utilities, gas and electric	145	-
Nucor	Metals	98	-
Sonic Automotive	Automotive retailing, services	300	-
Truist Financial	Superregional banks	155	-

Note: (1) Companies that produce a 10-K are ranked 1 to 500 based on 2021 revenue; (2) All private companies with at least $2 billion in annual revenue through the end of their most current fiscal year are ranked 1 to 246; companies listed are headquartered in the city; dashes indicate no ranking
Source: Fortune, "Fortune 500," 2022; Forbes, "America's Largest Private Companies," 2022

Fastest-Growing Businesses

According to *Inc.*, Charlotte is home to two of America's 500 fastest-growing private companies: **Carewell** (#248); **Let's Talk Interactive** (#496). Criteria: must be an independent, privately-held, for-profit, U.S. corporation, proprietorship or partnership as of December 31, 2021; revenues must be at least $100,000 in 2018 and $2 million in 2021; must have four-year operating/sales history. *Inc., "America's 500 Fastest-Growing Private Companies," 2022*

According to Deloitte, Charlotte is home to one of North America's 500 fastest-growing high-technology companies: **MedShift** (#265). Companies are ranked by percentage growth in revenue over a four-year period. Criteria for inclusion: company must be headquartered within North America; must own proprietary intellectual property or technology that is sold to customers in products that contributes to a significant portion of the company's operating revenue; must have been in business for a minumum of four years with 2018 operating revenues of at least $50,000 USD/CD and 2021 operating revenues of at least $5 million USD/CD. *Deloitte, 2022 Technology Fast 500™*

Living Environment

COST OF LIVING

Cost of Living Index

Composite Index	Groceries	Housing	Utilities	Trans- portation	Health Care	Misc. Goods/ Services
97.9	97.4	88.9	91.6	93.4	112.6	106.3

Note: The Cost of Living Index measures regional differences in the cost of consumer goods and services, excluding taxes and non-consumer expenditures, for professional and managerial households in the top income quintile. It is based on more than 50,000 prices covering almost 60 different items for which prices are collected three times a year by chambers of commerce, economic development organizations or university applied economic centers in each participating urban area. The numbers shown should be read as a percentage above or below the national average of 100. For example, a value of 115.4 in the groceries column indicates that grocery prices are 15.4% higher than the national average. Small differences in the index numbers should not be interpreted as significant; Figures cover the Charlotte NC urban area.
Source: The Council for Community and Economic Research, Cost of Living Index, 2022

Grocery Prices

Area[1]	T-Bone Steak ($/pound)	Frying Chicken ($/pound)	Whole Milk ($/half gal.)	Eggs ($/dozen)	Orange Juice ($/64 oz.)	Coffee ($/11.5 oz.)
City[2]	13.63	1.23	2.11	2.12	3.68	5.31
Avg.	13.81	1.59	2.43	2.25	3.85	4.95
Min.	10.17	0.90	1.51	1.30	2.90	3.46
Max.	19.35	3.30	4.32	4.32	5.31	8.59

Note: (1) Values for the local area are compared with the average, minimum and maximum values for all 286 areas in the Cost of Living Index; (2) Figures cover the Charlotte NC urban area; T-Bone Steak (price per pound); Frying Chicken (price per pound, whole fryer); Whole Milk (half gallon carton); Eggs (price per dozen, Grade A, large); Orange Juice (64 oz. Tropicana or Florida Natural); Coffee (11.5 oz. can, vacuum-packed, Maxwell House, Hills Bros, or Folgers).
Source: The Council for Community and Economic Research, Cost of Living Index, 2022

Housing and Utility Costs

Area[1]	New Home Price ($)	Apartment Rent ($/month)	All Electric ($/month)	Part Electric ($/month)	Other Energy ($/month)	Telephone ($/month)
City[2]	377,295	1,498	155.34	-	-	184.19
Avg.	450,913	1,371	176.41	99.93	76.96	190.22
Min.	229,283	546	100.84	31.56	27.15	174.27
Max.	2,434,977	4,569	356.86	249.59	272.24	208.31

Note: (1) Values for the local area are compared with the average, minimum and maximum values for all 286 areas in the Cost of Living Index; (2) Figures cover the Charlotte NC urban area; New Home Price (2,400 sf living area, 8,000 sf lot, in urban area with full utilities); Apartment Rent (950 sf 2 bedroom/1.5 or 2 bath, unfurnished, excluding all utilities except water); All Electric (average monthly cost for an all-electric home); Part Electric (average monthly cost for a part-electric home); Other Energy (average monthly cost for natural gas, fuel oil, coal, wood, and any other forms of energy except electricity); Telephone (price includes the base monthly rate plus taxes and fees for three lines of mobile phone service).
Source: The Council for Community and Economic Research, Cost of Living Index, 2022

Health Care, Transportation, and Other Costs

Area[1]	Doctor ($/visit)	Dentist ($/visit)	Optometrist ($/visit)	Gasoline ($/gallon)	Beauty Salon ($/visit)	Men's Shirt ($)
City[2]	140.33	135.13	125.78	3.68	31.70	49.35
Avg.	124.91	107.77	117.66	3.86	43.31	34.21
Min.	36.61	58.25	51.79	2.90	22.18	13.05
Max.	250.21	162.58	371.96	5.54	85.61	63.54

Note: (1) Values for the local area are compared with the average, minimum and maximum values for all 286 areas in the Cost of Living Index; (2) Figures cover the Charlotte NC urban area; Doctor (general practitioners routine exam of an established patient); Dentist (adult teeth cleaning and periodic oral examination); Optometrist (full vision eye exam for established adult patient); Gasoline (one gallon regular unleaded, national brand, including all taxes, cash price at self-service pump if available); Beauty Salon (woman's shampoo, trim, and blow-dry); Men's Shirt (cotton/polyester dress shirt, pinpoint weave, long sleeves).
Source: The Council for Community and Economic Research, Cost of Living Index, 2022

HOUSING

Homeownership Rate

Area	2015 (%)	2016 (%)	2017 (%)	2018 (%)	2019 (%)	2020 (%)	2021 (%)	2022 (%)
MSA[1]	62.3	66.2	64.6	67.9	72.3	73.3	70.0	68.7
U.S.	63.7	63.4	63.9	64.4	64.6	66.6	65.5	65.8

Note: (1) Figures cover the Charlotte-Concord-Gastonia, NC-SC Metropolitan Statistical Area
Source: U.S. Census Bureau, Housing Vacancies and Homeownership Annual Statistics: 2015-2022

House Price Index (HPI)

Area	National Ranking[2]	Quarterly Change (%)	One-Year Change (%)	Five-Year Change (%)	Since 1991Q1 (%)
MSA[1]	19	0.48	18.66	78.79	310.41
U.S.[3]	–	0.34	8.41	58.44	289.08

Note: The HPI is a weighted repeat sales index. It measures average price changes in repeat sales or refinancings on the same properties. This information is obtained by reviewing repeat mortgage transactions on single-family properties whose mortgages have been purchased or securitized by Fannie Mae or Freddie Mac since January 1975; (1) Figures cover the Charlotte-Concord-Gastonia, NC-SC Metropolitan Statistical Area; (2) Rankings are based on annual percentage change for all metro areas containing at least 15,000 transactions over the last 10 years and ranges from 1 to 257; (3) figures based on a weighted average of Census Division estimates using a seasonally adjusted, purchase-only index; all figures are for the period ending December 31, 2022
Source: Federal Housing Finance Agency, Change in FHFA Metropolitan Area House Price Indexes, 2022Q4

Median Single-Family Home Prices

Area	2020	2021	2022p	Percent Change 2021 to 2022
MSA[1]	296.2	354.1	397.7	12.3
U.S. Average	300.2	357.1	392.6	9.9

Note: Figures are median sales prices of existing single-family homes in thousands of dollars; (p) preliminary; (1) Figures cover the Charlotte-Concord-Gastonia, NC-SC Metropolitan Statistical Area
Source: National Association of Realtors, Median Sales Price of Existing Single-Family Homes for Metropolitan Areas, 4th Quarter 2022

Qualifying Income Based on Median Sales Price of Existing Single-Family Homes

Area	With 5% Down ($)	With 10% Down ($)	With 20% Down ($)
MSA[1]	118,327	112,099	99,644
U.S. Average	112,234	106,237	94,513

Note: Figures are preliminary; Qualifying income is based on a mortgage rate of 6.77%. Monthly principal and interest payment is limited to 25% of income; (1) Figures cover the Charlotte-Concord-Gastonia, NC-SC Metropolitan Statistical Area
Source: National Association of Realtors, Qualifying Income Based on Median Sales Price of Existing Single-Family Homes for Metropolitan Areas, 4th Quarter 2022

Home Value

Area	Under $100,000	$100,000 -$199,999	$200,000 -$299,999	$300,000 -$399,999	$400,000 -$499,999	$500,000 -$999,999	$1,000,000 or more	Median ($)
City	7.8	27.5	23.8	14.8	8.8	13.3	4.0	258,000
MSA[1]	13.0	27.8	23.7	15.3	8.0	10.0	2.3	237,300
U.S.	16.2	24.2	20.1	13.6	8.3	13.6	4.1	244,900

Note: Figures are percentages except for median and cover owner-occupied housing units; (1) Figures cover the Charlotte-Concord-Gastonia, NC-SC Metropolitan Statistical Area
Source: U.S. Census Bureau, 2017-2021 American Community Survey 5-Year Estimates

Year Housing Structure Built

Area	2020 or Later	2010 -2019	2000 -2009	1990 -1999	1980 -1989	1970 -1979	1960 -1969	1950 -1959	1940 -1949	Before 1940	Median Year
City	0.2	13.2	21.5	19.3	14.4	11.2	8.7	6.3	2.5	2.7	1992
MSA[1]	0.2	13.6	22.6	18.9	12.9	10.8	7.7	6.3	2.9	4.1	1993
U.S.	0.2	7.3	13.6	13.6	13.2	14.8	10.3	10.0	4.7	12.2	1979

Note: Figures are percentages except for Median Year; Note: (1) Figures cover the Charlotte-Concord-Gastonia, NC-SC Metropolitan Statistical Area
Source: U.S. Census Bureau, 2017-2021 American Community Survey 5-Year Estimates

Gross Monthly Rent

Area	Under $500	$500 -$999	$1,000 -$1,499	$1,500 -$1,999	$2,000 -$2,499	$2,500 -$2,999	$3,000 and up	Median ($)
City	3.4	19.6	48.2	21.7	4.5	1.5	1.2	1,260
MSA[1]	4.8	31.3	41.3	16.7	3.6	1.2	1.0	1,147
U.S.	8.1	30.5	30.8	16.8	7.3	3.1	3.5	1,163

Note: Figures are percentages except for median; Gross rent is the contract rent plus the estimated average monthly cost of utilities (electricity, gas, and water and sewer) and fuels (oil, coal, kerosene, wood, etc.) if these are paid by the renter (or paid for the renter by someone else); (1) Figures cover the Charlotte-Concord-Gastonia, NC-SC Metropolitan Statistical Area
Source: U.S. Census Bureau, 2017-2021 American Community Survey 5-Year Estimates

HEALTH

Health Risk Factors

Category	MSA[1] (%)	U.S. (%)
Adults aged 18–64 who have any kind of health care coverage	89.0	90.9
Adults who reported being in good or better health	88.1	85.2
Adults who have been told they have high blood cholesterol	38.2	35.7
Adults who have been told they have high blood pressure	32.5	32.4
Adults who are current smokers	13.9	14.4
Adults who currently use e-cigarettes	6.2	6.7
Adults who currently use chewing tobacco, snuff, or snus	3.8	3.5
Adults who are heavy drinkers[2]	4.8	6.3
Adults who are binge drinkers[3]	15.8	15.4
Adults who are overweight (BMI 25.0 - 29.9)	33.3	34.4
Adults who are obese (BMI 30.0 - 99.8)	34.5	33.9
Adults who participated in any physical activities in the past month	78.5	76.3

Note: (1) Figures cover the Charlotte-Concord-Gastonia, NC-SC Metropolitan Statistical Area; (2) Heavy drinkers are classified as adult men having more than 14 drinks per week and adult women having more than 7 drinks per week; (3) Binge drinkers are classified as males having five or more drinks on one occasion or females having four or more drinks on one occasion
Source: Centers for Disease Control and Prevention, Behaviorial Risk Factor Surveillance System, SMART: Selected Metropolitan Area Risk Trends, 2021

Acute and Chronic Health Conditions

Category	MSA[1] (%)	U.S. (%)
Adults who have ever been told they had a heart attack	3.8	4.0
Adults who have ever been told they have angina or coronary heart disease	4.3	3.8
Adults who have ever been told they had a stroke	3.8	3.0
Adults who have ever been told they have asthma	12.4	14.9
Adults who have ever been told they have arthritis	25.1	25.8
Adults who have ever been told they have diabetes[2]	12.8	10.9
Adults who have ever been told they had skin cancer	6.3	6.6
Adults who have ever been told they had any other types of cancer	5.4	7.5
Adults who have ever been told they have COPD	6.9	6.1
Adults who have ever been told they have kidney disease	2.7	3.0
Adults who have ever been told they have a form of depression	19.5	20.5

Note: (1) Figures cover the Charlotte-Concord-Gastonia, NC-SC Metropolitan Statistical Area; (2) Figures do not include pregnancy-related, borderline, or pre-diabetes
Source: Centers for Disease Control and Prevention, Behaviorial Risk Factor Surveillance System, SMART: Selected Metropolitan Area Risk Trends, 2021

Health Screening and Vaccination Rates

Category	MSA[1] (%)	U.S. (%)
Adults who have ever been tested for HIV	38.4	34.9
Adults who have had their blood cholesterol checked within the last five years	87.3	85.2
Adults aged 65+ who have had flu shot within the past year	69.0	68.6
Adults aged 65+ who have ever had a pneumonia vaccination	74.9	71.0

Note: (1) Figures cover the Charlotte-Concord-Gastonia, NC-SC Metropolitan Statistical Area.
Source: Centers for Disease Control and Prevention, Behaviorial Risk Factor Surveillance System, SMART: Selected Metropolitan Area Risk Trends, 2021

Disability Status

Category	MSA[1] (%)	U.S. (%)
Adults who reported being deaf	7.5	7.2
Are you blind or have serious difficulty seeing, even when wearing glasses?	5.8	4.8
Are you limited in any way in any of your usual activities due to arthritis?	8.9	11.1
Do you have difficulty doing errands alone?	5.6	7.0
Do you have difficulty dressing or bathing?	3.0	3.6
Do you have serious difficulty concentrating/remembering/making decisions?	11.0	12.1
Do you have serious difficulty walking or climbing stairs?	12.6	12.8

Note: (1) Figures cover the Charlotte-Concord-Gastonia, NC-SC Metropolitan Statistical Area.
Source: Centers for Disease Control and Prevention, Behaviorial Risk Factor Surveillance System, SMART: Selected Metropolitan Area Risk Trends, 2021

Mortality Rates for the Top 10 Causes of Death in the U.S.

ICD-10[a] Sub-Chapter	ICD-10[a] Code	Crude Mortality Rate[1] per 100,000 population	
		County[2]	U.S.
Malignant neoplasms	C00-C97	121.3	182.6
Ischaemic heart diseases	I20-I25	44.9	113.1
Other forms of heart disease	I30-I51	51.7	64.4
Other degenerative diseases of the nervous system	G30-G31	49.5	51.0
Cerebrovascular diseases	I60-I69	34.7	47.8
Other external causes of accidental injury	W00-X59	31.7	46.4
Chronic lower respiratory diseases	J40-J47	20.9	45.7
Organic, including symptomatic, mental disorders	F01-F09	24.9	35.9
Hypertensive diseases	I10-I15	18.9	35.0
Diabetes mellitus	E10-E14	19.7	29.6

Note: (a) ICD-10 = International Classification of Diseases 10th Revision; (1) Crude mortality rates are a three-year average covering 2019-2021; (2) Figures cover Mecklenburg County.
Source: Centers for Disease Control and Prevention, National Center for Health Statistics. National Vital Statistics System, Mortality 2018-2021 on CDC WONDER Online Database

Mortality Rates for Selected Causes of Death

ICD-10[a] Sub-Chapter	ICD-10[a] Code	Crude Mortality Rate[1] per 100,000 population	
		County[2]	U.S.
Assault	X85-Y09	10.1	7.0
Diseases of the liver	K70-K76	12.3	19.8
Human immunodeficiency virus (HIV) disease	B20-B24	2.3	1.5
Influenza and pneumonia	J09-J18	7.6	14.7
Intentional self-harm	X60-X84	9.8	14.3
Malnutrition	E40-E46	9.5	4.3
Obesity and other hyperalimentation	E65-E68	2.6	3.0
Renal failure	N17-N19	15.0	15.7
Transport accidents	V01-V99	10.5	13.6
Viral hepatitis	B15-B19	0.8	1.2

Note: (a) ICD-10 = International Classification of Diseases 10th Revision; (1) Crude mortality rates are a three-year average covering 2019-2021; (2) Figures cover Mecklenburg County; Data are suppressed when the data meet the criteria for confidentiality constraints; Crude mortality rates are flagged as unreliable when the rate would be calculated with a numerator of 20 or less.
Source: Centers for Disease Control and Prevention, National Center for Health Statistics. National Vital Statistics System, Mortality 2018-2021 on CDC WONDER Online Database

Health Insurance Coverage

Area	With Health Insurance	With Private Health Insurance	With Public Health Insurance	Without Health Insurance	Population Under Age 19 Without Health Insurance
City	87.2	68.2	26.4	12.8	7.7
MSA[1]	89.7	70.1	29.6	10.3	5.5
U.S.	91.2	67.8	35.4	8.8	5.3

Note: Figures are percentages that cover the civilian noninstitutionalized population; (1) Figures cover the Charlotte-Concord-Gastonia, NC-SC Metropolitan Statistical Area
Source: U.S. Census Bureau, 2017-2021 American Community Survey 5-Year Estimates

Number of Medical Professionals

Area	MDs[3]	DOs[3,4]	Dentists	Podiatrists	Chiropractors	Optometrists
County[1] (number)	3,836	189	808	42	395	163
County[1] (rate[2])	343.0	16.9	72.0	3.7	35.2	14.5
U.S. (rate[2])	289.3	23.5	72.5	6.2	28.7	17.4

Note: Data as of 2021 unless noted; (1) Data covers Mecklenburg County; (2) Rate per 100,000 population; (3) Data as of 2020 and includes all active, non-federal physicians; (4) Doctor of Osteopathic Medicine
Source: U.S. Department of Health and Human Services, Health Resources and Services Administration, Bureau of Health Professions, Area Resource File (ARF) 2021-2022

Best Hospitals

According to *U.S. News*, the Charlotte-Concord-Gastonia, NC-SC metro area is home to one of the best hospitals in the U.S.: **Atrium Health Carolinas Rehabilitation** (1 adult specialty). The hospital listed was nationally ranked in at least one of 15 adult or 10 pediatric specialties. The number of specialties shown cover the parent hospital. Only 164 U.S. hospitals performed well enough to be nationally ranked in one or more specialties. Twenty hospitals in the U.S. made the Honor Roll. The Best Hospitals Honor Roll takes both the national rankings and the procedure and condition ratings into account. Hospitals received points if they were nationally ranked in one of the 15 adult specialties—the higher they ranked, the more points they got—and how many ratings of "high performing" they earned in the 17 procedures and conditions. *U.S. News Online, "America's Best Hospitals 2022-23"*

According to *U.S. News,* the Charlotte-Concord-Gastonia, NC-SC metro area is home to one of the best children's hospitals in the U.S.: **Levine Children's Hospital** (8 pediatric specialties). The hospital listed was highly ranked in at least one of 10 pediatric specialties. Eighty-six children's hospitals in the U.S. were nationally ranked in at least one specialty. Hospitals received points for being ranked in a specialty, and the 10 hospitals with the most points across the 10 specialties make up the Honor Roll. *U.S. News Online, "America's Best Children's Hospitals 2022-23"*

EDUCATION

Public School District Statistics

District Name	Schls	Pupils	Pupil/ Teacher Ratio	Minority Pupils[1] (%)	LEP/ELL[2] (%)	IEP[3] (%)
Charlotte-Mecklenburg Schools	180	143,244	15.9	75.5	13.2	9.9

Note: Table includes school districts with 2,000 or more students; (1) Percentage of students that are not non-Hispanic white; (2) Percentage of students that are Limited English Proficient or English Language Learners (2018-19); (3) Percentage of students that have an Individualized Education Program (2019-20).
Source: U.S. Department of Education, National Center for Education Statistics, Common Core of Data, Local Education Agency (School District) Universe Survey: School Year 2021-2022

Highest Level of Education

Area	Less than H.S.	H.S. Diploma	Some College, No Deg.	Associate Degree	Bachelor's Degree	Master's Degree	Prof. School Degree	Doctorate Degree
City	10.3	16.9	19.2	7.9	29.5	12.2	2.9	1.2
MSA[1]	10.1	22.9	20.5	9.4	24.5	9.7	2.0	0.9
U.S.	11.1	26.5	20.0	8.7	20.6	9.3	2.2	1.5

Note: Figures cover persons age 25 and over; (1) Figures cover the Charlotte-Concord-Gastonia, NC-SC Metropolitan Statistical Area
Source: U.S. Census Bureau, 2017-2021 American Community Survey 5-Year Estimates

Educational Attainment by Race

Area	High School Graduate or Higher (%)					Bachelor's Degree or Higher (%)				
	Total	White	Black	Asian	Hisp.[2]	Total	White	Black	Asian	Hisp.[2]
City	89.7	94.7	91.2	84.3	60.8	45.7	59.2	30.8	61.5	19.1
MSA[1]	89.9	92.2	89.9	86.7	65.7	37.1	40.0	28.1	60.8	20.5
U.S.	88.9	91.4	87.2	87.6	71.2	33.7	35.5	23.3	55.6	18.4

Note: Figures shown cover persons 25 years old and over; (1) Figures cover the Charlotte-Concord-Gastonia, NC-SC Metropolitan Statistical Area; (2) People of Hispanic origin can be of any race
Source: U.S. Census Bureau, 2017-2021 American Community Survey 5-Year Estimates

School Enrollment by Grade and Control

Area	Preschool (%)		Kindergarten (%)		Grades 1 - 4 (%)		Grades 5 - 8 (%)		Grades 9 - 12 (%)	
	Public	Private	Public	Private	Public	Private	Public	Private	Public	Private
City	48.9	51.1	86.9	13.1	89.2	10.8	85.8	14.2	89.3	10.7
MSA[1]	50.3	49.7	87.4	12.6	89.5	10.5	87.5	12.5	89.9	10.1
U.S.	58.8	41.2	86.3	13.7	88.3	11.7	88.6	11.4	89.4	10.6

Note: Figures shown cover persons 3 years old and over; (1) Figures cover the Charlotte-Concord-Gastonia, NC-SC Metropolitan Statistical Area
Source: U.S. Census Bureau, 2017-2021 American Community Survey 5-Year Estimates

Higher Education

Four-Year Colleges			Two-Year Colleges			Medical Schools[1]	Law Schools[2]	Voc/ Tech[3]
Public	Private Non-profit	Private For-profit	Public	Private Non-profit	Private For-profit			
3	12	2	7	0	3	0	0	9

Note: Figures cover institutions located within the Charlotte-Concord-Gastonia, NC-SC Metropolitan Statistical Area and include main campuses only; (1) includes schools accredited by the Liaison Committee on Medical Education and the American Osteopathic Association's Commission on Osteopathic College Accreditation; (2) includes ABA-accredited schools, schools with provisional ABA accreditation, and state accredited schools; (3) includes all schools with programs that are less than 2 years.
Source: National Center for Education Statistics, Integrated Postsecondary Education System (IPEDS), 2021-22; Wikipedia, List of Medical Schools in the United States, accessed April 10, 2023; Wikipedia, List of Law Schools in the United States, accessed April 10, 2023

According to *U.S. News & World Report,* the Charlotte-Concord-Gastonia, NC-SC metro area is home to one of the top 100 liberal arts colleges in the U.S.: **Davidson College** (#15 tie). The indicators used to capture academic quality fall into a number of categories: assessment by administrators at peer institutions; retention of students; faculty resources; student selectivity; financial resources;

alumni giving; high school counselor ratings of colleges; and graduation rate. *U.S. News & World Report, "America's Best Colleges 2023"*

EMPLOYERS

Major Employers

Company Name	Industry
Bank of America, National Association	National commercial banks
Carlisle Companies Incorporated	Fabricated rubber products
Carolina Medical Center Northeast	General medical & surgical hospitals
Carolina Medical Center Union	General medical & surgical hospitals
Charlotte Mecklenburg Hospital Authority	General medical & surgical hospitals
Compass Group North America	Services
Duke Energy	Electric services
IBM	Office equipment
Insource Performance Solutions	Help supply services
Medcath Incorporated	Specialty hospitals, except psychiatric
Merchandising Corporation of America	Business consulting
Microsoft	Computer peripheral equipment
Polymer Group	Nonwoven fabrics
Presbyterian Hospital	General medical & surgical hospitals
RohrCredit Corporation	Aircraft engines & engine parts
University of NC at Chapel Hill	Colleges & universities
Wachovia Corporation	National commercial banks
Wells Fargo	Banking and financial services

Note: Companies shown are located within the Charlotte-Concord-Gastonia, NC-SC Metropolitan Statistical Area.
Source: Hoovers.com; Wikipedia

Best Companies to Work For

Bank of America, headquartered in Charlotte, is among "The 100 Best Companies to Work For." To pick the best companies, *Fortune* partnered with the Great Place to Work Institute. Two-thirds of a company's score is based on the results of the Institute's Trust Index survey, which is sent to a random sample of employees from each company. The questions related to attitudes about management's credibility, job satisfaction, and camaraderie. The other third of the scoring is based on the company's responses to the Institute's Culture Audit, which includes detailed questions about pay and benefit programs, and a series of open-ended questions about hiring practices, internal communication, training, recognition programs, and diversity efforts. Any company that is at least five years old with more than 1,000 U.S. employees is eligible. *Fortune, "The 100 Best Companies to Work For," 2023*

Bank of America; Cardinal Financial, headquartered in Charlotte, are among "Fortune's Best Workplaces for Women." To pick the best companies, *Fortune* partnered with the Great Place to Work Institute. To be considered for the list, companies must be Great Place To Work-Certified. Companies must also employ at least 50 women, at least 20% of their non-executive managers must be female, and at least one executive must be female. To determine the Best Workplaces for Women, Great Place To Work measured the differences in women's survey responses to those of their peers and assesses the impact of demographics and roles on the quality and consistency of women's experiences. Great Place To Work also analyzed the gender balance of each workplace, how it compared to each company's industry, and patterns in representation as women rise from front-line positions to the board of directors. *Fortune, "Best Workplaces for Women," 2022*

Bank of America, headquartered in Charlotte, is among "Fortune's Best Workplaces for Parents." To pick the best companies, *Fortune* partnered with the Great Place to Work Institute. To be considered for the list, companies must be Great Place To Work-Certified and have at least 50 responses from parents in the US. The survey enables employees to share confidential quantitative and qualitative feedback about their organization's culture by responding to 60 statements on a 5-point scale and answering two open-ended questions. Collectively, these statements describe a great employee experience, defined by high levels of trust, respect, credibility, fairness, pride, and camaraderie. In addition, companies provide organizational data like size, location, industry, demographics, roles, and levels; and provide information about parental leave, adoption, flexible schedule, childcare and dependent health care benefits. *Fortune, "Best Workplaces for Parents," 2022*

Atrium Health, headquartered in Charlotte, is among the "100 Best Places to Work in IT." To qualify, companies had to have a minimum of 100 total employees and five IT employees. The best places to work were selected based on DEI (diversity, equity, and inclusion) practices; IT turnover, promotions, and growth; IT retention and engagement programs; remote/hybrid working; benefits and perks (such as elder care and child care, flextime, and reimbursement for college tuition); and training and career development opportunities. *Computerworld, "Best Places to Work in IT," 2023*

88 Charlotte, North Carolina

PUBLIC SAFETY

Crime Rate

Area	Total Crime	Violent Crime Rate				Property Crime Rate		
		Murder	Rape[3]	Robbery	Aggrav. Assault	Burglary	Larceny -Theft	Motor Vehicle Theft
City	4,076.6	12.4	25.6	184.0	614.4	449.9	2,478.9	311.4
Suburbs[1]	n/a	n/a	n/a	n/a	n/a	n/a	n/a	n/a
Metro[2]	n/a	n/a	n/a	n/a	n/a	n/a	n/a	n/a
U.S.	2,356.7	6.5	38.4	73.9	279.7	314.2	1,398.0	246.0

Note: Figures are crimes per 100,000 population; (1) All areas within the metro area that are located outside the city limits; (2) Figures cover the Charlotte-Concord-Gastonia, NC-SC Metropolitan Statistical Area; n/a not available; (3) All figures shown were reported using the revised Uniform Crime Reporting (UCR) definition of rape; Due to the transition to the National Incident-Based Reporting System (NIBRS), limited city and metro area data was released for 2021.
Source: FBI Uniform Crime Reports, 2020

Hate Crimes

Area	Number of Quarters Reported	Number of Incidents per Bias Motivation					
		Race/Ethnicity/ Ancestry	Religion	Sexual Orientation	Disability	Gender	Gender Identity
City	4	13	0	5	0	0	0
U.S.	4	5,227	1,244	1,110	130	75	266

Note: Due to the transition to the National Incident-Based Reporting System (NIBRS), limited crime data was released for 2021.
Source: Federal Bureau of Investigation, Hate Crime Statistics 2020

Identity Theft Consumer Reports

Area	Reports	Reports per 100,000 Population	Rank[2]
MSA[1]	11,806	455	24
U.S.	1,108,609	339	-

Note: (1) Figures cover the Charlotte-Concord-Gastonia, NC-SC Metropolitan Statistical Area; (2) Rank ranges from 1 to 391 where 1 indicates greatest number of identity theft reports per 100,000 population
Source: Federal Trade Commission, Consumer Sentinel Network Data Book 2022

Fraud and Other Consumer Reports

Area	Reports	Reports per 100,000 Population	Rank[2]
MSA[1]	34,570	1,332	23
U.S.	4,064,520	1,245	-

Note: (1) Figures cover the Charlotte-Concord-Gastonia, NC-SC Metropolitan Statistical Area; (2) Rank ranges from 1 to 391 where 1 indicates greatest number of fraud and other consumer reports per 100,000 population
Source: Federal Trade Commission, Consumer Sentinel Network Data Book 2022

POLITICS

2020 Presidential Election Results

Area	Biden	Trump	Jorgensen	Hawkins	Other
Mecklenburg County	66.7	31.6	1.0	0.3	0.5
U.S.	51.3	46.8	1.2	0.3	0.5

Note: Results are percentages and may not add to 100% due to rounding
Source: Dave Leip's Atlas of U.S. Presidential Elections

SPORTS

Professional Sports Teams

Team Name	League	Year Established
Carolina Panthers	National Football League (NFL)	1995
Charlotte FC	Major League Soccer (MLS)	2022
Charlotte Hornets	National Basketball Association (NBA)	2004

Note: Includes teams located in the Charlotte-Concord-Gastonia, NC-SC Metropolitan Statistical Area.
Source: Wikipedia, Major Professional Sports Teams of the United States and Canada, April 12, 2023

Charlotte, North Carolina **89**

CLIMATE

Average and Extreme Temperatures

Temperature	Jan	Feb	Mar	Apr	May	Jun	Jul	Aug	Sep	Oct	Nov	Dec	Yr.
Extreme High (°F)	78	81	86	93	97	103	103	103	104	98	85	77	104
Average High (°F)	51	54	62	72	80	86	89	88	82	72	62	53	71
Average Temp. (°F)	41	44	51	61	69	76	79	78	72	61	51	43	61
Average Low (°F)	31	33	40	48	57	65	69	68	62	50	40	33	50
Extreme Low (°F)	-5	5	4	25	32	45	53	53	39	24	11	2	-5

Note: Figures cover the years 1948-1990
Source: National Climatic Data Center, International Station Meteorological Climate Summary, 9/96

Average Precipitation/Snowfall/Humidity

Precip./Humidity	Jan	Feb	Mar	Apr	May	Jun	Jul	Aug	Sep	Oct	Nov	Dec	Yr.
Avg. Precip. (in.)	3.6	3.8	4.5	3.0	3.7	3.4	3.9	3.9	3.4	3.2	3.1	3.4	42.8
Avg. Snowfall (in.)	2	2	1	Tr	0	0	0	0	0	0	Tr	1	6
Avg. Rel. Hum. 7am (%)	78	77	78	78	82	83	86	89	89	87	83	79	82
Avg. Rel. Hum. 4pm (%)	53	49	46	43	49	51	54	55	54	50	50	54	51

Note: Figures cover the years 1948-1990; Tr = Trace amounts (<0.05 in. of rain; <0.5 in. of snow)
Source: National Climatic Data Center, International Station Meteorological Climate Summary, 9/96

Weather Conditions

Temperature			Daytime Sky			Precipitation		
10°F & below	32°F & below	90°F & above	Clear	Partly cloudy	Cloudy	0.01 inch or more precip.	0.1 inch or more snow/ice	Thunder-storms
1	65	44	98	142	125	113	3	41

Note: Figures are average number of days per year and cover the years 1948-1990
Source: National Climatic Data Center, International Station Meteorological Climate Summary, 9/96

HAZARDOUS WASTE

Superfund Sites

The Charlotte-Concord-Gastonia, NC-SC metro area is home to 12 sites on the EPA's Superfund National Priorities List: **Bypass 601 Ground Water Contamination** (final); **Carolawn, Inc.** (final); **Davis Park Road Tce** (final); **FCX, Inc. (Statesville Plant)** (final); **Hemphill Road Tce** (final); **Jadco-Hughes Facility** (final); **Leonard Chemical Co., Inc.** (final); **National Starch & Chemical Corp.** (final); **North Belmont Pce** (final); **Ram Leather Care Site** (final); **Rock Hill Chemical Co.** (final); **Sigmon's Septic Tank Service** (final). There are a total of 1,165 Superfund sites with a status of proposed or final on the list in the U.S. *U.S. Environmental Protection Agency, National Priorities List, April 12, 2023*

AIR QUALITY

Air Quality Trends: Ozone

	1990	1995	2000	2005	2010	2015	2018	2019	2020	2021
MSA[1]	0.094	0.091	0.099	0.089	0.082	0.071	0.070	0.073	0.060	0.067
U.S.	0.087	0.089	0.081	0.080	0.072	0.067	0.069	0.065	0.065	0.067

Note: (1) Data covers the Charlotte-Concord-Gastonia, NC-SC Metropolitan Statistical Area. The values shown are the composite ozone concentration averages among trend sites based on the highest fourth daily maximum 8-hour concentration in parts per million. These trends are based on sites having an adequate record of monitoring data during the trend period. Data from exceptional events are included.
Source: U.S. Environmental Protection Agency, Air Quality Monitoring Information, "Air Quality Trends by City, 1990-2021"

Air Quality Index

Area	Percent of Days when Air Quality was...[2]					AQI Statistics[2]	
	Good	Moderate	Unhealthy for Sensitive Groups	Unhealthy	Very Unhealthy	Maximum	Median
MSA[1]	64.4	34.8	0.8	0.0	0.0	128	46

Note: (1) Data covers the Charlotte-Concord-Gastonia, NC-SC Metropolitan Statistical Area; (2) Based on 365 days with AQI data in 2021. Air Quality Index (AQI) is an index for reporting daily air quality. EPA calculates the AQI for five major air pollutants regulated by the Clean Air Act: ground-level ozone, particle pollution (aka particulate matter), carbon monoxide, sulfur dioxide, and nitrogen dioxide. The AQI runs from 0 to 500. The higher the AQI value, the greater the level of air pollution and the greater the health concern. There are six AQI categories: "Good" AQI is between 0 and 50. Air quality is considered satisfactory; "Moderate" AQI is between 51 and 100. Air quality is acceptable; "Unhealthy for Sensitive Groups" When AQI values are between 101 and 150, members of sensitive groups may experience health effects; "Unhealthy" When AQI values are between 151 and 200 everyone may begin to experience health effects; "Very Unhealthy" AQI values between 201 and 300 trigger a health alert; "Hazardous" AQI values over 300 trigger warnings of emergency conditions (not shown).
Source: U.S. Environmental Protection Agency, Air Quality Index Report, 2021

Air Quality Index Pollutants

Area	Percent of Days when AQI Pollutant was...[2]					
	Carbon Monoxide	Nitrogen Dioxide	Ozone	Sulfur Dioxide	Particulate Matter 2.5	Particulate Matter 10
MSA[1]	0.0	0.3	59.2	(3)	40.5	0.0

Note: (1) Data covers the Charlotte-Concord-Gastonia, NC-SC Metropolitan Statistical Area; (2) Based on 365 days with AQI data in 2021. The Air Quality Index (AQI) is an index for reporting daily air quality. EPA calculates the AQI for five major air pollutants regulated by the Clean Air Act: ground-level ozone, particle pollution (also known as particulate matter), carbon monoxide, sulfur dioxide, and nitrogen dioxide. The AQI runs from 0 to 500. The higher the AQI value, the greater the level of air pollution and the greater the health concern; (3) Sulfur dioxide is no longer included in this table (as of December 8, 2021) because SO_2 concentrations tend to be very localized and not necessarily representative of broad geographical areas like counties and CBSAs.
Source: U.S. Environmental Protection Agency, Air Quality Index Report, 2021

Maximum Air Pollutant Concentrations: Particulate Matter, Ozone, CO and Lead

	Particulate Matter 10 (ug/m^3)	Particulate Matter 2.5 Wtd AM (ug/m^3)	Particulate Matter 2.5 24-Hr (ug/m^3)	Ozone (ppm)	Carbon Monoxide (ppm)	Lead (ug/m^3)
MSA[1] Level	39	9.3	21	0.067	1	n/a
NAAQS[2]	150	15	35	0.075	9	0.15
Met NAAQS[2]	Yes	Yes	Yes	Yes	Yes	n/a

Note: (1) Data covers the Charlotte-Concord-Gastonia, NC-SC Metropolitan Statistical Area; Data from exceptional events are included; (2) National Ambient Air Quality Standards; ppm = parts per million; ug/m^3 = micrograms per cubic meter; n/a not available.
Concentrations: Particulate Matter 10 (coarse particulate)—highest second maximum 24-hour concentration; Particulate Matter 2.5 Wtd AM (fine particulate)—highest weighted annual mean concentration; Particulate Matter 2.5 24-Hour (fine particulate)—highest 98th percentile 24-hour concentration; Ozone—highest fourth daily maximum 8-hour concentration; Carbon Monoxide—highest second maximum non-overlapping 8-hour concentration; Lead—maximum running 3-month average
Source: U.S. Environmental Protection Agency, Air Quality Monitoring Information, "Air Quality Statistics by City, 2021"

Maximum Air Pollutant Concentrations: Nitrogen Dioxide and Sulfur Dioxide

	Nitrogen Dioxide AM (ppb)	Nitrogen Dioxide 1-Hr (ppb)	Sulfur Dioxide AM (ppb)	Sulfur Dioxide 1-Hr (ppb)	Sulfur Dioxide 24-Hr (ppb)
MSA[1] Level	7	37	n/a	2	n/a
NAAQS[2]	53	100	30	75	140
Met NAAQS[2]	Yes	Yes	n/a	Yes	n/a

Note: (1) Data covers the Charlotte-Concord-Gastonia, NC-SC Metropolitan Statistical Area; Data from exceptional events are included; (2) National Ambient Air Quality Standards; ppm = parts per million; ug/m^3 = micrograms per cubic meter; n/a not available.
Concentrations: Nitrogen Dioxide AM—highest arithmetic mean concentration; Nitrogen Dioxide 1-Hr—highest 98th percentile 1-hour daily maximum concentration; Sulfur Dioxide AM—highest annual mean concentration; Sulfur Dioxide 1-Hr—highest 99th percentile 1-hour daily maximum concentration; Sulfur Dioxide 24-Hr—highest second maximum 24-hour concentration
Source: U.S. Environmental Protection Agency, Air Quality Monitoring Information, "Air Quality Statistics by City, 2021"

Cincinnati, Ohio

Background

Cincinnati's name has a long history. After the American Revolution, former Continental Army soldiers formed a fraternal organization called the Society of Cincinnati, alluding to the Roman General Lucius Quinctius Cincinnatus. In 1790, General Arthur St. Clair, a member of that society and the first governor of the Northwest Territory, felt that this lovely city overlooking the Ohio River could only be called Cincinnati. As if that were not enough, he had to pay homage to fellow fraternal member Alexander Hamilton, so St. Clair named the county in which Cincinnati lies after him.

Since its incorporation as a city in 1819, the Miami and Erie canals have played great roles in Cincinnati's economic growth. Because of these waterways, farmers had the transportation necessary to sell their produce in town. From there, businesses would process the farmers' wares such as corn, pigs, and wheat into whiskey, pork, and flour.

Incidentally, the South, which was Cincinnati's greatest market for pork, made the city's loyalties difficult to declare during the Civil War. Cincinnati finally chose sides when it became a major station of the Underground Railroad, as well as the haven where Harriet Beecher Stowe would write her classic, *Uncle Tom's Cabin*. The National Underground Railroad Freedom Center in the city offers programs and exhibits highlighting the Railroad's true stories of courage in the quest for freedom.

Today, the city's major economic sectors include aerospace, automotive, chemistry and plastics, and financial services, although newer sectors are emerging such as advanced energy and consumer products. The city is home to the University of Cincinnati and Xavier University and six Fortune 500 corporate headquarters. Major employers headquartered here include Proctor & Gamble and The Kroger Company. Five interstate highways converge at Cincinnati, providing present-day transportation access just as the canals did early in the city's growth. Amtrak is on the verge of a 10-year project that will connect Cincinnati, Cleveland, Columbus, and Dayton.

The city blends Old World charm with modern business savvy. Investments of more than $700 million in the first decades of the 21st century are drawing tourists, conventioneers, and residents downtown—the Cincinnati Center City Development Corp., charged with supporting the area's renaissance, has seen to that. Improvements include new entertainment districts, called The Banks and Over the Rhine. New hotels that have opened in recent years include 21c Museum Hotel, which has an 8,000 square-foot art museum. Horseshoe Casino Cincinnati, which opened in March 2013, boasts a 31-table World Series Poker Room in addition to entertainment venues and restaurants. Not far from these are the Duke Energy Convention Center and the city's two professional sports stadiums: the Cincinnati Reds MLB team plays at the Great American Ball Park and the NFL's Cincinnati Bengals call the Paul Brown Stadium home.

The arts thrive in Cincinnati. The Rosenthal Center for Contemporary Art celebrated its 80th anniversary in 2019 and is housed in an acclaimed, Zaha Hadid-designed building; she won the Pritzker Architecture Award in 2004, the year after the building opened. The famed Cincinnati Opera, founded in 1920 and the second-oldest opera company in the U.S., features a complete season of productions as well as a summer program. The Cincinnati Symphony Orchestra, founded in 1905, is the nation's fifth-oldest orchestra. Both organizations perform in the historic Music Hall, whose Springer Auditorium is renowned for its acoustics.

To celebrate its German heritage, Cincinnati hosts the second largest Oktoberfest in the world.

But perhaps Cincinnati most celebrated tradition is its chili, unique in that it's served over spaghetti or as a "coney" sauce on a hotdog. It's a staple in many city restaurants, including Skyline Chili, Empress, and Gold Star.

Cincinnati experiences a rather wide range of temperatures from winter to summer. Summers are warm and quite humid, with brief periods of very high temperatures every two or three years. Winters are moderately cold with numerous periods of extensive cloudiness.

Rankings

General Rankings

- In their ninth annual survey, Livability.com looked at data for more than 2,300 mid-sized U.S. cities to determine the rankings for Livability's "Top 100 Best Places to Live" in 2022. Cincinnati ranked #42. Criteria: housing and economy; social and civic engagement; education; demographics; health care options; transportation & infrastructure; and community amenities. *Livability.com, "Top 100 Best Places to Live 2022" July 19, 2022*

Business/Finance Rankings

- Based on metro area social media reviews, the employment opinion group Glassdoor surveyed 50 of the most populous U.S. metro areas and equally weighed cost of living, hiring opportunity, and job satisfaction to compose a list of "25 Best Cities for Jobs." Median pay and home value, and number of active job openings were also factored in. The Cincinnati metro area was ranked #9 in overall job satisfaction. *www.glassdoor.com, "Best Cities for Jobs," February 25, 2020*

- The Brookings Institution ranked the nation's largest cities based on income inequality. Cincinnati was ranked #12 (#1 = greatest inequality). Criteria: the "95/20 ratio," a figure representing the income at which a household earns more than 95 percent of all other households, divided by the income at which a household earns more than only 20 percent of all other households. *Brookings Institution, "Household Income Inequality, Largest Cities of 97 Large U.S. Metro Areas, 2014-2016," February 5, 2018*

- The Brookings Institution ranked the 100 largest metro areas in the U.S. based on income inequality. Cincinnati was ranked #40 (#1 = greatest inequality). Criteria: the "95/20 ratio," a figure representing the income at which a household earns more than 95 percent of all other households, divided by the income at which a household earns more than only 20 percent of all other households. *Brookings Institution, "Household Income Inequality, 100 Largest U.S. Metro Areas, 2014-2016," February 5, 2018*

- Payscale.com ranked the 32 largest metro areas in terms of wage growth. The Cincinnati metro area ranked #13. Criteria: quarterly changes in private industry employee and education professional wage growth from the previous year. *PayScale, "Wage Trends by Metro Area-1st Quarter," April 20, 2023*

- Cincinnati was identified as one of America's most frugal metro areas by *Coupons.com*. The city ranked #24 out of 25. Criteria: digital coupon usage. *Coupons.com, "America's Most Frugal Cities of 2017," March 22, 2018*

- Cincinnati was cited as one of America's top metros for total corporate facility investment in 2022. The area ranked #9 in the large metro area category (population over 1 million). *Site Selection, "Top Metros of 2022," March 2023*

- Livability.com rated Cincinnati as #7 of ten cities where new college grads' job prospects are brightest. Criteria included: number of 22- to 29-year olds; good job opportunities; affordable housing options; public transportation users; educational attainment; variety of fun things to do. *Livability.com, "2018 Top 10 Best Cities for Recent College Grads," April 26, 2018*

- The Cincinnati metro area appeared on the Milken Institute "2022 Best Performing Cities" list. Rank: #111 out of 200 large metro areas (population over 250,000). Criteria: job growth; wage and salary growth; high-tech output growth; housing affordability; household broadband access. *Milken Institute, "Best-Performing Cities 2022," March 28, 2022*

- *Forbes* ranked the 200 most populous metro areas to determine the nation's "Best Places for Business and Careers." The Cincinnati metro area was ranked #44. Criteria: costs (business and living); job growth (past and projected); income growth; quality of life; educational attainment (college and high school); projected economic growth; cultural and leisure opportunities; workplace tolerance laws; net migration patterns. *Forbes, "The Best Places for Business and Careers 2019: Seattle Still On Top," October 30, 2019*

Children/Family Rankings

- Cincinnati was selected as one of the most playful cities in the U.S. by KaBOOM! The organization's Playful City USA initiative honors cities and towns across the nation that have made their communities more playable. Criteria: pledging to integrate play as a solution to challenges in their communities; making it easy for children to get active and balanced play; creating more family-friendly and innovative communities as a result. *KaBOOM! National Campaign for Play, "2017 Playful City USA Communities"*

Culture/Performing Arts Rankings

- Cincinnati was selected as one of the 25 best cities for moviemakers in North America. Great film cities are places where filmmaking dreams can come true, that offer more creative space, lower costs, and great outdoor locations. NYC & LA were intentionally excluded. Criteria: longstanding reputations as film-friendly communities; film community and culture; affordability; and quality of life. The city was ranked #11. *MovieMaker Magazine, "Best Places to Live and Work as a Moviemaker, 2023," January 18, 2023*

Dating/Romance Rankings

- *Apartment List* conducted its Annual Renter Satisfaction Survey and asked renters "how satisfied are you with opportunities for dating in your current city." The cities were ranked from highest to lowest based on their satisfaction scores. Cincinnati ranked #1 out of 85 cities. *Apartment List, "Best Cities for Dating 2022 with Local Dating Insights from Bumble," February 7, 2022*

- Cincinnati was ranked #5 out of 25 cities that stood out for inspiring romance and attracting diners on the website OpenTable.com. Criteria: percentage of people who dined out on Valentine's Day in 2018; percentage of romantic restaurants as rated by OpenTable diner reviews; and percentage of tables seated for two. *OpenTable, "25 Most Romantic Cities in America for 2019," February 7, 2019*

- Cincinnati was selected as one of the nation's most romantic cities with 100,000 or more residents by Amazon.com. The city ranked #7 of 20. Criteria: per capita sales of romance novels, relationship books, romantic comedy movies, romantic music, and sexual wellness products. *Amazon.com, "Top 20 Most Romantic Cities in the U.S.," February 1, 2017*

Education Rankings

- Personal finance website *WalletHub* analyzed the 150 largest U.S. metropolitan statistical areas to determine where the most educated Americans are putting their degrees to work. Criteria: education levels; percentage of workers with degrees; education quality and attainment gap; public school quality rankings; quality and enrollment of each metro area's universities. Cincinnati was ranked #56 (#1 = most educated city). *www.WalletHub.com, "Most & Least Educated Cities in America," July 18, 2022*

- Cincinnati was selected as one of America's most literate cities. The city ranked #7 out of the 84 largest U.S. cities. Criteria: number of booksellers; library resources; Internet resources; educational attainment; periodical publishing resources; newspaper circulation. *Central Connecticut State University, "America's Most Literate Cities, 2018," February 2019*

Environmental Rankings

- The U.S. Environmental Protection Agency (EPA) released its list of U.S. metropolitan areas with the most ENERGY STAR certified buildings in 2022. The Cincinnati metro area was ranked #25 out of 25. *U.S. Environmental Protection Agency, "2023 Energy Star Top Cities," April 26, 2023*

- Cincinnati was highlighted as one of the 25 metro areas most polluted by year-round particle pollution (Annual PM 2.5) in the U.S. during 2019 through 2021. The area ranked #18. *American Lung Association, "State of the Air 2023," April 19, 2023*

Health/Fitness Rankings

- For each of the 100 largest cities in the United States, the American Fitness Index®, compiled in partnership between the American College of Sports Medicine and the Elevance Health Foundation, evaluated community infrastructure and 34 health behaviors including preventive health, levels of chronic disease conditions, food insecurity, sleep quality, pedestrian safety, air quality, and community/environment resources that support physical activity. Cincinnati ranked #68 for "community fitness." *americanfitnessindex.org, "2022 ACSM American Fitness Index Summary Report," July 12, 2022*

- The Cincinnati metro area was identified as one of the worst cities for bed bugs in America by pest control company Orkin. The area ranked #13 out of 50 based on the number of bed bug treatments Orkin performed from December 2021 to November 2022. *Orkin, "The Windy City Can't Blow Bed Bugs Away: Chicago Ranks #1 For Third Consecutive Year On Orkin's Bed Bug Cities List," January 9, 2023*

- Cincinnati was identified as a "2022 Spring Allergy Capital." The area ranked #65 out of 100. Three groups of factors were used to identify the most challenging cities for people with allergies during the spring season: annual spring pollen scores; over the counter allergy medicine use; number of board-certified allergy specialists. *Asthma and Allergy Foundation of America, "Spring Allergy Capitals 2022," March 2, 2022*

- Cincinnati was identified as a "2022 Fall Allergy Capital." The area ranked #74 out of 100. Three groups of factors were used to identify the most challenging cities for people with allergies during the fall season: annual fall pollen scores; over the counter allergy medicine use; number of board-certified allergy specialists. *Asthma and Allergy Foundation of America, "Fall Allergy Capitals 2022," March 2, 2022*

- Cincinnati was identified as a "2022 Asthma Capital." The area ranked #26 out of the nation's 100 largest metropolitan areas. Criteria: estimated asthma prevalence; asthma-related mortality; and ER visits due to asthma. Risk factors analyzed but not factored in the rankings: annual pollen score; annual air quality; public smoking laws; access to board-certified asthma specialists; rescue and controller medication use; uninsured rate; poverty rate. *Asthma and Allergy Foundation of America, "Asthma Capitals 2022: The Most Challenging Places to Live With Asthma," September 14, 2022*

Real Estate Rankings

- *WalletHub* compared the most populated U.S. cities to determine which had the best markets for real estate agents. Cincinnati ranked #111 where demand was high and pay was the best. Criteria: sales per agent; annual median wage for real-estate agents; monthly average starting salary for real estate agents; real estate job density and competition; unemployment rate; home turnover rate; housing-market health index; and other relevant metrics. *www.WalletHub.com, "2021 Best Places to Be a Real Estate Agent," May 12, 2021*

- The Cincinnati metro area was identified as one of the nations's 20 hottest housing markets in 2023. Criteria: listing views as an indicator of demand and number of days on the market as an indicator of pace. The area ranked #14. *Realtor.com, "January 2023 Top 20 Hottest Housing Markets," February 23, 2023*

- Cincinnati was ranked #33 out of 235 metro areas in terms of housing affordability in 2022 by the National Association of Home Builders (#1 = most affordable). Criteria: the share of homes sold in that area affordable to a family earning the local median income, based on standard mortgage underwriting criteria. *National Association of Home Builders®, NAHB-Wells Fargo Housing Opportunity Index, 4th Quarter 2022*

Safety Rankings

- Allstate ranked the 200 largest cities in America in terms of driver safety. Cincinnati ranked #173. Criteria: internal property damage claims over a two-year period from January 2016 to December 2017. The report helps increase the importance of safety and awareness behind the wheel. *Allstate, "Allstate America's Best Drivers Report, 2019" June 24, 2019*

Seniors/Retirement Rankings

- From its Best Cities for Successful Aging indexes, the Milken Institute generated rankings for metropolitan areas, weighing data in nine categories—health care, wellness, living arrangements, transportation and convenience, financial characteristics, education, employment, community engagement, and overall livability. The Cincinnati metro area was ranked #50 overall in the large metro area category. *Milken Institute, "Best Cities for Successful Aging, 2017" March 14, 2017*

Women/Minorities Rankings

- Cincinnati was selected as one of the queerest cities in America by *The Advocate*. The city ranked #7 out of 25. Criteria, among many: Trans Pride parades/festivals; gay rugby teams; lesbian bars; LGBTQ centers; theater screenings of "Moonlight"; LGBTQ-inclusive nondiscrimination ordinances; and gay bowling teams. *The Advocate, "Queerest Cities in America 2017" January 12, 2017*

- Personal finance website *WalletHub* compared more than 180 U.S. cities across two key dimensions, "Hispanic Business-Friendliness" and "Hispanic Purchasing Power," to arrive at the most favorable conditions for Hispanic entrepreneurs. Cincinnati was ranked #99 out of 182. Criteria includes: share of Hispanic-Owned Businesses; Hispanic entrepreneurship rate to median annual income of Hispanics; Small Business-Friendliness score; cost of living; and number of Hispanics with at least a bachelor's degree. *WalletHub.com, "2019's Best Cities for Hispanic Entrepreneurs," May 1, 2019*

Miscellaneous Rankings

- The watchdog site, Charity Navigator, conducted a study of charities in major markets both to analyze statistical differences in their financial, accountability, and transparency practices and to track year-to-year variations in individual philanthropic communities. The Cincinnati metro area was ranked #30 among the 30 metro markets in the rating category of Overall Score. *www.charitynavigator.org, "2017 Metro Market Study," May 1, 2017*

- In *Condé Nast Traveler* magazine's 2022 Readers' Choice Survey, Cincinnati made the top ten list of friendliest American cities. Cincinnati ranked #10. *www.cntraveler.com, "The 10 Friendliest Cities in the U.S.," December 20, 2022*

- *WalletHub* compared the 150 most populated U.S. cities to determine their operating efficiency. A "Quality of Services" score was constructed for each city and then divided by the total budget per capita to reveal which were managed the best. Cincinnati ranked #110. Criteria: financial stability; economy; education; safety; health; infrastructure and pollution. *www.WalletHub.com, "2022's Best-& Worst-Run Cities in America," June 21, 2022*

Business Environment

DEMOGRAPHICS

Population Growth

Area	1990 Census	2000 Census	2010 Census	2020 Census	Population Growth (%) 1990-2020	Population Growth (%) 2010-2020
City	363,974	331,285	296,943	309,317	-15.0	4.2
MSA[1]	1,844,917	2,009,632	2,130,151	2,256,884	22.3	5.9
U.S.	248,709,873	281,421,906	308,745,538	331,449,281	33.3	7.4

Note: (1) Figures cover the Cincinnati, OH-KY-IN Metropolitan Statistical Area
Source: U.S. Census Bureau, 1990 Census, 2000 Census, 2010 Census, 2020 Census

Race

Area	White Alone[2] (%)	Black Alone[2] (%)	Asian Alone[2] (%)	AIAN[3] Alone[2] (%)	NHOPI[4] Alone[2] (%)	Other Race Alone[2] (%)	Two or More Races (%)
City	47.7	40.6	2.5	0.3	0.1	3.0	5.8
MSA[1]	76.7	12.1	3.0	0.3	0.1	2.1	5.7
U.S.	61.6	12.4	6.0	1.1	0.2	8.4	10.2

Note: (1) Figures cover the Cincinnati, OH-KY-IN Metropolitan Statistical Area; (2) Alone is defined as not being in combination with one or more other races; (3) American Indian and Alaska Native; (4) Native Hawaiian and Other Pacific Islander
Source: U.S. Census Bureau, 2020 Census

Hispanic or Latino Origin

Area	Total (%)	Mexican (%)	Puerto Rican (%)	Cuban (%)	Other (%)
City	4.4	1.4	0.6	0.2	2.2
MSA[1]	3.5	1.6	0.4	0.1	1.4
U.S.	18.4	11.2	1.8	0.7	4.7

Note: Persons of Hispanic or Latino origin can be of any race; (1) Figures cover the Cincinnati, OH-KY-IN Metropolitan Statistical Area
Source: U.S. Census Bureau, 2017-2021 American Community Survey 5-Year Estimates

Age

Area	Percent of Population Under Age 5	Age 5–19	Age 20–34	Age 35–44	Age 45–54	Age 55–64	Age 65–74	Age 75–84	Age 85+	Median Age
City	6.1	18.3	29.2	11.9	10.0	11.5	8.0	3.3	1.7	32.7
MSA[1]	5.9	20.1	19.8	12.4	12.3	13.4	9.7	4.5	1.8	38.2
U.S.	5.6	19.2	20.2	12.7	12.4	13.1	10.0	4.9	1.9	38.8

Note: (1) Figures cover the Cincinnati, OH-KY-IN Metropolitan Statistical Area
Source: U.S. Census Bureau, 2020 Census

Disability by Age

Area	All Ages	Under 18 Years Old	18 to 64 Years Old	65 Years and Over
City	12.8	5.2	11.8	32.0
MSA[1]	12.4	5.0	10.6	31.8
U.S.	12.6	4.4	10.3	33.4

Note: Figures show percent of the civilian noninstitutionalized population that reported having a disability. Disability status is determined from six types of difficulty: vision, hearing, cognitive, ambulatory, self-care, and independent living. For children under 5 years old, hearing and vision difficulty are used to determine disability status. For children between the ages of 5 and 14, disability status is determined from hearing, vision, cognitive, ambulatory, and self-care difficulties. For people aged 15 years and older, they are considered to have a disability if they have difficulty with any one of the six difficulty types; Note: (1) Figures cover the Cincinnati, OH-KY-IN Metropolitan Statistical Area
Source: U.S. Census Bureau, 2017-2021 American Community Survey 5-Year Estimates

Ancestry

Area	German	Irish	English	American	Italian	Polish	French[2]	Scottish	Dutch
City	17.3	9.4	6.2	3.5	3.8	1.6	1.4	1.1	0.9
MSA[1]	26.1	13.2	10.0	6.2	4.0	1.6	1.8	1.8	1.0
U.S.	12.8	9.6	8.1	5.7	5.0	2.7	2.2	1.6	1.1

Note: Figures are the percentage of the total population reporting a particular ancestry. The nine most commonly reported ancestries in the U.S. are shown. Figures include multiple ancestries (e.g. if a person reported being Irish and Italian, they were included in both columns); (1) Figures cover the Cincinnati, OH-KY-IN Metropolitan Statistical Area; (2) Excludes Basque
Source: U.S. Census Bureau, 2017-2021 American Community Survey 5-Year Estimates

Foreign-born Population

Area	Any Foreign Country	Asia	Mexico	Europe	Caribbean	Central America[2]	South America	Africa	Canada
				Percent of Population Born in					
City	6.6	1.9	0.4	0.9	0.2	0.8	0.3	2.0	0.1
MSA[1]	5.1	2.2	0.5	0.7	0.1	0.4	0.2	0.8	0.1
U.S.	13.6	4.2	3.3	1.5	1.4	1.1	1.1	0.8	0.2

Note: (1) Figures cover the Cincinnati, OH-KY-IN Metropolitan Statistical Area; (2) Excludes Mexico.
Source: U.S. Census Bureau, 2017-2021 American Community Survey 5-Year Estimates

Household Size

Area	One	Two	Three	Four	Five	Six	Seven or More	Average Household Size
			Persons in Household (%)					
City	44.6	30.3	11.4	8.5	3.1	1.3	0.9	2.10
MSA[1]	29.3	34.0	15.1	12.8	5.5	2.1	1.1	2.50
U.S.	28.1	33.8	15.5	12.9	6.0	2.3	1.4	2.60

Note: (1) Figures cover the Cincinnati, OH-KY-IN Metropolitan Statistical Area
Source: U.S. Census Bureau, 2017-2021 American Community Survey 5-Year Estimates

Household Relationships

Area	House-holder	Opposite-sex Spouse	Same-sex Spouse	Opposite-sex Unmarried Partner	Same-sex Unmarried Partner	Child[2]	Grand-child	Other Relatives	Non-relatives
City	45.1	10.2	0.3	3.4	0.3	24.6	2.2	3.4	5.3
MSA[1]	39.5	18.1	0.2	2.7	0.1	28.9	2.3	3.2	2.9
U.S.	38.3	17.5	0.2	2.5	0.2	28.3	2.4	4.8	3.4

Note: Figures are percent of the total population; (1) Figures cover the Cincinnati, OH-KY-IN Metropolitan Statistical Area; (2) Includes biological, adopted, and stepchildren of the householder
Source: U.S. Census Bureau, 2020 Census

Gender

Area	Males	Females	Males per 100 Females
City	149,736	159,581	93.8
MSA[1]	1,107,410	1,149,474	96.3
U.S.	162,685,811	168,763,470	96.4

Note: (1) Figures cover the Cincinnati, OH-KY-IN Metropolitan Statistical Area
Source: U.S. Census Bureau, 2020 Census

Marital Status

Area	Never Married	Now Married[2]	Separated	Widowed	Divorced
City	52.6	29.1	2.2	4.5	11.7
MSA[1]	32.8	48.7	1.5	5.6	11.4
U.S.	33.8	48.0	1.8	5.6	10.8

Note: Figures are percentages and cover the population 15 years of age and older; (1) Figures cover the Cincinnati, OH-KY-IN Metropolitan Statistical Area; (2) Excludes separated
Source: U.S. Census Bureau, 2017-2021 American Community Survey 5-Year Estimates

Religious Groups by Family

Area	Catholic	Baptist	Methodist	LDS[2]	Pentecostal	Lutheran	Islam	Adventist	Other
MSA[1]	17.0	5.7	2.3	0.6	1.5	0.8	1.1	0.7	21.8
U.S.	18.7	7.3	3.0	2.0	1.8	1.7	1.3	1.3	11.6

Note: Figures are the number of adherents as a percentage of the total population and cover the eight largest religious groups in the U.S; (1) Figures cover the Cincinnati, OH-KY-IN Metropolitan Statistical Area; (2) Church of Jesus Christ of Latter-day Saints
Sources: 2020 U.S. Religion Census, Association of Statisticians of American Religious Bodies; The Association of Religion Data Archives (ARDA)

Religious Groups by Tradition

Area	Catholic	Evangelical Protestant	Mainline Protestant	Black Protestant	Islam	Judaism	Hinduism	Orthodox	Buddhism
MSA[1]	17.0	24.9	4.1	2.0	1.1	0.4	0.3	0.3	0.1
U.S.	18.7	16.5	5.2	2.3	1.3	0.6	0.4	0.4	0.3

Note: Figures are the number of adherents as a percentage of the total population; (1) Figures cover the Cincinnati, OH-KY-IN Metropolitan Statistical Area
Sources: 2020 U.S. Religion Census, Association of Statisticians of American Religious Bodies; The Association of Religion Data Archives (ARDA)

ECONOMY

Gross Metropolitan Product

Area	2020	2021	2022	2023	Rank[2]
MSA[1]	152.1	165.2	178.8	190.5	27

Note: Figures are in billions of dollars; (1) Figures cover the Cincinnati, OH-KY-IN Metropolitan Statistical Area; (2) Rank is based on 2021 data and ranges from 1 to 381
Source: U.S. Conference of Mayors, U.S. Metro Economies: U.S. Metros Compared to Global and State Economies, June 2022

Economic Growth

Area	2018-20 (%)	2021 (%)	2022 (%)	2023 (%)	Rank[2]
MSA[1]	0.0	4.2	2.4	3.3	145
U.S.	-0.6	5.7	3.1	2.9	

Note: Figures are real gross metropolitan product (GMP) growth rates and represent average annual percent change; (1) Figures cover the Cincinnati, OH-KY-IN Metropolitan Statistical Area; (2) Rank is based on 2020 2-year average annual percent change and ranges from 1 to 381
Source: U.S. Conference of Mayors, U.S. Metro Economies: U.S. Metros Compared to Global and State Economies, June 2022

Metropolitan Area Exports

Area	2016	2017	2018	2019	2020	2021	Rank[2]
MSA[1]	26,326.2	28,581.8	27,396.3	28,778.3	21,002.2	23,198.7	19

Note: Figures are in millions of dollars; (1) Figures cover the Cincinnati, OH-KY-IN Metropolitan Statistical Area; (2) Rank is based on 2021 data and ranges from 1 to 388
Source: U.S. Department of Commerce, International Trade Administration, Office of Trade and Economic Analysis, Industry and Analysis, Exports by Metropolitan Area, data extracted March 16, 2023

Building Permits

Area	Single-Family			Multi-Family			Total		
	2021	2022	Pct. Chg.	2021	2022	Pct. Chg.	2021	2022	Pct. Chg.
City	206	104	-49.5	932	689	-26.1	1,138	793	-30.3
MSA[1]	5,358	4,126	-23.0	3,071	2,084	-32.1	8,429	6,210	-26.3
U.S.	1,115,400	975,600	-12.5	621,600	689,500	10.9	1,737,000	1,665,100	-4.1

Note: (1) Figures cover the Cincinnati, OH-KY-IN Metropolitan Statistical Area; Figures represent new, privately-owned housing units authorized (unadjusted data); All permit data are based on estimates with imputation
Source: U.S. Census Bureau, Manufacturing, Mining, and Construction Statistics, Building Permits, 2021, 2022

Bankruptcy Filings

Area	Business Filings			Nonbusiness Filings		
	2021	2022	% Chg.	2021	2022	% Chg.
Hamilton County	28	25	-10.7	1,500	1,164	-22.4
U.S.	14,347	13,481	-6.0	399,269	374,240	-6.3

Note: Business filings include Chapter 7, Chapter 9, Chapter 11, Chapter 12, Chapter 13, Chapter 15, and Section 304; Nonbusiness filings include Chapter 7, Chapter 11, and Chapter 13
Source: Administrative Office of the U.S. Courts, Business and Nonbusiness Bankruptcy, County Cases Commenced by Chapter of the Bankruptcy Code, During the 12-Month Period Ending December 31, 2021 and Business and Nonbusiness Bankruptcy, County Cases Commenced by Chapter of the Bankruptcy Code, During the 12-Month Period Ending December 31, 2022

Housing Vacancy Rates

Area	Gross Vacancy Rate[2] (%)			Year-Round Vacancy Rate[3] (%)			Rental Vacancy Rate[4] (%)			Homeowner Vacancy Rate[5] (%)		
	2020	2021	2022	2020	2021	2022	2020	2021	2022	2020	2021	2022
MSA[1]	6.6	7.9	6.8	6.2	7.3	6.3	7.9	7.2	6.3	0.7	0.5	0.3
U.S.	10.6	10.8	10.5	8.2	8.4	8.2	6.3	6.1	5.8	1.0	0.9	0.8

Note: (1) Figures cover the Cincinnati, OH-KY-IN Metropolitan Statistical Area; (2) The percentage of the total housing inventory that is vacant; (3) The percentage of the housing inventory (excluding seasonal units) that is year-round vacant; (4) The percentage of rental inventory that is vacant for rent; (5) The percentage of homeowner inventory that is vacant for sale
Source: U.S. Census Bureau, Housing Vacancies and Homeownership Annual Statistics: 2020, 2021, 2022

INCOME

Income

Area	Per Capita ($)	Median Household ($)	Average Household ($)
City	34,060	45,235	73,412
MSA[1]	37,846	70,308	94,687
U.S.	37,638	69,021	97,196

Note: (1) Figures cover the Cincinnati, OH-KY-IN Metropolitan Statistical Area
Source: U.S. Census Bureau, 2017-2021 American Community Survey 5-Year Estimates

Household Income Distribution

Area	Percent of Households Earning							
	Under $15,000	$15,000 -$24,999	$25,000 -$34,999	$35,000 -$49,999	$50,000 -$74,999	$75,000 -$99,999	$100,000 -$149,999	$150,000 and up
City	18.0	11.9	10.5	12.6	15.3	10.1	10.6	11.0
MSA[1]	9.2	7.6	8.0	11.1	17.0	13.3	17.5	16.3
U.S.	9.4	7.8	8.2	11.4	16.8	12.8	16.3	17.3

Note: (1) Figures cover the Cincinnati, OH-KY-IN Metropolitan Statistical Area
Source: U.S. Census Bureau, 2017-2021 American Community Survey 5-Year Estimates

Poverty Rate

Area	All Ages	Under 18 Years Old	18 to 64 Years Old	65 Years and Over
City	24.7	37.4	22.3	14.7
MSA[1]	11.6	15.5	10.9	8.1
U.S.	12.6	17.0	11.8	9.6

Note: Figures are percentage of people whose income during the past 12 months was below the poverty level;
(1) Figures cover the Cincinnati, OH-KY-IN Metropolitan Statistical Area
Source: U.S. Census Bureau, 2017-2021 American Community Survey 5-Year Estimates

EMPLOYMENT

Labor Force and Employment

Area	Civilian Labor Force			Workers Employed		
	Dec. 2021	Dec. 2022	% Chg.	Dec. 2021	Dec. 2022	% Chg.
City	147,147	145,962	-0.8	141,899	140,924	-0.7
MSA[1]	1,123,242	1,116,215	-0.6	1,088,875	1,082,108	-0.6
U.S.	161,696,000	164,224,000	1.6	155,732,000	158,872,000	2.0

Note: Data is not seasonally adjusted and covers workers 16 years of age and older; (1) Figures cover the
Cincinnati, OH-KY-IN Metropolitan Statistical Area
Source: Bureau of Labor Statistics, Local Area Unemployment Statistics

Unemployment Rate

Area	2022											
	Jan.	Feb.	Mar.	Apr.	May	Jun.	Jul.	Aug.	Sep.	Oct.	Nov.	Dec.
City	4.6	4.2	3.8	3.5	3.5	4.6	4.8	4.8	3.9	4.2	3.3	3.5
MSA[1]	3.9	3.8	3.5	3.0	3.0	3.9	3.9	3.8	3.3	3.6	3.0	3.1
U.S.	4.4	4.1	3.8	3.3	3.4	3.8	3.8	3.8	3.3	3.4	3.4	3.3

Note: Data is not seasonally adjusted and covers workers 16 years of age and older; (1) Figures cover the
Cincinnati, OH-KY-IN Metropolitan Statistical Area
Source: Bureau of Labor Statistics, Local Area Unemployment Statistics

Average Wages

Occupation	$/Hr.	Occupation	$/Hr.
Accountants and Auditors	38.18	Maintenance and Repair Workers	23.48
Automotive Mechanics	21.73	Marketing Managers	69.92
Bookkeepers	22.50	Network and Computer Systems Admin.	46.45
Carpenters	26.23	Nurses, Licensed Practical	25.99
Cashiers	12.78	Nurses, Registered	38.82
Computer Programmers	44.15	Nursing Assistants	16.53
Computer Systems Analysts	50.79	Office Clerks, General	19.80
Computer User Support Specialists	25.81	Physical Therapists	45.46
Construction Laborers	24.39	Physicians	108.34
Cooks, Restaurant	15.01	Plumbers, Pipefitters and Steamfitters	31.67
Customer Service Representatives	19.74	Police and Sheriff's Patrol Officers	33.83
Dentists	86.77	Postal Service Mail Carriers	28.15
Electricians	28.47	Real Estate Sales Agents	27.69
Engineers, Electrical	48.44	Retail Salespersons	16.23
Fast Food and Counter Workers	12.33	Sales Representatives, Technical/Scientific	51.86
Financial Managers	74.98	Secretaries, Exc. Legal/Medical/Executive	20.51
First-Line Supervisors of Office Workers	31.83	Security Guards	17.09
General and Operations Managers	54.62	Surgeons	184.17
Hairdressers/Cosmetologists	19.64	Teacher Assistants, Exc. Postsecondary*	16.00
Home Health and Personal Care Aides	13.84	Teachers, Secondary School, Exc. Sp. Ed.*	33.81
Janitors and Cleaners	15.79	Telemarketers	14.72
Landscaping/Groundskeeping Workers	16.69	Truck Drivers, Heavy/Tractor-Trailer	26.16
Lawyers	64.18	Truck Drivers, Light/Delivery Services	21.77
Maids and Housekeeping Cleaners	13.58	Waiters and Waitresses	14.51

Note: Wage data covers the Cincinnati, OH-KY-IN Metropolitan Statistical Area; (*) Hourly wages were
calculated from annual wage data based on a 40 hour work week; n/a not available.
Source: Bureau of Labor Statistics, Metro Area Occupational Employment & Wage Estimates, May 2022

Employment by Industry

Sector	MSA[1]		U.S.
	Number of Employees	Percent of Total	Percent of Total
Construction, Mining, and Logging	52,200	4.5	5.4
Private Education and Health Services	169,300	14.7	16.1
Financial Activities	78,700	6.8	5.9
Government	129,100	11.2	14.5
Information	13,900	1.2	2.0
Leisure and Hospitality	120,000	10.4	10.3
Manufacturing	120,000	10.4	8.4
Other Services	40,100	3.5	3.7
Professional and Business Services	186,200	16.2	14.7
Retail Trade	108,300	9.4	10.2
Transportation, Warehousing, and Utilities	73,900	6.4	4.9
Wholesale Trade	58,400	5.1	3.9

Note: Figures are non-farm employment as of December 2022. Figures are not seasonally adjusted and include workers 16 years of age and older; (1) Figures cover the Cincinnati, OH-KY-IN Metropolitan Statistical Area
Source: Bureau of Labor Statistics, Current Employment Statistics, Employment, Hours, and Earnings

Employment by Occupation

Occupation Classification	City (%)	MSA[1] (%)	U.S. (%)
Management, Business, Science, and Arts	44.1	42.0	40.3
Natural Resources, Construction, and Maintenance	4.4	6.8	8.7
Production, Transportation, and Material Moving	13.4	14.4	13.1
Sales and Office	20.0	21.4	20.9
Service	18.1	15.5	17.0

Note: Figures cover employed civilians 16 years of age and older; (1) Figures cover the Cincinnati, OH-KY-IN Metropolitan Statistical Area
Source: U.S. Census Bureau, 2017-2021 American Community Survey 5-Year Estimates

Occupations with Greatest Projected Employment Growth: 2022 – 2024

Occupation[1]	2022 Employment	2024 Projected Employment	Numeric Employment Change	Percent Employment Change
Stockers and Order Fillers	110,530	116,860	6,330	5.7
Laborers and Freight, Stock, and Material Movers, Hand	111,490	117,260	5,770	5.2
Industrial Truck and Tractor Operators	37,740	41,280	3,540	9.4
Heavy and Tractor-Trailer Truck Drivers	93,730	97,190	3,460	3.7
Cooks, Restaurant	49,740	52,350	2,610	5.2
Light Truck or Delivery Services Drivers	34,850	37,020	2,170	6.2
Construction Laborers	40,690	42,580	1,890	4.6
Landscaping and Groundskeeping Workers	42,810	44,630	1,820	4.3
Retail Salespersons	126,620	128,200	1,580	1.2
Janitors and Cleaners, Except Maids and Housekeeping Cleaners	75,960	77,460	1,500	2.0

Note: Projections cover Ohio; (1) Sorted by numeric employment change
Source: www.projectionscentral.com, State Occupational Projections, 2022–2024 Short-Term Projections

Fastest-Growing Occupations: 2022 – 2024

Occupation[1]	2022 Employment	2024 Projected Employment	Numeric Employment Change	Percent Employment Change
Statisticians	630	690	60	9.5
Industrial Truck and Tractor Operators	37,740	41,280	3,540	9.4
Machine Feeders and Offbearers	2,290	2,480	190	8.3
Nurse Practitioners	10,530	11,380	850	8.1
Information Security Analysts (SOC 2018)	4,290	4,610	320	7.5
Aerospace Engineering and Operations Technicians	980	1,050	70	7.1
Taxi Drivers	3,820	4,090	270	7.1
Logisticians	7,900	8,420	520	6.6
Amusement and Recreation Attendants	9,160	9,740	580	6.3
Light Truck or Delivery Services Drivers	34,850	37,020	2,170	6.2

Note: Projections cover Ohio; (1) Sorted by percent employment change and excludes occupations with numeric employment change less than 50
Source: www.projectionscentral.com, State Occupational Projections, 2022–2024 Short-Term Projections

Cincinnati, Ohio **101**

CITY FINANCES

City Government Finances

Component	2020 ($000)	2020 ($ per capita)
Total Revenues	1,073,301	3,531
Total Expenditures	1,083,355	3,564
Debt Outstanding	1,199,504	3,947
Cash and Securities[1]	1,068,971	3,517

Note: (1) Cash and security holdings of a government at the close of its fiscal year, including those of its dependent agencies, utilities, and liquor stores.
Source: U.S. Census Bureau, State & Local Government Finances 2020

City Government Revenue by Source

Source	2020 ($000)	2020 ($ per capita)	2020 (%)
General Revenue			
From Federal Government	22,334	73	2.1
From State Government	237,080	780	22.1
From Local Governments	0	0	0.0
Taxes			
Property	66,133	218	6.2
Sales and Gross Receipts	10,383	34	1.0
Personal Income	370,150	1,218	34.5
Corporate Income	46,936	154	4.4
Motor Vehicle License	2,581	8	0.2
Other Taxes	28,377	93	2.6
Current Charges	83,627	275	7.8
Liquor Store	0	0	0.0
Utility	173,934	572	16.2

Source: U.S. Census Bureau, State & Local Government Finances 2020

City Government Expenditures by Function

Function	2020 ($000)	2020 ($ per capita)	2020 (%)
General Direct Expenditures			
Air Transportation	1,254	4	0.1
Corrections	0	0	0.0
Education	0	0	0.0
Employment Security Administration	0	0	0.0
Financial Administration	11,142	36	1.0
Fire Protection	122,794	404	11.3
General Public Buildings	9,249	30	0.9
Governmental Administration, Other	29,710	97	2.7
Health	53,873	177	5.0
Highways	77,857	256	7.2
Hospitals	0	0	0.0
Housing and Community Development	85,826	282	7.9
Interest on General Debt	31,423	103	2.9
Judicial and Legal	8,532	28	0.8
Libraries	0	0	0.0
Parking	11,147	36	1.0
Parks and Recreation	75,793	249	7.0
Police Protection	161,671	531	14.9
Public Welfare	0	0	0.0
Sewerage	30,276	99	2.8
Solid Waste Management	37,673	123	3.5
Veterans' Services	0	0	0.0
Liquor Store	0	0	0.0
Utility	171,667	564	15.8

Source: U.S. Census Bureau, State & Local Government Finances 2020

TAXES

State Corporate Income Tax Rates

State	Tax Rate (%)	Income Brackets ($)	Num. of Brackets	Financial Institution Tax Rate (%)[a]	Federal Income Tax Ded.
Ohio	(r)	–	–	(r)	No

Note: Tax rates as of January 1, 2023; (a) Rates listed are the corporate income tax rate applied to financial institutions or excise taxes based on income. Some states have other taxes based upon the value of deposits or shares; (r) Ohio no longer levies a tax based on income (except for a particular subset of corporations), but instead imposes a Commercial Activity Tax (CAT) equal to $150 for gross receipts sitused to Ohio of between $150,000 and $1 million, plus 0.26% of gross receipts over $1 million. Banks continue to pay a franchise tax of 1.3% of net worth. For those few corporations for whom the franchise tax on net worth or net income still applies, a litter tax also applies.
Source: Federation of Tax Administrators, State Corporate Income Tax Rates, January 1, 2023

State Individual Income Tax Rates

State	Tax Rate (%)	Income Brackets ($)	Personal Exemptions ($)			Standard Ded. ($)	
			Single	Married	Depend.	Single	Married
Ohio (a)	0.0 - 3.99	26,050 - 115,300	1,900	3,800	1,900 (u)	–	–

Note: Tax rates as of January 1, 2023; Local- and county-level taxes are not included; Federal income tax is not deductible on state income tax returns; (a) 16 states have statutory provision for automatically adjusting to the rate of inflation the dollar values of the income tax brackets, standard deductions, and/or personal exemptions. Oregon does not index the income brackets for $125,000 and over; (u) Ohio provides an additional tax credit of $20 per exemption. Exemption amounts reduced for higher income taxpayers. Business income taxes at a flat 3% rate.
Source: Federation of Tax Administrators, State Individual Income Tax Rates, January 1, 2023

Various State Sales and Excise Tax Rates

State	State Sales Tax (%)	Gasoline[1] ($/gal.)	Cigarette[2] ($/pack)	Spirits[3] ($/gal.)	Wine[4] ($/gal.)	Beer[5] ($/gal.)	Recreational Marijuana (%)
Ohio	5.75	0.3851	1.60	11.38	0.32	0.18	Not legal

Note: All tax rates as of January 1, 2023; (1) The American Petroleum Institute has developed a methodology for determining the average tax rate on a gallon of fuel. Rates may include any of the following: excise taxes, environmental fees, storage tank fees, other fees or taxes, general sales tax, and local taxes; (2) The federal excise tax of $1.0066 per pack and local taxes are not included; (3) Rates are those applicable to off-premise sales of 40% alcohol by volume (a.b.v.) distilled spirits in 750ml containers. Local excise taxes are excluded; (4) Rates are those applicable to off-premise sales of 11% a.b.v. non-carbonated wine in 750ml containers; (5) Rates are those applicable to off-premise sales of 4.7% a.b.v. beer in 12 ounce containers.
Source: Tax Foundation, 2023 Facts & Figures: How Does Your State Compare?

State Business Tax Climate Index Rankings

State	Overall Rank	Corporate Tax Rank	Individual Income Tax Rank	Sales Tax Rank	Property Tax Rank	Unemployment Insurance Tax Rank
Ohio	37	39	41	36	6	13

Note: The index is a measure of how each state's tax laws affect economic performance. The lower the rank, the more favorable a state's tax system is for business. States without a given tax are given a ranking of 1. The scores/rankings for the District of Columbia do not affect other states. The 2023 index represents the tax climate as of July 1, 2022.
Source: Tax Foundation, State Business Tax Climate Index 2023

TRANSPORTATION

Means of Transportation to Work

Area	Car/Truck/Van		Public Transportation			Bicycle	Walked	Other Means	Worked at Home
	Drove Alone	Car-pooled	Bus	Subway	Railroad				
City	69.0	8.5	6.1	0.0	0.0	0.3	5.5	1.4	9.2
MSA[1]	78.8	7.7	1.4	0.0	0.0	0.2	1.9	0.9	9.1
U.S.	73.2	8.6	2.0	1.6	0.5	0.5	2.5	1.5	9.7

Note: Figures are percentages and cover workers 16 years of age and older; (1) Figures cover the Cincinnati, OH-KY-IN Metropolitan Statistical Area
Source: U.S. Census Bureau, 2017-2021 American Community Survey 5-Year Estimates

Travel Time to Work

Area	Less Than 10 Minutes	10 to 19 Minutes	20 to 29 Minutes	30 to 44 Minutes	45 to 59 Minutes	60 to 89 Minutes	90 Minutes or More
City	11.4	33.0	26.8	19.1	4.3	3.2	2.1
MSA[1]	10.9	28.2	25.2	23.1	7.5	3.5	1.6
U.S.	12.4	28.5	21.0	20.9	8.2	6.2	2.9

Note: Note: Figures are percentages and include workers 16 years old and over; (1) Figures cover the Cincinnati, OH-KY-IN Metropolitan Statistical Area
Source: U.S. Census Bureau, 2017-2021 American Community Survey 5-Year Estimates

Key Congestion Measures

Measure	1990	2000	2010	2015	2020
Annual Hours of Delay, Total (000)	17,369	37,540	44,108	53,591	28,436
Annual Hours of Delay, Per Auto Commuter	26	38	41	50	26
Annual Congestion Cost, Per Auto Commuter ($)	646	1,046	977	1,097	608

Note: Covers the Cincinnati OH-KY-IN urban area
Source: Texas A&M Transportation Institute, 2021 Urban Mobility Report

Freeway Travel Time Index

Measure	1985	1990	1995	2000	2005	2010	2015	2020
Urban Area Index[1]	1.06	1.11	1.15	1.17	1.17	1.16	1.17	1.06
Urban Area Rank[1,2]	53	42	36	36	49	54	46	75

Note: Freeway Travel Time Index—the ratio of travel time in the peak period to the travel time at free-flow conditions. For example, a value of 1.30 indicates a 20-minute free-flow trip takes 26 minutes in the peak (20 minutes x 1.30 = 26 minutes); (1) Covers the Cincinnati OH-KY-IN urban area; (2) Rank is based on 101 larger urban areas (#1 = highest travel time index)
Source: Texas A&M Transportation Institute, 2021 Urban Mobility Report

Public Transportation

Agency Name / Mode of Transportation	Vehicles Operated in Maximum Service[1]	Annual Unlinked Passenger Trips[2] (in thous.)	Annual Passenger Miles[3] (in thous.)
Southwest Ohio Regional Transit Authority (SORTA/Metro)			
Bus (directly operated)	286	9,600.3	51,828.6
Demand Response (directly operated)	40	130.4	1,243.6

Note: (1) Number of revenue vehicles operated by the given mode and type of service to meet the annual maximum service requirement. This is the revenue vehicle count during the peak season of the year; on the week and day that maximum service is provided. Vehicles operated in maximum service (VOMS) exclude atypical days and one-time special events; (2) Number of passengers who boarded public transportation vehicles. Passengers are counted each time they board a vehicle no matter how many vehicles they use to travel from their origin to their destination. (3) Sum of the distances ridden by all passengers during the entire fiscal year.
Source: Federal Transit Administration, National Transit Database, 2021

Air Transportation

Airport Name and Code / Type of Service	Passenger Airlines[1]	Passenger Enplanements	Freight Carriers[2]	Freight (lbs)
Cincinnati-Northern Kentucky International (CVG)				
Domestic service (U.S. carriers - 2022)	32	3,645,686	20	1,195,709,239
International service (U.S. carriers - 2021)	3	11,206	9	285,354,773

Note: (1) Includes all U.S.-based major, minor and commuter airlines that carried at least one passenger during the year; (2) Includes all U.S.-based airlines and freight carriers that transported at least one pound of freight during the year.
Source: Bureau of Transportation Statistics, The Intermodal Transportation Database, Air Carriers: T-100 Domestic Market (U.S. Carriers), 2022; Bureau of Transportation Statistics, The Intermodal Transportation Database, Air Carriers: T-100 International Market (U.S. Carriers), 2021

BUSINESSES

Major Business Headquarters

Company Name	Industry	Rankings	
		Fortune[1]	Forbes[2]
American Financial Group	Insurance, property and casualty (stock)	454	-
Cintas	Diversified outsourcing services	470	-
Fifth Third Bancorp	Commercial banks	415	-
Kroger	Food and drug stores	21	-
Macy's	General merchandisers	144	-
Procter & Gamble	Household and personal products	47	-
Western and Southern Financial Group	Financial services	372	-

Note: (1) Companies that produce a 10-K are ranked 1 to 500 based on 2021 revenue; (2) All private companies with at least $2 billion in annual revenue through the end of their most current fiscal year are ranked 1 to 246; companies listed are headquartered in the city; dashes indicate no ranking
Source: Fortune, "Fortune 500," 2022; Forbes, "America's Largest Private Companies," 2022

Fastest-Growing Businesses

According to *Inc.*, Cincinnati is home to one of America's 500 fastest-growing private companies: **ProLink Staffing** (#206). Criteria: must be an independent, privately-held, for-profit, U.S. corporation, proprietorship or partnership as of December 31, 2021; revenues must be at least $100,000 in 2018 and $2 million in 2021; must have four-year operating/sales history. *Inc., "America's 500 Fastest-Growing Private Companies," 2022*

According to *Initiative for a Competitive Inner City (ICIC)*, Cincinnati is home to two of America's 100 fastest-growing "inner city" companies: **Custom Pro Logistics** (#48); **Swath Design** (#63). Criteria for inclusion: company must be headquartered in or have 51 percent or more of its physical operations in an economically distressed urban area; must be an independent, for-profit corporation, partnership or proprietorship; must have 10 or more employees and have a five-year sales history that includes sales of at least $200,000 in the base year and at least $1 million in the current year with no decrease in sales over the two most recent years. Companies were ranked overall by revenue growth over the five-year period between 2017 and 2021. *Initiative for a Competitive Inner City (ICIC), "Inner City 100 Companies," 2022*

Living Environment

COST OF LIVING

Cost of Living Index

Composite Index	Groceries	Housing	Utilities	Transportation	Health Care	Misc. Goods/ Services
96.4	100.9	81.1	92.6	110.8	101.3	103.7

Note: The Cost of Living Index measures regional differences in the cost of consumer goods and services, excluding taxes and non-consumer expenditures, for professional and managerial households in the top income quintile. It is based on more than 50,000 prices covering almost 60 different items for which prices are collected three times a year by chambers of commerce, economic development organizations or university applied economic centers in each participating urban area. The numbers shown should be read as a percentage above or below the national average of 100. For example, a value of 115.4 in the groceries column indicates that grocery prices are 15.4% higher than the national average. Small differences in the index numbers should not be interpreted as significant; Figures cover the Cincinnati OH urban area.
Source: The Council for Community and Economic Research, Cost of Living Index, 2022

Grocery Prices

Area[1]	T-Bone Steak ($/pound)	Frying Chicken ($/pound)	Whole Milk ($/half gal.)	Eggs ($/dozen)	Orange Juice ($/64 oz.)	Coffee ($/11.5 oz.)
City[2]	13.66	2.66	2.15	1.68	3.92	6.05
Avg.	13.81	1.59	2.43	2.25	3.85	4.95
Min.	10.17	0.90	1.51	1.30	2.90	3.46
Max.	19.35	3.30	4.32	4.32	5.31	8.59

Note: (1) Values for the local area are compared with the average, minimum and maximum values for all 286 areas in the Cost of Living Index; (2) Figures cover the Cincinnati OH urban area; *T-Bone Steak* (price per pound); *Frying Chicken* (price per pound, whole fryer); *Whole Milk* (half gallon carton); *Eggs* (price per dozen, Grade A, large); *Orange Juice* (64 oz. Tropicana or Florida Natural); *Coffee* (11.5 oz. can, vacuum-packed, Maxwell House, Hills Bros, or Folgers).
Source: The Council for Community and Economic Research, Cost of Living Index, 2022

Housing and Utility Costs

Area[1]	New Home Price ($)	Apartment Rent ($/month)	All Electric ($/month)	Part Electric ($/month)	Other Energy ($/month)	Telephone ($/month)
City[2]	368,833	1,083	-	76.34	81.75	184.60
Avg.	450,913	1,371	176.41	99.93	76.96	190.22
Min.	229,283	546	100.84	31.56	27.15	174.27
Max.	2,434,977	4,569	356.86	249.59	272.24	208.31

Note: (1) Values for the local area are compared with the average, minimum and maximum values for all 286 areas in the Cost of Living Index; (2) Figures cover the Cincinnati OH urban area; *New Home Price* (2,400 sf living area, 8,000 sf lot, in urban area with full utilities); *Apartment Rent* (950 sf 2 bedroom/1.5 or 2 bath, unfurnished, excluding all utilities except water); *All Electric* (average monthly cost for an all-electric home); *Part Electric* (average monthly cost for a part-electric home); *Other Energy* (average monthly cost for natural gas, fuel oil, coal, wood, and any other forms of energy except electricity); *Telephone* (price includes the base monthly rate plus taxes and fees for three lines of mobile phone service).
Source: The Council for Community and Economic Research, Cost of Living Index, 2022

Health Care, Transportation, and Other Costs

Area[1]	Doctor ($/visit)	Dentist ($/visit)	Optometrist ($/visit)	Gasoline ($/gallon)	Beauty Salon ($/visit)	Men's Shirt ($)
City[2]	142.44	100.47	107.60	4.01	43.10	45.33
Avg.	124.91	107.77	117.66	3.86	43.31	34.21
Min.	36.61	58.25	51.79	2.90	22.18	13.05
Max.	250.21	162.58	371.96	5.54	85.61	63.54

Note: (1) Values for the local area are compared with the average, minimum and maximum values for all 286 areas in the Cost of Living Index; (2) Figures cover the Cincinnati OH urban area; *Doctor* (general practitioners routine exam of an established patient); *Dentist* (adult teeth cleaning and periodic oral examination); *Optometrist* (full vision eye exam for established adult patient); *Gasoline* (one gallon regular unleaded, national brand, including all taxes, cash price at self-service pump if available); *Beauty Salon* (woman's shampoo, trim, and blow-dry); *Men's Shirt* (cotton/polyester dress shirt, pinpoint weave, long sleeves).
Source: The Council for Community and Economic Research, Cost of Living Index, 2022

HOUSING

Homeownership Rate

Area	2015 (%)	2016 (%)	2017 (%)	2018 (%)	2019 (%)	2020 (%)	2021 (%)	2022 (%)
MSA[1]	65.9	64.9	65.7	67.3	67.4	71.1	72.1	67.1
U.S.	63.7	63.4	63.9	64.4	64.6	66.6	65.5	65.8

Note: (1) Figures cover the Cincinnati, OH-KY-IN Metropolitan Statistical Area
Source: U.S. Census Bureau, Housing Vacancies and Homeownership Annual Statistics: 2015-2022

House Price Index (HPI)

Area	National Ranking[2]	Quarterly Change (%)	One-Year Change (%)	Five-Year Change (%)	Since 1991Q1 (%)
MSA[1]	96	-0.52	12.38	55.37	199.65
U.S.[3]	–	0.34	8.41	58.44	289.08

Note: The HPI is a weighted repeat sales index. It measures average price changes in repeat sales or refinancings on the same properties. This information is obtained by reviewing repeat mortgage transactions on single-family properties whose mortgages have been purchased or securitized by Fannie Mae or Freddie Mac since January 1975; (1) Figures cover the Cincinnati, OH-KY-IN Metropolitan Statistical Area; (2) Rankings are based on annual percentage change for all metro areas containing at least 15,000 transactions over the last 10 years and ranges from 1 to 257; (3) figures based on a weighted average of Census Division estimates using a seasonally adjusted, purchase-only index; all figures are for the period ending December 31, 2022
Source: Federal Housing Finance Agency, Change in FHFA Metropolitan Area House Price Indexes, 2022Q4

Median Single-Family Home Prices

Area	2020	2021	2022p	Percent Change 2021 to 2022
MSA[1]	208.9	243.4	263.0	8.1
U.S. Average	300.2	357.1	392.6	9.9

Note: Figures are median sales prices of existing single-family homes in thousands of dollars; (p) preliminary; (1) Figures cover the Cincinnati, OH-KY-IN Metropolitan Statistical Area
Source: National Association of Realtors, Median Sales Price of Existing Single-Family Homes for Metropolitan Areas, 4th Quarter 2022

Qualifying Income Based on Median Sales Price of Existing Single-Family Homes

Area	With 5% Down ($)	With 10% Down ($)	With 20% Down ($)
MSA[1]	76,382	72,362	64,321
U.S. Average	112,234	106,237	94,513

Note: Figures are preliminary; Qualifying income is based on a mortgage rate of 6.77%. Monthly principal and interest payment is limited to 25% of income; (1) Figures cover the Cincinnati, OH-KY-IN Metropolitan Statistical Area
Source: National Association of Realtors, Qualifying Income Based on Median Sales Price of Existing Single-Family Homes for Metropolitan Areas, 4th Quarter 2022

Home Value

Area	Under $100,000	$100,000 -$199,999	$200,000 -$299,999	$300,000 -$399,999	$400,000 -$499,999	$500,000 -$999,999	$1,000,000 or more	Median ($)
City	24.5	35.2	17.3	9.2	4.7	7.2	1.8	162,300
MSA[1]	16.4	37.7	23.2	11.6	4.9	5.4	0.9	187,000
U.S.	16.2	24.2	20.1	13.6	8.3	13.6	4.1	244,900

Note: Figures are percentages except for median and cover owner-occupied housing units; (1) Figures cover the Cincinnati, OH-KY-IN Metropolitan Statistical Area
Source: U.S. Census Bureau, 2017-2021 American Community Survey 5-Year Estimates

Year Housing Structure Built

Area	2020 or Later	2010 -2019	2000 -2009	1990 -1999	1980 -1989	1970 -1979	1960 -1969	1950 -1959	1940 -1949	Before 1940	Median Year
City	0.1	3.3	3.7	4.2	6.0	9.4	12.2	11.5	8.4	41.4	1950
MSA[1]	0.1	5.3	12.0	13.8	10.7	13.8	10.5	11.6	4.8	17.3	1974
U.S.	0.2	7.3	13.6	13.6	13.2	14.8	10.3	10.0	4.7	12.2	1979

Note: Figures are percentages except for Median Year; Note: (1) Figures cover the Cincinnati, OH-KY-IN Metropolitan Statistical Area
Source: U.S. Census Bureau, 2017-2021 American Community Survey 5-Year Estimates

Gross Monthly Rent

Area	Under $500	$500 -$999	$1,000 -$1,499	$1,500 -$1,999	$2,000 -$2,499	$2,500 -$2,999	$3,000 and up	Median ($)
City	15.9	52.7	21.5	6.4	2.1	0.7	0.7	814
MSA[1]	10.6	49.6	28.4	7.8	2.1	0.7	0.8	906
U.S.	8.1	30.5	30.8	16.8	7.3	3.1	3.5	1,163

Note: Figures are percentages except for median; Gross rent is the contract rent plus the estimated average monthly cost of utilities (electricity, gas, and water and sewer) and fuels (oil, coal, kerosene, wood, etc.) if these are paid by the renter (or paid for the renter by someone else); (1) Figures cover the Cincinnati, OH-KY-IN Metropolitan Statistical Area
Source: U.S. Census Bureau, 2017-2021 American Community Survey 5-Year Estimates

HEALTH

Health Risk Factors

Category	MSA[1] (%)	U.S. (%)
Adults aged 18–64 who have any kind of health care coverage	92.9	90.9
Adults who reported being in good or better health	84.2	85.2
Adults who have been told they have high blood cholesterol	35.4	35.7
Adults who have been told they have high blood pressure	38.3	32.4
Adults who are current smokers	17.1	14.4
Adults who currently use e-cigarettes	9.2	6.7
Adults who currently use chewing tobacco, snuff, or snus	3.7	3.5
Adults who are heavy drinkers[2]	6.7	6.3
Adults who are binge drinkers[3]	19.2	15.4
Adults who are overweight (BMI 25.0 - 29.9)	34.5	34.4
Adults who are obese (BMI 30.0 - 99.8)	36.1	33.9
Adults who participated in any physical activities in the past month	74.9	76.3

Note: (1) Figures cover the Cincinnati, OH-KY-IN Metropolitan Statistical Area; (2) Heavy drinkers are classified as adult men having more than 14 drinks per week and adult women having more than 7 drinks per week; (3) Binge drinkers are classified as males having five or more drinks on one occasion or females having four or more drinks on one occasion
Source: Centers for Disease Control and Prevention, Behaviorial Risk Factor Surveillance System, SMART: Selected Metropolitan Area Risk Trends, 2021

Acute and Chronic Health Conditions

Category	MSA[1] (%)	U.S. (%)
Adults who have ever been told they had a heart attack	4.7	4.0
Adults who have ever been told they have angina or coronary heart disease	4.6	3.8
Adults who have ever been told they had a stroke	4.1	3.0
Adults who have ever been told they have asthma	14.8	14.9
Adults who have ever been told they have arthritis	26.3	25.8
Adults who have ever been told they have diabetes[2]	12.5	10.9
Adults who have ever been told they had skin cancer	7.4	6.6
Adults who have ever been told they had any other types of cancer	6.8	7.5
Adults who have ever been told they have COPD	7.4	6.1
Adults who have ever been told they have kidney disease	3.6	3.0
Adults who have ever been told they have a form of depression	22.3	20.5

Note: (1) Figures cover the Cincinnati, OH-KY-IN Metropolitan Statistical Area; (2) Figures do not include pregnancy-related, borderline, or pre-diabetes
Source: Centers for Disease Control and Prevention, Behaviorial Risk Factor Surveillance System, SMART: Selected Metropolitan Area Risk Trends, 2021

Health Screening and Vaccination Rates

Category	MSA[1] (%)	U.S. (%)
Adults who have ever been tested for HIV	33.1	34.9
Adults who have had their blood cholesterol checked within the last five years	86.8	85.2
Adults aged 65+ who have had flu shot within the past year	71.0	68.6
Adults aged 65+ who have ever had a pneumonia vaccination	69.0	71.0

Note: (1) Figures cover the Cincinnati, OH-KY-IN Metropolitan Statistical Area.
Source: Centers for Disease Control and Prevention, Behaviorial Risk Factor Surveillance System, SMART: Selected Metropolitan Area Risk Trends, 2021

Disability Status

Category	MSA[1] (%)	U.S. (%)
Adults who reported being deaf	6.8	7.2
Are you blind or have serious difficulty seeing, even when wearing glasses?	5.3	4.8
Are you limited in any way in any of your usual activities due to arthritis?	8.9	11.1
Do you have difficulty doing errands alone?	8.5	7.0
Do you have difficulty dressing or bathing?	3.2	3.6
Do you have serious difficulty concentrating/remembering/making decisions?	12.8	12.1
Do you have serious difficulty walking or climbing stairs?	12.8	12.8

Note: (1) Figures cover the Cincinnati, OH-KY-IN Metropolitan Statistical Area.
Source: Centers for Disease Control and Prevention, Behaviorial Risk Factor Surveillance System, SMART: Selected Metropolitan Area Risk Trends, 2021

Mortality Rates for the Top 10 Causes of Death in the U.S.

ICD-10[a] Sub-Chapter	ICD-10[a] Code	Crude Mortality Rate[1] per 100,000 population	
		County[2]	U.S.
Malignant neoplasms	C00-C97	192.1	182.6
Ischaemic heart diseases	I20-I25	101.1	113.1
Other forms of heart disease	I30-I51	89.1	64.4
Other degenerative diseases of the nervous system	G30-G31	52.7	51.0
Cerebrovascular diseases	I60-I69	61.9	47.8
Other external causes of accidental injury	W00-X59	63.9	46.4
Chronic lower respiratory diseases	J40-J47	41.9	45.7
Organic, including symptomatic, mental disorders	F01-F09	42.0	35.9
Hypertensive diseases	I10-I15	32.2	35.0
Diabetes mellitus	E10-E14	29.6	29.6

Note: (a) ICD-10 = International Classification of Diseases 10th Revision; (1) Crude mortality rates are a three-year average covering 2019-2021; (2) Figures cover Hamilton County.
Source: Centers for Disease Control and Prevention, National Center for Health Statistics. National Vital Statistics System, Mortality 2018-2021 on CDC WONDER Online Database

Mortality Rates for Selected Causes of Death

ICD-10[a] Sub-Chapter	ICD-10[a] Code	Crude Mortality Rate[1] per 100,000 population	
		County[2]	U.S.
Assault	X85-Y09	12.6	7.0
Diseases of the liver	K70-K76	18.0	19.8
Human immunodeficiency virus (HIV) disease	B20-B24	1.6	1.5
Influenza and pneumonia	J09-J18	15.8	14.7
Intentional self-harm	X60-X84	13.3	14.3
Malnutrition	E40-E46	11.1	4.3
Obesity and other hyperalimentation	E65-E68	2.0	3.0
Renal failure	N17-N19	23.6	15.7
Transport accidents	V01-V99	8.9	13.6
Viral hepatitis	B15-B19	Unreliable	1.2

Note: (a) ICD-10 = International Classification of Diseases 10th Revision; (1) Crude mortality rates are a three-year average covering 2019-2021; (2) Figures cover Hamilton County; Data are suppressed when the data meet the criteria for confidentiality constraints; Crude mortality rates are flagged as unreliable when the rate would be calculated with a numerator of 20 or less.
Source: Centers for Disease Control and Prevention, National Center for Health Statistics. National Vital Statistics System, Mortality 2018-2021 on CDC WONDER Online Database

Health Insurance Coverage

Area	With Health Insurance	With Private Health Insurance	With Public Health Insurance	Without Health Insurance	Population Under Age 19 Without Health Insurance
City	92.7	60.4	40.5	7.3	5.2
MSA[1]	94.6	72.7	33.0	5.4	3.5
U.S.	91.2	67.8	35.4	8.8	5.3

Note: Figures are percentages that cover the civilian noninstitutionalized population; (1) Figures cover the Cincinnati, OH-KY-IN Metropolitan Statistical Area
Source: U.S. Census Bureau, 2017-2021 American Community Survey 5-Year Estimates

Number of Medical Professionals

Area	MDs[3]	DOs[3,4]	Dentists	Podiatrists	Chiropractors	Optometrists
County[1] (number)	5,103	215	629	84	169	188
County[1] (rate[2])	614.9	25.9	76.1	10.2	20.5	22.8
U.S. (rate[2])	289.3	23.5	72.5	6.2	28.7	17.4

Note: Data as of 2021 unless noted; (1) Data covers Hamilton County; (2) Rate per 100,000 population; (3) Data as of 2020 and includes all active, non-federal physicians; (4) Doctor of Osteopathic Medicine
Source: U.S. Department of Health and Human Services, Health Resources and Services Administration, Bureau of Health Professions, Area Resource File (ARF) 2021-2022

Best Hospitals

According to *U.S. News,* the Cincinnati, OH-KY-IN metro area is home to one of the best hospitals in the U.S.: **Atrium Medical Center-Middletown** (1 adult specialty). The hospital listed was nationally ranked in at least one of 15 adult or 10 pediatric specialties. The number of specialties shown cover the parent hospital. Only 164 U.S. hospitals performed well enough to be nationally ranked in one or more specialties. Twenty hospitals in the U.S. made the Honor Roll. The Best Hospitals Honor Roll takes both the national rankings and the procedure and condition ratings into account. Hospitals received points if they were nationally ranked in one of the 15 adult specialties—the higher they ranked, the more points they got—and how many ratings of "high performing" they earned in the 17 procedures and conditions. *U.S. News Online, "America's Best Hospitals 2022-23"*

108 Cincinnati, Ohio

According to *U.S. News,* the Cincinnati, OH-KY-IN metro area is home to one of the best children's hospitals in the U.S.: **Cincinnati Children's Hospital Medical Center** (Honor Roll/10 pediatric specialties). The hospital listed was highly ranked in at least one of 10 pediatric specialties. Eighty-six children's hospitals in the U.S. were nationally ranked in at least one specialty. Hospitals received points for being ranked in a specialty, and the 10 hospitals with the most points across the 10 specialties make up the Honor Roll. *U.S. News Online, "America's Best Children's Hospitals 2022-23"*

EDUCATION

Public School District Statistics

District Name	Schls	Pupils	Pupil/ Teacher Ratio	Minority Pupils[1] (%)	LEP/ELL[2] (%)	IEP[3] (%)
Cincinnati Public Schools	65	35,820	17.9	78.9	6.6	20.9

Note: Table includes school districts with 2,000 or more students; (1) Percentage of students that are not non-Hispanic white; (2) Percentage of students that are Limited English Proficient or English Language Learners (2018-19); (3) Percentage of students that have an Individualized Education Program (2019-20).
Source: U.S. Department of Education, National Center for Education Statistics, Common Core of Data, Local Education Agency (School District) Universe Survey: School Year 2021-2022

Best High Schools

According to *U.S. News,* Cincinnati is home to four of the top 500 high schools in the U.S.: **Walnut Hills High School** (#139); **Indian Hill High School** (#198); **Madeira High School** (#206); **Turpin High School** (#416). Nearly 18,000 public, magnet and charter schools were ranked based on their performance on state assessments and how well they prepare students for college. *U.S. News & World Report, "Best High Schools 2022"*

Highest Level of Education

Area	Less than H.S.	H.S. Diploma	Some College, No Deg.	Associate Degree	Bachelor's Degree	Master's Degree	Prof. School Degree	Doctorate Degree
City	11.4	24.0	17.6	7.4	23.0	11.0	3.4	2.2
MSA[1]	8.2	29.3	18.7	8.4	21.9	9.8	2.1	1.5
U.S.	11.1	26.5	20.0	8.7	20.6	9.3	2.2	1.5

Note: Figures cover persons age 25 and over; (1) Figures cover the Cincinnati, OH-KY-IN Metropolitan Statistical Area
Source: U.S. Census Bureau, 2017-2021 American Community Survey 5-Year Estimates

Educational Attainment by Race

Area	High School Graduate or Higher (%)					Bachelor's Degree or Higher (%)				
	Total	White	Black	Asian	Hisp.[2]	Total	White	Black	Asian	Hisp.[2]
City	88.6	92.9	83.1	94.7	76.9	39.6	54.9	16.8	80.3	33.3
MSA[1]	91.8	92.7	87.3	89.4	77.4	35.4	36.4	21.6	65.9	29.4
U.S.	88.9	91.4	87.2	87.6	71.2	33.7	35.5	23.3	55.6	18.4

Note: Figures shown cover persons 25 years old and over; (1) Figures cover the Cincinnati, OH-KY-IN Metropolitan Statistical Area; (2) People of Hispanic origin can be of any race
Source: U.S. Census Bureau, 2017-2021 American Community Survey 5-Year Estimates

School Enrollment by Grade and Control

Area	Preschool (%)		Kindergarten (%)		Grades 1 - 4 (%)		Grades 5 - 8 (%)		Grades 9 - 12 (%)	
	Public	Private	Public	Private	Public	Private	Public	Private	Public	Private
City	64.4	35.6	70.7	29.3	76.8	23.2	78.9	21.1	80.3	19.7
MSA[1]	53.2	46.8	79.7	20.3	82.8	17.2	83.5	16.5	82.3	17.7
U.S.	58.8	41.2	86.3	13.7	88.3	11.7	88.6	11.4	89.4	10.6

Note: Figures shown cover persons 3 years old and over; (1) Figures cover the Cincinnati, OH-KY-IN Metropolitan Statistical Area
Source: U.S. Census Bureau, 2017-2021 American Community Survey 5-Year Estimates

Higher Education

Four-Year Colleges			Two-Year Colleges			Medical Schools[1]	Law Schools[2]	Voc/ Tech[3]
Public	Private Non-profit	Private For-profit	Public	Private Non-profit	Private For-profit			
8	11	2	1	1	6	1	2	14

Note: Figures cover institutions located within the Cincinnati, OH-KY-IN Metropolitan Statistical Area and include main campuses only; (1) includes schools accredited by the Liaison Committee on Medical Education and the American Osteopathic Association's Commission on Osteopathic College Accreditation; (2) includes ABA-accredited schools, schools with provisional ABA accreditation, and state accredited schools; (3) includes all schools with programs that are less than 2 years.
Source: National Center for Education Statistics, Integrated Postsecondary Education System (IPEDS), 2021-22; Wikipedia, List of Medical Schools in the United States, accessed April 10, 2023; Wikipedia, List of Law Schools in the United States, accessed April 10, 2023

According to *U.S. News & World Report,* the Cincinnati, OH-KY-IN metro area is home to three of the top 200 national universities in the U.S.: **Miami University—Oxford** (#105 tie); **University of Cincinnati** (#151 tie); **Xavier University** (#166 tie). The indicators used to capture academic quality fall into a number of categories: assessment by administrators at peer institutions; retention of students; faculty resources; student selectivity; financial resources; alumni giving; high school counselor ratings of colleges; and graduation rate. *U.S. News & World Report, "America's Best Colleges 2023"*

According to *U.S. News & World Report,* the Cincinnati, OH-KY-IN metro area is home to one of the top 100 law schools in the U.S.: **University of Cincinnati** (#88 tie). The rankings are based on a weighted average of 12 measures of quality: peer assessment score; assessment score by lawyers/judges; median LSAT scores; median undergrad GPA; acceptance rate; employment rates for graduates; placement success; bar passage rate; faculty resources; expenditures per student; student/faculty ratio; and library resources. *U.S. News & World Report, "America's Best Graduate Schools, Law, 2023"*

According to *U.S. News & World Report,* the Cincinnati, OH-KY-IN metro area is home to one of the top 75 medical schools for research in the U.S.: **University of Cincinnati** (#43 tie). The rankings are based on a weighted average of 11 measures of quality: quality assessment; peer assessment score; assessment score by residency directors; research activity; total research activity; average research activity per faculty member; student selectivity; median MCAT total score; median undergraduate GPA; acceptance rate; and faculty resources. *U.S. News & World Report, "America's Best Graduate Schools, Medical, 2023"*

EMPLOYERS

Major Employers

Company Name	Industry
Cincinnati Children's Hospital Medical Ctr	Medical
Cleveland Clinic Foundation	Medical
General Electric Company	Conglomerate
Giant Eagle	Grocery stores
Golden Gate Capital LP/Bob Evans	Restaurants
Home Depot	Retail
Honda Motor Co.	Automotive
JP Morgan Chase & Co.	Banking and financial services
Kettering Health Network	Healthcare
Kroger Co.	Grocery stores
Mercy Health	Healthcare
Nationwide Mutual Insurance Company	Insurance
Ohio Health	Healthcare
Ohio State University	Colleges & universities
Premier Health Partners	Healthcare
ProMedica Health System	Healthcare
United Parcel Service	Package delivery services
University Hospitals Health System	Healthcare
Wal-Mart Stores	Retail
Wright-Patterson Air Force Base	Military

Note: Companies shown are located within the Cincinnati, OH-KY-IN Metropolitan Statistical Area.
Source: Hoovers.com; Wikipedia

Best Companies to Work For

Total Quality Logistics, headquartered in Cincinnati, is among "The 100 Best Companies to Work For." To pick the best companies, *Fortune* partnered with the Great Place to Work Institute. Two-thirds of a company's score is based on the results of the Institute's Trust Index survey, which is sent to a random sample of employees from each company. The questions related to attitudes about management's credibility, job satisfaction, and camaraderie. The other third of the scoring is based on the company's responses to the Institute's Culture Audit, which includes detailed questions about pay and benefit programs, and a series of open-ended questions about hiring practices, internal communication, training, recognition programs, and diversity efforts. Any company that is at least five years old with more than 1,000 U.S. employees is eligible. *Fortune, "The 100 Best Companies to Work For," 2023*

The Kroger Co; Total Quality Logistics, headquartered in Cincinnati, are among the "100 Best Places to Work in IT." To qualify, companies had to have a minimum of 100 total employees and five IT employees. The best places to work were selected based on DEI (diversity, equity, and inclusion) practices; IT turnover, promotions, and growth; IT retention and engagement programs; remote/hybrid working; benefits and perks (such as elder care and child care, flextime, and reimbursement for college tuition); and training and career development opportunities. *Computerworld, "Best Places to Work in IT," 2023*

PUBLIC SAFETY

Crime Rate

Area	Total Crime	Violent Crime Rate				Property Crime Rate		
		Murder	Rape[3]	Robbery	Aggrav. Assault	Burglary	Larceny -Theft	Motor Vehicle Theft
City	4,576.3	30.2	70.6	246.1	546.1	762.0	2,427.1	494.2
Suburbs[1]	1,469.5	1.9	27.0	24.3	78.3	177.6	1,049.2	111.1
Metro[2]	1,894.4	5.7	33.0	54.6	142.3	257.5	1,237.7	163.5
U.S.	2,356.7	6.5	38.4	73.9	279.7	314.2	1,398.0	246.0

Note: Figures are crimes per 100,000 population; (1) All areas within the metro area that are located outside the city limits; (2) Figures cover the Cincinnati, OH-KY-IN Metropolitan Statistical Area; (3) All figures shown were reported using the revised Uniform Crime Reporting (UCR) definition of rape; Due to the transition to the National Incident-Based Reporting System (NIBRS), limited city and metro area data was released for 2021.
Source: FBI Uniform Crime Reports, 2020

Hate Crimes

Area	Number of Quarters Reported	Number of Incidents per Bias Motivation					
		Race/Ethnicity/ Ancestry	Religion	Sexual Orientation	Disability	Gender	Gender Identity
City	4	29	2	3	2	0	0
U.S.	4	5,227	1,244	1,110	130	75	266

Note: Due to the transition to the National Incident-Based Reporting System (NIBRS), limited crime data was released for 2021.
Source: Federal Bureau of Investigation, Hate Crime Statistics 2020

Identity Theft Consumer Reports

Area	Reports	Reports per 100,000 Population	Rank[2]
MSA[1]	4,302	194	177
U.S.	1,108,609	339	-

Note: (1) Figures cover the Cincinnati, OH-KY-IN Metropolitan Statistical Area; (2) Rank ranges from 1 to 391 where 1 indicates greatest number of identity theft reports per 100,000 population
Source: Federal Trade Commission, Consumer Sentinel Network Data Book 2022

Fraud and Other Consumer Reports

Area	Reports	Reports per 100,000 Population	Rank[2]
MSA[1]	19,036	860	175
U.S.	4,064,520	1,245	-

Note: (1) Figures cover the Cincinnati, OH-KY-IN Metropolitan Statistical Area; (2) Rank ranges from 1 to 391 where 1 indicates greatest number of fraud and other consumer reports per 100,000 population
Source: Federal Trade Commission, Consumer Sentinel Network Data Book 2022

POLITICS

2020 Presidential Election Results

Area	Biden	Trump	Jorgensen	Hawkins	Other
Hamilton County	57.1	41.3	1.2	0.3	0.0
U.S.	51.3	46.8	1.2	0.3	0.5

Note: Results are percentages and may not add to 100% due to rounding
Source: Dave Leip's Atlas of U.S. Presidential Elections

SPORTS

Professional Sports Teams

Team Name	League	Year Established
Cincinnati Bengals	National Football League (NFL)	1968
Cincinnati Reds	Major League Baseball (MLB)	1882
FC Cincinnati	Major League Soccer (MLS)	2019

Note: Includes teams located in the Cincinnati, OH-KY-IN Metropolitan Statistical Area.
Source: Wikipedia, Major Professional Sports Teams of the United States and Canada, April 12, 2023

CLIMATE

Average and Extreme Temperatures

Temperature	Jan	Feb	Mar	Apr	May	Jun	Jul	Aug	Sep	Oct	Nov	Dec	Yr.
Extreme High (°F)	74	72	84	89	93	102	103	102	102	89	81	75	103
Average High (°F)	38	42	52	64	74	82	86	85	78	67	53	42	64
Average Temp. (°F)	30	33	43	54	63	72	76	74	68	56	44	34	54
Average Low (°F)	21	24	33	43	52	61	65	63	56	45	35	26	44
Extreme Low (°F)	-25	-15	-11	17	27	39	47	43	33	16	0	-20	-25

Note: Figures cover the years 1948-1990
Source: National Climatic Data Center, International Station Meteorological Climate Summary, 9/96

Cincinnati, Ohio 111

Average Precipitation/Snowfall/Humidity

Precip./Humidity	Jan	Feb	Mar	Apr	May	Jun	Jul	Aug	Sep	Oct	Nov	Dec	Yr.
Avg. Precip. (in.)	3.2	2.9	3.9	3.5	4.0	3.9	4.2	3.1	2.8	2.8	3.4	3.1	40.9
Avg. Snowfall (in.)	7	5	4	1	Tr	0	0	0	0	Tr	2	4	23
Avg. Rel. Hum. 7am (%)	79	78	77	76	79	82	85	87	87	83	79	79	81
Avg. Rel. Hum. 4pm (%)	65	60	55	50	51	53	54	52	52	51	58	65	55

Note: Figures cover the years 1948-1990; Tr = Trace amounts (<0.05 in. of rain; <0.5 in. of snow)
Source: National Climatic Data Center, International Station Meteorological Climate Summary, 9/96

Weather Conditions

Temperature			Daytime Sky			Precipitation		
10°F & below	32°F & below	90°F & above	Clear	Partly cloudy	Cloudy	0.01 inch or more precip.	0.1 inch or more snow/ice	Thunder-storms
14	107	23	80	126	159	127	25	39

Note: Figures are average number of days per year and cover the years 1948-1990
Source: National Climatic Data Center, International Station Meteorological Climate Summary, 9/96

HAZARDOUS WASTE

Superfund Sites

The Cincinnati, OH-KY-IN metro area is home to six sites on the EPA's Superfund National Priorities List: **Armco Incorporation-Hamilton Plant** (proposed); **Chem-Dyne** (final); **Milford Contaminated Aquifer** (final); **Peters Cartridge Factory** (final); **Pristine, Inc.** (final); **Skinner Landfill** (final). There are a total of 1,165 Superfund sites with a status of proposed or final on the list in the U.S. *U.S. Environmental Protection Agency, National Priorities List, April 12, 2023*

AIR QUALITY

Air Quality Trends: Ozone

	1990	1995	2000	2005	2010	2015	2018	2019	2020	2021
MSA[1]	0.083	0.082	0.074	0.075	0.069	0.069	0.073	0.067	0.067	0.065
U.S.	0.087	0.089	0.081	0.080	0.072	0.067	0.069	0.065	0.065	0.067

Note: (1) Data covers the Cincinnati, OH-KY-IN Metropolitan Statistical Area. The values shown are the composite ozone concentration averages among trend sites based on the highest fourth daily maximum 8-hour concentration in parts per million. These trends are based on sites having an adequate record of monitoring data during the trend period. Data from exceptional events are included.
Source: U.S. Environmental Protection Agency, Air Quality Monitoring Information, "Air Quality Trends by City, 1990-2021"

Air Quality Index

Area	Percent of Days when Air Quality was...[2]					AQI Statistics[2]	
	Good	Moderate	Unhealthy for Sensitive Groups	Unhealthy	Very Unhealthy	Maximum	Median
MSA[1]	45.8	52.1	2.2	0.0	0.0	140	52

Note: (1) Data covers the Cincinnati, OH-KY-IN Metropolitan Statistical Area; (2) Based on 365 days with AQI data in 2021. Air Quality Index (AQI) is an index for reporting daily air quality. EPA calculates the AQI for five major air pollutants regulated by the Clean Air Act: ground-level ozone, particle pollution (aka particulate matter), carbon monoxide, sulfur dioxide, and nitrogen dioxide. The AQI runs from 0 to 500. The higher the AQI value, the greater the level of air pollution and the greater the health concern. There are six AQI categories: "Good" AQI is between 0 and 50. Air quality is considered satisfactory; "Moderate" AQI is between 51 and 100. Air quality is acceptable; "Unhealthy for Sensitive Groups" When AQI values are between 101 and 150, members of sensitive groups may experience health effects; "Unhealthy" When AQI values are between 151 and 200 everyone may begin to experience health effects; "Very Unhealthy" AQI values between 201 and 300 trigger a health alert; "Hazardous" AQI values over 300 trigger warnings of emergency conditions (not shown).
Source: U.S. Environmental Protection Agency, Air Quality Index Report, 2021

Air Quality Index Pollutants

Area	Percent of Days when AQI Pollutant was...[2]					
	Carbon Monoxide	Nitrogen Dioxide	Ozone	Sulfur Dioxide	Particulate Matter 2.5	Particulate Matter 10
MSA[1]	0.0	3.0	28.8	(3)	64.1	4.1

Note: (1) Data covers the Cincinnati, OH-KY-IN Metropolitan Statistical Area; (2) Based on 365 days with AQI data in 2021. The Air Quality Index (AQI) is an index for reporting daily air quality. EPA calculates the AQI for five major air pollutants regulated by the Clean Air Act: ground-level ozone, particle pollution (also known as particulate matter), carbon monoxide, sulfur dioxide, and nitrogen dioxide. The AQI runs from 0 to 500. The higher the AQI value, the greater the level of air pollution and the greater the health concern; (3) Sulfur dioxide is no longer included in this table (as of December 8, 2021) because SO_2 concentrations tend to be very localized and not necessarily representative of broad geographical areas like counties and CBSAs.
Source: U.S. Environmental Protection Agency, Air Quality Index Report, 2021

Maximum Air Pollutant Concentrations: Particulate Matter, Ozone, CO and Lead

	Particulate Matter 10 (ug/m^3)	Particulate Matter 2.5 Wtd AM (ug/m^3)	Particulate Matter 2.5 24-Hr (ug/m^3)	Ozone (ppm)	Carbon Monoxide (ppm)	Lead (ug/m^3)
MSA[1] Level	178	12.1	27	0.07	2	n/a
NAAQS[2]	150	15	35	0.075	9	0.15
Met NAAQS[2]	No	Yes	Yes	Yes	Yes	n/a

Note: (1) Data covers the Cincinnati, OH-KY-IN Metropolitan Statistical Area; Data from exceptional events are included; (2) National Ambient Air Quality Standards; ppm = parts per million; ug/m^3 = micrograms per cubic meter; n/a not available.
Concentrations: Particulate Matter 10 (coarse particulate)—highest second maximum 24-hour concentration; Particulate Matter 2.5 Wtd AM (fine particulate)—highest weighted annual mean concentration; Particulate Matter 2.5 24-Hour (fine particulate)—highest 98th percentile 24-hour concentration; Ozone—highest fourth daily maximum 8-hour concentration; Carbon Monoxide—highest second maximum non-overlapping 8-hour concentration; Lead—maximum running 3-month average
Source: U.S. Environmental Protection Agency, Air Quality Monitoring Information, "Air Quality Statistics by City, 2021"

Maximum Air Pollutant Concentrations: Nitrogen Dioxide and Sulfur Dioxide

	Nitrogen Dioxide AM (ppb)	Nitrogen Dioxide 1-Hr (ppb)	Sulfur Dioxide AM (ppb)	Sulfur Dioxide 1-Hr (ppb)	Sulfur Dioxide 24-Hr (ppb)
MSA[1] Level	16	49	n/a	28	n/a
NAAQS[2]	53	100	30	75	140
Met NAAQS[2]	Yes	Yes	n/a	Yes	n/a

Note: (1) Data covers the Cincinnati, OH-KY-IN Metropolitan Statistical Area; Data from exceptional events are included; (2) National Ambient Air Quality Standards; ppm = parts per million; ug/m^3 = micrograms per cubic meter; n/a not available.
Concentrations: Nitrogen Dioxide AM—highest arithmetic mean concentration; Nitrogen Dioxide 1-Hr—highest 98th percentile 1-hour daily maximum concentration; Sulfur Dioxide AM—highest annual mean concentration; Sulfur Dioxide 1-Hr—highest 99th percentile 1-hour daily maximum concentration; Sulfur Dioxide 24-Hr—highest second maximum 24-hour concentration
Source: U.S. Environmental Protection Agency, Air Quality Monitoring Information, "Air Quality Statistics by City, 2021"

Cleveland, Ohio

Background

Cleveland is located on the south shore of Lake Erie in northeastern Ohio and is bisected by the Cuyahoga River. The metro area has a frontage of 31 miles.

The city began with very modest resources. It was founded in 1796 by General Moses Cleveland, on what was known as the Western Reserve of Connecticut. The completion of the Erie and Ohio canals brought people and industry to this area, and by the 1840s, the population had grown by 500 percent from the prior decade. While neighborhoods fell along racial and ethnic lines, the children of these immigrants intermarried and surpassed their parents on socioeconomic levels. Cleveland was a place where the American dream could be realized.

During World War I, a new wave of job seekers flooded Cleveland. These were largely African Americans from Southern rural areas, and poor whites from Kentucky, Tennessee, and West Virginia filling in for a shortage of workers in war goods production. After the war, the next group of job seekers was unskilled and did not have the same opportunities as did their predecessors, thus making job competition difficult. These collapsing economic conditions set the stage for the urban unrest of the 1960s.

In the 1990s, Cleveland enjoyed an economic renaissance with several projects representing more than $9 billion in capital investment. A public-private partnership was responsible for a new downtown Gateway sports complex (1994), the Rock & Roll Hall of Fame (1998) designed by I.M. Pei, and a vibrant new entertainment district.

The biomed/biotechnology industry has been important in recent years, with the Cleveland Clinic recording 8.7 million patient visits in 2021, and employing 68,700, alongside other area universities and foundations. A leading national research center, it receives millions of dollars annually from the National Institutes of Health and was ranked No. 2 in the nation in *U.S. News and World Report* 2021-22 Best Hospitals, and No. 1 for heart care.

The city's Euclid Corridor Transportation Project, designed to improve public transportation between downtown and the University Circle, was completed in 2008 with increased ridership ever since, and Amtrak is on track to expand routes that will connect Cleveland, Cincinnati, Columbus, and Dayton.

The Port of Cleveland is the largest for overseas general cargo on Lake Erie, and the third largest on any of the Great Lakes. It generates roughly a billion dollars annually in trade.

Progressive Field is home to the MLB Cleveland Indians, and the Quicken Loans Arena hosts the Cavaliers basketball team. Both venues were extensively improved in recent years, and both teams have seen recent success, with the Indians advancing to the World Series in 2016 and the Cavaliers playing in the NBA Finals every year from 2015 to 2018, winning a championship in 2016, behind superstar forward LeBron James.

Increasingly, the northeastern Ohio economy is driven by research and specialized service industries, and Cleveland is considered one of the best metro areas in the U.S. for attracting expanded business facilities. Cleveland is especially prominent in the field of health-related technology. Altogether, nearly 200 tech companies operate in the Cleveland area. Other fields in which the city's economy thrives include banking, education, insurance, and healthcare. Cleveland's two largest employers are Cleveland Clinic and University Hospitals.

Few cities of its size offer the array of arts and cultural opportunities afforded by the Greater Cleveland area. The University Circle area is home to more than 70 cultural, educational, science, medical, and religious institutions, including the home of the renowned Cleveland Orchestra. Playhouse Square offers Broadway shows, plays, opera, ballet, and contemporary performing arts. Cleveland also has one of the six Second City comedy theaters in the nation, and is home to the Cleveland Museum of Natural History. The Cleveland Metroparks Zoo houses the biggest collection of primates in North America and has an indoor rainforest. Nearby is the Great Lakes Science center, which features an OMNIMAX(r) theater, and the Museum of Contemporary Art (MoCA).

Cleveland experiences a continental-like climate that brings great extremes in temperature throughout the year. Summers can be very warm with temperatures often exceeding 90 degrees, and winters are frequently below freezing with significant snowfall.

Rankings

Business/Finance Rankings

- Based on metro area social media reviews, the employment opinion group Glassdoor surveyed 50 of the most populous U.S. metro areas and equally weighed cost of living, hiring opportunity, and job satisfaction to compose a list of "25 Best Cities for Jobs." Median pay and home value, and number of active job openings were also factored in. The Cleveland metro area was ranked #5 in overall job satisfaction. *www.glassdoor.com, "Best Cities for Jobs," February 25, 2020*

- The Brookings Institution ranked the nation's largest cities based on income inequality. Cleveland was ranked #23 (#1 = greatest inequality). Criteria: the "95/20 ratio," a figure representing the income at which a household earns more than 95 percent of all other households, divided by the income at which a household earns more than only 20 percent of all other households. *Brookings Institution, "Household Income Inequality, Largest Cities of 97 Large U.S. Metro Areas, 2014-2016," February 5, 2018*

- The Brookings Institution ranked the 100 largest metro areas in the U.S. based on income inequality. Cleveland was ranked #18 (#1 = greatest inequality). Criteria: the "95/20 ratio," a figure representing the income at which a household earns more than 95 percent of all other households, divided by the income at which a household earns more than only 20 percent of all other households. *Brookings Institution, "Household Income Inequality, 100 Largest U.S. Metro Areas, 2014-2016," February 5, 2018*

- Payscale.com ranked the 32 largest metro areas in terms of wage growth. The Cleveland metro area ranked #9. Criteria: quarterly changes in private industry employee and education professional wage growth from the previous year. *PayScale, "Wage Trends by Metro Area-1st Quarter," April 20, 2023*

- Cleveland was identified as one of America's most frugal metro areas by *Coupons.com*. The city ranked #10 out of 25. Criteria: digital coupon usage. *Coupons.com, "America's Most Frugal Cities of 2017," March 22, 2018*

- The Cleveland metro area appeared on the Milken Institute "2022 Best Performing Cities" list. Rank: #162 out of 200 large metro areas (population over 250,000). Criteria: job growth; wage and salary growth; high-tech output growth; housing affordability; household broadband access. *Milken Institute, "Best-Performing Cities 2022," March 28, 2022*

- *Forbes* ranked the 200 most populous metro areas to determine the nation's "Best Places for Business and Careers." The Cleveland metro area was ranked #135. Criteria: costs (business and living); job growth (past and projected); income growth; quality of life; educational attainment (college and high school); projected economic growth; cultural and leisure opportunities; workplace tolerance laws; net migration patterns. *Forbes, "The Best Places for Business and Careers 2019: Seattle Still On Top," October 30, 2019*

- Mercer Human Resources Consulting ranked 227 cities worldwide in terms of cost-of-living. Cleveland ranked #112 (the lower the ranking, the higher the cost-of-living). The survey measured the comparative cost of over 200 items (such as housing, food, clothing, domestic supplies, transportation, and recreation/entertainment) in each location. *Mercer, "2022 Cost of Living City Ranking," June 29, 2022*

Culture/Performing Arts Rankings

- Cleveland was selected as one of the 25 best cities for moviemakers in North America. Great film cities are places where filmmaking dreams can come true, that offer more creative space, lower costs, and great outdoor locations. NYC & LA were intentionally excluded. Criteria: longstanding reputations as film-friendly communities; film community and culture; affordability; and quality of life. The city was ranked #18. *MovieMaker Magazine, "Best Places to Live and Work as a Moviemaker, 2023," January 18, 2023*

Education Rankings

- Personal finance website *WalletHub* analyzed the 150 largest U.S. metropolitan statistical areas to determine where the most educated Americans are putting their degrees to work. Criteria: education levels; percentage of workers with degrees; education quality and attainment gap; public school quality rankings; quality and enrollment of each metro area's universities. Cleveland was ranked #86 (#1 = most educated city). *www.WalletHub.com, "Most & Least Educated Cities in America," July 18, 2022*

- Cleveland was selected as one of America's most literate cities. The city ranked #17 out of the 84 largest U.S. cities. Criteria: number of booksellers; library resources; Internet resources; educational attainment; periodical publishing resources; newspaper circulation. *Central Connecticut State University, "America's Most Literate Cities, 2018," February 2019*

Environmental Rankings

- Niche compiled a list of the nation's snowiest cities, based on the National Oceanic and Atmospheric Administration's 30-year average snowfall data. Among cities with a population of at least 50,000, Cleveland ranked #9. *Niche.com, Top 25 Snowiest Cities in America, December 10, 2018*

Food/Drink Rankings

- Progressive Field was selected as one of PETA's "Top 10 Vegan-Friendly Ballparks" for 2019. The park ranked #5. *People for the Ethical Treatment of Animals, "Top 10 Vegan-Friendly Ballparks," May 23, 2019*

Health/Fitness Rankings

- For each of the 100 largest cities in the United States, the American Fitness Index®, compiled in partnership between the American College of Sports Medicine and the Elevance Health Foundation, evaluated community infrastructure and 34 health behaviors including preventive health, levels of chronic disease conditions, food insecurity, sleep quality, pedestrian safety, air quality, and community/environment resources that support physical activity. Cleveland ranked #55 for "community fitness." *americanfitnessindex.org, "2022 ACSM American Fitness Index Summary Report," July 12, 2022*

- The Cleveland metro area was identified as one of the worst cities for bed bugs in America by pest control company Orkin. The area ranked #4 out of 50 based on the number of bed bug treatments Orkin performed from December 2021 to November 2022. *Orkin, "The Windy City Can't Blow Bed Bugs Away: Chicago Ranks #1 For Third Consecutive Year On Orkin's Bed Bug Cities List," January 9, 2023*

- Cleveland was identified as a "2022 Spring Allergy Capital." The area ranked #43 out of 100. Three groups of factors were used to identify the most challenging cities for people with allergies during the spring season: annual spring pollen scores; over the counter allergy medicine use; number of board-certified allergy specialists. *Asthma and Allergy Foundation of America, "Spring Allergy Capitals 2022," March 2, 2022*

- Cleveland was identified as a "2022 Fall Allergy Capital." The area ranked #54 out of 100. Three groups of factors were used to identify the most challenging cities for people with allergies during the fall season: annual fall pollen scores; over the counter allergy medicine use; number of board-certified allergy specialists. *Asthma and Allergy Foundation of America, "Fall Allergy Capitals 2022," March 2, 2022*

- Cleveland was identified as a "2022 Asthma Capital." The area ranked #2 out of the nation's 100 largest metropolitan areas. Criteria: estimated asthma prevalence; asthma-related mortality; and ER visits due to asthma. Risk factors analyzed but not factored in the rankings: annual pollen score; annual air quality; public smoking laws; access to board-certified asthma specialists; rescue and controller medication use; uninsured rate; poverty rate. *Asthma and Allergy Foundation of America, "Asthma Capitals 2022: The Most Challenging Places to Live With Asthma," September 14, 2022*

Real Estate Rankings

- *WalletHub* compared the most populated U.S. cities to determine which had the best markets for real estate agents. Cleveland ranked #141 where demand was high and pay was the best. Criteria: sales per agent; annual median wage for real-estate agents; monthly average starting salary for real estate agents; real estate job density and competition; unemployment rate; home turnover rate; housing-market health index; and other relevant metrics. *www.WalletHub.com, "2021 Best Places to Be a Real Estate Agent," May 12, 2021*

- Cleveland was ranked #29 out of 235 metro areas in terms of housing affordability in 2022 by the National Association of Home Builders (#1 = most affordable). Criteria: the share of homes sold in that area affordable to a family earning the local median income, based on standard mortgage underwriting criteria. *National Association of Home Builders®, NAHB-Wells Fargo Housing Opportunity Index, 4th Quarter 2022*

- The nation's largest metro areas were analyzed in terms of the percentage of households entering some stage of foreclosure in 2022. The Cleveland metro area ranked #1 out of 8 (#1 = highest foreclosure rate). *ATTOM Data Solutions, "2022 Year-End U.S. Foreclosure Market Report™," January 12, 2023*

Safety Rankings

- To identify the most dangerous cities in America, *24/7 Wall St.* focused on violent crime categories—murder, non-negligent manslaughter, rape, robbery, and aggravated assault—as reported for every 100,000 residents using data from the FBI's 2020 annual Uniform Crime Report. For cities with populations over 25,000, Cleveland was ranked #12. *247wallst.com, "America's Most Dangerous Cities" November 12, 2021*

- Allstate ranked the 200 largest cities in America in terms of driver safety. Cleveland ranked #107. Criteria: internal property damage claims over a two-year period from January 2016 to December 2017. The report helps increase the importance of safety and awareness behind the wheel. *Allstate, "Allstate America's Best Drivers Report, 2019" June 24, 2019*

- Cleveland was identified as one of the most dangerous cities in America by NeighborhoodScout. The city ranked #11 out of 100 (#1 = most dangerous). Criteria: number of violent crimes per 1,000 residents. The editors evaluated cities with 25,000 or more residents. *NeighborhoodScout.com, "2023 Top 100 Most Dangerous Cities in the U.S.," January 12, 2023*

- The National Insurance Crime Bureau ranked 390 metro areas in the U.S. in terms of per capita rates of vehicle theft. The Cleveland metro area ranked #96 (#1 = highest rate). Criteria: number of vehicle theft offenses per 100,000 inhabitants in 2021. *National Insurance Crime Bureau, "Hot Spots 2021," September 1, 2022*

Seniors/Retirement Rankings

- From its Best Cities for Successful Aging indexes, the Milken Institute generated rankings for metropolitan areas, weighing data in nine categories—health care, wellness, living arrangements, transportation and convenience, financial characteristics, education, employment, community engagement, and overall livability. The Cleveland metro area was ranked #36 overall in the large metro area category. *Milken Institute, "Best Cities for Successful Aging, 2017" March 14, 2017*

Sports/Recreation Rankings

- Cleveland was chosen as one of America's best cities for bicycling. The city ranked #29 out of 50. Criteria: cycling infrastructure that is safe and friendly for all ages; energy and bike culture. The editors evaluated cities with populations of 100,000 or more. *Bicycling, "The 50 Best Bike Cities in America," October 10, 2018*

Women/Minorities Rankings

- Personal finance website *WalletHub* compared more than 180 U.S. cities across two key dimensions, "Hispanic Business-Friendliness" and "Hispanic Purchasing Power," to arrive at the most favorable conditions for Hispanic entrepreneurs. Cleveland was ranked #178 out of 182. Criteria includes: share of Hispanic-Owned Businesses; Hispanic entrepreneurship rate to median annual income of Hispanics; Small Business-Friendliness score; cost of living; and number of Hispanics with at least a bachelor's degree. *WalletHub.com, "2019's Best Cities for Hispanic Entrepreneurs," May 1, 2019*

Miscellaneous Rankings

- *MoveHub* ranked 446 hipster cities across 20 countries, using its new and improved *alternative* Hipster Index and Cleveland came out as #36 among the top 50. Criteria: population over 150,000; number of vintage boutiques; density of tattoo parlors; vegan places to eat; coffee shops; and density of vinyl record stores. *www.movehub.com, "The Hipster Index: Brighton Pips Portland to Global Top Spot," July 28, 2021*

- In its roundup of St. Patrick's Day parades "Gayot" listed the best festivals and parades of all things Irish. The festivities in Cleveland as among the best in North America. *www.gayot.com, "Best St. Patrick's Day Parades," March 2023*

- The watchdog site, Charity Navigator, conducted a study of charities in major markets both to analyze statistical differences in their financial, accountability, and transparency practices and to track year-to-year variations in individual philanthropic communities. The Cleveland metro area was ranked #6 among the 30 metro markets in the rating category of Overall Score. *www.charitynavigator.org, "2017 Metro Market Study," May 1, 2017*

- *WalletHub* compared the 150 most populated U.S. cities to determine their operating efficiency. A "Quality of Services" score was constructed for each city and then divided by the total budget per capita to reveal which were managed the best. Cleveland ranked #146. Criteria: financial stability; economy; education; safety; health; infrastructure and pollution. *www.WalletHub.com, "2022's Best- & Worst-Run Cities in America," June 21, 2022*

- Cleveland was selected as one of "America's Friendliest Cities." The city ranked #14 in the "Friendliest" category. Respondents to an online survey were asked to rate 38 top urban destinations in the United States as to general friendliness, as well as manners, politeness and warm disposition. *Travel + Leisure, "America's Friendliest Cities," October 20, 2017*

Business Environment

DEMOGRAPHICS

Population Growth

Area	1990 Census	2000 Census	2010 Census	2020 Census	Population Growth (%) 1990-2020	Population Growth (%) 2010-2020
City	505,333	478,403	396,815	372,624	-26.3	-6.1
MSA[1]	2,102,219	2,148,143	2,077,240	2,088,251	-0.7	0.5
U.S.	248,709,873	281,421,906	308,745,538	331,449,281	33.3	7.4

Note: (1) Figures cover the Cleveland-Elyria, OH Metropolitan Statistical Area
Source: U.S. Census Bureau, 1990 Census, 2000 Census, 2010 Census, 2020 Census

Race

Area	White Alone[2] (%)	Black Alone[2] (%)	Asian Alone[2] (%)	AIAN[3] Alone[2] (%)	NHOPI[4] Alone[2] (%)	Other Race Alone[2] (%)	Two or More Races (%)
City	34.5	48.4	2.8	0.4	0.0	6.3	7.6
MSA[1]	68.9	19.6	2.6	0.2	0.0	2.6	6.0
U.S.	61.6	12.4	6.0	1.1	0.2	8.4	10.2

Note: (1) Figures cover the Cleveland-Elyria, OH Metropolitan Statistical Area; (2) Alone is defined as not being in combination with one or more other races; (3) American Indian and Alaska Native; (4) Native Hawaiian and Other Pacific Islander
Source: U.S. Census Bureau, 2020 Census

Hispanic or Latino Origin

Area	Total (%)	Mexican (%)	Puerto Rican (%)	Cuban (%)	Other (%)
City	12.2	1.6	8.6	0.2	1.8
MSA[1]	6.2	1.4	3.5	0.1	1.1
U.S.	18.4	11.2	1.8	0.7	4.7

Note: Persons of Hispanic or Latino origin can be of any race; (1) Figures cover the Cleveland-Elyria, OH Metropolitan Statistical Area
Source: U.S. Census Bureau, 2017-2021 American Community Survey 5-Year Estimates

Age

Area	Percent of Population Under Age 5	Age 5–19	Age 20–34	Age 35–44	Age 45–54	Age 55–64	Age 65–74	Age 75–84	Age 85+	Median Age
City	6.0	18.2	24.2	11.8	11.5	13.9	9.0	3.9	1.7	36.1
MSA[1]	5.2	17.7	18.8	11.7	12.4	14.6	11.3	5.6	2.5	41.7
U.S.	5.6	19.2	20.2	12.7	12.4	13.1	10.0	4.9	1.9	38.8

Note: (1) Figures cover the Cleveland-Elyria, OH Metropolitan Statistical Area
Source: U.S. Census Bureau, 2020 Census

Disability by Age

Area	All Ages	Under 18 Years Old	18 to 64 Years Old	65 Years and Over
City	19.5	8.4	18.5	41.9
MSA[1]	14.0	5.0	11.6	32.6
U.S.	12.6	4.4	10.3	33.4

Note: Figures show percent of the civilian noninstitutionalized population that reported having a disability. Disability status is determined from six types of difficulty: vision, hearing, cognitive, ambulatory, self-care, and independent living. For children under 5 years old, hearing and vision difficulty are used to determine disability status. For children between the ages of 5 and 14, disability status is determined from hearing, vision, cognitive, ambulatory, and self-care difficulties. For people aged 15 years and older, they are considered to have a disability if they have difficulty with any one of the six difficulty types; Note: (1) Figures cover the Cleveland-Elyria, OH Metropolitan Statistical Area
Source: U.S. Census Bureau, 2017-2021 American Community Survey 5-Year Estimates

Ancestry

Area	German	Irish	English	American	Italian	Polish	French[2]	Scottish	Dutch
City	9.5	8.5	3.2	2.2	4.6	3.9	0.9	0.6	0.5
MSA[1]	18.7	13.4	7.7	4.2	9.4	7.4	1.5	1.4	0.8
U.S.	12.8	9.6	8.1	5.7	5.0	2.7	2.2	1.6	1.1

Note: Figures are the percentage of the total population reporting a particular ancestry. The nine most commonly reported ancestries in the U.S. are shown. Figures include multiple ancestries (e.g. if a person reported being Irish and Italian, they were included in both columns); (1) Figures cover the Cleveland-Elyria, OH Metropolitan Statistical Area; (2) Excludes Basque
Source: U.S. Census Bureau, 2017-2021 American Community Survey 5-Year Estimates

Foreign-born Population

Area	Percent of Population Born in								
	Any Foreign Country	Asia	Mexico	Europe	Caribbean	Central America[2]	South America	Africa	Canada
City	6.0	2.4	0.4	1.1	0.6	0.4	0.3	0.7	0.1
MSA[1]	6.0	2.2	0.4	2.2	0.2	0.2	0.2	0.4	0.2
U.S.	13.6	4.2	3.3	1.5	1.4	1.1	0.9	0.8	0.2

Note: (1) Figures cover the Cleveland-Elyria, OH Metropolitan Statistical Area; (2) Excludes Mexico.
Source: U.S. Census Bureau, 2017-2021 American Community Survey 5-Year Estimates

Household Size

Area	Persons in Household (%)							Average Household Size
	One	Two	Three	Four	Five	Six	Seven or More	
City	46.1	27.9	12.1	7.4	3.8	1.7	1.0	2.20
MSA[1]	34.9	33.6	13.9	10.6	4.6	1.6	0.9	2.30
U.S.	28.1	33.8	15.5	12.9	6.0	2.3	1.4	2.60

Note: (1) Figures cover the Cleveland-Elyria, OH Metropolitan Statistical Area
Source: U.S. Census Bureau, 2017-2021 American Community Survey 5-Year Estimates

Household Relationships

Area	House-holder	Opposite-sex Spouse	Same-sex Spouse	Opposite-sex Unmarried Partner	Same-sex Unmarried Partner	Child[2]	Grand-child	Other Relatives	Non-relatives
City	45.0	8.5	0.2	3.5	0.3	27.0	3.3	5.0	3.8
MSA[1]	42.5	17.1	0.1	2.7	0.1	27.7	2.1	3.3	2.3
U.S.	38.3	17.5	0.2	2.5	0.2	28.3	2.4	4.8	3.4

Note: Figures are percent of the total population; (1) Figures cover the Cleveland-Elyria, OH Metropolitan Statistical Area; (2) Includes biological, adopted, and stepchildren of the householder
Source: U.S. Census Bureau, 2020 Census

Gender

Area	Males	Females	Males per 100 Females
City	180,991	191,633	94.4
MSA[1]	1,008,568	1,079,683	93.4
U.S.	162,685,811	168,763,470	96.4

Note: (1) Figures cover the Cleveland-Elyria, OH Metropolitan Statistical Area
Source: U.S. Census Bureau, 2020 Census

Marital Status

Area	Never Married	Now Married[2]	Separated	Widowed	Divorced
City	53.1	24.0	2.9	5.9	14.1
MSA[1]	35.8	44.4	1.5	6.3	11.9
U.S.	33.8	48.0	1.8	5.6	10.8

Note: Figures are percentages and cover the population 15 years of age and older; (1) Figures cover the Cleveland-Elyria, OH Metropolitan Statistical Area; (2) Excludes separated
Source: U.S. Census Bureau, 2017-2021 American Community Survey 5-Year Estimates

Religious Groups by Family

Area	Catholic	Baptist	Methodist	LDS[2]	Pentecostal	Lutheran	Islam	Adventist	Other
MSA[1]	26.1	4.3	2.3	0.4	1.5	1.8	1.1	1.3	16.8
U.S.	18.7	7.3	3.0	2.0	1.8	1.7	1.3	1.3	11.6

Note: Figures are the number of adherents as a percentage of the total population and cover the eight largest religious groups in the U.S; (1) Figures cover the Cleveland-Elyria, OH Metropolitan Statistical Area; (2) Church of Jesus Christ of Latter-day Saints
Sources: 2020 U.S. Religion Census, Association of Statisticians of American Religious Bodies; The Association of Religion Data Archives (ARDA)

Religious Groups by Tradition

Area	Catholic	Evangelical Protestant	Mainline Protestant	Black Protestant	Islam	Judaism	Hinduism	Orthodox	Buddhism
MSA[1]	26.1	15.1	5.6	3.5	1.1	1.3	0.3	0.8	0.2
U.S.	18.7	16.5	5.2	2.3	1.3	0.6	0.4	0.4	0.3

Note: Figures are the number of adherents as a percentage of the total population; (1) Figures cover the Cleveland-Elyria, OH Metropolitan Statistical Area
Sources: 2020 U.S. Religion Census, Association of Statisticians of American Religious Bodies; The Association of Religion Data Archives (ARDA)

120   Cleveland, Ohio

ECONOMY

Gross Metropolitan Product

Area	2020	2021	2022	2023	Rank[2]
MSA[1]	133.6	144.9	157.7	167.2	35

Note: Figures are in billions of dollars; (1) Figures cover the Cleveland-Elyria, OH Metropolitan Statistical Area; (2) Rank is based on 2021 data and ranges from 1 to 381
Source: U.S. Conference of Mayors, U.S. Metro Economies: U.S. Metros Compared to Global and State Economies, June 2022

Economic Growth

Area	2018-20 (%)	2021 (%)	2022 (%)	2023 (%)	Rank[2]
MSA[1]	-1.3	4.3	3.1	2.7	238
U.S.	-0.6	5.7	3.1	2.9	—

Note: Figures are real gross metropolitan product (GMP) growth rates and represent average annual percent change; (1) Figures cover the Cleveland-Elyria, OH Metropolitan Statistical Area; (2) Rank is based on 2020 2-year average annual percent change and ranges from 1 to 381
Source: U.S. Conference of Mayors, U.S. Metro Economies: U.S. Metros Compared to Global and State Economies, June 2022

Metropolitan Area Exports

Area	2016	2017	2018	2019	2020	2021	Rank[2]
MSA[1]	8,752.9	8,944.9	9,382.9	8,829.9	7,415.8	8,560.4	41

Note: Figures are in millions of dollars; (1) Figures cover the Cleveland-Elyria, OH Metropolitan Statistical Area; (2) Rank is based on 2021 data and ranges from 1 to 388
Source: U.S. Department of Commerce, International Trade Administration, Office of Trade and Economic Analysis, Industry and Analysis, Exports by Metropolitan Area, data extracted March 16, 2023

Building Permits

Area	Single-Family			Multi-Family			Total		
	2021	2022	Pct. Chg.	2021	2022	Pct. Chg.	2021	2022	Pct. Chg.
City	104	158	51.9	27	363	1,244.4	131	521	297.7
MSA[1]	2,949	2,915	-1.2	391	820	109.7	3,340	3,735	11.8
U.S.	1,115,400	975,600	-12.5	621,600	689,500	10.9	1,737,000	1,665,100	-4.1

Note: (1) Figures cover the Cleveland-Elyria, OH Metropolitan Statistical Area; Figures represent new, privately-owned housing units authorized (unadjusted data); All permit data are based on estimates with imputation
Source: U.S. Census Bureau, Manufacturing, Mining, and Construction Statistics, Building Permits, 2021, 2022

Bankruptcy Filings

Area	Business Filings			Nonbusiness Filings		
	2021	2022	% Chg.	2021	2022	% Chg.
Cuyahoga County	48	53	10.4	3,240	2,994	-7.6
U.S.	14,347	13,481	-6.0	399,269	374,240	-6.3

Note: Business filings include Chapter 7, Chapter 9, Chapter 11, Chapter 12, Chapter 13, Chapter 15, and Section 304; Nonbusiness filings include Chapter 7, Chapter 11, and Chapter 13
Source: Administrative Office of the U.S. Courts, Business and Nonbusiness Bankruptcy, County Cases Commenced by Chapter of the Bankruptcy Code, During the 12-Month Period Ending December 31, 2021 and Business and Nonbusiness Bankruptcy, County Cases Commenced by Chapter of the Bankruptcy Code, During the 12-Month Period Ending December 31, 2022

Housing Vacancy Rates

Area	Gross Vacancy Rate[2] (%)			Year-Round Vacancy Rate[3] (%)			Rental Vacancy Rate[4] (%)			Homeowner Vacancy Rate[5] (%)		
	2020	2021	2022	2020	2021	2022	2020	2021	2022	2020	2021	2022
MSA[1]	9.3	7.7	7.0	8.8	7.5	6.8	5.5	3.6	3.2	0.7	0.4	1.0
U.S.	10.6	10.8	10.5	8.2	8.4	8.2	6.3	6.1	5.8	1.0	0.9	0.8

Note: (1) Figures cover the Cleveland-Elyria, OH Metropolitan Statistical Area; (2) The percentage of the total housing inventory that is vacant; (3) The percentage of the housing inventory (excluding seasonal units) that is year-round vacant; (4) The percentage of rental inventory that is vacant for rent; (5) The percentage of homeowner inventory that is vacant for sale
Source: U.S. Census Bureau, Housing Vacancies and Homeownership Annual Statistics: 2020, 2021, 2022

INCOME

Income

Area	Per Capita ($)	Median Household ($)	Average Household ($)
City	23,415	33,678	49,942
MSA[1]	36,907	61,320	85,864
U.S.	37,638	69,021	97,196

Note: (1) Figures cover the Cleveland-Elyria, OH Metropolitan Statistical Area
Source: U.S. Census Bureau, 2017-2021 American Community Survey 5-Year Estimates

Cleveland, Ohio 121

Household Income Distribution

Area	Percent of Households Earning							
	Under $15,000	$15,000 -$24,999	$25,000 -$34,999	$35,000 -$49,999	$50,000 -$74,999	$75,000 -$99,999	$100,000 -$149,999	$150,000 and up
City	25.4	13.8	12.4	13.8	14.7	8.7	7.0	4.4
MSA[1]	11.6	8.6	9.0	12.5	17.2	12.7	15.0	13.5
U.S.	9.4	7.8	8.2	11.4	16.8	12.8	16.3	17.3

Note: (1) Figures cover the Cleveland-Elyria, OH Metropolitan Statistical Area
Source: U.S. Census Bureau, 2017-2021 American Community Survey 5-Year Estimates

Poverty Rate

Area	All Ages	Under 18 Years Old	18 to 64 Years Old	65 Years and Over
City	31.4	45.7	28.3	22.8
MSA[1]	13.7	19.6	12.8	9.7
U.S.	12.6	17.0	11.8	9.6

Note: Figures are percentage of people whose income during the past 12 months was below the poverty level;
(1) Figures cover the Cleveland-Elyria, OH Metropolitan Statistical Area
Source: U.S. Census Bureau, 2017-2021 American Community Survey 5-Year Estimates

EMPLOYMENT

Labor Force and Employment

Area	Civilian Labor Force			Workers Employed		
	Dec. 2021	Dec. 2022	% Chg.	Dec. 2021	Dec. 2022	% Chg.
City	154,230	153,656	-0.4	144,455	146,635	1.5
MSA[1]	1,006,515	1,010,141	0.4	963,990	975,650	1.2
U.S.	161,696,000	164,224,000	1.6	155,732,000	158,872,000	2.0

Note: Data is not seasonally adjusted and covers workers 16 years of age and older; (1) Figures cover the
Cleveland-Elyria, OH Metropolitan Statistical Area
Source: Bureau of Labor Statistics, Local Area Unemployment Statistics

Unemployment Rate

Area	2022											
	Jan.	Feb.	Mar.	Apr.	May	Jun.	Jul.	Aug.	Sep.	Oct.	Nov.	Dec.
City	7.7	8.0	8.2	7.5	7.2	7.7	6.5	6.0	5.9	6.4	5.8	4.6
MSA[1]	5.6	6.0	5.6	4.8	4.9	5.3	4.9	4.5	4.1	3.9	3.6	3.4
U.S.	4.4	4.1	3.8	3.3	3.4	3.8	3.8	3.8	3.3	3.4	3.4	3.3

Note: Data is not seasonally adjusted and covers workers 16 years of age and older; (1) Figures cover the
Cleveland-Elyria, OH Metropolitan Statistical Area
Source: Bureau of Labor Statistics, Local Area Unemployment Statistics

Average Wages

Occupation	$/Hr.	Occupation	$/Hr.
Accountants and Auditors	39.26	Maintenance and Repair Workers	23.06
Automotive Mechanics	22.70	Marketing Managers	69.27
Bookkeepers	22.17	Network and Computer Systems Admin.	45.69
Carpenters	27.47	Nurses, Licensed Practical	26.09
Cashiers	12.94	Nurses, Registered	38.95
Computer Programmers	40.92	Nursing Assistants	17.21
Computer Systems Analysts	48.16	Office Clerks, General	20.05
Computer User Support Specialists	26.60	Physical Therapists	47.43
Construction Laborers	26.17	Physicians	79.22
Cooks, Restaurant	15.16	Plumbers, Pipefitters and Steamfitters	31.97
Customer Service Representatives	20.42	Police and Sheriff's Patrol Officers	34.02
Dentists	78.04	Postal Service Mail Carriers	27.79
Electricians	29.88	Real Estate Sales Agents	20.71
Engineers, Electrical	46.94	Retail Salespersons	16.56
Fast Food and Counter Workers	12.12	Sales Representatives, Technical/Scientific	52.20
Financial Managers	74.24	Secretaries, Exc. Legal/Medical/Executive	20.38
First-Line Supervisors of Office Workers	31.50	Security Guards	17.47
General and Operations Managers	57.05	Surgeons	n/a
Hairdressers/Cosmetologists	17.94	Teacher Assistants, Exc. Postsecondary*	16.13
Home Health and Personal Care Aides	13.45	Teachers, Secondary School, Exc. Sp. Ed.*	35.16
Janitors and Cleaners	16.17	Telemarketers	14.85
Landscaping/Groundskeeping Workers	17.23	Truck Drivers, Heavy/Tractor-Trailer	25.57
Lawyers	64.28	Truck Drivers, Light/Delivery Services	20.45
Maids and Housekeeping Cleaners	14.02	Waiters and Waitresses	14.38

Note: Wage data covers the Cleveland-Elyria, OH Metropolitan Statistical Area; (*) Hourly wages were
calculated from annual wage data based on a 40 hour work week; n/a not available.
Source: Bureau of Labor Statistics, Metro Area Occupational Employment & Wage Estimates, May 2022

Employment by Industry

Sector	MSA[1]		U.S.
	Number of Employees	Percent of Total	Percent of Total
Construction, Mining, and Logging	39,300	3.7	5.4
Private Education and Health Services	204,500	19.4	16.1
Financial Activities	73,600	7.0	5.9
Government	129,600	12.3	14.5
Information	16,000	1.5	2.0
Leisure and Hospitality	94,600	9.0	10.3
Manufacturing	120,200	11.4	8.4
Other Services	38,000	3.6	3.7
Professional and Business Services	151,600	14.4	14.7
Retail Trade	96,200	9.1	10.2
Transportation, Warehousing, and Utilities	37,800	3.6	4.9
Wholesale Trade	53,200	5.0	3.9

Note: Figures are non-farm employment as of December 2022. Figures are not seasonally adjusted and include workers 16 years of age and older; (1) Figures cover the Cleveland-Elyria, OH Metropolitan Statistical Area
Source: Bureau of Labor Statistics, Current Employment Statistics, Employment, Hours, and Earnings

Employment by Occupation

Occupation Classification	City (%)	MSA[1] (%)	U.S. (%)
Management, Business, Science, and Arts	31.4	41.0	40.3
Natural Resources, Construction, and Maintenance	5.8	6.5	8.7
Production, Transportation, and Material Moving	18.0	14.1	13.1
Sales and Office	21.1	21.8	20.9
Service	23.7	16.6	17.0

Note: Figures cover employed civilians 16 years of age and older; (1) Figures cover the Cleveland-Elyria, OH Metropolitan Statistical Area
Source: U.S. Census Bureau, 2017-2021 American Community Survey 5-Year Estimates

Occupations with Greatest Projected Employment Growth: 2022 – 2024

Occupation[1]	2022 Employment	2024 Projected Employment	Numeric Employment Change	Percent Employment Change
Stockers and Order Fillers	110,530	116,860	6,330	5.7
Laborers and Freight, Stock, and Material Movers, Hand	111,490	117,260	5,770	5.2
Industrial Truck and Tractor Operators	37,740	41,280	3,540	9.4
Heavy and Tractor-Trailer Truck Drivers	93,730	97,190	3,460	3.7
Cooks, Restaurant	49,740	52,350	2,610	5.2
Light Truck or Delivery Services Drivers	34,850	37,020	2,170	6.2
Construction Laborers	40,690	42,580	1,890	4.6
Landscaping and Groundskeeping Workers	42,810	44,630	1,820	4.3
Retail Salespersons	126,620	128,200	1,580	1.2
Janitors and Cleaners, Except Maids and Housekeeping Cleaners	75,960	77,460	1,500	2.0

Note: Projections cover Ohio; (1) Sorted by numeric employment change
Source: www.projectionscentral.com, State Occupational Projections, 2022–2024 Short-Term Projections

Fastest-Growing Occupations: 2022 – 2024

Occupation[1]	2022 Employment	2024 Projected Employment	Numeric Employment Change	Percent Employment Change
Statisticians	630	690	60	9.5
Industrial Truck and Tractor Operators	37,740	41,280	3,540	9.4
Machine Feeders and Offbearers	2,290	2,480	190	8.3
Nurse Practitioners	10,530	11,380	850	8.1
Information Security Analysts (SOC 2018)	4,290	4,610	320	7.5
Aerospace Engineering and Operations Technicians	980	1,050	70	7.1
Taxi Drivers	3,820	4,090	270	7.1
Logisticians	7,900	8,420	520	6.6
Amusement and Recreation Attendants	9,160	9,740	580	6.3
Light Truck or Delivery Services Drivers	34,850	37,020	2,170	6.2

Note: Projections cover Ohio; (1) Sorted by percent employment change and excludes occupations with numeric employment change less than 50
Source: www.projectionscentral.com, State Occupational Projections, 2022–2024 Short-Term Projections

CITY FINANCES

City Government Finances

Component	2020 ($000)	2020 ($ per capita)
Total Revenues	1,589,570	4,172
Total Expenditures	1,615,125	4,239
Debt Outstanding	2,157,233	5,662
Cash and Securities[1]	1,801,038	4,727

Note: (1) Cash and security holdings of a government at the close of its fiscal year, including those of its dependent agencies, utilities, and liquor stores.
Source: U.S. Census Bureau, State & Local Government Finances 2020

City Government Revenue by Source

Source	2020 ($000)	2020 ($ per capita)	2020 (%)
General Revenue			
From Federal Government	45,120	118	2.8
From State Government	108,466	285	6.8
From Local Governments	2,286	6	0.1
Taxes			
Property	57,580	151	3.6
Sales and Gross Receipts	47,304	124	3.0
Personal Income	486,792	1,278	30.6
Corporate Income	0	0	0.0
Motor Vehicle License	3,504	9	0.2
Other Taxes	21,893	57	1.4
Current Charges	234,168	615	14.7
Liquor Store	0	0	0.0
Utility	528,080	1,386	33.2

Source: U.S. Census Bureau, State & Local Government Finances 2020

City Government Expenditures by Function

Function	2020 ($000)	2020 ($ per capita)	2020 (%)
General Direct Expenditures			
Air Transportation	120,822	317	7.5
Corrections	5,200	13	0.3
Education	0	0	0.0
Employment Security Administration	0	0	0.0
Financial Administration	27,982	73	1.7
Fire Protection	99,613	261	6.2
General Public Buildings	8,265	21	0.5
Governmental Administration, Other	16,370	43	1.0
Health	58,612	153	3.6
Highways	102,315	268	6.3
Hospitals	0	0	0.0
Housing and Community Development	55,575	145	3.4
Interest on General Debt	62,190	163	3.9
Judicial and Legal	56,788	149	3.5
Libraries	0	0	0.0
Parking	5,079	13	0.3
Parks and Recreation	40,907	107	2.5
Police Protection	216,180	567	13.4
Public Welfare	0	0	0.0
Sewerage	43,140	113	2.7
Solid Waste Management	30,442	79	1.9
Veterans' Services	0	0	0.0
Liquor Store	0	0	0.0
Utility	520,359	1,365	32.2

Source: U.S. Census Bureau, State & Local Government Finances 2020

TAXES

State Corporate Income Tax Rates

State	Tax Rate (%)	Income Brackets ($)	Num. of Brackets	Financial Institution Tax Rate (%)[a]	Federal Income Tax Ded.
Ohio	(r)	–	–	(r)	No

Note: Tax rates as of January 1, 2023; (a) Rates listed are the corporate income tax rate applied to financial institutions or excise taxes based on income. Some states have other taxes based upon the value of deposits or shares; (r) Ohio no longer levies a tax based on income (except for a particular subset of corporations), but instead imposes a Commercial Activity Tax (CAT) equal to $150 for gross receipts sitused to Ohio of between $150,000 and $1 million, plus 0.26% of gross receipts over $1 million. Banks continue to pay a franchise tax of 1.3% of net worth. For those few corporations for whom the franchise tax on net worth or net income still applies, a litter tax also applies.
Source: Federation of Tax Administrators, State Corporate Income Tax Rates, January 1, 2023

State Individual Income Tax Rates

State	Tax Rate (%)	Income Brackets ($)	Personal Exemptions ($)			Standard Ded. ($)	
			Single	Married	Depend.	Single	Married
Ohio (a)	0.0 - 3.99	26,050 - 115,300	1,900		3,800	1,900 (u)	–	–

Note: Tax rates as of January 1, 2023; Local- and county-level taxes are not included; Federal income tax is not deductible on state income tax returns; (a) 16 states have statutory provision for automatically adjusting to the rate of inflation the dollar values of the income tax brackets, standard deductions, and/or personal exemptions. Oregon does not index the income brackets for $125,000 and over; (u) Ohio provides an additional tax credit of $20 per exemption. Exemption amounts reduced for higher income taxpayers. Business income taxes at a flat 3% rate.
Source: Federation of Tax Administrators, State Individual Income Tax Rates, January 1, 2023

Various State Sales and Excise Tax Rates

State	State Sales Tax (%)	Gasoline[1] ($/gal.)	Cigarette[2] ($/pack)	Spirits[3] ($/gal.)	Wine[4] ($/gal.)	Beer[5] ($/gal.)	Recreational Marijuana (%)
Ohio	5.75	0.3851	1.60	11.38	0.32	0.18	Not legal

Note: All tax rates as of January 1, 2023; (1) The American Petroleum Institute has developed a methodology for determining the average tax rate on a gallon of fuel. Rates may include any of the following: excise taxes, environmental fees, storage tank fees, other fees or taxes, general sales tax, and local taxes; (2) The federal excise tax of $1.0066 per pack and local taxes are not included; (3) Rates are those applicable to off-premise sales of 40% alcohol by volume (a.b.v.) distilled spirits in 750ml containers. Local excise taxes are excluded; (4) Rates are those applicable to off-premise sales of 11% a.b.v. non-carbonated wine in 750ml containers; (5) Rates are those applicable to off-premise sales of 4.7% a.b.v. beer in 12 ounce containers.
Source: Tax Foundation, 2023 Facts & Figures: How Does Your State Compare?

State Business Tax Climate Index Rankings

State	Overall Rank	Corporate Tax Rank	Individual Income Tax Rank	Sales Tax Rank	Property Tax Rank	Unemployment Insurance Tax Rank
Ohio	37	39	41	36	6	13

Note: The index is a measure of how each state's tax laws affect economic performance. The lower the rank, the more favorable a state's tax system is for business. States without a given tax are given a ranking of 1. The scores/rankings for the District of Columbia do not affect other states. The 2023 index represents the tax climate as of July 1, 2022.
Source: Tax Foundation, State Business Tax Climate Index 2023

TRANSPORTATION

Means of Transportation to Work

Area	Car/Truck/Van		Public Transportation			Bicycle	Walked	Other Means	Worked at Home
	Drove Alone	Car-pooled	Bus	Subway	Railroad				
City	68.6	9.9	7.3	0.4	0.1	0.5	4.7	1.7	6.9
MSA[1]	77.9	7.4	2.1	0.1	0.0	0.3	2.1	1.2	8.8
U.S.	73.2	8.6	2.0	1.6	0.5	0.5	2.5	1.5	9.7

Note: Figures are percentages and cover workers 16 years of age and older; (1) Figures cover the Cleveland-Elyria, OH Metropolitan Statistical Area
Source: U.S. Census Bureau, 2017-2021 American Community Survey 5-Year Estimates

Travel Time to Work

Area	Less Than 10 Minutes	10 to 19 Minutes	20 to 29 Minutes	30 to 44 Minutes	45 to 59 Minutes	60 to 89 Minutes	90 Minutes or More
City	10.2	34.0	27.0	20.0	3.9	3.0	2.1
MSA[1]	11.6	28.2	25.9	23.2	6.7	2.9	1.6
U.S.	12.4	28.5	21.0	20.9	8.2	6.2	2.9

Note: Note: Figures are percentages and include workers 16 years old and over; (1) Figures cover the Cleveland-Elyria, OH Metropolitan Statistical Area
Source: U.S. Census Bureau, 2017-2021 American Community Survey 5-Year Estimates

Key Congestion Measures

Measure	1990	2000	2010	2015	2020
Annual Hours of Delay, Total (000)	19,599	37,731	43,033	49,262	33,300
Annual Hours of Delay, Per Auto Commuter	21	35	39	44	29
Annual Congestion Cost, Per Auto Commuter ($)	698	1,011	916	968	686

Note: Covers the Cleveland OH urban area
Source: Texas A&M Transportation Institute, 2021 Urban Mobility Report

Freeway Travel Time Index

Measure	1985	1990	1995	2000	2005	2010	2015	2020
Urban Area Index[1]	1.04	1.08	1.14	1.14	1.14	1.14	1.15	1.08
Urban Area Rank[1,2]	81	62	41	62	73	71	67	44

Note: Freeway Travel Time Index—the ratio of travel time in the peak period to the travel time at free-flow conditions. For example, a value of 1.30 indicates a 20-minute free-flow trip takes 26 minutes in the peak (20 minutes x 1.30 = 26 minutes); (1) Covers the Cleveland OH urban area; (2) Rank is based on 101 larger urban areas (#1 = highest travel time index)
Source: Texas A&M Transportation Institute, 2021 Urban Mobility Report

Public Transportation

Agency Name / Mode of Transportation	Vehicles Operated in Maximum Service[1]	Annual Unlinked Passenger Trips[2] (in thous.)	Annual Passenger Miles[3] (in thous.)
The Greater Cleveland Regional Transit Authority (GCRTA)			
Bus (directly operated)	213	11,184.7	44,453.4
Bus Rapid Transit (directly operated)	11	1,411.8	3,644.6
Demand Response (directly operated)	52	208.5	1,676.9
Demand Response (purchased transportation)	57	182.7	1,564.9
Heavy Rail (directly operated)	18	2,420.1	14,341.6
Light Rail (directly operated)	5	465.1	2,520.9

Note: (1) Number of revenue vehicles operated by the given mode and type of service to meet the annual maximum service requirement. This is the revenue vehicle count during the peak season of the year; on the week and day that maximum service is provided. Vehicles operated in maximum service (VOMS) exclude atypical days and one-time special events; (2) Number of passengers who boarded public transportation vehicles. Passengers are counted each time they board a vehicle no matter how many vehicles they use to travel from their origin to their destination. (3) Sum of the distances ridden by all passengers during the entire fiscal year.
Source: Federal Transit Administration, National Transit Database, 2021

Air Transportation

Airport Name and Code / Type of Service	Passenger Airlines[1]	Passenger Enplanements	Freight Carriers[2]	Freight (lbs)
Cleveland-Hopkins International (CLE)				
Domestic service (U.S. carriers - 2022)	30	4,159,322	13	83,611,887
International service (U.S. carriers - 2021)	5	28,874	1	8,221

Note: (1) Includes all U.S.-based major, minor and commuter airlines that carried at least one passenger during the year; (2) Includes all U.S.-based airlines and freight carriers that transported at least one pound of freight during the year.
Source: Bureau of Transportation Statistics, The Intermodal Transportation Database, Air Carriers: T-100 Domestic Market (U.S. Carriers), 2022; Bureau of Transportation Statistics, The Intermodal Transportation Database, Air Carriers: T-100 International Market (U.S. Carriers), 2021

BUSINESSES

Major Business Headquarters

Company Name	Industry	Rankings	
		Fortune[1]	Forbes[2]
Cleveland-Cliffs	Iron ore and steel	171	-
Jones Day	Services	-	228
KeyCorp	Commercial banks	449	-
Parker-Hannifin	Industrial machinery	253	-
Sherwin-Williams	Chemicals	175	-

Note: (1) Companies that produce a 10-K are ranked 1 to 500 based on 2021 revenue; (2) All private companies with at least $2 billion in annual revenue through the end of their most current fiscal year are ranked 1 to 246; companies listed are headquartered in the city; dashes indicate no ranking
Source: Fortune, "Fortune 500," 2022; Forbes, "America's Largest Private Companies," 2022

Fastest-Growing Businesses

According to *Inc.*, Cleveland is home to one of America's 500 fastest-growing private companies: **Cleveland Kitchen** (#430). Criteria: must be an independent, privately-held, for-profit, U.S. corporation, proprietorship or partnership as of December 31, 2021; revenues must be at least $100,000 in 2018 and $2 million in 2021; must have four-year operating/sales history. *Inc., "America's 500 Fastest-Growing Private Companies," 2022*

According to *Initiative for a Competitive Inner City (ICIC)*, Cleveland is home to one of America's 100 fastest-growing "inner city" companies: **Muse** (#19). Criteria for inclusion: company must be headquartered in or have 51 percent or more of its physical operations in an economically distressed urban area; must be an independent, for-profit corporation, partnership or proprietorship; must have 10 or more employees and have a five-year sales history that includes sales of at least $200,000 in the base year and at least $1 million in the current year with no decrease in sales over the two most recent years. Companies were ranked overall by revenue growth over the five-year period between 2017 and 2021. *Initiative for a Competitive Inner City (ICIC), "Inner City 100 Companies," 2022*

According to Deloitte, Cleveland is home to one of North America's 500 fastest-growing high-technology companies: **Remesh** (#330). Companies are ranked by percentage growth in revenue over a four-year period. Criteria for inclusion: company must be headquartered within North America; must own proprietary intellectual property or technology that is sold to customers in products that contributes to a significant portion of the company's operating revenue; must have been in business for a minumum of four years with 2018 operating revenues of at least $50,000 USD/CD and 2021 operating revenues of at least $5 million USD/CD. *Deloitte, 2022 Technology Fast 500*™

Living Environment

COST OF LIVING

Cost of Living Index

Composite Index	Groceries	Housing	Utilities	Trans-portation	Health Care	Misc. Goods/Services
93.9	105.0	82.9	97.8	94.4	99.0	95.9

Note: The Cost of Living Index measures regional differences in the cost of consumer goods and services, excluding taxes and non-consumer expenditures, for professional and managerial households in the top income quintile. It is based on more than 50,000 prices covering almost 60 different items for which prices are collected three times a year by chambers of commerce, economic development organizations or university applied economic centers in each participating urban area. The numbers shown should be read as a percentage above or below the national average of 100. For example, a value of 115.4 in the groceries column indicates that grocery prices are 15.4% higher than the national average. Small differences in the index numbers should not be interpreted as significant; Figures cover the Cleveland OH urban area.
Source: The Council for Community and Economic Research, Cost of Living Index, 2022

Grocery Prices

Area[1]	T-Bone Steak ($/pound)	Frying Chicken ($/pound)	Whole Milk ($/half gal.)	Eggs ($/dozen)	Orange Juice ($/64 oz.)	Coffee ($/11.5 oz.)
City[2]	16.00	2.16	1.86	2.08	3.91	4.91
Avg.	13.81	1.59	2.43	2.25	3.85	4.95
Min.	10.17	0.90	1.51	1.30	2.90	3.46
Max.	19.35	3.30	4.32	4.32	5.31	8.59

Note: (1) Values for the local area are compared with the average, minimum and maximum values for all 286 areas in the Cost of Living Index; (2) Figures cover the Cleveland OH urban area; T-Bone Steak (price per pound); Frying Chicken (price per pound, whole fryer); Whole Milk (half gallon carton); Eggs (price per dozen, Grade A, large); Orange Juice (64 oz. Tropicana or Florida Natural); Coffee (11.5 oz. can, vacuum-packed, Maxwell House, Hills Bros, or Folgers).
Source: The Council for Community and Economic Research, Cost of Living Index, 2022

Housing and Utility Costs

Area[1]	New Home Price ($)	Apartment Rent ($/month)	All Electric ($/month)	Part Electric ($/month)	Other Energy ($/month)	Telephone ($/month)
City[2]	347,809	1,302	-	89.55	82.10	188.12
Avg.	450,913	1,371	176.41	99.93	76.96	190.22
Min.	229,283	546	100.84	31.56	27.15	174.27
Max.	2,434,977	4,569	356.86	249.59	272.24	208.31

Note: (1) Values for the local area are compared with the average, minimum and maximum values for all 286 areas in the Cost of Living Index; (2) Figures cover the Cleveland OH urban area; New Home Price (2,400 sf living area, 8,000 sf lot, in urban area with full utilities); Apartment Rent (950 sf 2 bedroom/1.5 or 2 bath, unfurnished, excluding all utilities except water); All Electric (average monthly cost for an all-electric home); Part Electric (average monthly cost for a part-electric home); Other Energy (average monthly cost for natural gas, fuel oil, coal, wood, and any other forms of energy except electricity); Telephone (price includes the base monthly rate plus taxes and fees for three lines of mobile phone service).
Source: The Council for Community and Economic Research, Cost of Living Index, 2022

Health Care, Transportation, and Other Costs

Area[1]	Doctor ($/visit)	Dentist ($/visit)	Optometrist ($/visit)	Gasoline ($/gallon)	Beauty Salon ($/visit)	Men's Shirt ($)
City[2]	113.00	109.47	94.21	3.86	35.71	41.99
Avg.	124.91	107.77	117.66	3.86	43.31	34.21
Min.	36.61	58.25	51.79	2.90	22.18	13.05
Max.	250.21	162.58	371.96	5.54	85.61	63.54

Note: (1) Values for the local area are compared with the average, minimum and maximum values for all 286 areas in the Cost of Living Index; (2) Figures cover the Cleveland OH urban area; Doctor (general practitioners routine exam of an established patient); Dentist (adult teeth cleaning and periodic oral examination); Optometrist (full vision eye exam for established adult patient); Gasoline (one gallon regular unleaded, national brand, including all taxes, cash price at self-service pump if available); Beauty Salon (woman's shampoo, trim, and blow-dry); Men's Shirt (cotton/polyester dress shirt, pinpoint weave, long sleeves).
Source: The Council for Community and Economic Research, Cost of Living Index, 2022

HOUSING

Homeownership Rate

Area	2015 (%)	2016 (%)	2017 (%)	2018 (%)	2019 (%)	2020 (%)	2021 (%)	2022 (%)
MSA[1]	68.4	64.8	66.6	66.7	64.4	66.3	64.7	63.0
U.S.	63.7	63.4	63.9	64.4	64.6	66.6	65.5	65.8

Note: (1) Figures cover the Cleveland-Elyria, OH Metropolitan Statistical Area
Source: U.S. Census Bureau, Housing Vacancies and Homeownership Annual Statistics: 2015-2022

House Price Index (HPI)

Area	National Ranking[2]	Quarterly Change (%)	One-Year Change (%)	Five-Year Change (%)	Since 1991Q1 (%)
MSA[1]	189	-1.76	9.23	49.32	153.83
U.S.[3]	–	0.34	8.41	58.44	289.08

Note: The HPI is a weighted repeat sales index. It measures average price changes in repeat sales or refinancings on the same properties. This information is obtained by reviewing repeat mortgage transactions on single-family properties whose mortgages have been purchased or securitized by Fannie Mae or Freddie Mac since January 1975; (1) Figures cover the Cleveland-Elyria, OH Metropolitan Statistical Area; (2) Rankings are based on annual percentage change for all metro areas containing at least 15,000 transactions over the last 10 years and ranges from 1 to 257; (3) figures based on a weighted average of Census Division estimates using a seasonally adjusted, purchase-only index; all figures are for the period ending December 31, 2022
Source: Federal Housing Finance Agency, Change in FHFA Metropolitan Area House Price Indexes, 2022Q4

Median Single-Family Home Prices

Area	2020	2021	2022[p]	Percent Change 2021 to 2022
MSA[1]	179.5	198.8	215.7	8.5
U.S. Average	300.2	357.1	392.6	9.9

Note: Figures are median sales prices of existing single-family homes in thousands of dollars; (p) preliminary; (1) Figures cover the Cleveland-Elyria, OH Metropolitan Statistical Area
Source: National Association of Realtors, Median Sales Price of Existing Single-Family Homes for Metropolitan Areas, 4th Quarter 2022

Qualifying Income Based on Median Sales Price of Existing Single-Family Homes

Area	With 5% Down ($)	With 10% Down ($)	With 20% Down ($)
MSA[1]	62,440	59,153	52,581
U.S. Average	112,234	106,237	94,513

Note: Figures are preliminary; Qualifying income is based on a mortgage rate of 6.77%. Monthly principal and interest payment is limited to 25% of income; (1) Figures cover the Cleveland-Elyria, OH Metropolitan Statistical Area
Source: National Association of Realtors, Qualifying Income Based on Median Sales Price of Existing Single-Family Homes for Metropolitan Areas, 4th Quarter 2022

Home Value

Area	Under $100,000	$100,000 -$199,999	$200,000 -$299,999	$300,000 -$399,999	$400,000 -$499,999	$500,000 -$999,999	$1,000,000 or more	Median ($)
City	67.7	23.2	4.6	2.2	0.7	1.3	0.2	74,700
MSA[1]	23.8	37.8	20.5	9.2	4.1	3.9	0.6	164,400
U.S.	16.2	24.2	20.1	13.6	8.3	13.6	4.1	244,900

Note: Figures are percentages except for median and cover owner-occupied housing units; (1) Figures cover the Cleveland-Elyria, OH Metropolitan Statistical Area
Source: U.S. Census Bureau, 2017-2021 American Community Survey 5-Year Estimates

Year Housing Structure Built

Area	2020 or Later	2010 -2019	2000 -2009	1990 -1999	1980 -1989	1970 -1979	1960 -1969	1950 -1959	1940 -1949	Before 1940	Median Year
City	0.1	2.9	3.5	3.4	2.8	5.5	7.8	12.7	11.2	50.0	<1940
MSA[1]	0.1	3.4	6.8	8.9	6.9	12.4	13.6	17.7	7.6	22.5	1962
U.S.	0.2	7.3	13.6	13.6	13.2	14.8	10.3	10.0	4.7	12.2	1979

Note: Figures are percentages except for Median Year; Note: (1) Figures cover the Cleveland-Elyria, OH Metropolitan Statistical Area
Source: U.S. Census Bureau, 2017-2021 American Community Survey 5-Year Estimates

Gross Monthly Rent

Area	Under $500	$500 -$999	$1,000 -$1,499	$1,500 -$1,999	$2,000 -$2,499	$2,500 -$2,999	$3,000 and up	Median ($)
City	20.3	53.7	19.1	4.7	1.3	0.6	0.4	774
MSA[1]	11.5	52.2	27.1	6.5	1.4	0.5	0.8	880
U.S.	8.1	30.5	30.8	16.8	7.3	3.1	3.5	1,163

Note: Figures are percentages except for median; Gross rent is the contract rent plus the estimated average monthly cost of utilities (electricity, gas, and water and sewer) and fuels (oil, coal, kerosene, wood, etc.) if these are paid by the renter (or paid for the renter by someone else); (1) Figures cover the Cleveland-Elyria, OH Metropolitan Statistical Area
Source: U.S. Census Bureau, 2017-2021 American Community Survey 5-Year Estimates

HEALTH

Health Risk Factors

Category	MSA[1] (%)	U.S. (%)
Adults aged 18–64 who have any kind of health care coverage	93.5	90.9
Adults who reported being in good or better health	82.3	85.2
Adults who have been told they have high blood cholesterol	34.2	35.7
Adults who have been told they have high blood pressure	33.7	32.4
Adults who are current smokers	17.6	14.4
Adults who currently use e-cigarettes	6.0	6.7
Adults who currently use chewing tobacco, snuff, or snus	2.3	3.5
Adults who are heavy drinkers[2]	6.8	6.3
Adults who are binge drinkers[3]	17.7	15.4
Adults who are overweight (BMI 25.0 - 29.9)	35.4	34.4
Adults who are obese (BMI 30.0 - 99.8)	32.8	33.9
Adults who participated in any physical activities in the past month	77.5	76.3

Note: (1) Figures cover the Cleveland-Elyria, OH Metropolitan Statistical Area; (2) Heavy drinkers are classified as adult men having more than 14 drinks per week and adult women having more than 7 drinks per week; (3) Binge drinkers are classified as males having five or more drinks on one occasion or females having four or more drinks on one occasion
Source: Centers for Disease Control and Prevention, Behaviorial Risk Factor Surveillance System, SMART: Selected Metropolitan Area Risk Trends, 2021

Acute and Chronic Health Conditions

Category	MSA[1] (%)	U.S. (%)
Adults who have ever been told they had a heart attack	5.0	4.0
Adults who have ever been told they have angina or coronary heart disease	4.6	3.8
Adults who have ever been told they had a stroke	3.6	3.0
Adults who have ever been told they have asthma	15.0	14.9
Adults who have ever been told they have arthritis	33.2	25.8
Adults who have ever been told they have diabetes[2]	10.7	10.9
Adults who have ever been told they had skin cancer	5.0	6.6
Adults who have ever been told they had any other types of cancer	8.1	7.5
Adults who have ever been told they have COPD	9.1	6.1
Adults who have ever been told they have kidney disease	3.1	3.0
Adults who have ever been told they have a form of depression	20.3	20.5

Note: (1) Figures cover the Cleveland-Elyria, OH Metropolitan Statistical Area; (2) Figures do not include pregnancy-related, borderline, or pre-diabetes
Source: Centers for Disease Control and Prevention, Behaviorial Risk Factor Surveillance System, SMART: Selected Metropolitan Area Risk Trends, 2021

Health Screening and Vaccination Rates

Category	MSA[1] (%)	U.S. (%)
Adults who have ever been tested for HIV	36.8	34.9
Adults who have had their blood cholesterol checked within the last five years	88.5	85.2
Adults aged 65+ who have had flu shot within the past year	68.5	68.6
Adults aged 65+ who have ever had a pneumonia vaccination	70.9	71.0

Note: (1) Figures cover the Cleveland-Elyria, OH Metropolitan Statistical Area.
Source: Centers for Disease Control and Prevention, Behaviorial Risk Factor Surveillance System, SMART: Selected Metropolitan Area Risk Trends, 2021

Disability Status

Category	MSA[1] (%)	U.S. (%)
Adults who reported being deaf	5.8	7.2
Are you blind or have serious difficulty seeing, even when wearing glasses?	4.4	4.8
Are you limited in any way in any of your usual activities due to arthritis?	13.4	11.1
Do you have difficulty doing errands alone?	7.0	7.0
Do you have difficulty dressing or bathing?	3.7	3.6
Do you have serious difficulty concentrating/remembering/making decisions?	12.6	12.1
Do you have serious difficulty walking or climbing stairs?	15.0	12.8

Note: (1) Figures cover the Cleveland-Elyria, OH Metropolitan Statistical Area.
Source: Centers for Disease Control and Prevention, Behaviorial Risk Factor Surveillance System, SMART: Selected Metropolitan Area Risk Trends, 2021

Mortality Rates for the Top 10 Causes of Death in the U.S.

ICD-10[a] Sub-Chapter	ICD-10[a] Code	Crude Mortality Rate[1] per 100,000 population	
		County[2]	U.S.
Malignant neoplasms	C00-C97	230.7	182.6
Ischaemic heart diseases	I20-I25	147.8	113.1
Other forms of heart disease	I30-I51	107.5	64.4
Other degenerative diseases of the nervous system	G30-G31	43.5	51.0
Cerebrovascular diseases	I60-I69	57.2	47.8
Other external causes of accidental injury	W00-X59	69.6	46.4
Chronic lower respiratory diseases	J40-J47	50.9	45.7
Organic, including symptomatic, mental disorders	F01-F09	67.5	35.9
Hypertensive diseases	I10-I15	47.8	35.0
Diabetes mellitus	E10-E14	33.1	29.6

Note: (a) ICD-10 = International Classification of Diseases 10th Revision; (1) Crude mortality rates are a three-year average covering 2019-2021; (2) Figures cover Cuyahoga County.
Source: Centers for Disease Control and Prevention, National Center for Health Statistics. National Vital Statistics System, Mortality 2018-2021 on CDC WONDER Online Database

Mortality Rates for Selected Causes of Death

ICD-10[a] Sub-Chapter	ICD-10[a] Code	Crude Mortality Rate[1] per 100,000 population	
		County[2]	U.S.
Assault	X85-Y09	17.1	7.0
Diseases of the liver	K70-K76	21.4	19.8
Human immunodeficiency virus (HIV) disease	B20-B24	1.8	1.5
Influenza and pneumonia	J09-J18	14.7	14.7
Intentional self-harm	X60-X84	14.2	14.3
Malnutrition	E40-E46	4.6	4.3
Obesity and other hyperalimentation	E65-E68	2.8	3.0
Renal failure	N17-N19	22.1	15.7
Transport accidents	V01-V99	10.4	13.6
Viral hepatitis	B15-B19	1.1	1.2

Note: (a) ICD-10 = International Classification of Diseases 10th Revision; (1) Crude mortality rates are a three-year average covering 2019-2021; (2) Figures cover Cuyahoga County; Data are suppressed when the data meet the criteria for confidentiality constraints; Crude mortality rates are flagged as unreliable when the rate would be calculated with a numerator of 20 or less.
Source: Centers for Disease Control and Prevention, National Center for Health Statistics. National Vital Statistics System, Mortality 2018-2021 on CDC WONDER Online Database

Health Insurance Coverage

Area	With Health Insurance	With Private Health Insurance	With Public Health Insurance	Without Health Insurance	Population Under Age 19 Without Health Insurance
City	92.5	44.5	56.6	7.5	3.3
MSA[1]	94.6	68.7	38.7	5.4	3.4
U.S.	91.2	67.8	35.4	8.8	5.3

Note: Figures are percentages that cover the civilian noninstitutionalized population; (1) Figures cover the Cleveland-Elyria, OH Metropolitan Statistical Area
Source: U.S. Census Bureau, 2017-2021 American Community Survey 5-Year Estimates

Number of Medical Professionals

Area	MDs[3]	DOs[3,4]	Dentists	Podiatrists	Chiropractors	Optometrists
County[1] (number)	9,027	645	1,375	236	239	216
County[1] (rate[2])	715.5	51.1	110.1	18.9	19.1	17.3
U.S. (rate[2])	289.3	23.5	72.5	6.2	28.7	17.4

Note: Data as of 2021 unless noted; (1) Data covers Cuyahoga County; (2) Rate per 100,000 population; (3) Data as of 2020 and includes all active, non-federal physicians; (4) Doctor of Osteopathic Medicine
Source: U.S. Department of Health and Human Services, Health Resources and Services Administration, Bureau of Health Professions, Area Resource File (ARF) 2021-2022

Best Hospitals

According to *U.S. News,* the Cleveland-Elyria, OH metro area is home to eight of the best hospitals in the U.S.: **Cleveland Clinic Fairview Hospital** (1 adult specialty); **Cleveland Clinic Hillcrest Hospital** (3 adult specialties); **Cleveland Clinic South Pointe Hospital** (1 adult specialty); **Cleveland Clinic** (Honor Roll/13 adult specialties and 9 pediatric specialties); **Cole Eye Institute at Cleveland Clinic** (Honor Roll/13 adult specialties and 9 pediatric specialties); **MetroHealth Medical Center** (1 adult specialty); **University Hospitals Cleveland Medical Center** (4 adult specialties and 9 pediatric specialties); **University Hospitals Harrington Heart & Vascular Institute** (4 adult specialties and 9 pediatric specialties). The hospitals listed were nationally ranked in at least one of 15 adult or 10 pediatric specialties. The number of specialties shown cover the parent hospital. Only 164 U.S. hospitals performed well enough to be nationally ranked in one or more specialties. Twenty hospitals in the U.S. made the Honor Roll. The Best Hospitals Honor Roll takes both the national rankings and the procedure and condition ratings into account. Hospitals received points if they were nationally ranked in one of the 15 adult specialties—the higher they ranked, the more points they got—and how many ratings of "high performing" they earned in the 17 procedures and conditions. *U.S. News Online, "America's Best Hospitals 2022-23"*

According to *U.S. News,* the Cleveland-Elyria, OH metro area is home to two of the best children's hospitals in the U.S.: **Cleveland Clinic Children's Hospital** (9 pediatric specialties); **Rainbow Babies and Children's Hospital** (9 pediatric specialties). The hospitals listed were highly ranked in at least one of 10 pediatric specialties. Eighty-six children's hospitals in the U.S. were nationally ranked in at least one specialty. Hospitals received points for being ranked in a specialty, and the 10 hospitals with the most points across the 10 specialties make up the Honor Roll. *U.S. News Online, "America's Best Children's Hospitals 2022-23"*

EDUCATION

Public School District Statistics

District Name	Schls	Pupils	Pupil/ Teacher Ratio	Minority Pupils[1] (%)	LEP/ELL[2] (%)	IEP[3] (%)
Cleveland Municipal	96	35,319	14.5	85.5	9.3	23.3
Ohio Connections Academy Inc	1	5,473	41.4	29.9	0.4	12.9
Orange City	4	2,005	n/a	31.6	2.1	15.2

Note: Table includes school districts with 2,000 or more students; (1) Percentage of students that are not non-Hispanic white; (2) Percentage of students that are Limited English Proficient or English Language Learners (2018-19); (3) Percentage of students that have an Individualized Education Program (2019-20).
Source: U.S. Department of Education, National Center for Education Statistics, Common Core of Data, Local Education Agency (School District) Universe Survey: School Year 2021-2022

Highest Level of Education

Area	Less than H.S.	H.S. Diploma	Some College, No Deg.	Associate Degree	Bachelor's Degree	Master's Degree	Prof. School Degree	Doctorate Degree
City	17.4	33.3	22.8	7.4	11.4	5.2	1.7	0.8
MSA[1]	8.6	28.5	21.3	8.8	19.8	9.2	2.5	1.3
U.S.	11.1	26.5	20.0	8.7	20.6	9.3	2.2	1.5

Note: Figures cover persons age 25 and over; (1) Figures cover the Cleveland-Elyria, OH Metropolitan Statistical Area
Source: U.S. Census Bureau, 2017-2021 American Community Survey 5-Year Estimates

Educational Attainment by Race

Area	High School Graduate or Higher (%)					Bachelor's Degree or Higher (%)				
	Total	White	Black	Asian	Hisp.[2]	Total	White	Black	Asian	Hisp.[2]
City	82.6	85.7	81.1	75.3	71.4	19.2	27.6	11.2	46.9	9.2
MSA[1]	91.4	93.3	86.1	86.8	77.9	32.7	36.2	16.8	63.5	17.6
U.S.	88.9	91.4	87.2	87.6	71.2	33.7	35.5	23.3	55.6	18.4

Note: Figures shown cover persons 25 years old and over; (1) Figures cover the Cleveland-Elyria, OH Metropolitan Statistical Area; (2) People of Hispanic origin can be of any race
Source: U.S. Census Bureau, 2017-2021 American Community Survey 5-Year Estimates

School Enrollment by Grade and Control

Area	Preschool (%)		Kindergarten (%)		Grades 1 - 4 (%)		Grades 5 - 8 (%)		Grades 9 - 12 (%)	
	Public	Private	Public	Private	Public	Private	Public	Private	Public	Private
City	71.3	28.7	80.0	20.0	81.4	18.6	78.8	21.2	78.0	22.0
MSA[1]	52.8	47.2	79.0	21.0	81.1	18.9	82.0	18.0	82.4	17.6
U.S.	58.8	41.2	86.3	13.7	88.3	11.7	88.6	11.4	89.4	10.6

Note: Figures shown cover persons 3 years old and over; (1) Figures cover the Cleveland-Elyria, OH Metropolitan Statistical Area
Source: U.S. Census Bureau, 2017-2021 American Community Survey 5-Year Estimates

Higher Education

Four-Year Colleges			Two-Year Colleges			Medical Schools[1]	Law Schools[2]	Voc/ Tech[3]
Public	Private Non-profit	Private For-profit	Public	Private Non-profit	Private For-profit			
3	11	2	2	2	11	1	2	12

Note: Figures cover institutions located within the Cleveland-Elyria, OH Metropolitan Statistical Area and include main campuses only; (1) includes schools accredited by the Liaison Committee on Medical Education and the American Osteopathic Association's Commission on Osteopathic College Accreditation; (2) includes ABA-accredited schools, schools with provisional ABA accreditation, and state accredited schools; (3) includes all schools with programs that are less than 2 years.
Source: National Center for Education Statistics, Integrated Postsecondary Education System (IPEDS), 2021-22; Wikipedia, List of Medical Schools in the United States, accessed April 10, 2023; Wikipedia, List of Law Schools in the United States, accessed April 10, 2023

According to *U.S. News & World Report,* the Cleveland-Elyria, OH metro area is home to one of the top 200 national universities in the U.S.: **Case Western Reserve University** (#44 tie). The indicators used to capture academic quality fall into a number of categories: assessment by administrators at peer institutions; retention of students; faculty resources; student selectivity; financial resources; alumni giving; high school counselor ratings of colleges; and graduation rate. *U.S. News & World Report, "America's Best Colleges 2023"*

According to *U.S. News & World Report,* the Cleveland-Elyria, OH metro area is home to one of the top 100 liberal arts colleges in the U.S.: **Oberlin College and Conservatory** (#39 tie). The indicators used to capture academic quality fall into a number of categories: assessment by administrators at peer institutions; retention of students; faculty resources; student selectivity; financial resources; alumni giving; high school counselor ratings of colleges; and graduation rate. *U.S. News & World Report, "America's Best Colleges 2023"*

According to *U.S. News & World Report,* the Cleveland-Elyria, OH metro area is home to one of the top 100 law schools in the U.S.: **Case Western Reserve University** (#78 tie). The rankings are based on a weighted average of 12 measures of quality: peer assessment score; assessment score by lawyers/judges; median LSAT scores; median undergrad GPA; acceptance rate; employment rates for graduates; placement success; bar passage rate; faculty resources; expenditures per student; student/faculty ratio; and library resources. *U.S. News & World Report, "America's Best Graduate Schools, Law, 2023"*

According to *U.S. News & World Report,* the Cleveland-Elyria, OH metro area is home to one of the top 75 medical schools for research in the U.S.: **Case Western Reserve University** (#24). The rankings are based on a weighted average of 11 measures of quality: quality assessment; peer assessment score; assessment score by residency directors; research activity; total research activity; average research activity per faculty member; student selectivity; median MCAT total score; median undergraduate GPA; acceptance rate; and faculty resources. *U.S. News & World Report, "America's Best Graduate Schools, Medical, 2023"*

EMPLOYERS

Major Employers

Company Name	Industry
Case Western Reserve University	Educational services
City of Cleveland	Municipal government
Cleveland Clinic	Health care
Cleveland Metropolitan School District	Educational services
Cuyahoga County	Government
KeyCorp	Finance
Metro Health System	Health care
Sherwin-Williams Co.	Retail
U.S. Office of Personnel Management	Government
University Hospitals	Health care

Note: Companies shown are located within the Cleveland-Elyria, OH Metropolitan Statistical Area.
Source: Hoovers.com; Wikipedia

Best Companies to Work For

AMS, headquartered in Cleveland, is among "Fortune's Best Workplaces for Women." To pick the best companies, *Fortune* partnered with the Great Place to Work Institute. To be considered for the list, companies must be Great Place To Work-Certified. Companies must also employ at least 50 women, at least 20% of their non-executive managers must be female, and at least one executive must be female. To determine the Best Workplaces for Women, Great Place To Work measured the differences in women's survey responses to those of their peers and assesses the impact of demographics and roles on the quality and consistency of women's experiences. Great Place To Work also analyzed the gender balance of each workplace, how it compared to each company's industry, and patterns in representation as women rise from front-line positions to the board of directors. *Fortune, "Best Workplaces for Women," 2022*

Cleveland, Ohio   133

PUBLIC SAFETY

Crime Rate

Area	Total Crime	Violent Crime Rate				Property Crime Rate		
		Murder	Rape[3]	Robbery	Aggrav. Assault	Burglary	Larceny -Theft	Motor Vehicle Theft
City	5,727.5	42.2	103.7	420.2	1,090.7	973.8	2,321.2	775.7
Suburbs[1]	1,328.9	3.0	20.9	35.0	104.7	154.4	907.3	103.7
Metro[2]	2,145.2	10.3	36.2	106.5	287.7	306.5	1,169.7	228.4
U.S.	2,356.7	6.5	38.4	73.9	279.7	314.2	1,398.0	246.0

Note: Figures are crimes per 100,000 population; (1) All areas within the metro area that are located outside the city limits; (2) Figures cover the Cleveland-Elyria, OH Metropolitan Statistical Area; (3) All figures shown were reported using the revised Uniform Crime Reporting (UCR) definition of rape; Due to the transition to the National Incident-Based Reporting System (NIBRS), limited city and metro area data was released for 2021.
Source: FBI Uniform Crime Reports, 2020

Hate Crimes

Area	Number of Quarters Reported	Number of Incidents per Bias Motivation					
		Race/Ethnicity/ Ancestry	Religion	Sexual Orientation	Disability	Gender	Gender Identity
City[1]	4	64	13	14	6	3	19
U.S.	4	5,227	1,244	1,110	130	75	266

Note: (1) Figures include one incident reported with more than one bias motivation; Due to the transition to the National Incident-Based Reporting System (NIBRS), limited crime data was released for 2021.
Source: Federal Bureau of Investigation, Hate Crime Statistics 2020

Identity Theft Consumer Reports

Area	Reports	Reports per 100,000 Population	Rank[2]
MSA[1]	7,693	375	37
U.S.	1,108,609	339	-

Note: (1) Figures cover the Cleveland-Elyria, OH Metropolitan Statistical Area; (2) Rank ranges from 1 to 391 where 1 indicates greatest number of identity theft reports per 100,000 population
Source: Federal Trade Commission, Consumer Sentinel Network Data Book 2022

Fraud and Other Consumer Reports

Area	Reports	Reports per 100,000 Population	Rank[2]
MSA[1]	24,010	1,169	45
U.S.	4,064,520	1,245	-

Note: (1) Figures cover the Cleveland-Elyria, OH Metropolitan Statistical Area; (2) Rank ranges from 1 to 391 where 1 indicates greatest number of fraud and other consumer reports per 100,000 population
Source: Federal Trade Commission, Consumer Sentinel Network Data Book 2022

POLITICS

2020 Presidential Election Results

Area	Biden	Trump	Jorgensen	Hawkins	Other
Cuyahoga County	66.4	32.3	0.7	0.3	0.3
U.S.	51.3	46.8	1.2	0.3	0.5

Note: Results are percentages and may not add to 100% due to rounding
Source: Dave Leip's Atlas of U.S. Presidential Elections

SPORTS

Professional Sports Teams

Team Name	League	Year Established
Cleveland Browns	National Football League (NFL)	1946
Cleveland Cavaliers	National Basketball Association (NBA)	1970
Cleveland Indians	Major League Baseball (MLB)	1900

Note: Includes teams located in the Cleveland-Elyria, OH Metropolitan Statistical Area.
Source: Wikipedia, Major Professional Sports Teams of the United States and Canada, April 12, 2023

CLIMATE

Average and Extreme Temperatures

Temperature	Jan	Feb	Mar	Apr	May	Jun	Jul	Aug	Sep	Oct	Nov	Dec	Yr.
Extreme High (°F)	73	69	82	88	92	104	100	102	101	89	82	77	104
Average High (°F)	33	36	46	58	69	79	83	81	74	63	50	38	59
Average Temp. (°F)	26	28	37	49	59	68	73	71	64	54	43	31	50
Average Low (°F)	19	20	28	38	48	58	62	61	54	44	35	24	41
Extreme Low (°F)	-19	-15	-5	10	25	31	41	38	34	19	3	-15	-19

Note: Figures cover the years 1948-1990
Source: National Climatic Data Center, International Station Meteorological Climate Summary, 9/96

Average Precipitation/Snowfall/Humidity

Precip./Humidity	Jan	Feb	Mar	Apr	May	Jun	Jul	Aug	Sep	Oct	Nov	Dec	Yr.
Avg. Precip. (in.)	2.4	2.3	3.1	3.4	3.5	3.5	3.5	3.4	3.2	2.6	3.2	2.9	37.1
Avg. Snowfall (in.)	13	12	10	2	Tr	0	0	0	0	1	5	12	55
Avg. Rel. Hum. 7am (%)	79	79	78	76	77	78	81	85	84	81	78	78	79
Avg. Rel. Hum. 4pm (%)	70	67	62	56	54	55	55	58	58	58	65	70	61

Note: Figures cover the years 1948-1990; Tr = Trace amounts (<0.05 in. of rain; <0.5 in. of snow)
Source: National Climatic Data Center, International Station Meteorological Climate Summary, 9/96

Weather Conditions

Temperature			Daytime Sky			Precipitation		
5°F & below	32°F & below	90°F & above	Clear	Partly cloudy	Cloudy	0.01 inch or more precip.	0.1 inch or more snow/ice	Thunder-storms
11	123	12	63	127	175	157	48	34

Note: Figures are average number of days per year and cover the years 1948-1990
Source: National Climatic Data Center, International Station Meteorological Climate Summary, 9/96

HAZARDOUS WASTE

Superfund Sites

The Cleveland-Elyria, OH metro area has no sites on the EPA's Superfund Final National Priorities List. There are a total of 1,165 Superfund sites with a status of proposed or final on the list in the U.S.
U.S. Environmental Protection Agency, National Priorities List, April 12, 2023

AIR QUALITY

Air Quality Trends: Ozone

	1990	1995	2000	2005	2010	2015	2018	2019	2020	2021
MSA[1]	0.084	0.090	0.079	0.084	0.074	0.069	0.072	0.067	0.069	0.066
U.S.	0.087	0.089	0.081	0.080	0.072	0.067	0.069	0.065	0.065	0.067

Note: (1) Data covers the Cleveland-Elyria, OH Metropolitan Statistical Area. The values shown are the composite ozone concentration averages among trend sites based on the highest fourth daily maximum 8-hour concentration in parts per million. These trends are based on sites having an adequate record of monitoring data during the trend period. Data from exceptional events are included.
Source: U.S. Environmental Protection Agency, Air Quality Monitoring Information, "Air Quality Trends by City, 1990-2021"

Air Quality Index

Area	Percent of Days when Air Quality was...[2]					AQI Statistics[2]	
	Good	Moderate	Unhealthy for Sensitive Groups	Unhealthy	Very Unhealthy	Maximum	Median
MSA[1]	47.4	50.4	2.2	0.0	0.0	122	52

Note: (1) Data covers the Cleveland-Elyria, OH Metropolitan Statistical Area; (2) Based on 365 days with AQI data in 2021. Air Quality Index (AQI) is an index for reporting daily air quality. EPA calculates the AQI for five major air pollutants regulated by the Clean Air Act: ground-level ozone, particle pollution (aka particulate matter), carbon monoxide, sulfur dioxide, and nitrogen dioxide. The AQI runs from 0 to 500. The higher the AQI value, the greater the level of air pollution and the greater the health concern. There are six AQI categories: "Good" AQI is between 0 and 50. Air quality is considered satisfactory; "Moderate" AQI is between 51 and 100. Air quality is acceptable; "Unhealthy for Sensitive Groups" When AQI values are between 101 and 150, members of sensitive groups may experience health effects; "Unhealthy" When AQI values are between 151 and 200 everyone may begin to experience health effects; "Very Unhealthy" AQI values between 201 and 300 trigger a health alert; "Hazardous" AQI values over 300 trigger warnings of emergency conditions (not shown).
Source: U.S. Environmental Protection Agency, Air Quality Index Report, 2021

Air Quality Index Pollutants

Area	Percent of Days when AQI Pollutant was...[2]					
	Carbon Monoxide	Nitrogen Dioxide	Ozone	Sulfur Dioxide	Particulate Matter 2.5	Particulate Matter 10
MSA[1]	0.0	1.4	35.9	(3)	60.8	1.9

Note: (1) Data covers the Cleveland-Elyria, OH Metropolitan Statistical Area; (2) Based on 365 days with AQI data in 2021. The Air Quality Index (AQI) is an index for reporting daily air quality. EPA calculates the AQI for five major air pollutants regulated by the Clean Air Act: ground-level ozone, particle pollution (also known as particulate matter), carbon monoxide, sulfur dioxide, and nitrogen dioxide. The AQI runs from 0 to 500. The higher the AQI value, the greater the level of air pollution and the greater the health concern; (3) Sulfur dioxide is no longer included in this table (as of December 8, 2021) because SO_2 concentrations tend to be very localized and not necessarily representative of broad geographical areas like counties and CBSAs.
Source: U.S. Environmental Protection Agency, Air Quality Index Report, 2021

Maximum Air Pollutant Concentrations: Particulate Matter, Ozone, CO and Lead

	Particulate Matter 10 (ug/m^3)	Particulate Matter 2.5 Wtd AM (ug/m^3)	Particulate Matter 2.5 24-Hr (ug/m^3)	Ozone (ppm)	Carbon Monoxide (ppm)	Lead (ug/m^3)
MSA[1] Level	89	12.6	29	0.072	2	0.01
NAAQS[2]	150	15	35	0.075	9	0.15
Met NAAQS[2]	Yes	Yes	Yes	Yes	Yes	Yes

Note: (1) Data covers the Cleveland-Elyria, OH Metropolitan Statistical Area; Data from exceptional events are included; (2) National Ambient Air Quality Standards; ppm = parts per million; ug/m^3 = micrograms per cubic meter; n/a not available.
Concentrations: Particulate Matter 10 (coarse particulate)—highest second maximum 24-hour concentration; Particulate Matter 2.5 Wtd AM (fine particulate)—highest weighted annual mean concentration; Particulate Matter 2.5 24-Hour (fine particulate)—highest 98th percentile 24-hour concentration; Ozone—highest fourth daily maximum 8-hour concentration; Carbon Monoxide—highest second maximum non-overlapping 8-hour concentration; Lead—maximum running 3-month average
Source: U.S. Environmental Protection Agency, Air Quality Monitoring Information, "Air Quality Statistics by City, 2021"

Maximum Air Pollutant Concentrations: Nitrogen Dioxide and Sulfur Dioxide

	Nitrogen Dioxide AM (ppb)	Nitrogen Dioxide 1-Hr (ppb)	Sulfur Dioxide AM (ppb)	Sulfur Dioxide 1-Hr (ppb)	Sulfur Dioxide 24-Hr (ppb)
MSA[1] Level	9	38	n/a	39	n/a
NAAQS[2]	53	100	30	75	140
Met NAAQS[2]	Yes	Yes	n/a	Yes	n/a

Note: (1) Data covers the Cleveland-Elyria, OH Metropolitan Statistical Area; Data from exceptional events are included; (2) National Ambient Air Quality Standards; ppm = parts per million; ug/m^3 = micrograms per cubic meter; n/a not available.
Concentrations: Nitrogen Dioxide AM—highest arithmetic mean concentration; Nitrogen Dioxide 1-Hr—highest 98th percentile 1-hour daily maximum concentration; Sulfur Dioxide AM—highest annual mean concentration; Sulfur Dioxide 1-Hr—highest 99th percentile 1-hour daily maximum concentration; Sulfur Dioxide 24-Hr—highest second maximum 24-hour concentration
Source: U.S. Environmental Protection Agency, Air Quality Monitoring Information, "Air Quality Statistics by City, 2021"

Columbus, Ohio

Background

Columbus is the capital of Ohio, and centrally located in the watershed of the Ohio River. The largest city in the state, it was not the first choice for the capital, but in 1812, residents of Franklinton, a county seat in the heart of Ohio, offered the government 1,200 acres of land and $50,000 to build a capitol building and state penitentiary.

Columbus grew steadily throughout the nineteenth century, its prosperity bolstered by the construction of a feeder link into the Ohio and Erie canals, which connected the town to the Great Lakes system and the Ohio River. By 1834, Columbus had attained a population of about 20,000. The railroad was established in 1850, bringing trade opportunities from the East.

Columbus became a major staging area for Union armies during the Civil War and was also home to Camp Chase, the largest military prison for Rebel soldiers. Both before and after the war, manufacturing in the city developed dramatically, based primarily on agricultural processing and packing, shoes, hardware, and heavy equipment. A specialty of Columbus was the buggy, and the Iron Buggy Company was the largest of its kind in the world.

Ohio State University, originally Ohio Agricultural and Mechanical University (1870), is in Columbus, and other colleges and universities include Franklin University (1902), Capital University (1830), Ohio Dominican University (1911), the Columbus College of Art and Design (1879), and Pontifical College Josephinum (1888). One of the first schools for the blind in the U.S., the Ohio State School for the Blind, was founded in Columbus in 1832.

Cultural resources include the Wexner Center for the Arts of Ohio State University, noted for its innovative architecture, and the Columbus Museum of Art, housing one of the nation's finest collections of 19th and 20th-century paintings. Columbus is also home to a symphony orchestra, and opera and ballet companies. The Columbus Zoo is nationally famous both for its success in the breeding of endangered species and for its large coral reef aquarium. And a National Veteran's Memorial and Museum opened in 2018.

Columbus fans support Ohio State University's Buckeye football, a major league soccer team (Columbus Crew), an expansion National Hockey League franchise (Columbus Blue Jackets), and a minor league baseball team (Columbus Clippers). The Clippers played in Cooper Stadium from 1977 to the 2008 season. April 2009 marked the opening of the new ballpark, Huntington Park. Bodybuilding has long played an important role in Columbus sports, and the Arnold Fitness Weekend bodybuilding and fitness competition is an annual event, named for actor/politician Arnold Schwarzenegger.

The largest employers in Columbus are state government and Ohio State University. Other major employers include Nationwide Insurance, and Proctor & Gamble Company. Columbus is a digital city, home to the Online Computer Library Center, CompuServe (a subsidiary of AOL) and the world's largest databases of chemical information. The area's multi-jurisdictional 315 Research + Technology Corridor was designed to achieve national and international recognition like Research Triangle Park in North Carolina.

Columbus has a widespread municipal bus service. Amtrak is planning a 10-year project to connect Ohio's major cities, including Columbus. Port Columbus International Airport, built in the 1920s, today serves national and international carriers. Rickenbacker Airport, named for famed Columbus resident Eddie Rickenbacker, World War I ace and airline pioneer, is a major center for air cargo. Columbus has also been home to other famous Americans, most notably Red Barber, beloved sports announcer, and James Thurber, perhaps the nation's most widely read humorist after Mark Twain. In *More Alarms at Night*, Thurber wrote of Columbus: "It's a town in which almost anything is likely to happen, and in which almost everything has."

Columbus has the usual four seasons associated with a continental climate, but extremes of high and low temperatures are possible. Summers are pleasant and mild. Though variable from year to year, rainfall is slightly more than the national average, and flooding is not unusual.

Rankings

General Rankings

- *Insider* listed 23 places in the U.S. that travel industry trends reveal would be popular destinations in 2023. This year the list trends towards cultural and historical happenings, sports events, wellness experiences and invigorating outdoor escapes. According to the website insider.com Columbus is a place to visit in 2023. *Insider, "23 of the Best Places You Should Travel to in the U.S. in 2023," December 17, 2022*

- The Columbus metro area was identified as one of America's fastest-growing areas in terms of population and business growth by *MagnifyMoney*. The area ranked #34 out of 35. The 100 most populous metro areas in the U.S. were evaluated on their change from 2011 to 2016 in the following categories: people and housing; workforce and employment opportunities; growing industry. *www.businessinsider.com, "The 35 Cities in the US with the Biggest Influx of People, the Most Work Opportunities, and the Hottest Business Growth," August 12, 2018*

Business/Finance Rankings

- Based on metro area social media reviews, the employment opinion group Glassdoor surveyed 50 of the most populous U.S. metro areas and equally weighed cost of living, hiring opportunity, and job satisfaction to compose a list of "25 Best Cities for Jobs." Median pay and home value, and number of active job openings were also factored in. The Columbus metro area was ranked #14 in overall job satisfaction. *www.glassdoor.com, "Best Cities for Jobs," February 25, 2020*

- The Brookings Institution ranked the nation's largest cities based on income inequality. Columbus was ranked #90 (#1 = greatest inequality). Criteria: the "95/20 ratio," a figure representing the income at which a household earns more than 95 percent of all other households, divided by the income at which a household earns more than only 20 percent of all other households. *Brookings Institution, "Household Income Inequality, Largest Cities of 97 Large U.S. Metro Areas, 2014-2016," February 5, 2018*

- The Brookings Institution ranked the 100 largest metro areas in the U.S. based on income inequality. Columbus was ranked #62 (#1 = greatest inequality). Criteria: the "95/20 ratio," a figure representing the income at which a household earns more than 95 percent of all other households, divided by the income at which a household earns more than only 20 percent of all other households. *Brookings Institution, "Household Income Inequality, 100 Largest U.S. Metro Areas, 2014-2016," February 5, 2018*

- Columbus was identified as one of America's most frugal metro areas by *Coupons.com*. The city ranked #20 out of 25. Criteria: digital coupon usage. *Coupons.com, "America's Most Frugal Cities of 2017," March 22, 2018*

- The Columbus metro area appeared on the Milken Institute "2022 Best Performing Cities" list. Rank: #80 out of 200 large metro areas (population over 250,000). Criteria: job growth; wage and salary growth; high-tech output growth; housing affordability; household broadband access. *Milken Institute, "Best-Performing Cities 2022," March 28, 2022*

- *Forbes* ranked the 200 most populous metro areas to determine the nation's "Best Places for Business and Careers." The Columbus metro area was ranked #28. Criteria: costs (business and living); job growth (past and projected); income growth; quality of life; educational attainment (college and high school); projected economic growth; cultural and leisure opportunities; workplace tolerance laws; net migration patterns. *Forbes, "The Best Places for Business and Careers 2019: Seattle Still On Top," October 30, 2019*

Education Rankings

- Personal finance website *WalletHub* analyzed the 150 largest U.S. metropolitan statistical areas to determine where the most educated Americans are putting their degrees to work. Criteria: education levels; percentage of workers with degrees; education quality and attainment gap; public school quality rankings; quality and enrollment of each metro area's universities. Columbus was ranked #46 (#1 = most educated city). *www.WalletHub.com, "Most & Least Educated Cities in America," July 18, 2022*

- Columbus was selected as one of America's most literate cities. The city ranked #25 out of the 84 largest U.S. cities. Criteria: number of booksellers; library resources; Internet resources; educational attainment; periodical publishing resources; newspaper circulation. *Central Connecticut State University, "America's Most Literate Cities, 2018," February 2019*

Environmental Rankings

- Sperling's BestPlaces assessed the 50 largest metropolitan areas of the United States for the likelihood of dangerously extreme weather events or earthquakes. In general the Southeast and South-Central regions have the highest risk of weather extremes and earthquakes, while the Pacific Northwest enjoys the lowest risk. Of the least risky metropolitan areas, the Columbus metro area was ranked #10. *www.bestplaces.net, "Avoid Natural Disasters: BestPlaces Reveals The Top 10 Safest Places to Live," October 25, 2017*

Food/Drink Rankings

- The U.S. Chamber of Commerce Foundation conducted an in-depth study on local food truck regulations, surveyed 288 food truck owners, and ranked 20 major American cities based on how friendly they are for operating a food truck. The compiled index assessed the following: procedures for obtaining permits and licenses; complying with restrictions; and financial obligations associated with operating a food truck. Columbus ranked #15 overall (1 being the best). *www.foodtrucknation.us, "Food Truck Nation," March 20, 2018*

Health/Fitness Rankings

- For each of the 100 largest cities in the United States, the American Fitness Index®, compiled in partnership between the American College of Sports Medicine and the Elevance Health Foundation, evaluated community infrastructure and 34 health behaviors including preventive health, levels of chronic disease conditions, food insecurity, sleep quality, pedestrian safety, air quality, and community/environment resources that support physical activity. Columbus ranked #76 for "community fitness." *americanfitnessindex.org, "2022 ACSM American Fitness Index Summary Report," July 12, 2022*

- The Columbus metro area was identified as one of the worst cities for bed bugs in America by pest control company Orkin. The area ranked #10 out of 50 based on the number of bed bug treatments Orkin performed from December 2021 to November 2022. *Orkin, "The Windy City Can't Blow Bed Bugs Away: Chicago Ranks #1 For Third Consecutive Year On Orkin's Bed Bug Cities List," January 9, 2023*

- Columbus was identified as a "2022 Spring Allergy Capital." The area ranked #36 out of 100. Three groups of factors were used to identify the most challenging cities for people with allergies during the spring season: annual spring pollen scores; over the counter allergy medicine use; number of board-certified allergy specialists. *Asthma and Allergy Foundation of America, "Spring Allergy Capitals 2022," March 2, 2022*

- Columbus was identified as a "2022 Fall Allergy Capital." The area ranked #42 out of 100. Three groups of factors were used to identify the most challenging cities for people with allergies during the fall season: annual fall pollen scores; over the counter allergy medicine use; number of board-certified allergy specialists. *Asthma and Allergy Foundation of America, "Fall Allergy Capitals 2022," March 2, 2022*

- Columbus was identified as a "2022 Asthma Capital." The area ranked #11 out of the nation's 100 largest metropolitan areas. Criteria: estimated asthma prevalence; asthma-related mortality; and ER visits due to asthma. Risk factors analyzed but not factored in the rankings: annual pollen score; annual air quality; public smoking laws; access to board-certified asthma specialists; rescue and controller medication use; uninsured rate; poverty rate. *Asthma and Allergy Foundation of America, "Asthma Capitals 2022: The Most Challenging Places to Live With Asthma," September 14, 2022*

Real Estate Rankings

- *WalletHub* compared the most populated U.S. cities to determine which had the best markets for real estate agents. Columbus ranked #116 where demand was high and pay was the best. Criteria: sales per agent; annual median wage for real-estate agents; monthly average starting salary for real estate agents; real estate job density and competition; unemployment rate; home turnover rate; housing-market health index; and other relevant metrics. *www.WalletHub.com, "2021 Best Places to Be a Real Estate Agent," May 12, 2021*

- The Columbus metro area was identified as one of the nations's 20 hottest housing markets in 2023. Criteria: listing views as an indicator of demand and number of days on the market as an indicator of pace. The area ranked #3. *Realtor.com, "January 2023 Top 20 Hottest Housing Markets," February 23, 2023*

- Columbus was ranked #99 out of 235 metro areas in terms of housing affordability in 2022 by the National Association of Home Builders (#1 = most affordable). Criteria: the share of homes sold in that area affordable to a family earning the local median income, based on standard mortgage underwriting criteria. *National Association of Home Builders®, NAHB-Wells Fargo Housing Opportunity Index, 4th Quarter 2022*

Safety Rankings

- Allstate ranked the 200 largest cities in America in terms of driver safety. Columbus ranked #141. Criteria: internal property damage claims over a two-year period from January 2016 to December 2017. The report helps increase the importance of safety and awareness behind the wheel. *Allstate, "Allstate America's Best Drivers Report, 2019" June 24, 2019*

- The National Insurance Crime Bureau ranked 390 metro areas in the U.S. in terms of per capita rates of vehicle theft. The Columbus metro area ranked #65 (#1 = highest rate). Criteria: number of vehicle theft offenses per 100,000 inhabitants in 2021. *National Insurance Crime Bureau, "Hot Spots 2021," September 1, 2022*

Seniors/Retirement Rankings

- From its Best Cities for Successful Aging indexes, the Milken Institute generated rankings for metropolitan areas, weighing data in nine categories—health care, wellness, living arrangements, transportation and convenience, financial characteristics, education, employment, community engagement, and overall livability. The Columbus metro area was ranked #49 overall in the large metro area category. *Milken Institute, "Best Cities for Successful Aging, 2017" March 14, 2017*

Sports/Recreation Rankings

- Columbus was chosen as one of America's best cities for bicycling. The city ranked #39 out of 50. Criteria: cycling infrastructure that is safe and friendly for all ages; energy and bike culture. The editors evaluated cities with populations of 100,000 or more. *Bicycling, "The 50 Best Bike Cities in America," October 10, 2018*

Women/Minorities Rankings

- Personal finance website *WalletHub* compared more than 180 U.S. cities across two key dimensions, "Hispanic Business-Friendliness" and "Hispanic Purchasing Power," to arrive at the most favorable conditions for Hispanic entrepreneurs. Columbus was ranked #113 out of 182. Criteria includes: share of Hispanic-Owned Businesses; Hispanic entrepreneurship rate to median annual income of Hispanics; Small Business-Friendliness score; cost of living; and number of Hispanics with at least a bachelor's degree. *WalletHub.com, "2019's Best Cities for Hispanic Entrepreneurs," May 1, 2019*

Miscellaneous Rankings

- *WalletHub* compared the 150 most populated U.S. cities to determine their operating efficiency. A "Quality of Services" score was constructed for each city and then divided by the total budget per capita to reveal which were managed the best. Columbus ranked #92. Criteria: financial stability; economy; education; safety; health; infrastructure and pollution. *www.WalletHub.com, "2022's Best- & Worst-Run Cities in America," June 21, 2022*

Business Environment

DEMOGRAPHICS

Population Growth

Area	1990 Census	2000 Census	2010 Census	2020 Census	Population Growth (%) 1990-2020	Population Growth (%) 2010-2020
City	648,656	711,470	787,033	905,748	39.6	15.1
MSA[1]	1,405,176	1,612,694	1,836,536	2,138,926	52.2	16.5
U.S.	248,709,873	281,421,906	308,745,538	331,449,281	33.3	7.4

Note: (1) Figures cover the Columbus, OH Metropolitan Statistical Area
Source: U.S. Census Bureau, 1990 Census, 2000 Census, 2010 Census, 2020 Census

Race

Area	White Alone[2] (%)	Black Alone[2] (%)	Asian Alone[2] (%)	AIAN[3] Alone[2] (%)	NHOPI[4] Alone[2] (%)	Other Race Alone[2] (%)	Two or More Races (%)
City	53.2	28.6	6.2	0.4	0.0	4.3	7.2
MSA[1]	70.1	15.7	4.9	0.3	0.0	2.7	6.3
U.S.	61.6	12.4	6.0	1.1	0.2	8.4	10.2

Note: (1) Figures cover the Columbus, OH Metropolitan Statistical Area; (2) Alone is defined as not being in combination with one or more other races; (3) American Indian and Alaska Native; (4) Native Hawaiian and Other Pacific Islander
Source: U.S. Census Bureau, 2020 Census

Hispanic or Latino Origin

Area	Total (%)	Mexican (%)	Puerto Rican (%)	Cuban (%)	Other (%)
City	6.5	3.1	1.0	0.1	2.3
MSA[1]	4.5	2.1	0.8	0.1	1.6
U.S.	18.4	11.2	1.8	0.7	4.7

Note: Persons of Hispanic or Latino origin can be of any race; (1) Figures cover the Columbus, OH Metropolitan Statistical Area
Source: U.S. Census Bureau, 2017-2021 American Community Survey 5-Year Estimates

Age

Area	Percent of Population Under Age 5	Age 5–19	Age 20–34	Age 35–44	Age 45–54	Age 55–64	Age 65–74	Age 75–84	Age 85+	Median Age
City	6.6	18.1	30.0	13.4	10.7	10.3	6.9	2.9	1.2	32.3
MSA[1]	6.2	19.8	22.2	13.4	12.3	12.0	8.6	3.9	1.5	36.2
U.S.	5.6	19.2	20.2	12.7	12.4	13.1	10.0	4.9	1.9	38.8

Note: (1) Figures cover the Columbus, OH Metropolitan Statistical Area
Source: U.S. Census Bureau, 2020 Census

Disability by Age

Area	All Ages	Under 18 Years Old	18 to 64 Years Old	65 Years and Over
City	11.6	5.2	10.3	34.5
MSA[1]	11.9	5.0	10.1	32.7
U.S.	12.6	4.4	10.3	33.4

Note: Figures show percent of the civilian noninstitutionalized population that reported having a disability. Disability status is determined from six types of difficulty: vision, hearing, cognitive, ambulatory, self-care, and independent living. For children under 5 years old, hearing and vision difficulty are used to determine disability status. For children between the ages of 5 and 14, disability status is determined from hearing, vision, cognitive, ambulatory, and self-care difficulties. For people aged 15 years and older, they are considered to have a disability if they have difficulty with any one of the six difficulty types; Note: (1) Figures cover the Columbus, OH Metropolitan Statistical Area
Source: U.S. Census Bureau, 2017-2021 American Community Survey 5-Year Estimates

Ancestry

Area	German	Irish	English	American	Italian	Polish	French[2]	Scottish	Dutch
City	15.2	10.2	6.9	4.0	4.9	2.1	1.3	1.6	0.8
MSA[1]	20.7	12.7	9.6	5.7	5.2	2.3	1.7	2.1	1.1
U.S.	12.8	9.6	8.1	5.7	5.0	2.7	2.2	1.6	1.1

Note: Figures are the percentage of the total population reporting a particular ancestry. The nine most commonly reported ancestries in the U.S. are shown. Figures include multiple ancestries (e.g. if a person reported being Irish and Italian, they were included in both columns); (1) Figures cover the Columbus, OH Metropolitan Statistical Area; (2) Excludes Basque
Source: U.S. Census Bureau, 2017-2021 American Community Survey 5-Year Estimates

Foreign-born Population

Area	Percent of Population Born in								
	Any Foreign Country	Asia	Mexico	Europe	Caribbean	Central America[2]	South America	Africa	Canada
City	13.3	5.0	1.1	0.9	0.5	0.8	0.4	4.7	0.1
MSA[1]	8.8	3.7	0.7	0.8	0.3	0.4	0.3	2.4	0.1
U.S.	13.6	4.2	3.3	1.5	1.4	1.1	1.1	0.8	0.2

Note: (1) Figures cover the Columbus, OH Metropolitan Statistical Area; (2) Excludes Mexico.
Source: U.S. Census Bureau, 2017-2021 American Community Survey 5-Year Estimates

Household Size

Area	Persons in Household (%)							Average Household Size
	One	Two	Three	Four	Five	Six	Seven or More	
City	35.8	32.7	13.4	10.2	4.9	1.7	1.3	2.30
MSA[1]	28.8	33.9	15.3	12.9	5.9	2.1	1.2	2.50
U.S.	28.1	33.8	15.5	12.9	6.0	2.3	1.4	2.60

Note: (1) Figures cover the Columbus, OH Metropolitan Statistical Area
Source: U.S. Census Bureau, 2017-2021 American Community Survey 5-Year Estimates

Household Relationships

Area	House-holder	Opposite-sex Spouse	Same-sex Spouse	Opposite-sex Unmarried Partner	Same-sex Unmarried Partner	Child[2]	Grand-child	Other Relatives	Non-relatives
City	42.2	12.9	0.3	3.6	0.3	26.2	2.1	4.4	5.2
MSA[1]	39.4	17.4	0.2	2.9	0.2	28.5	2.0	3.5	3.3
U.S.	38.3	17.5	0.2	2.5	0.2	28.3	2.4	4.8	3.4

Note: Figures are percent of the total population; (1) Figures cover the Columbus, OH Metropolitan Statistical Area; (2) Includes biological, adopted, and stepchildren of the householder
Source: U.S. Census Bureau, 2020 Census

Gender

Area	Males	Females	Males per 100 Females
City	441,869	463,879	95.3
MSA[1]	1,050,767	1,088,159	96.6
U.S.	162,685,811	168,763,470	96.4

Note: (1) Figures cover the Columbus, OH Metropolitan Statistical Area
Source: U.S. Census Bureau, 2020 Census

Marital Status

Area	Never Married	Now Married[2]	Separated	Widowed	Divorced
City	45.4	36.7	2.1	4.2	11.6
MSA[1]	34.8	47.6	1.7	4.8	11.1
U.S.	33.8	48.0	1.8	5.6	10.8

Note: Figures are percentages and cover the population 15 years of age and older; (1) Figures cover the Columbus, OH Metropolitan Statistical Area; (2) Excludes separated
Source: U.S. Census Bureau, 2017-2021 American Community Survey 5-Year Estimates

Religious Groups by Family

Area	Catholic	Baptist	Methodist	LDS[2]	Pentecostal	Lutheran	Islam	Adventist	Other
MSA[1]	11.7	3.4	3.0	0.8	1.9	1.7	2.1	0.9	17.5
U.S.	18.7	7.3	3.0	2.0	1.8	1.7	1.3	1.3	11.6

Note: Figures are the number of adherents as a percentage of the total population and cover the eight largest religious groups in the U.S; (1) Figures cover the Columbus, OH Metropolitan Statistical Area; (2) Church of Jesus Christ of Latter-day Saints
Sources: 2020 U.S. Religion Census, Association of Statisticians of American Religious Bodies; The Association of Religion Data Archives (ARDA)

Religious Groups by Tradition

Area	Catholic	Evangelical Protestant	Mainline Protestant	Black Protestant	Islam	Judaism	Hinduism	Orthodox	Buddhism
MSA[1]	11.7	18.1	6.8	1.5	2.1	0.4	0.4	0.5	0.2
U.S.	18.7	16.5	5.2	2.3	1.3	0.6	0.4	0.4	0.3

Note: Figures are the number of adherents as a percentage of the total population; (1) Figures cover the Columbus, OH Metropolitan Statistical Area
Sources: 2020 U.S. Religion Census, Association of Statisticians of American Religious Bodies; The Association of Religion Data Archives (ARDA)

Columbus, Ohio **143**

ECONOMY

Gross Metropolitan Product

Area	2020	2021	2022	2023	Rank[2]
MSA[1]	137.3	151.0	164.2	175.3	33

Note: Figures are in billions of dollars; (1) Figures cover the Columbus, OH Metropolitan Statistical Area; (2) Rank is based on 2021 data and ranges from 1 to 381
Source: U.S. Conference of Mayors, U.S. Metro Economies: U.S. Metros Compared to Global and State Economies, June 2022

Economic Growth

Area	2018-20 (%)	2021 (%)	2022 (%)	2023 (%)	Rank[2]
MSA[1]	0.1	5.8	3.1	3.5	136
U.S.	-0.6	5.7	3.1	2.9	–

Note: Figures are real gross metropolitan product (GMP) growth rates and represent average annual percent change; (1) Figures cover the Columbus, OH Metropolitan Statistical Area; (2) Rank is based on 2020 2-year average annual percent change and ranges from 1 to 381
Source: U.S. Conference of Mayors, U.S. Metro Economies: U.S. Metros Compared to Global and State Economies, June 2022

Metropolitan Area Exports

Area	2016	2017	2018	2019	2020	2021	Rank[2]
MSA[1]	5,675.4	5,962.2	7,529.5	7,296.6	6,304.8	6,557.9	51

Note: Figures are in millions of dollars; (1) Figures cover the Columbus, OH Metropolitan Statistical Area; (2) Rank is based on 2021 data and ranges from 1 to 388
Source: U.S. Department of Commerce, International Trade Administration, Office of Trade and Economic Analysis, Industry and Analysis, Exports by Metropolitan Area, data extracted March 16, 2023

Building Permits

Area	Single-Family			Multi-Family			Total		
	2021	2022	Pct. Chg.	2021	2022	Pct. Chg.	2021	2022	Pct. Chg.
City	913	642	-29.7	3,555	5,535	55.7	4,468	6,177	38.2
MSA[1]	6,844	5,623	-17.8	5,218	6,472	24.0	12,062	12,095	0.3
U.S.	1,115,400	975,600	-12.5	621,600	689,500	10.9	1,737,000	1,665,100	-4.1

Note: (1) Figures cover the Columbus, OH Metropolitan Statistical Area; Figures represent new, privately-owned housing units authorized (unadjusted data); All permit data are based on estimates with imputation
Source: U.S. Census Bureau, Manufacturing, Mining, and Construction Statistics, Building Permits, 2021, 2022

Bankruptcy Filings

Area	Business Filings			Nonbusiness Filings		
	2021	2022	% Chg.	2021	2022	% Chg.
Franklin County	128	38	-70.3	2,223	2,029	-8.7
U.S.	14,347	13,481	-6.0	399,269	374,240	-6.3

Note: Business filings include Chapter 7, Chapter 9, Chapter 11, Chapter 12, Chapter 13, Chapter 15, and Section 304; Nonbusiness filings include Chapter 7, Chapter 11, and Chapter 13
Source: Administrative Office of the U.S. Courts, Business and Nonbusiness Bankruptcy, County Cases Commenced by Chapter of the Bankruptcy Code, During the 12-Month Period Ending December 31, 2021 and Business and Nonbusiness Bankruptcy, County Cases Commenced by Chapter of the Bankruptcy Code, During the 12-Month Period Ending December 31, 2022

Housing Vacancy Rates

Area	Gross Vacancy Rate[2] (%)			Year-Round Vacancy Rate[3] (%)			Rental Vacancy Rate[4] (%)			Homeowner Vacancy Rate[5] (%)		
	2020	2021	2022	2020	2021	2022	2020	2021	2022	2020	2021	2022
MSA[1]	4.7	6.8	5.6	4.5	6.6	5.4	5.9	6.5	3.8	0.3	0.8	0.8
U.S.	10.6	10.8	10.5	8.2	8.4	8.2	6.3	6.1	5.8	1.0	0.9	0.8

Note: (1) Figures cover the Columbus, OH Metropolitan Statistical Area; (2) The percentage of the total housing inventory that is vacant; (3) The percentage of the housing inventory (excluding seasonal units) that is year-round vacant; (4) The percentage of rental inventory that is vacant for rent; (5) The percentage of homeowner inventory that is vacant for sale
Source: U.S. Census Bureau, Housing Vacancies and Homeownership Annual Statistics: 2020, 2021, 2022

INCOME

Income

Area	Per Capita ($)	Median Household ($)	Average Household ($)
City	32,481	58,575	75,482
MSA[1]	38,167	71,020	95,315
U.S.	37,638	69,021	97,196

Note: (1) Figures cover the Columbus, OH Metropolitan Statistical Area
Source: U.S. Census Bureau, 2017-2021 American Community Survey 5-Year Estimates

144 Columbus, Ohio

Household Income Distribution

Area	Percent of Households Earning							
	Under $15,000	$15,000 -$24,999	$25,000 -$34,999	$35,000 -$49,999	$50,000 -$74,999	$75,000 -$99,999	$100,000 -$149,999	$150,000 and up
City	10.8	8.4	9.5	13.6	19.5	13.5	15.3	9.5
MSA[1]	8.1	7.0	7.9	11.6	17.9	13.3	17.6	16.6
U.S.	9.4	7.8	8.2	11.4	16.8	12.8	16.3	17.3

Note: (1) Figures cover the Columbus, OH Metropolitan Statistical Area
Source: U.S. Census Bureau, 2017-2021 American Community Survey 5-Year Estimates

Poverty Rate

Area	All Ages	Under 18 Years Old	18 to 64 Years Old	65 Years and Over
City	18.4	27.1	16.5	11.6
MSA[1]	12.3	17.0	11.5	7.7
U.S.	12.6	17.0	11.8	9.6

Note: Figures are percentage of people whose income during the past 12 months was below the poverty level;
(1) Figures cover the Columbus, OH Metropolitan Statistical Area
Source: U.S. Census Bureau, 2017-2021 American Community Survey 5-Year Estimates

EMPLOYMENT

Labor Force and Employment

Area	Civilian Labor Force			Workers Employed		
	Dec. 2021	Dec. 2022	% Chg.	Dec. 2021	Dec. 2022	% Chg.
City	484,399	482,990	-0.3	469,341	467,547	-0.4
MSA[1]	1,121,138	1,118,600	-0.2	1,088,089	1,084,246	-0.4
U.S.	161,696,000	164,224,000	1.6	155,732,000	158,872,000	2.0

Note: Data is not seasonally adjusted and covers workers 16 years of age and older; (1) Figures cover the Columbus, OH Metropolitan Statistical Area
Source: Bureau of Labor Statistics, Local Area Unemployment Statistics

Unemployment Rate

Area	2022											
	Jan.	Feb.	Mar.	Apr.	May	Jun.	Jul.	Aug.	Sep.	Oct.	Nov.	Dec.
City	3.9	3.8	3.4	3.1	3.1	3.9	3.8	4.0	3.4	3.7	2.9	3.2
MSA[1]	3.8	3.7	3.3	2.9	2.9	3.8	3.7	3.8	3.3	3.5	2.7	3.1
U.S.	4.4	4.1	3.8	3.3	3.4	3.8	3.8	3.8	3.3	3.4	3.4	3.3

Note: Data is not seasonally adjusted and covers workers 16 years of age and older; (1) Figures cover the Columbus, OH Metropolitan Statistical Area
Source: Bureau of Labor Statistics, Local Area Unemployment Statistics

Average Wages

Occupation	$/Hr.	Occupation	$/Hr.
Accountants and Auditors	38.54	Maintenance and Repair Workers	23.16
Automotive Mechanics	23.63	Marketing Managers	69.18
Bookkeepers	22.84	Network and Computer Systems Admin.	47.97
Carpenters	26.80	Nurses, Licensed Practical	26.41
Cashiers	12.98	Nurses, Registered	38.80
Computer Programmers	44.12	Nursing Assistants	16.67
Computer Systems Analysts	48.82	Office Clerks, General	20.13
Computer User Support Specialists	26.03	Physical Therapists	48.56
Construction Laborers	26.04	Physicians	102.84
Cooks, Restaurant	15.34	Plumbers, Pipefitters and Steamfitters	31.99
Customer Service Representatives	20.25	Police and Sheriff's Patrol Officers	37.43
Dentists	69.07	Postal Service Mail Carriers	27.37
Electricians	29.48	Real Estate Sales Agents	21.29
Engineers, Electrical	53.22	Retail Salespersons	16.00
Fast Food and Counter Workers	12.65	Sales Representatives, Technical/Scientific	58.13
Financial Managers	71.54	Secretaries, Exc. Legal/Medical/Executive	20.96
First-Line Supervisors of Office Workers	32.35	Security Guards	17.83
General and Operations Managers	57.91	Surgeons	n/a
Hairdressers/Cosmetologists	20.68	Teacher Assistants, Exc. Postsecondary*	16.49
Home Health and Personal Care Aides	13.75	Teachers, Secondary School, Exc. Sp. Ed.*	34.42
Janitors and Cleaners	16.00	Telemarketers	15.65
Landscaping/Groundskeeping Workers	17.46	Truck Drivers, Heavy/Tractor-Trailer	26.61
Lawyers	65.26	Truck Drivers, Light/Delivery Services	22.93
Maids and Housekeeping Cleaners	13.91	Waiters and Waitresses	15.07

Note: Wage data covers the Columbus, OH Metropolitan Statistical Area; (*) Hourly wages were calculated from annual wage data based on a 40 hour work week; n/a not available.
Source: Bureau of Labor Statistics, Metro Area Occupational Employment & Wage Estimates, May 2022

Employment by Industry

Sector	MSA[1]		U.S.
	Number of Employees	Percent of Total	Percent of Total
Construction, Mining, and Logging	47,800	4.2	5.4
Private Education and Health Services	161,900	14.1	16.1
Financial Activities	83,900	7.3	5.9
Government	184,300	16.0	14.5
Information	18,000	1.6	2.0
Leisure and Hospitality	105,100	9.1	10.3
Manufacturing	73,700	6.4	8.4
Other Services	43,200	3.8	3.7
Professional and Business Services	190,300	16.5	14.7
Retail Trade	103,700	9.0	10.2
Transportation, Warehousing, and Utilities	97,900	8.5	4.9
Wholesale Trade	41,100	3.6	3.9

Note: Figures are non-farm employment as of December 2022. Figures are not seasonally adjusted and include workers 16 years of age and older; (1) Figures cover the Columbus, OH Metropolitan Statistical Area
Source: Bureau of Labor Statistics, Current Employment Statistics, Employment, Hours, and Earnings

Employment by Occupation

Occupation Classification	City (%)	MSA[1] (%)	U.S. (%)
Management, Business, Science, and Arts	42.6	44.5	40.3
Natural Resources, Construction, and Maintenance	4.9	6.0	8.7
Production, Transportation, and Material Moving	14.2	13.4	13.1
Sales and Office	21.4	20.8	20.9
Service	16.9	15.3	17.0

Note: Figures cover employed civilians 16 years of age and older; (1) Figures cover the Columbus, OH Metropolitan Statistical Area
Source: U.S. Census Bureau, 2017-2021 American Community Survey 5-Year Estimates

Occupations with Greatest Projected Employment Growth: 2022 – 2024

Occupation[1]	2022 Employment	2024 Projected Employment	Numeric Employment Change	Percent Employment Change
Stockers and Order Fillers	110,530	116,860	6,330	5.7
Laborers and Freight, Stock, and Material Movers, Hand	111,490	117,260	5,770	5.2
Industrial Truck and Tractor Operators	37,740	41,280	3,540	9.4
Heavy and Tractor-Trailer Truck Drivers	93,730	97,190	3,460	3.7
Cooks, Restaurant	49,740	52,350	2,610	5.2
Light Truck or Delivery Services Drivers	34,850	37,020	2,170	6.2
Construction Laborers	40,690	42,580	1,890	4.6
Landscaping and Groundskeeping Workers	42,810	44,630	1,820	4.3
Retail Salespersons	126,620	128,200	1,580	1.2
Janitors and Cleaners, Except Maids and Housekeeping Cleaners	75,960	77,460	1,500	2.0

Note: Projections cover Ohio; (1) Sorted by numeric employment change
Source: www.projectionscentral.com, State Occupational Projections, 2022–2024 Short-Term Projections

Fastest-Growing Occupations: 2022 – 2024

Occupation[1]	2022 Employment	2024 Projected Employment	Numeric Employment Change	Percent Employment Change
Statisticians	630	690	60	9.5
Industrial Truck and Tractor Operators	37,740	41,280	3,540	9.4
Machine Feeders and Offbearers	2,290	2,480	190	8.3
Nurse Practitioners	10,530	11,380	850	8.1
Information Security Analysts (SOC 2018)	4,290	4,610	320	7.5
Aerospace Engineering and Operations Technicians	980	1,050	70	7.1
Taxi Drivers	3,820	4,090	270	7.1
Logisticians	7,900	8,420	520	6.6
Amusement and Recreation Attendants	9,160	9,740	580	6.3
Light Truck or Delivery Services Drivers	34,850	37,020	2,170	6.2

Note: Projections cover Ohio; (1) Sorted by percent employment change and excludes occupations with numeric employment change less than 50
Source: www.projectionscentral.com, State Occupational Projections, 2022–2024 Short-Term Projections

146   Columbus, Ohio

CITY FINANCES

City Government Finances

Component	2020 ($000)	2020 ($ per capita)
Total Revenues	2,214,896	2,465
Total Expenditures	2,384,118	2,653
Debt Outstanding	4,667,973	5,195
Cash and Securities[1]	2,114,374	2,353

Note: (1) Cash and security holdings of a government at the close of its fiscal year, including those of its dependent agencies, utilities, and liquor stores.
Source: U.S. Census Bureau, State & Local Government Finances 2020

City Government Revenue by Source

Source	2020 ($000)	2020 ($ per capita)	2020 (%)
General Revenue			
From Federal Government	146,731	163	6.6
From State Government	59,458	66	2.7
From Local Governments	38,136	42	1.7
Taxes			
Property	51,087	57	2.3
Sales and Gross Receipts	36,926	41	1.7
Personal Income	941,819	1,048	42.5
Corporate Income	0	0	0.0
Motor Vehicle License	0	0	0.0
Other Taxes	33,890	38	1.5
Current Charges	454,000	505	20.5
Liquor Store	0	0	0.0
Utility	279,932	312	12.6

Source: U.S. Census Bureau, State & Local Government Finances 2020

City Government Expenditures by Function

Function	2020 ($000)	2020 ($ per capita)	2020 (%)
General Direct Expenditures			
Air Transportation	0	0	0.0
Corrections	0	0	0.0
Education	6,496	7	0.3
Employment Security Administration	0	0	0.0
Financial Administration	61,836	68	2.6
Fire Protection	292,243	325	12.3
General Public Buildings	17,335	19	0.7
Governmental Administration, Other	47,530	52	2.0
Health	61,321	68	2.6
Highways	230,402	256	9.7
Hospitals	0	0	0.0
Housing and Community Development	35,406	39	1.5
Interest on General Debt	123,797	137	5.2
Judicial and Legal	54,487	60	2.3
Libraries	0	0	0.0
Parking	6,544	7	0.3
Parks and Recreation	192,023	213	8.1
Police Protection	361,860	402	15.2
Public Welfare	0	0	0.0
Sewerage	311,860	347	13.1
Solid Waste Management	49,503	55	2.1
Veterans' Services	0	0	0.0
Liquor Store	0	0	0.0
Utility	335,068	372	14.1

Source: U.S. Census Bureau, State & Local Government Finances 2020

TAXES

State Corporate Income Tax Rates

State	Tax Rate (%)	Income Brackets ($)	Num. of Brackets	Financial Institution Tax Rate (%)[a]	Federal Income Tax Ded.
Ohio	(r)	—	—	(r)	No

Note: Tax rates as of January 1, 2023; (a) Rates listed are the corporate income tax rate applied to financial institutions or excise taxes based on income. Some states have other taxes based upon the value of deposits or shares; (r) Ohio no longer levies a tax based on income (except for a particular subset of corporations), but instead imposes a Commercial Activity Tax (CAT) equal to $150 for gross receipts sitused to Ohio of between $150,000 and $1 million, plus 0.26% of gross receipts over $1 million. Banks continue to pay a franchise tax of 1.3% of net worth. For those few corporations for whom the franchise tax on net worth or net income still applies, a litter tax also applies.
Source: Federation of Tax Administrators, State Corporate Income Tax Rates, January 1, 2023

State Individual Income Tax Rates

State	Tax Rate (%)	Income Brackets ($)	Personal Exemptions ($)			Standard Ded. ($)	
			Single	Married	Depend.	Single	Married
Ohio (a)	0.0 - 3.99	26,050 - 115,300	1,900	3,800	1,900 (u)	–	–

Note: Tax rates as of January 1, 2023; Local- and county-level taxes are not included; Federal income tax is not deductible on state income tax returns; (a) 16 states have statutory provision for automatically adjusting to the rate of inflation the dollar values of the income tax brackets, standard deductions, and/or personal exemptions. Oregon does not index the income brackets for $125,000 and over; (u) Ohio provides an additional tax credit of $20 per exemption. Exemption amounts reduced for higher income taxpayers. Business income taxes at a flat 3% rate.
Source: Federation of Tax Administrators, State Individual Income Tax Rates, January 1, 2023

Various State Sales and Excise Tax Rates

State	State Sales Tax (%)	Gasoline[1] ($/gal.)	Cigarette[2] ($/pack)	Spirits[3] ($/gal.)	Wine[4] ($/gal.)	Beer[5] ($/gal.)	Recreational Marijuana (%)
Ohio	5.75	0.3851	1.60	11.38	0.32	0.18	Not legal

Note: All tax rates as of January 1, 2023; (1) The American Petroleum Institute has developed a methodology for determining the average tax rate on a gallon of fuel. Rates may include any of the following: excise taxes, environmental fees, storage tank fees, other fees or taxes, general sales tax, and local taxes; (2) The federal excise tax of $1.0066 per pack and local taxes are not included; (3) Rates are those applicable to off-premise sales of 40% alcohol by volume (a.b.v.) distilled spirits in 750ml containers. Local excise taxes are excluded; (4) Rates are those applicable to off-premise sales of 11% a.b.v. non-carbonated wine in 750ml containers; (5) Rates are those applicable to off-premise sales of 4.7% a.b.v. beer in 12 ounce containers.
Source: Tax Foundation, 2023 Facts & Figures: How Does Your State Compare?

State Business Tax Climate Index Rankings

State	Overall Rank	Corporate Tax Rank	Individual Income Tax Rank	Sales Tax Rank	Property Tax Rank	Unemployment Insurance Tax Rank
Ohio	37	39	41	36	6	13

Note: The index is a measure of how each state's tax laws affect economic performance. The lower the rank, the more favorable a state's tax system is for business. States without a given tax are given a ranking of 1. The scores/rankings for the District of Columbia do not affect other states. The 2023 index represents the tax climate as of July 1, 2022.
Source: Tax Foundation, State Business Tax Climate Index 2023

TRANSPORTATION

Means of Transportation to Work

Area	Car/Truck/Van		Public Transportation			Bicycle	Walked	Other Means	Worked at Home
	Drove Alone	Car-pooled	Bus	Subway	Railroad				
City	75.0	7.2	2.5	0.0	0.0	0.4	2.7	1.1	11.0
MSA[1]	77.1	6.7	1.3	0.0	0.0	0.3	2.0	1.0	11.6
U.S.	73.2	8.6	2.0	1.6	0.5	0.5	2.5	1.5	9.7

Note: Figures are percentages and cover workers 16 years of age and older; (1) Figures cover the Columbus, OH Metropolitan Statistical Area
Source: U.S. Census Bureau, 2017-2021 American Community Survey 5-Year Estimates

Travel Time to Work

Area	Less Than 10 Minutes	10 to 19 Minutes	20 to 29 Minutes	30 to 44 Minutes	45 to 59 Minutes	60 to 89 Minutes	90 Minutes or More
City	10.3	34.2	30.4	18.7	3.2	1.9	1.3
MSA[1]	11.4	29.5	26.7	21.7	6.1	3.1	1.5
U.S.	12.4	28.5	21.0	20.9	8.2	6.2	2.9

Note: Note: Figures are percentages and include workers 16 years old and over; (1) Figures cover the Columbus, OH Metropolitan Statistical Area
Source: U.S. Census Bureau, 2017-2021 American Community Survey 5-Year Estimates

Key Congestion Measures

Measure	1990	2000	2010	2015	2020
Annual Hours of Delay, Total (000)	12,273	25,284	35,331	43,524	26,055
Annual Hours of Delay, Per Auto Commuter	27	38	41	47	27
Annual Congestion Cost, Per Auto Commuter ($)	536	827	919	1,045	645

Note: Covers the Columbus OH urban area
Source: Texas A&M Transportation Institute, 2021 Urban Mobility Report

Freeway Travel Time Index

Measure	1985	1990	1995	2000	2005	2010	2015	2020
Urban Area Index[1]	1.09	1.12	1.15	1.17	1.18	1.17	1.18	1.08
Urban Area Rank[1,2]	36	35	36	36	41	41	41	44

Note: Freeway Travel Time Index—the ratio of travel time in the peak period to the travel time at free-flow conditions. For example, a value of 1.30 indicates a 20-minute free-flow trip takes 26 minutes in the peak (20 minutes x 1.30 = 26 minutes); (1) Covers the Columbus OH urban area; (2) Rank is based on 101 larger urban areas (#1 = highest travel time index)
Source: Texas A&M Transportation Institute, 2021 Urban Mobility Report

Public Transportation

Agency Name / Mode of Transportation	Vehicles Operated in Maximum Service[1]	Annual Unlinked Passenger Trips[2] (in thous.)	Annual Passenger Miles[3] (in thous.)
Central Ohio Transit Authority (COTA)			
Bus (directly operated)	219	8,899.8	36,048.9
Demand Response (directly operated)	17	50.8	189.4
Demand Response (purchased transportation)	47	191.7	2,279.6

Note: (1) Number of revenue vehicles operated by the given mode and type of service to meet the annual maximum service requirement. This is the revenue vehicle count during the peak season of the year; on the week and day that maximum service is provided. Vehicles operated in maximum service (VOMS) exclude atypical days and one-time special events; (2) Number of passengers who boarded public transportation vehicles. Passengers are counted each time they board a vehicle no matter how many vehicles they use to travel from their origin to their destination. (3) Sum of the distances ridden by all passengers during the entire fiscal year.
Source: Federal Transit Administration, National Transit Database, 2021

Air Transportation

Airport Name and Code / Type of Service	Passenger Airlines[1]	Passenger Enplanements	Freight Carriers[2]	Freight (lbs)
Port Columbus International (CMH)				
Domestic service (U.S. carriers - 2022)	32	3,582,631	11	4,395,569
International service (U.S. carriers - 2021)	3	5,682	0	0

Note: (1) Includes all U.S.-based major, minor and commuter airlines that carried at least one passenger during the year; (2) Includes all U.S.-based airlines and freight carriers that transported at least one pound of freight during the year.
Source: Bureau of Transportation Statistics, The Intermodal Transportation Database, Air Carriers: T-100 Domestic Market (U.S. Carriers), 2022; Bureau of Transportation Statistics, The Intermodal Transportation Database, Air Carriers: T-100 International Market (U.S. Carriers), 2021

BUSINESSES

Major Business Headquarters

Company Name	Industry	Rankings	
		Fortune[1]	Forbes[2]
American Electric Power	Utilities, gas and electric	219	-
Bath & Body Works	Specialty retailers, apparel	435	-
Nationwide	Insurance, property and casualty (mutual)	80	-

Note: (1) Companies that produce a 10-K are ranked 1 to 500 based on 2021 revenue; (2) All private companies with at least $2 billion in annual revenue through the end of their most current fiscal year are ranked 1 to 246; companies listed are headquartered in the city; dashes indicate no ranking
Source: Fortune, "Fortune 500," 2022; Forbes, "America's Largest Private Companies," 2022

Fastest-Growing Businesses

According to *Initiative for a Competitive Inner City (ICIC)*, Columbus is home to one of America's 100 fastest-growing "inner city" companies: **Dos Hermanos Taco Truck** (#41). Criteria for inclusion: company must be headquartered in or have 51 percent or more of its physical operations in an economically distressed urban area; must be an independent, for-profit corporation, partnership or proprietorship; must have 10 or more employees and have a five-year sales history that includes sales of at least $200,000 in the base year and at least $1 million in the current year with no decrease in sales over the two most recent years. Companies were ranked overall by revenue growth over the five-year period between 2017 and 2021. *Initiative for a Competitive Inner City (ICIC), "Inner City 100 Companies," 2022*

According to Deloitte, Columbus is home to one of North America's 500 fastest-growing high-technology companies: **Beam Benefits** (#189). Companies are ranked by percentage growth in revenue over a four-year period. Criteria for inclusion: company must be headquartered within North America; must own proprietary intellectual property or technology that is sold to customers in products that contributes to a significant portion of the company's operating revenue; must have been in business for a minumum of four years with 2018 operating revenues of at least $50,000 USD/CD and 2021 operating revenues of at least $5 million USD/CD. *Deloitte, 2022 Technology Fast 500[TM]*

Living Environment

COST OF LIVING

Cost of Living Index

Composite Index	Groceries	Housing	Utilities	Trans-portation	Health Care	Misc. Goods/ Services
89.7	96.7	79.6	93.4	89.6	86.5	94.3

Note: The Cost of Living Index measures regional differences in the cost of consumer goods and services, excluding taxes and non-consumer expenditures, for professional and managerial households in the top income quintile. It is based on more than 50,000 prices covering almost 60 different items for which prices are collected three times a year by chambers of commerce, economic development organizations or university applied economic centers in each participating urban area. The numbers shown should be read as a percentage above or below the national average of 100. For example, a value of 115.4 in the groceries column indicates that grocery prices are 15.4% higher than the national average. Small differences in the index numbers should not be interpreted as significant; Figures cover the Columbus OH urban area.
Source: The Council for Community and Economic Research, Cost of Living Index, 2022

Grocery Prices

Area[1]	T-Bone Steak ($/pound)	Frying Chicken ($/pound)	Whole Milk ($/half gal.)	Eggs ($/dozen)	Orange Juice ($/64 oz.)	Coffee ($/11.5 oz.)
City[2]	14.20	1.44	1.93	1.99	4.00	5.76
Avg.	13.81	1.59	2.43	2.25	3.85	4.95
Min.	10.17	0.90	1.51	1.30	2.90	3.46
Max.	19.35	3.30	4.32	4.32	5.31	8.59

*Note: (1) Values for the local area are compared with the average, minimum and maximum values for all 286 areas in the Cost of Living Index; (2) Figures cover the Columbus OH urban area; **T-Bone Steak** (price per pound); **Frying Chicken** (price per pound, whole fryer); **Whole Milk** (half gallon carton); **Eggs** (price per dozen, Grade A, large); **Orange Juice** (64 oz. Tropicana or Florida Natural); **Coffee** (11.5 oz. can, vacuum-packed, Maxwell House, Hills Bros, or Folgers).*
Source: The Council for Community and Economic Research, Cost of Living Index, 2022

Housing and Utility Costs

Area[1]	New Home Price ($)	Apartment Rent ($/month)	All Electric ($/month)	Part Electric ($/month)	Other Energy ($/month)	Telephone ($/month)
City[2]	366,506	1,200	-	88.37	72.63	184.15
Avg.	450,913	1,371	176.41	99.93	76.96	190.22
Min.	229,283	546	100.84	31.56	27.15	174.27
Max.	2,434,977	4,569	356.86	249.59	272.24	208.31

*Note: (1) Values for the local area are compared with the average, minimum and maximum values for all 286 areas in the Cost of Living Index; (2) Figures cover the Columbus OH urban area; **New Home Price** (2,400 sf living area, 8,000 sf lot, in urban area with full utilities); **Apartment Rent** (950 sf 2 bedroom/1.5 or 2 bath, unfurnished, excluding all utilities except water); **All Electric** (average monthly cost for an all-electric home); **Part Electric** (average monthly cost for a part-electric home); **Other Energy** (average monthly cost for natural gas, fuel oil, coal, wood, and any other forms of energy except electricity); **Telephone** (price includes the base monthly rate plus taxes and fees for three lines of mobile phone service).*
Source: The Council for Community and Economic Research, Cost of Living Index, 2022

Health Care, Transportation, and Other Costs

Area[1]	Doctor ($/visit)	Dentist ($/visit)	Optometrist ($/visit)	Gasoline ($/gallon)	Beauty Salon ($/visit)	Men's Shirt ($)
City[2]	118.38	87.19	61.70	3.77	42.53	38.24
Avg.	124.91	107.77	117.66	3.86	43.31	34.21
Min.	36.61	58.25	51.79	2.90	22.18	13.05
Max.	250.21	162.58	371.96	5.54	85.61	63.54

*Note: (1) Values for the local area are compared with the average, minimum and maximum values for all 286 areas in the Cost of Living Index; (2) Figures cover the Columbus OH urban area; **Doctor** (general practitioners routine exam of an established patient); **Dentist** (adult teeth cleaning and periodic oral examination); **Optometrist** (full vision eye exam for established adult patient); **Gasoline** (one gallon regular unleaded, national brand, including all taxes, cash price at self-service pump if available); **Beauty Salon** (woman's shampoo, trim, and blow-dry); **Men's Shirt** (cotton/polyester dress shirt, pinpoint weave, long sleeves).*
Source: The Council for Community and Economic Research, Cost of Living Index, 2022

HOUSING

Homeownership Rate

Area	2015 (%)	2016 (%)	2017 (%)	2018 (%)	2019 (%)	2020 (%)	2021 (%)	2022 (%)
MSA[1]	59.0	57.5	57.9	64.8	65.7	65.6	64.6	61.5
U.S.	63.7	63.4	63.9	64.4	64.6	66.6	65.5	65.8

Note: (1) Figures cover the Columbus, OH Metropolitan Statistical Area
Source: U.S. Census Bureau, Housing Vacancies and Homeownership Annual Statistics: 2015-2022

House Price Index (HPI)

Area	National Ranking[2]	Quarterly Change (%)	One-Year Change (%)	Five-Year Change (%)	Since 1991Q1 (%)
MSA[1]	94	-1.27	12.41	59.08	243.03
U.S.[3]	—	0.34	8.41	58.44	289.08

Note: The HPI is a weighted repeat sales index. It measures average price changes in repeat sales or refinancings on the same properties. This information is obtained by reviewing repeat mortgage transactions on single-family properties whose mortgages have been purchased or securitized by Fannie Mae or Freddie Mac since January 1975; (1) Figures cover the Columbus, OH Metropolitan Statistical Area; (2) Rankings are based on annual percentage change for all metro areas containing at least 15,000 transactions over the last 10 years and ranges from 1 to 257; (3) figures based on a weighted average of Census Division estimates using a seasonally adjusted, purchase-only index; all figures are for the period ending December 31, 2022
Source: Federal Housing Finance Agency, Change in FHFA Metropolitan Area House Price Indexes, 2022Q4

Median Single-Family Home Prices

Area	2020	2021	2022[p]	Percent Change 2021 to 2022
MSA[1]	240.8	274.1	301.1	9.9
U.S. Average	300.2	357.1	392.6	9.9

Note: Figures are median sales prices of existing single-family homes in thousands of dollars; (p) preliminary; (1) Figures cover the Columbus, OH Metropolitan Statistical Area
Source: National Association of Realtors, Median Sales Price of Existing Single-Family Homes for Metropolitan Areas, 4th Quarter 2022

Qualifying Income Based on Median Sales Price of Existing Single-Family Homes

Area	With 5% Down ($)	With 10% Down ($)	With 20% Down ($)
MSA[1]	85,776	81,261	72,232
U.S. Average	112,234	106,237	94,513

Note: Figures are preliminary; Qualifying income is based on a mortgage rate of 6.77%. Monthly principal and interest payment is limited to 25% of income; (1) Figures cover the Columbus, OH Metropolitan Statistical Area
Source: National Association of Realtors, Qualifying Income Based on Median Sales Price of Existing Single-Family Homes for Metropolitan Areas, 4th Quarter 2022

Home Value

Area	Under $100,000	$100,000 -$199,999	$200,000 -$299,999	$300,000 -$399,999	$400,000 -$499,999	$500,000 -$999,999	$1,000,000 or more	Median ($)
City	19.2	40.1	25.2	9.3	2.9	2.8	0.5	174,400
MSA[1]	14.2	32.0	25.3	14.2	6.8	6.6	0.9	213,600
U.S.	16.2	24.2	20.1	13.6	8.3	13.6	4.1	244,900

Note: Figures are percentages except for median and cover owner-occupied housing units; (1) Figures cover the Columbus, OH Metropolitan Statistical Area
Source: U.S. Census Bureau, 2017-2021 American Community Survey 5-Year Estimates

Year Housing Structure Built

Area	2020 or Later	2010 -2019	2000 -2009	1990 -1999	1980 -1989	1970 -1979	1960 -1969	1950 -1959	1940 -1949	Before 1940	Median Year
City	0.1	8.0	11.7	15.1	12.9	14.3	11.5	10.4	4.3	11.8	1978
MSA[1]	0.2	8.0	14.2	15.9	11.6	13.8	10.7	9.8	3.7	12.2	1980
U.S.	0.2	7.3	13.6	13.6	13.2	14.8	10.3	10.0	4.7	12.2	1979

Note: Figures are percentages except for Median Year; Note: (1) Figures cover the Columbus, OH Metropolitan Statistical Area
Source: U.S. Census Bureau, 2017-2021 American Community Survey 5-Year Estimates

Gross Monthly Rent

Area	Under $500	$500 -$999	$1,000 -$1,499	$1,500 -$1,999	$2,000 -$2,499	$2,500 -$2,999	$3,000 and up	Median ($)
City	5.2	37.8	43.6	10.1	2.3	0.4	0.6	1,061
MSA[1]	6.0	38.6	41.3	10.3	2.4	0.7	0.6	1,049
U.S.	8.1	30.5	30.8	16.8	7.3	3.1	3.5	1,163

Note: Figures are percentages except for median; Gross rent is the contract rent plus the estimated average monthly cost of utilities (electricity, gas, and water and sewer) and fuels (oil, coal, kerosene, wood, etc.) if these are paid by the renter (or paid for the renter by someone else); (1) Figures cover the Columbus, OH Metropolitan Statistical Area
Source: U.S. Census Bureau, 2017-2021 American Community Survey 5-Year Estimates

HEALTH

Health Risk Factors

Category	MSA[1] (%)	U.S. (%)
Adults aged 18–64 who have any kind of health care coverage	90.6	90.9
Adults who reported being in good or better health	86.5	85.2
Adults who have been told they have high blood cholesterol	33.3	35.7
Adults who have been told they have high blood pressure	32.7	32.4
Adults who are current smokers	14.9	14.4
Adults who currently use e-cigarettes	8.1	6.7
Adults who currently use chewing tobacco, snuff, or snus	3.3	3.5
Adults who are heavy drinkers[2]	6.4	6.3
Adults who are binge drinkers[3]	17.7	15.4
Adults who are overweight (BMI 25.0 - 29.9)	34.1	34.4
Adults who are obese (BMI 30.0 - 99.8)	36.5	33.9
Adults who participated in any physical activities in the past month	76.6	76.3

Note: (1) Figures cover the Columbus, OH Metropolitan Statistical Area; (2) Heavy drinkers are classified as adult men having more than 14 drinks per week and adult women having more than 7 drinks per week; (3) Binge drinkers are classified as males having five or more drinks on one occasion or females having four or more drinks on one occasion
Source: Centers for Disease Control and Prevention, Behaviorial Risk Factor Surveillance System, SMART: Selected Metropolitan Area Risk Trends, 2021

Acute and Chronic Health Conditions

Category	MSA[1] (%)	U.S. (%)
Adults who have ever been told they had a heart attack	4.1	4.0
Adults who have ever been told they have angina or coronary heart disease	3.7	3.8
Adults who have ever been told they had a stroke	3.7	3.0
Adults who have ever been told they have asthma	15.7	14.9
Adults who have ever been told they have arthritis	25.8	25.8
Adults who have ever been told they have diabetes[2]	12.4	10.9
Adults who have ever been told they had skin cancer	5.5	6.6
Adults who have ever been told they had any other types of cancer	8.0	7.5
Adults who have ever been told they have COPD	7.0	6.1
Adults who have ever been told they have kidney disease	3.9	3.0
Adults who have ever been told they have a form of depression	22.3	20.5

Note: (1) Figures cover the Columbus, OH Metropolitan Statistical Area; (2) Figures do not include pregnancy-related, borderline, or pre-diabetes
Source: Centers for Disease Control and Prevention, Behaviorial Risk Factor Surveillance System, SMART: Selected Metropolitan Area Risk Trends, 2021

Health Screening and Vaccination Rates

Category	MSA[1] (%)	U.S. (%)
Adults who have ever been tested for HIV	35.4	34.9
Adults who have had their blood cholesterol checked within the last five years	85.9	85.2
Adults aged 65+ who have had flu shot within the past year	70.2	68.6
Adults aged 65+ who have ever had a pneumonia vaccination	75.4	71.0

Note: (1) Figures cover the Columbus, OH Metropolitan Statistical Area.
Source: Centers for Disease Control and Prevention, Behaviorial Risk Factor Surveillance System, SMART: Selected Metropolitan Area Risk Trends, 2021

Disability Status

Category	MSA[1] (%)	U.S. (%)
Adults who reported being deaf	6.1	7.2
Are you blind or have serious difficulty seeing, even when wearing glasses?	2.8	4.8
Are you limited in any way in any of your usual activities due to arthritis?	10.3	11.1
Do you have difficulty doing errands alone?	5.8	7.0
Do you have difficulty dressing or bathing?	2.8	3.6
Do you have serious difficulty concentrating/remembering/making decisions?	12.6	12.1
Do you have serious difficulty walking or climbing stairs?	12.6	12.8

Note: (1) Figures cover the Columbus, OH Metropolitan Statistical Area.
Source: Centers for Disease Control and Prevention, Behaviorial Risk Factor Surveillance System, SMART: Selected Metropolitan Area Risk Trends, 2021

Mortality Rates for the Top 10 Causes of Death in the U.S.

ICD-10[a] Sub-Chapter	ICD-10[a] Code	Crude Mortality Rate[1] per 100,000 population	
		County[2]	U.S.
Malignant neoplasms	C00-C97	146.5	182.6
Ischaemic heart diseases	I20-I25	77.0	113.1
Other forms of heart disease	I30-I51	60.6	64.4
Other degenerative diseases of the nervous system	G30-G31	41.5	51.0
Cerebrovascular diseases	I60-I69	39.5	47.8
Other external causes of accidental injury	W00-X59	73.7	46.4
Chronic lower respiratory diseases	J40-J47	39.5	45.7
Organic, including symptomatic, mental disorders	F01-F09	34.8	35.9
Hypertensive diseases	I10-I15	32.8	35.0
Diabetes mellitus	E10-E14	23.7	29.6

Note: (a) ICD-10 = International Classification of Diseases 10th Revision; (1) Crude mortality rates are a three-year average covering 2019-2021; (2) Figures cover Franklin County.
Source: Centers for Disease Control and Prevention, National Center for Health Statistics. National Vital Statistics System, Mortality 2018-2021 on CDC WONDER Online Database

Mortality Rates for Selected Causes of Death

ICD-10[a] Sub-Chapter	ICD-10[a] Code	Crude Mortality Rate[1] per 100,000 population	
		County[2]	U.S.
Assault	X85-Y09	12.9	7.0
Diseases of the liver	K70-K76	16.3	19.8
Human immunodeficiency virus (HIV) disease	B20-B24	1.0	1.5
Influenza and pneumonia	J09-J18	12.9	14.7
Intentional self-harm	X60-X84	11.7	14.3
Malnutrition	E40-E46	4.4	4.3
Obesity and other hyperalimentation	E65-E68	2.2	3.0
Renal failure	N17-N19	12.3	15.7
Transport accidents	V01-V99	11.2	13.6
Viral hepatitis	B15-B19	1.0	1.2

Note: (a) ICD-10 = International Classification of Diseases 10th Revision; (1) Crude mortality rates are a three-year average covering 2019-2021; (2) Figures cover Franklin County; Data are suppressed when the data meet the criteria for confidentiality constraints; Crude mortality rates are flagged as unreliable when the rate would be calculated with a numerator of 20 or less.
Source: Centers for Disease Control and Prevention, National Center for Health Statistics. National Vital Statistics System, Mortality 2018-2021 on CDC WONDER Online Database

Health Insurance Coverage

Area	With Health Insurance	With Private Health Insurance	With Public Health Insurance	Without Health Insurance	Population Under Age 19 Without Health Insurance
City	90.7	63.4	34.7	9.3	5.6
MSA[1]	93.0	71.1	31.8	7.0	4.5
U.S.	91.2	67.8	35.4	8.8	5.3

Note: Figures are percentages that cover the civilian noninstitutionalized population; (1) Figures cover the Columbus, OH Metropolitan Statistical Area
Source: U.S. Census Bureau, 2017-2021 American Community Survey 5-Year Estimates

Number of Medical Professionals

Area	MDs[3]	DOs[3,4]	Dentists	Podiatrists	Chiropractors	Optometrists
County[1] (number)	5,859	828	1,237	100	335	378
County[1] (rate[2])	442.5	62.5	93.6	7.6	25.4	28.6
U.S. (rate[2])	289.3	23.5	72.5	6.2	28.7	17.4

Note: Data as of 2021 unless noted; (1) Data covers Franklin County; (2) Rate per 100,000 population; (3) Data as of 2020 and includes all active, non-federal physicians; (4) Doctor of Osteopathic Medicine
Source: U.S. Department of Health and Human Services, Health Resources and Services Administration, Bureau of Health Professions, Area Resource File (ARF) 2021-2022

Best Hospitals

According to *U.S. News,* the Columbus, OH metro area is home to three of the best hospitals in the U.S.: **Ohio State University James Cancer Hospital** (1 adult specialty); **Ohio State University Wexner Medical Center** (9 adult specialties); **OhioHealth Rehabilitation Hospital** (1 adult specialty). The hospitals listed were nationally ranked in at least one of 15 adult or 10 pediatric specialties. The number of specialties shown cover the parent hospital. Only 164 U.S. hospitals performed well enough to be nationally ranked in one or more specialties. Twenty hospitals in the U.S. made the Honor Roll. The Best Hospitals Honor Roll takes both the national rankings and the procedure and condition ratings into account. Hospitals received points if they were nationally ranked in one of the 15 adult specialties—the higher they ranked, the more points they got—and how many ratings of "high performing" they earned in the 17 procedures and conditions. *U.S. News Online, "America's Best Hospitals 2022-23"*

According to *U.S. News,* the Columbus, OH metro area is home to one of the best children's hospitals in the U.S.: **Nationwide Children's Hospital** (Honor Roll/10 pediatric specialties). The hospital listed was highly ranked in at least one of 10 pediatric specialties. Eighty-six children's hospitals in the U.S. were nationally ranked in at least one specialty. Hospitals received points for being ranked in a specialty, and the 10 hospitals with the most points across the 10 specialties make up the Honor Roll. *U.S. News Online, "America's Best Children's Hospitals 2022-23"*

EDUCATION

Public School District Statistics

District Name	Schls	Pupils	Pupil/ Teacher Ratio	Minority Pupils[1] (%)	LEP/ELL[2] (%)	IEP[3] (%)
Columbus City School District	117	45,547	14.5	79.0	16.1	19.4
Hamilton Local	5	2,940	20.7	28.1	1.8	13.0
Hilliard City	24	16,068	17.2	30.4	7.5	15.0

Note: Table includes school districts with 2,000 or more students; (1) Percentage of students that are not non-Hispanic white; (2) Percentage of students that are Limited English Proficient or English Language Learners (2018-19); (3) Percentage of students that have an Individualized Education Program (2019-20). Source: U.S. Department of Education, National Center for Education Statistics, Common Core of Data, Local Education Agency (School District) Universe Survey: School Year 2021-2022

Best High Schools

According to *U.S. News,* Columbus is home to one of the top 500 high schools in the U.S.: **Grandview Heights High School** (#427). Nearly 18,000 public, magnet and charter schools were ranked based on their performance on state assessments and how well they prepare students for college. *U.S. News & World Report, "Best High Schools 2022"*

Highest Level of Education

Area	Less than H.S.	H.S. Diploma	Some College, No Deg.	Associate Degree	Bachelor's Degree	Master's Degree	Prof. School Degree	Doctorate Degree
City	9.7	24.8	20.3	7.4	24.3	10.0	2.1	1.6
MSA[1]	7.9	26.7	19.4	7.6	24.0	10.4	2.5	1.5
U.S.	11.1	26.5	20.0	8.7	20.6	9.3	2.2	1.5

Note: Figures cover persons age 25 and over; (1) Figures cover the Columbus, OH Metropolitan Statistical Area Source: U.S. Census Bureau, 2017-2021 American Community Survey 5-Year Estimates

Educational Attainment by Race

Area	High School Graduate or Higher (%)					Bachelor's Degree or Higher (%)				
	Total	White	Black	Asian	Hisp.[2]	Total	White	Black	Asian	Hisp.[2]
City	90.3	93.0	87.0	86.5	73.5	37.9	44.5	20.1	60.7	24.1
MSA[1]	92.1	93.6	87.6	88.4	76.8	38.4	40.3	22.7	64.1	27.4
U.S.	88.9	91.4	87.2	87.6	71.2	33.7	35.5	23.3	55.6	18.4

Note: Figures shown cover persons 25 years old and over; (1) Figures cover the Columbus, OH Metropolitan Statistical Area; (2) People of Hispanic origin can be of any race Source: U.S. Census Bureau, 2017-2021 American Community Survey 5-Year Estimates

School Enrollment by Grade and Control

Area	Preschool (%)		Kindergarten (%)		Grades 1 - 4 (%)		Grades 5 - 8 (%)		Grades 9 - 12 (%)	
	Public	Private	Public	Private	Public	Private	Public	Private	Public	Private
City	63.4	36.6	78.5	21.5	84.4	15.6	84.8	15.2	86.2	13.8
MSA[1]	57.3	42.7	82.1	17.9	87.4	12.6	87.9	12.1	88.7	11.3
U.S.	58.8	41.2	86.3	13.7	88.3	11.7	88.6	11.4	89.4	10.6

Note: Figures shown cover persons 3 years old and over; (1) Figures cover the Columbus, OH Metropolitan Statistical Area Source: U.S. Census Bureau, 2017-2021 American Community Survey 5-Year Estimates

Higher Education

Four-Year Colleges			Two-Year Colleges			Medical Schools[1]	Law Schools[2]	Voc/ Tech[3]
Public	Private Non-profit	Private For-profit	Public	Private Non-profit	Private For-profit			
3	12	4	2	1	9	1	2	7

Note: Figures cover institutions located within the Columbus, OH Metropolitan Statistical Area and include main campuses only; (1) includes schools accredited by the Liaison Committee on Medical Education and the American Osteopathic Association's Commission on Osteopathic College Accreditation; (2) includes ABA-accredited schools, schools with provisional ABA accreditation, and state accredited schools; (3) includes all schools with programs that are less than 2 years.
Source: National Center for Education Statistics, Integrated Postsecondary Education System (IPEDS), 2021-22; Wikipedia, List of Medical Schools in the United States, accessed April 10, 2023; Wikipedia, List of Law Schools in the United States, accessed April 10, 2023

According to *U.S. News & World Report*, the Columbus, OH metro area is home to one of the top 200 national universities in the U.S.: **The Ohio State University** (#49 tie). The indicators used to capture academic quality fall into a number of categories: assessment by administrators at peer institutions; retention of students; faculty resources; student selectivity; financial resources; alumni giving; high school counselor ratings of colleges; and graduation rate. *U.S. News & World Report, "America's Best Colleges 2023"*

According to *U.S. News & World Report*, the Columbus, OH metro area is home to one of the top 100 liberal arts colleges in the U.S.: **Denison University** (#39 tie). The indicators used to capture academic quality fall into a number of categories: assessment by administrators at peer institutions; retention of students; faculty resources; student selectivity; financial resources; alumni giving; high school counselor ratings of colleges; and graduation rate. *U.S. News & World Report, "America's Best Colleges 2023"*

According to *U.S. News & World Report*, the Columbus, OH metro area is home to one of the top 100 law schools in the U.S.: **Ohio State University (Moritz)** (#30 tie). The rankings are based on a weighted average of 12 measures of quality: peer assessment score; assessment score by lawyers/judges; median LSAT scores; median undergrad GPA; acceptance rate; employment rates for graduates; placement success; bar passage rate; faculty resources; expenditures per student; student/faculty ratio; and library resources. *U.S. News & World Report, "America's Best Graduate Schools, Law, 2023"*

According to *U.S. News & World Report*, the Columbus, OH metro area is home to one of the top 75 medical schools for research in the U.S.: **Ohio State University** (#30 tie). The rankings are based on a weighted average of 11 measures of quality: quality assessment; peer assessment score; assessment score by residency directors; research activity; total research activity; average research activity per faculty member; student selectivity; median MCAT total score; median undergraduate GPA; acceptance rate; and faculty resources. *U.S. News & World Report, "America's Best Graduate Schools, Medical, 2023"*

According to *U.S. News & World Report*, the Columbus, OH metro area is home to one of the top 75 business schools in the U.S.: **Ohio State University (Fisher)** (#39). The rankings are based on a weighted average of the following nine measures: quality assessment; peer assessment; recruiter assessment; placement success; mean starting salary and bonus; student selectivity; mean GMAT and GRE scores; mean undergraduate GPA; and acceptance rate. *U.S. News & World Report, "America's Best Graduate Schools, Business, 2023"*

EMPLOYERS

Major Employers

Company Name	Industry
Abbott Labs, Ross Products Division	Manufacturing
American Electric Power	Utilities
AT&T Ohio	Information
Battelle Memorial Institute	Professional services
Big Lots	Corp. mgt./retail trade
City of Columbus	Municipal government
Columbus City Schools	Public education
Franklin County	Government
Honda of America Manufacturing	Manufacturing
Huntington Bancshares	Financial activities
JPMorgan Chase	Financial activities
Kroger Company	Retail grocery
Limited Brands	Corp. mgt./retail trade
Medco Health Solutions	Health care/wholesale trade
Mount Carmel Health System	Health care
Nationwide	Financial activities
Nationwide Children's Hospital	Health care
OhioHealth	Health care
Retail Ventures	Corp. mgt./retail trade
South-Western City School District	Public education
State of Ohio	State government
The Ohio State University	Public education
United States Government	Federal government
Wal-Mart Stores	Retail trade
Wendy's International	Corp. mgt./retail trade

Note: Companies shown are located within the Columbus, OH Metropolitan Statistical Area.
Source: Hoovers.com; Wikipedia

Best Companies to Work For

Nationwide Mutual Insurance Company, headquartered in Columbus, is among "The 100 Best Companies to Work For." To pick the best companies, *Fortune* partnered with the Great Place to Work Institute. Two-thirds of a company's score is based on the results of the Institute's Trust Index survey, which is sent to a random sample of employees from each company. The questions related to attitudes about management's credibility, job satisfaction, and camaraderie. The other third of the scoring is based on the company's responses to the Institute's Culture Audit, which includes detailed questions about pay and benefit programs, and a series of open-ended questions about hiring practices, internal communication, training, recognition programs, and diversity efforts. Any company that is at least five years old with more than 1,000 U.S. employees is eligible. *Fortune, "The 100 Best Companies to Work For," 2023*

Nationwide Mutual Insurance Company, headquartered in Columbus, is among "Fortune's Best Workplaces for Women." To pick the best companies, *Fortune* partnered with the Great Place to Work Institute. To be considered for the list, companies must be Great Place To Work-Certified. Companies must also employ at least 50 women, at least 20% of their non-executive managers must be female, and at least one executive must be female. To determine the Best Workplaces for Women, Great Place To Work measured the differences in women's survey responses to those of their peers and assesses the impact of demographics and roles on the quality and consistency of women's experiences. Great Place To Work also analyzed the gender balance of each workplace, how it compared to each company's industry, and patterns in representation as women rise from front-line positions to the board of directors. *Fortune, "Best Workplaces for Women," 2022*

ARC Healthcare; OhioHealth, headquartered in Columbus, are among "Best Workplaces in Health Care." To determine the Best Workplaces in Health Care list, Great Place To Work analyzed the survey responses of over 161,000 employees from Great Place To Work-Certified companies in the health care industry. Survey data analysis and company-provided datapoints are then factored into a combined score to compare and rank the companies that create the most consistently positive experience for all employees in this industry. *Fortune, "Best Workplaces in Health Care," 2022*

Nationwide Mutual Insurance Company, headquartered in Columbus, is among "Fortune's Best Workplaces for Parents." To pick the best companies, *Fortune* partnered with the Great Place to Work Institute. To be considered for the list, companies must be Great Place To Work-Certified and have at least 50 responses from parents in the US. The survey enables employees to share confidential quantitative and qualitative feedback about their organization's culture by responding to 60 statements on a 5-point scale and answering two open-ended questions. Collectively, these statements describe a great employee experience, defined by high levels of trust, respect, credibility, fairness, pride, and camaraderie. In addition, companies provide organizational data like size, location, industry, demographics, roles, and levels; and provide information about parental leave, adoption, flexible schedule, childcare and dependent health care benefits. *Fortune, "Best Workplaces for Parents," 2022*

Avaap; Worthington Industries, headquartered in Columbus, are among the "100 Best Places to Work in IT." To qualify, companies had to have a minimum of 100 total employees and five IT employees. The best places to work were selected based on DEI (diversity, equity, and inclusion) practices; IT turnover, promotions, and growth; IT retention and engagement programs; remote/hybrid working; benefits and perks (such as elder care and child care, flextime, and reimbursement for college tuition); and training and career development opportunities. *Computerworld, "Best Places to Work in IT," 2023*

PUBLIC SAFETY

Crime Rate

Area	Total Crime	Violent Crime Rate				Property Crime Rate		
		Murder	Rape[3]	Robbery	Aggrav. Assault	Burglary	Larceny -Theft	Motor Vehicle Theft
City	3,686.0	19.1	89.5	197.1	249.9	609.1	2,180.6	340.7
Suburbs[1]	1,664.0	1.5	28.2	27.2	77.2	205.1	1,223.7	101.1
Metro[2]	2,523.0	9.0	54.3	99.3	150.6	376.7	1,630.2	202.9
U.S.	2,356.7	6.5	38.4	73.9	279.7	314.2	1,398.0	246.0

Note: Figures are crimes per 100,000 population; (1) All areas within the metro area that are located outside the city limits; (2) Figures cover the Columbus, OH Metropolitan Statistical Area; (3) All figures shown were reported using the revised Uniform Crime Reporting (UCR) definition of rape; Due to the transition to the National Incident-Based Reporting System (NIBRS), limited city and metro area data was released for 2021.
Source: FBI Uniform Crime Reports, 2020

Hate Crimes

Area	Number of Quarters Reported	Number of Incidents per Bias Motivation					
		Race/Ethnicity/ Ancestry	Religion	Sexual Orientation	Disability	Gender	Gender Identity
City[1]	4	56	7	16	1	0	6
U.S.	4	5,227	1,244	1,110	130	75	266

Note: (1) Figures include one incident reported with more than one bias motivation; Due to the transition to the National Incident-Based Reporting System (NIBRS), limited crime data was released for 2021.
Source: Federal Bureau of Investigation, Hate Crime Statistics 2020

Identity Theft Consumer Reports

Area	Reports	Reports per 100,000 Population	Rank[2]
MSA[1]	7,641	364	42
U.S.	1,108,609	339	-

Note: (1) Figures cover the Columbus, OH Metropolitan Statistical Area; (2) Rank ranges from 1 to 391 where 1 indicates greatest number of identity theft reports per 100,000 population
Source: Federal Trade Commission, Consumer Sentinel Network Data Book 2022

Fraud and Other Consumer Reports

Area	Reports	Reports per 100,000 Population	Rank[2]
MSA[1]	21,512	1,024	88
U.S.	4,064,520	1,245	-

Note: (1) Figures cover the Columbus, OH Metropolitan Statistical Area; (2) Rank ranges from 1 to 391 where 1 indicates greatest number of fraud and other consumer reports per 100,000 population
Source: Federal Trade Commission, Consumer Sentinel Network Data Book 2022

POLITICS

2020 Presidential Election Results

Area	Biden	Trump	Jorgensen	Hawkins	Other
Franklin County	64.7	33.4	1.2	0.3	0.4
U.S.	51.3	46.8	1.2	0.3	0.5

Note: Results are percentages and may not add to 100% due to rounding
Source: Dave Leip's Atlas of U.S. Presidential Elections

SPORTS

Professional Sports Teams

Team Name	League	Year Established
Columbus Blue Jackets	National Hockey League (NHL)	2000
Columbus Crew	Major League Soccer (MLS)	1996

Note: Includes teams located in the Columbus, OH Metropolitan Statistical Area.
Source: Wikipedia, Major Professional Sports Teams of the United States and Canada, April 12, 2023

Columbus, Ohio   157

CLIMATE

Average and Extreme Temperatures

Temperature	Jan	Feb	Mar	Apr	May	Jun	Jul	Aug	Sep	Oct	Nov	Dec	Yr.
Extreme High (°F)	74	73	82	89	93	101	104	101	100	90	80	76	104
Average High (°F)	36	39	50	62	73	82	85	83	77	65	51	40	62
Average Temp. (°F)	28	31	41	52	62	70	74	73	66	54	43	32	52
Average Low (°F)	20	22	31	40	50	59	63	62	55	43	34	24	42
Extreme Low (°F)	-19	-13	-6	14	25	35	43	39	31	17	-4	-17	-19

Note: Figures cover the years 1948-1990
Source: National Climatic Data Center, International Station Meteorological Climate Summary, 9/96

Average Precipitation/Snowfall/Humidity

Precip./Humidity	Jan	Feb	Mar	Apr	May	Jun	Jul	Aug	Sep	Oct	Nov	Dec	Yr.
Avg. Precip. (in.)	2.8	2.4	3.1	3.3	3.9	4.0	4.3	3.3	2.7	2.1	3.0	2.8	37.9
Avg. Snowfall (in.)	8	6	5	1	Tr	0	0	0	Tr	Tr	2	6	28
Avg. Rel. Hum. 7am (%)	78	78	76	76	79	81	84	87	87	83	80	79	81
Avg. Rel. Hum. 4pm (%)	66	62	55	51	52	53	53	54	53	53	61	68	57

Note: Figures cover the years 1948-1990; Tr = Trace amounts (<0.05 in. of rain; <0.5 in. of snow)
Source: National Climatic Data Center, International Station Meteorological Climate Summary, 9/96

Weather Conditions

Temperature			Daytime Sky			Precipitation		
5°F & below	32°F & below	90°F & above	Clear	Partly cloudy	Cloudy	0.01 inch or more precip.	0.1 inch or more snow/ice	Thunder-storms
10	118	19	72	137	156	136	29	40

Note: Figures are average number of days per year and cover the years 1948-1990
Source: National Climatic Data Center, International Station Meteorological Climate Summary, 9/96

HAZARDOUS WASTE

Superfund Sites

The Columbus, OH metro area is home to one site on the EPA's Superfund National Priorities List: **Air Force Plant 85** (proposed). There are a total of 1,165 Superfund sites with a status of proposed or final on the list in the U.S. *U.S. Environmental Protection Agency, National Priorities List, April 12, 2023*

AIR QUALITY

Air Quality Trends: Ozone

	1990	1995	2000	2005	2010	2015	2018	2019	2020	2021
MSA[1]	0.090	0.091	0.085	0.084	0.073	0.066	0.062	0.060	0.062	0.061
U.S.	0.087	0.089	0.081	0.080	0.072	0.067	0.069	0.065	0.065	0.067

Note: (1) Data covers the Columbus, OH Metropolitan Statistical Area. The values shown are the composite ozone concentration averages among trend sites based on the highest fourth daily maximum 8-hour concentration in parts per million. These trends are based on sites having an adequate record of monitoring data during the trend period. Data from exceptional events are included.
Source: U.S. Environmental Protection Agency, Air Quality Monitoring Information, "Air Quality Trends by City, 1990-2021"

Air Quality Index

Area	Percent of Days when Air Quality was...[2]					AQI Statistics[2]	
	Good	Moderate	Unhealthy for Sensitive Groups	Unhealthy	Very Unhealthy	Maximum	Median
MSA[1]	71.2	28.8	0.0	0.0	0.0	100	43

Note: (1) Data covers the Columbus, OH Metropolitan Statistical Area; (2) Based on 365 days with AQI data in 2021. Air Quality Index (AQI) is an index for reporting daily air quality. EPA calculates the AQI for five major air pollutants regulated by the Clean Air Act: ground-level ozone, particle pollution (aka particulate matter), carbon monoxide, sulfur dioxide, and nitrogen dioxide. The AQI runs from 0 to 500. The higher the AQI value, the greater the level of air pollution and the greater the health concern. There are six AQI categories: "Good" AQI is between 0 and 50. Air quality is considered satisfactory; "Moderate" AQI is between 51 and 100. Air quality is acceptable; "Unhealthy for Sensitive Groups" When AQI values are between 101 and 150, members of sensitive groups may experience health effects; "Unhealthy" When AQI values are between 151 and 200 everyone may begin to experience health effects; "Very Unhealthy" AQI values between 201 and 300 trigger a health alert; "Hazardous" AQI values over 300 trigger warnings of emergency conditions (not shown).
Source: U.S. Environmental Protection Agency, Air Quality Index Report, 2021

Air Quality Index Pollutants

Area	Percent of Days when AQI Pollutant was...[2]					
	Carbon Monoxide	Nitrogen Dioxide	Ozone	Sulfur Dioxide	Particulate Matter 2.5	Particulate Matter 10
MSA[1]	0.0	2.7	44.7	(3)	52.6	0.0

Note: (1) Data covers the Columbus, OH Metropolitan Statistical Area; (2) Based on 365 days with AQI data in 2021. The Air Quality Index (AQI) is an index for reporting daily air quality. EPA calculates the AQI for five major air pollutants regulated by the Clean Air Act: ground-level ozone, particle pollution (also known as particulate matter), carbon monoxide, sulfur dioxide, and nitrogen dioxide. The AQI runs from 0 to 500. The higher the AQI value, the greater the level of air pollution and the greater the health concern; (3) Sulfur dioxide is no longer included in this table (as of December 8, 2021) because SO_2 concentrations tend to be very localized and not necessarily representative of broad geographical areas like counties and CBSAs.
Source: U.S. Environmental Protection Agency, Air Quality Index Report, 2021

Maximum Air Pollutant Concentrations: Particulate Matter, Ozone, CO and Lead

	Particulate Matter 10 (ug/m^3)	Particulate Matter 2.5 Wtd AM (ug/m^3)	Particulate Matter 2.5 24-Hr (ug/m^3)	Ozone (ppm)	Carbon Monoxide (ppm)	Lead (ug/m^3)
MSA[1] Level	32	9.9	24	0.064	1	n/a
NAAQS[2]	150	15	35	0.075	9	0.15
Met NAAQS[2]	Yes	Yes	Yes	Yes	Yes	n/a

Note: (1) Data covers the Columbus, OH Metropolitan Statistical Area; Data from exceptional events are included; (2) National Ambient Air Quality Standards; ppm = parts per million; ug/m^3 = micrograms per cubic meter; n/a not available.
Concentrations: Particulate Matter 10 (coarse particulate)—highest second maximum 24-hour concentration; Particulate Matter 2.5 Wtd AM (fine particulate)—highest weighted annual mean concentration; Particulate Matter 2.5 24-Hour (fine particulate)—highest 98th percentile 24-hour concentration; Ozone—highest fourth daily maximum 8-hour concentration; Carbon Monoxide—highest second maximum non-overlapping 8-hour concentration; Lead—maximum running 3-month average
Source: U.S. Environmental Protection Agency, Air Quality Monitoring Information, "Air Quality Statistics by City, 2021"

Maximum Air Pollutant Concentrations: Nitrogen Dioxide and Sulfur Dioxide

	Nitrogen Dioxide AM (ppb)	Nitrogen Dioxide 1-Hr (ppb)	Sulfur Dioxide AM (ppb)	Sulfur Dioxide 1-Hr (ppb)	Sulfur Dioxide 24-Hr (ppb)
MSA[1] Level	10	47	n/a	2	n/a
NAAQS[2]	53	100	30	75	140
Met NAAQS[2]	Yes	Yes	n/a	Yes	n/a

Note: (1) Data covers the Columbus, OH Metropolitan Statistical Area; Data from exceptional events are included; (2) National Ambient Air Quality Standards; ppm = parts per million; ug/m^3 = micrograms per cubic meter; n/a not available.
Concentrations: Nitrogen Dioxide AM—highest arithmetic mean concentration; Nitrogen Dioxide 1-Hr—highest 98th percentile 1-hour daily maximum concentration; Sulfur Dioxide AM—highest annual mean concentration; Sulfur Dioxide 1-Hr—highest 99th percentile 1-hour daily maximum concentration; Sulfur Dioxide 24-Hr—highest second maximum 24-hour concentration
Source: U.S. Environmental Protection Agency, Air Quality Monitoring Information, "Air Quality Statistics by City, 2021"

Durham, North Carolina

Background

Durham, on the Eno River in north-central North Carolina, is known as the "City of Medicine," and forms a corner of the region's famous Research Triangle, one of the nation's earliest and most successful planned centers for research and development. The economy is deeply interlinked with area universities and businesses specializing in medicine, biopharmaceuticals, computer technology and software, and telecommunications.

The original inhabitants of the area were Eno and Occaneechi Indians, who were mostly settled, horticulturist villagers. English explorer John Lawson visited the site in 1701, and called it the "flower of the Carolinas" for its scenic beauty. By the mid-eighteenth century, Scottish, Irish, and English settlers had established farms in the site of the present city.

Durham began as a station for the North Carolina Railroad, which had been built on land originally owned by the city's namesake, Bartlett Durham. Prior to the Civil War, several extensive plantations were established in the area.

Throughout the prewar period and beyond, Durham continued its growth as a center for tobacco farming and processing, with emphasis on "brightleaf" tobacco. Tobacco entrepreneur Washington Duke was of particular importance to the growth of Durham, and his efforts helped established Durham as a major regional economic center. The textile industry also grew and prospered Durham in the post-Civil War years, giving rise to many clothing innovations, including the nation's first denim and sheer hosiery mills.

In 1910, the popular B.C. Headache Powders were produced in Durham and the city's connection with health care deepened considerably when Duke University's Medical School opened in 1939. Durham's current economy is both high-tech and broad-based. Hundreds of private companies in the area employ thousands of highly skilled workers in a variety of high-technology enterprises.

Durham boasts a vibrant African American community, the center of which was an area once known as Hayti, just south of the center of town, where some of the most prominent and successful black-owned businesses in the country were established during the early 20th century. Portions of the Hayti district, along with large parts of other historic neighborhoods, were demolished for the construction of the Durham Freeway during the late 1960s. Although downtown revitalization heated up in the '70s and '80s, economic progress continues to butt heads with historic preservation.

Durham's downtown draws many residents and out-of-town visitors for its architecture, shops, and restaurants. Former tobacco warehouses and factories are converted to residential, office, retail, and entertainment uses. The American Tobacco Company Historic District now features historic preservation projects, as well as offices, restaurants, stores, and residences. At the center of Durham's cultural scene is The Carolina Theatre, a historic building currently owned by the city and maintained by The Carolina Theatre of Durham Inc. Durham is home to the renowned annual Full Frame Documentary Film Festival, which celebrated its 25th year in 2022.

Beyond the influence of the historic theater, Durham maintains a vibrant arts scene. Many of Durham's substantial cultural assets are linked to Duke University, including the Nasher Museum of Art at Duke University, whose Rafael Vinoly-designed building hosts traveling exhibitions from cutting-edge contemporary artists. Duke University also hosts The American Dance Festival each summer.

The city is also home to North Carolina Central University (1910), the nation's first publicly supported liberal arts college for African Americans.

In 2020, Durham residents elected its first Muslim American women to the city commission.

Durham is serviced by the 5,000-acre Raleigh-Durham International Airport, one of the country's fastest-growing terminals, now with two passenger terminals.

Durham lies between coastal plain and piedmont plateau, giving it a moderate climate. The mountains to the west partially protect the area from excess cold winter winds, although temperatures fall below freezing some days. Summers are hot and humid. July and August see the most rain, often in the form of thunderstorms, while October and November see the least amount of rainfall.

Rankings

General Rankings

- *US News & World Report* conducted a survey of more than 3,600 people and analyzed the 150 largest metropolitan areas to determine what matters most when selecting where to settle down. Durham ranked #6 out of the top 25 as having the best combination of desirable factors. Criteria: cost of living; quality of life and education; net migration; job market; desirability; and other factors. *money.usnews.com, "The 25 Best Places to Live in the U.S. in 2022-2023," May 17, 2022*

- The Durham metro area was identified as one of America's fastest-growing areas in terms of population and business growth by *MagnifyMoney*. The area ranked #16 out of 35. The 100 most populous metro areas in the U.S. were evaluated on their change from 2011 to 2016 in the following categories: people and housing; workforce and employment opportunities; growing industry. *www.businessinsider.com, "The 35 Cities in the US with the Biggest Influx of People, the Most Work Opportunities, and the Hottest Business Growth," August 12, 2018*

- In their ninth annual survey, Livability.com looked at data for more than 2,300 mid-sized U.S. cities to determine the rankings for Livability's "Top 100 Best Places to Live" in 2022. Durham ranked #45. Criteria: housing and economy; social and civic engagement; education; demographics; health care options; transportation & infrastructure; and community amenities. *Livability.com, "Top 100 Best Places to Live 2022" July 19, 2022*

Business/Finance Rankings

- *24/7 Wall St.* used metro data from the Bureau of Labor Statistics' Occupational Employment database to identify the cities with the highest percentage of those employed in jobs requiring knowledge in the science, technology, engineering, and math (STEM) fields as well as average wages for STEM jobs. The Durham metro area was #5. *247wallst.com, "15 Cities with the Most High-Tech Jobs," January 11, 2020*

- The Durham metro area appeared on the Milken Institute "2022 Best Performing Cities" list. Rank: #11 out of 200 large metro areas (population over 250,000). Criteria: job growth; wage and salary growth; high-tech output growth; housing affordability; household broadband access. *Milken Institute, "Best-Performing Cities 2022," March 28, 2022*

- *Forbes* ranked the 200 most populous metro areas to determine the nation's "Best Places for Business and Careers." The Durham metro area was ranked #17. Criteria: costs (business and living); job growth (past and projected); income growth; quality of life; educational attainment (college and high school); projected economic growth; cultural and leisure opportunities; workplace tolerance laws; net migration patterns. *Forbes, "The Best Places for Business and Careers 2019: Seattle Still On Top," October 30, 2019*

Children/Family Rankings

- Durham was selected as one of the most playful cities in the U.S. by KaBOOM! The organization's Playful City USA initiative honors cities and towns across the nation that have made their communities more playable. Criteria: pledging to integrate play as a solution to challenges in their communities; making it easy for children to get active and balanced play; creating more family-friendly and innovative communities as a result. *KaBOOM! National Campaign for Play, "2017 Playful City USA Communities"*

Education Rankings

- Personal finance website *WalletHub* analyzed the 150 largest U.S. metropolitan statistical areas to determine where the most educated Americans are putting their degrees to work. Criteria: education levels; percentage of workers with degrees; education quality and attainment gap; public school quality rankings; quality and enrollment of each metro area's universities. Durham was ranked #7 (#1 = most educated city). *www.WalletHub.com, "Most & Least Educated Cities in America," July 18, 2022*

- Durham was selected as one of America's most literate cities. The city ranked #16 out of the 84 largest U.S. cities. Criteria: number of booksellers; library resources; Internet resources; educational attainment; periodical publishing resources; newspaper circulation. *Central Connecticut State University, "America's Most Literate Cities, 2018," February 2019*

Environmental Rankings

- Durham was highlighted as one of the cleanest metro areas for ozone air pollution in the U.S. during 2019 through 2021. The list represents cities with no monitored ozone air pollution in unhealthful ranges. *American Lung Association, "State of the Air 2023," April 19, 2023*

Health/Fitness Rankings

- For each of the 100 largest cities in the United States, the American Fitness Index®, compiled in partnership between the American College of Sports Medicine and the Elevance Health Foundation, evaluated community infrastructure and 34 health behaviors including preventive health, levels of chronic disease conditions, food insecurity, sleep quality, pedestrian safety, air quality, and community/environment resources that support physical activity. Durham ranked #37 for "community fitness." *americanfitnessindex.org, "2022 ACSM American Fitness Index Summary Report," July 12, 2022*

- The Durham metro area was identified as one of the worst cities for bed bugs in America by pest control company Orkin. The area ranked #20 out of 50 based on the number of bed bug treatments Orkin performed from December 2021 to November 2022. *Orkin, "The Windy City Can't Blow Bed Bugs Away: Chicago Ranks #1 For Third Consecutive Year On Orkin's Bed Bug Cities List," January 9, 2023*

- Durham was identified as a "2022 Spring Allergy Capital." The area ranked #100 out of 100. Three groups of factors were used to identify the most challenging cities for people with allergies during the spring season: annual spring pollen scores; over the counter allergy medicine use; number of board-certified allergy specialists. *Asthma and Allergy Foundation of America, "Spring Allergy Capitals 2022," March 2, 2022*

- Durham was identified as a "2022 Fall Allergy Capital." The area ranked #98 out of 100. Three groups of factors were used to identify the most challenging cities for people with allergies during the fall season: annual fall pollen scores; over the counter allergy medicine use; number of board-certified allergy specialists. *Asthma and Allergy Foundation of America, "Fall Allergy Capitals 2022," March 2, 2022*

- Durham was identified as a "2022 Asthma Capital." The area ranked #92 out of the nation's 100 largest metropolitan areas. Criteria: estimated asthma prevalence; asthma-related mortality; and ER visits due to asthma. Risk factors analyzed but not factored in the rankings: annual pollen score; annual air quality; public smoking laws; access to board-certified asthma specialists; rescue and controller medication use; uninsured rate; poverty rate. *Asthma and Allergy Foundation of America, "Asthma Capitals 2022: The Most Challenging Places to Live With Asthma," September 14, 2022*

Real Estate Rankings

- *WalletHub* compared the most populated U.S. cities to determine which had the best markets for real estate agents. Durham ranked #25 where demand was high and pay was the best. Criteria: sales per agent; annual median wage for real-estate agents; monthly average starting salary for real estate agents; real estate job density and competition; unemployment rate; home turnover rate; housing-market health index; and other relevant metrics. *www.WalletHub.com, "2021 Best Places to Be a Real Estate Agent," May 12, 2021*

- Durham was ranked #143 out of 235 metro areas in terms of housing affordability in 2022 by the National Association of Home Builders (#1 = most affordable). Criteria: the share of homes sold in that area affordable to a family earning the local median income, based on standard mortgage underwriting criteria. *National Association of Home Builders®, NAHB-Wells Fargo Housing Opportunity Index, 4th Quarter 2022*

Safety Rankings

- Allstate ranked the 200 largest cities in America in terms of driver safety. Durham ranked #73. Criteria: internal property damage claims over a two-year period from January 2016 to December 2017. The report helps increase the importance of safety and awareness behind the wheel. *Allstate, "Allstate America's Best Drivers Report, 2019" June 24, 2019*

- The National Insurance Crime Bureau ranked 390 metro areas in the U.S. in terms of per capita rates of vehicle theft. The Durham metro area ranked #200 (#1 = highest rate). Criteria: number of vehicle theft offenses per 100,000 inhabitants in 2021. *National Insurance Crime Bureau, "Hot Spots 2021," September 1, 2022*

Seniors/Retirement Rankings

- From its Best Cities for Successful Aging indexes, the Milken Institute generated rankings for metropolitan areas, weighing data in nine categories—health care, wellness, living arrangements, transportation and convenience, financial characteristics, education, employment, community engagement, and overall livability. The Durham metro area was ranked #3 overall in the large metro area category. *Milken Institute, "Best Cities for Successful Aging, 2017" March 14, 2017*

Women/Minorities Rankings

- *Women's Health*, together with the site Yelp, identified the 15 "Wellthiest" spots in the U.S. Durham appeared among the top for happiest, healthiest, outdoorsiest and Zen-iest. *Women's Health, "The 15 Wellthiest Cities in the U.S." July 5, 2017*

- Durham was selected as one of the queerest cities in America by *The Advocate.* The city ranked #15 out of 25. Criteria, among many: Trans Pride parades/festivals; gay rugby teams; lesbian bars; LGBTQ centers; theater screenings of "Moonlight"; LGBTQ-inclusive nondiscrimination ordinances; and gay bowling teams. *The Advocate, "Queerest Cities in America 2017" January 12, 2017*

- Personal finance website *WalletHub* compared more than 180 U.S. cities across two key dimensions, "Hispanic Business-Friendliness" and "Hispanic Purchasing Power," to arrive at the most favorable conditions for Hispanic entrepreneurs. Durham was ranked #64 out of 182. Criteria includes: share of Hispanic-Owned Businesses; Hispanic entrepreneurship rate to median annual income of Hispanics; Small Business-Friendliness score; cost of living; and number of Hispanics with at least a bachelor's degree. *WalletHub.com, "2019's Best Cities for Hispanic Entrepreneurs," May 1, 2019*

Miscellaneous Rankings

- Durham was selected as a 2022 Digital Cities Survey winner. The city ranked #3 in the large city (250,000 to 499,999 population) category. The survey examined and assessed how city governments are utilizing technology to continue innovation, engage with residents, and persevere through the challenges of the pandemic. Survey questions focused on ten initiatives: cybersecurity; citizen experience; disaster recovery; business intelligence; IT personnel; data governance; business automation; IT governance; infrastructure modernization; and broadband connectivity. *Center for Digital Government, "2022 Digital Cities Survey," November 10, 2022*

- *WalletHub* compared the 150 most populated U.S. cities to determine their operating efficiency. A "Quality of Services" score was constructed for each city and then divided by the total budget per capita to reveal which were managed the best. Durham ranked #10. Criteria: financial stability; economy; education; safety; health; infrastructure and pollution. *www.WalletHub.com, "2022's Best-& Worst-Run Cities in America," June 21, 2022*

Business Environment

DEMOGRAPHICS

Population Growth

Area	1990 Census	2000 Census	2010 Census	2020 Census	Population Growth (%) 1990-2020	Population Growth (%) 2010-2020
City	151,737	187,035	228,330	283,506	86.8	24.2
MSA[1]	344,646	426,493	504,357	649,903	88.6	28.9
U.S.	248,709,873	281,421,906	308,745,538	331,449,281	33.3	7.4

Note: (1) Figures cover the Durham-Chapel Hill, NC Metropolitan Statistical Area
Source: U.S. Census Bureau, 1990 Census, 2000 Census, 2010 Census, 2020 Census

Race

Area	White Alone[2] (%)	Black Alone[2] (%)	Asian Alone[2] (%)	AIAN[3] Alone[2] (%)	NHOPI[4] Alone[2] (%)	Other Race Alone[2] (%)	Two or More Races (%)
City	40.2	36.2	5.6	0.7	0.0	9.8	7.4
MSA[1]	54.3	25.0	4.9	0.7	0.0	7.9	7.2
U.S.	61.6	12.4	6.0	1.1	0.2	8.4	10.2

Note: (1) Figures cover the Durham-Chapel Hill, NC Metropolitan Statistical Area; (2) Alone is defined as not being in combination with one or more other races; (3) American Indian and Alaska Native; (4) Native Hawaiian and Other Pacific Islander
Source: U.S. Census Bureau, 2020 Census

Hispanic or Latino Origin

Area	Total (%)	Mexican (%)	Puerto Rican (%)	Cuban (%)	Other (%)
City	13.2	6.4	0.9	0.3	5.7
MSA[1]	11.3	5.9	0.8	0.3	4.3
U.S.	18.4	11.2	1.8	0.7	4.7

Note: Persons of Hispanic or Latino origin can be of any race; (1) Figures cover the Durham-Chapel Hill, NC Metropolitan Statistical Area
Source: U.S. Census Bureau, 2017-2021 American Community Survey 5-Year Estimates

Age

Area	Under Age 5	Age 5–19	Age 20–34	Age 35–44	Age 45–54	Age 55–64	Age 65–74	Age 75–84	Age 85+	Median Age
City	6.0	17.6	28.2	13.9	11.1	10.4	8.1	3.4	1.3	33.9
MSA[1]	5.2	18.4	23.1	12.7	12.1	12.3	9.9	4.6	1.6	37.4
U.S.	5.6	19.2	20.2	12.7	12.4	13.1	10.0	4.9	1.9	38.8

Note: (1) Figures cover the Durham-Chapel Hill, NC Metropolitan Statistical Area
Source: U.S. Census Bureau, 2020 Census

Disability by Age

Area	All Ages	Under 18 Years Old	18 to 64 Years Old	65 Years and Over
City	9.6	3.0	7.6	31.7
MSA[1]	11.0	3.4	8.6	30.7
U.S.	12.6	4.4	10.3	33.4

Note: Figures show percent of the civilian noninstitutionalized population that reported having a disability. Disability status is determined from six types of difficulty: vision, hearing, cognitive, ambulatory, self-care, and independent living. For children under 5 years old, hearing and vision difficulty are used to determine disability status. For children between the ages of 5 and 14, disability status is determined from hearing, vision, cognitive, ambulatory, and self-care difficulties. For people aged 15 years and older, they are considered to have a disability if they have difficulty with any one of the six difficulty types; Note: (1) Figures cover the Durham-Chapel Hill, NC Metropolitan Statistical Area
Source: U.S. Census Bureau, 2017-2021 American Community Survey 5-Year Estimates

Ancestry

Area	German	Irish	English	American	Italian	Polish	French[2]	Scottish	Dutch
City	8.1	6.5	9.4	3.7	3.3	1.7	1.6	1.6	0.6
MSA[1]	9.3	8.0	11.1	5.4	3.5	1.8	1.7	2.1	0.7
U.S.	12.8	9.6	8.1	5.7	5.0	2.7	2.2	1.6	1.1

Note: Figures are the percentage of the total population reporting a particular ancestry. The nine most commonly reported ancestries in the U.S. are shown. Figures include multiple ancestries (e.g. if a person reported being Irish and Italian, they were included in both columns); (1) Figures cover the Durham-Chapel Hill, NC Metropolitan Statistical Area; (2) Excludes Basque
Source: U.S. Census Bureau, 2017-2021 American Community Survey 5-Year Estimates

Foreign-born Population

Area	Percent of Population Born in								
	Any Foreign Country	Asia	Mexico	Europe	Caribbean	Central America[2]	South America	Africa	Canada
City	14.6	4.4	2.8	1.4	0.6	2.7	0.7	1.5	0.3
MSA[1]	11.8	3.6	2.7	1.4	0.4	1.8	0.6	1.0	0.3
U.S.	13.6	4.2	3.3	1.5	1.4	1.1	1.1	0.8	0.2

Note: (1) Figures cover the Durham-Chapel Hill, NC Metropolitan Statistical Area; (2) Excludes Mexico.
Source: U.S. Census Bureau, 2017-2021 American Community Survey 5-Year Estimates

Household Size

Area	Persons in Household (%)							Average Household Size
	One	Two	Three	Four	Five	Six	Seven or More	
City	35.6	34.0	14.1	9.6	4.3	1.6	0.7	2.30
MSA[1]	30.7	36.0	15.0	11.2	4.8	1.5	0.7	2.40
U.S.	28.1	33.8	15.5	12.9	6.0	2.3	1.4	2.60

Note: (1) Figures cover the Durham-Chapel Hill, NC Metropolitan Statistical Area
Source: U.S. Census Bureau, 2017-2021 American Community Survey 5-Year Estimates

Household Relationships

Area	House-holder	Opposite-sex Spouse	Same-sex Spouse	Opposite-sex Unmarried Partner	Same-sex Unmarried Partner	Child[2]	Grand-child	Other Relatives	Non-relatives
City	42.0	14.8	0.4	2.9	0.3	24.6	1.8	4.4	4.6
MSA[1]	40.3	17.2	0.3	2.5	0.2	25.1	1.9	3.8	3.9
U.S.	38.3	17.5	0.2	2.5	0.2	28.3	2.4	4.8	3.4

Note: Figures are percent of the total population; (1) Figures cover the Durham-Chapel Hill, NC Metropolitan Statistical Area; (2) Includes biological, adopted, and stepchildren of the householder
Source: U.S. Census Bureau, 2020 Census

Gender

Area	Males	Females	Males per 100 Females
City	133,353	150,153	88.8
MSA[1]	312,256	337,647	92.5
U.S.	162,685,811	168,763,470	96.4

Note: (1) Figures cover the Durham-Chapel Hill, NC Metropolitan Statistical Area
Source: U.S. Census Bureau, 2020 Census

Marital Status

Area	Never Married	Now Married[2]	Separated	Widowed	Divorced
City	43.1	40.7	2.2	4.1	9.9
MSA[1]	37.3	46.1	2.0	4.8	9.8
U.S.	33.8	48.0	1.8	5.6	10.8

Note: Figures are percentages and cover the population 15 years of age and older; (1) Figures cover the Durham-Chapel Hill, NC Metropolitan Statistical Area; (2) Excludes separated
Source: U.S. Census Bureau, 2017-2021 American Community Survey 5-Year Estimates

Religious Groups by Family

Area	Catholic	Baptist	Methodist	LDS[2]	Pentecostal	Lutheran	Islam	Adventist	Other
MSA[1]	8.5	12.3	6.5	0.9	1.3	0.3	1.5	1.1	13.7
U.S.	18.7	7.3	3.0	2.0	1.8	1.7	1.3	1.3	11.6

Note: Figures are the number of adherents as a percentage of the total population and cover the eight largest religious groups in the U.S; (1) Figures cover the Durham-Chapel Hill, NC Metropolitan Statistical Area; (2) Church of Jesus Christ of Latter-day Saints
Sources: 2020 U.S. Religion Census, Association of Statisticians of American Religious Bodies; The Association of Religion Data Archives (ARDA)

Religious Groups by Tradition

Area	Catholic	Evangelical Protestant	Mainline Protestant	Black Protestant	Islam	Judaism	Hinduism	Orthodox	Buddhism
MSA[1]	8.5	20.0	8.8	4.3	1.5	0.5	0.1	0.3	0.1
U.S.	18.7	16.5	5.2	2.3	1.3	0.6	0.4	0.4	0.3

Note: Figures are the number of adherents as a percentage of the total population; (1) Figures cover the Durham-Chapel Hill, NC Metropolitan Statistical Area
Sources: 2020 U.S. Religion Census, Association of Statisticians of American Religious Bodies; The Association of Religion Data Archives (ARDA)

Durham, North Carolina 165

ECONOMY

Gross Metropolitan Product

Area	2020	2021	2022	2023	Rank[2]
MSA[1]	51.6	57.3	61.8	65.6	60

Note: Figures are in billions of dollars; (1) Figures cover the Durham-Chapel Hill, NC Metropolitan Statistical Area; (2) Rank is based on 2021 data and ranges from 1 to 381
Source: U.S. Conference of Mayors, U.S. Metro Economies: U.S. Metros Compared to Global and State Economies, June 2022

Economic Growth

Area	2018-20 (%)	2021 (%)	2022 (%)	2023 (%)	Rank[2]
MSA[1]	2.7	6.7	2.5	2.9	19
U.S.	-0.6	5.7	3.1	2.9	–

Note: Figures are real gross metropolitan product (GMP) growth rates and represent average annual percent change; (1) Figures cover the Durham-Chapel Hill, NC Metropolitan Statistical Area; (2) Rank is based on 2020 2-year average annual percent change and ranges from 1 to 381
Source: U.S. Conference of Mayors, U.S. Metro Economies: U.S. Metros Compared to Global and State Economies, June 2022

Metropolitan Area Exports

Area	2016	2017	2018	2019	2020	2021	Rank[2]
MSA[1]	2,937.4	3,128.4	3,945.8	4,452.9	3,359.3	3,326.4	78

Note: Figures are in millions of dollars; (1) Figures cover the Durham-Chapel Hill, NC Metropolitan Statistical Area; (2) Rank is based on 2021 data and ranges from 1 to 388
Source: U.S. Department of Commerce, International Trade Administration, Office of Trade and Economic Analysis, Industry and Analysis, Exports by Metropolitan Area, data extracted March 16, 2023

Building Permits

Area	Single-Family			Multi-Family			Total		
	2021	2022	Pct. Chg.	2021	2022	Pct. Chg.	2021	2022	Pct. Chg.
City	1,960	1,595	-18.6	1,361	2,771	103.6	3,321	4,366	31.5
MSA[1]	3,735	3,170	-15.1	2,165	3,222	48.8	5,900	6,392	8.3
U.S.	1,115,400	975,600	-12.5	621,600	689,500	10.9	1,737,000	1,665,100	-4.1

Note: (1) Figures cover the Durham-Chapel Hill, NC Metropolitan Statistical Area; Figures represent new, privately-owned housing units authorized (unadjusted data); All permit data are based on estimates with imputation
Source: U.S. Census Bureau, Manufacturing, Mining, and Construction Statistics, Building Permits, 2021, 2022

Bankruptcy Filings

Area	Business Filings			Nonbusiness Filings		
	2021	2022	% Chg.	2021	2022	% Chg.
Durham County	10	5	-50.0	175	143	-18.3
U.S.	14,347	13,481	-6.0	399,269	374,240	-6.3

Note: Business filings include Chapter 7, Chapter 9, Chapter 11, Chapter 12, Chapter 13, Chapter 15, and Section 304; Nonbusiness filings include Chapter 7, Chapter 11, and Chapter 13
Source: Administrative Office of the U.S. Courts, Business and Nonbusiness Bankruptcy, County Cases Commenced by Chapter of the Bankruptcy Code, During the 12-Month Period Ending December 31, 2021 and Business and Nonbusiness Bankruptcy, County Cases Commenced by Chapter of the Bankruptcy Code, During the 12-Month Period Ending December 31, 2022

Housing Vacancy Rates

Area	Gross Vacancy Rate[2] (%)			Year-Round Vacancy Rate[3] (%)			Rental Vacancy Rate[4] (%)			Homeowner Vacancy Rate[5] (%)		
	2020	2021	2022	2020	2021	2022	2020	2021	2022	2020	2021	2022
MSA[1]	n/a	n/a	n/a	n/a	n/a	n/a	n/a	n/a	n/a	n/a	n/a	n/a
U.S.	10.6	10.8	10.5	8.2	8.4	8.2	6.3	6.1	5.8	1.0	0.9	0.8

Note: (1) Figures cover the Durham-Chapel Hill, NC Metropolitan Statistical Area; (2) The percentage of the total housing inventory that is vacant; (3) The percentage of the housing inventory (excluding seasonal units) that is year-round vacant; (4) The percentage of rental inventory that is vacant for rent; (5) The percentage of homeowner inventory that is vacant for sale; n/a not available
Source: U.S. Census Bureau, Housing Vacancies and Homeownership Annual Statistics: 2020, 2021, 2022

INCOME

Income

Area	Per Capita ($)	Median Household ($)	Average Household ($)
City	39,496	66,623	91,960
MSA[1]	40,502	68,913	99,164
U.S.	37,638	69,021	97,196

Note: (1) Figures cover the Durham-Chapel Hill, NC Metropolitan Statistical Area
Source: U.S. Census Bureau, 2017-2021 American Community Survey 5-Year Estimates

166 Durham, North Carolina

Household Income Distribution

Area	Percent of Households Earning							
	Under $15,000	$15,000 -$24,999	$25,000 -$34,999	$35,000 -$49,999	$50,000 -$74,999	$75,000 -$99,999	$100,000 -$149,999	$150,000 and up
City	8.9	6.8	9.7	12.2	17.2	13.1	15.7	16.4
MSA[1]	9.2	7.1	9.1	11.5	16.4	12.4	15.6	18.8
U.S.	9.4	7.8	8.2	11.4	16.8	12.8	16.3	17.3

Note: (1) Figures cover the Durham-Chapel Hill, NC Metropolitan Statistical Area
Source: U.S. Census Bureau, 2017-2021 American Community Survey 5-Year Estimates

Poverty Rate

Area	All Ages	Under 18 Years Old	18 to 64 Years Old	65 Years and Over
City	13.5	19.6	12.5	8.9
MSA[1]	13.2	17.8	12.9	8.2
U.S.	12.6	17.0	11.8	9.6

Note: Figures are percentage of people whose income during the past 12 months was below the poverty level;
(1) Figures cover the Durham-Chapel Hill, NC Metropolitan Statistical Area
Source: U.S. Census Bureau, 2017-2021 American Community Survey 5-Year Estimates

EMPLOYMENT

Labor Force and Employment

Area	Civilian Labor Force			Workers Employed		
	Dec. 2021	Dec. 2022	% Chg.	Dec. 2021	Dec. 2022	% Chg.
City	155,641	159,589	2.5	151,405	155,264	2.5
MSA[1]	311,304	319,367	2.6	303,354	310,936	2.5
U.S.	161,696,000	164,224,000	1.6	155,732,000	158,872,000	2.0

Note: Data is not seasonally adjusted and covers workers 16 years of age and older; (1) Figures cover the
Durham-Chapel Hill, NC Metropolitan Statistical Area
Source: Bureau of Labor Statistics, Local Area Unemployment Statistics

Unemployment Rate

Area	2022											
	Jan.	Feb.	Mar.	Apr.	May	Jun.	Jul.	Aug.	Sep.	Oct.	Nov.	Dec.
City	3.2	3.0	3.0	2.9	3.1	3.5	3.1	3.3	2.7	3.4	3.2	2.7
MSA[1]	3.0	2.9	2.8	2.8	3.0	3.4	3.1	3.2	2.7	3.3	3.2	2.6
U.S.	4.4	4.1	3.8	3.3	3.4	3.8	3.8	3.8	3.3	3.4	3.4	3.3

Note: Data is not seasonally adjusted and covers workers 16 years of age and older; (1) Figures cover the
Durham-Chapel Hill, NC Metropolitan Statistical Area
Source: Bureau of Labor Statistics, Local Area Unemployment Statistics

Average Wages

Occupation	$/Hr.	Occupation	$/Hr.
Accountants and Auditors	42.03	Maintenance and Repair Workers	23.68
Automotive Mechanics	24.33	Marketing Managers	75.77
Bookkeepers	23.51	Network and Computer Systems Admin.	48.52
Carpenters	22.09	Nurses, Licensed Practical	26.52
Cashiers	12.86	Nurses, Registered	n/a
Computer Programmers	51.67	Nursing Assistants	16.82
Computer Systems Analysts	48.44	Office Clerks, General	19.49
Computer User Support Specialists	31.57	Physical Therapists	40.71
Construction Laborers	18.55	Physicians	n/a
Cooks, Restaurant	15.87	Plumbers, Pipefitters and Steamfitters	26.00
Customer Service Representatives	19.93	Police and Sheriff's Patrol Officers	25.40
Dentists	106.19	Postal Service Mail Carriers	27.82
Electricians	27.22	Real Estate Sales Agents	26.02
Engineers, Electrical	56.69	Retail Salespersons	15.72
Fast Food and Counter Workers	13.08	Sales Representatives, Technical/Scientific	58.46
Financial Managers	84.49	Secretaries, Exc. Legal/Medical/Executive	21.42
First-Line Supervisors of Office Workers	31.92	Security Guards	18.04
General and Operations Managers	70.01	Surgeons	n/a
Hairdressers/Cosmetologists	22.31	Teacher Assistants, Exc. Postsecondary*	13.63
Home Health and Personal Care Aides	13.24	Teachers, Secondary School, Exc. Sp. Ed.*	26.62
Janitors and Cleaners	16.43	Telemarketers	15.07
Landscaping/Groundskeeping Workers	17.41	Truck Drivers, Heavy/Tractor-Trailer	24.94
Lawyers	73.85	Truck Drivers, Light/Delivery Services	19.89
Maids and Housekeeping Cleaners	14.21	Waiters and Waitresses	14.16

Note: Wage data covers the Durham-Chapel Hill, NC Metropolitan Statistical Area; (*) Hourly wages were
calculated from annual wage data based on a 40 hour work week; n/a not available.
Source: Bureau of Labor Statistics, Metro Area Occupational Employment & Wage Estimates, May 2022

Employment by Industry

Sector	MSA[1]		U.S.
	Number of Employees	Percent of Total	Percent of Total
Construction, Mining, and Logging	9,900	2.9	5.4
Private Education and Health Services	75,200	21.9	16.1
Financial Activities	16,500	4.8	5.9
Government	65,000	18.9	14.5
Information	6,200	1.8	2.0
Leisure and Hospitality	26,600	7.7	10.3
Manufacturing	29,300	8.5	8.4
Other Services	11,600	3.4	3.7
Professional and Business Services	60,200	17.5	14.7
Retail Trade	24,400	7.1	10.2
Transportation, Warehousing, and Utilities	8,700	2.5	4.9
Wholesale Trade	9,700	2.8	3.9

Note: Figures are non-farm employment as of December 2022. Figures are not seasonally adjusted and include workers 16 years of age and older; (1) Figures cover the Durham-Chapel Hill, NC Metropolitan Statistical Area
Source: Bureau of Labor Statistics, Current Employment Statistics, Employment, Hours, and Earnings

Employment by Occupation

Occupation Classification	City (%)	MSA[1] (%)	U.S. (%)
Management, Business, Science, and Arts	54.0	51.4	40.3
Natural Resources, Construction, and Maintenance	6.1	7.3	8.7
Production, Transportation, and Material Moving	7.7	9.0	13.1
Sales and Office	17.0	17.2	20.9
Service	15.2	15.0	17.0

Note: Figures cover employed civilians 16 years of age and older; (1) Figures cover the Durham-Chapel Hill, NC Metropolitan Statistical Area
Source: U.S. Census Bureau, 2017-2021 American Community Survey 5-Year Estimates

Occupations with Greatest Projected Employment Growth: 2022 – 2024

Occupation[1]	2022 Employment	2024 Projected Employment	Numeric Employment Change	Percent Employment Change
Cooks, Restaurant	45,830	53,440	7,610	16.6
Waiters and Waitresses	65,770	72,960	7,190	10.9
Software Developers	55,450	62,610	7,160	12.9
Cooks, Fast Food	82,470	88,860	6,390	7.7
Fast Food and Counter Workers	68,750	75,030	6,280	9.1
Laborers and Freight, Stock, and Material Movers, Hand	100,780	106,480	5,700	5.7
Retail Salespersons	125,490	130,210	4,720	3.8
General and Operations Managers	87,450	92,120	4,670	5.3
First-Line Supervisors of Food Preparation and Serving Workers	42,440	47,070	4,630	10.9
Stockers and Order Fillers	88,320	92,930	4,610	5.2

Note: Projections cover North Carolina; (1) Sorted by numeric employment change
Source: www.projectionscentral.com, State Occupational Projections, 2022–2024 Short-Term Projections

Fastest-Growing Occupations: 2022 – 2024

Occupation[1]	2022 Employment	2024 Projected Employment	Numeric Employment Change	Percent Employment Change
Cooks, Restaurant	45,830	53,440	7,610	16.6
Solar Photovoltaic Installers	390	450	60	15.4
Statisticians	1,710	1,960	250	14.6
Medical Scientists, Except Epidemiologists	3,630	4,160	530	14.6
Actuaries	950	1,080	130	13.7
Data Scientists	5,390	6,100	710	13.2
Soil and Plant Scientists	2,160	2,440	280	13.0
Software Developers	55,450	62,610	7,160	12.9
Software Quality Assurance Analysts and Testers	8,850	9,950	1,100	12.4
Bartenders	14,560	16,360	1,800	12.4

Note: Projections cover North Carolina; (1) Sorted by percent employment change and excludes occupations with numeric employment change less than 50
Source: www.projectionscentral.com, State Occupational Projections, 2022–2024 Short-Term Projections

CITY FINANCES

City Government Finances

Component	2020 ($000)	2020 ($ per capita)
Total Revenues	492,749	1,766
Total Expenditures	547,178	1,961
Debt Outstanding	635,428	2,278
Cash and Securities[1]	12,163	44

Note: (1) Cash and security holdings of a government at the close of its fiscal year, including those of its dependent agencies, utilities, and liquor stores.
Source: U.S. Census Bureau, State & Local Government Finances 2020

City Government Revenue by Source

Source	2020 ($000)	2020 ($ per capita)	2020 (%)
General Revenue			
From Federal Government	14,401	52	2.9
From State Government	44,443	159	9.0
From Local Governments	7,505	27	1.5
Taxes			
Property	193,562	694	39.3
Sales and Gross Receipts	51,592	185	10.5
Personal Income	0	0	0.0
Corporate Income	0	0	0.0
Motor Vehicle License	3,155	11	0.6
Other Taxes	871	3	0.2
Current Charges	102,006	366	20.7
Liquor Store	0	0	0.0
Utility	54,002	194	11.0

Source: U.S. Census Bureau, State & Local Government Finances 2020

City Government Expenditures by Function

Function	2020 ($000)	2020 ($ per capita)	2020 (%)
General Direct Expenditures			
Air Transportation	13	< 1	< 0.1
Corrections	0	0	0.0
Education	0	0	0.0
Employment Security Administration	0	0	0.0
Financial Administration	8,530	30	1.6
Fire Protection	37,253	133	6.8
General Public Buildings	13,559	48	2.5
Governmental Administration, Other	19,998	71	3.7
Health	0	0	0.0
Highways	38,111	136	7.0
Hospitals	0	0	0.0
Housing and Community Development	31,782	113	5.8
Interest on General Debt	13,145	47	2.4
Judicial and Legal	1,919	6	0.4
Libraries	0	0	0.0
Parking	7,512	26	1.4
Parks and Recreation	21,925	78	4.0
Police Protection	75,965	272	13.9
Public Welfare	0	0	0.0
Sewerage	105,819	379	19.3
Solid Waste Management	23,841	85	4.4
Veterans' Services	0	0	0.0
Liquor Store	0	0	0.0
Utility	122,867	440	22.5

Source: U.S. Census Bureau, State & Local Government Finances 2020

TAXES

State Corporate Income Tax Rates

State	Tax Rate (%)	Income Brackets ($)	Num. of Brackets	Financial Institution Tax Rate (%)[a]	Federal Income Tax Ded.
North Carolina	2.5	Flat rate	1	2.5	No

Note: Tax rates as of January 1, 2023; (a) Rates listed are the corporate income tax rate applied to financial institutions or excise taxes based on income. Some states have other taxes based upon the value of deposits or shares.
Source: Federation of Tax Administrators, State Corporate Income Tax Rates, January 1, 2023

State Individual Income Tax Rates

State	Tax Rate (%)	Income Brackets ($)	Personal Exemptions ($)			Standard Ded. ($)	
			Single	Married	Depend.	Single	Married
North Carolina	4.75	Flat rate	None	None	None	10,750	21,500

Note: Tax rates as of January 1, 2023; Local- and county-level taxes are not included; Federal income tax is not deductible on state income tax returns
Source: Federation of Tax Administrators, State Individual Income Tax Rates, January 1, 2023

Various State Sales and Excise Tax Rates

State	State Sales Tax (%)	Gasoline[1] ($/gal.)	Cigarette[2] ($/pack)	Spirits[3] ($/gal.)	Wine[4] ($/gal.)	Beer[5] ($/gal.)	Recreational Marijuana (%)
North Carolina	4.75	0.3875	0.45	16.40	1.00	0.62	Not legal

Note: All tax rates as of January 1, 2023; (1) The American Petroleum Institute has developed a methodology for determining the average tax rate on a gallon of fuel. Rates may include any of the following: excise taxes, environmental fees, storage tank fees, other fees or taxes, general sales tax, and local taxes; (2) The federal excise tax of $1.0066 per pack and local taxes are not included; (3) Rates are those applicable to off-premise sales of 40% alcohol by volume (a.b.v.) distilled spirits in 750ml containers. Local excise taxes are excluded; (4) Rates are those applicable to off-premise sales of 11% a.b.v. non-carbonated wine in 750ml containers; (5) Rates are those applicable to off-premise sales of 4.7% a.b.v. beer in 12 ounce containers.
Source: Tax Foundation, 2023 Facts & Figures: How Does Your State Compare?

State Business Tax Climate Index Rankings

State	Overall Rank	Corporate Tax Rank	Individual Income Tax Rank	Sales Tax Rank	Property Tax Rank	Unemployment Insurance Tax Rank
North Carolina	10	5	17	20	13	10

Note: The index is a measure of how each state's tax laws affect economic performance. The lower the rank, the more favorable a state's tax system is for business. States without a given tax are given a ranking of 1. The scores/rankings for the District of Columbia do not affect other states. The 2023 index represents the tax climate as of July 1, 2022.
Source: Tax Foundation, State Business Tax Climate Index 2023

TRANSPORTATION

Means of Transportation to Work

Area	Car/Truck/Van		Public Transportation			Bicycle	Walked	Other Means	Worked at Home
	Drove Alone	Car-pooled	Bus	Subway	Railroad				
City	70.7	8.0	2.6	0.0	0.0	0.5	2.2	1.3	14.6
MSA[1]	70.8	7.7	2.6	0.0	0.0	0.6	2.3	1.3	14.5
U.S.	73.2	8.6	2.0	1.6	0.5	0.5	2.5	1.5	9.7

Note: Figures are percentages and cover workers 16 years of age and older; (1) Figures cover the Durham-Chapel Hill, NC Metropolitan Statistical Area
Source: U.S. Census Bureau, 2017-2021 American Community Survey 5-Year Estimates

Travel Time to Work

Area	Less Than 10 Minutes	10 to 19 Minutes	20 to 29 Minutes	30 to 44 Minutes	45 to 59 Minutes	60 to 89 Minutes	90 Minutes or More
City	9.2	38.4	25.5	17.9	4.8	2.7	1.4
MSA[1]	9.8	31.4	24.8	21.0	7.3	4.2	1.5
U.S.	12.4	28.5	21.0	20.9	8.2	6.2	2.9

Note: Note: Figures are percentages and include workers 16 years old and over; (1) Figures cover the Durham-Chapel Hill, NC Metropolitan Statistical Area
Source: U.S. Census Bureau, 2017-2021 American Community Survey 5-Year Estimates

Key Congestion Measures

Measure	1990	2000	2010	2015	2020
Annual Hours of Delay, Total (000)	n/a	n/a	n/a	11,811	6,841
Annual Hours of Delay, Per Auto Commuter	n/a	n/a	n/a	32	18
Annual Congestion Cost, Per Auto Commuter ($)	n/a	n/a	n/a	646	401

Note: n/a not available
Source: Texas A&M Transportation Institute, 2021 Urban Mobility Report

Freeway Travel Time Index

Measure	1985	1990	1995	2000	2005	2010	2015	2020
Urban Area Index[1]	n/a	n/a	n/a	n/a	n/a	n/a	1.15	1.10
Urban Area Rank[1,2]	n/a	n/a	n/a	n/a	n/a	n/a	n/a	n/a

Note: Freeway Travel Time Index—the ratio of travel time in the peak period to the travel time at free-flow conditions. For example, a value of 1.30 indicates a 20-minute free-flow trip takes 26 minutes in the peak (20 minutes x 1.30 = 26 minutes); (1) Covers the Durham NC urban area; (2) Rank is based on 101 larger urban areas (#1 = highest travel time index); n/a not available
Source: Texas A&M Transportation Institute, 2021 Urban Mobility Report

Public Transportation

Agency Name / Mode of Transportation	Vehicles Operated in Maximum Service[1]	Annual Unlinked Passenger Trips[2] (in thous.)	Annual Passenger Miles[3] (in thous.)
Durham Area Transit Authority (DATA)			
Bus (purchased transportation)	43	4,403.7	14,213.3
Demand Response (purchased transportation)	32	115.3	1,013.5

Note: (1) Number of revenue vehicles operated by the given mode and type of service to meet the annual maximum service requirement. This is the revenue vehicle count during the peak season of the year; on the week and day that maximum service is provided. Vehicles operated in maximum service (VOMS) exclude atypical days and one-time special events; (2) Number of passengers who boarded public transportation vehicles. Passengers are counted each time they board a vehicle no matter how many vehicles they use to travel from their origin to their destination. (3) Sum of the distances ridden by all passengers during the entire fiscal year.
Source: Federal Transit Administration, National Transit Database, 2021

Air Transportation

Airport Name and Code / Type of Service	Passenger Airlines[1]	Passenger Enplanements	Freight Carriers[2]	Freight (lbs)
Raleigh-Durham International (RDU)				
Domestic service (U.S. carriers - 2022)	32	5,713,482	13	91,381,469
International service (U.S. carriers - 2021)	4	29,848	3	250,550

Note: (1) Includes all U.S.-based major, minor and commuter airlines that carried at least one passenger during the year; (2) Includes all U.S.-based airlines and freight carriers that transported at least one pound of freight during the year.
Source: Bureau of Transportation Statistics, The Intermodal Transportation Database, Air Carriers: T-100 Domestic Market (U.S. Carriers), 2022; Bureau of Transportation Statistics, The Intermodal Transportation Database, Air Carriers: T-100 International Market (U.S. Carriers), 2021

BUSINESSES

Major Business Headquarters

Company Name	Industry	Rankings	
		Fortune[1]	Forbes[2]
IQVIA Holdings	Pharmaceutical services	269	-

Note: (1) Companies that produce a 10-K are ranked 1 to 500 based on 2021 revenue; (2) All private companies with at least $2 billion in annual revenue through the end of their most current fiscal year are ranked 1 to 246; companies listed are headquartered in the city; dashes indicate no ranking
Source: Fortune, "Fortune 500," 2022; Forbes, "America's Largest Private Companies," 2022

Fastest-Growing Businesses

According to Deloitte, Durham is home to three of North America's 500 fastest-growing high-technology companies: **Precision Biosciences** (#150); **Aerie Pharmaceuticals** (#216); **Biocryst Pharmaceuticals** (#229). Companies are ranked by percentage growth in revenue over a four-year period. Criteria for inclusion: company must be headquartered within North America; must own proprietary intellectual property or technology that is sold to customers in products that contributes to a significant portion of the company's operating revenue; must have been in business for a minumum of four years with 2018 operating revenues of at least $50,000 USD/CD and 2021 operating revenues of at least $5 million USD/CD. *Deloitte, 2022 Technology Fast 500™*

Living Environment

COST OF LIVING

Cost of Living Index

Composite Index	Groceries	Housing	Utilities	Trans-portation	Health Care	Misc. Goods/Services
101.8	101.0	120.1	87.4	93.3	106.5	92.2

Note: The Cost of Living Index measures regional differences in the cost of consumer goods and services, excluding taxes and non-consumer expenditures, for professional and managerial households in the top income quintile. It is based on more than 50,000 prices covering almost 60 different items for which prices are collected three times a year by chambers of commerce, economic development organizations or university applied economic centers in each participating urban area. The numbers shown should be read as a percentage above or below the national average of 100. For example, a value of 115.4 in the groceries column indicates that grocery prices are 15.4% higher than the national average. Small differences in the index numbers should not be interpreted as significant; Figures cover the Chapel Hill NC urban area.
Source: The Council for Community and Economic Research, Cost of Living Index, 2022

Grocery Prices

Area[1]	T-Bone Steak ($/pound)	Frying Chicken ($/pound)	Whole Milk ($/half gal.)	Eggs ($/dozen)	Orange Juice ($/64 oz.)	Coffee ($/11.5 oz.)
City[2]	13.15	1.77	1.97	2.14	4.23	5.04
Avg.	13.81	1.59	2.43	2.25	3.85	4.95
Min.	10.17	0.90	1.51	1.30	2.90	3.46
Max.	19.35	3.30	4.32	4.32	5.31	8.59

*Note: (1) Values for the local area are compared with the average, minimum and maximum values for all 286 areas in the Cost of Living Index; (2) Figures cover the Chapel Hill NC urban area; **T-Bone Steak** (price per pound); **Frying Chicken** (price per pound, whole fryer); **Whole Milk** (half gallon carton); **Eggs** (price per dozen, Grade A, large); **Orange Juice** (64 oz. Tropicana or Florida Natural); **Coffee** (11.5 oz. can, vacuum-packed, Maxwell House, Hills Bros, or Folgers).*
Source: The Council for Community and Economic Research, Cost of Living Index, 2022

Housing and Utility Costs

Area[1]	New Home Price ($)	Apartment Rent ($/month)	All Electric ($/month)	Part Electric ($/month)	Other Energy ($/month)	Telephone ($/month)
City[2]	582,565	1,411	-	85.31	62.68	176.30
Avg.	450,913	1,371	176.41	99.93	76.96	190.22
Min.	229,283	546	100.84	31.56	27.15	174.27
Max.	2,434,977	4,569	356.86	249.59	272.24	208.31

*Note: (1) Values for the local area are compared with the average, minimum and maximum values for all 286 areas in the Cost of Living Index; (2) Figures cover the Chapel Hill NC urban area; **New Home Price** (2,400 sf living area, 8,000 sf lot, in urban area with full utilities); **Apartment Rent** (950 sf 2 bedroom/1.5 or 2 bath, unfurnished, excluding all utilities except water); **All Electric** (average monthly cost for an all-electric home); **Part Electric** (average monthly cost for a part-electric home); **Other Energy** (average monthly cost for natural gas, fuel oil, coal, wood, and any other forms of energy except electricity); **Telephone** (price includes the base monthly rate plus taxes and fees for three lines of mobile phone service).*
Source: The Council for Community and Economic Research, Cost of Living Index, 2022

Health Care, Transportation, and Other Costs

Area[1]	Doctor ($/visit)	Dentist ($/visit)	Optometrist ($/visit)	Gasoline ($/gallon)	Beauty Salon ($/visit)	Men's Shirt ($)
City[2]	143.27	113.91	132.86	3.70	53.11	22.22
Avg.	124.91	107.77	117.66	3.86	43.31	34.21
Min.	36.61	58.25	51.79	2.90	22.18	13.05
Max.	250.21	162.58	371.96	5.54	85.61	63.54

*Note: (1) Values for the local area are compared with the average, minimum and maximum values for all 286 areas in the Cost of Living Index; (2) Figures cover the Chapel Hill NC urban area; **Doctor** (general practitioners routine exam of an established patient); **Dentist** (adult teeth cleaning and periodic oral examination); **Optometrist** (full vision eye exam for established adult patient); **Gasoline** (one gallon regular unleaded, national brand, including all taxes, cash price at self-service pump if available); **Beauty Salon** (woman's shampoo, trim, and blow-dry); **Men's Shirt** (cotton/polyester dress shirt, pinpoint weave, long sleeves).*
Source: The Council for Community and Economic Research, Cost of Living Index, 2022

HOUSING

Homeownership Rate

Area	2015 (%)	2016 (%)	2017 (%)	2018 (%)	2019 (%)	2020 (%)	2021 (%)	2022 (%)
MSA[1]	n/a	n/a	n/a	n/a	n/a	n/a	n/a	n/a
U.S.	63.7	63.4	63.9	64.4	64.6	66.6	65.5	65.8

Note: (1) Figures cover the Durham-Chapel Hill, NC Metropolitan Statistical Area; n/a not available
Source: U.S. Census Bureau, Housing Vacancies and Homeownership Annual Statistics: 2015-2022

House Price Index (HPI)

Area	National Ranking[2]	Quarterly Change (%)	One-Year Change (%)	Five-Year Change (%)	Since 1991Q1 (%)
MSA[1]	45	-3.85	15.68	66.89	294.13
U.S.[3]	–	0.34	8.41	58.44	289.08

Note: The HPI is a weighted repeat sales index. It measures average price changes in repeat sales or refinancings on the same properties. This information is obtained by reviewing repeat mortgage transactions on single-family properties whose mortgages have been purchased or securitized by Fannie Mae or Freddie Mac since January 1975; (1) Figures cover the Durham-Chapel Hill, NC Metropolitan Statistical Area; (2) Rankings are based on annual percentage change for all metro areas containing at least 15,000 transactions over the last 10 years and ranges from 1 to 257; (3) figures based on a weighted average of Census Division estimates using a seasonally adjusted, purchase-only index; all figures are for the period ending December 31, 2022
Source: Federal Housing Finance Agency, Change in FHFA Metropolitan Area House Price Indexes, 2022Q4

Median Single-Family Home Prices

Area	2020	2021	2022[p]	Percent Change 2021 to 2022
MSA[1]	326.3	397.9	453.6	14.0
U.S. Average	300.2	357.1	392.6	9.9

Note: Figures are median sales prices of existing single-family homes in thousands of dollars; (p) preliminary; (1) Figures cover the Durham-Chapel Hill, NC Metropolitan Statistical Area
Source: National Association of Realtors, Median Sales Price of Existing Single-Family Homes for Metropolitan Areas, 4th Quarter 2022

Qualifying Income Based on Median Sales Price of Existing Single-Family Homes

Area	With 5% Down ($)	With 10% Down ($)	With 20% Down ($)
MSA[1]	127,333	120,631	107,227
U.S. Average	112,234	106,237	94,513

Note: Figures are preliminary; Qualifying income is based on a mortgage rate of 6.77%. Monthly principal and interest payment is limited to 25% of income; (1) Figures cover the Durham-Chapel Hill, NC Metropolitan Statistical Area
Source: National Association of Realtors, Qualifying Income Based on Median Sales Price of Existing Single-Family Homes for Metropolitan Areas, 4th Quarter 2022

Home Value

Area	Under $100,000	$100,000 -$199,999	$200,000 -$299,999	$300,000 -$399,999	$400,000 -$499,999	$500,000 -$999,999	$1,000,000 or more	Median ($)
City	5.0	24.8	31.4	20.4	8.2	9.0	1.1	264,100
MSA[1]	10.6	23.8	24.0	17.7	9.2	12.7	1.9	264,400
U.S.	16.2	24.2	20.1	13.6	8.3	13.6	4.1	244,900

Note: Figures are percentages except for median and cover owner-occupied housing units; (1) Figures cover the Durham-Chapel Hill, NC Metropolitan Statistical Area
Source: U.S. Census Bureau, 2017-2021 American Community Survey 5-Year Estimates

Year Housing Structure Built

Area	2020 or Later	2010 -2019	2000 -2009	1990 -1999	1980 -1989	1970 -1979	1960 -1969	1950 -1959	1940 -1949	Before 1940	Median Year
City	0.4	17.0	17.9	16.6	14.6	10.4	8.1	5.7	3.3	5.9	1991
MSA[1]	0.5	13.4	17.9	18.2	15.3	12.0	8.4	6.1	2.9	5.3	1990
U.S.	0.2	7.3	13.6	13.6	13.2	14.8	10.3	10.0	4.7	12.2	1979

Note: Figures are percentages except for Median Year; Note: (1) Figures cover the Durham-Chapel Hill, NC Metropolitan Statistical Area
Source: U.S. Census Bureau, 2017-2021 American Community Survey 5-Year Estimates

Gross Monthly Rent

Area	Under $500	$500 -$999	$1,000 -$1,499	$1,500 -$1,999	$2,000 -$2,499	$2,500 -$2,999	$3,000 and up	Median ($)
City	6.7	26.5	44.8	17.4	3.1	0.4	1.1	1,157
MSA[1]	6.6	30.7	41.7	15.5	3.6	0.7	1.3	1,127
U.S.	8.1	30.5	30.8	16.8	7.3	3.1	3.5	1,163

Note: Figures are percentages except for median; Gross rent is the contract rent plus the estimated average monthly cost of utilities (electricity, gas, and water and sewer) and fuels (oil, coal, kerosene, wood, etc.) if these are paid by the renter (or paid for the renter by someone else); (1) Figures cover the Durham-Chapel Hill, NC Metropolitan Statistical Area
Source: U.S. Census Bureau, 2017-2021 American Community Survey 5-Year Estimates

HEALTH

Health Risk Factors

Category	MSA[1] (%)	U.S. (%)
Adults aged 18–64 who have any kind of health care coverage	n/a	90.9
Adults who reported being in good or better health	n/a	85.2
Adults who have been told they have high blood cholesterol	n/a	35.7
Adults who have been told they have high blood pressure	n/a	32.4
Adults who are current smokers	n/a	14.4
Adults who currently use e-cigarettes	n/a	6.7
Adults who currently use chewing tobacco, snuff, or snus	n/a	3.5
Adults who are heavy drinkers[2]	n/a	6.3
Adults who are binge drinkers[3]	n/a	15.4
Adults who are overweight (BMI 25.0 - 29.9)	n/a	34.4
Adults who are obese (BMI 30.0 - 99.8)	n/a	33.9
Adults who participated in any physical activities in the past month	n/a	76.3

Note: (1) Figures for the Durham-Chapel Hill, NC Metropolitan Statistical Area were not available.
(2) Heavy drinkers are classified as adult men having more than 14 drinks per week and adult women having more than 7 drinks per week; (3) Binge drinkers are classified as males having five or more drinks on one occasion or females having four or more drinks on one occasion
Source: Centers for Disease Control and Prevention, Behaviorial Risk Factor Surveillance System, SMART: Selected Metropolitan Area Risk Trends, 2021

Acute and Chronic Health Conditions

Category	MSA[1] (%)	U.S. (%)
Adults who have ever been told they had a heart attack	n/a	4.0
Adults who have ever been told they have angina or coronary heart disease	n/a	3.8
Adults who have ever been told they had a stroke	n/a	3.0
Adults who have ever been told they have asthma	n/a	14.9
Adults who have ever been told they have arthritis	n/a	25.8
Adults who have ever been told they have diabetes[2]	n/a	10.9
Adults who have ever been told they had skin cancer	n/a	6.6
Adults who have ever been told they had any other types of cancer	n/a	7.5
Adults who have ever been told they have COPD	n/a	6.1
Adults who have ever been told they have kidney disease	n/a	3.0
Adults who have ever been told they have a form of depression	n/a	20.5

Note: (1) Figures for the Durham-Chapel Hill, NC Metropolitan Statistical Area were not available.
(2) Figures do not include pregnancy-related, borderline, or pre-diabetes
Source: Centers for Disease Control and Prevention, Behaviorial Risk Factor Surveillance System, SMART: Selected Metropolitan Area Risk Trends, 2021

Health Screening and Vaccination Rates

Category	MSA[1] (%)	U.S. (%)
Adults who have ever been tested for HIV	n/a	34.9
Adults who have had their blood cholesterol checked within the last five years	n/a	85.2
Adults aged 65+ who have had flu shot within the past year	n/a	68.6
Adults aged 65+ who have ever had a pneumonia vaccination	n/a	71.0

Note: (1) Figures for the Durham-Chapel Hill, NC Metropolitan Statistical Area were not available.
Source: Centers for Disease Control and Prevention, Behaviorial Risk Factor Surveillance System, SMART: Selected Metropolitan Area Risk Trends, 2021

Disability Status

Category	MSA[1] (%)	U.S. (%)
Adults who reported being deaf	n/a	7.2
Are you blind or have serious difficulty seeing, even when wearing glasses?	n/a	4.8
Are you limited in any way in any of your usual activities due to arthritis?	n/a	11.1
Do you have difficulty doing errands alone?	n/a	7.0
Do you have difficulty dressing or bathing?	n/a	3.6
Do you have serious difficulty concentrating/remembering/making decisions?	n/a	12.1
Do you have serious difficulty walking or climbing stairs?	n/a	12.8

Note: (1) Figures for the Durham-Chapel Hill, NC Metropolitan Statistical Area were not available.
Source: Centers for Disease Control and Prevention, Behaviorial Risk Factor Surveillance System, SMART: Selected Metropolitan Area Risk Trends, 2021

174   Durham, North Carolina

Mortality Rates for the Top 10 Causes of Death in the U.S.

ICD-10[a] Sub-Chapter	ICD-10[a] Code	Crude Mortality Rate[1] per 100,000 population	
		County[2]	U.S.
Malignant neoplasms	C00-C97	141.9	182.6
Ischaemic heart diseases	I20-I25	59.2	113.1
Other forms of heart disease	I30-I51	48.6	64.4
Other degenerative diseases of the nervous system	G30-G31	32.8	51.0
Cerebrovascular diseases	I60-I69	31.2	47.8
Other external causes of accidental injury	W00-X59	43.3	46.4
Chronic lower respiratory diseases	J40-J47	25.2	45.7
Organic, including symptomatic, mental disorders	F01-F09	50.6	35.9
Hypertensive diseases	I10-I15	17.2	35.0
Diabetes mellitus	E10-E14	19.2	29.6

Note: (a) ICD-10 = International Classification of Diseases 10th Revision; (1) Crude mortality rates are a three-year average covering 2019-2021; (2) Figures cover Durham County.
Source: Centers for Disease Control and Prevention, National Center for Health Statistics. National Vital Statistics System, Mortality 2018-2021 on CDC WONDER Online Database

Mortality Rates for Selected Causes of Death

ICD-10[a] Sub-Chapter	ICD-10[a] Code	Crude Mortality Rate[1] per 100,000 population	
		County[2]	U.S.
Assault	X85-Y09	11.8	7.0
Diseases of the liver	K70-K76	14.2	19.8
Human immunodeficiency virus (HIV) disease	B20-B24	Unreliable	1.5
Influenza and pneumonia	J09-J18	6.3	14.7
Intentional self-harm	X60-X84	9.4	14.3
Malnutrition	E40-E46	4.9	4.3
Obesity and other hyperalimentation	E65-E68	3.3	3.0
Renal failure	N17-N19	16.3	15.7
Transport accidents	V01-V99	11.1	13.6
Viral hepatitis	B15-B19	Suppressed	1.2

Note: (a) ICD-10 = International Classification of Diseases 10th Revision; (1) Crude mortality rates are a three-year average covering 2019-2021; (2) Figures cover Durham County; Data are suppressed when the data meet the criteria for confidentiality constraints; Crude mortality rates are flagged as unreliable when the rate would be calculated with a numerator of 20 or less.
Source: Centers for Disease Control and Prevention, National Center for Health Statistics. National Vital Statistics System, Mortality 2018-2021 on CDC WONDER Online Database

Health Insurance Coverage

Area	With Health Insurance	With Private Health Insurance	With Public Health Insurance	Without Health Insurance	Population Under Age 19 Without Health Insurance
City	88.1	69.6	27.9	11.9	7.7
MSA[1]	90.0	71.8	30.0	10.0	5.7
U.S.	91.2	67.8	35.4	8.8	5.3

Note: Figures are percentages that cover the civilian noninstitutionalized population; (1) Figures cover the Durham-Chapel Hill, NC Metropolitan Statistical Area
Source: U.S. Census Bureau, 2017-2021 American Community Survey 5-Year Estimates

Number of Medical Professionals

Area	MDs[3]	DOs[3,4]	Dentists	Podiatrists	Chiropractors	Optometrists
County[1] (number)	3,681	53	246	14	65	46
County[1] (rate[2])	1,130.5	16.3	75.4	4.3	19.9	14.1
U.S. (rate[2])	289.3	23.5	72.5	6.2	28.7	17.4

Note: Data as of 2021 unless noted; (1) Data covers Durham County; (2) Rate per 100,000 population; (3) Data as of 2020 and includes all active, non-federal physicians; (4) Doctor of Osteopathic Medicine
Source: U.S. Department of Health and Human Services, Health Resources and Services Administration, Bureau of Health Professions, Area Resource File (ARF) 2021-2022

Best Hospitals

According to *U.S. News,* the Durham-Chapel Hill, NC metro area is home to two of the best hospitals in the U.S.: **Duke University Hospital** (11 adult specialties and 9 pediatric specialties); **UNC Hospitals** (4 adult specialties and 8 pediatric specialties). The hospitals listed were nationally ranked in at least one of 15 adult or 10 pediatric specialties. The number of specialties shown cover the parent hospital. Only 164 U.S. hospitals performed well enough to be nationally ranked in one or more specialties. Twenty hospitals in the U.S. made the Honor Roll. The Best Hospitals Honor Roll takes both the national rankings and the procedure and condition ratings into account. Hospitals received points if they were nationally ranked in one of the 15 adult specialties—the higher they ranked, the more points they got—and how many ratings of "high performing" they earned in the 17 procedures and conditions. *U.S. News Online, "America's Best Hospitals 2022-23"*

According to *U.S. News,* the Durham-Chapel Hill, NC metro area is home to two of the best children's hospitals in the U.S.: **North Carolina Children's Hospital at UNC** (8 pediatric specialties); **Duke Children's Hospital and Health Center** (9 pediatric specialties). The hospitals listed were highly ranked in at least one of 10 pediatric specialties. Eighty-six children's hospitals in the U.S. were nationally ranked in at least one specialty. Hospitals received points for being ranked in a specialty, and the 10 hospitals with the most points across the 10 specialties make up the Honor Roll. *U.S. News Online, "America's Best Children's Hospitals 2022-23"*

EDUCATION

Public School District Statistics

District Name	Schls	Pupils	Pupil/ Teacher Ratio	Minority Pupils[1] (%)	LEP/ELL[2] (%)	IEP[3] (%)
Durham Public Schools	55	31,754	13.1	80.8	15.3	14.3
NC Connections Academy	1	2,815	28.4	54.4	1.4	12.4
NC Virtual Academy	1	3,403	23.3	55.1	0.4	14.0

Note: Table includes school districts with 2,000 or more students; (1) Percentage of students that are not non-Hispanic white; (2) Percentage of students that are Limited English Proficient or English Language Learners (2018-19); (3) Percentage of students that have an Individualized Education Program (2019-20).
Source: U.S. Department of Education, National Center for Education Statistics, Common Core of Data, Local Education Agency (School District) Universe Survey: School Year 2021-2022

Highest Level of Education

Area	Less than H.S.	H.S. Diploma	Some College, No Deg.	Associate Degree	Bachelor's Degree	Master's Degree	Prof. School Degree	Doctorate Degree
City	9.4	16.2	14.7	6.9	27.7	15.8	4.3	5.0
MSA[1]	9.9	19.0	15.8	7.9	24.4	14.1	4.1	4.8
U.S.	11.1	26.5	20.0	8.7	20.6	9.3	2.2	1.5

Note: Figures cover persons age 25 and over; (1) Figures cover the Durham-Chapel Hill, NC Metropolitan Statistical Area
Source: U.S. Census Bureau, 2017-2021 American Community Survey 5-Year Estimates

Educational Attainment by Race

Area	High School Graduate or Higher (%)					Bachelor's Degree or Higher (%)				
	Total	White	Black	Asian	Hisp.[2]	Total	White	Black	Asian	Hisp.[2]
City	90.6	93.8	90.0	93.0	54.7	52.8	65.7	35.4	77.8	19.8
MSA[1]	90.1	93.0	87.9	92.8	56.5	47.4	54.2	30.3	77.1	21.3
U.S.	88.9	91.4	87.2	87.6	71.2	33.7	35.5	23.3	55.6	18.4

Note: Figures shown cover persons 25 years old and over; (1) Figures cover the Durham-Chapel Hill, NC Metropolitan Statistical Area; (2) People of Hispanic origin can be of any race
Source: U.S. Census Bureau, 2017-2021 American Community Survey 5-Year Estimates

School Enrollment by Grade and Control

Area	Preschool (%)		Kindergarten (%)		Grades 1 - 4 (%)		Grades 5 - 8 (%)		Grades 9 - 12 (%)	
	Public	Private	Public	Private	Public	Private	Public	Private	Public	Private
City	53.6	46.4	84.7	15.3	89.3	10.7	84.4	15.6	88.5	11.5
MSA[1]	47.9	52.1	81.8	18.2	88.9	11.1	86.0	14.0	90.4	9.6
U.S.	58.8	41.2	86.3	13.7	88.3	11.7	88.6	11.4	89.4	10.6

Note: Figures shown cover persons 3 years old and over; (1) Figures cover the Durham-Chapel Hill, NC Metropolitan Statistical Area
Source: U.S. Census Bureau, 2017-2021 American Community Survey 5-Year Estimates

Higher Education

Four-Year Colleges			Two-Year Colleges			Medical Schools[1]	Law Schools[2]	Voc/ Tech[3]
Public	Private Non-profit	Private For-profit	Public	Private Non-profit	Private For-profit			
2	2	0	2	0	0	2	3	3

Note: Figures cover institutions located within the Durham-Chapel Hill, NC Metropolitan Statistical Area and include main campuses only; (1) includes schools accredited by the Liaison Committee on Medical Education and the American Osteopathic Association's Commission on Osteopathic College Accreditation; (2) includes ABA-accredited schools, schools with provisional ABA accreditation, and state accredited schools; (3) includes all schools with programs that are less than 2 years.
Source: National Center for Education Statistics, Integrated Postsecondary Education System (IPEDS), 2021-22; Wikipedia, List of Medical Schools in the United States, accessed April 10, 2023; Wikipedia, List of Law Schools in the United States, accessed April 10, 2023

According to *U.S. News & World Report,* the Durham-Chapel Hill, NC metro area is home to two of the top 200 national universities in the U.S.: **Duke University** (#10 tie); **University of North**

Carolina at Chapel Hill (#29 tie). The indicators used to capture academic quality fall into a number of categories: assessment by administrators at peer institutions; retention of students; faculty resources; student selectivity; financial resources; alumni giving; high school counselor ratings of colleges; and graduation rate. *U.S. News & World Report, "America's Best Colleges 2023"*

According to *U.S. News & World Report,* the Durham-Chapel Hill, NC metro area is home to two of the top 100 law schools in the U.S.: **Duke University** (#11); **University of North Carolina—Chapel Hill** (#23 tie). The rankings are based on a weighted average of 12 measures of quality: peer assessment score; assessment score by lawyers/judges; median LSAT scores; median undergrad GPA; acceptance rate; employment rates for graduates; placement success; bar passage rate; faculty resources; expenditures per student; student/faculty ratio; and library resources. *U.S. News & World Report, "America's Best Graduate Schools, Law, 2023"*

According to *U.S. News & World Report,* the Durham-Chapel Hill, NC metro area is home to two of the top 75 medical schools for research in the U.S.: **Duke University** (#6 tie); **University of North Carolina—Chapel Hill** (#25 tie). The rankings are based on a weighted average of 11 measures of quality: quality assessment; peer assessment score; assessment score by residency directors; research activity; total research activity; average research activity per faculty member; student selectivity; median MCAT total score; median undergraduate GPA; acceptance rate; and faculty resources. *U.S. News & World Report, "America's Best Graduate Schools, Medical, 2023"*

According to *U.S. News & World Report,* the Durham-Chapel Hill, NC metro area is home to two of the top 75 business schools in the U.S.: **Duke University (Fuqua)** (#12 tie); **University of North Carolina—Chapel Hill (Kenan-Flagler)** (#19 tie). The rankings are based on a weighted average of the following nine measures: quality assessment; peer assessment; recruiter assessment; placement success; mean starting salary and bonus; student selectivity; mean GMAT and GRE scores; mean undergraduate GPA; and acceptance rate. *U.S. News & World Report, "America's Best Graduate Schools, Business, 2023"*

EMPLOYERS

Major Employers

Company Name	Industry
CISCO Systems	Data conversion equipment, media-to-media: computer
City of Durham	Municipal government
Duke University	Colleges & universities
Duke University Health System	General medical & surgical hospitals
Durham County Hospital Corporation	General medical & surgical hospitals
Environmental Protection Agency	Environmental protection agency, government
IBM	Computer peripheral equipment
National Institutes of Health	Environmental health program administration, govt
Netapp	Computer integrated systems design
North Carolina Central University	Colleges & universities
Patheon	Pharmaceutical preparations
Phyamerica Government Services	Hospital management
Research Triangle Institute	Commercial physical research
Sports Endeavors	Sporting goods & bicycle shops
University of NC at Chapel Hill	University
University of North Carolina Hospitals	General medical & surgical hospitals

Note: Companies shown are located within the Durham-Chapel Hill, NC Metropolitan Statistical Area. Source: Hoovers.com; Wikipedia

Best Companies to Work For

Matchwell, headquartered in Durham, is among "Best Workplaces in Health Care." To determine the Best Workplaces in Health Care list, Great Place To Work analyzed the survey responses of over 161,000 employees from Great Place To Work-Certified companies in the health care industry. Survey data analysis and company-provided datapoints are then factored into a combined score to compare and rank the companies that create the most consistently positive experience for all employees in this industry. *Fortune, "Best Workplaces in Health Care," 2022*

Blue Cross Blue Shield of North Carolina, headquartered in Durham, is among the "100 Best Places to Work in IT." To qualify, companies had to have a minimum of 100 total employees and five IT employees. The best places to work were selected based on DEI (diversity, equity, and inclusion) practices; IT turnover, promotions, and growth; IT retention and engagement programs; remote/hybrid working; benefits and perks (such as elder care and child care, flextime, and reimbursement for college tuition); and training and career development opportunities. *Computerworld, "Best Places to Work in IT," 2023*

Durham, North Carolina 177

PUBLIC SAFETY

Crime Rate

Area	Total Crime	Violent Crime Rate				Property Crime Rate		
		Murder	Rape[3]	Robbery	Aggrav. Assault	Burglary	Larceny -Theft	Motor Vehicle Theft
City	4,596.6	12.6	43.9	219.7	582.6	668.9	2,730.2	338.7
Suburbs[1]	1,768.6	4.6	17.6	32.3	169.1	319.6	1,113.7	111.7
Metro[2]	3,000.9	8.1	29.1	113.9	349.3	471.8	1,818.1	210.6
U.S.	2,356.7	6.5	38.4	73.9	279.7	314.2	1,398.0	246.0

Note: Figures are crimes per 100,000 population; (1) All areas within the metro area that are located outside the city limits; (2) Figures cover the Durham-Chapel Hill, NC Metropolitan Statistical Area; (3) All figures shown were reported using the revised Uniform Crime Reporting (UCR) definition of rape; Due to the transition to the National Incident-Based Reporting System (NIBRS), limited city and metro area data was released for 2021.
Source: FBI Uniform Crime Reports, 2020

Hate Crimes

Area	Number of Quarters Reported	Number of Incidents per Bias Motivation					
		Race/Ethnicity/ Ancestry	Religion	Sexual Orientation	Disability	Gender	Gender Identity
City	4	12	1	2	0	0	0
U.S.	4	5,227	1,244	1,110	130	75	266

Note: Due to the transition to the National Incident-Based Reporting System (NIBRS), limited crime data was released for 2021.
Source: Federal Bureau of Investigation, Hate Crime Statistics 2020

Identity Theft Consumer Reports

Area	Reports	Reports per 100,000 Population	Rank[2]
MSA[1]	1,598	251	105
U.S.	1,108,609	339	-

Note: (1) Figures cover the Durham-Chapel Hill, NC Metropolitan Statistical Area; (2) Rank ranges from 1 to 391 where 1 indicates greatest number of identity theft reports per 100,000 population
Source: Federal Trade Commission, Consumer Sentinel Network Data Book 2022

Fraud and Other Consumer Reports

Area	Reports	Reports per 100,000 Population	Rank[2]
MSA[1]	6,284	988	104
U.S.	4,064,520	1,245	-

Note: (1) Figures cover the Durham-Chapel Hill, NC Metropolitan Statistical Area; (2) Rank ranges from 1 to 391 where 1 indicates greatest number of fraud and other consumer reports per 100,000 population
Source: Federal Trade Commission, Consumer Sentinel Network Data Book 2022

POLITICS

2020 Presidential Election Results

Area	Biden	Trump	Jorgensen	Hawkins	Other
Durham County	80.4	18.0	0.8	0.3	0.4
U.S.	51.3	46.8	1.2	0.3	0.5

Note: Results are percentages and may not add to 100% due to rounding
Source: Dave Leip's Atlas of U.S. Presidential Elections

SPORTS

Professional Sports Teams

Team Name	League	Year Established
Carolina Hurricanes	National Hockey League (NHL)	1997

Note: Includes teams located in the Durham-Chapel Hill, NC Metropolitan Statistical Area.
Source: Wikipedia, Major Professional Sports Teams of the United States and Canada, April 12, 2023

CLIMATE

Average and Extreme Temperatures

Temperature	Jan	Feb	Mar	Apr	May	Jun	Jul	Aug	Sep	Oct	Nov	Dec	Yr.
Extreme High (°F)	79	84	90	95	97	104	105	105	104	98	88	79	105
Average High (°F)	50	53	61	72	79	86	89	87	81	72	62	53	71
Average Temp. (°F)	40	43	50	59	67	75	78	77	71	60	51	42	60
Average Low (°F)	29	31	38	46	55	63	68	67	60	48	39	32	48
Extreme Low (°F)	-9	5	11	23	29	38	48	46	37	19	11	4	-9

Note: Figures cover the years 1948-1990
Source: National Climatic Data Center, International Station Meteorological Climate Summary, 9/96

178   Durham, North Carolina

Average Precipitation/Snowfall/Humidity

Precip./Humidity	Jan	Feb	Mar	Apr	May	Jun	Jul	Aug	Sep	Oct	Nov	Dec	Yr.
Avg. Precip. (in.)	3.4	3.6	3.6	2.9	3.9	3.6	4.4	4.4	3.2	2.9	3.0	3.1	42.0
Avg. Snowfall (in.)	2	3	1	Tr	0	0	0	0	0	0	Tr	1	8
Avg. Rel. Hum. 7am (%)	79	79	79	80	84	86	88	91	91	90	84	81	84
Avg. Rel. Hum. 4pm (%)	53	49	46	43	51	54	57	59	57	53	51	53	52

Note: Figures cover the years 1948-1990; Tr = Trace amounts (<0.05 in. of rain; <0.5 in. of snow)
Source: National Climatic Data Center, International Station Meteorological Climate Summary, 9/96

Weather Conditions

Temperature			Daytime Sky			Precipitation		
32°F & below	45°F & below	90°F & above	Clear	Partly cloudy	Cloudy	0.01 inch or more precip.	0.1 inch or more snow/ice	Thunder-storms
77	160	39	98	143	124	110	3	42

Note: Figures are average number of days per year and cover the years 1948-1990
Source: National Climatic Data Center, International Station Meteorological Climate Summary, 9/96

HAZARDOUS WASTE

Superfund Sites

The Durham-Chapel Hill, NC metro area is home to one site on the EPA's Superfund National Priorities List: **GMH Electronics** (final). There are a total of 1,165 Superfund sites with a status of proposed or final on the list in the U.S. *U.S. Environmental Protection Agency, National Priorities List, April 12, 2023*

AIR QUALITY

Air Quality Trends: Ozone

	1990	1995	2000	2005	2010	2015	2018	2019	2020	2021
MSA[1]	0.078	0.080	0.082	0.079	0.074	0.061	0.063	0.063	0.051	0.063
U.S.	0.087	0.089	0.081	0.080	0.072	0.067	0.069	0.065	0.065	0.067

Note: (1) Data covers the Durham-Chapel Hill, NC Metropolitan Statistical Area. The values shown are the composite ozone concentration averages among trend sites based on the highest fourth daily maximum 8-hour concentration in parts per million. These trends are based on sites having an adequate record of monitoring data during the trend period. Data from exceptional events are included.
Source: U.S. Environmental Protection Agency, Air Quality Monitoring Information, "Air Quality Trends by City, 1990-2021"

Air Quality Index

Area	Percent of Days when Air Quality was...[2]					AQI Statistics[2]	
	Good	Moderate	Unhealthy for Sensitive Groups	Unhealthy	Very Unhealthy	Maximum	Median
MSA[1]	81.6	18.4	0.0	0.0	0.0	90	40

Note: (1) Data covers the Durham-Chapel Hill, NC Metropolitan Statistical Area; (2) Based on 365 days with AQI data in 2021. Air Quality Index (AQI) is an index for reporting daily air quality. EPA calculates the AQI for five major air pollutants regulated by the Clean Air Act: ground-level ozone, particle pollution (aka particulate matter), carbon monoxide, sulfur dioxide, and nitrogen dioxide. The AQI runs from 0 to 500. The higher the AQI value, the greater the level of air pollution and the greater the health concern. There are six AQI categories: "Good" AQI is between 0 and 50. Air quality is considered satisfactory; "Moderate" AQI is between 51 and 100. Air quality is acceptable; "Unhealthy for Sensitive Groups" When AQI values are between 101 and 150, members of sensitive groups may experience health effects; "Unhealthy" When AQI values are between 151 and 200 everyone may begin to experience health effects; "Very Unhealthy" AQI values between 201 and 300 trigger a health alert; "Hazardous" AQI values over 300 trigger warnings of emergency conditions (not shown).
Source: U.S. Environmental Protection Agency, Air Quality Index Report, 2021

Air Quality Index Pollutants

Area	Percent of Days when AQI Pollutant was...[2]					
	Carbon Monoxide	Nitrogen Dioxide	Ozone	Sulfur Dioxide	Particulate Matter 2.5	Particulate Matter 10
MSA[1]	0.0	0.0	51.8	(3)	48.2	0.0

Note: (1) Data covers the Durham-Chapel Hill, NC Metropolitan Statistical Area; (2) Based on 365 days with AQI data in 2021. The Air Quality Index (AQI) is an index for reporting daily air quality. EPA calculates the AQI for five major air pollutants regulated by the Clean Air Act: ground-level ozone, particle pollution (also known as particulate matter), carbon monoxide, sulfur dioxide, and nitrogen dioxide. The AQI runs from 0 to 500. The higher the AQI value, the greater the level of air pollution and the greater the health concern; (3) Sulfur dioxide is no longer included in this table (as of December 8, 2021) because SO_2 concentrations tend to be very localized and not necessarily representative of broad geographical areas like counties and CBSAs.
Source: U.S. Environmental Protection Agency, Air Quality Index Report, 2021

Maximum Air Pollutant Concentrations: Particulate Matter, Ozone, CO and Lead

	Particulate Matter 10 (ug/m^3)	Particulate Matter 2.5 Wtd AM (ug/m^3)	Particulate Matter 2.5 24-Hr (ug/m^3)	Ozone (ppm)	Carbon Monoxide (ppm)	Lead (ug/m^3)
MSA[1] Level	40	8	18	0.063	n/a	n/a
NAAQS[2]	150	15	35	0.075	9	0.15
Met NAAQS[2]	Yes	Yes	Yes	Yes	n/a	n/a

Note: (1) Data covers the Durham-Chapel Hill, NC Metropolitan Statistical Area; Data from exceptional events are included; (2) National Ambient Air Quality Standards; ppm = parts per million; ug/m^3 = micrograms per cubic meter; n/a not available.
Concentrations: Particulate Matter 10 (coarse particulate)—highest second maximum 24-hour concentration; Particulate Matter 2.5 Wtd AM (fine particulate)—highest weighted annual mean concentration; Particulate Matter 2.5 24-Hour (fine particulate)—highest 98th percentile 24-hour concentration; Ozone—highest fourth daily maximum 8-hour concentration; Carbon Monoxide—highest second maximum non-overlapping 8-hour concentration; Lead—maximum running 3-month average
Source: U.S. Environmental Protection Agency, Air Quality Monitoring Information, "Air Quality Statistics by City, 2021"

Maximum Air Pollutant Concentrations: Nitrogen Dioxide and Sulfur Dioxide

	Nitrogen Dioxide AM (ppb)	Nitrogen Dioxide 1-Hr (ppb)	Sulfur Dioxide AM (ppb)	Sulfur Dioxide 1-Hr (ppb)	Sulfur Dioxide 24-Hr (ppb)
MSA[1] Level	n/a	n/a	n/a	1	n/a
NAAQS[2]	53	100	30	75	140
Met NAAQS[2]	n/a	n/a	n/a	Yes	n/a

Note: (1) Data covers the Durham-Chapel Hill, NC Metropolitan Statistical Area; Data from exceptional events are included; (2) National Ambient Air Quality Standards; ppm = parts per million; ug/m^3 = micrograms per cubic meter; n/a not available.
Concentrations: Nitrogen Dioxide AM—highest arithmetic mean concentration; Nitrogen Dioxide 1-Hr—highest 98th percentile 1-hour daily maximum concentration; Sulfur Dioxide AM—highest annual mean concentration; Sulfur Dioxide 1-Hr—highest 99th percentile 1-hour daily maximum concentration; Sulfur Dioxide 24-Hr—highest second maximum 24-hour concentration
Source: U.S. Environmental Protection Agency, Air Quality Monitoring Information, "Air Quality Statistics by City, 2021"

Edison, New Jersey

Background

Edison, previously known as Raritan Township, earned its eponymous name from the inventor, Thomas Alva Edison. In 1876, Edison set up his home and research laboratory on the site of an unsuccessful real estate development in Raritan Township called Menlo Park. Edison came up with his most famous inventions, including the phonograph and the incandescent light bulb, in his Menlo Park lab. In just over a decade Edison's Menlo Park laboratory expanded to consume two city blocks. In 1954, town fathers changed the name of the city to honor the inventor. Today, the Thomas Edison Center at Menlo Park includes new and restored exhibits and detailed tours of the surrounding grounds and facilities.

Edison, six miles from New Brunswick and 20 miles from Newark, has a growing Indian community. To reflect Edison's large Indian and Chinese populations, the city has sister-city arrangements with Shijiazhuang, China, and Baroda, India.

In recent years, Edison has been named one of the most livable/best/safest small cities and one of the ten best places to grow up.

Crowded industrial parks, including Raritan Center, the state's largest, help provide Edison with one of the largest municipal tax bases in New Jersey. Majesco Entertainment, Zylog Systems, Boxed, and Bare Necessities all have headquarters in the city. Italian food producer and importer Colavita, JFK Medical Center, FedEx, UPS, and Newegg have warehouse operations in Edison.

Edison's Sugarloaf Craft Festivals, operated annually since 1974, comprise about a dozen festivals that focus on immersing independent artisans, collectors, and enthusiasts into a vibrant art scene. The 2023 festivals, in November, will showcase 200-450 emerging, carefully curated and juried artisans that showcase the region's diverse culture through the arts, and consistently ranks as one of the country's top 50 craft shows.

The Sergeant Joyce Kilmer U.S. Army Reserve Center is also located in Edison. The township was once home to two large military bases, Raritan Arsenal and Camp Kilmer, both of which closed in the 1960s. Today Raritan Center and Middlesex County College stand on the Raritan Arsenal land. Camp Kilmer became Rutgers University's Livingston College and the Sutton Industrial Campus. Residents are served by a community college, Middlesex County College, which houses the Middlesex County Academy for Science, Mathematics, and Engineering Technologies. The engineering-based high school is free for all Middlesex County residents, with admission based on academics and extra-curricular activities.

The Plainfield Country Club in the city hosted the PGA Tour FedEx Cup playoff most recently in 2015, among other golf events. The 57th Annual Memorial Day Parade celebration took place in 2019. Edison station, located in South Edison, has New Jersey Transit trains to New York City, and the town is connected to nearly every major highway in the state.

Bounded by the Atlantic Ocean and the Delaware River, most of New Jersey has a moderate climate with cold winters and warm, humid summers. Occasional tornadoes, violent spring storms, and floods are not uncommon. A serious drought occurs, on average, about once every 15 years.

Rankings

Business/Finance Rankings

- The Brookings Institution ranked the 100 largest metro areas in the U.S. based on income inequality. New York was ranked #2 (#1 = greatest inequality). Criteria: the "95/20 ratio," a figure representing the income at which a household earns more than 95 percent of all other households, divided by the income at which a household earns more than only 20 percent of all other households. *Brookings Institution, "Household Income Inequality, 100 Largest U.S. Metro Areas, 2014-2016," February 5, 2018*

- Payscale.com ranked the 32 largest metro areas in terms of wage growth. The New York metro area ranked #30. Criteria: quarterly changes in private industry employee and education professional wage growth from the previous year. *PayScale, "Wage Trends by Metro Area-1st Quarter," April 20, 2023*

- The New York metro area was identified as one of the most debt-ridden places in America by the finance site Credit.com. The metro area was ranked #3. Criteria: residents' average credit card debt as well as median income. *Credit.com, "25 Cities With the Most Credit Card Debt," February 28, 2018*

- New York was identified as one of America's most frugal metro areas by *Coupons.com*. The city ranked #15 out of 25. Criteria: digital coupon usage. *Coupons.com, "America's Most Frugal Cities of 2017," March 22, 2018*

- New York was cited as one of America's top metros for total corporate facility investment in 2022. The area ranked #4 in the large metro area category (population over 1 million). *Site Selection, "Top Metros of 2022," March 2023*

- The New York metro area appeared on the Milken Institute "2022 Best Performing Cities" list. Rank: #116 out of 200 large metro areas (population over 250,000). Criteria: job growth; wage and salary growth; high-tech output growth; housing affordability; household broadband access. *Milken Institute, "Best-Performing Cities 2022," March 28, 2022*

- *Forbes* ranked the 200 most populous metro areas to determine the nation's "Best Places for Business and Careers." The New York metro area was ranked #115. Criteria: costs (business and living); job growth (past and projected); income growth; quality of life; educational attainment (college and high school); projected economic growth; cultural and leisure opportunities; workplace tolerance laws; net migration patterns. *Forbes, "The Best Places for Business and Careers 2019: Seattle Still On Top," October 30, 2019*

Education Rankings

- Personal finance website *WalletHub* analyzed the 150 largest U.S. metropolitan statistical areas to determine where the most educated Americans are putting their degrees to work. Criteria: education levels; percentage of workers with degrees; education quality and attainment gap; public school quality rankings; quality and enrollment of each metro area's universities. New York was ranked #25 (#1 = most educated city). *www.WalletHub.com, "Most & Least Educated Cities in America," July 18, 2022*

Environmental Rankings

- The U.S. Environmental Protection Agency (EPA) released its list of U.S. metropolitan areas with the most ENERGY STAR certified buildings in 2022. The New York metro area was ranked #5 out of 25. *U.S. Environmental Protection Agency, "2023 Energy Star Top Cities," April 26, 2023*

- New York was highlighted as one of the 25 most ozone-polluted metro areas in the U.S. during 2019 through 2021. The area ranked #12. *American Lung Association, "State of the Air 2023," April 19, 2023*

Health/Fitness Rankings

- The New York metro area was identified as one of the worst cities for bed bugs in America by pest control company Orkin. The area ranked #2 out of 50 based on the number of bed bug treatments Orkin performed from December 2021 to November 2022. *Orkin, "The Windy City Can't Blow Bed Bugs Away: Chicago Ranks #1 For Third Consecutive Year On Orkin's Bed Bug Cities List," January 9, 2023*

- New York was identified as a "2022 Spring Allergy Capital." The area ranked #54 out of 100. Three groups of factors were used to identify the most challenging cities for people with allergies during the spring season: annual spring pollen scores; over the counter allergy medicine use; number of board-certified allergy specialists. *Asthma and Allergy Foundation of America, "Spring Allergy Capitals 2022," March 2, 2022*

- New York was identified as a "2022 Fall Allergy Capital." The area ranked #75 out of 100. Three groups of factors were used to identify the most challenging cities for people with allergies during the fall season: annual fall pollen scores; over the counter allergy medicine use; number of board-certified allergy specialists. *Asthma and Allergy Foundation of America, "Fall Allergy Capitals 2022," March 2, 2022*

- New York was identified as a "2022 Asthma Capital." The area ranked #21 out of the nation's 100 largest metropolitan areas. Criteria: estimated asthma prevalence; asthma-related mortality; and ER visits due to asthma. Risk factors analyzed but not factored in the rankings: annual pollen score; annual air quality; public smoking laws; access to board-certified asthma specialists; rescue and controller medication use; uninsured rate; poverty rate. *Asthma and Allergy Foundation of America, "Asthma Capitals 2022: The Most Challenging Places to Live With Asthma," September 14, 2022*

- The Sharecare Community Well-Being Index evaluates 10 individual and social health factors in order to measure what matters to Americans in the communities in which they live. The New York metro area ranked #7 in the top 10 across all 10 domains. Criteria: access to healthcare, food, and community resources; housng and transportation; economic security; feeling of purpose; physical, financial, social, and community well-being. *www.sharecare.com, "Community Well-Being Index: 2020 Metro Area & County Rankings Report," August 30, 2021*

Real Estate Rankings

- The New York metro area was identified as one of the 20 least affordable housing markets in the U.S. in 2022. The area ranked #172 out of 186 markets. Criteria: qualification for a mortgage loan with a 10 percent down payment on a typical home. *National Association of Realtors®, Qualifying Income Based on Sales Price of Existing Single-Family Homes for Metropolitan Areas, 2022*

- New York was ranked #210 out of 235 metro areas in terms of housing affordability in 2022 by the National Association of Home Builders (#1 = most affordable). Criteria: the share of homes sold in that area affordable to a family earning the local median income, based on standard mortgage underwriting criteria. *National Association of Home Builders®, NAHB-Wells Fargo Housing Opportunity Index, 4th Quarter 2022*

Safety Rankings

- The National Insurance Crime Bureau ranked 390 metro areas in the U.S. in terms of per capita rates of vehicle theft. The New York metro area ranked #273 (#1 = highest rate). Criteria: number of vehicle theft offenses per 100,000 inhabitants in 2021. *National Insurance Crime Bureau, "Hot Spots 2021," September 1, 2022*

Seniors/Retirement Rankings

- From its Best Cities for Successful Aging indexes, the Milken Institute generated rankings for metropolitan areas, weighing data in nine categories—health care, wellness, living arrangements, transportation and convenience, financial characteristics, education, employment, community engagement, and overall livability. The New York metro area was ranked #73 overall in the large metro area category. *Milken Institute, "Best Cities for Successful Aging, 2017" March 14, 2017*

Transportation Rankings

- New York was identified as one of the most congested metro areas in the U.S. The area ranked #9 out of 10. Criteria: yearly delay per auto commuter in hours. *Texas A&M Transportation Institute, "2021 Urban Mobility Report," June 2021*

- According to the INRIX "2022 Global Traffic Scorecard," New York was identified as one of the most congested metro areas in the U.S. The area ranked #3 out of 25. Criteria: average annual time spent in traffic and average cost of congestion per motorist. *Inrix.com, "Return to Work, Higher Gas Prices & Inflation Drove Americans to Spend Hundreds More in Time and Money Commuting," January 10, 2023*

Women/Minorities Rankings

- The *Houston Chronicle* listed the New York metro area as #4 in top places for young Latinos to live in the U.S. Research was largely based on housing and occupational data from the largest metropolitan areas performed by *Forbes* and NBC Universo. Criteria: percentage of 18-34 year-olds; Latino college grad rates; and diversity. *blog.chron.com, "The 15 Best Big Cities for Latino Millenials," January 26, 2016*

Miscellaneous Rankings

- The watchdog site, Charity Navigator, conducted a study of charities in major markets both to analyze statistical differences in their financial, accountability, and transparency practices and to track year-to-year variations in individual philanthropic communities. The New York metro area was ranked #19 among the 30 metro markets in the rating category of Overall Score. *www.charitynavigator.org, "2017 Metro Market Study," May 1, 2017*

- The National Alliance to End Homelessness listed the 25 most populous metro areas with the highest rate of homelessness. The New York metro area had a high rate of homelessness. Criteria: number of homeless people per 10,000 population in 2016. *National Alliance to End Homelessness, "Homelessness in the 25 Most Populous U.S. Metro Areas," September 1, 2017*

Business Environment

DEMOGRAPHICS

Population Growth

Area	1990 Census	2000 Census	2010 Census	2020 Census	Population Growth (%) 1990-2020	Population Growth (%) 2010-2020
City	88,680	97,687	99,967	107,588	21.3	7.6
MSA[1]	16,845,992	18,323,002	18,897,109	20,140,470	19.6	6.6
U.S.	248,709,873	281,421,906	308,745,538	331,449,281	33.3	7.4

Note: (1) Figures cover the New York-Newark-Jersey City, NY-NJ-PA Metropolitan Statistical Area
Source: U.S. Census Bureau, 1990 Census, 2000 Census, 2010 Census, 2020 Census

Race

Area	White Alone[2] (%)	Black Alone[2] (%)	Asian Alone[2] (%)	AIAN[3] Alone[2] (%)	NHOPI[4] Alone[2] (%)	Other Race Alone[2] (%)	Two or More Races (%)
City	28.1	7.6	53.7	0.4	0.0	4.7	5.5
MSA[1]	46.5	16.1	12.5	0.8	0.1	14.1	10.0
U.S.	61.6	12.4	6.0	1.1	0.2	8.4	10.2

Note: (1) Figures cover the New York-Newark-Jersey City, NY-NJ-PA Metropolitan Statistical Area; (2) Alone is defined as not being in combination with one or more other races; (3) American Indian and Alaska Native; (4) Native Hawaiian and Other Pacific Islander
Source: U.S. Census Bureau, 2020 Census

Hispanic or Latino Origin

Area	Total (%)	Mexican (%)	Puerto Rican (%)	Cuban (%)	Other (%)
City	10.8	1.4	2.8	0.7	6.0
MSA[1]	24.8	2.9	5.9	0.8	15.3
U.S.	18.4	11.2	1.8	0.7	4.7

Note: Persons of Hispanic or Latino origin can be of any race; (1) Figures cover the New York-Newark-Jersey City, NY-NJ-PA Metropolitan Statistical Area
Source: U.S. Census Bureau, 2017-2021 American Community Survey 5-Year Estimates

Age

Area	Under Age 5	Age 5–19	Age 20–34	Age 35–44	Age 45–54	Age 55–64	Age 65–74	Age 75–84	Age 85+	Median Age
City	5.3	19.7	18.1	16.5	13.3	12.2	8.9	4.2	1.9	39.0
MSA[1]	5.4	18.0	21.5	13.3	12.8	13.0	9.2	4.7	2.1	38.7
U.S.	5.6	19.2	20.2	12.7	12.4	13.1	10.0	4.9	1.9	38.8

Note: (1) Figures cover the New York-Newark-Jersey City, NY-NJ-PA Metropolitan Statistical Area
Source: U.S. Census Bureau, 2020 Census

Disability by Age

Area	All Ages	Under 18 Years Old	18 to 64 Years Old	65 Years and Over
City	7.6	4.2	4.5	26.9
MSA[1]	10.1	3.3	7.3	30.5
U.S.	12.6	4.4	10.3	33.4

Note: Figures show percent of the civilian noninstitutionalized population that reported having a disability. Disability status is determined from six types of difficulty: vision, hearing, cognitive, ambulatory, self-care, and independent living. For children under 5 years old, hearing and vision difficulty are used to determine disability status. For children between the ages of 5 and 14, disability status is determined from hearing, vision, cognitive, ambulatory, and self-care difficulties. For people aged 15 years and older, they are considered to have a disability if they have difficulty with any one of the six difficulty types; Note: (1) Figures cover the New York-Newark-Jersey City, NY-NJ-PA Metropolitan Statistical Area
Source: U.S. Census Bureau, 2017-2021 American Community Survey 5-Year Estimates

Ancestry

Area	German	Irish	English	American	Italian	Polish	French[2]	Scottish	Dutch
City	4.4	5.8	1.6	1.7	7.8	3.3	1.0	0.5	0.2
MSA[1]	6.0	8.9	2.9	4.0	11.6	3.7	0.9	0.6	0.5
U.S.	12.8	9.6	8.1	5.7	5.0	2.7	2.2	1.6	1.1

Note: Figures are the percentage of the total population reporting a particular ancestry. The nine most commonly reported ancestries in the U.S. are shown. Figures include multiple ancestries (e.g. if a person reported being Irish and Italian, they were included in both columns); (1) Figures cover the New York-Newark-Jersey City, NY-NJ-PA Metropolitan Statistical Area; (2) Excludes Basque
Source: U.S. Census Bureau, 2017-2021 American Community Survey 5-Year Estimates

Foreign-born Population

Area	Any Foreign Country	Asia	Mexico	Europe	Caribbean	Central America[2]	South America	Africa	Canada
City	46.1	37.1	0.5	2.2	1.8	0.6	1.8	1.8	0.3
MSA[1]	29.4	8.7	1.4	4.3	6.9	1.9	4.5	1.4	0.2
U.S.	13.6	4.2	3.3	1.5	1.4	1.1	1.1	0.8	0.2

Note: (1) Figures cover the New York-Newark-Jersey City, NY-NJ-PA Metropolitan Statistical Area;
(2) Excludes Mexico.
Source: U.S. Census Bureau, 2017-2021 American Community Survey 5-Year Estimates

Household Size

Area	Persons in Household (%)							Average Household Size
	One	Two	Three	Four	Five	Six	Seven or More	
City	17.7	28.6	20.6	22.7	6.4	2.3	1.7	2.90
MSA[1]	28.0	29.6	17.0	14.4	6.5	2.6	1.9	2.70
U.S.	28.1	33.8	15.5	12.9	6.0	2.3	1.4	2.60

Note: (1) Figures cover the New York-Newark-Jersey City, NY-NJ-PA Metropolitan Statistical Area
Source: U.S. Census Bureau, 2017-2021 American Community Survey 5-Year Estimates

Household Relationships

Area	House-holder	Opposite-sex Spouse	Same-sex Spouse	Opposite-sex Unmarried Partner	Same-sex Unmarried Partner	Child[2]	Grand-child	Other Relatives	Non-relatives
City	34.3	21.2	0.1	1.1	0.1	32.2	1.4	6.8	1.9
MSA[1]	36.8	15.8	0.2	2.0	0.2	29.7	2.1	7.1	4.1
U.S.	38.3	17.5	0.2	2.5	0.2	28.3	2.4	4.8	3.4

Note: Figures are percent of the total population; (1) Figures cover the New York-Newark-Jersey City,
NY-NJ-PA Metropolitan Statistical Area; (2) Includes biological, adopted, and stepchildren of the householder
Source: U.S. Census Bureau, 2020 Census

Gender

Area	Males	Females	Males per 100 Females
City	53,123	54,465	97.5
MSA[1]	9,693,702	10,446,768	92.8
U.S.	162,685,811	168,763,470	96.4

Note: (1) Figures cover the New York-Newark-Jersey City, NY-NJ-PA Metropolitan Statistical Area
Source: U.S. Census Bureau, 2020 Census

Marital Status

Area	Never Married	Now Married[2]	Separated	Widowed	Divorced
City	26.3	61.4	0.8	5.3	6.1
MSA[1]	38.1	46.1	2.2	5.5	8.1
U.S.	33.8	48.0	1.8	5.6	10.8

Note: Figures are percentages and cover the population 15 years of age and older; (1) Figures cover the New
York-Newark-Jersey City, NY-NJ-PA Metropolitan Statistical Area; (2) Excludes separated
Source: U.S. Census Bureau, 2017-2021 American Community Survey 5-Year Estimates

Religious Groups by Family

Area	Catholic	Baptist	Methodist	LDS[2]	Pentecostal	Lutheran	Islam	Adventist	Other
MSA[1]	32.5	1.7	1.2	0.3	0.9	0.5	4.5	1.4	10.6
U.S.	18.7	7.3	3.0	2.0	1.8	1.7	1.3	1.3	11.6

Note: Figures are the number of adherents as a percentage of the total population and cover the eight largest
religious groups in the U.S; (1) Figures cover the New York-Newark-Jersey City, NY-NJ-PA Metropolitan
Statistical Area; (2) Church of Jesus Christ of Latter-day Saints
Sources: 2020 U.S. Religion Census, Association of Statisticians of American Religious Bodies; The
Association of Religion Data Archives (ARDA)

Religious Groups by Tradition

Area	Catholic	Evangelical Protestant	Mainline Protestant	Black Protestant	Islam	Judaism	Hinduism	Orthodox	Buddhism
MSA[1]	32.5	4.4	3.0	1.5	4.5	4.4	1.0	0.8	0.3
U.S.	18.7	16.5	5.2	2.3	1.3	0.6	0.4	0.4	0.3

Note: Figures are the number of adherents as a percentage of the total population; (1) Figures cover the New
York-Newark-Jersey City, NY-NJ-PA Metropolitan Statistical Area
Sources: 2020 U.S. Religion Census, Association of Statisticians of American Religious Bodies; The
Association of Religion Data Archives (ARDA)

Edison, New Jersey   187

ECONOMY

Gross Metropolitan Product

Area	2020	2021	2022	2023	Rank[2]
MSA[1]	1,844.7	1,993.2	2,157.6	2,278.7	1

Note: Figures are in billions of dollars; (1) Figures cover the New York-Newark-Jersey City, NY-NJ-PA Metropolitan Statistical Area; (2) Rank is based on 2021 data and ranges from 1 to 381
Source: U.S. Conference of Mayors, U.S. Metro Economies: U.S. Metros Compared to Global and State Economies, June 2022

Economic Growth

Area	2018-20 (%)	2021 (%)	2022 (%)	2023 (%)	Rank[2]
MSA[1]	-1.5	5.6	3.3	2.4	250
U.S.	-0.6	5.7	3.1	2.9	–

Note: Figures are real gross metropolitan product (GMP) growth rates and represent average annual percent change; (1) Figures cover the New York-Newark-Jersey City, NY-NJ-PA Metropolitan Statistical Area; (2) Rank is based on 2020 2-year average annual percent change and ranges from 1 to 381
Source: U.S. Conference of Mayors, U.S. Metro Economies: U.S. Metros Compared to Global and State Economies, June 2022

Metropolitan Area Exports

Area	2016	2017	2018	2019	2020	2021	Rank[2]
MSA[1]	89,649.5	93,693.7	97,692.4	87,365.7	75,745.4	103,930.9	2

Note: Figures are in millions of dollars; (1) Figures cover the New York-Newark-Jersey City, NY-NJ-PA Metropolitan Statistical Area; (2) Rank is based on 2021 data and ranges from 1 to 388
Source: U.S. Department of Commerce, International Trade Administration, Office of Trade and Economic Analysis, Industry and Analysis, Exports by Metropolitan Area, data extracted March 16, 2023

Building Permits

Area	Single-Family			Multi-Family			Total		
	2021	2022	Pct. Chg.	2021	2022	Pct. Chg.	2021	2022	Pct. Chg.
City	105	104	-1.0	250	17	-93.2	355	121	-65.9
MSA[1]	12,947	12,089	-6.6	43,714	46,323	6.0	56,661	58,412	3.1
U.S.	1,115,400	975,600	-12.5	621,600	689,500	10.9	1,737,000	1,665,100	-4.1

Note: (1) Figures cover the New York-Newark-Jersey City, NY-NJ-PA Metropolitan Statistical Area; Figures represent new, privately-owned housing units authorized (unadjusted data); All permit data are based on estimates with imputation
Source: U.S. Census Bureau, Manufacturing, Mining, and Construction Statistics, Building Permits, 2021, 2022

Bankruptcy Filings

Area	Business Filings			Nonbusiness Filings		
	2021	2022	% Chg.	2021	2022	% Chg.
Middlesex County	45	30	-33.3	843	746	-11.5
U.S.	14,347	13,481	-6.0	399,269	374,240	-6.3

Note: Business filings include Chapter 7, Chapter 9, Chapter 11, Chapter 12, Chapter 13, Chapter 15, and Section 304; Nonbusiness filings include Chapter 7, Chapter 11, and Chapter 13
Source: Administrative Office of the U.S. Courts, Business and Nonbusiness Bankruptcy, County Cases Commenced by Chapter of the Bankruptcy Code, During the 12-Month Period Ending December 31, 2021 and Business and Nonbusiness Bankruptcy, County Cases Commenced by Chapter of the Bankruptcy Code, During the 12-Month Period Ending December 31, 2022

Housing Vacancy Rates

Area	Gross Vacancy Rate[2] (%)			Year-Round Vacancy Rate[3] (%)			Rental Vacancy Rate[4] (%)			Homeowner Vacancy Rate[5] (%)		
	2020	2021	2022	2020	2021	2022	2020	2021	2022	2020	2021	2022
MSA[1]	9.1	9.8	8.2	7.8	8.7	7.0	4.5	5.2	3.5	1.3	1.2	1.0
U.S.	10.6	10.8	10.5	8.2	8.4	8.2	6.3	6.1	5.8	1.0	0.9	0.8

Note: (1) Figures cover the New York-Newark-Jersey City, NY-NJ-PA Metropolitan Statistical Area; (2) The percentage of the total housing inventory that is vacant; (3) The percentage of the housing inventory (excluding seasonal units) that is year-round vacant; (4) The percentage of rental inventory that is vacant for rent; (5) The percentage of homeowner inventory that is vacant for sale
Source: U.S. Census Bureau, Housing Vacancies and Homeownership Annual Statistics: 2020, 2021, 2022

INCOME

Income

Area	Per Capita ($)	Median Household ($)	Average Household ($)
City	47,410	110,896	136,606
MSA[1]	47,591	86,445	127,555
U.S.	37,638	69,021	97,196

Note: (1) Figures cover the New York-Newark-Jersey City, NY-NJ-PA Metropolitan Statistical Area
Source: U.S. Census Bureau, 2017-2021 American Community Survey 5-Year Estimates

Household Income Distribution

Area	Percent of Households Earning							
	Under $15,000	$15,000 -$24,999	$25,000 -$34,999	$35,000 -$49,999	$50,000 -$74,999	$75,000 -$99,999	$100,000 -$149,999	$150,000 and up
City	4.6	3.4	3.5	7.2	13.3	12.4	21.8	34.0
MSA[1]	9.7	6.6	6.3	8.6	13.3	11.2	16.7	27.5
U.S.	9.4	7.8	8.2	11.4	16.8	12.8	16.3	17.3

Note: (1) Figures cover the New York-Newark-Jersey City, NY-NJ-PA Metropolitan Statistical Area
Source: U.S. Census Bureau, 2017-2021 American Community Survey 5-Year Estimates

Poverty Rate

Area	All Ages	Under 18 Years Old	18 to 64 Years Old	65 Years and Over
City	5.8	7.1	5.1	6.6
MSA[1]	12.3	16.6	10.8	12.1
U.S.	12.6	17.0	11.8	9.6

Note: Figures are percentage of people whose income during the past 12 months was below the poverty level;
(1) Figures cover the New York-Newark-Jersey City, NY-NJ-PA Metropolitan Statistical Area
Source: U.S. Census Bureau, 2017-2021 American Community Survey 5-Year Estimates

EMPLOYMENT

Labor Force and Employment

Area	Civilian Labor Force			Workers Employed		
	Dec. 2021	Dec. 2022	% Chg.	Dec. 2021	Dec. 2022	% Chg.
City	55,370	56,778	2.5	53,727	55,594	3.5
MD[1]	6,978,612	7,057,593	1.1	6,599,840	6,759,099	2.4
U.S.	161,696,000	164,224,000	1.6	155,732,000	158,872,000	2.0

Note: Data is not seasonally adjusted and covers workers 16 years of age and older; (1) Figures cover the New York-Jersey City-White Plains, NY-NJ Metropolitan Division
Source: Bureau of Labor Statistics, Local Area Unemployment Statistics

Unemployment Rate

Area	2022											
	Jan.	Feb.	Mar.	Apr.	May	Jun.	Jul.	Aug.	Sep.	Oct.	Nov.	Dec.
City	3.3	3.0	2.9	2.5	2.5	2.8	2.7	2.6	2.0	2.1	2.1	2.1
MD[1]	6.1	5.6	5.1	4.7	4.6	4.9	5.3	5.4	4.1	4.1	4.2	4.2
U.S.	4.4	4.1	3.8	3.3	3.4	3.8	3.8	3.8	3.3	3.4	3.4	3.3

Note: Data is not seasonally adjusted and covers workers 16 years of age and older; (1) Figures cover the New York-Jersey City-White Plains, NY-NJ Metropolitan Division
Source: Bureau of Labor Statistics, Local Area Unemployment Statistics

Average Wages

Occupation	$/Hr.	Occupation	$/Hr.
Accountants and Auditors	54.94	Maintenance and Repair Workers	26.67
Automotive Mechanics	26.81	Marketing Managers	93.41
Bookkeepers	26.44	Network and Computer Systems Admin.	55.75
Carpenters	37.06	Nurses, Licensed Practical	30.31
Cashiers	16.55	Nurses, Registered	50.41
Computer Programmers	57.97	Nursing Assistants	21.50
Computer Systems Analysts	60.54	Office Clerks, General	21.90
Computer User Support Specialists	35.55	Physical Therapists	53.25
Construction Laborers	30.93	Physicians	128.42
Cooks, Restaurant	19.55	Plumbers, Pipefitters and Steamfitters	42.38
Customer Service Representatives	23.75	Police and Sheriff's Patrol Officers	42.43
Dentists	89.01	Postal Service Mail Carriers	27.72
Electricians	41.22	Real Estate Sales Agents	47.01
Engineers, Electrical	53.37	Retail Salespersons	19.51
Fast Food and Counter Workers	16.08	Sales Representatives, Technical/Scientific	63.64
Financial Managers	110.67	Secretaries, Exc. Legal/Medical/Executive	23.24
First-Line Supervisors of Office Workers	38.32	Security Guards	19.89
General and Operations Managers	83.82	Surgeons	149.60
Hairdressers/Cosmetologists	20.85	Teacher Assistants, Exc. Postsecondary*	18.07
Home Health and Personal Care Aides	17.10	Teachers, Secondary School, Exc. Sp. Ed.*	45.24
Janitors and Cleaners	20.14	Telemarketers	20.35
Landscaping/Groundskeeping Workers	20.81	Truck Drivers, Heavy/Tractor-Trailer	29.43
Lawyers	92.92	Truck Drivers, Light/Delivery Services	23.63
Maids and Housekeeping Cleaners	21.40	Waiters and Waitresses	23.01

Note: Wage data covers the New York-Newark-Jersey City, NY-NJ-PA Metropolitan Statistical Area;
(*) Hourly wages were calculated from annual wage data based on a 40 hour work week; n/a not available.
Source: Bureau of Labor Statistics, Metro Area Occupational Employment & Wage Estimates, May 2022

Employment by Industry

Sector	MD[1]		U.S.
	Number of Employees	Percent of Total	Percent of Total
Construction, Mining, and Logging	267,500	3.6	5.4
Private Education and Health Services	1,672,200	22.7	16.1
Financial Activities	660,600	9.0	5.9
Government	915,600	12.4	14.5
Information	288,400	3.9	2.0
Leisure and Hospitality	655,900	8.9	10.3
Manufacturing	193,700	2.6	8.4
Other Services	292,300	4.0	3.7
Professional and Business Services	1,215,400	16.5	14.7
Retail Trade	613,100	8.3	10.2
Transportation, Warehousing, and Utilities	312,800	4.3	4.9
Wholesale Trade	270,500	3.7	3.9

Note: Figures are non-farm employment as of December 2022. Figures are not seasonally adjusted and include workers 16 years of age and older; (1) Figures cover the New York-Jersey City-White Plains, NY-NJ Metropolitan Division
Source: Bureau of Labor Statistics, Current Employment Statistics, Employment, Hours, and Earnings

Employment by Occupation

Occupation Classification	City (%)	MSA[1] (%)	U.S. (%)
Management, Business, Science, and Arts	57.1	45.3	40.3
Natural Resources, Construction, and Maintenance	3.2	6.5	8.7
Production, Transportation, and Material Moving	10.6	9.6	13.1
Sales and Office	18.5	20.3	20.9
Service	10.5	18.2	17.0

Note: Figures cover employed civilians 16 years of age and older; (1) Figures cover the New York-Newark-Jersey City, NY-NJ-PA Metropolitan Statistical Area
Source: U.S. Census Bureau, 2017-2021 American Community Survey 5-Year Estimates

Occupations with Greatest Projected Employment Growth: 2020 – 2030

Occupation[1]	2020 Employment	2030 Projected Employment	Numeric Employment Change	Percent Employment Change
Laborers and Freight, Stock, and Material Movers, Hand	116,850	139,630	22,780	19.5
Fast Food and Counter Workers	60,660	80,300	19,640	32.4
Home Health and Personal Care Aides	59,610	76,930	17,320	29.1
Waiters and Waitresses	45,030	61,460	16,430	36.5
Software Developers and Software Quality Assurance Analysts and Testers	59,300	73,160	13,860	23.4
Packers and Packagers, Hand	58,150	68,740	10,590	18.2
Cooks, Restaurant	14,320	23,870	9,550	66.7
Hairdressers, Hairstylists, and Cosmetologists	26,680	35,480	8,800	33.0
Light Truck or Delivery Services Drivers	32,180	39,820	7,640	23.7
Retail Salespersons	105,150	112,550	7,400	7.0

Note: Projections cover New Jersey; Short-term projections for 2022-2024 were not available at time of publication; (1) Sorted by numeric employment change
Source: www.projectionscentral.com, State Occupational Projections, 2020–2030 Long-Term Projections

190   Edison, New Jersey

Fastest-Growing Occupations: 2020 – 2030

Occupation[1]	2020 Employment	2030 Projected Employment	Numeric Employment Change	Percent Employment Change
Athletes and Sports Competitors	560	950	390	69.6
Gaming and Sports Book Writers and Runners	130	220	90	69.2
Fitness Trainers and Aerobics Instructors	10,360	17,430	7,070	68.2
Cooks, Restaurant	14,320	23,870	9,550	66.7
Actors	330	540	210	63.6
Nurse Practitioners	6,150	9,920	3,770	61.3
Tour and Travel Guides	510	810	300	58.8
Amusement and Recreation Attendants	5,750	9,070	3,320	57.7
Locker Room, Coatroom, and Dressing Room Attendants	400	620	220	55.0
Agents and Business Managers of Artists, Performers, and Athletes	130	200	70	53.8

Note: Projections cover New Jersey; Short-term projections for 2022-2024 were not available at time of publication; (1) Sorted by percent employment change and excludes occupations with numeric employment change less than 50
Source: www.projectionscentral.com, State Occupational Projections, 2020–2030 Long-Term Projections

CITY FINANCES

City Government Finances

Component	2020 ($000)	2020 ($ per capita)
Total Revenues	321,495	3,223
Total Expenditures	404,882	4,059
Debt Outstanding	26,620	267
Cash and Securities[1]	130,845	1,312

Note: (1) Cash and security holdings of a government at the close of its fiscal year, including those of its dependent agencies, utilities, and liquor stores.
Source: U.S. Census Bureau, State & Local Government Finances 2020

City Government Revenue by Source

Source	2020 ($000)	2020 ($ per capita)	2020 (%)
General Revenue			
From Federal Government	0	0	0.0
From State Government	53,429	536	16.6
From Local Governments	282	3	0.1
Taxes			
Property	224,701	2,252	69.9
Sales and Gross Receipts	1,410	14	0.4
Personal Income	0	0	0.0
Corporate Income	0	0	0.0
Motor Vehicle License	0	0	0.0
Other Taxes	8,146	82	2.5
Current Charges	25,706	258	8.0
Liquor Store	0	0	0.0
Utility	89	1	0.0

Source: U.S. Census Bureau, State & Local Government Finances 2020

City Government Expenditures by Function

Function	2020 ($000)	2020 ($ per capita)	2020 (%)
General Direct Expenditures			
Air Transportation	0	0	0.0
Corrections	0	0	0.0
Education	262,720	2,633	64.9
Employment Security Administration	0	0	0.0
Financial Administration	1,219	12	0.3
Fire Protection	21,833	218	5.4
General Public Buildings	2,162	21	0.5
Governmental Administration, Other	1,474	14	0.4
Health	1,544	15	0.4
Highways	3,781	37	0.9
Hospitals	0	0	0.0
Housing and Community Development	0	0	0.0
Interest on General Debt	3,358	33	0.8
Judicial and Legal	617	6	0.2
Libraries	4,797	48	1.2
Parking	0	0	0.0
Parks and Recreation	2,977	29	0.7
Police Protection	28,423	284	7.0
Public Welfare	373	3	0.1
Sewerage	20,353	204	5.0
Solid Waste Management	806	8	0.2
Veterans' Services	0	0	0.0
Liquor Store	0	0	0.0
Utility	89	< 1	< 0.1

Source: U.S. Census Bureau, State & Local Government Finances 2020

TAXES

State Corporate Income Tax Rates

State	Tax Rate (%)	Income Brackets ($)	Num. of Brackets	Financial Institution Tax Rate (%)[a]	Federal Income Tax Ded.
New Jersey	9.0 (o)	Flat rate	1	9.0 (o)	No

Note: Tax rates as of January 1, 2023; (a) Rates listed are the corporate income tax rate applied to financial institutions or excise taxes based on income. Some states have other taxes based upon the value of deposits or shares; (o) New Jersey also imposes a 2.5% surtax on taxpayers with income over $1 million in tax year 2023. Small businesses with annual entire net income under $100,000 pay a tax rate of 7.5%; businesses with income under $50,000 pay 6.5%. The minimum Corporation Business Tax is based on New Jersey gross receipts. It ranges from $500 for a corporation with gross receipts less than $100,000, to $2,000 for a corporation with gross receipts of $1 million or more.
Source: Federation of Tax Administrators, State Corporate Income Tax Rates, January 1, 2023

State Individual Income Tax Rates

State	Tax Rate (%)	Income Brackets ($)	Personal Exemptions ($)			Standard Ded. ($)	
			Single	Married	Depend.	Single	Married
New Jersey	1.4 - 10.75	20,000 - 1 million (q)	1,000	2,000	1,500	–	–

Note: Tax rates as of January 1, 2023; Local- and county-level taxes are not included; Federal income tax is not deductible on state income tax returns; (q) The New Jersey rates reported are for single individuals. For married couples filing jointly, the tax rates also range from 1.4% to 10.75%, with 8 brackets and the same high and low income ranges.
Source: Federation of Tax Administrators, State Individual Income Tax Rates, January 1, 2023

Various State Sales and Excise Tax Rates

State	State Sales Tax (%)	Gasoline[1] ($/gal.)	Cigarette[2] ($/pack)	Spirits[3] ($/gal.)	Wine[4] ($/gal.)	Beer[5] ($/gal.)	Recreational Marijuana (%)
New Jersey	6.625	0.414	2.70	5.50	0.88	0.12	(m)

Note: All tax rates as of January 1, 2023; (1) The American Petroleum Institute has developed a methodology for determining the average tax rate on a gallon of fuel. Rates may include any of the following: excise taxes, environmental fees, storage tank fees, other fees or taxes, general sales tax, and local taxes; (2) The federal excise tax of $1.0066 per pack and local taxes are not included; (3) Rates are those applicable to off-premise sales of 40% alcohol by volume (a.b.v.) distilled spirits in 750ml containers. Local excise taxes are excluded; (4) Rates are those applicable to off-premise sales of 11% a.b.v. non-carbonated wine in 750ml containers; (5) Rates are those applicable to off-premise sales of 4.7% a.b.v. beer in 12 ounce containers; (m) Up to $10 per ounce, if the average retail price of an ounce of usable cannabis was $350 or more; up to $30 per ounce, if the average retail price of an ounce of usable cannabis was less than $350 but at least $250; up to $40 per ounce, if the average retail price of an ounce of usable cannabis was less than $250 but at least $200; up to $60 per ounce, if the average retail price of an ounce of usable cannabis was less than $200
Source: Tax Foundation, 2023 Facts & Figures: How Does Your State Compare?

Edison, New Jersey

State Business Tax Climate Index Rankings

State	Overall Rank	Corporate Tax Rank	Individual Income Tax Rank	Sales Tax Rank	Property Tax Rank	Unemployment Insurance Tax Rank
New Jersey	50	48	48	42	45	32

Note: The index is a measure of how each state's tax laws affect economic performance. The lower the rank, the more favorable a state's tax system is for business. States without a given tax are given a ranking of 1. The scores/rankings for the District of Columbia do not affect other states. The 2023 index represents the tax climate as of July 1, 2022.
Source: Tax Foundation, State Business Tax Climate Index 2023

TRANSPORTATION

Means of Transportation to Work

Area	Car/Truck/Van		Public Transportation			Bicycle	Walked	Other Means	Worked at Home
	Drove Alone	Car-pooled	Bus	Subway	Railroad				
City	64.0	8.1	0.7	0.5	9.9	0.1	1.1	1.3	14.1
MSA[1]	47.4	6.1	6.7	17.4	3.1	0.7	5.5	2.3	10.6
U.S.	73.2	8.6	2.0	1.6	0.5	0.5	2.5	1.5	9.7

Note: Figures are percentages and cover workers 16 years of age and older; (1) Figures cover the New York-Newark-Jersey City, NY-NJ-PA Metropolitan Statistical Area
Source: U.S. Census Bureau, 2017-2021 American Community Survey 5-Year Estimates

Travel Time to Work

Area	Less Than 10 Minutes	10 to 19 Minutes	20 to 29 Minutes	30 to 44 Minutes	45 to 59 Minutes	60 to 89 Minutes	90 Minutes or More
City	7.6	22.0	18.1	17.8	12.2	12.6	9.6
MSA[1]	7.0	18.5	16.3	24.0	12.7	14.7	6.8
U.S.	12.4	28.5	21.0	20.9	8.2	6.2	2.9

Note: Note: Figures are percentages and include workers 16 years old and over; (1) Figures cover the New York-Newark-Jersey City, NY-NJ-PA Metropolitan Statistical Area
Source: U.S. Census Bureau, 2017-2021 American Community Survey 5-Year Estimates

Key Congestion Measures

Measure	1990	2000	2010	2015	2020
Annual Hours of Delay, Total (000)	275,610	480,809	688,933	778,986	494,268
Annual Hours of Delay, Per Auto Commuter	43	62	78	87	56
Annual Congestion Cost, Per Auto Commuter ($)	1,265	1,658	1,887	1,971	1,322

Note: Covers the New York-Newark NY-NJ-CT urban area
Source: Texas A&M Transportation Institute, 2021 Urban Mobility Report

Freeway Travel Time Index

Measure	1985	1990	1995	2000	2005	2010	2015	2020
Urban Area Index[1]	1.16	1.20	1.24	1.29	1.33	1.33	1.35	1.17
Urban Area Rank[1,2]	10	9	7	6	6	7	7	1

Note: Freeway Travel Time Index—the ratio of travel time in the peak period to the travel time at free-flow conditions. For example, a value of 1.30 indicates a 20-minute free-flow trip takes 26 minutes in the peak (20 minutes x 1.30 = 26 minutes); (1) Covers the New York-Newark NY-NJ-CT urban area; (2) Rank is based on 101 larger urban areas (#1 = highest travel time index)
Source: Texas A&M Transportation Institute, 2021 Urban Mobility Report

Public Transportation

Agency Name / Mode of Transportation	Vehicles Operated in Maximum Service[1]	Annual Unlinked Passenger Trips[2] (in thous.)	Annual Passenger Miles[3] (in thous.)
New Jersey Transit Corporation			
Bus (directly operated)	1,894	71,310.0	501,249.9
Bus (purchased transportation)	182	6,194.0	27,712.0
Commuter Rail (directly operated)	897	19,096.9	529,338.5
Demand Response (purchased transportation)	334	1,076.2	6,722.6
Hybrid Rail (purchased transportation)	16	1,476.1	21,234.6
Light Rail (directly operated)	15	2,681.2	6,137.3
Light Rail (purchased transportation)	42	7,748.9	32,256.5
Vanpool (purchased transportation)	114	178.7	3,647.0

Note: (1) Number of revenue vehicles operated by the given mode and type of service to meet the annual maximum service requirement. This is the revenue vehicle count during the peak season of the year; on the week and day that maximum service is provided. Vehicles operated in maximum service (VOMS) exclude atypical days and one-time special events; (2) Number of passengers who boarded public transportation vehicles. Passengers are counted each time they board a vehicle no matter how many vehicles they use to travel from their origin to their destination. (3) Sum of the distances ridden by all passengers during the entire fiscal year.
Source: Federal Transit Administration, National Transit Database, 2021

Air Transportation

Airport Name and Code / Type of Service	Passenger Airlines[1]	Passenger Enplanements	Freight Carriers[2]	Freight (lbs)
Newark International (EWR)				
Domestic service (U.S. carriers - 2022)	30	15,510,932	17	534,832,694
International service (U.S. carriers - 2021)	8	2,548,014	4	115,568,069

Note: (1) Includes all U.S.-based major, minor and commuter airlines that carried at least one passenger during the year; (2) Includes all U.S.-based airlines and freight carriers that transported at least one pound of freight during the year.
Source: Bureau of Transportation Statistics, The Intermodal Transportation Database, Air Carriers: T-100 Domestic Market (U.S. Carriers), 2022; Bureau of Transportation Statistics, The Intermodal Transportation Database, Air Carriers: T-100 International Market (U.S. Carriers), 2021

BUSINESSES

Major Business Headquarters

Company Name	Industry	Rankings	
		Fortune[1]	Forbes[2]
JM Huber	Chemicals	-	162

Note: (1) Companies that produce a 10-K are ranked 1 to 500 based on 2021 revenue; (2) All private companies with at least $2 billion in annual revenue through the end of their most current fiscal year are ranked 1 to 246; companies listed are headquartered in the city; dashes indicate no ranking
Source: Fortune, "Fortune 500," 2022; Forbes, "America's Largest Private Companies," 2022

Fastest-Growing Businesses

According to *Inc.*, Edison is home to one of America's 500 fastest-growing private companies: **Nutrifresh Holdings** (#200). Criteria: must be an independent, privately-held, for-profit, U.S. corporation, proprietorship or partnership as of December 31, 2021; revenues must be at least $100,000 in 2018 and $2 million in 2021; must have four-year operating/sales history. *Inc., "America's 500 Fastest-Growing Private Companies," 2022*

Living Environment

COST OF LIVING

Cost of Living Index

Composite Index	Groceries	Housing	Utilities	Trans-portation	Health Care	Misc. Goods/Services
n/a	n/a	n/a	n/a	n/a	n/a	n/a

Note: The Cost of Living Index measures regional differences in the cost of consumer goods and services, excluding taxes and non-consumer expenditures, for professional and managerial households in the top income quintile. It is based on more than 50,000 prices covering almost 60 different items for which prices are collected three times a year by chambers of commerce, economic development organizations or university applied economic centers in each participating urban area. The numbers shown should be read as a percentage above or below the national average of 100. For example, a value of 115.4 in the groceries column indicates that grocery prices are 15.4% higher than the national average. Small differences in the index numbers should not be interpreted as significant; n/a not available.
Source: The Council for Community and Economic Research, Cost of Living Index, 2022

Grocery Prices

Area[1]	T-Bone Steak ($/pound)	Frying Chicken ($/pound)	Whole Milk ($/half gal.)	Eggs ($/dozen)	Orange Juice ($/64 oz.)	Coffee ($/11.5 oz.)
City[2]	n/a	n/a	n/a	n/a	n/a	n/a
Avg.	13.81	1.59	2.43	2.25	3.85	4.95
Min.	10.17	0.90	1.51	1.30	2.90	3.46
Max.	19.35	3.30	4.32	4.32	5.31	8.59

Note: (1) Values for the local area are compared with the average, minimum and maximum values for all 286 areas in the Cost of Living Index; (2) Figures cover the Edison NJ urban area; n/a not available; **T-Bone Steak** (price per pound); **Frying Chicken** (price per pound, whole fryer); **Whole Milk** (half gallon carton); **Eggs** (price per dozen, Grade A, large); **Orange Juice** (64 oz. Tropicana or Florida Natural); **Coffee** (11.5 oz. can, vacuum-packed, Maxwell House, Hills Bros, or Folgers).
Source: The Council for Community and Economic Research, Cost of Living Index, 2022

Housing and Utility Costs

Area[1]	New Home Price ($)	Apartment Rent ($/month)	All Electric ($/month)	Part Electric ($/month)	Other Energy ($/month)	Telephone ($/month)
City[2]	n/a	n/a	n/a	n/a	n/a	n/a
Avg.	450,913	1,371	176.41	99.93	76.96	190.22
Min.	229,283	546	100.84	31.56	27.15	174.27
Max.	2,434,977	4,569	356.86	249.59	272.24	208.31

Note: (1) Values for the local area are compared with the average, minimum and maximum values for all 286 areas in the Cost of Living Index; (2) Figures cover the Edison NJ urban area; n/a not available; **New Home Price** (2,400 sf living area, 8,000 sf lot, in urban area with full utilities); **Apartment Rent** (950 sf 2 bedroom/1.5 or 2 bath, unfurnished, excluding all utilities except water); **All Electric** (average monthly cost for an all-electric home); **Part Electric** (average monthly cost for a part-electric home); **Other Energy** (average monthly cost for natural gas, fuel oil, coal, wood, and any other forms of energy except electricity); **Telephone** (price includes the base monthly rate plus taxes and fees for three lines of mobile phone service).
Source: The Council for Community and Economic Research, Cost of Living Index, 2022

Health Care, Transportation, and Other Costs

Area[1]	Doctor ($/visit)	Dentist ($/visit)	Optometrist ($/visit)	Gasoline ($/gallon)	Beauty Salon ($/visit)	Men's Shirt ($)
City[2]	n/a	n/a	n/a	n/a	n/a	n/a
Avg.	124.91	107.77	117.66	3.86	43.31	34.21
Min.	36.61	58.25	51.79	2.90	22.18	13.05
Max.	250.21	162.58	371.96	5.54	85.61	63.54

Note: (1) Values for the local area are compared with the average, minimum and maximum values for all 286 areas in the Cost of Living Index; (2) Figures cover the Edison NJ urban area; n/a not available; **Doctor** (general practitioners routine exam of an established patient); **Dentist** (adult teeth cleaning and periodic oral examination); **Optometrist** (full vision eye exam for established adult patient); **Gasoline** (one gallon regular unleaded, national brand, including all taxes, cash price at self-service pump if available); **Beauty Salon** (woman's shampoo, trim, and blow-dry); **Men's Shirt** (cotton/polyester dress shirt, pinpoint weave, long sleeves).
Source: The Council for Community and Economic Research, Cost of Living Index, 2022

HOUSING

Homeownership Rate

Area	2015 (%)	2016 (%)	2017 (%)	2018 (%)	2019 (%)	2020 (%)	2021 (%)	2022 (%)
MSA[1]	49.9	50.4	49.9	49.7	50.4	50.9	50.7	50.5
U.S.	63.7	63.4	63.9	64.4	64.6	66.6	65.5	65.8

Note: (1) Figures cover the New York-Newark-Jersey City, NY-NJ-PA Metropolitan Statistical Area
Source: U.S. Census Bureau, Housing Vacancies and Homeownership Annual Statistics: 2015-2022

House Price Index (HPI)

Area	National Ranking[2]	Quarterly Change (%)	One-Year Change (%)	Five-Year Change (%)	Since 1991Q1 (%)
MD[1]	212	-0.09	8.22	34.61	258.57
U.S.[3]	–	0.34	8.41	58.44	289.08

Note: The HPI is a weighted repeat sales index. It measures average price changes in repeat sales or refinancings on the same properties. This information is obtained by reviewing repeat mortgage transactions on single-family properties whose mortgages have been purchased or securitized by Fannie Mae or Freddie Mac since January 1975; (1) Figures cover the New York-Jersey City-White Plains, NY-NJ Metropolitan Division; (2) Rankings are based on annual percentage change for all metro areas containing at least 15,000 transactions over the last 10 years and ranges from 1 to 257; (3) figures based on a weighted average of Census Division estimates using a seasonally adjusted, purchase-only index; all figures are for the period ending December 31, 2022
Source: Federal Housing Finance Agency, Change in FHFA Metropolitan Area House Price Indexes, 2022Q4

Median Single-Family Home Prices

Area	2020	2021	2022p	Percent Change 2021 to 2022
MD[1]	442.4	535.8	589.2	10.0
U.S. Average	300.2	357.1	392.6	9.9

Note: Figures are median sales prices of existing single-family homes in thousands of dollars; (p) preliminary; (1) Figures cover the New York-Jersey City-White Plains, NY-NJ Metropolitan Division
Source: National Association of Realtors, Median Sales Price of Existing Single-Family Homes for Metropolitan Areas, 4th Quarter 2022

Qualifying Income Based on Median Sales Price of Existing Single-Family Homes

Area	With 5% Down ($)	With 10% Down ($)	With 20% Down ($)
MD[1]	172,719	163,628	145,447
U.S. Average	112,234	106,237	94,513

Note: Figures are preliminary; Qualifying income is based on a mortgage rate of 6.77%. Monthly principal and interest payment is limited to 25% of income; (1) Figures cover the New York-Jersey City-White Plains, NY-NJ Metropolitan Division
Source: National Association of Realtors, Qualifying Income Based on Median Sales Price of Existing Single-Family Homes for Metropolitan Areas, 4th Quarter 2022

Home Value

Area	Under $100,000	$100,000 -$199,999	$200,000 -$299,999	$300,000 -$399,999	$400,000 -$499,999	$500,000 -$999,999	$1,000,000 or more	Median ($)
City	3.9	3.9	14.5	26.0	20.3	29.1	2.3	408,100
MSA[1]	3.5	5.2	11.1	16.7	16.1	36.2	11.2	483,500
U.S.	16.2	24.2	20.1	13.6	8.3	13.6	4.1	244,900

Note: Figures are percentages except for median and cover owner-occupied housing units; (1) Figures cover the New York-Newark-Jersey City, NY-NJ-PA Metropolitan Statistical Area
Source: U.S. Census Bureau, 2017-2021 American Community Survey 5-Year Estimates

Year Housing Structure Built

Area	2020 or Later	2010 -2019	2000 -2009	1990 -1999	1980 -1989	1970 -1979	1960 -1969	1950 -1959	1940 -1949	Before 1940	Median Year
City	0.1	2.5	5.7	9.8	24.2	11.6	18.6	17.8	4.0	5.5	1973
MSA[1]	0.1	4.1	6.5	6.2	7.8	9.7	13.5	15.6	8.5	28.1	1959
U.S.	0.2	7.3	13.6	13.6	13.2	14.8	10.3	10.0	4.7	12.2	1979

Note: Figures are percentages except for Median Year; Note: (1) Figures cover the New York-Newark-Jersey City, NY-NJ-PA Metropolitan Statistical Area
Source: U.S. Census Bureau, 2017-2021 American Community Survey 5-Year Estimates

Gross Monthly Rent

Area	Under $500	$500 -$999	$1,000 -$1,499	$1,500 -$1,999	$2,000 -$2,499	$2,500 -$2,999	$3,000 and up	Median ($)
City	3.2	3.3	26.6	39.0	22.8	4.0	1.1	1,716
MSA[1]	8.4	11.4	26.5	24.9	13.4	6.3	9.1	1,573
U.S.	8.1	30.5	30.8	16.8	7.3	3.1	3.5	1,163

Note: Figures are percentages except for median; Gross rent is the contract rent plus the estimated average monthly cost of utilities (electricity, gas, and water and sewer) and fuels (oil, coal, kerosene, wood, etc.) if these are paid by the renter (or paid for the renter by someone else); (1) Figures cover the New York-Newark-Jersey City, NY-NJ-PA Metropolitan Statistical Area
Source: U.S. Census Bureau, 2017-2021 American Community Survey 5-Year Estimates

HEALTH

Health Risk Factors

Category	MD[1] (%)	U.S. (%)
Adults aged 18–64 who have any kind of health care coverage	90.1	90.9
Adults who reported being in good or better health	84.7	85.2
Adults who have been told they have high blood cholesterol	35.6	35.7
Adults who have been told they have high blood pressure	28.3	32.4
Adults who are current smokers	10.0	14.4
Adults who currently use e-cigarettes	4.5	6.7
Adults who currently use chewing tobacco, snuff, or snus	1.6	3.5
Adults who are heavy drinkers[2]	4.6	6.3
Adults who are binge drinkers[3]	14.8	15.4
Adults who are overweight (BMI 25.0 - 29.9)	34.7	34.4
Adults who are obese (BMI 30.0 - 99.8)	25.5	33.9
Adults who participated in any physical activities in the past month	72.7	76.3

Note: (1) Figures cover the New York-Jersey City-White Plains, NY-NJ Metropolitan Division; (2) Heavy drinkers are classified as adult men having more than 14 drinks per week and adult women having more than 7 drinks per week; (3) Binge drinkers are classified as males having five or more drinks on one occasion or females having four or more drinks on one occasion
Source: Centers for Disease Control and Prevention, Behaviorial Risk Factor Surveillance System, SMART: Selected Metropolitan Area Risk Trends, 2021

Acute and Chronic Health Conditions

Category	MD[1] (%)	U.S. (%)
Adults who have ever been told they had a heart attack	3.0	4.0
Adults who have ever been told they have angina or coronary heart disease	3.2	3.8
Adults who have ever been told they had a stroke	2.1	3.0
Adults who have ever been told they have asthma	12.8	14.9
Adults who have ever been told they have arthritis	20.0	25.8
Adults who have ever been told they have diabetes[2]	11.3	10.9
Adults who have ever been told they had skin cancer	3.3	6.6
Adults who have ever been told they had any other types of cancer	5.3	7.5
Adults who have ever been told they have COPD	4.0	6.1
Adults who have ever been told they have kidney disease	2.6	3.0
Adults who have ever been told they have a form of depression	15.0	20.5

Note: (1) Figures cover the New York-Jersey City-White Plains, NY-NJ Metropolitan Division; (2) Figures do not include pregnancy-related, borderline, or pre-diabetes
Source: Centers for Disease Control and Prevention, Behaviorial Risk Factor Surveillance System, SMART: Selected Metropolitan Area Risk Trends, 2021

Health Screening and Vaccination Rates

Category	MD[1] (%)	U.S. (%)
Adults who have ever been tested for HIV	50.1	34.9
Adults who have had their blood cholesterol checked within the last five years	90.8	85.2
Adults aged 65+ who have had flu shot within the past year	65.1	68.6
Adults aged 65+ who have ever had a pneumonia vaccination	60.1	71.0

Note: (1) Figures cover the New York-Jersey City-White Plains, NY-NJ Metropolitan Division.
Source: Centers for Disease Control and Prevention, Behaviorial Risk Factor Surveillance System, SMART: Selected Metropolitan Area Risk Trends, 2021

Disability Status

Category	MD[1] (%)	U.S. (%)
Adults who reported being deaf	4.9	7.2
Are you blind or have serious difficulty seeing, even when wearing glasses?	5.8	4.8
Are you limited in any way in any of your usual activities due to arthritis?	7.8	11.1
Do you have difficulty doing errands alone?	7.3	7.0
Do you have difficulty dressing or bathing?	4.3	3.6
Do you have serious difficulty concentrating/remembering/making decisions?	10.6	12.1
Do you have serious difficulty walking or climbing stairs?	14.3	12.8

Note: (1) Figures cover the New York-Jersey City-White Plains, NY-NJ Metropolitan Division.
Source: Centers for Disease Control and Prevention, Behaviorial Risk Factor Surveillance System, SMART: Selected Metropolitan Area Risk Trends, 2021

Mortality Rates for the Top 10 Causes of Death in the U.S.

ICD-10[a] Sub-Chapter	ICD-10[a] Code	Crude Mortality Rate[1] per 100,000 population	
		County[2]	U.S.
Malignant neoplasms	C00-C97	151.2	182.6
Ischaemic heart diseases	I20-I25	95.0	113.1
Other forms of heart disease	I30-I51	64.3	64.4
Other degenerative diseases of the nervous system	G30-G31	27.6	51.0
Cerebrovascular diseases	I60-I69	33.4	47.8
Other external causes of accidental injury	W00-X59	38.4	46.4
Chronic lower respiratory diseases	J40-J47	22.9	45.7
Organic, including symptomatic, mental disorders	F01-F09	35.3	35.9
Hypertensive diseases	I10-I15	19.5	35.0
Diabetes mellitus	E10-E14	21.2	29.6

Note: (a) ICD-10 = International Classification of Diseases 10th Revision; (1) Crude mortality rates are a three-year average covering 2019-2021; (2) Figures cover Middlesex County.
Source: Centers for Disease Control and Prevention, National Center for Health Statistics. National Vital Statistics System, Mortality 2018-2021 on CDC WONDER Online Database

Mortality Rates for Selected Causes of Death

ICD-10[a] Sub-Chapter	ICD-10[a] Code	Crude Mortality Rate[1] per 100,000 population	
		County[2]	U.S.
Assault	X85-Y09	2.3	7.0
Diseases of the liver	K70-K76	13.6	19.8
Human immunodeficiency virus (HIV) disease	B20-B24	1.0	1.5
Influenza and pneumonia	J09-J18	14.7	14.7
Intentional self-harm	X60-X84	6.6	14.3
Malnutrition	E40-E46	2.3	4.3
Obesity and other hyperalimentation	E65-E68	2.1	3.0
Renal failure	N17-N19	15.3	15.7
Transport accidents	V01-V99	7.2	13.6
Viral hepatitis	B15-B19	Suppressed	1.2

Note: (a) ICD-10 = International Classification of Diseases 10th Revision; (1) Crude mortality rates are a three-year average covering 2019-2021; (2) Figures cover Middlesex County; Data are suppressed when the data meet the criteria for confidentiality constraints; Crude mortality rates are flagged as unreliable when the rate would be calculated with a numerator of 20 or less.
Source: Centers for Disease Control and Prevention, National Center for Health Statistics. National Vital Statistics System, Mortality 2018-2021 on CDC WONDER Online Database

Health Insurance Coverage

Area	With Health Insurance	With Private Health Insurance	With Public Health Insurance	Without Health Insurance	Population Under Age 19 Without Health Insurance
City	95.2	80.5	23.8	4.8	1.9
MSA[1]	93.2	67.3	36.5	6.8	3.0
U.S.	91.2	67.8	35.4	8.8	5.3

Note: Figures are percentages that cover the civilian noninstitutionalized population; (1) Figures cover the New York-Newark-Jersey City, NY-NJ-PA Metropolitan Statistical Area
Source: U.S. Census Bureau, 2017-2021 American Community Survey 5-Year Estimates

Number of Medical Professionals

Area	MDs[3]	DOs[3,4]	Dentists	Podiatrists	Chiropractors	Optometrists
County[1] (number)	3,252	174	761	85	214	172
County[1] (rate[2])	377.3	20.2	88.4	9.9	24.9	20.0
U.S. (rate[2])	289.3	23.5	72.5	6.2	28.7	17.4

Note: Data as of 2021 unless noted; (1) Data covers Middlesex County; (2) Rate per 100,000 population; (3) Data as of 2020 and includes all active, non-federal physicians; (4) Doctor of Osteopathic Medicine
Source: U.S. Department of Health and Human Services, Health Resources and Services Administration, Bureau of Health Professions, Area Resource File (ARF) 2021-2022

Best Hospitals

According to *U.S. News,* the New York-Jersey City-White Plains, NY-NJ metro area is home to 16 of the best hospitals in the U.S.: **Hackensack University Medical Center at Hackensack Meridian Health** (4 adult specialties and 1 pediatric specialty); **Hospital for Special Surgery** (2 adult specialties and 1 pediatric specialty); **Lenox Hill Hospital at Northwell Health** (9 adult specialties); **Manhattan Eye Ear & Throat Hospital** (9 adult specialties); **Memorial Sloan Kettering Cancer Center** (7 adult specialties and 1 pediatric specialty); **Montefiore Medical Center** (6 adult specialties and 3 pediatric specialties); **Mount Sinai Beth Israel Hospital** (2 adult specialties); **Mount Sinai Hospital** (Honor Roll/11 adult specialties and 3 pediatric specialties); **Mount Sinai Morningside and Mount Sinai West Hospitals** (2 adult specialties); **NYU Langone Hospitals** (Honor Roll/14 adult specialties and 3 pediatric specialties); **NYU Langone Orthopedic Hospital at NYU Langone Hospitals** (Honor Roll/14 adult specialties and 3 pediatric specialties); **New York Eye and Ear Infirmary of Mount Sinai** (1 adult specialty); **New York-Presbyterian Brooklyn Methodist Hospital** (2 adult specialties); **New York-Presbyterian Hospital-Columbia and Cornell** (Honor Roll/14 adult specialties and 10 pediatric specialties); **Perlmutter Cancer Center at NYU Langone Hospitals** (Honor Roll/14 adult specialties and 3 pediatric specialties); **Rusk Rehabilitation at NYU Langone Hospitals** (Honor Roll/14 adult specialties and 3 pediatric specialties). The hospitals listed were nationally ranked in at least one of 15 adult or 10 pediatric specialties. The number of specialties shown cover the parent hospital. Only 164 U.S. hospitals performed well enough to be nationally ranked in one or more specialties. Twenty hospitals in the U.S. made the Honor Roll. The Best Hospitals Honor Roll takes both the national rankings and the procedure and condition ratings into account. Hospitals received points if they were nationally ranked in one of the 15 adult specialties—the higher they ranked, the more points they got—and how many ratings of "high performing" they earned in the 17 procedures and conditions. *U.S. News Online, "America's Best Hospitals 2022-23"*

According to *U.S. News,* the New York-Jersey City-White Plains, NY-NJ metro area is home to five of the best children's hospitals in the U.S.: **New York-Presbyterian Children's Hospital-Columbia and Cornell** (10 pediatric specialties); **Hassenfeld Children's Hospital at NYU Langone** (3 pediatric specialties); **Children's Hospital at Montefiore** (3 pediatric specialties); **Hackensack Meridian Health JM Sanzari and K Hovnanian Children's Hospitals** (1 pediatric specialty); **Mount Sinai Kravis Children's Hospital** (3 pediatric specialties). The hospitals listed were highly ranked in at least one of 10 pediatric specialties. Eighty-six children's hospitals in the U.S. were nationally ranked in at least one specialty. Hospitals received points for being ranked in a specialty, and the 10 hospitals with the most points across the 10 specialties make up the Honor Roll. *U.S. News Online, "America's Best Children's Hospitals 2022-23"*

EDUCATION

Public School District Statistics

District Name	Schls	Pupils	Pupil/ Teacher Ratio	Minority Pupils[1] (%)	LEP/ELL[2] (%)	IEP[3] (%)
Edison Township School District	19	16,268	13.4	89.6	2.5	11.5

Note: Table includes school districts with 2,000 or more students; (1) Percentage of students that are not non-Hispanic white; (2) Percentage of students that are Limited English Proficient or English Language Learners (2018-19); (3) Percentage of students that have an Individualized Education Program (2019-20).
Source: U.S. Department of Education, National Center for Education Statistics, Common Core of Data, Local Education Agency (School District) Universe Survey: School Year 2021-2022

Best High Schools

According to *U.S. News,* Edison is home to one of the top 500 high schools in the U.S.: **Middlesex County Academy for Science Mathematics and Engineering Technologies** (#23). Nearly 18,000 public, magnet and charter schools were ranked based on their performance on state assessments and how well they prepare students for college. *U.S. News & World Report, "Best High Schools 2022"*

Highest Level of Education

Area	Less than H.S.	H.S. Diploma	Some College, No Deg.	Associate Degree	Bachelor's Degree	Master's Degree	Prof. School Degree	Doctorate Degree
City	7.9	18.1	11.9	5.8	30.1	21.4	2.6	2.3
MSA[1]	12.7	24.0	14.4	6.8	24.2	12.7	3.4	1.7
U.S.	11.1	26.5	20.0	8.7	20.6	9.3	2.2	1.5

Note: Figures cover persons age 25 and over; (1) Figures cover the New York-Newark-Jersey City, NY-NJ-PA Metropolitan Statistical Area
Source: U.S. Census Bureau, 2017-2021 American Community Survey 5-Year Estimates

Educational Attainment by Race

Area	High School Graduate or Higher (%)					Bachelor's Degree or Higher (%)				
	Total	White	Black	Asian	Hisp.[2]	Total	White	Black	Asian	Hisp.[2]
City	92.1	94.0	95.0	92.0	86.3	56.4	38.6	43.0	76.2	25.0
MSA[1]	87.3	92.2	86.3	84.1	73.1	42.0	49.1	26.8	56.0	21.3
U.S.	88.9	91.4	87.2	87.6	71.2	33.7	35.5	23.3	55.6	18.4

Note: Figures shown cover persons 25 years old and over; (1) Figures cover the New York-Newark-Jersey City, NY-NJ-PA Metropolitan Statistical Area; (2) People of Hispanic origin can be of any race
Source: U.S. Census Bureau, 2017-2021 American Community Survey 5-Year Estimates

School Enrollment by Grade and Control

Area	Preschool (%)		Kindergarten (%)		Grades 1 - 4 (%)		Grades 5 - 8 (%)		Grades 9 - 12 (%)	
	Public	Private	Public	Private	Public	Private	Public	Private	Public	Private
City	18.4	81.6	71.4	28.6	88.2	11.8	89.7	10.3	91.9	8.1
MSA[1]	56.6	43.4	81.6	18.4	84.6	15.4	84.8	15.2	84.1	15.9
U.S.	58.8	41.2	86.3	13.7	88.3	11.7	88.6	11.4	89.4	10.6

Note: Figures shown cover persons 3 years old and over; (1) Figures cover the New York-Newark-Jersey City, NY-NJ-PA Metropolitan Statistical Area
Source: U.S. Census Bureau, 2017-2021 American Community Survey 5-Year Estimates

Higher Education

Four-Year Colleges			Two-Year Colleges			Medical Schools[1]	Law Schools[2]	Voc/ Tech[3]
Public	Private Non-profit	Private For-profit	Public	Private Non-profit	Private For-profit			
30	153	19	23	20	30	16	13	96

Note: Figures cover institutions located within the New York-Newark-Jersey City, NY-NJ-PA Metropolitan Statistical Area and include main campuses only; (1) includes schools accredited by the Liaison Committee on Medical Education and the American Osteopathic Association's Commission on Osteopathic College Accreditation; (2) includes ABA-accredited schools, schools with provisional ABA accreditation, and state accredited schools; (3) includes all schools with programs that are less than 2 years.
Source: National Center for Education Statistics, Integrated Postsecondary Education System (IPEDS), 2021-22; Wikipedia, List of Medical Schools in the United States, accessed April 10, 2023; Wikipedia, List of Law Schools in the United States, accessed April 10, 2023

According to *U.S. News & World Report,* the New York-Jersey City-White Plains, NY-NJ metro division is home to 10 of the top 200 national universities in the U.S.: **Columbia University** (#18 tie); **New York University** (#25 tie); **Rutgers University—New Brunswick** (#55 tie); **Yeshiva University** (#67 tie); **Fordham University** (#72 tie); **Stevens Institute of Technology** (#83 tie); **The New School** (#127 tie); **CUNY—City College** (#151 tie); **St. John's University (NY)** (#166 tie); **Touro University** (#182 tie). The indicators used to capture academic quality fall into a number of categories: assessment by administrators at peer institutions; retention of students; faculty resources; student selectivity; financial resources; alumni giving; high school counselor ratings of colleges; and graduation rate. *U.S. News & World Report, "America's Best Colleges 2023"*

According to *U.S. News & World Report,* the New York-Jersey City-White Plains, NY-NJ metro division is home to three of the top 100 liberal arts colleges in the U.S.: **United States Military Academy at West Point** (#9 tie); **Barnard College** (#18 tie); **Sarah Lawrence College** (#72 tie). The indicators used to capture academic quality fall into a number of categories: assessment by administrators at peer institutions; retention of students; faculty resources; student selectivity; financial resources; alumni giving; high school counselor ratings of colleges; and graduation rate. *U.S. News & World Report, "America's Best Colleges 2023"*

According to *U.S. News & World Report,* the New York-Jersey City-White Plains, NY-NJ metro division is home to six of the top 100 law schools in the U.S.: **Columbia University** (#4 tie); **New York University** (#7); **Fordham University** (#37 tie); **Yeshiva University (Cardozo)** (#52 tie); **St. John's University** (#84 tie); **Brooklyn Law School** (#98 tie). The rankings are based on a weighted average of 12 measures of quality: peer assessment score; assessment score by lawyers/judges; median LSAT scores; median undergrad GPA; acceptance rate; employment rates for graduates; placement success; bar passage rate; faculty resources; expenditures per student; student/faculty ratio; and library resources. *U.S. News & World Report, "America's Best Graduate Schools, Law, 2023"*

According to *U.S. News & World Report,* the New York-Jersey City-White Plains, NY-NJ metro division is home to six of the top 75 medical schools for research in the U.S.: **New York University (Grossman)** (#2); **Columbia University** (#3 tie); **Icahn School of Medicine at Mount Sinai** (#11 tie); **Cornell University (Weill)** (#14 tie); **Albert Einstein College of Medicine** (#37 tie); **Rutgers Robert Wood Johnson Medical School—New Brunswick (Johnson)** (#68 tie). The rankings are based on a weighted average of 11 measures of quality: quality assessment; peer assessment score; assessment score by residency directors; research activity; total research activity; average research activity per faculty member; student selectivity; median MCAT total score; median undergraduate GPA; acceptance rate; and faculty resources. *U.S. News & World Report, "America's Best Graduate Schools, Medical, 2023"*

According to *U.S. News & World Report,* the New York-Jersey City-White Plains, NY-NJ metro division is home to four of the top 75 business schools in the U.S.: **Columbia University** (#8 tie); **New York University (Stern)** (#12 tie); **CUNY Bernard M. Baruch College (Zicklin)** (#62 tie); **Fordham University (Gabelli)** (#64 tie). The rankings are based on a weighted average of the following nine measures: quality assessment; peer assessment; recruiter assessment; placement success; mean starting salary and bonus; student selectivity; mean GMAT and GRE scores; mean undergraduate GPA; and acceptance rate. *U.S. News & World Report, "America's Best Graduate Schools, Business, 2023"*

EMPLOYERS

Major Employers

Company Name	Industry
American Express Company	Personal credit institutions
American International Group	Life insurance
Deloitte Consulting	Management consulting services
Hackensack University Medical Center	University
Merrill Lynch and Co	Security brokers & dealers
Mount Sinai Hospital	General medical & surgical hospitals
Mount Sinai School of Medicine	Medical training services
New York-Presbyterian Hospital	General medical & surgical hospitals
NYC Health and Hospitals Corp	Psychiatric hospitals
NYU School of Medicine	Offices & clinics of medical doctors
Paramount Comm Acq Corp	Investment holding companies, except banks
Patriarch Partners	Investment offices
Rutgers, The State Univ of NJ	Colleges & universities
Standard Americas	Agencies of foreign banks
The Long Island Rail Road Company	Local & suburban transit
UMASS Memorial Health Care	Psychiatrist
United States Postal Service	U.S. postal service
University of Med and Dentistry of NJ	Colleges & universities
Wellchoice	Health insurance carriers

Note: Companies shown are located within the New York-Newark-Jersey City, NY-NJ-PA Metropolitan Statistical Area.
Source: Hoovers.com; Wikipedia

PUBLIC SAFETY

Crime Rate

Area	Total Crime	Violent Crime Rate				Property Crime Rate		
		Murder	Rape[3]	Robbery	Aggrav. Assault	Burglary	Larceny -Theft	Motor Vehicle Theft
City	1,242.2	1.0	9.0	31.1	62.3	131.5	889.7	117.5
Suburbs[1]	n/a	n/a	n/a	n/a	n/a	n/a	n/a	n/a
Metro[2]	n/a	n/a	n/a	n/a	n/a	n/a	n/a	n/a
U.S.	2,356.7	6.5	38.4	73.9	279.7	314.2	1,398.0	246.0

Note: Figures are crimes per 100,000 population; (1) All areas within the metro area that are located outside the city limits; (2) Figures cover the New York-Jersey City-White Plains, NY-NJ Metropolitan Division; n/a not available; (3) All figures shown were reported using the revised Uniform Crime Reporting (UCR) definition of rape; Due to the transition to the National Incident-Based Reporting System (NIBRS), limited city and metro area data was released for 2021.
Source: FBI Uniform Crime Reports, 2020

Hate Crimes

Area	Number of Quarters Reported	Number of Incidents per Bias Motivation					
		Race/Ethnicity/ Ancestry	Religion	Sexual Orientation	Disability	Gender	Gender Identity
City	4	3	1	0	0	0	0
U.S.	4	5,227	1,244	1,110	130	75	266

Note: Due to the transition to the National Incident-Based Reporting System (NIBRS), limited crime data was released for 2021.
Source: Federal Bureau of Investigation, Hate Crime Statistics 2020

Identity Theft Consumer Reports

Area	Reports	Reports per 100,000 Population	Rank[2]
MSA[1]	69,873	363	43
U.S.	1,108,609	339	-

Note: (1) Figures cover the New York-Newark-Jersey City, NY-NJ-PA Metropolitan Statistical Area; (2) Rank ranges from 1 to 391 where 1 indicates greatest number of identity theft reports per 100,000 population
Source: Federal Trade Commission, Consumer Sentinel Network Data Book 2022

Fraud and Other Consumer Reports

Area	Reports	Reports per 100,000 Population	Rank[2]
MSA[1]	202,205	1,050	79
U.S.	4,064,520	1,245	-

Note: (1) Figures cover the New York-Newark-Jersey City, NY-NJ-PA Metropolitan Statistical Area; (2) Rank ranges from 1 to 391 where 1 indicates greatest number of fraud and other consumer reports per 100,000 population
Source: Federal Trade Commission, Consumer Sentinel Network Data Book 2022

POLITICS

2020 Presidential Election Results

Area	Biden	Trump	Jorgensen	Hawkins	Other
Middlesex County	60.2	38.2	0.7	0.3	0.6
U.S.	51.3	46.8	1.2	0.3	0.5

Note: Results are percentages and may not add to 100% due to rounding
Source: Dave Leip's Atlas of U.S. Presidential Elections

SPORTS

Professional Sports Teams

Team Name	League	Year Established
Brooklyn Nets	National Basketball Association (NBA)	1967
New Jersey Devils	National Hockey League (NHL)	1982
New York City FC	Major League Soccer (MLS)	2015
New York Giants	National Football League (NFL)	1925
New York Islanders	National Hockey League (NHL)	1972
New York Jets	National Football League (NFL)	1960
New York Knicks	National Basketball Association (NBA)	1946
New York Mets	Major League Baseball (MLB)	1962
New York Rangers	National Hockey League (NHL)	1926
New York Red Bulls	Major League Soccer (MLS)	1996
New York Yankees	Major League Baseball (MLB)	1903

Note: Includes teams located in the New York-Newark-Jersey City, NY-NJ-PA Metropolitan Statistical Area.
Source: Wikipedia, Major Professional Sports Teams of the United States and Canada, April 12, 2023

CLIMATE

Average and Extreme Temperatures

Temperature	Jan	Feb	Mar	Apr	May	Jun	Jul	Aug	Sep	Oct	Nov	Dec	Yr.
Extreme High (°F)	74	76	89	94	98	102	105	103	105	93	85	72	105
Average High (°F)	38	41	50	61	72	81	86	84	77	66	54	42	63
Average Temp. (°F)	32	33	42	52	63	72	77	76	68	57	47	36	55
Average Low (°F)	24	25	33	43	53	62	68	67	59	48	39	28	46
Extreme Low (°F)	-8	-7	6	16	33	41	52	45	35	25	15	-1	-8

Note: Figures cover the years 1935-1995
Source: National Climatic Data Center, International Station Meteorological Climate Summary, 9/96

Average Precipitation/Snowfall/Humidity

Precip./Humidity	Jan	Feb	Mar	Apr	May	Jun	Jul	Aug	Sep	Oct	Nov	Dec	Yr.
Avg. Precip. (in.)	3.4	3.0	4.0	3.7	3.9	3.3	4.2	4.1	3.6	3.0	3.8	3.4	43.5
Avg. Snowfall (in.)	8	8	5	1	Tr	0	0	0	0	Tr	1	5	27
Avg. Rel. Hum. 7am (%)	73	71	69	67	70	71	72	76	79	78	76	74	73
Avg. Rel. Hum. 4pm (%)	58	54	51	48	51	51	52	54	55	53	57	59	54

Note: Figures cover the years 1935-1995; Tr = Trace amounts (<0.05 in. of rain; <0.5 in. of snow)
Source: National Climatic Data Center, International Station Meteorological Climate Summary, 9/96

Weather Conditions

Temperature			Daytime Sky			Precipitation		
5°F & below	32°F & below	90°F & above	Clear	Partly cloudy	Cloudy	0.01 inch or more precip.	0.1 inch or more snow/ice	Thunder-storms
2	90	24	80	146	139	122	16	46

Note: Figures are average number of days per year and cover the years 1935-1995
Source: National Climatic Data Center, International Station Meteorological Climate Summary, 9/96

HAZARDOUS WASTE

Superfund Sites

The New York-Jersey City-White Plains, NY-NJ metro division is home to 40 sites on the EPA's Superfund National Priorities List: **Atlantic Resources** (final); **Bog Creek Farm** (final); **Brick Township Landfill** (final); **Burnt Fly Bog** (final); **Carroll & Dubies Sewage Disposal** (final); **Chemical Insecticide Corp.** (final); **Chemsol, Inc.** (final); **Ciba-Geigy Corp.** (final); **Cornell Dubilier Electronics Inc.** (final); **CPS/Madison Industries** (final); **Curcio Scrap Metal, Inc.** (final); **Diamond Head Oil Refinery Division** (final); **Evor Phillips Leasing** (final); **Fair Lawn Well Field** (final); **Fried Industries** (final); **Garfield Ground Water Contamination** (final); **Global Sanitary Landfill** (final); **Goose Farm** (final); **Gowanus Canal** (final); **Horseshoe Road** (final); **Imperial Oil Co., Inc./Champion Chemicals** (final); **JIS Landfill** (final); **Kin-Buc Landfill** (final); **Lone Pine Landfill** (final); **Lower Hackensack River** (final); **Magna Metals** (final); **Maywood Chemical Co.** (final); **Meeker Avenue Plume** (final); **Middlesex Sampling Plant (USDOE)** (final); **Monitor Devices, Inc./Intercircuits, Inc.** (final); **Naval Air Engineering Center** (final); **Naval Weapons Station Earle (Site A)** (final); **Nepera Chemical Co., Inc.** (final); **Newtown Creek** (final); **PJP Landfill** (final); **Quanta Resources** (final); **Ramapo Landfill** (final); **Raritan Bay Slag**

202   Edison, New Jersey

(final); **Ringwood Mines/Landfill** (final); **Scientific Chemical Processing** (final). There are a total of 1,165 Superfund sites with a status of proposed or final on the list in the U.S. *U.S. Environmental Protection Agency, National Priorities List, April 12, 2023*

AIR QUALITY

Air Quality Trends: Ozone

	1990	1995	2000	2005	2010	2015	2018	2019	2020	2021
MSA[1]	0.101	0.105	0.089	0.090	0.080	0.074	0.073	0.067	0.064	0.069
U.S.	0.087	0.089	0.081	0.080	0.072	0.067	0.069	0.065	0.065	0.067

Note: (1) Data covers the New York-Newark-Jersey City, NY-NJ-PA Metropolitan Statistical Area. The values shown are the composite ozone concentration averages among trend sites based on the highest fourth daily maximum 8-hour concentration in parts per million. These trends are based on sites having an adequate record of monitoring data during the trend period. Data from exceptional events are included.
Source: U.S. Environmental Protection Agency, Air Quality Monitoring Information, "Air Quality Trends by City, 1990-2021"

Air Quality Index

Area	Percent of Days when Air Quality was...[2]					AQI Statistics[2]	
	Good	Moderate	Unhealthy for Sensitive Groups	Unhealthy	Very Unhealthy	Maximum	Median
MSA[1]	54.8	39.5	4.9	0.8	0.0	154	49

Note: (1) Data covers the New York-Newark-Jersey City, NY-NJ-PA Metropolitan Statistical Area; (2) Based on 365 days with AQI data in 2021. Air Quality Index (AQI) is an index for reporting daily air quality. EPA calculates the AQI for five major air pollutants regulated by the Clean Air Act: ground-level ozone, particle pollution (aka particulate matter), carbon monoxide, sulfur dioxide, and nitrogen dioxide. The AQI runs from 0 to 500. The higher the AQI value, the greater the level of air pollution and the greater the health concern. There are six AQI categories: "Good" AQI is between 0 and 50. Air quality is considered satisfactory; "Moderate" AQI is between 51 and 100. Air quality is acceptable; "Unhealthy for Sensitive Groups" When AQI values are between 101 and 150, members of sensitive groups may experience health effects; "Unhealthy" When AQI values are between 151 and 200 everyone may begin to experience health effects; "Very Unhealthy" AQI values between 201 and 300 trigger a health alert; "Hazardous" AQI values over 300 trigger warnings of emergency conditions (not shown).
Source: U.S. Environmental Protection Agency, Air Quality Index Report, 2021

Air Quality Index Pollutants

Area	Percent of Days when AQI Pollutant was...[2]					
	Carbon Monoxide	Nitrogen Dioxide	Ozone	Sulfur Dioxide	Particulate Matter 2.5	Particulate Matter 10
MSA[1]	0.0	12.3	41.4	(3)	46.3	0.0

Note: (1) Data covers the New York-Newark-Jersey City, NY-NJ-PA Metropolitan Statistical Area; (2) Based on 365 days with AQI data in 2021. The Air Quality Index (AQI) is an index for reporting daily air quality. EPA calculates the AQI for five major air pollutants regulated by the Clean Air Act: ground-level ozone, particle pollution (also known as particulate matter), carbon monoxide, sulfur dioxide, and nitrogen dioxide. The AQI runs from 0 to 500. The higher the AQI value, the greater the level of air pollution and the greater the health concern; (3) Sulfur dioxide is no longer included in this table (as of December 8, 2021) because SO_2 concentrations tend to be very localized and not necessarily representative of broad geographical areas like counties and CBSAs.
Source: U.S. Environmental Protection Agency, Air Quality Index Report, 2021

Maximum Air Pollutant Concentrations: Particulate Matter, Ozone, CO and Lead

	Particulate Matter 10 (ug/m^3)	Particulate Matter 2.5 Wtd AM (ug/m^3)	Particulate Matter 2.5 24-Hr (ug/m^3)	Ozone (ppm)	Carbon Monoxide (ppm)	Lead (ug/m^3)
MSA[1] Level	40	9.8	26	0.079	2	n/a
NAAQS[2]	150	15	35	0.075	9	0.15
Met NAAQS[2]	Yes	Yes	Yes	No	Yes	n/a

Note: (1) Data covers the New York-Newark-Jersey City, NY-NJ-PA Metropolitan Statistical Area; Data from exceptional events are included; (2) National Ambient Air Quality Standards; ppm = parts per million; ug/m^3 = micrograms per cubic meter; n/a not available.
Concentrations: Particulate Matter 10 (coarse particulate)—highest second maximum 24-hour concentration; Particulate Matter 2.5 Wtd AM (fine particulate)—highest weighted annual mean concentration; Particulate Matter 2.5 24-Hour (fine particulate)—highest 98th percentile 24-hour concentration; Ozone—highest fourth daily maximum 8-hour concentration; Carbon Monoxide—highest second maximum non-overlapping 8-hour concentration; Lead—maximum running 3-month average
Source: U.S. Environmental Protection Agency, Air Quality Monitoring Information, "Air Quality Statistics by City, 2021"

Maximum Air Pollutant Concentrations: Nitrogen Dioxide and Sulfur Dioxide

	Nitrogen Dioxide AM (ppb)	Nitrogen Dioxide 1-Hr (ppb)	Sulfur Dioxide AM (ppb)	Sulfur Dioxide 1-Hr (ppb)	Sulfur Dioxide 24-Hr (ppb)
MSA[1] Level	19	65	n/a	17	n/a
NAAQS[2]	53	100	30	75	140
Met NAAQS[2]	Yes	Yes	n/a	Yes	n/a

Note: (1) Data covers the New York-Newark-Jersey City, NY-NJ-PA Metropolitan Statistical Area; Data from exceptional events are included; (2) National Ambient Air Quality Standards; ppm = parts per million; ug/m³ = micrograms per cubic meter; n/a not available.
Concentrations: Nitrogen Dioxide AM—highest arithmetic mean concentration; Nitrogen Dioxide 1-Hr—highest 98th percentile 1-hour daily maximum concentration; Sulfur Dioxide AM—highest annual mean concentration; Sulfur Dioxide 1-Hr—highest 99th percentile 1-hour daily maximum concentration; Sulfur Dioxide 24-Hr—highest second maximum 24-hour concentration
Source: U.S. Environmental Protection Agency, Air Quality Monitoring Information, "Air Quality Statistics by City, 2021"

Greensboro, North Carolina

Background

Greensboro is a quiet community in northern North Carolina. It, along with Winston-Salem and High Point, is part of an urban triangle. The city was the site of the Battle of Guilford Courthouse on March 15, 1781, during the American Revolution, as well as the birthplace of such notable Americans as Dolly Madison, wife of James Madison, the fourth president of the United States, and William Sydney Porter, otherwise known as author O. Henry.

During the mid- to late nineteenth century, the economy of the city was largely based upon textile production. While that still remains a vital role in Greensboro, petroleum, pharmaceutical products, and furniture have come into prominence as well.

The birth of the American Civil Rights movement can be traced to 1960 in Greensboro when four students from the historically black North Carolina A&T State sat at the white-only lunch counter at Greensboro's downtown Woolworth's department store. Their violent removal led to sit-ins all over the south. In 1979, several Ku Klux Klan (KKK) members traded gunfire with members of the Communist Workers Party (CWP) who were holding an anti-KKK rally. Five CWP members were killed and the event became known as the Greensboro Massacre. Today, the former Woolworth Building houses the Civil Rights Center and Museum.

Greensboro is one of the anchors of the center for business opportunities in North Carolina, the Piedmont Triad. Along with Winston-Salem and High Point, it has become a major metro area for attracting new plants and facilities. FedEx has a Mid-Atlantic air-cargo package-sorting hub in Greensboro, which is also home to the Gateway University Research Park, consisting of two 75-acre campuses focusing on nanotechnology, biotechnology, biochemistry, electronics, artificial intelligence, environmental sciences, food and nutrition, health genetics, materials science and engineering, alternate and renewable energy and social sciences.

Greensboro has a thriving cultural scene. The Green Hill Center for North Carolina Art Gallery promotes the visual arts and includes ArtQuest, an interactive gallery. The Greensboro Ballet provides performances, educational programs, the Summer Ballet Festival, and houses student and professional studios. The Greensboro Symphony Orchestra's Masterworks and Chamber Series concerts feature guest artists from around the world.

Greensboro College, Guilford College, University of North Carolina at Greensboro, North Carolina A&T State, and Bennett College for Women all reside in Greensboro. The Eastern Music Festival and School, part of Guilford College, offers a summer concert series. Elon University School of Law is in the heart of downtown.

In the past 30 years, Greensboro has grown into an internationally diverse community. Today, the city is home to large populations of Vietnamese, West African, and Latino immigrants. Such diverse communities have contributed to the local cuisine and flavor, and authentic international specialty stores and restaurants are not hard to come by.

Downtown development, such as the NewBridge Bank Park minor league baseball stadium, and a variety of residential options, have helped transform the city center. The revitalized Southside neighborhood is touted as one of the best planned re-developments in the U.S. The city is famous to college sports fans as the home to the Atlantic Coast Conference. The annual ACC basketball tournament in March often airs from the Greensboro Coliseum Complex.

The Greensboro Parks & Recreation Department has acquired over 3,200 acres of land, with more than 170 parks and special facilities recognized internationally for their culturally diverse athletic, historical, and arts programs. The Bog Garden features more than 8,000 individually labeled trees, shrubs, ferns, bamboo, and wildflowers. Wet 'n' Wild Emerald Pointe Water Park offers one of only four tsunami (giant wave) pools in the U.S. Greensboro Historical Museum, located downtown in a building dating back to 1900, is listed on the National Register of Historic Places. The Battle of Guilford Courthouse National Military Park, with 220 acres of historic fields and forests, monuments, and graves, was the first national park established at a Revolutionary War site.

For children, Greensboro hosts a Science Center and Zoo, and a Children's Museum with a 30-foot climbing structure.

Greensboro is the largest city in the Piedmont Triad region. Both winter temperatures and rainfall are modified by the Blue Ridge Mountain barrier on the northwest. The summer temperatures vary with cloudiness and shower activity, but are generally mild. Northwesterly winds rarely bring heavy or prolonged winter rain or snow. Damaging storms are infrequent, however, strong tornadoes have struck the area in the late 1990s, 2008, 2010, and most recently, in 2018.

Rankings

General Rankings

- In their ninth annual survey, Livability.com looked at data for more than 2,300 mid-sized U.S. cities to determine the rankings for Livability's "Top 100 Best Places to Live" in 2022. Greensboro ranked #72. Criteria: housing and economy; social and civic engagement; education; demographics; health care options; transportation & infrastructure; and community amenities. *Livability.com, "Top 100 Best Places to Live 2022" July 19, 2022*

Business/Finance Rankings

- The Brookings Institution ranked the nation's largest cities based on income inequality. Greensboro was ranked #32 (#1 = greatest inequality). Criteria: the "95/20 ratio," a figure representing the income at which a household earns more than 95 percent of all other households, divided by the income at which a household earns more than only 20 percent of all other households. *Brookings Institution, "Household Income Inequality, Largest Cities of 97 Large U.S. Metro Areas, 2014-2016," February 5, 2018*

- The Brookings Institution ranked the 100 largest metro areas in the U.S. based on income inequality. Greensboro was ranked #25 (#1 = greatest inequality). Criteria: the "95/20 ratio," a figure representing the income at which a household earns more than 95 percent of all other households, divided by the income at which a household earns more than only 20 percent of all other households. *Brookings Institution, "Household Income Inequality, 100 Largest U.S. Metro Areas, 2014-2016," February 5, 2018*

- Greensboro was cited as one of America's top metros for total major capital investment facility projects in 2022. The area ranked #8 in the mid-sized metro area category (population 200,000 to 1 million). *Site Selection, "Top Metros of 2022," March 2023*

- Greensboro was identified as one of the unhappiest cities to work in by CareerBliss.com, an online community for career advancement. The city ranked #3 out of 5. Criteria: an employee's relationship with his or her boss and co-workers; general work environment; compensation; opportunities for advancement; company culture and job reputation; and resources. *Businesswire.com, "CareerBliss Unhappiest Cities to Work 2019," February 12, 2019*

- The Greensboro metro area appeared on the Milken Institute "2022 Best Performing Cities" list. Rank: #138 out of 200 large metro areas (population over 250,000). Criteria: job growth; wage and salary growth; high-tech output growth; housing affordability; household broadband access. *Milken Institute, "Best-Performing Cities 2022," March 28, 2022*

- *Forbes* ranked the 200 most populous metro areas to determine the nation's "Best Places for Business and Careers." The Greensboro metro area was ranked #66. Criteria: costs (business and living); job growth (past and projected); income growth; quality of life; educational attainment (college and high school); projected economic growth; cultural and leisure opportunities; workplace tolerance laws; net migration patterns. *Forbes, "The Best Places for Business and Careers 2019: Seattle Still On Top," October 30, 2019*

Dating/Romance Rankings

- Greensboro was ranked #8 out of 25 cities that stood out for inspiring romance and attracting diners on the website OpenTable.com. Criteria: percentage of people who dined out on Valentine's Day in 2018; percentage of romantic restaurants as rated by OpenTable diner reviews; and percentage of tables seated for two. *OpenTable, "25 Most Romantic Cities in America for 2019," February 7, 2019*

Education Rankings

- Personal finance website *WalletHub* analyzed the 150 largest U.S. metropolitan statistical areas to determine where the most educated Americans are putting their degrees to work. Criteria: education levels; percentage of workers with degrees; education quality and attainment gap; public school quality rankings; quality and enrollment of each metro area's universities. Greensboro was ranked #101 (#1 = most educated city). *www.WalletHub.com, "Most & Least Educated Cities in America," July 18, 2022*

- Greensboro was selected as one of America's most literate cities. The city ranked #45 out of the 84 largest U.S. cities. Criteria: number of booksellers; library resources; Internet resources; educational attainment; periodical publishing resources; newspaper circulation. *Central Connecticut State University, "America's Most Literate Cities, 2018," February 2019*

Environmental Rankings

- Greensboro was highlighted as one of the cleanest metro areas for ozone air pollution in the U.S. during 2019 through 2021. The list represents cities with no monitored ozone air pollution in unhealthful ranges. *American Lung Association, "State of the Air 2023," April 19, 2023*

Health/Fitness Rankings

- For each of the 100 largest cities in the United States, the American Fitness Index®, compiled in partnership between the American College of Sports Medicine and the Elevance Health Foundation, evaluated community infrastructure and 34 health behaviors including preventive health, levels of chronic disease conditions, food insecurity, sleep quality, pedestrian safety, air quality, and community/environment resources that support physical activity. Greensboro ranked #72 for "community fitness." *americanfitnessindex.org, "2022 ACSM American Fitness Index Summary Report," July 12, 2022*

- The Greensboro metro area was identified as one of the worst cities for bed bugs in America by pest control company Orkin. The area ranked #43 out of 50 based on the number of bed bug treatments Orkin performed from December 2021 to November 2022. *Orkin, "The Windy City Can't Blow Bed Bugs Away: Chicago Ranks #1 For Third Consecutive Year On Orkin's Bed Bug Cities List," January 9, 2023*

- Greensboro was identified as a "2022 Spring Allergy Capital." The area ranked #33 out of 100. Three groups of factors were used to identify the most challenging cities for people with allergies during the spring season: annual spring pollen scores; over the counter allergy medicine use; number of board-certified allergy specialists. *Asthma and Allergy Foundation of America, "Spring Allergy Capitals 2022," March 2, 2022*

- Greensboro was identified as a "2022 Fall Allergy Capital." The area ranked #34 out of 100. Three groups of factors were used to identify the most challenging cities for people with allergies during the fall season: annual fall pollen scores; over the counter allergy medicine use; number of board-certified allergy specialists. *Asthma and Allergy Foundation of America, "Fall Allergy Capitals 2022," March 2, 2022*

- Greensboro was identified as a "2022 Asthma Capital." The area ranked #89 out of the nation's 100 largest metropolitan areas. Criteria: estimated asthma prevalence; asthma-related mortality; and ER visits due to asthma. Risk factors analyzed but not factored in the rankings: annual pollen score; annual air quality; public smoking laws; access to board-certified asthma specialists; rescue and controller medication use; uninsured rate; poverty rate. *Asthma and Allergy Foundation of America, "Asthma Capitals 2022: The Most Challenging Places to Live With Asthma," September 14, 2022*

Real Estate Rankings

- *WalletHub* compared the most populated U.S. cities to determine which had the best markets for real estate agents. Greensboro ranked #161 where demand was high and pay was the best. Criteria: sales per agent; annual median wage for real-estate agents; monthly average starting salary for real estate agents; real estate job density and competition; unemployment rate; home turnover rate; housing-market health index; and other relevant metrics. *www.WalletHub.com, "2021 Best Places to Be a Real Estate Agent," May 12, 2021*

- Greensboro was ranked #9 in the top 20 out of the 100 largest metro areas in terms of house price appreciation in 2022 (#1 = highest rate). *Federal Housing Finance Agency, House Price Index, 4th Quarter 2022*

- The Greensboro metro area was identified as one of the 20 best housing markets in the U.S. in 2022. The area ranked #4 out of 187 markets. Criteria: year-over-year change of median sales price of existing single-family homes between the 4th quarter of 2021 and the 4th quarter of 2022. *National Association of Realtors®, Median Sales Price of Existing Single-Family Homes for Metropolitan Areas, 4th Quarter 2022*

- The Greensboro metro area was identified as one of the 10 best condo markets in the U.S. in 2022. The area ranked #9 out of 63 markets. Criteria: year-over-year change of median sales price of existing apartment condo-coop homes between the 4th quarter of 2021 and the 4th quarter of 2022. *National Association of Realtors®, Median Sales Price of Existing Apartment Condo-Coops Homes for Metropolitan Areas, 4th Quarter 2022*

- Greensboro was ranked #106 out of 235 metro areas in terms of housing affordability in 2022 by the National Association of Home Builders (#1 = most affordable). Criteria: the share of homes sold in that area affordable to a family earning the local median income, based on standard mortgage underwriting criteria. *National Association of Home Builders®, NAHB-Wells Fargo Housing Opportunity Index, 4th Quarter 2022*

Safety Rankings

- Allstate ranked the 200 largest cities in America in terms of driver safety. Greensboro ranked #77. Criteria: internal property damage claims over a two-year period from January 2016 to December 2017. The report helps increase the importance of safety and awareness behind the wheel. *Allstate, "Allstate America's Best Drivers Report, 2019" June 24, 2019*

- The National Insurance Crime Bureau ranked 390 metro areas in the U.S. in terms of per capita rates of vehicle theft. The Greensboro metro area ranked #119 (#1 = highest rate). Criteria: number of vehicle theft offenses per 100,000 inhabitants in 2021. *National Insurance Crime Bureau, "Hot Spots 2021," September 1, 2022*

Seniors/Retirement Rankings

- From its Best Cities for Successful Aging indexes, the Milken Institute generated rankings for metropolitan areas, weighing data in nine categories—health care, wellness, living arrangements, transportation and convenience, financial characteristics, education, employment, community engagement, and overall livability. The Greensboro metro area was ranked #92 overall in the large metro area category. *Milken Institute, "Best Cities for Successful Aging, 2017" March 14, 2017*

Women/Minorities Rankings

- Greensboro was selected as one of the queerest cities in America by *The Advocate*. The city ranked #18 out of 25. Criteria, among many: Trans Pride parades/festivals; gay rugby teams; lesbian bars; LGBTQ centers; theater screenings of "Moonlight"; LGBTQ-inclusive nondiscrimination ordinances; and gay bowling teams. *The Advocate, "Queerest Cities in America 2017" January 12, 2017*

- Personal finance website *WalletHub* compared more than 180 U.S. cities across two key dimensions, "Hispanic Business-Friendliness" and "Hispanic Purchasing Power," to arrive at the most favorable conditions for Hispanic entrepreneurs. Greensboro was ranked #88 out of 182. Criteria includes: share of Hispanic-Owned Businesses; Hispanic entrepreneurship rate to median annual income of Hispanics; Small Business-Friendliness score; cost of living; and number of Hispanics with at least a bachelor's degree. *WalletHub.com, "2019's Best Cities for Hispanic Entrepreneurs," May 1, 2019*

Miscellaneous Rankings

- *WalletHub* compared the 150 most populated U.S. cities to determine their operating efficiency. A "Quality of Services" score was constructed for each city and then divided by the total budget per capita to reveal which were managed the best. Greensboro ranked #27. Criteria: financial stability; economy; education; safety; health; infrastructure and pollution. *www.WalletHub.com, "2022's Best- & Worst-Run Cities in America," June 21, 2022*

Business Environment

DEMOGRAPHICS

Population Growth

Area	1990 Census	2000 Census	2010 Census	2020 Census	Population Growth (%)	
					1990-2020	2010-2020
City	193,389	223,891	269,666	299,035	54.6	10.9
MSA[1]	540,257	643,430	723,801	776,566	43.7	7.3
U.S.	248,709,873	281,421,906	308,745,538	331,449,281	33.3	7.4

Note: (1) Figures cover the Greensboro-High Point, NC Metropolitan Statistical Area
Source: U.S. Census Bureau, 1990 Census, 2000 Census, 2010 Census, 2020 Census

Race

Area	White Alone[2] (%)	Black Alone[2] (%)	Asian Alone[2] (%)	AIAN[3] Alone[2] (%)	NHOPI[4] Alone[2] (%)	Other Race Alone[2] (%)	Two or More Races (%)
City	40.0	42.0	5.1	0.6	0.0	5.6	6.6
MSA[1]	56.7	26.7	4.1	0.6	0.0	5.5	6.4
U.S.	61.6	12.4	6.0	1.1	0.2	8.4	10.2

Note: (1) Figures cover the Greensboro-High Point, NC Metropolitan Statistical Area; (2) Alone is defined as not being in combination with one or more other races; (3) American Indian and Alaska Native; (4) Native Hawaiian and Other Pacific Islander
Source: U.S. Census Bureau, 2020 Census

Hispanic or Latino Origin

Area	Total (%)	Mexican (%)	Puerto Rican (%)	Cuban (%)	Other (%)
City	8.4	4.5	1.1	0.2	2.6
MSA[1]	8.8	5.7	1.0	0.2	1.9
U.S.	18.4	11.2	1.8	0.7	4.7

Note: Persons of Hispanic or Latino origin can be of any race; (1) Figures cover the Greensboro-High Point, NC Metropolitan Statistical Area
Source: U.S. Census Bureau, 2017-2021 American Community Survey 5-Year Estimates

Age

Area	Percent of Population									Median Age
	Under Age 5	Age 5–19	Age 20–34	Age 35–44	Age 45–54	Age 55–64	Age 65–74	Age 75–84	Age 85+	
City	5.5	20.0	24.9	12.1	11.5	11.3	8.7	4.2	1.8	34.7
MSA[1]	5.3	19.6	19.9	11.7	12.9	13.2	10.2	5.1	1.9	39.4
U.S.	5.6	19.2	20.2	12.7	12.4	13.1	10.0	4.9	1.9	38.8

Note: (1) Figures cover the Greensboro-High Point, NC Metropolitan Statistical Area
Source: U.S. Census Bureau, 2020 Census

Disability by Age

Area	All Ages	Under 18 Years Old	18 to 64 Years Old	65 Years and Over
City	11.1	4.9	8.9	32.1
MSA[1]	13.1	4.9	10.9	32.7
U.S.	12.6	4.4	10.3	33.4

Note: Figures show percent of the civilian noninstitutionalized population that reported having a disability. Disability status is determined from six types of difficulty: vision, hearing, cognitive, ambulatory, self-care, and independent living. For children under 5 years old, hearing and vision difficulty are used to determine disability status. For children between the ages of 5 and 14, disability status is determined from hearing, vision, cognitive, ambulatory, and self-care difficulties. For people aged 15 years and older, they are considered to have a disability if they have difficulty with any one of the six difficulty types; Note: (1) Figures cover the Greensboro-High Point, NC Metropolitan Statistical Area
Source: U.S. Census Bureau, 2017-2021 American Community Survey 5-Year Estimates

Ancestry

Area	German	Irish	English	American	Italian	Polish	French[2]	Scottish	Dutch
City	6.5	5.5	8.6	4.4	2.4	1.0	1.2	1.6	0.5
MSA[1]	8.5	7.0	9.4	7.3	2.4	1.1	1.3	2.1	0.8
U.S.	12.8	9.6	8.1	5.7	5.0	2.7	2.2	1.6	1.1

Note: Figures are the percentage of the total population reporting a particular ancestry. The nine most commonly reported ancestries in the U.S. are shown. Figures include multiple ancestries (e.g. if a person reported being Irish and Italian, they were included in both columns); (1) Figures cover the Greensboro-High Point, NC Metropolitan Statistical Area; (2) Excludes Basque
Source: U.S. Census Bureau, 2017-2021 American Community Survey 5-Year Estimates

Greensboro, North Carolina

Foreign-born Population

Area	Any Foreign Country	Asia	Mexico	Europe	Caribbean	Central America[2]	South America	Africa	Canada
City	12.1	4.1	1.8	1.2	0.7	0.5	0.7	2.9	0.2
MSA[1]	9.1	3.0	2.4	0.8	0.4	0.5	0.5	1.4	0.1
U.S.	13.6	4.2	3.3	1.5	1.4	1.1	1.1	0.8	0.2

Note: (1) Figures cover the Greensboro-High Point, NC Metropolitan Statistical Area; (2) Excludes Mexico.
Source: U.S. Census Bureau, 2017-2021 American Community Survey 5-Year Estimates

Household Size

Area	Persons in Household (%)							Average Household Size
	One	Two	Three	Four	Five	Six	Seven or More	
City	35.2	31.9	15.6	10.3	4.5	1.5	1.0	2.40
MSA[1]	30.0	34.5	16.1	11.5	5.0	1.9	1.0	2.50
U.S.	28.1	33.8	15.5	12.9	6.0	2.3	1.4	2.60

Note: (1) Figures cover the Greensboro-High Point, NC Metropolitan Statistical Area
Source: U.S. Census Bureau, 2017-2021 American Community Survey 5-Year Estimates

Household Relationships

Area	House-holder	Opposite-sex Spouse	Same-sex Spouse	Opposite-sex Unmarried Partner	Same-sex Unmarried Partner	Child[2]	Grand-child	Other Relatives	Non-relatives
City	40.9	13.6	0.2	2.6	0.2	26.4	2.0	4.1	3.6
MSA[1]	40.2	17.1	0.2	2.4	0.2	27.4	2.3	3.9	2.6
U.S.	38.3	17.5	0.2	2.5	0.2	28.3	2.4	4.8	3.4

Note: Figures are percent of the total population; (1) Figures cover the Greensboro-High Point, NC Metropolitan Statistical Area; (2) Includes biological, adopted, and stepchildren of the householder
Source: U.S. Census Bureau, 2020 Census

Gender

Area	Males	Females	Males per 100 Females
City	138,465	160,570	86.2
MSA[1]	370,483	406,083	91.2
U.S.	162,685,811	168,763,470	96.4

Note: (1) Figures cover the Greensboro-High Point, NC Metropolitan Statistical Area
Source: U.S. Census Bureau, 2020 Census

Marital Status

Area	Never Married	Now Married[2]	Separated	Widowed	Divorced
City	43.8	36.8	2.6	5.9	11.0
MSA[1]	34.1	45.5	2.8	6.2	11.4
U.S.	33.8	48.0	1.8	5.6	10.8

Note: Figures are percentages and cover the population 15 years of age and older; (1) Figures cover the Greensboro-High Point, NC Metropolitan Statistical Area; (2) Excludes separated
Source: U.S. Census Bureau, 2017-2021 American Community Survey 5-Year Estimates

Religious Groups by Family

Area	Catholic	Baptist	Methodist	LDS[2]	Pentecostal	Lutheran	Islam	Adventist	Other
MSA[1]	7.9	10.0	8.0	0.7	2.8	0.4	1.5	1.4	17.8
U.S.	18.7	7.3	3.0	2.0	1.8	1.7	1.3	1.3	11.6

Note: Figures are the number of adherents as a percentage of the total population and cover the eight largest religious groups in the U.S; (1) Figures cover the Greensboro-High Point, NC Metropolitan Statistical Area; (2) Church of Jesus Christ of Latter-day Saints
Sources: 2020 U.S. Religion Census, Association of Statisticians of American Religious Bodies; The Association of Religion Data Archives (ARDA)

Religious Groups by Tradition

Area	Catholic	Evangelical Protestant	Mainline Protestant	Black Protestant	Islam	Judaism	Hinduism	Orthodox	Buddhism
MSA[1]	7.9	24.9	10.1	3.5	1.5	0.3	0.3	0.1	0.1
U.S.	18.7	16.5	5.2	2.3	1.3	0.6	0.4	0.4	0.3

Note: Figures are the number of adherents as a percentage of the total population; (1) Figures cover the Greensboro-High Point, NC Metropolitan Statistical Area
Sources: 2020 U.S. Religion Census, Association of Statisticians of American Religious Bodies; The Association of Religion Data Archives (ARDA)

Greensboro, North Carolina   211

ECONOMY

Gross Metropolitan Product

Area	2020	2021	2022	2023	Rank[2]
MSA[1]	42.0	46.1	49.5	51.7	75

Note: Figures are in billions of dollars; (1) Figures cover the Greensboro-High Point, NC Metropolitan Statistical Area; (2) Rank is based on 2021 data and ranges from 1 to 381
Source: U.S. Conference of Mayors, U.S. Metro Economies: U.S. Metros Compared to Global and State Economies, June 2022

Economic Growth

Area	2018-20 (%)	2021 (%)	2022 (%)	2023 (%)	Rank[2]
MSA[1]	-2.2	5.4	1.5	1.4	302
U.S.	-0.6	5.7	3.1	2.9	–

Note: Figures are real gross metropolitan product (GMP) growth rates and represent average annual percent change; (1) Figures cover the Greensboro-High Point, NC Metropolitan Statistical Area; (2) Rank is based on 2020 2-year average annual percent change and ranges from 1 to 381
Source: U.S. Conference of Mayors, U.S. Metro Economies: U.S. Metros Compared to Global and State Economies, June 2022

Metropolitan Area Exports

Area	2016	2017	2018	2019	2020	2021	Rank[2]
MSA[1]	3,730.4	3,537.9	3,053.5	2,561.8	2,007.3	2,356.2	97

Note: Figures are in millions of dollars; (1) Figures cover the Greensboro-High Point, NC Metropolitan Statistical Area; (2) Rank is based on 2021 data and ranges from 1 to 388
Source: U.S. Department of Commerce, International Trade Administration, Office of Trade and Economic Analysis, Industry and Analysis, Exports by Metropolitan Area, data extracted March 16, 2023

Building Permits

Area	Single-Family			Multi-Family			Total		
	2021	2022	Pct. Chg.	2021	2022	Pct. Chg.	2021	2022	Pct. Chg.
City	529	467	-11.7	1,363	676	-50.4	1,892	1,143	-39.6
MSA[1]	2,593	2,161	-16.7	1,371	832	-39.3	3,964	2,993	-24.5
U.S.	1,115,400	975,600	-12.5	621,600	689,500	10.9	1,737,000	1,665,100	-4.1

Note: (1) Figures cover the Greensboro-High Point, NC Metropolitan Statistical Area; Figures represent new, privately-owned housing units authorized (unadjusted data); All permit data are based on estimates with imputation
Source: U.S. Census Bureau, Manufacturing, Mining, and Construction Statistics, Building Permits, 2021, 2022

Bankruptcy Filings

Area	Business Filings			Nonbusiness Filings		
	2021	2022	% Chg.	2021	2022	% Chg.
Guilford County	23	8	-65.2	369	336	-8.9
U.S.	14,347	13,481	-6.0	399,269	374,240	-6.3

Note: Business filings include Chapter 7, Chapter 9, Chapter 11, Chapter 12, Chapter 13, Chapter 15, and Section 304; Nonbusiness filings include Chapter 7, Chapter 11, and Chapter 13
Source: Administrative Office of the U.S. Courts, Business and Nonbusiness Bankruptcy, County Cases Commenced by Chapter of the Bankruptcy Code, During the 12-Month Period Ending December 31, 2021 and Business and Nonbusiness Bankruptcy, County Cases Commenced by Chapter of the Bankruptcy Code, During the 12-Month Period Ending December 31, 2022

Housing Vacancy Rates

Area	Gross Vacancy Rate[2] (%)			Year-Round Vacancy Rate[3] (%)			Rental Vacancy Rate[4] (%)			Homeowner Vacancy Rate[5] (%)		
	2020	2021	2022	2020	2021	2022	2020	2021	2022	2020	2021	2022
MSA[1]	8.3	5.9	8.7	8.2	5.9	8.7	7.2	2.7	10.2	0.7	0.5	0.7
U.S.	10.6	10.8	10.5	8.2	8.4	8.2	6.3	6.1	5.8	1.0	0.9	0.8

Note: (1) Figures cover the Greensboro-High Point, NC Metropolitan Statistical Area; (2) The percentage of the total housing inventory that is vacant; (3) The percentage of the housing inventory (excluding seasonal units) that is year-round vacant; (4) The percentage of rental inventory that is vacant for rent; (5) The percentage of homeowner inventory that is vacant for sale
Source: U.S. Census Bureau, Housing Vacancies and Homeownership Annual Statistics: 2020, 2021, 2022

INCOME

Income

Area	Per Capita ($)	Median Household ($)	Average Household ($)
City	31,812	51,667	76,282
MSA[1]	31,655	55,544	77,839
U.S.	37,638	69,021	97,196

Note: (1) Figures cover the Greensboro-High Point, NC Metropolitan Statistical Area
Source: U.S. Census Bureau, 2017-2021 American Community Survey 5-Year Estimates

Household Income Distribution

Area	Percent of Households Earning							
	Under $15,000	$15,000 -$24,999	$25,000 -$34,999	$35,000 -$49,999	$50,000 -$74,999	$75,000 -$99,999	$100,000 -$149,999	$150,000 and up
City	12.2	9.7	10.9	15.7	17.5	11.3	12.7	9.9
MSA[1]	11.3	9.5	10.3	14.5	17.9	12.1	13.8	10.5
U.S.	9.4	7.8	8.2	11.4	16.8	12.8	16.3	17.3

Note: (1) Figures cover the Greensboro-High Point, NC Metropolitan Statistical Area
Source: U.S. Census Bureau, 2017-2021 American Community Survey 5-Year Estimates

Poverty Rate

Area	All Ages	Under 18 Years Old	18 to 64 Years Old	65 Years and Over
City	17.4	24.3	15.9	13.0
MSA[1]	15.1	21.5	14.0	10.3
U.S.	12.6	17.0	11.8	9.6

Note: Figures are percentage of people whose income during the past 12 months was below the poverty level;
(1) Figures cover the Greensboro-High Point, NC Metropolitan Statistical Area
Source: U.S. Census Bureau, 2017-2021 American Community Survey 5-Year Estimates

EMPLOYMENT

Labor Force and Employment

Area	Civilian Labor Force			Workers Employed		
	Dec. 2021	Dec. 2022	% Chg.	Dec. 2021	Dec. 2022	% Chg.
City	143,008	144,251	0.9	137,220	138,826	1.2
MSA[1]	360,317	364,357	1.1	347,114	351,304	1.2
U.S.	161,696,000	164,224,000	1.6	155,732,000	158,872,000	2.0

Note: Data is not seasonally adjusted and covers workers 16 years of age and older; (1) Figures cover the
Greensboro-High Point, NC Metropolitan Statistical Area
Source: Bureau of Labor Statistics, Local Area Unemployment Statistics

Unemployment Rate

Area	2022											
	Jan.	Feb.	Mar.	Apr.	May	Jun.	Jul.	Aug.	Sep.	Oct.	Nov.	Dec.
City	4.6	4.5	4.4	4.3	4.3	4.8	4.6	4.8	4.0	4.5	4.4	3.8
MSA[1]	4.2	4.1	4.0	3.8	4.0	4.5	4.2	4.4	3.7	4.3	4.1	3.6
U.S.	4.4	4.1	3.8	3.3	3.4	3.8	3.8	3.8	3.3	3.4	3.4	3.3

Note: Data is not seasonally adjusted and covers workers 16 years of age and older; (1) Figures cover the
Greensboro-High Point, NC Metropolitan Statistical Area
Source: Bureau of Labor Statistics, Local Area Unemployment Statistics

Average Wages

Occupation	$/Hr.	Occupation	$/Hr.
Accountants and Auditors	39.53	Maintenance and Repair Workers	21.27
Automotive Mechanics	23.26	Marketing Managers	64.13
Bookkeepers	20.74	Network and Computer Systems Admin.	41.11
Carpenters	21.12	Nurses, Licensed Practical	25.19
Cashiers	11.95	Nurses, Registered	38.59
Computer Programmers	47.79	Nursing Assistants	14.93
Computer Systems Analysts	44.56	Office Clerks, General	17.77
Computer User Support Specialists	25.86	Physical Therapists	45.22
Construction Laborers	17.39	Physicians	n/a
Cooks, Restaurant	14.20	Plumbers, Pipefitters and Steamfitters	23.39
Customer Service Representatives	18.33	Police and Sheriff's Patrol Officers	24.52
Dentists	85.11	Postal Service Mail Carriers	27.21
Electricians	24.46	Real Estate Sales Agents	26.84
Engineers, Electrical	46.74	Retail Salespersons	15.24
Fast Food and Counter Workers	11.81	Sales Representatives, Technical/Scientific	42.34
Financial Managers	73.43	Secretaries, Exc. Legal/Medical/Executive	19.33
First-Line Supervisors of Office Workers	28.58	Security Guards	14.54
General and Operations Managers	57.79	Surgeons	n/a
Hairdressers/Cosmetologists	18.33	Teacher Assistants, Exc. Postsecondary*	12.50
Home Health and Personal Care Aides	12.20	Teachers, Secondary School, Exc. Sp. Ed.*	24.32
Janitors and Cleaners	13.36	Telemarketers	18.68
Landscaping/Groundskeeping Workers	15.69	Truck Drivers, Heavy/Tractor-Trailer	24.84
Lawyers	66.92	Truck Drivers, Light/Delivery Services	18.97
Maids and Housekeeping Cleaners	13.04	Waiters and Waitresses	12.88

Note: Wage data covers the Greensboro-High Point, NC Metropolitan Statistical Area; (*) Hourly wages were
calculated from annual wage data based on a 40 hour work week; n/a not available.
Source: Bureau of Labor Statistics, Metro Area Occupational Employment & Wage Estimates, May 2022

Employment by Industry

Sector	MSA[1]		U.S.
	Number of Employees	Percent of Total	Percent of Total
Construction, Mining, and Logging	17,700	4.8	5.4
Private Education and Health Services	53,900	14.6	16.1
Financial Activities	16,800	4.6	5.9
Government	43,900	11.9	14.5
Information	3,900	1.1	2.0
Leisure and Hospitality	36,300	9.9	10.3
Manufacturing	50,800	13.8	8.4
Other Services	12,600	3.4	3.7
Professional and Business Services	46,500	12.6	14.7
Retail Trade	41,300	11.2	10.2
Transportation, Warehousing, and Utilities	23,100	6.3	4.9
Wholesale Trade	21,200	5.8	3.9

Note: Figures are non-farm employment as of December 2022. Figures are not seasonally adjusted and include workers 16 years of age and older; (1) Figures cover the Greensboro-High Point, NC Metropolitan Statistical Area
Source: Bureau of Labor Statistics, Current Employment Statistics, Employment, Hours, and Earnings

Employment by Occupation

Occupation Classification	City (%)	MSA[1] (%)	U.S. (%)
Management, Business, Science, and Arts	38.6	36.4	40.3
Natural Resources, Construction, and Maintenance	5.3	8.0	8.7
Production, Transportation, and Material Moving	15.8	17.6	13.1
Sales and Office	23.1	21.8	20.9
Service	17.2	16.2	17.0

Note: Figures cover employed civilians 16 years of age and older; (1) Figures cover the Greensboro-High Point, NC Metropolitan Statistical Area
Source: U.S. Census Bureau, 2017-2021 American Community Survey 5-Year Estimates

Occupations with Greatest Projected Employment Growth: 2022 – 2024

Occupation[1]	2022 Employment	2024 Projected Employment	Numeric Employment Change	Percent Employment Change
Cooks, Restaurant	45,830	53,440	7,610	16.6
Waiters and Waitresses	65,770	72,960	7,190	10.9
Software Developers	55,450	62,610	7,160	12.9
Cooks, Fast Food	82,470	88,860	6,390	7.7
Fast Food and Counter Workers	68,750	75,030	6,280	9.1
Laborers and Freight, Stock, and Material Movers, Hand	100,780	106,480	5,700	5.7
Retail Salespersons	125,490	130,210	4,720	3.8
General and Operations Managers	87,450	92,120	4,670	5.3
First-Line Supervisors of Food Preparation and Serving Workers	42,440	47,070	4,630	10.9
Stockers and Order Fillers	88,320	92,930	4,610	5.2

Note: Projections cover North Carolina; (1) Sorted by numeric employment change
Source: www.projectionscentral.com, State Occupational Projections, 2022–2024 Short-Term Projections

Fastest-Growing Occupations: 2022 – 2024

Occupation[1]	2022 Employment	2024 Projected Employment	Numeric Employment Change	Percent Employment Change
Cooks, Restaurant	45,830	53,440	7,610	16.6
Solar Photovoltaic Installers	390	450	60	15.4
Statisticians	1,710	1,960	250	14.6
Medical Scientists, Except Epidemiologists	3,630	4,160	530	14.6
Actuaries	950	1,080	130	13.7
Data Scientists	5,390	6,100	710	13.2
Soil and Plant Scientists	2,160	2,440	280	13.0
Software Developers	55,450	62,610	7,160	12.9
Software Quality Assurance Analysts and Testers	8,850	9,950	1,100	12.4
Bartenders	14,560	16,360	1,800	12.4

Note: Projections cover North Carolina; (1) Sorted by percent employment change and excludes occupations with numeric employment change less than 50
Source: www.projectionscentral.com, State Occupational Projections, 2022–2024 Short-Term Projections

214   Greensboro, North Carolina

CITY FINANCES

City Government Finances

Component	2020 ($000)	2020 ($ per capita)
Total Revenues	551,822	1,860
Total Expenditures	681,184	2,296
Debt Outstanding	522,951	1,762
Cash and Securities[1]	n/a	n/a

Note: (1) Cash and security holdings of a government at the close of its fiscal year, including those of its dependent agencies, utilities, and liquor stores; n/a not available.
Source: U.S. Census Bureau, State & Local Government Finances 2020

City Government Revenue by Source

Source	2020 ($000)	2020 ($ per capita)	2020 (%)
General Revenue			
From Federal Government	24,223	82	4.4
From State Government	37,752	127	6.8
From Local Governments	3,291	11	0.6
Taxes			
Property	157,092	529	28.5
Sales and Gross Receipts	67,598	228	12.3
Personal Income	0	0	0.0
Corporate Income	0	0	0.0
Motor Vehicle License	1,055	4	0.2
Other Taxes	144	0	0.0
Current Charges	125,822	424	22.8
Liquor Store	40,439	136	7.3
Utility	67,700	228	12.3

Source: U.S. Census Bureau, State & Local Government Finances 2020

City Government Expenditures by Function

Function	2020 ($000)	2020 ($ per capita)	2020 (%)
General Direct Expenditures			
Air Transportation	0	0	0.0
Corrections	0	0	0.0
Education	0	0	0.0
Employment Security Administration	0	0	0.0
Financial Administration	8,204	27	1.2
Fire Protection	58,098	195	8.5
General Public Buildings	15,049	50	2.2
Governmental Administration, Other	5,639	19	0.8
Health	253	< 1	< 0.1
Highways	44,768	150	6.6
Hospitals	0	0	0.0
Housing and Community Development	22,286	75	3.3
Interest on General Debt	15,711	53	2.3
Judicial and Legal	1,420	4	0.2
Libraries	9,656	32	1.4
Parking	7,986	26	1.2
Parks and Recreation	106,224	358	15.6
Police Protection	82,740	278	12.1
Public Welfare	0	0	0.0
Sewerage	81,208	273	11.9
Solid Waste Management	35,950	121	5.3
Veterans' Services	0	0	0.0
Liquor Store	36,262	122	5.3
Utility	133,370	449	19.6

Source: U.S. Census Bureau, State & Local Government Finances 2020

TAXES

State Corporate Income Tax Rates

State	Tax Rate (%)	Income Brackets ($)	Num. of Brackets	Financial Institution Tax Rate (%)[a]	Federal Income Tax Ded.
North Carolina	2.5	Flat rate	1	2.5	No

Note: Tax rates as of January 1, 2023; (a) Rates listed are the corporate income tax rate applied to financial institutions or excise taxes based on income. Some states have other taxes based upon the value of deposits or shares.
Source: Federation of Tax Administrators, State Corporate Income Tax Rates, January 1, 2023

State Individual Income Tax Rates

State	Tax Rate (%)	Income Brackets ($)	Personal Exemptions ($)			Standard Ded. ($)	
			Single	Married	Depend.	Single	Married
North Carolina	4.75	Flat rate	None	None	None	10,750	21,500

Note: Tax rates as of January 1, 2023; Local- and county-level taxes are not included; Federal income tax is not deductible on state income tax returns
Source: Federation of Tax Administrators, State Individual Income Tax Rates, January 1, 2023

Various State Sales and Excise Tax Rates

State	State Sales Tax (%)	Gasoline[1] ($/gal.)	Cigarette[2] ($/pack)	Spirits[3] ($/gal.)	Wine[4] ($/gal.)	Beer[5] ($/gal.)	Recreational Marijuana (%)
North Carolina	4.75	0.3875	0.45	16.40	1.00	0.62	Not legal

Note: All tax rates as of January 1, 2023; (1) The American Petroleum Institute has developed a methodology for determining the average tax rate on a gallon of fuel. Rates may include any of the following: excise taxes, environmental fees, storage tank fees, other fees or taxes, general sales tax, and local taxes; (2) The federal excise tax of $1.0066 per pack and local taxes are not included; (3) Rates are those applicable to off-premise sales of 40% alcohol by volume (a.b.v.) distilled spirits in 750ml containers. Local excise taxes are excluded; (4) Rates are those applicable to off-premise sales of 11% a.b.v. non-carbonated wine in 750ml containers; (5) Rates are those applicable to off-premise sales of 4.7% a.b.v. beer in 12 ounce containers.
Source: Tax Foundation, 2023 Facts & Figures: How Does Your State Compare?

State Business Tax Climate Index Rankings

State	Overall Rank	Corporate Tax Rank	Individual Income Tax Rank	Sales Tax Rank	Property Tax Rank	Unemployment Insurance Tax Rank
North Carolina	10	5	17	20	13	10

Note: The index is a measure of how each state's tax laws affect economic performance. The lower the rank, the more favorable a state's tax system is for business. States without a given tax are given a ranking of 1. The scores/rankings for the District of Columbia do not affect other states. The 2023 index represents the tax climate as of July 1, 2022.
Source: Tax Foundation, State Business Tax Climate Index 2023

TRANSPORTATION

Means of Transportation to Work

Area	Car/Truck/Van		Public Transportation			Bicycle	Walked	Other Means	Worked at Home
	Drove Alone	Car-pooled	Bus	Subway	Railroad				
City	78.2	7.7	2.3	0.0	0.0	0.2	2.3	1.0	8.3
MSA[1]	79.8	8.8	1.1	0.0	0.0	0.2	1.5	1.1	7.5
U.S.	73.2	8.6	2.0	1.6	0.5	0.5	2.5	1.5	9.7

Note: Figures are percentages and cover workers 16 years of age and older; (1) Figures cover the Greensboro-High Point, NC Metropolitan Statistical Area
Source: U.S. Census Bureau, 2017-2021 American Community Survey 5-Year Estimates

Travel Time to Work

Area	Less Than 10 Minutes	10 to 19 Minutes	20 to 29 Minutes	30 to 44 Minutes	45 to 59 Minutes	60 to 89 Minutes	90 Minutes or More
City	12.5	40.0	23.6	15.9	3.2	3.0	2.0
MSA[1]	12.8	34.6	24.4	18.6	4.8	3.0	1.9
U.S.	12.4	28.5	21.0	20.9	8.2	6.2	2.9

Note: Note: Figures are percentages and include workers 16 years old and over; (1) Figures cover the Greensboro-High Point, NC Metropolitan Statistical Area
Source: U.S. Census Bureau, 2017-2021 American Community Survey 5-Year Estimates

Key Congestion Measures

Measure	1990	2000	2010	2015	2020
Annual Hours of Delay, Total (000)	1,248	4,218	6,517	7,508	5,320
Annual Hours of Delay, Per Auto Commuter	11	26	32	37	25
Annual Congestion Cost, Per Auto Commuter ($)	196	485	599	636	463

Note: Covers the Greensboro NC urban area
Source: Texas A&M Transportation Institute, 2021 Urban Mobility Report

Freeway Travel Time Index

Measure	1985	1990	1995	2000	2005	2010	2015	2020
Urban Area Index[1]	1.02	1.03	1.07	1.08	1.09	1.10	1.12	1.11
Urban Area Rank[1,2]	96	96	87	97	98	98	92	20

Note: Freeway Travel Time Index—the ratio of travel time in the peak period to the travel time at free-flow conditions. For example, a value of 1.30 indicates a 20-minute free-flow trip takes 26 minutes in the peak (20 minutes x 1.30 = 26 minutes); (1) Covers the Greensboro NC urban area; (2) Rank is based on 101 larger urban areas (#1 = highest travel time index)
Source: Texas A&M Transportation Institute, 2021 Urban Mobility Report

Public Transportation

Agency Name / Mode of Transportation	Vehicles Operated in Maximum Service[1]	Annual Unlinked Passenger Trips[2] (in thous.)	Annual Passenger Miles[3] (in thous.)
Greensboro Transit Authority (GTA)			
Bus (purchased transportation)	41	1,799.1	6,028.8
Demand Response (purchased transportation)	35	161.8	1,203.4

Note: (1) Number of revenue vehicles operated by the given mode and type of service to meet the annual maximum service requirement. This is the revenue vehicle count during the peak season of the year; on the week and day that maximum service is provided. Vehicles operated in maximum service (VOMS) exclude atypical days and one-time special events; (2) Number of passengers who boarded public transportation vehicles. Passengers are counted each time they board a vehicle no matter how many vehicles they use to travel from their origin to their destination. (3) Sum of the distances ridden by all passengers during the entire fiscal year.
Source: Federal Transit Administration, National Transit Database, 2021

Air Transportation

Airport Name and Code / Type of Service	Passenger Airlines[1]	Passenger Enplanements	Freight Carriers[2]	Freight (lbs)
Piedmont Triad International (GSO)				
Domestic service (U.S. carriers - 2022)	20	792,106	13	157,492,875
International service (U.S. carriers - 2021)	0	0	2	99,193

Note: (1) Includes all U.S.-based major, minor and commuter airlines that carried at least one passenger during the year; (2) Includes all U.S.-based airlines and freight carriers that transported at least one pound of freight during the year.
Source: Bureau of Transportation Statistics, The Intermodal Transportation Database, Air Carriers: T-100 Domestic Market (U.S. Carriers), 2022; Bureau of Transportation Statistics, The Intermodal Transportation Database, Air Carriers: T-100 International Market (U.S. Carriers), 2021

BUSINESSES

Major Business Headquarters

Company Name	Industry	Rankings	
		Fortune[1]	Forbes[2]
VF	Apparel	380	-

Note: (1) Companies that produce a 10-K are ranked 1 to 500 based on 2021 revenue; (2) All private companies with at least $2 billion in annual revenue through the end of their most current fiscal year are ranked 1 to 246; companies listed are headquartered in the city; dashes indicate no ranking
Source: Fortune, "Fortune 500," 2022; Forbes, "America's Largest Private Companies," 2022

Living Environment

COST OF LIVING

Cost of Living Index

Composite Index	Groceries	Housing	Utilities	Trans-portation	Health Care	Misc. Goods/ Services
n/a	n/a	n/a	n/a	n/a	n/a	n/a

Note: The Cost of Living Index measures regional differences in the cost of consumer goods and services, excluding taxes and non-consumer expenditures, for professional and managerial households in the top income quintile. It is based on more than 50,000 prices covering almost 60 different items for which prices are collected three times a year by chambers of commerce, economic development organizations or university applied economic centers in each participating urban area. The numbers shown should be read as a percentage above or below the national average of 100. For example, a value of 115.4 in the groceries column indicates that grocery prices are 15.4% higher than the national average. Small differences in the index numbers should not be interpreted as significant; n/a not available.
Source: The Council for Community and Economic Research, Cost of Living Index, 2022

Grocery Prices

Area[1]	T-Bone Steak ($/pound)	Frying Chicken ($/pound)	Whole Milk ($/half gal.)	Eggs ($/dozen)	Orange Juice ($/64 oz.)	Coffee ($/11.5 oz.)
City[2]	n/a	n/a	n/a	n/a	n/a	n/a
Avg.	13.81	1.59	2.43	2.25	3.85	4.95
Min.	10.17	0.90	1.51	1.30	2.90	3.46
Max.	19.35	3.30	4.32	4.32	5.31	8.59

*Note: (1) Values for the local area are compared with the average, minimum and maximum values for all 286 areas in the Cost of Living Index; (2) Figures cover the Greensboro NC urban area; n/a not available; **T-Bone Steak** (price per pound); **Frying Chicken** (price per pound, whole fryer); **Whole Milk** (half gallon carton); **Eggs** (price per dozen, Grade A, large); **Orange Juice** (64 oz. Tropicana or Florida Natural); **Coffee** (11.5 oz. can, vacuum-packed, Maxwell House, Hills Bros, or Folgers).*
Source: The Council for Community and Economic Research, Cost of Living Index, 2022

Housing and Utility Costs

Area[1]	New Home Price ($)	Apartment Rent ($/month)	All Electric ($/month)	Part Electric ($/month)	Other Energy ($/month)	Telephone ($/month)
City[2]	n/a	n/a	n/a	n/a	n/a	n/a
Avg.	450,913	1,371	176.41	99.93	76.96	190.22
Min.	229,283	546	100.84	31.56	27.15	174.27
Max.	2,434,977	4,569	356.86	249.59	272.24	208.31

*Note: (1) Values for the local area are compared with the average, minimum and maximum values for all 286 areas in the Cost of Living Index; (2) Figures cover the Greensboro NC urban area; n/a not available; **New Home Price** (2,400 sf living area, 8,000 sf lot, in urban area with full utilities); **Apartment Rent** (950 sf 2 bedroom/1.5 or 2 bath, unfurnished, excluding all utilities except water); **All Electric** (average monthly cost for an all-electric home); **Part Electric** (average monthly cost for a part-electric home); **Other Energy** (average monthly cost for natural gas, fuel oil, coal, wood, and any other forms of energy except electricity); **Telephone** (price includes the base monthly rate plus taxes and fees for three lines of mobile phone service).*
Source: The Council for Community and Economic Research, Cost of Living Index, 2022

Health Care, Transportation, and Other Costs

Area[1]	Doctor ($/visit)	Dentist ($/visit)	Optometrist ($/visit)	Gasoline ($/gallon)	Beauty Salon ($/visit)	Men's Shirt ($)
City[2]	n/a	n/a	n/a	n/a	n/a	n/a
Avg.	124.91	107.77	117.66	3.86	43.31	34.21
Min.	36.61	58.25	51.79	2.90	22.18	13.05
Max.	250.21	162.58	371.96	5.54	85.61	63.54

*Note: (1) Values for the local area are compared with the average, minimum and maximum values for all 286 areas in the Cost of Living Index; (2) Figures cover the Greensboro NC urban area; n/a not available; **Doctor** (general practitioners routine exam of an established patient); **Dentist** (adult teeth cleaning and periodic oral examination); **Optometrist** (full vision eye exam for established adult patient); **Gasoline** (one gallon regular unleaded, national brand, including all taxes, cash price at self-service pump if available); **Beauty Salon** (woman's shampoo, trim, and blow-dry); **Men's Shirt** (cotton/polyester dress shirt, pinpoint weave, long sleeves).*
Source: The Council for Community and Economic Research, Cost of Living Index, 2022

HOUSING

Homeownership Rate

Area	2015 (%)	2016 (%)	2017 (%)	2018 (%)	2019 (%)	2020 (%)	2021 (%)	2022 (%)
MSA[1]	65.4	62.9	61.9	63.2	61.7	65.8	61.9	70.0
U.S.	63.7	63.4	63.9	64.4	64.6	66.6	65.5	65.8

Note: (1) Figures cover the Greensboro-High Point, NC Metropolitan Statistical Area
Source: U.S. Census Bureau, Housing Vacancies and Homeownership Annual Statistics: 2015-2022

House Price Index (HPI)

Area	National Ranking[2]	Quarterly Change (%)	One-Year Change (%)	Five-Year Change (%)	Since 1991Q1 (%)
MSA[1]	26	0.70	17.71	64.64	188.62
U.S.[3]	–	0.34	8.41	58.44	289.08

Note: The HPI is a weighted repeat sales index. It measures average price changes in repeat sales or refinancings on the same properties. This information is obtained by reviewing repeat mortgage transactions on single-family properties whose mortgages have been purchased or securitized by Fannie Mae or Freddie Mac since January 1975; (1) Figures cover the Greensboro-High Point, NC Metropolitan Statistical Area; (2) Rankings are based on annual percentage change for all metro areas containing at least 15,000 transactions over the last 10 years and ranges from 1 to 257; (3) figures based on a weighted average of Census Division estimates using a seasonally adjusted, purchase-only index; all figures are for the period ending December 31, 2022
Source: Federal Housing Finance Agency, Change in FHFA Metropolitan Area House Price Indexes, 2022Q4

Median Single-Family Home Prices

Area	2020	2021	2022p	Percent Change 2021 to 2022
MSA[1]	199.2	228.6	270.3	18.2
U.S. Average	300.2	357.1	392.6	9.9

Note: Figures are median sales prices of existing single-family homes in thousands of dollars; (p) preliminary; (1) Figures cover the Greensboro-High Point, NC Metropolitan Statistical Area
Source: National Association of Realtors, Median Sales Price of Existing Single-Family Homes for Metropolitan Areas, 4th Quarter 2022

Qualifying Income Based on Median Sales Price of Existing Single-Family Homes

Area	With 5% Down ($)	With 10% Down ($)	With 20% Down ($)
MSA[1]	82,605	78,257	69,562
U.S. Average	112,234	106,237	94,513

Note: Figures are preliminary; Qualifying income is based on a mortgage rate of 6.77%. Monthly principal and interest payment is limited to 25% of income; (1) Figures cover the Greensboro-High Point, NC Metropolitan Statistical Area
Source: National Association of Realtors, Qualifying Income Based on Median Sales Price of Existing Single-Family Homes for Metropolitan Areas, 4th Quarter 2022

Home Value

Area	Under $100,000	$100,000 -$199,999	$200,000 -$299,999	$300,000 -$399,999	$400,000 -$499,999	$500,000 -$999,999	$1,000,000 or more	Median ($)
City	19.7	40.5	20.3	9.3	4.4	4.8	1.0	169,100
MSA[1]	22.8	39.9	19.0	9.0	4.4	4.2	0.7	162,700
U.S.	16.2	24.2	20.1	13.6	8.3	13.6	4.1	244,900

Note: Figures are percentages except for median and cover owner-occupied housing units; (1) Figures cover the Greensboro-High Point, NC Metropolitan Statistical Area
Source: U.S. Census Bureau, 2017-2021 American Community Survey 5-Year Estimates

Year Housing Structure Built

Area	2020 or Later	2010 -2019	2000 -2009	1990 -1999	1980 -1989	1970 -1979	1960 -1969	1950 -1959	1940 -1949	Before 1940	Median Year
City	0.1	8.0	15.0	16.8	16.5	13.3	11.3	10.2	3.7	5.1	1984
MSA[1]	0.1	7.3	15.8	17.9	14.5	14.4	10.4	9.5	4.1	6.0	1984
U.S.	0.2	7.3	13.6	13.6	13.2	14.8	10.3	10.0	4.7	12.2	1979

Note: Figures are percentages except for Median Year; Note: (1) Figures cover the Greensboro-High Point, NC Metropolitan Statistical Area
Source: U.S. Census Bureau, 2017-2021 American Community Survey 5-Year Estimates

Gross Monthly Rent

Area	Under $500	$500 -$999	$1,000 -$1,499	$1,500 -$1,999	$2,000 -$2,499	$2,500 -$2,999	$3,000 and up	Median ($)
City	5.7	53.2	33.2	5.9	1.2	0.3	0.6	944
MSA[1]	9.0	55.6	28.9	4.6	1.1	0.3	0.6	900
U.S.	8.1	30.5	30.8	16.8	7.3	3.1	3.5	1,163

Note: Figures are percentages except for median; Gross rent is the contract rent plus the estimated average monthly cost of utilities (electricity, gas, and water and sewer) and fuels (oil, coal, kerosene, wood, etc.) if these are paid by the renter (or paid for the renter by someone else); (1) Figures cover the Greensboro-High Point, NC Metropolitan Statistical Area
Source: U.S. Census Bureau, 2017-2021 American Community Survey 5-Year Estimates

HEALTH

Health Risk Factors

Category	MSA[1] (%)	U.S. (%)
Adults aged 18–64 who have any kind of health care coverage	n/a	90.9
Adults who reported being in good or better health	n/a	85.2
Adults who have been told they have high blood cholesterol	n/a	35.7
Adults who have been told they have high blood pressure	n/a	32.4
Adults who are current smokers	n/a	14.4
Adults who currently use e-cigarettes	n/a	6.7
Adults who currently use chewing tobacco, snuff, or snus	n/a	3.5
Adults who are heavy drinkers[2]	n/a	6.3
Adults who are binge drinkers[3]	n/a	15.4
Adults who are overweight (BMI 25.0 - 29.9)	n/a	34.4
Adults who are obese (BMI 30.0 - 99.8)	n/a	33.9
Adults who participated in any physical activities in the past month	n/a	76.3

Note: (1) Figures for the Greensboro-High Point, NC Metropolitan Statistical Area were not available.
(2) Heavy drinkers are classified as adult men having more than 14 drinks per week and adult women having more than 7 drinks per week; (3) Binge drinkers are classified as males having five or more drinks on one occasion or females having four or more drinks on one occasion
Source: Centers for Disease Control and Prevention, Behaviorial Risk Factor Surveillance System, SMART: Selected Metropolitan Area Risk Trends, 2021

Acute and Chronic Health Conditions

Category	MSA[1] (%)	U.S. (%)
Adults who have ever been told they had a heart attack	n/a	4.0
Adults who have ever been told they have angina or coronary heart disease	n/a	3.8
Adults who have ever been told they had a stroke	n/a	3.0
Adults who have ever been told they have asthma	n/a	14.9
Adults who have ever been told they have arthritis	n/a	25.8
Adults who have ever been told they have diabetes[2]	n/a	10.9
Adults who have ever been told they had skin cancer	n/a	6.6
Adults who have ever been told they had any other types of cancer	n/a	7.5
Adults who have ever been told they have COPD	n/a	6.1
Adults who have ever been told they have kidney disease	n/a	3.0
Adults who have ever been told they have a form of depression	n/a	20.5

Note: (1) Figures for the Greensboro-High Point, NC Metropolitan Statistical Area were not available.
(2) Figures do not include pregnancy-related, borderline, or pre-diabetes
Source: Centers for Disease Control and Prevention, Behaviorial Risk Factor Surveillance System, SMART: Selected Metropolitan Area Risk Trends, 2021

Health Screening and Vaccination Rates

Category	MSA[1] (%)	U.S. (%)
Adults who have ever been tested for HIV	n/a	34.9
Adults who have had their blood cholesterol checked within the last five years	n/a	85.2
Adults aged 65+ who have had flu shot within the past year	n/a	68.6
Adults aged 65+ who have ever had a pneumonia vaccination	n/a	71.0

Note: (1) Figures for the Greensboro-High Point, NC Metropolitan Statistical Area were not available.
Source: Centers for Disease Control and Prevention, Behaviorial Risk Factor Surveillance System, SMART: Selected Metropolitan Area Risk Trends, 2021

Disability Status

Category	MSA[1] (%)	U.S. (%)
Adults who reported being deaf	n/a	7.2
Are you blind or have serious difficulty seeing, even when wearing glasses?	n/a	4.8
Are you limited in any way in any of your usual activities due to arthritis?	n/a	11.1
Do you have difficulty doing errands alone?	n/a	7.0
Do you have difficulty dressing or bathing?	n/a	3.6
Do you have serious difficulty concentrating/remembering/making decisions?	n/a	12.1
Do you have serious difficulty walking or climbing stairs?	n/a	12.8

Note: (1) Figures for the Greensboro-High Point, NC Metropolitan Statistical Area were not available.
Source: Centers for Disease Control and Prevention, Behaviorial Risk Factor Surveillance System, SMART: Selected Metropolitan Area Risk Trends, 2021

Mortality Rates for the Top 10 Causes of Death in the U.S.

ICD-10[a] Sub-Chapter	ICD-10[a] Code	Crude Mortality Rate[1] per 100,000 population	
		County[2]	U.S.
Malignant neoplasms	C00-C97	174.9	182.6
Ischaemic heart diseases	I20-I25	85.5	113.1
Other forms of heart disease	I30-I51	65.1	64.4
Other degenerative diseases of the nervous system	G30-G31	50.1	51.0
Cerebrovascular diseases	I60-I69	49.9	47.8
Other external causes of accidental injury	W00-X59	58.1	46.4
Chronic lower respiratory diseases	J40-J47	36.4	45.7
Organic, including symptomatic, mental disorders	F01-F09	55.3	35.9
Hypertensive diseases	I10-I15	24.8	35.0
Diabetes mellitus	E10-E14	31.8	29.6

Note: (a) ICD-10 = International Classification of Diseases 10th Revision; (1) Crude mortality rates are a three-year average covering 2019-2021; (2) Figures cover Guilford County.
Source: Centers for Disease Control and Prevention, National Center for Health Statistics. National Vital Statistics System, Mortality 2018-2021 on CDC WONDER Online Database

Mortality Rates for Selected Causes of Death

ICD-10[a] Sub-Chapter	ICD-10[a] Code	Crude Mortality Rate[1] per 100,000 population	
		County[2]	U.S.
Assault	X85-Y09	12.5	7.0
Diseases of the liver	K70-K76	17.5	19.8
Human immunodeficiency virus (HIV) disease	B20-B24	2.2	1.5
Influenza and pneumonia	J09-J18	17.1	14.7
Intentional self-harm	X60-X84	10.9	14.3
Malnutrition	E40-E46	4.9	4.3
Obesity and other hyperalimentation	E65-E68	3.8	3.0
Renal failure	N17-N19	22.2	15.7
Transport accidents	V01-V99	14.7	13.6
Viral hepatitis	B15-B19	1.2	1.2

Note: (a) ICD-10 = International Classification of Diseases 10th Revision; (1) Crude mortality rates are a three-year average covering 2019-2021; (2) Figures cover Guilford County; Data are suppressed when the data meet the criteria for confidentiality constraints; Crude mortality rates are flagged as unreliable when the rate would be calculated with a numerator of 20 or less.
Source: Centers for Disease Control and Prevention, National Center for Health Statistics. National Vital Statistics System, Mortality 2018-2021 on CDC WONDER Online Database

Health Insurance Coverage

Area	With Health Insurance	With Private Health Insurance	With Public Health Insurance	Without Health Insurance	Population Under Age 19 Without Health Insurance
City	90.3	66.3	34.1	9.7	4.1
MSA[1]	89.9	64.9	36.0	10.1	4.5
U.S.	91.2	67.8	35.4	8.8	5.3

Note: Figures are percentages that cover the civilian noninstitutionalized population; (1) Figures cover the Greensboro-High Point, NC Metropolitan Statistical Area
Source: U.S. Census Bureau, 2017-2021 American Community Survey 5-Year Estimates

Number of Medical Professionals

Area	MDs[3]	DOs[3,4]	Dentists	Podiatrists	Chiropractors	Optometrists
County[1] (number)	1,391	80	328	26	78	56
County[1] (rate[2])	257.0	14.8	60.5	4.8	14.4	10.3
U.S. (rate[2])	289.3	23.5	72.5	6.2	28.7	17.4

Note: Data as of 2021 unless noted; (1) Data covers Guilford County; (2) Rate per 100,000 population; (3) Data as of 2020 and includes all active, non-federal physicians; (4) Doctor of Osteopathic Medicine
Source: U.S. Department of Health and Human Services, Health Resources and Services Administration, Bureau of Health Professions, Area Resource File (ARF) 2021-2022

EDUCATION

Public School District Statistics

District Name	Schls	Pupils	Pupil/ Teacher Ratio	Minority Pupils[1] (%)	LEP/ELL[2] (%)	IEP[3] (%)
Guilford County Schools	127	69,173	14.5	72.1	9.3	13.8

Note: Table includes school districts with 2,000 or more students; (1) Percentage of students that are not non-Hispanic white; (2) Percentage of students that are Limited English Proficient or English Language Learners (2018-19); (3) Percentage of students that have an Individualized Education Program (2019-20).
Source: U.S. Department of Education, National Center for Education Statistics, Common Core of Data, Local Education Agency (School District) Universe Survey: School Year 2021-2022

Best High Schools

According to *U.S. News,* Greensboro is home to three of the top 500 high schools in the U.S.: **The Early College at Guilford** (#35); **STEM Early College at N.C. A&T** (#87); **Philip J. Weaver Ed Center** (#240). Nearly 18,000 public, magnet and charter schools were ranked based on their performance on state assessments and how well they prepare students for college. *U.S. News & World Report, "Best High Schools 2022"*

Highest Level of Education

Area	Less than H.S.	H.S. Diploma	Some College, No Deg.	Associate Degree	Bachelor's Degree	Master's Degree	Prof. School Degree	Doctorate Degree
City	9.8	21.3	20.4	9.0	24.5	10.7	2.4	1.9
MSA[1]	11.8	26.7	21.4	9.7	19.8	7.9	1.5	1.3
U.S.	11.1	26.5	20.0	8.7	20.6	9.3	2.2	1.5

Note: Figures cover persons age 25 and over; (1) Figures cover the Greensboro-High Point, NC Metropolitan Statistical Area
Source: U.S. Census Bureau, 2017-2021 American Community Survey 5-Year Estimates

Educational Attainment by Race

Area	High School Graduate or Higher (%)					Bachelor's Degree or Higher (%)				
	Total	White	Black	Asian	Hisp.[2]	Total	White	Black	Asian	Hisp.[2]
City	90.2	93.9	89.3	77.0	68.0	39.5	50.5	26.7	47.0	19.3
MSA[1]	88.2	90.3	87.8	78.5	61.1	30.5	32.9	24.1	47.0	14.3
U.S.	88.9	91.4	87.2	87.6	71.2	33.7	35.5	23.3	55.6	18.4

Note: Figures shown cover persons 25 years old and over; (1) Figures cover the Greensboro-High Point, NC Metropolitan Statistical Area; (2) People of Hispanic origin can be of any race
Source: U.S. Census Bureau, 2017-2021 American Community Survey 5-Year Estimates

School Enrollment by Grade and Control

Area	Preschool (%)		Kindergarten (%)		Grades 1 - 4 (%)		Grades 5 - 8 (%)		Grades 9 - 12 (%)	
	Public	Private	Public	Private	Public	Private	Public	Private	Public	Private
City	55.5	44.5	90.0	10.0	93.3	6.7	91.0	9.0	89.1	10.9
MSA[1]	55.7	44.3	86.7	13.3	88.5	11.5	88.1	11.9	88.2	11.8
U.S.	58.8	41.2	86.3	13.7	88.3	11.7	88.6	11.4	89.4	10.6

Note: Figures shown cover persons 3 years old and over; (1) Figures cover the Greensboro-High Point, NC Metropolitan Statistical Area
Source: U.S. Census Bureau, 2017-2021 American Community Survey 5-Year Estimates

Higher Education

Four-Year Colleges			Two-Year Colleges			Medical Schools[1]	Law Schools[2]	Voc/ Tech[3]
Public	Private Non-profit	Private For-profit	Public	Private Non-profit	Private For-profit			
2	4	2	3	0	1	0	1	2

Note: Figures cover institutions located within the Greensboro-High Point, NC Metropolitan Statistical Area and include main campuses only; (1) includes schools accredited by the Liaison Committee on Medical Education and the American Osteopathic Association's Commission on Osteopathic College Accreditation; (2) includes ABA-accredited schools, schools with provisional ABA accreditation, and state accredited schools; (3) includes all schools with programs that are less than 2 years.
Source: National Center for Education Statistics, Integrated Postsecondary Education System (IPEDS), 2021-22; Wikipedia, List of Medical Schools in the United States, accessed April 10, 2023; Wikipedia, List of Law Schools in the United States, accessed April 10, 2023

222 Greensboro, North Carolina

EMPLOYERS

Major Employers

Company Name	Industry
Bank of America	Financial services
CitiGroup	Financial services
City of Greensboro	Municipal government
City of High Point	Municipal government
Cone Denim	Denims
County of Guilford	County government
Daimler Trucks North America	Motor vehicles & car bodies
Gilbarco	Electronic computers
High Point Regional Health System	General medical & surgical hospitals
ITG Holdings	Denims
Kayser- Roth Corporation	Mens, boys, girls, hosiery
Klaussner Furniture Industries	Upholstered/household furniture
Lorillard Tobbacco Co	Cigarettes
NC Ag & Technical State University	University
Piedmont Express	Airline ticket offices
Ralph Lauren Corporation	Distribution/customer service
RF Micro Devices	Semiconductors & related devices
Technimark	Injection-molded plastics
The Fresh Market	Grocery stores
The Moses H Cone Memorial Hospital	General medical & surgical hospitals
The University of NC at Greensboro	Colleges & universities
Thomas Built Buses	Truck and bus bodies
Zen Hro	Employee leasing services

Note: Companies shown are located within the Greensboro-High Point, NC Metropolitan Statistical Area.
Source: Hoovers.com; Wikipedia

PUBLIC SAFETY

Crime Rate

Area	Total Crime	Violent Crime Rate				Property Crime Rate		
		Murder	Rape[3]	Robbery	Aggrav. Assault	Burglary	Larceny -Theft	Motor Vehicle Theft
City	4,513.0	19.7	31.7	193.7	656.6	737.6	2,501.9	371.8
Suburbs[1]	2,458.1	7.5	28.3	53.6	282.3	415.1	1,477.5	193.7
Metro[2]	3,250.8	12.2	29.6	107.7	426.7	539.5	1,872.7	262.4
U.S.	2,356.7	6.5	38.4	73.9	279.7	314.2	1,398.0	246.0

Note: Figures are crimes per 100,000 population; (1) All areas within the metro area that are located outside the city limits; (2) Figures cover the Greensboro-High Point, NC Metropolitan Statistical Area; (3) All figures shown were reported using the revised Uniform Crime Reporting (UCR) definition of rape; Due to the transition to the National Incident-Based Reporting System (NIBRS), limited city and metro area data was released for 2021.
Source: FBI Uniform Crime Reports, 2020

Hate Crimes

Area	Number of Quarters Reported	Number of Incidents per Bias Motivation					
		Race/Ethnicity/ Ancestry	Religion	Sexual Orientation	Disability	Gender	Gender Identity
City	4	11	1	4	0	0	0
U.S.	4	5,227	1,244	1,110	130	75	266

Note: Due to the transition to the National Incident-Based Reporting System (NIBRS), limited crime data was released for 2021.
Source: Federal Bureau of Investigation, Hate Crime Statistics 2020

Identity Theft Consumer Reports

Area	Reports	Reports per 100,000 Population	Rank[2]
MSA[1]	2,737	357	44
U.S.	1,108,609	339	-

Note: (1) Figures cover the Greensboro-High Point, NC Metropolitan Statistical Area; (2) Rank ranges from 1 to 391 where 1 indicates greatest number of identity theft reports per 100,000 population
Source: Federal Trade Commission, Consumer Sentinel Network Data Book 2022

Fraud and Other Consumer Reports

Area	Reports	Reports per 100,000 Population	Rank[2]
MSA[1]	8,149	1,062	72
U.S.	4,064,520	1,245	-

Note: (1) Figures cover the Greensboro-High Point, NC Metropolitan Statistical Area; (2) Rank ranges from 1 to 391 where 1 indicates greatest number of fraud and other consumer reports per 100,000 population
Source: Federal Trade Commission, Consumer Sentinel Network Data Book 2022

POLITICS

2020 Presidential Election Results

Area	Biden	Trump	Jorgensen	Hawkins	Other
Guilford County	60.8	37.7	0.8	0.2	0.4
U.S.	51.3	46.8	1.2	0.3	0.5

Note: Results are percentages and may not add to 100% due to rounding
Source: Dave Leip's Atlas of U.S. Presidential Elections

SPORTS

Professional Sports Teams

Team Name	League	Year Established

No teams are located in the metro area
Source: Wikipedia, Major Professional Sports Teams of the United States and Canada, April 12, 2023

CLIMATE

Average and Extreme Temperatures

Temperature	Jan	Feb	Mar	Apr	May	Jun	Jul	Aug	Sep	Oct	Nov	Dec	Yr.
Extreme High (°F)	78	81	89	91	96	102	102	103	100	95	85	78	103
Average High (°F)	48	51	60	70	78	84	87	86	80	70	60	50	69
Average Temp. (°F)	38	41	49	58	67	74	78	76	70	59	49	40	58
Average Low (°F)	28	30	37	46	55	63	67	66	59	47	37	30	47
Extreme Low (°F)	-8	-1	5	23	32	42	49	45	37	20	10	0	-8

Note: Figures cover the years 1948-1990
Source: National Climatic Data Center, International Station Meteorological Climate Summary, 9/96

Average Precipitation/Snowfall/Humidity

Precip./Humidity	Jan	Feb	Mar	Apr	May	Jun	Jul	Aug	Sep	Oct	Nov	Dec	Yr.
Avg. Precip. (in.)	3.2	3.4	3.7	3.1	3.7	3.8	4.5	4.2	3.4	3.4	2.9	3.3	42.5
Avg. Snowfall (in.)	4	3	2	Tr	0	0	0	0	0	0	Tr	1	10
Avg. Rel. Hum. 7am (%)	80	78	78	77	82	84	87	90	90	88	83	80	83
Avg. Rel. Hum. 4pm (%)	53	50	47	44	51	54	57	58	56	51	51	54	52

Note: Figures cover the years 1948-1990; Tr = Trace amounts (<0.05 in. of rain; <0.5 in. of snow)
Source: National Climatic Data Center, International Station Meteorological Climate Summary, 9/96

Weather Conditions

Temperature			Daytime Sky			Precipitation		
10°F & below	32°F & below	90°F & above	Clear	Partly cloudy	Cloudy	0.01 inch or more precip.	0.1 inch or more snow/ice	Thunder-storms
3	85	32	94	143	128	113	5	43

Note: Figures are average number of days per year and cover the years 1948-1990
Source: National Climatic Data Center, International Station Meteorological Climate Summary, 9/96

HAZARDOUS WASTE

Superfund Sites

The Greensboro-High Point, NC metro area has no sites on the EPA's Superfund Final National Priorities List. There are a total of 1,165 Superfund sites with a status of proposed or final on the list in the U.S. *U.S. Environmental Protection Agency, National Priorities List, April 12, 2023*

AIR QUALITY

Air Quality Trends: Ozone

	1990	1995	2000	2005	2010	2015	2018	2019	2020	2021
MSA[1]	0.097	0.089	0.089	0.082	0.076	0.064	0.067	0.064	0.057	0.066
U.S.	0.087	0.089	0.081	0.080	0.072	0.067	0.069	0.065	0.065	0.067

Note: (1) Data covers the Greensboro-High Point, NC Metropolitan Statistical Area. The values shown are the composite ozone concentration averages among trend sites based on the highest fourth daily maximum 8-hour concentration in parts per million. These trends are based on sites having an adequate record of monitoring data during the trend period. Data from exceptional events are included.
Source: U.S. Environmental Protection Agency, Air Quality Monitoring Information, "Air Quality Trends by City, 1990-2021"

Air Quality Index

Area	Percent of Days when Air Quality was...[2]					AQI Statistics[2]	
	Good	Moderate	Unhealthy for Sensitive Groups	Unhealthy	Very Unhealthy	Maximum	Median
MSA[1]	75.9	24.1	0.0	0.0	0.0	100	42

Note: (1) Data covers the Greensboro-High Point, NC Metropolitan Statistical Area; (2) Based on 365 days with AQI data in 2021. Air Quality Index (AQI) is an index for reporting daily air quality. EPA calculates the AQI for five major air pollutants regulated by the Clean Air Act: ground-level ozone, particle pollution (aka particulate matter), carbon monoxide, sulfur dioxide, and nitrogen dioxide. The AQI runs from 0 to 500. The higher the AQI value, the greater the level of air pollution and the greater the health concern. There are six AQI categories: "Good" AQI is between 0 and 50. Air quality is considered satisfactory; "Moderate" AQI is between 51 and 100. Air quality is acceptable; "Unhealthy for Sensitive Groups" When AQI values are between 101 and 150, members of sensitive groups may experience health effects; "Unhealthy" When AQI values are between 151 and 200 everyone may begin to experience health effects; "Very Unhealthy" AQI values between 201 and 300 trigger a health alert; "Hazardous" AQI values over 300 trigger warnings of emergency conditions (not shown).
Source: U.S. Environmental Protection Agency, Air Quality Index Report, 2021

Air Quality Index Pollutants

Area	Percent of Days when AQI Pollutant was...[2]					
	Carbon Monoxide	Nitrogen Dioxide	Ozone	Sulfur Dioxide	Particulate Matter 2.5	Particulate Matter 10
MSA[1]	0.0	0.0	52.9	(3)	46.3	0.8

Note: (1) Data covers the Greensboro-High Point, NC Metropolitan Statistical Area; (2) Based on 365 days with AQI data in 2021. The Air Quality Index (AQI) is an index for reporting daily air quality. EPA calculates the AQI for five major air pollutants regulated by the Clean Air Act: ground-level ozone, particle pollution (also known as particulate matter), carbon monoxide, sulfur dioxide, and nitrogen dioxide. The AQI runs from 0 to 500. The higher the AQI value, the greater the level of air pollution and the greater the health concern; (3) Sulfur dioxide is no longer included in this table (as of December 8, 2021) because SO_2 concentrations tend to be very localized and not necessarily representative of broad geographical areas like counties and CBSAs.
Source: U.S. Environmental Protection Agency, Air Quality Index Report, 2021

Maximum Air Pollutant Concentrations: Particulate Matter, Ozone, CO and Lead

	Particulate Matter 10 (ug/m³)	Particulate Matter 2.5 Wtd AM (ug/m³)	Particulate Matter 2.5 24-Hr (ug/m³)	Ozone (ppm)	Carbon Monoxide (ppm)	Lead (ug/m³)
MSA[1] Level	35	7.7	18	0.066	n/a	n/a
NAAQS[2]	150	15	35	0.075	9	0.15
Met NAAQS[2]	Yes	Yes	Yes	Yes	n/a	n/a

Note: (1) Data covers the Greensboro-High Point, NC Metropolitan Statistical Area; Data from exceptional events are included; (2) National Ambient Air Quality Standards; ppm = parts per million; ug/m³ = micrograms per cubic meter; n/a not available.
Concentrations: Particulate Matter 10 (coarse particulate)—highest second maximum 24-hour concentration; Particulate Matter 2.5 Wtd AM (fine particulate)—highest weighted annual mean concentration; Particulate Matter 2.5 24-Hour (fine particulate)—highest 98th percentile 24-hour concentration; Ozone—highest fourth daily maximum 8-hour concentration; Carbon Monoxide—highest second maximum non-overlapping 8-hour concentration; Lead—maximum running 3-month average
Source: U.S. Environmental Protection Agency, Air Quality Monitoring Information, "Air Quality Statistics by City, 2021"

Maximum Air Pollutant Concentrations: Nitrogen Dioxide and Sulfur Dioxide

	Nitrogen Dioxide AM (ppb)	Nitrogen Dioxide 1-Hr (ppb)	Sulfur Dioxide AM (ppb)	Sulfur Dioxide 1-Hr (ppb)	Sulfur Dioxide 24-Hr (ppb)
MSA[1] Level	n/a	n/a	n/a	n/a	n/a
NAAQS[2]	53	100	30	75	140
Met NAAQS[2]	n/a	n/a	n/a	n/a	n/a

Note: (1) Data covers the Greensboro-High Point, NC Metropolitan Statistical Area; Data from exceptional events are included; (2) National Ambient Air Quality Standards; ppm = parts per million; ug/m³ = micrograms per cubic meter; n/a not available.
Concentrations: Nitrogen Dioxide AM—highest arithmetic mean concentration; Nitrogen Dioxide 1-Hr—highest 98th percentile 1-hour daily maximum concentration; Sulfur Dioxide AM—highest annual mean concentration; Sulfur Dioxide 1-Hr—highest 99th percentile 1-hour daily maximum concentration; Sulfur Dioxide 24-Hr—highest second maximum 24-hour concentration
Source: U.S. Environmental Protection Agency, Air Quality Monitoring Information, "Air Quality Statistics by City, 2021"

Lexington, Kentucky

Background

Lexington has managed to combine the frenzied pace of a major city with the slow tempo of a small town without losing the traditions and gentility of its Southern heritage. It is situated in a scenic area of rolling plateaus and small creeks flowing into the Kentucky River.

Since its settlement in 1775, Lexington has grown to become Kentucky's second-largest city and the commercial center of the Bluegrass Region. The town was founded in 1779 and incorporated in 1832. Hemp was Lexington's major antebellum crop until the rope from which it was made was no longer used for ship rigging. After the Civil War the farmers in the area switched to tobacco as their primary crop. The city is also the chief producer of bluegrass seed and white barley in the United States.

Other products manufactured in Lexington include paper products, air-conditioning and heating equipment, electric typewriters, metal products, and bourbon whiskey.

Lexington was once known as the "Athens of the West" when many early American artists, poets, musicians, and architects settled here, all leaving their imprint on the city. The Actor's Guild of Lexington and the Studio Players, Lexington's oldest community theater (1953) reside in the city, as does the Chamber Music Society of Kentucky. The 1898 Fayette County Courthouse, which operated from 1901 to 2001, has been transformed into the Lexington History Museum.

No discussion of Lexington would be complete without mention of horse racing. Kentucky is synonymous with horses, especially the American Saddlebred—Kentucky's only native breed. The region, with its fertile soil and excellent pastureland, is perfectly suited for breeding horses. Horse racing in Kentucky dates to 1789, when the first course was laid out in Lexington. In 1787, The Commons, a park-like block near Race Street in Lexington, was used for horse racing, but complaints by citizens led to the formal development of a race meet, organized by Kentucky statesman Henry Clay, who also helped form the commonwealth's first jockey club, now known as the Kentucky Jockey Club. The Kentucky Horse Park, a 1,200-acre educational theme park, highlights 50 different horse breeds and allows visitors the opportunity to pet and ride the horses and talk with riders, while the International Museum of the Horse includes artifacts and exhibits (both in person and online). The American Saddle Horse Museum offers exciting exhibits showing the role of the saddle horse in American history.

In addition to racecourses, Lexington has its share of fine golf courses, and there are plenty of blues, country, and dance clubs for those who prefer musical nightlife. Lexington is home to many thriving arts organizations including a professional orchestra, two ballet companies, and several museums including a basketball museum, several choral organizations, and a highly respected opera program at the University of Kentucky. There are more than 200 churches and synagogues in Lexington, representing 38 denominations.

Regarding education in and around the city, Lexington built two new elementary schools in 2016 and a new high school in 2017. Institutions of higher learning include the University of Kentucky, Lexington Theological Seminary, the National College of Business and Technology, Georgetown College, Kentucky State University, and Transylvania University. Since its opening in 1982, the Kentucky World Trade Center has organized high-profile trade programs featuring business and political leaders from Asia, Europe, and the Middle East. The Commonwealth of Kentucky has emerged as a leader among the 50 states in expanding its international trade.

Hosted annually in June by the Lexington Pride Center, the Lexington Pride Festival celebrates the LGBTQ community in Central Kentucky, offering live music, crafts, food, and informational booths from diverse service organizations; 2023 is the festival's 15th year. In 2010, Jim Gray was elected as the first openly gay mayor of Lexington. He proclaimed June 29, 2013, as Pride Day.

Lexington has a definite continental climate, temperate and well-suited to a varied plant and animal life. The area is subject to sudden and sweeping temperature changes, generally of short duration. Temperatures below zero and above 100 degrees are relatively rare.

Rankings

General Rankings

- In their ninth annual survey, Livability.com looked at data for more than 2,300 mid-sized U.S. cities to determine the rankings for Livability's "Top 100 Best Places to Live" in 2022. Lexington ranked #93. Criteria: housing and economy; social and civic engagement; education; demographics; health care options; transportation & infrastructure; and community amenities. *Livability.com, "Top 100 Best Places to Live 2022" July 19, 2022*

Business/Finance Rankings

- Lexington was the #7-ranked city for savers, according to a study by the finance site GOBankingRates, which considered the prospects for people trying to save money. Criteria: average monthly cost of grocery items; median home listing price; median rent; median income; transportation costs; gas prices; and the cost of eating out for an inexpensive and mid-range meal in 100 U.S. cities. *www.gobankingrates.com, "The 20 Best (and Worst) Places to Live If You're Trying to Save Money," August 27, 2019*

- Lexington was ranked #7 among 100 U.S. cities for most difficult conditions for savers, according to a study by the finance site GOBankingRates. Criteria: average monthly cost of grocery items; median home listing price; median rent; median income; transportation costs; gas prices; and the cost of eating out for an inexpensive and mid-range meal. *www.gobankingrates.com, "The 20 Best (and Worst) Places to Live If You're Trying to Save Money," August 27, 2019*

- The Lexington metro area appeared on the Milken Institute "2022 Best Performing Cities" list. Rank: #163 out of 200 large metro areas (population over 250,000). Criteria: job growth; wage and salary growth; high-tech output growth; housing affordability; household broadband access. *Milken Institute, "Best-Performing Cities 2022," March 28, 2022*

- *Forbes* ranked the 200 most populous metro areas to determine the nation's "Best Places for Business and Careers." The Lexington metro area was ranked #33. Criteria: costs (business and living); job growth (past and projected); income growth; quality of life; educational attainment (college and high school); projected economic growth; cultural and leisure opportunities; workplace tolerance laws; net migration patterns. *Forbes, "The Best Places for Business and Careers 2019: Seattle Still On Top," October 30, 2019*

Children/Family Rankings

- Lexington was selected as one of the most playful cities in the U.S. by KaBOOM! The organization's Playful City USA initiative honors cities and towns across the nation that have made their communities more playable. Criteria: pledging to integrate play as a solution to challenges in their communities; making it easy for children to get active and balanced play; creating more family-friendly and innovative communities as a result. *KaBOOM! National Campaign for Play, "2017 Playful City USA Communities"*

- Lexington was selected as one of the best cities for newlyweds by *Rent.com*. The city ranked #14 of 15. Criteria: cost of living; availability of affordable rental inventory; annual household income; activities and restaurant options; percentage of married couples; concentration of millennials; safety. *Rent.com, "The 15 Best Cities for Newlyweds," December 11, 2018*

Education Rankings

- Personal finance website *WalletHub* analyzed the 150 largest U.S. metropolitan statistical areas to determine where the most educated Americans are putting their degrees to work. Criteria: education levels; percentage of workers with degrees; education quality and attainment gap; public school quality rankings; quality and enrollment of each metro area's universities. Lexington was ranked #24 (#1 = most educated city). *www.WalletHub.com, "Most & Least Educated Cities in America," July 18, 2022*

- Lexington was selected as one of America's most literate cities. The city ranked #26 out of the 84 largest U.S. cities. Criteria: number of booksellers; library resources; Internet resources; educational attainment; periodical publishing resources; newspaper circulation. *Central Connecticut State University, "America's Most Literate Cities, 2018," February 2019*

Environmental Rankings

- Lexington was highlighted as one of the top 59 cleanest metro areas for short-term particle pollution (24-hour PM 2.5) in the U.S. during 2019 through 2021. Monitors in these cities reported no days with unhealthful PM 2.5 levels. *American Lung Association, "State of the Air 2023," April 19, 2023*

Health/Fitness Rankings

- For each of the 100 largest cities in the United States, the American Fitness Index®, compiled in partnership between the American College of Sports Medicine and the Elevance Health Foundation, evaluated community infrastructure and 34 health behaviors including preventive health, levels of chronic disease conditions, food insecurity, sleep quality, pedestrian safety, air quality, and community/environment resources that support physical activity. Lexington ranked #92 for "community fitness." *americanfitnessindex.org, "2022 ACSM American Fitness Index Summary Report," July 12, 2022*

- The Lexington metro area was identified as one of the worst cities for bed bugs in America by pest control company Orkin. The area ranked #46 out of 50 based on the number of bed bug treatments Orkin performed from December 2021 to November 2022. *Orkin, "The Windy City Can't Blow Bed Bugs Away: Chicago Ranks #1 For Third Consecutive Year On Orkin's Bed Bug Cities List," January 9, 2023*

Real Estate Rankings

- *WalletHub* compared the most populated U.S. cities to determine which had the best markets for real estate agents. Lexington ranked #136 where demand was high and pay was the best. Criteria: sales per agent; annual median wage for real-estate agents; monthly average starting salary for real estate agents; real estate job density and competition; unemployment rate; home turnover rate; housing-market health index; and other relevant metrics. *www.WalletHub.com, "2021 Best Places to Be a Real Estate Agent," May 12, 2021*

Safety Rankings

- Allstate ranked the 200 largest cities in America in terms of driver safety. Lexington ranked #29. Criteria: internal property damage claims over a two-year period from January 2016 to December 2017. The report helps increase the importance of safety and awareness behind the wheel. *Allstate, "Allstate America's Best Drivers Report, 2019" June 24, 2019*

- The National Insurance Crime Bureau ranked 390 metro areas in the U.S. in terms of per capita rates of vehicle theft. The Lexington metro area ranked #172 (#1 = highest rate). Criteria: number of vehicle theft offenses per 100,000 inhabitants in 2021. *National Insurance Crime Bureau, "Hot Spots 2021," September 1, 2022*

Seniors/Retirement Rankings

- Lexington made *Southern Living's* list of southern places—by the beach, in the mountains, river or college town—to retire. From the incredible views and close knit communities, to the opportunities to put down new roots, and great places to eat and hike, these superb places are perfect for settling down. *Southern Living, "The Best Places to Retire in the South," March 7, 2022*

- From its Best Cities for Successful Aging indexes, the Milken Institute generated rankings for metropolitan areas, weighing data in nine categories—health care, wellness, living arrangements, transportation and convenience, financial characteristics, education, employment, community engagement, and overall livability. The Lexington metro area was ranked #60 overall in the small metro area category. *Milken Institute, "Best Cities for Successful Aging, 2017" March 14, 2017*

- Lexington made the 2022 *Forbes* list of "25 Best Places to Retire." Criteria, focused on overall affordability as well as quality of life indicators, include: housing/living costs compared to the national average and state taxes; air quality; crime rates; home price appreciation; risk associated with climate-change/natural hazards; availability of medical care; bikeability; walkability; healthy living. *Forbes.com, "The Best Places to Retire in 2022," May 13, 2022*

Women/Minorities Rankings

- *Travel + Leisure* listed the best cities in and around the U.S. for a memorable and fun girls' trip, even on a budget. Whether it is for a special occasion, to make new memories or just to get away, Lexington is sure to have something for all the ladies in your tribe. *Travel + Leisure, "25 Affordable Girls Weekend Getaways That Won't Break the Bank," November 25, 2022*

- Personal finance website *WalletHub* compared more than 180 U.S. cities across two key dimensions, "Hispanic Business-Friendliness" and "Hispanic Purchasing Power," to arrive at the most favorable conditions for Hispanic entrepreneurs. Lexington was ranked #142 out of 182. Criteria includes: share of Hispanic-Owned Businesses; Hispanic entrepreneurship rate to median annual income of Hispanics; Small Business-Friendliness score; cost of living; and number of Hispanics with at least a bachelor's degree. *WalletHub.com, "2019's Best Cities for Hispanic Entrepreneurs," May 1, 2019*

Miscellaneous Rankings

- *WalletHub* compared the 150 most populated U.S. cities to determine their operating efficiency. A "Quality of Services" score was constructed for each city and then divided by the total budget per capita to reveal which were managed the best. Lexington ranked #5. Criteria: financial stability; economy; education; safety; health; infrastructure and pollution. *www.WalletHub.com, "2022's Best-& Worst-Run Cities in America," June 21, 2022*

Business Environment

DEMOGRAPHICS

Population Growth

Area	1990 Census	2000 Census	2010 Census	2020 Census	Population Growth (%)	
					1990-2020	2010-2020
City	225,366	260,512	295,803	322,570	43.1	9.0
MSA[1]	348,428	408,326	472,099	516,811	48.3	9.5
U.S.	248,709,873	281,421,906	308,745,538	331,449,281	33.3	7.4

Note: (1) Figures cover the Lexington-Fayette, KY Metropolitan Statistical Area
Source: U.S. Census Bureau, 1990 Census, 2000 Census, 2010 Census, 2020 Census

Race

Area	White Alone[2] (%)	Black Alone[2] (%)	Asian Alone[2] (%)	AIAN[3] Alone[2] (%)	NHOPI[4] Alone[2] (%)	Other Race Alone[2] (%)	Two or More Races (%)
City	68.3	14.9	4.2	0.3	0.0	5.2	7.1
MSA[1]	74.9	11.1	2.9	0.3	0.0	4.2	6.6
U.S.	61.6	12.4	6.0	1.1	0.2	8.4	10.2

Note: (1) Figures cover the Lexington-Fayette, KY Metropolitan Statistical Area; (2) Alone is defined as not being in combination with one or more other races; (3) American Indian and Alaska Native; (4) Native Hawaiian and Other Pacific Islander
Source: U.S. Census Bureau, 2020 Census

Hispanic or Latino Origin

Area	Total (%)	Mexican (%)	Puerto Rican (%)	Cuban (%)	Other (%)
City	7.4	4.7	0.6	0.2	1.9
MSA[1]	6.3	4.2	0.5	0.1	1.5
U.S.	18.4	11.2	1.8	0.7	4.7

Note: Persons of Hispanic or Latino origin can be of any race; (1) Figures cover the Lexington-Fayette, KY Metropolitan Statistical Area
Source: U.S. Census Bureau, 2017-2021 American Community Survey 5-Year Estimates

Age

Area	Under Age 5	Age 5–19	Age 20–34	Age 35–44	Age 45–54	Age 55–64	Age 65–74	Age 75–84	Age 85+	Median Age
City	5.7	19.2	24.7	13.3	11.4	11.2	8.6	4.0	1.6	35.2
MSA[1]	5.9	19.7	22.2	13.2	12.1	12.1	9.2	4.2	1.6	36.5
U.S.	5.6	19.2	20.2	12.7	12.4	13.1	10.0	4.9	1.9	38.8

Note: (1) Figures cover the Lexington-Fayette, KY Metropolitan Statistical Area
Source: U.S. Census Bureau, 2020 Census

Disability by Age

Area	All Ages	Under 18 Years Old	18 to 64 Years Old	65 Years and Over
City	12.5	4.9	10.8	33.2
MSA[1]	13.5	5.2	11.8	34.2
U.S.	12.6	4.4	10.3	33.4

Note: Figures show percent of the civilian noninstitutionalized population that reported having a disability. Disability status is determined from six types of difficulty: vision, hearing, cognitive, ambulatory, self-care, and independent living. For children under 5 years old, hearing and vision difficulty are used to determine disability status. For children between the ages of 5 and 14, disability status is determined from hearing, vision, cognitive, ambulatory, and self-care difficulties. For people aged 15 years and older, they are considered to have a disability if they have difficulty with any one of the six difficulty types; Note: (1) Figures cover the Lexington-Fayette, KY Metropolitan Statistical Area
Source: U.S. Census Bureau, 2017-2021 American Community Survey 5-Year Estimates

Ancestry

Area	German	Irish	English	American	Italian	Polish	French[2]	Scottish	Dutch
City	13.1	11.0	12.1	8.2	3.1	1.6	1.6	2.6	1.1
MSA[1]	12.7	11.3	12.6	11.4	2.8	1.4	1.6	2.5	1.1
U.S.	12.8	9.6	8.1	5.7	5.0	2.7	2.2	1.6	1.1

Note: Figures are the percentage of the total population reporting a particular ancestry. The nine most commonly reported ancestries in the U.S. are shown. Figures include multiple ancestries (e.g. if a person reported being Irish and Italian, they were included in both columns); (1) Figures cover the Lexington-Fayette, KY Metropolitan Statistical Area; (2) Excludes Basque
Source: U.S. Census Bureau, 2017-2021 American Community Survey 5-Year Estimates

Foreign-born Population

Area	Percent of Population Born in								
	Any Foreign Country	Asia	Mexico	Europe	Caribbean	Central America[2]	South America	Africa	Canada
City	10.1	3.8	2.0	1.1	0.3	0.7	0.5	1.5	0.2
MSA[1]	7.6	2.6	1.7	1.0	0.2	0.5	0.3	1.1	0.2
U.S.	13.6	4.2	3.3	1.5	1.4	1.1	1.1	0.8	0.2

Note: (1) Figures cover the Lexington-Fayette, KY Metropolitan Statistical Area; (2) Excludes Mexico.
Source: U.S. Census Bureau, 2017-2021 American Community Survey 5-Year Estimates

Household Size

Area	Persons in Household (%)							Average Household Size
	One	Two	Three	Four	Five	Six	Seven or More	
City	33.1	34.3	14.3	11.4	4.3	1.8	0.8	2.30
MSA[1]	29.9	35.2	15.5	12.2	4.5	1.9	0.8	2.40
U.S.	28.1	33.8	15.5	12.9	6.0	2.3	1.4	2.60

Note: (1) Figures cover the Lexington-Fayette, KY Metropolitan Statistical Area
Source: U.S. Census Bureau, 2017-2021 American Community Survey 5-Year Estimates

Household Relationships

Area	House-holder	Opposite-sex Spouse	Same-sex Spouse	Opposite-sex Unmarried Partner	Same-sex Unmarried Partner	Child[2]	Grand-child	Other Relatives	Non-relatives
City	41.7	16.0	0.3	2.9	0.3	25.3	1.6	3.4	4.4
MSA[1]	40.5	17.4	0.2	2.8	0.2	26.5	2.0	3.4	3.7
U.S.	38.3	17.5	0.2	2.5	0.2	28.3	2.4	4.8	3.4

Note: Figures are percent of the total population; (1) Figures cover the Lexington-Fayette, KY Metropolitan Statistical Area; (2) Includes biological, adopted, and stepchildren of the householder
Source: U.S. Census Bureau, 2020 Census

Gender

Area	Males	Females	Males per 100 Females
City	155,876	166,694	93.5
MSA[1]	250,691	266,120	94.2
U.S.	162,685,811	168,763,470	96.4

Note: (1) Figures cover the Lexington-Fayette, KY Metropolitan Statistical Area
Source: U.S. Census Bureau, 2020 Census

Marital Status

Area	Never Married	Now Married[2]	Separated	Widowed	Divorced
City	38.6	43.4	1.5	4.6	11.8
MSA[1]	34.1	47.0	1.5	5.1	12.3
U.S.	33.8	48.0	1.8	5.6	10.8

Note: Figures are percentages and cover the population 15 years of age and older; (1) Figures cover the Lexington-Fayette, KY Metropolitan Statistical Area; (2) Excludes separated
Source: U.S. Census Bureau, 2017-2021 American Community Survey 5-Year Estimates

Religious Groups by Family

Area	Catholic	Baptist	Methodist	LDS[2]	Pentecostal	Lutheran	Islam	Adventist	Other
MSA[1]	5.8	14.9	5.5	1.2	1.6	0.3	0.5	1.2	16.6
U.S.	18.7	7.3	3.0	2.0	1.8	1.7	1.3	1.3	11.6

Note: Figures are the number of adherents as a percentage of the total population and cover the eight largest religious groups in the U.S; (1) Figures cover the Lexington-Fayette, KY Metropolitan Statistical Area; (2) Church of Jesus Christ of Latter-day Saints
Sources: 2020 U.S. Religion Census, Association of Statisticians of American Religious Bodies; The Association of Religion Data Archives (ARDA)

Religious Groups by Tradition

Area	Catholic	Evangelical Protestant	Mainline Protestant	Black Protestant	Islam	Judaism	Hinduism	Orthodox	Buddhism
MSA[1]	5.8	26.9	8.1	3.5	0.5	0.3	0.1	0.2	<0.1
U.S.	18.7	16.5	5.2	2.3	1.3	0.6	0.4	0.4	0.3

Note: Figures are the number of adherents as a percentage of the total population; (1) Figures cover the Lexington-Fayette, KY Metropolitan Statistical Area
Sources: 2020 U.S. Religion Census, Association of Statisticians of American Religious Bodies; The Association of Religion Data Archives (ARDA)

Lexington, Kentucky 231

ECONOMY

Gross Metropolitan Product

Area	2020	2021	2022	2023	Rank[2]
MSA[1]	29.8	32.5	35.1	36.8	103

Note: Figures are in billions of dollars; (1) Figures cover the Lexington-Fayette, KY Metropolitan Statistical Area; (2) Rank is based on 2021 data and ranges from 1 to 381
Source: U.S. Conference of Mayors, U.S. Metro Economies: U.S. Metros Compared to Global and State Economies, June 2022

Economic Growth

Area	2018-20 (%)	2021 (%)	2022 (%)	2023 (%)	Rank[2]
MSA[1]	-1.6	4.1	1.8	1.6	261
U.S.	-0.6	5.7	3.1	2.9	–

Note: Figures are real gross metropolitan product (GMP) growth rates and represent average annual percent change; (1) Figures cover the Lexington-Fayette, KY Metropolitan Statistical Area; (2) Rank is based on 2020 2-year average annual percent change and ranges from 1 to 381
Source: U.S. Conference of Mayors, U.S. Metro Economies: U.S. Metros Compared to Global and State Economies, June 2022

Metropolitan Area Exports

Area	2016	2017	2018	2019	2020	2021	Rank[2]
MSA[1]	2,069.6	2,119.8	2,148.0	2,093.8	1,586.3	1,880.0	113

Note: Figures are in millions of dollars; (1) Figures cover the Lexington-Fayette, KY Metropolitan Statistical Area; (2) Rank is based on 2021 data and ranges from 1 to 388
Source: U.S. Department of Commerce, International Trade Administration, Office of Trade and Economic Analysis, Industry and Analysis, Exports by Metropolitan Area, data extracted March 16, 2023

Building Permits

Area	Single-Family			Multi-Family			Total		
	2021	2022	Pct. Chg.	2021	2022	Pct. Chg.	2021	2022	Pct. Chg.
City	792	686	-13.4	863	1,045	21.1	1,655	1,731	4.6
MSA[1]	1,760	1,460	-17.0	1,183	1,249	5.6	2,943	2,709	-8.0
U.S.	1,115,400	975,600	-12.5	621,600	689,500	10.9	1,737,000	1,665,100	-4.1

Note: (1) Figures cover the Lexington-Fayette, KY Metropolitan Statistical Area; Figures represent new, privately-owned housing units authorized (unadjusted data); All permit data are based on estimates with imputation
Source: U.S. Census Bureau, Manufacturing, Mining, and Construction Statistics, Building Permits, 2021, 2022

Bankruptcy Filings

Area	Business Filings			Nonbusiness Filings		
	2021	2022	% Chg.	2021	2022	% Chg.
Fayette County	8	7	-12.5	450	410	-8.9
U.S.	14,347	13,481	-6.0	399,269	374,240	-6.3

Note: Business filings include Chapter 7, Chapter 9, Chapter 11, Chapter 12, Chapter 13, Chapter 15, and Section 304; Nonbusiness filings include Chapter 7, Chapter 11, and Chapter 13
Source: Administrative Office of the U.S. Courts, Business and Nonbusiness Bankruptcy, County Cases Commenced by Chapter of the Bankruptcy Code, During the 12-Month Period Ending December 31, 2021 and Business and Nonbusiness Bankruptcy, County Cases Commenced by Chapter of the Bankruptcy Code, During the 12-Month Period Ending December 31, 2022

Housing Vacancy Rates

Area	Gross Vacancy Rate[2] (%)			Year-Round Vacancy Rate[3] (%)			Rental Vacancy Rate[4] (%)			Homeowner Vacancy Rate[5] (%)		
	2020	2021	2022	2020	2021	2022	2020	2021	2022	2020	2021	2022
MSA[1]	n/a	n/a	n/a	n/a	n/a	n/a	n/a	n/a	n/a	n/a	n/a	n/a
U.S.	10.6	10.8	10.5	8.2	8.4	8.2	6.3	6.1	5.8	1.0	0.9	0.8

Note: (1) Figures cover the Lexington-Fayette, KY Metropolitan Statistical Area; (2) The percentage of the total housing inventory that is vacant; (3) The percentage of the housing inventory (excluding seasonal units) that is year-round vacant; (4) The percentage of rental inventory that is vacant for rent; (5) The percentage of homeowner inventory that is vacant for sale; n/a not available
Source: U.S. Census Bureau, Housing Vacancies and Homeownership Annual Statistics: 2020, 2021, 2022

INCOME

Income

Area	Per Capita ($)	Median Household ($)	Average Household ($)
City	37,475	61,526	88,901
MSA[1]	36,123	63,360	88,439
U.S.	37,638	69,021	97,196

Note: (1) Figures cover the Lexington-Fayette, KY Metropolitan Statistical Area
Source: U.S. Census Bureau, 2017-2021 American Community Survey 5-Year Estimates

Lexington, Kentucky

Household Income Distribution

Area	Percent of Households Earning							
	Under $15,000	$15,000 -$24,999	$25,000 -$34,999	$35,000 -$49,999	$50,000 -$74,999	$75,000 -$99,999	$100,000 -$149,999	$150,000 and up
City	10.6	8.9	9.5	12.1	17.6	12.3	14.9	14.1
MSA[1]	10.0	8.2	9.3	12.4	17.6	12.9	16.1	13.4
U.S.	9.4	7.8	8.2	11.4	16.8	12.8	16.3	17.3

Note: (1) Figures cover the Lexington-Fayette, KY Metropolitan Statistical Area
Source: U.S. Census Bureau, 2017-2021 American Community Survey 5-Year Estimates

Poverty Rate

Area	All Ages	Under 18 Years Old	18 to 64 Years Old	65 Years and Over
City	15.7	18.6	16.5	7.6
MSA[1]	14.1	17.2	14.4	8.3
U.S.	12.6	17.0	11.8	9.6

Note: Figures are percentage of people whose income during the past 12 months was below the poverty level;
(1) Figures cover the Lexington-Fayette, KY Metropolitan Statistical Area
Source: U.S. Census Bureau, 2017-2021 American Community Survey 5-Year Estimates

EMPLOYMENT

Labor Force and Employment

Area	Civilian Labor Force			Workers Employed		
	Dec. 2021	Dec. 2022	% Chg.	Dec. 2021	Dec. 2022	% Chg.
City	175,989	174,916	-0.6	170,668	170,430	-0.1
MSA[1]	275,622	274,006	-0.6	267,238	266,822	-0.2
U.S.	161,696,000	164,224,000	1.6	155,732,000	158,872,000	2.0

Note: Data is not seasonally adjusted and covers workers 16 years of age and older; (1) Figures cover the Lexington-Fayette, KY Metropolitan Statistical Area
Source: Bureau of Labor Statistics, Local Area Unemployment Statistics

Unemployment Rate

Area	2022											
	Jan.	Feb.	Mar.	Apr.	May	Jun.	Jul.	Aug.	Sep.	Oct.	Nov.	Dec.
City	3.3	3.0	3.1	2.8	2.9	3.5	3.3	3.0	2.8	3.3	3.1	2.6
MSA[1]	3.4	3.1	3.1	2.8	2.9	3.5	3.3	3.0	2.8	3.3	3.1	2.6
U.S.	4.4	4.1	3.8	3.3	3.4	3.8	3.8	3.8	3.3	3.4	3.4	3.3

Note: Data is not seasonally adjusted and covers workers 16 years of age and older; (1) Figures cover the Lexington-Fayette, KY Metropolitan Statistical Area
Source: Bureau of Labor Statistics, Local Area Unemployment Statistics

Average Wages

Occupation	$/Hr.	Occupation	$/Hr.
Accountants and Auditors	34.78	Maintenance and Repair Workers	22.07
Automotive Mechanics	19.88	Marketing Managers	55.36
Bookkeepers	21.74	Network and Computer Systems Admin.	38.28
Carpenters	24.79	Nurses, Licensed Practical	24.21
Cashiers	12.65	Nurses, Registered	37.36
Computer Programmers	41.29	Nursing Assistants	16.43
Computer Systems Analysts	41.63	Office Clerks, General	17.56
Computer User Support Specialists	25.84	Physical Therapists	40.93
Construction Laborers	20.07	Physicians	146.74
Cooks, Restaurant	14.54	Plumbers, Pipefitters and Steamfitters	29.90
Customer Service Representatives	17.87	Police and Sheriff's Patrol Officers	24.95
Dentists	n/a	Postal Service Mail Carriers	27.17
Electricians	25.25	Real Estate Sales Agents	27.67
Engineers, Electrical	44.15	Retail Salespersons	15.76
Fast Food and Counter Workers	11.82	Sales Representatives, Technical/Scientific	45.14
Financial Managers	65.06	Secretaries, Exc. Legal/Medical/Executive	20.09
First-Line Supervisors of Office Workers	29.85	Security Guards	14.57
General and Operations Managers	45.50	Surgeons	n/a
Hairdressers/Cosmetologists	13.22	Teacher Assistants, Exc. Postsecondary*	16.94
Home Health and Personal Care Aides	14.88	Teachers, Secondary School, Exc. Sp. Ed.*	29.65
Janitors and Cleaners	14.75	Telemarketers	n/a
Landscaping/Groundskeeping Workers	15.64	Truck Drivers, Heavy/Tractor-Trailer	26.48
Lawyers	51.22	Truck Drivers, Light/Delivery Services	21.58
Maids and Housekeeping Cleaners	12.88	Waiters and Waitresses	14.02

Note: Wage data covers the Lexington-Fayette, KY Metropolitan Statistical Area; (*) Hourly wages were calculated from annual wage data based on a 40 hour work week; n/a not available.
Source: Bureau of Labor Statistics, Metro Area Occupational Employment & Wage Estimates, May 2022

Employment by Industry

Sector	MSA[1]		U.S.
	Number of Employees	Percent of Total	Percent of Total
Construction, Mining, and Logging	14,000	4.8	5.4
Private Education and Health Services	38,100	13.0	16.1
Financial Activities	11,800	4.0	5.9
Government	55,500	19.0	14.5
Information	3,000	1.0	2.0
Leisure and Hospitality	32,500	11.1	10.3
Manufacturing	31,700	10.8	8.4
Other Services	12,800	4.4	3.7
Professional and Business Services	38,700	13.2	14.7
Retail Trade	29,700	10.2	10.2
Transportation, Warehousing, and Utilities	13,200	4.5	4.9
Wholesale Trade	11,200	3.8	3.9

Note: Figures are non-farm employment as of December 2022. Figures are not seasonally adjusted and include workers 16 years of age and older; (1) Figures cover the Lexington-Fayette, KY Metropolitan Statistical Area
Source: Bureau of Labor Statistics, Current Employment Statistics, Employment, Hours, and Earnings

Employment by Occupation

Occupation Classification	City (%)	MSA[1] (%)	U.S. (%)
Management, Business, Science, and Arts	45.9	42.7	40.3
Natural Resources, Construction, and Maintenance	5.6	7.0	8.7
Production, Transportation, and Material Moving	11.1	13.3	13.1
Sales and Office	21.0	21.1	20.9
Service	16.4	15.9	17.0

Note: Figures cover employed civilians 16 years of age and older; (1) Figures cover the Lexington-Fayette, KY Metropolitan Statistical Area
Source: U.S. Census Bureau, 2017-2021 American Community Survey 5-Year Estimates

Occupations with Greatest Projected Employment Growth: 2022 – 2024

Occupation[1]	2022 Employment	2024 Projected Employment	Numeric Employment Change	Percent Employment Change
Laborers and Freight, Stock, and Material Movers, Hand	64,300	66,790	2,490	3.9
Cooks, Restaurant	17,620	18,990	1,370	7.8
Home Health and Personal Care Aides	22,390	23,560	1,170	5.2
Stockers and Order Fillers	38,290	39,440	1,150	3.0
General and Operations Managers	46,980	47,930	950	2.0
Heavy and Tractor-Trailer Truck Drivers	31,920	32,870	950	3.0
Registered Nurses	40,910	41,740	830	2.0
Waiters and Waitresses	23,020	23,620	600	2.6
Industrial Truck and Tractor Operators	12,230	12,820	590	4.8
Light Truck or Delivery Services Drivers	16,050	16,610	560	3.5

Note: Projections cover Kentucky; (1) Sorted by numeric employment change
Source: www.projectionscentral.com, State Occupational Projections, 2022–2024 Short-Term Projections

Fastest-Growing Occupations: 2022 – 2024

Occupation[1]	2022 Employment	2024 Projected Employment	Numeric Employment Change	Percent Employment Change
Reservation and Transportation Ticket Agents and Travel Clerks	1,990	2,190	200	10.1
Nurse Practitioners	4,670	5,130	460	9.9
Logisticians	2,030	2,190	160	7.9
Hotel, Motel, and Resort Desk Clerks	3,820	4,120	300	7.9
Cooks, Restaurant	17,620	18,990	1,370	7.8
Sailors and Marine Oilers	1,680	1,810	130	7.7
Cargo and Freight Agents	2,850	3,060	210	7.4
Captains, Mates, and Pilots of Water Vessels	1,890	2,030	140	7.4
Farmworkers, Farm, Ranch, and Aquacultural Animals	1,960	2,100	140	7.1
Taxi Drivers	1,120	1,200	80	7.1

Note: Projections cover Kentucky; (1) Sorted by percent employment change and excludes occupations with numeric employment change less than 50
Source: www.projectionscentral.com, State Occupational Projections, 2022–2024 Short-Term Projections

234   Lexington, Kentucky

CITY FINANCES

City Government Finances

Component	2020 ($000)	2020 ($ per capita)
Total Revenues	691,628	2,140
Total Expenditures	498,043	1,541
Debt Outstanding	860,390	2,662
Cash and Securities[1]	768,783	2,379

Note: (1) Cash and security holdings of a government at the close of its fiscal year, including those of its dependent agencies, utilities, and liquor stores.
Source: U.S. Census Bureau, State & Local Government Finances 2020

City Government Revenue by Source

Source	2020 ($000)	2020 ($ per capita)	2020 (%)
General Revenue			
From Federal Government	57,522	178	8.3
From State Government	19,124	59	2.8
From Local Governments	17,123	53	2.5
Taxes			
Property	92,357	286	13.4
Sales and Gross Receipts	72,602	225	10.5
Personal Income	205,058	635	29.6
Corporate Income	37,941	117	5.5
Motor Vehicle License	219	1	0.0
Other Taxes	4,355	13	0.6
Current Charges	170,453	527	24.6
Liquor Store	0	0	0.0
Utility	3,367	10	0.5

Source: U.S. Census Bureau, State & Local Government Finances 2020

City Government Expenditures by Function

Function	2020 ($000)	2020 ($ per capita)	2020 (%)
General Direct Expenditures			
Air Transportation	14,487	44	2.9
Corrections	29,430	91	5.9
Education	0	0	0.0
Employment Security Administration	0	0	0.0
Financial Administration	0	0	0.0
Fire Protection	55,651	172	11.2
General Public Buildings	0	0	0.0
Governmental Administration, Other	45,441	140	9.1
Health	5,984	18	1.2
Highways	9,610	29	1.9
Hospitals	0	0	0.0
Housing and Community Development	3,342	10	0.7
Interest on General Debt	22,070	68	4.4
Judicial and Legal	2,349	7	0.5
Libraries	15,804	48	3.2
Parking	3,957	12	0.8
Parks and Recreation	56,952	176	11.4
Police Protection	50,011	154	10.0
Public Welfare	11,152	34	2.2
Sewerage	82,629	255	16.6
Solid Waste Management	42,273	130	8.5
Veterans' Services	0	0	0.0
Liquor Store	0	0	0.0
Utility	25,801	79	5.2

Source: U.S. Census Bureau, State & Local Government Finances 2020

TAXES

State Corporate Income Tax Rates

State	Tax Rate (%)	Income Brackets ($)	Num. of Brackets	Financial Institution Tax Rate (%)[a]	Federal Income Tax Ded.
Kentucky	5.0	Flat rate	1	5.0	No

Note: Tax rates as of January 1, 2023; (a) Rates listed are the corporate income tax rate applied to financial institutions or excise taxes based on income. Some states have other taxes based upon the value of deposits or shares.
Source: Federation of Tax Administrators, State Corporate Income Tax Rates, January 1, 2023

State Individual Income Tax Rates

State	Tax Rate (%)	Income Brackets ($)	Personal Exemptions ($)			Standard Ded. ($)	
			Single	Married	Depend.	Single	Married
Kentucky	4.5	Flat rate	None	None	None	2,980	5,960

Note: Tax rates as of January 1, 2023; Local- and county-level taxes are not included; Federal income tax is not deductible on state income tax returns
Source: Federation of Tax Administrators, State Individual Income Tax Rates, January 1, 2023

Various State Sales and Excise Tax Rates

State	State Sales Tax (%)	Gasoline[1] ($/gal.)	Cigarette[2] ($/pack)	Spirits[3] ($/gal.)	Wine[4] ($/gal.)	Beer[5] ($/gal.)	Recreational Marijuana (%)
Kentucky	6	0.26	1.10	9.25	3.58	0.93	Not legal

Note: All tax rates as of January 1, 2023; (1) The American Petroleum Institute has developed a methodology for determining the average tax rate on a gallon of fuel. Rates may include any of the following: excise taxes, environmental fees, storage tank fees, other fees or taxes, general sales tax, and local taxes; (2) The federal excise tax of $1.0066 per pack and local taxes are not included; (3) Rates are those applicable to off-premise sales of 40% alcohol by volume (a.b.v.) distilled spirits in 750ml containers. Local excise taxes are excluded; (4) Rates are those applicable to off-premise sales of 11% a.b.v. non-carbonated wine in 750ml containers; (5) Rates are those applicable to off-premise sales of 4.7% a.b.v. beer in 12 ounce containers.
Source: Tax Foundation, 2023 Facts & Figures: How Does Your State Compare?

State Business Tax Climate Index Rankings

State	Overall Rank	Corporate Tax Rank	Individual Income Tax Rank	Sales Tax Rank	Property Tax Rank	Unemployment Insurance Tax Rank
Kentucky	18	15	18	14	24	48

Note: The index is a measure of how each state's tax laws affect economic performance. The lower the rank, the more favorable a state's tax system is for business. States without a given tax are given a ranking of 1. The scores/rankings for the District of Columbia do not affect other states. The 2023 index represents the tax climate as of July 1, 2022.
Source: Tax Foundation, State Business Tax Climate Index 2023

TRANSPORTATION

Means of Transportation to Work

Area	Car/Truck/Van		Public Transportation			Bicycle	Walked	Other Means	Worked at Home
	Drove Alone	Car-pooled	Bus	Subway	Railroad				
City	77.0	8.1	1.7	0.0	0.0	0.6	3.5	1.1	8.2
MSA[1]	78.2	8.4	1.1	0.0	0.0	0.4	2.9	1.0	8.0
U.S.	73.2	8.6	2.0	1.6	0.5	0.5	2.5	1.5	9.7

Note: Figures are percentages and cover workers 16 years of age and older; (1) Figures cover the Lexington-Fayette, KY Metropolitan Statistical Area
Source: U.S. Census Bureau, 2017-2021 American Community Survey 5-Year Estimates

Travel Time to Work

Area	Less Than 10 Minutes	10 to 19 Minutes	20 to 29 Minutes	30 to 44 Minutes	45 to 59 Minutes	60 to 89 Minutes	90 Minutes or More
City	13.2	39.5	26.2	13.9	2.9	2.4	1.8
MSA[1]	14.5	35.6	24.5	16.8	4.3	2.6	1.7
U.S.	12.4	28.5	21.0	20.9	8.2	6.2	2.9

Note: Note: Figures are percentages and include workers 16 years old and over; (1) Figures cover the Lexington-Fayette, KY Metropolitan Statistical Area
Source: U.S. Census Bureau, 2017-2021 American Community Survey 5-Year Estimates

Key Congestion Measures

Measure	1990	2000	2010	2015	2020
Annual Hours of Delay, Total (000)	n/a	n/a	n/a	11,066	4,137
Annual Hours of Delay, Per Auto Commuter	n/a	n/a	n/a	36	13
Annual Congestion Cost, Per Auto Commuter ($)	n/a	n/a	n/a	776	308

Note: n/a not available
Source: Texas A&M Transportation Institute, 2021 Urban Mobility Report

Freeway Travel Time Index

Measure	1985	1990	1995	2000	2005	2010	2015	2020
Urban Area Index[1]	n/a	n/a	n/a	n/a	n/a	n/a	1.19	1.08
Urban Area Rank[1,2]	n/a	n/a	n/a	n/a	n/a	n/a	n/a	n/a

Note: Freeway Travel Time Index—the ratio of travel time in the peak period to the travel time at free-flow conditions. For example, a value of 1.30 indicates a 20-minute free-flow trip takes 26 minutes in the peak (20 minutes x 1.30 = 26 minutes); (1) Covers the Lexington-Fayette KY urban area; (2) Rank is based on 101 larger urban areas (#1 = highest travel time index); n/a not available
Source: Texas A&M Transportation Institute, 2021 Urban Mobility Report

Public Transportation

Agency Name / Mode of Transportation	Vehicles Operated in Maximum Service[1]	Annual Unlinked Passenger Trips[2] (in thous.)	Annual Passenger Miles[3] (in thous.)
Lexington Transit Authority (LexTran)			
Bus (directly operated)	51	2,383.8	9,191.1
Demand Response (purchased transportation)	42	159.5	1,183.3
Vanpool (purchased transportation)	6	6.3	278.2

Note: (1) Number of revenue vehicles operated by the given mode and type of service to meet the annual maximum service requirement. This is the revenue vehicle count during the peak season of the year; on the week and day that maximum service is provided. Vehicles operated in maximum service (VOMS) exclude atypical days and one-time special events; (2) Number of passengers who boarded public transportation vehicles. Passengers are counted each time they board a vehicle no matter how many vehicles they use to travel from their origin to their destination. (3) Sum of the distances ridden by all passengers during the entire fiscal year.
Source: Federal Transit Administration, National Transit Database, 2021

Air Transportation

Airport Name and Code / Type of Service	Passenger Airlines[1]	Passenger Enplanements	Freight Carriers[2]	Freight (lbs)
Bluegrass Airport (LEX)				
Domestic service (U.S. carriers - 2022)	23	576,634	9	117,736
International service (U.S. carriers - 2021)	0	0	0	0

Note: (1) Includes all U.S.-based major, minor and commuter airlines that carried at least one passenger during the year; (2) Includes all U.S.-based airlines and freight carriers that transported at least one pound of freight during the year.
Source: Bureau of Transportation Statistics, The Intermodal Transportation Database, Air Carriers: T-100 Domestic Market (U.S. Carriers), 2022; Bureau of Transportation Statistics, The Intermodal Transportation Database, Air Carriers: T-100 International Market (U.S. Carriers), 2021

BUSINESSES

Major Business Headquarters

Company Name	Industry	Rankings	
		Fortune[1]	Forbes[2]
Gray	Construction	-	202

Note: (1) Companies that produce a 10-K are ranked 1 to 500 based on 2021 revenue; (2) All private companies with at least $2 billion in annual revenue through the end of their most current fiscal year are ranked 1 to 246; companies listed are headquartered in the city; dashes indicate no ranking
Source: Fortune, "Fortune 500," 2022; Forbes, "America's Largest Private Companies," 2022

Fastest-Growing Businesses

According to *Inc.*, Lexington is home to one of America's 500 fastest-growing private companies: **Bitwerx** (#274). Criteria: must be an independent, privately-held, for-profit, U.S. corporation, proprietorship or partnership as of December 31, 2021; revenues must be at least $100,000 in 2018 and $2 million in 2021; must have four-year operating/sales history. *Inc., "America's 500 Fastest-Growing Private Companies," 2022*

Living Environment

COST OF LIVING

Cost of Living Index

Composite Index	Groceries	Housing	Utilities	Trans-portation	Health Care	Misc. Goods/Services
93.9	93.3	76.1	107.8	97.0	81.6	106.3

Note: The Cost of Living Index measures regional differences in the cost of consumer goods and services, excluding taxes and non-consumer expenditures, for professional and managerial households in the top income quintile. It is based on more than 50,000 prices covering almost 60 different items for which prices are collected three times a year by chambers of commerce, economic development organizations or university applied economic centers in each participating urban area. The numbers shown should be read as a percentage above or below the national average of 100. For example, a value of 115.4 in the groceries column indicates that grocery prices are 15.4% higher than the national average. Small differences in the index numbers should not be interpreted as significant; Figures cover the Lexington KY urban area.
Source: The Council for Community and Economic Research, Cost of Living Index, 2022

Grocery Prices

Area[1]	T-Bone Steak ($/pound)	Frying Chicken ($/pound)	Whole Milk ($/half gal.)	Eggs ($/dozen)	Orange Juice ($/64 oz.)	Coffee ($/11.5 oz.)
City[2]	13.65	1.26	2.02	1.80	3.65	4.54
Avg.	13.81	1.59	2.43	2.25	3.85	4.95
Min.	10.17	0.90	1.51	1.30	2.90	3.46
Max.	19.35	3.30	4.32	4.32	5.31	8.59

Note: (1) Values for the local area are compared with the average, minimum and maximum values for all 286 areas in the Cost of Living Index; (2) Figures cover the Lexington KY urban area; T-Bone Steak (price per pound); Frying Chicken (price per pound, whole fryer); Whole Milk (half gallon carton); Eggs (price per dozen, Grade A, large); Orange Juice (64 oz. Tropicana or Florida Natural); Coffee (11.5 oz. can, vacuum-packed, Maxwell House, Hills Bros, or Folgers).
Source: The Council for Community and Economic Research, Cost of Living Index, 2022

Housing and Utility Costs

Area[1]	New Home Price ($)	Apartment Rent ($/month)	All Electric ($/month)	Part Electric ($/month)	Other Energy ($/month)	Telephone ($/month)
City[2]	351,975	982	-	90.87	109.72	189.80
Avg.	450,913	1,371	176.41	99.93	76.96	190.22
Min.	229,283	546	100.84	31.56	27.15	174.27
Max.	2,434,977	4,569	356.86	249.59	272.24	208.31

Note: (1) Values for the local area are compared with the average, minimum and maximum values for all 286 areas in the Cost of Living Index; (2) Figures cover the Lexington KY urban area; New Home Price (2,400 sf living area, 8,000 sf lot, in urban area with full utilities); Apartment Rent (950 sf 2 bedroom/1.5 or 2 bath, unfurnished, excluding all utilities except water); All Electric (average monthly cost for an all-electric home); Part Electric (average monthly cost for a part-electric home); Other Energy (average monthly cost for natural gas, fuel oil, coal, wood, and any other forms of energy except electricity); Telephone (price includes the base monthly rate plus taxes and fees for three lines of mobile phone service).
Source: The Council for Community and Economic Research, Cost of Living Index, 2022

Health Care, Transportation, and Other Costs

Area[1]	Doctor ($/visit)	Dentist ($/visit)	Optometrist ($/visit)	Gasoline ($/gallon)	Beauty Salon ($/visit)	Men's Shirt ($)
City[2]	97.28	98.17	80.03	3.78	58.71	52.93
Avg.	124.91	107.77	117.66	3.86	43.31	34.21
Min.	36.61	58.25	51.79	2.90	22.18	13.05
Max.	250.21	162.58	371.96	5.54	85.61	63.54

Note: (1) Values for the local area are compared with the average, minimum and maximum values for all 286 areas in the Cost of Living Index; (2) Figures cover the Lexington KY urban area; Doctor (general practitioners routine exam of an established patient); Dentist (adult teeth cleaning and periodic oral examination); Optometrist (full vision eye exam for established adult patient); Gasoline (one gallon regular unleaded, national brand, including all taxes, cash price at self-service pump if available); Beauty Salon (woman's shampoo, trim, and blow-dry); Men's Shirt (cotton/polyester dress shirt, pinpoint weave, long sleeves).
Source: The Council for Community and Economic Research, Cost of Living Index, 2022

HOUSING

Homeownership Rate

Area	2015 (%)	2016 (%)	2017 (%)	2018 (%)	2019 (%)	2020 (%)	2021 (%)	2022 (%)
MSA[1]	n/a	n/a	n/a	n/a	n/a	n/a	n/a	n/a
U.S.	63.7	63.4	63.9	64.4	64.6	66.6	65.5	65.8

Note: (1) Figures cover the Lexington-Fayette, KY Metropolitan Statistical Area; n/a not available
Source: U.S. Census Bureau, Housing Vacancies and Homeownership Annual Statistics: 2015-2022

House Price Index (HPI)

Area	National Ranking[2]	Quarterly Change (%)	One-Year Change (%)	Five-Year Change (%)	Since 1991Q1 (%)
MSA[1]	72	0.70	13.70	53.19	235.38
U.S.[3]	–	0.34	8.41	58.44	289.08

Note: The HPI is a weighted repeat sales index. It measures average price changes in repeat sales or refinancings on the same properties. This information is obtained by reviewing repeat mortgage transactions on single-family properties whose mortgages have been purchased or securitized by Fannie Mae or Freddie Mac since January 1975; (1) Figures cover the Lexington-Fayette, KY Metropolitan Statistical Area; (2) Rankings are based on annual percentage change for all metro areas containing at least 15,000 transactions over the last 10 years and ranges from 1 to 257; (3) figures based on a weighted average of Census Division estimates using a seasonally adjusted, purchase-only index; all figures are for the period ending December 31, 2022
Source: Federal Housing Finance Agency, Change in FHFA Metropolitan Area House Price Indexes, 2022Q4

Median Single-Family Home Prices

Area	2020	2021	2022[p]	Percent Change 2021 to 2022
MSA[1]	201.2	224.2	242.5	8.2
U.S. Average	300.2	357.1	392.6	9.9

Note: Figures are median sales prices of existing single-family homes in thousands of dollars; (p) preliminary; (1) Figures cover the Lexington-Fayette, KY Metropolitan Statistical Area
Source: National Association of Realtors, Median Sales Price of Existing Single-Family Homes for Metropolitan Areas, 4th Quarter 2022

Qualifying Income Based on Median Sales Price of Existing Single-Family Homes

Area	With 5% Down ($)	With 10% Down ($)	With 20% Down ($)
MSA[1]	71,804	68,025	60,467
U.S. Average	112,234	106,237	94,513

Note: Figures are preliminary; Qualifying income is based on a mortgage rate of 6.77%. Monthly principal and interest payment is limited to 25% of income; (1) Figures cover the Lexington-Fayette, KY Metropolitan Statistical Area
Source: National Association of Realtors, Qualifying Income Based on Median Sales Price of Existing Single-Family Homes for Metropolitan Areas, 4th Quarter 2022

Home Value

Area	Under $100,000	$100,000 -$199,999	$200,000 -$299,999	$300,000 -$399,999	$400,000 -$499,999	$500,000 -$999,999	$1,000,000 or more	Median ($)
City	9.0	36.1	25.2	14.5	6.4	7.6	1.2	216,800
MSA[1]	10.9	37.5	24.2	13.2	6.0	7.1	1.2	206,000
U.S.	16.2	24.2	20.1	13.6	8.3	13.6	4.1	244,900

Note: Figures are percentages except for median and cover owner-occupied housing units; (1) Figures cover the Lexington-Fayette, KY Metropolitan Statistical Area
Source: U.S. Census Bureau, 2017-2021 American Community Survey 5-Year Estimates

Year Housing Structure Built

Area	2020 or Later	2010 -2019	2000 -2009	1990 -1999	1980 -1989	1970 -1979	1960 -1969	1950 -1959	1940 -1949	Before 1940	Median Year
City	0.2	8.4	14.2	16.5	13.2	15.2	13.5	8.9	2.9	7.1	1982
MSA[1]	0.2	8.7	16.1	17.4	13.4	14.8	11.1	7.7	3.0	7.6	1984
U.S.	0.2	7.3	13.6	13.6	13.2	14.8	10.3	10.0	4.7	12.2	1979

Note: Figures are percentages except for Median Year; Note: (1) Figures cover the Lexington-Fayette, KY Metropolitan Statistical Area
Source: U.S. Census Bureau, 2017-2021 American Community Survey 5-Year Estimates

Gross Monthly Rent

Area	Under $500	$500 -$999	$1,000 -$1,499	$1,500 -$1,999	$2,000 -$2,499	$2,500 -$2,999	$3,000 and up	Median ($)
City	6.4	47.7	34.5	8.1	2.3	0.5	0.4	967
MSA[1]	7.5	50.4	32.5	7.0	1.8	0.4	0.3	934
U.S.	8.1	30.5	30.8	16.8	7.3	3.1	3.5	1,163

Note: Figures are percentages except for median; Gross rent is the contract rent plus the estimated average monthly cost of utilities (electricity, gas, and water and sewer) and fuels (oil, coal, kerosene, wood, etc.) if these are paid by the renter (or paid for the renter by someone else); (1) Figures cover the Lexington-Fayette, KY Metropolitan Statistical Area
Source: U.S. Census Bureau, 2017-2021 American Community Survey 5-Year Estimates

HEALTH

Health Risk Factors

Category	MSA[1] (%)	U.S. (%)
Adults aged 18–64 who have any kind of health care coverage	n/a	90.9
Adults who reported being in good or better health	n/a	85.2
Adults who have been told they have high blood cholesterol	n/a	35.7
Adults who have been told they have high blood pressure	n/a	32.4
Adults who are current smokers	n/a	14.4
Adults who currently use e-cigarettes	n/a	6.7
Adults who currently use chewing tobacco, snuff, or snus	n/a	3.5
Adults who are heavy drinkers[2]	n/a	6.3
Adults who are binge drinkers[3]	n/a	15.4
Adults who are overweight (BMI 25.0 - 29.9)	n/a	34.4
Adults who are obese (BMI 30.0 - 99.8)	n/a	33.9
Adults who participated in any physical activities in the past month	n/a	76.3

Note: (1) Figures for the Lexington-Fayette, KY Metropolitan Statistical Area were not available.
(2) Heavy drinkers are classified as adult men having more than 14 drinks per week and adult women having more than 7 drinks per week; (3) Binge drinkers are classified as males having five or more drinks on one occasion or females having four or more drinks on one occasion
Source: Centers for Disease Control and Prevention, Behaviorial Risk Factor Surveillance System, SMART: Selected Metropolitan Area Risk Trends, 2021

Acute and Chronic Health Conditions

Category	MSA[1] (%)	U.S. (%)
Adults who have ever been told they had a heart attack	n/a	4.0
Adults who have ever been told they have angina or coronary heart disease	n/a	3.8
Adults who have ever been told they had a stroke	n/a	3.0
Adults who have ever been told they have asthma	n/a	14.9
Adults who have ever been told they have arthritis	n/a	25.8
Adults who have ever been told they have diabetes[2]	n/a	10.9
Adults who have ever been told they had skin cancer	n/a	6.6
Adults who have ever been told they had any other types of cancer	n/a	7.5
Adults who have ever been told they have COPD	n/a	6.1
Adults who have ever been told they have kidney disease	n/a	3.0
Adults who have ever been told they have a form of depression	n/a	20.5

Note: (1) Figures for the Lexington-Fayette, KY Metropolitan Statistical Area were not available.
(2) Figures do not include pregnancy-related, borderline, or pre-diabetes
Source: Centers for Disease Control and Prevention, Behaviorial Risk Factor Surveillance System, SMART: Selected Metropolitan Area Risk Trends, 2021

Health Screening and Vaccination Rates

Category	MSA[1] (%)	U.S. (%)
Adults who have ever been tested for HIV	n/a	34.9
Adults who have had their blood cholesterol checked within the last five years	n/a	85.2
Adults aged 65+ who have had flu shot within the past year	n/a	68.6
Adults aged 65+ who have ever had a pneumonia vaccination	n/a	71.0

Note: (1) Figures for the Lexington-Fayette, KY Metropolitan Statistical Area were not available.
Source: Centers for Disease Control and Prevention, Behaviorial Risk Factor Surveillance System, SMART: Selected Metropolitan Area Risk Trends, 2021

Disability Status

Category	MSA[1] (%)	U.S. (%)
Adults who reported being deaf	n/a	7.2
Are you blind or have serious difficulty seeing, even when wearing glasses?	n/a	4.8
Are you limited in any way in any of your usual activities due to arthritis?	n/a	11.1
Do you have difficulty doing errands alone?	n/a	7.0
Do you have difficulty dressing or bathing?	n/a	3.6
Do you have serious difficulty concentrating/remembering/making decisions?	n/a	12.1
Do you have serious difficulty walking or climbing stairs?	n/a	12.8

Note: (1) Figures for the Lexington-Fayette, KY Metropolitan Statistical Area were not available.
Source: Centers for Disease Control and Prevention, Behaviorial Risk Factor Surveillance System, SMART: Selected Metropolitan Area Risk Trends, 2021

Mortality Rates for the Top 10 Causes of Death in the U.S.

ICD-10[a] Sub-Chapter	ICD-10[a] Code	Crude Mortality Rate[1] per 100,000 population	
		County[2]	U.S.
Malignant neoplasms	C00-C97	151.8	182.6
Ischaemic heart diseases	I20-I25	66.8	113.1
Other forms of heart disease	I30-I51	62.5	64.4
Other degenerative diseases of the nervous system	G30-G31	47.9	51.0
Cerebrovascular diseases	I60-I69	41.1	47.8
Other external causes of accidental injury	W00-X59	60.9	46.4
Chronic lower respiratory diseases	J40-J47	42.1	45.7
Organic, including symptomatic, mental disorders	F01-F09	39.7	35.9
Hypertensive diseases	I10-I15	26.7	35.0
Diabetes mellitus	E10-E14	25.8	29.6

Note: (a) ICD-10 = International Classification of Diseases 10th Revision; (1) Crude mortality rates are a three-year average covering 2019-2021; (2) Figures cover Fayette County.
Source: Centers for Disease Control and Prevention, National Center for Health Statistics. National Vital Statistics System, Mortality 2018-2021 on CDC WONDER Online Database

Mortality Rates for Selected Causes of Death

ICD-10[a] Sub-Chapter	ICD-10[a] Code	Crude Mortality Rate[1] per 100,000 population	
		County[2]	U.S.
Assault	X85-Y09	9.9	7.0
Diseases of the liver	K70-K76	16.6	19.8
Human immunodeficiency virus (HIV) disease	B20-B24	Unreliable	1.5
Influenza and pneumonia	J09-J18	9.7	14.7
Intentional self-harm	X60-X84	13.6	14.3
Malnutrition	E40-E46	4.0	4.3
Obesity and other hyperalimentation	E65-E68	3.6	3.0
Renal failure	N17-N19	10.5	15.7
Transport accidents	V01-V99	9.5	13.6
Viral hepatitis	B15-B19	Unreliable	1.2

Note: (a) ICD-10 = International Classification of Diseases 10th Revision; (1) Crude mortality rates are a three-year average covering 2019-2021; (2) Figures cover Fayette County; Data are suppressed when the data meet the criteria for confidentiality constraints; Crude mortality rates are flagged as unreliable when the rate would be calculated with a numerator of 20 or less.
Source: Centers for Disease Control and Prevention, National Center for Health Statistics. National Vital Statistics System, Mortality 2018-2021 on CDC WONDER Online Database

Health Insurance Coverage

Area	With Health Insurance	With Private Health Insurance	With Public Health Insurance	Without Health Insurance	Population Under Age 19 Without Health Insurance
City	93.2	70.9	33.1	6.8	3.1
MSA[1]	93.9	71.2	34.6	6.1	3.4
U.S.	91.2	67.8	35.4	8.8	5.3

Note: Figures are percentages that cover the civilian noninstitutionalized population; (1) Figures cover the Lexington-Fayette, KY Metropolitan Statistical Area
Source: U.S. Census Bureau, 2017-2021 American Community Survey 5-Year Estimates

Number of Medical Professionals

Area	MDs[3]	DOs[3,4]	Dentists	Podiatrists	Chiropractors	Optometrists
County[1] (number)	2,464	123	472	25	79	85
County[1] (rate[2])	764.3	38.2	146.7	7.8	24.5	26.4
U.S. (rate[2])	289.3	23.5	72.5	6.2	28.7	17.4

Note: Data as of 2021 unless noted; (1) Data covers Fayette County; (2) Rate per 100,000 population; (3) Data as of 2020 and includes all active, non-federal physicians; (4) Doctor of Osteopathic Medicine
Source: U.S. Department of Health and Human Services, Health Resources and Services Administration, Bureau of Health Professions, Area Resource File (ARF) 2021-2022

Best Hospitals

According to *U.S. News,* the Lexington-Fayette, KY metro area is home to one of the best hospitals in the U.S.: **University of Kentucky Albert B. Chandler Hospital** (1 adult specialty and 2 pediatric specialties). The hospital listed was nationally ranked in at least one of 15 adult or 10 pediatric specialties. The number of specialties shown cover the parent hospital. Only 164 U.S. hospitals performed well enough to be nationally ranked in one or more specialties. Twenty hospitals in the U.S. made the Honor Roll. The Best Hospitals Honor Roll takes both the national rankings and the procedure and condition ratings into account. Hospitals received points if they were nationally ranked in one of the 15 adult specialties—the higher they ranked, the more points they got—and how many ratings of "high performing" they earned in the 17 procedures and conditions. *U.S. News Online, "America's Best Hospitals 2022-23"*

According to *U.S. News,* the Lexington-Fayette, KY metro area is home to one of the best children's hospitals in the U.S.: **Kentucky Children's Hospital** (2 pediatric specialties). The hospital listed was highly ranked in at least one of 10 pediatric specialties. Eighty-six children's hospitals in the U.S. were nationally ranked in at least one specialty. Hospitals received points for being ranked in a specialty, and the 10 hospitals with the most points across the 10 specialties make up the Honor Roll. *U.S. News Online, "America's Best Children's Hospitals 2022-23"*

EDUCATION

Public School District Statistics

District Name	Schls	Pupils	Pupil/ Teacher Ratio	Minority Pupils[1] (%)	LEP/ELL[2] (%)	IEP[3] (%)
Fayette County	80	41,415	13.5	53.9	12.0	11.7

Note: Table includes school districts with 2,000 or more students; (1) Percentage of students that are not non-Hispanic white; (2) Percentage of students that are Limited English Proficient or English Language Learners (2018-19); (3) Percentage of students that have an Individualized Education Program (2019-20). Source: U.S. Department of Education, National Center for Education Statistics, Common Core of Data, Local Education Agency (School District) Universe Survey: School Year 2021-2022

Highest Level of Education

Area	Less than H.S.	H.S. Diploma	Some College, No Deg.	Associate Degree	Bachelor's Degree	Master's Degree	Prof. School Degree	Doctorate Degree
City	7.6	18.9	20.0	7.9	25.9	12.2	4.2	3.4
MSA[1]	8.3	23.8	20.5	8.3	22.4	10.8	3.4	2.5
U.S.	11.1	26.5	20.0	8.7	20.6	9.3	2.2	1.5

Note: Figures cover persons age 25 and over; (1) Figures cover the Lexington-Fayette, KY Metropolitan Statistical Area Source: U.S. Census Bureau, 2017-2021 American Community Survey 5-Year Estimates

Educational Attainment by Race

Area	High School Graduate or Higher (%)					Bachelor's Degree or Higher (%)				
	Total	White	Black	Asian	Hisp.[2]	Total	White	Black	Asian	Hisp.[2]
City	92.4	94.8	88.9	89.4	64.1	45.6	49.7	23.7	69.0	25.3
MSA[1]	91.7	93.3	89.0	89.2	63.6	39.0	40.9	22.8	65.5	22.1
U.S.	88.9	91.4	87.2	87.6	71.2	33.7	35.5	23.3	55.6	18.4

Note: Figures shown cover persons 25 years old and over; (1) Figures cover the Lexington-Fayette, KY Metropolitan Statistical Area; (2) People of Hispanic origin can be of any race Source: U.S. Census Bureau, 2017-2021 American Community Survey 5-Year Estimates

School Enrollment by Grade and Control

Area	Preschool (%)		Kindergarten (%)		Grades 1 - 4 (%)		Grades 5 - 8 (%)		Grades 9 - 12 (%)	
	Public	Private	Public	Private	Public	Private	Public	Private	Public	Private
City	37.3	62.7	84.6	15.4	83.2	16.8	83.9	16.1	85.4	14.6
MSA[1]	44.3	55.7	82.5	17.5	85.0	15.0	84.0	16.0	86.6	13.4
U.S.	58.8	41.2	86.3	13.7	88.3	11.7	88.6	11.4	89.4	10.6

Note: Figures shown cover persons 3 years old and over; (1) Figures cover the Lexington-Fayette, KY Metropolitan Statistical Area Source: U.S. Census Bureau, 2017-2021 American Community Survey 5-Year Estimates

Higher Education

Four-Year Colleges			Two-Year Colleges			Medical Schools[1]	Law Schools[2]	Voc/ Tech[3]
Public	Private Non-profit	Private For-profit	Public	Private Non-profit	Private For-profit			
1	7	0	1	0	0	1	1	5

Note: Figures cover institutions located within the Lexington-Fayette, KY Metropolitan Statistical Area and include main campuses only; (1) includes schools accredited by the Liaison Committee on Medical Education and the American Osteopathic Association's Commission on Osteopathic College Accreditation; (2) includes ABA-accredited schools, schools with provisional ABA accreditation, and state accredited schools; (3) includes all schools with programs that are less than 2 years. Source: National Center for Education Statistics, Integrated Postsecondary Education System (IPEDS), 2021-22; Wikipedia, List of Medical Schools in the United States, accessed April 10, 2023; Wikipedia, List of Law Schools in the United States, accessed April 10, 2023

According to *U.S. News & World Report,* the Lexington-Fayette, KY metro area is home to one of the top 200 national universities in the U.S.: **University of Kentucky** (#137 tie). The indicators used to capture academic quality fall into a number of categories: assessment by administrators at peer institutions; retention of students; faculty resources; student selectivity; financial resources; alumni giving; high school counselor ratings of colleges; and graduation rate. *U.S. News & World Report, "America's Best Colleges 2023"*

According to *U.S. News & World Report,* the Lexington-Fayette, KY metro area is home to one of the top 100 law schools in the U.S.: **University of Kentucky (Rosenburg)** (#67 tie). The rankings are based on a weighted average of 12 measures of quality: peer assessment score; assessment score by lawyers/judges; median LSAT scores; median undergrad GPA; acceptance rate; employment rates for graduates; placement success; bar passage rate; faculty resources; expenditures per student; student/faculty ratio; and library resources. *U.S. News & World Report, "America's Best Graduate Schools, Law, 2023"*

According to *U.S. News & World Report,* the Lexington-Fayette, KY metro area is home to one of the top 75 medical schools for research in the U.S.: **University of Kentucky** (#64 tie). The rankings are based on a weighted average of 11 measures of quality: quality assessment; peer assessment score; assessment score by residency directors; research activity; total research activity; average research activity per faculty member; student selectivity; median MCAT total score; median undergraduate GPA; acceptance rate; and faculty resources. *U.S. News & World Report, "America's Best Graduate Schools, Medical, 2023"*

According to *U.S. News & World Report,* the Lexington-Fayette, KY metro area is home to one of the top 75 business schools in the U.S.: **University of Kentucky (Gatton)** (#72 tie). The rankings are based on a weighted average of the following nine measures: quality assessment; peer assessment; recruiter assessment; placement success; mean starting salary and bonus; student selectivity; mean GMAT and GRE scores; mean undergraduate GPA; and acceptance rate. *U.S. News & World Report, "America's Best Graduate Schools, Business, 2023"*

EMPLOYERS

Major Employers

Company Name	Industry
Amazon.com	Distribution
Baptist Health	Healthcare
Cardinal Hill Rehabilitation Hospital	Healthcare
Eastern Kentucky University	Education
Fayette County Public Schools	Education
Kentucky Health & Family Svcs Cabinet	Government
KentuckyOne Health	Healthcare
KY Dept for Workforce Inv	Government
Lexington-Fayette Urban County Govt	Government
Lexmark International	Enterprise software, hardware and services
Lockheed Martin	Manufacturing
Osram Sylvania	Manufacturing
Scott County Public Schools	Education
Tokico (USA) (Hitachi)	Manufacturing
Toyota Motor Manufacturing	Manufacturing
Transportation Cabinet of Kentucky	Government
University of Kentucky	Education
Veterans Medical Center	Healthcare
Wal-Mart Stores	Retail
Xerox	Outsourcing

Note: Companies shown are located within the Lexington-Fayette, KY Metropolitan Statistical Area.
Source: Hoovers.com; Wikipedia

PUBLIC SAFETY

Crime Rate

Area	Total Crime	Violent Crime Rate				Property Crime Rate		
		Murder	Rape[3]	Robbery	Aggrav. Assault	Burglary	Larceny -Theft	Motor Vehicle Theft
City	3,191.6	8.6	54.6	102.8	154.1	445.0	2,108.3	318.2
Suburbs[1]	2,178.6	1.5	29.6	28.6	75.6	317.7	1,508.9	216.6
Metro[2]	2,811.4	5.9	45.2	75.0	124.6	397.2	1,883.4	280.1
U.S.	2,356.7	6.5	38.4	73.9	279.7	314.2	1,398.0	246.0

Note: Figures are crimes per 100,000 population; (1) All areas within the metro area that are located outside the city limits; (2) Figures cover the Lexington-Fayette, KY Metropolitan Statistical Area; (3) All figures shown were reported using the revised Uniform Crime Reporting (UCR) definition of rape; Due to the transition to the National Incident-Based Reporting System (NIBRS), limited city and metro area data was released for 2021.
Source: FBI Uniform Crime Reports, 2020

Hate Crimes

Area	Number of Quarters Reported	Number of Incidents per Bias Motivation					
		Race/Ethnicity/ Ancestry	Religion	Sexual Orientation	Disability	Gender	Gender Identity
City[1]	4	18	5	6	0	0	2
U.S.	4	5,227	1,244	1,110	130	75	266

Note: (1) Figures include one incident reported with more than one bias motivation; Due to the transition to the National Incident-Based Reporting System (NIBRS), limited crime data was released for 2021.
Source: Federal Bureau of Investigation, Hate Crime Statistics 2020

Identity Theft Consumer Reports

Area	Reports	Reports per 100,000 Population	Rank[2]
MSA[1]	761	148	258
U.S.	1,108,609	339	-

Note: (1) Figures cover the Lexington-Fayette, KY Metropolitan Statistical Area; (2) Rank ranges from 1 to 391 where 1 indicates greatest number of identity theft reports per 100,000 population
Source: Federal Trade Commission, Consumer Sentinel Network Data Book 2022

Fraud and Other Consumer Reports

Area	Reports	Reports per 100,000 Population	Rank[2]
MSA[1]	4,263	829	196
U.S.	4,064,520	1,245	-

Note: (1) Figures cover the Lexington-Fayette, KY Metropolitan Statistical Area; (2) Rank ranges from 1 to 391 where 1 indicates greatest number of fraud and other consumer reports per 100,000 population
Source: Federal Trade Commission, Consumer Sentinel Network Data Book 2022

POLITICS

2020 Presidential Election Results

Area	Biden	Trump	Jorgensen	Hawkins	Other
Fayette County	59.2	38.5	1.6	0.1	0.6
U.S.	51.3	46.8	1.2	0.3	0.5

Note: Results are percentages and may not add to 100% due to rounding
Source: Dave Leip's Atlas of U.S. Presidential Elections

SPORTS

Professional Sports Teams

Team Name	League	Year Established

No teams are located in the metro area
Source: Wikipedia, Major Professional Sports Teams of the United States and Canada, April 12, 2023

CLIMATE

Average and Extreme Temperatures

Temperature	Jan	Feb	Mar	Apr	May	Jun	Jul	Aug	Sep	Oct	Nov	Dec	Yr.
Extreme High (°F)	76	75	82	88	92	101	103	103	103	91	83	75	103
Average High (°F)	40	44	54	66	75	83	86	85	79	68	55	44	65
Average Temp. (°F)	32	36	45	55	64	73	76	75	69	57	46	36	55
Average Low (°F)	24	26	34	44	54	62	66	65	58	46	36	28	45
Extreme Low (°F)	-21	-15	-2	18	26	39	47	42	35	20	-3	-19	-21

Note: Figures cover the years 1948-1990
Source: National Climatic Data Center, International Station Meteorological Climate Summary, 9/96

Average Precipitation/Snowfall/Humidity

Precip./Humidity	Jan	Feb	Mar	Apr	May	Jun	Jul	Aug	Sep	Oct	Nov	Dec	Yr.
Avg. Precip. (in.)	3.6	3.4	4.4	3.9	4.3	4.0	4.8	3.7	3.0	2.4	3.5	3.9	45.1
Avg. Snowfall (in.)	6	5	3	Tr	Tr	0	0	0	0	Tr	1	3	17
Avg. Rel. Hum. 7am (%)	81	80	77	75	78	80	83	85	85	83	81	81	81
Avg. Rel. Hum. 4pm (%)	67	61	55	51	54	54	56	55	54	53	60	66	57

Note: Figures cover the years 1948-1990; Tr = Trace amounts (<0.05 in. of rain; <0.5 in. of snow)
Source: National Climatic Data Center, International Station Meteorological Climate Summary, 9/96

Weather Conditions

Temperature			Daytime Sky			Precipitation		
10°F & below	32°F & below	90°F & above	Clear	Partly cloudy	Cloudy	0.01 inch or more precip.	0.1 inch or more snow/ice	Thunder-storms
11	96	22	86	136	143	129	17	44

Note: Figures are average number of days per year and cover the years 1948-1990
Source: National Climatic Data Center, International Station Meteorological Climate Summary, 9/96

HAZARDOUS WASTE

Superfund Sites

The Lexington-Fayette, KY metro area has no sites on the EPA's Superfund Final National Priorities List. There are a total of 1,165 Superfund sites with a status of proposed or final on the list in the U.S.
U.S. Environmental Protection Agency, National Priorities List, April 12, 2023

AIR QUALITY

Air Quality Trends: Ozone

	1990	1995	2000	2005	2010	2015	2018	2019	2020	2021
MSA[1]	0.078	0.088	0.077	0.078	0.070	0.069	0.063	0.059	0.060	0.064
U.S.	0.087	0.089	0.081	0.080	0.072	0.067	0.069	0.065	0.065	0.067

Note: (1) Data covers the Lexington-Fayette, KY Metropolitan Statistical Area. The values shown are the composite ozone concentration averages among trend sites based on the highest fourth daily maximum 8-hour concentration in parts per million. These trends are based on sites having an adequate record of monitoring data during the trend period. Data from exceptional events are included.
Source: U.S. Environmental Protection Agency, Air Quality Monitoring Information, "Air Quality Trends by City, 1990-2021"

Air Quality Index

Area	Percent of Days when Air Quality was...[2]					AQI Statistics[2]	
	Good	Moderate	Unhealthy for Sensitive Groups	Unhealthy	Very Unhealthy	Maximum	Median
MSA[1]	77.4	22.0	0.6	0.0	0.0	108	40

Note: (1) Data covers the Lexington-Fayette, KY Metropolitan Statistical Area; (2) Based on 363 days with AQI data in 2021. Air Quality Index (AQI) is an index for reporting daily air quality. EPA calculates the AQI for five major air pollutants regulated by the Clean Air Act: ground-level ozone, particle pollution (aka particulate matter), carbon monoxide, sulfur dioxide, and nitrogen dioxide. The AQI runs from 0 to 500. The higher the AQI value, the greater the level of air pollution and the greater the health concern. There are six AQI categories: "Good" AQI is between 0 and 50. Air quality is considered satisfactory; "Moderate" AQI is between 51 and 100. Air quality is acceptable; "Unhealthy for Sensitive Groups" When AQI values are between 101 and 150, members of sensitive groups may experience health effects; "Unhealthy" When AQI values are between 151 and 200 everyone may begin to experience health effects; "Very Unhealthy" AQI values between 201 and 300 trigger a health alert; "Hazardous" AQI values over 300 trigger warnings of emergency conditions (not shown).
Source: U.S. Environmental Protection Agency, Air Quality Index Report, 2021

Air Quality Index Pollutants

Area	Percent of Days when AQI Pollutant was...[2]					
	Carbon Monoxide	Nitrogen Dioxide	Ozone	Sulfur Dioxide	Particulate Matter 2.5	Particulate Matter 10
MSA[1]	0.0	5.5	38.3	(3)	55.9	0.3

Note: (1) Data covers the Lexington-Fayette, KY Metropolitan Statistical Area; (2) Based on 363 days with AQI data in 2021. The Air Quality Index (AQI) is an index for reporting daily air quality. EPA calculates the AQI for five major air pollutants regulated by the Clean Air Act: ground-level ozone, particle pollution (also known as particulate matter), carbon monoxide, sulfur dioxide, and nitrogen dioxide. The AQI runs from 0 to 500. The higher the AQI value, the greater the level of air pollution and the greater the health concern; (3) Sulfur dioxide is no longer included in this table (as of December 8, 2021) because SO_2 concentrations tend to be very localized and not necessarily representative of broad geographical areas like counties and CBSAs.
Source: U.S. Environmental Protection Agency, Air Quality Index Report, 2021

Maximum Air Pollutant Concentrations: Particulate Matter, Ozone, CO and Lead

	Particulate Matter 10 (ug/m^3)	Particulate Matter 2.5 Wtd AM (ug/m^3)	Particulate Matter 2.5 24-Hr (ug/m^3)	Ozone (ppm)	Carbon Monoxide (ppm)	Lead (ug/m^3)
MSA[1] Level	27	9.6	23	0.064	n/a	n/a
NAAQS[2]	150	15	35	0.075	9	0.15
Met NAAQS[2]	Yes	Yes	Yes	Yes	n/a	n/a

Note: (1) Data covers the Lexington-Fayette, KY Metropolitan Statistical Area; Data from exceptional events are included; (2) National Ambient Air Quality Standards; ppm = parts per million; ug/m³ = micrograms per cubic meter; n/a not available.
Concentrations: Particulate Matter 10 (coarse particulate)—highest second maximum 24-hour concentration; Particulate Matter 2.5 Wtd AM (fine particulate)—highest weighted annual mean concentration; Particulate Matter 2.5 24-Hour (fine particulate)—highest 98th percentile 24-hour concentration; Ozone—highest fourth daily maximum 8-hour concentration; Carbon Monoxide—highest second maximum non-overlapping 8-hour concentration; Lead—maximum running 3-month average
Source: U.S. Environmental Protection Agency, Air Quality Monitoring Information, "Air Quality Statistics by City, 2021"

Maximum Air Pollutant Concentrations: Nitrogen Dioxide and Sulfur Dioxide

	Nitrogen Dioxide AM (ppb)	Nitrogen Dioxide 1-Hr (ppb)	Sulfur Dioxide AM (ppb)	Sulfur Dioxide 1-Hr (ppb)	Sulfur Dioxide 24-Hr (ppb)
MSA[1] Level	6	n/a	n/a	5	n/a
NAAQS[2]	53	100	30	75	140
Met NAAQS[2]	Yes	n/a	n/a	Yes	n/a

Note: (1) Data covers the Lexington-Fayette, KY Metropolitan Statistical Area; Data from exceptional events are included; (2) National Ambient Air Quality Standards; ppm = parts per million; ug/m³ = micrograms per cubic meter; n/a not available.
Concentrations: Nitrogen Dioxide AM—highest arithmetic mean concentration; Nitrogen Dioxide 1-Hr—highest 98th percentile 1-hour daily maximum concentration; Sulfur Dioxide AM—highest annual mean concentration; Sulfur Dioxide 1-Hr—highest 99th percentile 1-hour daily maximum concentration; Sulfur Dioxide 24-Hr—highest second maximum 24-hour concentration
Source: U.S. Environmental Protection Agency, Air Quality Monitoring Information, "Air Quality Statistics by City, 2021"

Louisville, Kentucky

Background

Louisville was founded in 1778, when George Rogers Clark, on his way to capture British Fort Vincennes, established a base on an island above the Falls of the Ohio River. Shortly thereafter a settlement grew on the south side of the river. Two years later the Virginia state legislature named the town Louisville to pay homage to King Louis XVI of France, who had allied his country with America during the American Revolution.

The Falls forced people traveling down the Ohio to use the portage of Louisville, which helped the town grow in the early nineteenth century. Kentucky incorporated the town as a city in 1828. Two years later, the Portland Canal opened, allowing boats to go around the rapids, thereby increasing river traffic and assisting the city's growth. In the next several years, the arrival of the railroad would link the town to much of the South. The cultivation of tobacco became important to the state in the 1830s, when Louisville became a prominent processing site.

The Civil War was an interesting period in the city's history, as adherents to both the North and the South walked the city's streets. Yet the North had the upper hand, and Louisville quickly became a supply center for Union armies marching south.

The postwar period saw boom times for Louisville, and by the end of the nineteenth century the population topped 200,000. In 1937, after the Ohio River flooded the city's environs, a floodwall was built to prevent such a catastrophe from recurring. World War II saw Louisville rebound as it became an important center for munitions production. After the war, the city desegregated its schools in a calm fashion, without the trouble seen in so many other areas.

The Kentucky Derby horserace—the annual Run for the Roses—has been held at Churchill Downs in Louisville since 1875, earning the city the nickname, "Derby Town." The fabled track now includes the Grandstand Terrace and Rooftop Garden and close to 2,400 new seats. A new stadium for the city's pro soccer team opened in 2020.

The city serves as an important corporate command post, and a number of major companies do business there, including the United Postal Service, Ford Motor Company, Humana, Walmart, Amazon, and Spectrum. Louisville also produces one third of all bourbon whiskey. Major bourbon maker Brown-Forman is headquartered in the city, and in 2021 announced an expansion to double its distillery, with completion expected in 2024. Louisville also has an official Bourbon District, home to several other distilleries.

Louisville has maintained its importance as a vital center of transportation, with two ports on the Ohio River and three interstate highways intersecting the city. The Louisville International Airport serves as the international hub for United Parcel Service with a 10,000-foot taxiway. The Louisville metro area offers new businesses many incentives, including a foreign trade zone.

The "NuLu" District, formally called the East Market District, is hopping with shops, restaurants and breweries established in the old warehouse district. City attractions include the Kentucky Science Center with interactive exhibits and Science Education Wing, the Louisville Zoo, the Kentucky Derby Museum, Kentucky Kingdom and Hurricane Bay, the Louisville Slugger Museum & Factor (with the world's largest bat), and the Kentucky Exposition Center. The Speed Art Museum, the oldest (1927) and largest art museum in the state, reopened in 2016 with 220,000 of renovated space after a 3-year closure.

The city's climate is a typical continental one. Look for cool winters, warm summers, and thunderstorms with intense rainfall during spring and summer. Fall tends to be the driest, and snow can arrive anytime from November through March, although all precipitation varies from year to year.

Rankings

General Rankings

- For its "Best for Vets: Places to Live 2019" rankings, *Military Times* evaluated 599 cities (83 large, 234 medium, 282 small) and compared the locations across three broad categories: veteran and military culture/services; economic indicators; and livability factors such as health, crime, traffic, and school quality. Louisville ranked #19 out of the top 25, in the large city category (population of more than 250,000). Data points more specific to veterans and the military weighed more heavily than others. *rebootcamp.militarytimes.com, "Military Times Best Places to Live 2019," September 10, 2018*

- Louisville was selected as an "All-America City" by the National Civic League. The All-America City Award recognizes civic excellence and in 2022 honored 10 communities that best exemplify the spirit of grassroots citizen involvement and cross-sector collaborative problem solving to collectively tackle pressing and complex issues. This year's theme was: "Housing as a Platform to Promote Early School Success and Equitable Learning Recovery." *National Civic League, "2022 All-America City Awards," July 21, 2022*

- In their ninth annual survey, Livability.com looked at data for more than 2,300 mid-sized U.S. cities to determine the rankings for Livability's "Top 100 Best Places to Live" in 2022. Louisville ranked #55. Criteria: housing and economy; social and civic engagement; education; demographics; health care options; transportation & infrastructure; and community amenities. *Livability.com, "Top 100 Best Places to Live 2022" July 19, 2022*

Business/Finance Rankings

- Based on metro area social media reviews, the employment opinion group Glassdoor surveyed 50 of the most populous U.S. metro areas and equally weighed cost of living, hiring opportunity, and job satisfaction to compose a list of "25 Best Cities for Jobs." Median pay and home value, and number of active job openings were also factored in. The Louisville metro area was ranked #13 in overall job satisfaction. *www.glassdoor.com, "Best Cities for Jobs," February 25, 2020*

- The Brookings Institution ranked the nation's largest cities based on income inequality. Louisville was ranked #74 (#1 = greatest inequality). Criteria: the "95/20 ratio," a figure representing the income at which a household earns more than 95 percent of all other households, divided by the income at which a household earns more than only 20 percent of all other households. *Brookings Institution, "Household Income Inequality, Largest Cities of 97 Large U.S. Metro Areas, 2014-2016," February 5, 2018*

- The Brookings Institution ranked the 100 largest metro areas in the U.S. based on income inequality. Louisville was ranked #74 (#1 = greatest inequality). Criteria: the "95/20 ratio," a figure representing the income at which a household earns more than 95 percent of all other households, divided by the income at which a household earns more than only 20 percent of all other households. *Brookings Institution, "Household Income Inequality, 100 Largest U.S. Metro Areas, 2014-2016," February 5, 2018*

- The Louisville metro area appeared on the Milken Institute "2022 Best Performing Cities" list. Rank: #115 out of 200 large metro areas (population over 250,000). Criteria: job growth; wage and salary growth; high-tech output growth; housing affordability; household broadband access. *Milken Institute, "Best-Performing Cities 2022," March 28, 2022*

- *Forbes* ranked the 200 most populous metro areas to determine the nation's "Best Places for Business and Careers." The Louisville metro area was ranked #92. Criteria: costs (business and living); job growth (past and projected); income growth; quality of life; educational attainment (college and high school); projected economic growth; cultural and leisure opportunities; workplace tolerance laws; net migration patterns. *Forbes, "The Best Places for Business and Careers 2019: Seattle Still On Top," October 30, 2019*

Dating/Romance Rankings

- Louisville was ranked #14 out of 25 cities that stood out for inspiring romance and attracting diners on the website OpenTable.com. Criteria: percentage of people who dined out on Valentine's Day in 2018; percentage of romantic restaurants as rated by OpenTable diner reviews; and percentage of tables seated for two. *OpenTable, "25 Most Romantic Cities in America for 2019," February 7, 2019*

Education Rankings

- Personal finance website *WalletHub* analyzed the 150 largest U.S. metropolitan statistical areas to determine where the most educated Americans are putting their degrees to work. Criteria: education levels; percentage of workers with degrees; education quality and attainment gap; public school quality rankings; quality and enrollment of each metro area's universities. Louisville was ranked #94 (#1 = most educated city). *www.WalletHub.com, "Most & Least Educated Cities in America," July 18, 2022*

- Louisville was selected as one of America's most literate cities. The city ranked #44 out of the 84 largest U.S. cities. Criteria: number of booksellers; library resources; Internet resources; educational attainment; periodical publishing resources; newspaper circulation. *Central Connecticut State University, "America's Most Literate Cities, 2018," February 2019*

Environmental Rankings

- The U.S. Environmental Protection Agency (EPA) released its list of mid-size U.S. metropolitan areas with the most ENERGY STAR certified buildings in 2022. The Louisville metro area was ranked #5 out of 10. *U.S. Environmental Protection Agency, "2023 Energy Star Top Cities," April 26, 2023*

- The U.S. Conference of Mayors and Walmart Stores sponsor the Mayors' Climate Protection Awards Program which recognize mayors for outstanding and innovative practices that address the climate crisis: increase energy efficiency in their cities, reduce carbon emissions and expand renewable energy. Louisville received an Honorable Mention in the large city category. *U.S. Conference of Mayors, "2022 Mayors' Climate Protection Awards," June 3, 2022*

- Louisville was highlighted as one of the 25 metro areas most polluted by year-round particle pollution (Annual PM 2.5) in the U.S. during 2019 through 2021. The area ranked #22. *American Lung Association, "State of the Air 2023," April 19, 2023*

Health/Fitness Rankings

- For each of the 100 largest cities in the United States, the American Fitness Index®, compiled in partnership between the American College of Sports Medicine and the Elevance Health Foundation, evaluated community infrastructure and 34 health behaviors including preventive health, levels of chronic disease conditions, food insecurity, sleep quality, pedestrian safety, air quality, and community/environment resources that support physical activity. Louisville ranked #96 for "community fitness." *americanfitnessindex.org, "2022 ACSM American Fitness Index Summary Report," July 12, 2022*

- The Louisville metro area was identified as one of the worst cities for bed bugs in America by pest control company Orkin. The area ranked #49 out of 50 based on the number of bed bug treatments Orkin performed from December 2021 to November 2022. *Orkin, "The Windy City Can't Blow Bed Bugs Away: Chicago Ranks #1 For Third Consecutive Year On Orkin's Bed Bug Cities List," January 9, 2023*

- Louisville was identified as a "2022 Spring Allergy Capital." The area ranked #46 out of 100. Three groups of factors were used to identify the most challenging cities for people with allergies during the spring season: annual spring pollen scores; over the counter allergy medicine use; number of board-certified allergy specialists. *Asthma and Allergy Foundation of America, "Spring Allergy Capitals 2022," March 2, 2022*

- Louisville was identified as a "2022 Fall Allergy Capital." The area ranked #43 out of 100. Three groups of factors were used to identify the most challenging cities for people with allergies during the fall season: annual fall pollen scores; over the counter allergy medicine use; number of board-certified allergy specialists. *Asthma and Allergy Foundation of America, "Fall Allergy Capitals 2022," March 2, 2022*

- Louisville was identified as a "2022 Asthma Capital." The area ranked #17 out of the nation's 100 largest metropolitan areas. Criteria: estimated asthma prevalence; asthma-related mortality; and ER visits due to asthma. Risk factors analyzed but not factored in the rankings: annual pollen score; annual air quality; public smoking laws; access to board-certified asthma specialists; rescue and controller medication use; uninsured rate; poverty rate. *Asthma and Allergy Foundation of America, "Asthma Capitals 2022: The Most Challenging Places to Live With Asthma," September 14, 2022*

Real Estate Rankings

- *WalletHub* compared the most populated U.S. cities to determine which had the best markets for real estate agents. Louisville ranked #142 where demand was high and pay was the best. Criteria: sales per agent; annual median wage for real-estate agents; monthly average starting salary for real estate agents; real estate job density and competition; unemployment rate; home turnover rate; housing-market health index; and other relevant metrics. *www.WalletHub.com, "2021 Best Places to Be a Real Estate Agent," May 12, 2021*

- The Louisville metro area appeared on Realtor.com's list of hot housing markets to watch in 2023. The area ranked #3. Criteria: forecasted home price and sales growth; overall economy; population trends. *Realtor.com®, "Top 10 Housing Markets Positioned for Growth in 2023," December 7, 2022*
- Louisville was ranked #63 out of 235 metro areas in terms of housing affordability in 2022 by the National Association of Home Builders (#1 = most affordable). Criteria: the share of homes sold in that area affordable to a family earning the local median income, based on standard mortgage underwriting criteria. *National Association of Home Builders®, NAHB-Wells Fargo Housing Opportunity Index, 4th Quarter 2022*

Safety Rankings

- Allstate ranked the 200 largest cities in America in terms of driver safety. Louisville ranked #98. Criteria: internal property damage claims over a two-year period from January 2016 to December 2017. The report helps increase the importance of safety and awareness behind the wheel. *Allstate, "Allstate America's Best Drivers Report, 2019" June 24, 2019*
- Louisville was identified as one of the most dangerous cities in America by NeighborhoodScout. The city ranked #82 out of 100 (#1 = most dangerous). Criteria: number of violent crimes per 1,000 residents. The editors evaluated cities with 25,000 or more residents. *NeighborhoodScout.com, "2023 Top 100 Most Dangerous Cities in the U.S.," January 12, 2023*

Seniors/Retirement Rankings

- From its Best Cities for Successful Aging indexes, the Milken Institute generated rankings for metropolitan areas, weighing data in nine categories—health care, wellness, living arrangements, transportation and convenience, financial characteristics, education, employment, community engagement, and overall livability. The Louisville metro area was ranked #79 overall in the large metro area category. *Milken Institute, "Best Cities for Successful Aging, 2017" March 14, 2017*

Sports/Recreation Rankings

- Louisville was chosen as one of America's best cities for bicycling. The city ranked #37 out of 50. Criteria: cycling infrastructure that is safe and friendly for all ages; energy and bike culture. The editors evaluated cities with populations of 100,000 or more. *Bicycling, "The 50 Best Bike Cities in America," October 10, 2018*

Women/Minorities Rankings

- Personal finance website *WalletHub* compared more than 180 U.S. cities across two key dimensions, "Hispanic Business-Friendliness" and "Hispanic Purchasing Power," to arrive at the most favorable conditions for Hispanic entrepreneurs. Louisville was ranked #138 out of 182. Criteria includes: share of Hispanic-Owned Businesses; Hispanic entrepreneurship rate to median annual income of Hispanics; Small Business-Friendliness score; cost of living; and number of Hispanics with at least a bachelor's degree. *WalletHub.com, "2019's Best Cities for Hispanic Entrepreneurs," May 1, 2019*

Miscellaneous Rankings

- Louisville was selected as a 2022 Digital Cities Survey winner. The city ranked #7 in the large city (500,000 or more population) category. The survey examined and assessed how city governments are utilizing technology to continue innovation, engage with residents, and persevere through the challenges of the pandemic. Survey questions focused on ten initiatives: cybersecurity; citizen experience; disaster recovery; business intelligence; IT personnel; data governance; business automation; IT governance; infrastructure modernization; and broadband connectivity. *Center for Digital Government, "2022 Digital Cities Survey," November 10, 2022*
- *WalletHub* compared the 150 most populated U.S. cities to determine their operating efficiency. A "Quality of Services" score was constructed for each city and then divided by the total budget per capita to reveal which were managed the best. Louisville ranked #31. Criteria: financial stability; economy; education; safety; health; infrastructure and pollution. *www.WalletHub.com, "2022's Best- & Worst-Run Cities in America," June 21, 2022*
- Louisville was selected as one of "America's Friendliest Cities." The city ranked #8 in the "Friendliest" category. Respondents to an online survey were asked to rate 38 top urban destinations in the United States as to general friendliness, as well as manners, politeness and warm disposition. *Travel + Leisure, "America's Friendliest Cities," October 20, 2017*

Business Environment

DEMOGRAPHICS

Population Growth

Area	1990 Census	2000 Census	2010 Census	2020 Census	Population Growth (%)	
					1990-2020	2010-2020
City	269,160	256,231	597,337	386,884	43.7	-35.2
MSA[1]	1,055,973	1,161,975	1,283,566	1,285,439	21.7	0.1
U.S.	248,709,873	281,421,906	308,745,538	331,449,281	33.3	7.4

Note: (1) Figures cover the Louisville/Jefferson County, KY-IN Metropolitan Statistical Area
Source: U.S. Census Bureau, 1990 Census, 2000 Census, 2010 Census, 2020 Census

Race

Area	White Alone[2] (%)	Black Alone[2] (%)	Asian Alone[2] (%)	AIAN[3] Alone[2] (%)	NHOPI[4] Alone[2] (%)	Other Race Alone[2] (%)	Two or More Races (%)
City	66.3	17.5	3.5	0.3	0.1	4.2	8.0
MSA[1]	72.7	14.8	2.5	0.3	0.1	2.9	6.8
U.S.	61.6	12.4	6.0	1.1	0.2	8.4	10.2

Note: (1) Figures cover the Louisville/Jefferson County, KY-IN Metropolitan Statistical Area; (2) Alone is defined as not being in combination with one or more other races; (3) American Indian and Alaska Native; (4) Native Hawaiian and Other Pacific Islander
Source: U.S. Census Bureau, 2020 Census

Hispanic or Latino Origin

Area	Total (%)	Mexican (%)	Puerto Rican (%)	Cuban (%)	Other (%)
City	6.5	2.3	0.4	2.3	1.4
MSA[1]	5.3	2.4	0.4	1.3	1.1
U.S.	18.4	11.2	1.8	0.7	4.7

Note: Persons of Hispanic or Latino origin can be of any race; (1) Figures cover the Louisville/Jefferson County, KY-IN Metropolitan Statistical Area
Source: U.S. Census Bureau, 2017-2021 American Community Survey 5-Year Estimates

Age

Area	Percent of Population									Median Age
	Under Age 5	Age 5–19	Age 20–34	Age 35–44	Age 45–54	Age 55–64	Age 65–74	Age 75–84	Age 85+	
City	5.9	19.2	18.9	12.8	12.8	13.4	10.0	4.8	1.9	39.5
MSA[1]	5.8	18.9	19.5	12.9	12.6	13.6	10.2	4.7	1.8	39.3
U.S.	5.6	19.2	20.2	12.7	12.4	13.1	10.0	4.9	1.9	38.8

Note: (1) Figures cover the Louisville/Jefferson County, KY-IN Metropolitan Statistical Area
Source: U.S. Census Bureau, 2020 Census

Disability by Age

Area	All Ages	Under 18 Years Old	18 to 64 Years Old	65 Years and Over
City	14.3	4.5	12.8	35.6
MSA[1]	13.9	4.4	12.1	35.1
U.S.	12.6	4.4	10.3	33.4

Note: Figures show percent of the civilian noninstitutionalized population that reported having a disability. Disability status is determined from six types of difficulty: vision, hearing, cognitive, ambulatory, self-care, and independent living. For children under 5 years old, hearing and vision difficulty are used to determine disability status. For children between the ages of 5 and 14, disability status is determined from hearing, vision, cognitive, ambulatory, and self-care difficulties. For people aged 15 years and older, they are considered to have a disability if they have difficulty with any one of the six difficulty types; Note: (1) Figures cover the Louisville/Jefferson County, KY-IN Metropolitan Statistical Area
Source: U.S. Census Bureau, 2017-2021 American Community Survey 5-Year Estimates

Ancestry

Area	German	Irish	English	American	Italian	Polish	French[2]	Scottish	Dutch
City	15.2	11.5	9.3	6.5	2.6	1.1	1.7	1.6	0.9
MSA[1]	17.3	12.5	10.8	8.1	2.5	1.2	1.9	1.9	1.0
U.S.	12.8	9.6	8.1	5.7	5.0	2.7	2.2	1.6	1.1

Note: Figures are the percentage of the total population reporting a particular ancestry. The nine most commonly reported ancestries in the U.S. are shown. Figures include multiple ancestries (e.g. if a person reported being Irish and Italian, they were included in both columns); (1) Figures cover the Louisville/Jefferson County, KY-IN Metropolitan Statistical Area; (2) Excludes Basque
Source: U.S. Census Bureau, 2017-2021 American Community Survey 5-Year Estimates

Foreign-born Population

Area	Any Foreign Country	Asia	Mexico	Europe	Caribbean	Central America[2]	South America	Africa	Canada
							Percent of Population Born in		
City	8.6	2.6	0.8	0.9	2.0	0.5	0.3	1.4	0.2
MSA[1]	6.4	2.0	0.9	0.7	1.1	0.4	0.2	0.9	0.1
U.S.	13.6	4.2	3.3	1.5	1.4	1.1	1.1	0.8	0.2

Note: (1) Figures cover the Louisville/Jefferson County, KY-IN Metropolitan Statistical Area; (2) Excludes Mexico.
Source: U.S. Census Bureau, 2017-2021 American Community Survey 5-Year Estimates

Household Size

Area	One	Two	Three	Four	Five	Six	Seven or More	Average Household Size
			Persons in Household (%)					
City	33.8	33.0	15.1	10.7	5.0	1.4	0.9	2.40
MSA[1]	30.3	34.5	15.6	11.7	5.3	1.7	0.9	2.50
U.S.	28.1	33.8	15.5	12.9	6.0	2.3	1.4	2.60

Note: (1) Figures cover the Louisville/Jefferson County, KY-IN Metropolitan Statistical Area
Source: U.S. Census Bureau, 2017-2021 American Community Survey 5-Year Estimates

Household Relationships

Area	House-holder	Opposite-sex Spouse	Same-sex Spouse	Opposite-sex Unmarried Partner	Same-sex Unmarried Partner	Child[2]	Grand-child	Other Relatives	Non-relatives
City	40.0	18.0	0.2	2.9	0.2	28.8	2.6	4.2	2.7
MSA[1]	40.5	17.7	0.2	2.8	0.2	27.6	2.5	3.6	2.9
U.S.	38.3	17.5	0.2	2.5	0.2	28.3	2.4	4.8	3.4

Note: Figures are percent of the total population; (1) Figures cover the Louisville/Jefferson County, KY-IN Metropolitan Statistical Area; (2) Includes biological, adopted, and stepchildren of the householder
Source: U.S. Census Bureau, 2020 Census

Gender

Area	Males	Females	Males per 100 Females
City	186,813	200,071	93.4
MSA[1]	628,220	657,219	95.6
U.S.	162,685,811	168,763,470	96.4

Note: (1) Figures cover the Louisville/Jefferson County, KY-IN Metropolitan Statistical Area
Source: U.S. Census Bureau, 2020 Census

Marital Status

Area	Never Married	Now Married[2]	Separated	Widowed	Divorced
City	36.9	42.0	2.1	6.3	12.7
MSA[1]	31.9	47.5	1.8	6.0	12.9
U.S.	33.8	48.0	1.8	5.6	10.8

Note: Figures are percentages and cover the population 15 years of age and older; (1) Figures cover the Louisville/Jefferson County, KY-IN Metropolitan Statistical Area; (2) Excludes separated
Source: U.S. Census Bureau, 2017-2021 American Community Survey 5-Year Estimates

Religious Groups by Family

Area	Catholic	Baptist	Methodist	LDS[2]	Pentecostal	Lutheran	Islam	Adventist	Other
MSA[1]	11.9	14.5	3.2	0.8	0.9	0.5	1.0	1.0	12.4
U.S.	18.7	7.3	3.0	2.0	1.8	1.7	1.3	1.3	11.6

Note: Figures are the number of adherents as a percentage of the total population and cover the eight largest religious groups in the U.S; (1) Figures cover the Louisville/Jefferson County, KY-IN Metropolitan Statistical Area; (2) Church of Jesus Christ of Latter-day Saints
Sources: 2020 U.S. Religion Census, Association of Statisticians of American Religious Bodies; The Association of Religion Data Archives (ARDA)

Religious Groups by Tradition

Area	Catholic	Evangelical Protestant	Mainline Protestant	Black Protestant	Islam	Judaism	Hinduism	Orthodox	Buddhism
MSA[1]	11.9	21.1	5.0	4.6	1.0	0.2	0.4	0.2	0.2
U.S.	18.7	16.5	5.2	2.3	1.3	0.6	0.4	0.4	0.3

Note: Figures are the number of adherents as a percentage of the total population; (1) Figures cover the Louisville/Jefferson County, KY-IN Metropolitan Statistical Area
Sources: 2020 U.S. Religion Census, Association of Statisticians of American Religious Bodies; The Association of Religion Data Archives (ARDA)

Louisville, Kentucky   **253**

ECONOMY

Gross Metropolitan Product

Area	2020	2021	2022	2023	Rank[2]
MSA[1]	75.6	83.6	90.5	94.4	47

Note: Figures are in billions of dollars; (1) Figures cover the Louisville/Jefferson County, KY-IN Metropolitan Statistical Area; (2) Rank is based on 2021 data and ranges from 1 to 381
Source: U.S. Conference of Mayors, U.S. Metro Economies: U.S. Metros Compared to Global and State Economies, June 2022

Economic Growth

Area	2018-20 (%)	2021 (%)	2022 (%)	2023 (%)	Rank[2]
MSA[1]	-0.4	5.8	2.2	1.2	169
U.S.	-0.6	5.7	3.1	2.9	–

Note: Figures are real gross metropolitan product (GMP) growth rates and represent average annual percent change; (1) Figures cover the Louisville/Jefferson County, KY-IN Metropolitan Statistical Area; (2) Rank is based on 2020 2-year average annual percent change and ranges from 1 to 381
Source: U.S. Conference of Mayors, U.S. Metro Economies: U.S. Metros Compared to Global and State Economies, June 2022

Metropolitan Area Exports

Area	2016	2017	2018	2019	2020	2021	Rank[2]
MSA[1]	7,793.3	8,925.9	8,987.0	9,105.5	8,360.3	10,262.8	35

Note: Figures are in millions of dollars; (1) Figures cover the Louisville/Jefferson County, KY-IN Metropolitan Statistical Area; (2) Rank is based on 2021 data and ranges from 1 to 388
Source: U.S. Department of Commerce, International Trade Administration, Office of Trade and Economic Analysis, Industry and Analysis, Exports by Metropolitan Area, data extracted March 16, 2023

Building Permits

Area	Single-Family			Multi-Family			Total		
	2021	2022	Pct. Chg.	2021	2022	Pct. Chg.	2021	2022	Pct. Chg.
City	1,382	1,151	-16.7	466	1,637	251.3	1,848	2,788	50.9
MSA[1]	4,136	3,345	-19.1	1,372	2,111	53.9	5,508	5,456	-0.9
U.S.	1,115,400	975,600	-12.5	621,600	689,500	10.9	1,737,000	1,665,100	-4.1

Note: (1) Figures cover the Louisville/Jefferson County, KY-IN Metropolitan Statistical Area; Figures represent new, privately-owned housing units authorized (unadjusted data); All permit data are based on estimates with imputation
Source: U.S. Census Bureau, Manufacturing, Mining, and Construction Statistics, Building Permits, 2021, 2022

Bankruptcy Filings

Area	Business Filings			Nonbusiness Filings		
	2021	2022	% Chg.	2021	2022	% Chg.
Jefferson County	19	20	5.3	1,918	1,883	-1.8
U.S.	14,347	13,481	-6.0	399,269	374,240	-6.3

Note: Business filings include Chapter 7, Chapter 9, Chapter 11, Chapter 12, Chapter 13, Chapter 15, and Section 304; Nonbusiness filings include Chapter 7, Chapter 11, and Chapter 13
Source: Administrative Office of the U.S. Courts, Business and Nonbusiness Bankruptcy, County Cases Commenced by Chapter of the Bankruptcy Code, During the 12-Month Period Ending December 31, 2021 and Business and Nonbusiness Bankruptcy, County Cases Commenced by Chapter of the Bankruptcy Code, During the 12-Month Period Ending December 31, 2022

Housing Vacancy Rates

Area	Gross Vacancy Rate[2] (%)			Year-Round Vacancy Rate[3] (%)			Rental Vacancy Rate[4] (%)			Homeowner Vacancy Rate[5] (%)		
	2020	2021	2022	2020	2021	2022	2020	2021	2022	2020	2021	2022
MSA[1]	6.9	8.3	5.7	6.9	8.3	5.7	6.4	8.5	5.3	1.4	0.7	0.5
U.S.	10.6	10.8	10.5	8.2	8.4	8.2	6.3	6.1	5.8	1.0	0.9	0.8

Note: (1) Figures cover the Louisville/Jefferson County, KY-IN Metropolitan Statistical Area; (2) The percentage of the total housing inventory that is vacant; (3) The percentage of the housing inventory (excluding seasonal units) that is year-round vacant; (4) The percentage of rental inventory that is vacant for rent; (5) The percentage of homeowner inventory that is vacant for sale
Source: U.S. Census Bureau, Housing Vacancies and Homeownership Annual Statistics: 2020, 2021, 2022

INCOME

Income

Area	Per Capita ($)	Median Household ($)	Average Household ($)
City	34,195	58,357	81,393
MSA[1]	35,613	64,533	87,361
U.S.	37,638	69,021	97,196

Note: (1) Figures cover the Louisville/Jefferson County, KY-IN Metropolitan Statistical Area
Source: U.S. Census Bureau, 2017-2021 American Community Survey 5-Year Estimates

Household Income Distribution

Area	Percent of Households Earning							
	Under $15,000	$15,000 -$24,999	$25,000 -$34,999	$35,000 -$49,999	$50,000 -$74,999	$75,000 -$99,999	$100,000 -$149,999	$150,000 and up
City	11.2	8.8	9.5	13.3	18.5	12.3	14.3	11.9
MSA[1]	9.2	7.9	8.9	12.9	18.3	13.2	16.0	13.6
U.S.	9.4	7.8	8.2	11.4	16.8	12.8	16.3	17.3

Note: (1) Figures cover the Louisville/Jefferson County, KY-IN Metropolitan Statistical Area
Source: U.S. Census Bureau, 2017-2021 American Community Survey 5-Year Estimates

Poverty Rate

Area	All Ages	Under 18 Years Old	18 to 64 Years Old	65 Years and Over
City	15.2	22.6	14.0	9.4
MSA[1]	12.0	17.0	11.1	8.2
U.S.	12.6	17.0	11.8	9.6

Note: Figures are percentage of people whose income during the past 12 months was below the poverty level;
(1) Figures cover the Louisville/Jefferson County, KY-IN Metropolitan Statistical Area
Source: U.S. Census Bureau, 2017-2021 American Community Survey 5-Year Estimates

EMPLOYMENT

Labor Force and Employment

Area	Civilian Labor Force			Workers Employed		
	Dec. 2021	Dec. 2022	% Chg.	Dec. 2021	Dec. 2022	% Chg.
City	400,329	398,800	-0.4	384,379	387,119	0.7
MSA[1]	672,926	678,057	0.8	650,589	659,926	1.4
U.S.	161,696,000	164,224,000	1.6	155,732,000	158,872,000	2.0

Note: Data is not seasonally adjusted and covers workers 16 years of age and older; (1) Figures cover the Louisville/Jefferson County, KY-IN Metropolitan Statistical Area
Source: Bureau of Labor Statistics, Local Area Unemployment Statistics

Unemployment Rate

Area	2022											
	Jan.	Feb.	Mar.	Apr.	May	Jun.	Jul.	Aug.	Sep.	Oct.	Nov.	Dec.
City	4.7	3.9	4.7	3.1	4.1	3.8	4.1	3.4	3.0	3.5	3.3	2.9
MSA[1]	4.1	3.5	4.3	2.8	3.7	3.5	3.8	3.1	2.7	3.3	3.1	2.7
U.S.	4.4	4.1	3.8	3.3	3.4	3.8	3.8	3.8	3.3	3.4	3.4	3.3

Note: Data is not seasonally adjusted and covers workers 16 years of age and older; (1) Figures cover the Louisville/Jefferson County, KY-IN Metropolitan Statistical Area
Source: Bureau of Labor Statistics, Local Area Unemployment Statistics

Average Wages

Occupation	$/Hr.	Occupation	$/Hr.
Accountants and Auditors	37.30	Maintenance and Repair Workers	23.69
Automotive Mechanics	20.62	Marketing Managers	68.37
Bookkeepers	21.86	Network and Computer Systems Admin.	40.49
Carpenters	24.50	Nurses, Licensed Practical	25.32
Cashiers	12.91	Nurses, Registered	39.08
Computer Programmers	39.53	Nursing Assistants	16.62
Computer Systems Analysts	43.77	Office Clerks, General	18.11
Computer User Support Specialists	26.08	Physical Therapists	43.91
Construction Laborers	21.24	Physicians	144.45
Cooks, Restaurant	14.55	Plumbers, Pipefitters and Steamfitters	29.23
Customer Service Representatives	19.09	Police and Sheriff's Patrol Officers	25.96
Dentists	87.22	Postal Service Mail Carriers	27.28
Electricians	28.92	Real Estate Sales Agents	22.31
Engineers, Electrical	45.08	Retail Salespersons	15.89
Fast Food and Counter Workers	11.98	Sales Representatives, Technical/Scientific	49.19
Financial Managers	70.09	Secretaries, Exc. Legal/Medical/Executive	19.91
First-Line Supervisors of Office Workers	32.22	Security Guards	16.60
General and Operations Managers	48.89	Surgeons	194.02
Hairdressers/Cosmetologists	14.19	Teacher Assistants, Exc. Postsecondary*	15.01
Home Health and Personal Care Aides	15.29	Teachers, Secondary School, Exc. Sp. Ed.*	30.29
Janitors and Cleaners	14.97	Telemarketers	15.36
Landscaping/Groundskeeping Workers	16.00	Truck Drivers, Heavy/Tractor-Trailer	27.04
Lawyers	52.07	Truck Drivers, Light/Delivery Services	23.90
Maids and Housekeeping Cleaners	13.67	Waiters and Waitresses	13.48

Note: Wage data covers the Louisville/Jefferson County, KY-IN Metropolitan Statistical Area; (*) Hourly wages were calculated from annual wage data based on a 40 hour work week; n/a not available.
Source: Bureau of Labor Statistics, Metro Area Occupational Employment & Wage Estimates, May 2022

Employment by Industry

Sector	MSA[1]		U.S.
	Number of Employees	Percent of Total	Percent of Total
Construction, Mining, and Logging	29,900	4.3	5.4
Private Education and Health Services	101,100	14.7	16.1
Financial Activities	46,600	6.8	5.9
Government	72,100	10.5	14.5
Information	8,900	1.3	2.0
Leisure and Hospitality	64,200	9.3	10.3
Manufacturing	85,600	12.4	8.4
Other Services	25,300	3.7	3.7
Professional and Business Services	88,700	12.9	14.7
Retail Trade	64,800	9.4	10.2
Transportation, Warehousing, and Utilities	70,100	10.2	4.9
Wholesale Trade	32,000	4.6	3.9

Note: Figures are non-farm employment as of December 2022. Figures are not seasonally adjusted and include workers 16 years of age and older; (1) Figures cover the Louisville/Jefferson County, KY-IN Metropolitan Statistical Area
Source: Bureau of Labor Statistics, Current Employment Statistics, Employment, Hours, and Earnings

Employment by Occupation

Occupation Classification	City (%)	MSA[1] (%)	U.S. (%)
Management, Business, Science, and Arts	36.4	37.7	40.3
Natural Resources, Construction, and Maintenance	6.5	7.5	8.7
Production, Transportation, and Material Moving	19.9	18.9	13.1
Sales and Office	21.6	21.4	20.9
Service	15.6	14.5	17.0

Note: Figures cover employed civilians 16 years of age and older; (1) Figures cover the Louisville/Jefferson County, KY-IN Metropolitan Statistical Area
Source: U.S. Census Bureau, 2017-2021 American Community Survey 5-Year Estimates

Occupations with Greatest Projected Employment Growth: 2022 – 2024

Occupation[1]	2022 Employment	2024 Projected Employment	Numeric Employment Change	Percent Employment Change
Laborers and Freight, Stock, and Material Movers, Hand	64,300	66,790	2,490	3.9
Cooks, Restaurant	17,620	18,990	1,370	7.8
Home Health and Personal Care Aides	22,390	23,560	1,170	5.2
Stockers and Order Fillers	38,290	39,440	1,150	3.0
General and Operations Managers	46,980	47,930	950	2.0
Heavy and Tractor-Trailer Truck Drivers	31,920	32,870	950	3.0
Registered Nurses	40,910	41,740	830	2.0
Waiters and Waitresses	23,020	23,620	600	2.6
Industrial Truck and Tractor Operators	12,230	12,820	590	4.8
Light Truck or Delivery Services Drivers	16,050	16,610	560	3.5

Note: Projections cover Kentucky; (1) Sorted by numeric employment change
Source: www.projectionscentral.com, State Occupational Projections, 2022–2024 Short-Term Projections

Fastest-Growing Occupations: 2022 – 2024

Occupation[1]	2022 Employment	2024 Projected Employment	Numeric Employment Change	Percent Employment Change
Reservation and Transportation Ticket Agents and Travel Clerks	1,990	2,190	200	10.1
Nurse Practitioners	4,670	5,130	460	9.9
Logisticians	2,030	2,190	160	7.9
Hotel, Motel, and Resort Desk Clerks	3,820	4,120	300	7.9
Cooks, Restaurant	17,620	18,990	1,370	7.8
Sailors and Marine Oilers	1,680	1,810	130	7.7
Cargo and Freight Agents	2,850	3,060	210	7.4
Captains, Mates, and Pilots of Water Vessels	1,890	2,030	140	7.4
Farmworkers, Farm, Ranch, and Aquacultural Animals	1,960	2,100	140	7.1
Taxi Drivers	1,120	1,200	80	7.1

Note: Projections cover Kentucky; (1) Sorted by percent employment change and excludes occupations with numeric employment change less than 50
Source: www.projectionscentral.com, State Occupational Projections, 2022–2024 Short-Term Projections

256　Louisville, Kentucky

CITY FINANCES

City Government Finances

Component	2020 ($000)	2020 ($ per capita)
Total Revenues	1,602,491	2,090
Total Expenditures	2,042,942	2,664
Debt Outstanding	4,623,312	6,030
Cash and Securities[1]	1,844,416	2,405

Note: (1) Cash and security holdings of a government at the close of its fiscal year, including those of its dependent agencies, utilities, and liquor stores.
Source: U.S. Census Bureau, State & Local Government Finances 2020

City Government Revenue by Source

Source	2020 ($000)	2020 ($ per capita)	2020 (%)
General Revenue			
From Federal Government	178,199	232	11.1
From State Government	165,019	215	10.3
From Local Governments	84,570	110	5.3
Taxes			
Property	178,899	233	11.2
Sales and Gross Receipts	89,608	117	5.6
Personal Income	356,249	465	22.2
Corporate Income	53,371	70	3.3
Motor Vehicle License	369	0	0.0
Other Taxes	14,373	19	0.9
Current Charges	211,628	276	13.2
Liquor Store	0	0	0.0
Utility	211,431	276	13.2

Source: U.S. Census Bureau, State & Local Government Finances 2020

City Government Expenditures by Function

Function	2020 ($000)	2020 ($ per capita)	2020 (%)
General Direct Expenditures			
Air Transportation	111,775	145	5.5
Corrections	56,293	73	2.8
Education	58,528	76	2.9
Employment Security Administration	0	0	0.0
Financial Administration	47,105	61	2.3
Fire Protection	83,324	108	4.1
General Public Buildings	0	0	0.0
Governmental Administration, Other	54,294	70	2.7
Health	87,751	114	4.3
Highways	94,015	122	4.6
Hospitals	0	0	0.0
Housing and Community Development	52,877	69	2.6
Interest on General Debt	134,909	175	6.6
Judicial and Legal	12,039	15	0.6
Libraries	20,317	26	1.0
Parking	27,434	35	1.3
Parks and Recreation	60,105	78	2.9
Police Protection	173,719	226	8.5
Public Welfare	17,902	23	0.9
Sewerage	399,668	521	19.6
Solid Waste Management	33,301	43	1.6
Veterans' Services	0	0	0.0
Liquor Store	0	0	0.0
Utility	405,410	528	19.8

Source: U.S. Census Bureau, State & Local Government Finances 2020

TAXES

State Corporate Income Tax Rates

State	Tax Rate (%)	Income Brackets ($)	Num. of Brackets	Financial Institution Tax Rate (%)[a]	Federal Income Tax Ded.
Kentucky	5.0	Flat rate	1	5.0	No

Note: Tax rates as of January 1, 2023; (a) Rates listed are the corporate income tax rate applied to financial institutions or excise taxes based on income. Some states have other taxes based upon the value of deposits or shares.
Source: Federation of Tax Administrators, State Corporate Income Tax Rates, January 1, 2023

State Individual Income Tax Rates

State	Tax Rate (%)	Income Brackets ($)	Personal Exemptions ($)			Standard Ded. ($)	
			Single	Married	Depend.	Single	Married
Kentucky	4.5	Flat rate	None	None	None	2,980	5,960

Note: Tax rates as of January 1, 2023; Local- and county-level taxes are not included; Federal income tax is not deductible on state income tax returns
Source: Federation of Tax Administrators, State Individual Income Tax Rates, January 1, 2023

Various State Sales and Excise Tax Rates

State	State Sales Tax (%)	Gasoline[1] ($/gal.)	Cigarette[2] ($/pack)	Spirits[3] ($/gal.)	Wine[4] ($/gal.)	Beer[5] ($/gal.)	Recreational Marijuana (%)
Kentucky	6	0.26	1.10	9.25	3.58	0.93	Not legal

Note: All tax rates as of January 1, 2023; (1) The American Petroleum Institute has developed a methodology for determining the average tax rate on a gallon of fuel. Rates may include any of the following: excise taxes, environmental fees, storage tank fees, other fees or taxes, general sales tax, and local taxes; (2) The federal excise tax of $1.0066 per pack and local taxes are not included; (3) Rates are those applicable to off-premise sales of 40% alcohol by volume (a.b.v.) distilled spirits in 750ml containers. Local excise taxes are excluded; (4) Rates are those applicable to off-premise sales of 11% a.b.v. non-carbonated wine in 750ml containers; (5) Rates are those applicable to off-premise sales of 4.7% a.b.v. beer in 12 ounce containers.
Source: Tax Foundation, 2023 Facts & Figures: How Does Your State Compare?

State Business Tax Climate Index Rankings

State	Overall Rank	Corporate Tax Rank	Individual Income Tax Rank	Sales Tax Rank	Property Tax Rank	Unemployment Insurance Tax Rank
Kentucky	18	15	18	14	24	48

Note: The index is a measure of how each state's tax laws affect economic performance. The lower the rank, the more favorable a state's tax system is for business. States without a given tax are given a ranking of 1. The scores/rankings for the District of Columbia do not affect other states. The 2023 index represents the tax climate as of July 1, 2022.
Source: Tax Foundation, State Business Tax Climate Index 2023

TRANSPORTATION

Means of Transportation to Work

Area	Car/Truck/Van		Public Transportation			Bicycle	Walked	Other Means	Worked at Home
	Drove Alone	Car-pooled	Bus	Subway	Railroad				
City	76.6	8.4	2.6	0.0	0.0	0.3	1.9	1.6	8.5
MSA[1]	78.9	8.2	1.5	0.0	0.0	0.2	1.4	1.1	8.7
U.S.	73.2	8.6	2.0	1.6	0.5	0.5	2.5	1.5	9.7

Note: Figures are percentages and cover workers 16 years of age and older; (1) Figures cover the Louisville/Jefferson County, KY-IN Metropolitan Statistical Area
Source: U.S. Census Bureau, 2017-2021 American Community Survey 5-Year Estimates

Travel Time to Work

Area	Less Than 10 Minutes	10 to 19 Minutes	20 to 29 Minutes	30 to 44 Minutes	45 to 59 Minutes	60 to 89 Minutes	90 Minutes or More
City	9.6	32.6	31.4	19.1	3.9	2.0	1.4
MSA[1]	9.7	30.1	28.8	22.0	5.7	2.4	1.5
U.S.	12.4	28.5	21.0	20.9	8.2	6.2	2.9

Note: Note: Figures are percentages and include workers 16 years old and over; (1) Figures cover the Louisville/Jefferson County, KY-IN Metropolitan Statistical Area
Source: U.S. Census Bureau, 2017-2021 American Community Survey 5-Year Estimates

Key Congestion Measures

Measure	1990	2000	2010	2015	2020
Annual Hours of Delay, Total (000)	9,136	17,140	24,266	28,088	13,886
Annual Hours of Delay, Per Auto Commuter	26	32	37	43	22
Annual Congestion Cost, Per Auto Commuter ($)	432	608	685	732	386

Note: Covers the Louisville-Jefferson County KY-IN urban area
Source: Texas A&M Transportation Institute, 2021 Urban Mobility Report

Freeway Travel Time Index

Measure	1985	1990	1995	2000	2005	2010	2015	2020
Urban Area Index[1]	1.09	1.12	1.15	1.17	1.18	1.17	1.17	1.05
Urban Area Rank[1,2]	36	35	36	36	41	41	46	85

Note: Freeway Travel Time Index—the ratio of travel time in the peak period to the travel time at free-flow conditions. For example, a value of 1.30 indicates a 20-minute free-flow trip takes 26 minutes in the peak (20 minutes x 1.30 = 26 minutes); (1) Covers the Louisville-Jefferson County KY-IN urban area; (2) Rank is based on 101 larger urban areas (#1 = highest travel time index)
Source: Texas A&M Transportation Institute, 2021 Urban Mobility Report

Public Transportation

Agency Name / Mode of Transportation	Vehicles Operated in Maximum Service[1]	Annual Unlinked Passenger Trips[2] (in thous.)	Annual Passenger Miles[3] (in thous.)
Transit Authority of River City (TARC)			
Bus (directly operated)	174	4,396.8	18,686.3
Bus (purchased transportation)	2	6.0	15.2
Demand Response (purchased transportation)	38	127.5	1,203.0
Demand Response - Taxi	56	190.4	1,360.8

Note: (1) Number of revenue vehicles operated by the given mode and type of service to meet the annual maximum service requirement. This is the revenue vehicle count during the peak season of the year; on the week and day that maximum service is provided. Vehicles operated in maximum service (VOMS) exclude atypical days and one-time special events; (2) Number of passengers who boarded public transportation vehicles. Passengers are counted each time they board a vehicle no matter how many vehicles they use to travel from their origin to their destination. (3) Sum of the distances ridden by all passengers during the entire fiscal year.
Source: Federal Transit Administration, National Transit Database, 2021

Air Transportation

Airport Name and Code / Type of Service	Passenger Airlines[1]	Passenger Enplanements	Freight Carriers[2]	Freight (lbs)
Louisville International-Standiford Field (SDF)				
Domestic service (U.S. carriers - 2022)	30	1,892,605	20	3,006,625,840
International service (U.S. carriers - 2021)	1	82	6	242,324,059

Note: (1) Includes all U.S.-based major, minor and commuter airlines that carried at least one passenger during the year; (2) Includes all U.S.-based airlines and freight carriers that transported at least one pound of freight during the year.
Source: Bureau of Transportation Statistics, The Intermodal Transportation Database, Air Carriers: T-100 Domestic Market (U.S. Carriers), 2022; Bureau of Transportation Statistics, The Intermodal Transportation Database, Air Carriers: T-100 International Market (U.S. Carriers), 2021

BUSINESSES

Major Business Headquarters

Company Name	Industry	Rankings	
		Fortune[1]	Forbes[2]
Humana	Health care, insurance and managed care	40	-
Yum Brands	Food services	490	-

Note: (1) Companies that produce a 10-K are ranked 1 to 500 based on 2021 revenue; (2) All private companies with at least $2 billion in annual revenue through the end of their most current fiscal year are ranked 1 to 246; companies listed are headquartered in the city; dashes indicate no ranking
Source: Fortune, "Fortune 500," 2022; Forbes, "America's Largest Private Companies," 2022

Fastest-Growing Businesses

According to *Inc.*, Louisville is home to three of America's 500 fastest-growing private companies: **Guardian Baseball** (#180); **eBlu Solutions** (#189); **CRG Automation** (#387). Criteria: must be an independent, privately-held, for-profit, U.S. corporation, proprietorship or partnership as of December 31, 2021; revenues must be at least $100,000 in 2018 and $2 million in 2021; must have four-year operating/sales history. *Inc., "America's 500 Fastest-Growing Private Companies," 2022*

Living Environment

COST OF LIVING

Cost of Living Index

Composite Index	Groceries	Housing	Utilities	Trans-portation	Health Care	Misc. Goods/ Services
95.7	93.5	78.8	105.3	113.0	75.7	106.8

Note: The Cost of Living Index measures regional differences in the cost of consumer goods and services, excluding taxes and non-consumer expenditures, for professional and managerial households in the top income quintile. It is based on more than 50,000 prices covering almost 60 different items for which prices are collected three times a year by chambers of commerce, economic development organizations or university applied economic centers in each participating urban area. The numbers shown should be read as a percentage above or below the national average of 100. For example, a value of 115.4 in the groceries column indicates that grocery prices are 15.4% higher than the national average. Small differences in the index numbers should not be interpreted as significant; Figures cover the Louisville KY urban area.
Source: The Council for Community and Economic Research, Cost of Living Index, 2022

Grocery Prices

Area[1]	T-Bone Steak ($/pound)	Frying Chicken ($/pound)	Whole Milk ($/half gal.)	Eggs ($/dozen)	Orange Juice ($/64 oz.)	Coffee ($/11.5 oz.)
City[2]	14.49	1.35	1.51	1.48	3.61	4.28
Avg.	13.81	1.59	2.43	2.25	3.85	4.95
Min.	10.17	0.90	1.51	1.30	2.90	3.46
Max.	19.35	3.30	4.32	4.32	5.31	8.59

Note: (1) Values for the local area are compared with the average, minimum and maximum values for all 286 areas in the Cost of Living Index; (2) Figures cover the Louisville KY urban area; T-Bone Steak (price per pound); Frying Chicken (price per pound, whole fryer); Whole Milk (half gallon carton); Eggs (price per dozen, Grade A, large); Orange Juice (64 oz. Tropicana or Florida Natural); Coffee (11.5 oz. can, vacuum-packed, Maxwell House, Hills Bros, or Folgers).
Source: The Council for Community and Economic Research, Cost of Living Index, 2022

Housing and Utility Costs

Area[1]	New Home Price ($)	Apartment Rent ($/month)	All Electric ($/month)	Part Electric ($/month)	Other Energy ($/month)	Telephone ($/month)
City[2]	338,400	1,315	-	90.92	105.78	184.63
Avg.	450,913	1,371	176.41	99.93	76.96	190.22
Min.	229,283	546	100.84	31.56	27.15	174.27
Max.	2,434,977	4,569	356.86	249.59	272.24	208.31

Note: (1) Values for the local area are compared with the average, minimum and maximum values for all 286 areas in the Cost of Living Index; (2) Figures cover the Louisville KY urban area; New Home Price (2,400 sf living area, 8,000 sf lot, in urban area with full utilities); Apartment Rent (950 sf 2 bedroom/1.5 or 2 bath, unfurnished, excluding all utilities except water); All Electric (average monthly cost for an all-electric home); Part Electric (average monthly cost for a part-electric home); Other Energy (average monthly cost for natural gas, fuel oil, coal, wood, and any other forms of energy except electricity); Telephone (price includes the base monthly rate plus taxes and fees for three lines of mobile phone service).
Source: The Council for Community and Economic Research, Cost of Living Index, 2022

Health Care, Transportation, and Other Costs

Area[1]	Doctor ($/visit)	Dentist ($/visit)	Optometrist ($/visit)	Gasoline ($/gallon)	Beauty Salon ($/visit)	Men's Shirt ($)
City[2]	82.50	87.22	61.89	4.13	84.44	45.50
Avg.	124.91	107.77	117.66	3.86	43.31	34.21
Min.	36.61	58.25	51.79	2.90	22.18	13.05
Max.	250.21	162.58	371.96	5.54	85.61	63.54

Note: (1) Values for the local area are compared with the average, minimum and maximum values for all 286 areas in the Cost of Living Index; (2) Figures cover the Louisville KY urban area; Doctor (general practitioners routine exam of an established patient); Dentist (adult teeth cleaning and periodic oral examination); Optometrist (full vision eye exam for established adult patient); Gasoline (one gallon regular unleaded, national brand, including all taxes, cash price at self-service pump if available); Beauty Salon (woman's shampoo, trim, and blow-dry); Men's Shirt (cotton/polyester dress shirt, pinpoint weave, long sleeves).
Source: The Council for Community and Economic Research, Cost of Living Index, 2022

HOUSING

Homeownership Rate

Area	2015 (%)	2016 (%)	2017 (%)	2018 (%)	2019 (%)	2020 (%)	2021 (%)	2022 (%)
MSA[1]	67.7	67.6	71.7	67.9	64.9	69.3	71.4	71.7
U.S.	63.7	63.4	63.9	64.4	64.6	66.6	65.5	65.8

Note: (1) Figures cover the Louisville/Jefferson County, KY-IN Metropolitan Statistical Area
Source: U.S. Census Bureau, Housing Vacancies and Homeownership Annual Statistics: 2015-2022

House Price Index (HPI)

Area	National Ranking[2]	Quarterly Change (%)	One-Year Change (%)	Five-Year Change (%)	Since 1991Q1 (%)
MSA[1]	147	1.02	10.70	47.57	251.74
U.S.[3]	–	0.34	8.41	58.44	289.08

Note: The HPI is a weighted repeat sales index. It measures average price changes in repeat sales or refinancings on the same properties. This information is obtained by reviewing repeat mortgage transactions on single-family properties whose mortgages have been purchased or securitized by Fannie Mae or Freddie Mac since January 1975; (1) Figures cover the Louisville/Jefferson County, KY-IN Metropolitan Statistical Area; (2) Rankings are based on annual percentage change for all metro areas containing at least 15,000 transactions over the last 10 years and ranges from 1 to 257; (3) figures based on a weighted average of Census Division estimates using a seasonally adjusted, purchase-only index; all figures are for the period ending December 31, 2022
Source: Federal Housing Finance Agency, Change in FHFA Metropolitan Area House Price Indexes, 2022Q4

Median Single-Family Home Prices

Area	2020	2021	2022[p]	Percent Change 2021 to 2022
MSA[1]	212.1	235.6	254.2	7.9
U.S. Average	300.2	357.1	392.6	9.9

Note: Figures are median sales prices of existing single-family homes in thousands of dollars; (p) preliminary; (1) Figures cover the Louisville/Jefferson County, KY-IN Metropolitan Statistical Area
Source: National Association of Realtors, Median Sales Price of Existing Single-Family Homes for Metropolitan Areas, 4th Quarter 2022

Qualifying Income Based on Median Sales Price of Existing Single-Family Homes

Area	With 5% Down ($)	With 10% Down ($)	With 20% Down ($)
MSA[1]	75,155	71,199	63,288
U.S. Average	112,234	106,237	94,513

Note: Figures are preliminary; Qualifying income is based on a mortgage rate of 6.77%. Monthly principal and interest payment is limited to 25% of income; (1) Figures cover the Louisville/Jefferson County, KY-IN Metropolitan Statistical Area
Source: National Association of Realtors, Qualifying Income Based on Median Sales Price of Existing Single-Family Homes for Metropolitan Areas, 4th Quarter 2022

Home Value

Area	Under $100,000	$100,000 -$199,999	$200,000 -$299,999	$300,000 -$399,999	$400,000 -$499,999	$500,000 -$999,999	$1,000,000 or more	Median ($)
City	17.5	40.5	20.3	10.8	5.0	5.1	0.9	174,400
MSA[1]	15.4	37.8	23.3	12.0	5.0	5.4	0.9	189,900
U.S.	16.2	24.2	20.1	13.6	8.3	13.6	4.1	244,900

Note: Figures are percentages except for median and cover owner-occupied housing units; (1) Figures cover the Louisville/Jefferson County, KY-IN Metropolitan Statistical Area
Source: U.S. Census Bureau, 2017-2021 American Community Survey 5-Year Estimates

Year Housing Structure Built

Area	2020 or Later	2010 -2019	2000 -2009	1990 -1999	1980 -1989	1970 -1979	1960 -1969	1950 -1959	1940 -1949	Before 1940	Median Year
City	0.2	6.6	11.0	11.1	6.9	12.4	13.6	14.6	7.2	16.5	1969
MSA[1]	0.2	6.7	12.8	13.8	9.2	14.8	12.1	12.2	5.9	12.3	1975
U.S.	0.2	7.3	13.6	13.6	13.2	14.8	10.3	10.0	4.7	12.2	1979

Note: Figures are percentages except for Median Year; Note: (1) Figures cover the Louisville/Jefferson County, KY-IN Metropolitan Statistical Area
Source: U.S. Census Bureau, 2017-2021 American Community Survey 5-Year Estimates

Gross Monthly Rent

Area	Under $500	$500 -$999	$1,000 -$1,499	$1,500 -$1,999	$2,000 -$2,499	$2,500 -$2,999	$3,000 and up	Median ($)
City	11.4	47.2	32.6	6.8	1.2	0.2	0.6	931
MSA[1]	11.0	47.2	33.5	6.2	1.3	0.2	0.6	934
U.S.	8.1	30.5	30.8	16.8	7.3	3.1	3.5	1,163

Note: Figures are percentages except for median; Gross rent is the contract rent plus the estimated average monthly cost of utilities (electricity, gas, and water and sewer) and fuels (oil, coal, kerosene, wood, etc.) if these are paid by the renter (or paid for the renter by someone else); (1) Figures cover the Louisville/Jefferson County, KY-IN Metropolitan Statistical Area
Source: U.S. Census Bureau, 2017-2021 American Community Survey 5-Year Estimates

HEALTH

Health Risk Factors

Category	MSA[1] (%)	U.S. (%)
Adults aged 18–64 who have any kind of health care coverage	95.0	90.9
Adults who reported being in good or better health	81.1	85.2
Adults who have been told they have high blood cholesterol	35.9	35.7
Adults who have been told they have high blood pressure	36.2	32.4
Adults who are current smokers	15.8	14.4
Adults who currently use e-cigarettes	6.5	6.7
Adults who currently use chewing tobacco, snuff, or snus	2.9	3.5
Adults who are heavy drinkers[2]	3.9	6.3
Adults who are binge drinkers[3]	13.8	15.4
Adults who are overweight (BMI 25.0 - 29.9)	34.6	34.4
Adults who are obese (BMI 30.0 - 99.8)	36.7	33.9
Adults who participated in any physical activities in the past month	70.4	76.3

Note: (1) Figures cover the Louisville/Jefferson County, KY-IN Metropolitan Statistical Area; (2) Heavy drinkers are classified as adult men having more than 14 drinks per week and adult women having more than 7 drinks per week; (3) Binge drinkers are classified as males having five or more drinks on one occasion or females having four or more drinks on one occasion
Source: Centers for Disease Control and Prevention, Behaviorial Risk Factor Surveillance System, SMART: Selected Metropolitan Area Risk Trends, 2021

Acute and Chronic Health Conditions

Category	MSA[1] (%)	U.S. (%)
Adults who have ever been told they had a heart attack	5.9	4.0
Adults who have ever been told they have angina or coronary heart disease	5.3	3.8
Adults who have ever been told they had a stroke	3.8	3.0
Adults who have ever been told they have asthma	15.0	14.9
Adults who have ever been told they have arthritis	28.2	25.8
Adults who have ever been told they have diabetes[2]	13.9	10.9
Adults who have ever been told they had skin cancer	5.6	6.6
Adults who have ever been told they had any other types of cancer	6.0	7.5
Adults who have ever been told they have COPD	8.3	6.1
Adults who have ever been told they have kidney disease	2.8	3.0
Adults who have ever been told they have a form of depression	25.0	20.5

Note: (1) Figures cover the Louisville/Jefferson County, KY-IN Metropolitan Statistical Area; (2) Figures do not include pregnancy-related, borderline, or pre-diabetes
Source: Centers for Disease Control and Prevention, Behaviorial Risk Factor Surveillance System, SMART: Selected Metropolitan Area Risk Trends, 2021

Health Screening and Vaccination Rates

Category	MSA[1] (%)	U.S. (%)
Adults who have ever been tested for HIV	33.9	34.9
Adults who have had their blood cholesterol checked within the last five years	90.3	85.2
Adults aged 65+ who have had flu shot within the past year	68.2	68.6
Adults aged 65+ who have ever had a pneumonia vaccination	68.6	71.0

Note: (1) Figures cover the Louisville/Jefferson County, KY-IN Metropolitan Statistical Area.
Source: Centers for Disease Control and Prevention, Behaviorial Risk Factor Surveillance System, SMART: Selected Metropolitan Area Risk Trends, 2021

Disability Status

Category	MSA[1] (%)	U.S. (%)
Adults who reported being deaf	8.4	7.2
Are you blind or have serious difficulty seeing, even when wearing glasses?	6.5	4.8
Are you limited in any way in any of your usual activities due to arthritis?	13.6	11.1
Do you have difficulty doing errands alone?	9.2	7.0
Do you have difficulty dressing or bathing?	3.4	3.6
Do you have serious difficulty concentrating/remembering/making decisions?	15.7	12.1
Do you have serious difficulty walking or climbing stairs?	17.4	12.8

Note: (1) Figures cover the Louisville/Jefferson County, KY-IN Metropolitan Statistical Area.
Source: Centers for Disease Control and Prevention, Behaviorial Risk Factor Surveillance System, SMART: Selected Metropolitan Area Risk Trends, 2021

Mortality Rates for the Top 10 Causes of Death in the U.S.

ICD-10[a] Sub-Chapter	ICD-10[a] Code	Crude Mortality Rate[1] per 100,000 population	
		County[2]	U.S.
Malignant neoplasms	C00-C97	206.9	182.6
Ischaemic heart diseases	I20-I25	73.2	113.1
Other forms of heart disease	I30-I51	91.0	64.4
Other degenerative diseases of the nervous system	G30-G31	52.2	51.0
Cerebrovascular diseases	I60-I69	47.0	47.8
Other external causes of accidental injury	W00-X59	81.6	46.4
Chronic lower respiratory diseases	J40-J47	54.2	45.7
Organic, including symptomatic, mental disorders	F01-F09	76.9	35.9
Hypertensive diseases	I10-I15	62.7	35.0
Diabetes mellitus	E10-E14	29.5	29.6

Note: (a) ICD-10 = International Classification of Diseases 10th Revision; (1) Crude mortality rates are a three-year average covering 2019-2021; (2) Figures cover Jefferson County.
Source: Centers for Disease Control and Prevention, National Center for Health Statistics. National Vital Statistics System, Mortality 2018-2021 on CDC WONDER Online Database

Mortality Rates for Selected Causes of Death

ICD-10[a] Sub-Chapter	ICD-10[a] Code	Crude Mortality Rate[1] per 100,000 population	
		County[2]	U.S.
Assault	X85-Y09	20.4	7.0
Diseases of the liver	K70-K76	21.4	19.8
Human immunodeficiency virus (HIV) disease	B20-B24	2.0	1.5
Influenza and pneumonia	J09-J18	15.6	14.7
Intentional self-harm	X60-X84	16.8	14.3
Malnutrition	E40-E46	7.4	4.3
Obesity and other hyperalimentation	E65-E68	1.9	3.0
Renal failure	N17-N19	22.8	15.7
Transport accidents	V01-V99	16.0	13.6
Viral hepatitis	B15-B19	1.3	1.2

Note: (a) ICD-10 = International Classification of Diseases 10th Revision; (1) Crude mortality rates are a three-year average covering 2019-2021; (2) Figures cover Jefferson County; Data are suppressed when the data meet the criteria for confidentiality constraints; Crude mortality rates are flagged as unreliable when the rate would be calculated with a numerator of 20 or less.
Source: Centers for Disease Control and Prevention, National Center for Health Statistics. National Vital Statistics System, Mortality 2018-2021 on CDC WONDER Online Database

Health Insurance Coverage

Area	With Health Insurance	With Private Health Insurance	With Public Health Insurance	Without Health Insurance	Population Under Age 19 Without Health Insurance
City	94.4	66.2	41.2	5.6	3.4
MSA[1]	94.6	70.7	37.3	5.4	3.5
U.S.	91.2	67.8	35.4	8.8	5.3

Note: Figures are percentages that cover the civilian noninstitutionalized population; (1) Figures cover the Louisville/Jefferson County, KY-IN Metropolitan Statistical Area
Source: U.S. Census Bureau, 2017-2021 American Community Survey 5-Year Estimates

Number of Medical Professionals

Area	MDs[3]	DOs[3,4]	Dentists	Podiatrists	Chiropractors	Optometrists
County[1] (number)	3,754	146	816	63	216	129
County[1] (rate[2])	480.0	18.7	104.9	8.1	27.8	16.6
U.S. (rate[2])	289.3	23.5	72.5	6.2	28.7	17.4

Note: Data as of 2021 unless noted; (1) Data covers Jefferson County; (2) Rate per 100,000 population; (3) Data as of 2020 and includes all active, non-federal physicians; (4) Doctor of Osteopathic Medicine
Source: U.S. Department of Health and Human Services, Health Resources and Services Administration, Bureau of Health Professions, Area Resource File (ARF) 2021-2022

Best Hospitals

According to *U.S. News,* the Louisville/Jefferson County, KY-IN metro area is home to one of the best children's hospitals in the U.S.: **Norton Children's Hospital** (3 pediatric specialties). The hospital listed was highly ranked in at least one of 10 pediatric specialties. Eighty-six children's hospitals in the U.S. were nationally ranked in at least one specialty. Hospitals received points for being ranked in a specialty, and the 10 hospitals with the most points across the 10 specialties make up the Honor Roll. *U.S. News Online, "America's Best Children's Hospitals 2022-23"*

EDUCATION

Public School District Statistics

District Name	Schls	Pupils	Pupil/ Teacher Ratio	Minority Pupils[1] (%)	LEP/ELL[2] (%)	IEP[3] (%)
Jefferson County	170	94,393	15.2	61.4	9.2	12.7

Note: Table includes school districts with 2,000 or more students; (1) Percentage of students that are not non-Hispanic white; (2) Percentage of students that are Limited English Proficient or English Language Learners (2018-19); (3) Percentage of students that have an Individualized Education Program (2019-20).
Source: U.S. Department of Education, National Center for Education Statistics, Common Core of Data, Local Education Agency (School District) Universe Survey: School Year 2021-2022

Best High Schools

According to *U.S. News,* Louisville is home to three of the top 500 high schools in the U.S.: **Dupont Manual High School** (#47); **J. Graham Brown School** (#241); **Atherton High School** (#480). Nearly 18,000 public, magnet and charter schools were ranked based on their performance on state assessments and how well they prepare students for college. *U.S. News & World Report, "Best High Schools 2022"*

Highest Level of Education

Area	Less than H.S.	H.S. Diploma	Some College, No Deg.	Associate Degree	Bachelor's Degree	Master's Degree	Prof. School Degree	Doctorate Degree
City	9.8	28.2	22.1	8.3	18.9	9.0	2.1	1.5
MSA[1]	9.1	29.3	21.7	8.7	18.9	8.8	2.1	1.4
U.S.	11.1	26.5	20.0	8.7	20.6	9.3	2.2	1.5

Note: Figures cover persons age 25 and over; (1) Figures cover the Louisville/Jefferson County, KY-IN Metropolitan Statistical Area
Source: U.S. Census Bureau, 2017-2021 American Community Survey 5-Year Estimates

Educational Attainment by Race

Area	High School Graduate or Higher (%)					Bachelor's Degree or Higher (%)				
	Total	White	Black	Asian	Hisp.[2]	Total	White	Black	Asian	Hisp.[2]
City	90.2	91.8	88.2	80.0	77.1	31.6	35.2	18.8	50.7	24.4
MSA[1]	90.9	91.9	88.1	85.5	73.8	31.1	32.7	19.7	57.5	21.6
U.S.	88.9	91.4	87.2	87.6	71.2	33.7	35.5	23.3	55.6	18.4

Note: Figures shown cover persons 25 years old and over; (1) Figures cover the Louisville/Jefferson County, KY-IN Metropolitan Statistical Area; (2) People of Hispanic origin can be of any race
Source: U.S. Census Bureau, 2017-2021 American Community Survey 5-Year Estimates

School Enrollment by Grade and Control

Area	Preschool (%)		Kindergarten (%)		Grades 1 - 4 (%)		Grades 5 - 8 (%)		Grades 9 - 12 (%)	
	Public	Private	Public	Private	Public	Private	Public	Private	Public	Private
City	51.6	48.4	80.2	19.8	82.9	17.1	82.3	17.7	78.3	21.7
MSA[1]	52.4	47.6	81.8	18.2	82.3	17.7	82.4	17.6	80.7	19.3
U.S.	58.8	41.2	86.3	13.7	88.3	11.7	88.6	11.4	89.4	10.6

Note: Figures shown cover persons 3 years old and over; (1) Figures cover the Louisville/Jefferson County, KY-IN Metropolitan Statistical Area
Source: U.S. Census Bureau, 2017-2021 American Community Survey 5-Year Estimates

Higher Education

Four-Year Colleges			Two-Year Colleges			Medical Schools[1]	Law Schools[2]	Voc/ Tech[3]
Public	Private Non-profit	Private For-profit	Public	Private Non-profit	Private For-profit			
2	6	2	1	0	3	1	1	7

Note: Figures cover institutions located within the Louisville/Jefferson County, KY-IN Metropolitan Statistical Area and include main campuses only; (1) includes schools accredited by the Liaison Committee on Medical Education and the American Osteopathic Association's Commission on Osteopathic College Accreditation; (2) includes ABA-accredited schools, schools with provisional ABA accreditation, and state accredited schools; (3) includes all schools with programs that are less than 2 years.
Source: National Center for Education Statistics, Integrated Postsecondary Education System (IPEDS), 2021-22; Wikipedia, List of Medical Schools in the United States, accessed April 10, 2023; Wikipedia, List of Law Schools in the United States, accessed April 10, 2023

According to *U.S. News & World Report,* the Louisville/Jefferson County, KY-IN metro area is home to one of the top 200 national universities in the U.S.: **University of Louisville** (#182 tie). The indicators used to capture academic quality fall into a number of categories: assessment by administrators at peer institutions; retention of students; faculty resources; student selectivity; financial resources; alumni giving; high school counselor ratings of colleges; and graduation rate. *U.S. News & World Report, "America's Best Colleges 2023"*

According to *U.S. News & World Report,* the Louisville/Jefferson County, KY-IN metro area is home to one of the top 100 law schools in the U.S.: **University of Louisville (Brandeis)** (#94 tie). The rankings are based on a weighted average of 12 measures of quality: peer assessment score; assessment score by lawyers/judges; median LSAT scores; median undergrad GPA; acceptance rate; employment rates for graduates; placement success; bar passage rate; faculty resources; expenditures per student; student/faculty ratio; and library resources. *U.S. News & World Report, "America's Best Graduate Schools, Law, 2023"*

EMPLOYERS

Major Employers

Company Name	Industry
Baptist Healthcare Systems	Healthcare
BF Cos./ERJ Dining	Restaurants
Catholic Archdiocese of Louisville	Schools/churches/related activities
Clark Memorial Hospital	Healthcare
Floyd Memorial Hospital & Health Services	Healthcare
Ford Motor Co.	Automotive manufacturer
GE Appliances & Lighting	Home appliance/lighting products
Horseshoe Southern Indiana	Entertainment
Humana	Health insurance
Jefferson County Public Schools	K-12 public education
Kentucky State Government	Government
KentuckyOne Health	Healthcare
Kindred Healthcare	Healthcare
LG&E and KU Energy	Utility
Louisville/Jefferson County Metro Govt	Government
New Albany-Floyd County School Corp	K-12 public education
Norton Healthcare	Healthcare
Publishers Printing Co.	Printer
Robley Rex VA Medical Center	Healthcare
Securitas Security Services USA	Security services
U.S. Government	Government
United Parcel Services	Package delivery services
University of Louisville	Higher education
University of Louisville Hospital	Healthcare
Yum! Brands	Quick-service restaurants

Note: Companies shown are located within the Louisville/Jefferson County, KY-IN Metropolitan Statistical Area.
Source: Hoovers.com; Wikipedia

Best Companies to Work For

Norton Healthcare, headquartered in Louisville, is among the "100 Best Places to Work in IT." To qualify, companies had to have a minimum of 100 total employees and five IT employees. The best places to work were selected based on DEI (diversity, equity, and inclusion) practices; IT turnover, promotions, and growth; IT retention and engagement programs; remote/hybrid working; benefits and perks (such as elder care and child care, flextime, and reimbursement for college tuition); and training and career development opportunities. *Computerworld, "Best Places to Work in IT," 2023*

PUBLIC SAFETY

Crime Rate

Area	Total Crime	Violent Crime Rate				Property Crime Rate		
		Murder	Rape[3]	Robbery	Aggrav. Assault	Burglary	Larceny-Theft	Motor Vehicle Theft
City	4,578.4	13.9	29.8	149.2	494.0	638.9	2,670.2	582.4
Suburbs[1]	1,847.8	1.9	21.7	30.8	98.0	230.7	1,263.0	201.7
Metro[2]	3,300.8	8.3	26.0	93.8	308.7	447.9	2,011.8	404.3
U.S.	2,510.4	5.1	42.6	81.8	250.4	340.5	1,569.2	220.8

Note: Figures are crimes per 100,000 population; (1) All areas within the metro area that are located outside the city limits; (2) Figures cover the Louisville/Jefferson County, KY-IN Metropolitan Statistical Area; (3) All figures shown were reported using the revised Uniform Crime Reporting (UCR) definition of rape; Due to the transition to the National Incident-Based Reporting System (NIBRS), limited city and metro area data was released for 2021.
Source: FBI Uniform Crime Reports, 2019 (data for 2020 was not available)

Hate Crimes

Area	Number of Quarters Reported	Number of Incidents per Bias Motivation					
		Race/Ethnicity/ Ancestry	Religion	Sexual Orientation	Disability	Gender	Gender Identity
City	4	27	2	3	0	0	0
U.S.	4	5,227	1,244	1,110	130	75	266

Note: Due to the transition to the National Incident-Based Reporting System (NIBRS), limited crime data was released for 2021.
Source: Federal Bureau of Investigation, Hate Crime Statistics 2020

Identity Theft Consumer Reports

Area	Reports	Reports per 100,000 Population	Rank[2]
MSA[1]	2,071	164	218
U.S.	1,108,609	339	-

Note: (1) Figures cover the Louisville/Jefferson County, KY-IN Metropolitan Statistical Area; (2) Rank ranges from 1 to 391 where 1 indicates greatest number of identity theft reports per 100,000 population
Source: Federal Trade Commission, Consumer Sentinel Network Data Book 2022

Fraud and Other Consumer Reports

Area	Reports	Reports per 100,000 Population	Rank[2]
MSA[1]	11,224	889	154
U.S.	4,064,520	1,245	-

Note: (1) Figures cover the Louisville/Jefferson County, KY-IN Metropolitan Statistical Area; (2) Rank ranges from 1 to 391 where 1 indicates greatest number of fraud and other consumer reports per 100,000 population
Source: Federal Trade Commission, Consumer Sentinel Network Data Book 2022

POLITICS

2020 Presidential Election Results

Area	Biden	Trump	Jorgensen	Hawkins	Other
Jefferson County	58.9	38.8	1.2	0.1	1.0
U.S.	51.3	46.8	1.2	0.3	0.5

Note: Results are percentages and may not add to 100% due to rounding
Source: Dave Leip's Atlas of U.S. Presidential Elections

SPORTS

Professional Sports Teams

Team Name	League	Year Established
No teams are located in the metro area		

Source: Wikipedia, Major Professional Sports Teams of the United States and Canada, April 12, 2023

CLIMATE

Average and Extreme Temperatures

Temperature	Jan	Feb	Mar	Apr	May	Jun	Jul	Aug	Sep	Oct	Nov	Dec	Yr.
Extreme High (°F)	77	77	86	91	95	102	105	101	104	92	84	76	105
Average High (°F)	41	46	56	68	77	85	88	87	80	69	56	45	67
Average Temp. (°F)	33	37	46	57	66	74	78	77	70	58	47	37	57
Average Low (°F)	25	27	36	46	55	64	68	66	59	47	37	29	46
Extreme Low (°F)	-20	-9	-1	22	31	42	50	46	33	23	-1	-15	-20

Note: Figures cover the years 1948-1990
Source: National Climatic Data Center, International Station Meteorological Climate Summary, 9/96

Average Precipitation/Snowfall/Humidity

Precip./Humidity	Jan	Feb	Mar	Apr	May	Jun	Jul	Aug	Sep	Oct	Nov	Dec	Yr.
Avg. Precip. (in.)	3.4	3.5	4.5	4.0	4.5	3.7	4.2	3.2	3.0	2.6	3.7	3.6	43.9
Avg. Snowfall (in.)	5	4	3	Tr	Tr	0	0	0	0	Tr	1	2	17
Avg. Rel. Hum. 7am (%)	78	78	75	75	79	80	82	85	86	84	79	78	80
Avg. Rel. Hum. 4pm (%)	62	58	52	49	52	53	55	53	53	51	57	62	55

Note: Figures cover the years 1948-1990; Tr = Trace amounts (<0.05 in. of rain; <0.5 in. of snow)
Source: National Climatic Data Center, International Station Meteorological Climate Summary, 9/96

Weather Conditions

Temperature			Daytime Sky			Precipitation		
10°F & below	32°F & below	90°F & above	Clear	Partly cloudy	Cloudy	0.01 inch or more precip.	0.1 inch or more snow/ice	Thunder-storms
8	90	35	82	143	140	125	15	45

Note: Figures are average number of days per year and cover the years 1948-1990
Source: National Climatic Data Center, International Station Meteorological Climate Summary, 9/96

266 Louisville, Kentucky

HAZARDOUS WASTE

Superfund Sites

The Louisville/Jefferson County, KY-IN metro area is home to two sites on the EPA's Superfund National Priorities List: **Distler Farm** (final); **Smith's Farm** (final). There are a total of 1,165 Superfund sites with a status of proposed or final on the list in the U.S. *U.S. Environmental Protection Agency, National Priorities List, April 12, 2023*

AIR QUALITY

Air Quality Trends: Ozone

	1990	1995	2000	2005	2010	2015	2018	2019	2020	2021
MSA[1]	0.082	0.091	0.087	0.083	0.076	0.071	0.069	0.064	0.063	0.064
U.S.	0.087	0.089	0.081	0.080	0.072	0.067	0.069	0.065	0.065	0.067

Note: (1) Data covers the Louisville/Jefferson County, KY-IN Metropolitan Statistical Area. The values shown are the composite ozone concentration averages among trend sites based on the highest fourth daily maximum 8-hour concentration in parts per million. These trends are based on sites having an adequate record of monitoring data during the trend period. Data from exceptional events are included.
Source: U.S. Environmental Protection Agency, Air Quality Monitoring Information, "Air Quality Trends by City, 1990-2021"

Air Quality Index

Area	Percent of Days when Air Quality was...[2]					AQI Statistics[2]	
	Good	Moderate	Unhealthy for Sensitive Groups	Unhealthy	Very Unhealthy	Maximum	Median
MSA[1]	60.8	37.3	1.9	0.0	0.0	143	46

Note: (1) Data covers the Louisville/Jefferson County, KY-IN Metropolitan Statistical Area; (2) Based on 365 days with AQI data in 2021. Air Quality Index (AQI) is an index for reporting daily air quality. EPA calculates the AQI for five major air pollutants regulated by the Clean Air Act: ground-level ozone, particle pollution (aka particulate matter), carbon monoxide, sulfur dioxide, and nitrogen dioxide. The AQI runs from 0 to 500. The higher the AQI value, the greater the level of air pollution and the greater the health concern. There are six AQI categories: "Good" AQI is between 0 and 50. Air quality is considered satisfactory; "Moderate" AQI is between 51 and 100. Air quality is acceptable; "Unhealthy for Sensitive Groups" When AQI values are between 101 and 150, members of sensitive groups may experience health effects; "Unhealthy" When AQI values are between 151 and 200 everyone may begin to experience health effects; "Very Unhealthy" AQI values between 201 and 300 trigger a health alert; "Hazardous" AQI values over 300 trigger warnings of emergency conditions (not shown).
Source: U.S. Environmental Protection Agency, Air Quality Index Report, 2021

Air Quality Index Pollutants

Area	Percent of Days when AQI Pollutant was...[2]					
	Carbon Monoxide	Nitrogen Dioxide	Ozone	Sulfur Dioxide	Particulate Matter 2.5	Particulate Matter 10
MSA[1]	0.0	2.2	39.5	(3)	58.4	0.0

Note: (1) Data covers the Louisville/Jefferson County, KY-IN Metropolitan Statistical Area; (2) Based on 365 days with AQI data in 2021. The Air Quality Index (AQI) is an index for reporting daily air quality. EPA calculates the AQI for five major air pollutants regulated by the Clean Air Act: ground-level ozone, particle pollution (also known as particulate matter), carbon monoxide, sulfur dioxide, and nitrogen dioxide. The AQI runs from 0 to 500. The higher the AQI value, the greater the level of air pollution and the greater the health concern; (3) Sulfur dioxide is no longer included in this table (as of December 8, 2021) because SO_2 concentrations tend to be very localized and not necessarily representative of broad geographical areas like counties and CBSAs.
Source: U.S. Environmental Protection Agency, Air Quality Index Report, 2021

Maximum Air Pollutant Concentrations: Particulate Matter, Ozone, CO and Lead

	Particulate Matter 10 (ug/m^3)	Particulate Matter 2.5 Wtd AM (ug/m^3)	Particulate Matter 2.5 24-Hr (ug/m^3)	Ozone (ppm)	Carbon Monoxide (ppm)	Lead (ug/m^3)
MSA[1] Level	46	11.2	28	0.073	1	n/a
NAAQS[2]	150	15	35	0.075	9	0.15
Met NAAQS[2]	Yes	Yes	Yes	Yes	Yes	n/a

Note: (1) Data covers the Louisville/Jefferson County, KY-IN Metropolitan Statistical Area; Data from exceptional events are included; (2) National Ambient Air Quality Standards; ppm = parts per million; ug/m^3 = micrograms per cubic meter; n/a not available.
Concentrations: Particulate Matter 10 (coarse particulate)—highest second maximum 24-hour concentration; Particulate Matter 2.5 Wtd AM (fine particulate)—highest weighted annual mean concentration; Particulate Matter 2.5 24-Hour (fine particulate)—highest 98th percentile 24-hour concentration; Ozone—highest fourth daily maximum 8-hour concentration; Carbon Monoxide—highest second maximum non-overlapping 8-hour concentration; Lead—maximum running 3-month average
Source: U.S. Environmental Protection Agency, Air Quality Monitoring Information, "Air Quality Statistics by City, 2021"

Maximum Air Pollutant Concentrations: Nitrogen Dioxide and Sulfur Dioxide

	Nitrogen Dioxide AM (ppb)	Nitrogen Dioxide 1-Hr (ppb)	Sulfur Dioxide AM (ppb)	Sulfur Dioxide 1-Hr (ppb)	Sulfur Dioxide 24-Hr (ppb)
MSA[1] Level	15	50	n/a	13	n/a
NAAQS[2]	53	100	30	75	140
Met NAAQS[2]	Yes	Yes	n/a	Yes	n/a

Note: (1) Data covers the Louisville/Jefferson County, KY-IN Metropolitan Statistical Area; Data from exceptional events are included; (2) National Ambient Air Quality Standards; ppm = parts per million; ug/m^3 = micrograms per cubic meter; n/a not available.
Concentrations: Nitrogen Dioxide AM—highest arithmetic mean concentration; Nitrogen Dioxide 1-Hr—highest 98th percentile 1-hour daily maximum concentration; Sulfur Dioxide AM—highest annual mean concentration; Sulfur Dioxide 1-Hr—highest 99th percentile 1-hour daily maximum concentration; Sulfur Dioxide 24-Hr—highest second maximum 24-hour concentration
Source: U.S. Environmental Protection Agency, Air Quality Monitoring Information, "Air Quality Statistics by City, 2021"

Manchester, New Hampshire

Background

Manchester, the largest city in northern New England, lies along the Merrimack River in the southern part of the "Live Free or Die" state. Fifty-one miles northwest of Boston, Manchester is a major financial and manufacturing center in its region and a main stop on the way to New Hampshire's many vacation resorts.

Amoskeag Falls, on the Merrimack, had been an important Penacook Indian fishing site for many years prior to the arrival of the first Europeans, who came in 1636 on instructions from Massachusetts Governor John Winthrop. A schoolhouse was built in 1650 by the missionary John Elliot, but for many years the European population was limited to a small number of hunters, trappers, and fishermen. The first permanent settlement was established in 1722 by a tiny group from the Massachusetts Bay Colony. The town was known by a variety of names, including Old Harrytown, Tyngstown, and Derryfield.

For many years "Derryfield's" fortunes depended on lumber and fishing, but in 1810, cotton mills relying on waterpower from the Merrimack River became an economic mainstay. Though the town's population was then only 615, a local resident, Judge Samuel Blodgett, predicted that it would eventually grow to become a mighty center of industry, like England's Manchester. The name change was a result of this unlikely prediction, and by 1846, the new American Manchester had grown to a population of more than 10,000.

Manchester's early industrial history is inextricably linked to the history of the Amoskeag Manufacturing Company, whose 64 mills lined the banks of the river with what came to be the world's largest cotton milling operation. As Amoskeag thrived, so did Manchester. By the 1920s, however, Amoskeag had lost its leading edge, with obsolete machinery and alternatives to cotton, like silk and rayon. It declared bankruptcy in 1935, paving the way for cheaper facilities, particularly in the Southern states, and causing a decline in Manchester's jobs and population.

By the mid-1990s, Manchester recovered from its Depression-era difficulties to become the nation's fastest-growing city. A development company bought up the old mill buildings, restoring and adapting them to new commercial and residential uses. But the changes were not merely cosmetic; considering a lesson well-learned from its single-industry past, Manchester's economic renaissance was finely calibrated to fit in with regional and national trends.

In recent years the Neighborhood Initiative program has included streetscapes, infrastructure improvements and continued development of the Amoskeag Mill into high end condominiums. The city's downtown includes the tallest buildings north of Cambridge, MA. In 2022, Manchester launched NAACP-Community Loan Fund initiative to offer assistance, training, and financing to support the city's minority-owned businesses.

The economic attractiveness of the city today, and its overall affordability, is enhanced by New Hampshire's unique reluctance to institute any sales or income tax. Manchester has been recognized as "tax friendly" and one of the best places in America to launch a business. The city is home to Segway, Inc., manufacturers of the two-wheeled, self-balancing electric vehicle, as well as headquarters for Bank of America and Citizens Bank.

The city is served by the Manchester-Boston Regional Airport, one of the nation's fastest-growing. With its recent 74,000-square-foot addition, airport traffic continues to increase. In 2021, city leaders supported a downtown hybrid passenger rail station.

The cultural assets of Manchester include the Currier Museum of Art, and the New Hampshire Institute of Art. Another major attraction is the Manchester Historical Association's Millyard Museum founded in 1896. Institutions of higher education convenient to Manchester include St. Anselm College, Southern New Hampshire University, Franklin Pierce College, and the University of New Hampshire at Manchester, as well as a community college. SNHU's Arena is the centerpiece of the city's downtown, hosting concerts and other events.

There are four seasons in Manchester, and the climate can be characterized as typical of northern New England. Long winters with considerable snow are to be expected, as are lovely, cool springs and summers.

Rankings

Business/Finance Rankings

- The Manchester metro area appeared on the Milken Institute "2022 Best Performing Cities" list. Rank: #70 out of 200 large metro areas (population over 250,000). Criteria: job growth; wage and salary growth; high-tech output growth; housing affordability; household broadband access. *Milken Institute, "Best-Performing Cities 2022," March 28, 2022*

- *Forbes* ranked the 200 most populous metro areas to determine the nation's "Best Places for Business and Careers." The Manchester metro area was ranked #133. Criteria: costs (business and living); job growth (past and projected); income growth; quality of life; educational attainment (college and high school); projected economic growth; cultural and leisure opportunities; workplace tolerance laws; net migration patterns. *Forbes, "The Best Places for Business and Careers 2019: Seattle Still On Top," October 30, 2019*

Education Rankings

- Personal finance website *WalletHub* analyzed the 150 largest U.S. metropolitan statistical areas to determine where the most educated Americans are putting their degrees to work. Criteria: education levels; percentage of workers with degrees; education quality and attainment gap; public school quality rankings; quality and enrollment of each metro area's universities. Manchester was ranked #37 (#1 = most educated city). *www.WalletHub.com, "Most & Least Educated Cities in America," July 18, 2022*

Environmental Rankings

- Niche compiled a list of the nation's snowiest cities, based on the National Oceanic and Atmospheric Administration's 30-year average snowfall data. Among cities with a population of at least 50,000, Manchester ranked #23. *Niche.com, Top 25 Snowiest Cities in America, December 10, 2018*

Real Estate Rankings

- *WalletHub* compared the most populated U.S. cities to determine which had the best markets for real estate agents. Manchester ranked #31 where demand was high and pay was the best. Criteria: sales per agent; annual median wage for real-estate agents; monthly average starting salary for real estate agents; real estate job density and competition; unemployment rate; home turnover rate; housing-market health index; and other relevant metrics. *www.WalletHub.com, "2021 Best Places to Be a Real Estate Agent," May 12, 2021*

- The Manchester metro area was identified as one of the nations's 20 hottest housing markets in 2023. Criteria: listing views as an indicator of demand and number of days on the market as an indicator of pace. The area ranked #1. *Realtor.com, "January 2023 Top 20 Hottest Housing Markets," February 23, 2023*

- The Manchester metro area was identified as one of the 10 best condo markets in the U.S. in 2022. The area ranked #10 out of 63 markets. Criteria: year-over-year change of median sales price of existing apartment condo-coop homes between the 4th quarter of 2021 and the 4th quarter of 2022. *National Association of Realtors®, Median Sales Price of Existing Apartment Condo-Coops Homes for Metropolitan Areas, 4th Quarter 2022*

- Manchester was ranked #136 out of 235 metro areas in terms of housing affordability in 2022 by the National Association of Home Builders (#1 = most affordable). Criteria: the share of homes sold in that area affordable to a family earning the local median income, based on standard mortgage underwriting criteria. *National Association of Home Builders®, NAHB-Wells Fargo Housing Opportunity Index, 4th Quarter 2022*

Safety Rankings

- The National Insurance Crime Bureau ranked 390 metro areas in the U.S. in terms of per capita rates of vehicle theft. The Manchester metro area ranked #339 (#1 = highest rate). Criteria: number of vehicle theft offenses per 100,000 inhabitants in 2021. *National Insurance Crime Bureau, "Hot Spots 2021," September 1, 2022*

Seniors/Retirement Rankings

- From its Best Cities for Successful Aging indexes, the Milken Institute generated rankings for metropolitan areas, weighing data in nine categories—health care, wellness, living arrangements, transportation and convenience, financial characteristics, education, employment, community engagement, and overall livability. The Manchester metro area was ranked #181 overall in the small metro area category. *Milken Institute, "Best Cities for Successful Aging, 2017" March 14, 2017*

Women/Minorities Rankings

- Personal finance website *WalletHub* compared more than 180 U.S. cities across two key dimensions, "Hispanic Business-Friendliness" and "Hispanic Purchasing Power," to arrive at the most favorable conditions for Hispanic entrepreneurs. Manchester was ranked #163 out of 182. Criteria includes: share of Hispanic-Owned Businesses; Hispanic entrepreneurship rate to median annual income of Hispanics; Small Business-Friendliness score; cost of living; and number of Hispanics with at least a bachelor's degree. *WalletHub.com, "2019's Best Cities for Hispanic Entrepreneurs," May 1, 2019*

Miscellaneous Rankings

- *WalletHub* compared the 150 most populated U.S. cities to determine their operating efficiency. A "Quality of Services" score was constructed for each city and then divided by the total budget per capita to reveal which were managed the best. Manchester ranked #19. Criteria: financial stability; economy; education; safety; health; infrastructure and pollution. *www.WalletHub.com, "2022's Best-& Worst-Run Cities in America," June 21, 2022*

Business Environment

DEMOGRAPHICS

Population Growth

Area	1990 Census	2000 Census	2010 Census	2020 Census	Population Growth (%) 1990-2020	Population Growth (%) 2010-2020
City	99,567	107,006	109,565	115,644	16.1	5.5
MSA[1]	336,073	380,841	400,721	422,937	25.8	5.5
U.S.	248,709,873	281,421,906	308,745,538	331,449,281	33.3	7.4

Note: (1) Figures cover the Manchester-Nashua, NH Metropolitan Statistical Area
Source: U.S. Census Bureau, 1990 Census, 2000 Census, 2010 Census, 2020 Census

Race

Area	White Alone[2] (%)	Black Alone[2] (%)	Asian Alone[2] (%)	AIAN[3] Alone[2] (%)	NHOPI[4] Alone[2] (%)	Other Race Alone[2] (%)	Two or More Races (%)
City	76.7	5.5	4.2	0.3	0.0	5.2	7.9
MSA[1]	82.8	2.6	3.9	0.2	0.0	3.5	6.9
U.S.	61.6	12.4	6.0	1.1	0.2	8.4	10.2

Note: (1) Figures cover the Manchester-Nashua, NH Metropolitan Statistical Area; (2) Alone is defined as not being in combination with one or more other races; (3) American Indian and Alaska Native; (4) Native Hawaiian and Other Pacific Islander
Source: U.S. Census Bureau, 2020 Census

Hispanic or Latino Origin

Area	Total (%)	Mexican (%)	Puerto Rican (%)	Cuban (%)	Other (%)
City	11.0	1.6	3.9	0.1	5.4
MSA[1]	7.4	1.1	2.5	0.2	3.5
U.S.	18.4	11.2	1.8	0.7	4.7

Note: Persons of Hispanic or Latino origin can be of any race; (1) Figures cover the Manchester-Nashua, NH Metropolitan Statistical Area
Source: U.S. Census Bureau, 2017-2021 American Community Survey 5-Year Estimates

Age

Area	Under Age 5	Age 5–19	Age 20–34	Age 35–44	Age 45–54	Age 55–64	Age 65–74	Age 75–84	Age 85+	Median Age
City	5.3	15.7	26.0	12.6	12.1	13.4	9.0	3.9	2.0	37.0
MSA[1]	5.0	17.5	20.0	12.3	13.5	15.2	10.0	4.7	1.9	40.9
U.S.	5.6	19.2	20.2	12.7	12.4	13.1	10.0	4.9	1.9	38.8

Note: (1) Figures cover the Manchester-Nashua, NH Metropolitan Statistical Area
Source: U.S. Census Bureau, 2020 Census

Disability by Age

Area	All Ages	Under 18 Years Old	18 to 64 Years Old	65 Years and Over
City	13.9	6.6	11.8	34.7
MSA[1]	11.6	4.7	9.5	29.8
U.S.	12.6	4.4	10.3	33.4

Note: Figures show percent of the civilian noninstitutionalized population that reported having a disability. Disability status is determined from six types of difficulty: vision, hearing, cognitive, ambulatory, self-care, and independent living. For children under 5 years old, hearing and vision difficulty are used to determine disability status. For children between the ages of 5 and 14, disability status is determined from hearing, vision, cognitive, ambulatory, and self-care difficulties. For people aged 15 years and older, they are considered to have a disability if they have difficulty with any one of the six difficulty types; Note: (1) Figures cover the Manchester-Nashua, NH Metropolitan Statistical Area
Source: U.S. Census Bureau, 2017-2021 American Community Survey 5-Year Estimates

Ancestry

Area	German	Irish	English	American	Italian	Polish	French[2]	Scottish	Dutch
City	6.2	19.3	9.5	2.9	8.8	3.8	11.4	2.7	0.3
MSA[1]	8.0	20.7	13.9	3.3	9.8	4.0	11.2	3.3	0.7
U.S.	12.8	9.6	8.1	5.7	5.0	2.7	2.2	1.6	1.1

Note: Figures are the percentage of the total population reporting a particular ancestry. The nine most commonly reported ancestries in the U.S. are shown. Figures include multiple ancestries (e.g. if a person reported being Irish and Italian, they were included in both columns); (1) Figures cover the Manchester-Nashua, NH Metropolitan Statistical Area; (2) Excludes Basque
Source: U.S. Census Bureau, 2017-2021 American Community Survey 5-Year Estimates

Foreign-born Population

Area	Percent of Population Born in								
	Any Foreign Country	Asia	Mexico	Europe	Caribbean	Central America[2]	South America	Africa	Canada
City	14.6	4.3	0.5	2.7	1.7	1.4	1.0	2.1	1.0
MSA[1]	10.0	3.4	0.3	1.9	1.3	0.5	0.8	0.8	0.9
U.S.	13.6	4.2	3.3	1.5	1.4	1.1	1.1	0.8	0.2

Note: (1) Figures cover the Manchester-Nashua, NH Metropolitan Statistical Area; (2) Excludes Mexico.
Source: U.S. Census Bureau, 2017-2021 American Community Survey 5-Year Estimates

Household Size

Area	Persons in Household (%)							Average Household Size
	One	Two	Three	Four	Five	Six	Seven or More	
City	34.0	33.3	15.9	10.3	3.5	2.0	1.1	2.30
MSA[1]	27.1	35.7	16.3	13.1	4.8	2.1	0.8	2.50
U.S.	28.1	33.8	15.5	12.9	6.0	2.3	1.4	2.60

Note: (1) Figures cover the Manchester-Nashua, NH Metropolitan Statistical Area
Source: U.S. Census Bureau, 2017-2021 American Community Survey 5-Year Estimates

Household Relationships

Area	House-holder	Opposite-sex Spouse	Same-sex Spouse	Opposite-sex Unmarried Partner	Same-sex Unmarried Partner	Child[2]	Grand-child	Other Relatives	Non-relatives
City	42.5	14.9	0.3	4.3	0.2	24.3	1.6	4.3	4.7
MSA[1]	39.7	19.2	0.3	3.2	0.1	27.2	1.6	3.5	3.2
U.S.	38.3	17.5	0.2	2.5	0.2	28.3	2.4	4.8	3.4

Note: Figures are percent of the total population; (1) Figures cover the Manchester-Nashua, NH Metropolitan Statistical Area; (2) Includes biological, adopted, and stepchildren of the householder
Source: U.S. Census Bureau, 2020 Census

Gender

Area	Males	Females	Males per 100 Females
City	57,668	57,976	99.5
MSA[1]	209,879	213,058	98.5
U.S.	162,685,811	168,763,470	96.4

Note: (1) Figures cover the Manchester-Nashua, NH Metropolitan Statistical Area
Source: U.S. Census Bureau, 2020 Census

Marital Status

Area	Never Married	Now Married[2]	Separated	Widowed	Divorced
City	39.2	39.2	1.8	5.4	14.3
MSA[1]	31.3	50.2	1.2	5.1	12.1
U.S.	33.8	48.0	1.8	5.6	10.8

Note: Figures are percentages and cover the population 15 years of age and older; (1) Figures cover the Manchester-Nashua, NH Metropolitan Statistical Area; (2) Excludes separated
Source: U.S. Census Bureau, 2017-2021 American Community Survey 5-Year Estimates

Religious Groups by Family

Area	Catholic	Baptist	Methodist	LDS[2]	Pentecostal	Lutheran	Islam	Adventist	Other
MSA[1]	16.3	0.6	0.6	0.6	0.3	0.3	0.1	0.8	8.1
U.S.	18.7	7.3	3.0	2.0	1.8	1.7	1.3	1.3	11.6

Note: Figures are the number of adherents as a percentage of the total population and cover the eight largest religious groups in the U.S; (1) Figures cover the Manchester-Nashua, NH Metropolitan Statistical Area; (2) Church of Jesus Christ of Latter-day Saints
Sources: 2020 U.S. Religion Census, Association of Statisticians of American Religious Bodies; The Association of Religion Data Archives (ARDA)

Religious Groups by Tradition

Area	Catholic	Evangelical Protestant	Mainline Protestant	Black Protestant	Islam	Judaism	Hinduism	Orthodox	Buddhism
MSA[1]	16.3	5.8	2.7	n/a	0.1	0.3	<0.1	0.9	n/a
U.S.	18.7	16.5	5.2	2.3	1.3	0.6	0.4	0.4	0.3

Note: Figures are the number of adherents as a percentage of the total population; (1) Figures cover the Manchester-Nashua, NH Metropolitan Statistical Area
Sources: 2020 U.S. Religion Census, Association of Statisticians of American Religious Bodies; The Association of Religion Data Archives (ARDA)

274 Manchester, New Hampshire

ECONOMY

Gross Metropolitan Product

Area	2020	2021	2022	2023	Rank[2]
MSA[1]	28.8	32.2	34.1	35.6	104

Note: Figures are in billions of dollars; (1) Figures cover the Manchester-Nashua, NH Metropolitan Statistical Area; (2) Rank is based on 2021 data and ranges from 1 to 381
Source: U.S. Conference of Mayors, U.S. Metro Economies: U.S. Metros Compared to Global and State Economies, June 2022

Economic Growth

Area	2018-20 (%)	2021 (%)	2022 (%)	2023 (%)	Rank[2]
MSA[1]	0.9	8.3	1.2	1.0	78
U.S.	-0.6	5.7	3.1	2.9	—

Note: Figures are real gross metropolitan product (GMP) growth rates and represent average annual percent change; (1) Figures cover the Manchester-Nashua, NH Metropolitan Statistical Area; (2) Rank is based on 2020 2-year average annual percent change and ranges from 1 to 381
Source: U.S. Conference of Mayors, U.S. Metro Economies: U.S. Metros Compared to Global and State Economies, June 2022

Metropolitan Area Exports

Area	2016	2017	2018	2019	2020	2021	Rank[2]
MSA[1]	1,465.2	1,714.7	1,651.4	1,587.1	1,704.9	2,077.6	106

Note: Figures are in millions of dollars; (1) Figures cover the Manchester-Nashua, NH Metropolitan Statistical Area; (2) Rank is based on 2021 data and ranges from 1 to 388
Source: U.S. Department of Commerce, International Trade Administration, Office of Trade and Economic Analysis, Industry and Analysis, Exports by Metropolitan Area, data extracted March 16, 2023

Building Permits

Area	Single-Family			Multi-Family			Total		
	2021	2022	Pct. Chg.	2021	2022	Pct. Chg.	2021	2022	Pct. Chg.
City	126	132	4.8	8	6	-25.0	134	138	3.0
MSA[1]	683	623	-8.8	659	224	-66.0	1,342	847	-36.9
U.S.	1,115,400	975,600	-12.5	621,600	689,500	10.9	1,737,000	1,665,100	-4.1

Note: (1) Figures cover the Manchester-Nashua, NH Metropolitan Statistical Area; Figures represent new, privately-owned housing units authorized (unadjusted data); All permit data are based on estimates with imputation
Source: U.S. Census Bureau, Manufacturing, Mining, and Construction Statistics, Building Permits, 2021, 2022

Bankruptcy Filings

Area	Business Filings			Nonbusiness Filings		
	2021	2022	% Chg.	2021	2022	% Chg.
Hillsborough County	19	11	-42.1	253	204	-19.4
U.S.	14,347	13,481	-6.0	399,269	374,240	-6.3

Note: Business filings include Chapter 7, Chapter 9, Chapter 11, Chapter 12, Chapter 13, Chapter 15, and Section 304; Nonbusiness filings include Chapter 7, Chapter 11, and Chapter 13
Source: Administrative Office of the U.S. Courts, Business and Nonbusiness Bankruptcy, County Cases Commenced by Chapter of the Bankruptcy Code, During the 12-Month Period Ending December 31, 2021 and Business and Nonbusiness Bankruptcy, County Cases Commenced by Chapter of the Bankruptcy Code, During the 12-Month Period Ending December 31, 2022

Housing Vacancy Rates

Area	Gross Vacancy Rate[2] (%)			Year-Round Vacancy Rate[3] (%)			Rental Vacancy Rate[4] (%)			Homeowner Vacancy Rate[5] (%)		
	2020	2021	2022	2020	2021	2022	2020	2021	2022	2020	2021	2022
MSA[1]	n/a	n/a	n/a	n/a	n/a	n/a	n/a	n/a	n/a	n/a	n/a	n/a
U.S.	10.6	10.8	10.5	8.2	8.4	8.2	6.3	6.1	5.8	1.0	0.9	0.8

Note: (1) Figures cover the Manchester-Nashua, NH Metropolitan Statistical Area; (2) The percentage of the total housing inventory that is vacant; (3) The percentage of the housing inventory (excluding seasonal units) that is year-round vacant; (4) The percentage of rental inventory that is vacant for rent; (5) The percentage of homeowner inventory that is vacant for sale; n/a not available
Source: U.S. Census Bureau, Housing Vacancies and Homeownership Annual Statistics: 2020, 2021, 2022

INCOME

Income

Area	Per Capita ($)	Median Household ($)	Average Household ($)
City	36,440	66,929	83,913
MSA[1]	45,238	86,930	111,733
U.S.	37,638	69,021	97,196

Note: (1) Figures cover the Manchester-Nashua, NH Metropolitan Statistical Area
Source: U.S. Census Bureau, 2017-2021 American Community Survey 5-Year Estimates

Household Income Distribution

Area				Percent of Households Earning				
	Under $15,000	$15,000 -$24,999	$25,000 -$34,999	$35,000 -$49,999	$50,000 -$74,999	$75,000 -$99,999	$100,000 -$149,999	$150,000 and up
City	8.0	7.7	7.3	13.7	19.8	14.0	17.0	12.5
MSA[1]	5.4	5.5	6.2	10.2	15.7	13.2	20.1	23.7
U.S.	9.4	7.8	8.2	11.4	16.8	12.8	16.3	17.3

Note: (1) Figures cover the Manchester-Nashua, NH Metropolitan Statistical Area
Source: U.S. Census Bureau, 2017-2021 American Community Survey 5-Year Estimates

Poverty Rate

Area	All Ages	Under 18 Years Old	18 to 64 Years Old	65 Years and Over
City	12.5	22.1	10.7	8.6
MSA[1]	7.2	9.8	6.5	6.2
U.S.	12.6	17.0	11.8	9.6

Note: Figures are percentage of people whose income during the past 12 months was below the poverty level;
(1) Figures cover the Manchester-Nashua, NH Metropolitan Statistical Area
Source: U.S. Census Bureau, 2017-2021 American Community Survey 5-Year Estimates

EMPLOYMENT

Labor Force and Employment

Area	Civilian Labor Force			Workers Employed		
	Dec. 2021	Dec. 2022	% Chg.	Dec. 2021	Dec. 2022	% Chg.
City	63,249	66,044	4.4	61,619	64,357	4.4
NECTA[1]	118,844	124,173	4.5	116,140	121,300	4.4
U.S.	161,696,000	164,224,000	1.6	155,732,000	158,872,000	2.0

Note: Data is not seasonally adjusted and covers workers 16 years of age and older; (1) Figures cover the Manchester, NH New England City and Town Area
Source: Bureau of Labor Statistics, Local Area Unemployment Statistics

Unemployment Rate

Area	2022											
	Jan.	Feb.	Mar.	Apr.	May	Jun.	Jul.	Aug.	Sep.	Oct.	Nov.	Dec.
City	3.6	2.6	2.5	2.3	1.9	2.0	2.0	2.4	2.4	2.7	2.7	2.6
NECTA[1]	3.3	2.3	2.3	2.1	1.8	1.9	1.9	2.2	2.3	2.5	2.4	2.3
U.S.	4.4	4.1	3.8	3.3	3.4	3.8	3.8	3.8	3.3	3.4	3.4	3.3

Note: Data is not seasonally adjusted and covers workers 16 years of age and older; (1) Figures cover the Manchester, NH New England City and Town Area
Source: Bureau of Labor Statistics, Local Area Unemployment Statistics

Average Wages

Occupation	$/Hr.	Occupation	$/Hr.
Accountants and Auditors	38.41	Maintenance and Repair Workers	23.02
Automotive Mechanics	25.34	Marketing Managers	70.51
Bookkeepers	23.03	Network and Computer Systems Admin.	42.70
Carpenters	25.30	Nurses, Licensed Practical	31.39
Cashiers	13.47	Nurses, Registered	39.38
Computer Programmers	37.37	Nursing Assistants	18.40
Computer Systems Analysts	55.74	Office Clerks, General	22.10
Computer User Support Specialists	30.81	Physical Therapists	43.45
Construction Laborers	20.40	Physicians	n/a
Cooks, Restaurant	17.24	Plumbers, Pipefitters and Steamfitters	28.32
Customer Service Representatives	20.95	Police and Sheriff's Patrol Officers	30.78
Dentists	139.57	Postal Service Mail Carriers	27.77
Electricians	28.40	Real Estate Sales Agents	30.34
Engineers, Electrical	53.87	Retail Salespersons	16.93
Fast Food and Counter Workers	13.09	Sales Representatives, Technical/Scientific	41.73
Financial Managers	72.83	Secretaries, Exc. Legal/Medical/Executive	20.73
First-Line Supervisors of Office Workers	33.58	Security Guards	18.41
General and Operations Managers	67.22	Surgeons	n/a
Hairdressers/Cosmetologists	16.38	Teacher Assistants, Exc. Postsecondary*	16.19
Home Health and Personal Care Aides	15.63	Teachers, Secondary School, Exc. Sp. Ed.*	33.56
Janitors and Cleaners	17.06	Telemarketers	15.33
Landscaping/Groundskeeping Workers	19.05	Truck Drivers, Heavy/Tractor-Trailer	25.70
Lawyers	69.50	Truck Drivers, Light/Delivery Services	20.52
Maids and Housekeeping Cleaners	15.17	Waiters and Waitresses	16.61

Note: Wage data covers the Manchester, NH New England City and Town Area; (*) Hourly wages were calculated from annual wage data based on a 40 hour work week; n/a not available.
Source: Bureau of Labor Statistics, Metro Area Occupational Employment & Wage Estimates, May 2022

Employment by Industry

Sector	NECTA[1]		U.S.
	Number of Employees	Percent of Total	Percent of Total
Construction, Mining, and Logging	5,800	5.0	5.4
Private Education and Health Services	26,200	22.7	16.1
Financial Activities	7,500	6.5	5.9
Government	11,900	10.3	14.5
Information	2,500	2.2	2.0
Leisure and Hospitality	9,700	8.4	10.3
Manufacturing	8,000	6.9	8.4
Other Services	4,700	4.1	3.7
Professional and Business Services	18,700	16.2	14.7
Retail Trade	12,500	10.8	10.2
Transportation, Warehousing, and Utilities	3,500	3.0	4.9
Wholesale Trade	4,500	3.9	3.9

Note: Figures are non-farm employment as of December 2022. Figures are not seasonally adjusted and include workers 16 years of age and older; (1) Figures cover the Manchester, NH New England City and Town Area
Source: Bureau of Labor Statistics, Current Employment Statistics, Employment, Hours, and Earnings

Employment by Occupation

Occupation Classification	City (%)	MSA[1] (%)	U.S. (%)
Management, Business, Science, and Arts	36.0	43.8	40.3
Natural Resources, Construction, and Maintenance	7.4	7.9	8.7
Production, Transportation, and Material Moving	15.1	12.6	13.1
Sales and Office	23.5	21.4	20.9
Service	18.0	14.2	17.0

Note: Figures cover employed civilians 16 years of age and older; (1) Figures cover the Manchester-Nashua, NH Metropolitan Statistical Area
Source: U.S. Census Bureau, 2017-2021 American Community Survey 5-Year Estimates

Occupations with Greatest Projected Employment Growth: 2022 – 2024

Occupation[1]	2022 Employment	2024 Projected Employment	Numeric Employment Change	Percent Employment Change
General and Operations Managers	16,780	17,210	430	2.6
Software Developers	7,300	7,670	370	5.1
Home Health and Personal Care Aides	9,370	9,710	340	3.6
Cooks, Restaurant	6,150	6,490	340	5.5
Sales Representatives of Services, Except Advertising, Insurance, Financial Services, and Travel	7,310	7,600	290	4.0
Computer and Information Systems Managers	4,250	4,510	260	6.1
Market Research Analysts and Marketing Specialists	3,740	3,990	250	6.7
Landscaping and Groundskeeping Workers	8,140	8,390	250	3.1
Management Analysts	4,230	4,460	230	5.4
Financial Managers	4,440	4,650	210	4.7

Note: Projections cover New Hampshire; (1) Sorted by numeric employment change
Source: www.projectionscentral.com, State Occupational Projections, 2022–2024 Short-Term Projections

Fastest-Growing Occupations: 2022 – 2024

Occupation[1]	2022 Employment	2024 Projected Employment	Numeric Employment Change	Percent Employment Change
Information Security Analysts (SOC 2018)	530	580	50	9.4
Nurse Practitioners	1,410	1,540	130	9.2
Logisticians	840	910	70	8.3
Fitness Trainers and Aerobics Instructors	2,080	2,230	150	7.2
Market Research Analysts and Marketing Specialists	3,740	3,990	250	6.7
Software Quality Assurance Analysts and Testers	1,130	1,200	70	6.2
Computer and Information Systems Managers	4,250	4,510	260	6.1
Nonfarm Animal Caretakers	1,820	1,930	110	6.0
Self-Enrichment Education Teachers	2,220	2,350	130	5.9
Amusement and Recreation Attendants	1,580	1,670	90	5.7

Note: Projections cover New Hampshire; (1) Sorted by percent employment change and excludes occupations with numeric employment change less than 50
Source: www.projectionscentral.com, State Occupational Projections, 2022–2024 Short-Term Projections

Manchester, New Hampshire 277

CITY FINANCES

City Government Finances

Component	2020 ($000)	2020 ($ per capita)
Total Revenues	375,911	3,336
Total Expenditures	440,382	3,908
Debt Outstanding	417,560	3,706
Cash and Securities[1]	198,761	1,764

Note: (1) Cash and security holdings of a government at the close of its fiscal year, including those of its dependent agencies, utilities, and liquor stores.
Source: U.S. Census Bureau, State & Local Government Finances 2020

City Government Revenue by Source

Source	2020 ($000)	2020 ($ per capita)	2020 (%)
General Revenue			
From Federal Government	6,356	56	1.7
From State Government	127,928	1,135	34.0
From Local Governments	5,498	49	1.5
Taxes			
Property	120,728	1,071	32.1
Sales and Gross Receipts	1,757	16	0.5
Personal Income	0	0	0.0
Corporate Income	0	0	0.0
Motor Vehicle License	0	0	0.0
Other Taxes	5,234	46	1.4
Current Charges	66,166	587	17.6
Liquor Store	0	0	0.0
Utility	22,407	199	6.0

Source: U.S. Census Bureau, State & Local Government Finances 2020

City Government Expenditures by Function

Function	2020 ($000)	2020 ($ per capita)	2020 (%)
General Direct Expenditures			
Air Transportation	40,690	361	9.2
Corrections	0	0	0.0
Education	178,081	1,580	40.4
Employment Security Administration	0	0	0.0
Financial Administration	1,539	13	0.3
Fire Protection	20,893	185	4.7
General Public Buildings	6,894	61	1.6
Governmental Administration, Other	8,352	74	1.9
Health	2,311	20	0.5
Highways	16,014	142	3.6
Hospitals	0	0	0.0
Housing and Community Development	0	0	0.0
Interest on General Debt	15,858	140	3.6
Judicial and Legal	0	0	0.0
Libraries	2,066	18	0.5
Parking	2,250	20	0.5
Parks and Recreation	6,574	58	1.5
Police Protection	26,208	232	6.0
Public Welfare	904	8	0.2
Sewerage	10,330	91	2.3
Solid Waste Management	10,877	96	2.5
Veterans' Services	0	0	0.0
Liquor Store	0	0	0.0
Utility	40,057	355	9.1

Source: U.S. Census Bureau, State & Local Government Finances 2020

TAXES

State Corporate Income Tax Rates

State	Tax Rate (%)	Income Brackets ($)	Num. of Brackets	Financial Institution Tax Rate (%)[a]	Federal Income Tax Ded.
New Hampshire	7.5 (n)	Flat rate	1	7.5 (n)	No

Note: Tax rates as of January 1, 2023; (a) Rates listed are the corporate income tax rate applied to financial institutions or excise taxes based on income. Some states have other taxes based upon the value of deposits or shares; (n) New Hampshire's 7.5% [for tax years ending on or before 12/31/23] Business Profits Tax is imposed on both corporations and unincorporated associations with gross income over $50,000. In addition, New Hampshire levies a Business Enterprise Tax of 0.60% on the enterprise base (total compensation, interest and dividends paid) for businesses with gross receipts over $222,000 or enterprise base over $111,000, adjusted every biennium for CPI.
Source: Federation of Tax Administrators, State Corporate Income Tax Rates, January 1, 2023

State Individual Income Tax Rates

State	Tax Rate (%)	Income Brackets ($)	Personal Exemptions ($)			Standard Ded. ($)	
			Single	Married	Depend.	Single	Married
New Hampshire	– State income tax of 5% on dividends and interest income only –						

Note: Tax rates as of January 1, 2023; Local- and county-level taxes are not included; Federal income tax is not deductible on state income tax returns
Source: Federation of Tax Administrators, State Individual Income Tax Rates, January 1, 2023

Various State Sales and Excise Tax Rates

State	State Sales Tax (%)	Gasoline[1] ($/gal.)	Cigarette[2] ($/pack)	Spirits[3] ($/gal.)	Wine[4] ($/gal.)	Beer[5] ($/gal.)	Recreational Marijuana (%)
New Hampshire	None	0.2383	1.78	—	—	0.30	Not legal

Note: All tax rates as of January 1, 2023; (1) The American Petroleum Institute has developed a methodology for determining the average tax rate on a gallon of fuel. Rates may include any of the following: excise taxes, environmental fees, storage tank fees, other fees or taxes, general sales tax, and local taxes; (2) The federal excise tax of $1.0066 per pack and local taxes are not included; (3) Rates are those applicable to off-premise sales of 40% alcohol by volume (a.b.v.) distilled spirits in 750ml containers. Local excise taxes are excluded; (4) Rates are those applicable to off-premise sales of 11% a.b.v. non-carbonated wine in 750ml containers; (5) Rates are those applicable to off-premise sales of 4.7% a.b.v. beer in 12 ounce containers.
Source: Tax Foundation, 2023 Facts & Figures: How Does Your State Compare?

State Business Tax Climate Index Rankings

State	Overall Rank	Corporate Tax Rank	Individual Income Tax Rank	Sales Tax Rank	Property Tax Rank	Unemployment Insurance Tax Rank
New Hampshire	6	44	9	1	43	45

Note: The index is a measure of how each state's tax laws affect economic performance. The lower the rank, the more favorable a state's tax system is for business. States without a given tax are given a ranking of 1. The scores/rankings for the District of Columbia do not affect other states. The 2023 index represents the tax climate as of July 1, 2022.
Source: Tax Foundation, State Business Tax Climate Index 2023

TRANSPORTATION

Means of Transportation to Work

Area	Car/Truck/Van		Public Transportation			Bicycle	Walked	Other Means	Worked at Home
	Drove Alone	Car-pooled	Bus	Subway	Railroad				
City	77.8	8.9	0.5	0.0	0.0	0.2	2.6	1.2	8.8
MSA[1]	77.6	7.2	0.6	0.1	0.1	0.2	1.8	0.9	11.5
U.S.	73.2	8.6	2.0	1.6	0.5	0.5	2.5	1.5	9.7

Note: Figures are percentages and cover workers 16 years of age and older; (1) Figures cover the Manchester-Nashua, NH Metropolitan Statistical Area
Source: U.S. Census Bureau, 2017-2021 American Community Survey 5-Year Estimates

Travel Time to Work

Area	Less Than 10 Minutes	10 to 19 Minutes	20 to 29 Minutes	30 to 44 Minutes	45 to 59 Minutes	60 to 89 Minutes	90 Minutes or More
City	12.6	35.5	23.4	14.6	6.4	5.1	2.4
MSA[1]	10.9	29.7	21.2	19.5	8.7	6.7	3.4
U.S.	12.4	28.5	21.0	20.9	8.2	6.2	2.9

Note: Note: Figures are percentages and include workers 16 years old and over; (1) Figures cover the Manchester-Nashua, NH Metropolitan Statistical Area
Source: U.S. Census Bureau, 2017-2021 American Community Survey 5-Year Estimates

Key Congestion Measures

Measure	1990	2000	2010	2015	2020
Annual Hours of Delay, Total (000)	n/a	n/a	n/a	3,780	2,387
Annual Hours of Delay, Per Auto Commuter	n/a	n/a	n/a	22	13
Annual Congestion Cost, Per Auto Commuter ($)	n/a	n/a	n/a	457	302

Note: n/a not available
Source: Texas A&M Transportation Institute, 2021 Urban Mobility Report

Freeway Travel Time Index

Measure	1985	1990	1995	2000	2005	2010	2015	2020
Urban Area Index[1]	n/a	n/a	n/a	n/a	n/a	n/a	1.07	1.05
Urban Area Rank[1,2]	n/a	n/a	n/a	n/a	n/a	n/a	n/a	n/a

Note: Freeway Travel Time Index—the ratio of travel time in the peak period to the travel time at free-flow conditions. For example, a value of 1.30 indicates a 20-minute free-flow trip takes 26 minutes in the peak (20 minutes x 1.30 = 26 minutes); (1) Covers the Manchester NH urban area; (2) Rank is based on 101 larger urban areas (#1 = highest travel time index); n/a not available
Source: Texas A&M Transportation Institute, 2021 Urban Mobility Report

Public Transportation

Agency Name / Mode of Transportation	Vehicles Operated in Maximum Service[1]	Annual Unlinked Passenger Trips[2] (in thous.)	Annual Passenger Miles[3] (in thous.)
Manchester Transit Authority (MTA)			
Bus (directly operated)	14	234.9	n/a
Demand Response (directly operated)	6	12.2	n/a

Note: (1) Number of revenue vehicles operated by the given mode and type of service to meet the annual maximum service requirement. This is the revenue vehicle count during the peak season of the year; on the week and day that maximum service is provided. Vehicles operated in maximum service (VOMS) exclude atypical days and one-time special events; (2) Number of passengers who boarded public transportation vehicles. Passengers are counted each time they board a vehicle no matter how many vehicles they use to travel from their origin to their destination. (3) Sum of the distances ridden by all passengers during the entire fiscal year.
Source: Federal Transit Administration, National Transit Database, 2021

Air Transportation

Airport Name and Code / Type of Service	Passenger Airlines[1]	Passenger Enplanements	Freight Carriers[2]	Freight (lbs)
Manchester Municipal (MHT)				
Domestic service (U.S. carriers - 2022)	18	643,475	7	82,409,080
International service (U.S. carriers - 2021)	0	0	0	0

Note: (1) Includes all U.S.-based major, minor and commuter airlines that carried at least one passenger during the year; (2) Includes all U.S.-based airlines and freight carriers that transported at least one pound of freight during the year.
Source: Bureau of Transportation Statistics, The Intermodal Transportation Database, Air Carriers: T-100 Domestic Market (U.S. Carriers), 2022; Bureau of Transportation Statistics, The Intermodal Transportation Database, Air Carriers: T-100 International Market (U.S. Carriers), 2021

BUSINESSES

Major Business Headquarters

Company Name	Industry	Rankings	
		Fortune[1]	Forbes[2]
No companies listed	-	-	-

Note: (1) Companies that produce a 10-K are ranked 1 to 500 based on 2021 revenue; (2) All private companies with at least $2 billion in annual revenue through the end of their most current fiscal year are ranked 1 to 246; companies listed are headquartered in the city; dashes indicate no ranking
Source: Fortune, "Fortune 500," 2022; Forbes, "America's Largest Private Companies," 2022

Fastest-Growing Businesses

According to *Initiative for a Competitive Inner City (ICIC)*, Manchester is home to one of America's 100 fastest-growing "inner city" companies: **Cookson Communications** (#87). Criteria for inclusion: company must be headquartered in or have 51 percent or more of its physical operations in an economically distressed urban area; must be an independent, for-profit corporation, partnership or proprietorship; must have 10 or more employees and have a five-year sales history that includes sales of at least $200,000 in the base year and at least $1 million in the current year with no decrease in sales over the two most recent years. Companies were ranked overall by revenue growth over the five-year period between 2017 and 2021. *Initiative for a Competitive Inner City (ICIC), "Inner City 100 Companies," 2022*

Living Environment

COST OF LIVING

Cost of Living Index

Composite Index	Groceries	Housing	Utilities	Trans-portation	Health Care	Misc. Goods/ Services
116.1	105.2	109.9	114.9	106.7	130.1	127.0

Note: The Cost of Living Index measures regional differences in the cost of consumer goods and services, excluding taxes and non-consumer expenditures, for professional and managerial households in the top income quintile. It is based on more than 50,000 prices covering almost 60 different items for which prices are collected three times a year by chambers of commerce, economic development organizations or university applied economic centers in each participating urban area. The numbers shown should be read as a percentage above or below the national average of 100. For example, a value of 115.4 in the groceries column indicates that grocery prices are 15.4% higher than the national average. Small differences in the index numbers should not be interpreted as significant; Figures cover the Manchester NH urban area.
Source: The Council for Community and Economic Research, Cost of Living Index, 2022

Grocery Prices

Area[1]	T-Bone Steak ($/pound)	Frying Chicken ($/pound)	Whole Milk ($/half gal.)	Eggs ($/dozen)	Orange Juice ($/64 oz.)	Coffee ($/11.5 oz.)
City[2]	16.69	1.85	2.66	2.57	4.36	5.25
Avg.	13.81	1.59	2.43	2.25	3.85	4.95
Min.	10.17	0.90	1.51	1.30	2.90	3.46
Max.	19.35	3.30	4.32	4.32	5.31	8.59

*Note: (1) Values for the local area are compared with the average, minimum and maximum values for all 286 areas in the Cost of Living Index; (2) Figures cover the Manchester NH urban area; **T-Bone Steak** (price per pound); **Frying Chicken** (price per pound, whole fryer); **Whole Milk** (half gallon carton); **Eggs** (price per dozen, Grade A, large); **Orange Juice** (64 oz. Tropicana or Florida Natural); **Coffee** (11.5 oz. can, vacuum-packed, Maxwell House, Hills Bros, or Folgers).*
Source: The Council for Community and Economic Research, Cost of Living Index, 2022

Housing and Utility Costs

Area[1]	New Home Price ($)	Apartment Rent ($/month)	All Electric ($/month)	Part Electric ($/month)	Other Energy ($/month)	Telephone ($/month)
City[2]	441,922	2,064	-	107.51	118.35	184.25
Avg.	450,913	1,371	176.41	99.93	76.96	190.22
Min.	229,283	546	100.84	31.56	27.15	174.27
Max.	2,434,977	4,569	356.86	249.59	272.24	208.31

*Note: (1) Values for the local area are compared with the average, minimum and maximum values for all 286 areas in the Cost of Living Index; (2) Figures cover the Manchester NH urban area; **New Home Price** (2,400 sf living area, 8,000 sf lot, in urban area with full utilities); **Apartment Rent** (950 sf 2 bedroom/1.5 or 2 bath, unfurnished, excluding all utilities except water); **All Electric** (average monthly cost for an all-electric home); **Part Electric** (average monthly cost for a part-electric home); **Other Energy** (average monthly cost for natural gas, fuel oil, coal, wood, and any other forms of energy except electricity); **Telephone** (price includes the base monthly rate plus taxes and fees for three lines of mobile phone service).*
Source: The Council for Community and Economic Research, Cost of Living Index, 2022

Health Care, Transportation, and Other Costs

Area[1]	Doctor ($/visit)	Dentist ($/visit)	Optometrist ($/visit)	Gasoline ($/gallon)	Beauty Salon ($/visit)	Men's Shirt ($)
City[2]	175.70	152.18	115.00	4.03	59.17	41.12
Avg.	124.91	107.77	117.66	3.86	43.31	34.21
Min.	36.61	58.25	51.79	2.90	22.18	13.05
Max.	250.21	162.58	371.96	5.54	85.61	63.54

*Note: (1) Values for the local area are compared with the average, minimum and maximum values for all 286 areas in the Cost of Living Index; (2) Figures cover the Manchester NH urban area; **Doctor** (general practitioners routine exam of an established patient); **Dentist** (adult teeth cleaning and periodic oral examination); **Optometrist** (full vision eye exam for established adult patient); **Gasoline** (one gallon regular unleaded, national brand, including all taxes, cash price at self-service pump if available); **Beauty Salon** (woman's shampoo, trim, and blow-dry); **Men's Shirt** (cotton/polyester dress shirt, pinpoint weave, long sleeves).*
Source: The Council for Community and Economic Research, Cost of Living Index, 2022

HOUSING

Homeownership Rate

Area	2015 (%)	2016 (%)	2017 (%)	2018 (%)	2019 (%)	2020 (%)	2021 (%)	2022 (%)
MSA[1]	n/a	n/a	n/a	n/a	n/a	n/a	n/a	n/a
U.S.	63.7	63.4	63.9	64.4	64.6	66.6	65.5	65.8

Note: (1) Figures cover the Manchester-Nashua, NH Metropolitan Statistical Area; n/a not available
Source: U.S. Census Bureau, Housing Vacancies and Homeownership Annual Statistics: 2015-2022

House Price Index (HPI)

Area	National Ranking[2]	Quarterly Change (%)	One-Year Change (%)	Five-Year Change (%)	Since 1991Q1 (%)
MSA[1]	126	-0.32	11.34	59.79	253.04
U.S.[3]	–	0.34	8.41	58.44	289.08

Note: The HPI is a weighted repeat sales index. It measures average price changes in repeat sales or refinancings on the same properties. This information is obtained by reviewing repeat mortgage transactions on single-family properties whose mortgages have been purchased or securitized by Fannie Mae or Freddie Mac since January 1975; (1) Figures cover the Manchester-Nashua, NH Metropolitan Statistical Area; (2) Rankings are based on annual percentage change for all metro areas containing at least 15,000 transactions over the last 10 years and ranges from 1 to 257; (3) figures based on a weighted average of Census Division estimates using a seasonally adjusted, purchase-only index; all figures are for the period ending December 31, 2022
Source: Federal Housing Finance Agency, Change in FHFA Metropolitan Area House Price Indexes, 2022Q4

Median Single-Family Home Prices

Area	2020	2021	2022p	Percent Change 2021 to 2022
MSA[1]	357.8	412.6	466.0	12.9
U.S. Average	300.2	357.1	392.6	9.9

Note: Figures are median sales prices of existing single-family homes in thousands of dollars; (p) preliminary; (1) Figures cover the Manchester-Nashua, NH Metropolitan Statistical Area
Source: National Association of Realtors, Median Sales Price of Existing Single-Family Homes for Metropolitan Areas, 4th Quarter 2022

Qualifying Income Based on Median Sales Price of Existing Single-Family Homes

Area	With 5% Down ($)	With 10% Down ($)	With 20% Down ($)
MSA[1]	135,859	128,709	114,408
U.S. Average	112,234	106,237	94,513

Note: Figures are preliminary; Qualifying income is based on a mortgage rate of 6.77%. Monthly principal and interest payment is limited to 25% of income; (1) Figures cover the Manchester-Nashua, NH Metropolitan Statistical Area
Source: National Association of Realtors, Qualifying Income Based on Median Sales Price of Existing Single-Family Homes for Metropolitan Areas, 4th Quarter 2022

Home Value

Area	Under $100,000	$100,000 -$199,999	$200,000 -$299,999	$300,000 -$399,999	$400,000 -$499,999	$500,000 -$999,999	$1,000,000 or more	Median ($)
City	4.7	21.9	39.9	23.6	6.6	3.1	0.1	258,100
MSA[1]	4.2	13.5	30.7	27.5	12.9	10.7	0.5	306,000
U.S.	16.2	24.2	20.1	13.6	8.3	13.6	4.1	244,900

Note: Figures are percentages except for median and cover owner-occupied housing units; (1) Figures cover the Manchester-Nashua, NH Metropolitan Statistical Area
Source: U.S. Census Bureau, 2017-2021 American Community Survey 5-Year Estimates

Year Housing Structure Built

Area	2020 or Later	2010 -2019	2000 -2009	1990 -1999	1980 -1989	1970 -1979	1960 -1969	1950 -1959	1940 -1949	Before 1940	Median Year
City	0.3	2.5	6.2	8.3	16.3	11.9	8.1	10.1	7.2	29.1	1965
MSA[1]	0.1	4.2	9.7	10.9	20.4	15.6	9.5	7.0	3.8	18.8	1977
U.S.	0.2	7.3	13.6	13.6	13.2	14.8	10.3	10.0	4.7	12.2	1979

Note: Figures are percentages except for Median Year; Note: (1) Figures cover the Manchester-Nashua, NH Metropolitan Statistical Area
Source: U.S. Census Bureau, 2017-2021 American Community Survey 5-Year Estimates

Gross Monthly Rent

Area	Under $500	$500 -$999	$1,000 -$1,499	$1,500 -$1,999	$2,000 -$2,499	$2,500 -$2,999	$3,000 and up	Median ($)
City	7.0	21.3	43.4	20.8	5.4	1.4	0.8	1,220
MSA[1]	6.7	18.6	40.2	24.7	6.8	1.9	1.1	1,305
U.S.	8.1	30.5	30.8	16.8	7.3	3.1	3.5	1,163

Note: Figures are percentages except for median; Gross rent is the contract rent plus the estimated average monthly cost of utilities (electricity, gas, and water and sewer) and fuels (oil, coal, kerosene, wood, etc.) if these are paid by the renter (or paid for the renter by someone else); (1) Figures cover the Manchester-Nashua, NH Metropolitan Statistical Area
Source: U.S. Census Bureau, 2017-2021 American Community Survey 5-Year Estimates

HEALTH

Health Risk Factors

Category	MSA[1] (%)	U.S. (%)
Adults aged 18–64 who have any kind of health care coverage	n/a	90.9
Adults who reported being in good or better health	n/a	85.2
Adults who have been told they have high blood cholesterol	n/a	35.7
Adults who have been told they have high blood pressure	n/a	32.4
Adults who are current smokers	n/a	14.4
Adults who currently use e-cigarettes	n/a	6.7
Adults who currently use chewing tobacco, snuff, or snus	n/a	3.5
Adults who are heavy drinkers[2]	n/a	6.3
Adults who are binge drinkers[3]	n/a	15.4
Adults who are overweight (BMI 25.0 - 29.9)	n/a	34.4
Adults who are obese (BMI 30.0 - 99.8)	n/a	33.9
Adults who participated in any physical activities in the past month	n/a	76.3

Note: (1) Figures for the Manchester-Nashua, NH Metropolitan Statistical Area were not available.
(2) Heavy drinkers are classified as adult men having more than 14 drinks per week and adult women having more than 7 drinks per week; (3) Binge drinkers are classified as males having five or more drinks on one occasion or females having four or more drinks on one occasion
Source: Centers for Disease Control and Prevention, Behaviorial Risk Factor Surveillance System, SMART: Selected Metropolitan Area Risk Trends, 2021

Acute and Chronic Health Conditions

Category	MSA[1] (%)	U.S. (%)
Adults who have ever been told they had a heart attack	n/a	4.0
Adults who have ever been told they have angina or coronary heart disease	n/a	3.8
Adults who have ever been told they had a stroke	n/a	3.0
Adults who have ever been told they have asthma	n/a	14.9
Adults who have ever been told they have arthritis	n/a	25.8
Adults who have ever been told they have diabetes[2]	n/a	10.9
Adults who have ever been told they had skin cancer	n/a	6.6
Adults who have ever been told they had any other types of cancer	n/a	7.5
Adults who have ever been told they have COPD	n/a	6.1
Adults who have ever been told they have kidney disease	n/a	3.0
Adults who have ever been told they have a form of depression	n/a	20.5

Note: (1) Figures for the Manchester-Nashua, NH Metropolitan Statistical Area were not available.
(2) Figures do not include pregnancy-related, borderline, or pre-diabetes
Source: Centers for Disease Control and Prevention, Behaviorial Risk Factor Surveillance System, SMART: Selected Metropolitan Area Risk Trends, 2021

Health Screening and Vaccination Rates

Category	MSA[1] (%)	U.S. (%)
Adults who have ever been tested for HIV	n/a	34.9
Adults who have had their blood cholesterol checked within the last five years	n/a	85.2
Adults aged 65+ who have had flu shot within the past year	n/a	68.6
Adults aged 65+ who have ever had a pneumonia vaccination	n/a	71.0

Note: (1) Figures for the Manchester-Nashua, NH Metropolitan Statistical Area were not available.
Source: Centers for Disease Control and Prevention, Behaviorial Risk Factor Surveillance System, SMART: Selected Metropolitan Area Risk Trends, 2021

Disability Status

Category	MSA[1] (%)	U.S. (%)
Adults who reported being deaf	n/a	7.2
Are you blind or have serious difficulty seeing, even when wearing glasses?	n/a	4.8
Are you limited in any way in any of your usual activities due to arthritis?	n/a	11.1
Do you have difficulty doing errands alone?	n/a	7.0
Do you have difficulty dressing or bathing?	n/a	3.6
Do you have serious difficulty concentrating/remembering/making decisions?	n/a	12.1
Do you have serious difficulty walking or climbing stairs?	n/a	12.8

Note: (1) Figures for the Manchester-Nashua, NH Metropolitan Statistical Area were not available.
Source: Centers for Disease Control and Prevention, Behaviorial Risk Factor Surveillance System, SMART: Selected Metropolitan Area Risk Trends, 2021

Mortality Rates for the Top 10 Causes of Death in the U.S.

ICD-10[a] Sub-Chapter	ICD-10[a] Code	Crude Mortality Rate[1] per 100,000 population	
		County[2]	U.S.
Malignant neoplasms	C00-C97	177.6	182.6
Ischaemic heart diseases	I20-I25	92.9	113.1
Other forms of heart disease	I30-I51	70.7	64.4
Other degenerative diseases of the nervous system	G30-G31	34.6	51.0
Cerebrovascular diseases	I60-I69	33.8	47.8
Other external causes of accidental injury	W00-X59	54.7	46.4
Chronic lower respiratory diseases	J40-J47	43.9	45.7
Organic, including symptomatic, mental disorders	F01-F09	64.1	35.9
Hypertensive diseases	I10-I15	20.2	35.0
Diabetes mellitus	E10-E14	25.6	29.6

Note: (a) ICD-10 = International Classification of Diseases 10th Revision; (1) Crude mortality rates are a three-year average covering 2019-2021; (2) Figures cover Hillsborough County.
Source: Centers for Disease Control and Prevention, National Center for Health Statistics. National Vital Statistics System, Mortality 2018-2021 on CDC WONDER Online Database

Mortality Rates for Selected Causes of Death

ICD-10[a] Sub-Chapter	ICD-10[a] Code	Crude Mortality Rate[1] per 100,000 population	
		County[2]	U.S.
Assault	X85-Y09	1.7	7.0
Diseases of the liver	K70-K76	19.8	19.8
Human immunodeficiency virus (HIV) disease	B20-B24	Suppressed	1.5
Influenza and pneumonia	J09-J18	10.5	14.7
Intentional self-harm	X60-X84	18.8	14.3
Malnutrition	E40-E46	3.1	4.3
Obesity and other hyperalimentation	E65-E68	4.3	3.0
Renal failure	N17-N19	12.7	15.7
Transport accidents	V01-V99	9.2	13.6
Viral hepatitis	B15-B19	Unreliable	1.2

Note: (a) ICD-10 = International Classification of Diseases 10th Revision; (1) Crude mortality rates are a three-year average covering 2019-2021; (2) Figures cover Hillsborough County; Data are suppressed when the data meet the criteria for confidentiality constraints; Crude mortality rates are flagged as unreliable when the rate would be calculated with a numerator of 20 or less.
Source: Centers for Disease Control and Prevention, National Center for Health Statistics. National Vital Statistics System, Mortality 2018-2021 on CDC WONDER Online Database

Health Insurance Coverage

Area	With Health Insurance	With Private Health Insurance	With Public Health Insurance	Without Health Insurance	Population Under Age 19 Without Health Insurance
City	90.9	65.9	35.1	9.1	3.8
MSA[1]	93.8	77.2	28.7	6.2	3.4
U.S.	91.2	67.8	35.4	8.8	5.3

Note: Figures are percentages that cover the civilian noninstitutionalized population; (1) Figures cover the Manchester-Nashua, NH Metropolitan Statistical Area
Source: U.S. Census Bureau, 2017-2021 American Community Survey 5-Year Estimates

Number of Medical Professionals

Area	MDs[3]	DOs[3,4]	Dentists	Podiatrists	Chiropractors	Optometrists
County[1] (number)	1,018	103	351	24	111	93
County[1] (rate[2])	240.8	24.4	82.8	5.7	26.2	21.9
U.S. (rate[2])	289.3	23.5	72.5	6.2	28.7	17.4

Note: Data as of 2021 unless noted; (1) Data covers Hillsborough County; (2) Rate per 100,000 population; (3) Data as of 2020 and includes all active, non-federal physicians; (4) Doctor of Osteopathic Medicine
Source: U.S. Department of Health and Human Services, Health Resources and Services Administration, Bureau of Health Professions, Area Resource File (ARF) 2021-2022

EDUCATION

Public School District Statistics

District Name	Schls	Pupils	Pupil/ Teacher Ratio	Minority Pupils[1] (%)	LEP/ELL[2] (%)	IEP[3] (%)
Manchester School District	21	12,510	12.4	49.0	14.4	20.4

Note: Table includes school districts with 2,000 or more students; (1) Percentage of students that are not non-Hispanic white; (2) Percentage of students that are Limited English Proficient or English Language Learners (2018-19); (3) Percentage of students that have an Individualized Education Program (2019-20).
Source: U.S. Department of Education, National Center for Education Statistics, Common Core of Data, Local Education Agency (School District) Universe Survey: School Year 2021-2022

Highest Level of Education

Area	Less than H.S.	H.S. Diploma	Some College, No Deg.	Associate Degree	Bachelor's Degree	Master's Degree	Prof. School Degree	Doctorate Degree
City	11.4	28.8	18.8	9.1	21.5	8.0	1.5	1.0
MSA[1]	7.1	25.6	17.7	9.9	25.0	11.4	1.7	1.6
U.S.	11.1	26.5	20.0	8.7	20.6	9.3	2.2	1.5

Note: Figures cover persons age 25 and over; (1) Figures cover the Manchester-Nashua, NH Metropolitan Statistical Area
Source: U.S. Census Bureau, 2017-2021 American Community Survey 5-Year Estimates

Educational Attainment by Race

Area	High School Graduate or Higher (%)					Bachelor's Degree or Higher (%)				
	Total	White	Black	Asian	Hisp.[2]	Total	White	Black	Asian	Hisp.[2]
City	88.6	90.4	78.2	81.0	67.1	31.9	32.9	17.6	40.8	13.0
MSA[1]	92.9	93.8	82.8	89.8	73.6	39.6	39.8	20.5	62.1	19.0
U.S.	88.9	91.4	87.2	87.6	71.2	33.7	35.5	23.3	55.6	18.4

Note: Figures shown cover persons 25 years old and over; (1) Figures cover the Manchester-Nashua, NH Metropolitan Statistical Area; (2) People of Hispanic origin can be of any race
Source: U.S. Census Bureau, 2017-2021 American Community Survey 5-Year Estimates

School Enrollment by Grade and Control

Area	Preschool (%)		Kindergarten (%)		Grades 1 - 4 (%)		Grades 5 - 8 (%)		Grades 9 - 12 (%)	
	Public	Private	Public	Private	Public	Private	Public	Private	Public	Private
City	58.7	41.3	86.5	13.5	89.0	11.0	93.0	7.0	92.0	8.0
MSA[1]	49.7	50.3	81.7	18.3	87.4	12.6	87.8	12.2	88.9	11.1
U.S.	58.8	41.2	86.3	13.7	88.3	11.7	88.6	11.4	89.4	10.6

Note: Figures shown cover persons 3 years old and over; (1) Figures cover the Manchester-Nashua, NH Metropolitan Statistical Area
Source: U.S. Census Bureau, 2017-2021 American Community Survey 5-Year Estimates

Higher Education

Four-Year Colleges			Two-Year Colleges			Medical Schools[1]	Law Schools[2]	Voc/ Tech[3]
Public	Private Non-profit	Private For-profit	Public	Private Non-profit	Private For-profit			
1	3	0	2	1	0	0	0	5

Note: Figures cover institutions located within the Manchester-Nashua, NH Metropolitan Statistical Area and include main campuses only; (1) includes schools accredited by the Liaison Committee on Medical Education and the American Osteopathic Association's Commission on Osteopathic College Accreditation; (2) includes ABA-accredited schools, schools with provisional ABA accreditation, and state accredited schools; (3) includes all schools with programs that are less than 2 years.
Source: National Center for Education Statistics, Integrated Postsecondary Education System (IPEDS), 2021-22; Wikipedia, List of Medical Schools in the United States, accessed April 10, 2023; Wikipedia, List of Law Schools in the United States, accessed April 10, 2023

EMPLOYERS

Major Employers

Company Name	Industry
C & S Wholesale Grocers Inc	Grocery stores
Concord Hospital	Healthcare
Dartmouth-Hitchcock Medical Center	Healthcare
Elliot Hospital	Healthcare
Fidelity Investments	Financial services
Freudenberg-Nok	Healthcare
Hypertherm	Technology
J Jill	Retailer
Liberty Life Assurance Co	Insurance companies/services
Southern New Hampshire Health	Healthcare
St. Joseph's Hospital	Healthcare
Sturm Ruger & Co. Inc	Firearms
Trustees of Dartmouth College	Education
UA Local 788 Marine Pipefitter	Union
United Physical Therapy	Healthcare
University of New Hampshire	Education
University System of NH	Education

Note: Companies shown are located within the Manchester-Nashua, NH Metropolitan Statistical Area.
Source: Hoovers.com; Wikipedia

Manchester, New Hampshire   285

PUBLIC SAFETY

Crime Rate

Area	Total Crime	Violent Crime Rate				Property Crime Rate		
		Murder	Rape[3]	Robbery	Aggrav. Assault	Burglary	Larceny -Theft	Motor Vehicle Theft
City	2,858.0	4.4	64.6	97.3	426.5	253.9	1,854.6	156.6
Suburbs[1]	801.4	0.0	34.0	8.8	36.6	64.3	609.1	48.6
Metro[2]	1,355.7	1.2	42.2	32.7	141.6	115.4	944.8	77.7
U.S.	2,356.7	6.5	38.4	73.9	279.7	314.2	1,398.0	246.0

Note: Figures are crimes per 100,000 population; (1) All areas within the metro area that are located outside the city limits; (2) Figures cover the Manchester-Nashua, NH Metropolitan Statistical Area; (3) All figures shown were reported using the revised Uniform Crime Reporting (UCR) definition of rape; Due to the transition to the National Incident-Based Reporting System (NIBRS), limited city and metro area data was released for 2021.
Source: FBI Uniform Crime Reports, 2020

Hate Crimes

Area	Number of Quarters Reported	Number of Incidents per Bias Motivation					
		Race/Ethnicity/ Ancestry	Religion	Sexual Orientation	Disability	Gender	Gender Identity
City	4	0	0	1	0	0	0
U.S.	4	5,227	1,244	1,110	130	75	266

Note: Due to the transition to the National Incident-Based Reporting System (NIBRS), limited crime data was released for 2021.
Source: Federal Bureau of Investigation, Hate Crime Statistics 2020

Identity Theft Consumer Reports

Area	Reports	Reports per 100,000 Population	Rank[2]
MSA[1]	720	173	202
U.S.	1,108,609	339	-

Note: (1) Figures cover the Manchester-Nashua, NH Metropolitan Statistical Area; (2) Rank ranges from 1 to 391 where 1 indicates greatest number of identity theft reports per 100,000 population
Source: Federal Trade Commission, Consumer Sentinel Network Data Book 2022

Fraud and Other Consumer Reports

Area	Reports	Reports per 100,000 Population	Rank[2]
MSA[1]	3,757	905	144
U.S.	4,064,520	1,245	-

Note: (1) Figures cover the Manchester-Nashua, NH Metropolitan Statistical Area; (2) Rank ranges from 1 to 391 where 1 indicates greatest number of fraud and other consumer reports per 100,000 population
Source: Federal Trade Commission, Consumer Sentinel Network Data Book 2022

POLITICS

2020 Presidential Election Results

Area	Biden	Trump	Jorgensen	Hawkins	Other
Hillsborough County	52.8	45.2	1.7	0.0	0.3
U.S.	51.3	46.8	1.2	0.3	0.5

Note: Results are percentages and may not add to 100% due to rounding
Source: Dave Leip's Atlas of U.S. Presidential Elections

SPORTS

Professional Sports Teams

Team Name	League	Year Established

No teams are located in the metro area
Source: Wikipedia, Major Professional Sports Teams of the United States and Canada, April 12, 2023

CLIMATE

Average and Extreme Temperatures

Temperature	Jan	Feb	Mar	Apr	May	Jun	Jul	Aug	Sep	Oct	Nov	Dec	Yr.
Extreme High (°F)	68	66	85	95	97	98	102	101	98	90	80	68	102
Average High (°F)	31	34	43	57	69	77	83	80	72	61	48	35	57
Average Temp. (°F)	20	23	33	44	56	65	70	68	59	48	38	25	46
Average Low (°F)	9	11	22	32	42	51	57	55	46	35	28	15	34
Extreme Low (°F)	-33	-27	-16	8	21	30	35	29	22	10	-5	-22	-33

Note: Figures cover the years 1948-1990
Source: National Climatic Data Center, International Station Meteorological Climate Summary, 9/96

Average Precipitation/Snowfall/Humidity

Precip./Humidity	Jan	Feb	Mar	Apr	May	Jun	Jul	Aug	Sep	Oct	Nov	Dec	Yr.
Avg. Precip. (in.)	2.8	2.5	2.9	3.1	3.2	3.1	3.1	3.3	2.9	3.1	3.8	3.2	36.9
Avg. Snowfall (in.)	18	15	11	2	Tr	0	0	0	0	Tr	4	14	63
Avg. Rel. Hum. 7am (%)	76	76	76	75	75	80	82	87	89	86	83	79	80
Avg. Rel. Hum. 4pm (%)	59	55	52	46	47	52	51	53	55	53	61	63	54

Note: Figures cover the years 1948-1990; Tr = Trace amounts (<0.05 in. of rain; <0.5 in. of snow)
Source: National Climatic Data Center, International Station Meteorological Climate Summary, 9/96

Weather Conditions

Temperature			Daytime Sky			Precipitation		
5°F & below	32°F & below	90°F & above	Clear	Partly cloudy	Cloudy	0.01 inch or more precip.	0.1 inch or more snow/ice	Thunder-storms
32	171	12	87	131	147	125	32	19

Note: Figures are average number of days per year and cover the years 1948-1990
Source: National Climatic Data Center, International Station Meteorological Climate Summary, 9/96

HAZARDOUS WASTE

Superfund Sites

The Manchester-Nashua, NH metro area is home to five sites on the EPA's Superfund National Priorities List: **Fletcher's Paint Works & Storage** (final); **Mohawk Tannery** (proposed); **New Hampshire Plating Co.** (final); **Savage Municipal Water Supply** (final); **South Municipal Water Supply Well** (final). There are a total of 1,165 Superfund sites with a status of proposed or final on the list in the U.S. *U.S. Environmental Protection Agency, National Priorities List, April 12, 2023*

AIR QUALITY

Air Quality Trends: Ozone

	1990	1995	2000	2005	2010	2015	2018	2019	2020	2021
MSA[1]	0.085	0.088	0.070	0.082	0.067	0.061	0.066	0.054	0.055	0.061
U.S.	0.087	0.089	0.081	0.080	0.072	0.067	0.069	0.065	0.065	0.067

Note: (1) Data covers the Manchester-Nashua, NH Metropolitan Statistical Area. The values shown are the composite ozone concentration averages among trend sites based on the highest fourth daily maximum 8-hour concentration in parts per million. These trends are based on sites having an adequate record of monitoring data during the trend period. Data from exceptional events are included.
Source: U.S. Environmental Protection Agency, Air Quality Monitoring Information, "Air Quality Trends by City, 1990-2021"

Air Quality Index

Area	Percent of Days when Air Quality was...[2]					AQI Statistics[2]	
	Good	Moderate	Unhealthy for Sensitive Groups	Unhealthy	Very Unhealthy	Maximum	Median
MSA[1]	91.8	7.7	0.5	0.0	0.0	144	36

Note: (1) Data covers the Manchester-Nashua, NH Metropolitan Statistical Area; (2) Based on 365 days with AQI data in 2021. Air Quality Index (AQI) is an index for reporting daily air quality. EPA calculates the AQI for five major air pollutants regulated by the Clean Air Act: ground-level ozone, particle pollution (aka particulate matter), carbon monoxide, sulfur dioxide, and nitrogen dioxide. The AQI runs from 0 to 500. The higher the AQI value, the greater the level of air pollution and the greater the health concern. There are six AQI categories: "Good" AQI is between 0 and 50. Air quality is considered satisfactory; "Moderate" AQI is between 51 and 100. Air quality is acceptable; "Unhealthy for Sensitive Groups" When AQI values are between 101 and 150, members of sensitive groups may experience health effects; "Unhealthy" When AQI values are between 151 and 200 everyone may begin to experience health effects; "Very Unhealthy" AQI values between 201 and 300 trigger a health alert; "Hazardous" AQI values over 300 trigger warnings of emergency conditions (not shown).
Source: U.S. Environmental Protection Agency, Air Quality Index Report, 2021

Air Quality Index Pollutants

Area	Percent of Days when AQI Pollutant was...[2]					
	Carbon Monoxide	Nitrogen Dioxide	Ozone	Sulfur Dioxide	Particulate Matter 2.5	Particulate Matter 10
MSA[1]	0.0	0.0	92.1	(3)	7.9	0.0

Note: (1) Data covers the Manchester-Nashua, NH Metropolitan Statistical Area; (2) Based on 365 days with AQI data in 2021. The Air Quality Index (AQI) is an index for reporting daily air quality. EPA calculates the AQI for five major air pollutants regulated by the Clean Air Act: ground-level ozone, particle pollution (also known as particulate matter), carbon monoxide, sulfur dioxide, and nitrogen dioxide. The AQI runs from 0 to 500. The higher the AQI value, the greater the level of air pollution and the greater the health concern; (3) Sulfur dioxide is no longer included in this table (as of December 8, 2021) because SO_2 concentrations tend to be very localized and not necessarily representative of broad geographical areas like counties and CBSAs.
Source: U.S. Environmental Protection Agency, Air Quality Index Report, 2021

Maximum Air Pollutant Concentrations: Particulate Matter, Ozone, CO and Lead

	Particulate Matter 10 (ug/m^3)	Particulate Matter 2.5 Wtd AM (ug/m^3)	Particulate Matter 2.5 24-Hr (ug/m^3)	Ozone (ppm)	Carbon Monoxide (ppm)	Lead (ug/m^3)
MSA[1] Level	n/a	4.5	13	0.062	1	n/a
NAAQS[2]	150	15	35	0.075	9	0.15
Met NAAQS[2]	n/a	Yes	Yes	Yes	Yes	n/a

Note: (1) Data covers the Manchester-Nashua, NH Metropolitan Statistical Area; Data from exceptional events are included; (2) National Ambient Air Quality Standards; ppm = parts per million; ug/m^3 = micrograms per cubic meter; n/a not available.
Concentrations: Particulate Matter 10 (coarse particulate)—highest second maximum 24-hour concentration; Particulate Matter 2.5 Wtd AM (fine particulate)—highest weighted annual mean concentration; Particulate Matter 2.5 24-Hour (fine particulate)—highest 98th percentile 24-hour concentration; Ozone—highest fourth daily maximum 8-hour concentration; Carbon Monoxide—highest second maximum non-overlapping 8-hour concentration; Lead—maximum running 3-month average
Source: U.S. Environmental Protection Agency, Air Quality Monitoring Information, "Air Quality Statistics by City, 2021"

Maximum Air Pollutant Concentrations: Nitrogen Dioxide and Sulfur Dioxide

	Nitrogen Dioxide AM (ppb)	Nitrogen Dioxide 1-Hr (ppb)	Sulfur Dioxide AM (ppb)	Sulfur Dioxide 1-Hr (ppb)	Sulfur Dioxide 24-Hr (ppb)
MSA[1] Level	n/a	n/a	n/a	1	n/a
NAAQS[2]	53	100	30	75	140
Met NAAQS[2]	n/a	n/a	n/a	Yes	n/a

Note: (1) Data covers the Manchester-Nashua, NH Metropolitan Statistical Area; Data from exceptional events are included; (2) National Ambient Air Quality Standards; ppm = parts per million; ug/m^3 = micrograms per cubic meter; n/a not available.
Concentrations: Nitrogen Dioxide AM—highest arithmetic mean concentration; Nitrogen Dioxide 1-Hr—highest 98th percentile 1-hour daily maximum concentration; Sulfur Dioxide AM—highest annual mean concentration; Sulfur Dioxide 1-Hr—highest 99th percentile 1-hour daily maximum concentration; Sulfur Dioxide 24-Hr—highest second maximum 24-hour concentration
Source: U.S. Environmental Protection Agency, Air Quality Monitoring Information, "Air Quality Statistics by City, 2021"

New Haven, Connecticut

Background

New Haven is coastal city along on the northern shore of Long Island Sound in central Connecticut originally laid out in a grid of nine square blocks, with the central square—the green—left open, which remains the social center of the city to this day. New Haven was nicknamed "The Elm City" for its canopy of trees, the result of the first public tree planting program in America.

One of the main cities in New Haven County, it is the principal municipality of the Greater New Haven area, as well part of the larger New York City metropolitan area. The city is drained by three rivers, the West, the Mill, and the Quinnipiac, which flow into the New Haven and West Haven Harbors.

Originally home to the Quinnipiac tribe, the area that became New Haven was first visited by Dutch traders in 1614 and then in 1637 by a group of English Puritans who had left the Massachusetts Bay Colony. These Puritans purchased the land occupied by the Quinnipiacs in exchange for protection against the rival Pequot tribe and set up a theocratic government in what was called the New Haven Colony and which, in 1664, became part of the Connecticut Colony. In 1716, the city received a major cultural boost when the Collegiate School moved from Old Saybrook to New Haven. Two years later, it took on its current name, Yale, when a wealthy merchant named Elihu Yale made a large donation to the school that set it on its current path.

Incorporated as a city in 1784, New Haven quickly became a leading industrial center thanks largely to the efforts of Yale alumni Eli Whitney who developed the cotton gin and established a gun-making factory in the city. New Haven's status as a gun manufacturing center was cemented during the Civil War when demand for firearms significantly increased and the New Haven Arms Company (later the Winchester Repeating Arms Company) was founded. The number of residents grew steadily after the war, with increased immigration from Italy and Eastern Europe swelling the population, which doubled between 1870 and 1900.

New Haven continued to grow throughout the first half of the 20th century with large populations of African Americans and Puerto Ricans moving to the city. During the 1950s, New Haven suffered from a mass exodus of white middle-class workers. Thanks to policies such as redlining and rezoning, as well as the departure of the city's industrial base, conditions in the city began to deteriorate.

Since 2000, several revitalization projects have brought new life to downtown New Haven, transforming it into a desirable place for people to live. Community policing resulted in crime rates dropping at the beginning of the 21st century, and the growth of Yale University helped create a service sector economy, particularly in education and healthcare. In 2018, the city instituted Bike New Haven bike share program.

Today, economically, New Haven is dominated by Yale University, the largest employer and taxpayer in the city. Other large employers include Yale-New Haven Hospital, Southern Connecticut State University, and Alexion Pharmaceuticals. Once an industrial center, New Haven has largely moved away from its manufacturing tradition, and is now a burgeoning center for healthcare, biotechnology, professional services, financial services, and retail, with clothing stores Gant and Ann Taylor founded in the city. It's also one of the top cities in the country for launching tech startups.

Culturally, New Haven is extraordinarily rich, largely thanks again to Yale. Among the numerous world-class museums are the Beinecke Rare Book and Manuscript Library, the Yale University Art Gallery, and the New Haven Museum and Historical Society. The Yale Repertory Theater, the Long Wharf Theater, and the Shubert Theater are among the city's numerous venues for plays and performing arts. The city is served musically by the New Haven Symphony Orchestra which occasionally performs for free on the New Haven Green. The Yale School of Music also offers free concerts to residents. The New Haven Jazz Festival, revived in 2008, is a popular annual event.

New Haven is a culinary hotspot, with nearly 60 Zagat-rated restaurants. Excelling in both fine dining and lowbrow treats, its signature New Haven style pizza is served up in classic neighborhood joints like the legendary Pepe's. And Louis Lassan, the founder of Louis' Lunch, is credited by the Library of Congress as having invented the hamburger and steak sandwich.

New Haven experiences a temperate climate, marked by hot, humid summers and moderately cold winters. Average temperatures exceed 80 degrees 70 days a year. In January, the average high is 37.8 degrees and the average low 22.2 degrees. Although extreme weather is rare, hurricanes have struck New Haven on several occasions.

Rankings

General Rankings

- New Haven was selected as an "All-America City" by the National Civic League. The All-America City Award recognizes civic excellence and in 2022 honored 10 communities that best exemplify the spirit of grassroots citizen involvement and cross-sector collaborative problem solving to collectively tackle pressing and complex issues. This year's theme was: "Housing as a Platform to Promote Early School Success and Equitable Learning Recovery." *National Civic League, "2022 All-America City Awards," July 21, 2022*

Business/Finance Rankings

- The Brookings Institution ranked the nation's largest cities based on income inequality. New Haven was ranked #35 (#1 = greatest inequality). Criteria: the "95/20 ratio," a figure representing the income at which a household earns more than 95 percent of all other households, divided by the income at which a household earns more than only 20 percent of all other households. *Brookings Institution, "Household Income Inequality, Largest Cities of 97 Large U.S. Metro Areas, 2014-2016," February 5, 2018*

- The Brookings Institution ranked the 100 largest metro areas in the U.S. based on income inequality. New Haven was ranked #30 (#1 = greatest inequality). Criteria: the "95/20 ratio," a figure representing the income at which a household earns more than 95 percent of all other households, divided by the income at which a household earns more than only 20 percent of all other households. *Brookings Institution, "Household Income Inequality, 100 Largest U.S. Metro Areas, 2014-2016," February 5, 2018*

- The New Haven metro area appeared on the Milken Institute "2022 Best Performing Cities" list. Rank: #117 out of 200 large metro areas (population over 250,000). Criteria: job growth; wage and salary growth; high-tech output growth; housing affordability; household broadband access. *Milken Institute, "Best-Performing Cities 2022," March 28, 2022*

- *Forbes* ranked the 200 most populous metro areas to determine the nation's "Best Places for Business and Careers." The New Haven metro area was ranked #169. Criteria: costs (business and living); job growth (past and projected); income growth; quality of life; educational attainment (college and high school); projected economic growth; cultural and leisure opportunities; workplace tolerance laws; net migration patterns. *Forbes, "The Best Places for Business and Careers 2019: Seattle Still On Top," October 30, 2019*

Education Rankings

- Personal finance website *WalletHub* analyzed the 150 largest U.S. metropolitan statistical areas to determine where the most educated Americans are putting their degrees to work. Criteria: education levels; percentage of workers with degrees; education quality and attainment gap; public school quality rankings; quality and enrollment of each metro area's universities. New Haven was ranked #43 (#1 = most educated city). *www.WalletHub.com, "Most & Least Educated Cities in America," July 18, 2022*

Health/Fitness Rankings

- New Haven was identified as a "2022 Spring Allergy Capital." The area ranked #5 out of 100. Three groups of factors were used to identify the most challenging cities for people with allergies during the spring season: annual spring pollen scores; over the counter allergy medicine use; number of board-certified allergy specialists. *Asthma and Allergy Foundation of America, "Spring Allergy Capitals 2022," March 2, 2022*

- New Haven was identified as a "2022 Fall Allergy Capital." The area ranked #9 out of 100. Three groups of factors were used to identify the most challenging cities for people with allergies during the fall season: annual fall pollen scores; over the counter allergy medicine use; number of board-certified allergy specialists. *Asthma and Allergy Foundation of America, "Fall Allergy Capitals 2022," March 2, 2022*

- New Haven was identified as a "2022 Asthma Capital." The area ranked #90 out of the nation's 100 largest metropolitan areas. Criteria: estimated asthma prevalence; asthma-related mortality; and ER visits due to asthma. Risk factors analyzed but not factored in the rankings: annual pollen score; annual air quality; public smoking laws; access to board-certified asthma specialists; rescue and controller medication use; uninsured rate; poverty rate. *Asthma and Allergy Foundation of America, "Asthma Capitals 2022: The Most Challenging Places to Live With Asthma," September 14, 2022*

Real Estate Rankings

- *WalletHub* compared the most populated U.S. cities to determine which had the best markets for real estate agents. New Haven ranked #168 where demand was high and pay was the best. Criteria: sales per agent; annual median wage for real-estate agents; monthly average starting salary for real estate agents; real estate job density and competition; unemployment rate; home turnover rate; housing-market health index; and other relevant metrics. *www.WalletHub.com, "2021 Best Places to Be a Real Estate Agent," May 12, 2021*

- New Haven was ranked #90 out of 235 metro areas in terms of housing affordability in 2022 by the National Association of Home Builders (#1 = most affordable). Criteria: the share of homes sold in that area affordable to a family earning the local median income, based on standard mortgage underwriting criteria. *National Association of Home Builders®, NAHB-Wells Fargo Housing Opportunity Index, 4th Quarter 2022*

Safety Rankings

- The National Insurance Crime Bureau ranked 390 metro areas in the U.S. in terms of per capita rates of vehicle theft. The New Haven metro area ranked #90 (#1 = highest rate). Criteria: number of vehicle theft offenses per 100,000 inhabitants in 2021. *National Insurance Crime Bureau, "Hot Spots 2021," September 1, 2022*

Seniors/Retirement Rankings

- From its Best Cities for Successful Aging indexes, the Milken Institute generated rankings for metropolitan areas, weighing data in nine categories—health care, wellness, living arrangements, transportation and convenience, financial characteristics, education, employment, community engagement, and overall livability. The New Haven metro area was ranked #78 overall in the large metro area category. *Milken Institute, "Best Cities for Successful Aging, 2017" March 14, 2017*

Transportation Rankings

- The business website *24/7 Wall St.* reviewed U.S. Census data to identify the 25 cities where the largest share of households do not own a vehicle. New Haven held the #7 position. *247wallst.com, "Cities Where No One Wants to Drive," January 12, 2020*

Women/Minorities Rankings

- Personal finance website *WalletHub* compared more than 180 U.S. cities across two key dimensions, "Hispanic Business-Friendliness" and "Hispanic Purchasing Power," to arrive at the most favorable conditions for Hispanic entrepreneurs. New Haven was ranked #179 out of 182. Criteria includes: share of Hispanic-Owned Businesses; Hispanic entrepreneurship rate to median annual income of Hispanics; Small Business-Friendliness score; cost of living; and number of Hispanics with at least a bachelor's degree. *WalletHub.com, "2019's Best Cities for Hispanic Entrepreneurs," May 1, 2019*

Miscellaneous Rankings

- *WalletHub* compared the 150 most populated U.S. cities to determine their operating efficiency. A "Quality of Services" score was constructed for each city and then divided by the total budget per capita to reveal which were managed the best. New Haven ranked #131. Criteria: financial stability; economy; education; safety; health; infrastructure and pollution. *www.WalletHub.com, "2022's Best- & Worst-Run Cities in America," June 21, 2022*

Business Environment

DEMOGRAPHICS

Population Growth

Area	1990 Census	2000 Census	2010 Census	2020 Census	Population Growth (%)	
					1990-2020	2010-2020
City	130,474	123,626	129,779	134,023	2.7	3.3
MSA[1]	804,219	824,008	862,477	864,835	7.5	0.3
U.S.	248,709,873	281,421,906	308,745,538	331,449,281	33.3	7.4

Note: (1) Figures cover the New Haven-Milford, CT Metropolitan Statistical Area
Source: U.S. Census Bureau, 1990 Census, 2000 Census, 2010 Census, 2020 Census

Race

Area	White Alone[2] (%)	Black Alone[2] (%)	Asian Alone[2] (%)	AIAN[3] Alone[2] (%)	NHOPI[4] Alone[2] (%)	Other Race Alone[2] (%)	Two or More Races (%)
City	32.7	32.2	6.8	1.0	0.1	15.3	12.0
MSA[1]	62.9	13.8	4.3	0.5	0.1	9.0	9.5
U.S.	61.6	12.4	6.0	1.1	0.2	8.4	10.2

Note: (1) Figures cover the New Haven-Milford, CT Metropolitan Statistical Area; (2) Alone is defined as not being in combination with one or more other races; (3) American Indian and Alaska Native; (4) Native Hawaiian and Other Pacific Islander
Source: U.S. Census Bureau, 2020 Census

Hispanic or Latino Origin

Area	Total (%)	Mexican (%)	Puerto Rican (%)	Cuban (%)	Other (%)
City	30.3	5.3	16.5	0.4	8.1
MSA[1]	19.2	2.2	10.6	0.4	6.0
U.S.	18.4	11.2	1.8	0.7	4.7

Note: Persons of Hispanic or Latino origin can be of any race; (1) Figures cover the New Haven-Milford, CT Metropolitan Statistical Area
Source: U.S. Census Bureau, 2017-2021 American Community Survey 5-Year Estimates

Age

Area	Percent of Population									Median Age
	Under Age 5	Age 5–19	Age 20–34	Age 35–44	Age 45–54	Age 55–64	Age 65–74	Age 75–84	Age 85+	
City	5.6	20.8	30.4	12.8	10.0	9.4	6.6	3.1	1.2	31.0
MSA[1]	4.9	18.1	20.3	11.9	12.6	14.1	10.4	5.3	2.5	40.4
U.S.	5.6	19.2	20.2	12.7	12.4	13.1	10.0	4.9	1.9	38.8

Note: (1) Figures cover the New Haven-Milford, CT Metropolitan Statistical Area
Source: U.S. Census Bureau, 2020 Census

Disability by Age

Area	All Ages	Under 18 Years Old	18 to 64 Years Old	65 Years and Over
City	10.3	4.2	8.8	33.4
MSA[1]	11.6	3.7	9.2	29.9
U.S.	12.6	4.4	10.3	33.4

Note: Figures show percent of the civilian noninstitutionalized population that reported having a disability. Disability status is determined from six types of difficulty: vision, hearing, cognitive, ambulatory, self-care, and independent living. For children under 5 years old, hearing and vision difficulty are used to determine disability status. For children between the ages of 5 and 14, disability status is determined from hearing, vision, cognitive, ambulatory, and self-care difficulties. For people aged 15 years and older, they are considered to have a disability if they have difficulty with any one of the six difficulty types; Note: (1) Figures cover the New Haven-Milford, CT Metropolitan Statistical Area
Source: U.S. Census Bureau, 2017-2021 American Community Survey 5-Year Estimates

Ancestry

Area	German	Irish	English	American	Italian	Polish	French[2]	Scottish	Dutch
City	3.9	6.2	3.2	2.0	8.2	2.0	1.2	0.5	0.5
MSA[1]	7.5	14.2	7.1	2.9	19.9	5.4	3.0	1.0	0.5
U.S.	12.8	9.6	8.1	5.7	5.0	2.7	2.2	1.6	1.1

Note: Figures are the percentage of the total population reporting a particular ancestry. The nine most commonly reported ancestries in the U.S. are shown. Figures include multiple ancestries (e.g. if a person reported being Irish and Italian, they were included in both columns); (1) Figures cover the New Haven-Milford, CT Metropolitan Statistical Area; (2) Excludes Basque
Source: U.S. Census Bureau, 2017-2021 American Community Survey 5-Year Estimates

Foreign-born Population

Area	Any Foreign Country	Asia	Mexico	Europe	Caribbean	Central America[2]	South America	Africa	Canada
City	17.4	4.2	2.7	2.4	2.6	1.3	2.3	1.5	0.3
MSA[1]	13.4	3.2	1.1	2.9	2.1	0.6	2.1	1.0	0.3
U.S.	13.6	4.2	3.3	1.5	1.4	1.1	1.1	0.8	0.2

Note: (1) Figures cover the New Haven-Milford, CT Metropolitan Statistical Area; (2) Excludes Mexico.
Source: U.S. Census Bureau, 2017-2021 American Community Survey 5-Year Estimates

Household Size

Area	Persons in Household (%)							Average Household Size
	One	Two	Three	Four	Five	Six	Seven or More	
City	36.7	29.2	16.2	9.1	5.3	2.1	1.4	2.50
MSA[1]	30.7	33.2	16.5	12.3	4.8	1.6	1.0	2.50
U.S.	28.1	33.8	15.5	12.9	6.0	2.3	1.4	2.60

Note: (1) Figures cover the New Haven-Milford, CT Metropolitan Statistical Area
Source: U.S. Census Bureau, 2017-2021 American Community Survey 5-Year Estimates

Household Relationships

Area	House-holder	Opposite-sex Spouse	Same-sex Spouse	Opposite-sex Unmarried Partner	Same-sex Unmarried Partner	Child[2]	Grand-child	Other Relatives	Non-relatives
City	39.0	9.4	0.3	2.9	0.2	27.0	2.5	5.0	5.7
MSA[1]	39.7	16.5	0.2	2.6	0.2	28.1	2.0	4.4	2.9
U.S.	38.3	17.5	0.2	2.5	0.2	28.3	2.4	4.8	3.4

Note: Figures are percent of the total population; (1) Figures cover the New Haven-Milford, CT Metropolitan Statistical Area; (2) Includes biological, adopted, and stepchildren of the householder
Source: U.S. Census Bureau, 2020 Census

Gender

Area	Males	Females	Males per 100 Females
City	64,141	69,882	91.8
MSA[1]	415,391	449,444	92.4
U.S.	162,685,811	168,763,470	96.4

Note: (1) Figures cover the New Haven-Milford, CT Metropolitan Statistical Area
Source: U.S. Census Bureau, 2020 Census

Marital Status

Area	Never Married	Now Married[2]	Separated	Widowed	Divorced
City	59.1	25.5	2.4	3.9	9.1
MSA[1]	38.2	43.7	1.6	5.7	10.8
U.S.	33.8	48.0	1.8	5.6	10.8

Note: Figures are percentages and cover the population 15 years of age and older; (1) Figures cover the New Haven-Milford, CT Metropolitan Statistical Area; (2) Excludes separated
Source: U.S. Census Bureau, 2017-2021 American Community Survey 5-Year Estimates

Religious Groups by Family

Area	Catholic	Baptist	Methodist	LDS[2]	Pentecostal	Lutheran	Islam	Adventist	Other
MSA[1]	29.9	1.4	1.2	0.4	1.2	0.4	0.9	1.2	9.9
U.S.	18.7	7.3	3.0	2.0	1.8	1.7	1.3	1.3	11.6

Note: Figures are the number of adherents as a percentage of the total population and cover the eight largest religious groups in the U.S; (1) Figures cover the New Haven-Milford, CT Metropolitan Statistical Area; (2) Church of Jesus Christ of Latter-day Saints
Sources: 2020 U.S. Religion Census, Association of Statisticians of American Religious Bodies; The Association of Religion Data Archives (ARDA)

Religious Groups by Tradition

Area	Catholic	Evangelical Protestant	Mainline Protestant	Black Protestant	Islam	Judaism	Hinduism	Orthodox	Buddhism
MSA[1]	29.9	6.4	4.4	1.4	0.9	1.0	0.3	0.5	0.4
U.S.	18.7	16.5	5.2	2.3	1.3	0.6	0.4	0.4	0.3

Note: Figures are the number of adherents as a percentage of the total population; (1) Figures cover the New Haven-Milford, CT Metropolitan Statistical Area
Sources: 2020 U.S. Religion Census, Association of Statisticians of American Religious Bodies; The Association of Religion Data Archives (ARDA)

294   New Haven, Connecticut

ECONOMY

Gross Metropolitan Product

Area	2020	2021	2022	2023	Rank[2]
MSA[1]	53.0	57.1	61.7	64.7	61

Note: Figures are in billions of dollars; (1) Figures cover the New Haven-Milford, CT Metropolitan Statistical Area; (2) Rank is based on 2021 data and ranges from 1 to 381
Source: U.S. Conference of Mayors, U.S. Metro Economies: U.S. Metros Compared to Global and State Economies, June 2022

Economic Growth

Area	2018-20 (%)	2021 (%)	2022 (%)	2023 (%)	Rank[2]
MSA[1]	-0.9	4.6	2.8	1.7	206
U.S.	-0.6	5.7	3.1	2.9	

Note: Figures are real gross metropolitan product (GMP) growth rates and represent average annual percent change; (1) Figures cover the New Haven-Milford, CT Metropolitan Statistical Area; (2) Rank is based on 2020 2-year average annual percent change and ranges from 1 to 381
Source: U.S. Conference of Mayors, U.S. Metro Economies: U.S. Metros Compared to Global and State Economies, June 2022

Metropolitan Area Exports

Area	2016	2017	2018	2019	2020	2021	Rank[2]
MSA[1]	1,819.8	1,876.3	2,082.3	2,133.8	2,330.5	2,667.5	91

Note: Figures are in millions of dollars; (1) Figures cover the New Haven-Milford, CT Metropolitan Statistical Area; (2) Rank is based on 2021 data and ranges from 1 to 388
Source: U.S. Department of Commerce, International Trade Administration, Office of Trade and Economic Analysis, Industry and Analysis, Exports by Metropolitan Area, data extracted March 16, 2023

Building Permits

Area	Single-Family			Multi-Family			Total		
	2021	2022	Pct. Chg.	2021	2022	Pct. Chg.	2021	2022	Pct. Chg.
City	13	10	-23.1	286	491	71.7	299	501	67.6
MSA[1]	497	493	-0.8	486	770	58.4	983	1,263	28.5
U.S.	1,115,400	975,600	-12.5	621,600	689,500	10.9	1,737,000	1,665,100	-4.1

Note: (1) Figures cover the New Haven-Milford, CT Metropolitan Statistical Area; Figures represent new, privately-owned housing units authorized (unadjusted data); All permit data are based on estimates with imputation
Source: U.S. Census Bureau, Manufacturing, Mining, and Construction Statistics, Building Permits, 2021, 2022

Bankruptcy Filings

Area	Business Filings			Nonbusiness Filings		
	2021	2022	% Chg.	2021	2022	% Chg.
New Haven County	14	12	-14.3	864	719	-16.8
U.S.	14,347	13,481	-6.0	399,269	374,240	-6.3

Note: Business filings include Chapter 7, Chapter 9, Chapter 11, Chapter 12, Chapter 13, Chapter 15, and Section 304; Nonbusiness filings include Chapter 7, Chapter 11, and Chapter 13
Source: Administrative Office of the U.S. Courts, Business and Nonbusiness Bankruptcy, County Cases Commenced by Chapter of the Bankruptcy Code, During the 12-Month Period Ending December 31, 2021 and Business and Nonbusiness Bankruptcy, County Cases Commenced by Chapter of the Bankruptcy Code, During the 12-Month Period Ending December 31, 2022

Housing Vacancy Rates

Area	Gross Vacancy Rate[2] (%)			Year-Round Vacancy Rate[3] (%)			Rental Vacancy Rate[4] (%)			Homeowner Vacancy Rate[5] (%)		
	2020	2021	2022	2020	2021	2022	2020	2021	2022	2020	2021	2022
MSA[1]	9.4	7.9	6.8	8.4	7.2	6.4	7.8	5.4	2.6	0.2	0.5	1.1
U.S.	10.6	10.8	10.5	8.2	8.4	8.2	6.3	6.1	5.8	1.0	0.9	0.8

Note: (1) Figures cover the New Haven-Milford, CT Metropolitan Statistical Area; (2) The percentage of the total housing inventory that is vacant; (3) The percentage of the housing inventory (excluding seasonal units) that is year-round vacant; (4) The percentage of rental inventory that is vacant for rent; (5) The percentage of homeowner inventory that is vacant for sale
Source: U.S. Census Bureau, Housing Vacancies and Homeownership Annual Statistics: 2020, 2021, 2022

INCOME

Income

Area	Per Capita ($)	Median Household ($)	Average Household ($)
City	29,348	48,973	73,450
MSA[1]	41,192	75,043	102,367
U.S.	37,638	69,021	97,196

Note: (1) Figures cover the New Haven-Milford, CT Metropolitan Statistical Area
Source: U.S. Census Bureau, 2017-2021 American Community Survey 5-Year Estimates

New Haven, Connecticut 295

Household Income Distribution

Area	Under $15,000	$15,000 -$24,999	$25,000 -$34,999	$35,000 -$49,999	$50,000 -$74,999	$75,000 -$99,999	$100,000 -$149,999	$150,000 and up
				Percent of Households Earning				
City	18.5	11.0	9.8	11.2	17.2	10.3	11.4	10.6
MSA[1]	9.4	7.6	6.9	10.1	15.8	12.5	17.1	20.4
U.S.	9.4	7.8	8.2	11.4	16.8	12.8	16.3	17.3

Note: (1) Figures cover the New Haven-Milford, CT Metropolitan Statistical Area
Source: U.S. Census Bureau, 2017-2021 American Community Survey 5-Year Estimates

Poverty Rate

Area	All Ages	Under 18 Years Old	18 to 64 Years Old	65 Years and Over
City	24.6	31.4	23.3	17.4
MSA[1]	11.5	15.8	11.1	7.9
U.S.	12.6	17.0	11.8	9.6

Note: Figures are percentage of people whose income during the past 12 months was below the poverty level;
(1) Figures cover the New Haven-Milford, CT Metropolitan Statistical Area
Source: U.S. Census Bureau, 2017-2021 American Community Survey 5-Year Estimates

EMPLOYMENT

Labor Force and Employment

Area	Civilian Labor Force			Workers Employed		
	Dec. 2021	Dec. 2022	% Chg.	Dec. 2021	Dec. 2022	% Chg.
City	65,615	66,515	1.4	62,503	64,310	2.9
NECTA[1]	327,755	334,058	1.9	315,344	324,400	2.9
U.S.	161,696,000	164,224,000	1.6	155,732,000	158,872,000	2.0

Note: Data is not seasonally adjusted and covers workers 16 years of age and older; (1) Figures cover the New Haven, CT New England City and Town Area
Source: Bureau of Labor Statistics, Local Area Unemployment Statistics

Unemployment Rate

Area	2022											
	Jan.	Feb.	Mar.	Apr.	May	Jun.	Jul.	Aug.	Sep.	Oct.	Nov.	Dec.
City	5.5	5.4	4.4	4.1	4.8	5.0	5.6	5.4	4.7	4.7	4.0	3.3
NECTA[1]	4.6	4.6	3.9	3.5	3.8	3.9	4.2	4.1	3.7	3.7	3.3	2.9
U.S.	4.4	4.1	3.8	3.3	3.4	3.8	3.8	3.8	3.3	3.4	3.4	3.3

Note: Data is not seasonally adjusted and covers workers 16 years of age and older; (1) Figures cover the New Haven, CT New England City and Town Area
Source: Bureau of Labor Statistics, Local Area Unemployment Statistics

Average Wages

Occupation	$/Hr.	Occupation	$/Hr.
Accountants and Auditors	40.18	Maintenance and Repair Workers	24.69
Automotive Mechanics	25.11	Marketing Managers	71.85
Bookkeepers	25.93	Network and Computer Systems Admin.	45.08
Carpenters	29.63	Nurses, Licensed Practical	30.20
Cashiers	14.82	Nurses, Registered	46.18
Computer Programmers	46.28	Nursing Assistants	18.43
Computer Systems Analysts	50.48	Office Clerks, General	21.09
Computer User Support Specialists	31.79	Physical Therapists	48.79
Construction Laborers	25.19	Physicians	130.80
Cooks, Restaurant	17.29	Plumbers, Pipefitters and Steamfitters	34.63
Customer Service Representatives	21.99	Police and Sheriff's Patrol Officers	36.86
Dentists	95.87	Postal Service Mail Carriers	26.76
Electricians	33.24	Real Estate Sales Agents	29.22
Engineers, Electrical	50.00	Retail Salespersons	18.46
Fast Food and Counter Workers	14.76	Sales Representatives, Technical/Scientific	45.89
Financial Managers	71.48	Secretaries, Exc. Legal/Medical/Executive	26.88
First-Line Supervisors of Office Workers	34.08	Security Guards	18.52
General and Operations Managers	70.00	Surgeons	n/a
Hairdressers/Cosmetologists	18.17	Teacher Assistants, Exc. Postsecondary*	18.30
Home Health and Personal Care Aides	16.48	Teachers, Secondary School, Exc. Sp. Ed.*	36.32
Janitors and Cleaners	18.12	Telemarketers	23.10
Landscaping/Groundskeeping Workers	20.86	Truck Drivers, Heavy/Tractor-Trailer	26.23
Lawyers	73.87	Truck Drivers, Light/Delivery Services	21.59
Maids and Housekeeping Cleaners	15.86	Waiters and Waitresses	19.08

Note: Wage data covers the New Haven, CT New England City and Town Area; (*) Hourly wages were calculated from annual wage data based on a 40 hour work week; n/a not available.
Source: Bureau of Labor Statistics, Metro Area Occupational Employment & Wage Estimates, May 2022

Employment by Industry

Sector	NECTA[1]		U.S.
	Number of Employees	Percent of Total	Percent of Total
Construction, Mining, and Logging	11,300	3.7	5.4
Private Education and Health Services	88,300	29.2	16.1
Financial Activities	11,900	3.9	5.9
Government	36,100	11.9	14.5
Information	3,800	1.3	2.0
Leisure and Hospitality	26,400	8.7	10.3
Manufacturing	23,600	7.8	8.4
Other Services	10,600	3.5	3.7
Professional and Business Services	31,600	10.4	14.7
Retail Trade	27,200	9.0	10.2
Transportation, Warehousing, and Utilities	20,200	6.7	4.9
Wholesale Trade	11,800	3.9	3.9

Note: Figures are non-farm employment as of December 2022. Figures are not seasonally adjusted and include workers 16 years of age and older; (1) Figures cover the New Haven, CT New England City and Town Area
Source: Bureau of Labor Statistics, Current Employment Statistics, Employment, Hours, and Earnings

Employment by Occupation

Occupation Classification	City (%)	MSA[1] (%)	U.S. (%)
Management, Business, Science, and Arts	41.7	43.4	40.3
Natural Resources, Construction, and Maintenance	6.5	7.6	8.7
Production, Transportation, and Material Moving	12.6	11.7	13.1
Sales and Office	16.3	19.9	20.9
Service	22.9	17.4	17.0

Note: Figures cover employed civilians 16 years of age and older; (1) Figures cover the New Haven-Milford, CT Metropolitan Statistical Area
Source: U.S. Census Bureau, 2017-2021 American Community Survey 5-Year Estimates

Occupations with Greatest Projected Employment Growth: 2022 – 2024

Occupation[1]	2022 Employment	2024 Projected Employment	Numeric Employment Change	Percent Employment Change
Home Health and Personal Care Aides	45,380	47,930	2,550	5.6
Laborers and Freight, Stock, and Material Movers, Hand	26,590	27,860	1,270	4.8
Registered Nurses	35,090	36,230	1,140	3.2
General and Operations Managers	39,300	40,420	1,120	2.8
Order Clerks	9,990	11,090	1,100	11.0
Cooks, Restaurant	12,080	13,090	1,010	8.4
Stockers and Order Fillers	25,760	26,720	960	3.7
Software Developers and Software Quality Assurance Analysts and Testers	20,800	21,690	890	4.3
Janitors and Cleaners, Except Maids and Housekeeping Cleaners	33,990	34,780	790	2.3
Fast Food and Counter Workers	27,740	28,470	730	2.6

Note: Projections cover Connecticut; (1) Sorted by numeric employment change
Source: www.projectionscentral.com, State Occupational Projections, 2022–2024 Short-Term Projections

Fastest-Growing Occupations: 2022 – 2024

Occupation[1]	2022 Employment	2024 Projected Employment	Numeric Employment Change	Percent Employment Change
Ushers, Lobby Attendants, and Ticket Takers	280	330	50	17.9
Crossing Guards	1,730	1,950	220	12.7
Farmers, Ranchers, and Other Agricultural Managers	1,290	1,450	160	12.4
Athletes and Sports Competitors	700	780	80	11.4
Sailors and Marine Oilers	440	490	50	11.4
Order Clerks	9,990	11,090	1,100	11.0
Farmworkers and Laborers, Crop, Nursery, and Greenhouse	2,730	3,020	290	10.6
Nurse Practitioners	2,840	3,120	280	9.9
Biological Technicians	920	1,010	90	9.8
Directors, Religious Activities and Education	1,020	1,120	100	9.8

Note: Projections cover Connecticut; (1) Sorted by percent employment change and excludes occupations with numeric employment change less than 50
Source: www.projectionscentral.com, State Occupational Projections, 2022–2024 Short-Term Projections

New Haven, Connecticut   297

CITY FINANCES

City Government Finances

Component	2020 ($000)	2020 ($ per capita)
Total Revenues	967,534	7,428
Total Expenditures	864,441	6,637
Debt Outstanding	742,277	5,699
Cash and Securities[1]	227,193	1,744

Note: (1) Cash and security holdings of a government at the close of its fiscal year, including those of its dependent agencies, utilities, and liquor stores.
Source: U.S. Census Bureau, State & Local Government Finances 2020

City Government Revenue by Source

Source	2020 ($000)	2020 ($ per capita)	2020 (%)
General Revenue			
From Federal Government	10,120	78	1.0
From State Government	574,137	4,408	59.3
From Local Governments	2,324	18	0.2
Taxes			
Property	282,790	2,171	29.2
Sales and Gross Receipts	0	0	0.0
Personal Income	0	0	0.0
Corporate Income	0	0	0.0
Motor Vehicle License	0	0	0.0
Other Taxes	24,927	191	2.6
Current Charges	40,881	314	4.2
Liquor Store	0	0	0.0
Utility	0	0	0.0

Source: U.S. Census Bureau, State & Local Government Finances 2020

City Government Expenditures by Function

Function	2020 ($000)	2020 ($ per capita)	2020 (%)
General Direct Expenditures			
Air Transportation	0	0	0.0
Corrections	0	0	0.0
Education	380,201	2,919	44.0
Employment Security Administration	0	0	0.0
Financial Administration	12,163	93	1.4
Fire Protection	34,978	268	4.0
General Public Buildings	0	0	0.0
Governmental Administration, Other	52,412	402	6.1
Health	0	0	0.0
Highways	25,017	192	2.9
Hospitals	0	0	0.0
Housing and Community Development	0	0	0.0
Interest on General Debt	29,423	225	3.4
Judicial and Legal	2,462	18	0.3
Libraries	3,879	29	0.4
Parking	22,498	172	2.6
Parks and Recreation	0	0	0.0
Police Protection	76,887	590	8.9
Public Welfare	0	0	0.0
Sewerage	0	0	0.0
Solid Waste Management	7,593	58	0.9
Veterans' Services	0	0	0.0
Liquor Store	0	0	0.0
Utility	0	0	0.0

Source: U.S. Census Bureau, State & Local Government Finances 2020

TAXES

State Corporate Income Tax Rates

State	Tax Rate (%)	Income Brackets ($)	Num. of Brackets	Financial Institution Tax Rate (%)[a]	Federal Income Tax Ded.
Connecticut	7.5 (c)	Flat rate	1	7.5 (c)	No

Note: Tax rates as of January 1, 2023; (a) Rates listed are the corporate income tax rate applied to financial institutions or excise taxes based on income. Some states have other taxes based upon the value of deposits or shares; (c) Connecticut's tax is the greater of the 7.5% tax on net income, a 0.31% tax on capital stock and surplus (maximum tax of $1 million), or $250 (the minimum tax).
Source: Federation of Tax Administrators, State Corporate Income Tax Rates, January 1, 2023

State Individual Income Tax Rates

State	Tax Rate (%)	Income Brackets ($)	Personal Exemptions ($)			Standard Ded. ($)	
			Single	Married	Depend.	Single	Married
Connecticut	3.0 - 6.99	10,000 - 500,000 (b)	15,000	24,000	0	(h)	(h)

Note: Tax rates as of January 1, 2023; Local- and county-level taxes are not included; Federal income tax is not deductible on state income tax returns; (b) For joint returns, taxes are twice the tax on half the couple's income; (h) Connecticut's personal exemption incorporates a standard deduction. An additional tax credit is allowed ranging from 75% to 0% based on state adjusted gross income. Exemption amounts and 3% rate are phased out for higher income taxpayers until they are eliminated for households earning over $101,500.
Source: Federation of Tax Administrators, State Individual Income Tax Rates, January 1, 2023

Various State Sales and Excise Tax Rates

State	State Sales Tax (%)	Gasoline[1] ($/gal.)	Cigarette[2] ($/pack)	Spirits[3] ($/gal.)	Wine[4] ($/gal.)	Beer[5] ($/gal.)	Recreational Marijuana (%)
Connecticut	6.35	0.5335	4.35	5.94	0.792	0.23	(e)

Note: All tax rates as of January 1, 2023; (1) The American Petroleum Institute has developed a methodology for determining the average tax rate on a gallon of fuel. Rates may include any of the following: excise taxes, environmental fees, storage tank fees, other fees or taxes, general sales tax, and local taxes; (2) The federal excise tax of $1.0066 per pack and local taxes are not included; (3) Rates are those applicable to off-premise sales of 40% alcohol by volume (a.b.v.) distilled spirits in 750ml containers. Local excise taxes are excluded; (4) Rates are those applicable to off-premise sales of 11% a.b.v. non-carbonated wine in 750ml containers; (5) Rates are those applicable to off-premise sales of 4.7% a.b.v. beer in 12 ounce containers; (e) 3% excise tax (retail price); $0.00625 per milligram of THC in flower; $0.00275 per milligram of THC in edibles; $0.009 per milligram of THC in other cannabis products
Source: Tax Foundation, 2023 Facts & Figures: How Does Your State Compare?

State Business Tax Climate Index Rankings

State	Overall Rank	Corporate Tax Rank	Individual Income Tax Rank	Sales Tax Rank	Property Tax Rank	Unemployment Insurance Tax Rank
Connecticut	47	27	47	23	50	23

Note: The index is a measure of how each state's tax laws affect economic performance. The lower the rank, the more favorable a state's tax system is for business. States without a given tax are given a ranking of 1. The scores/rankings for the District of Columbia do not affect other states. The 2023 index represents the tax climate as of July 1, 2022.
Source: Tax Foundation, State Business Tax Climate Index 2023

TRANSPORTATION

Means of Transportation to Work

Area	Car/Truck/Van		Public Transportation			Bicycle	Walked	Other Means	Worked at Home
	Drove Alone	Car-pooled	Bus	Subway	Railroad				
City	58.6	8.0	7.5	0.1	1.1	2.1	11.6	1.9	9.1
MSA[1]	74.9	8.1	2.3	0.1	0.7	0.4	3.4	1.3	8.7
U.S.	73.2	8.6	2.0	1.6	0.5	0.5	2.5	1.5	9.7

Note: Figures are percentages and cover workers 16 years of age and older; (1) Figures cover the New Haven-Milford, CT Metropolitan Statistical Area
Source: U.S. Census Bureau, 2017-2021 American Community Survey 5-Year Estimates

Travel Time to Work

Area	Less Than 10 Minutes	10 to 19 Minutes	20 to 29 Minutes	30 to 44 Minutes	45 to 59 Minutes	60 to 89 Minutes	90 Minutes or More
City	13.2	40.4	21.6	13.6	4.5	4.2	2.5
MSA[1]	11.7	31.6	23.1	19.7	6.3	4.6	3.0
U.S.	12.4	28.5	21.0	20.9	8.2	6.2	2.9

Note: Note: Figures are percentages and include workers 16 years old and over; (1) Figures cover the New Haven-Milford, CT Metropolitan Statistical Area
Source: U.S. Census Bureau, 2017-2021 American Community Survey 5-Year Estimates

Key Congestion Measures

Measure	1990	2000	2010	2015	2020
Annual Hours of Delay, Total (000)	5,080	10,842	13,337	14,932	10,778
Annual Hours of Delay, Per Auto Commuter	22	36	40	44	31
Annual Congestion Cost, Per Auto Commuter ($)	481	770	751	776	583

Note: Covers the New Haven CT urban area
Source: Texas A&M Transportation Institute, 2021 Urban Mobility Report

Freeway Travel Time Index

Measure	1985	1990	1995	2000	2005	2010	2015	2020
Urban Area Index[1]	1.06	1.09	1.13	1.16	1.17	1.16	1.16	1.10
Urban Area Rank[1,2]	53	56	47	43	49	54	57	29

Note: Freeway Travel Time Index—the ratio of travel time in the peak period to the travel time at free-flow conditions. For example, a value of 1.30 indicates a 20-minute free-flow trip takes 26 minutes in the peak (20 minutes x 1.30 = 26 minutes); (1) Covers the New Haven CT urban area; (2) Rank is based on 101 larger urban areas (#1 = highest travel time index)
Source: Texas A&M Transportation Institute, 2021 Urban Mobility Report

Public Transportation

Agency Name / Mode of Transportation	Vehicles Operated in Maximum Service[1]	Annual Unlinked Passenger Trips[2] (in thous.)	Annual Passenger Miles[3] (in thous.)
CTTRANSIT New Haven Division			
Bus (directly operated)	99	4,962.7	16,699.7
The Greater New Haven Transit District			
Demand Response (directly operated)	47	158.0	1,031.6

Note: (1) Number of revenue vehicles operated by the given mode and type of service to meet the annual maximum service requirement. This is the revenue vehicle count during the peak season of the year; on the week and day that maximum service is provided. Vehicles operated in maximum service (VOMS) exclude atypical days and one-time special events; (2) Number of passengers who boarded public transportation vehicles. Passengers are counted each time they board a vehicle no matter how many vehicles they use to travel from their origin to their destination. (3) Sum of the distances ridden by all passengers during the entire fiscal year.
Source: Federal Transit Administration, National Transit Database, 2021

Air Transportation

Airport Name and Code / Type of Service	Passenger Airlines[1]	Passenger Enplanements	Freight Carriers[2]	Freight (lbs)
Bradley International Airport (BDL)				
Domestic service (U.S. carriers - 2022)	28	2,816,447	14	158,345,190
International service (U.S. carriers - 2021)	5	25,109	0	0
Tweed New Haven Airport (HVN)				
Domestic service (U.S. carriers - 2022)	6	345,242	0	0
International service (U.S. carriers - 2021)	1	12	0	0

Note: (1) Includes all U.S.-based major, minor and commuter airlines that carried at least one passenger during the year; (2) Includes all U.S.-based airlines and freight carriers that transported at least one pound of freight during the year.
Source: Bureau of Transportation Statistics, The Intermodal Transportation Database, Air Carriers: T-100 Domestic Market (U.S. Carriers), 2022; Bureau of Transportation Statistics, The Intermodal Transportation Database, Air Carriers: T-100 International Market (U.S. Carriers), 2021

BUSINESSES

Major Business Headquarters

Company Name	Industry	Rankings	
		Fortune[1]	Forbes[2]
No companies listed	-	-	-

Note: (1) Companies that produce a 10-K are ranked 1 to 500 based on 2021 revenue; (2) All private companies with at least $2 billion in annual revenue through the end of their most current fiscal year are ranked 1 to 246; companies listed are headquartered in the city; dashes indicate no ranking
Source: Fortune, "Fortune 500," 2022; Forbes, "America's Largest Private Companies," 2022

Living Environment

COST OF LIVING

Cost of Living Index

Composite Index	Groceries	Housing	Utilities	Trans-portation	Health Care	Misc. Goods/Services
113.8	99.2	114.8	133.7	110.6	111.9	115.6

Note: The Cost of Living Index measures regional differences in the cost of consumer goods and services, excluding taxes and non-consumer expenditures, for professional and managerial households in the top income quintile. It is based on more than 50,000 prices covering almost 60 different items for which prices are collected three times a year by chambers of commerce, economic development organizations or university applied economic centers in each participating urban area. The numbers shown should be read as a percentage above or below the national average of 100. For example, a value of 115.4 in the groceries column indicates that grocery prices are 15.4% higher than the national average. Small differences in the index numbers should not be interpreted as significant; Figures cover the New Haven CT urban area.
Source: The Council for Community and Economic Research, Cost of Living Index, 2022

Grocery Prices

Area[1]	T-Bone Steak ($/pound)	Frying Chicken ($/pound)	Whole Milk ($/half gal.)	Eggs ($/dozen)	Orange Juice ($/64 oz.)	Coffee ($/11.5 oz.)
City[2]	13.03	1.44	2.84	2.53	3.81	4.79
Avg.	13.81	1.59	2.43	2.25	3.85	4.95
Min.	10.17	0.90	1.51	1.30	2.90	3.46
Max.	19.35	3.30	4.32	4.32	5.31	8.59

*Note: (1) Values for the local area are compared with the average, minimum and maximum values for all 286 areas in the Cost of Living Index; (2) Figures cover the New Haven CT urban area; **T-Bone Steak** (price per pound); **Frying Chicken** (price per pound, whole fryer); **Whole Milk** (half gallon carton); **Eggs** (price per dozen, Grade A, large); **Orange Juice** (64 oz. Tropicana or Florida Natural); **Coffee** (11.5 oz. can, vacuum-packed, Maxwell House, Hills Bros, or Folgers).*
Source: The Council for Community and Economic Research, Cost of Living Index, 2022

Housing and Utility Costs

Area[1]	New Home Price ($)	Apartment Rent ($/month)	All Electric ($/month)	Part Electric ($/month)	Other Energy ($/month)	Telephone ($/month)
City[2]	434,014	2,127	-	166.18	115.11	186.44
Avg.	450,913	1,371	176.41	99.93	76.96	190.22
Min.	229,283	546	100.84	31.56	27.15	174.27
Max.	2,434,977	4,569	356.86	249.59	272.24	208.31

*Note: (1) Values for the local area are compared with the average, minimum and maximum values for all 286 areas in the Cost of Living Index; (2) Figures cover the New Haven CT urban area; **New Home Price** (2,400 sf living area, 8,000 sf lot, in urban area with full utilities); **Apartment Rent** (950 sf 2 bedroom/1.5 or 2 bath, unfurnished, excluding all utilities except water); **All Electric** (average monthly cost for an all-electric home); **Part Electric** (average monthly cost for a part-electric home); **Other Energy** (average monthly cost for natural gas, fuel oil, coal, wood, and any other forms of energy except electricity); **Telephone** (price includes the base monthly rate plus taxes and fees for three lines of mobile phone service).*
Source: The Council for Community and Economic Research, Cost of Living Index, 2022

Health Care, Transportation, and Other Costs

Area[1]	Doctor ($/visit)	Dentist ($/visit)	Optometrist ($/visit)	Gasoline ($/gallon)	Beauty Salon ($/visit)	Men's Shirt ($)
City[2]	146.79	125.96	131.33	4.04	46.14	28.74
Avg.	124.91	107.77	117.66	3.86	43.31	34.21
Min.	36.61	58.25	51.79	2.90	22.18	13.05
Max.	250.21	162.58	371.96	5.54	85.61	63.54

*Note: (1) Values for the local area are compared with the average, minimum and maximum values for all 286 areas in the Cost of Living Index; (2) Figures cover the New Haven CT urban area; **Doctor** (general practitioners routine exam of an established patient); **Dentist** (adult teeth cleaning and periodic oral examination); **Optometrist** (full vision eye exam for established adult patient); **Gasoline** (one gallon regular unleaded, national brand, including all taxes, cash price at self-service pump if available); **Beauty Salon** (woman's shampoo, trim, and blow-dry); **Men's Shirt** (cotton/polyester dress shirt, pinpoint weave, long sleeves).*
Source: The Council for Community and Economic Research, Cost of Living Index, 2022

HOUSING

Homeownership Rate

Area	2015 (%)	2016 (%)	2017 (%)	2018 (%)	2019 (%)	2020 (%)	2021 (%)	2022 (%)
MSA[1]	64.6	59.4	58.7	65.0	65.1	63.4	61.0	63.3
U.S.	63.7	63.4	63.9	64.4	64.6	66.6	65.5	65.8

Note: (1) Figures cover the New Haven-Milford, CT Metropolitan Statistical Area
Source: U.S. Census Bureau, Housing Vacancies and Homeownership Annual Statistics: 2015-2022

House Price Index (HPI)

Area	National Ranking[2]	Quarterly Change (%)	One-Year Change (%)	Five-Year Change (%)	Since 1991Q1 (%)
MSA[1]	113	0.91	11.80	48.13	135.81
U.S.[3]	–	0.34	8.41	58.44	289.08

Note: The HPI is a weighted repeat sales index. It measures average price changes in repeat sales or refinancings on the same properties. This information is obtained by reviewing repeat mortgage transactions on single-family properties whose mortgages have been purchased or securitized by Fannie Mae or Freddie Mac since January 1975; (1) Figures cover the New Haven-Milford, CT Metropolitan Statistical Area; (2) Rankings are based on annual percentage change for all metro areas containing at least 15,000 transactions over the last 10 years and ranges from 1 to 257; (3) figures based on a weighted average of Census Division estimates using a seasonally adjusted, purchase-only index; all figures are for the period ending December 31, 2022
Source: Federal Housing Finance Agency, Change in FHFA Metropolitan Area House Price Indexes, 2022Q4

Median Single-Family Home Prices

Area	2020	2021	2022p	Percent Change 2021 to 2022
MSA[1]	265.9	300.0	339.0	13.0
U.S. Average	300.2	357.1	392.6	9.9

Note: Figures are median sales prices of existing single-family homes in thousands of dollars; (p) preliminary; (1) Figures cover the New Haven-Milford, CT Metropolitan Statistical Area
Source: National Association of Realtors, Median Sales Price of Existing Single-Family Homes for Metropolitan Areas, 4th Quarter 2022

Qualifying Income Based on Median Sales Price of Existing Single-Family Homes

Area	With 5% Down ($)	With 10% Down ($)	With 20% Down ($)
MSA[1]	98,611	93,421	83,041
U.S. Average	112,234	106,237	94,513

Note: Figures are preliminary; Qualifying income is based on a mortgage rate of 6.77%. Monthly principal and interest payment is limited to 25% of income; (1) Figures cover the New Haven-Milford, CT Metropolitan Statistical Area
Source: National Association of Realtors, Qualifying Income Based on Median Sales Price of Existing Single-Family Homes for Metropolitan Areas, 4th Quarter 2022

Home Value

Area	Under $100,000	$100,000 -$199,999	$200,000 -$299,999	$300,000 -$399,999	$400,000 -$499,999	$500,000 -$999,999	$1,000,000 or more	Median ($)
City	11.0	36.4	29.4	10.5	5.4	5.7	1.6	207,600
MSA[1]	6.4	25.9	29.4	18.7	10.0	8.3	1.2	259,400
U.S.	16.2	24.2	20.1	13.6	8.3	13.6	4.1	244,900

Note: Figures are percentages except for median and cover owner-occupied housing units; (1) Figures cover the New Haven-Milford, CT Metropolitan Statistical Area
Source: U.S. Census Bureau, 2017-2021 American Community Survey 5-Year Estimates

Year Housing Structure Built

Area	2020 or Later	2010 -2019	2000 -2009	1990 -1999	1980 -1989	1970 -1979	1960 -1969	1950 -1959	1940 -1949	Before 1940	Median Year
City	0.0	3.8	4.6	3.1	6.8	9.5	11.2	10.3	7.4	43.2	1949
MSA[1]	<0.1	2.5	5.8	7.4	12.6	13.6	12.2	14.8	7.1	23.9	1963
U.S.	0.2	7.3	13.6	13.6	13.2	14.8	10.3	10.0	4.7	12.2	1979

Note: Figures are percentages except for Median Year; Note: (1) Figures cover the New Haven-Milford, CT Metropolitan Statistical Area
Source: U.S. Census Bureau, 2017-2021 American Community Survey 5-Year Estimates

Gross Monthly Rent

Area	Under $500	$500 -$999	$1,000 -$1,499	$1,500 -$1,999	$2,000 -$2,499	$2,500 -$2,999	$3,000 and up	Median ($)
City	13.5	14.2	40.8	20.6	7.4	2.4	1.1	1,267
MSA[1]	10.6	19.5	41.4	19.9	5.6	1.6	1.4	1,223
U.S.	8.1	30.5	30.8	16.8	7.3	3.1	3.5	1,163

Note: Figures are percentages except for median; Gross rent is the contract rent plus the estimated average monthly cost of utilities (electricity, gas, and water and sewer) and fuels (oil, coal, kerosene, wood, etc.) if these are paid by the renter (or paid for the renter by someone else); (1) Figures cover the New Haven-Milford, CT Metropolitan Statistical Area
Source: U.S. Census Bureau, 2017-2021 American Community Survey 5-Year Estimates

HEALTH

Health Risk Factors

Category	MSA[1] (%)	U.S. (%)
Adults aged 18–64 who have any kind of health care coverage	n/a	90.9
Adults who reported being in good or better health	n/a	85.2
Adults who have been told they have high blood cholesterol	n/a	35.7
Adults who have been told they have high blood pressure	n/a	32.4
Adults who are current smokers	n/a	14.4
Adults who currently use e-cigarettes	n/a	6.7
Adults who currently use chewing tobacco, snuff, or snus	n/a	3.5
Adults who are heavy drinkers[2]	n/a	6.3
Adults who are binge drinkers[3]	n/a	15.4
Adults who are overweight (BMI 25.0 - 29.9)	n/a	34.4
Adults who are obese (BMI 30.0 - 99.8)	n/a	33.9
Adults who participated in any physical activities in the past month	n/a	76.3

Note: (1) Figures for the New Haven-Milford, CT Metropolitan Statistical Area were not available.
(2) Heavy drinkers are classified as adult men having more than 14 drinks per week and adult women having more than 7 drinks per week; (3) Binge drinkers are classified as males having five or more drinks on one occasion or females having four or more drinks on one occasion
Source: Centers for Disease Control and Prevention, Behaviorial Risk Factor Surveillance System, SMART: Selected Metropolitan Area Risk Trends, 2021

Acute and Chronic Health Conditions

Category	MSA[1] (%)	U.S. (%)
Adults who have ever been told they had a heart attack	n/a	4.0
Adults who have ever been told they have angina or coronary heart disease	n/a	3.8
Adults who have ever been told they had a stroke	n/a	3.0
Adults who have ever been told they have asthma	n/a	14.9
Adults who have ever been told they have arthritis	n/a	25.8
Adults who have ever been told they have diabetes[2]	n/a	10.9
Adults who have ever been told they had skin cancer	n/a	6.6
Adults who have ever been told they had any other types of cancer	n/a	7.5
Adults who have ever been told they have COPD	n/a	6.1
Adults who have ever been told they have kidney disease	n/a	3.0
Adults who have ever been told they have a form of depression	n/a	20.5

Note: (1) Figures for the New Haven-Milford, CT Metropolitan Statistical Area were not available.
(2) Figures do not include pregnancy-related, borderline, or pre-diabetes
Source: Centers for Disease Control and Prevention, Behaviorial Risk Factor Surveillance System, SMART: Selected Metropolitan Area Risk Trends, 2021

Health Screening and Vaccination Rates

Category	MSA[1] (%)	U.S. (%)
Adults who have ever been tested for HIV	n/a	34.9
Adults who have had their blood cholesterol checked within the last five years	n/a	85.2
Adults aged 65+ who have had flu shot within the past year	n/a	68.6
Adults aged 65+ who have ever had a pneumonia vaccination	n/a	71.0

Note: (1) Figures for the New Haven-Milford, CT Metropolitan Statistical Area were not available.
Source: Centers for Disease Control and Prevention, Behaviorial Risk Factor Surveillance System, SMART: Selected Metropolitan Area Risk Trends, 2021

Disability Status

Category	MSA[1] (%)	U.S. (%)
Adults who reported being deaf	n/a	7.2
Are you blind or have serious difficulty seeing, even when wearing glasses?	n/a	4.8
Are you limited in any way in any of your usual activities due to arthritis?	n/a	11.1
Do you have difficulty doing errands alone?	n/a	7.0
Do you have difficulty dressing or bathing?	n/a	3.6
Do you have serious difficulty concentrating/remembering/making decisions?	n/a	12.1
Do you have serious difficulty walking or climbing stairs?	n/a	12.8

Note: (1) Figures for the New Haven-Milford, CT Metropolitan Statistical Area were not available.
Source: Centers for Disease Control and Prevention, Behaviorial Risk Factor Surveillance System, SMART: Selected Metropolitan Area Risk Trends, 2021

Mortality Rates for the Top 10 Causes of Death in the U.S.

ICD-10[a] Sub-Chapter	ICD-10[a] Code	Crude Mortality Rate[1] per 100,000 population	
		County[2]	U.S.
Malignant neoplasms	C00-C97	191.9	182.6
Ischaemic heart diseases	I20-I25	98.7	113.1
Other forms of heart disease	I30-I51	80.6	64.4
Other degenerative diseases of the nervous system	G30-G31	43.7	51.0
Cerebrovascular diseases	I60-I69	47.1	47.8
Other external causes of accidental injury	W00-X59	70.8	46.4
Chronic lower respiratory diseases	J40-J47	36.6	45.7
Organic, including symptomatic, mental disorders	F01-F09	61.5	35.9
Hypertensive diseases	I10-I15	24.1	35.0
Diabetes mellitus	E10-E14	24.5	29.6

Note: (a) ICD-10 = International Classification of Diseases 10th Revision; (1) Crude mortality rates are a three-year average covering 2019-2021; (2) Figures cover New Haven County.
Source: Centers for Disease Control and Prevention, National Center for Health Statistics. National Vital Statistics System, Mortality 2018-2021 on CDC WONDER Online Database

Mortality Rates for Selected Causes of Death

ICD-10[a] Sub-Chapter	ICD-10[a] Code	Crude Mortality Rate[1] per 100,000 population	
		County[2]	U.S.
Assault	X85-Y09	5.4	7.0
Diseases of the liver	K70-K76	18.5	19.8
Human immunodeficiency virus (HIV) disease	B20-B24	2.0	1.5
Influenza and pneumonia	J09-J18	12.8	14.7
Intentional self-harm	X60-X84	10.7	14.3
Malnutrition	E40-E46	3.2	4.3
Obesity and other hyperalimentation	E65-E68	3.2	3.0
Renal failure	N17-N19	19.7	15.7
Transport accidents	V01-V99	9.9	13.6
Viral hepatitis	B15-B19	1.1	1.2

Note: (a) ICD-10 = International Classification of Diseases 10th Revision; (1) Crude mortality rates are a three-year average covering 2019-2021; (2) Figures cover New Haven County; Data are suppressed when the data meet the criteria for confidentiality constraints; Crude mortality rates are flagged as unreliable when the rate would be calculated with a numerator of 20 or less.
Source: Centers for Disease Control and Prevention, National Center for Health Statistics. National Vital Statistics System, Mortality 2018-2021 on CDC WONDER Online Database

Health Insurance Coverage

Area	With Health Insurance	With Private Health Insurance	With Public Health Insurance	Without Health Insurance	Population Under Age 19 Without Health Insurance
City	92.2	51.9	46.3	7.8	3.1
MSA[1]	94.9	66.9	39.6	5.1	2.5
U.S.	91.2	67.8	35.4	8.8	5.3

Note: Figures are percentages that cover the civilian noninstitutionalized population; (1) Figures cover the New Haven-Milford, CT Metropolitan Statistical Area
Source: U.S. Census Bureau, 2017-2021 American Community Survey 5-Year Estimates

Number of Medical Professionals

Area	MDs[3]	DOs[3,4]	Dentists	Podiatrists	Chiropractors	Optometrists
County[1] (number)	4,985	89	671	83	235	143
County[1] (rate[2])	577.3	10.3	77.7	9.6	27.2	16.6
U.S. (rate[2])	289.3	23.5	72.5	6.2	28.7	17.4

Note: Data as of 2021 unless noted; (1) Data covers New Haven County; (2) Rate per 100,000 population; (3) Data as of 2020 and includes all active, non-federal physicians; (4) Doctor of Osteopathic Medicine
Source: U.S. Department of Health and Human Services, Health Resources and Services Administration, Bureau of Health Professions, Area Resource File (ARF) 2021-2022

Best Hospitals

According to *U.S. News,* the New Haven-Milford, CT metro area is home to one of the best hospitals in the U.S.: **Yale New Haven Hospital** (9 adult specialties and 8 pediatric specialties). The hospital listed was nationally ranked in at least one of 15 adult or 10 pediatric specialties. The number of specialties shown cover the parent hospital. Only 164 U.S. hospitals performed well enough to be nationally ranked in one or more specialties. Twenty hospitals in the U.S. made the Honor Roll. The Best Hospitals Honor Roll takes both the national rankings and the procedure and condition ratings into account. Hospitals received points if they were nationally ranked in one of the 15 adult specialties—the higher they ranked, the more points they got—and how many ratings of "high performing" they earned in the 17 procedures and conditions. *U.S. News Online, "America's Best Hospitals 2022-23"*

According to *U.S. News,* the New Haven-Milford, CT metro area is home to one of the best children's hospitals in the U.S.: **Yale New Haven Children's Hospital** (8 pediatric specialties). The hospital listed was highly ranked in at least one of 10 pediatric specialties. Eighty-six children's hospitals in the U.S. were nationally ranked in at least one specialty. Hospitals received points for being ranked in a specialty, and the 10 hospitals with the most points across the 10 specialties make up the Honor Roll. *U.S. News Online, "America's Best Children's Hospitals 2022-23"*

EDUCATION

Public School District Statistics

District Name	Schls	Pupils	Pupil/ Teacher Ratio	Minority Pupils[1] (%)	LEP/ELL[2] (%)	IEP[3] (%)
New Haven School District	37	19,216	12.6	89.0	16.7	16.7

Note: Table includes school districts with 2,000 or more students; (1) Percentage of students that are not non-Hispanic white; (2) Percentage of students that are Limited English Proficient or English Language Learners (2018-19); (3) Percentage of students that have an Individualized Education Program (2019-20). Source: U.S. Department of Education, National Center for Education Statistics, Common Core of Data, Local Education Agency (School District) Universe Survey: School Year 2021-2022

Highest Level of Education

Area	Less than H.S.	H.S. Diploma	Some College, No Deg.	Associate Degree	Bachelor's Degree	Master's Degree	Prof. School Degree	Doctorate Degree
City	14.6	30.2	14.2	4.6	16.3	11.9	4.0	4.3
MSA[1]	9.7	29.6	16.7	7.3	19.4	11.9	3.2	2.2
U.S.	11.1	26.5	20.0	8.7	20.6	9.3	2.2	1.5

Note: Figures cover persons age 25 and over; (1) Figures cover the New Haven-Milford, CT Metropolitan Statistical Area Source: U.S. Census Bureau, 2017-2021 American Community Survey 5-Year Estimates

Educational Attainment by Race

Area	High School Graduate or Higher (%)					Bachelor's Degree or Higher (%)				
	Total	White	Black	Asian	Hisp.[2]	Total	White	Black	Asian	Hisp.[2]
City	85.4	87.2	87.3	94.8	71.6	36.5	49.2	22.5	78.5	14.5
MSA[1]	90.3	92.7	88.2	89.7	74.5	36.6	39.8	23.0	64.1	15.6
U.S.	88.9	91.4	87.2	87.6	71.2	33.7	35.5	23.3	55.6	18.4

Note: Figures shown cover persons 25 years old and over; (1) Figures cover the New Haven-Milford, CT Metropolitan Statistical Area; (2) People of Hispanic origin can be of any race Source: U.S. Census Bureau, 2017-2021 American Community Survey 5-Year Estimates

School Enrollment by Grade and Control

Area	Preschool (%)		Kindergarten (%)		Grades 1 - 4 (%)		Grades 5 - 8 (%)		Grades 9 - 12 (%)	
	Public	Private	Public	Private	Public	Private	Public	Private	Public	Private
City	80.4	19.6	89.7	10.3	95.2	4.8	93.4	6.6	92.5	7.5
MSA[1]	65.6	34.4	93.4	6.6	92.1	7.9	90.4	9.6	88.9	11.1
U.S.	58.8	41.2	86.3	13.7	88.3	11.7	88.6	11.4	89.4	10.6

Note: Figures shown cover persons 3 years old and over; (1) Figures cover the New Haven-Milford, CT Metropolitan Statistical Area Source: U.S. Census Bureau, 2017-2021 American Community Survey 5-Year Estimates

Higher Education

Four-Year Colleges			Two-Year Colleges			Medical Schools[1]	Law Schools[2]	Voc/ Tech[3]
Public	Private Non-profit	Private For-profit	Public	Private Non-profit	Private For-profit			
2	4	2	2	0	2	2	2	10

Note: Figures cover institutions located within the New Haven-Milford, CT Metropolitan Statistical Area and include main campuses only; (1) includes schools accredited by the Liaison Committee on Medical Education and the American Osteopathic Association's Commission on Osteopathic College Accreditation; (2) includes ABA-accredited schools, schools with provisional ABA accreditation, and state accredited schools; (3) includes all schools with programs that are less than 2 years. Source: National Center for Education Statistics, Integrated Postsecondary Education System (IPEDS), 2021-22; Wikipedia, List of Medical Schools in the United States, accessed April 10, 2023; Wikipedia, List of Law Schools in the United States, accessed April 10, 2023

According to *U.S. News & World Report,* the New Haven-Milford, CT metro area is home to two of the top 200 national universities in the U.S.: **Yale University** (#3 tie); **Quinnipiac University** (#166 tie). The indicators used to capture academic quality fall into a number of categories: assessment by administrators at peer institutions; retention of students; faculty resources; student selectivity; financial resources; alumni giving; high school counselor ratings of colleges; and graduation rate. *U.S. News & World Report, "America's Best Colleges 2023"*

According to *U.S. News & World Report*, the New Haven-Milford, CT metro area is home to one of the top 100 law schools in the U.S.: **Yale University** (#1). The rankings are based on a weighted average of 12 measures of quality: peer assessment score; assessment score by lawyers/judges; median LSAT scores; median undergrad GPA; acceptance rate; employment rates for graduates; placement success; bar passage rate; faculty resources; expenditures per student; student/faculty ratio; and library resources. *U.S. News & World Report, "America's Best Graduate Schools, Law, 2023"*

According to *U.S. News & World Report*, the New Haven-Milford, CT metro area is home to one of the top 75 medical schools for research in the U.S.: **Yale University** (#10). The rankings are based on a weighted average of 11 measures of quality: quality assessment; peer assessment score; assessment score by residency directors; research activity; total research activity; average research activity per faculty member; student selectivity; median MCAT total score; median undergraduate GPA; acceptance rate; and faculty resources. *U.S. News & World Report, "America's Best Graduate Schools, Medical, 2023"*

According to *U.S. News & World Report*, the New Haven-Milford, CT metro area is home to one of the top 75 business schools in the U.S.: **Yale University** (#7). The rankings are based on a weighted average of the following nine measures: quality assessment; peer assessment; recruiter assessment; placement success; mean starting salary and bonus; student selectivity; mean GMAT and GRE scores; mean undergraduate GPA; and acceptance rate. *U.S. News & World Report, "America's Best Graduate Schools, Business, 2023"*

EMPLOYERS

Major Employers

Company Name	Industry
Bozzuto's	Distribution centers, wholesale
Connecticut Education Association	Schools
Covidien-Surgical Devices	Physicians & surgeons equip & supls-whls
General Counselors Office	Business services nec
Grandview Adult Behavioral Health	Mental health services
Griffin Hospital	Hospitals
LATICRETE International	Adhesives & glues, wholesale
Masonicare Health Center	Hospitals
Medtronic	Hospital equipment & supplies, wholesale
Saint Mary's Hospital	Hospitals
Southbury Training School	Junior-community college-tech institutes
Southern CT State University	Schools-universities & colleges academic
VA Connecticut Healthcare System	Health care management
Waterbury Board of Education	Boards of education
Waterbury Hospital	Hospitals
Yale New Haven Health System	Health care management

Note: Companies shown are located within the New Haven-Milford, CT Metropolitan Statistical Area.
Source: Hoovers.com; Wikipedia

PUBLIC SAFETY

Crime Rate

Area	Total Crime	Violent Crime Rate				Property Crime Rate		
		Murder	Rape[3]	Robbery	Aggrav. Assault	Burglary	Larceny -Theft	Motor Vehicle Theft
City	4,218.8	16.1	22.3	257.9	411.4	419.8	2,507.3	584.0
Suburbs[1]	2,076.3	4.2	20.2	61.1	82.9	193.7	1,413.6	300.7
Metro[2]	2,425.5	6.1	20.5	93.2	136.5	230.5	1,591.8	346.9
U.S.	2,356.7	6.5	38.4	73.9	279.7	314.2	1,398.0	246.0

Note: Figures are crimes per 100,000 population; (1) All areas within the metro area that are located outside the city limits; (2) Figures cover the New Haven-Milford, CT Metropolitan Statistical Area; (3) All figures shown were reported using the revised Uniform Crime Reporting (UCR) definition of rape; Due to the transition to the National Incident-Based Reporting System (NIBRS), limited city and metro area data was released for 2021.
Source: FBI Uniform Crime Reports, 2020

Hate Crimes

Area	Number of Quarters Reported	Number of Incidents per Bias Motivation					
		Race/Ethnicity/ Ancestry	Religion	Sexual Orientation	Disability	Gender	Gender Identity
City	4	7	3	1	0	0	0
U.S.	4	5,227	1,244	1,110	130	75	266

Note: Due to the transition to the National Incident-Based Reporting System (NIBRS), limited crime data was released for 2021.
Source: Federal Bureau of Investigation, Hate Crime Statistics 2020

Identity Theft Consumer Reports

Area	Reports	Reports per 100,000 Population	Rank[2]
MSA[1]	2,069	242	114
U.S.	1,108,609	339	-

Note: (1) Figures cover the New Haven-Milford, CT Metropolitan Statistical Area; (2) Rank ranges from 1 to 391 where 1 indicates greatest number of identity theft reports per 100,000 population
Source: Federal Trade Commission, Consumer Sentinel Network Data Book 2022

Fraud and Other Consumer Reports

Area	Reports	Reports per 100,000 Population	Rank[2]
MSA[1]	8,407	982	105
U.S.	4,064,520	1,245	-

Note: (1) Figures cover the New Haven-Milford, CT Metropolitan Statistical Area; (2) Rank ranges from 1 to 391 where 1 indicates greatest number of fraud and other consumer reports per 100,000 population
Source: Federal Trade Commission, Consumer Sentinel Network Data Book 2022

POLITICS

2020 Presidential Election Results

Area	Biden	Trump	Jorgensen	Hawkins	Other
New Haven County	58.0	40.6	0.9	0.4	0.0
U.S.	51.3	46.8	1.2	0.3	0.5

Note: Results are percentages and may not add to 100% due to rounding
Source: Dave Leip's Atlas of U.S. Presidential Elections

SPORTS

Professional Sports Teams

Team Name	League	Year Established

No teams are located in the metro area
Source: Wikipedia, Major Professional Sports Teams of the United States and Canada, April 12, 2023

CLIMATE

Average and Extreme Temperatures

Temperature	Jan	Feb	Mar	Apr	May	Jun	Jul	Aug	Sep	Oct	Nov	Dec	Yr.
Extreme High (°F)	65	67	84	91	92	96	103	100	99	85	78	65	103
Average High (°F)	37	38	46	57	67	76	82	81	74	64	53	41	60
Average Temp. (°F)	30	32	39	49	59	68	74	73	66	56	46	35	52
Average Low (°F)	23	24	31	40	50	59	65	65	57	47	38	27	44
Extreme Low (°F)	-7	-5	4	18	31	41	49	44	36	26	16	-4	-7

Note: Figures cover the years 1948-1992
Source: National Climatic Data Center, International Station Meteorological Climate Summary, 9/96

Average Precipitation/Snowfall/Humidity

Precip./Humidity	Jan	Feb	Mar	Apr	May	Jun	Jul	Aug	Sep	Oct	Nov	Dec	Yr.
Avg. Precip. (in.)	3.2	2.9	3.7	3.7	3.7	3.1	3.7	3.8	3.0	3.2	3.8	3.5	41.4
Avg. Snowfall (in.)	7	7	5	1	Tr	0	0	0	0	Tr	1	5	25
Avg. Rel. Hum. 7am (%)	73	72	72	72	76	77	79	80	81	79	77	74	76
Avg. Rel. Hum. 4pm (%)	61	59	56	55	59	60	60	61	60	60	62	63	60

Note: Figures cover the years 1948-1992; Tr = Trace amounts (<0.05 in. of rain; <0.5 in. of snow)
Source: National Climatic Data Center, International Station Meteorological Climate Summary, 9/96

Weather Conditions

Temperature			Daytime Sky			Precipitation		
32°F & below	45°F & below	90°F & above	Clear	Partly cloudy	Cloudy	0.01 inch or more precip.	0.1 inch or more snow/ice	Thunder-storms
100	193	7	80	146	139	118	17	22

Note: Figures are average number of days per year and cover the years 1948-1992
Source: National Climatic Data Center, International Station Meteorological Climate Summary, 9/96

HAZARDOUS WASTE

Superfund Sites

The New Haven-Milford, CT metro area is home to three sites on the EPA's Superfund National Priorities List: **Beacon Heights Landfill** (final); **Laurel Park, Inc.** (final); **Scovill Industrial Landfill** (final). There are a total of 1,165 Superfund sites with a status of proposed or final on the list in the U.S. *U.S. Environmental Protection Agency, National Priorities List, April 12, 2023*

AIR QUALITY

Air Quality Trends: Ozone

	1990	1995	2000	2005	2010	2015	2018	2019	2020	2021
MSA[1]	0.121	0.117	0.087	0.092	0.079	0.081	0.077	0.084	0.080	0.083
U.S.	0.087	0.089	0.081	0.080	0.072	0.067	0.069	0.065	0.065	0.067

Note: (1) Data covers the New Haven-Milford, CT Metropolitan Statistical Area. The values shown are the composite ozone concentration averages among trend sites based on the highest fourth daily maximum 8-hour concentration in parts per million. These trends are based on sites having an adequate record of monitoring data during the trend period. Data from exceptional events are included.
Source: U.S. Environmental Protection Agency, Air Quality Monitoring Information, "Air Quality Trends by City, 1990-2021"

Air Quality Index

Area	Percent of Days when Air Quality was...[2]					AQI Statistics[2]	
	Good	Moderate	Unhealthy for Sensitive Groups	Unhealthy	Very Unhealthy	Maximum	Median
MSA[1]	77.0	19.2	3.3	0.5	0.0	159	40

Note: (1) Data covers the New Haven-Milford, CT Metropolitan Statistical Area; (2) Based on 365 days with AQI data in 2021. Air Quality Index (AQI) is an index for reporting daily air quality. EPA calculates the AQI for five major air pollutants regulated by the Clean Air Act: ground-level ozone, particle pollution (aka particulate matter), carbon monoxide, sulfur dioxide, and nitrogen dioxide. The AQI runs from 0 to 500. The higher the AQI value, the greater the level of air pollution and the greater the health concern. There are six AQI categories: "Good" AQI is between 0 and 50. Air quality is considered satisfactory; "Moderate" AQI is between 51 and 100. Air quality is acceptable; "Unhealthy for Sensitive Groups" When AQI values are between 101 and 150, members of sensitive groups may experience health effects; "Unhealthy" When AQI values are between 151 and 200 everyone may begin to experience health effects; "Very Unhealthy" AQI values between 201 and 300 trigger a health alert; "Hazardous" AQI values over 300 trigger warnings of emergency conditions (not shown).
Source: U.S. Environmental Protection Agency, Air Quality Index Report, 2021

Air Quality Index Pollutants

Area	Percent of Days when AQI Pollutant was...[2]					
	Carbon Monoxide	Nitrogen Dioxide	Ozone	Sulfur Dioxide	Particulate Matter 2.5	Particulate Matter 10
MSA[1]	0.0	5.2	55.9	(3)	37.5	1.4

Note: (1) Data covers the New Haven-Milford, CT Metropolitan Statistical Area; (2) Based on 365 days with AQI data in 2021. The Air Quality Index (AQI) is an index for reporting daily air quality. EPA calculates the AQI for five major air pollutants regulated by the Clean Air Act: ground-level ozone, particle pollution (also known as particulate matter), carbon monoxide, sulfur dioxide, and nitrogen dioxide. The AQI runs from 0 to 500. The higher the AQI value, the greater the level of air pollution and the greater the health concern; (3) Sulfur dioxide is no longer included in this table (as of December 8, 2021) because SO_2 concentrations tend to be very localized and not necessarily representative of broad geographical areas like counties and CBSAs.
Source: U.S. Environmental Protection Agency, Air Quality Index Report, 2021

Maximum Air Pollutant Concentrations: Particulate Matter, Ozone, CO and Lead

	Particulate Matter 10 (ug/m^3)	Particulate Matter 2.5 Wtd AM (ug/m^3)	Particulate Matter 2.5 24-Hr (ug/m^3)	Ozone (ppm)	Carbon Monoxide (ppm)	Lead (ug/m^3)
MSA[1] Level	68	8.8	22	0.083	1	n/a
NAAQS[2]	150	15	35	0.075	9	0.15
Met NAAQS[2]	Yes	Yes	Yes	No	Yes	n/a

Note: (1) Data covers the New Haven-Milford, CT Metropolitan Statistical Area; Data from exceptional events are included; (2) National Ambient Air Quality Standards; ppm = parts per million; ug/m^3 = micrograms per cubic meter; n/a not available.
Concentrations: Particulate Matter 10 (coarse particulate)—highest second maximum 24-hour concentration; Particulate Matter 2.5 Wtd AM (fine particulate)—highest weighted annual mean concentration; Particulate Matter 2.5 24-Hour (fine particulate)—highest 98th percentile 24-hour concentration; Ozone—highest fourth daily maximum 8-hour concentration; Carbon Monoxide—highest second maximum non-overlapping 8-hour concentration; Lead—maximum running 3-month average
Source: U.S. Environmental Protection Agency, Air Quality Monitoring Information, "Air Quality Statistics by City, 2021"

Maximum Air Pollutant Concentrations: Nitrogen Dioxide and Sulfur Dioxide

	Nitrogen Dioxide AM (ppb)	Nitrogen Dioxide 1-Hr (ppb)	Sulfur Dioxide AM (ppb)	Sulfur Dioxide 1-Hr (ppb)	Sulfur Dioxide 24-Hr (ppb)
MSA[1] Level	12	48	n/a	3	n/a
NAAQS[2]	53	100	30	75	140
Met NAAQS[2]	Yes	Yes	n/a	Yes	n/a

Note: (1) Data covers the New Haven-Milford, CT Metropolitan Statistical Area; Data from exceptional events are included; (2) National Ambient Air Quality Standards; ppm = parts per million; ug/m^3 = micrograms per cubic meter; n/a not available.
Concentrations: Nitrogen Dioxide AM—highest arithmetic mean concentration; Nitrogen Dioxide 1-Hr—highest 98th percentile 1-hour daily maximum concentration; Sulfur Dioxide AM—highest annual mean concentration; Sulfur Dioxide 1-Hr—highest 99th percentile 1-hour daily maximum concentration; Sulfur Dioxide 24-Hr—highest second maximum 24-hour concentration
Source: U.S. Environmental Protection Agency, Air Quality Monitoring Information, "Air Quality Statistics by City, 2021"

New York, New York

Background

Few cities in the world can compare with New York's frenetic excitement. Known for its dramatic skyline and famous bridges and historic buildings, the city is beautiful, mighty, inspiring, loaded with attitude and home to 8.8 million people speaking 800 languages within its five boroughs—Bronx, Brooklyn, Queens, Manhattan, and Staten Island.

New York is the largest city in New York State, in the U.S., and one of the largest cities in the world. Located at the mouth of the Hudson River, the area was first explored by Giovanni da Verrazzano in 1524, and then by Henry Hudson in 1609. In 1625, it became New Amsterdam and a year later, as the story goes, Peter Minuit purchased the island of Manhattan from local Native Americans for the equivalent of $24.00.

The city offers the best in the arts—Metropolitan Museum of Art, Museum of Modern Art, Guggenheim Museum, among thousands of others; education—New York University and Columbia University; finance—the New York and the American stock exchanges; plus fashion, theaters, restaurants, political activism, and more. As a major cultural, financial and media center, it significantly influences commence, entertainment, research, technology, education, politics, tourism, dining, art, fashion, and sports and is the most photographed city in the world

The city is home to the highest number of Fortune 500 companies (42) and to the second highest number of billionaires of any city in the world.

New York is home to The Alvin Ailey American Dance Theater, American Ballet Theater, Brooklyn Academy of Music, Carnegie Hall, and Cunningham Dance Company, among many other world-famous artistic centers.

Professional sports abound in the city, including New York Giants and Jets football teams, New York Red Bulls soccer team, Knicks basketball team, and New York Yankees and Mets baseball teams. The Giants' MetLife Stadium hosted the Super Bowl in 2014, the first outdoor, cold-weather Super Bowl. In addition, Barclays Arena in Brooklyn is home to the New Jersey Nets basketball team, the New York Islanders hockey team, and hosts world-class entertainment.

New York City is also an international business capital, with its entrepreneurial spirit, highly educated workforce, first-rate transportation system, unequaled telecommunications infrastructure, and lowest crime rate of any big city in America.

On September 11, 2001, New York became the site of the deadliest terrorist attack ever to occur in the United States. Two hijacked commercial airplanes were flown into the Twin Towers and demolished the complex of seven buildings at the World Trade Center, killing more than 3,500 people. The grieving city immediately began the monumental task of moving forward. The new 8-acre World Trade Center Complex consists of seven office buildings, a Memorial, and Museum. The Memorial, which opened on the 10th anniversary of the attacks, consists of two massive pools in the footprints of the Twin Towers, with the largest manmade waterfalls in the country. The World Trade Center Transportation Hub opened in 2016, replacing the Hudson Terminal which was destroyed in the attacks.

The New York metropolitan area is home to a prominent LBGTQ+ community. More than 600,000 strong, it's the largest in the country. The annual New York City Pride March traverses southward down Fifth Avenue and ends at Greenwich Village in Lower Manhattan, attracting tens of thousands of participants and millions of sidewalk spectators each June.

The New York metro area is close to the path of most storm and frontal systems which move across the continent. The city can experience very high temperatures in summer and very low in winter, despite its coastal location. The passage of many weather systems helps to reduce the duration of both cold and warm spells, circulate the air, and reduce stagnation. The most recent major weather event occurred in 2012, as Hurricane Sandy flooded subways and tunnels, shut down hospitals and the New York Stock Exchange.

Rankings

General Rankings

- The human resources consulting firm Mercer ranked 231 major cities worldwide in terms of overall quality of life. New York ranked #44. Criteria: political, social, economic, and socio-cultural factors; medical and health considerations; schools and education; public services and transportation; recreation; consumer goods; housing; and natural environment. *Mercer, "Mercer 2019 Quality of Living Survey," March 13, 2019*

- New York appeared on *Travel + Leisure's* list of "The 15 Best Cities in the United States." The city was ranked #6. Criteria: sights/landmarks; culture; food; friendliness; shopping; and overall value. *Travel + Leisure, "The World's Best Awards 2022" July 12, 2022*

- For its 35th annual "Readers' Choice Awards" survey, *Condé Nast Traveler* ranked its readers' favorite cities in the U.S. Whether it be a longed-for visit or a first on the list, these are the places that inspired a return to travel. The list was broken into large cities and cities under 250,000. New York ranked #5 in the big city category. *Condé Nast Traveler, Readers' Choice Awards 2022, "Best Big Cities in the U.S." October 4, 2022*

Business/Finance Rankings

- The Brookings Institution ranked the nation's largest cities based on income inequality. New York was ranked #8 (#1 = greatest inequality). Criteria: the "95/20 ratio," a figure representing the income at which a household earns more than 95 percent of all other households, divided by the income at which a household earns more than only 20 percent of all other households. *Brookings Institution, "Household Income Inequality, Largest Cities of 97 Large U.S. Metro Areas, 2014-2016," February 5, 2018*

- The Brookings Institution ranked the 100 largest metro areas in the U.S. based on income inequality. New York was ranked #2 (#1 = greatest inequality). Criteria: the "95/20 ratio," a figure representing the income at which a household earns more than 95 percent of all other households, divided by the income at which a household earns more than only 20 percent of all other households. *Brookings Institution, "Household Income Inequality, 100 Largest U.S. Metro Areas, 2014-2016," February 5, 2018*

- Payscale.com ranked the 32 largest metro areas in terms of wage growth. The New York metro area ranked #30. Criteria: quarterly changes in private industry employee and education professional wage growth from the previous year. *PayScale, "Wage Trends by Metro Area-1st Quarter," April 20, 2023*

- The New York metro area was identified as one of the most debt-ridden places in America by the finance site Credit.com. The metro area was ranked #3. Criteria: residents' average credit card debt as well as median income. *Credit.com, "25 Cities With the Most Credit Card Debt," February 28, 2018*

- For its annual survey of the "Most Expensive U.S. Cities to Live In," Kiplinger applied Cost of Living Index statistics developed by the Council for Community and Economic Research to U.S. Census Bureau population and median household income data for 265 urban areas. New York ranked #4 among the most expensive in the country. *Kiplinger.com, "The 11 Most Expensive Cities to Live in the U.S.," April 15, 2023*

- New York was identified as one of America's most frugal metro areas by *Coupons.com.* The city ranked #15 out of 25. Criteria: digital coupon usage. *Coupons.com, "America's Most Frugal Cities of 2017," March 22, 2018*

- New York was cited as one of America's top metros for total corporate facility investment in 2022. The area ranked #4 in the large metro area category (population over 1 million). *Site Selection, "Top Metros of 2022," March 2023*

- New York was identified as one of the happiest cities to work in by CareerBliss.com, an online community for career advancement. The city ranked #5 out of 10. Criteria: an employee's relationship with his or her boss and co-workers; daily tasks; general work environment; compensation; opportunities for advancement; company culture and job reputation; and resources. *Businesswire.com, "CareerBliss Happiest Cities to Work 2019," February 12, 2019*

- The New York metro area appeared on the Milken Institute "2022 Best Performing Cities" list. Rank: #116 out of 200 large metro areas (population over 250,000). Criteria: job growth; wage and salary growth; high-tech output growth; housing affordability; household broadband access. *Milken Institute, "Best-Performing Cities 2022," March 28, 2022*

- *Forbes* ranked the 200 most populous metro areas to determine the nation's "Best Places for Business and Careers." The New York metro area was ranked #115. Criteria: costs (business and living); job growth (past and projected); income growth; quality of life; educational attainment (college and high school); projected economic growth; cultural and leisure opportunities; workplace tolerance laws; net migration patterns. *Forbes, "The Best Places for Business and Careers 2019: Seattle Still On Top," October 30, 2019*

- Mercer Human Resources Consulting ranked 227 cities worldwide in terms of cost-of-living. New York ranked #7 (the lower the ranking, the higher the cost-of-living). The survey measured the comparative cost of over 200 items (such as housing, food, clothing, domestic supplies, transportation, and recreation/entertainment) in each location. *Mercer, "2022 Cost of Living City Ranking," June 29, 2022*

Dating/Romance Rankings

- New York was ranked #17 out of 25 cities that stood out for inspiring romance and attracting diners on the website OpenTable.com. Criteria: percentage of people who dined out on Valentine's Day in 2018; percentage of romantic restaurants as rated by OpenTable diner reviews; and percentage of tables seated for two. *OpenTable, "25 Most Romantic Cities in America for 2019," February 7, 2019*

Education Rankings

- Personal finance website *WalletHub* analyzed the 150 largest U.S. metropolitan statistical areas to determine where the most educated Americans are putting their degrees to work. Criteria: education levels; percentage of workers with degrees; education quality and attainment gap; public school quality rankings; quality and enrollment of each metro area's universities. New York was ranked #25 (#1 = most educated city). *www.WalletHub.com, "Most & Least Educated Cities in America," July 18, 2022*

- New York was selected as one of America's most literate cities. The city ranked #22 out of the 84 largest U.S. cities. Criteria: number of booksellers; library resources; Internet resources; educational attainment; periodical publishing resources; newspaper circulation. *Central Connecticut State University, "America's Most Literate Cities, 2018," February 2019*

Environmental Rankings

- The U.S. Environmental Protection Agency (EPA) released its list of U.S. metropolitan areas with the most ENERGY STAR certified buildings in 2022. The New York metro area was ranked #5 out of 25. *U.S. Environmental Protection Agency, "2023 Energy Star Top Cities," April 26, 2023*

- New York was highlighted as one of the 25 most ozone-polluted metro areas in the U.S. during 2019 through 2021. The area ranked #12. *American Lung Association, "State of the Air 2023," April 19, 2023*

Food/Drink Rankings

- The U.S. Chamber of Commerce Foundation conducted an in-depth study on local food truck regulations, surveyed 288 food truck owners, and ranked 20 major American cities based on how friendly they are for operating a food truck. The compiled index assessed the following: procedures for obtaining permits and licenses; complying with restrictions; and financial obligations associated with operating a food truck. New York ranked #9 overall (1 being the best). *www.foodtrucknation.us, "Food Truck Nation," March 20, 2018*

- New York was identified as one of the cities in America ordering the most vegan food options by GrubHub.com. The city ranked #2 out of 5. Criteria: percentage of vegan, vegetarian and plant-based food orders compared to the overall number of orders. *GrubHub.com, "State of the Plate Report 2021: Top Cities for Vegans," June 20, 2021*

- Yankee Stadium was selected as one of PETA's "Top 10 Vegan-Friendly Ballparks" for 2019. The park ranked #6. *People for the Ethical Treatment of Animals, "Top 10 Vegan-Friendly Ballparks," May 23, 2019*

Health/Fitness Rankings

- For each of the 100 largest cities in the United States, the American Fitness Index®, compiled in partnership between the American College of Sports Medicine and the Elevance Health Foundation, evaluated community infrastructure and 34 health behaviors including preventive health, levels of chronic disease conditions, food insecurity, sleep quality, pedestrian safety, air quality, and community/environment resources that support physical activity. New York ranked #17 for "community fitness." *americanfitnessindex.org, "2022 ACSM American Fitness Index Summary Report," July 12, 2022*

- New York was identified as one of the 10 most walkable cities in the U.S. by Walk Score. The city ranked #1. Walk Score measures walkability by analyzing hundreds of walking routes to nearby amenities, and also measures pedestrian friendliness by analyzing population density and road metrics such as block length and intersection density. *WalkScore.com, April 13, 2021*

- The New York metro area was identified as one of the worst cities for bed bugs in America by pest control company Orkin. The area ranked #2 out of 50 based on the number of bed bug treatments Orkin performed from December 2021 to November 2022. *Orkin, "The Windy City Can't Blow Bed Bugs Away: Chicago Ranks #1 For Third Consecutive Year On Orkin's Bed Bug Cities List," January 9, 2023*

- New York was identified as a "2022 Spring Allergy Capital." The area ranked #54 out of 100. Three groups of factors were used to identify the most challenging cities for people with allergies during the spring season: annual spring pollen scores; over the counter allergy medicine use; number of board-certified allergy specialists. *Asthma and Allergy Foundation of America, "Spring Allergy Capitals 2022," March 2, 2022*

- New York was identified as a "2022 Fall Allergy Capital." The area ranked #75 out of 100. Three groups of factors were used to identify the most challenging cities for people with allergies during the fall season: annual fall pollen scores; over the counter allergy medicine use; number of board-certified allergy specialists. *Asthma and Allergy Foundation of America, "Fall Allergy Capitals 2022," March 2, 2022*

- New York was identified as a "2022 Asthma Capital." The area ranked #21 out of the nation's 100 largest metropolitan areas. Criteria: estimated asthma prevalence; asthma-related mortality; and ER visits due to asthma. Risk factors analyzed but not factored in the rankings: annual pollen score; annual air quality; public smoking laws; access to board-certified asthma specialists; rescue and controller medication use; uninsured rate; poverty rate. *Asthma and Allergy Foundation of America, "Asthma Capitals 2022: The Most Challenging Places to Live With Asthma," September 14, 2022*

- The Sharecare Community Well-Being Index evaluates 10 individual and social health factors in order to measure what matters to Americans in the communities in which they live. The New York metro area ranked #7 in the top 10 across all 10 domains. Criteria: access to healthcare, food, and community resources; housng and transportation; economic security; feeling of purpose; physical, financial, social, and community well-being. *www.sharecare.com, "Community Well-Being Index: 2020 Metro Area & County Rankings Report," August 30, 2021*

Real Estate Rankings

- *WalletHub* compared the most populated U.S. cities to determine which had the best markets for real estate agents. New York ranked #98 where demand was high and pay was the best. Criteria: sales per agent; annual median wage for real-estate agents; monthly average starting salary for real estate agents; real estate job density and competition; unemployment rate; home turnover rate; housing-market health index; and other relevant metrics. *www.WalletHub.com, "2021 Best Places to Be a Real Estate Agent," May 12, 2021*

- The New York metro area was identified as one of the 20 least affordable housing markets in the U.S. in 2022. The area ranked #172 out of 186 markets. Criteria: qualification for a mortgage loan with a 10 percent down payment on a typical home. *National Association of Realtors®, Qualifying Income Based on Sales Price of Existing Single-Family Homes for Metropolitan Areas, 2022*

- New York was ranked #210 out of 235 metro areas in terms of housing affordability in 2022 by the National Association of Home Builders (#1 = most affordable). Criteria: the share of homes sold in that area affordable to a family earning the local median income, based on standard mortgage underwriting criteria. *National Association of Home Builders®, NAHB-Wells Fargo Housing Opportunity Index, 4th Quarter 2022*

Safety Rankings

- Allstate ranked the 200 largest cities in America in terms of driver safety. New York ranked #111. Criteria: internal property damage claims over a two-year period from January 2016 to December 2017. The report helps increase the importance of safety and awareness behind the wheel. *Allstate, "Allstate America's Best Drivers Report, 2019" June 24, 2019*

- The National Insurance Crime Bureau ranked 390 metro areas in the U.S. in terms of per capita rates of vehicle theft. The New York metro area ranked #273 (#1 = highest rate). Criteria: number of vehicle theft offenses per 100,000 inhabitants in 2021. *National Insurance Crime Bureau, "Hot Spots 2021," September 1, 2022*

Seniors/Retirement Rankings

- From its Best Cities for Successful Aging indexes, the Milken Institute generated rankings for metropolitan areas, weighing data in nine categories—health care, wellness, living arrangements, transportation and convenience, financial characteristics, education, employment, community engagement, and overall livability. The New York metro area was ranked #73 overall in the large metro area category. *Milken Institute, "Best Cities for Successful Aging, 2017" March 14, 2017*

Sports/Recreation Rankings

- New York was chosen as one of America's best cities for bicycling. The city ranked #9 out of 50. Criteria: cycling infrastructure that is safe and friendly for all ages; energy and bike culture. The editors evaluated cities with populations of 100,000 or more. *Bicycling, "The 50 Best Bike Cities in America," October 10, 2018*

Transportation Rankings

- Business Insider presented an AllTransit Performance Score ranking of public transportation in major U.S. cities and towns, with populations over 250,000, in which New York earned the #2-ranked "Transit Score," awarded for frequency of service, access to jobs, quality and number of stops, and affordability. *www.businessinsider.com, "The 17 Major U.S. Cities with the Best Public Transportation," April 17, 2018*

- The business website *24/7 Wall St.* reviewed U.S. Census data to identify the 25 cities where the largest share of households do not own a vehicle. New York held the #1 position. *247wallst.com, "Cities Where No One Wants to Drive," January 12, 2020*

- New York was identified as one of the most congested metro areas in the U.S. The area ranked #9 out of 10. Criteria: yearly delay per auto commuter in hours. *Texas A&M Transportation Institute, "2021 Urban Mobility Report," June 2021*

- According to the INRIX "2022 Global Traffic Scorecard," New York was identified as one of the most congested metro areas in the U.S. The area ranked #3 out of 25. Criteria: average annual time spent in traffic and average cost of congestion per motorist. *Inrix.com, "Return to Work, Higher Gas Prices & Inflation Drove Americans to Spend Hundreds More in Time and Money Commuting," January 10, 2023*

Women/Minorities Rankings

- *Travel + Leisure* listed the best cities in and around the U.S. for a memorable and fun girls' trip, even on a budget. Whether it is for a special occasion, to make new memories or just to get away, New York is sure to have something for all the ladies in your tribe. *Travel + Leisure, "25 Affordable Girls Weekend Getaways That Won't Break the Bank," November 25, 2022*

- The *Houston Chronicle* listed the New York metro area as #4 in top places for young Latinos to live in the U.S. Research was largely based on housing and occupational data from the largest metropolitan areas performed by *Forbes* and NBC Universo. Criteria: percentage of 18-34 year-olds; Latino college grad rates; and diversity. *blog.chron.com, "The 15 Best Big Cities for Latino Millenials," January 26, 2016*

- Personal finance website *WalletHub* compared more than 180 U.S. cities across two key dimensions, "Hispanic Business-Friendliness" and "Hispanic Purchasing Power," to arrive at the most favorable conditions for Hispanic entrepreneurs. New York was ranked #160 out of 182. Criteria includes: share of Hispanic-Owned Businesses; Hispanic entrepreneurship rate to median annual income of Hispanics; Small Business-Friendliness score; cost of living; and number of Hispanics with at least a bachelor's degree. *WalletHub.com, "2019's Best Cities for Hispanic Entrepreneurs," May 1, 2019*

Miscellaneous Rankings

- In its roundup of St. Patrick's Day parades "Gayot" listed the best festivals and parades of all things Irish. The festivities in New York as among the best in North America. *www.gayot.com, "Best St. Patrick's Day Parades," March 2023*

- The watchdog site, Charity Navigator, conducted a study of charities in major markets both to analyze statistical differences in their financial, accountability, and transparency practices and to track year-to-year variations in individual philanthropic communities. The New York metro area was ranked #19 among the 30 metro markets in the rating category of Overall Score. *www.charitynavigator.org, "2017 Metro Market Study," May 1, 2017*

- *WalletHub* compared the 150 most populated U.S. cities to determine their operating efficiency. A "Quality of Services" score was constructed for each city and then divided by the total budget per capita to reveal which were managed the best. New York ranked #148. Criteria: financial stability; economy; education; safety; health; infrastructure and pollution. *www.WalletHub.com, "2022's Best- & Worst-Run Cities in America," June 21, 2022*

- The National Alliance to End Homelessness listed the 25 most populous metro areas with the highest rate of homelessness. The New York metro area had a high rate of homelessness. Criteria: number of homeless people per 10,000 population in 2016. *National Alliance to End Homelessness, "Homelessness in the 25 Most Populous U.S. Metro Areas," September 1, 2017*

Business Environment

DEMOGRAPHICS

Population Growth

Area	1990 Census	2000 Census	2010 Census	2020 Census	Population Growth (%)	
					1990-2020	2010-2020
City	7,322,552	8,008,278	8,175,133	8,804,190	20.2	7.7
MSA[1]	16,845,992	18,323,002	18,897,109	20,140,470	19.6	6.6
U.S.	248,709,873	281,421,906	308,745,538	331,449,281	33.3	7.4

Note: (1) Figures cover the New York-Newark-Jersey City, NY-NJ-PA Metropolitan Statistical Area
Source: U.S. Census Bureau, 1990 Census, 2000 Census, 2010 Census, 2020 Census

Race

Area	White Alone[2] (%)	Black Alone[2] (%)	Asian Alone[2] (%)	AIAN[3] Alone[2] (%)	NHOPI[4] Alone[2] (%)	Other Race Alone[2] (%)	Two or More Races (%)
City	34.1	22.1	15.7	1.0	0.1	17.0	10.1
MSA[1]	46.5	16.1	12.5	0.8	0.1	14.1	10.0
U.S.	61.6	12.4	6.0	1.1	0.2	8.4	10.2

Note: (1) Figures cover the New York-Newark-Jersey City, NY-NJ-PA Metropolitan Statistical Area; (2) Alone is defined as not being in combination with one or more other races; (3) American Indian and Alaska Native; (4) Native Hawaiian and Other Pacific Islander
Source: U.S. Census Bureau, 2020 Census

Hispanic or Latino Origin

Area	Total (%)	Mexican (%)	Puerto Rican (%)	Cuban (%)	Other (%)
City	28.9	3.8	7.7	0.5	16.9
MSA[1]	24.8	2.9	5.9	0.8	15.3
U.S.	18.4	11.2	1.8	0.7	4.7

Note: Persons of Hispanic or Latino origin can be of any race; (1) Figures cover the New York-Newark-Jersey City, NY-NJ-PA Metropolitan Statistical Area
Source: U.S. Census Bureau, 2017-2021 American Community Survey 5-Year Estimates

Age

Area	Percent of Population									Median Age
	Under Age 5	Age 5–19	Age 20–34	Age 35–44	Age 45–54	Age 55–64	Age 65–74	Age 75–84	Age 85+	
City	5.4	16.7	24.8	13.9	12.2	12.0	8.7	4.4	1.9	36.8
MSA[1]	5.4	18.0	21.5	13.3	12.8	13.0	9.2	4.7	2.1	38.7
U.S.	5.6	19.2	20.2	12.7	12.4	13.1	10.0	4.9	1.9	38.8

Note: (1) Figures cover the New York-Newark-Jersey City, NY-NJ-PA Metropolitan Statistical Area
Source: U.S. Census Bureau, 2020 Census

Disability by Age

Area	All Ages	Under 18 Years Old	18 to 64 Years Old	65 Years and Over
City	10.9	3.6	8.0	33.9
MSA[1]	10.1	3.3	7.3	30.5
U.S.	12.6	4.4	10.3	33.4

Note: Figures show percent of the civilian noninstitutionalized population that reported having a disability. Disability status is determined from six types of difficulty: vision, hearing, cognitive, ambulatory, self-care, and independent living. For children under 5 years old, hearing and vision difficulty are used to determine disability status. For children between the ages of 5 and 14, disability status is determined from hearing, vision, cognitive, ambulatory, and self-care difficulties. For people aged 15 years and older, they are considered to have a disability if they have difficulty with any one of the six difficulty types; Note: (1) Figures cover the New York-Newark-Jersey City, NY-NJ-PA Metropolitan Statistical Area
Source: U.S. Census Bureau, 2017-2021 American Community Survey 5-Year Estimates

Ancestry

Area	German	Irish	English	American	Italian	Polish	French[2]	Scottish	Dutch
City	2.9	4.4	1.9	3.8	6.1	2.3	0.8	0.5	0.3
MSA[1]	6.0	8.9	2.9	4.0	11.6	3.7	0.9	0.6	0.5
U.S.	12.8	9.6	8.1	5.7	5.0	2.7	2.2	1.6	1.1

Note: Figures are the percentage of the total population reporting a particular ancestry. The nine most commonly reported ancestries in the U.S. are shown. Figures include multiple ancestries (e.g. if a person reported being Irish and Italian, they were included in both columns); (1) Figures cover the New York-Newark-Jersey City, NY-NJ-PA Metropolitan Statistical Area; (2) Excludes Basque
Source: U.S. Census Bureau, 2017-2021 American Community Survey 5-Year Estimates

Foreign-born Population

Area	Any Foreign Country	Asia	Mexico	Europe	Caribbean	Central America[2]	South America	Africa	Canada
City	36.3	10.8	1.8	5.2	9.9	1.4	4.9	1.7	0.3
MSA[1]	29.4	8.7	1.4	4.3	6.9	1.9	4.5	1.4	0.2
U.S.	13.6	4.2	3.3	1.5	1.4	1.1	1.1	0.8	0.2

Note: (1) Figures cover the New York-Newark-Jersey City, NY-NJ-PA Metropolitan Statistical Area;
(2) Excludes Mexico.
Source: U.S. Census Bureau, 2017-2021 American Community Survey 5-Year Estimates

Household Size

Area	One	Two	Three	Four	Five	Six	Seven or More	Average Household Size
City	32.5	28.7	16.3	12.2	5.8	2.5	2.0	2.60
MSA[1]	28.0	29.6	17.0	14.4	6.5	2.6	1.9	2.70
U.S.	28.1	33.8	15.5	12.9	6.0	2.3	1.4	2.60

Note: (1) Figures cover the New York-Newark-Jersey City, NY-NJ-PA Metropolitan Statistical Area
Source: U.S. Census Bureau, 2017-2021 American Community Survey 5-Year Estimates

Household Relationships

Area	House-holder	Opposite-sex Spouse	Same-sex Spouse	Opposite-sex Unmarried Partner	Same-sex Unmarried Partner	Child[2]	Grand-child	Other Relatives	Non-relatives
City	38.3	12.7	0.3	2.2	0.2	27.6	2.5	8.3	5.3
MSA[1]	36.8	15.8	0.2	2.0	0.2	29.7	2.1	7.1	4.1
U.S.	38.3	17.5	0.2	2.5	0.2	28.3	2.4	4.8	3.4

Note: Figures are percent of the total population; (1) Figures cover the New York-Newark-Jersey City,
NY-NJ-PA Metropolitan Statistical Area; (2) Includes biological, adopted, and stepchildren of the householder
Source: U.S. Census Bureau, 2020 Census

Gender

Area	Males	Females	Males per 100 Females
City	4,184,548	4,619,642	90.6
MSA[1]	9,693,702	10,446,768	92.8
U.S.	162,685,811	168,763,470	96.4

Note: (1) Figures cover the New York-Newark-Jersey City, NY-NJ-PA Metropolitan Statistical Area
Source: U.S. Census Bureau, 2020 Census

Marital Status

Area	Never Married	Now Married[2]	Separated	Widowed	Divorced
City	43.8	39.9	2.9	5.3	8.1
MSA[1]	38.1	46.1	2.2	5.5	8.1
U.S.	33.8	48.0	1.8	5.6	10.8

Note: Figures are percentages and cover the population 15 years of age and older; (1) Figures cover the New
York-Newark-Jersey City, NY-NJ-PA Metropolitan Statistical Area; (2) Excludes separated
Source: U.S. Census Bureau, 2017-2021 American Community Survey 5-Year Estimates

Religious Groups by Family

Area	Catholic	Baptist	Methodist	LDS[2]	Pentecostal	Lutheran	Islam	Adventist	Other
MSA[1]	32.5	1.7	1.2	0.3	0.9	0.5	4.5	1.4	10.6
U.S.	18.7	7.3	3.0	2.0	1.8	1.7	1.3	1.3	11.6

Note: Figures are the number of adherents as a percentage of the total population and cover the eight largest
religious groups in the U.S; (1) Figures cover the New York-Newark-Jersey City, NY-NJ-PA Metropolitan
Statistical Area; (2) Church of Jesus Christ of Latter-day Saints
Sources: 2020 U.S. Religion Census, Association of Statisticians of American Religious Bodies; The
Association of Religion Data Archives (ARDA)

Religious Groups by Tradition

Area	Catholic	Evangelical Protestant	Mainline Protestant	Black Protestant	Islam	Judaism	Hinduism	Orthodox	Buddhism
MSA[1]	32.5	4.4	3.0	1.5	4.5	4.4	1.0	0.8	0.3
U.S.	18.7	16.5	5.2	2.3	1.3	0.6	0.4	0.4	0.3

Note: Figures are the number of adherents as a percentage of the total population; (1) Figures cover the New
York-Newark-Jersey City, NY-NJ-PA Metropolitan Statistical Area
Sources: 2020 U.S. Religion Census, Association of Statisticians of American Religious Bodies; The
Association of Religion Data Archives (ARDA)

ECONOMY

Gross Metropolitan Product

Area	2020	2021	2022	2023	Rank[2]
MSA[1]	1,844.7	1,993.2	2,157.6	2,278.7	1

Note: Figures are in billions of dollars; (1) Figures cover the New York-Newark-Jersey City, NY-NJ-PA Metropolitan Statistical Area; (2) Rank is based on 2021 data and ranges from 1 to 381
Source: U.S. Conference of Mayors, U.S. Metro Economies: U.S. Metros Compared to Global and State Economies, June 2022

Economic Growth

Area	2018-20 (%)	2021 (%)	2022 (%)	2023 (%)	Rank[2]
MSA[1]	-1.5	5.6	3.3	2.4	250
U.S.	-0.6	5.7	3.1	2.9	–

Note: Figures are real gross metropolitan product (GMP) growth rates and represent average annual percent change; (1) Figures cover the New York-Newark-Jersey City, NY-NJ-PA Metropolitan Statistical Area; (2) Rank is based on 2020 2-year average annual percent change and ranges from 1 to 381
Source: U.S. Conference of Mayors, U.S. Metro Economies: U.S. Metros Compared to Global and State Economies, June 2022

Metropolitan Area Exports

Area	2016	2017	2018	2019	2020	2021	Rank[2]
MSA[1]	89,649.5	93,693.7	97,692.4	87,365.7	75,745.4	103,930.9	2

Note: Figures are in millions of dollars; (1) Figures cover the New York-Newark-Jersey City, NY-NJ-PA Metropolitan Statistical Area; (2) Rank is based on 2021 data and ranges from 1 to 388
Source: U.S. Department of Commerce, International Trade Administration, Office of Trade and Economic Analysis, Industry and Analysis, Exports by Metropolitan Area, data extracted March 16, 2023

Building Permits

Area	Single-Family			Multi-Family			Total		
	2021	2022	Pct. Chg.	2021	2022	Pct. Chg.	2021	2022	Pct. Chg.
City	151	61	-59.6	19,772	21,429	8.4	19,923	21,490	7.9
MSA[1]	12,947	12,089	-6.6	43,714	46,323	6.0	56,661	58,412	3.1
U.S.	1,115,400	975,600	-12.5	621,600	689,500	10.9	1,737,000	1,665,100	-4.1

Note: (1) Figures cover the New York-Newark-Jersey City, NY-NJ-PA Metropolitan Statistical Area; Figures represent new, privately-owned housing units authorized (unadjusted data); All permit data are based on estimates with imputation
Source: U.S. Census Bureau, Manufacturing, Mining, and Construction Statistics, Building Permits, 2021, 2022

Bankruptcy Filings

Area	Business Filings			Nonbusiness Filings		
	2021	2022	% Chg.	2021	2022	% Chg.
Bronx County	23	27	17.4	1,219	862	-29.3
Kings County	108	212	96.3	1,238	1,062	-14.2
New York County	398	240	-39.7	721	595	-17.5
Queens County	82	126	53.7	1,447	1,478	2.1
Richmond County	24	25	4.2	310	352	13.5
U.S.	14,347	13,481	-6.0	399,269	374,240	-6.3

Note: Business filings include Chapter 7, Chapter 9, Chapter 11, Chapter 12, Chapter 13, Chapter 15, and Section 304; Nonbusiness filings include Chapter 7, Chapter 11, and Chapter 13
Source: Administrative Office of the U.S. Courts, Business and Nonbusiness Bankruptcy, County Cases Commenced by Chapter of the Bankruptcy Code, During the 12-Month Period Ending December 31, 2021 and Business and Nonbusiness Bankruptcy, County Cases Commenced by Chapter of the Bankruptcy Code, During the 12-Month Period Ending December 31, 2022

Housing Vacancy Rates

Area	Gross Vacancy Rate[2] (%)			Year-Round Vacancy Rate[3] (%)			Rental Vacancy Rate[4] (%)			Homeowner Vacancy Rate[5] (%)		
	2020	2021	2022	2020	2021	2022	2020	2021	2022	2020	2021	2022
MSA[1]	9.1	9.8	8.2	7.8	8.7	7.0	4.5	5.2	3.5	1.3	1.2	1.0
U.S.	10.6	10.8	10.5	8.2	8.4	8.2	6.3	6.1	5.8	1.0	0.9	0.8

Note: (1) Figures cover the New York-Newark-Jersey City, NY-NJ-PA Metropolitan Statistical Area; (2) The percentage of the total housing inventory that is vacant; (3) The percentage of the housing inventory (excluding seasonal units) that is year-round vacant; (4) The percentage of rental inventory that is vacant for rent; (5) The percentage of homeowner inventory that is vacant for sale
Source: U.S. Census Bureau, Housing Vacancies and Homeownership Annual Statistics: 2020, 2021, 2022

INCOME

Income

Area	Per Capita ($)	Median Household ($)	Average Household ($)
City	43,952	70,663	113,315
MSA[1]	47,591	86,445	127,555
U.S.	37,638	69,021	97,196

Note: (1) Figures cover the New York-Newark-Jersey City, NY-NJ-PA Metropolitan Statistical Area
Source: U.S. Census Bureau, 2017-2021 American Community Survey 5-Year Estimates

Household Income Distribution

Area	Percent of Households Earning							
	Under $15,000	$15,000 -$24,999	$25,000 -$34,999	$35,000 -$49,999	$50,000 -$74,999	$75,000 -$99,999	$100,000 -$149,999	$150,000 and up
City	13.2	8.0	7.3	9.6	14.0	11.0	15.0	21.9
MSA[1]	9.7	6.6	6.3	8.6	13.3	11.2	16.7	27.5
U.S.	9.4	7.8	8.2	11.4	16.8	12.8	16.3	17.3

Note: (1) Figures cover the New York-Newark-Jersey City, NY-NJ-PA Metropolitan Statistical Area
Source: U.S. Census Bureau, 2017-2021 American Community Survey 5-Year Estimates

Poverty Rate

Area	All Ages	Under 18 Years Old	18 to 64 Years Old	65 Years and Over
City	17.0	23.2	14.7	17.8
MSA[1]	12.3	16.6	10.8	12.1
U.S.	12.6	17.0	11.8	9.6

Note: Figures are percentage of people whose income during the past 12 months was below the poverty level;
(1) Figures cover the New York-Newark-Jersey City, NY-NJ-PA Metropolitan Statistical Area
Source: U.S. Census Bureau, 2017-2021 American Community Survey 5-Year Estimates

EMPLOYMENT

Labor Force and Employment

Area	Civilian Labor Force			Workers Employed		
	Dec. 2021	Dec. 2022	% Chg.	Dec. 2021	Dec. 2022	% Chg.
City	4,085,159	4,113,259	0.7	3,782,405	3,907,975	3.3
MD[1]	6,978,612	7,057,593	1.1	6,599,840	6,759,099	2.4
U.S.	161,696,000	164,224,000	1.6	155,732,000	158,872,000	2.0

Note: Data is not seasonally adjusted and covers workers 16 years of age and older; (1) Figures cover the New York-Jersey City-White Plains, NY-NJ Metropolitan Division
Source: Bureau of Labor Statistics, Local Area Unemployment Statistics

Unemployment Rate

Area	2022											
	Jan.	Feb.	Mar.	Apr.	May	Jun.	Jul.	Aug.	Sep.	Oct.	Nov.	Dec.
City	7.8	7.2	6.3	5.7	5.4	5.5	5.4	5.2	4.5	5.0	5.0	5.0
MD[1]	6.1	5.6	5.1	4.7	4.6	4.9	5.3	5.4	4.1	4.1	4.2	4.2
U.S.	4.4	4.1	3.8	3.3	3.4	3.8	3.8	3.8	3.3	3.4	3.4	3.3

Note: Data is not seasonally adjusted and covers workers 16 years of age and older; (1) Figures cover the New York-Jersey City-White Plains, NY-NJ Metropolitan Division
Source: Bureau of Labor Statistics, Local Area Unemployment Statistics

Average Wages

Occupation	$/Hr.	Occupation	$/Hr.
Accountants and Auditors	54.94	Maintenance and Repair Workers	26.67
Automotive Mechanics	26.81	Marketing Managers	93.41
Bookkeepers	26.44	Network and Computer Systems Admin.	55.75
Carpenters	37.06	Nurses, Licensed Practical	30.31
Cashiers	16.55	Nurses, Registered	50.41
Computer Programmers	57.97	Nursing Assistants	21.50
Computer Systems Analysts	60.54	Office Clerks, General	21.90
Computer User Support Specialists	35.55	Physical Therapists	53.25
Construction Laborers	30.93	Physicians	128.42
Cooks, Restaurant	19.55	Plumbers, Pipefitters and Steamfitters	42.38
Customer Service Representatives	23.75	Police and Sheriff's Patrol Officers	42.43
Dentists	89.01	Postal Service Mail Carriers	27.72
Electricians	41.22	Real Estate Sales Agents	47.01
Engineers, Electrical	53.37	Retail Salespersons	19.51
Fast Food and Counter Workers	16.08	Sales Representatives, Technical/Scientific	63.64
Financial Managers	110.67	Secretaries, Exc. Legal/Medical/Executive	23.24
First-Line Supervisors of Office Workers	38.32	Security Guards	19.89
General and Operations Managers	83.82	Surgeons	149.60
Hairdressers/Cosmetologists	20.85	Teacher Assistants, Exc. Postsecondary*	18.07
Home Health and Personal Care Aides	17.10	Teachers, Secondary School, Exc. Sp. Ed.*	45.24
Janitors and Cleaners	20.14	Telemarketers	20.35
Landscaping/Groundskeeping Workers	20.81	Truck Drivers, Heavy/Tractor-Trailer	29.43
Lawyers	92.92	Truck Drivers, Light/Delivery Services	23.63
Maids and Housekeeping Cleaners	21.40	Waiters and Waitresses	23.01

Note: Wage data covers the New York-Newark-Jersey City, NY-NJ-PA Metropolitan Statistical Area;
(*) Hourly wages were calculated from annual wage data based on a 40 hour work week; n/a not available.
Source: Bureau of Labor Statistics, Metro Area Occupational Employment & Wage Estimates, May 2022

Employment by Industry

Sector	MD[1]		U.S.
	Number of Employees	Percent of Total	Percent of Total
Construction, Mining, and Logging	267,500	3.6	5.4
Private Education and Health Services	1,672,200	22.7	16.1
Financial Activities	660,600	9.0	5.9
Government	915,600	12.4	14.5
Information	288,400	3.9	2.0
Leisure and Hospitality	655,900	8.9	10.3
Manufacturing	193,700	2.6	8.4
Other Services	292,300	4.0	3.7
Professional and Business Services	1,215,400	16.5	14.7
Retail Trade	613,100	8.3	10.2
Transportation, Warehousing, and Utilities	312,800	4.3	4.9
Wholesale Trade	270,500	3.7	3.9

Note: Figures are non-farm employment as of December 2022. Figures are not seasonally adjusted and include workers 16 years of age and older; (1) Figures cover the New York-Jersey City-White Plains, NY-NJ Metropolitan Division
Source: Bureau of Labor Statistics, Current Employment Statistics, Employment, Hours, and Earnings

Employment by Occupation

Occupation Classification	City (%)	MSA[1] (%)	U.S. (%)
Management, Business, Science, and Arts	44.0	45.3	40.3
Natural Resources, Construction, and Maintenance	5.8	6.5	8.7
Production, Transportation, and Material Moving	8.9	9.6	13.1
Sales and Office	19.3	20.3	20.9
Service	22.0	18.2	17.0

Note: Figures cover employed civilians 16 years of age and older; (1) Figures cover the New York-Newark-Jersey City, NY-NJ-PA Metropolitan Statistical Area
Source: U.S. Census Bureau, 2017-2021 American Community Survey 5-Year Estimates

Occupations with Greatest Projected Employment Growth: 2022 – 2024

Occupation[1]	2022 Employment	2024 Projected Employment	Numeric Employment Change	Percent Employment Change
Home Health and Personal Care Aides	553,830	585,130	31,300	5.7
Fast Food and Counter Workers	201,510	211,420	9,910	4.9
Cooks, Restaurant	71,380	79,220	7,840	11.0
Waiters and Waitresses	112,740	119,660	6,920	6.1
Software Developers	92,920	96,920	4,000	4.3
First-Line Supervisors of Food Preparation and Serving Workers	59,180	62,960	3,780	6.4
Registered Nurses	200,950	203,720	2,770	1.4
Market Research Analysts and Marketing Specialists	85,250	87,700	2,450	2.9
Fitness Trainers and Aerobics Instructors	21,540	23,720	2,180	10.1
Maids and Housekeeping Cleaners	61,160	63,300	2,140	3.5

Note: Projections cover New York; (1) Sorted by numeric employment change
Source: www.projectionscentral.com, State Occupational Projections, 2022–2024 Short-Term Projections

Fastest-Growing Occupations: 2022 – 2024

Occupation[1]	2022 Employment	2024 Projected Employment	Numeric Employment Change	Percent Employment Change
Amusement and Recreation Attendants	12,490	14,170	1,680	13.5
Gaming Dealers	2,800	3,140	340	12.1
Cooks, Restaurant	71,380	79,220	7,840	11.0
First-Line Supervisors of Gambling Services Workers	1,020	1,130	110	10.8
Fitness Trainers and Aerobics Instructors	21,540	23,720	2,180	10.1
Hotel, Motel, and Resort Desk Clerks	8,600	9,340	740	8.6
Lodging Managers	3,480	3,760	280	8.0
Gaming Change Persons and Booth Cashiers	630	680	50	7.9
Lifeguards, Ski Patrol, and Other Recreational Protective Service Workers	5,630	6,060	430	7.6
Bartenders	26,230	28,200	1,970	7.5

Note: Projections cover New York; (1) Sorted by percent employment change and excludes occupations with numeric employment change less than 50
Source: www.projectionscentral.com, State Occupational Projections, 2022–2024 Short-Term Projections

CITY FINANCES

City Government Finances

Component	2020 ($000)	2020 ($ per capita)
Total Revenues	122,816,406	14,732
Total Expenditures	124,755,775	14,964
Debt Outstanding	149,657,240	17,951
Cash and Securities[1]	46,772,346	5,610

Note: (1) Cash and security holdings of a government at the close of its fiscal year, including those of its dependent agencies, utilities, and liquor stores.
Source: U.S. Census Bureau, State & Local Government Finances 2020

City Government Revenue by Source

Source	2020 ($000)	2020 ($ per capita)	2020 (%)
General Revenue			
From Federal Government	8,481,350	1,017	6.9
From State Government	27,437,603	3,291	22.3
From Local Governments	3,269,079	392	2.7
Taxes			
Property	28,815,935	3,456	23.5
Sales and Gross Receipts	9,378,842	1,125	7.6
Personal Income	14,247,844	1,709	11.6
Corporate Income	6,486,597	778	5.3
Motor Vehicle License	92,221	11	0.1
Other Taxes	2,754,023	330	2.2
Current Charges	10,618,436	1,274	8.6
Liquor Store	0	0	0.0
Utility	6,185,124	742	5.0

Source: U.S. Census Bureau, State & Local Government Finances 2020

City Government Expenditures by Function

Function	2020 ($000)	2020 ($ per capita)	2020 (%)
General Direct Expenditures			
Air Transportation	0	0	0.0
Corrections	1,420,580	170	1.1
Education	35,711,176	4,283	28.6
Employment Security Administration	0	0	0.0
Financial Administration	595,674	71	0.5
Fire Protection	2,259,911	271	1.8
General Public Buildings	468,116	56	0.4
Governmental Administration, Other	302,702	36	0.2
Health	1,339,297	160	1.1
Highways	2,310,300	277	1.9
Hospitals	8,619,606	1,033	6.9
Housing and Community Development	6,589,174	790	5.3
Interest on General Debt	7,093,148	850	5.7
Judicial and Legal	1,060,292	127	0.8
Libraries	429,980	51	0.3
Parking	44,830	5	0.0
Parks and Recreation	1,398,134	167	1.1
Police Protection	6,113,179	733	4.9
Public Welfare	9,267,595	1,111	7.4
Sewerage	2,232,419	267	1.8
Solid Waste Management	2,159,333	259	1.7
Veterans' Services	0	0	0.0
Liquor Store	0	0	0.0
Utility	15,252,482	1,829	12.2

Source: U.S. Census Bureau, State & Local Government Finances 2020

TAXES

State Corporate Income Tax Rates

State	Tax Rate (%)	Income Brackets ($)	Num. of Brackets	Financial Institution Tax Rate (%)[a]	Federal Income Tax Ded.
New York	6.5 (p)	Flat rate	1	6.5 (p)	No

Note: Tax rates as of January 1, 2023; (a) Rates listed are the corporate income tax rate applied to financial institutions or excise taxes based on income. Some states have other taxes based upon the value of deposits or shares; (p) Plus a Corporate Stocks Tax of 0.1875% for tax years 2022 & 2023. A top bracket of 7.25% is imposed on income over $5 million for 2022 & 2023. A minimum tax ranges from $25 to $200,000, depending on receipts ($250 minimum for banks). Certain qualified New York manufacturers pay 0%.
Source: Federation of Tax Administrators, State Corporate Income Tax Rates, January 1, 2023

State Individual Income Tax Rates

State	Tax Rate (%)	Income Brackets ($)	Personal Exemptions ($)			Standard Ded. ($)	
			Single	Married	Depend.	Single	Married
New York (a)	4.0 - 10.9	8,500 - 25 mil. (s)	0	0	1,000	8,000	16,050

Note: Tax rates as of January 1, 2023; Local- and county-level taxes are not included; Federal income tax is not deductible on state income tax returns; (a) 16 states have statutory provision for automatically adjusting to the rate of inflation the dollar values of the income tax brackets, standard deductions, and/or personal exemptions. Oregon does not index the income brackets for $125,000 and over; (s) The income brackets reported for New York are for single individuals. For married couples filing jointly, the same tax rates apply to income brackets ranging from $17,150 to $25 million.
Source: Federation of Tax Administrators, State Individual Income Tax Rates, January 1, 2023

Various State Sales and Excise Tax Rates

State	State Sales Tax (%)	Gasoline[1] ($/gal.)	Cigarette[2] ($/pack)	Spirits[3] ($/gal.)	Wine[4] ($/gal.)	Beer[5] ($/gal.)	Recreational Marijuana (%)
New York	4	0.5655	4.35	6.44	0.30	0.14	(o)

Note: All tax rates as of January 1, 2023; (1) The American Petroleum Institute has developed a methodology for determining the average tax rate on a gallon of fuel. Rates may include any of the following: excise taxes, environmental fees, storage tank fees, other fees or taxes, general sales tax, and local taxes; (2) The federal excise tax of $1.0066 per pack and local taxes are not included; (3) Rates are those applicable to off-premise sales of 40% alcohol by volume (a.b.v.) distilled spirits in 750ml containers. Local excise taxes are excluded; (4) Rates are those applicable to off-premise sales of 11% a.b.v. non-carbonated wine in 750ml containers; (5) Rates are those applicable to off-premise sales of 4.7% a.b.v. beer in 12 ounce containers; (o) $0.005 per milligram of THC in flower; $0.008 per milligram of THC in concentrates; $0.03 per milligram of THC in edibles; 9% of retail
Source: Tax Foundation, 2023 Facts & Figures: How Does Your State Compare?

State Business Tax Climate Index Rankings

State	Overall Rank	Corporate Tax Rank	Individual Income Tax Rank	Sales Tax Rank	Property Tax Rank	Unemployment Insurance Tax Rank
New York	49	24	50	43	49	40

Note: The index is a measure of how each state's tax laws affect economic performance. The lower the rank, the more favorable a state's tax system is for business. States without a given tax are given a ranking of 1. The scores/rankings for the District of Columbia do not affect other states. The 2023 index represents the tax climate as of July 1, 2022.
Source: Tax Foundation, State Business Tax Climate Index 2023

TRANSPORTATION

Means of Transportation to Work

Area	Car/Truck/Van		Public Transportation			Bicycle	Walked	Other Means	Worked at Home
	Drove Alone	Car-pooled	Bus	Subway	Railroad				
City	22.4	4.4	9.7	38.4	1.2	1.4	9.5	2.5	10.7
MSA[1]	47.4	6.1	6.7	17.4	3.1	0.7	5.5	2.3	10.6
U.S.	73.2	8.6	2.0	1.6	0.5	0.5	2.5	1.5	9.7

Note: Figures are percentages and cover workers 16 years of age and older; (1) Figures cover the New York-Newark-Jersey City, NY-NJ-PA Metropolitan Statistical Area
Source: U.S. Census Bureau, 2017-2021 American Community Survey 5-Year Estimates

Travel Time to Work

Area	Less Than 10 Minutes	10 to 19 Minutes	20 to 29 Minutes	30 to 44 Minutes	45 to 59 Minutes	60 to 89 Minutes	90 Minutes or More
City	4.0	12.3	13.5	27.1	16.3	19.2	7.6
MSA[1]	7.0	18.5	16.3	24.0	12.7	14.7	6.8
U.S.	12.4	28.5	21.0	20.9	8.2	6.2	2.9

Note: Note: Figures are percentages and include workers 16 years old and over; (1) Figures cover the New York-Newark-Jersey City, NY-NJ-PA Metropolitan Statistical Area
Source: U.S. Census Bureau, 2017-2021 American Community Survey 5-Year Estimates

Key Congestion Measures

Measure	1990	2000	2010	2015	2020
Annual Hours of Delay, Total (000)	275,610	480,809	688,933	778,986	494,268
Annual Hours of Delay, Per Auto Commuter	43	62	78	87	56
Annual Congestion Cost, Per Auto Commuter ($)	1,265	1,658	1,887	1,971	1,322

Note: Covers the New York-Newark NY-NJ-CT urban area
Source: Texas A&M Transportation Institute, 2021 Urban Mobility Report

Freeway Travel Time Index

Measure	1985	1990	1995	2000	2005	2010	2015	2020
Urban Area Index[1]	1.16	1.20	1.24	1.29	1.33	1.33	1.35	1.17
Urban Area Rank[1,2]	10	9	7	6	6	7	7	1

Note: Freeway Travel Time Index—the ratio of travel time in the peak period to the travel time at free-flow conditions. For example, a value of 1.30 indicates a 20-minute free-flow trip takes 26 minutes in the peak (20 minutes x 1.30 = 26 minutes); (1) Covers the New York-Newark NY-NJ-CT urban area; (2) Rank is based on 101 larger urban areas (#1 = highest travel time index)
Source: Texas A&M Transportation Institute, 2021 Urban Mobility Report

Public Transportation

Agency Name / Mode of Transportation	Vehicles Operated in Maximum Service[1]	Annual Unlinked Passenger Trips[2] (in thous.)	Annual Passenger Miles[3] (in thous.)
MTA New York City Transit (NYCT)			
Bus (directly operated)	3,223	393,017.8	925,195.5
Bus Rapid Transit (directly operated)	131	15,797.5	31,595.0
Commuter Bus (directly operated)	433	4,985.7	75,937.8
Demand Response (purchased transportation)	878	2,378.7	22,109.1
Heavy Rail (directly operated)	5,410	1,311,224.6	5,668,693.5
MTA Metro-North Railroad (MTA-MNCR)			
Bus (purchased transportation)	9	90.2	75.4
Commuter Rail (directly operated)	1,128	32,254.1	737,084.8
Ferryboat (purchased transportation)	2	16.2	61.9
MTA Long Island Railroad (MTA-LIRR)			
Commuter Rail (directly operated)	882	49,167.6	1,420,978.6
MTA Staten Island Railway (SIRTOA)			
Heavy Rail (directly operated)	44	2,776.3	17,315.5
New York City Department of Transportation (NYCDOT)			
Commuter Bus (purchased transportation)	9	63.5	2,090.3
Ferryboat (directly operated)	4	7,561.4	39,319.1
Port Authority Trans-Hudson Corporation (PATH)			
Heavy Rail (directly operated)	282	32,073.7	161,154.7

Note: (1) Number of revenue vehicles operated by the given mode and type of service to meet the annual maximum service requirement. This is the revenue vehicle count during the peak season of the year; on the week and day that maximum service is provided. Vehicles operated in maximum service (VOMS) exclude atypical days and one-time special events; (2) Number of passengers who boarded public transportation vehicles. Passengers are counted each time they board a vehicle no matter how many vehicles they use to travel from their origin to their destination. (3) Sum of the distances ridden by all passengers during the entire fiscal year.
Source: Federal Transit Administration, National Transit Database, 2021

Air Transportation

Airport Name and Code / Type of Service	Passenger Airlines[1]	Passenger Enplanements	Freight Carriers[2]	Freight (lbs)
John F. Kennedy International (JFK)				
Domestic service (U.S. carriers - 2022)	19	13,969,297	18	374,335,582
International service (U.S. carriers - 2021)	5	3,608,667	12	156,710,274
La Guardia International (LGA)				
Domestic service (U.S. carriers - 2022)	18	13,700,063	4	6,164,079
International service (U.S. carriers - 2021)	5	37,365	0	0
Newark International (EWR)				
Domestic service (U.S. carriers - 2022)	30	15,510,932	17	534,832,694
International service (U.S. carriers - 2021)	8	2,548,014	4	115,568,069

Note: (1) Includes all U.S.-based major, minor and commuter airlines that carried at least one passenger during the year; (2) Includes all U.S.-based airlines and freight carriers that transported at least one pound of freight during the year.
Source: Bureau of Transportation Statistics, The Intermodal Transportation Database, Air Carriers: T-100 Domestic Market (U.S. Carriers), 2022; Bureau of Transportation Statistics, The Intermodal Transportation Database, Air Carriers: T-100 International Market (U.S. Carriers), 2021

BUSINESSES

Major Business Headquarters

Company Name	Industry	Rankings	
		Fortune[1]	Forbes[2]
AIG	Finance and insurance	67	-
Alcoa	Metals	312	-
Alleghany	Insurance, property and casualty (stock)	318	-
Altice USA	Telecommunications	355	-
AmTrust Financial Services	Insurance and financial services	-	100
American Express	Commercial banks	85	-
Apollo Global Management	Asset management	386	-
Assurant	Insurance, property and casualty (stock)	325	-
Bank of New York Mellon	Commercial banks	229	-
BlackRock	Securities	184	-
Blackstone	Financial services	159	-
Bloomberg	Business services & supplies	-	32
Breakthru Beverage Group	Food, drink & tobacco	-	76
Bristol-Myers Squibb	Pharmaceuticals	82	-
Citigroup	Commercial banks	44	-
Colgate-Palmolive	Household and personal products	211	-
Compass	Internet services and retailing	495	

Company	Industry		
Consolidated Edison	Utilities, gas and electric	276	-
Equitable Holdings	Insurance, life and health (stock)	336	-
Estée Lauder	Cosmetics	228	-
Foot Locker	Specialty retailers, apparel	390	-
Fox	Entertainment	287	-
Goldman Sachs Group	Commercial banks	57	-
Guardian Life Ins. Co. of America	Insurance, life and health (mutual)	247	-
Hearst	Media	-	36
Hess	Mining and crude oil production	447	-
Icahn Enterprises	Petroleum refining	328	-
International Flavors & Fragrances	Specialty chemicals	322	-
Interpublic Group	Advertising, marketing	353	-
J. Crew	Retailing	-	234
JPMorgan Chase	Commercial banks	24	-
Jefferies Financial Group	Diversified financials	387	-
KKR	Securities	138	-
Latham & Watkins	Services	-	92
Loews	Insurance, property and casualty (stock)	246	-
Marsh & McLennan	Diversified financials	177	-
McKinsey & Company	Business services & supplies	-	29
MetLife	Insurance, life and health (stock)	50	-
Morgan Stanley	Commercial banks	61	-
New York Life Insurance	Insurance, life and health (mutual)	72	-
News Corp.	Publishing, printing	374	-
Omnicom Group	Advertising, marketing	255	-
PVH	Apparel	385	-
Paramount Global	Media and entertainment	116	-
Pfizer	Pharmaceuticals	43	-
Red Apple Group	Oil & gas operations	-	74
Renco Group	Materials	-	108
S&P Global	Financial data services	417	-
STO Building Group	Construction	-	50
Simpson Thacher & Bartlett	Services	-	241
Skadden, Arps, Slate, Meagher & Flom	Services	-	185
Standard Industries	Manufacturing	-	46
StoneX Group	Financial services	87	-
TIAA	Insurance, life and health (mutual)	90	-
Trammo	Trading companies	-	133
Travelers	Insurance and financial services	103	-
Verizon Communications	Telecommunications	23	-
Warner Bros. Discovery	Media and entertainment	310	-
White & Case	Services	-	189

Note: (1) Companies that produce a 10-K are ranked 1 to 500 based on 2021 revenue; (2) All private companies with at least $2 billion in annual revenue through the end of their most current fiscal year are ranked 1 to 246; companies listed are headquartered in the city; dashes indicate no ranking
Source: Fortune, "Fortune 500," 2022; Forbes, "America's Largest Private Companies," 2022

Fastest-Growing Businesses

According to *Inc.*, New York is home to 31 of America's 500 fastest-growing private companies: **The Newsette** (#16); **Capital Rx** (#33); **Thesis** (#34); **Partake Foods** (#45); **MATTIO Communications** (#69); **Bearaby** (#82); **Athena Club** (#84); **Little Spoon** (#91); **Piece Of Cake Moving and Storage** (#104); **Hero Cosmetics** (#132); **Ribbon** (#161); **Orchard** (#226); **Audigent** (#249); **Lovebug Probiotics** (#253); **Unite Us** (#294); **Tomorrow** (#296); **Feltman's of Coney Island** (#297); **Ragnarok** (#320); **Prose** (#337); **Casely** (#354); **Snappy App** (#356); **Qloo** (#360); **Rightway** (#362); **Morty** (#363); **Mixlab** (#394); **LeafLink** (#408); **i80 Group** (#421); **Vestwell** (#435); **Octane Lending** (#462); **WhiteCap Search** (#463); **ClearDoc** (#489). Criteria: must be an independent, privately-held, for-profit, U.S. corporation, proprietorship or partnership as of December 31, 2021; revenues must be at least $100,000 in 2018 and $2 million in 2021; must have four-year operating/sales history. *Inc., "America's 500 Fastest-Growing Private Companies," 2022*

According to *Initiative for a Competitive Inner City (ICIC)*, New York is home to seven of America's 100 fastest-growing "inner city" companies: **City Safe Partners Security** (#15); **Epiphany Blue** (#27); **Ombligo** (#67); **Urbantech Consulting Engineering** (#69); **Infopeople Corporation** (#77); **Tempco Glass Fabrication** (#95); **Creative Business** (#100). Criteria for inclusion: company must be headquartered in or have 51 percent or more of its physical operations in an economically distressed urban area; must be an independent, for-profit corporation, partnership or proprietorship; must have 10 or more employees and have a five-year sales history that includes sales of at least $200,000 in the base year and at least $1 million in the current year with no decrease in sales over the two most recent years. Companies were ranked overall by revenue growth over the five-year period between 2017 and 2021. *Initiative for a Competitive Inner City (ICIC), "Inner City 100 Companies," 2022*

According to Deloitte, New York is home to 42 of North America's 500 fastest-growing high-technology companies: **Axonius** (#3); **VAST Data** (#5); **Capital Rx** (#15); **BigID** (#21); **Audigent** (#79); **Unite Us** (#86); **LeafLink** (#98); **OpenReel** (#112); **Bowery Valuation** (#113); **Unqork** (#119); **Claroty** (#128); **ConsenSys Software** (#136); **LifeMD** (#140); **Biz2Credit** (#144); **Noom** (#156); **Onna** (#160); **FuboTV** (#197); **Glia** (#219); **BlueVoyant** (#222); **Cyware** (#224); **TheGuarantors** (#227); **Electric** (#239); **Chainalysis** (#245); **DataDome** (#247); **SmartAsset** (#250); **Roc360** (#302); **Prove** (#305); **HiredScore** (#313); **Datadog** (#334); **Braze** (#344); **Aircall** (#354); **Olo** (#371); **RethinkFirst** (#377); **Slice** (#405); **ATSG** (#430); **Stensul** (#441); **AppViewX** (#446); **Fund That Flip** (#447); **Magnite** (#451); **COTA** (#454); **Microblink** (#469); **Territory Foods** (#489). Companies are ranked by percentage growth in revenue over a four-year period. Criteria for inclusion: company must be headquartered within North America; must own proprietary intellectual property or technology that is sold to customers in products that contributes to a significant portion of the company's operating revenue; must have been in business for a minumum of four years with 2018 operating revenues of at least $50,000 USD/CD and 2021 operating revenues of at least $5 million USD/CD. *Deloitte, 2022 Technology Fast 500*[TM]

Living Environment

COST OF LIVING

Cost of Living Index

Composite Index	Groceries	Housing	Utilities	Trans-portation	Health Care	Misc. Goods/Services
168.7	122.3	293.1	106.6	113.9	105.4	126.4

Note: The Cost of Living Index measures regional differences in the cost of consumer goods and services, excluding taxes and non-consumer expenditures, for professional and managerial households in the top income quintile. It is based on more than 50,000 prices covering almost 60 different items for which prices are collected three times a year by chambers of commerce, economic development organizations or university applied economic centers in each participating urban area. The numbers shown should be read as a percentage above or below the national average of 100. For example, a value of 115.4 in the groceries column indicates that grocery prices are 15.4% higher than the national average. Small differences in the index numbers should not be interpreted as significant; Figures cover the Brooklyn NY urban area.
Source: The Council for Community and Economic Research, Cost of Living Index, 2022

Grocery Prices

Area[1]	T-Bone Steak ($/pound)	Frying Chicken ($/pound)	Whole Milk ($/half gal.)	Eggs ($/dozen)	Orange Juice ($/64 oz.)	Coffee ($/11.5 oz.)
City[2]	16.18	1.70	2.88	2.77	4.42	4.89
Avg.	13.81	1.59	2.43	2.25	3.85	4.95
Min.	10.17	0.90	1.51	1.30	2.90	3.46
Max.	19.35	3.30	4.32	4.32	5.31	8.59

Note: (1) Values for the local area are compared with the average, minimum and maximum values for all 286 areas in the Cost of Living Index; (2) Figures cover the Brooklyn NY urban area; T-Bone Steak (price per pound); Frying Chicken (price per pound, whole fryer); Whole Milk (half gallon carton); Eggs (price per dozen, Grade A, large); Orange Juice (64 oz. Tropicana or Florida Natural); Coffee (11.5 oz. can, vacuum-packed, Maxwell House, Hills Bros, or Folgers).
Source: The Council for Community and Economic Research, Cost of Living Index, 2022

Housing and Utility Costs

Area[1]	New Home Price ($)	Apartment Rent ($/month)	All Electric ($/month)	Part Electric ($/month)	Other Energy ($/month)	Telephone ($/month)
City[2]	1,349,755	3,727	-	106.15	87.34	195.04
Avg.	450,913	1,371	176.41	99.93	76.96	190.22
Min.	229,283	546	100.84	31.56	27.15	174.27
Max.	2,434,977	4,569	356.86	249.59	272.24	208.31

Note: (1) Values for the local area are compared with the average, minimum and maximum values for all 286 areas in the Cost of Living Index; (2) Figures cover the Brooklyn NY urban area; New Home Price (2,400 sf living area, 8,000 sf lot, in urban area with full utilities); Apartment Rent (950 sf 2 bedroom/1.5 or 2 bath, unfurnished, excluding all utilities except water); All Electric (average monthly cost for an all-electric home); Part Electric (average monthly cost for a part-electric home); Other Energy (average monthly cost for natural gas, fuel oil, coal, wood, and any other forms of energy except electricity); Telephone (price includes the base monthly rate plus taxes and fees for three lines of mobile phone service).
Source: The Council for Community and Economic Research, Cost of Living Index, 2022

Health Care, Transportation, and Other Costs

Area[1]	Doctor ($/visit)	Dentist ($/visit)	Optometrist ($/visit)	Gasoline ($/gallon)	Beauty Salon ($/visit)	Men's Shirt ($)
City[2]	124.61	125.08	113.20	4.34	68.52	42.89
Avg.	124.91	107.77	117.66	3.86	43.31	34.21
Min.	36.61	58.25	51.79	2.90	22.18	13.05
Max.	250.21	162.58	371.96	5.54	85.61	63.54

Note: (1) Values for the local area are compared with the average, minimum and maximum values for all 286 areas in the Cost of Living Index; (2) Figures cover the Brooklyn NY urban area; Doctor (general practitioners routine exam of an established patient); Dentist (adult teeth cleaning and periodic oral examination); Optometrist (full vision eye exam for established adult patient); Gasoline (one gallon regular unleaded, national brand, including all taxes, cash price at self-service pump if available); Beauty Salon (woman's shampoo, trim, and blow-dry); Men's Shirt (cotton/polyester dress shirt, pinpoint weave, long sleeves).
Source: The Council for Community and Economic Research, Cost of Living Index, 2022

HOUSING

Homeownership Rate

Area	2015 (%)	2016 (%)	2017 (%)	2018 (%)	2019 (%)	2020 (%)	2021 (%)	2022 (%)
MSA[1]	49.9	50.4	49.9	49.7	50.4	50.9	50.7	50.5
U.S.	63.7	63.4	63.9	64.4	64.6	66.6	65.5	65.8

Note: (1) Figures cover the New York-Newark-Jersey City, NY-NJ-PA Metropolitan Statistical Area
Source: U.S. Census Bureau, Housing Vacancies and Homeownership Annual Statistics: 2015-2022

House Price Index (HPI)

Area	National Ranking[2]	Quarterly Change (%)	One-Year Change (%)	Five-Year Change (%)	Since 1991Q1 (%)
MD[1]	212	-0.09	8.22	34.61	258.57
U.S.[3]	–	0.34	8.41	58.44	289.08

Note: The HPI is a weighted repeat sales index. It measures average price changes in repeat sales or refinancings on the same properties. This information is obtained by reviewing repeat mortgage transactions on single-family properties whose mortgages have been purchased or securitized by Fannie Mae or Freddie Mac since January 1975; (1) Figures cover the New York-Jersey City-White Plains, NY-NJ Metropolitan Division; (2) Rankings are based on annual percentage change for all metro areas containing at least 15,000 transactions over the last 10 years and ranges from 1 to 257; (3) figures based on a weighted average of Census Division estimates using a seasonally adjusted, purchase-only index; all figures are for the period ending December 31, 2022
Source: Federal Housing Finance Agency, Change in FHFA Metropolitan Area House Price Indexes, 2022Q4

Median Single-Family Home Prices

Area	2020	2021	2022p	Percent Change 2021 to 2022
MD[1]	442.4	535.8	589.2	10.0
U.S. Average	300.2	357.1	392.6	9.9

Note: Figures are median sales prices of existing single-family homes in thousands of dollars; (p) preliminary; (1) Figures cover the New York-Jersey City-White Plains, NY-NJ Metropolitan Division
Source: National Association of Realtors, Median Sales Price of Existing Single-Family Homes for Metropolitan Areas, 4th Quarter 2022

Qualifying Income Based on Median Sales Price of Existing Single-Family Homes

Area	With 5% Down ($)	With 10% Down ($)	With 20% Down ($)
MD[1]	172,719	163,628	145,447
U.S. Average	112,234	106,237	94,513

Note: Figures are preliminary; Qualifying income is based on a mortgage rate of 6.77%. Monthly principal and interest payment is limited to 25% of income; (1) Figures cover the New York-Jersey City-White Plains, NY-NJ Metropolitan Division
Source: National Association of Realtors, Qualifying Income Based on Median Sales Price of Existing Single-Family Homes for Metropolitan Areas, 4th Quarter 2022

Home Value

Area	Under $100,000	$100,000 -$199,999	$200,000 -$299,999	$300,000 -$399,999	$400,000 -$499,999	$500,000 -$999,999	$1,000,000 or more	Median ($)
City	4.3	3.6	5.5	8.2	10.8	44.7	22.9	660,700
MSA[1]	3.5	5.2	11.1	16.7	16.1	36.2	11.2	483,500
U.S.	16.2	24.2	20.1	13.6	8.3	13.6	4.1	244,900

Note: Figures are percentages except for median and cover owner-occupied housing units; (1) Figures cover the New York-Newark-Jersey City, NY-NJ-PA Metropolitan Statistical Area
Source: U.S. Census Bureau, 2017-2021 American Community Survey 5-Year Estimates

Year Housing Structure Built

Area	2020 or Later	2010 -2019	2000 -2009	1990 -1999	1980 -1989	1970 -1979	1960 -1969	1950 -1959	1940 -1949	Before 1940	Median Year
City	<0.1	4.1	5.4	3.8	4.9	7.0	12.5	12.9	9.5	39.9	1950
MSA[1]	0.1	4.1	6.5	6.2	7.8	9.7	13.5	15.6	8.5	28.1	1959
U.S.	0.2	7.3	13.6	13.6	13.2	14.8	10.3	10.0	4.7	12.2	1979

Note: Figures are percentages except for Median Year; Note: (1) Figures cover the New York-Newark-Jersey City, NY-NJ-PA Metropolitan Statistical Area
Source: U.S. Census Bureau, 2017-2021 American Community Survey 5-Year Estimates

Gross Monthly Rent

Area	Under $500	$500 -$999	$1,000 -$1,499	$1,500 -$1,999	$2,000 -$2,499	$2,500 -$2,999	$3,000 and up	Median ($)
City	9.5	12.4	24.4	23.3	13.3	6.6	10.5	1,579
MSA[1]	8.4	11.4	26.5	24.9	13.4	6.3	9.1	1,573
U.S.	8.1	30.5	30.8	16.8	7.3	3.1	3.5	1,163

Note: Figures are percentages except for median; Gross rent is the contract rent plus the estimated average monthly cost of utilities (electricity, gas, and water and sewer) and fuels (oil, coal, kerosene, wood, etc.) if these are paid by the renter (or paid for the renter by someone else); (1) Figures cover the New York-Newark-Jersey City, NY-NJ-PA Metropolitan Statistical Area
Source: U.S. Census Bureau, 2017-2021 American Community Survey 5-Year Estimates

HEALTH

Health Risk Factors

Category	MD[1] (%)	U.S. (%)
Adults aged 18–64 who have any kind of health care coverage	90.1	90.9
Adults who reported being in good or better health	84.7	85.2
Adults who have been told they have high blood cholesterol	35.6	35.7
Adults who have been told they have high blood pressure	28.3	32.4
Adults who are current smokers	10.0	14.4
Adults who currently use e-cigarettes	4.5	6.7
Adults who currently use chewing tobacco, snuff, or snus	1.6	3.5
Adults who are heavy drinkers[2]	4.6	6.3
Adults who are binge drinkers[3]	14.8	15.4
Adults who are overweight (BMI 25.0 - 29.9)	34.7	34.4
Adults who are obese (BMI 30.0 - 99.8)	25.5	33.9
Adults who participated in any physical activities in the past month	72.7	76.3

Note: (1) Figures cover the New York-Jersey City-White Plains, NY-NJ Metropolitan Division; (2) Heavy drinkers are classified as adult men having more than 14 drinks per week and adult women having more than 7 drinks per week; (3) Binge drinkers are classified as males having five or more drinks on one occasion or females having four or more drinks on one occasion
Source: Centers for Disease Control and Prevention, Behaviorial Risk Factor Surveillance System, SMART: Selected Metropolitan Area Risk Trends, 2021

Acute and Chronic Health Conditions

Category	MD[1] (%)	U.S. (%)
Adults who have ever been told they had a heart attack	3.0	4.0
Adults who have ever been told they have angina or coronary heart disease	3.2	3.8
Adults who have ever been told they had a stroke	2.1	3.0
Adults who have ever been told they have asthma	12.8	14.9
Adults who have ever been told they have arthritis	20.0	25.8
Adults who have ever been told they have diabetes[2]	11.3	10.9
Adults who have ever been told they had skin cancer	3.3	6.6
Adults who have ever been told they had any other types of cancer	5.3	7.5
Adults who have ever been told they have COPD	4.0	6.1
Adults who have ever been told they have kidney disease	2.6	3.0
Adults who have ever been told they have a form of depression	15.0	20.5

Note: (1) Figures cover the New York-Jersey City-White Plains, NY-NJ Metropolitan Division; (2) Figures do not include pregnancy-related, borderline, or pre-diabetes
Source: Centers for Disease Control and Prevention, Behaviorial Risk Factor Surveillance System, SMART: Selected Metropolitan Area Risk Trends, 2021

Health Screening and Vaccination Rates

Category	MD[1] (%)	U.S. (%)
Adults who have ever been tested for HIV	50.1	34.9
Adults who have had their blood cholesterol checked within the last five years	90.8	85.2
Adults aged 65+ who have had flu shot within the past year	65.1	68.6
Adults aged 65+ who have ever had a pneumonia vaccination	60.1	71.0

Note: (1) Figures cover the New York-Jersey City-White Plains, NY-NJ Metropolitan Division.
Source: Centers for Disease Control and Prevention, Behaviorial Risk Factor Surveillance System, SMART: Selected Metropolitan Area Risk Trends, 2021

Disability Status

Category	MD[1] (%)	U.S. (%)
Adults who reported being deaf	4.9	7.2
Are you blind or have serious difficulty seeing, even when wearing glasses?	5.8	4.8
Are you limited in any way in any of your usual activities due to arthritis?	7.8	11.1
Do you have difficulty doing errands alone?	7.3	7.0
Do you have difficulty dressing or bathing?	4.3	3.6
Do you have serious difficulty concentrating/remembering/making decisions?	10.6	12.1
Do you have serious difficulty walking or climbing stairs?	14.3	12.8

Note: (1) Figures cover the New York-Jersey City-White Plains, NY-NJ Metropolitan Division.
Source: Centers for Disease Control and Prevention, Behaviorial Risk Factor Surveillance System, SMART: Selected Metropolitan Area Risk Trends, 2021

Mortality Rates for the Top 10 Causes of Death in the U.S. (Bronx)

ICD-10[a] Sub-Chapter	ICD-10[a] Code	Crude Mortality Rate[1] per 100,000 population	
		County[2]	U.S.
Malignant neoplasms	C00-C97	133.8	182.6
Ischaemic heart diseases	I20-I25	157.1	113.1
Other forms of heart disease	I30-I51	21.3	64.4
Other degenerative diseases of the nervous system	G30-G31	20.7	51.0
Cerebrovascular diseases	I60-I69	30.3	47.8
Other external causes of accidental injury	W00-X59	51.4	46.4
Chronic lower respiratory diseases	J40-J47	25.6	45.7
Organic, including symptomatic, mental disorders	F01-F09	18.1	35.9
Hypertensive diseases	I10-I15	59.4	35.0
Diabetes mellitus	E10-E14	29.1	29.6

Note: (a) ICD-10 = International Classification of Diseases 10th Revision; (1) Crude mortality rates are a three-year average covering 2019-2021; (2) Figures cover Bronx County
Source: Centers for Disease Control and Prevention, National Center for Health Statistics. National Vital Statistics System, Mortality 2018-2021 on CDC WONDER Online Database

Mortality Rates for the Top 10 Causes of Death in the U.S. (Brooklyn)

ICD-10[a] Sub-Chapter	ICD-10[a] Code	Crude Mortality Rate[1] per 100,000 population	
		County[2]	U.S.
Malignant neoplasms	C00-C97	126.0	182.6
Ischaemic heart diseases	I20-I25	169.4	113.1
Other forms of heart disease	I30-I51	19.3	64.4
Other degenerative diseases of the nervous system	G30-G31	15.0	51.0
Cerebrovascular diseases	I60-I69	22.3	47.8
Other external causes of accidental injury	W00-X59	26.4	46.4
Chronic lower respiratory diseases	J40-J47	17.3	45.7
Organic, including symptomatic, mental disorders	F01-F09	13.2	35.9
Hypertensive diseases	I10-I15	52.1	35.0
Diabetes mellitus	E10-E14	25.2	29.6

Note: (a) ICD-10 = International Classification of Diseases 10th Revision; (1) Crude mortality rates are a three-year average covering 2019-2021; (2) Figures cover Kings County
Source: Centers for Disease Control and Prevention, National Center for Health Statistics. National Vital Statistics System, Mortality 2018-2021 on CDC WONDER Online Database

Mortality Rates for the Top 10 Causes of Death in the U.S. (Manhattan)

ICD-10[a] Sub-Chapter	ICD-10[a] Code	Crude Mortality Rate[1] per 100,000 population	
		County[2]	U.S.
Malignant neoplasms	C00-C97	138.7	182.6
Ischaemic heart diseases	I20-I25	128.3	113.1
Other forms of heart disease	I30-I51	24.1	64.4
Other degenerative diseases of the nervous system	G30-G31	27.8	51.0
Cerebrovascular diseases	I60-I69	25.5	47.8
Other external causes of accidental injury	W00-X59	34.9	46.4
Chronic lower respiratory diseases	J40-J47	18.9	45.7
Organic, including symptomatic, mental disorders	F01-F09	22.5	35.9
Hypertensive diseases	I10-I15	45.9	35.0
Diabetes mellitus	E10-E14	17.6	29.6

Note: (a) ICD-10 = International Classification of Diseases 10th Revision; (1) Crude mortality rates are a three-year average covering 2019-2021; (2) Figures cover New York County
Source: Centers for Disease Control and Prevention, National Center for Health Statistics. National Vital Statistics System, Mortality 2018-2021 on CDC WONDER Online Database

Mortality Rates for the Top 10 Causes of Death in the U.S. (Queens)

ICD-10[a] Sub-Chapter	ICD-10[a] Code	Crude Mortality Rate[1] per 100,000 population	
		County[2]	U.S.
Malignant neoplasms	C00-C97	136.5	182.6
Ischaemic heart diseases	I20-I25	179.3	113.1
Other forms of heart disease	I30-I51	21.4	64.4
Other degenerative diseases of the nervous system	G30-G31	23.4	51.0
Cerebrovascular diseases	I60-I69	27.4	47.8
Other external causes of accidental injury	W00-X59	26.0	46.4
Chronic lower respiratory diseases	J40-J47	18.3	45.7
Organic, including symptomatic, mental disorders	F01-F09	14.8	35.9
Hypertensive diseases	I10-I15	44.1	35.0
Diabetes mellitus	E10-E14	20.9	29.6

Note: (a) ICD-10 = International Classification of Diseases 10th Revision; (1) Crude mortality rates are a three-year average covering 2019-2021; (2) Figures cover Queens County
Source: Centers for Disease Control and Prevention, National Center for Health Statistics. National Vital Statistics System, Mortality 2018-2021 on CDC WONDER Online Database

Mortality Rates for the Top 10 Causes of Death in the U.S. (Staten Island)

ICD-10[a] Sub-Chapter	ICD-10[a] Code	Crude Mortality Rate[1] per 100,000 population	
		County[2]	U.S.
Malignant neoplasms	C00-C97	175.4	182.6
Ischaemic heart diseases	I20-I25	228.7	113.1
Other forms of heart disease	I30-I51	22.1	64.4
Other degenerative diseases of the nervous system	G30-G31	32.8	51.0
Cerebrovascular diseases	I60-I69	21.8	47.8
Other external causes of accidental injury	W00-X59	37.8	46.4
Chronic lower respiratory diseases	J40-J47	32.7	45.7
Organic, including symptomatic, mental disorders	F01-F09	12.8	35.9
Hypertensive diseases	I10-I15	57.3	35.0
Diabetes mellitus	E10-E14	31.3	29.6

Note: (a) ICD-10 = International Classification of Diseases 10th Revision; (1) Crude mortality rates are a three-year average covering 2019-2021; (2) Figures cover Richmond County
Source: Centers for Disease Control and Prevention, National Center for Health Statistics. National Vital Statistics System, Mortality 2018-2021 on CDC WONDER Online Database

Mortality Rates for Selected Causes of Death (Bronx)

ICD-10[a] Sub-Chapter	ICD-10[a] Code	Crude Mortality Rate[1] per 100,000 population	
		County[2]	U.S.
Assault	X85-Y09	8.5	7.0
Diseases of the liver	K70-K76	11.4	19.8
Human immunodeficiency virus (HIV) disease	B20-B24	8.2	1.5
Influenza and pneumonia	J09-J18	28.2	14.7
Intentional self-harm	X60-X84	5.3	14.3
Malnutrition	E40-E46	Unreliable	4.3
Obesity and other hyperalimentation	E65-E68	2.2	3.0
Renal failure	N17-N19	7.5	15.7
Transport accidents	V01-V99	5.3	13.6
Viral hepatitis	B15-B19	2.1	1.2

Note: (a) ICD-10 = International Classification of Diseases 10th Revision; (1) Crude mortality rates are a three-year average covering 2019-2021; (2) Figures cover Bronx County; Data are suppressed when the data meet the criteria for confidentiality constraints; Crude mortality rates are flagged as unreliable when the rate would be calculated with a numerator of 20 or less.
Source: Centers for Disease Control and Prevention, National Center for Health Statistics. National Vital Statistics System, Mortality 2018-2021 on CDC WONDER Online Database

Mortality Rates for Selected Causes of Death (Brooklyn)

ICD-10[a] Sub-Chapter	ICD-10[a] Code	Crude Mortality Rate[1] per 100,000 population	
		County[2]	U.S.
Assault	X85-Y09	5.4	7.0
Diseases of the liver	K70-K76	7.6	19.8
Human immunodeficiency virus (HIV) disease	B20-B24	3.8	1.5
Influenza and pneumonia	J09-J18	23.0	14.7
Intentional self-harm	X60-X84	5.6	14.3
Malnutrition	E40-E46	0.9	4.3
Obesity and other hyperalimentation	E65-E68	2.1	3.0
Renal failure	N17-N19	9.4	15.7
Transport accidents	V01-V99	4.7	13.6
Viral hepatitis	B15-B19	1.3	1.2

Note: (a) ICD-10 = International Classification of Diseases 10th Revision; (1) Crude mortality rates are a three-year average covering 2019-2021; (2) Figures cover Kings County; Data are suppressed when the data meet the criteria for confidentiality constraints; Crude mortality rates are flagged as unreliable when the rate would be calculated with a numerator of 20 or less.
Source: Centers for Disease Control and Prevention, National Center for Health Statistics. National Vital Statistics System, Mortality 2018-2021 on CDC WONDER Online Database

Mortality Rates for Selected Causes of Death (Manhattan)

ICD-10[a] Sub-Chapter	ICD-10[a] Code	Crude Mortality Rate[1] per 100,000 population	
		County[2]	U.S.
Assault	X85-Y09	3.6	7.0
Diseases of the liver	K70-K76	7.5	19.8
Human immunodeficiency virus (HIV) disease	B20-B24	3.9	1.5
Influenza and pneumonia	J09-J18	15.6	14.7
Intentional self-harm	X60-X84	8.0	14.3
Malnutrition	E40-E46	1.6	4.3
Obesity and other hyperalimentation	E65-E68	1.6	3.0
Renal failure	N17-N19	7.3	15.7
Transport accidents	V01-V99	3.5	13.6
Viral hepatitis	B15-B19	1.2	1.2

Note: (a) ICD-10 = International Classification of Diseases 10th Revision; (1) Crude mortality rates are a three-year average covering 2019-2021; (2) Figures cover New York County; Data are suppressed when the data meet the criteria for confidentiality constraints; Crude mortality rates are flagged as unreliable when the rate would be calculated with a numerator of 20 or less.
Source: Centers for Disease Control and Prevention, National Center for Health Statistics. National Vital Statistics System, Mortality 2018-2021 on CDC WONDER Online Database

Mortality Rates for Selected Causes of Death (Queens)

ICD-10[a] Sub-Chapter	ICD-10[a] Code	Crude Mortality Rate[1] per 100,000 population	
		County[2]	U.S.
Assault	X85-Y09	3.3	7.0
Diseases of the liver	K70-K76	9.3	19.8
Human immunodeficiency virus (HIV) disease	B20-B24	1.8	1.5
Influenza and pneumonia	J09-J18	22.0	14.7
Intentional self-harm	X60-X84	6.4	14.3
Malnutrition	E40-E46	0.8	4.3
Obesity and other hyperalimentation	E65-E68	1.7	3.0
Renal failure	N17-N19	7.2	15.7
Transport accidents	V01-V99	4.6	13.6
Viral hepatitis	B15-B19	0.9	1.2

Note: (a) ICD-10 = International Classification of Diseases 10th Revision; (1) Crude mortality rates are a three-year average covering 2019-2021; (2) Figures cover Queens County; Data are suppressed when the data meet the criteria for confidentiality constraints; Crude mortality rates are flagged as unreliable when the rate would be calculated with a numerator of 20 or less.
Source: Centers for Disease Control and Prevention, National Center for Health Statistics. National Vital Statistics System, Mortality 2018-2021 on CDC WONDER Online Database

Mortality Rates for Selected Causes of Death (Staten Island)

ICD-10[a] Sub-Chapter	ICD-10[a] Code	Crude Mortality Rate[1] per 100,000 population	
		County[2]	U.S.
Assault	X85-Y09	3.9	7.0
Diseases of the liver	K70-K76	9.2	19.8
Human immunodeficiency virus (HIV) disease	B20-B24	Unreliable	1.5
Influenza and pneumonia	J09-J18	16.3	14.7
Intentional self-harm	X60-X84	6.9	14.3
Malnutrition	E40-E46	Unreliable	4.3
Obesity and other hyperalimentation	E65-E68	2.7	3.0
Renal failure	N17-N19	7.1	15.7
Transport accidents	V01-V99	4.7	13.6
Viral hepatitis	B15-B19	Unreliable	1.2

Note: (a) ICD-10 = International Classification of Diseases 10th Revision; (1) Crude mortality rates are a three-year average covering 2019-2021; (2) Figures cover Richmond County; Data are suppressed when the data meet the criteria for confidentiality constraints; Crude mortality rates are flagged as unreliable when the rate would be calculated with a numerator of 20 or less.
Source: Centers for Disease Control and Prevention, National Center for Health Statistics. National Vital Statistics System, Mortality 2018-2021 on CDC WONDER Online Database

Health Insurance Coverage

Area	With Health Insurance	With Private Health Insurance	With Public Health Insurance	Without Health Insurance	Population Under Age 19 Without Health Insurance
City	93.1	58.8	43.6	6.9	2.4
MSA[1]	93.2	67.3	36.5	6.8	3.0
U.S.	91.2	67.8	35.4	8.8	5.3

Note: Figures are percentages that cover the civilian noninstitutionalized population; (1) Figures cover the New York-Newark-Jersey City, NY-NJ-PA Metropolitan Statistical Area
Source: U.S. Census Bureau, 2017-2021 American Community Survey 5-Year Estimates

Number of Medical Professionals

Area	MDs[3]	DOs[3,4]	Dentists	Podiatrists	Chiropractors	Optometrists
City[1] (number)	41,389	1,472	7,404	1,133	1,383	1,540
City[1] (rate[2])	471.8	16.8	87.4	13.4	16.3	18.2
U.S. (rate[2])	289.3	23.5	72.5	6.2	28.7	17.4

Note: Data as of 2021 unless noted; (1) Data covers New York City; (2) Rate per 100,000 population; (3) Data as of 2020 and includes all active, non-federal physicians; (4) Doctor of Osteopathic Medicine
Source: U.S. Department of Health and Human Services, Health Resources and Services Administration, Bureau of Health Professions, Area Resource File (ARF) 2021-2022

Best Hospitals

According to *U.S. News,* the New York-Jersey City-White Plains, NY-NJ metro area is home to 16 of the best hospitals in the U.S.: **Hackensack University Medical Center at Hackensack Meridian Health** (4 adult specialties and 1 pediatric specialty); **Hospital for Special Surgery** (2 adult specialties and 1 pediatric specialty); **Lenox Hill Hospital at Northwell Health** (9 adult specialties); **Manhattan Eye Ear & Throat Hospital** (9 adult specialties); **Memorial Sloan Kettering Cancer Center** (7 adult specialties and 1 pediatric specialty); **Montefiore Medical Center** (6 adult specialties and 3 pediatric specialties); **Mount Sinai Beth Israel Hospital** (2 adult specialties); **Mount Sinai Hospital** (Honor Roll/11 adult specialties and 3 pediatric specialties); **Mount Sinai Morningside and Mount Sinai West Hospitals** (2 adult specialties); **NYU Langone Hospitals** (Honor Roll/14 adult specialties and 3 pediatric specialties); **NYU Langone Orthopedic Hospital at NYU Langone Hospitals** (Honor Roll/14 adult specialties and 3 pediatric specialties); **New York Eye and Ear Infirmary of Mount Sinai** (1 adult specialty); **New York-Presbyterian Brooklyn Methodist Hospital** (2 adult specialties); **New York-Presbyterian Hospital-Columbia and Cornell** (Honor Roll/14 adult specialties and 10 pediatric specialties); **Perlmutter Cancer Center at NYU Langone Hospitals** (Honor Roll/14 adult specialties and 3 pediatric specialties); **Rusk Rehabilitation at NYU Langone Hospitals** (Honor Roll/14 adult specialties and 3 pediatric specialties). The hospitals listed were nationally ranked in at least one of 15 adult or 10 pediatric specialties. The number of specialties shown cover the parent hospital. Only 164 U.S. hospitals performed well enough to be nationally ranked in one or more specialties. Twenty hospitals in the U.S. made the Honor Roll. The Best Hospitals Honor Roll takes both the national rankings and the procedure and condition ratings into account. Hospitals received points if they were nationally ranked in one of the 15 adult specialties—the higher they ranked, the more points they got—and how many ratings of "high performing" they earned in the 17 procedures and conditions. *U.S. News Online, "America's Best Hospitals 2022-23"*

According to *U.S. News,* the New York-Jersey City-White Plains, NY-NJ metro area is home to five of the best children's hospitals in the U.S.: **New York-Presbyterian Children's Hospital-Columbia and Cornell** (10 pediatric specialties); **Hassenfeld Children's Hospital at NYU Langone** (3 pediatric specialties); **Children's Hospital at Montefiore** (3 pediatric specialties); **Hackensack Meridian**

Health JM Sanzari and K Hovnanian Children's Hospitals (1 pediatric specialty); **Mount Sinai Kravis Children's Hospital** (3 pediatric specialties). The hospitals listed were highly ranked in at least one of 10 pediatric specialties. Eighty-six children's hospitals in the U.S. were nationally ranked in at least one specialty. Hospitals received points for being ranked in a specialty, and the 10 hospitals with the most points across the 10 specialties make up the Honor Roll. *U.S. News Online, "America's Best Children's Hospitals 2022-23"*

EDUCATION

Public School District Statistics

District Name	Schls	Pupils	Pupil/ Teacher Ratio	Minority Pupils[1] (%)	LEP/ELL[2] (%)	IEP[3] (%)
NYC Geo Dist #01 (Manhattan)	27	9,969	11.0	82.1	8.8	24.9
NYC Geo Dist #02 (Manhattan)	118	56,893	12.1	74.3	7.9	19.9
NYC Geo Dist #03 (Manhattan)	44	19,316	11.6	67.8	4.7	23.9
NYC Geo Dist #04 (Manhattan)	29	11,524	11.2	94.4	10.0	32.6
NYC Geo Dist #05 (Manhattan)	28	9,784	9.8	93.3	9.2	45.6
NYC Geo Dist #06 (Manhattan)	46	18,394	11.8	93.8	27.5	29.3
NYC Geo Dist #07 (Bronx)	40	16,211	10.1	98.4	16.6	35.8
NYC Geo Dist #08 (Bronx)	51	24,528	11.7	94.6	14.0	34.5
NYC Geo Dist #09 (Bronx)	69	28,607	11.6	98.5	23.3	33.4
NYC Geo Dist #10 (Bronx)	84	46,525	11.3	94.2	21.5	27.0
NYC Geo Dist #11 (Bronx)	62	33,849	11.1	91.1	12.3	30.1
NYC Geo Dist #12 (Bronx)	46	18,447	9.8	98.6	20.8	33.7
NYC Geo Dist #13 (Brooklyn)	40	19,887	12.3	81.9	4.2	18.9
NYC Geo Dist #14 (Brooklyn)	38	15,762	10.5	84.3	10.9	30.5
NYC Geo Dist #15 (Brooklyn)	48	28,165	10.8	70.8	14.8	25.3
NYC Geo Dist #16 (Brooklyn)	23	6,091	11.5	95.9	5.3	40.6
NYC Geo Dist #17 (Brooklyn)	49	18,836	12.0	95.6	10.7	36.4
NYC Geo Dist #18 (Brooklyn)	33	11,429	11.7	95.9	7.7	31.9
NYC Geo Dist #19 (Brooklyn)	52	20,068	10.9	97.9	14.2	33.3
NYC Geo Dist #20 (Brooklyn)	45	47,493	13.8	76.8	23.3	28.1
NYC Geo Dist #21 (Brooklyn)	40	33,455	12.5	68.9	18.1	32.1
NYC Geo Dist #22 (Brooklyn)	40	31,137	13.9	68.7	12.1	33.2
NYC Geo Dist #23 (Brooklyn)	28	8,012	10.3	98.3	5.5	38.7
NYC Geo Dist #24 (Corona)	56	51,878	12.2	87.9	22.8	21.5
NYC Geo Dist #25 (Flushing)	46	34,608	13.1	89.6	19.1	19.3
NYC Geo Dist #26 (Bayside)	34	29,600	11.8	86.4	8.4	17.0
NYC Geo Dist #27 (Ozone Park)	63	41,220	13.4	90.3	11.1	25.2
NYC Geo Dist #28 (Jamaica)	50	37,531	13.7	85.7	11.3	20.4
NYC Geo Dist #29 (Queens Village)	46	23,673	13.8	97.7	9.1	25.0
NYC Geo Dist #30 (Long Island City)	50	35,787	13.7	82.6	17.1	19.8
NYC Geo Dist #31 (Staten Island)	72	60,749	12.8	59.3	6.5	30.3
NYC Geo Dist #32 (Brooklyn)	27	10,086	11.7	96.9	20.3	27.5

Note: Table includes school districts with 2,000 or more students; (1) Percentage of students that are not non-Hispanic white; (2) Percentage of students that are Limited English Proficient or English Language Learners (2018-19); (3) Percentage of students that have an Individualized Education Program (2019-20). Source: U.S. Department of Education, National Center for Education Statistics, Common Core of Data, Local Education Agency (School District) Universe Survey: School Year 2021-2022

Best High Schools

According to *U.S. News,* New York is home to 28 of the top 500 high schools in the U.S.: **Townsend Harris High School** (#19); **Queens High School for the Sciences at York College** (#25); **Stuyvesant High School** (#36); **High School Math Science and Engineering at CCNY** (#38); **Bronx High School of Science** (#41); **Brooklyn Technical High School** (#46); **Staten Island Technical High School** (#63); **High School of American Studies at Lehman College** (#64); **Brooklyn Latin School** (#79); **High School for Dual Language and Asian Studies** (#89); **Baccalaureate School for Global Education** (#98); **Eleanor Roosevelt High School** (#108); **Millennium High School** (#152); **Manhattan Village Academy** (#179); **Columbia Secondary School** (#218); **Success Academy Charter School-Harlem 1** (#233); **Fiorello H Laguardia High School** (#250); **Scholars' Academy** (#265); **New Explorations Into Science Tech and Math High School** (#288); **Millennium Brooklyn High School** (#307); **Leon M. Goldstein High School for the Sciences** (#321); **Baruch College Campus High School** (#342); **Manhattan Bridges High School** (#360); **NYC iSchool** (#373); **Manhattan Center for Science and Mathematics** (#381); **Beacon High School** (#382); **All City Leadership Secondary School** (#446); **Manhattan/Hunter Science High School** (#500). Nearly 18,000 public, magnet and charter schools were ranked based on their performance on state assessments and how well they prepare students for college. *U.S. News & World Report, "Best High Schools 2022"*

Highest Level of Education

Area	Less than H.S.	H.S. Diploma	Some College, No Deg.	Associate Degree	Bachelor's Degree	Master's Degree	Prof. School Degree	Doctorate Degree
City	16.8	23.6	13.5	6.5	22.9	11.8	3.3	1.6
MSA[1]	12.7	24.0	14.4	6.8	24.2	12.7	3.4	1.7
U.S.	11.1	26.5	20.0	8.7	20.6	9.3	2.2	1.5

Note: Figures cover persons age 25 and over; (1) Figures cover the New York-Newark-Jersey City, NY-NJ-PA Metropolitan Statistical Area
Source: U.S. Census Bureau, 2017-2021 American Community Survey 5-Year Estimates

Educational Attainment by Race

Area	High School Graduate or Higher (%)					Bachelor's Degree or Higher (%)				
	Total	White	Black	Asian	Hisp.[2]	Total	White	Black	Asian	Hisp.[2]
City	83.2	90.5	84.7	76.8	70.8	39.6	54.6	25.3	44.0	20.1
MSA[1]	87.3	92.2	86.3	84.1	73.1	42.0	49.1	26.8	56.0	21.3
U.S.	88.9	91.4	87.2	87.6	71.2	33.7	35.5	23.3	55.6	18.4

Note: Figures shown cover persons 25 years old and over; (1) Figures cover the New York-Newark-Jersey City, NY-NJ-PA Metropolitan Statistical Area; (2) People of Hispanic origin can be of any race
Source: U.S. Census Bureau, 2017-2021 American Community Survey 5-Year Estimates

School Enrollment by Grade and Control

Area	Preschool (%)		Kindergarten (%)		Grades 1 - 4 (%)		Grades 5 - 8 (%)		Grades 9 - 12 (%)	
	Public	Private	Public	Private	Public	Private	Public	Private	Public	Private
City	63.8	36.2	79.0	21.0	81.8	18.2	80.9	19.1	80.3	19.7
MSA[1]	56.6	43.4	81.6	18.4	84.6	15.4	84.8	15.2	84.1	15.9
U.S.	58.8	41.2	86.3	13.7	88.3	11.7	88.6	11.4	89.4	10.6

Note: Figures shown cover persons 3 years old and over; (1) Figures cover the New York-Newark-Jersey City, NY-NJ-PA Metropolitan Statistical Area
Source: U.S. Census Bureau, 2017-2021 American Community Survey 5-Year Estimates

Higher Education

Four-Year Colleges			Two-Year Colleges			Medical Schools[1]	Law Schools[2]	Voc/ Tech[3]
Public	Private Non-profit	Private For-profit	Public	Private Non-profit	Private For-profit			
30	153	19	23	20	30	16	13	96

Note: Figures cover institutions located within the New York-Newark-Jersey City, NY-NJ-PA Metropolitan Statistical Area and include main campuses only; (1) includes schools accredited by the Liaison Committee on Medical Education and the American Osteopathic Association's Commission on Osteopathic College Accreditation; (2) includes ABA-accredited schools, schools with provisional ABA accreditation, and state accredited schools; (3) includes all schools with programs that are less than 2 years.
Source: National Center for Education Statistics, Integrated Postsecondary Education System (IPEDS), 2021-22; Wikipedia, List of Medical Schools in the United States, accessed April 10, 2023; Wikipedia, List of Law Schools in the United States, accessed April 10, 2023

According to *U.S. News & World Report,* the New York-Jersey City-White Plains, NY-NJ metro division is home to 10 of the top 200 national universities in the U.S.: **Columbia University** (#18 tie); **New York University** (#25 tie); **Rutgers University—New Brunswick** (#55 tie); **Yeshiva University** (#67 tie); **Fordham University** (#72 tie); **Stevens Institute of Technology** (#83 tie); **The New School** (#127 tie); **CUNY—City College** (#151 tie); **St. John's University (NY)** (#166 tie); **Touro University** (#182 tie). The indicators used to capture academic quality fall into a number of categories: assessment by administrators at peer institutions; retention of students; faculty resources; student selectivity; financial resources; alumni giving; high school counselor ratings of colleges; and graduation rate. *U.S. News & World Report, "America's Best Colleges 2023"*

According to *U.S. News & World Report,* the New York-Jersey City-White Plains, NY-NJ metro division is home to three of the top 100 liberal arts colleges in the U.S.: **United States Military Academy at West Point** (#9 tie); **Barnard College** (#18 tie); **Sarah Lawrence College** (#72 tie). The indicators used to capture academic quality fall into a number of categories: assessment by administrators at peer institutions; retention of students; faculty resources; student selectivity; financial resources; alumni giving; high school counselor ratings of colleges; and graduation rate. *U.S. News & World Report, "America's Best Colleges 2023"*

According to *U.S. News & World Report,* the New York-Jersey City-White Plains, NY-NJ metro division is home to six of the top 100 law schools in the U.S.: **Columbia University** (#4 tie); **New York University** (#7); **Fordham University** (#37 tie); **Yeshiva University (Cardozo)** (#52 tie); **St. John's University** (#84 tie); **Brooklyn Law School** (#98 tie). The rankings are based on a weighted average of 12 measures of quality: peer assessment score; assessment score by lawyers/judges; median LSAT scores; median undergrad GPA; acceptance rate; employment rates for graduates; placement success; bar passage rate; faculty resources; expenditures per student; student/faculty ratio; and library resources. *U.S. News & World Report, "America's Best Graduate Schools, Law, 2023"*

According to *U.S. News & World Report,* the New York-Jersey City-White Plains, NY-NJ metro division is home to six of the top 75 medical schools for research in the U.S.: **New York University (Grossman) (#2); Columbia University (#3 tie); Icahn School of Medicine at Mount Sinai (#11 tie); Cornell University (Weill) (#14 tie); Albert Einstein College of Medicine (#37 tie); Rutgers Robert Wood Johnson Medical School—New Brunswick (Johnson)** (#68 tie). The rankings are based on a weighted average of 11 measures of quality: quality assessment; peer assessment score; assessment score by residency directors; research activity; total research activity; average research activity per faculty member; student selectivity; median MCAT total score; median undergraduate GPA; acceptance rate; and faculty resources. *U.S. News & World Report, "America's Best Graduate Schools, Medical, 2023"*

According to *U.S. News & World Report,* the New York-Jersey City-White Plains, NY-NJ metro division is home to four of the top 75 business schools in the U.S.: **Columbia University (#8 tie); New York University (Stern) (#12 tie); CUNY Bernard M. Baruch College (Zicklin) (#62 tie); Fordham University (Gabelli)** (#64 tie). The rankings are based on a weighted average of the following nine measures: quality assessment; peer assessment; recruiter assessment; placement success; mean starting salary and bonus; student selectivity; mean GMAT and GRE scores; mean undergraduate GPA; and acceptance rate. *U.S. News & World Report, "America's Best Graduate Schools, Business, 2023"*

EMPLOYERS

Major Employers

Company Name	Industry
American Express Company	Personal credit institutions
American International Group	Life insurance
Deloitte Consulting	Management consulting services
Hackensack University Medical Center	University
Merrill Lynch and Co	Security brokers & dealers
Mount Sinai Hospital	General medical & surgical hospitals
Mount Sinai School of Medicine	Medical training services
New York-Presbyterian Hospital	General medical & surgical hospitals
NYC Health and Hospitals Corp	Psychiatric hospitals
NYU School of Medicine	Offices & clinics of medical doctors
Paramount Comm Acq Corp	Investment holding companies, except banks
Patriarch Partners	Investment offices
Rutgers, The State Univ of NJ	Colleges & universities
Standard Americas	Agencies of foreign banks
The Long Island Rail Road Company	Local & suburban transit
UMASS Memorial Health Care	Psychiatrist
United States Postal Service	U.S. postal service
University of Med and Dentistry of NJ	Colleges & universities
Wellchoice	Health insurance carriers

Note: Companies shown are located within the New York-Newark-Jersey City, NY-NJ-PA Metropolitan Statistical Area.
Source: Hoovers.com; Wikipedia

Best Companies to Work For

Accenture; American Express; Deloitte; EY; KPMG; MetLife; PricewaterhouseCoopers, headquartered in New York, are among "The 100 Best Companies to Work For." To pick the best companies, *Fortune* partnered with the Great Place to Work Institute. Two-thirds of a company's score is based on the results of the Institute's Trust Index survey, which is sent to a random sample of employees from each company. The questions related to attitudes about management's credibility, job satisfaction, and camaraderie. The other third of the scoring is based on the company's responses to the Institute's Culture Audit, which includes detailed questions about pay and benefit programs, and a series of open-ended questions about hiring practices, internal communication, training, recognition programs, and diversity efforts. Any company that is at least five years old with more than 1,000 U.S. employees is eligible. *Fortune, "The 100 Best Companies to Work For," 2023*

Accenture; American Express; Braze; Deloitte; Greenhouse; KPMG; Maven Clinic; PricewaterhouseCoopers; White Glove Community Care; White Glove Placement, headquartered in New York, are among "Fortune's Best Workplaces for Women." To pick the best companies, *Fortune* partnered with the Great Place to Work Institute. To be considered for the list, companies must be Great Place To Work-Certified. Companies must also employ at least 50 women, at least 20% of their non-executive managers must be female, and at least one executive must be female. To determine the Best Workplaces for Women, Great Place To Work measured the differences in women's survey responses to those of their peers and assesses the impact of demographics and roles on the quality and consistency of women's experiences. Great Place To Work also analyzed the gender balance of each workplace, how it compared to each company's industry, and patterns in representation as women rise from front-line positions to the board of directors. *Fortune, "Best Workplaces for Women," 2022*

AbleTo; CAIPA MSO; EHE Health; Maven Clinic; Ophelia; Ro; Thirty Madison; Unite Us; White Glove Placement, headquartered in New York, are among "Best Workplaces in Health Care." To determine the Best Workplaces in Health Care list, Great Place To Work analyzed the survey responses of over 161,000 employees from Great Place To Work-Certified companies in the health care industry. Survey data analysis and company-provided datapoints are then factored into a combined score to compare and rank the companies that create the most consistently positive experience for all employees in this industry. *Fortune, "Best Workplaces in Health Care," 2022*

Accenture; American Express; Braze; Collibra; Deloitte; EY; Greenhouse; Horizon Media; KPMG; Maven Clinic; monday.com; PricewaterhouseCoopers; Ro, headquartered in New York, are among "Fortune's Best Workplaces for Parents." To pick the best companies, *Fortune* partnered with the Great Place to Work Institute. To be considered for the list, companies must be Great Place To Work-Certified and have at least 50 responses from parents in the US. The survey enables employees to share confidential quantitative and qualitative feedback about their organization's culture by responding to 60 statements on a 5-point scale and answering two open-ended questions. Collectively, these statements describe a great employee experience, defined by high levels of trust, respect, credibility, fairness, pride, and camaraderie. In addition, companies provide organizational data like size, location, industry, demographics, roles, and levels; and provide information about parental leave, adoption, flexible schedule, childcare and dependent health care benefits. *Fortune, "Best Workplaces for Parents," 2022*

PUBLIC SAFETY

Crime Rate

Area	Total Crime	Violent Crime Rate				Property Crime Rate		
		Murder	Rape[3]	Robbery	Aggrav. Assault	Burglary	Larceny -Theft	Motor Vehicle Theft
City	2,136.3	5.6	27.1	158.8	386.2	167.5	1,279.4	111.5
Suburbs[1]	n/a	n/a	n/a	n/a	n/a	n/a	n/a	n/a
Metro[2]	n/a	n/a	n/a	n/a	n/a	n/a	n/a	n/a
U.S.	2,356.7	6.5	38.4	73.9	279.7	314.2	1,398.0	246.0

Note: Figures are crimes per 100,000 population; (1) All areas within the metro area that are located outside the city limits; (2) Figures cover the New York-Jersey City-White Plains, NY-NJ Metropolitan Division; n/a not available; (3) All figures shown were reported using the revised Uniform Crime Reporting (UCR) definition of rape; Due to the transition to the National Incident-Based Reporting System (NIBRS), limited city and metro area data was released for 2021.
Source: FBI Uniform Crime Reports, 2020

Hate Crimes

Area	Number of Quarters Reported	Number of Incidents per Bias Motivation					
		Race/Ethnicity/ Ancestry	Religion	Sexual Orientation	Disability	Gender	Gender Identity
City	4	84	144	24	0	7	11
U.S.	4	5,227	1,244	1,110	130	75	266

Note: Due to the transition to the National Incident-Based Reporting System (NIBRS), limited crime data was released for 2021.
Source: Federal Bureau of Investigation, Hate Crime Statistics 2020

Identity Theft Consumer Reports

Area	Reports	Reports per 100,000 Population	Rank[2]
MSA[1]	69,873	363	43
U.S.	1,108,609	339	-

Note: (1) Figures cover the New York-Newark-Jersey City, NY-NJ-PA Metropolitan Statistical Area; (2) Rank ranges from 1 to 391 where 1 indicates greatest number of identity theft reports per 100,000 population
Source: Federal Trade Commission, Consumer Sentinel Network Data Book 2022

Fraud and Other Consumer Reports

Area	Reports	Reports per 100,000 Population	Rank[2]
MSA[1]	202,205	1,050	79
U.S.	4,064,520	1,245	-

Note: (1) Figures cover the New York-Newark-Jersey City, NY-NJ-PA Metropolitan Statistical Area; (2) Rank ranges from 1 to 391 where 1 indicates greatest number of fraud and other consumer reports per 100,000 population
Source: Federal Trade Commission, Consumer Sentinel Network Data Book 2022

POLITICS

2020 Presidential Election Results

Area	Biden	Trump	Jorgensen	Hawkins	Other
Bronx County	83.3	15.9	0.2	0.3	0.3
Kings County	76.8	22.1	0.3	0.4	0.4
New York County	86.4	12.2	0.5	0.4	0.5
Queens County	72.0	26.9	0.3	0.4	0.4
Richmond County	42.0	56.9	0.4	0.3	0.4
U.S.	51.3	46.8	1.2	0.3	0.5

Note: Results are percentages and may not add to 100% due to rounding
Source: Dave Leip's Atlas of U.S. Presidential Elections

SPORTS

Professional Sports Teams

Team Name	League	Year Established
Brooklyn Nets	National Basketball Association (NBA)	1967
New Jersey Devils	National Hockey League (NHL)	1982
New York City FC	Major League Soccer (MLS)	2015
New York Giants	National Football League (NFL)	1925
New York Islanders	National Hockey League (NHL)	1972
New York Jets	National Football League (NFL)	1960
New York Knicks	National Basketball Association (NBA)	1946
New York Mets	Major League Baseball (MLB)	1962
New York Rangers	National Hockey League (NHL)	1926
New York Red Bulls	Major League Soccer (MLS)	1996
New York Yankees	Major League Baseball (MLB)	1903

Note: Includes teams located in the New York-Newark-Jersey City, NY-NJ-PA Metropolitan Statistical Area.
Source: Wikipedia, Major Professional Sports Teams of the United States and Canada, April 12, 2023

CLIMATE

Average and Extreme Temperatures

Temperature	Jan	Feb	Mar	Apr	May	Jun	Jul	Aug	Sep	Oct	Nov	Dec	Yr.
Extreme High (°F)	68	75	85	96	97	101	104	99	99	88	81	72	104
Average High (°F)	38	41	50	61	72	80	85	84	76	65	54	43	62
Average Temp. (°F)	32	34	43	53	63	72	77	76	68	58	48	37	55
Average Low (°F)	26	27	35	44	54	63	68	67	60	49	41	31	47
Extreme Low (°F)	-2	-2	8	21	36	46	53	50	40	29	17	-1	-2

Note: Figures cover the years 1962-1992
Source: National Climatic Data Center, International Station Meteorological Climate Summary, 9/96

Average Precipitation/Snowfall/Humidity

Precip./Humidity	Jan	Feb	Mar	Apr	May	Jun	Jul	Aug	Sep	Oct	Nov	Dec	Yr.
Avg. Precip. (in.)	3.5	3.1	4.0	3.9	4.5	3.8	4.5	4.1	4.1	3.3	4.5	3.8	47.0
Avg. Snowfall (in.)	7	8	4	Tr	Tr	0	0	0	0	Tr	Tr	3	23
Avg. Rel. Hum. 7am (%)	67	67	66	64	72	74	74	76	78	75	72	69	71
Avg. Rel. Hum. 4pm (%)	55	53	50	45	52	55	53	54	56	55	57	58	53

Note: Figures cover the years 1962-1992; Tr = Trace amounts (<0.05 in. of rain; <0.5 in. of snow)
Source: National Climatic Data Center, International Station Meteorological Climate Summary, 9/96

Weather Conditions

Temperature			Daytime Sky			Precipitation		
32°F & below	45°F & below	90°F & above	Clear	Partly cloudy	Cloudy	0.01 inch or more precip.	0.1 inch or more snow/ice	Thunder-storms
75	170	18	85	166	114	120	11	20

Note: Figures are average number of days per year and cover the years 1962-1992
Source: National Climatic Data Center, International Station Meteorological Climate Summary, 9/96

HAZARDOUS WASTE

Superfund Sites

The New York-Jersey City-White Plains, NY-NJ metro division is home to 40 sites on the EPA's Superfund National Priorities List: **Atlantic Resources** (final); **Bog Creek Farm** (final); **Brick Township Landfill** (final); **Burnt Fly Bog** (final); **Carroll & Dubies Sewage Disposal** (final); **Chemical Insecticide Corp.** (final); **Chemsol, Inc.** (final); **Ciba-Geigy Corp.** (final); **Cornell Dubilier Electronics Inc.** (final); **CPS/Madison Industries** (final); **Curcio Scrap Metal, Inc.** (final); **Diamond Head Oil Refinery Division** (final); **Evor Phillips Leasing** (final); **Fair Lawn Well Field** (final); **Fried Industries** (final); **Garfield Ground Water Contamination** (final); **Global Sanitary Landfill** (final); **Goose Farm** (final); **Gowanus Canal** (final); **Horseshoe Road** (final); **Imperial Oil Co., Inc./Champion Chemicals** (final); **JIS Landfill** (final); **Kin-Buc Landfill** (final); **Lone Pine Landfill** (final); **Lower Hackensack River** (final); **Magna Metals** (final); **Maywood Chemical Co.** (final); **Meeker Avenue Plume** (final); **Middlesex Sampling Plant (USDOE)** (final);

Monitor Devices, Inc./Intercircuits, Inc. (final); **Naval Air Engineering Center** (final); **Naval Weapons Station Earle (Site A)** (final); **Nepera Chemical Co., Inc.** (final); **Newtown Creek** (final); **PJP Landfill** (final); **Quanta Resources** (final); **Ramapo Landfill** (final); **Raritan Bay Slag** (final); **Ringwood Mines/Landfill** (final); **Scientific Chemical Processing** (final). There are a total of 1,165 Superfund sites with a status of proposed or final on the list in the U.S. *U.S. Environmental Protection Agency, National Priorities List, April 12, 2023*

AIR QUALITY

Air Quality Trends: Ozone

	1990	1995	2000	2005	2010	2015	2018	2019	2020	2021
MSA[1]	0.101	0.105	0.089	0.090	0.080	0.074	0.073	0.067	0.064	0.069
U.S.	0.087	0.089	0.081	0.080	0.072	0.067	0.069	0.065	0.065	0.067

Note: (1) Data covers the New York-Newark-Jersey City, NY-NJ-PA Metropolitan Statistical Area. The values shown are the composite ozone concentration averages among trend sites based on the highest fourth daily maximum 8-hour concentration in parts per million. These trends are based on sites having an adequate record of monitoring data during the trend period. Data from exceptional events are included.
Source: U.S. Environmental Protection Agency, Air Quality Monitoring Information, "Air Quality Trends by City, 1990-2021"

Air Quality Index

Area	Percent of Days when Air Quality was...[2]					AQI Statistics[2]	
	Good	Moderate	Unhealthy for Sensitive Groups	Unhealthy	Very Unhealthy	Maximum	Median
MSA[1]	54.8	39.5	4.9	0.8	0.0	154	49

Note: (1) Data covers the New York-Newark-Jersey City, NY-NJ-PA Metropolitan Statistical Area; (2) Based on 365 days with AQI data in 2021. Air Quality Index (AQI) is an index for reporting daily air quality. EPA calculates the AQI for five major air pollutants regulated by the Clean Air Act: ground-level ozone, particle pollution (aka particulate matter), carbon monoxide, sulfur dioxide, and nitrogen dioxide. The AQI runs from 0 to 500. The higher the AQI value, the greater the level of air pollution and the greater the health concern. There are six AQI categories: "Good" AQI is between 0 and 50. Air quality is considered satisfactory; "Moderate" AQI is between 51 and 100. Air quality is acceptable; "Unhealthy for Sensitive Groups" When AQI values are between 101 and 150, members of sensitive groups may experience health effects; "Unhealthy" When AQI values are between 151 and 200 everyone may begin to experience health effects; "Very Unhealthy" AQI values between 201 and 300 trigger a health alert; "Hazardous" AQI values over 300 trigger warnings of emergency conditions (not shown).
Source: U.S. Environmental Protection Agency, Air Quality Index Report, 2021

Air Quality Index Pollutants

Area	Percent of Days when AQI Pollutant was...[2]					
	Carbon Monoxide	Nitrogen Dioxide	Ozone	Sulfur Dioxide	Particulate Matter 2.5	Particulate Matter 10
MSA[1]	0.0	12.3	41.4	(3)	46.3	0.0

Note: (1) Data covers the New York-Newark-Jersey City, NY-NJ-PA Metropolitan Statistical Area; (2) Based on 365 days with AQI data in 2021. The Air Quality Index (AQI) is an index for reporting daily air quality. EPA calculates the AQI for five major air pollutants regulated by the Clean Air Act: ground-level ozone, particle pollution (also known as particulate matter), carbon monoxide, sulfur dioxide, and nitrogen dioxide. The AQI runs from 0 to 500. The higher the AQI value, the greater the level of air pollution and the greater the health concern; (3) Sulfur dioxide is no longer included in this table (as of December 8, 2021) because SO_2 concentrations tend to be very localized and not necessarily representative of broad geographical areas like counties and CBSAs.
Source: U.S. Environmental Protection Agency, Air Quality Index Report, 2021

Maximum Air Pollutant Concentrations: Particulate Matter, Ozone, CO and Lead

	Particulate Matter 10 (ug/m^3)	Particulate Matter 2.5 Wtd AM (ug/m^3)	Particulate Matter 2.5 24-Hr (ug/m^3)	Ozone (ppm)	Carbon Monoxide (ppm)	Lead (ug/m^3)
MSA[1] Level	40	9.8	26	0.079	2	n/a
NAAQS[2]	150	15	35	0.075	9	0.15
Met NAAQS[2]	Yes	Yes	Yes	No	Yes	n/a

Note: (1) Data covers the New York-Newark-Jersey City, NY-NJ-PA Metropolitan Statistical Area; Data from exceptional events are included; (2) National Ambient Air Quality Standards; ppm = parts per million; ug/m^3 = micrograms per cubic meter; n/a not available.
Concentrations: Particulate Matter 10 (coarse particulate)—highest second maximum 24-hour concentration; Particulate Matter 2.5 Wtd AM (fine particulate)—highest weighted annual mean concentration; Particulate Matter 2.5 24-Hour (fine particulate)—highest 98th percentile 24-hour concentration; Ozone—highest fourth daily maximum 8-hour concentration; Carbon Monoxide—highest second maximum non-overlapping 8-hour concentration; Lead—maximum running 3-month average
Source: U.S. Environmental Protection Agency, Air Quality Monitoring Information, "Air Quality Statistics by City, 2021"

Maximum Air Pollutant Concentrations: Nitrogen Dioxide and Sulfur Dioxide

	Nitrogen Dioxide AM (ppb)	Nitrogen Dioxide 1-Hr (ppb)	Sulfur Dioxide AM (ppb)	Sulfur Dioxide 1-Hr (ppb)	Sulfur Dioxide 24-Hr (ppb)
MSA[1] Level	19	65	n/a	17	n/a
NAAQS[2]	53	100	30	75	140
Met NAAQS[2]	Yes	Yes	n/a	Yes	n/a

Note: (1) Data covers the New York-Newark-Jersey City, NY-NJ-PA Metropolitan Statistical Area; Data from exceptional events are included; (2) National Ambient Air Quality Standards; ppm = parts per million; ug/m^3 = micrograms per cubic meter; n/a not available.
Concentrations: Nitrogen Dioxide AM—highest arithmetic mean concentration; Nitrogen Dioxide 1-Hr—highest 98th percentile 1-hour daily maximum concentration; Sulfur Dioxide AM—highest annual mean concentration; Sulfur Dioxide 1-Hr—highest 99th percentile 1-hour daily maximum concentration; Sulfur Dioxide 24-Hr—highest second maximum 24-hour concentration
Source: U.S. Environmental Protection Agency, Air Quality Monitoring Information, "Air Quality Statistics by City, 2021"

Philadelphia, Pennsylvania

Background

Philadelphia, "The City of Brotherly Love," was not founded upon brotherly love at all. The largest city in Pennsylvania was settled by Swedes and Finns in 1638, in a settlement known as New Sweden, seized in 1655 by Peter Stuyvesant, director general of New Amsterdam for the Dutch crown. Inconsiderate of any previous claims by the Dutch, King Charles II of England conferred land between the Connecticut and Delaware rivers upon his brother, the duke of York. Naturally, the two countries went to war. Thanks to a generous loan by Admiral Sir William Penn, the land fell permanently into English hands. To repay the loan, the king gave Sir William's son, also named William, sole proprietorship of the state of present-day Pennsylvania, probably glad to be rid of a subject heavily influenced by a dissenting religious sect known as the Society of Friends, or the Quakers.

Pennsylvania's landlord had the vision and the financial means to carry out a simple but radical experiment for the times: a city built upon religious tolerance, and this place of religious outcasts prospered. Thanks to forests abundant in natural resources, and ports busy with international trade, Philadelphia, in the state's southeast corner, was a bustling, ideal American city.

The service sector has emerged as the predominant economic force driving current and future growth in the city. Greater Philadelphia has one of the largest health care industries in the nation. It has become a major materials development and processing center, with more than 100,000 working in the manufacture of chemicals, advanced materials, glass, plastics, industrial gases, metals, composites, and textiles. Philadelphia is also a national leader in the biotech field. Its "knowledge industry," with over 80 colleges and universities helps to supply a skilled workforce for the growing technical and bio-industries. Because of Philadelphia's importance as a mecca for medical research, the region is a major center for the pharmaceutical industry.

The city claimed firsts in many cultural, educational, and political arenas. The Pennsylvania Academy of Fine Arts is the oldest museum and fine arts school in the country. The University of Pennsylvania, which Benjamin Franklin helped found, is the oldest university in the country. And on July 4, 1776, the United States was born when "longhaired radicals" such as Thomas Jefferson, George Washington, and John Hancock signed the Declaration of Independence in Philadelphia, breaking away from the mother country forever.

The city offers a thriving cultural scene with something for everyone, from chamber music to jazz, historic Society Hill to South Philadelphia, home of the open-air Italian Market and famous Philly cheesesteak. The waterfront district has many colonial-era homes and cobblestone streets, as well as the Liberty Bell, Independence Hall and Independence National Historic Park.

The Avenue of the Arts is home to several theaters. The Kimmel Center for the Performing Arts and the Academy of Music serve as home to a number of resident performing arts companies, including The Philadelphia Orchestra, Opera Company of Philadelphia, Pennsylvania Ballet, Chamber Orchestra of Philadelphia, American Theater Arts for Youth, PHILADANCO, Philadelphia Chamber Music Society, and Peter Nero and the Philly Pops. The Walnut Street Theater, a National Historical Landmark, and the oldest (1809) and most subscribed theater in the English-speaking world, completed a $39 million expansion and renovation to both public and nonpublic spaces in 2022.

The National Constitution Center Museum, devoted to exploring the role and meaning of the United States Constitution, is a glass, steel, and limestone building designed by Pei, Cobb Freed, and Partners, built in 2003. That same year, a new Liberty Bell Center, designed to enhance the viewing of the nation's iconic Liberty Bell, also opened.

Sports venues include Lincoln Financial Field for the Philadelphia Eagles NFL football team, who won Super Bowl LI in 2018, and Citizens Bank Park for Major League Baseball's Philadelphia Phillies, who won the World Series in 2008. These replace the 33-year-old Veterans Stadium, which was razed in a sentimental farewell ceremony. The Wells Fargo Center along the Delaware River hosts the Philadelphia Flyers professional ice hockey team and the Philadelphia 76ers professional basketball team.

The Appalachian Mountains to the west and the Atlantic Ocean to the east have a moderating effect on the city's climate and temperatures. Summer does bring humid days, owing to proximity to the ocean. Precipitation is evenly distributed throughout the year, but there are variations within the city. Summer rains and winter snows are sometimes heavier in suburbs to the north and west, with their higher elevations, than in the south and east.

Rankings

General Rankings

- Philadelphia was selected as one of the best places to live in America by *Outside Magazine*. Criteria centered on diversity; sustainability; outdoor equity; and affordability. Local experts shared highlights from hands-on experience in each location. *Outside Magazine, "The 20 Most Livable Towns and Cities in America," October 15, 2021*

- The human resources consulting firm Mercer ranked 231 major cities worldwide in terms of overall quality of life. Philadelphia ranked #54. Criteria: political, social, economic, and socio-cultural factors; medical and health considerations; schools and education; public services and transportation; recreation; consumer goods; housing; and natural environment. *Mercer, "Mercer 2019 Quality of Living Survey," March 13, 2019*

Business/Finance Rankings

- The Brookings Institution ranked the nation's largest cities based on income inequality. Philadelphia was ranked #20 (#1 = greatest inequality). Criteria: the "95/20 ratio," a figure representing the income at which a household earns more than 95 percent of all other households, divided by the income at which a household earns more than only 20 percent of all other households. *Brookings Institution, "Household Income Inequality, Largest Cities of 97 Large U.S. Metro Areas, 2014-2016," February 5, 2018*

- The Brookings Institution ranked the 100 largest metro areas in the U.S. based on income inequality. Philadelphia was ranked #12 (#1 = greatest inequality). Criteria: the "95/20 ratio," a figure representing the income at which a household earns more than 95 percent of all other households, divided by the income at which a household earns more than only 20 percent of all other households. *Brookings Institution, "Household Income Inequality, 100 Largest U.S. Metro Areas, 2014-2016," February 5, 2018*

- The Philadelphia metro area was identified as one of the most debt-ridden places in America by the finance site Credit.com. The metro area was ranked #11. Criteria: residents' average credit card debt as well as median income. *Credit.com, "25 Cities With the Most Credit Card Debt," February 28, 2018*

- Philadelphia was identified as one of America's most frugal metro areas by *Coupons.com*. The city ranked #6 out of 25. Criteria: digital coupon usage. *Coupons.com, "America's Most Frugal Cities of 2017," March 22, 2018*

- Philadelphia was identified as one of the happiest cities to work in by CareerBliss.com, an online community for career advancement. The city ranked #8 out of 10. Criteria: an employee's relationship with his or her boss and co-workers; daily tasks; general work environment; compensation; opportunities for advancement; company culture and job reputation; and resources. *Businesswire.com, "CareerBliss Happiest Cities to Work 2019," February 12, 2019*

- *Forbes* ranked the 200 most populous metro areas to determine the nation's "Best Places for Business and Careers." The Philadelphia metro area was ranked #88. Criteria: costs (business and living); job growth (past and projected); income growth; quality of life; educational attainment (college and high school); projected economic growth; cultural and leisure opportunities; workplace tolerance laws; net migration patterns. *Forbes, "The Best Places for Business and Careers 2019: Seattle Still On Top," October 30, 2019*

- Mercer Human Resources Consulting ranked 227 cities worldwide in terms of cost-of-living. Philadelphia ranked #70 (the lower the ranking, the higher the cost-of-living). The survey measured the comparative cost of over 200 items (such as housing, food, clothing, domestic supplies, transportation, and recreation/entertainment) in each location. *Mercer, "2022 Cost of Living City Ranking," June 29, 2022*

Culture/Performing Arts Rankings

- Philadelphia was selected as one of the 25 best cities for moviemakers in North America. Great film cities are places where filmmaking dreams can come true, that offer more creative space, lower costs, and great outdoor locations. NYC & LA were intentionally excluded. Criteria: longstanding reputations as film-friendly communities; film community and culture; affordability; and quality of life. The city was ranked #9. *MovieMaker Magazine, "Best Places to Live and Work as a Moviemaker, 2023," January 18, 2023*

- Philadelphia was selected as one of "America's Favorite Cities." The city ranked #9 in the "Architecture " category. Respondents to an online survey were asked to rate their favorite place (population over 100,000) in over 65 categories. *Travelandleisure.com, "America's Favorite Cities for Architecture 2016," March 2, 2017*

Education Rankings

- Philadelphia was selected as one of America's most literate cities. The city ranked #26 out of the 84 largest U.S. cities. Criteria: number of booksellers; library resources; Internet resources; educational attainment; periodical publishing resources; newspaper circulation. *Central Connecticut State University, "America's Most Literate Cities, 2018," February 2019*

Environmental Rankings

- The U.S. Environmental Protection Agency (EPA) released its list of U.S. metropolitan areas with the most ENERGY STAR certified buildings in 2022. The Philadelphia metro area was ranked #22 out of 25. *U.S. Environmental Protection Agency, "2023 Energy Star Top Cities," April 26, 2023*

Food/Drink Rankings

- The U.S. Chamber of Commerce Foundation conducted an in-depth study on local food truck regulations, surveyed 288 food truck owners, and ranked 20 major American cities based on how friendly they are for operating a food truck. The compiled index assessed the following: procedures for obtaining permits and licenses; complying with restrictions; and financial obligations associated with operating a food truck. Philadelphia ranked #4 overall (1 being the best). *www.foodtrucknation.us, "Food Truck Nation," March 20, 2018*

- Philadelphia was identified as one of the cities in America ordering the most vegan food options by GrubHub.com. The city ranked #5 out of 5. Criteria: percentage of vegan, vegetarian and plant-based food orders compared to the overall number of orders. *GrubHub.com, "State of the Plate Report 2021: Top Cities for Vegans," June 20, 2021*

Health/Fitness Rankings

- For each of the 100 largest cities in the United States, the American Fitness Index®, compiled in partnership between the American College of Sports Medicine and the Elevance Health Foundation, evaluated community infrastructure and 34 health behaviors including preventive health, levels of chronic disease conditions, food insecurity, sleep quality, pedestrian safety, air quality, and community/environment resources that support physical activity. Philadelphia ranked #62 for "community fitness." *americanfitnessindex.org, "2022 ACSM American Fitness Index Summary Report," July 12, 2022*

- Philadelphia was identified as one of the 10 most walkable cities in the U.S. by Walk Score. The city ranked #4. Walk Score measures walkability by analyzing hundreds of walking routes to nearby amenities, and also measures pedestrian friendliness by analyzing population density and road metrics such as block length and intersection density. *WalkScore.com, April 13, 2021*

- Philadelphia was identified as a "2022 Spring Allergy Capital." The area ranked #34 out of 100. Three groups of factors were used to identify the most challenging cities for people with allergies during the spring season: annual spring pollen scores; over the counter allergy medicine use; number of board-certified allergy specialists. *Asthma and Allergy Foundation of America, "Spring Allergy Capitals 2022," March 2, 2022*

- Philadelphia was identified as a "2022 Fall Allergy Capital." The area ranked #49 out of 100. Three groups of factors were used to identify the most challenging cities for people with allergies during the fall season: annual fall pollen scores; over the counter allergy medicine use; number of board-certified allergy specialists. *Asthma and Allergy Foundation of America, "Fall Allergy Capitals 2022," March 2, 2022*

- Philadelphia was identified as a "2022 Asthma Capital." The area ranked #9 out of the nation's 100 largest metropolitan areas. Criteria: estimated asthma prevalence; asthma-related mortality; and ER visits due to asthma. Risk factors analyzed but not factored in the rankings: annual pollen score; annual air quality; public smoking laws; access to board-certified asthma specialists; rescue and controller medication use; uninsured rate; poverty rate. *Asthma and Allergy Foundation of America, "Asthma Capitals 2022: The Most Challenging Places to Live With Asthma," September 14, 2022*

Real Estate Rankings

- *WalletHub* compared the most populated U.S. cities to determine which had the best markets for real estate agents. Philadelphia ranked #144 where demand was high and pay was the best. Criteria: sales per agent; annual median wage for real-estate agents; monthly average starting salary for real estate agents; real estate job density and competition; unemployment rate; home turnover rate; housing-market health index; and other relevant metrics. *www.WalletHub.com, "2021 Best Places to Be a Real Estate Agent," May 12, 2021*

Safety Rankings

- Allstate ranked the 200 largest cities in America in terms of driver safety. Philadelphia ranked #190. Criteria: internal property damage claims over a two-year period from January 2016 to December 2017. The report helps increase the importance of safety and awareness behind the wheel. *Allstate, "Allstate America's Best Drivers Report, 2019" June 24, 2019*

Seniors/Retirement Rankings

- *AARP the Magazine* selected Philadelphia as one of the great places in the United States for seniors, as well as younger generations, that represent "a place to call home." For the list, the magazine recognized the change in criteria due to the pandemic, and looked for cities with easy access to exercise/outdoors, quality healthcare, sense of community, relatively affordable housing costs, job markets that accommodate working from home, and reliable internet access. *www.aarp.org/magazine, "Best Places to Live and Retire Now," November 29, 2021*

Sports/Recreation Rankings

- Philadelphia was chosen as one of America's best cities for bicycling. The city ranked #26 out of 50. Criteria: cycling infrastructure that is safe and friendly for all ages; energy and bike culture. The editors evaluated cities with populations of 100,000 or more. *Bicycling, "The 50 Best Bike Cities in America," October 10, 2018*

Transportation Rankings

- Business Insider presented an AllTransit Performance Score ranking of public transportation in major U.S. cities and towns, with populations over 250,000, in which Philadelphia earned the #7-ranked "Transit Score," awarded for frequency of service, access to jobs, quality and number of stops, and affordability. *www.businessinsider.com, "The 17 Major U.S. Cities with the Best Public Transportation," April 17, 2018*

- The business website *24/7 Wall St.* reviewed U.S. Census data to identify the 25 cities where the largest share of households do not own a vehicle. Philadelphia held the #6 position. *247wallst.com, "Cities Where No One Wants to Drive," January 12, 2020*

- According to the INRIX "2022 Global Traffic Scorecard," Philadelphia was identified as one of the most congested metro areas in the U.S. The area ranked #4 out of 25. Criteria: average annual time spent in traffic and average cost of congestion per motorist. *Inrix.com, "Return to Work, Higher Gas Prices & Inflation Drove Americans to Spend Hundreds More in Time and Money Commuting," January 10, 2023*

Women/Minorities Rankings

- Personal finance website *WalletHub* compared more than 180 U.S. cities across two key dimensions, "Hispanic Business-Friendliness" and "Hispanic Purchasing Power," to arrive at the most favorable conditions for Hispanic entrepreneurs. Philadelphia was ranked #174 out of 182. Criteria includes: share of Hispanic-Owned Businesses; Hispanic entrepreneurship rate to median annual income of Hispanics; Small Business-Friendliness score; cost of living; and number of Hispanics with at least a bachelor's degree. *WalletHub.com, "2019's Best Cities for Hispanic Entrepreneurs," May 1, 2019*

Miscellaneous Rankings

- In its roundup of St. Patrick's Day parades "Gayot" listed the best festivals and parades of all things Irish. The festivities in Philadelphia as among the best in North America. *www.gayot.com, "Best St. Patrick's Day Parades," March 2023*

- The watchdog site, Charity Navigator, conducted a study of charities in major markets both to analyze statistical differences in their financial, accountability, and transparency practices and to track year-to-year variations in individual philanthropic communities. The Philadelphia metro area was ranked #20 among the 30 metro markets in the rating category of Overall Score. *www.charitynavigator.org, "2017 Metro Market Study," May 1, 2017*

- *WalletHub* compared the 150 most populated U.S. cities to determine their operating efficiency. A "Quality of Services" score was constructed for each city and then divided by the total budget per capita to reveal which were managed the best. Philadelphia ranked #134. Criteria: financial stability; economy; education; safety; health; infrastructure and pollution. *www.WalletHub.com, "2022's Best- & Worst-Run Cities in America," June 21, 2022*

Business Environment

DEMOGRAPHICS

Population Growth

Area	1990 Census	2000 Census	2010 Census	2020 Census	Population Growth (%)	
					1990-2020	2010-2020
City	1,585,577	1,517,550	1,526,006	1,603,797	1.1	5.1
MSA[1]	5,435,470	5,687,147	5,965,343	6,245,051	14.9	4.7
U.S.	248,709,873	281,421,906	308,745,538	331,449,281	33.3	7.4

Note: (1) Figures cover the Philadelphia-Camden-Wilmington, PA-NJ-DE-MD Metropolitan Statistical Area
Source: U.S. Census Bureau, 1990 Census, 2000 Census, 2010 Census, 2020 Census

Race

Area	White Alone[2] (%)	Black Alone[2] (%)	Asian Alone[2] (%)	AIAN[3] Alone[2] (%)	NHOPI[4] Alone[2] (%)	Other Race Alone[2] (%)	Two or More Races (%)
City	36.3	39.3	8.3	0.4	0.1	8.7	6.9
MSA[1]	60.7	20.4	6.6	0.3	0.0	5.1	6.8
U.S.	61.6	12.4	6.0	1.1	0.2	8.4	10.2

Note: (1) Figures cover the Philadelphia-Camden-Wilmington, PA-NJ-DE-MD Metropolitan Statistical Area;
(2) Alone is defined as not being in combination with one or more other races; (3) American Indian and Alaska
Native; (4) Native Hawaiian and Other Pacific Islander
Source: U.S. Census Bureau, 2020 Census

Hispanic or Latino Origin

Area	Total (%)	Mexican (%)	Puerto Rican (%)	Cuban (%)	Other (%)
City	15.4	1.3	8.7	0.3	5.1
MSA[1]	9.9	1.9	4.6	0.3	3.2
U.S.	18.4	11.2	1.8	0.7	4.7

Note: Persons of Hispanic or Latino origin can be of any race; (1) Figures cover the
Philadelphia-Camden-Wilmington, PA-NJ-DE-MD Metropolitan Statistical Area
Source: U.S. Census Bureau, 2017-2021 American Community Survey 5-Year Estimates

Age

Area	Percent of Population									Median Age
	Under Age 5	Age 5–19	Age 20–34	Age 35–44	Age 45–54	Age 55–64	Age 65–74	Age 75–84	Age 85+	
City	5.5	17.6	27.2	12.9	10.9	11.6	8.5	4.0	1.7	34.8
MSA[1]	5.3	18.7	20.7	12.6	12.4	13.7	9.8	4.8	2.1	39.1
U.S.	5.6	19.2	20.2	12.7	12.4	13.1	10.0	4.9	1.9	38.8

Note: (1) Figures cover the Philadelphia-Camden-Wilmington, PA-NJ-DE-MD Metropolitan Statistical Area
Source: U.S. Census Bureau, 2020 Census

Disability by Age

Area	All Ages	Under 18 Years Old	18 to 64 Years Old	65 Years and Over
City	16.9	7.0	15.0	42.0
MSA[1]	12.7	5.1	10.5	32.2
U.S.	12.6	4.4	10.3	33.4

Note: Figures show percent of the civilian noninstitutionalized population that reported having a disability.
Disability status is determined from six types of difficulty: vision, hearing, cognitive, ambulatory, self-care, and
independent living. For children under 5 years old, hearing and vision difficulty are used to determine
disability status. For children between the ages of 5 and 14, disability status is determined from hearing, vision,
cognitive, ambulatory, and self-care difficulties. For people aged 15 years and older, they are considered to
have a disability if they have difficulty with any one of the six difficulty types; Note: (1) Figures cover the
Philadelphia-Camden-Wilmington, PA-NJ-DE-MD Metropolitan Statistical Area
Source: U.S. Census Bureau, 2017-2021 American Community Survey 5-Year Estimates

Ancestry

Area	German	Irish	English	American	Italian	Polish	French[2]	Scottish	Dutch
City	6.7	9.9	2.8	2.5	6.9	3.1	0.8	0.6	0.3
MSA[1]	14.1	17.4	7.4	3.2	12.4	4.7	1.2	1.2	0.7
U.S.	12.8	9.6	8.1	5.7	5.0	2.7	2.2	1.6	1.1

Note: Figures are the percentage of the total population reporting a particular ancestry. The nine most
commonly reported ancestries in the U.S. are shown. Figures include multiple ancestries (e.g. if a person
reported being Irish and Italian, they were included in both columns); (1) Figures cover the
Philadelphia-Camden-Wilmington, PA-NJ-DE-MD Metropolitan Statistical Area; (2) Excludes Basque
Source: U.S. Census Bureau, 2017-2021 American Community Survey 5-Year Estimates

Foreign-born Population

Area	Percent of Population Born in								
	Any Foreign Country	Asia	Mexico	Europe	Caribbean	Central America[2]	South America	Africa	Canada
City	14.3	5.5	0.5	2.1	2.9	0.7	0.9	1.6	0.1
MSA[1]	11.2	4.6	0.8	1.9	1.4	0.5	0.7	1.2	0.2
U.S.	13.6	4.2	3.3	1.5	1.4	1.1	1.1	0.8	0.2

Note: (1) Figures cover the Philadelphia-Camden-Wilmington, PA-NJ-DE-MD Metropolitan Statistical Area; (2) Excludes Mexico.
Source: U.S. Census Bureau, 2017-2021 American Community Survey 5-Year Estimates

Household Size

Area	Persons in Household (%)							Average Household Size
	One	Two	Three	Four	Five	Six	Seven or More	
City	37.2	29.5	15.0	10.3	4.8	1.9	1.4	2.40
MSA[1]	29.3	32.2	16.2	13.5	5.7	2.0	1.1	2.50
U.S.	28.1	33.8	15.5	12.9	6.0	2.3	1.4	2.60

Note: (1) Figures cover the Philadelphia-Camden-Wilmington, PA-NJ-DE-MD Metropolitan Statistical Area
Source: U.S. Census Bureau, 2017-2021 American Community Survey 5-Year Estimates

Household Relationships

Area	House-holder	Opposite-sex Spouse	Same-sex Spouse	Opposite-sex Unmarried Partner	Same-sex Unmarried Partner	Child[2]	Grand-child	Other Relatives	Non-relatives
City	41.0	10.9	0.3	3.1	0.3	26.8	3.6	5.9	5.2
MSA[1]	38.7	16.9	0.2	2.5	0.2	29.2	2.5	4.4	3.0
U.S.	38.3	17.5	0.2	2.5	0.2	28.3	2.4	4.8	3.4

Note: Figures are percent of the total population; (1) Figures cover the Philadelphia-Camden-Wilmington, PA-NJ-DE-MD Metropolitan Statistical Area; (2) Includes biological, adopted, and stepchildren of the householder
Source: U.S. Census Bureau, 2020 Census

Gender

Area	Males	Females	Males per 100 Females
City	760,383	843,414	90.2
MSA[1]	3,015,319	3,229,732	93.4
U.S.	162,685,811	168,763,470	96.4

Note: (1) Figures cover the Philadelphia-Camden-Wilmington, PA-NJ-DE-MD Metropolitan Statistical Area
Source: U.S. Census Bureau, 2020 Census

Marital Status

Area	Never Married	Now Married[2]	Separated	Widowed	Divorced
City	50.5	31.5	3.0	5.7	9.2
MSA[1]	37.3	45.8	2.0	5.7	9.2
U.S.	33.8	48.0	1.8	5.6	10.8

Note: Figures are percentages and cover the population 15 years of age and older; (1) Figures cover the Philadelphia-Camden-Wilmington, PA-NJ-DE-MD Metropolitan Statistical Area; (2) Excludes separated
Source: U.S. Census Bureau, 2017-2021 American Community Survey 5-Year Estimates

Religious Groups by Family

Area	Catholic	Baptist	Methodist	LDS[2]	Pentecostal	Lutheran	Islam	Adventist	Other
MSA[1]	26.8	3.3	2.4	0.3	1.0	1.2	2.6	1.0	10.5
U.S.	18.7	7.3	3.0	2.0	1.8	1.7	1.3	1.3	11.6

Note: Figures are the number of adherents as a percentage of the total population and cover the eight largest religious groups in the U.S; (1) Figures cover the Philadelphia-Camden-Wilmington, PA-NJ-DE-MD Metropolitan Statistical Area; (2) Church of Jesus Christ of Latter-day Saints
Sources: 2020 U.S. Religion Census, Association of Statisticians of American Religious Bodies; The Association of Religion Data Archives (ARDA)

Religious Groups by Tradition

Area	Catholic	Evangelical Protestant	Mainline Protestant	Black Protestant	Islam	Judaism	Hinduism	Orthodox	Buddhism
MSA[1]	26.8	7.3	6.6	2.2	2.6	1.1	0.6	0.4	0.4
U.S.	18.7	16.5	5.2	2.3	1.3	0.6	0.4	0.4	0.3

Note: Figures are the number of adherents as a percentage of the total population; (1) Figures cover the Philadelphia-Camden-Wilmington, PA-NJ-DE-MD Metropolitan Statistical Area
Sources: 2020 U.S. Religion Census, Association of Statisticians of American Religious Bodies; The Association of Religion Data Archives (ARDA)

Philadelphia, Pennsylvania   347

ECONOMY

Gross Metropolitan Product

Area	2020	2021	2022	2023	Rank[2]
MSA[1]	439.1	478.2	521.7	553.7	9

Note: Figures are in billions of dollars; (1) Figures cover the Philadelphia-Camden-Wilmington, PA-NJ-DE-MD Metropolitan Statistical Area; (2) Rank is based on 2021 data and ranges from 1 to 381
Source: U.S. Conference of Mayors, U.S. Metro Economies: U.S. Metros Compared to Global and State Economies, June 2022

Economic Growth

Area	2018-20 (%)	2021 (%)	2022 (%)	2023 (%)	Rank[2]
MSA[1]	-1.2	4.9	3.3	2.8	235
U.S.	-0.6	5.7	3.1	2.9	–

Note: Figures are real gross metropolitan product (GMP) growth rates and represent average annual percent change; (1) Figures cover the Philadelphia-Camden-Wilmington, PA-NJ-DE-MD Metropolitan Statistical Area; (2) Rank is based on 2020 2-year average annual percent change and ranges from 1 to 381
Source: U.S. Conference of Mayors, U.S. Metro Economies: U.S. Metros Compared to Global and State Economies, June 2022

Metropolitan Area Exports

Area	2016	2017	2018	2019	2020	2021	Rank[2]
MSA[1]	21,359.9	21,689.7	23,663.2	24,721.3	23,022.1	28,724.4	15

Note: Figures are in millions of dollars; (1) Figures cover the Philadelphia-Camden-Wilmington, PA-NJ-DE-MD Metropolitan Statistical Area; (2) Rank is based on 2021 data and ranges from 1 to 388
Source: U.S. Department of Commerce, International Trade Administration, Office of Trade and Economic Analysis, Industry and Analysis, Exports by Metropolitan Area, data extracted March 16, 2023

Building Permits

Area	Single-Family			Multi-Family			Total		
	2021	2022	Pct. Chg.	2021	2022	Pct. Chg.	2021	2022	Pct. Chg.
City	1,553	478	-69.2	23,704	2,745	-88.4	25,257	3,223	-87.2
MSA[1]	8,868	8,532	-3.8	27,439	5,881	-78.6	36,307	14,413	-60.3
U.S.	1,115,400	975,600	-12.5	621,600	689,500	10.9	1,737,000	1,665,100	-4.1

Note: (1) Figures cover the Philadelphia-Camden-Wilmington, PA-NJ-DE-MD Metropolitan Statistical Area; Figures represent new, privately-owned housing units authorized (unadjusted data); All permit data are based on estimates with imputation
Source: U.S. Census Bureau, Manufacturing, Mining, and Construction Statistics, Building Permits, 2021, 2022

Bankruptcy Filings

Area	Business Filings			Nonbusiness Filings		
	2021	2022	% Chg.	2021	2022	% Chg.
Philadelphia County	31	28	-9.7	741	952	28.5
U.S.	14,347	13,481	-6.0	399,269	374,240	-6.3

Note: Business filings include Chapter 7, Chapter 9, Chapter 11, Chapter 12, Chapter 13, Chapter 15, and Section 304; Nonbusiness filings include Chapter 7, Chapter 11, and Chapter 13
Source: Administrative Office of the U.S. Courts, Business and Nonbusiness Bankruptcy, County Cases Commenced by Chapter of the Bankruptcy Code, During the 12-Month Period Ending December 31, 2021 and Business and Nonbusiness Bankruptcy, County Cases Commenced by Chapter of the Bankruptcy Code, During the 12-Month Period Ending December 31, 2022

Housing Vacancy Rates

Area	Gross Vacancy Rate[2] (%)			Year-Round Vacancy Rate[3] (%)			Rental Vacancy Rate[4] (%)			Homeowner Vacancy Rate[5] (%)		
	2020	2021	2022	2020	2021	2022	2020	2021	2022	2020	2021	2022
MSA[1]	6.0	6.1	5.5	5.8	5.9	5.4	5.4	4.8	4.2	0.7	0.5	1.0
U.S.	10.6	10.8	10.5	8.2	8.4	8.2	6.3	6.1	5.8	1.0	0.9	0.8

Note: (1) Figures cover the Philadelphia-Camden-Wilmington, PA-NJ-DE-MD Metropolitan Statistical Area; (2) The percentage of the total housing inventory that is vacant; (3) The percentage of the housing inventory (excluding seasonal units) that is year-round vacant; (4) The percentage of rental inventory that is vacant for rent; (5) The percentage of homeowner inventory that is vacant for sale
Source: U.S. Census Bureau, Housing Vacancies and Homeownership Annual Statistics: 2020, 2021, 2022

INCOME

Income

Area	Per Capita ($)	Median Household ($)	Average Household ($)
City	32,344	52,649	77,454
MSA[1]	43,195	79,070	109,757
U.S.	37,638	69,021	97,196

Note: (1) Figures cover the Philadelphia-Camden-Wilmington, PA-NJ-DE-MD Metropolitan Statistical Area
Source: U.S. Census Bureau, 2017-2021 American Community Survey 5-Year Estimates

Household Income Distribution

Area	Percent of Households Earning							
	Under $15,000	$15,000 -$24,999	$25,000 -$34,999	$35,000 -$49,999	$50,000 -$74,999	$75,000 -$99,999	$100,000 -$149,999	$150,000 and up
City	17.1	9.8	9.2	12.0	16.4	11.3	12.4	11.7
MSA[1]	9.3	6.7	7.1	9.7	15.1	12.5	17.3	22.5
U.S.	9.4	7.8	8.2	11.4	16.8	12.8	16.3	17.3

Note: (1) Figures cover the Philadelphia-Camden-Wilmington, PA-NJ-DE-MD Metropolitan Statistical Area
Source: U.S. Census Bureau, 2017-2021 American Community Survey 5-Year Estimates

Poverty Rate

Area	All Ages	Under 18 Years Old	18 to 64 Years Old	65 Years and Over
City	22.8	31.9	20.6	18.9
MSA[1]	11.7	16.0	10.9	9.2
U.S.	12.6	17.0	11.8	9.6

Note: Figures are percentage of people whose income during the past 12 months was below the poverty level;
(1) Figures cover the Philadelphia-Camden-Wilmington, PA-NJ-DE-MD Metropolitan Statistical Area
Source: U.S. Census Bureau, 2017-2021 American Community Survey 5-Year Estimates

EMPLOYMENT

Labor Force and Employment

Area	Civilian Labor Force			Workers Employed		
	Dec. 2021	Dec. 2022	% Chg.	Dec. 2021	Dec. 2022	% Chg.
City	712,569	723,233	1.5	667,785	690,464	3.4
MD[1]	1,004,235	1,021,788	1.7	946,859	979,293	3.4
U.S.	161,696,000	164,224,000	1.6	155,732,000	158,872,000	2.0

Note: Data is not seasonally adjusted and covers workers 16 years of age and older; (1) Figures cover the
Philadelphia, PA Metropolitan Division
Source: Bureau of Labor Statistics, Local Area Unemployment Statistics

Unemployment Rate

Area	2022											
	Jan.	Feb.	Mar.	Apr.	May	Jun.	Jul.	Aug.	Sep.	Oct.	Nov.	Dec.
City	7.7	6.8	6.3	6.0	5.7	6.2	6.2	6.4	4.9	4.7	4.8	4.5
MD[1]	7.0	6.2	5.7	5.5	5.2	5.7	5.7	5.9	4.5	4.3	4.4	4.2
U.S.	4.4	4.1	3.8	3.3	3.4	3.8	3.8	3.8	3.3	3.4	3.4	3.3

Note: Data is not seasonally adjusted and covers workers 16 years of age and older; (1) Figures cover the
Philadelphia, PA Metropolitan Division
Source: Bureau of Labor Statistics, Local Area Unemployment Statistics

Average Wages

Occupation	$/Hr.	Occupation	$/Hr.
Accountants and Auditors	41.83	Maintenance and Repair Workers	23.49
Automotive Mechanics	25.23	Marketing Managers	71.68
Bookkeepers	23.94	Network and Computer Systems Admin.	47.15
Carpenters	30.34	Nurses, Licensed Practical	28.52
Cashiers	13.39	Nurses, Registered	42.23
Computer Programmers	48.86	Nursing Assistants	18.17
Computer Systems Analysts	51.32	Office Clerks, General	21.08
Computer User Support Specialists	31.04	Physical Therapists	48.69
Construction Laborers	26.48	Physicians	n/a
Cooks, Restaurant	16.51	Plumbers, Pipefitters and Steamfitters	34.76
Customer Service Representatives	21.24	Police and Sheriff's Patrol Officers	37.93
Dentists	93.37	Postal Service Mail Carriers	27.23
Electricians	38.35	Real Estate Sales Agents	27.12
Engineers, Electrical	53.63	Retail Salespersons	16.66
Fast Food and Counter Workers	13.26	Sales Representatives, Technical/Scientific	57.64
Financial Managers	78.78	Secretaries, Exc. Legal/Medical/Executive	21.81
First-Line Supervisors of Office Workers	33.31	Security Guards	18.05
General and Operations Managers	68.82	Surgeons	196.21
Hairdressers/Cosmetologists	17.70	Teacher Assistants, Exc. Postsecondary*	16.04
Home Health and Personal Care Aides	14.31	Teachers, Secondary School, Exc. Sp. Ed.*	35.76
Janitors and Cleaners	17.24	Telemarketers	16.16
Landscaping/Groundskeeping Workers	18.71	Truck Drivers, Heavy/Tractor-Trailer	27.40
Lawyers	76.88	Truck Drivers, Light/Delivery Services	22.39
Maids and Housekeeping Cleaners	15.47	Waiters and Waitresses	15.81

Note: Wage data covers the Philadelphia-Camden-Wilmington, PA-NJ-DE-MD Metropolitan Statistical Area;
(*) Hourly wages were calculated from annual wage data based on a 40 hour work week; n/a not available.
Source: Bureau of Labor Statistics, Metro Area Occupational Employment & Wage Estimates, May 2022

Employment by Industry

Sector	MD[1]		U.S.
	Number of Employees	Percent of Total	Percent of Total
Construction, Mining, and Logging	25,600	2.5	5.4
Private Education and Health Services	317,800	31.6	16.1
Financial Activities	65,100	6.5	5.9
Government	127,900	12.7	14.5
Information	19,700	2.0	2.0
Leisure and Hospitality	91,800	9.1	10.3
Manufacturing	32,800	3.3	8.4
Other Services	40,200	4.0	3.7
Professional and Business Services	146,200	14.5	14.7
Retail Trade	74,400	7.4	10.2
Transportation, Warehousing, and Utilities	41,800	4.2	4.9
Wholesale Trade	23,800	2.4	3.9

Note: Figures are non-farm employment as of December 2022. Figures are not seasonally adjusted and include workers 16 years of age and older; (1) Figures cover the Philadelphia, PA Metropolitan Division
Source: Bureau of Labor Statistics, Current Employment Statistics, Employment, Hours, and Earnings

Employment by Occupation

Occupation Classification	City (%)	MSA[1] (%)	U.S. (%)
Management, Business, Science, and Arts	41.9	46.1	40.3
Natural Resources, Construction, and Maintenance	5.2	6.6	8.7
Production, Transportation, and Material Moving	12.0	10.6	13.1
Sales and Office	19.1	20.7	20.9
Service	21.7	16.0	17.0

Note: Figures cover employed civilians 16 years of age and older; (1) Figures cover the Philadelphia-Camden-Wilmington, PA-NJ-DE-MD Metropolitan Statistical Area
Source: U.S. Census Bureau, 2017-2021 American Community Survey 5-Year Estimates

Occupations with Greatest Projected Employment Growth: 2022 – 2024

Occupation[1]	2022 Employment	2024 Projected Employment	Numeric Employment Change	Percent Employment Change
Home Health and Personal Care Aides	194,980	205,150	10,170	5.2
Laborers and Freight, Stock, and Material Movers, Hand	150,480	158,160	7,680	5.1
Stockers and Order Fillers	100,260	104,570	4,310	4.3
Industrial Truck and Tractor Operators	31,030	33,930	2,900	9.3
General and Operations Managers	114,430	116,380	1,950	1.7
Heavy and Tractor-Trailer Truck Drivers	88,610	90,560	1,950	2.2
Cooks, Restaurant	49,280	51,090	1,810	3.7
Registered Nurses	148,910	150,170	1,260	0.8
Market Research Analysts and Marketing Specialists	29,510	30,730	1,220	4.1
Light Truck or Delivery Services Drivers	44,200	45,390	1,190	2.7

Note: Projections cover Pennsylvania; (1) Sorted by numeric employment change
Source: www.projectionscentral.com, State Occupational Projections, 2022–2024 Short-Term Projections

Fastest-Growing Occupations: 2022 – 2024

Occupation[1]	2022 Employment	2024 Projected Employment	Numeric Employment Change	Percent Employment Change
Nurse Practitioners	8,090	8,990	900	11.1
Weighers, Measurers, Checkers, and Samplers, Recordkeeping	2,480	2,720	240	9.7
Machine Feeders and Offbearers	3,430	3,760	330	9.6
Industrial Truck and Tractor Operators	31,030	33,930	2,900	9.3
Occupational Therapy Assistants	2,740	2,940	200	7.3
Statisticians	2,840	3,040	200	7.0
Logisticians	8,310	8,880	570	6.9
Physical Therapist Assistants	5,700	6,090	390	6.8
Information Security Analysts (SOC 2018)	3,780	4,020	240	6.3
Physician Assistants	7,730	8,200	470	6.1

Note: Projections cover Pennsylvania; (1) Sorted by percent employment change and excludes occupations with numeric employment change less than 50
Source: www.projectionscentral.com, State Occupational Projections, 2022–2024 Short-Term Projections

350　Philadelphia, Pennsylvania

CITY FINANCES

City Government Finances

Component	2020 ($000)	2020 ($ per capita)
Total Revenues	9,635,644	6,083
Total Expenditures	9,023,862	5,697
Debt Outstanding	5,348,516	3,376
Cash and Securities[1]	3,655,526	2,308

Note: (1) Cash and security holdings of a government at the close of its fiscal year, including those of its dependent agencies, utilities, and liquor stores.
Source: U.S. Census Bureau, State & Local Government Finances 2020

City Government Revenue by Source

Source	2020 ($000)	2020 ($ per capita)	2020 (%)
General Revenue			
From Federal Government	772,995	488	8.0
From State Government	2,004,897	1,266	20.8
From Local Governments	61,936	39	0.6
Taxes			
Property	696,907	440	7.2
Sales and Gross Receipts	734,860	464	7.6
Personal Income	2,110,662	1,332	21.9
Corporate Income	590,369	373	6.1
Motor Vehicle License	0	0	0.0
Other Taxes	400,439	253	4.2
Current Charges	975,203	616	10.1
Liquor Store	0	0	0.0
Utility	1,119,325	707	11.6

Source: U.S. Census Bureau, State & Local Government Finances 2020

City Government Expenditures by Function

Function	2020 ($000)	2020 ($ per capita)	2020 (%)
General Direct Expenditures			
Air Transportation	388,363	245	4.3
Corrections	361,000	227	4.0
Education	0	0	0.0
Employment Security Administration	0	0	0.0
Financial Administration	101,538	64	1.1
Fire Protection	308,088	194	3.4
General Public Buildings	174,502	110	1.9
Governmental Administration, Other	158,151	99	1.8
Health	1,914,977	1,208	21.2
Highways	235,209	148	2.6
Hospitals	0	0	0.0
Housing and Community Development	462,982	292	5.1
Interest on General Debt	225,046	142	2.5
Judicial and Legal	358,014	226	4.0
Libraries	50,732	32	0.6
Parking	0	0	0.0
Parks and Recreation	74,632	47	0.8
Police Protection	745,747	470	8.3
Public Welfare	218,670	138	2.4
Sewerage	438,297	276	4.9
Solid Waste Management	161,869	102	1.8
Veterans' Services	0	0	0.0
Liquor Store	0	0	0.0
Utility	982,699	620	10.9

Source: U.S. Census Bureau, State & Local Government Finances 2020

TAXES

State Corporate Income Tax Rates

State	Tax Rate (%)	Income Brackets ($)	Num. of Brackets	Financial Institution Tax Rate (%)[a]	Federal Income Tax Ded.
Pennsylvania	8.99	Flat rate	1	(a)	No

Note: Tax rates as of January 1, 2023; (a) Rates listed are the corporate income tax rate applied to financial institutions or excise taxes based on income. Some states have other taxes based upon the value of deposits or shares.
Source: Federation of Tax Administrators, State Corporate Income Tax Rates, January 1, 2023

State Individual Income Tax Rates

State	Tax Rate (%)	Income Brackets ($)	Personal Exemptions ($)			Standard Ded. ($)	
			Single	Married	Depend.	Single	Married
Pennsylvania	3.07	Flat rate	None	None	None	–	–

Note: Tax rates as of January 1, 2023; Local- and county-level taxes are not included; Federal income tax is not deductible on state income tax returns
Source: Federation of Tax Administrators, State Individual Income Tax Rates, January 1, 2023

Various State Sales and Excise Tax Rates

State	State Sales Tax (%)	Gasoline[1] ($/gal.)	Cigarette[2] ($/pack)	Spirits[3] ($/gal.)	Wine[4] ($/gal.)	Beer[5] ($/gal.)	Recreational Marijuana (%)
Pennsylvania	6	0.622	2.60	7.41	–	0.08	Not legal

Note: All tax rates as of January 1, 2023; (1) The American Petroleum Institute has developed a methodology for determining the average tax rate on a gallon of fuel. Rates may include any of the following: excise taxes, environmental fees, storage tank fees, other fees or taxes, general sales tax, and local taxes; (2) The federal excise tax of $1.0066 per pack and local taxes are not included; (3) Rates are those applicable to off-premise sales of 40% alcohol by volume (a.b.v.) distilled spirits in 750ml containers. Local excise taxes are excluded; (4) Rates are those applicable to off-premise sales of 11% a.b.v. non-carbonated wine in 750ml containers; (5) Rates are those applicable to off-premise sales of 4.7% a.b.v. beer in 12 ounce containers.
Source: Tax Foundation, 2023 Facts & Figures: How Does Your State Compare?

State Business Tax Climate Index Rankings

State	Overall Rank	Corporate Tax Rank	Individual Income Tax Rank	Sales Tax Rank	Property Tax Rank	Unemployment Insurance Tax Rank
Pennsylvania	33	42	20	16	16	22

Note: The index is a measure of how each state's tax laws affect economic performance. The lower the rank, the more favorable a state's tax system is for business. States without a given tax are given a ranking of 1. The scores/rankings for the District of Columbia do not affect other states. The 2023 index represents the tax climate as of July 1, 2022.
Source: Tax Foundation, State Business Tax Climate Index 2023

TRANSPORTATION

Means of Transportation to Work

Area	Car/Truck/Van		Public Transportation			Bicycle	Walked	Other Means	Worked at Home
	Drove Alone	Car-pooled	Bus	Subway	Railroad				
City	48.3	7.8	13.5	5.2	2.2	2.0	7.6	2.7	10.8
MSA[1]	68.2	7.1	4.2	1.7	1.7	0.6	3.2	1.5	11.7
U.S.	73.2	8.6	2.0	1.6	0.5	0.5	2.5	1.5	9.7

Note: Figures are percentages and cover workers 16 years of age and older; (1) Figures cover the Philadelphia-Camden-Wilmington, PA-NJ-DE-MD Metropolitan Statistical Area
Source: U.S. Census Bureau, 2017-2021 American Community Survey 5-Year Estimates

Travel Time to Work

Area	Less Than 10 Minutes	10 to 19 Minutes	20 to 29 Minutes	30 to 44 Minutes	45 to 59 Minutes	60 to 89 Minutes	90 Minutes or More
City	6.1	19.2	20.2	28.1	12.9	9.5	4.0
MSA[1]	9.6	23.9	20.6	24.0	11.1	7.8	3.1
U.S.	12.4	28.5	21.0	20.9	8.2	6.2	2.9

Note: Note: Figures are percentages and include workers 16 years old and over; (1) Figures cover the Philadelphia-Camden-Wilmington, PA-NJ-DE-MD Metropolitan Statistical Area
Source: U.S. Census Bureau, 2017-2021 American Community Survey 5-Year Estimates

Key Congestion Measures

Measure	1990	2000	2010	2015	2020
Annual Hours of Delay, Total (000)	61,560	111,501	149,593	163,314	100,726
Annual Hours of Delay, Per Auto Commuter	30	41	50	58	37
Annual Congestion Cost, Per Auto Commuter ($)	830	1,130	1,204	1,215	789

Note: Covers the Philadelphia PA-NJ-DE-MD urban area
Source: Texas A&M Transportation Institute, 2021 Urban Mobility Report

Freeway Travel Time Index

Measure	1985	1990	1995	2000	2005	2010	2015	2020
Urban Area Index[1]	1.12	1.15	1.18	1.21	1.25	1.24	1.24	1.12
Urban Area Rank[1,2]	21	22	26	27	25	24	26	10

Note: Freeway Travel Time Index—the ratio of travel time in the peak period to the travel time at free-flow conditions. For example, a value of 1.30 indicates a 20-minute free-flow trip takes 26 minutes in the peak (20 minutes x 1.30 = 26 minutes); (1) Covers the Philadelphia PA-NJ-DE-MD urban area; (2) Rank is based on 101 larger urban areas (#1 = highest travel time index)
Source: Texas A&M Transportation Institute, 2021 Urban Mobility Report

Public Transportation

Agency Name / Mode of Transportation	Vehicles Operated in Maximum Service[1]	Annual Unlinked Passenger Trips[2] (in thous.)	Annual Passenger Miles[3] (in thous.)
Southeastern Pennsylvania Transportation Authority (SEPTA)			
Bus (directly operated)	1,212	60,285.7	187,793.7
Bus (purchased transportation)	3	21.5	141.6
Commuter Rail (directly operated)	286	6,871.3	92,146.4
Demand Response (purchased transportation)	175	511.6	3,164.7
Heavy Rail (directly operated)	286	28,642.8	126,097.6
Streetcar Rail (directly operated)	108	7,452.8	19,033.1
Trolleybus (directly operated)	29	2,026.4	4,132.8

Note: (1) Number of revenue vehicles operated by the given mode and type of service to meet the annual maximum service requirement. This is the revenue vehicle count during the peak season of the year; on the week and day that maximum service is provided. Vehicles operated in maximum service (VOMS) exclude atypical days and one-time special events; (2) Number of passengers who boarded public transportation vehicles. Passengers are counted each time they board a vehicle no matter how many vehicles they use to travel from their origin to their destination. (3) Sum of the distances ridden by all passengers during the entire fiscal year.
Source: Federal Transit Administration, National Transit Database, 2021

Air Transportation

Airport Name and Code / Type of Service	Passenger Airlines[1]	Passenger Enplanements	Freight Carriers[2]	Freight (lbs)
Philadelphia International (PHL)				
Domestic service (U.S. carriers - 2022)	34	10,889,630	20	462,647,489
International service (U.S. carriers - 2021)	11	431,485	3	113,010,277

Note: (1) Includes all U.S.-based major, minor and commuter airlines that carried at least one passenger during the year; (2) Includes all U.S.-based airlines and freight carriers that transported at least one pound of freight during the year.
Source: Bureau of Transportation Statistics, The Intermodal Transportation Database, Air Carriers: T-100 Domestic Market (U.S. Carriers), 2022; Bureau of Transportation Statistics, The Intermodal Transportation Database, Air Carriers: T-100 International Market (U.S. Carriers), 2021

BUSINESSES

Major Business Headquarters

Company Name	Industry	Rankings	
		Fortune[1]	Forbes[2]
Aramark	Diversified outsourcing services	314	-
Comcast	Telecommunications	28	-
Day & Zimmermann	Construction	-	200
Morgan Lewis & Bockius	Services	-	212

Note: (1) Companies that produce a 10-K are ranked 1 to 500 based on 2021 revenue; (2) All private companies with at least $2 billion in annual revenue through the end of their most current fiscal year are ranked 1 to 246; companies listed are headquartered in the city; dashes indicate no ranking
Source: Fortune, "Fortune 500," 2022; Forbes, "America's Largest Private Companies," 2022

Fastest-Growing Businesses

According to *Inc.*, Philadelphia is home to three of America's 500 fastest-growing private companies: **Printfresh** (#103); **Exyn Technologies** (#177); **PatientWing** (#348). Criteria: must be an independent, privately-held, for-profit, U.S. corporation, proprietorship or partnership as of December 31, 2021; revenues must be at least $100,000 in 2018 and $2 million in 2021; must have four-year operating/sales history. *Inc., "America's 500 Fastest-Growing Private Companies," 2022*

According to *Initiative for a Competitive Inner City (ICIC)*, Philadelphia is home to eight of America's 100 fastest-growing "inner city" companies: **Printfresh** (#1); **Somerset Academy Early Learning Center** (#9); **Sarah Car Care** (#13); **Bennett Compost** (#32); **The Tactile Group** (#35); **Seer Interactive** (#57); **Appletree Childcare & Learning Center** (#78); **Pixel Parlor** (#84). Criteria for inclusion: company must be headquartered in or have 51 percent or more of its physical operations in an economically distressed urban area; must be an independent, for-profit corporation, partnership or proprietorship; must have 10 or more employees and have a five-year sales history that includes sales of at least $200,000 in the base year and at least $1 million in the current year with no decrease in sales over the two most recent years. Companies were ranked overall by revenue growth over the five-year period between 2017 and 2021. *Initiative for a Competitive Inner City (ICIC), "Inner City 100 Companies," 2022*

According to Deloitte, Philadelphia is home to one of North America's 500 fastest-growing high-technology companies: **dbt Labs** (#237). Companies are ranked by percentage growth in revenue over a four-year period. Criteria for inclusion: company must be headquartered within North America; must own proprietary intellectual property or technology that is sold to customers in products that contributes to a significant portion of the company's operating revenue; must have been in business for a minumum of four years with 2018 operating revenues of at least $50,000 USD/CD and 2021 operating revenues of at least $5 million USD/CD. *Deloitte, 2022 Technology Fast 500*[TM]

Living Environment

COST OF LIVING

Cost of Living Index

Composite Index	Groceries	Housing	Utilities	Transportation	Health Care	Misc. Goods/ Services
104.5	117.4	100.0	111.9	109.0	97.1	100.3

Note: The Cost of Living Index measures regional differences in the cost of consumer goods and services, excluding taxes and non-consumer expenditures, for professional and managerial households in the top income quintile. It is based on more than 50,000 prices covering almost 60 different items for which prices are collected three times a year by chambers of commerce, economic development organizations or university applied economic centers in each participating urban area. The numbers shown should be read as a percentage above or below the national average of 100. For example, a value of 115.4 in the groceries column indicates that grocery prices are 15.4% higher than the national average. Small differences in the index numbers should not be interpreted as significant; Figures cover the Philadelphia PA urban area.
Source: The Council for Community and Economic Research, Cost of Living Index, 2022

Grocery Prices

Area[1]	T-Bone Steak ($/pound)	Frying Chicken ($/pound)	Whole Milk ($/half gal.)	Eggs ($/dozen)	Orange Juice ($/64 oz.)	Coffee ($/11.5 oz.)
City[2]	16.43	1.91	2.57	2.47	4.19	5.67
Avg.	13.81	1.59	2.43	2.25	3.85	4.95
Min.	10.17	0.90	1.51	1.30	2.90	3.46
Max.	19.35	3.30	4.32	4.32	5.31	8.59

Note: (1) Values for the local area are compared with the average, minimum and maximum values for all 286 areas in the Cost of Living Index; (2) Figures cover the Philadelphia PA urban area; T-Bone Steak (price per pound); Frying Chicken (price per pound, whole fryer); Whole Milk (half gallon carton); Eggs (price per dozen, Grade A, large); Orange Juice (64 oz. Tropicana or Florida Natural); Coffee (11.5 oz. can, vacuum-packed, Maxwell House, Hills Bros, or Folgers).
Source: The Council for Community and Economic Research, Cost of Living Index, 2022

Housing and Utility Costs

Area[1]	New Home Price ($)	Apartment Rent ($/month)	All Electric ($/month)	Part Electric ($/month)	Other Energy ($/month)	Telephone ($/month)
City[2]	430,067	1,542	-	105.62	103.27	196.34
Avg.	450,913	1,371	176.41	99.93	76.96	190.22
Min.	229,283	546	100.84	31.56	27.15	174.27
Max.	2,434,977	4,569	356.86	249.59	272.24	208.31

Note: (1) Values for the local area are compared with the average, minimum and maximum values for all 286 areas in the Cost of Living Index; (2) Figures cover the Philadelphia PA urban area; New Home Price (2,400 sf living area, 8,000 sf lot, in urban area with full utilities); Apartment Rent (950 sf 2 bedroom/1.5 or 2 bath, unfurnished, excluding all utilities except water); All Electric (average monthly cost for an all-electric home); Part Electric (average monthly cost for a part-electric home); Other Energy (average monthly cost for natural gas, fuel oil, coal, wood, and any other forms of energy except electricity); Telephone (price includes the base monthly rate plus taxes and fees for three lines of mobile phone service).
Source: The Council for Community and Economic Research, Cost of Living Index, 2022

Health Care, Transportation, and Other Costs

Area[1]	Doctor ($/visit)	Dentist ($/visit)	Optometrist ($/visit)	Gasoline ($/gallon)	Beauty Salon ($/visit)	Men's Shirt ($)
City[2]	136.17	96.17	118.67	4.19	63.11	34.67
Avg.	124.91	107.77	117.66	3.86	43.31	34.21
Min.	36.61	58.25	51.79	2.90	22.18	13.05
Max.	250.21	162.58	371.96	5.54	85.61	63.54

Note: (1) Values for the local area are compared with the average, minimum and maximum values for all 286 areas in the Cost of Living Index; (2) Figures cover the Philadelphia PA urban area; Doctor (general practitioners routine exam of an established patient); Dentist (adult teeth cleaning and periodic oral examination); Optometrist (full vision eye exam for established adult patient); Gasoline (one gallon regular unleaded, national brand, including all taxes, cash price at self-service pump if available); Beauty Salon (woman's shampoo, trim, and blow-dry); Men's Shirt (cotton/polyester dress shirt, pinpoint weave, long sleeves).
Source: The Council for Community and Economic Research, Cost of Living Index, 2022

HOUSING

Homeownership Rate

Area	2015 (%)	2016 (%)	2017 (%)	2018 (%)	2019 (%)	2020 (%)	2021 (%)	2022 (%)
MSA[1]	67.0	64.7	65.6	67.4	67.4	69.2	69.8	68.2
U.S.	63.7	63.4	63.9	64.4	64.6	66.6	65.5	65.8

Note: (1) Figures cover the Philadelphia-Camden-Wilmington, PA-NJ-DE-MD Metropolitan Statistical Area
Source: U.S. Census Bureau, Housing Vacancies and Homeownership Annual Statistics: 2015-2022

House Price Index (HPI)

Area	National Ranking[2]	Quarterly Change (%)	One-Year Change (%)	Five-Year Change (%)	Since 1991Q1 (%)
MD[1]	187	1.72	9.32	47.35	257.72
U.S.[3]	–	0.34	8.41	58.44	289.08

Note: The HPI is a weighted repeat sales index. It measures average price changes in repeat sales or refinancings on the same properties. This information is obtained by reviewing repeat mortgage transactions on single-family properties whose mortgages have been purchased or securitized by Fannie Mae or Freddie Mac since January 1975; (1) Figures cover the Philadelphia, PA Metropolitan Division; (2) Rankings are based on annual percentage change for all metro areas containing at least 15,000 transactions over the last 10 years and ranges from 1 to 257; (3) figures based on a weighted average of Census Division estimates using a seasonally adjusted, purchase-only index; all figures are for the period ending December 31, 2022
Source: Federal Housing Finance Agency, Change in FHFA Metropolitan Area House Price Indexes, 2022Q4

Median Single-Family Home Prices

Area	2020	2021	2022p	Percent Change 2021 to 2022
MSA[1]	272.9	305.0	333.1	9.2
U.S. Average	300.2	357.1	392.6	9.9

Note: Figures are median sales prices of existing single-family homes in thousands of dollars; (p) preliminary; (1) Figures cover the Philadelphia-Camden-Wilmington, PA-NJ-DE-MD Metropolitan Statistical Area
Source: National Association of Realtors, Median Sales Price of Existing Single-Family Homes for Metropolitan Areas, 4th Quarter 2022

Qualifying Income Based on Median Sales Price of Existing Single-Family Homes

Area	With 5% Down ($)	With 10% Down ($)	With 20% Down ($)
MSA[1]	98,581	93,393	83,016
U.S. Average	112,234	106,237	94,513

Note: Figures are preliminary; Qualifying income is based on a mortgage rate of 6.77%. Monthly principal and interest payment is limited to 25% of income; (1) Figures cover the Philadelphia-Camden-Wilmington, PA-NJ-DE-MD Metropolitan Statistical Area
Source: National Association of Realtors, Qualifying Income Based on Median Sales Price of Existing Single-Family Homes for Metropolitan Areas, 4th Quarter 2022

Home Value

Area	Under $100,000	$100,000 -$199,999	$200,000 -$299,999	$300,000 -$399,999	$400,000 -$499,999	$500,000 -$999,999	$1,000,000 or more	Median ($)
City	21.6	33.0	22.8	10.0	4.6	6.6	1.4	184,100
MSA[1]	9.6	21.9	25.7	18.4	10.4	12.1	1.8	270,400
U.S.	16.2	24.2	20.1	13.6	8.3	13.6	4.1	244,900

Note: Figures are percentages except for median and cover owner-occupied housing units; (1) Figures cover the Philadelphia-Camden-Wilmington, PA-NJ-DE-MD Metropolitan Statistical Area
Source: U.S. Census Bureau, 2017-2021 American Community Survey 5-Year Estimates

Year Housing Structure Built

Area	2020 or Later	2010 -2019	2000 -2009	1990 -1999	1980 -1989	1970 -1979	1960 -1969	1950 -1959	1940 -1949	Before 1940	Median Year
City	0.1	3.6	3.0	3.2	4.0	7.4	11.1	15.7	11.2	40.7	1948
MSA[1]	0.1	4.3	7.9	9.4	9.8	12.0	12.0	15.3	7.2	22.0	1965
U.S.	0.2	7.3	13.6	13.6	13.2	14.8	10.3	10.0	4.7	12.2	1979

Note: Figures are percentages except for Median Year; Note: (1) Figures cover the Philadelphia-Camden-Wilmington, PA-NJ-DE-MD Metropolitan Statistical Area
Source: U.S. Census Bureau, 2017-2021 American Community Survey 5-Year Estimates

Gross Monthly Rent

Area	Under $500	$500 -$999	$1,000 -$1,499	$1,500 -$1,999	$2,000 -$2,499	$2,500 -$2,999	$3,000 and up	Median ($)
City	9.3	27.7	38.4	15.3	5.5	2.0	1.8	1,149
MSA[1]	7.2	22.3	40.2	19.2	6.7	2.3	2.0	1,230
U.S.	8.1	30.5	30.8	16.8	7.3	3.1	3.5	1,163

Note: Figures are percentages except for median; Gross rent is the contract rent plus the estimated average monthly cost of utilities (electricity, gas, and water and sewer) and fuels (oil, coal, kerosene, wood, etc.) if these are paid by the renter (or paid for the renter by someone else); (1) Figures cover the Philadelphia-Camden-Wilmington, PA-NJ-DE-MD Metropolitan Statistical Area
Source: U.S. Census Bureau, 2017-2021 American Community Survey 5-Year Estimates

HEALTH

Health Risk Factors

Category	MD[1] (%)	U.S. (%)
Adults aged 18–64 who have any kind of health care coverage	92.3	90.9
Adults who reported being in good or better health	80.9	85.2
Adults who have been told they have high blood cholesterol	31.7	35.7
Adults who have been told they have high blood pressure	33.7	32.4
Adults who are current smokers	15.3	14.4
Adults who currently use e-cigarettes	6.4	6.7
Adults who currently use chewing tobacco, snuff, or snus	3.3	3.5
Adults who are heavy drinkers[2]	7.5	6.3
Adults who are binge drinkers[3]	15.0	15.4
Adults who are overweight (BMI 25.0 - 29.9)	31.2	34.4
Adults who are obese (BMI 30.0 - 99.8)	31.9	33.9
Adults who participated in any physical activities in the past month	72.9	76.3

Note: (1) Figures cover the Philadelphia, PA Metropolitan Division; (2) Heavy drinkers are classified as adult men having more than 14 drinks per week and adult women having more than 7 drinks per week; (3) Binge drinkers are classified as males having five or more drinks on one occasion or females having four or more drinks on one occasion
Source: Centers for Disease Control and Prevention, Behaviorial Risk Factor Surveillance System, SMART: Selected Metropolitan Area Risk Trends, 2021

Acute and Chronic Health Conditions

Category	MD[1] (%)	U.S. (%)
Adults who have ever been told they had a heart attack	4.0	4.0
Adults who have ever been told they have angina or coronary heart disease	3.6	3.8
Adults who have ever been told they had a stroke	4.1	3.0
Adults who have ever been told they have asthma	16.3	14.9
Adults who have ever been told they have arthritis	25.2	25.8
Adults who have ever been told they have diabetes[2]	12.6	10.9
Adults who have ever been told they had skin cancer	3.7	6.6
Adults who have ever been told they had any other types of cancer	8.2	7.5
Adults who have ever been told they have COPD	6.9	6.1
Adults who have ever been told they have kidney disease	4.4	3.0
Adults who have ever been told they have a form of depression	19.8	20.5

Note: (1) Figures cover the Philadelphia, PA Metropolitan Division; (2) Figures do not include pregnancy-related, borderline, or pre-diabetes
Source: Centers for Disease Control and Prevention, Behaviorial Risk Factor Surveillance System, SMART: Selected Metropolitan Area Risk Trends, 2021

Health Screening and Vaccination Rates

Category	MD[1] (%)	U.S. (%)
Adults who have ever been tested for HIV	47.7	34.9
Adults who have had their blood cholesterol checked within the last five years	87.2	85.2
Adults aged 65+ who have had flu shot within the past year	65.0	68.6
Adults aged 65+ who have ever had a pneumonia vaccination	68.2	71.0

Note: (1) Figures cover the Philadelphia, PA Metropolitan Division.
Source: Centers for Disease Control and Prevention, Behaviorial Risk Factor Surveillance System, SMART: Selected Metropolitan Area Risk Trends, 2021

Disability Status

Category	MD[1] (%)	U.S. (%)
Adults who reported being deaf	3.9	7.2
Are you blind or have serious difficulty seeing, even when wearing glasses?	5.4	4.8
Are you limited in any way in any of your usual activities due to arthritis?	12.0	11.1
Do you have difficulty doing errands alone?	10.7	7.0
Do you have difficulty dressing or bathing?	5.9	3.6
Do you have serious difficulty concentrating/remembering/making decisions?	14.7	12.1
Do you have serious difficulty walking or climbing stairs?	16.1	12.8

Note: (1) Figures cover the Philadelphia, PA Metropolitan Division.
Source: Centers for Disease Control and Prevention, Behaviorial Risk Factor Surveillance System, SMART: Selected Metropolitan Area Risk Trends, 2021

Mortality Rates for the Top 10 Causes of Death in the U.S.

ICD-10[a] Sub-Chapter	ICD-10[a] Code	Crude Mortality Rate[1] per 100,000 population County[2]	U.S.
Malignant neoplasms	C00-C97	181.7	182.6
Ischaemic heart diseases	I20-I25	123.1	113.1
Other forms of heart disease	I30-I51	65.1	64.4
Other degenerative diseases of the nervous system	G30-G31	23.7	51.0
Cerebrovascular diseases	I60-I69	47.3	47.8
Other external causes of accidental injury	W00-X59	86.7	46.4
Chronic lower respiratory diseases	J40-J47	33.2	45.7
Organic, including symptomatic, mental disorders	F01-F09	32.7	35.9
Hypertensive diseases	I10-I15	38.5	35.0
Diabetes mellitus	E10-E14	26.8	29.6

Note: (a) ICD-10 = International Classification of Diseases 10th Revision; (1) Crude mortality rates are a three-year average covering 2019-2021; (2) Figures cover Philadelphia County.
Source: Centers for Disease Control and Prevention, National Center for Health Statistics. National Vital Statistics System, Mortality 2018-2021 on CDC WONDER Online Database

Mortality Rates for Selected Causes of Death

ICD-10[a] Sub-Chapter	ICD-10[a] Code	Crude Mortality Rate[1] per 100,000 population County[2]	U.S.
Assault	X85-Y09	29.4	7.0
Diseases of the liver	K70-K76	13.1	19.8
Human immunodeficiency virus (HIV) disease	B20-B24	2.4	1.5
Influenza and pneumonia	J09-J18	14.0	14.7
Intentional self-harm	X60-X84	10.9	14.3
Malnutrition	E40-E46	3.3	4.3
Obesity and other hyperalimentation	E65-E68	3.4	3.0
Renal failure	N17-N19	21.1	15.7
Transport accidents	V01-V99	9.9	13.6
Viral hepatitis	B15-B19	1.7	1.2

Note: (a) ICD-10 = International Classification of Diseases 10th Revision; (1) Crude mortality rates are a three-year average covering 2019-2021; (2) Figures cover Philadelphia County; Data are suppressed when the data meet the criteria for confidentiality constraints; Crude mortality rates are flagged as unreliable when the rate would be calculated with a numerator of 20 or less.
Source: Centers for Disease Control and Prevention, National Center for Health Statistics. National Vital Statistics System, Mortality 2018-2021 on CDC WONDER Online Database

Health Insurance Coverage

Area	With Health Insurance	With Private Health Insurance	With Public Health Insurance	Without Health Insurance	Population Under Age 19 Without Health Insurance
City	92.6	57.7	45.8	7.4	4.1
MSA[1]	94.7	73.0	34.8	5.3	3.2
U.S.	91.2	67.8	35.4	8.8	5.3

Note: Figures are percentages that cover the civilian noninstitutionalized population; (1) Figures cover the Philadelphia-Camden-Wilmington, PA-NJ-DE-MD Metropolitan Statistical Area
Source: U.S. Census Bureau, 2017-2021 American Community Survey 5-Year Estimates

Number of Medical Professionals

Area	MDs[3]	DOs[3,4]	Dentists	Podiatrists	Chiropractors	Optometrists
County[1] (number)	9,411	698	1,286	265	242	300
County[1] (rate[2])	587.8	43.6	81.6	16.8	15.4	19.0
U.S. (rate[2])	289.3	23.5	72.5	6.2	28.7	17.4

Note: Data as of 2021 unless noted; (1) Data covers Philadelphia County; (2) Rate per 100,000 population; (3) Data as of 2020 and includes all active, non-federal physicians; (4) Doctor of Osteopathic Medicine
Source: U.S. Department of Health and Human Services, Health Resources and Services Administration, Bureau of Health Professions, Area Resource File (ARF) 2021-2022

Best Hospitals

According to *U.S. News,* the Philadelphia, PA metro area is home to 10 of the best hospitals in the U.S.: **Fox Chase Cancer Center** (1 adult specialty); **Hospitals of the University of Pennsylvania-Penn Presbyterian** (Honor Roll/12 adult specialties); **Jefferson Health-Thomas Jefferson University Hospitals** (9 adult specialties); **Main Line Health Lankenau Medical Center** (1 adult specialty); **MossRehab** (1 adult specialty); **Rothman Orthopaedics at Thomas Jefferson University Hospitals** (9 adult specialties); **Thomas Jefferson University Hospitals-Jane and Leonard Korman Respiratory Institute** (9 adult specialties); **Thomas Jefferson University Hospitals-Sidney Kimmel Cancer Center** (9 adult specialties); **Thomas Jefferson University Hospitals-Vickie and Jack Farber Institute for Neuroscience** (9 adult specialties); **Wills Eye Hospital at Thomas**

358   Philadelphia, Pennsylvania

Jefferson University Hospitals (1 adult specialty). The hospitals listed were nationally ranked in at least one of 15 adult or 10 pediatric specialties. The number of specialties shown cover the parent hospital. Only 164 U.S. hospitals performed well enough to be nationally ranked in one or more specialties. Twenty hospitals in the U.S. made the Honor Roll. The Best Hospitals Honor Roll takes both the national rankings and the procedure and condition ratings into account. Hospitals received points if they were nationally ranked in one of the 15 adult specialties—the higher they ranked, the more points they got—and how many ratings of "high performing" they earned in the 17 procedures and conditions. *U.S. News Online, "America's Best Hospitals 2022-23"*

According to *U.S. News,* the Philadelphia, PA metro area is home to one of the best children's hospitals in the U.S.: **Children's Hospital of Philadelphia** (Honor Roll/10 pediatric specialties). The hospital listed was highly ranked in at least one of 10 pediatric specialties. Eighty-six children's hospitals in the U.S. were nationally ranked in at least one specialty. Hospitals received points for being ranked in a specialty, and the 10 hospitals with the most points across the 10 specialties make up the Honor Roll. *U.S. News Online, "America's Best Children's Hospitals 2022-23"*

EDUCATION

Public School District Statistics

District Name	Schls	Pupils	Pupil/ Teacher Ratio	Minority Pupils[1] (%)	LEP/ELL[2] (%)	IEP[3] (%)
Philadelphia City SD	218	118,053	14.8	85.6	11.7	19.4
Philadelphia Performing Arts CS	1	2,487	15.2	62.4	4.1	16.5

Note: Table includes school districts with 2,000 or more students; (1) Percentage of students that are not non-Hispanic white; (2) Percentage of students that are Limited English Proficient or English Language Learners (2018-19); (3) Percentage of students that have an Individualized Education Program (2019-20).
Source: U.S. Department of Education, National Center for Education Statistics, Common Core of Data, Local Education Agency (School District) Universe Survey: School Year 2021-2022

Best High Schools

According to *U.S. News,* Philadelphia is home to two of the top 500 high schools in the U.S.: **Julia R. Masterman Secondary School** (#10); **Central High School** (#290). Nearly 18,000 public, magnet and charter schools were ranked based on their performance on state assessments and how well they prepare students for college. *U.S. News & World Report, "Best High Schools 2022"*

Highest Level of Education

Area	Less than H.S.	H.S. Diploma	Some College, No Deg.	Associate Degree	Bachelor's Degree	Master's Degree	Prof. School Degree	Doctorate Degree
City	13.4	31.4	16.7	6.0	18.4	9.3	3.0	1.8
MSA[1]	8.4	27.9	16.5	7.3	23.3	11.5	2.9	2.0
U.S.	11.1	26.5	20.0	8.7	20.6	9.3	2.2	1.5

Note: Figures cover persons age 25 and over; (1) Figures cover the Philadelphia-Camden-Wilmington, PA-NJ-DE-MD Metropolitan Statistical Area
Source: U.S. Census Bureau, 2017-2021 American Community Survey 5-Year Estimates

Educational Attainment by Race

Area	High School Graduate or Higher (%)					Bachelor's Degree or Higher (%)				
	Total	White	Black	Asian	Hisp.[2]	Total	White	Black	Asian	Hisp.[2]
City	86.6	91.8	86.9	73.2	71.9	32.5	46.4	19.3	41.4	18.1
MSA[1]	91.6	94.4	89.0	84.5	73.0	39.8	44.5	23.0	58.3	20.7
U.S.	88.9	91.4	87.2	87.6	71.2	33.7	35.5	23.3	55.6	18.4

Note: Figures shown cover persons 25 years old and over; (1) Figures cover the Philadelphia-Camden-Wilmington, PA-NJ-DE-MD Metropolitan Statistical Area; (2) People of Hispanic origin can be of any race
Source: U.S. Census Bureau, 2017-2021 American Community Survey 5-Year Estimates

School Enrollment by Grade and Control

Area	Preschool (%)		Kindergarten (%)		Grades 1 - 4 (%)		Grades 5 - 8 (%)		Grades 9 - 12 (%)	
	Public	Private	Public	Private	Public	Private	Public	Private	Public	Private
City	54.6	45.4	78.1	21.9	79.2	20.8	80.8	19.2	79.4	20.6
MSA[1]	46.2	53.8	81.2	18.8	84.8	15.2	84.6	15.4	83.3	16.7
U.S.	58.8	41.2	86.3	13.7	88.3	11.7	88.6	11.4	89.4	10.6

Note: Figures shown cover persons 3 years old and over; (1) Figures cover the Philadelphia-Camden-Wilmington, PA-NJ-DE-MD Metropolitan Statistical Area
Source: U.S. Census Bureau, 2017-2021 American Community Survey 5-Year Estimates

Higher Education

Four-Year Colleges			Two-Year Colleges			Medical Schools[1]	Law Schools[2]	Voc/ Tech[3]
Public	Private Non-profit	Private For-profit	Public	Private Non-profit	Private For-profit			
7	46	5	9	6	12	7	6	34

Note: Figures cover institutions located within the Philadelphia-Camden-Wilmington, PA-NJ-DE-MD Metropolitan Statistical Area and include main campuses only; (1) includes schools accredited by the Liaison Committee on Medical Education and the American Osteopathic Association's Commission on Osteopathic College Accreditation; (2) includes ABA-accredited schools, schools with provisional ABA accreditation, and state accredited schools; (3) includes all schools with programs that are less than 2 years.
Source: National Center for Education Statistics, Integrated Postsecondary Education System (IPEDS), 2021-22; Wikipedia, List of Medical Schools in the United States, accessed April 10, 2023; Wikipedia, List of Law Schools in the United States, accessed April 10, 2023

According to *U.S. News & World Report,* the Philadelphia, PA metro division is home to five of the top 200 national universities in the U.S.: **University of Pennsylvania** (#7 tie); **Villanova University** (#51 tie); **Drexel University** (#105 tie); **Temple University** (#121 tie); **Thomas Jefferson University** (#127 tie). The indicators used to capture academic quality fall into a number of categories: assessment by administrators at peer institutions; retention of students; faculty resources; student selectivity; financial resources; alumni giving; high school counselor ratings of colleges; and graduation rate. *U.S. News & World Report, "America's Best Colleges 2023"*

According to *U.S. News & World Report,* the Philadelphia, PA metro division is home to two of the top 100 liberal arts colleges in the U.S.: **Swarthmore College** (#4); **Haverford College** (#18 tie). The indicators used to capture academic quality fall into a number of categories: assessment by administrators at peer institutions; retention of students; faculty resources; student selectivity; financial resources; alumni giving; high school counselor ratings of colleges; and graduation rate. *U.S. News & World Report, "America's Best Colleges 2023"*

According to *U.S. News & World Report,* the Philadelphia, PA metro division is home to four of the top 100 law schools in the U.S.: **University of Pennsylvania (Carey)** (#6); **Villanova University (Widger)** (#56 tie); **Temple University (Beasley)** (#63); **Drexel University (Kline)** (#78 tie). The rankings are based on a weighted average of 12 measures of quality: peer assessment score; assessment score by lawyers/judges; median LSAT scores; median undergrad GPA; acceptance rate; employment rates for graduates; placement success; bar passage rate; faculty resources; expenditures per student; student/faculty ratio; and library resources. *U.S. News & World Report, "America's Best Graduate Schools, Law, 2023"*

According to *U.S. News & World Report,* the Philadelphia, PA metro division is home to three of the top 75 medical schools for research in the U.S.: **University of Pennsylvania (Perelman)** (#6 tie); **Thomas Jefferson University (Kimmel)** (#56 tie); **Temple University (Katz)** (#68 tie). The rankings are based on a weighted average of 11 measures of quality: quality assessment; peer assessment score; assessment score by residency directors; research activity; total research activity; average research activity per faculty member; student selectivity; median MCAT total score; median undergraduate GPA; acceptance rate; and faculty resources. *U.S. News & World Report, "America's Best Graduate Schools, Medical, 2023"*

According to *U.S. News & World Report,* the Philadelphia, PA metro division is home to one of the top 75 business schools in the U.S.: **University of Pennsylvania (Wharton)** (#1 tie). The rankings are based on a weighted average of the following nine measures: quality assessment; peer assessment; recruiter assessment; placement success; mean starting salary and bonus; student selectivity; mean GMAT and GRE scores; mean undergraduate GPA; and acceptance rate. *U.S. News & World Report, "America's Best Graduate Schools, Business, 2023"*

360 Philadelphia, Pennsylvania

EMPLOYERS

Major Employers

Company Name	Industry
Abington Memorial Hospital	General medical & surgical hospitals
AstraZeneca Pharmaceuticals	Pharmaceutical preparations
City of Philadelphia	Municipal government
Comcast Holdings Corporation	Cable & other pay television services
Cooper Health Care	Hospital management
E.I. du Pont de Nemours and Company	Agricultural chemicals
Einstein Community Health Associates	Offices & clinics of medical doctors
Glaxosmithkline	Commerical physical research
Lockheed Martin Corporation	Defense systems & equipment
Mercy Health System of SE Pennsylvania	General medical & surgical hospitals
On Time Staffing	Employment agencies
Richlieu Associates	Apartment building operators
Temple University	General medical & surgical hospitals
The University of Pennsylvania	Colleges & universities
The Vanguard Group	Management, investment, open-end
Thomas Jefferson University Hospital	General medical & surgical hospitals
Trustees of the University of Penn	General medical & surgical hospitals
U.S. Navy	U.S. military
Unisys Corporation	Computer integrated systems design
University of Delaware	Colleges & universities

Note: Companies shown are located within the Philadelphia-Camden-Wilmington, PA-NJ-DE-MD Metropolitan Statistical Area.
Source: Hoovers.com; Wikipedia

Best Companies to Work For

Comcast NBCUniversal, headquartered in Philadelphia, is among "The 100 Best Companies to Work For." To pick the best companies, *Fortune* partnered with the Great Place to Work Institute. Two-thirds of a company's score is based on the results of the Institute's Trust Index survey, which is sent to a random sample of employees from each company. The questions related to attitudes about management's credibility, job satisfaction, and camaraderie. The other third of the scoring is based on the company's responses to the Institute's Culture Audit, which includes detailed questions about pay and benefit programs, and a series of open-ended questions about hiring practices, internal communication, training, recognition programs, and diversity efforts. Any company that is at least five years old with more than 1,000 U.S. employees is eligible. *Fortune, "The 100 Best Companies to Work For," 2023*

Comcast NBCUniversal; Dechert, headquartered in Philadelphia, are among "Fortune's Best Workplaces for Women." To pick the best companies, *Fortune* partnered with the Great Place to Work Institute. To be considered for the list, companies must be Great Place To Work-Certified. Companies must also employ at least 50 women, at least 20% of their non-executive managers must be female, and at least one executive must be female. To determine the Best Workplaces for Women, Great Place To Work measured the differences in women's survey responses to those of their peers and assesses the impact of demographics and roles on the quality and consistency of women's experiences. Great Place To Work also analyzed the gender balance of each workplace, how it compared to each company's industry, and patterns in representation as women rise from front-line positions to the board of directors. *Fortune, "Best Workplaces for Women," 2022*

Comcast NBCUniversal; Dechert, headquartered in Philadelphia, are among "Fortune's Best Workplaces for Parents." To pick the best companies, *Fortune* partnered with the Great Place to Work Institute. To be considered for the list, companies must be Great Place To Work-Certified and have at least 50 responses from parents in the US. The survey enables employees to share confidential quantitative and qualitative feedback about their organization's culture by responding to 60 statements on a 5-point scale and answering two open-ended questions. Collectively, these statements describe a great employee experience, defined by high levels of trust, respect, credibility, fairness, pride, and camaraderie. In addition, companies provide organizational data like size, location, industry, demographics, roles, and levels; and provide information about parental leave, adoption, flexible schedule, childcare and dependent health care benefits. *Fortune, "Best Workplaces for Parents," 2022*

Janney Montgomery Scott; TMNA Services (TMNAS), headquartered in Philadelphia, are among the "100 Best Places to Work in IT." To qualify, companies had to have a minimum of 100 total employees and five IT employees. The best places to work were selected based on DEI (diversity, equity, and inclusion) practices; IT turnover, promotions, and growth; IT retention and engagement programs; remote/hybrid working; benefits and perks (such as elder care and child care, flextime, and reimbursement for college tuition); and training and career development opportunities. *Computerworld, "Best Places to Work in IT," 2023*

Philadelphia, Pennsylvania **361**

PUBLIC SAFETY

Crime Rate

Area	Total Crime	Violent Crime Rate				Property Crime Rate		
		Murder	Rape[3]	Robbery	Aggrav. Assault	Burglary	Larceny -Theft	Motor Vehicle Theft
City	4,005.6	22.1	69.0	331.6	486.0	409.4	2,329.5	357.9
Suburbs[1]	1,935.5	7.6	16.3	96.8	235.8	202.8	1,235.3	140.9
Metro[2]	3,462.1	18.3	55.2	270.0	420.3	355.2	2,042.3	300.9
U.S.	2,593.1	5.0	44.0	86.1	248.2	378.0	1,601.6	230.2

Note: Figures are crimes per 100,000 population; (1) All areas within the metro area that are located outside the city limits; (2) Figures cover the Philadelphia, PA Metropolitan Division; (3) All figures shown were reported using the revised Uniform Crime Reporting (UCR) definition of rape; Due to the transition to the National Incident-Based Reporting System (NIBRS), limited city and metro area data was released for 2021.
Source: FBI Uniform Crime Reports, 2018 (data for 2020 was not available)

Hate Crimes

Area	Number of Quarters Reported	Number of Incidents per Bias Motivation					
		Race/Ethnicity/ Ancestry	Religion	Sexual Orientation	Disability	Gender	Gender Identity
City	4	36	9	3	0	0	2
U.S.	4	5,227	1,244	1,110	130	75	266

Note: Due to the transition to the National Incident-Based Reporting System (NIBRS), limited crime data was released for 2021.
Source: Federal Bureau of Investigation, Hate Crime Statistics 2020

Identity Theft Consumer Reports

Area	Reports	Reports per 100,000 Population	Rank[2]
MSA[1]	34,557	567	11
U.S.	1,108,609	339	-

Note: (1) Figures cover the Philadelphia-Camden-Wilmington, PA-NJ-DE-MD Metropolitan Statistical Area; (2) Rank ranges from 1 to 391 where 1 indicates greatest number of identity theft reports per 100,000 population
Source: Federal Trade Commission, Consumer Sentinel Network Data Book 2022

Fraud and Other Consumer Reports

Area	Reports	Reports per 100,000 Population	Rank[2]
MSA[1]	98,616	1,619	5
U.S.	4,064,520	1,245	-

Note: (1) Figures cover the Philadelphia-Camden-Wilmington, PA-NJ-DE-MD Metropolitan Statistical Area; (2) Rank ranges from 1 to 391 where 1 indicates greatest number of fraud and other consumer reports per 100,000 population
Source: Federal Trade Commission, Consumer Sentinel Network Data Book 2022

POLITICS

2020 Presidential Election Results

Area	Biden	Trump	Jorgensen	Hawkins	Other
Philadelphia County	81.2	17.9	0.7	0.1	0.2
U.S.	51.3	46.8	1.2	0.3	0.5

Note: Results are percentages and may not add to 100% due to rounding
Source: Dave Leip's Atlas of U.S. Presidential Elections

SPORTS

Professional Sports Teams

Team Name	League	Year Established
Philadelphia 76ers	National Basketball Association (NBA)	1963
Philadelphia Eagles	National Football League (NFL)	1933
Philadelphia Flyers	National Hockey League (NHL)	1967
Philadelphia Phillies	Major League Baseball (MLB)	1883
Philadelphia Union	Major League Soccer (MLS)	2010

Note: Includes teams located in the Philadelphia-Camden-Wilmington, PA-NJ-DE-MD Metropolitan Statistical Area.
Source: Wikipedia, Major Professional Sports Teams of the United States and Canada, April 12, 2023

362   Philadelphia, Pennsylvania

CLIMATE

Average and Extreme Temperatures

Temperature	Jan	Feb	Mar	Apr	May	Jun	Jul	Aug	Sep	Oct	Nov	Dec	Yr.
Extreme High (°F)	74	74	85	94	96	100	104	101	100	89	84	72	104
Average High (°F)	39	42	51	63	73	82	86	85	78	67	55	43	64
Average Temp. (°F)	32	34	42	53	63	72	77	76	68	57	47	36	55
Average Low (°F)	24	26	33	43	53	62	67	66	59	47	38	28	45
Extreme Low (°F)	-7	-4	7	19	28	44	51	44	35	25	15	1	-7

Note: Figures cover the years 1948-1990
Source: National Climatic Data Center, International Station Meteorological Climate Summary, 9/96

Average Precipitation/Snowfall/Humidity

Precip./Humidity	Jan	Feb	Mar	Apr	May	Jun	Jul	Aug	Sep	Oct	Nov	Dec	Yr.
Avg. Precip. (in.)	3.2	2.8	3.7	3.5	3.7	3.6	4.1	4.0	3.3	2.7	3.4	3.3	41.4
Avg. Snowfall (in.)	7	7	4	Tr	Tr	0	0	0	0	Tr	1	4	22
Avg. Rel. Hum. 7am (%)	74	73	73	72	75	77	80	82	84	83	79	75	77
Avg. Rel. Hum. 4pm (%)	60	55	51	48	51	52	54	55	55	54	57	60	54

Note: Figures cover the years 1948-1990; Tr = Trace amounts (<0.05 in. of rain; <0.5 in. of snow)
Source: National Climatic Data Center, International Station Meteorological Climate Summary, 9/96

Weather Conditions

Temperature			Daytime Sky			Precipitation		
10°F & below	32°F & below	90°F & above	Clear	Partly cloudy	Cloudy	0.01 inch or more precip.	0.1 inch or more snow/ice	Thunderstorms
5	94	23	81	146	138	117	14	27

Note: Figures are average number of days per year and cover the years 1948-1990
Source: National Climatic Data Center, International Station Meteorological Climate Summary, 9/96

HAZARDOUS WASTE

Superfund Sites

The Philadelphia, PA metro division is home to five sites on the EPA's Superfund National Priorities List: **Franklin Slag Pile (MDC)** (final); **Havertown Pcp** (final); **Lower Darby Creek Area** (final); **Metal Bank** (final); **Metro Container Corporation** (final). There are a total of 1,165 Superfund sites with a status of proposed or final on the list in the U.S. *U.S. Environmental Protection Agency, National Priorities List, April 12, 2023*

AIR QUALITY

Air Quality Trends: Ozone

	1990	1995	2000	2005	2010	2015	2018	2019	2020	2021
MSA[1]	0.102	0.109	0.099	0.091	0.083	0.074	0.075	0.067	0.065	0.068
U.S.	0.087	0.089	0.081	0.080	0.072	0.067	0.069	0.065	0.065	0.067

Note: (1) Data covers the Philadelphia-Camden-Wilmington, PA-NJ-DE-MD Metropolitan Statistical Area. The values shown are the composite ozone concentration averages among trend sites based on the highest fourth daily maximum 8-hour concentration in parts per million. These trends are based on sites having an adequate record of monitoring data during the trend period. Data from exceptional events are included.
Source: U.S. Environmental Protection Agency, Air Quality Monitoring Information, "Air Quality Trends by City, 1990-2021"

Air Quality Index

Area	Percent of Days when Air Quality was...[2]					AQI Statistics[2]	
	Good	Moderate	Unhealthy for Sensitive Groups	Unhealthy	Very Unhealthy	Maximum	Median
MSA[1]	49.9	46.0	3.6	0.5	0.0	152	51

Note: (1) Data covers the Philadelphia-Camden-Wilmington, PA-NJ-DE-MD Metropolitan Statistical Area; (2) Based on 365 days with AQI data in 2021. Air Quality Index (AQI) is an index for reporting daily air quality. EPA calculates the AQI for five major air pollutants regulated by the Clean Air Act: ground-level ozone, particle pollution (aka particulate matter), carbon monoxide, sulfur dioxide, and nitrogen dioxide. The AQI runs from 0 to 500. The higher the AQI value, the greater the level of air pollution and the greater the health concern. There are six AQI categories: "Good" AQI is between 0 and 50. Air quality is considered satisfactory; "Moderate" AQI is between 51 and 100. Air quality is acceptable; "Unhealthy for Sensitive Groups" When AQI values are between 101 and 150, members of sensitive groups may experience health effects; "Unhealthy" When AQI values are between 151 and 200 everyone may begin to experience health effects; "Very Unhealthy" AQI values between 201 and 300 trigger a health alert; "Hazardous" AQI values over 300 trigger warnings of emergency conditions (not shown).
Source: U.S. Environmental Protection Agency, Air Quality Index Report, 2021

Air Quality Index Pollutants

Area	Percent of Days when AQI Pollutant was...[2]					
	Carbon Monoxide	Nitrogen Dioxide	Ozone	Sulfur Dioxide	Particulate Matter 2.5	Particulate Matter 10
MSA[1]	0.0	6.0	39.7	(3)	54.0	0.3

Note: (1) Data covers the Philadelphia-Camden-Wilmington, PA-NJ-DE-MD Metropolitan Statistical Area; (2) Based on 365 days with AQI data in 2021. The Air Quality Index (AQI) is an index for reporting daily air quality. EPA calculates the AQI for five major air pollutants regulated by the Clean Air Act: ground-level ozone, particle pollution (also known as particulate matter), carbon monoxide, sulfur dioxide, and nitrogen dioxide. The AQI runs from 0 to 500. The higher the AQI value, the greater the level of air pollution and the greater the health concern; (3) Sulfur dioxide is no longer included in this table (as of December 8, 2021) because SO_2 concentrations tend to be very localized and not necessarily representative of broad geographical areas like counties and CBSAs.
Source: U.S. Environmental Protection Agency, Air Quality Index Report, 2021

Maximum Air Pollutant Concentrations: Particulate Matter, Ozone, CO and Lead

	Particulate Matter 10 (ug/m^3)	Particulate Matter 2.5 Wtd AM (ug/m^3)	Particulate Matter 2.5 24-Hr (ug/m^3)	Ozone (ppm)	Carbon Monoxide (ppm)	Lead (ug/m^3)
MSA[1] Level	60	10.1	25	0.077	1	0
NAAQS[2]	150	15	35	0.075	9	0.15
Met NAAQS[2]	Yes	Yes	Yes	No	Yes	Yes

Note: (1) Data covers the Philadelphia-Camden-Wilmington, PA-NJ-DE-MD Metropolitan Statistical Area; Data from exceptional events are included; (2) National Ambient Air Quality Standards; ppm = parts per million; ug/m^3 = micrograms per cubic meter; n/a not available.
Concentrations: Particulate Matter 10 (coarse particulate)—highest second maximum 24-hour concentration; Particulate Matter 2.5 Wtd AM (fine particulate)—highest weighted annual mean concentration; Particulate Matter 2.5 24-Hour (fine particulate)—highest 98th percentile 24-hour concentration; Ozone—highest fourth daily maximum 8-hour concentration; Carbon Monoxide—highest second maximum non-overlapping 8-hour concentration; Lead—maximum running 3-month average
Source: U.S. Environmental Protection Agency, Air Quality Monitoring Information, "Air Quality Statistics by City, 2021"

Maximum Air Pollutant Concentrations: Nitrogen Dioxide and Sulfur Dioxide

	Nitrogen Dioxide AM (ppb)	Nitrogen Dioxide 1-Hr (ppb)	Sulfur Dioxide AM (ppb)	Sulfur Dioxide 1-Hr (ppb)	Sulfur Dioxide 24-Hr (ppb)
MSA[1] Level	14	54	n/a	6	n/a
NAAQS[2]	53	100	30	75	140
Met NAAQS[2]	Yes	Yes	n/a	Yes	n/a

Note: (1) Data covers the Philadelphia-Camden-Wilmington, PA-NJ-DE-MD Metropolitan Statistical Area; Data from exceptional events are included; (2) National Ambient Air Quality Standards; ppm = parts per million; ug/m^3 = micrograms per cubic meter; n/a not available.
Concentrations: Nitrogen Dioxide AM—highest arithmetic mean concentration; Nitrogen Dioxide 1-Hr—highest 98th percentile 1-hour daily maximum concentration; Sulfur Dioxide AM—highest annual mean concentration; Sulfur Dioxide 1-Hr—highest 99th percentile 1-hour daily maximum concentration; Sulfur Dioxide 24-Hr—highest second maximum 24-hour concentration
Source: U.S. Environmental Protection Agency, Air Quality Monitoring Information, "Air Quality Statistics by City, 2021"

Pittsburgh, Pennsylvania

Background

Pittsburgh was once the creaking, croaking, belching giant of heavy industry. Thanks to a plentiful supply of bituminous coal beds and limestone deposits nearby, the city forged a prosperous economy based on steel, glass, rubber, petroleum, and machinery. Unregulated spews of soot into the air by these factories earned Pittsburgh the title of "Smoky City," prompting concerned citizens and politicians to pass smoke-control laws. Today, Pittsburgh's renaissance is a result of its citizens' unflagging faith.

In the eighteenth century, the area in and around the Ohio Valley and the Allegheny River, where present-day Pittsburgh lies, was claimed by both the British and the French. After being lobbed back and forth between the two, the land finally fell into British hands. The city was named Pittsborough, for the British prime minister at the time, William Pitt.

Almost immediately, the city showed signs of what it was to become. In 1792, the first blast furnace was built by George Anschulz. In 1797, the first glass factory was opened, and in 1804, the first cotton factory. Irish, Scottish, and a smattering of English immigrants provided the labor pool for these factories. During the Civil War, a wave of German immigrant workers swept in. During the late nineteenth century, Poles, Czechs, Slovaks, Italians, Russians, and Hungarians completed the picture in the colorful quilt of Pittsburgh's workforce. The last wave particularly contributed their sweat and toil to the fortunes of captains of industry such as Andrew Carnegie, Henry Clay Frick, and Charles M. Schwab.

Fortunately for Pittsburgh, these industrialists gave back to the city in the form of their cultural and educational patronage. The Carnegie Museum of Natural History has an extensive dinosaur collection and ancient Egypt wing. The Frick Art & Historical Center holds a noted private collection featuring such artists as Rubens, Tintoretto, Fragonard, and Boucher. Other educational and cultural attractions include the Pittsburgh Ballet Theatre, Pittsburgh Opera, Pittsburgh Civic Light Opera, Pittsburgh Symphony Orchestra, Pittsburgh Broadway Across America series, Carnegie Science Center, Phipps Conservatory and Botanical Gardens, Pittsburgh Zoo and PPG Aquarium, Children's Museum of Pittsburgh, Johnstown Flood Museum, Rachel Carson Homestead, and the Andy Warhol Museum.

By the late 1990s, Pittsburgh was showing tremendous growth. Technology and health care services, their manufacturing counterparts, and financial institutions were dominant forces behind a steadily diversifying economy. Today, the city's economy depends on services, medicine, higher education, tourism, banking, and technology. Although the city has no steel mills within its limits, Pittsburgh-based companies US Steel, Ampco Pittsburgh, and Allegheny Technologies own working mills in the Pittsburgh metro area. The city was the site of the 2009 G-20 summit as its transformation is an example of a 21st century economy, and is home to eight Fortune 500 companies.

An incredible amount of downtown building has occurred in recent years. Two downtown stadiums were opened in 2001: PNC Park for the Pittsburgh Pirates baseball team, and Heinz Field for the Steelers football team, 2009 Superbowl XLII champions. PNC Park is built along the lines of traditional two-tier ballparks, providing spectators intimate contact with the game. Heinz Field is an open, natural-turf field with stands in a horseshoe shape, the open-end affording visitors a magnificent view of the Pittsburgh skyline.

In September 2003, the city inaugurated its handsome riverfront David L. Lawrence Convention Center, the first and largest certified "green" convention center, which provides 330,000 square feet of exhibition space, meeting rooms, two lecture halls, and a 35,000 square-foot ballroom. The Pittsburgh Cultural Trust completed 700 residential units and multiple towers. This area is home to the PPG Place gothic glass skyscraper complex as well as resident condo towers that comprise both new construction and conversion of historic office towers. Downtown is serviced by a subway, buses and multiple bridges leading north and south.

Pittsburgh has ranked high in several "Most Livable City" lists for nearly 40 years, with criteria including cost of living, crime, and cultural opportunities. Pittsburgh has a low cost of living compared to other northeastern U.S. cities. Pittsburgh has five city parks and several others managed by the Nature Conservancy. Birding enthusiasts love to visit the Clayton Hill area of Frick Park, where well over 100 species of birds have been recorded

Pittsburgh is a little over 100 miles southeast of Lake Erie. Its nearness to the Great Lakes and to the Atlantic Seaboard helps to modify its humid, continental climate. Winter is influenced primarily by Canadian air masses. During the summer, Gulf air brings warm, humid weather. Once every four years, the Monongahela and Ohio rivers combine, causing the Ohio River to reach flood stage.

Rankings

General Rankings

- The human resources consulting firm Mercer ranked 231 major cities worldwide in terms of overall quality of life. Pittsburgh ranked #59. Criteria: political, social, economic, and socio-cultural factors; medical and health considerations; schools and education; public services and transportation; recreation; consumer goods; housing; and natural environment. *Mercer, "Mercer 2019 Quality of Living Survey," March 13, 2019*

- In their ninth annual survey, Livability.com looked at data for more than 2,300 mid-sized U.S. cities to determine the rankings for Livability's "Top 100 Best Places to Live" in 2022. Pittsburgh ranked #9. Criteria: housing and economy; social and civic engagement; education; demographics; health care options; transportation & infrastructure; and community amenities. *Livability.com, "Top 100 Best Places to Live 2022" July 19, 2022*

Business/Finance Rankings

- WalletHub's latest report ranked over 2,500 cities by the average credit score of its residents. Pittsburgh was ranked #4 among the ten cities with the lowest average credit score, based on TransUnion data as of October 2022. *www.wallethub.com, "2023's Cities With the Highest & Lowest Credit Scores," March 29, 2023*

- Based on metro area social media reviews, the employment opinion group Glassdoor surveyed 50 of the most populous U.S. metro areas and equally weighed cost of living, hiring opportunity, and job satisfaction to compose a list of "25 Best Cities for Jobs." Median pay and home value, and number of active job openings were also factored in. The Pittsburgh metro area was ranked #2 in overall job satisfaction. *www.glassdoor.com, "Best Cities for Jobs," February 25, 2020*

- The Brookings Institution ranked the nation's largest cities based on income inequality. Pittsburgh was ranked #27 (#1 = greatest inequality). Criteria: the "95/20 ratio," a figure representing the income at which a household earns more than 95 percent of all other households, divided by the income at which a household earns more than only 20 percent of all other households. *Brookings Institution, "Household Income Inequality, Largest Cities of 97 Large U.S. Metro Areas, 2014-2016," February 5, 2018*

- The Brookings Institution ranked the 100 largest metro areas in the U.S. based on income inequality. Pittsburgh was ranked #34 (#1 = greatest inequality). Criteria: the "95/20 ratio," a figure representing the income at which a household earns more than 95 percent of all other households, divided by the income at which a household earns more than only 20 percent of all other households. *Brookings Institution, "Household Income Inequality, 100 Largest U.S. Metro Areas, 2014-2016," February 5, 2018*

- Payscale.com ranked the 32 largest metro areas in terms of wage growth. The Pittsburgh metro area ranked #20. Criteria: quarterly changes in private industry employee and education professional wage growth from the previous year. *PayScale, "Wage Trends by Metro Area-1st Quarter," April 20, 2023*

- Pittsburgh was identified as one of America's most frugal metro areas by *Coupons.com*. The city ranked #25 out of 25. Criteria: digital coupon usage. *Coupons.com, "America's Most Frugal Cities of 2017," March 22, 2018*

- The Pittsburgh metro area appeared on the Milken Institute "2022 Best Performing Cities" list. Rank: #153 out of 200 large metro areas (population over 250,000). Criteria: job growth; wage and salary growth; high-tech output growth; housing affordability; household broadband access. *Milken Institute, "Best-Performing Cities 2022," March 28, 2022*

- *Forbes* ranked the 200 most populous metro areas to determine the nation's "Best Places for Business and Careers." The Pittsburgh metro area was ranked #114. Criteria: costs (business and living); job growth (past and projected); income growth; quality of life; educational attainment (college and high school); projected economic growth; cultural and leisure opportunities; workplace tolerance laws; net migration patterns. *Forbes, "The Best Places for Business and Careers 2019: Seattle Still On Top," October 30, 2019*

- Mercer Human Resources Consulting ranked 227 cities worldwide in terms of cost-of-living. Pittsburgh ranked #82 (the lower the ranking, the higher the cost-of-living). The survey measured the comparative cost of over 200 items (such as housing, food, clothing, domestic supplies, transportation, and recreation/entertainment) in each location. *Mercer, "2022 Cost of Living City Ranking," June 29, 2022*

Children/Family Rankings

- Pittsburgh was selected as one of the most playful cities in the U.S. by KaBOOM! The organization's Playful City USA initiative honors cities and towns across the nation that have made their communities more playable. Criteria: pledging to integrate play as a solution to challenges in their communities; making it easy for children to get active and balanced play; creating more family-friendly and innovative communities as a result. *KaBOOM! National Campaign for Play, "2017 Playful City USA Communities"*

Culture/Performing Arts Rankings

- Pittsburgh was selected as one of the 25 best cities for moviemakers in North America. Great film cities are places where filmmaking dreams can come true, that offer more creative space, lower costs, and great outdoor locations. NYC & LA were intentionally excluded. Criteria: longstanding reputations as film-friendly communities; film community and culture; affordability; and quality of life. The city was ranked #10. *MovieMaker Magazine, "Best Places to Live and Work as a Moviemaker, 2023," January 18, 2023*

- Pittsburgh was selected as one of "America's Favorite Cities." The city ranked #11 in the "Architecture " category. Respondents to an online survey were asked to rate their favorite place (population over 100,000) in over 65 categories. *Travelandleisure.com, "America's Favorite Cities for Architecture 2016," March 2, 2017*

Dating/Romance Rankings

- Pittsburgh was selected as one of the nation's most romantic cities with 100,000 or more residents by Amazon.com. The city ranked #8 of 20. Criteria: per capita sales of romance novels, relationship books, romantic comedy movies, romantic music, and sexual wellness products. *Amazon.com, "Top 20 Most Romantic Cities in the U.S.," February 1, 2017*

Education Rankings

- Personal finance website *WalletHub* analyzed the 150 largest U.S. metropolitan statistical areas to determine where the most educated Americans are putting their degrees to work. Criteria: education levels; percentage of workers with degrees; education quality and attainment gap; public school quality rankings; quality and enrollment of each metro area's universities. Pittsburgh was ranked #33 (#1 = most educated city). *www.WalletHub.com, "Most & Least Educated Cities in America, " July 18, 2022*

- Pittsburgh was selected as one of America's most literate cities. The city ranked #9 out of the 84 largest U.S. cities. Criteria: number of booksellers; library resources; Internet resources; educational attainment; periodical publishing resources; newspaper circulation. *Central Connecticut State University, "America's Most Literate Cities, 2018," February 2019*

Environmental Rankings

- Pittsburgh was highlighted as one of the 25 metro areas most polluted by year-round particle pollution (Annual PM 2.5) in the U.S. during 2019 through 2021. The area ranked #14. *American Lung Association, "State of the Air 2023," April 19, 2023*

- Pittsburgh was highlighted as one of the 25 metro areas most polluted by short-term particle pollution (24-hour PM 2.5) in the U.S. during 2019 through 2021. The area ranked #20. *American Lung Association, "State of the Air 2023," April 19, 2023*

Health/Fitness Rankings

- For each of the 100 largest cities in the United States, the American Fitness Index®, compiled in partnership between the American College of Sports Medicine and the Elevance Health Foundation, evaluated community infrastructure and 34 health behaviors including preventive health, levels of chronic disease conditions, food insecurity, sleep quality, pedestrian safety, air quality, and community/environment resources that support physical activity. Pittsburgh ranked #38 for "community fitness." *americanfitnessindex.org, "2022 ACSM American Fitness Index Summary Report," July 12, 2022*

- The Pittsburgh metro area was identified as one of the worst cities for bed bugs in America by pest control company Orkin. The area ranked #18 out of 50 based on the number of bed bug treatments Orkin performed from December 2021 to November 2022. *Orkin, "The Windy City Can't Blow Bed Bugs Away: Chicago Ranks #1 For Third Consecutive Year On Orkin's Bed Bug Cities List," January 9, 2023*

- Pittsburgh was identified as a "2022 Spring Allergy Capital." The area ranked #27 out of 100. Three groups of factors were used to identify the most challenging cities for people with allergies during the spring season: annual spring pollen scores; over the counter allergy medicine use; number of board-certified allergy specialists. *Asthma and Allergy Foundation of America, "Spring Allergy Capitals 2022," March 2, 2022*

- Pittsburgh was identified as a "2022 Fall Allergy Capital." The area ranked #24 out of 100. Three groups of factors were used to identify the most challenging cities for people with allergies during the fall season: annual fall pollen scores; over the counter allergy medicine use; number of board-certified allergy specialists. *Asthma and Allergy Foundation of America, "Fall Allergy Capitals 2022," March 2, 2022*

- Pittsburgh was identified as a "2022 Asthma Capital." The area ranked #50 out of the nation's 100 largest metropolitan areas. Criteria: estimated asthma prevalence; asthma-related mortality; and ER visits due to asthma. Risk factors analyzed but not factored in the rankings: annual pollen score; annual air quality; public smoking laws; access to board-certified asthma specialists; rescue and controller medication use; uninsured rate; poverty rate. *Asthma and Allergy Foundation of America, "Asthma Capitals 2022: The Most Challenging Places to Live With Asthma," September 14, 2022*

Real Estate Rankings

- *WalletHub* compared the most populated U.S. cities to determine which had the best markets for real estate agents. Pittsburgh ranked #112 where demand was high and pay was the best. Criteria: sales per agent; annual median wage for real-estate agents; monthly average starting salary for real estate agents; real estate job density and competition; unemployment rate; home turnover rate; housing-market health index; and other relevant metrics. *www.WalletHub.com, "2021 Best Places to Be a Real Estate Agent," May 12, 2021*

- Pittsburgh was ranked #22 out of 235 metro areas in terms of housing affordability in 2022 by the National Association of Home Builders (#1 = most affordable). Criteria: the share of homes sold in that area affordable to a family earning the local median income, based on standard mortgage underwriting criteria. *National Association of Home Builders®, NAHB-Wells Fargo Housing Opportunity Index, 4th Quarter 2022*

Safety Rankings

- Allstate ranked the 200 largest cities in America in terms of driver safety. Pittsburgh ranked #167. Criteria: internal property damage claims over a two-year period from January 2016 to December 2017. The report helps increase the importance of safety and awareness behind the wheel. *Allstate, "Allstate America's Best Drivers Report, 2019" June 24, 2019*

- The National Insurance Crime Bureau ranked 390 metro areas in the U.S. in terms of per capita rates of vehicle theft. The Pittsburgh metro area ranked #341 (#1 = highest rate). Criteria: number of vehicle theft offenses per 100,000 inhabitants in 2021. *National Insurance Crime Bureau, "Hot Spots 2021," September 1, 2022*

Seniors/Retirement Rankings

- From its Best Cities for Successful Aging indexes, the Milken Institute generated rankings for metropolitan areas, weighing data in nine categories—health care, wellness, living arrangements, transportation and convenience, financial characteristics, education, employment, community engagement, and overall livability. The Pittsburgh metro area was ranked #44 overall in the large metro area category. *Milken Institute, "Best Cities for Successful Aging, 2017" March 14, 2017*

- Pittsburgh made the 2022 *Forbes* list of "25 Best Places to Retire." Criteria, focused on overall affordability as well as quality of life indicators, include: housing/living costs compared to the national average and state taxes; air quality; crime rates; home price appreciation; risk associated with climate-change/natural hazards; availability of medical care; bikeability; walkability; healthy living. *Forbes.com, "The Best Places to Retire in 2022," May 13, 2022*

Sports/Recreation Rankings

- Pittsburgh was chosen as one of America's best cities for bicycling. The city ranked #40 out of 50. Criteria: cycling infrastructure that is safe and friendly for all ages; energy and bike culture. The editors evaluated cities with populations of 100,000 or more. *Bicycling, "The 50 Best Bike Cities in America," October 10, 2018*

Transportation Rankings

- Business Insider presented an AllTransit Performance Score ranking of public transportation in major U.S. cities and towns, with populations over 250,000, in which Pittsburgh earned the #15-ranked "Transit Score," awarded for frequency of service, access to jobs, quality and number of stops, and affordability. *www.businessinsider.com, "The 17 Major U.S. Cities with the Best Public Transportation," April 17, 2018*

Women/Minorities Rankings

- Pittsburgh was selected as one of the queerest cities in America by *The Advocate*. The city ranked #8 out of 25. Criteria, among many: Trans Pride parades/festivals; gay rugby teams; lesbian bars; LGBTQ centers; theater screenings of "Moonlight"; LGBTQ-inclusive nondiscrimination ordinances; and gay bowling teams. *The Advocate, "Queerest Cities in America 2017" January 12, 2017*

- Personal finance website *WalletHub* compared more than 180 U.S. cities across two key dimensions, "Hispanic Business-Friendliness" and "Hispanic Purchasing Power," to arrive at the most favorable conditions for Hispanic entrepreneurs. Pittsburgh was ranked #97 out of 182. Criteria includes: share of Hispanic-Owned Businesses; Hispanic entrepreneurship rate to median annual income of Hispanics; Small Business-Friendliness score; cost of living; and number of Hispanics with at least a bachelor's degree. *WalletHub.com, "2019's Best Cities for Hispanic Entrepreneurs," May 1, 2019*

Miscellaneous Rankings

- *MoveHub* ranked 446 hipster cities across 20 countries, using its new and improved *alternative* Hipster Index and Pittsburgh came out as #18 among the top 50. Criteria: population over 150,000; number of vintage boutiques; density of tattoo parlors; vegan places to eat; coffee shops; and density of vinyl record stores. *www.movehub.com, "The Hipster Index: Brighton Pips Portland to Global Top Spot," July 28, 2021*

- The watchdog site, Charity Navigator, conducted a study of charities in major markets both to analyze statistical differences in their financial, accountability, and transparency practices and to track year-to-year variations in individual philanthropic communities. The Pittsburgh metro area was ranked #27 among the 30 metro markets in the rating category of Overall Score. *www.charitynavigator.org, "2017 Metro Market Study," May 1, 2017*

- *WalletHub* compared the 150 most populated U.S. cities to determine their operating efficiency. A "Quality of Services" score was constructed for each city and then divided by the total budget per capita to reveal which were managed the best. Pittsburgh ranked #120. Criteria: financial stability; economy; education; safety; health; infrastructure and pollution. *www.WalletHub.com, "2022's Best- & Worst-Run Cities in America," June 21, 2022*

- Pittsburgh was selected as one of "America's Friendliest Cities." The city ranked #12 in the "Friendliest" category. Respondents to an online survey were asked to rate 38 top urban destinations in the United States as to general friendliness, as well as manners, politeness and warm disposition. *Travel + Leisure, "America's Friendliest Cities," October 20, 2017*

Business Environment

370 Pittsburgh, Pennsylvania

DEMOGRAPHICS

Population Growth

Area	1990 Census	2000 Census	2010 Census	2020 Census	Population Growth (%)	
					1990-2020	2010-2020
City	369,785	334,563	305,704	302,971	-18.1	-0.9
MSA[1]	2,468,289	2,431,087	2,356,285	2,370,930	-3.9	0.6
U.S.	248,709,873	281,421,906	308,745,538	331,449,281	33.3	7.4

Note: (1) Figures cover the Pittsburgh, PA Metropolitan Statistical Area
Source: U.S. Census Bureau, 1990 Census, 2000 Census, 2010 Census, 2020 Census

Race

Area	White Alone[2] (%)	Black Alone[2] (%)	Asian Alone[2] (%)	AIAN[3] Alone[2] (%)	NHOPI[4] Alone[2] (%)	Other Race Alone[2] (%)	Two or More Races (%)
City	62.7	22.8	6.5	0.2	0.0	1.8	5.9
MSA[1]	82.7	8.4	2.9	0.1	0.0	0.9	4.9
U.S.	61.6	12.4	6.0	1.1	0.2	8.4	10.2

Note: (1) Figures cover the Pittsburgh, PA Metropolitan Statistical Area; (2) Alone is defined as not being in combination with one or more other races; (3) American Indian and Alaska Native; (4) Native Hawaiian and Other Pacific Islander
Source: U.S. Census Bureau, 2020 Census

Hispanic or Latino Origin

Area	Total (%)	Mexican (%)	Puerto Rican (%)	Cuban (%)	Other (%)
City	3.5	1.2	0.7	0.1	1.6
MSA[1]	1.9	0.6	0.5	0.1	0.7
U.S.	18.4	11.2	1.8	0.7	4.7

Note: Persons of Hispanic or Latino origin can be of any race; (1) Figures cover the Pittsburgh, PA Metropolitan Statistical Area
Source: U.S. Census Bureau, 2017-2021 American Community Survey 5-Year Estimates

Age

Area	Percent of Population									Median Age
	Under Age 5	Age 5–19	Age 20–34	Age 35–44	Age 45–54	Age 55–64	Age 65–74	Age 75–84	Age 85+	
City	4.4	14.5	34.3	11.5	8.8	11.1	9.1	4.2	2.0	33.0
MSA[1]	4.9	16.3	19.3	11.8	12.1	14.9	12.0	5.9	2.8	42.9
U.S.	5.6	19.2	20.2	12.7	12.4	13.1	10.0	4.9	1.9	38.8

Note: (1) Figures cover the Pittsburgh, PA Metropolitan Statistical Area
Source: U.S. Census Bureau, 2020 Census

Disability by Age

Area	All Ages	Under 18 Years Old	18 to 64 Years Old	65 Years and Over
City	14.3	7.7	11.3	35.4
MSA[1]	14.4	5.7	11.3	32.5
U.S.	12.6	4.4	10.3	33.4

Note: Figures show percent of the civilian noninstitutionalized population that reported having a disability. Disability status is determined from six types of difficulty: vision, hearing, cognitive, ambulatory, self-care, and independent living. For children under 5 years old, hearing and vision difficulty are used to determine disability status. For children between the ages of 5 and 14, disability status is determined from hearing, vision, cognitive, ambulatory, and self-care difficulties. For people aged 15 years and older, they are considered to have a disability if they have difficulty with any one of the six difficulty types; Note: (1) Figures cover the Pittsburgh, PA Metropolitan Statistical Area
Source: U.S. Census Bureau, 2017-2021 American Community Survey 5-Year Estimates

Ancestry

Area	German	Irish	English	American	Italian	Polish	French[2]	Scottish	Dutch
City	17.9	13.8	5.4	3.0	12.1	6.7	1.4	1.3	0.5
MSA[1]	25.1	17.0	8.6	3.3	15.2	8.1	1.6	1.9	1.0
U.S.	12.8	9.6	8.1	5.7	5.0	2.7	2.2	1.6	1.1

Note: Figures are the percentage of the total population reporting a particular ancestry. The nine most commonly reported ancestries in the U.S. are shown. Figures include multiple ancestries (e.g. if a person reported being Irish and Italian, they were included in both columns); (1) Figures cover the Pittsburgh, PA Metropolitan Statistical Area; (2) Excludes Basque
Source: U.S. Census Bureau, 2017-2021 American Community Survey 5-Year Estimates

Foreign-born Population

Area	Percent of Population Born in								
	Any Foreign Country	Asia	Mexico	Europe	Caribbean	Central America[2]	South America	Africa	Canada
City	9.0	4.5	0.3	1.8	0.4	0.1	0.5	1.0	0.3
MSA[1]	4.1	2.0	0.1	0.9	0.2	0.1	0.2	0.3	0.1
U.S.	13.6	4.2	3.3	1.5	1.4	1.1	1.1	0.8	0.2

Note: (1) Figures cover the Pittsburgh, PA Metropolitan Statistical Area; (2) Excludes Mexico.
Source: U.S. Census Bureau, 2017-2021 American Community Survey 5-Year Estimates

Household Size

Area	Persons in Household (%)							Average Household Size
	One	Two	Three	Four	Five	Six	Seven or More	
City	44.2	32.4	12.4	6.8	2.5	1.1	0.6	2.00
MSA[1]	33.8	35.4	14.1	10.7	4.1	1.3	0.5	2.30
U.S.	28.1	33.8	15.5	12.9	6.0	2.3	1.4	2.60

Note: (1) Figures cover the Pittsburgh, PA Metropolitan Statistical Area
Source: U.S. Census Bureau, 2017-2021 American Community Survey 5-Year Estimates

Household Relationships

Area	House-holder	Opposite-sex Spouse	Same-sex Spouse	Opposite-sex Unmarried Partner	Same-sex Unmarried Partner	Child[2]	Grand-child	Other Relatives	Non-relatives
City	46.1	11.5	0.3	3.6	0.4	19.3	1.7	3.1	6.7
MSA[1]	43.2	19.0	0.2	2.8	0.2	25.6	1.6	2.6	2.4
U.S.	38.3	17.5	0.2	2.5	0.2	28.3	2.4	4.8	3.4

Note: Figures are percent of the total population; (1) Figures cover the Pittsburgh, PA Metropolitan Statistical Area; (2) Includes biological, adopted, and stepchildren of the householder
Source: U.S. Census Bureau, 2020 Census

Gender

Area	Males	Females	Males per 100 Females
City	148,157	154,814	95.7
MSA[1]	1,157,964	1,212,966	95.5
U.S.	162,685,811	168,763,470	96.4

Note: (1) Figures cover the Pittsburgh, PA Metropolitan Statistical Area
Source: U.S. Census Bureau, 2020 Census

Marital Status

Area	Never Married	Now Married[2]	Separated	Widowed	Divorced
City	53.1	30.4	1.9	5.4	9.2
MSA[1]	32.6	48.7	1.7	6.9	10.1
U.S.	33.8	48.0	1.8	5.6	10.8

Note: Figures are percentages and cover the population 15 years of age and older; (1) Figures cover the Pittsburgh, PA Metropolitan Statistical Area; (2) Excludes separated
Source: U.S. Census Bureau, 2017-2021 American Community Survey 5-Year Estimates

Religious Groups by Family

Area	Catholic	Baptist	Methodist	LDS[2]	Pentecostal	Lutheran	Islam	Adventist	Other
MSA[1]	30.6	1.9	4.3	0.4	1.3	2.5	0.6	0.6	12.5
U.S.	18.7	7.3	3.0	2.0	1.8	1.7	1.3	1.3	11.6

Note: Figures are the number of adherents as a percentage of the total population and cover the eight largest religious groups in the U.S; (1) Figures cover the Pittsburgh, PA Metropolitan Statistical Area; (2) Church of Jesus Christ of Latter-day Saints
Sources: 2020 U.S. Religion Census, Association of Statisticians of American Religious Bodies; The Association of Religion Data Archives (ARDA)

Religious Groups by Tradition

Area	Catholic	Evangelical Protestant	Mainline Protestant	Black Protestant	Islam	Judaism	Hinduism	Orthodox	Buddhism
MSA[1]	30.6	8.8	10.1	1.3	0.6	0.6	1.2	0.6	0.1
U.S.	18.7	16.5	5.2	2.3	1.3	0.6	0.4	0.4	0.3

Note: Figures are the number of adherents as a percentage of the total population; (1) Figures cover the Pittsburgh, PA Metropolitan Statistical Area
Sources: 2020 U.S. Religion Census, Association of Statisticians of American Religious Bodies; The Association of Religion Data Archives (ARDA)

372 Pittsburgh, Pennsylvania

ECONOMY

Gross Metropolitan Product

Area	2020	2021	2022	2023	Rank[2]
MSA[1]	153.4	165.5	178.3	189.7	26

Note: Figures are in billions of dollars; (1) Figures cover the Pittsburgh, PA Metropolitan Statistical Area; (2) Rank is based on 2021 data and ranges from 1 to 381
Source: U.S. Conference of Mayors, U.S. Metro Economies: U.S. Metros Compared to Global and State Economies, June 2022

Economic Growth

Area	2018-20 (%)	2021 (%)	2022 (%)	2023 (%)	Rank[2]
MSA[1]	-1.6	3.8	1.9	3.1	257
U.S.	-0.6	5.7	3.1	2.9	—

Note: Figures are real gross metropolitan product (GMP) growth rates and represent average annual percent change; (1) Figures cover the Pittsburgh, PA Metropolitan Statistical Area; (2) Rank is based on 2020 2-year average annual percent change and ranges from 1 to 381
Source: U.S. Conference of Mayors, U.S. Metro Economies: U.S. Metros Compared to Global and State Economies, June 2022

Metropolitan Area Exports

Area	2016	2017	2018	2019	2020	2021	Rank[2]
MSA[1]	7,971.0	9,322.7	9,824.2	9,672.9	7,545.1	9,469.6	36

Note: Figures are in millions of dollars; (1) Figures cover the Pittsburgh, PA Metropolitan Statistical Area; (2) Rank is based on 2021 data and ranges from 1 to 388
Source: U.S. Department of Commerce, International Trade Administration, Office of Trade and Economic Analysis, Industry and Analysis, Exports by Metropolitan Area, data extracted March 16, 2023

Building Permits

Area	Single-Family			Multi-Family			Total		
	2021	2022	Pct. Chg.	2021	2022	Pct. Chg.	2021	2022	Pct. Chg.
City	198	115	-41.9	617	1,913	210.0	815	2,028	148.8
MSA[1]	3,891	3,184	-18.2	1,332	2,481	86.3	5,223	5,665	8.5
U.S.	1,115,400	975,600	-12.5	621,600	689,500	10.9	1,737,000	1,665,100	-4.1

Note: (1) Figures cover the Pittsburgh, PA Metropolitan Statistical Area; Figures represent new, privately-owned housing units authorized (unadjusted data); All permit data are based on estimates with imputation
Source: U.S. Census Bureau, Manufacturing, Mining, and Construction Statistics, Building Permits, 2021, 2022

Bankruptcy Filings

Area	Business Filings			Nonbusiness Filings		
	2021	2022	% Chg.	2021	2022	% Chg.
Allegheny County	79	72	-8.9	1,266	1,135	-10.3
U.S.	14,347	13,481	-6.0	399,269	374,240	-6.3

Note: Business filings include Chapter 7, Chapter 9, Chapter 11, Chapter 12, Chapter 13, Chapter 15, and Section 304; Nonbusiness filings include Chapter 7, Chapter 11, and Chapter 13
Source: Administrative Office of the U.S. Courts, Business and Nonbusiness Bankruptcy, County Cases Commenced by Chapter of the Bankruptcy Code, During the 12-Month Period Ending December 31, 2021 and Business and Nonbusiness Bankruptcy, County Cases Commenced by Chapter of the Bankruptcy Code, During the 12-Month Period Ending December 31, 2022

Housing Vacancy Rates

Area	Gross Vacancy Rate[2] (%)			Year-Round Vacancy Rate[3] (%)			Rental Vacancy Rate[4] (%)			Homeowner Vacancy Rate[5] (%)		
	2020	2021	2022	2020	2021	2022	2020	2021	2022	2020	2021	2022
MSA[1]	11.5	11.4	11.5	11.3	10.8	11.0	9.3	9.4	8.3	1.0	0.4	0.7
U.S.	10.6	10.8	10.5	8.2	8.4	8.2	6.3	6.1	5.8	1.0	0.9	0.8

Note: (1) Figures cover the Pittsburgh, PA Metropolitan Statistical Area; (2) The percentage of the total housing inventory that is vacant; (3) The percentage of the housing inventory (excluding seasonal units) that is year-round vacant; (4) The percentage of rental inventory that is vacant for rent; (5) The percentage of homeowner inventory that is vacant for sale
Source: U.S. Census Bureau, Housing Vacancies and Homeownership Annual Statistics: 2020, 2021, 2022

INCOME

Income

Area	Per Capita ($)	Median Household ($)	Average Household ($)
City	37,655	54,306	80,248
MSA[1]	39,416	65,894	90,001
U.S.	37,638	69,021	97,196

Note: (1) Figures cover the Pittsburgh, PA Metropolitan Statistical Area
Source: U.S. Census Bureau, 2017-2021 American Community Survey 5-Year Estimates

Household Income Distribution

Area	Percent of Households Earning							
	Under $15,000	$15,000 -$24,999	$25,000 -$34,999	$35,000 -$49,999	$50,000 -$74,999	$75,000 -$99,999	$100,000 -$149,999	$150,000 and up
City	16.3	9.8	9.6	11.2	16.1	11.7	12.6	12.8
MSA[1]	9.7	8.4	8.7	11.8	17.0	12.9	16.5	14.9
U.S.	9.4	7.8	8.2	11.4	16.8	12.8	16.3	17.3

Note: (1) Figures cover the Pittsburgh, PA Metropolitan Statistical Area
Source: U.S. Census Bureau, 2017-2021 American Community Survey 5-Year Estimates

Poverty Rate

Area	All Ages	Under 18 Years Old	18 to 64 Years Old	65 Years and Over
City	19.7	28.8	19.0	14.0
MSA[1]	10.7	14.2	10.3	8.3
U.S.	12.6	17.0	11.8	9.6

Note: Figures are percentage of people whose income during the past 12 months was below the poverty level;
(1) Figures cover the Pittsburgh, PA Metropolitan Statistical Area
Source: U.S. Census Bureau, 2017-2021 American Community Survey 5-Year Estimates

EMPLOYMENT

Labor Force and Employment

Area	Civilian Labor Force			Workers Employed		
	Dec. 2021	Dec. 2022	% Chg.	Dec. 2021	Dec. 2022	% Chg.
City	148,500	152,028	2.4	142,551	147,423	3.4
MSA[1]	1,147,805	1,177,164	2.6	1,096,709	1,134,155	3.4
U.S.	161,696,000	164,224,000	1.6	155,732,000	158,872,000	2.0

Note: Data is not seasonally adjusted and covers workers 16 years of age and older; (1) Figures cover the
Pittsburgh, PA Metropolitan Statistical Area
Source: Bureau of Labor Statistics, Local Area Unemployment Statistics

Unemployment Rate

Area	2022											
	Jan.	Feb.	Mar.	Apr.	May	Jun.	Jul.	Aug.	Sep.	Oct.	Nov.	Dec.
City	4.9	4.1	4.0	3.8	3.9	4.3	4.4	4.4	3.2	3.1	3.0	3.0
MSA[1]	5.8	5.1	4.6	4.2	4.0	4.6	4.7	4.8	3.4	3.3	3.5	3.7
U.S.	4.4	4.1	3.8	3.3	3.4	3.8	3.8	3.8	3.3	3.4	3.4	3.3

Note: Data is not seasonally adjusted and covers workers 16 years of age and older; (1) Figures cover the
Pittsburgh, PA Metropolitan Statistical Area
Source: Bureau of Labor Statistics, Local Area Unemployment Statistics

Average Wages

Occupation	$/Hr.	Occupation	$/Hr.
Accountants and Auditors	36.77	Maintenance and Repair Workers	22.49
Automotive Mechanics	22.54	Marketing Managers	60.70
Bookkeepers	21.77	Network and Computer Systems Admin.	45.38
Carpenters	27.30	Nurses, Licensed Practical	25.74
Cashiers	12.18	Nurses, Registered	36.65
Computer Programmers	44.53	Nursing Assistants	17.51
Computer Systems Analysts	44.54	Office Clerks, General	19.95
Computer User Support Specialists	29.16	Physical Therapists	45.42
Construction Laborers	24.33	Physicians	59.50
Cooks, Restaurant	14.67	Plumbers, Pipefitters and Steamfitters	34.72
Customer Service Representatives	19.68	Police and Sheriff's Patrol Officers	36.66
Dentists	68.86	Postal Service Mail Carriers	26.80
Electricians	34.15	Real Estate Sales Agents	30.60
Engineers, Electrical	49.62	Retail Salespersons	15.60
Fast Food and Counter Workers	11.65	Sales Representatives, Technical/Scientific	50.53
Financial Managers	73.72	Secretaries, Exc. Legal/Medical/Executive	19.68
First-Line Supervisors of Office Workers	29.71	Security Guards	16.59
General and Operations Managers	55.74	Surgeons	n/a
Hairdressers/Cosmetologists	16.69	Teacher Assistants, Exc. Postsecondary*	15.05
Home Health and Personal Care Aides	13.88	Teachers, Secondary School, Exc. Sp. Ed.*	39.73
Janitors and Cleaners	16.22	Telemarketers	16.91
Landscaping/Groundskeeping Workers	16.84	Truck Drivers, Heavy/Tractor-Trailer	25.67
Lawyers	66.28	Truck Drivers, Light/Delivery Services	20.10
Maids and Housekeeping Cleaners	14.29	Waiters and Waitresses	14.85

Note: Wage data covers the Pittsburgh, PA Metropolitan Statistical Area; (*) Hourly wages were calculated
from annual wage data based on a 40 hour work week; n/a not available.
Source: Bureau of Labor Statistics, Metro Area Occupational Employment & Wage Estimates, May 2022

Employment by Industry

Sector	MSA[1]		U.S.
	Number of Employees	Percent of Total	Percent of Total
Construction	55,100	4.7	5.0
Private Education and Health Services	246,900	21.2	16.1
Financial Activities	75,700	6.5	5.9
Government	112,600	9.7	14.5
Information	21,800	1.9	2.0
Leisure and Hospitality	111,600	9.6	10.3
Manufacturing	83,500	7.2	8.4
Mining and Logging	8,100	0.7	0.4
Other Services	46,400	4.0	3.7
Professional and Business Services	193,300	16.6	14.7
Retail Trade	117,600	10.1	10.2
Transportation, Warehousing, and Utilities	51,100	4.4	4.9
Wholesale Trade	41,800	3.6	3.9

Note: Figures are non-farm employment as of December 2022. Figures are not seasonally adjusted and include workers 16 years of age and older; (1) Figures cover the Pittsburgh, PA Metropolitan Statistical Area
Source: Bureau of Labor Statistics, Current Employment Statistics, Employment, Hours, and Earnings

Employment by Occupation

Occupation Classification	City (%)	MSA[1] (%)	U.S. (%)
Management, Business, Science, and Arts	51.4	43.4	40.3
Natural Resources, Construction, and Maintenance	4.2	7.8	8.7
Production, Transportation, and Material Moving	7.8	11.8	13.1
Sales and Office	18.3	20.9	20.9
Service	18.2	16.2	17.0

Note: Figures cover employed civilians 16 years of age and older; (1) Figures cover the Pittsburgh, PA Metropolitan Statistical Area
Source: U.S. Census Bureau, 2017-2021 American Community Survey 5-Year Estimates

Occupations with Greatest Projected Employment Growth: 2022 – 2024

Occupation[1]	2022 Employment	2024 Projected Employment	Numeric Employment Change	Percent Employment Change
Home Health and Personal Care Aides	194,980	205,150	10,170	5.2
Laborers and Freight, Stock, and Material Movers, Hand	150,480	158,160	7,680	5.1
Stockers and Order Fillers	100,260	104,570	4,310	4.3
Industrial Truck and Tractor Operators	31,030	33,930	2,900	9.3
General and Operations Managers	114,430	116,380	1,950	1.7
Heavy and Tractor-Trailer Truck Drivers	88,610	90,560	1,950	2.2
Cooks, Restaurant	49,280	51,090	1,810	3.7
Registered Nurses	148,910	150,170	1,260	0.8
Market Research Analysts and Marketing Specialists	29,510	30,730	1,220	4.1
Light Truck or Delivery Services Drivers	44,200	45,390	1,190	2.7

Note: Projections cover Pennsylvania; (1) Sorted by numeric employment change
Source: www.projectionscentral.com, State Occupational Projections, 2022–2024 Short-Term Projections

Fastest-Growing Occupations: 2022 – 2024

Occupation[1]	2022 Employment	2024 Projected Employment	Numeric Employment Change	Percent Employment Change
Nurse Practitioners	8,090	8,990	900	11.1
Weighers, Measurers, Checkers, and Samplers, Recordkeeping	2,480	2,720	240	9.7
Machine Feeders and Offbearers	3,430	3,760	330	9.6
Industrial Truck and Tractor Operators	31,030	33,930	2,900	9.3
Occupational Therapy Assistants	2,740	2,940	200	7.3
Statisticians	2,840	3,040	200	7.0
Logisticians	8,310	8,880	570	6.9
Physical Therapist Assistants	5,700	6,090	390	6.8
Information Security Analysts (SOC 2018)	3,780	4,020	240	6.3
Physician Assistants	7,730	8,200	470	6.1

Note: Projections cover Pennsylvania; (1) Sorted by percent employment change and excludes occupations with numeric employment change less than 50
Source: www.projectionscentral.com, State Occupational Projections, 2022–2024 Short-Term Projections

CITY FINANCES

City Government Finances

Component	2020 ($000)	2020 ($ per capita)
Total Revenues	628,984	2,095
Total Expenditures	751,228	2,502
Debt Outstanding	428,512	1,427
Cash and Securities[1]	270,728	902

Note: (1) Cash and security holdings of a government at the close of its fiscal year, including those of its dependent agencies, utilities, and liquor stores.
Source: U.S. Census Bureau, State & Local Government Finances 2020

City Government Revenue by Source

Source	2020 ($000)	2020 ($ per capita)	2020 (%)
General Revenue			
From Federal Government	24,415	81	3.9
From State Government	54,600	182	8.7
From Local Governments	9,468	32	1.5
Taxes			
Property	147,859	492	23.5
Sales and Gross Receipts	150,103	500	23.9
Personal Income	109,822	366	17.5
Corporate Income	0	0	0.0
Motor Vehicle License	0	0	0.0
Other Taxes	70,165	234	11.2
Current Charges	42,273	141	6.7
Liquor Store	0	0	0.0
Utility	0	0	0.0

Source: U.S. Census Bureau, State & Local Government Finances 2020

City Government Expenditures by Function

Function	2020 ($000)	2020 ($ per capita)	2020 (%)
General Direct Expenditures			
Air Transportation	0	0	0.0
Corrections	0	0	0.0
Education	0	0	0.0
Employment Security Administration	0	0	0.0
Financial Administration	20,964	69	2.8
Fire Protection	80,743	268	10.7
General Public Buildings	16,086	53	2.1
Governmental Administration, Other	70,324	234	9.4
Health	32,152	107	4.3
Highways	122,100	406	16.3
Hospitals	0	0	0.0
Housing and Community Development	11,311	37	1.5
Interest on General Debt	20,725	69	2.8
Judicial and Legal	2,096	7	0.3
Libraries	0	0	0.0
Parking	0	0	0.0
Parks and Recreation	10,613	35	1.4
Police Protection	130,597	434	17.4
Public Welfare	0	0	0.0
Sewerage	0	0	0.0
Solid Waste Management	22,868	76	3.0
Veterans' Services	0	0	0.0
Liquor Store	0	0	0.0
Utility	0	0	0.0

Source: U.S. Census Bureau, State & Local Government Finances 2020

TAXES

State Corporate Income Tax Rates

State	Tax Rate (%)	Income Brackets ($)	Num. of Brackets	Financial Institution Tax Rate (%)[a]	Federal Income Tax Ded.
Pennsylvania	8.99	Flat rate	1	(a)	No

Note: Tax rates as of January 1, 2023; (a) Rates listed are the corporate income tax rate applied to financial institutions or excise taxes based on income. Some states have other taxes based upon the value of deposits or shares.
Source: Federation of Tax Administrators, State Corporate Income Tax Rates, January 1, 2023

State Individual Income Tax Rates

State	Tax Rate (%)	Income Brackets ($)	Personal Exemptions ($)			Standard Ded. ($)	
			Single	Married	Depend.	Single	Married
Pennsylvania	3.07	Flat rate	None	None	None	–	–

Note: Tax rates as of January 1, 2023; Local- and county-level taxes are not included; Federal income tax is not deductible on state income tax returns
Source: Federation of Tax Administrators, State Individual Income Tax Rates, January 1, 2023

Various State Sales and Excise Tax Rates

State	State Sales Tax (%)	Gasoline[1] ($/gal.)	Cigarette[2] ($/pack)	Spirits[3] ($/gal.)	Wine[4] ($/gal.)	Beer[5] ($/gal.)	Recreational Marijuana (%)
Pennsylvania	6	0.622	2.60	7.41	–	0.08	Not legal

Note: All tax rates as of January 1, 2023; (1) The American Petroleum Institute has developed a methodology for determining the average tax rate on a gallon of fuel. Rates may include any of the following: excise taxes, environmental fees, storage tank fees, other fees or taxes, general sales tax, and local taxes; (2) The federal excise tax of $1.0066 per pack and local taxes are not included; (3) Rates are those applicable to off-premise sales of 40% alcohol by volume (a.b.v.) distilled spirits in 750ml containers. Local excise taxes are excluded; (4) Rates are those applicable to off-premise sales of 11% a.b.v. non-carbonated wine in 750ml containers; (5) Rates are those applicable to off-premise sales of 4.7% a.b.v. beer in 12 ounce containers.
Source: Tax Foundation, 2023 Facts & Figures: How Does Your State Compare?

State Business Tax Climate Index Rankings

State	Overall Rank	Corporate Tax Rank	Individual Income Tax Rank	Sales Tax Rank	Property Tax Rank	Unemployment Insurance Tax Rank
Pennsylvania	33	42	20	16	16	22

Note: The index is a measure of how each state's tax laws affect economic performance. The lower the rank, the more favorable a state's tax system is for business. States without a given tax are given a ranking of 1. The scores/rankings for the District of Columbia do not affect other states. The 2023 index represents the tax climate as of July 1, 2022.
Source: Tax Foundation, State Business Tax Climate Index 2023

TRANSPORTATION

Means of Transportation to Work

Area	Car/Truck/Van		Public Transportation			Bicycle	Walked	Other Means	Worked at Home
	Drove Alone	Car-pooled	Bus	Subway	Railroad				
City	52.1	6.6	14.5	0.3	0.0	1.2	9.7	1.8	13.9
MSA[1]	73.0	7.4	4.2	0.2	0.0	0.2	3.0	1.3	10.8
U.S.	73.2	8.6	2.0	1.6	0.5	0.5	2.5	1.5	9.7

Note: Figures are percentages and cover workers 16 years of age and older; (1) Figures cover the Pittsburgh, PA Metropolitan Statistical Area
Source: U.S. Census Bureau, 2017-2021 American Community Survey 5-Year Estimates

Travel Time to Work

Area	Less Than 10 Minutes	10 to 19 Minutes	20 to 29 Minutes	30 to 44 Minutes	45 to 59 Minutes	60 to 89 Minutes	90 Minutes or More
City	9.4	32.3	26.6	21.8	4.6	3.6	1.7
MSA[1]	11.8	27.0	21.3	22.9	9.1	5.8	2.1
U.S.	12.4	28.5	21.0	20.9	8.2	6.2	2.9

Note: Note: Figures are percentages and include workers 16 years old and over; (1) Figures cover the Pittsburgh, PA Metropolitan Statistical Area
Source: U.S. Census Bureau, 2017-2021 American Community Survey 5-Year Estimates

Key Congestion Measures

Measure	1990	2000	2010	2015	2020
Annual Hours of Delay, Total (000)	19,803	30,888	37,291	43,037	24,743
Annual Hours of Delay, Per Auto Commuter	25	33	39	45	25
Annual Congestion Cost, Per Auto Commuter ($)	756	890	853	910	552

Note: Covers the Pittsburgh PA urban area
Source: Texas A&M Transportation Institute, 2021 Urban Mobility Report

Freeway Travel Time Index

Measure	1985	1990	1995	2000	2005	2010	2015	2020
Urban Area Index[1]	1.08	1.13	1.15	1.16	1.18	1.17	1.19	1.08
Urban Area Rank[1,2]	40	34	36	43	41	41	38	44

Note: Freeway Travel Time Index—the ratio of travel time in the peak period to the travel time at free-flow conditions. For example, a value of 1.30 indicates a 20-minute free-flow trip takes 26 minutes in the peak (20 minutes x 1.30 = 26 minutes); (1) Covers the Pittsburgh PA urban area; (2) Rank is based on 101 larger urban areas (#1 = highest travel time index)
Source: Texas A&M Transportation Institute, 2021 Urban Mobility Report

Public Transportation

Agency Name / Mode of Transportation	Vehicles Operated in Maximum Service[1]	Annual Unlinked Passenger Trips[2] (in thous.)	Annual Passenger Miles[3] (in thous.)
Port Authority of Allegheny County			
Bus (directly operated)	561	20,136.0	82,792.9
Demand Response (purchased transportation)	194	667.1	4,479.5
Inclined Plane (directly operated)	2	204.8	23.9
Light Rail (directly operated)	24	1,460.1	5,707.4

Note: (1) Number of revenue vehicles operated by the given mode and type of service to meet the annual maximum service requirement. This is the revenue vehicle count during the peak season of the year; on the week and day that maximum service is provided. Vehicles operated in maximum service (VOMS) exclude atypical days and one-time special events; (2) Number of passengers who boarded public transportation vehicles. Passengers are counted each time they board a vehicle no matter how many vehicles they use to travel from their origin to their destination. (3) Sum of the distances ridden by all passengers during the entire fiscal year.
Source: Federal Transit Administration, National Transit Database, 2021

Air Transportation

Airport Name and Code / Type of Service	Passenger Airlines[1]	Passenger Enplanements	Freight Carriers[2]	Freight (lbs)
Pittsburgh International Airport (PIT)				
Domestic service (U.S. carriers - 2022)	35	3,853,670	15	86,556,135
International service (U.S. carriers - 2021)	5	15,394	0	0

Note: (1) Includes all U.S.-based major, minor and commuter airlines that carried at least one passenger during the year; (2) Includes all U.S.-based airlines and freight carriers that transported at least one pound of freight during the year.
Source: Bureau of Transportation Statistics, The Intermodal Transportation Database, Air Carriers: T-100 Domestic Market (U.S. Carriers), 2022; Bureau of Transportation Statistics, The Intermodal Transportation Database, Air Carriers: T-100 International Market (U.S. Carriers), 2021

BUSINESSES

Major Business Headquarters

Company Name	Industry	Rankings	
		Fortune[1]	Forbes[2]
Arconic	Metals	452	-
Armada	Business services & supplies	-	131
Giant Eagle	Food markets	-	39
Kraft Heinz	Food consumer products	139	-
PNC Financial Services	Financial services	178	-
PPG Industries	Chemicals	218	-
United States Steel	Metals	172	-
WESCO International	Wholesalers, diversified	200	-
Westinghouse Air Break Technologies	Industrial machinery	439	-

Note: (1) Companies that produce a 10-K are ranked 1 to 500 based on 2021 revenue; (2) All private companies with at least $2 billion in annual revenue through the end of their most current fiscal year are ranked 1 to 246; companies listed are headquartered in the city; dashes indicate no ranking
Source: Fortune, "Fortune 500," 2022; Forbes, "America's Largest Private Companies," 2022

Living Environment

378 Pittsburgh, Pennsylvania

COST OF LIVING

Cost of Living Index

Composite Index	Groceries	Housing	Utilities	Trans-portation	Health Care	Misc. Goods/ Services
100.4	107.9	93.0	131.3	103.4	94.6	94.9

Note: The Cost of Living Index measures regional differences in the cost of consumer goods and services, excluding taxes and non-consumer expenditures, for professional and managerial households in the top income quintile. It is based on more than 50,000 prices covering almost 60 different items for which prices are collected three times a year by chambers of commerce, economic development organizations or university applied economic centers in each participating urban area. The numbers shown should be read as a percentage above or below the national average of 100. For example, a value of 115.4 in the groceries column indicates that grocery prices are 15.4% higher than the national average. Small differences in the index numbers should not be interpreted as significant; Figures cover the Pittsburgh PA urban area.
Source: The Council for Community and Economic Research, Cost of Living Index, 2022

Grocery Prices

Area[1]	T-Bone Steak ($/pound)	Frying Chicken ($/pound)	Whole Milk ($/half gal.)	Eggs ($/dozen)	Orange Juice ($/64 oz.)	Coffee ($/11.5 oz.)
City[2]	16.67	2.16	2.50	1.93	3.90	5.33
Avg.	13.81	1.59	2.43	2.25	3.85	4.95
Min.	10.17	0.90	1.51	1.30	2.90	3.46
Max.	19.35	3.30	4.32	4.32	5.31	8.59

*Note: (1) Values for the local area are compared with the average, minimum and maximum values for all 286 areas in the Cost of Living Index; (2) Figures cover the Pittsburgh PA urban area; **T-Bone Steak** (price per pound); **Frying Chicken** (price per pound, whole fryer); **Whole Milk** (half gallon carton); **Eggs** (price per dozen, Grade A, large); **Orange Juice** (64 oz. Tropicana or Florida Natural); **Coffee** (11.5 oz. can, vacuum-packed, Maxwell House, Hills Bros, or Folgers).*
Source: The Council for Community and Economic Research, Cost of Living Index, 2022

Housing and Utility Costs

Area[1]	New Home Price ($)	Apartment Rent ($/month)	All Electric ($/month)	Part Electric ($/month)	Other Energy ($/month)	Telephone ($/month)
City[2]	418,872	1,281	-	118.68	149.99	194.84
Avg.	450,913	1,371	176.41	99.93	76.96	190.22
Min.	229,283	546	100.84	31.56	27.15	174.27
Max.	2,434,977	4,569	356.86	249.59	272.24	208.31

*Note: (1) Values for the local area are compared with the average, minimum and maximum values for all 286 areas in the Cost of Living Index; (2) Figures cover the Pittsburgh PA urban area; **New Home Price** (2,400 sf living area, 8,000 sf lot, in urban area with full utilities); **Apartment Rent** (950 sf 2 bedroom/1.5 or 2 bath, unfurnished, excluding all utilities except water); **All Electric** (average monthly cost for an all-electric home); **Part Electric** (average monthly cost for a part-electric home); **Other Energy** (average monthly cost for natural gas, fuel oil, coal, wood, and any other forms of energy except electricity); **Telephone** (price includes the base monthly rate plus taxes and fees for three lines of mobile phone service).*
Source: The Council for Community and Economic Research, Cost of Living Index, 2022

Health Care, Transportation, and Other Costs

Area[1]	Doctor ($/visit)	Dentist ($/visit)	Optometrist ($/visit)	Gasoline ($/gallon)	Beauty Salon ($/visit)	Men's Shirt ($)
City[2]	98.25	112.80	96.58	3.99	37.03	20.62
Avg.	124.91	107.77	117.66	3.86	43.31	34.21
Min.	36.61	58.25	51.79	2.90	22.18	13.05
Max.	250.21	162.58	371.96	5.54	85.61	63.54

*Note: (1) Values for the local area are compared with the average, minimum and maximum values for all 286 areas in the Cost of Living Index; (2) Figures cover the Pittsburgh PA urban area; **Doctor** (general practitioners routine exam of an established patient); **Dentist** (adult teeth cleaning and periodic oral examination); **Optometrist** (full vision eye exam for established adult patient); **Gasoline** (one gallon regular unleaded, national brand, including all taxes, cash price at self-service pump if available); **Beauty Salon** (woman's shampoo, trim, and blow-dry); **Men's Shirt** (cotton/polyester dress shirt, pinpoint weave, long sleeves).*
Source: The Council for Community and Economic Research, Cost of Living Index, 2022

HOUSING

Homeownership Rate

Area	2015 (%)	2016 (%)	2017 (%)	2018 (%)	2019 (%)	2020 (%)	2021 (%)	2022 (%)
MSA[1]	71.0	72.2	72.7	71.7	71.5	69.8	69.1	72.7
U.S.	63.7	63.4	63.9	64.4	64.6	66.6	65.5	65.8

Note: (1) Figures cover the Pittsburgh, PA Metropolitan Statistical Area
Source: U.S. Census Bureau, Housing Vacancies and Homeownership Annual Statistics: 2015-2022

House Price Index (HPI)

Area	National Ranking[2]	Quarterly Change (%)	One-Year Change (%)	Five-Year Change (%)	Since 1991Q1 (%)
MSA[1]	224	-1.54	7.43	42.48	223.87
U.S.[3]	–	0.34	8.41	58.44	289.08

Note: The HPI is a weighted repeat sales index. It measures average price changes in repeat sales or refinancings on the same properties. This information is obtained by reviewing repeat mortgage transactions on single-family properties whose mortgages have been purchased or securitized by Fannie Mae or Freddie Mac since January 1975; (1) Figures cover the Pittsburgh, PA Metropolitan Statistical Area; (2) Rankings are based on annual percentage change for all metro areas containing at least 15,000 transactions over the last 10 years and ranges from 1 to 257; (3) figures based on a weighted average of Census Division estimates using a seasonally adjusted, purchase-only index; all figures are for the period ending December 31, 2022
Source: Federal Housing Finance Agency, Change in FHFA Metropolitan Area House Price Indexes, 2022Q4

Median Single-Family Home Prices

Area	2020	2021	2022p	Percent Change 2021 to 2022
MSA[1]	n/a	n/a	n/a	n/a
U.S. Average	300.2	357.1	392.6	9.9

Note: Figures are median sales prices of existing single-family homes in thousands of dollars; (p) preliminary; n/a not available; (1) Figures cover the Pittsburgh, PA Metropolitan Statistical Area
Source: National Association of Realtors, Median Sales Price of Existing Single-Family Homes for Metropolitan Areas, 4th Quarter 2022

Qualifying Income Based on Median Sales Price of Existing Single-Family Homes

Area	With 5% Down ($)	With 10% Down ($)	With 20% Down ($)
MSA[1]	n/a	n/a	n/a
U.S. Average	112,234	106,237	94,513

Note: Figures are preliminary; Qualifying income is based on a mortgage rate of 6.77%. Monthly principal and interest payment is limited to 25% of income; n/a not available; (1) Figures cover the Pittsburgh, PA Metropolitan Statistical Area
Source: National Association of Realtors, Qualifying Income Based on Median Sales Price of Existing Single-Family Homes for Metropolitan Areas, 4th Quarter 2022

Home Value

Area	Under $100,000	$100,000 -$199,999	$200,000 -$299,999	$300,000 -$399,999	$400,000 -$499,999	$500,000 -$999,999	$1,000,000 or more	Median ($)
City	33.7	31.4	13.9	7.9	4.8	7.2	1.1	147,600
MSA[1]	25.5	34.6	19.9	9.9	4.5	4.9	0.7	167,500
U.S.	16.2	24.2	20.1	13.6	8.3	13.6	4.1	244,900

Note: Figures are percentages except for median and cover owner-occupied housing units; (1) Figures cover the Pittsburgh, PA Metropolitan Statistical Area
Source: U.S. Census Bureau, 2017-2021 American Community Survey 5-Year Estimates

Year Housing Structure Built

Area	2020 or Later	2010 -2019	2000 -2009	1990 -1999	1980 -1989	1970 -1979	1960 -1969	1950 -1959	1940 -1949	Before 1940	Median Year
City	0.1	3.9	3.0	3.6	4.4	6.6	8.3	13.2	8.3	48.8	1941
MSA[1]	0.1	4.0	6.2	7.6	7.7	12.0	11.4	16.5	8.6	25.9	1959
U.S.	0.2	7.3	13.6	13.6	13.2	14.8	10.3	10.0	4.7	12.2	1979

Note: Figures are percentages except for Median Year; Note: (1) Figures cover the Pittsburgh, PA Metropolitan Statistical Area
Source: U.S. Census Bureau, 2017-2021 American Community Survey 5-Year Estimates

Gross Monthly Rent

Area	Under $500	$500 -$999	$1,000 -$1,499	$1,500 -$1,999	$2,000 -$2,499	$2,500 -$2,999	$3,000 and up	Median ($)
City	13.0	33.7	31.0	13.9	5.5	2.0	0.9	1,043
MSA[1]	14.0	47.0	26.4	7.9	2.9	0.9	0.9	892
U.S.	8.1	30.5	30.8	16.8	7.3	3.1	3.5	1,163

Note: Figures are percentages except for median; Gross rent is the contract rent plus the estimated average monthly cost of utilities (electricity, gas, and water and sewer) and fuels (oil, coal, kerosene, wood, etc.) if these are paid by the renter (or paid for the renter by someone else); (1) Figures cover the Pittsburgh, PA Metropolitan Statistical Area
Source: U.S. Census Bureau, 2017-2021 American Community Survey 5-Year Estimates

HEALTH

Health Risk Factors

Category	MSA[1] (%)	U.S. (%)
Adults aged 18–64 who have any kind of health care coverage	96.5	90.9
Adults who reported being in good or better health	85.0	85.2
Adults who have been told they have high blood cholesterol	33.1	35.7
Adults who have been told they have high blood pressure	34.0	32.4
Adults who are current smokers	15.0	14.4
Adults who currently use e-cigarettes	6.4	6.7
Adults who currently use chewing tobacco, snuff, or snus	3.7	3.5
Adults who are heavy drinkers[2]	6.7	6.3
Adults who are binge drinkers[3]	18.4	15.4
Adults who are overweight (BMI 25.0 - 29.9)	32.6	34.4
Adults who are obese (BMI 30.0 - 99.8)	31.1	33.9
Adults who participated in any physical activities in the past month	77.8	76.3

Note: (1) Figures cover the Pittsburgh, PA Metropolitan Statistical Area; (2) Heavy drinkers are classified as adult men having more than 14 drinks per week and adult women having more than 7 drinks per week; (3) Binge drinkers are classified as males having five or more drinks on one occasion or females having four or more drinks on one occasion
Source: Centers for Disease Control and Prevention, Behaviorial Risk Factor Surveillance System, SMART: Selected Metropolitan Area Risk Trends, 2021

Acute and Chronic Health Conditions

Category	MSA[1] (%)	U.S. (%)
Adults who have ever been told they had a heart attack	4.2	4.0
Adults who have ever been told they have angina or coronary heart disease	4.0	3.8
Adults who have ever been told they had a stroke	3.0	3.0
Adults who have ever been told they have asthma	15.6	14.9
Adults who have ever been told they have arthritis	30.1	25.8
Adults who have ever been told they have diabetes[2]	9.7	10.9
Adults who have ever been told they had skin cancer	7.5	6.6
Adults who have ever been told they had any other types of cancer	8.2	7.5
Adults who have ever been told they have COPD	7.1	6.1
Adults who have ever been told they have kidney disease	3.5	3.0
Adults who have ever been told they have a form of depression	19.1	20.5

Note: (1) Figures cover the Pittsburgh, PA Metropolitan Statistical Area; (2) Figures do not include pregnancy-related, borderline, or pre-diabetes
Source: Centers for Disease Control and Prevention, Behaviorial Risk Factor Surveillance System, SMART: Selected Metropolitan Area Risk Trends, 2021

Health Screening and Vaccination Rates

Category	MSA[1] (%)	U.S. (%)
Adults who have ever been tested for HIV	26.8	34.9
Adults who have had their blood cholesterol checked within the last five years	89.0	85.2
Adults aged 65+ who have had flu shot within the past year	75.5	68.6
Adults aged 65+ who have ever had a pneumonia vaccination	71.0	71.0

Note: (1) Figures cover the Pittsburgh, PA Metropolitan Statistical Area.
Source: Centers for Disease Control and Prevention, Behaviorial Risk Factor Surveillance System, SMART: Selected Metropolitan Area Risk Trends, 2021

Disability Status

Category	MSA[1] (%)	U.S. (%)
Adults who reported being deaf	8.2	7.2
Are you blind or have serious difficulty seeing, even when wearing glasses?	3.1	4.8
Are you limited in any way in any of your usual activities due to arthritis?	11.2	11.1
Do you have difficulty doing errands alone?	6.4	7.0
Do you have difficulty dressing or bathing?	3.9	3.6
Do you have serious difficulty concentrating/remembering/making decisions?	10.6	12.1
Do you have serious difficulty walking or climbing stairs?	12.1	12.8

Note: (1) Figures cover the Pittsburgh, PA Metropolitan Statistical Area.
Source: Centers for Disease Control and Prevention, Behaviorial Risk Factor Surveillance System, SMART: Selected Metropolitan Area Risk Trends, 2021

Mortality Rates for the Top 10 Causes of Death in the U.S.

ICD-10[a] Sub-Chapter	ICD-10[a] Code	Crude Mortality Rate[1] per 100,000 population	
		County[2]	U.S.
Malignant neoplasms	C00-C97	224.7	182.6
Ischaemic heart diseases	I20-I25	173.5	113.1
Other forms of heart disease	I30-I51	90.1	64.4
Other degenerative diseases of the nervous system	G30-G31	48.0	51.0
Cerebrovascular diseases	I60-I69	52.9	47.8
Other external causes of accidental injury	W00-X59	78.7	46.4
Chronic lower respiratory diseases	J40-J47	49.2	45.7
Organic, including symptomatic, mental disorders	F01-F09	64.2	35.9
Hypertensive diseases	I10-I15	28.9	35.0
Diabetes mellitus	E10-E14	27.8	29.6

Note: (a) ICD-10 = International Classification of Diseases 10th Revision; (1) Crude mortality rates are a three-year average covering 2019-2021; (2) Figures cover Allegheny County.
Source: Centers for Disease Control and Prevention, National Center for Health Statistics. National Vital Statistics System, Mortality 2018-2021 on CDC WONDER Online Database

Mortality Rates for Selected Causes of Death

ICD-10[a] Sub-Chapter	ICD-10[a] Code	Crude Mortality Rate[1] per 100,000 population	
		County[2]	U.S.
Assault	X85-Y09	8.3	7.0
Diseases of the liver	K70-K76	20.5	19.8
Human immunodeficiency virus (HIV) disease	B20-B24	0.5	1.5
Influenza and pneumonia	J09-J18	18.6	14.7
Intentional self-harm	X60-X84	13.7	14.3
Malnutrition	E40-E46	6.0	4.3
Obesity and other hyperalimentation	E65-E68	2.5	3.0
Renal failure	N17-N19	23.6	15.7
Transport accidents	V01-V99	7.2	13.6
Viral hepatitis	B15-B19	0.8	1.2

Note: (a) ICD-10 = International Classification of Diseases 10th Revision; (1) Crude mortality rates are a three-year average covering 2019-2021; (2) Figures cover Allegheny County; Data are suppressed when the data meet the criteria for confidentiality constraints; Crude mortality rates are flagged as unreliable when the rate would be calculated with a numerator of 20 or less.
Source: Centers for Disease Control and Prevention, National Center for Health Statistics. National Vital Statistics System, Mortality 2018-2021 on CDC WONDER Online Database

Health Insurance Coverage

Area	With Health Insurance	With Private Health Insurance	With Public Health Insurance	Without Health Insurance	Population Under Age 19 Without Health Insurance
City	94.5	73.0	33.7	5.5	3.9
MSA[1]	96.3	76.2	36.5	3.7	1.9
U.S.	91.2	67.8	35.4	8.8	5.3

Note: Figures are percentages that cover the civilian noninstitutionalized population; (1) Figures cover the Pittsburgh, PA Metropolitan Statistical Area
Source: U.S. Census Bureau, 2017-2021 American Community Survey 5-Year Estimates

Number of Medical Professionals

Area	MDs[3]	DOs[3,4]	Dentists	Podiatrists	Chiropractors	Optometrists
County[1] (number)	7,993	553	1,202	114	545	256
County[1] (rate[2])	640.1	44.3	97.1	9.2	44.0	20.7
U.S. (rate[2])	289.3	23.5	72.5	6.2	28.7	17.4

Note: Data as of 2021 unless noted; (1) Data covers Allegheny County; (2) Rate per 100,000 population; (3) Data as of 2020 and includes all active, non-federal physicians; (4) Doctor of Osteopathic Medicine
Source: U.S. Department of Health and Human Services, Health Resources and Services Administration, Bureau of Health Professions, Area Resource File (ARF) 2021-2022

Best Hospitals

According to *U.S. News,* the Pittsburgh, PA metro area is home to four of the best hospitals in the U.S.: **UPMC Magee-Womens Hospital** (1 adult specialty); **UPMC Mercy** (1 adult specialty); **UPMC Presbyterian Shadyside** (9 adult specialties); **West Penn Hospital** (1 adult specialty). The hospitals listed were nationally ranked in at least one of 15 adult or 10 pediatric specialties. The number of specialties shown cover the parent hospital. Only 164 U.S. hospitals performed well enough to be nationally ranked in one or more specialties. Twenty hospitals in the U.S. made the Honor Roll. The Best Hospitals Honor Roll takes both the national rankings and the procedure and condition ratings into account. Hospitals received points if they were nationally ranked in one of the 15 adult specialties—the higher they ranked, the more points they got—and how many ratings of "high performing" they earned in the 17 procedures and conditions. *U.S. News Online, "America's Best Hospitals 2022-23"*

According to *U.S. News,* the Pittsburgh, PA metro area is home to one of the best children's hospitals in the U.S.: **UPMC Children's Hospital of Pittsburgh** (Honor Roll/10 pediatric specialties). The hospital listed was highly ranked in at least one of 10 pediatric specialties. Eighty-six children's hospitals in the U.S. were nationally ranked in at least one specialty. Hospitals received points for being ranked in a specialty, and the 10 hospitals with the most points across the 10 specialties make up the Honor Roll. *U.S. News Online, "America's Best Children's Hospitals 2022-23"*

EDUCATION

Public School District Statistics

District Name	Schls	Pupils	Pupil/ Teacher Ratio	Minority Pupils[1] (%)	LEP/ELL[2] (%)	IEP[3] (%)
Baldwin-Whitehall SD	4	4,432	14.4	33.7	7.2	12.1
Chartiers Valley SD	4	3,341	14.0	21.5	4.3	13.9
Fox Chapel Area SD	6	4,158	13.0	21.2	1.2	13.2
Mount Lebanon SD	10	5,397	13.5	16.2	2.4	13.6
North Allegheny SD	11	8,467	14.1	27.5	1.4	13.2
North Hills SD	6	4,554	13.6	16.8	1.9	16.2
Penn Hills SD	3	3,067	16.2	75.5	0.9	27.5
Pittsburgh SD	56	20,105	10.7	69.5	4.5	22.4
Upper Saint Clair SD	6	3,934	14.1	19.8	1.8	13.8

Note: Table includes school districts with 2,000 or more students; (1) Percentage of students that are not non-Hispanic white; (2) Percentage of students that are Limited English Proficient or English Language Learners (2018-19); (3) Percentage of students that have an Individualized Education Program (2019-20).
Source: U.S. Department of Education, National Center for Education Statistics, Common Core of Data, Local Education Agency (School District) Universe Survey: School Year 2021-2022

Highest Level of Education

Area	Less than H.S.	H.S. Diploma	Some College, No Deg.	Associate Degree	Bachelor's Degree	Master's Degree	Prof. School Degree	Doctorate Degree
City	6.5	24.7	14.9	8.2	23.5	13.7	4.6	3.9
MSA[1]	5.5	31.4	16.0	10.5	22.2	10.3	2.3	1.7
U.S.	11.1	26.5	20.0	8.7	20.6	9.3	2.2	1.5

Note: Figures cover persons age 25 and over; (1) Figures cover the Pittsburgh, PA Metropolitan Statistical Area
Source: U.S. Census Bureau, 2017-2021 American Community Survey 5-Year Estimates

Educational Attainment by Race

Area	High School Graduate or Higher (%)					Bachelor's Degree or Higher (%)				
	Total	White	Black	Asian	Hisp.[2]	Total	White	Black	Asian	Hisp.[2]
City	93.5	95.0	89.1	92.5	87.3	45.7	51.2	19.8	77.7	49.3
MSA[1]	94.5	95.1	90.8	87.5	88.5	36.6	37.0	21.6	69.2	37.5
U.S.	88.9	91.4	87.2	87.6	71.2	33.7	35.5	23.3	55.6	18.4

Note: Figures shown cover persons 25 years old and over; (1) Figures cover the Pittsburgh, PA Metropolitan Statistical Area; (2) People of Hispanic origin can be of any race
Source: U.S. Census Bureau, 2017-2021 American Community Survey 5-Year Estimates

School Enrollment by Grade and Control

Area	Preschool (%)		Kindergarten (%)		Grades 1 - 4 (%)		Grades 5 - 8 (%)		Grades 9 - 12 (%)	
	Public	Private	Public	Private	Public	Private	Public	Private	Public	Private
City	50.4	49.6	76.4	23.6	76.9	23.1	76.5	23.5	79.5	20.5
MSA[1]	50.8	49.2	82.7	17.3	88.7	11.3	89.0	11.0	89.6	10.4
U.S.	58.8	41.2	86.3	13.7	88.3	11.7	88.6	11.4	89.4	10.6

Note: Figures shown cover persons 3 years old and over; (1) Figures cover the Pittsburgh, PA Metropolitan Statistical Area
Source: U.S. Census Bureau, 2017-2021 American Community Survey 5-Year Estimates

Higher Education

Four-Year Colleges			Two-Year Colleges			Medical Schools[1]	Law Schools[2]	Voc/ Tech[3]
Public	Private Non-profit	Private For-profit	Public	Private Non-profit	Private For-profit			
4	16	0	4	9	11	1	2	18

Note: Figures cover institutions located within the Pittsburgh, PA Metropolitan Statistical Area and include main campuses only; (1) includes schools accredited by the Liaison Committee on Medical Education and the American Osteopathic Association's Commission on Osteopathic College Accreditation; (2) includes ABA-accredited schools, schools with provisional ABA accreditation, and state accredited schools; (3) includes all schools with programs that are less than 2 years.
Source: National Center for Education Statistics, Integrated Postsecondary Education System (IPEDS), 2021-22; Wikipedia, List of Medical Schools in the United States, accessed April 10, 2023; Wikipedia, List of Law Schools in the United States, accessed April 10, 2023

According to *U.S. News & World Report,* the Pittsburgh, PA metro area is home to five of the top 200 national universities in the U.S.: **Carnegie Mellon University** (#22 tie); **University of Pittsburgh** (#62 tie); **Duquesne University** (#151 tie); **Chatham University** (#194 tie); **Robert Morris University** (#194 tie). The indicators used to capture academic quality fall into a number of categories: assessment by administrators at peer institutions; retention of students; faculty resources; student selectivity; financial resources; alumni giving; high school counselor ratings of colleges; and graduation rate. *U.S. News & World Report, "America's Best Colleges 2023"*

According to *U.S. News & World Report,* the Pittsburgh, PA metro area is home to one of the top 100 liberal arts colleges in the U.S.: **Washington & Jefferson College** (#94 tie). The indicators used to capture academic quality fall into a number of categories: assessment by administrators at peer institutions; retention of students; faculty resources; student selectivity; financial resources; alumni giving; high school counselor ratings of colleges; and graduation rate. *U.S. News & World Report, "America's Best Colleges 2023"*

According to *U.S. News & World Report,* the Pittsburgh, PA metro area is home to one of the top 100 law schools in the U.S.: **University of Pittsburgh** (#78 tie). The rankings are based on a weighted average of 12 measures of quality: peer assessment score; assessment score by lawyers/judges; median LSAT scores; median undergrad GPA; acceptance rate; employment rates for graduates; placement success; bar passage rate; faculty resources; expenditures per student; student/faculty ratio; and library resources. *U.S. News & World Report, "America's Best Graduate Schools, Law, 2023"*

According to *U.S. News & World Report,* the Pittsburgh, PA metro area is home to one of the top 75 medical schools for research in the U.S.: **University of Pittsburgh** (#14 tie). The rankings are based on a weighted average of 11 measures of quality: quality assessment; peer assessment score; assessment score by residency directors; research activity; total research activity; average research activity per faculty member; student selectivity; median MCAT total score; median undergraduate GPA; acceptance rate; and faculty resources. *U.S. News & World Report, "America's Best Graduate Schools, Medical, 2023"*

According to *U.S. News & World Report,* the Pittsburgh, PA metro area is home to two of the top 75 business schools in the U.S.: **Carnegie Mellon University (Tepper)** (#16); **University of Pittsburgh (Katz)** (#55 tie). The rankings are based on a weighted average of the following nine measures: quality assessment; peer assessment; recruiter assessment; placement success; mean starting salary and bonus; student selectivity; mean GMAT and GRE scores; mean undergraduate GPA; and acceptance rate. *U.S. News & World Report, "America's Best Graduate Schools, Business, 2023"*

EMPLOYERS

Major Employers

Company Name	Industry
Allegheny General Hospital	Extended care facility
Associated Cleaning Consultants	Janitorial service, contract basis
Bayer Corporation	Pharmaceutical preparations
Children's Hospital of Pittsburgh	Specialty hospitals, except psychiatric
Duquesne University of the Holy Spirit	Colleges & universities
Highmark	Hospital & medical services plans
Jefferson Regional Medical Center	General medical & surgical hospitals
Magee-Womens Hospital of UPMC	Hospital, affiliated with ama residency
Mercy Life Center Corporation	Mental health clinic, outpatient
PNC Bank	National trust companies with deposits, commercial
U.S. Dept of Energy	Noncommercial research organizations
United States Steel Corporation	Blast furnaces & steel mills
United States Steel International	Steel
University of Pittsburgh	Colleges & universities
UPMC Mercy	General medical & surgical hospitals
UPMC Shadyside	General medical & surgical hospitals
Veterans Health Administration	Administration of veterans' affairs
West Penn Allegheny Health System	Management services

Note: Companies shown are located within the Pittsburgh, PA Metropolitan Statistical Area.
Source: Hoovers.com; Wikipedia

Best Companies to Work For

PPG, headquartered in Pittsburgh, is among the "100 Best Places to Work in IT." To qualify, companies had to have a minimum of 100 total employees and five IT employees. The best places to work were selected based on DEI (diversity, equity, and inclusion) practices; IT turnover, promotions, and growth; IT retention and engagement programs; remote/hybrid working; benefits and perks (such as elder care and child care, flextime, and reimbursement for college tuition); and training and career development opportunities. *Computerworld, "Best Places to Work in IT," 2023*

PUBLIC SAFETY

Crime Rate

Area	Total Crime	Violent Crime Rate				Property Crime Rate		
		Murder	Rape[3]	Robbery	Aggrav. Assault	Burglary	Larceny -Theft	Motor Vehicle Theft
City	3,594.8	18.8	40.0	230.0	289.9	443.2	2,331.9	241.0
Suburbs[1]	1,402.7	3.5	23.7	33.2	168.7	159.1	958.5	55.9
Metro[2]	1,687.7	5.5	25.8	58.8	184.5	196.1	1,137.0	80.0
U.S.	2,593.1	5.0	44.0	86.1	248.2	378.0	1,601.6	230.2

Note: Figures are crimes per 100,000 population; (1) All areas within the metro area that are located outside the city limits; (2) Figures cover the Pittsburgh, PA Metropolitan Statistical Area; (3) All figures shown were reported using the revised Uniform Crime Reporting (UCR) definition of rape; Due to the transition to the National Incident-Based Reporting System (NIBRS), limited city and metro area data was released for 2021.
Source: FBI Uniform Crime Reports, 2018 (data for 2020 was not available)

Hate Crimes

Area	Number of Quarters Reported	Number of Incidents per Bias Motivation					
		Race/Ethnicity/ Ancestry	Religion	Sexual Orientation	Disability	Gender	Gender Identity
City	4	3	2	0	0	0	0
U.S.	4	5,227	1,244	1,110	130	75	266

Note: Due to the transition to the National Incident-Based Reporting System (NIBRS), limited crime data was released for 2021.
Source: Federal Bureau of Investigation, Hate Crime Statistics 2020

Identity Theft Consumer Reports

Area	Reports	Reports per 100,000 Population	Rank[2]
MSA[1]	7,114	306	65
U.S.	1,108,609	339	-

Note: (1) Figures cover the Pittsburgh, PA Metropolitan Statistical Area; (2) Rank ranges from 1 to 391 where 1 indicates greatest number of identity theft reports per 100,000 population
Source: Federal Trade Commission, Consumer Sentinel Network Data Book 2022

Fraud and Other Consumer Reports

Area	Reports	Reports per 100,000 Population	Rank[2]
MSA[1]	24,896	1,071	70
U.S.	4,064,520	1,245	-

Note: (1) Figures cover the Pittsburgh, PA Metropolitan Statistical Area; (2) Rank ranges from 1 to 391 where 1 indicates greatest number of fraud and other consumer reports per 100,000 population
Source: Federal Trade Commission, Consumer Sentinel Network Data Book 2022

POLITICS

2020 Presidential Election Results

Area	Biden	Trump	Jorgensen	Hawkins	Other
Allegheny County	59.4	39.0	1.2	0.0	0.4
U.S.	51.3	46.8	1.2	0.3	0.5

Note: Results are percentages and may not add to 100% due to rounding
Source: Dave Leip's Atlas of U.S. Presidential Elections

SPORTS

Professional Sports Teams

Team Name	League	Year Established
Pittsburgh Penguins	National Hockey League (NHL)	1967
Pittsburgh Pirates	Major League Baseball (MLB)	1882
Pittsburgh Steelers	National Football League (NFL)	1933

Note: Includes teams located in the Pittsburgh, PA Metropolitan Statistical Area.
Source: Wikipedia, Major Professional Sports Teams of the United States and Canada, April 12, 2023

CLIMATE

Average and Extreme Temperatures

Temperature	Jan	Feb	Mar	Apr	May	Jun	Jul	Aug	Sep	Oct	Nov	Dec	Yr.
Extreme High (°F)	75	69	83	89	91	98	103	100	97	89	82	74	103
Average High (°F)	35	38	48	61	71	79	83	81	75	63	50	39	60
Average Temp. (°F)	28	30	39	50	60	68	73	71	64	53	42	32	51
Average Low (°F)	20	22	29	39	49	57	62	61	54	43	34	25	41
Extreme Low (°F)	-18	-12	-1	14	26	34	42	39	31	16	-1	-12	-18

Note: Figures cover the years 1948-1990
Source: National Climatic Data Center, International Station Meteorological Climate Summary, 9/96

Average Precipitation/Snowfall/Humidity

Precip./Humidity	Jan	Feb	Mar	Apr	May	Jun	Jul	Aug	Sep	Oct	Nov	Dec	Yr.
Avg. Precip. (in.)	2.8	2.4	3.4	3.3	3.6	3.9	3.8	3.2	2.8	2.4	2.7	2.8	37.1
Avg. Snowfall (in.)	11	9	8	2	Tr	0	0	0	0	Tr	4	8	43
Avg. Rel. Hum. 7am (%)	76	75	75	73	76	79	82	86	85	81	78	77	79
Avg. Rel. Hum. 4pm (%)	64	60	54	49	50	51	53	54	55	53	60	66	56

Note: Figures cover the years 1948-1990; Tr = Trace amounts (<0.05 in. of rain; <0.5 in. of snow)
Source: National Climatic Data Center, International Station Meteorological Climate Summary, 9/96

Weather Conditions

Temperature			Daytime Sky			Precipitation		
5°F & below	32°F & below	90°F & above	Clear	Partly cloudy	Cloudy	0.01 inch or more precip.	0.1 inch or more snow/ice	Thunder-storms
9	121	8	62	137	166	154	42	35

Note: Figures are average number of days per year and cover the years 1948-1990
Source: National Climatic Data Center, International Station Meteorological Climate Summary, 9/96

HAZARDOUS WASTE

Superfund Sites

The Pittsburgh, PA metro area is home to three sites on the EPA's Superfund National Priorities List: **Breslube-Penn, Inc.** (final); **Lindane Dump** (final); **Ohio River Park** (final). There are a total of 1,165 Superfund sites with a status of proposed or final on the list in the U.S. *U.S. Environmental Protection Agency, National Priorities List, April 12, 2023*

386   Pittsburgh, Pennsylvania

AIR QUALITY

Air Quality Trends: Ozone

	1990	1995	2000	2005	2010	2015	2018	2019	2020	2021
MSA[1]	0.080	0.100	0.084	0.083	0.077	0.070	0.070	0.062	0.066	0.066
U.S.	0.087	0.089	0.081	0.080	0.072	0.067	0.069	0.065	0.065	0.067

Note: (1) Data covers the Pittsburgh, PA Metropolitan Statistical Area. The values shown are the composite ozone concentration averages among trend sites based on the highest fourth daily maximum 8-hour concentration in parts per million. These trends are based on sites having an adequate record of monitoring data during the trend period. Data from exceptional events are included.
Source: U.S. Environmental Protection Agency, Air Quality Monitoring Information, "Air Quality Trends by City, 1990-2021"

Air Quality Index

Area	Percent of Days when Air Quality was...[2]					AQI Statistics[2]	
	Good	Moderate	Unhealthy for Sensitive Groups	Unhealthy	Very Unhealthy	Maximum	Median
MSA[1]	44.9	52.6	2.2	0.3	0.0	153	53

Note: (1) Data covers the Pittsburgh, PA Metropolitan Statistical Area; (2) Based on 365 days with AQI data in 2021. Air Quality Index (AQI) is an index for reporting daily air quality. EPA calculates the AQI for five major air pollutants regulated by the Clean Air Act: ground-level ozone, particle pollution (aka particulate matter), carbon monoxide, sulfur dioxide, and nitrogen dioxide. The AQI runs from 0 to 500. The higher the AQI value, the greater the level of air pollution and the greater the health concern. There are six AQI categories: "Good" AQI is between 0 and 50. Air quality is considered satisfactory; "Moderate" AQI is between 51 and 100. Air quality is acceptable; "Unhealthy for Sensitive Groups" When AQI values are between 101 and 150, members of sensitive groups may experience health effects; "Unhealthy" When AQI values are between 151 and 200 everyone may begin to experience health effects; "Very Unhealthy" AQI values between 201 and 300 trigger a health alert; "Hazardous" AQI values over 300 trigger warnings of emergency conditions (not shown).
Source: U.S. Environmental Protection Agency, Air Quality Index Report, 2021

Air Quality Index Pollutants

Area	Percent of Days when AQI Pollutant was...[2]					
	Carbon Monoxide	Nitrogen Dioxide	Ozone	Sulfur Dioxide	Particulate Matter 2.5	Particulate Matter 10
MSA[1]	0.0	0.3	32.6	(3)	67.1	0.0

Note: (1) Data covers the Pittsburgh, PA Metropolitan Statistical Area; (2) Based on 365 days with AQI data in 2021. The Air Quality Index (AQI) is an index for reporting daily air quality. EPA calculates the AQI for five major air pollutants regulated by the Clean Air Act: ground-level ozone, particle pollution (also known as particulate matter), carbon monoxide, sulfur dioxide, and nitrogen dioxide. The AQI runs from 0 to 500. The higher the AQI value, the greater the level of air pollution and the greater the health concern; (3) Sulfur dioxide is no longer included in this table (as of December 8, 2021) because SO_2 concentrations tend to be very localized and not necessarily representative of broad geographical areas like counties and CBSAs.
Source: U.S. Environmental Protection Agency, Air Quality Index Report, 2021

Maximum Air Pollutant Concentrations: Particulate Matter, Ozone, CO and Lead

	Particulate Matter 10 (ug/m^3)	Particulate Matter 2.5 Wtd AM (ug/m^3)	Particulate Matter 2.5 24-Hr (ug/m^3)	Ozone (ppm)	Carbon Monoxide (ppm)	Lead (ug/m^3)
MSA[1] Level	81	11.8	30	0.068	4	0
NAAQS[2]	150	15	35	0.075	9	0.15
Met NAAQS[2]	Yes	Yes	Yes	Yes	Yes	Yes

Note: (1) Data covers the Pittsburgh, PA Metropolitan Statistical Area; Data from exceptional events are included; (2) National Ambient Air Quality Standards; ppm = parts per million; ug/m^3 = micrograms per cubic meter; n/a not available.
Concentrations: Particulate Matter 10 (coarse particulate)—highest second maximum 24-hour concentration; Particulate Matter 2.5 Wtd AM (fine particulate)—highest weighted annual mean concentration; Particulate Matter 2.5 24-Hour (fine particulate)—highest 98th percentile 24-hour concentration; Ozone—highest fourth daily maximum 8-hour concentration; Carbon Monoxide—highest second maximum non-overlapping 8-hour concentration; Lead—maximum running 3-month average
Source: U.S. Environmental Protection Agency, Air Quality Monitoring Information, "Air Quality Statistics by City, 2021"

Maximum Air Pollutant Concentrations: Nitrogen Dioxide and Sulfur Dioxide

	Nitrogen Dioxide AM (ppb)	Nitrogen Dioxide 1-Hr (ppb)	Sulfur Dioxide AM (ppb)	Sulfur Dioxide 1-Hr (ppb)	Sulfur Dioxide 24-Hr (ppb)
MSA[1] Level	10	36	n/a	54	n/a
NAAQS[2]	53	100	30	75	140
Met NAAQS[2]	Yes	Yes	n/a	Yes	n/a

Note: (1) Data covers the Pittsburgh, PA Metropolitan Statistical Area; Data from exceptional events are included; (2) National Ambient Air Quality Standards; ppm = parts per million; ug/m³ = micrograms per cubic meter; n/a not available.
Concentrations: Nitrogen Dioxide AM—highest arithmetic mean concentration; Nitrogen Dioxide 1-Hr—highest 98th percentile 1-hour daily maximum concentration; Sulfur Dioxide AM—highest annual mean concentration; Sulfur Dioxide 1-Hr—highest 99th percentile 1-hour daily maximum concentration; Sulfur Dioxide 24-Hr—highest second maximum 24-hour concentration
Source: U.S. Environmental Protection Agency, Air Quality Monitoring Information, "Air Quality Statistics by City, 2021"

Providence, Rhode Island

Background

Providence is the capital of Rhode Island. At the head of Narragansett Bay, it's one of the nation's most historic cities as well as one of its most inviting, recognized as having big city qualities on a small city scale.

Providence was founded in 1636 by Roger Williams, the Massachusetts preacher exiled by the Puritans for his radical religious ideas. In a reversal of the usual procedure, Williams first obtained title to the land directly from the Narragansett tribe, and subsequently, in 1644, received a Royal Charter from London for the settlement.

Though the economy originally depended on agriculture, trade soon dominated. Whaling, a related maritime activity, was as important in Providence as it was to all of Rhode Island's ports. During this trade, several Rhode Islanders amassed considerable wealth and endowed many of Providence's enduring public and cultural institutions, including Brown University, one of the nation's oldest.

After the Revolution, Providence industrialized and became a major center for the textile, silver, and jewelry trades. Innovations born from Providence workshops include plating base metals with gold or silver. By the time of the Civil War, the economy had shifted from mercantile shipping to the fully industrial, making the city a major economic resource to the Union during the Civil War.

By the mid-twentieth century, Providence's population had declined and government mismanagement, along with the national decline of heavy industry, combined to blemish the city. Since the 1980s, however, reforms and improvements have brought to Providence a renaissance of jobs, city services, downtown revitalization, and cultural assets. The city is now regarded, particularly by younger professionals, as one of the most desirable urban locations on the East Coast. Educational and cultural assets include museums, theaters, an award-winning zoo, highly acclaimed restaurants, and renowned venues for arts and entertainment. Providence and the surrounding areas have been a backdrop for several movies and television series and the city remains invested in luring filmmakers by offering a tax credit to motion picture companies.

A living testament to Providence's renaissance is WaterFire, a fire sculpture installation by Barnaby Evans which burns anew each spring on downtown Providence's three rivers. Waterplace Park and Riverwalk was perhaps the most important revitalization project to happen in Providence for many years. Parts of the river that had long been paved over were reopened, and park areas were created along the banks. The picturesque river is now used routinely for boating and sculling and by the Brown University rowing crews.

Downtown Providence offers the Providence Place Mall, a state-of-the-art emporium that mirrors the historically mercantile character of the city, the Arcade, built in 1828 and America's first indoor shopping mall, and the famous 1922 Biltmore Hotel. A favorite Providence neighborhood is College Hill, which connects the campuses of Brown University and the Rhode Island School of Design with cafes, restaurants, shops, and street vendors.

Getting around Providence is getting easier. In 2020, Providence's public transit system expanded service in the city, and Transit Master Plan 2040 will see improvements or expansions to all aspects of public transportation. Construction is underway on developing 60 miles of bike paths, bike lanes, and greenways.

The city is considered one of the most active gay communities in the Northeast. Former mayor David Cicilline ran as openly gay, and former Mayor Cianci instituted the position of Mayor's Liaison to the Gay and Lesbian community in the 1990s.

The energy of Providence is apparent in its choice of sports. The city is home to the American Hockey League's Providence Bruins, and it was host to Gravity Games in 1999, 2000, and 2001. Providence is also the 1995 birthplace of ESPN's X Games.

Providence enjoys variable southern New England weather with temperatures slightly moderated by the city's proximity to Narragansett Bay and the Atlantic Ocean. The weather is changeable, due to the convergence of weather systems from the west, the Gulf of Mexico, and the North Atlantic. Precipitation is evenly distributed throughout the year. In October 2012, the city was hit by Hurricane Sandy, resulting in storm surges, power outages, and interrupted transportation.

Rankings

Business/Finance Rankings

- The Brookings Institution ranked the nation's largest cities based on income inequality. Providence was ranked #3 (#1 = greatest inequality). Criteria: the "95/20 ratio," a figure representing the income at which a household earns more than 95 percent of all other households, divided by the income at which a household earns more than only 20 percent of all other households. *Brookings Institution, "Household Income Inequality, Largest Cities of 97 Large U.S. Metro Areas, 2014-2016," February 5, 2018*

- The Brookings Institution ranked the 100 largest metro areas in the U.S. based on income inequality. Providence was ranked #20 (#1 = greatest inequality). Criteria: the "95/20 ratio," a figure representing the income at which a household earns more than 95 percent of all other households, divided by the income at which a household earns more than only 20 percent of all other households. *Brookings Institution, "Household Income Inequality, 100 Largest U.S. Metro Areas, 2014-2016," February 5, 2018*

- Providence was identified as one of America's most frugal metro areas by *Coupons.com.* The city ranked #22 out of 25. Criteria: digital coupon usage. *Coupons.com, "America's Most Frugal Cities of 2017," March 22, 2018*

- The Providence metro area appeared on the Milken Institute "2022 Best Performing Cities" list. Rank: #157 out of 200 large metro areas (population over 250,000). Criteria: job growth; wage and salary growth; high-tech output growth; housing affordability; household broadband access. *Milken Institute, "Best-Performing Cities 2022," March 28, 2022*

- *Forbes* ranked the 200 most populous metro areas to determine the nation's "Best Places for Business and Careers." The Providence metro area was ranked #124. Criteria: costs (business and living); job growth (past and projected); income growth; quality of life; educational attainment (college and high school); projected economic growth; cultural and leisure opportunities; workplace tolerance laws; net migration patterns. *Forbes, "The Best Places for Business and Careers 2019: Seattle Still On Top," October 30, 2019*

Children/Family Rankings

- Providence was selected as one of the most playful cities in the U.S. by KaBOOM! The organization's Playful City USA initiative honors cities and towns across the nation that have made their communities more playable. Criteria: pledging to integrate play as a solution to challenges in their communities; making it easy for children to get active and balanced play; creating more family-friendly and innovative communities as a result. *KaBOOM! National Campaign for Play, "2017 Playful City USA Communities"*

Culture/Performing Arts Rankings

- Providence was selected as one of "America's Favorite Cities." The city ranked #4 in the "Architecture" category. Respondents to an online survey were asked to rate their favorite place (population over 100,000) in over 65 categories. *Travelandleisure.com, "America's Favorite Cities for Architecture 2016," March 2, 2017*

Dating/Romance Rankings

- Providence was ranked #20 out of 25 cities that stood out for inspiring romance and attracting diners on the website OpenTable.com. Criteria: percentage of people who dined out on Valentine's Day in 2018; percentage of romantic restaurants as rated by OpenTable diner reviews; and percentage of tables seated for two. *OpenTable, "25 Most Romantic Cities in America for 2019," February 7, 2019*

Education Rankings

- Personal finance website *WalletHub* analyzed the 150 largest U.S. metropolitan statistical areas to determine where the most educated Americans are putting their degrees to work. Criteria: education levels; percentage of workers with degrees; education quality and attainment gap; public school quality rankings; quality and enrollment of each metro area's universities. Providence was ranked #91 (#1 = most educated city). *www.WalletHub.com, "Most & Least Educated Cities in America," July 18, 2022*

Environmental Rankings

- Sperling's BestPlaces assessed the 50 largest metropolitan areas of the United States for the likelihood of dangerously extreme weather events or earthquakes. In general the Southeast and South-Central regions have the highest risk of weather extremes and earthquakes, while the Pacific Northwest enjoys the lowest risk. Of the least risky metropolitan areas, the Providence metro area was ranked #9. *www.bestplaces.net, "Avoid Natural Disasters: BestPlaces Reveals The Top 10 Safest Places to Live," October 25, 2017*

Health/Fitness Rankings

- Providence was identified as a "2022 Spring Allergy Capital." The area ranked #66 out of 100. Three groups of factors were used to identify the most challenging cities for people with allergies during the spring season: annual spring pollen scores; over the counter allergy medicine use; number of board-certified allergy specialists. *Asthma and Allergy Foundation of America, "Spring Allergy Capitals 2022," March 2, 2022*

- Providence was identified as a "2022 Fall Allergy Capital." The area ranked #71 out of 100. Three groups of factors were used to identify the most challenging cities for people with allergies during the fall season: annual fall pollen scores; over the counter allergy medicine use; number of board-certified allergy specialists. *Asthma and Allergy Foundation of America, "Fall Allergy Capitals 2022," March 2, 2022*

- Providence was identified as a "2022 Asthma Capital." The area ranked #58 out of the nation's 100 largest metropolitan areas. Criteria: estimated asthma prevalence; asthma-related mortality; and ER visits due to asthma. Risk factors analyzed but not factored in the rankings: annual pollen score; annual air quality; public smoking laws; access to board-certified asthma specialists; rescue and controller medication use; uninsured rate; poverty rate. *Asthma and Allergy Foundation of America, "Asthma Capitals 2022: The Most Challenging Places to Live With Asthma," September 14, 2022*

Real Estate Rankings

- *WalletHub* compared the most populated U.S. cities to determine which had the best markets for real estate agents. Providence ranked #152 where demand was high and pay was the best. Criteria: sales per agent; annual median wage for real-estate agents; monthly average starting salary for real estate agents; real estate job density and competition; unemployment rate; home turnover rate; housing-market health index; and other relevant metrics. *www.WalletHub.com, "2021 Best Places to Be a Real Estate Agent," May 12, 2021*

- The Providence metro area was identified as one of the nations's 20 hottest housing markets in 2023. Criteria: listing views as an indicator of demand and number of days on the market as an indicator of pace. The area ranked #7. *Realtor.com, "January 2023 Top 20 Hottest Housing Markets," February 23, 2023*

- Providence was ranked #156 out of 235 metro areas in terms of housing affordability in 2022 by the National Association of Home Builders (#1 = most affordable). Criteria: the share of homes sold in that area affordable to a family earning the local median income, based on standard mortgage underwriting criteria. *National Association of Home Builders®, NAHB-Wells Fargo Housing Opportunity Index, 4th Quarter 2022*

Safety Rankings

- Allstate ranked the 200 largest cities in America in terms of driver safety. Providence ranked #193. Criteria: internal property damage claims over a two-year period from January 2016 to December 2017. The report helps increase the importance of safety and awareness behind the wheel. *Allstate, "Allstate America's Best Drivers Report, 2019" June 24, 2019*

Seniors/Retirement Rankings

- From its Best Cities for Successful Aging indexes, the Milken Institute generated rankings for metropolitan areas, weighing data in nine categories—health care, wellness, living arrangements, transportation and convenience, financial characteristics, education, employment, community engagement, and overall livability. The Providence metro area was ranked #70 overall in the large metro area category. *Milken Institute, "Best Cities for Successful Aging, 2017" March 14, 2017*

Transportation Rankings

- According to the INRIX "2022 Global Traffic Scorecard," Providence was identified as one of the most congested metro areas in the U.S. The area ranked #21 out of 25. Criteria: average annual time spent in traffic and average cost of congestion per motorist. *Inrix.com, "Return to Work, Higher Gas Prices & Inflation Drove Americans to Spend Hundreds More in Time and Money Commuting," January 10, 2023*

Women/Minorities Rankings

- Personal finance website *WalletHub* compared more than 180 U.S. cities across two key dimensions, "Hispanic Business-Friendliness" and "Hispanic Purchasing Power," to arrive at the most favorable conditions for Hispanic entrepreneurs. Providence was ranked #182 out of 182. Criteria includes: share of Hispanic-Owned Businesses; Hispanic entrepreneurship rate to median annual income of Hispanics; Small Business-Friendliness score; cost of living; and number of Hispanics with at least a bachelor's degree. *WalletHub.com, "2019's Best Cities for Hispanic Entrepreneurs," May 1, 2019*

Miscellaneous Rankings

- *MoveHub* ranked 446 hipster cities across 20 countries, using its new and improved *alternative* Hipster Index and Providence came out as #33 among the top 50. Criteria: population over 150,000; number of vintage boutiques; density of tattoo parlors; vegan places to eat; coffee shops; and density of vinyl record stores. *www.movehub.com, "The Hipster Index: Brighton Pips Portland to Global Top Spot," July 28, 2021*

- *WalletHub* compared the 150 most populated U.S. cities to determine their operating efficiency. A "Quality of Services" score was constructed for each city and then divided by the total budget per capita to reveal which were managed the best. Providence ranked #96. Criteria: financial stability; economy; education; safety; health; infrastructure and pollution. *www.WalletHub.com, "2022's Best- & Worst-Run Cities in America," June 21, 2022*

Business Environment

DEMOGRAPHICS

Population Growth

Area	1990 Census	2000 Census	2010 Census	2020 Census	Population Growth (%)	
					1990-2020	2010-2020
City	160,734	173,618	178,042	190,934	18.8	7.2
MSA[1]	1,509,789	1,582,997	1,600,852	1,676,579	11.0	4.7
U.S.	248,709,873	281,421,906	308,745,538	331,449,281	33.3	7.4

Note: (1) Figures cover the Providence-Warwick, RI-MA Metropolitan Statistical Area
Source: U.S. Census Bureau, 1990 Census, 2000 Census, 2010 Census, 2020 Census

Race

Area	White Alone[2] (%)	Black Alone[2] (%)	Asian Alone[2] (%)	AIAN[3] Alone[2] (%)	NHOPI[4] Alone[2] (%)	Other Race Alone[2] (%)	Two or More Races (%)
City	37.7	13.5	6.1	1.5	0.1	26.9	14.2
MSA[1]	73.9	5.2	3.1	0.6	0.0	8.0	9.1
U.S.	61.6	12.4	6.0	1.1	0.2	8.4	10.2

Note: (1) Figures cover the Providence-Warwick, RI-MA Metropolitan Statistical Area; (2) Alone is defined as not being in combination with one or more other races; (3) American Indian and Alaska Native; (4) Native Hawaiian and Other Pacific Islander
Source: U.S. Census Bureau, 2020 Census

Hispanic or Latino Origin

Area	Total (%)	Mexican (%)	Puerto Rican (%)	Cuban (%)	Other (%)
City	42.9	1.3	7.9	0.3	33.4
MSA[1]	13.7	0.9	4.4	0.2	8.3
U.S.	18.4	11.2	1.8	0.7	4.7

Note: Persons of Hispanic or Latino origin can be of any race; (1) Figures cover the Providence-Warwick, RI-MA Metropolitan Statistical Area
Source: U.S. Census Bureau, 2017-2021 American Community Survey 5-Year Estimates

Age

Area	Percent of Population									Median Age
	Under Age 5	Age 5–19	Age 20–34	Age 35–44	Age 45–54	Age 55–64	Age 65–74	Age 75–84	Age 85+	
City	5.6	21.3	29.4	12.4	10.4	9.8	6.6	3.0	1.4	30.9
MSA[1]	4.8	17.9	20.0	12.1	12.8	14.5	10.6	5.2	2.4	40.8
U.S.	5.6	19.2	20.2	12.7	12.4	13.1	10.0	4.9	1.9	38.8

Note: (1) Figures cover the Providence-Warwick, RI-MA Metropolitan Statistical Area
Source: U.S. Census Bureau, 2020 Census

Disability by Age

Area	All Ages	Under 18 Years Old	18 to 64 Years Old	65 Years and Over
City	13.6	5.9	12.4	36.4
MSA[1]	13.7	5.4	11.5	31.9
U.S.	12.6	4.4	10.3	33.4

Note: Figures show percent of the civilian noninstitutionalized population that reported having a disability. Disability status is determined from six types of difficulty: vision, hearing, cognitive, ambulatory, self-care, and independent living. For children under 5 years old, hearing and vision difficulty are used to determine disability status. For children between the ages of 5 and 14, disability status is determined from hearing, vision, cognitive, ambulatory, and self-care difficulties. For people aged 15 years and older, they are considered to have a disability if they have difficulty with any one of the six difficulty types; Note: (1) Figures cover the Providence-Warwick, RI-MA Metropolitan Statistical Area
Source: U.S. Census Bureau, 2017-2021 American Community Survey 5-Year Estimates

Ancestry

Area	German	Irish	English	American	Italian	Polish	French[2]	Scottish	Dutch
City	3.7	8.0	3.9	2.1	6.9	1.4	2.9	0.8	0.3
MSA[1]	4.5	17.2	10.7	3.2	13.1	3.4	8.6	1.5	0.4
U.S.	12.8	9.6	8.1	5.7	5.0	2.7	2.2	1.6	1.1

Note: Figures are the percentage of the total population reporting a particular ancestry. The nine most commonly reported ancestries in the U.S. are shown. Figures include multiple ancestries (e.g. if a person reported being Irish and Italian, they were included in both columns); (1) Figures cover the Providence-Warwick, RI-MA Metropolitan Statistical Area; (2) Excludes Basque
Source: U.S. Census Bureau, 2017-2021 American Community Survey 5-Year Estimates

Foreign-born Population

Area	Any Foreign Country	Asia	Mexico	Europe	Caribbean	Central America[2]	South America	Africa	Canada
City	30.7	3.8	0.3	2.5	13.9	5.4	1.2	3.1	0.4
MSA[1]	13.9	2.3	0.3	4.1	2.6	1.6	1.2	1.6	0.2
U.S.	13.6	4.2	3.3	1.4	1.1	1.1	1.1	0.8	0.2

Above the area/detail columns: Percent of Population Born in

Note: (1) Figures cover the Providence-Warwick, RI-MA Metropolitan Statistical Area; (2) Excludes Mexico.
Source: U.S. Census Bureau, 2017-2021 American Community Survey 5-Year Estimates

Household Size

Area	One	Two	Three	Four	Five	Six	Seven or More	Average Household Size
City	33.7	29.1	15.5	11.1	7.1	1.9	1.6	2.60
MSA[1]	29.6	33.1	16.7	12.8	5.2	1.7	0.9	2.50
U.S.	28.1	33.8	15.5	12.9	6.0	2.3	1.4	2.60

Persons in Household (%) spans the One–Seven or More columns.

Note: (1) Figures cover the Providence-Warwick, RI-MA Metropolitan Statistical Area
Source: U.S. Census Bureau, 2017-2021 American Community Survey 5-Year Estimates

Household Relationships

Area	House-holder	Opposite-sex Spouse	Same-sex Spouse	Opposite-sex Unmarried Partner	Same-sex Unmarried Partner	Child[2]	Grand-child	Other Relatives	Non-relatives
City	36.5	10.5	0.3	2.9	0.3	27.3	1.9	5.7	6.1
MSA[1]	40.0	16.9	0.2	3.0	0.2	27.2	1.9	4.1	3.0
U.S.	38.3	17.5	0.2	2.5	0.2	28.3	2.4	4.8	3.4

Note: Figures are percent of the total population; (1) Figures cover the Providence-Warwick, RI-MA Metropolitan Statistical Area; (2) Includes biological, adopted, and stepchildren of the householder
Source: U.S. Census Bureau, 2020 Census

Gender

Area	Males	Females	Males per 100 Females
City	92,861	98,073	94.7
MSA[1]	812,496	864,083	94.0
U.S.	162,685,811	168,763,470	96.4

Note: (1) Figures cover the Providence-Warwick, RI-MA Metropolitan Statistical Area
Source: U.S. Census Bureau, 2020 Census

Marital Status

Area	Never Married	Now Married[2]	Separated	Widowed	Divorced
City	53.6	31.9	2.0	4.2	8.4
MSA[1]	36.5	45.0	1.5	5.9	11.1
U.S.	33.8	48.0	1.8	5.6	10.8

Note: Figures are percentages and cover the population 15 years of age and older; (1) Figures cover the Providence-Warwick, RI-MA Metropolitan Statistical Area; (2) Excludes separated
Source: U.S. Census Bureau, 2017-2021 American Community Survey 5-Year Estimates

Religious Groups by Family

Area	Catholic	Baptist	Methodist	LDS[2]	Pentecostal	Lutheran	Islam	Adventist	Other
MSA[1]	37.9	0.9	0.6	0.3	0.6	0.3	0.5	0.9	6.1
U.S.	18.7	7.3	3.0	2.0	1.8	1.7	1.3	1.3	11.6

Note: Figures are the number of adherents as a percentage of the total population and cover the eight largest religious groups in the U.S; (1) Figures cover the Providence-Warwick, RI-MA Metropolitan Statistical Area; (2) Church of Jesus Christ of Latter-day Saints
Sources: 2020 U.S. Religion Census, Association of Statisticians of American Religious Bodies; The Association of Religion Data Archives (ARDA)

Religious Groups by Tradition

Area	Catholic	Evangelical Protestant	Mainline Protestant	Black Protestant	Islam	Judaism	Hinduism	Orthodox	Buddhism
MSA[1]	37.9	4.0	3.2	0.1	0.5	0.6	0.1	0.5	0.2
U.S.	18.7	16.5	5.2	2.3	1.3	0.6	0.4	0.4	0.3

Note: Figures are the number of adherents as a percentage of the total population; (1) Figures cover the Providence-Warwick, RI-MA Metropolitan Statistical Area
Sources: 2020 U.S. Religion Census, Association of Statisticians of American Religious Bodies; The Association of Religion Data Archives (ARDA)

ECONOMY

Gross Metropolitan Product

Area	2020	2021	2022	2023	Rank[2]
MSA[1]	87.9	95.6	104.0	109.3	45

Note: Figures are in billions of dollars; (1) Figures cover the Providence-Warwick, RI-MA Metropolitan Statistical Area; (2) Rank is based on 2021 data and ranges from 1 to 381
Source: U.S. Conference of Mayors, U.S. Metro Economies: U.S. Metros Compared to Global and State Economies, June 2022

Economic Growth

Area	2018-20 (%)	2021 (%)	2022 (%)	2023 (%)	Rank[2]
MSA[1]	-1.1	5.6	3.4	1.9	224
U.S.	-0.6	5.7	3.1	2.9	–

Note: Figures are real gross metropolitan product (GMP) growth rates and represent average annual percent change; (1) Figures cover the Providence-Warwick, RI-MA Metropolitan Statistical Area; (2) Rank is based on 2020 2-year average annual percent change and ranges from 1 to 381
Source: U.S. Conference of Mayors, U.S. Metro Economies: U.S. Metros Compared to Global and State Economies, June 2022

Metropolitan Area Exports

Area	2016	2017	2018	2019	2020	2021	Rank[2]
MSA[1]	6,595.7	7,125.4	6,236.6	7,424.8	6,685.2	6,708.2	49

Note: Figures are in millions of dollars; (1) Figures cover the Providence-Warwick, RI-MA Metropolitan Statistical Area; (2) Rank is based on 2021 data and ranges from 1 to 388
Source: U.S. Department of Commerce, International Trade Administration, Office of Trade and Economic Analysis, Industry and Analysis, Exports by Metropolitan Area, data extracted March 16, 2023

Building Permits

Area	Single-Family			Multi-Family			Total		
	2021	2022	Pct. Chg.	2021	2022	Pct. Chg.	2021	2022	Pct. Chg.
City	1	28	2,700.0	53	271	411.3	54	299	453.7
MSA[1]	1,788	1,559	-12.8	470	563	19.8	2,258	2,122	-6.0
U.S.	1,115,400	975,600	-12.5	621,600	689,500	10.9	1,737,000	1,665,100	-4.1

Note: (1) Figures cover the Providence-Warwick, RI-MA Metropolitan Statistical Area; Figures represent new, privately-owned housing units authorized (unadjusted data); All permit data are based on estimates with imputation
Source: U.S. Census Bureau, Manufacturing, Mining, and Construction Statistics, Building Permits, 2021, 2022

Bankruptcy Filings

Area	Business Filings			Nonbusiness Filings		
	2021	2022	% Chg.	2021	2022	% Chg.
Providence County	16	21	31.3	638	507	-20.5
U.S.	14,347	13,481	-6.0	399,269	374,240	-6.3

Note: Business filings include Chapter 7, Chapter 9, Chapter 11, Chapter 12, Chapter 13, Chapter 15, and Section 304; Nonbusiness filings include Chapter 7, Chapter 11, and Chapter 13
Source: Administrative Office of the U.S. Courts, Business and Nonbusiness Bankruptcy, County Cases Commenced by Chapter of the Bankruptcy Code, During the 12-Month Period Ending December 31, 2021 and Business and Nonbusiness Bankruptcy, County Cases Commenced by Chapter of the Bankruptcy Code, During the 12-Month Period Ending December 31, 2022

Housing Vacancy Rates

Area	Gross Vacancy Rate[2] (%)			Year-Round Vacancy Rate[3] (%)			Rental Vacancy Rate[4] (%)			Homeowner Vacancy Rate[5] (%)		
	2020	2021	2022	2020	2021	2022	2020	2021	2022	2020	2021	2022
MSA[1]	8.7	7.9	9.5	6.6	5.8	7.6	3.5	2.7	4.5	0.8	0.7	0.4
U.S.	10.6	10.8	10.5	8.2	8.4	8.2	6.3	6.1	5.8	1.0	0.9	0.8

Note: (1) Figures cover the Providence-Warwick, RI-MA Metropolitan Statistical Area; (2) The percentage of the total housing inventory that is vacant; (3) The percentage of the housing inventory (excluding seasonal units) that is year-round vacant; (4) The percentage of rental inventory that is vacant for rent; (5) The percentage of homeowner inventory that is vacant for sale
Source: U.S. Census Bureau, Housing Vacancies and Homeownership Annual Statistics: 2020, 2021, 2022

INCOME

Income

Area	Per Capita ($)	Median Household ($)	Average Household ($)
City	31,757	55,787	83,046
MSA[1]	39,267	74,422	97,540
U.S.	37,638	69,021	97,196

Note: (1) Figures cover the Providence-Warwick, RI-MA Metropolitan Statistical Area
Source: U.S. Census Bureau, 2017-2021 American Community Survey 5-Year Estimates

Providence, Rhode Island

Household Income Distribution

Area	Percent of Households Earning							
	Under $15,000	$15,000 -$24,999	$25,000 -$34,999	$35,000 -$49,999	$50,000 -$74,999	$75,000 -$99,999	$100,000 -$149,999	$150,000 and up
City	15.7	10.6	8.8	11.3	17.4	11.9	12.0	12.4
MSA[1]	9.7	7.9	7.3	10.1	15.2	13.2	18.2	18.3
U.S.	9.4	7.8	8.2	11.4	16.8	12.8	16.3	17.3

Note: (1) Figures cover the Providence-Warwick, RI-MA Metropolitan Statistical Area
Source: U.S. Census Bureau, 2017-2021 American Community Survey 5-Year Estimates

Poverty Rate

Area	All Ages	Under 18 Years Old	18 to 64 Years Old	65 Years and Over
City	21.5	30.3	18.8	19.5
MSA[1]	11.2	15.2	10.3	9.6
U.S.	12.6	17.0	11.8	9.6

Note: Figures are percentage of people whose income during the past 12 months was below the poverty level;
(1) Figures cover the Providence-Warwick, RI-MA Metropolitan Statistical Area
Source: U.S. Census Bureau, 2017-2021 American Community Survey 5-Year Estimates

EMPLOYMENT

Labor Force and Employment

Area	Civilian Labor Force			Workers Employed		
	Dec. 2021	Dec. 2022	% Chg.	Dec. 2021	Dec. 2022	% Chg.
City	88,878	88,200	-0.8	85,136	85,603	0.5
NECTA[1]	706,157	698,803	-1.0	679,845	680,282	0.1
U.S.	161,696,000	164,224,000	1.6	155,732,000	158,872,000	2.0

Note: Data is not seasonally adjusted and covers workers 16 years of age and older; (1) Figures cover the Providence-Warwick, RI-MA New England City and Town Area
Source: Bureau of Labor Statistics, Local Area Unemployment Statistics

Unemployment Rate

Area	2022											
	Jan.	Feb.	Mar.	Apr.	May	Jun.	Jul.	Aug.	Sep.	Oct.	Nov.	Dec.
City	5.5	5.3	3.7	3.3	3.5	3.5	4.0	5.0	4.3	4.1	4.3	2.9
NECTA[1]	4.9	4.7	3.4	3.0	2.9	3.0	3.3	4.0	3.4	3.3	3.4	2.7
U.S.	4.4	4.1	3.8	3.3	3.4	3.8	3.8	3.8	3.3	3.4	3.4	3.3

Note: Data is not seasonally adjusted and covers workers 16 years of age and older; (1) Figures cover the Providence-Warwick, RI-MA New England City and Town Area
Source: Bureau of Labor Statistics, Local Area Unemployment Statistics

Average Wages

Occupation	$/Hr.	Occupation	$/Hr.
Accountants and Auditors	44.90	Maintenance and Repair Workers	24.78
Automotive Mechanics	22.35	Marketing Managers	79.73
Bookkeepers	24.22	Network and Computer Systems Admin.	51.47
Carpenters	29.76	Nurses, Licensed Practical	31.28
Cashiers	14.61	Nurses, Registered	42.39
Computer Programmers	43.32	Nursing Assistants	18.87
Computer Systems Analysts	51.67	Office Clerks, General	21.07
Computer User Support Specialists	29.79	Physical Therapists	45.70
Construction Laborers	26.46	Physicians	100.09
Cooks, Restaurant	17.00	Plumbers, Pipefitters and Steamfitters	32.22
Customer Service Representatives	21.03	Police and Sheriff's Patrol Officers	34.35
Dentists	97.31	Postal Service Mail Carriers	27.29
Electricians	30.94	Real Estate Sales Agents	35.48
Engineers, Electrical	54.51	Retail Salespersons	17.17
Fast Food and Counter Workers	14.82	Sales Representatives, Technical/Scientific	39.71
Financial Managers	81.58	Secretaries, Exc. Legal/Medical/Executive	22.88
First-Line Supervisors of Office Workers	34.07	Security Guards	17.75
General and Operations Managers	65.29	Surgeons	n/a
Hairdressers/Cosmetologists	15.61	Teacher Assistants, Exc. Postsecondary*	17.68
Home Health and Personal Care Aides	17.07	Teachers, Secondary School, Exc. Sp. Ed.*	36.31
Janitors and Cleaners	17.99	Telemarketers	16.60
Landscaping/Groundskeeping Workers	20.58	Truck Drivers, Heavy/Tractor-Trailer	27.14
Lawyers	74.38	Truck Drivers, Light/Delivery Services	22.45
Maids and Housekeeping Cleaners	16.14	Waiters and Waitresses	16.64

Note: Wage data covers the Providence-Warwick, RI-MA New England City and Town Area; (*) Hourly wages were calculated from annual wage data based on a 40 hour work week; n/a not available.
Source: Bureau of Labor Statistics, Metro Area Occupational Employment & Wage Estimates, May 2022

Employment by Industry

Sector	NECTA[1]		U.S.
	Number of Employees	Percent of Total	Percent of Total
Construction	28,400	4.8	5.0
Private Education and Health Services	124,100	20.8	16.1
Financial Activities	38,400	6.4	5.9
Government	76,200	12.8	14.5
Information	6,900	1.2	2.0
Leisure and Hospitality	63,000	10.6	10.3
Manufacturing	51,300	8.6	8.4
Mining and Logging	200	<0.1	0.4
Other Services	26,400	4.4	3.7
Professional and Business Services	76,000	12.7	14.7
Retail Trade	65,300	10.9	10.2
Transportation, Warehousing, and Utilities	20,200	3.4	4.9
Wholesale Trade	20,000	3.4	3.9

Note: Figures are non-farm employment as of December 2022. Figures are not seasonally adjusted and include workers 16 years of age and older; (1) Figures cover the Providence-Warwick, RI-MA New England City and Town Area
Source: Bureau of Labor Statistics, Current Employment Statistics, Employment, Hours, and Earnings

Employment by Occupation

Occupation Classification	City (%)	MSA[1] (%)	U.S. (%)
Management, Business, Science, and Arts	37.5	39.9	40.3
Natural Resources, Construction, and Maintenance	4.9	8.3	8.7
Production, Transportation, and Material Moving	16.5	12.2	13.1
Sales and Office	19.2	21.3	20.9
Service	21.9	18.3	17.0

Note: Figures cover employed civilians 16 years of age and older; (1) Figures cover the Providence-Warwick, RI-MA Metropolitan Statistical Area
Source: U.S. Census Bureau, 2017-2021 American Community Survey 5-Year Estimates

Occupations with Greatest Projected Employment Growth: 2022 – 2024

Occupation[1]	2022 Employment	2024 Projected Employment	Numeric Employment Change	Percent Employment Change
Cooks, Restaurant	6,170	7,080	910	14.7
Fast Food and Counter Workers	9,060	9,750	690	7.6
Waiters and Waitresses	6,820	7,490	670	9.8
Home Health and Personal Care Aides	8,760	9,220	460	5.3
Landscaping and Groundskeeping Workers	5,610	6,070	460	8.2
Carpenters	5,060	5,510	450	8.9
Laborers and Freight, Stock, and Material Movers, Hand	7,020	7,430	410	5.8
Fitness Trainers and Aerobics Instructors	1,360	1,750	390	28.7
Software Developers and Software Quality Assurance Analysts and Testers	5,100	5,460	360	7.1
Construction Laborers	3,730	4,070	340	9.1

Note: Projections cover Rhode Island; (1) Sorted by numeric employment change
Source: www.projectionscentral.com, State Occupational Projections, 2022–2024 Short-Term Projections

Fastest-Growing Occupations: 2022 – 2024

Occupation[1]	2022 Employment	2024 Projected Employment	Numeric Employment Change	Percent Employment Change
Fitness Trainers and Aerobics Instructors	1,360	1,750	390	28.7
Amusement and Recreation Attendants	1,050	1,300	250	23.8
Hotel, Motel, and Resort Desk Clerks	620	730	110	17.7
Motorboat Mechanics and Service Technicians	530	620	90	17.0
Musicians and Singers	370	430	60	16.2
Cooks, Restaurant	6,170	7,080	910	14.7
First-Line Supervisors of Personal Service & Entertainment and Recreation Workers, Exc Gambling Ser	630	710	80	12.7
Nonfarm Animal Caretakers	1,480	1,650	170	11.5
Bartenders	2,370	2,640	270	11.4
Dining Room and Cafeteria Attendants and Bartender Helpers	1,920	2,130	210	10.9

Note: Projections cover Rhode Island; (1) Sorted by percent employment change and excludes occupations with numeric employment change less than 50
Source: www.projectionscentral.com, State Occupational Projections, 2022–2024 Short-Term Projections

CITY FINANCES

City Government Finances

Component	2020 ($000)	2020 ($ per capita)
Total Revenues	1,034,558	5,751
Total Expenditures	937,541	5,212
Debt Outstanding	837,615	4,656
Cash and Securities[1]	335,527	1,865

Note: (1) Cash and security holdings of a government at the close of its fiscal year, including those of its dependent agencies, utilities, and liquor stores.
Source: U.S. Census Bureau, State & Local Government Finances 2020

City Government Revenue by Source

Source	2020 ($000)	2020 ($ per capita)	2020 (%)
General Revenue			
From Federal Government	8,435	47	0.8
From State Government	420,281	2,336	40.6
From Local Governments	49,349	274	4.8
Taxes			
Property	352,750	1,961	34.1
Sales and Gross Receipts	7,100	39	0.7
Personal Income	0	0	0.0
Corporate Income	0	0	0.0
Motor Vehicle License	0	0	0.0
Other Taxes	7,744	43	0.7
Current Charges	89,694	499	8.7
Liquor Store	0	0	0.0
Utility	69,796	388	6.7

Source: U.S. Census Bureau, State & Local Government Finances 2020

City Government Expenditures by Function

Function	2020 ($000)	2020 ($ per capita)	2020 (%)
General Direct Expenditures			
Air Transportation	0	0	0.0
Corrections	0	0	0.0
Education	454,543	2,526	48.5
Employment Security Administration	0	0	0.0
Financial Administration	11,769	65	1.3
Fire Protection	68,989	383	7.4
General Public Buildings	39,018	216	4.2
Governmental Administration, Other	12,601	70	1.3
Health	0	0	0.0
Highways	7,852	43	0.8
Hospitals	0	0	0.0
Housing and Community Development	10,967	61	1.2
Interest on General Debt	45,850	254	4.9
Judicial and Legal	8,839	49	0.9
Libraries	4,275	23	0.5
Parking	571	3	0.1
Parks and Recreation	9,892	55	1.1
Police Protection	107,251	596	11.4
Public Welfare	826	4	0.1
Sewerage	899	5	0.1
Solid Waste Management	11,649	64	1.2
Veterans' Services	0	0	0.0
Liquor Store	0	0	0.0
Utility	76,795	426	8.2

Source: U.S. Census Bureau, State & Local Government Finances 2020

TAXES

State Corporate Income Tax Rates

State	Tax Rate (%)	Income Brackets ($)	Num. of Brackets	Financial Institution Tax Rate (%)[a]	Federal Income Tax Ded.
Rhode Island	7.0 (b)	Flat rate	1	9.0 (b)	No

Note: Tax rates as of January 1, 2023; (a) Rates listed are the corporate income tax rate applied to financial institutions or excise taxes based on income. Some states have other taxes based upon the value of deposits or shares; (b) Minimum tax is $800 in California, $250 in District of Columbia, $50 in Arizona and North Dakota (banks), $400 ($100 banks) in Rhode Island, $200 per location in South Dakota (banks), $100 in Utah, $300 in Vermont.
Source: Federation of Tax Administrators, State Corporate Income Tax Rates, January 1, 2023

State Individual Income Tax Rates

State	Tax Rate (%)	Income Brackets ($)	Personal Exemptions ($)			Standard Ded. ($)	
			Single	Married	Depend.	Single	Married
Rhode Island (a)	3.75 - 5.99	73,450 - 166,950	4,350	8,700	4,350	9,300	18,600 (z)

Note: Tax rates as of January 1, 2023; Local- and county-level taxes are not included; Federal income tax is not deductible on state income tax returns; (a) 16 states have statutory provision for automatically adjusting to the rate of inflation the dollar values of the income tax brackets, standard deductions, and/or personal exemptions. Oregon does not index the income brackets for $125,000 and over; (z) Alabama standard deduction is phased out for incomes over $25,000. Rhode Island exemptions & standard deductions phased out for incomes over $233,750; Wisconsin standard deduciton phases out for income over $16,989.
Source: Federation of Tax Administrators, State Individual Income Tax Rates, January 1, 2023

Various State Sales and Excise Tax Rates

State	State Sales Tax (%)	Gasoline[1] ($/gal.)	Cigarette[2] ($/pack)	Spirits[3] ($/gal.)	Wine[4] ($/gal.)	Beer[5] ($/gal.)	Recreational Marijuana (%)
Rhode Island	7	0.35	4.25	5.40	1.40	0.12	(q)

Note: All tax rates as of January 1, 2023; (1) The American Petroleum Institute has developed a methodology for determining the average tax rate on a gallon of fuel. Rates may include any of the following: excise taxes, environmental fees, storage tank fees, other fees or taxes, general sales tax, and local taxes; (2) The federal excise tax of $1.0066 per pack and local taxes are not included; (3) Rates are those applicable to off-premise sales of 40% alcohol by volume (a.b.v.) distilled spirits in 750ml containers. Local excise taxes are excluded; (4) Rates are those applicable to off-premise sales of 11% a.b.v. non-carbonated wine in 750ml containers; (5) Rates are those applicable to off-premise sales of 4.7% a.b.v. beer in 12 ounce containers; (q) 10% excise tax (retail price)
Source: Tax Foundation, 2023 Facts & Figures: How Does Your State Compare?

State Business Tax Climate Index Rankings

State	Overall Rank	Corporate Tax Rank	Individual Income Tax Rank	Sales Tax Rank	Property Tax Rank	Unemployment Insurance Tax Rank
Rhode Island	42	40	33	24	41	49

Note: The index is a measure of how each state's tax laws affect economic performance. The lower the rank, the more favorable a state's tax system is for business. States without a given tax are given a ranking of 1. The scores/rankings for the District of Columbia do not affect other states. The 2023 index represents the tax climate as of July 1, 2022.
Source: Tax Foundation, State Business Tax Climate Index 2023

TRANSPORTATION

Means of Transportation to Work

| Area | Car/Truck/Van | | Public Transportation | | | Bicycle | Walked | Other Means | Worked at Home |
	Drove Alone	Car-pooled	Bus	Subway	Railroad				
City	64.0	11.3	3.3	0.1	1.0	0.9	7.3	1.7	10.4
MSA[1]	77.8	8.3	1.2	0.1	0.7	0.2	2.7	1.0	7.8
U.S.	73.2	8.6	2.0	1.6	0.5	0.5	2.5	1.5	9.7

Note: Figures are percentages and cover workers 16 years of age and older; (1) Figures cover the Providence-Warwick, RI-MA Metropolitan Statistical Area
Source: U.S. Census Bureau, 2017-2021 American Community Survey 5-Year Estimates

Travel Time to Work

Area	Less Than 10 Minutes	10 to 19 Minutes	20 to 29 Minutes	30 to 44 Minutes	45 to 59 Minutes	60 to 89 Minutes	90 Minutes or More
City	10.3	40.4	19.4	15.3	6.2	5.5	2.8
MSA[1]	11.7	30.4	21.3	19.8	7.8	6.2	2.8
U.S.	12.4	28.5	21.0	20.9	8.2	6.2	2.9

Note: Note: Figures are percentages and include workers 16 years old and over; (1) Figures cover the Providence-Warwick, RI-MA Metropolitan Statistical Area
Source: U.S. Census Bureau, 2017-2021 American Community Survey 5-Year Estimates

Key Congestion Measures

Measure	1990	2000	2010	2015	2020
Annual Hours of Delay, Total (000)	9,641	24,093	31,473	36,249	26,373
Annual Hours of Delay, Per Auto Commuter	17	36	41	46	33
Annual Congestion Cost, Per Auto Commuter ($)	401	750	778	827	630

Note: Covers the Providence RI-MA urban area
Source: Texas A&M Transportation Institute, 2021 Urban Mobility Report

Freeway Travel Time Index

Measure	1985	1990	1995	2000	2005	2010	2015	2020
Urban Area Index[1]	1.04	1.08	1.12	1.16	1.19	1.17	1.17	1.13
Urban Area Rank[1,2]	81	62	57	43	38	41	46	6

Note: Freeway Travel Time Index—the ratio of travel time in the peak period to the travel time at free-flow conditions. For example, a value of 1.30 indicates a 20-minute free-flow trip takes 26 minutes in the peak (20 minutes x 1.30 = 26 minutes); (1) Covers the Providence RI-MA urban area; (2) Rank is based on 101 larger urban areas (#1 = highest travel time index)
Source: Texas A&M Transportation Institute, 2021 Urban Mobility Report

Public Transportation

Agency Name / Mode of Transportation	Vehicles Operated in Maximum Service[1]	Annual Unlinked Passenger Trips[2] (in thous.)	Annual Passenger Miles[3] (in thous.)
Rhode Island Public Transit Authority (RIPTA)			
Bus (directly operated)	203	7,712.5	41,486.1
Demand Response (directly operated)	50	177.5	2,634.6
Demand Response - Taxi	3	1.2	26.6
Vanpool (purchased transportation)	41	76.3	3,051.3

Note: (1) Number of revenue vehicles operated by the given mode and type of service to meet the annual maximum service requirement. This is the revenue vehicle count during the peak season of the year; on the week and day that maximum service is provided. Vehicles operated in maximum service (VOMS) exclude atypical days and one-time special events; (2) Number of passengers who boarded public transportation vehicles. Passengers are counted each time they board a vehicle no matter how many vehicles they use to travel from their origin to their destination. (3) Sum of the distances ridden by all passengers during the entire fiscal year.
Source: Federal Transit Administration, National Transit Database, 2021

Air Transportation

Airport Name and Code / Type of Service	Passenger Airlines[1]	Passenger Enplanements	Freight Carriers[2]	Freight (lbs)
Theodore Francis Green State Airport (PVD)				
Domestic service (U.S. carriers - 2022)	31	1,570,418	10	12,153,026
International service (U.S. carriers - 2021)	1	11	0	0

Note: (1) Includes all U.S.-based major, minor and commuter airlines that carried at least one passenger during the year; (2) Includes all U.S.-based airlines and freight carriers that transported at least one pound of freight during the year.
Source: Bureau of Transportation Statistics, The Intermodal Transportation Database, Air Carriers: T-100 Domestic Market (U.S. Carriers), 2022; Bureau of Transportation Statistics, The Intermodal Transportation Database, Air Carriers: T-100 International Market (U.S. Carriers), 2021

BUSINESSES

Major Business Headquarters

Company Name	Industry	Rankings	
		Fortune[1]	Forbes[2]
Citizens Financial Group	Commercial banks	473	-
Gilbane	Construction	-	80
Textron	Aerospace and defense	302	-
United Natural Foods	Wholesalers, food and grocery	132	-

Note: (1) Companies that produce a 10-K are ranked 1 to 500 based on 2021 revenue; (2) All private companies with at least $2 billion in annual revenue through the end of their most current fiscal year are ranked 1 to 246; companies listed are headquartered in the city; dashes indicate no ranking
Source: Fortune, "Fortune 500," 2022; Forbes, "America's Largest Private Companies," 2022

Living Environment

COST OF LIVING

Cost of Living Index

Composite Index	Groceries	Housing	Utilities	Trans-portation	Health Care	Misc. Goods/ Services
112.9	98.3	118.1	125.3	109.1	102.9	114.5

Note: The Cost of Living Index measures regional differences in the cost of consumer goods and services, excluding taxes and non-consumer expenditures, for professional and managerial households in the top income quintile. It is based on more than 50,000 prices covering almost 60 different items for which prices are collected three times a year by chambers of commerce, economic development organizations or university applied economic centers in each participating urban area. The numbers shown should be read as a percentage above or below the national average of 100. For example, a value of 115.4 in the groceries column indicates that grocery prices are 15.4% higher than the national average. Small differences in the index numbers should not be interpreted as significant; Figures cover the Providence RI urban area.
Source: The Council for Community and Economic Research, Cost of Living Index, 2022

Grocery Prices

Area[1]	T-Bone Steak ($/pound)	Frying Chicken ($/pound)	Whole Milk ($/half gal.)	Eggs ($/dozen)	Orange Juice ($/64 oz.)	Coffee ($/11.5 oz.)
City[2]	15.73	1.68	2.42	2.52	3.90	3.94
Avg.	13.81	1.59	2.43	2.25	3.85	4.95
Min.	10.17	0.90	1.51	1.30	2.90	3.46
Max.	19.35	3.30	4.32	4.32	5.31	8.59

Note: (1) Values for the local area are compared with the average, minimum and maximum values for all 286 areas in the Cost of Living Index; (2) Figures cover the Providence RI urban area; **T-Bone Steak** (price per pound); **Frying Chicken** (price per pound, whole fryer); **Whole Milk** (half gallon carton); **Eggs** (price per dozen, Grade A, large); **Orange Juice** (64 oz. Tropicana or Florida Natural); **Coffee** (11.5 oz. can, vacuum-packed, Maxwell House, Hills Bros, or Folgers).
Source: The Council for Community and Economic Research, Cost of Living Index, 2022

Housing and Utility Costs

Area[1]	New Home Price ($)	Apartment Rent ($/month)	All Electric ($/month)	Part Electric ($/month)	Other Energy ($/month)	Telephone ($/month)
City[2]	462,061	2,085	-	132.22	119.10	193.25
Avg.	450,913	1,371	176.41	99.93	76.96	190.22
Min.	229,283	546	100.84	31.56	27.15	174.27
Max.	2,434,977	4,569	356.86	249.59	272.24	208.31

Note: (1) Values for the local area are compared with the average, minimum and maximum values for all 286 areas in the Cost of Living Index; (2) Figures cover the Providence RI urban area; **New Home Price** (2,400 sf living area, 8,000 sf lot, in urban area with full utilities); **Apartment Rent** (950 sf 2 bedroom/1.5 or 2 bath, unfurnished, excluding all utilities except water); **All Electric** (average monthly cost for an all-electric home); **Part Electric** (average monthly cost for a part-electric home); **Other Energy** (average monthly cost for natural gas, fuel oil, coal, wood, and any other forms of energy except electricity); **Telephone** (price includes the base monthly rate plus taxes and fees for three lines of mobile phone service).
Source: The Council for Community and Economic Research, Cost of Living Index, 2022

Health Care, Transportation, and Other Costs

Area[1]	Doctor ($/visit)	Dentist ($/visit)	Optometrist ($/visit)	Gasoline ($/gallon)	Beauty Salon ($/visit)	Men's Shirt ($)
City[2]	143.54	117.33	120.06	3.98	51.00	34.08
Avg.	124.91	107.77	117.66	3.86	43.31	34.21
Min.	36.61	58.25	51.79	2.90	22.18	13.05
Max.	250.21	162.58	371.96	5.54	85.61	63.54

Note: (1) Values for the local area are compared with the average, minimum and maximum values for all 286 areas in the Cost of Living Index; (2) Figures cover the Providence RI urban area; **Doctor** (general practitioners routine exam of an established patient); **Dentist** (adult teeth cleaning and periodic oral examination); **Optometrist** (full vision eye exam for established adult patient); **Gasoline** (one gallon regular unleaded, national brand, including all taxes, cash price at self-service pump if available); **Beauty Salon** (woman's shampoo, trim, and blow-dry); **Men's Shirt** (cotton/polyester dress shirt, pinpoint weave, long sleeves).
Source: The Council for Community and Economic Research, Cost of Living Index, 2022

HOUSING

Homeownership Rate

Area	2015 (%)	2016 (%)	2017 (%)	2018 (%)	2019 (%)	2020 (%)	2021 (%)	2022 (%)
MSA[1]	60.0	57.5	58.6	61.3	63.5	64.8	64.1	66.3
U.S.	63.7	63.4	63.9	64.4	64.6	66.6	65.5	65.8

Note: (1) Figures cover the Providence-Warwick, RI-MA Metropolitan Statistical Area
Source: U.S. Census Bureau, Housing Vacancies and Homeownership Annual Statistics: 2015-2022

House Price Index (HPI)

Area	National Ranking[2]	Quarterly Change (%)	One-Year Change (%)	Five-Year Change (%)	Since 1991Q1 (%)
MSA[1]	153	-0.93	10.48	54.47	232.15
U.S.[3]	–	0.34	8.41	58.44	289.08

Note: The HPI is a weighted repeat sales index. It measures average price changes in repeat sales or refinancings on the same properties. This information is obtained by reviewing repeat mortgage transactions on single-family properties whose mortgages have been purchased or securitized by Fannie Mae or Freddie Mac since January 1975; (1) Figures cover the Providence-Warwick, RI-MA Metropolitan Statistical Area; (2) Rankings are based on annual percentage change for all metro areas containing at least 15,000 transactions over the last 10 years and ranges from 1 to 257; (3) figures based on a weighted average of Census Division estimates using a seasonally adjusted, purchase-only index; all figures are for the period ending December 31, 2022
Source: Federal Housing Finance Agency, Change in FHFA Metropolitan Area House Price Indexes, 2022Q4

Median Single-Family Home Prices

Area	2020	2021	2022p	Percent Change 2021 to 2022
MSA[1]	347.3	396.1	440.9	11.3
U.S. Average	300.2	357.1	392.6	9.9

Note: Figures are median sales prices of existing single-family homes in thousands of dollars; (p) preliminary; (1) Figures cover the Providence-Warwick, RI-MA Metropolitan Statistical Area
Source: National Association of Realtors, Median Sales Price of Existing Single-Family Homes for Metropolitan Areas, 4th Quarter 2022

Qualifying Income Based on Median Sales Price of Existing Single-Family Homes

Area	With 5% Down ($)	With 10% Down ($)	With 20% Down ($)
MSA[1]	129,158	122,360	108,764
U.S. Average	112,234	106,234	94,513

Note: Figures are preliminary; Qualifying income is based on a mortgage rate of 6.77%. Monthly principal and interest payment is limited to 25% of income; (1) Figures cover the Providence-Warwick, RI-MA Metropolitan Statistical Area
Source: National Association of Realtors, Qualifying Income Based on Median Sales Price of Existing Single-Family Homes for Metropolitan Areas, 4th Quarter 2022

Home Value

Area	Under $100,000	$100,000 -$199,999	$200,000 -$299,999	$300,000 -$399,999	$400,000 -$499,999	$500,000 -$999,999	$1,000,000 or more	Median ($)
City	4.9	27.5	34.7	14.0	4.1	11.6	3.2	248,900
MSA[1]	3.5	12.7	31.4	24.1	12.7	13.5	2.1	309,600
U.S.	16.2	24.2	20.1	13.6	8.3	13.6	4.1	244,900

Note: Figures are percentages except for median and cover owner-occupied housing units; (1) Figures cover the Providence-Warwick, RI-MA Metropolitan Statistical Area
Source: U.S. Census Bureau, 2017-2021 American Community Survey 5-Year Estimates

Year Housing Structure Built

Area	2020 or Later	2010 -2019	2000 -2009	1990 -1999	1980 -1989	1970 -1979	1960 -1969	1950 -1959	1940 -1949	Before 1940	Median Year
City	0.1	1.2	4.6	4.6	5.7	7.9	5.4	7.1	5.7	57.7	<1940
MSA[1]	0.1	2.7	6.1	8.1	11.2	12.1	10.7	11.5	6.0	31.4	1961
U.S.	0.2	7.3	13.6	13.6	13.2	14.8	10.3	10.0	4.7	12.2	1979

Note: Figures are percentages except for Median Year; Note: (1) Figures cover the Providence-Warwick, RI-MA Metropolitan Statistical Area
Source: U.S. Census Bureau, 2017-2021 American Community Survey 5-Year Estimates

Gross Monthly Rent

Area	Under $500	$500 -$999	$1,000 -$1,499	$1,500 -$1,999	$2,000 -$2,499	$2,500 -$2,999	$3,000 and up	Median ($)
City	19.3	21.5	38.2	14.8	3.7	1.3	1.2	1,098
MSA[1]	14.9	29.3	35.5	14.2	4.1	1.0	0.9	1,066
U.S.	8.1	30.5	30.8	16.8	7.3	3.1	3.5	1,163

Note: Figures are percentages except for median; Gross rent is the contract rent plus the estimated average monthly cost of utilities (electricity, gas, and water and sewer) and fuels (oil, coal, kerosene, wood, etc.) if these are paid by the renter (or paid for the renter by someone else); (1) Figures cover the Providence-Warwick, RI-MA Metropolitan Statistical Area
Source: U.S. Census Bureau, 2017-2021 American Community Survey 5-Year Estimates

HEALTH

Health Risk Factors

Category	MSA[1] (%)	U.S. (%)
Adults aged 18–64 who have any kind of health care coverage	95.1	90.9
Adults who reported being in good or better health	86.4	85.2
Adults who have been told they have high blood cholesterol	35.5	35.7
Adults who have been told they have high blood pressure	32.9	32.4
Adults who are current smokers	13.5	14.4
Adults who currently use e-cigarettes	6.2	6.7
Adults who currently use chewing tobacco, snuff, or snus	1.4	3.5
Adults who are heavy drinkers[2]	7.5	6.3
Adults who are binge drinkers[3]	16.9	15.4
Adults who are overweight (BMI 25.0 - 29.9)	37.2	34.4
Adults who are obese (BMI 30.0 - 99.8)	29.5	33.9
Adults who participated in any physical activities in the past month	74.3	76.3

Note: (1) Figures cover the Providence-Warwick, RI-MA Metropolitan Statistical Area; (2) Heavy drinkers are classified as adult men having more than 14 drinks per week and adult women having more than 7 drinks per week; (3) Binge drinkers are classified as males having five or more drinks on one occasion or females having four or more drinks on one occasion
Source: Centers for Disease Control and Prevention, Behaviorial Risk Factor Surveillance System, SMART: Selected Metropolitan Area Risk Trends, 2021

Acute and Chronic Health Conditions

Category	MSA[1] (%)	U.S. (%)
Adults who have ever been told they had a heart attack	4.4	4.0
Adults who have ever been told they have angina or coronary heart disease	3.7	3.8
Adults who have ever been told they had a stroke	2.6	3.0
Adults who have ever been told they have asthma	17.9	14.9
Adults who have ever been told they have arthritis	28.3	25.8
Adults who have ever been told they have diabetes[2]	10.4	10.9
Adults who have ever been told they had skin cancer	7.5	6.6
Adults who have ever been told they had any other types of cancer	7.4	7.5
Adults who have ever been told they have COPD	6.7	6.1
Adults who have ever been told they have kidney disease	3.1	3.0
Adults who have ever been told they have a form of depression	21.4	20.5

Note: (1) Figures cover the Providence-Warwick, RI-MA Metropolitan Statistical Area; (2) Figures do not include pregnancy-related, borderline, or pre-diabetes
Source: Centers for Disease Control and Prevention, Behaviorial Risk Factor Surveillance System, SMART: Selected Metropolitan Area Risk Trends, 2021

Health Screening and Vaccination Rates

Category	MSA[1] (%)	U.S. (%)
Adults who have ever been tested for HIV	38.8	34.9
Adults who have had their blood cholesterol checked within the last five years	91.6	85.2
Adults aged 65+ who have had flu shot within the past year	72.4	68.6
Adults aged 65+ who have ever had a pneumonia vaccination	73.5	71.0

Note: (1) Figures cover the Providence-Warwick, RI-MA Metropolitan Statistical Area.
Source: Centers for Disease Control and Prevention, Behaviorial Risk Factor Surveillance System, SMART: Selected Metropolitan Area Risk Trends, 2021

Disability Status

Category	MSA[1] (%)	U.S. (%)
Adults who reported being deaf	6.7	7.2
Are you blind or have serious difficulty seeing, even when wearing glasses?	5.3	4.8
Are you limited in any way in any of your usual activities due to arthritis?	9.9	11.1
Do you have difficulty doing errands alone?	7.0	7.0
Do you have difficulty dressing or bathing?	3.7	3.6
Do you have serious difficulty concentrating/remembering/making decisions?	12.6	12.1
Do you have serious difficulty walking or climbing stairs?	12.4	12.8

Note: (1) Figures cover the Providence-Warwick, RI-MA Metropolitan Statistical Area.
Source: Centers for Disease Control and Prevention, Behaviorial Risk Factor Surveillance System, SMART: Selected Metropolitan Area Risk Trends, 2021

Mortality Rates for the Top 10 Causes of Death in the U.S.

ICD-10[a] Sub-Chapter	ICD-10[a] Code	Crude Mortality Rate[1] per 100,000 population	
		County[2]	U.S.
Malignant neoplasms	C00-C97	179.4	182.6
Ischaemic heart diseases	I20-I25	132.5	113.1
Other forms of heart disease	I30-I51	51.0	64.4
Other degenerative diseases of the nervous system	G30-G31	48.7	51.0
Cerebrovascular diseases	I60-I69	34.0	47.8
Other external causes of accidental injury	W00-X59	65.3	46.4
Chronic lower respiratory diseases	J40-J47	38.7	45.7
Organic, including symptomatic, mental disorders	F01-F09	54.1	35.9
Hypertensive diseases	I10-I15	28.4	35.0
Diabetes mellitus	E10-E14	28.4	29.6

Note: (a) ICD-10 = International Classification of Diseases 10th Revision; (1) Crude mortality rates are a three-year average covering 2019-2021; (2) Figures cover Providence County.
Source: Centers for Disease Control and Prevention, National Center for Health Statistics. National Vital Statistics System, Mortality 2018-2021 on CDC WONDER Online Database

Mortality Rates for Selected Causes of Death

ICD-10[a] Sub-Chapter	ICD-10[a] Code	Crude Mortality Rate[1] per 100,000 population	
		County[2]	U.S.
Assault	X85-Y09	4.0	7.0
Diseases of the liver	K70-K76	19.3	19.8
Human immunodeficiency virus (HIV) disease	B20-B24	Unreliable	1.5
Influenza and pneumonia	J09-J18	11.6	14.7
Intentional self-harm	X60-X84	9.6	14.3
Malnutrition	E40-E46	1.4	4.3
Obesity and other hyperalimentation	E65-E68	3.7	3.0
Renal failure	N17-N19	14.5	15.7
Transport accidents	V01-V99	7.7	13.6
Viral hepatitis	B15-B19	1.2	1.2

Note: (a) ICD-10 = International Classification of Diseases 10th Revision; (1) Crude mortality rates are a three-year average covering 2019-2021; (2) Figures cover Providence County; Data are suppressed when the data meet the criteria for confidentiality constraints; Crude mortality rates are flagged as unreliable when the rate would be calculated with a numerator of 20 or less.
Source: Centers for Disease Control and Prevention, National Center for Health Statistics. National Vital Statistics System, Mortality 2018-2021 on CDC WONDER Online Database

Health Insurance Coverage

Area	With Health Insurance	With Private Health Insurance	With Public Health Insurance	Without Health Insurance	Population Under Age 19 Without Health Insurance
City	93.2	55.8	45.4	6.8	3.9
MSA[1]	96.0	70.2	39.4	4.0	2.2
U.S.	91.2	67.8	35.4	8.8	5.3

Note: Figures are percentages that cover the civilian noninstitutionalized population; (1) Figures cover the Providence-Warwick, RI-MA Metropolitan Statistical Area
Source: U.S. Census Bureau, 2017-2021 American Community Survey 5-Year Estimates

Number of Medical Professionals

Area	MDs[3]	DOs[3,4]	Dentists	Podiatrists	Chiropractors	Optometrists
County[1] (number)	3,233	113	384	64	139	142
County[1] (rate[2])	489.8	17.1	58.3	9.7	21.1	21.6
U.S. (rate[2])	289.3	23.5	72.5	6.2	28.7	17.4

Note: Data as of 2021 unless noted; (1) Data covers Providence County; (2) Rate per 100,000 population; (3) Data as of 2020 and includes all active, non-federal physicians; (4) Doctor of Osteopathic Medicine
Source: U.S. Department of Health and Human Services, Health Resources and Services Administration, Bureau of Health Professions, Area Resource File (ARF) 2021-2022

EDUCATION

Public School District Statistics

District Name	Schls	Pupils	Pupil/ Teacher Ratio	Minority Pupils[1] (%)	LEP/ELL[2] (%)	IEP[3] (%)
Providence	40	21,656	13.9	92.1	29.4	16.5

Note: Table includes school districts with 2,000 or more students; (1) Percentage of students that are not non-Hispanic white; (2) Percentage of students that are Limited English Proficient or English Language Learners (2018-19); (3) Percentage of students that have an Individualized Education Program (2019-20).
Source: U.S. Department of Education, National Center for Education Statistics, Common Core of Data, Local Education Agency (School District) Universe Survey: School Year 2021-2022

Best High Schools

According to *U.S. News,* Providence is home to one of the top 500 high schools in the U.S.: **Classical High School** (#91). Nearly 18,000 public, magnet and charter schools were ranked based on their performance on state assessments and how well they prepare students for college. *U.S. News & World Report, "Best High Schools 2022"*

Highest Level of Education

Area	Less than H.S.	H.S. Diploma	Some College, No Deg.	Associate Degree	Bachelor's Degree	Master's Degree	Prof. School Degree	Doctorate Degree
City	16.5	30.6	14.6	5.1	17.4	9.5	3.5	2.9
MSA[1]	12.0	28.7	17.5	8.6	20.2	9.4	2.0	1.6
U.S.	11.1	26.5	20.0	8.7	20.6	9.3	2.2	1.5

Note: Figures cover persons age 25 and over; (1) Figures cover the Providence-Warwick, RI-MA Metropolitan Statistical Area
Source: U.S. Census Bureau, 2017-2021 American Community Survey 5-Year Estimates

Educational Attainment by Race

Area	High School Graduate or Higher (%)					Bachelor's Degree or Higher (%)				
	Total	White	Black	Asian	Hisp.[2]	Total	White	Black	Asian	Hisp.[2]
City	83.5	88.8	85.7	84.1	73.3	33.3	41.9	27.0	50.4	12.3
MSA[1]	88.0	89.8	84.7	86.4	73.3	33.2	34.9	25.8	53.2	15.5
U.S.	88.9	91.4	87.2	87.6	71.2	33.7	35.5	23.3	55.6	18.4

Note: Figures shown cover persons 25 years old and over; (1) Figures cover the Providence-Warwick, RI-MA Metropolitan Statistical Area; (2) People of Hispanic origin can be of any race
Source: U.S. Census Bureau, 2017-2021 American Community Survey 5-Year Estimates

School Enrollment by Grade and Control

Area	Preschool (%)		Kindergarten (%)		Grades 1 - 4 (%)		Grades 5 - 8 (%)		Grades 9 - 12 (%)	
	Public	Private	Public	Private	Public	Private	Public	Private	Public	Private
City	56.9	43.1	80.9	19.1	88.4	11.6	84.5	15.5	89.6	10.4
MSA[1]	56.5	43.5	88.3	11.7	90.4	9.6	89.4	10.6	88.4	11.6
U.S.	58.8	41.2	86.3	13.7	88.3	11.7	88.6	11.4	89.4	10.6

Note: Figures shown cover persons 3 years old and over; (1) Figures cover the Providence-Warwick, RI-MA Metropolitan Statistical Area
Source: U.S. Census Bureau, 2017-2021 American Community Survey 5-Year Estimates

Higher Education

Four-Year Colleges			Two-Year Colleges			Medical Schools[1]	Law Schools[2]	Voc/ Tech[3]
Public	Private Non-profit	Private For-profit	Public	Private Non-profit	Private For-profit			
3	13	0	2	1	0	1	2	12

Note: Figures cover institutions located within the Providence-Warwick, RI-MA Metropolitan Statistical Area and include main campuses only; (1) includes schools accredited by the Liaison Committee on Medical Education and the American Osteopathic Association's Commission on Osteopathic College Accreditation; (2) includes ABA-accredited schools, schools with provisional ABA accreditation, and state accredited schools; (3) includes all schools with programs that are less than 2 years.
Source: National Center for Education Statistics, Integrated Postsecondary Education System (IPEDS), 2021-22; Wikipedia, List of Medical Schools in the United States, accessed April 10, 2023; Wikipedia, List of Law Schools in the United States, accessed April 10, 2023

According to *U.S. News & World Report,* the Providence-Warwick, RI-MA metro area is home to two of the top 200 national universities in the U.S.: **Brown University** (#13 tie); **University of Rhode Island** (#182 tie). The indicators used to capture academic quality fall into a number of categories: assessment by administrators at peer institutions; retention of students; faculty resources; student selectivity; financial resources; alumni giving; high school counselor ratings of colleges; and graduation rate. *U.S. News & World Report, "America's Best Colleges 2023"*

According to *U.S. News & World Report,* the Providence-Warwick, RI-MA metro area is home to two of the top 100 liberal arts colleges in the U.S.: **Stonehill College** (#89 tie); **Wheaton College (MA)** (#89 tie). The indicators used to capture academic quality fall into a number of categories: assessment by administrators at peer institutions; retention of students; faculty resources; student selectivity; financial resources; alumni giving; high school counselor ratings of colleges; and graduation rate. *U.S. News & World Report, "America's Best Colleges 2023"*

According to *U.S. News & World Report,* the Providence-Warwick, RI-MA metro area is home to one of the top 75 medical schools for research in the U.S.: **Brown University (Alpert)** (#35 tie). The rankings are based on a weighted average of 11 measures of quality: quality assessment; peer assessment score; assessment score by residency directors; research activity; total research activity; average research activity per faculty member; student selectivity; median MCAT total score; median undergraduate GPA; acceptance rate; and faculty resources. *U.S. News & World Report, "America's Best Graduate Schools, Medical, 2023"*

EMPLOYERS

Major Employers

Company Name	Industry
A&M Special Purchasing	Payroll accounting service
Acushnet Company	Sporting & recreation goods
Brown University	Colleges & universities
Charlton Memorial Hospital	General medical & surgical hospitals
City of Fall River	Public elementary & secondary schools
City of Providence	Municipal government
CVS Pharmacy	Drug stores
Hasbro	Games, toys, & children's vehicles
Hasbro Managerial Services	Management services
Kent Hospital	General medical & surgical hospitals
Providence School Department	Public elementary & secondary schools
Rhode Island Hospital	General medical & surgical hospitals
Roman Catholic Diocese of Fall River	Catholic church
Saint Luke's Hospital of New Bedford	General medical & surgical hospitals
Samsonite International S.A.	Luggage
Southcoast Hospitals Group	General medical & surgical hospitals
U.S. Navy	U.S. military
University of Rhode Island	Colleges & universities
Women & Infants Hospital of Rhode Island	Specialty outpatient clinics, nec

Note: Companies shown are located within the Providence-Warwick, RI-MA Metropolitan Statistical Area.
Source: Hoovers.com; Wikipedia

PUBLIC SAFETY

Crime Rate

Area	Total Crime	Violent Crime Rate				Property Crime Rate		
		Murder	Rape[3]	Robbery	Aggrav. Assault	Burglary	Larceny -Theft	Motor Vehicle Theft
City	2,900.8	9.5	36.7	101.9	338.0	335.2	1,776.7	302.9
Suburbs[1]	1,264.5	1.7	40.2	29.7	189.1	149.7	749.5	104.7
Metro[2]	1,445.8	2.5	39.8	37.7	205.6	170.2	863.3	126.6
U.S.	2,356.7	6.5	38.4	73.9	279.7	314.2	1,398.0	246.0

Note: Figures are crimes per 100,000 population; (1) All areas within the metro area that are located outside the city limits; (2) Figures cover the Providence-Warwick, RI-MA Metropolitan Statistical Area; (3) All figures shown were reported using the revised Uniform Crime Reporting (UCR) definition of rape; Due to the transition to the National Incident-Based Reporting System (NIBRS), limited city and metro area data was released for 2021.
Source: FBI Uniform Crime Reports, 2020

Hate Crimes

Area	Number of Quarters Reported	Number of Incidents per Bias Motivation					
		Race/Ethnicity/ Ancestry	Religion	Sexual Orientation	Disability	Gender	Gender Identity
City	4	1	0	0	0	0	0
U.S.	4	5,227	1,244	1,110	130	75	266

Note: Due to the transition to the National Incident-Based Reporting System (NIBRS), limited crime data was released for 2021.
Source: Federal Bureau of Investigation, Hate Crime Statistics 2020

Identity Theft Consumer Reports

Area	Reports	Reports per 100,000 Population	Rank[2]
MSA[1]	3,834	237	121
U.S.	1,108,609	339	-

Note: (1) Figures cover the Providence-Warwick, RI-MA Metropolitan Statistical Area; (2) Rank ranges from 1 to 391 where 1 indicates greatest number of identity theft reports per 100,000 population
Source: Federal Trade Commission, Consumer Sentinel Network Data Book 2022

Fraud and Other Consumer Reports

Area	Reports	Reports per 100,000 Population	Rank[2]
MSA[1]	13,537	835	191
U.S.	4,064,520	1,245	-

Note: (1) Figures cover the Providence-Warwick, RI-MA Metropolitan Statistical Area; (2) Rank ranges from 1 to 391 where 1 indicates greatest number of fraud and other consumer reports per 100,000 population
Source: Federal Trade Commission, Consumer Sentinel Network Data Book 2022

Providence, Rhode Island

POLITICS

2020 Presidential Election Results

Area	Biden	Trump	Jorgensen	Hawkins	Other
Providence County	60.5	37.6	0.8	0.0	1.0
U.S.	51.3	46.8	1.2	0.3	0.5

Note: Results are percentages and may not add to 100% due to rounding
Source: Dave Leip's Atlas of U.S. Presidential Elections

SPORTS

Professional Sports Teams

Team Name	League	Year Established

No teams are located in the metro area
Source: Wikipedia, Major Professional Sports Teams of the United States and Canada, April 12, 2023

CLIMATE

Average and Extreme Temperatures

Temperature	Jan	Feb	Mar	Apr	May	Jun	Jul	Aug	Sep	Oct	Nov	Dec	Yr.
Extreme High (°F)	66	72	80	98	94	97	102	104	100	88	81	70	104
Average High (°F)	37	39	46	58	68	77	82	80	73	63	52	41	60
Average Temp. (°F)	29	30	38	48	58	67	73	71	64	54	44	33	51
Average Low (°F)	20	22	29	39	48	57	63	62	54	43	35	25	42
Extreme Low (°F)	-13	-7	1	14	29	41	48	40	32	20	6	-10	-13

Note: Figures cover the years 1948-1992
Source: National Climatic Data Center, International Station Meteorological Climate Summary, 9/96

Average Precipitation/Snowfall/Humidity

Precip./Humidity	Jan	Feb	Mar	Apr	May	Jun	Jul	Aug	Sep	Oct	Nov	Dec	Yr.
Avg. Precip. (in.)	3.9	3.6	4.2	4.1	3.7	2.9	3.2	4.0	3.5	3.6	4.5	4.3	45.3
Avg. Snowfall (in.)	10	10	7	1	Tr	0	0	0	0	Tr	1	7	35
Avg. Rel. Hum. 7am (%)	71	71	71	70	73	75	78	81	83	81	78	74	75
Avg. Rel. Hum. 4pm (%)	58	56	54	51	55	58	58	60	60	58	60	60	57

Note: Figures cover the years 1948-1992; Tr = Trace amounts (<0.05 in. of rain; <0.5 in. of snow)
Source: National Climatic Data Center, International Station Meteorological Climate Summary, 9/96

Weather Conditions

Temperature			Daytime Sky			Precipitation		
5°F & below	32°F & below	90°F & above	Clear	Partly cloudy	Cloudy	0.01 inch or more precip.	0.1 inch or more snow/ice	Thunder-storms
6	117	9	85	134	146	123	21	21

Note: Figures are average number of days per year and cover the years 1948-1992
Source: National Climatic Data Center, International Station Meteorological Climate Summary, 9/96

HAZARDOUS WASTE

Superfund Sites

The Providence-Warwick, RI-MA metro area is home to 12 sites on the EPA's Superfund National Priorities List: **Atlas Tack Corp.** (final); **Central Landfill** (final); **Centredale Manor Restoration Project** (final); **Davis Liquid Waste** (final); **Davisville Naval Construction Battalion Center** (final); **Landfill & Resource Recovery, Inc. (L&RR)** (final); **New Bedford** (final); **Newport Naval Education & Training Center** (final); **Peterson/Puritan, Inc.** (final); **Picillo Farm** (final); **Re-Solve, Inc.** (final); **Rose Hill Regional Landfill** (final). There are a total of 1,165 Superfund sites with a status of proposed or final on the list in the U.S. *U.S. Environmental Protection Agency, National Priorities List, April 12, 2023*

AIR QUALITY

Air Quality Trends: Ozone

	1990	1995	2000	2005	2010	2015	2018	2019	2020	2021
MSA[1]	0.106	0.107	0.087	0.090	0.072	0.070	0.074	0.064	0.065	0.067
U.S.	0.087	0.089	0.081	0.080	0.072	0.067	0.069	0.065	0.065	0.067

Note: (1) Data covers the Providence-Warwick, RI-MA Metropolitan Statistical Area. The values shown are the composite ozone concentration averages among trend sites based on the highest fourth daily maximum 8-hour concentration in parts per million. These trends are based on sites having an adequate record of monitoring data during the trend period. Data from exceptional events are included.
Source: U.S. Environmental Protection Agency, Air Quality Monitoring Information, "Air Quality Trends by City, 1990-2021"

Air Quality Index

Area	Percent of Days when Air Quality was...[2]					AQI Statistics[2]	
	Good	Moderate	Unhealthy for Sensitive Groups	Unhealthy	Very Unhealthy	Maximum	Median
MSA[1]	76.2	22.7	1.1	0.0	0.0	147	41

Note: (1) Data covers the Providence-Warwick, RI-MA Metropolitan Statistical Area; (2) Based on 365 days with AQI data in 2021. Air Quality Index (AQI) is an index for reporting daily air quality. EPA calculates the AQI for five major air pollutants regulated by the Clean Air Act: ground-level ozone, particle pollution (aka particulate matter), carbon monoxide, sulfur dioxide, and nitrogen dioxide. The AQI runs from 0 to 500. The higher the AQI value, the greater the level of air pollution and the greater the health concern. There are six AQI categories: "Good" AQI is between 0 and 50. Air quality is considered satisfactory; "Moderate" AQI is between 51 and 100. Air quality is acceptable; "Unhealthy for Sensitive Groups" When AQI values are between 101 and 150, members of sensitive groups may experience health effects; "Unhealthy" When AQI values are between 151 and 200 everyone may begin to experience health effects; "Very Unhealthy" AQI values between 201 and 300 trigger a health alert; "Hazardous" AQI values over 300 trigger warnings of emergency conditions (not shown).
Source: U.S. Environmental Protection Agency, Air Quality Index Report, 2021

Air Quality Index Pollutants

Area	Percent of Days when AQI Pollutant was...[2]					
	Carbon Monoxide	Nitrogen Dioxide	Ozone	Sulfur Dioxide	Particulate Matter 2.5	Particulate Matter 10
MSA[1]	0.0	2.2	63.0	(3)	34.8	0.0

Note: (1) Data covers the Providence-Warwick, RI-MA Metropolitan Statistical Area; (2) Based on 365 days with AQI data in 2021. The Air Quality Index (AQI) is an index for reporting daily air quality. EPA calculates the AQI for five major air pollutants regulated by the Clean Air Act: ground-level ozone, particle pollution (also known as particulate matter), carbon monoxide, sulfur dioxide, and nitrogen dioxide. The AQI runs from 0 to 500. The higher the AQI value, the greater the level of air pollution and the greater the health concern; (3) Sulfur dioxide is no longer included in this table (as of December 8, 2021) because SO_2 concentrations tend to be very localized and not necessarily representative of broad geographical areas like counties and CBSAs.
Source: U.S. Environmental Protection Agency, Air Quality Index Report, 2021

Maximum Air Pollutant Concentrations: Particulate Matter, Ozone, CO and Lead

	Particulate Matter 10 (ug/m^3)	Particulate Matter 2.5 Wtd AM (ug/m^3)	Particulate Matter 2.5 24-Hr (ug/m^3)	Ozone (ppm)	Carbon Monoxide (ppm)	Lead (ug/m^3)
MSA[1] Level	29	9.3	21	0.069	1	n/a
NAAQS[2]	150	15	35	0.075	9	0.15
Met NAAQS[2]	Yes	Yes	Yes	Yes	Yes	n/a

Note: (1) Data covers the Providence-Warwick, RI-MA Metropolitan Statistical Area; Data from exceptional events are included; (2) National Ambient Air Quality Standards; ppm = parts per million; ug/m^3 = micrograms per cubic meter; n/a not available.
Concentrations: Particulate Matter 10 (coarse particulate)—highest second maximum 24-hour concentration; Particulate Matter 2.5 Wtd AM (fine particulate)—highest weighted annual mean concentration; Particulate Matter 2.5 24-Hour (fine particulate)—highest 98th percentile 24-hour concentration; Ozone—highest fourth daily maximum 8-hour concentration; Carbon Monoxide—highest second maximum non-overlapping 8-hour concentration; Lead—maximum running 3-month average
Source: U.S. Environmental Protection Agency, Air Quality Monitoring Information, "Air Quality Statistics by City, 2021"

Maximum Air Pollutant Concentrations: Nitrogen Dioxide and Sulfur Dioxide

	Nitrogen Dioxide AM (ppb)	Nitrogen Dioxide 1-Hr (ppb)	Sulfur Dioxide AM (ppb)	Sulfur Dioxide 1-Hr (ppb)	Sulfur Dioxide 24-Hr (ppb)
MSA[1] Level	16	36	n/a	3	n/a
NAAQS[2]	53	100	30	75	140
Met NAAQS[2]	Yes	Yes	n/a	Yes	n/a

Note: (1) Data covers the Providence-Warwick, RI-MA Metropolitan Statistical Area; Data from exceptional events are included; (2) National Ambient Air Quality Standards; ppm = parts per million; ug/m^3 = micrograms per cubic meter; n/a not available.
Concentrations: Nitrogen Dioxide AM—highest arithmetic mean concentration; Nitrogen Dioxide 1-Hr—highest 98th percentile 1-hour daily maximum concentration; Sulfur Dioxide AM—highest annual mean concentration; Sulfur Dioxide 1-Hr—highest 99th percentile 1-hour daily maximum concentration; Sulfur Dioxide 24-Hr—highest second maximum 24-hour concentration
Source: U.S. Environmental Protection Agency, Air Quality Monitoring Information, "Air Quality Statistics by City, 2021"

Raleigh, North Carolina

Background

Raleigh is named for Queen Elizabeth I's swashbuckling favorite, Sir Walter Raleigh. In her name, he plundered Spanish ships for gold in the New World and founded the first English settlement along the North Carolina coast. His excessive piracy led to his execution in 1618.

Raleigh is the capital of North Carolina, and its cultural and educational center. Located 120 miles west of the Atlantic Ocean, Raleigh is the retail and wholesale center of eastern North Carolina. Its top industries are manufacturing, trade, information, finance, professional services, education and health services, and government. Apple is planning to to invest over $1 billion into a new campus and engineering hub in the Raleigh-Durham area.

The city boasts first-rate universities such as North Carolina State, Duke University, and the University of North Carolina. The Research Triangle Park—one of the largest university-affiliated research parks in the world, comprising Raleigh, Durham, and Chapel Hill—continues to pump money into the local economy.

The region has a high business startup rate, a low unemployment rate, and average wages above the state level. North Carolina State University's Centennial Campus has also encouraged major corporations to relocate, bringing with them thousands of jobs.

Called the "City of Oaks," for its tree-lined streets, architecture in Raleigh ranges from the modern architecture of the North Carolina Museum of Art, designed by Edward Durrell Stone (architect of Washington DC's John F. Kennedy Center), to the antebellum structures such as the Greek Revival Capitol Building. The city's street grid simplifies exploration of Raleigh's downtown, which continues to prosper and develop. In 2009, Raleigh became one of three United States cities participating in Project Get Ready—a non-profit program led by the Rocky Mountain Institute (RMI) to advance Electric Vehicle policies. Today, Raleigh operates a diverse fleet of nearly 1,000 electric vehicles. The city's climate action goal is an 80 percent reduction in greenhouse gases by 2050.

Cultural attractions include the North Carolina Symphony, the Opera Company of North Carolina, and the Carolina Ballet, all of which perform at the Progress Energy Center for the Performing Arts. There are numerous other musical, dance and theater groups in the city and the City of Raleigh Arts Commission actively supports the arts. Children enjoy the Marbles Kids Museum & Wachovia IMAX® Theatre.

The Coastal Credit Union Music Park at Walnut Creek hosts major international touring acts. The Downtown Raleigh Amphitheater (aka the Red Hat Amphitheater) hosts numerous concerts in the summer months. An additional amphitheater sits on the grounds of the North Carolina Museum of Art, which hosts summer concerts and outdoor movies.

Because it is centrally located between the mountains on the west and the coast on the south and east, the Raleigh area enjoys a pleasant climate. The mountains form a partial barrier to cold air masses moving from the west. As a result, there are few seriously cold winter days. In the summer, tropical air is present over the eastern and central sections of North Carolina, bringing warm temperatures and high humidity to the area. Raleigh usually is not dangerously affected by coastal storms. In April 2011, a devastating tornado hit the city, killing 24 people. While snow and sleet usually occur each year, excessive accumulations of snow are rare.

Rankings

General Rankings

- For its "Best for Vets: Places to Live 2019" rankings, *Military Times* evaluated 599 cities (83 large, 234 medium, 282 small) and compared the locations across three broad categories: veteran and military culture/services; economic indicators; and livability factors such as health, crime, traffic, and school quality. Raleigh ranked #23 out of the top 25, in the large city category (population of more than 250,000). Data points more specific to veterans and the military weighed more heavily than others. *rebootcamp.militarytimes.com, "Military Times Best Places to Live 2019," September 10, 2018*

- *US News & World Report* conducted a survey of more than 3,600 people and analyzed the 150 largest metropolitan areas to determine what matters most when selecting where to settle down. Raleigh ranked #6 out of the top 25 as having the best combination of desirable factors. Criteria: cost of living; quality of life and education; net migration; job market; desirability; and other factors. *money.usnews.com, "The 25 Best Places to Live in the U.S. in 2022-2023," May 17, 2022*

- The Raleigh metro area was identified as one of America's fastest-growing areas in terms of population and business growth by *MagnifyMoney*. The area ranked #3 out of 35. The 100 most populous metro areas in the U.S. were evaluated on their change from 2011 to 2016 in the following categories: people and housing; workforce and employment opportunities; growing industry. *www.businessinsider.com, "The 35 Cities in the US with the Biggest Influx of People, the Most Work Opportunities, and the Hottest Business Growth," August 12, 2018*

- The Raleigh metro area was identified as one of America's fastest-growing areas in terms of population and economy by *Forbes*. The area ranked #15 out of 25. The 100 most populous metro areas in the U.S. were evaluated on the following criteria: estimated population growth; employment; economic output; wages; home values. *Forbes, "America's Fastest-Growing Cities 2018," February 28, 2018*

- Raleigh was selected as one of the best places to live in the United States by *Money* magazine. The city ranked #4 out of 50. This year's list focused on cities that would be welcoming to a broader group of people and with populations of at least 20,000. Beginning with a pool of 1,370 candidates, editors looked at 350 data points, organized into the these nine categories: income and personal finance, cost of living, economic opportunity, housing market, fun and amenities, health and safety, education, diversity, and quality of life. *Money, "The 50 Best Places to Live in the U.S. in 2022-2023" September 29, 2022*

- In their ninth annual survey, Livability.com looked at data for more than 2,300 mid-sized U.S. cities to determine the rankings for Livability's "Top 100 Best Places to Live" in 2022. Raleigh ranked #14. Criteria: housing and economy; social and civic engagement; education; demographics; health care options; transportation & infrastructure; and community amenities. *Livability.com, "Top 100 Best Places to Live 2022" July 19, 2022*

Business/Finance Rankings

- According to *Business Insider*, the Raleigh metro area is a prime place to run a startup or move an existing business to. The area ranked #16. More than 300 metro areas were analyzed for factors that were of top concern to new business owners. Data was based on the 2019 U.S. Census Bureau American Community Survey, statistics from the CDC, Bureau of Labor Statistics employment report, and University of Chicago analysis. Criteria: business formations; percentage of vaccinated population; percentage of households with internet subscriptions; median household income; and share of work that can be done from home. *www.businessinsider.com, "The 20 Best Cities for Starting a Business in 2022 Include Baltimore, Boulder, and Boston," January 5, 2022*

- *24/7 Wall St.* used metro data from the Bureau of Labor Statistics' Occupational Employment database to identify the cities with the highest percentage of those employed in jobs requiring knowledge in the science, technology, engineering, and math (STEM) fields as well as average wages for STEM jobs. The Raleigh metro area was #8. *247wallst.com, "15 Cities with the Most High-Tech Jobs," January 11, 2020*

- Based on metro area social media reviews, the employment opinion group Glassdoor surveyed 50 of the most populous U.S. metro areas and equally weighed cost of living, hiring opportunity, and job satisfaction to compose a list of "25 Best Cities for Jobs." Median pay and home value, and number of active job openings were also factored in. The Raleigh metro area was ranked #1 in overall job satisfaction. *www.glassdoor.com, "Best Cities for Jobs," February 25, 2020*

- The Brookings Institution ranked the nation's largest cities based on income inequality. Raleigh was ranked #84 (#1 = greatest inequality). Criteria: the "95/20 ratio," a figure representing the income at which a household earns more than 95 percent of all other households, divided by the income at which a household earns more than only 20 percent of all other households. *Brookings Institution, "Household Income Inequality, Largest Cities of 97 Large U.S. Metro Areas, 2014-2016," February 5, 2018*

- The Brookings Institution ranked the 100 largest metro areas in the U.S. based on income inequality. Raleigh was ranked #80 (#1 = greatest inequality). Criteria: the "95/20 ratio," a figure representing the income at which a household earns more than 95 percent of all other households, divided by the income at which a household earns more than only 20 percent of all other households. *Brookings Institution, "Household Income Inequality, 100 Largest U.S. Metro Areas, 2014-2016," February 5, 2018*

- Payscale.com ranked the 32 largest metro areas in terms of wage growth. The Raleigh metro area ranked #13. Criteria: quarterly changes in private industry employee and education professional wage growth from the previous year. *PayScale, "Wage Trends by Metro Area-1st Quarter," April 20, 2023*

- Raleigh was identified as one of America's most frugal metro areas by *Coupons.com.* The city ranked #3 out of 25. Criteria: digital coupon usage. *Coupons.com, "America's Most Frugal Cities of 2017," March 22, 2018*

- The Raleigh metro area appeared on the Milken Institute "2022 Best Performing Cities" list. Rank: #16 out of 200 large metro areas (population over 250,000). Criteria: job growth; wage and salary growth; high-tech output growth; housing affordability; household broadband access. *Milken Institute, "Best-Performing Cities 2022," March 28, 2022*

- *Forbes* ranked the 200 most populous metro areas to determine the nation's "Best Places for Business and Careers." The Raleigh metro area was ranked #3. Criteria: costs (business and living); job growth (past and projected); income growth; quality of life; educational attainment (college and high school); projected economic growth; cultural and leisure opportunities; workplace tolerance laws; net migration patterns. *Forbes, "The Best Places for Business and Careers 2019: Seattle Still On Top," October 30, 2019*

Children/Family Rankings

- Raleigh was selected as one of the most playful cities in the U.S. by KaBOOM! The organization's Playful City USA initiative honors cities and towns across the nation that have made their communities more playable. Criteria: pledging to integrate play as a solution to challenges in their communities; making it easy for children to get active and balanced play; creating more family-friendly and innovative communities as a result. *KaBOOM! National Campaign for Play, "2017 Playful City USA Communities"*

Education Rankings

- Personal finance website *WalletHub* analyzed the 150 largest U.S. metropolitan statistical areas to determine where the most educated Americans are putting their degrees to work. Criteria: education levels; percentage of workers with degrees; education quality and attainment gap; public school quality rankings; quality and enrollment of each metro area's universities. Raleigh was ranked #8 (#1 = most educated city). *www.WalletHub.com, "Most & Least Educated Cities in America," July 18, 2022*

- Raleigh was selected as one of the best cities for post grads by *Rent.com.* The city ranked among the top 10. Criteria: jobs per capita; unemployment rate; mean annual income; cost of living; rental inventory. *Rent.com, "Best Cities for College Grads," December 11, 2018*

- Raleigh was selected as one of America's most literate cities. The city ranked #14 out of the 84 largest U.S. cities. Criteria: number of booksellers; library resources; Internet resources; educational attainment; periodical publishing resources; newspaper circulation. *Central Connecticut State University, "America's Most Literate Cities, 2018," February 2019*

Environmental Rankings

- The U.S. Environmental Protection Agency (EPA) released its list of U.S. metropolitan areas with the most ENERGY STAR certified buildings in 2022. The Raleigh metro area was ranked #25 out of 25. *U.S. Environmental Protection Agency, "2023 Energy Star Top Cities," April 26, 2023*

- The U.S. Environmental Protection Agency (EPA) released its list of mid-size U.S. metropolitan areas with the most ENERGY STAR certified buildings in 2022. The Raleigh metro area was ranked #1 out of 10. *U.S. Environmental Protection Agency, "2023 Energy Star Top Cities," April 26, 2023*

- Raleigh was highlighted as one of the cleanest metro areas for ozone air pollution in the U.S. during 2019 through 2021. The list represents cities with no monitored ozone air pollution in unhealthful ranges. *American Lung Association, "State of the Air 2023," April 19, 2023*

Food/Drink Rankings

- The U.S. Chamber of Commerce Foundation conducted an in-depth study on local food truck regulations, surveyed 288 food truck owners, and ranked 20 major American cities based on how friendly they are for operating a food truck. The compiled index assessed the following: procedures for obtaining permits and licenses; complying with restrictions; and financial obligations associated with operating a food truck. Raleigh ranked #11 overall (1 being the best). *www.foodtrucknation.us, "Food Truck Nation," March 20, 2018*

Health/Fitness Rankings

- For each of the 100 largest cities in the United States, the American Fitness Index®, compiled in partnership between the American College of Sports Medicine and the Elevance Health Foundation, evaluated community infrastructure and 34 health behaviors including preventive health, levels of chronic disease conditions, food insecurity, sleep quality, pedestrian safety, air quality, and community/environment resources that support physical activity. Raleigh ranked #34 for "community fitness." *americanfitnessindex.org, "2022 ACSM American Fitness Index Summary Report," July 12, 2022*

- The Raleigh metro area was identified as one of the worst cities for bed bugs in America by pest control company Orkin. The area ranked #20 out of 50 based on the number of bed bug treatments Orkin performed from December 2021 to November 2022. *Orkin, "The Windy City Can't Blow Bed Bugs Away: Chicago Ranks #1 For Third Consecutive Year On Orkin's Bed Bug Cities List," January 9, 2023*

- Raleigh was identified as a "2022 Spring Allergy Capital." The area ranked #80 out of 100. Three groups of factors were used to identify the most challenging cities for people with allergies during the spring season: annual spring pollen scores; over the counter allergy medicine use; number of board-certified allergy specialists. *Asthma and Allergy Foundation of America, "Spring Allergy Capitals 2022," March 2, 2022*

- Raleigh was identified as a "2022 Fall Allergy Capital." The area ranked #78 out of 100. Three groups of factors were used to identify the most challenging cities for people with allergies during the fall season: annual fall pollen scores; over the counter allergy medicine use; number of board-certified allergy specialists. *Asthma and Allergy Foundation of America, "Fall Allergy Capitals 2022," March 2, 2022*

- Raleigh was identified as a "2022 Asthma Capital." The area ranked #97 out of the nation's 100 largest metropolitan areas. Criteria: estimated asthma prevalence; asthma-related mortality; and ER visits due to asthma. Risk factors analyzed but not factored in the rankings: annual pollen score; annual air quality; public smoking laws; access to board-certified asthma specialists; rescue and controller medication use; uninsured rate; poverty rate. *Asthma and Allergy Foundation of America, "Asthma Capitals 2022: The Most Challenging Places to Live With Asthma," September 14, 2022*

Real Estate Rankings

- *WalletHub* compared the most populated U.S. cities to determine which had the best markets for real estate agents. Raleigh ranked #54 where demand was high and pay was the best. Criteria: sales per agent; annual median wage for real-estate agents; monthly average starting salary for real estate agents; real estate job density and competition; unemployment rate; home turnover rate; housing-market health index; and other relevant metrics. *www.WalletHub.com, "2021 Best Places to Be a Real Estate Agent," May 12, 2021*

- Raleigh was ranked #137 out of 235 metro areas in terms of housing affordability in 2022 by the National Association of Home Builders (#1 = most affordable). Criteria: the share of homes sold in that area affordable to a family earning the local median income, based on standard mortgage underwriting criteria. *National Association of Home Builders®, NAHB-Wells Fargo Housing Opportunity Index, 4th Quarter 2022*

Safety Rankings

- Allstate ranked the 200 largest cities in America in terms of driver safety. Raleigh ranked #81. Criteria: internal property damage claims over a two-year period from January 2016 to December 2017. The report helps increase the importance of safety and awareness behind the wheel. *Allstate, "Allstate America's Best Drivers Report, 2019" June 24, 2019*

- The National Insurance Crime Bureau ranked 390 metro areas in the U.S. in terms of per capita rates of vehicle theft. The Raleigh metro area ranked #246 (#1 = highest rate). Criteria: number of vehicle theft offenses per 100,000 inhabitants in 2021. *National Insurance Crime Bureau, "Hot Spots 2021," September 1, 2022*

Seniors/Retirement Rankings

- From its Best Cities for Successful Aging indexes, the Milken Institute generated rankings for metropolitan areas, weighing data in nine categories—health care, wellness, living arrangements, transportation and convenience, financial characteristics, education, employment, community engagement, and overall livability. The Raleigh metro area was ranked #42 overall in the large metro area category. *Milken Institute, "Best Cities for Successful Aging, 2017" March 14, 2017*

Women/Minorities Rankings

- Personal finance website *WalletHub* compared more than 180 U.S. cities across two key dimensions, "Hispanic Business-Friendliness" and "Hispanic Purchasing Power," to arrive at the most favorable conditions for Hispanic entrepreneurs. Raleigh was ranked #56 out of 182. Criteria includes: share of Hispanic-Owned Businesses; Hispanic entrepreneurship rate to median annual income of Hispanics; Small Business-Friendliness score; cost of living; and number of Hispanics with at least a bachelor's degree. *WalletHub.com, "2019's Best Cities for Hispanic Entrepreneurs," May 1, 2019*

Miscellaneous Rankings

- *WalletHub* compared the 150 most populated U.S. cities to determine their operating efficiency. A "Quality of Services" score was constructed for each city and then divided by the total budget per capita to reveal which were managed the best. Raleigh ranked #13. Criteria: financial stability; economy; education; safety; health; infrastructure and pollution. *www.WalletHub.com, "2022's Best- & Worst-Run Cities in America," June 21, 2022*

416   Raleigh, North Carolina

Business Environment

DEMOGRAPHICS

Population Growth

Area	1990 Census	2000 Census	2010 Census	2020 Census	Population Growth (%)	
					1990-2020	2010-2020
City	226,841	276,093	403,892	467,665	106.2	15.8
MSA[1]	541,081	797,071	1,130,490	1,413,982	161.3	25.1
U.S.	248,709,873	281,421,906	308,745,538	331,449,281	33.3	7.4

Note: (1) Figures cover the Raleigh-Cary, NC Metropolitan Statistical Area
Source: U.S. Census Bureau, 1990 Census, 2000 Census, 2010 Census, 2020 Census

Race

Area	White Alone[2] (%)	Black Alone[2] (%)	Asian Alone[2] (%)	AIAN[3] Alone[2] (%)	NHOPI[4] Alone[2] (%)	Other Race Alone[2] (%)	Two or More Races (%)
City	53.3	26.3	5.0	0.6	0.1	7.5	7.4
MSA[1]	60.1	18.3	7.0	0.6	0.0	6.4	7.6
U.S.	61.6	12.4	6.0	1.1	0.2	8.4	10.2

Note: (1) Figures cover the Raleigh-Cary, NC Metropolitan Statistical Area; (2) Alone is defined as not being in combination with one or more other races; (3) American Indian and Alaska Native; (4) Native Hawaiian and Other Pacific Islander
Source: U.S. Census Bureau, 2020 Census

Hispanic or Latino Origin

Area	Total (%)	Mexican (%)	Puerto Rican (%)	Cuban (%)	Other (%)
City	11.3	5.0	1.4	0.4	4.5
MSA[1]	10.8	5.6	1.4	0.4	3.5
U.S.	18.4	11.2	1.8	0.7	4.7

Note: Persons of Hispanic or Latino origin can be of any race; (1) Figures cover the Raleigh-Cary, NC Metropolitan Statistical Area
Source: U.S. Census Bureau, 2017-2021 American Community Survey 5-Year Estimates

Age

Area	Percent of Population									Median Age
	Under Age 5	Age 5–19	Age 20–34	Age 35–44	Age 45–54	Age 55–64	Age 65–74	Age 75–84	Age 85+	
City	5.5	18.5	28.0	14.0	12.1	10.1	7.0	3.3	1.4	33.7
MSA[1]	5.8	21.0	20.5	14.3	13.8	11.7	8.0	3.6	1.2	36.8
U.S.	5.6	19.2	20.2	12.7	12.4	13.1	10.0	4.9	1.9	38.8

Note: (1) Figures cover the Raleigh-Cary, NC Metropolitan Statistical Area
Source: U.S. Census Bureau, 2020 Census

Disability by Age

Area	All Ages	Under 18 Years Old	18 to 64 Years Old	65 Years and Over
City	9.0	4.2	7.2	30.1
MSA[1]	9.7	3.9	7.9	30.4
U.S.	12.6	4.4	10.3	33.4

Note: Figures show percent of the civilian noninstitutionalized population that reported having a disability. Disability status is determined from six types of difficulty: vision, hearing, cognitive, ambulatory, self-care, and independent living. For children under 5 years old, hearing and vision difficulty are used to determine disability status. For children between the ages of 5 and 14, disability status is determined from hearing, vision, cognitive, ambulatory, and self-care difficulties. For people aged 15 years and older, they are considered to have a disability if they have difficulty with any one of the six difficulty types; Note: (1) Figures cover the Raleigh-Cary, NC Metropolitan Statistical Area
Source: U.S. Census Bureau, 2017-2021 American Community Survey 5-Year Estimates

Ancestry

Area	German	Irish	English	American	Italian	Polish	French[2]	Scottish	Dutch
City	9.0	8.1	10.4	8.4	3.9	2.0	1.7	2.3	0.9
MSA[1]	9.9	9.1	11.6	8.2	4.6	2.1	1.8	2.4	0.8
U.S.	12.8	9.6	8.1	5.7	5.0	2.7	2.2	1.6	1.1

Note: Figures are the percentage of the total population reporting a particular ancestry. The nine most commonly reported ancestries in the U.S. are shown. Figures include multiple ancestries (e.g. if a person reported being Irish and Italian, they were included in both columns); (1) Figures cover the Raleigh-Cary, NC Metropolitan Statistical Area; (2) Excludes Basque
Source: U.S. Census Bureau, 2017-2021 American Community Survey 5-Year Estimates

Foreign-born Population

Area	Any Foreign Country	Asia	Mexico	Europe	Caribbean	Central America[2]	South America	Africa	Canada
City	13.0	3.9	2.4	1.2	0.9	1.2	0.8	2.3	0.2
MSA[1]	12.2	4.7	2.4	1.3	0.6	0.9	0.6	1.2	0.3
U.S.	13.6	4.2	3.3	1.4	1.1	1.1	1.1	0.8	0.2

Note: (1) Figures cover the Raleigh-Cary, NC Metropolitan Statistical Area; (2) Excludes Mexico.
Source: U.S. Census Bureau, 2017-2021 American Community Survey 5-Year Estimates

Household Size

Area	One	Two	Three	Four	Five	Six	Seven or More	Average Household Size
City	34.6	32.8	14.4	12.1	4.3	1.2	0.6	2.40
MSA[1]	25.4	34.2	16.7	14.8	6.0	2.0	0.9	2.60
U.S.	28.1	33.8	15.5	12.9	6.0	2.3	1.4	2.60

Note: (1) Figures cover the Raleigh-Cary, NC Metropolitan Statistical Area
Source: U.S. Census Bureau, 2017-2021 American Community Survey 5-Year Estimates

Household Relationships

Area	House-holder	Opposite-sex Spouse	Same-sex Spouse	Opposite-sex Unmarried Partner	Same-sex Unmarried Partner	Child[2]	Grand-child	Other Relatives	Non-relatives
City	41.8	15.1	0.2	2.9	0.2	25.5	1.4	3.9	5.0
MSA[1]	38.4	19.2	0.2	2.2	0.2	30.0	1.5	3.7	3.0
U.S.	38.3	17.5	0.2	2.5	0.2	28.3	2.4	4.8	3.4

Note: Figures are percent of the total population; (1) Figures cover the Raleigh-Cary, NC Metropolitan Statistical Area; (2) Includes biological, adopted, and stepchildren of the householder
Source: U.S. Census Bureau, 2020 Census

Gender

Area	Males	Females	Males per 100 Females
City	224,994	242,671	92.7
MSA[1]	687,440	726,542	94.6
U.S.	162,685,811	168,763,470	96.4

Note: (1) Figures cover the Raleigh-Cary, NC Metropolitan Statistical Area
Source: U.S. Census Bureau, 2020 Census

Marital Status

Area	Never Married	Now Married[2]	Separated	Widowed	Divorced
City	43.2	40.0	2.1	3.8	11.0
MSA[1]	32.2	51.9	2.0	4.2	9.7
U.S.	33.8	48.0	1.8	5.6	10.8

Note: Figures are percentages and cover the population 15 years of age and older; (1) Figures cover the Raleigh-Cary, NC Metropolitan Statistical Area; (2) Excludes separated
Source: U.S. Census Bureau, 2017-2021 American Community Survey 5-Year Estimates

Religious Groups by Family

Area	Catholic	Baptist	Methodist	LDS[2]	Pentecostal	Lutheran	Islam	Adventist	Other
MSA[1]	12.4	9.8	5.4	1.2	1.9	0.7	3.2	1.5	12.8
U.S.	18.7	7.3	3.0	2.0	1.8	1.7	1.3	1.3	11.6

Note: Figures are the number of adherents as a percentage of the total population and cover the eight largest religious groups in the U.S; (1) Figures cover the Raleigh-Cary, NC Metropolitan Statistical Area; (2) Church of Jesus Christ of Latter-day Saints
Sources: 2020 U.S. Religion Census, Association of Statisticians of American Religious Bodies; The Association of Religion Data Archives (ARDA)

Religious Groups by Tradition

Area	Catholic	Evangelical Protestant	Mainline Protestant	Black Protestant	Islam	Judaism	Hinduism	Orthodox	Buddhism
MSA[1]	12.4	19.3	7.4	2.8	3.2	0.2	0.4	0.3	0.4
U.S.	18.7	16.5	5.2	2.3	1.3	0.6	0.4	0.4	0.3

Note: Figures are the number of adherents as a percentage of the total population; (1) Figures cover the Raleigh-Cary, NC Metropolitan Statistical Area
Sources: 2020 U.S. Religion Census, Association of Statisticians of American Religious Bodies; The Association of Religion Data Archives (ARDA)

418 Raleigh, North Carolina

ECONOMY

Gross Metropolitan Product

Area	2020	2021	2022	2023	Rank[2]
MSA[1]	95.3	106.6	117.3	125.7	39

Note: Figures are in billions of dollars; (1) Figures cover the Raleigh-Cary, NC Metropolitan Statistical Area; (2) Rank is based on 2021 data and ranges from 1 to 381
Source: U.S. Conference of Mayors, U.S. Metro Economies: U.S. Metros Compared to Global and State Economies, June 2022

Economic Growth

Area	2018-20 (%)	2021 (%)	2022 (%)	2023 (%)	Rank[2]
MSA[1]	-0.1	7.7	4.4	4.0	148
U.S.	-0.6	5.7	3.1	2.9	—

Note: Figures are real gross metropolitan product (GMP) growth rates and represent average annual percent change; (1) Figures cover the Raleigh-Cary, NC Metropolitan Statistical Area; (2) Rank is based on 2020 2-year average annual percent change and ranges from 1 to 381
Source: U.S. Conference of Mayors, U.S. Metro Economies: U.S. Metros Compared to Global and State Economies, June 2022

Metropolitan Area Exports

Area	2016	2017	2018	2019	2020	2021	Rank[2]
MSA[1]	2,620.4	2,865.8	3,193.2	3,546.8	3,372.0	3,962.7	71

Note: Figures are in millions of dollars; (1) Figures cover the Raleigh-Cary, NC Metropolitan Statistical Area; (2) Rank is based on 2021 data and ranges from 1 to 388
Source: U.S. Department of Commerce, International Trade Administration, Office of Trade and Economic Analysis, Industry and Analysis, Exports by Metropolitan Area, data extracted March 16, 2023

Building Permits

Area	Single-Family			Multi-Family			Total		
	2021	2022	Pct. Chg.	2021	2022	Pct. Chg.	2021	2022	Pct. Chg.
City	1,354	1,875	38.5	5,133	6,760	31.7	6,487	8,635	33.1
MSA[1]	14,227	12,488	-12.2	7,422	9,080	22.3	21,649	21,568	-0.4
U.S.	1,115,400	975,600	-12.5	621,600	689,500	10.9	1,737,000	1,665,100	-4.1

Note: (1) Figures cover the Raleigh-Cary, NC Metropolitan Statistical Area; Figures represent new, privately-owned housing units authorized (unadjusted data); All permit data are based on estimates with imputation
Source: U.S. Census Bureau, Manufacturing, Mining, and Construction Statistics, Building Permits, 2021, 2022

Bankruptcy Filings

Area	Business Filings			Nonbusiness Filings		
	2021	2022	% Chg.	2021	2022	% Chg.
Wake County	53	50	-5.7	614	536	-12.7
U.S.	14,347	13,481	-6.0	399,269	374,240	-6.3

Note: Business filings include Chapter 7, Chapter 9, Chapter 11, Chapter 12, Chapter 13, Chapter 15, and Section 304; Nonbusiness filings include Chapter 7, Chapter 11, and Chapter 13
Source: Administrative Office of the U.S. Courts, Business and Nonbusiness Bankruptcy, County Cases Commenced by Chapter of the Bankruptcy Code, During the 12-Month Period Ending December 31, 2021 and Business and Nonbusiness Bankruptcy, County Cases Commenced by Chapter of the Bankruptcy Code, During the 12-Month Period Ending December 31, 2022

Housing Vacancy Rates

Area	Gross Vacancy Rate[2] (%)			Year-Round Vacancy Rate[3] (%)			Rental Vacancy Rate[4] (%)			Homeowner Vacancy Rate[5] (%)		
	2020	2021	2022	2020	2021	2022	2020	2021	2022	2020	2021	2022
MSA[1]	4.6	6.3	7.4	4.5	6.3	7.3	2.3	2.9	7.1	0.4	1.1	0.5
U.S.	10.6	10.8	10.5	8.2	8.4	8.2	6.3	6.1	5.8	1.0	0.9	0.8

Note: (1) Figures cover the Raleigh-Cary, NC Metropolitan Statistical Area; (2) The percentage of the total housing inventory that is vacant; (3) The percentage of the housing inventory (excluding seasonal units) that is year-round vacant; (4) The percentage of rental inventory that is vacant for rent; (5) The percentage of homeowner inventory that is vacant for sale
Source: U.S. Census Bureau, Housing Vacancies and Homeownership Annual Statistics: 2020, 2021, 2022

INCOME

Income

Area	Per Capita ($)	Median Household ($)	Average Household ($)
City	42,632	72,996	102,100
MSA[1]	42,554	83,581	110,195
U.S.	37,638	69,021	97,196

Note: (1) Figures cover the Raleigh-Cary, NC Metropolitan Statistical Area
Source: U.S. Census Bureau, 2017-2021 American Community Survey 5-Year Estimates

Household Income Distribution

Area	Percent of Households Earning							
	Under $15,000	$15,000 -$24,999	$25,000 -$34,999	$35,000 -$49,999	$50,000 -$74,999	$75,000 -$99,999	$100,000 -$149,999	$150,000 and up
City	7.5	6.5	8.7	12.1	16.7	12.9	17.0	18.8
MSA[1]	6.3	6.0	7.0	10.4	15.8	12.8	19.5	22.3
U.S.	9.4	7.8	8.2	11.4	16.8	12.8	16.3	17.3

Note: (1) Figures cover the Raleigh-Cary, NC Metropolitan Statistical Area
Source: U.S. Census Bureau, 2017-2021 American Community Survey 5-Year Estimates

Poverty Rate

Area	All Ages	Under 18 Years Old	18 to 64 Years Old	65 Years and Over
City	12.1	15.8	11.8	7.2
MSA[1]	9.3	12.1	8.7	6.9
U.S.	12.6	17.0	11.8	9.6

Note: Figures are percentage of people whose income during the past 12 months was below the poverty level;
(1) Figures cover the Raleigh-Cary, NC Metropolitan Statistical Area
Source: U.S. Census Bureau, 2017-2021 American Community Survey 5-Year Estimates

EMPLOYMENT

Labor Force and Employment

Area	Civilian Labor Force			Workers Employed		
	Dec. 2021	Dec. 2022	% Chg.	Dec. 2021	Dec. 2022	% Chg.
City	255,398	264,381	3.5	247,896	256,967	3.7
MSA[1]	737,649	764,883	3.7	718,092	744,560	3.7
U.S.	161,696,000	164,224,000	1.6	155,732,000	158,872,000	2.0

Note: Data is not seasonally adjusted and covers workers 16 years of age and older; (1) Figures cover the
Raleigh-Cary, NC Metropolitan Statistical Area
Source: Bureau of Labor Statistics, Local Area Unemployment Statistics

Unemployment Rate

Area	2022											
	Jan.	Feb.	Mar.	Apr.	May	Jun.	Jul.	Aug.	Sep.	Oct.	Nov.	Dec.
City	3.3	3.3	3.2	3.1	3.3	3.6	3.4	3.5	3.0	3.5	3.4	2.8
MSA[1]	3.1	3.0	2.9	2.9	3.1	3.4	3.1	3.3	2.8	3.3	3.2	2.7
U.S.	4.4	4.1	3.8	3.3	3.4	3.8	3.8	3.8	3.3	3.4	3.4	3.3

Note: Data is not seasonally adjusted and covers workers 16 years of age and older; (1) Figures cover the
Raleigh-Cary, NC Metropolitan Statistical Area
Source: Bureau of Labor Statistics, Local Area Unemployment Statistics

Average Wages

Occupation	$/Hr.	Occupation	$/Hr.
Accountants and Auditors	40.68	Maintenance and Repair Workers	22.67
Automotive Mechanics	23.79	Marketing Managers	71.21
Bookkeepers	21.92	Network and Computer Systems Admin.	45.26
Carpenters	22.09	Nurses, Licensed Practical	26.69
Cashiers	12.55	Nurses, Registered	37.82
Computer Programmers	51.36	Nursing Assistants	16.03
Computer Systems Analysts	48.99	Office Clerks, General	19.56
Computer User Support Specialists	31.64	Physical Therapists	42.43
Construction Laborers	18.40	Physicians	140.14
Cooks, Restaurant	15.45	Plumbers, Pipefitters and Steamfitters	24.57
Customer Service Representatives	19.52	Police and Sheriff's Patrol Officers	26.56
Dentists	107.63	Postal Service Mail Carriers	27.38
Electricians	24.71	Real Estate Sales Agents	27.61
Engineers, Electrical	52.39	Retail Salespersons	16.28
Fast Food and Counter Workers	12.10	Sales Representatives, Technical/Scientific	55.59
Financial Managers	74.45	Secretaries, Exc. Legal/Medical/Executive	20.25
First-Line Supervisors of Office Workers	29.75	Security Guards	15.48
General and Operations Managers	64.48	Surgeons	n/a
Hairdressers/Cosmetologists	21.68	Teacher Assistants, Exc. Postsecondary*	12.44
Home Health and Personal Care Aides	13.39	Teachers, Secondary School, Exc. Sp. Ed.*	25.67
Janitors and Cleaners	14.13	Telemarketers	15.51
Landscaping/Groundskeeping Workers	17.40	Truck Drivers, Heavy/Tractor-Trailer	24.80
Lawyers	67.47	Truck Drivers, Light/Delivery Services	19.06
Maids and Housekeeping Cleaners	14.15	Waiters and Waitresses	14.41

Note: Wage data covers the Raleigh-Cary, NC Metropolitan Statistical Area; (*) Hourly wages were calculated
from annual wage data based on a 40 hour work week; n/a not available.
Source: Bureau of Labor Statistics, Metro Area Occupational Employment & Wage Estimates, May 2022

Employment by Industry

Sector	MSA[1]		U.S.
	Number of Employees	Percent of Total	Percent of Total
Construction, Mining, and Logging	47,600	6.6	5.4
Private Education and Health Services	93,500	13.0	16.1
Financial Activities	40,800	5.7	5.9
Government	98,800	13.8	14.5
Information	25,800	3.6	2.0
Leisure and Hospitality	74,700	10.4	10.3
Manufacturing	33,900	4.7	8.4
Other Services	28,400	4.0	3.7
Professional and Business Services	146,800	20.4	14.7
Retail Trade	73,300	10.2	10.2
Transportation, Warehousing, and Utilities	25,300	3.5	4.9
Wholesale Trade	29,400	4.1	3.9

Note: Figures are non-farm employment as of December 2022. Figures are not seasonally adjusted and include workers 16 years of age and older; (1) Figures cover the Raleigh-Cary, NC Metropolitan Statistical Area
Source: Bureau of Labor Statistics, Current Employment Statistics, Employment, Hours, and Earnings

Employment by Occupation

Occupation Classification	City (%)	MSA[1] (%)	U.S. (%)
Management, Business, Science, and Arts	50.2	51.2	40.3
Natural Resources, Construction, and Maintenance	5.8	6.8	8.7
Production, Transportation, and Material Moving	8.2	8.8	13.1
Sales and Office	21.7	20.3	20.9
Service	14.0	13.0	17.0

Note: Figures cover employed civilians 16 years of age and older; (1) Figures cover the Raleigh-Cary, NC Metropolitan Statistical Area
Source: U.S. Census Bureau, 2017-2021 American Community Survey 5-Year Estimates

Occupations with Greatest Projected Employment Growth: 2022 – 2024

Occupation[1]	2022 Employment	2024 Projected Employment	Numeric Employment Change	Percent Employment Change
Cooks, Restaurant	45,830	53,440	7,610	16.6
Waiters and Waitresses	65,770	72,960	7,190	10.9
Software Developers	55,450	62,610	7,160	12.9
Cooks, Fast Food	82,470	88,860	6,390	7.7
Fast Food and Counter Workers	68,750	75,030	6,280	9.1
Laborers and Freight, Stock, and Material Movers, Hand	100,780	106,480	5,700	5.7
Retail Salespersons	125,490	130,210	4,720	3.8
General and Operations Managers	87,450	92,120	4,670	5.3
First-Line Supervisors of Food Preparation and Serving Workers	42,440	47,070	4,630	10.9
Stockers and Order Fillers	88,320	92,930	4,610	5.2

Note: Projections cover North Carolina; (1) Sorted by numeric employment change
Source: www.projectionscentral.com, State Occupational Projections, 2022–2024 Short-Term Projections

Fastest-Growing Occupations: 2022 – 2024

Occupation[1]	2022 Employment	2024 Projected Employment	Numeric Employment Change	Percent Employment Change
Cooks, Restaurant	45,830	53,440	7,610	16.6
Solar Photovoltaic Installers	390	450	60	15.4
Statisticians	1,710	1,960	250	14.6
Medical Scientists, Except Epidemiologists	3,630	4,160	530	14.6
Actuaries	950	1,080	130	13.7
Data Scientists	5,390	6,100	710	13.2
Soil and Plant Scientists	2,160	2,440	280	13.0
Software Developers	55,450	62,610	7,160	12.9
Software Quality Assurance Analysts and Testers	8,850	9,950	1,100	12.4
Bartenders	14,560	16,360	1,800	12.4

Note: Projections cover North Carolina; (1) Sorted by percent employment change and excludes occupations with numeric employment change less than 50
Source: www.projectionscentral.com, State Occupational Projections, 2022–2024 Short-Term Projections

CITY FINANCES

City Government Finances

Component	2020 ($000)	2020 ($ per capita)
Total Revenues	970,815	2,048
Total Expenditures	943,401	1,990
Debt Outstanding	1,508,441	3,182
Cash and Securities[1]	1,267,633	2,674

Note: (1) Cash and security holdings of a government at the close of its fiscal year, including those of its dependent agencies, utilities, and liquor stores.
Source: U.S. Census Bureau, State & Local Government Finances 2020

City Government Revenue by Source

Source	2020 ($000)	2020 ($ per capita)	2020 (%)
General Revenue			
From Federal Government	15,079	32	1.6
From State Government	55,562	117	5.7
From Local Governments	60,500	128	6.2
Taxes			
Property	270,851	571	27.9
Sales and Gross Receipts	108,261	228	11.2
Personal Income	0	0	0.0
Corporate Income	0	0	0.0
Motor Vehicle License	10,535	22	1.1
Other Taxes	24,205	51	2.5
Current Charges	264,012	557	27.2
Liquor Store	0	0	0.0
Utility	116,800	246	12.0

Source: U.S. Census Bureau, State & Local Government Finances 2020

City Government Expenditures by Function

Function	2020 ($000)	2020 ($ per capita)	2020 (%)
General Direct Expenditures			
Air Transportation	0	0	0.0
Corrections	0	0	0.0
Education	0	0	0.0
Employment Security Administration	0	0	0.0
Financial Administration	11,334	23	1.2
Fire Protection	72,169	152	7.6
General Public Buildings	21,411	45	2.3
Governmental Administration, Other	8,865	18	0.9
Health	0	0	0.0
Highways	61,110	128	6.5
Hospitals	0	0	0.0
Housing and Community Development	25,484	53	2.7
Interest on General Debt	40,536	85	4.3
Judicial and Legal	4,054	8	0.4
Libraries	0	0	0.0
Parking	8,314	17	0.9
Parks and Recreation	106,341	224	11.3
Police Protection	130,049	274	13.8
Public Welfare	0	0	0.0
Sewerage	174,810	368	18.5
Solid Waste Management	35,490	74	3.8
Veterans' Services	0	0	0.0
Liquor Store	0	0	0.0
Utility	185,001	390	19.6

Source: U.S. Census Bureau, State & Local Government Finances 2020

TAXES

State Corporate Income Tax Rates

State	Tax Rate (%)	Income Brackets ($)	Num. of Brackets	Financial Institution Tax Rate (%)[a]	Federal Income Tax Ded.
North Carolina	2.5	Flat rate	1	2.5	No

Note: Tax rates as of January 1, 2023; (a) Rates listed are the corporate income tax rate applied to financial institutions or excise taxes based on income. Some states have other taxes based upon the value of deposits or shares.
Source: Federation of Tax Administrators, State Corporate Income Tax Rates, January 1, 2023

State Individual Income Tax Rates

State	Tax Rate (%)	Income Brackets ($)	Personal Exemptions ($)			Standard Ded. ($)	
			Single	Married	Depend.	Single	Married
North Carolina	4.75	Flat rate	None	None	None	10,750	21,500

Note: Tax rates as of January 1, 2023; Local- and county-level taxes are not included; Federal income tax is not deductible on state income tax returns
Source: Federation of Tax Administrators, State Individual Income Tax Rates, January 1, 2023

Various State Sales and Excise Tax Rates

State	State Sales Tax (%)	Gasoline[1] ($/gal.)	Cigarette[2] ($/pack)	Spirits[3] ($/gal.)	Wine[4] ($/gal.)	Beer[5] ($/gal.)	Recreational Marijuana (%)
North Carolina	4.75	0.3875	0.45	16.40	1.00	0.62	Not legal

Note: All tax rates as of January 1, 2023; (1) The American Petroleum Institute has developed a methodology for determining the average tax rate on a gallon of fuel. Rates may include any of the following: excise taxes, environmental fees, storage tank fees, other fees or taxes, general sales tax, and local taxes; (2) The federal excise tax of $1.0066 per pack and local taxes are not included; (3) Rates are those applicable to off-premise sales of 40% alcohol by volume (a.b.v.) distilled spirits in 750ml containers. Local excise taxes are excluded; (4) Rates are those applicable to off-premise sales of 11% a.b.v. non-carbonated wine in 750ml containers; (5) Rates are those applicable to off-premise sales of 4.7% a.b.v. beer in 12 ounce containers.
Source: Tax Foundation, 2023 Facts & Figures: How Does Your State Compare?

State Business Tax Climate Index Rankings

State	Overall Rank	Corporate Tax Rank	Individual Income Tax Rank	Sales Tax Rank	Property Tax Rank	Unemployment Insurance Tax Rank
North Carolina	10	5	17	20	13	10

Note: The index is a measure of how each state's tax laws affect economic performance. The lower the rank, the more favorable a state's tax system is for business. States without a given tax are given a ranking of 1. The scores/rankings for the District of Columbia do not affect other states. The 2023 index represents the tax climate as of July 1, 2022.
Source: Tax Foundation, State Business Tax Climate Index 2023

TRANSPORTATION

Means of Transportation to Work

Area	Car/Truck/Van		Public Transportation			Bicycle	Walked	Other Means	Worked at Home
	Drove Alone	Car-pooled	Bus	Subway	Railroad				
City	70.9	7.1	1.7	0.0	0.0	0.2	1.4	1.4	17.2
MSA[1]	72.9	7.4	0.7	0.0	0.0	0.1	1.1	1.0	16.8
U.S.	73.2	8.6	2.0	1.6	0.5	0.5	2.5	1.5	9.7

Note: Figures are percentages and cover workers 16 years of age and older; (1) Figures cover the Raleigh-Cary, NC Metropolitan Statistical Area
Source: U.S. Census Bureau, 2017-2021 American Community Survey 5-Year Estimates

Travel Time to Work

Area	Less Than 10 Minutes	10 to 19 Minutes	20 to 29 Minutes	30 to 44 Minutes	45 to 59 Minutes	60 to 89 Minutes	90 Minutes or More
City	9.3	32.4	27.0	20.8	5.7	3.0	1.8
MSA[1]	8.6	26.7	24.4	24.4	9.1	4.9	1.9
U.S.	12.4	28.5	21.0	20.9	8.2	6.2	2.9

Note: Note: Figures are percentages and include workers 16 years old and over; (1) Figures cover the Raleigh-Cary, NC Metropolitan Statistical Area
Source: U.S. Census Bureau, 2017-2021 American Community Survey 5-Year Estimates

Key Congestion Measures

Measure	1990	2000	2010	2015	2020
Annual Hours of Delay, Total (000)	5,670	13,776	21,618	25,692	11,144
Annual Hours of Delay, Per Auto Commuter	20	28	34	39	17
Annual Congestion Cost, Per Auto Commuter ($)	320	577	722	792	361

Note: Covers the Raleigh NC urban area
Source: Texas A&M Transportation Institute, 2021 Urban Mobility Report

Freeway Travel Time Index

Measure	1985	1990	1995	2000	2005	2010	2015	2020
Urban Area Index[1]	1.06	1.10	1.12	1.14	1.16	1.16	1.17	1.05
Urban Area Rank[1,2]	53	47	57	62	57	54	46	85

Note: Freeway Travel Time Index—the ratio of travel time in the peak period to the travel time at free-flow conditions. For example, a value of 1.30 indicates a 20-minute free-flow trip takes 26 minutes in the peak (20 minutes x 1.30 = 26 minutes); (1) Covers the Raleigh NC urban area; (2) Rank is based on 101 larger urban areas (#1 = highest travel time index)
Source: Texas A&M Transportation Institute, 2021 Urban Mobility Report

Public Transportation

Agency Name / Mode of Transportation	Vehicles Operated in Maximum Service[1]	Annual Unlinked Passenger Trips[2] (in thous.)	Annual Passenger Miles[3] (in thous.)
Capital Area Transit (CAT)			
Bus (purchased transportation)	75	3,412.7	12,931.3
Demand Response - Taxi	178	469.8	3,027.9

Note: (1) Number of revenue vehicles operated by the given mode and type of service to meet the annual maximum service requirement. This is the revenue vehicle count during the peak season of the year; on the week and day that maximum service is provided. Vehicles operated in maximum service (VOMS) exclude atypical days and one-time special events; (2) Number of passengers who boarded public transportation vehicles. Passengers are counted each time they board a vehicle no matter how many vehicles they use to travel from their origin to their destination. (3) Sum of the distances ridden by all passengers during the entire fiscal year.
Source: Federal Transit Administration, National Transit Database, 2021

Air Transportation

Airport Name and Code / Type of Service	Passenger Airlines[1]	Passenger Enplanements	Freight Carriers[2]	Freight (lbs)
Raleigh-Durham International (RDU)				
Domestic service (U.S. carriers - 2022)	32	5,713,482	13	91,381,469
International service (U.S. carriers - 2021)	4	29,848	3	250,550

Note: (1) Includes all U.S.-based major, minor and commuter airlines that carried at least one passenger during the year; (2) Includes all U.S.-based airlines and freight carriers that transported at least one pound of freight during the year.
Source: Bureau of Transportation Statistics, The Intermodal Transportation Database, Air Carriers: T-100 Domestic Market (U.S. Carriers), 2022; Bureau of Transportation Statistics, The Intermodal Transportation Database, Air Carriers: T-100 International Market (U.S. Carriers), 2021

BUSINESSES

Major Business Headquarters

Company Name	Industry	Rankings	
		Fortune[1]	Forbes[2]
No companies listed	-	-	-

Note: (1) Companies that produce a 10-K are ranked 1 to 500 based on 2021 revenue; (2) All private companies with at least $2 billion in annual revenue through the end of their most current fiscal year are ranked 1 to 246; companies listed are headquartered in the city; dashes indicate no ranking
Source: Fortune, "Fortune 500," 2022; Forbes, "America's Largest Private Companies," 2022

Fastest-Growing Businesses

According to *Inc.*, Raleigh is home to five of America's 500 fastest-growing private companies: **Industrial Automation Co.** (#110); **Custom Patch Hats** (#140); **ACHUTI** (#178); **Givebacks** (#375); **World Headquarters of Awesome** (#436). Criteria: must be an independent, privately-held, for-profit, U.S. corporation, proprietorship or partnership as of December 31, 2021; revenues must be at least $100,000 in 2018 and $2 million in 2021; must have four-year operating/sales history. *Inc., "America's 500 Fastest-Growing Private Companies," 2022*

According to *Initiative for a Competitive Inner City (ICIC)*, Raleigh is home to one of America's 100 fastest-growing "inner city" companies: **Southeastern Healthcare of North Carolina** (#28). Criteria for inclusion: company must be headquartered in or have 51 percent or more of its physical operations in an economically distressed urban area; must be an independent, for-profit corporation, partnership or proprietorship; must have 10 or more employees and have a five-year sales history that includes sales of at least $200,000 in the base year and at least $1 million in the current year with no decrease in sales over the two most recent years. Companies were ranked overall by revenue growth over the five-year period between 2017 and 2021. *Initiative for a Competitive Inner City (ICIC), "Inner City 100 Companies," 2022*

According to Deloitte, Raleigh is home to two of North America's 500 fastest-growing high-technology companies: **Pendo** (#351); **FM:Systems** (#462). Companies are ranked by percentage growth in revenue over a four-year period. Criteria for inclusion: company must be headquartered within North America; must own proprietary intellectual property or technology that is sold to customers in products that contributes to a significant portion of the company's operating revenue; must have been in business for a minumum of four years with 2018 operating revenues of at least $50,000 USD/CD and 2021 operating revenues of at least $5 million USD/CD. *Deloitte, 2022 Technology Fast 500*[TM]

Living Environment

COST OF LIVING

Cost of Living Index

Composite Index	Groceries	Housing	Utilities	Trans-portation	Health Care	Misc. Goods/Services
96.1	91.6	97.5	102.0	94.5	102.6	94.9

Note: The Cost of Living Index measures regional differences in the cost of consumer goods and services, excluding taxes and non-consumer expenditures, for professional and managerial households in the top income quintile. It is based on more than 50,000 prices covering almost 60 different items for which prices are collected three times a year by chambers of commerce, economic development organizations or university applied economic centers in each participating urban area. The numbers shown should be read as a percentage above or below the national average of 100. For example, a value of 115.4 in the groceries column indicates that grocery prices are 15.4% higher than the national average. Small differences in the index numbers should not be interpreted as significant; Figures cover the Raleigh NC urban area.
Source: The Council for Community and Economic Research, Cost of Living Index, 2022

Grocery Prices

Area[1]	T-Bone Steak ($/pound)	Frying Chicken ($/pound)	Whole Milk ($/half gal.)	Eggs ($/dozen)	Orange Juice ($/64 oz.)	Coffee ($/11.5 oz.)
City[2]	11.98	1.14	1.99	1.71	4.00	3.54
Avg.	13.81	1.59	2.43	2.25	3.85	4.95
Min.	10.17	0.90	1.51	1.30	2.90	3.46
Max.	19.35	3.30	4.32	4.32	5.31	8.59

Note: (1) Values for the local area are compared with the average, minimum and maximum values for all 286 areas in the Cost of Living Index; (2) Figures cover the Raleigh NC urban area; T-Bone Steak (price per pound); Frying Chicken (price per pound, whole fryer); Whole Milk (half gallon carton); Eggs (price per dozen, Grade A, large); Orange Juice (64 oz. Tropicana or Florida Natural); Coffee (11.5 oz. can, vacuum-packed, Maxwell House, Hills Bros, or Folgers).
Source: The Council for Community and Economic Research, Cost of Living Index, 2022

Housing and Utility Costs

Area[1]	New Home Price ($)	Apartment Rent ($/month)	All Electric ($/month)	Part Electric ($/month)	Other Energy ($/month)	Telephone ($/month)
City[2]	400,445	1,614	-	112.40	74.47	184.19
Avg.	450,913	1,371	176.41	99.93	76.96	190.22
Min.	229,283	546	100.84	31.56	27.15	174.27
Max.	2,434,977	4,569	356.86	249.59	272.24	208.31

Note: (1) Values for the local area are compared with the average, minimum and maximum values for all 286 areas in the Cost of Living Index; (2) Figures cover the Raleigh NC urban area; New Home Price (2,400 sf living area, 8,000 sf lot, in urban area with full utilities); Apartment Rent (950 sf 2 bedroom/1.5 or 2 bath, unfurnished, excluding all utilities except water); All Electric (average monthly cost for an all-electric home); Part Electric (average monthly cost for a part-electric home); Other Energy (average monthly cost for natural gas, fuel oil, coal, wood, and any other forms of energy except electricity); Telephone (price includes the base monthly rate plus taxes and fees for three lines of mobile phone service).
Source: The Council for Community and Economic Research, Cost of Living Index, 2022

Health Care, Transportation, and Other Costs

Area[1]	Doctor ($/visit)	Dentist ($/visit)	Optometrist ($/visit)	Gasoline ($/gallon)	Beauty Salon ($/visit)	Men's Shirt ($)
City[2]	121.09	115.41	113.39	3.86	50.42	26.62
Avg.	124.91	107.77	117.66	3.86	43.31	34.21
Min.	36.61	58.25	51.79	2.90	22.18	13.05
Max.	250.21	162.58	371.96	5.54	85.61	63.54

Note: (1) Values for the local area are compared with the average, minimum and maximum values for all 286 areas in the Cost of Living Index; (2) Figures cover the Raleigh NC urban area; Doctor (general practitioners routine exam of an established patient); Dentist (adult teeth cleaning and periodic oral examination); Optometrist (full vision eye exam for established adult patient); Gasoline (one gallon regular unleaded, national brand, including all taxes, cash price at self-service pump if available); Beauty Salon (woman's shampoo, trim, and blow-dry); Men's Shirt (cotton/polyester dress shirt, pinpoint weave, long sleeves).
Source: The Council for Community and Economic Research, Cost of Living Index, 2022

HOUSING

Homeownership Rate

Area	2015 (%)	2016 (%)	2017 (%)	2018 (%)	2019 (%)	2020 (%)	2021 (%)	2022 (%)
MSA[1]	67.4	65.9	68.2	64.9	63.0	68.2	62.7	65.1
U.S.	63.7	63.4	63.9	64.4	64.6	66.6	65.5	65.8

Note: (1) Figures cover the Raleigh-Cary, NC Metropolitan Statistical Area
Source: U.S. Census Bureau, Housing Vacancies and Homeownership Annual Statistics: 2015-2022

House Price Index (HPI)

Area	National Ranking[2]	Quarterly Change (%)	One-Year Change (%)	Five-Year Change (%)	Since 1991Q1 (%)
MSA[1]	57	-2.71	14.97	69.49	298.33
U.S.[3]	–	0.34	8.41	58.44	289.08

Note: The HPI is a weighted repeat sales index. It measures average price changes in repeat sales or refinancings on the same properties. This information is obtained by reviewing repeat mortgage transactions on single-family properties whose mortgages have been purchased or securitized by Fannie Mae or Freddie Mac since January 1975; (1) Figures cover the Raleigh, NC Metropolitan Statistical Area; (2) Rankings are based on annual percentage change for all metro areas containing at least 15,000 transactions over the last 10 years and ranges from 1 to 257; (3) figures based on a weighted average of Census Division estimates using a seasonally adjusted, purchase-only index; all figures are for the period ending December 31, 2022
Source: Federal Housing Finance Agency, Change in FHFA Metropolitan Area House Price Indexes, 2022Q4

Median Single-Family Home Prices

Area	2020	2021	2022p	Percent Change 2021 to 2022
MSA[1]	325.2	392.8	455.3	15.9
U.S. Average	300.2	357.1	392.6	9.9

Note: Figures are median sales prices of existing single-family homes in thousands of dollars; (p) preliminary; (1) Figures cover the Raleigh-Cary, NC Metropolitan Statistical Area
Source: National Association of Realtors, Median Sales Price of Existing Single-Family Homes for Metropolitan Areas, 4th Quarter 2022

Qualifying Income Based on Median Sales Price of Existing Single-Family Homes

Area	With 5% Down ($)	With 10% Down ($)	With 20% Down ($)
MSA[1]	128,948	122,161	108,588
U.S. Average	112,234	106,237	94,513

Note: Figures are preliminary; Qualifying income is based on a mortgage rate of 6.77%. Monthly principal and interest payment is limited to 25% of income; (1) Figures cover the Raleigh-Cary, NC Metropolitan Statistical Area
Source: National Association of Realtors, Qualifying Income Based on Median Sales Price of Existing Single-Family Homes for Metropolitan Areas, 4th Quarter 2022

Home Value

Area	Under $100,000	$100,000 -$199,999	$200,000 -$299,999	$300,000 -$399,999	$400,000 -$499,999	$500,000 -$999,999	$1,000,000 or more	Median ($)
City	4.0	21.6	28.3	18.3	11.0	14.2	2.7	285,400
MSA[1]	7.0	20.0	25.5	20.2	12.4	13.2	1.7	289,700
U.S.	16.2	24.2	20.1	13.6	8.3	13.6	4.1	244,900

Note: Figures are percentages except for median and cover owner-occupied housing units; (1) Figures cover the Raleigh-Cary, NC Metropolitan Statistical Area
Source: U.S. Census Bureau, 2017-2021 American Community Survey 5-Year Estimates

Year Housing Structure Built

Area	2020 or Later	2010 -2019	2000 -2009	1990 -1999	1980 -1989	1970 -1979	1960 -1969	1950 -1959	1940 -1949	Before 1940	Median Year
City	0.3	14.6	23.4	18.5	16.8	9.9	7.6	4.2	1.6	3.1	1994
MSA[1]	0.5	17.9	23.9	21.6	14.6	8.6	5.4	3.4	1.4	2.7	1996
U.S.	0.2	7.3	13.6	13.6	13.2	14.8	10.3	10.0	4.7	12.2	1979

Note: Figures are percentages except for Median Year; Note: (1) Figures cover the Raleigh-Cary, NC Metropolitan Statistical Area
Source: U.S. Census Bureau, 2017-2021 American Community Survey 5-Year Estimates

Gross Monthly Rent

Area	Under $500	$500 -$999	$1,000 -$1,499	$1,500 -$1,999	$2,000 -$2,499	$2,500 -$2,999	$3,000 and up	Median ($)
City	3.2	19.5	52.4	19.0	4.3	0.9	0.9	1,237
MSA[1]	4.4	22.5	46.4	19.1	5.2	1.2	1.2	1,230
U.S.	8.1	30.5	30.8	16.8	7.3	3.1	3.5	1,163

Note: Figures are percentages except for median; Gross rent is the contract rent plus the estimated average monthly cost of utilities (electricity, gas, and water and sewer) and fuels (oil, coal, kerosene, wood, etc.) if these are paid by the renter (or paid for the renter by someone else); (1) Figures cover the Raleigh-Cary, NC Metropolitan Statistical Area
Source: U.S. Census Bureau, 2017-2021 American Community Survey 5-Year Estimates

HEALTH

Health Risk Factors

Category	MSA[1] (%)	U.S. (%)
Adults aged 18–64 who have any kind of health care coverage	86.1	90.9
Adults who reported being in good or better health	88.0	85.2
Adults who have been told they have high blood cholesterol	32.5	35.7
Adults who have been told they have high blood pressure	29.8	32.4
Adults who are current smokers	8.9	14.4
Adults who currently use e-cigarettes	5.2	6.7
Adults who currently use chewing tobacco, snuff, or snus	2.3	3.5
Adults who are heavy drinkers[2]	6.8	6.3
Adults who are binge drinkers[3]	19.2	15.4
Adults who are overweight (BMI 25.0 - 29.9)	34.7	34.4
Adults who are obese (BMI 30.0 - 99.8)	33.7	33.9
Adults who participated in any physical activities in the past month	84.2	76.3

Note: (1) Figures cover the Raleigh, NC Metropolitan Statistical Area; (2) Heavy drinkers are classified as adult men having more than 14 drinks per week and adult women having more than 7 drinks per week; (3) Binge drinkers are classified as males having five or more drinks on one occasion or females having four or more drinks on one occasion
Source: Centers for Disease Control and Prevention, Behaviorial Risk Factor Surveillance System, SMART: Selected Metropolitan Area Risk Trends, 2021

Acute and Chronic Health Conditions

Category	MSA[1] (%)	U.S. (%)
Adults who have ever been told they had a heart attack	n/a	4.0
Adults who have ever been told they have angina or coronary heart disease	n/a	3.8
Adults who have ever been told they had a stroke	4.4	3.0
Adults who have ever been told they have asthma	12.3	14.9
Adults who have ever been told they have arthritis	24.0	25.8
Adults who have ever been told they have diabetes[2]	11.1	10.9
Adults who have ever been told they had skin cancer	5.4	6.6
Adults who have ever been told they had any other types of cancer	6.7	7.5
Adults who have ever been told they have COPD	5.2	6.1
Adults who have ever been told they have kidney disease	n/a	3.0
Adults who have ever been told they have a form of depression	17.1	20.5

Note: (1) Figures cover the Raleigh, NC Metropolitan Statistical Area; (2) Figures do not include pregnancy-related, borderline, or pre-diabetes
Source: Centers for Disease Control and Prevention, Behaviorial Risk Factor Surveillance System, SMART: Selected Metropolitan Area Risk Trends, 2021

Health Screening and Vaccination Rates

Category	MSA[1] (%)	U.S. (%)
Adults who have ever been tested for HIV	40.2	34.9
Adults who have had their blood cholesterol checked within the last five years	88.2	85.2
Adults aged 65+ who have had flu shot within the past year	76.2	68.6
Adults aged 65+ who have ever had a pneumonia vaccination	80.3	71.0

Note: (1) Figures cover the Raleigh, NC Metropolitan Statistical Area.
Source: Centers for Disease Control and Prevention, Behaviorial Risk Factor Surveillance System, SMART: Selected Metropolitan Area Risk Trends, 2021

Disability Status

Category	MSA[1] (%)	U.S. (%)
Adults who reported being deaf	8.1	7.2
Are you blind or have serious difficulty seeing, even when wearing glasses?	4.0	4.8
Are you limited in any way in any of your usual activities due to arthritis?	9.7	11.1
Do you have difficulty doing errands alone?	5.0	7.0
Do you have difficulty dressing or bathing?	n/a	3.6
Do you have serious difficulty concentrating/remembering/making decisions?	11.1	12.1
Do you have serious difficulty walking or climbing stairs?	9.7	12.8

Note: (1) Figures cover the Raleigh, NC Metropolitan Statistical Area.
Source: Centers for Disease Control and Prevention, Behaviorial Risk Factor Surveillance System, SMART: Selected Metropolitan Area Risk Trends, 2021

Mortality Rates for the Top 10 Causes of Death in the U.S.

ICD-10[a] Sub-Chapter	ICD-10[a] Code	Crude Mortality Rate[1] per 100,000 population	
		County[2]	U.S.
Malignant neoplasms	C00-C97	117.6	182.6
Ischaemic heart diseases	I20-I25	50.6	113.1
Other forms of heart disease	I30-I51	39.5	64.4
Other degenerative diseases of the nervous system	G30-G31	31.8	51.0
Cerebrovascular diseases	I60-I69	43.1	47.8
Other external causes of accidental injury	W00-X59	31.6	46.4
Chronic lower respiratory diseases	J40-J47	19.9	45.7
Organic, including symptomatic, mental disorders	F01-F09	27.6	35.9
Hypertensive diseases	I10-I15	15.1	35.0
Diabetes mellitus	E10-E14	17.1	29.6

Note: (a) ICD-10 = International Classification of Diseases 10th Revision; (1) Crude mortality rates are a three-year average covering 2019-2021; (2) Figures cover Wake County.
Source: Centers for Disease Control and Prevention, National Center for Health Statistics. National Vital Statistics System, Mortality 2018-2021 on CDC WONDER Online Database

Mortality Rates for Selected Causes of Death

ICD-10[a] Sub-Chapter	ICD-10[a] Code	Crude Mortality Rate[1] per 100,000 population	
		County[2]	U.S.
Assault	X85-Y09	3.9	7.0
Diseases of the liver	K70-K76	11.5	19.8
Human immunodeficiency virus (HIV) disease	B20-B24	1.4	1.5
Influenza and pneumonia	J09-J18	5.4	14.7
Intentional self-harm	X60-X84	8.8	14.3
Malnutrition	E40-E46	2.8	4.3
Obesity and other hyperalimentation	E65-E68	1.8	3.0
Renal failure	N17-N19	11.4	15.7
Transport accidents	V01-V99	8.8	13.6
Viral hepatitis	B15-B19	0.8	1.2

Note: (a) ICD-10 = International Classification of Diseases 10th Revision; (1) Crude mortality rates are a three-year average covering 2019-2021; (2) Figures cover Wake County; Data are suppressed when the data meet the criteria for confidentiality constraints; Crude mortality rates are flagged as unreliable when the rate would be calculated with a numerator of 20 or less.
Source: Centers for Disease Control and Prevention, National Center for Health Statistics. National Vital Statistics System, Mortality 2018-2021 on CDC WONDER Online Database

Health Insurance Coverage

Area	With Health Insurance	With Private Health Insurance	With Public Health Insurance	Without Health Insurance	Population Under Age 19 Without Health Insurance
City	89.6	74.3	24.5	10.4	6.1
MSA[1]	90.9	75.9	25.2	9.1	5.2
U.S.	91.2	67.8	35.4	8.8	5.3

Note: Figures are percentages that cover the civilian noninstitutionalized population; (1) Figures cover the Raleigh-Cary, NC Metropolitan Statistical Area
Source: U.S. Census Bureau, 2017-2021 American Community Survey 5-Year Estimates

Number of Medical Professionals

Area	MDs[3]	DOs[3,4]	Dentists	Podiatrists	Chiropractors	Optometrists
County[1] (number)	3,281	141	836	43	326	193
County[1] (rate[2])	289.4	12.4	72.7	3.7	28.3	16.8
U.S. (rate[2])	289.3	23.5	72.5	6.2	28.7	17.4

Note: Data as of 2021 unless noted; (1) Data covers Wake County; (2) Rate per 100,000 population; (3) Data as of 2020 and includes all active, non-federal physicians; (4) Doctor of Osteopathic Medicine
Source: U.S. Department of Health and Human Services, Health Resources and Services Administration, Bureau of Health Professions, Area Resource File (ARF) 2021-2022

Best Hospitals

According to *U.S. News,* the Raleigh-Cary, NC metro area is home to one of the best hospitals in the U.S.: **WakeMed Raleigh Campus** (1 adult specialty). The hospital listed was nationally ranked in at least one of 15 adult or 10 pediatric specialties. The number of specialties shown cover the parent hospital. Only 164 U.S. hospitals performed well enough to be nationally ranked in one or more specialties. Twenty hospitals in the U.S. made the Honor Roll. The Best Hospitals Honor Roll takes both the national rankings and the procedure and condition ratings into account. Hospitals received points if they were nationally ranked in one of the 15 adult specialties—the higher they ranked, the more points they got—and how many ratings of "high performing" they earned in the 17 procedures and conditions. *U.S. News Online, "America's Best Hospitals 2022-23"*

428 Raleigh, North Carolina

EDUCATION

Public School District Statistics

District Name	Schls	Pupils	Pupil/ Teacher Ratio	Minority Pupils[1] (%)	LEP/ELL[2] (%)	IEP[3] (%)
Wake County Schools	193	160,099	14.6	56.5	8.7	12.3

Note: Table includes school districts with 2,000 or more students; (1) Percentage of students that are not non-Hispanic white; (2) Percentage of students that are Limited English Proficient or English Language Learners (2018-19); (3) Percentage of students that have an Individualized Education Program (2019-20).
Source: U.S. Department of Education, National Center for Education Statistics, Common Core of Data, Local Education Agency (School District) Universe Survey: School Year 2021-2022

Best High Schools

According to *U.S. News,* Raleigh is home to two of the top 500 high schools in the U.S.: **Raleigh Charter High School** (#123); **Wake NCSU STEM Early College High School** (#257). Nearly 18,000 public, magnet and charter schools were ranked based on their performance on state assessments and how well they prepare students for college. *U.S. News & World Report, "Best High Schools 2022"*

Highest Level of Education

Area	Less than H.S.	H.S. Diploma	Some College, No Deg.	Associate Degree	Bachelor's Degree	Master's Degree	Prof. School Degree	Doctorate Degree
City	7.7	15.7	16.9	7.3	32.7	13.7	3.5	2.5
MSA[1]	7.4	17.3	17.7	9.0	30.1	13.6	2.6	2.3
U.S.	11.1	26.5	20.0	8.7	20.6	9.3	2.2	1.5

Note: Figures cover persons age 25 and over; (1) Figures cover the Raleigh-Cary, NC Metropolitan Statistical Area
Source: U.S. Census Bureau, 2017-2021 American Community Survey 5-Year Estimates

Educational Attainment by Race

Area	High School Graduate or Higher (%)					Bachelor's Degree or Higher (%)				
	Total	White	Black	Asian	Hisp.[2]	Total	White	Black	Asian	Hisp.[2]
City	92.3	96.3	91.6	89.4	62.6	52.4	64.4	32.6	61.7	23.0
MSA[1]	92.6	95.1	91.1	92.7	65.6	48.6	52.8	32.3	75.7	21.1
U.S.	88.9	91.4	87.2	87.6	71.2	33.7	35.5	23.3	55.6	18.4

Note: Figures shown cover persons 25 years old and over; (1) Figures cover the Raleigh-Cary, NC Metropolitan Statistical Area; (2) People of Hispanic origin can be of any race
Source: U.S. Census Bureau, 2017-2021 American Community Survey 5-Year Estimates

School Enrollment by Grade and Control

Area	Preschool (%)		Kindergarten (%)		Grades 1 - 4 (%)		Grades 5 - 8 (%)		Grades 9 - 12 (%)	
	Public	Private	Public	Private	Public	Private	Public	Private	Public	Private
City	37.3	62.7	87.2	12.8	85.6	14.4	87.7	12.3	87.7	12.3
MSA[1]	33.6	66.4	84.1	15.9	86.7	13.3	86.5	13.5	88.1	11.9
U.S.	58.8	41.2	86.3	13.7	88.3	11.7	88.6	11.4	89.4	10.6

Note: Figures shown cover persons 3 years old and over; (1) Figures cover the Raleigh-Cary, NC Metropolitan Statistical Area
Source: U.S. Census Bureau, 2017-2021 American Community Survey 5-Year Estimates

Higher Education

Four-Year Colleges			Two-Year Colleges			Medical Schools[1]	Law Schools[2]	Voc/ Tech[3]
Public	Private Non-profit	Private For-profit	Public	Private Non-profit	Private For-profit			
1	7	1	2	1	1	0	1	4

Note: Figures cover institutions located within the Raleigh-Cary, NC Metropolitan Statistical Area and include main campuses only; (1) includes schools accredited by the Liaison Committee on Medical Education and the American Osteopathic Association's Commission on Osteopathic College Accreditation; (2) includes ABA-accredited schools, schools with provisional ABA accreditation, and state accredited schools; (3) includes all schools with programs that are less than 2 years.
Source: National Center for Education Statistics, Integrated Postsecondary Education System (IPEDS), 2021-22; Wikipedia, List of Medical Schools in the United States, accessed April 10, 2023; Wikipedia, List of Law Schools in the United States, accessed April 10, 2023

According to *U.S. News & World Report,* the Raleigh-Cary, NC metro area is home to one of the top 200 national universities in the U.S.: **North Carolina State University** (#72 tie). The indicators used to capture academic quality fall into a number of categories: assessment by administrators at peer institutions; retention of students; faculty resources; student selectivity; financial resources; alumni giving; high school counselor ratings of colleges; and graduation rate. *U.S. News & World Report, "America's Best Colleges 2023"*

According to *U.S. News & World Report,* the Raleigh-Cary, NC metro area is home to one of the top 75 business schools in the U.S.: **North Carolina State University (Poole)** (#67 tie). The rankings are based on a weighted average of the following nine measures: quality assessment; peer assessment; recruiter assessment; placement success; mean starting salary and bonus; student selectivity; mean GMAT and GRE scores; mean undergraduate GPA; and acceptance rate. *U.S. News & World Report, "America's Best Graduate Schools, Business, 2023"*

EMPLOYERS

Major Employers

Company Name	Industry
Cisco Systems	Software
City of Raleigh	Municipal government
Duke Energy	Electric services
Fidelity Investments	Financial services
GlaxoSmithKline	Healthcare
IBM	Technology
Lenovo	Technology
N.C. DHHS	Government
North Carolina State University	Education
Rex Healthcare	Healthcare
RTI International	Research & development
SAS Institute	Data management
State of North Carolina	State government
Wake County Government	Government
Wake County Public School System	Education
Wake Technical Community College	Education
WakeMed Health & Hospitals	Education
Wells Fargo	Financial services

Note: Companies shown are located within the Raleigh-Cary, NC Metropolitan Statistical Area.
Source: Hoovers.com; Wikipedia

Best Companies to Work For

Kimley-Horn and Associates; Red Hat, headquartered in Raleigh, are among "The 100 Best Companies to Work For." To pick the best companies, *Fortune* partnered with the Great Place to Work Institute. Two-thirds of a company's score is based on the results of the Institute's Trust Index survey, which is sent to a random sample of employees from each company. The questions related to attitudes about management's credibility, job satisfaction, and camaraderie. The other third of the scoring is based on the company's responses to the Institute's Culture Audit, which includes detailed questions about pay and benefit programs, and a series of open-ended questions about hiring practices, internal communication, training, recognition programs, and diversity efforts. Any company that is at least five years old with more than 1,000 U.S. employees is eligible. *Fortune, "The 100 Best Companies to Work For," 2023*

Kimley-Horn and Associates, headquartered in Raleigh, is among "Fortune's Best Workplaces for Women." To pick the best companies, *Fortune* partnered with the Great Place to Work Institute. To be considered for the list, companies must be Great Place To Work-Certified. Companies must also employ at least 50 women, at least 20% of their non-executive managers must be female, and at least one executive must be female. To determine the Best Workplaces for Women, Great Place To Work measured the differences in women's survey responses to those of their peers and assesses the impact of demographics and roles on the quality and consistency of women's experiences. Great Place To Work also analyzed the gender balance of each workplace, how it compared to each company's industry, and patterns in representation as women rise from front-line positions to the board of directors. *Fortune, "Best Workplaces for Women," 2022*

Merz Aesthetics, headquartered in Raleigh, is among "Best Workplaces in Health Care." To determine the Best Workplaces in Health Care list, Great Place To Work analyzed the survey responses of over 161,000 employees from Great Place To Work-Certified companies in the health care industry. Survey data analysis and company-provided datapoints are then factored into a combined score to compare and rank the companies that create the most consistently positive experience for all employees in this industry. *Fortune, "Best Workplaces in Health Care," 2022*

First Citizens Bank; Red Hat, headquartered in Raleigh, are among the "100 Best Places to Work in IT." To qualify, companies had to have a minimum of 100 total employees and five IT employees. The best places to work were selected based on DEI (diversity, equity, and inclusion) practices; IT turnover, promotions, and growth; IT retention and engagement programs; remote/hybrid working; benefits and perks (such as elder care and child care, flextime, and reimbursement for college tuition); and training and career development opportunities. *Computerworld, "Best Places to Work in IT," 2023*

430 Raleigh, North Carolina

PUBLIC SAFETY

Crime Rate

Area	Total Crime	Violent Crime Rate				Property Crime Rate		
		Murder	Rape[3]	Robbery	Aggrav. Assault	Burglary	Larceny -Theft	Motor Vehicle Theft
City	2,412.8	4.4	34.2	97.0	256.5	270.0	1,468.3	282.4
Suburbs[1]	1,376.5	2.8	12.2	21.8	100.3	201.3	956.0	82.2
Metro[2]	1,727.9	3.3	19.7	47.3	153.3	224.6	1,129.7	150.1
U.S.	2,356.7	6.5	38.4	73.9	279.7	314.2	1,398.0	246.0

Note: Figures are crimes per 100,000 population; (1) All areas within the metro area that are located outside the city limits; (2) Figures cover the Raleigh, NC Metropolitan Statistical Area; (3) All figures shown were reported using the revised Uniform Crime Reporting (UCR) definition of rape; Due to the transition to the National Incident-Based Reporting System (NIBRS), limited city and metro area data was released for 2021.
Source: FBI Uniform Crime Reports, 2020

Hate Crimes

Area	Number of Quarters Reported	Number of Incidents per Bias Motivation					
		Race/Ethnicity/ Ancestry	Religion	Sexual Orientation	Disability	Gender	Gender Identity
City	4	16	0	1	0	0	0
U.S.	4	5,227	1,244	1,110	130	75	266

Note: Due to the transition to the National Incident-Based Reporting System (NIBRS), limited crime data was released for 2021.
Source: Federal Bureau of Investigation, Hate Crime Statistics 2020

Identity Theft Consumer Reports

Area	Reports	Reports per 100,000 Population	Rank[2]
MSA[1]	4,480	329	53
U.S.	1,108,609	339	-

Note: (1) Figures cover the Raleigh-Cary, NC Metropolitan Statistical Area; (2) Rank ranges from 1 to 391 where 1 indicates greatest number of identity theft reports per 100,000 population
Source: Federal Trade Commission, Consumer Sentinel Network Data Book 2022

Fraud and Other Consumer Reports

Area	Reports	Reports per 100,000 Population	Rank[2]
MSA[1]	16,234	1,191	43
U.S.	4,064,520	1,245	-

Note: (1) Figures cover the Raleigh-Cary, NC Metropolitan Statistical Area; (2) Rank ranges from 1 to 391 where 1 indicates greatest number of fraud and other consumer reports per 100,000 population
Source: Federal Trade Commission, Consumer Sentinel Network Data Book 2022

POLITICS

2020 Presidential Election Results

Area	Biden	Trump	Jorgensen	Hawkins	Other
Wake County	62.3	35.8	1.2	0.3	0.5
U.S.	51.3	46.8	1.2	0.3	0.5

Note: Results are percentages and may not add to 100% due to rounding
Source: Dave Leip's Atlas of U.S. Presidential Elections

SPORTS

Professional Sports Teams

Team Name	League	Year Established
Carolina Hurricanes	National Hockey League (NHL)	1997

Note: Includes teams located in the Raleigh-Cary, NC Metropolitan Statistical Area.
Source: Wikipedia, Major Professional Sports Teams of the United States and Canada, April 12, 2023

CLIMATE

Average and Extreme Temperatures

Temperature	Jan	Feb	Mar	Apr	May	Jun	Jul	Aug	Sep	Oct	Nov	Dec	Yr.
Extreme High (°F)	79	84	90	95	97	104	105	105	104	98	88	79	105
Average High (°F)	50	53	61	72	79	86	89	87	81	72	62	53	71
Average Temp. (°F)	40	43	50	59	67	75	78	77	71	60	51	42	60
Average Low (°F)	29	31	38	46	55	63	68	67	60	48	39	32	48
Extreme Low (°F)	-9	5	11	23	29	38	48	46	37	19	11	4	-9

Note: Figures cover the years 1948-1990
Source: National Climatic Data Center, International Station Meteorological Climate Summary, 9/96

Average Precipitation/Snowfall/Humidity

Precip./Humidity	Jan	Feb	Mar	Apr	May	Jun	Jul	Aug	Sep	Oct	Nov	Dec	Yr.
Avg. Precip. (in.)	3.4	3.6	3.6	2.9	3.9	3.6	4.4	4.4	3.2	2.9	3.0	3.1	42.0
Avg. Snowfall (in.)	2	3	1	Tr	0	0	0	0	0	0	Tr	1	8
Avg. Rel. Hum. 7am (%)	79	79	79	80	84	86	88	91	91	90	84	81	84
Avg. Rel. Hum. 4pm (%)	53	49	46	43	51	54	57	59	57	53	51	53	52

Note: Figures cover the years 1948-1990; Tr = Trace amounts (<0.05 in. of rain; <0.5 in. of snow)
Source: National Climatic Data Center, International Station Meteorological Climate Summary, 9/96

Weather Conditions

Temperature			Daytime Sky			Precipitation		
32°F & below	45°F & below	90°F & above	Clear	Partly cloudy	Cloudy	0.01 inch or more precip.	0.1 inch or more snow/ice	Thunder-storms
77	160	39	98	143	124	110	3	42

Note: Figures are average number of days per year and cover the years 1948-1990
Source: National Climatic Data Center, International Station Meteorological Climate Summary, 9/96

HAZARDOUS WASTE

Superfund Sites

The Raleigh-Cary, NC metro area is home to two sites on the EPA's Superfund National Priorities List: **Koppers Co., Inc. (Morrisville Plant)** (final); **North Carolina State University (Lot 86, Farm Unit #1)** (final). There are a total of 1,165 Superfund sites with a status of proposed or final on the list in the U.S. *U.S. Environmental Protection Agency, National Priorities List, April 12, 2023*

AIR QUALITY

Air Quality Trends: Ozone

	1990	1995	2000	2005	2010	2015	2018	2019	2020	2021
MSA[1]	0.093	0.081	0.087	0.082	0.071	0.065	0.063	0.064	0.054	0.062
U.S.	0.087	0.089	0.081	0.080	0.072	0.067	0.069	0.065	0.065	0.067

Note: (1) Data covers the Raleigh-Cary, NC Metropolitan Statistical Area. The values shown are the composite ozone concentration averages among trend sites based on the highest fourth daily maximum 8-hour concentration in parts per million. These trends are based on sites having an adequate record of monitoring data during the trend period. Data from exceptional events are included.
Source: U.S. Environmental Protection Agency, Air Quality Monitoring Information, "Air Quality Trends by City, 1990-2021"

Air Quality Index

Area	Percent of Days when Air Quality was...[2]					AQI Statistics[2]	
	Good	Moderate	Unhealthy for Sensitive Groups	Unhealthy	Very Unhealthy	Maximum	Median
MSA[1]	71.0	29.0	0.0	0.0	0.0	97	43

Note: (1) Data covers the Raleigh-Cary, NC Metropolitan Statistical Area; (2) Based on 365 days with AQI data in 2021. Air Quality Index (AQI) is an index for reporting daily air quality. EPA calculates the AQI for five major air pollutants regulated by the Clean Air Act: ground-level ozone, particle pollution (aka particulate matter), carbon monoxide, sulfur dioxide, and nitrogen dioxide. The AQI runs from 0 to 500. The higher the AQI value, the greater the level of air pollution and the greater the health concern. There are six AQI categories: "Good" AQI is between 0 and 50. Air quality is considered satisfactory; "Moderate" AQI is between 51 and 100. Air quality is acceptable; "Unhealthy for Sensitive Groups" When AQI values are between 101 and 150, members of sensitive groups may experience health effects; "Unhealthy" When AQI values are between 151 and 200 everyone may begin to experience health effects; "Very Unhealthy" AQI values between 201 and 300 trigger a health alert; "Hazardous" AQI values over 300 trigger warnings of emergency conditions (not shown).
Source: U.S. Environmental Protection Agency, Air Quality Index Report, 2021

Air Quality Index Pollutants

Area	Percent of Days when AQI Pollutant was...[2]					
	Carbon Monoxide	Nitrogen Dioxide	Ozone	Sulfur Dioxide	Particulate Matter 2.5	Particulate Matter 10
MSA[1]	0.0	0.5	53.7	(3)	45.8	0.0

Note: (1) Data covers the Raleigh-Cary, NC Metropolitan Statistical Area; (2) Based on 365 days with AQI data in 2021. The Air Quality Index (AQI) is an index for reporting daily air quality. EPA calculates the AQI for five major air pollutants regulated by the Clean Air Act: ground-level ozone, particle pollution (also known as particulate matter), carbon monoxide, sulfur dioxide, and nitrogen dioxide. The AQI runs from 0 to 500. The higher the AQI value, the greater the level of air pollution and the greater the health concern; (3) Sulfur dioxide is no longer included in this table (as of December 8, 2021) because SO_2 concentrations tend to be very localized and not necessarily representative of broad geographical areas like counties and CBSAs.
Source: U.S. Environmental Protection Agency, Air Quality Index Report, 2021

Maximum Air Pollutant Concentrations: Particulate Matter, Ozone, CO and Lead

	Particulate Matter 10 (ug/m³)	Particulate Matter 2.5 Wtd AM (ug/m³)	Particulate Matter 2.5 24-Hr (ug/m³)	Ozone (ppm)	Carbon Monoxide (ppm)	Lead (ug/m³)
MSA[1] Level	56	9.2	22	0.066	1	n/a
NAAQS[2]	150	15	35	0.075	9	0.15
Met NAAQS[2]	Yes	Yes	Yes	Yes	Yes	n/a

Note: (1) Data covers the Raleigh-Cary, NC Metropolitan Statistical Area; Data from exceptional events are included; (2) National Ambient Air Quality Standards; ppm = parts per million; ug/m³ = micrograms per cubic meter; n/a not available.
Concentrations: Particulate Matter 10 (coarse particulate)—highest second maximum 24-hour concentration; Particulate Matter 2.5 Wtd AM (fine particulate)—highest weighted annual mean concentration; Particulate Matter 2.5 24-Hour (fine particulate)—highest 98th percentile 24-hour concentration; Ozone—highest fourth daily maximum 8-hour concentration; Carbon Monoxide—highest second maximum non-overlapping 8-hour concentration; Lead—maximum running 3-month average
Source: U.S. Environmental Protection Agency, Air Quality Monitoring Information, "Air Quality Statistics by City, 2021"

Maximum Air Pollutant Concentrations: Nitrogen Dioxide and Sulfur Dioxide

	Nitrogen Dioxide AM (ppb)	Nitrogen Dioxide 1-Hr (ppb)	Sulfur Dioxide AM (ppb)	Sulfur Dioxide 1-Hr (ppb)	Sulfur Dioxide 24-Hr (ppb)
MSA[1] Level	8	31	n/a	2	n/a
NAAQS[2]	53	100	30	75	140
Met NAAQS[2]	Yes	Yes	n/a	Yes	n/a

Note: (1) Data covers the Raleigh-Cary, NC Metropolitan Statistical Area; Data from exceptional events are included; (2) National Ambient Air Quality Standards; ppm = parts per million; ug/m³ = micrograms per cubic meter; n/a not available.
Concentrations: Nitrogen Dioxide AM—highest arithmetic mean concentration; Nitrogen Dioxide 1-Hr—highest 98th percentile 1-hour daily maximum concentration; Sulfur Dioxide AM—highest annual mean concentration; Sulfur Dioxide 1-Hr—highest 99th percentile 1-hour daily maximum concentration; Sulfur Dioxide 24-Hr—highest second maximum 24-hour concentration
Source: U.S. Environmental Protection Agency, Air Quality Monitoring Information, "Air Quality Statistics by City, 2021"

Richmond, Virginia

Background

Richmond is the capital of Virginia and is located on the James River. Home to blue-blooded old families such as the Byrds and Lees, the city played a central role in both U.S. and Confederate histories.

John Smith and Christopher Newport first claimed Richmond in 1607 as English territory. In 1679, the area was granted to William Byrd I, with the understanding that he establish a settlement. His son, William Byrd II, continued his father's work and along with William Mayo surveyed lots for what was to be named Richmond. During the Revolutionary War, Richmond played host to two Virginia Conventions, which gathered founding fathers such as George Washington, Thomas Jefferson, and Patrick Henry in the same room, ans ratified the Constitution as the law of the land for the emerging nation. In 1775, Patrick Henry delivered his famous "Give me Liberty or Give me Death" speech in the city's St. John's Church.

Not long after the United States congealed as a nation, however, dissension caused fragmentation and Richmond became the Confederate States' capital. From its Roman temple-inspired capitol designed by Thomas Jefferson, Jefferson Davis presided over the Confederacy.

Not surprisingly, today Richmond is home to authoritative repositories of both Southern and Virginia history, which include the Virginia State Library, the Museum of the Confederacy, and the Virginia Historical Society.

Today, government and higher education are economic mainstays for the city, with Virginia Commonwealth University, the Medical College of Virginia, the University of Richmond, and Virginia Union University all located within the city limits. The Virginia BioTechnology Research Park houses more than 60 life sciences organizations in 1.3 million square feet of research and office space adjacent to the VCU Medical Center. Companies located there include government and VCU labs, young companies, international bioscience companies, and headquarters of several major companies. Banking and telecommunications sectors are also well represented in the city's economy. Major employers include Brink's, CarMax and Mead/Westvaco.

The city's James River waterfront, with a multimillion-dollar flood wall to protect it from the frequent rising waters of the river, is now home to much of Richmond's entertainment, dining, and nightlife, bolstered by the creation of a Canal Walk along the city's former industrial canals. In 2018, the city's first rapid transit system began operating.

Richmond's cultural offerings include the Richmond Symphony, Richmond Ballet, and the Virginia Museum of Fine Arts, known for its fine travelling Faberge collection. A variety of murals from internationally recognized street artists have appeared throughout the city as a result of the efforts of Art Whino and *RVA Magazine* with The Richmond Mural Project and the RVA Street Art Festival. After some controversy, a bronze statue of African American Richmond native and tennis star Arthur Ashe was completed on the city's Monument Avenue.

Richmond's Northside is home to several historic districts, including Chestnut Hill-Plateau and Barton Heights. The affluent West End is home to the University of Richmond and the Country Club of Virginia.

Richmond's climate is classified as modified continental with its warm summer and humid, mild winters. Snow remains on the ground for only a day or so. Ice storms are not uncommon but usually do not cause considerable damage. Hurricanes and tropical storms, when they occur, are responsible for flooding during the summer and early fall months. Tornadoes are infrequent, but some notable occurrences have been observed in the vicinity.

Rankings

Business/Finance Rankings

- Based on metro area social media reviews, the employment opinion group Glassdoor surveyed 50 of the most populous U.S. metro areas and equally weighed cost of living, hiring opportunity, and job satisfaction to compose a list of "25 Best Cities for Jobs." Median pay and home value, and number of active job openings were also factored in. The Richmond metro area was ranked #22 in overall job satisfaction. *www.glassdoor.com, "Best Cities for Jobs," February 25, 2020*

- The Brookings Institution ranked the nation's largest cities based on income inequality. Richmond was ranked #14 (#1 = greatest inequality). Criteria: the "95/20 ratio," a figure representing the income at which a household earns more than 95 percent of all other households, divided by the income at which a household earns more than only 20 percent of all other households. *Brookings Institution, "Household Income Inequality, Largest Cities of 97 Large U.S. Metro Areas, 2014-2016," February 5, 2018*

- The Brookings Institution ranked the 100 largest metro areas in the U.S. based on income inequality. Richmond was ranked #75 (#1 = greatest inequality). Criteria: the "95/20 ratio," a figure representing the income at which a household earns more than 95 percent of all other households, divided by the income at which a household earns more than only 20 percent of all other households. *Brookings Institution, "Household Income Inequality, 100 Largest U.S. Metro Areas, 2014-2016," February 5, 2018*

- The Richmond metro area appeared on the Milken Institute "2022 Best Performing Cities" list. Rank: #123 out of 200 large metro areas (population over 250,000). Criteria: job growth; wage and salary growth; high-tech output growth; housing affordability; household broadband access. *Milken Institute, "Best-Performing Cities 2022," March 28, 2022*

- *Forbes* ranked the 200 most populous metro areas to determine the nation's "Best Places for Business and Careers." The Richmond metro area was ranked #55. Criteria: costs (business and living); job growth (past and projected); income growth; quality of life; educational attainment (college and high school); projected economic growth; cultural and leisure opportunities; workplace tolerance laws; net migration patterns. *Forbes, "The Best Places for Business and Careers 2019: Seattle Still On Top," October 30, 2019*

Children/Family Rankings

- Richmond was selected as one of the most playful cities in the U.S. by KaBOOM! The organization's Playful City USA initiative honors cities and towns across the nation that have made their communities more playable. Criteria: pledging to integrate play as a solution to challenges in their communities; making it easy for children to get active and balanced play; creating more family-friendly and innovative communities as a result. *KaBOOM! National Campaign for Play, "2017 Playful City USA Communities"*

Culture/Performing Arts Rankings

- Richmond was selected as one of "America's Favorite Cities." The city ranked #12 in the "Architecture" category. Respondents to an online survey were asked to rate their favorite place (population over 100,000) in over 65 categories. *Travelandleisure.com, "America's Favorite Cities for Architecture 2016," March 2, 2017*

Education Rankings

- Personal finance website *WalletHub* analyzed the 150 largest U.S. metropolitan statistical areas to determine where the most educated Americans are putting their degrees to work. Criteria: education levels; percentage of workers with degrees; education quality and attainment gap; public school quality rankings; quality and enrollment of each metro area's universities. Richmond was ranked #36 (#1 = most educated city). *www.WalletHub.com, "Most & Least Educated Cities in America," July 18, 2022*

Environmental Rankings

- Sperling's BestPlaces assessed the 50 largest metropolitan areas of the United States for the likelihood of dangerously extreme weather events or earthquakes. In general the Southeast and South-Central regions have the highest risk of weather extremes and earthquakes, while the Pacific Northwest enjoys the lowest risk. Of the least risky metropolitan areas, the Richmond metro area was ranked #8. *www.bestplaces.net, "Avoid Natural Disasters: BestPlaces Reveals The Top 10 Safest Places to Live," October 25, 2017*

Health/Fitness Rankings

- For each of the 100 largest cities in the United States, the American Fitness Index®, compiled in partnership between the American College of Sports Medicine and the Elevance Health Foundation, evaluated community infrastructure and 34 health behaviors including preventive health, levels of chronic disease conditions, food insecurity, sleep quality, pedestrian safety, air quality, and community/environment resources that support physical activity. Richmond ranked #36 for "community fitness." *americanfitnessindex.org, "2022 ACSM American Fitness Index Summary Report," July 12, 2022*

- The Richmond metro area was identified as one of the worst cities for bed bugs in America by pest control company Orkin. The area ranked #26 out of 50 based on the number of bed bug treatments Orkin performed from December 2021 to November 2022. *Orkin, "The Windy City Can't Blow Bed Bugs Away: Chicago Ranks #1 For Third Consecutive Year On Orkin's Bed Bug Cities List," January 9, 2023*

- Richmond was identified as a "2022 Spring Allergy Capital." The area ranked #2 out of 100. Three groups of factors were used to identify the most challenging cities for people with allergies during the spring season: annual spring pollen scores; over the counter allergy medicine use; number of board-certified allergy specialists. *Asthma and Allergy Foundation of America, "Spring Allergy Capitals 2022," March 2, 2022*

- Richmond was identified as a "2022 Fall Allergy Capital." The area ranked #10 out of 100. Three groups of factors were used to identify the most challenging cities for people with allergies during the fall season: annual fall pollen scores; over the counter allergy medicine use; number of board-certified allergy specialists. *Asthma and Allergy Foundation of America, "Fall Allergy Capitals 2022," March 2, 2022*

- Richmond was identified as a "2022 Asthma Capital." The area ranked #12 out of the nation's 100 largest metropolitan areas. Criteria: estimated asthma prevalence; asthma-related mortality; and ER visits due to asthma. Risk factors analyzed but not factored in the rankings: annual pollen score; annual air quality; public smoking laws; access to board-certified asthma specialists; rescue and controller medication use; uninsured rate; poverty rate. *Asthma and Allergy Foundation of America, "Asthma Capitals 2022: The Most Challenging Places to Live With Asthma," September 14, 2022*

Real Estate Rankings

- *WalletHub* compared the most populated U.S. cities to determine which had the best markets for real estate agents. Richmond ranked #77 where demand was high and pay was the best. Criteria: sales per agent; annual median wage for real-estate agents; monthly average starting salary for real estate agents; real estate job density and competition; unemployment rate; home turnover rate; housing-market health index; and other relevant metrics. *www.WalletHub.com, "2021 Best Places to Be a Real Estate Agent," May 12, 2021*

- Richmond was ranked #95 out of 235 metro areas in terms of housing affordability in 2022 by the National Association of Home Builders (#1 = most affordable). Criteria: the share of homes sold in that area affordable to a family earning the local median income, based on standard mortgage underwriting criteria. *National Association of Home Builders®, NAHB-Wells Fargo Housing Opportunity Index, 4th Quarter 2022*

Safety Rankings

- Allstate ranked the 200 largest cities in America in terms of driver safety. Richmond ranked #113. Criteria: internal property damage claims over a two-year period from January 2016 to December 2017. The report helps increase the importance of safety and awareness behind the wheel. *Allstate, "Allstate America's Best Drivers Report, 2019" June 24, 2019*

- The National Insurance Crime Bureau ranked 390 metro areas in the U.S. in terms of per capita rates of vehicle theft. The Richmond metro area ranked #199 (#1 = highest rate). Criteria: number of vehicle theft offenses per 100,000 inhabitants in 2021. *National Insurance Crime Bureau, "Hot Spots 2021," September 1, 2022*

Seniors/Retirement Rankings

- From its Best Cities for Successful Aging indexes, the Milken Institute generated rankings for metropolitan areas, weighing data in nine categories—health care, wellness, living arrangements, transportation and convenience, financial characteristics, education, employment, community engagement, and overall livability. The Richmond metro area was ranked #32 overall in the large metro area category. *Milken Institute, "Best Cities for Successful Aging, 2017" March 14, 2017*

Sports/Recreation Rankings

- Richmond was chosen as one of America's best cities for bicycling. The city ranked #34 out of 50. Criteria: cycling infrastructure that is safe and friendly for all ages; energy and bike culture. The editors evaluated cities with populations of 100,000 or more. *Bicycling, "The 50 Best Bike Cities in America," October 10, 2018*

Women/Minorities Rankings

- Personal finance website *WalletHub* compared more than 180 U.S. cities across two key dimensions, "Hispanic Business-Friendliness" and "Hispanic Purchasing Power," to arrive at the most favorable conditions for Hispanic entrepreneurs. Richmond was ranked #152 out of 182. Criteria includes: share of Hispanic-Owned Businesses; Hispanic entrepreneurship rate to median annual income of Hispanics; Small Business-Friendliness score; cost of living; and number of Hispanics with at least a bachelor's degree. *WalletHub.com, "2019's Best Cities for Hispanic Entrepreneurs," May 1, 2019*

Miscellaneous Rankings

- *MoveHub* ranked 446 hipster cities across 20 countries, using its new and improved *alternative* Hipster Index and Richmond came out as #20 among the top 50. Criteria: population over 150,000; number of vintage boutiques; density of tattoo parlors; vegan places to eat; coffee shops; and density of vinyl record stores. *www.movehub.com, "The Hipster Index: Brighton Pips Portland to Global Top Spot," July 28, 2021*

- *WalletHub* compared the 150 most populated U.S. cities to determine their operating efficiency. A "Quality of Services" score was constructed for each city and then divided by the total budget per capita to reveal which were managed the best. Richmond ranked #98. Criteria: financial stability; economy; education; safety; health; infrastructure and pollution. *www.WalletHub.com, "2022's Best- & Worst-Run Cities in America," June 21, 2022*

Business Environment

DEMOGRAPHICS

Population Growth

Area	1990 Census	2000 Census	2010 Census	2020 Census	Population Growth (%)	
					1990-2020	2010-2020
City	202,783	197,790	204,214	226,610	11.7	11.0
MSA[1]	949,244	1,096,957	1,258,251	1,314,434	38.5	4.5
U.S.	248,709,873	281,421,906	308,745,538	331,449,281	33.3	7.4

Note: (1) Figures cover the Richmond, VA Metropolitan Statistical Area
Source: U.S. Census Bureau, 1990 Census, 2000 Census, 2010 Census, 2020 Census

Race

Area	White Alone[2] (%)	Black Alone[2] (%)	Asian Alone[2] (%)	AIAN[3] Alone[2] (%)	NHOPI[4] Alone[2] (%)	Other Race Alone[2] (%)	Two or More Races (%)
City	43.3	40.4	2.8	0.4	0.1	6.8	6.2
MSA[1]	56.5	27.7	4.3	0.5	0.1	4.4	6.4
U.S.	61.6	12.4	6.0	1.1	0.2	8.4	10.2

Note: (1) Figures cover the Richmond, VA Metropolitan Statistical Area; (2) Alone is defined as not being in combination with one or more other races; (3) American Indian and Alaska Native; (4) Native Hawaiian and Other Pacific Islander
Source: U.S. Census Bureau, 2020 Census

Hispanic or Latino Origin

Area	Total (%)	Mexican (%)	Puerto Rican (%)	Cuban (%)	Other (%)
City	7.3	1.3	0.8	0.3	4.9
MSA[1]	6.7	1.6	1.0	0.2	3.8
U.S.	18.4	11.2	1.8	0.7	4.7

Note: Persons of Hispanic or Latino origin can be of any race; (1) Figures cover the Richmond, VA Metropolitan Statistical Area
Source: U.S. Census Bureau, 2017-2021 American Community Survey 5-Year Estimates

Age

Area	Percent of Population									Median Age
	Under Age 5	Age 5–19	Age 20–34	Age 35–44	Age 45–54	Age 55–64	Age 65–74	Age 75–84	Age 85+	
City	5.5	15.8	33.4	12.0	9.3	10.8	8.2	3.4	1.5	32.4
MSA[1]	5.5	18.9	20.8	12.7	12.3	13.3	10.1	4.6	1.8	38.6
U.S.	5.6	19.2	20.2	12.7	12.4	13.1	10.0	4.9	1.9	38.8

Note: (1) Figures cover the Richmond, VA Metropolitan Statistical Area
Source: U.S. Census Bureau, 2020 Census

Disability by Age

Area	All Ages	Under 18 Years Old	18 to 64 Years Old	65 Years and Over
City	14.2	6.5	12.1	35.7
MSA[1]	12.8	5.3	10.5	32.1
U.S.	12.6	4.4	10.3	33.4

Note: Figures show percent of the civilian noninstitutionalized population that reported having a disability. Disability status is determined from six types of difficulty: vision, hearing, cognitive, ambulatory, self-care, and independent living. For children under 5 years old, hearing and vision difficulty are used to determine disability status. For children between the ages of 5 and 14, disability status is determined from hearing, vision, cognitive, ambulatory, and self-care difficulties. For people aged 15 years and older, they are considered to have a disability if they have difficulty with any one of the six difficulty types; Note: (1) Figures cover the Richmond, VA Metropolitan Statistical Area
Source: U.S. Census Bureau, 2017-2021 American Community Survey 5-Year Estimates

Ancestry

Area	German	Irish	English	American	Italian	Polish	French[2]	Scottish	Dutch
City	7.3	7.0	8.9	4.5	3.5	1.4	1.5	1.9	0.5
MSA[1]	9.0	7.9	11.7	6.7	3.8	1.5	1.5	1.9	0.7
U.S.	12.8	9.6	8.1	5.7	5.0	2.7	2.2	1.6	1.1

Note: Figures are the percentage of the total population reporting a particular ancestry. The nine most commonly reported ancestries in the U.S. are shown. Figures include multiple ancestries (e.g. if a person reported being Irish and Italian, they were included in both columns); (1) Figures cover the Richmond, VA Metropolitan Statistical Area; (2) Excludes Basque
Source: U.S. Census Bureau, 2017-2021 American Community Survey 5-Year Estimates

Foreign-born Population

Area	Percent of Population Born in								
	Any Foreign Country	Asia	Mexico	Europe	Caribbean	Central America[2]	South America	Africa	Canada
City	7.5	1.6	0.6	0.8	0.6	2.7	0.4	0.7	0.1
MSA[1]	8.1	3.1	0.6	1.0	0.4	1.6	0.5	0.7	0.1
U.S.	13.6	4.2	3.3	1.4	1.4	1.1	1.1	0.8	0.2

Note: (1) Figures cover the Richmond, VA Metropolitan Statistical Area; (2) Excludes Mexico.
Source: U.S. Census Bureau, 2017-2021 American Community Survey 5-Year Estimates

Household Size

Area	Persons in Household (%)							Average Household Size
	One	Two	Three	Four	Five	Six	Seven or More	
City	42.5	33.1	12.0	7.7	2.9	1.3	0.6	2.20
MSA[1]	29.4	34.6	15.8	12.4	5.3	1.7	0.8	2.50
U.S.	28.1	33.8	15.5	12.9	6.0	2.3	1.4	2.60

Note: (1) Figures cover the Richmond, VA Metropolitan Statistical Area
Source: U.S. Census Bureau, 2017-2021 American Community Survey 5-Year Estimates

Household Relationships

Area	House-holder	Opposite-sex Spouse	Same-sex Spouse	Opposite-sex Unmarried Partner	Same-sex Unmarried Partner	Child[2]	Grand-child	Other Relatives	Non-relatives
City	45.2	10.4	0.4	4.0	0.4	20.8	2.1	4.3	7.4
MSA[1]	39.5	17.3	0.2	2.5	0.2	27.7	2.4	4.0	3.3
U.S.	38.3	17.5	0.2	2.5	0.2	28.3	2.4	4.8	3.4

Note: Figures are percent of the total population; (1) Figures cover the Richmond, VA Metropolitan Statistical Area; (2) Includes biological, adopted, and stepchildren of the householder
Source: U.S. Census Bureau, 2020 Census

Gender

Area	Males	Females	Males per 100 Females
City	107,678	118,932	90.5
MSA[1]	632,849	681,585	92.8
U.S.	162,685,811	168,763,470	96.4

Note: (1) Figures cover the Richmond, VA Metropolitan Statistical Area
Source: U.S. Census Bureau, 2020 Census

Marital Status

Area	Never Married	Now Married[2]	Separated	Widowed	Divorced
City	51.2	29.4	2.8	5.2	11.4
MSA[1]	34.7	46.7	2.3	5.6	10.7
U.S.	33.8	48.0	1.8	5.6	10.8

Note: Figures are percentages and cover the population 15 years of age and older; (1) Figures cover the Richmond, VA Metropolitan Statistical Area; (2) Excludes separated
Source: U.S. Census Bureau, 2017-2021 American Community Survey 5-Year Estimates

Religious Groups by Family

Area	Catholic	Baptist	Methodist	LDS[2]	Pentecostal	Lutheran	Islam	Adventist	Other
MSA[1]	12.3	14.2	4.8	0.9	3.2	0.5	2.1	1.2	14.8
U.S.	18.7	7.3	3.0	2.0	1.8	1.7	1.3	1.3	11.6

Note: Figures are the number of adherents as a percentage of the total population and cover the eight largest religious groups in the U.S; (1) Figures cover the Richmond, VA Metropolitan Statistical Area; (2) Church of Jesus Christ of Latter-day Saints
Sources: 2020 U.S. Religion Census, Association of Statisticians of American Religious Bodies; The Association of Religion Data Archives (ARDA)

Religious Groups by Tradition

Area	Catholic	Evangelical Protestant	Mainline Protestant	Black Protestant	Islam	Judaism	Hinduism	Orthodox	Buddhism
MSA[1]	12.3	23.1	9.3	3.1	2.1	0.3	1.3	0.4	0.2
U.S.	18.7	16.5	5.2	2.3	1.3	0.6	0.4	0.4	0.3

Note: Figures are the number of adherents as a percentage of the total population; (1) Figures cover the Richmond, VA Metropolitan Statistical Area
Sources: 2020 U.S. Religion Census, Association of Statisticians of American Religious Bodies; The Association of Religion Data Archives (ARDA)

ECONOMY

Gross Metropolitan Product

Area	2020	2021	2022	2023	Rank[2]
MSA[1]	91.2	97.3	104.5	110.5	44

Note: Figures are in billions of dollars; (1) Figures cover the Richmond, VA Metropolitan Statistical Area; (2) Rank is based on 2021 data and ranges from 1 to 381
Source: U.S. Conference of Mayors, U.S. Metro Economies: U.S. Metros Compared to Global and State Economies, June 2022

Economic Growth

Area	2018-20 (%)	2021 (%)	2022 (%)	2023 (%)	Rank[2]
MSA[1]	-0.3	3.0	1.7	2.3	160
U.S.	-0.6	5.7	3.1	2.9	–

Note: Figures are real gross metropolitan product (GMP) growth rates and represent average annual percent change; (1) Figures cover the Richmond, VA Metropolitan Statistical Area; (2) Rank is based on 2020 2-year average annual percent change and ranges from 1 to 381
Source: U.S. Conference of Mayors, U.S. Metro Economies: U.S. Metros Compared to Global and State Economies, June 2022

Metropolitan Area Exports

Area	2016	2017	2018	2019	2020	2021	Rank[2]
MSA[1]	3,525.7	3,663.7	3,535.0	3,203.2	2,719.1	3,010.7	84

Note: Figures are in millions of dollars; (1) Figures cover the Richmond, VA Metropolitan Statistical Area; (2) Rank is based on 2021 data and ranges from 1 to 388
Source: U.S. Department of Commerce, International Trade Administration, Office of Trade and Economic Analysis, Industry and Analysis, Exports by Metropolitan Area, data extracted March 16, 2023

Building Permits

Area	Single-Family			Multi-Family			Total		
	2021	2022	Pct. Chg.	2021	2022	Pct. Chg.	2021	2022	Pct. Chg.
City	502	457	-9.0	565	2,192	288.0	1,067	2,649	148.3
MSA[1]	5,946	4,503	-24.3	3,601	5,911	64.1	9,547	10,414	9.1
U.S.	1,115,400	975,600	-12.5	621,600	689,500	10.9	1,737,000	1,665,100	-4.1

Note: (1) Figures cover the Richmond, VA Metropolitan Statistical Area; Figures represent new, privately-owned housing units authorized (unadjusted data); All permit data are based on estimates with imputation
Source: U.S. Census Bureau, Manufacturing, Mining, and Construction Statistics, Building Permits, 2021, 2022

Bankruptcy Filings

Area	Business Filings			Nonbusiness Filings		
	2021	2022	% Chg.	2021	2022	% Chg.
Richmond city	21	6	-71.4	590	511	-13.4
U.S.	14,347	13,481	-6.0	399,269	374,240	-6.3

Note: Business filings include Chapter 7, Chapter 9, Chapter 11, Chapter 12, Chapter 13, Chapter 15, and Section 304; Nonbusiness filings include Chapter 7, Chapter 11, and Chapter 13
Source: Administrative Office of the U.S. Courts, Business and Nonbusiness Bankruptcy, County Cases Commenced by Chapter of the Bankruptcy Code, During the 12-Month Period Ending December 31, 2021 and Business and Nonbusiness Bankruptcy, County Cases Commenced by Chapter of the Bankruptcy Code, During the 12-Month Period Ending December 31, 2022

Housing Vacancy Rates

Area	Gross Vacancy Rate[2] (%)			Year-Round Vacancy Rate[3] (%)			Rental Vacancy Rate[4] (%)			Homeowner Vacancy Rate[5] (%)		
	2020	2021	2022	2020	2021	2022	2020	2021	2022	2020	2021	2022
MSA[1]	6.0	5.8	6.1	6.0	5.8	6.1	2.7	1.8	3.0	0.9	1.0	0.7
U.S.	10.6	10.8	10.5	8.2	8.4	8.2	6.3	6.1	5.8	1.0	0.9	0.8

Note: (1) Figures cover the Richmond, VA Metropolitan Statistical Area; (2) The percentage of the total housing inventory that is vacant; (3) The percentage of the housing inventory (excluding seasonal units) that is year-round vacant; (4) The percentage of rental inventory that is vacant for rent; (5) The percentage of homeowner inventory that is vacant for sale
Source: U.S. Census Bureau, Housing Vacancies and Homeownership Annual Statistics: 2020, 2021, 2022

INCOME

Income

Area	Per Capita ($)	Median Household ($)	Average Household ($)
City	38,132	54,795	82,939
MSA[1]	40,254	74,592	100,389
U.S.	37,638	69,021	97,196

Note: (1) Figures cover the Richmond, VA Metropolitan Statistical Area
Source: U.S. Census Bureau, 2017-2021 American Community Survey 5-Year Estimates

Richmond, Virginia

Household Income Distribution

Area	Percent of Households Earning							
	Under $15,000	$15,000 -$24,999	$25,000 -$34,999	$35,000 -$49,999	$50,000 -$74,999	$75,000 -$99,999	$100,000 -$149,999	$150,000 and up
City	14.1	9.6	9.4	13.7	17.4	11.3	11.7	12.7
MSA[1]	7.9	6.7	7.2	11.2	17.2	13.1	18.3	18.3
U.S.	9.4	7.8	8.2	11.4	16.8	12.8	16.3	17.3

Note: (1) Figures cover the Richmond, VA Metropolitan Statistical Area
Source: U.S. Census Bureau, 2017-2021 American Community Survey 5-Year Estimates

Poverty Rate

Area	All Ages	Under 18 Years Old	18 to 64 Years Old	65 Years and Over
City	19.8	30.2	18.3	13.5
MSA[1]	10.2	14.1	9.4	7.7
U.S.	12.6	17.0	11.8	9.6

Note: Figures are percentage of people whose income during the past 12 months was below the poverty level;
(1) Figures cover the Richmond, VA Metropolitan Statistical Area
Source: U.S. Census Bureau, 2017-2021 American Community Survey 5-Year Estimates

EMPLOYMENT

Labor Force and Employment

Area	Civilian Labor Force			Workers Employed		
	Dec. 2021	Dec. 2022	% Chg.	Dec. 2021	Dec. 2022	% Chg.
City	115,165	116,068	0.8	110,750	112,086	1.2
MSA[1]	664,206	670,336	0.9	643,038	650,950	1.2
U.S.	161,696,000	164,224,000	1.6	155,732,000	158,872,000	2.0

Note: Data is not seasonally adjusted and covers workers 16 years of age and older; (1) Figures cover the Richmond, VA Metropolitan Statistical Area
Source: Bureau of Labor Statistics, Local Area Unemployment Statistics

Unemployment Rate

Area	2022											
	Jan.	Feb.	Mar.	Apr.	May	Jun.	Jul.	Aug.	Sep.	Oct.	Nov.	Dec.
City	4.6	4.1	3.7	3.5	3.9	3.8	3.7	4.1	3.4	3.5	3.9	3.4
MSA[1]	3.7	3.2	2.9	2.8	3.2	3.2	3.1	3.4	2.8	3.0	3.2	2.9
U.S.	4.4	4.1	3.8	3.3	3.4	3.8	3.8	3.8	3.3	3.4	3.4	3.3

Note: Data is not seasonally adjusted and covers workers 16 years of age and older; (1) Figures cover the Richmond, VA Metropolitan Statistical Area
Source: Bureau of Labor Statistics, Local Area Unemployment Statistics

Average Wages

Occupation	$/Hr.	Occupation	$/Hr.
Accountants and Auditors	39.80	Maintenance and Repair Workers	22.55
Automotive Mechanics	24.06	Marketing Managers	72.33
Bookkeepers	22.01	Network and Computer Systems Admin.	48.67
Carpenters	22.95	Nurses, Licensed Practical	25.75
Cashiers	13.04	Nurses, Registered	39.75
Computer Programmers	46.05	Nursing Assistants	15.79
Computer Systems Analysts	49.01	Office Clerks, General	18.79
Computer User Support Specialists	28.49	Physical Therapists	46.28
Construction Laborers	17.43	Physicians	79.68
Cooks, Restaurant	15.43	Plumbers, Pipefitters and Steamfitters	25.66
Customer Service Representatives	18.72	Police and Sheriff's Patrol Officers	29.03
Dentists	79.72	Postal Service Mail Carriers	26.92
Electricians	27.27	Real Estate Sales Agents	35.50
Engineers, Electrical	50.41	Retail Salespersons	15.56
Fast Food and Counter Workers	12.47	Sales Representatives, Technical/Scientific	47.20
Financial Managers	80.46	Secretaries, Exc. Legal/Medical/Executive	19.90
First-Line Supervisors of Office Workers	31.31	Security Guards	17.63
General and Operations Managers	59.05	Surgeons	n/a
Hairdressers/Cosmetologists	18.60	Teacher Assistants, Exc. Postsecondary*	14.32
Home Health and Personal Care Aides	13.05	Teachers, Secondary School, Exc. Sp. Ed.*	37.47
Janitors and Cleaners	14.79	Telemarketers	n/a
Landscaping/Groundskeeping Workers	16.43	Truck Drivers, Heavy/Tractor-Trailer	24.27
Lawyers	80.05	Truck Drivers, Light/Delivery Services	20.61
Maids and Housekeeping Cleaners	13.35	Waiters and Waitresses	16.35

Note: Wage data covers the Richmond, VA Metropolitan Statistical Area; (*) Hourly wages were calculated from annual wage data based on a 40 hour work week; n/a not available.
Source: Bureau of Labor Statistics, Metro Area Occupational Employment & Wage Estimates, May 2022

Employment by Industry

Sector	MSA[1]		U.S.
	Number of Employees	Percent of Total	Percent of Total
Construction, Mining, and Logging	41,200	5.8	5.4
Private Education and Health Services	99,300	14.1	16.1
Financial Activities	56,600	8.0	5.9
Government	114,300	16.2	14.5
Information	6,600	0.9	2.0
Leisure and Hospitality	65,100	9.2	10.3
Manufacturing	32,800	4.6	8.4
Other Services	31,600	4.5	3.7
Professional and Business Services	125,200	17.7	14.7
Retail Trade	67,600	9.6	10.2
Transportation, Warehousing, and Utilities	38,400	5.4	4.9
Wholesale Trade	28,000	4.0	3.9

Note: Figures are non-farm employment as of December 2022. Figures are not seasonally adjusted and include workers 16 years of age and older; (1) Figures cover the Richmond, VA Metropolitan Statistical Area
Source: Bureau of Labor Statistics, Current Employment Statistics, Employment, Hours, and Earnings

Employment by Occupation

Occupation Classification	City (%)	MSA[1] (%)	U.S. (%)
Management, Business, Science, and Arts	44.5	43.9	40.3
Natural Resources, Construction, and Maintenance	6.2	7.8	8.7
Production, Transportation, and Material Moving	10.2	11.2	13.1
Sales and Office	19.1	21.1	20.9
Service	19.9	15.9	17.0

Note: Figures cover employed civilians 16 years of age and older; (1) Figures cover the Richmond, VA Metropolitan Statistical Area
Source: U.S. Census Bureau, 2017-2021 American Community Survey 5-Year Estimates

Occupations with Greatest Projected Employment Growth: 2022 – 2024

Occupation[1]	2022 Employment	2024 Projected Employment	Numeric Employment Change	Percent Employment Change
Software Developers and Software Quality Assurance Analysts and Testers	86,590	90,990	4,400	5.1
Laborers and Freight, Stock, and Material Movers, Hand	65,350	68,080	2,730	4.2
Management Analysts	64,340	67,000	2,660	4.1
Stockers and Order Fillers	55,280	57,410	2,130	3.9
Cooks, Restaurant	29,990	31,930	1,940	6.5
Janitors and Cleaners, Except Maids and Housekeeping Cleaners	63,330	64,950	1,620	2.6
Retail Salespersons	101,360	102,940	1,580	1.6
Home Health and Personal Care Aides	54,320	55,870	1,550	2.9
General and Operations Managers	53,920	55,420	1,500	2.8
Accountants and Auditors	46,230	47,600	1,370	3.0

Note: Projections cover Virginia; (1) Sorted by numeric employment change
Source: www.projectionscentral.com, State Occupational Projections, 2022–2024 Short-Term Projections

Fastest-Growing Occupations: 2022 – 2024

Occupation[1]	2022 Employment	2024 Projected Employment	Numeric Employment Change	Percent Employment Change
Travel Agents	1,150	1,310	160	13.9
Nurse Practitioners	5,040	5,620	580	11.5
Ushers, Lobby Attendants, and Ticket Takers	1,740	1,920	180	10.3
Statisticians	1,360	1,480	120	8.8
Economists	1,430	1,550	120	8.4
Information Security Analysts (SOC 2018)	15,400	16,610	1,210	7.9
Medical Scientists, Except Epidemiologists	2,060	2,200	140	6.8
Physician Assistants	2,660	2,840	180	6.8
Fitness Trainers and Aerobics Instructors	14,290	15,250	960	6.7
Cooks, Restaurant	29,990	31,930	1,940	6.5

Note: Projections cover Virginia; (1) Sorted by percent employment change and excludes occupations with numeric employment change less than 50
Source: www.projectionscentral.com, State Occupational Projections, 2022–2024 Short-Term Projections

442   Richmond, Virginia

CITY FINANCES

City Government Finances

Component	2020 ($000)	2020 ($ per capita)
Total Revenues	1,503,940	6,526
Total Expenditures	1,506,250	6,537
Debt Outstanding	1,755,026	7,616
Cash and Securities[1]	752,608	3,266

Note: (1) Cash and security holdings of a government at the close of its fiscal year, including those of its dependent agencies, utilities, and liquor stores.
Source: U.S. Census Bureau, State & Local Government Finances 2020

City Government Revenue by Source

Source	2020 ($000)	2020 ($ per capita)	2020 (%)
General Revenue			
From Federal Government	67,074	291	4.5
From State Government	358,443	1,555	23.8
From Local Governments	23,387	101	1.6
Taxes			
Property	391,525	1,699	26.0
Sales and Gross Receipts	121,248	526	8.1
Personal Income	0	0	0.0
Corporate Income	0	0	0.0
Motor Vehicle License	7,204	31	0.5
Other Taxes	57,530	250	3.8
Current Charges	189,746	823	12.6
Liquor Store	0	0	0.0
Utility	245,295	1,064	16.3

Source: U.S. Census Bureau, State & Local Government Finances 2020

City Government Expenditures by Function

Function	2020 ($000)	2020 ($ per capita)	2020 (%)
General Direct Expenditures			
Air Transportation	0	0	0.0
Corrections	41,120	178	2.7
Education	385,171	1,671	25.6
Employment Security Administration	0	0	0.0
Financial Administration	15,940	69	1.1
Fire Protection	54,972	238	3.6
General Public Buildings	4,763	20	0.3
Governmental Administration, Other	19,364	84	1.3
Health	94,540	410	6.3
Highways	61,972	268	4.1
Hospitals	0	0	0.0
Housing and Community Development	94,328	409	6.3
Interest on General Debt	41,942	182	2.8
Judicial and Legal	25,730	111	1.7
Libraries	5,796	25	0.4
Parking	11,459	49	0.8
Parks and Recreation	24,361	105	1.6
Police Protection	111,766	485	7.4
Public Welfare	58,392	253	3.9
Sewerage	86,456	375	5.7
Solid Waste Management	0	0	0.0
Veterans' Services	0	0	0.0
Liquor Store	0	0	0.0
Utility	283,769	1,231	18.8

Source: U.S. Census Bureau, State & Local Government Finances 2020

TAXES

State Corporate Income Tax Rates

State	Tax Rate (%)	Income Brackets ($)	Num. of Brackets	Financial Institution Tax Rate (%)[a]	Federal Income Tax Ded.
Virginia	6.0	Flat rate	1	6.0	No

Note: Tax rates as of January 1, 2023; (a) Rates listed are the corporate income tax rate applied to financial institutions or excise taxes based on income. Some states have other taxes based upon the value of deposits or shares.
Source: Federation of Tax Administrators, State Corporate Income Tax Rates, January 1, 2023

State Individual Income Tax Rates

State	Tax Rate (%)	Income Brackets ($)	Personal Exemptions ($)			Standard Ded. ($)	
			Single	Married	Depend.	Single	Married
Virginia	2.0 - 5.75	3,000 - 17,001	930	1,860	930	7,500	15,000

Note: Tax rates as of January 1, 2023; Local- and county-level taxes are not included; Federal income tax is not deductible on state income tax returns
Source: Federation of Tax Administrators, State Individual Income Tax Rates, January 1, 2023

Various State Sales and Excise Tax Rates

State	State Sales Tax (%)	Gasoline[1] ($/gal.)	Cigarette[2] ($/pack)	Spirits[3] ($/gal.)	Wine[4] ($/gal.)	Beer[5] ($/gal.)	Recreational Marijuana (%)
Virginia	5.3	0.362	0.60	22.06	1.51	0.26	(s)

Note: All tax rates as of January 1, 2023; (1) The American Petroleum Institute has developed a methodology for determining the average tax rate on a gallon of fuel. Rates may include any of the following: excise taxes, environmental fees, storage tank fees, other fees or taxes, general sales tax, and local taxes; (2) The federal excise tax of $1.0066 per pack and local taxes are not included; (3) Rates are those applicable to off-premise sales of 40% alcohol by volume (a.b.v.) distilled spirits in 750ml containers. Local excise taxes are excluded; (4) Rates are those applicable to off-premise sales of 11% a.b.v. non-carbonated wine in 750ml containers; (5) Rates are those applicable to off-premise sales of 4.7% a.b.v. beer in 12 ounce containers; (s) 21% excise tax (retail price)
Source: Tax Foundation, 2023 Facts & Figures: How Does Your State Compare?

State Business Tax Climate Index Rankings

State	Overall Rank	Corporate Tax Rank	Individual Income Tax Rank	Sales Tax Rank	Property Tax Rank	Unemployment Insurance Tax Rank
Virginia	26	17	34	12	29	39

Note: The index is a measure of how each state's tax laws affect economic performance. The lower the rank, the more favorable a state's tax system is for business. States without a given tax are given a ranking of 1. The scores/rankings for the District of Columbia do not affect other states. The 2023 index represents the tax climate as of July 1, 2022.
Source: Tax Foundation, State Business Tax Climate Index 2023

TRANSPORTATION

Means of Transportation to Work

Area	Car/Truck/Van		Public Transportation			Bicycle	Walked	Other Means	Worked at Home
	Drove Alone	Car-pooled	Bus	Subway	Railroad				
City	67.8	8.5	4.2	0.1	0.0	1.8	4.5	1.6	11.5
MSA[1]	76.2	7.7	1.2	0.0	0.1	0.4	1.4	1.1	11.9
U.S.	73.2	8.6	2.0	1.6	0.5	0.5	2.5	1.5	9.7

Note: Figures are percentages and cover workers 16 years of age and older; (1) Figures cover the Richmond, VA Metropolitan Statistical Area
Source: U.S. Census Bureau, 2017-2021 American Community Survey 5-Year Estimates

Travel Time to Work

Area	Less Than 10 Minutes	10 to 19 Minutes	20 to 29 Minutes	30 to 44 Minutes	45 to 59 Minutes	60 to 89 Minutes	90 Minutes or More
City	11.4	37.4	27.3	16.8	2.9	2.7	1.5
MSA[1]	9.3	28.8	26.7	23.5	6.6	3.1	2.1
U.S.	12.4	28.5	21.0	20.9	8.2	6.2	2.9

Note: Note: Figures are percentages and include workers 16 years old and over; (1) Figures cover the Richmond, VA Metropolitan Statistical Area
Source: U.S. Census Bureau, 2017-2021 American Community Survey 5-Year Estimates

Key Congestion Measures

Measure	1990	2000	2010	2015	2020
Annual Hours of Delay, Total (000)	5,569	10,256	20,216	23,120	15,862
Annual Hours of Delay, Per Auto Commuter	16	23	28	31	24
Annual Congestion Cost, Per Auto Commuter ($)	282	385	607	638	482

Note: Covers the Richmond VA urban area
Source: Texas A&M Transportation Institute, 2021 Urban Mobility Report

Freeway Travel Time Index

Measure	1985	1990	1995	2000	2005	2010	2015	2020
Urban Area Index[1]	1.04	1.06	1.09	1.09	1.11	1.12	1.12	1.07
Urban Area Rank[1,2]	81	85	77	92	92	89	92	57

Note: Freeway Travel Time Index—the ratio of travel time in the peak period to the travel time at free-flow conditions. For example, a value of 1.30 indicates a 20-minute free-flow trip takes 26 minutes in the peak (20 minutes x 1.30 = 26 minutes); (1) Covers the Richmond VA urban area; (2) Rank is based on 101 larger urban areas (#1 = highest travel time index)
Source: Texas A&M Transportation Institute, 2021 Urban Mobility Report

Public Transportation

Agency Name / Mode of Transportation	Vehicles Operated in Maximum Service[1]	Annual Unlinked Passenger Trips[2] (in thous.)	Annual Passenger Miles[3] (in thous.)
Greater Richmond Transit Company (GRTC)			
Bus (directly operated)	104	6,124.5	30,464.6
Bus (purchased transportation)	18	11.8	131.8
Bus Rapid Transit (directly operated)	9	1,345.8	4,158.8
Demand Response (purchased transportation)	41	211.3	2,476.8
Vanpool (purchased transportation)	89	117.1	7,117.1

Note: (1) Number of revenue vehicles operated by the given mode and type of service to meet the annual maximum service requirement. This is the revenue vehicle count during the peak season of the year; on the week and day that maximum service is provided. Vehicles operated in maximum service (VOMS) exclude atypical days and one-time special events; (2) Number of passengers who boarded public transportation vehicles. Passengers are counted each time they board a vehicle no matter how many vehicles they use to travel from their origin to their destination. (3) Sum of the distances ridden by all passengers during the entire fiscal year.
Source: Federal Transit Administration, National Transit Database, 2021

Air Transportation

Airport Name and Code / Type of Service	Passenger Airlines[1]	Passenger Enplanements	Freight Carriers[2]	Freight (lbs)
Richmond International (RIC)				
Domestic service (U.S. carriers - 2022)	28	2,042,363	15	63,882,844
International service (U.S. carriers - 2021)	2	140		9,892

Note: (1) Includes all U.S.-based major, minor and commuter airlines that carried at least one passenger during the year; (2) Includes all U.S.-based airlines and freight carriers that transported at least one pound of freight during the year.
Source: Bureau of Transportation Statistics, The Intermodal Transportation Database, Air Carriers: T-100 Domestic Market (U.S. Carriers), 2022; Bureau of Transportation Statistics, The Intermodal Transportation Database, Air Carriers: T-100 International Market (U.S. Carriers), 2021

BUSINESSES

Major Business Headquarters

Company Name	Industry	Rankings	
		Fortune[1]	Forbes[2]
ARKO	Specialty retailers, other	498	-
AltriaGroup	Tobacco	165	-
CarMax	Automotive retailing, services	174	-
Dominion Energy	Utilities, gas and electric	257	-
Estes Express Lines	Transportation	-	129
Genworth Financial	Insurance, life and health (stock)	434	-
Performance Food Group	Wholesalers, food and grocery	112	-

Note: (1) Companies that produce a 10-K are ranked 1 to 500 based on 2021 revenue; (2) All private companies with at least $2 billion in annual revenue through the end of their most current fiscal year are ranked 1 to 246; companies listed are headquartered in the city; dashes indicate no ranking
Source: Fortune, "Fortune 500," 2022; Forbes, "America's Largest Private Companies," 2022

Fastest-Growing Businesses

According to *Inc.*, Richmond is home to two of America's 500 fastest-growing private companies: **Summit Human Capital** (#20); **Git The Trucking Commercial Tires** (#485). Criteria: must be an independent, privately-held, for-profit, U.S. corporation, proprietorship or partnership as of December 31, 2021; revenues must be at least $100,000 in 2018 and $2 million in 2021; must have four-year operating/sales history. *Inc., "America's 500 Fastest-Growing Private Companies," 2022*

According to *Initiative for a Competitive Inner City (ICIC)*, Richmond is home to two of America's 100 fastest-growing "inner city" companies: **Astyra Corporation** (#23); **Heaven Sent Child Care** (#61). Criteria for inclusion: company must be headquartered in or have 51 percent or more of its physical operations in an economically distressed urban area; must be an independent, for-profit corporation, partnership or proprietorship; must have 10 or more employees and have a five-year sales history that includes sales of at least $200,000 in the base year and at least $1 million in the current year with no decrease in sales over the two most recent years. Companies were ranked overall by revenue growth over the five-year period between 2017 and 2021. *Initiative for a Competitive Inner City (ICIC), "Inner City 100 Companies," 2022*

Living Environment

COST OF LIVING

Cost of Living Index

Composite Index	Groceries	Housing	Utilities	Trans-portation	Health Care	Misc. Goods/ Services
96.8	94.1	88.1	104.3	95.9	103.2	102.7

Note: The Cost of Living Index measures regional differences in the cost of consumer goods and services, excluding taxes and non-consumer expenditures, for professional and managerial households in the top income quintile. It is based on more than 50,000 prices covering almost 60 different items for which prices are collected three times a year by chambers of commerce, economic development organizations or university applied economic centers in each participating urban area. The numbers shown should be read as a percentage above or below the national average of 100. For example, a value of 115.4 in the groceries column indicates that grocery prices are 15.4% higher than the national average. Small differences in the index numbers should not be interpreted as significant; Figures cover the Richmond VA urban area.
Source: The Council for Community and Economic Research, Cost of Living Index, 2022

Grocery Prices

Area[1]	T-Bone Steak ($/pound)	Frying Chicken ($/pound)	Whole Milk ($/half gal.)	Eggs ($/dozen)	Orange Juice ($/64 oz.)	Coffee ($/11.5 oz.)
City[2]	12.49	1.38	2.09	1.44	3.87	4.49
Avg.	13.81	1.59	2.43	2.25	3.85	4.95
Min.	10.17	0.90	1.51	1.30	2.90	3.46
Max.	19.35	3.30	4.32	4.32	5.31	8.59

Note: (1) Values for the local area are compared with the average, minimum and maximum values for all 286 areas in the Cost of Living Index; (2) Figures cover the Richmond VA urban area; T-Bone Steak (price per pound); Frying Chicken (price per pound, whole fryer); Whole Milk (half gallon carton); Eggs (price per dozen, Grade A, large); Orange Juice (64 oz. Tropicana or Florida Natural); Coffee (11.5 oz. can, vacuum-packed, Maxwell House, Hills Bros, or Folgers).
Source: The Council for Community and Economic Research, Cost of Living Index, 2022

Housing and Utility Costs

Area[1]	New Home Price ($)	Apartment Rent ($/month)	All Electric ($/month)	Part Electric ($/month)	Other Energy ($/month)	Telephone ($/month)
City[2]	383,637	1,334	-	95.49	99.23	182.67
Avg.	450,913	1,371	176.41	99.93	76.96	190.22
Min.	229,283	546	100.84	31.56	27.15	174.27
Max.	2,434,977	4,569	356.86	249.59	272.24	208.31

Note: (1) Values for the local area are compared with the average, minimum and maximum values for all 286 areas in the Cost of Living Index; (2) Figures cover the Richmond VA urban area; New Home Price (2,400 sf living area, 8,000 sf lot, in urban area with full utilities); Apartment Rent (950 sf 2 bedroom/1.5 or 2 bath, unfurnished, excluding all utilities except water); All Electric (average monthly cost for an all-electric home); Part Electric (average monthly cost for a part-electric home); Other Energy (average monthly cost for natural gas, fuel oil, coal, wood, and any other forms of energy except electricity); Telephone (price includes the base monthly rate plus taxes and fees for three lines of mobile phone service).
Source: The Council for Community and Economic Research, Cost of Living Index, 2022

Health Care, Transportation, and Other Costs

Area[1]	Doctor ($/visit)	Dentist ($/visit)	Optometrist ($/visit)	Gasoline ($/gallon)	Beauty Salon ($/visit)	Men's Shirt ($)
City[2]	145.32	104.74	115.73	3.61	49.08	29.41
Avg.	124.91	107.77	117.66	3.86	43.31	34.21
Min.	36.61	58.25	51.79	2.90	22.18	13.05
Max.	250.21	162.58	371.96	5.54	85.61	63.54

Note: (1) Values for the local area are compared with the average, minimum and maximum values for all 286 areas in the Cost of Living Index; (2) Figures cover the Richmond VA urban area; Doctor (general practitioners routine exam of an established patient); Dentist (adult teeth cleaning and periodic oral examination); Optometrist (full vision eye exam for established adult patient); Gasoline (one gallon regular unleaded, national brand, including all taxes, cash price at self-service pump if available); Beauty Salon (woman's shampoo, trim, and blow-dry); Men's Shirt (cotton/polyester dress shirt, pinpoint weave, long sleeves).
Source: The Council for Community and Economic Research, Cost of Living Index, 2022

HOUSING

Homeownership Rate

Area	2015 (%)	2016 (%)	2017 (%)	2018 (%)	2019 (%)	2020 (%)	2021 (%)	2022 (%)
MSA[1]	67.4	61.7	63.1	62.9	66.4	66.5	64.9	66.3
U.S.	63.7	63.4	63.9	64.4	64.6	66.6	65.5	65.8

Note: (1) Figures cover the Richmond, VA Metropolitan Statistical Area
Source: U.S. Census Bureau, Housing Vacancies and Homeownership Annual Statistics: 2015-2022

House Price Index (HPI)

Area	National Ranking[2]	Quarterly Change (%)	One-Year Change (%)	Five-Year Change (%)	Since 1991Q1 (%)
MSA[1]	79	-0.25	13.11	53.64	254.70
U.S.[3]	—	0.34	8.41	58.44	289.08

Note: The HPI is a weighted repeat sales index. It measures average price changes in repeat sales or refinancings on the same properties. This information is obtained by reviewing repeat mortgage transactions on single-family properties whose mortgages have been purchased or securitized by Fannie Mae or Freddie Mac since January 1975; (1) Figures cover the Richmond, VA Metropolitan Statistical Area; (2) Rankings are based on annual percentage change for all metro areas containing at least 15,000 transactions over the last 10 years and ranges from 1 to 257; (3) figures based on a weighted average of Census Division estimates using a seasonally adjusted, purchase-only index; all figures are for the period ending December 31, 2022
Source: Federal Housing Finance Agency, Change in FHFA Metropolitan Area House Price Indexes, 2022Q4

Median Single-Family Home Prices

Area	2020	2021	2022[p]	Percent Change 2021 to 2022
MSA[1]	303.4	342.8	374.0	9.1
U.S. Average	300.2	357.1	392.6	9.9

Note: Figures are median sales prices of existing single-family homes in thousands of dollars; (p) preliminary; (1) Figures cover the Richmond, VA Metropolitan Statistical Area
Source: National Association of Realtors, Median Sales Price of Existing Single-Family Homes for Metropolitan Areas, 4th Quarter 2022

Qualifying Income Based on Median Sales Price of Existing Single-Family Homes

Area	With 5% Down ($)	With 10% Down ($)	With 20% Down ($)
MSA[1]	109,202	103,455	91,960
U.S. Average	112,234	106,237	94,513

Note: Figures are preliminary; Qualifying income is based on a mortgage rate of 6.77%. Monthly principal and interest payment is limited to 25% of income; (1) Figures cover the Richmond, VA Metropolitan Statistical Area
Source: National Association of Realtors, Qualifying Income Based on Median Sales Price of Existing Single-Family Homes for Metropolitan Areas, 4th Quarter 2022

Home Value

Area	Under $100,000	$100,000 -$199,999	$200,000 -$299,999	$300,000 -$399,999	$400,000 -$499,999	$500,000 -$999,999	$1,000,000 or more	Median ($)
City	9.5	26.4	21.0	16.5	8.6	14.2	3.8	263,000
MSA[1]	6.4	24.3	29.8	18.4	9.3	10.4	1.5	262,900
U.S.	16.2	24.2	20.1	13.6	8.3	13.6	4.1	244,900

Note: Figures are percentages except for median and cover owner-occupied housing units; (1) Figures cover the Richmond, VA Metropolitan Statistical Area
Source: U.S. Census Bureau, 2017-2021 American Community Survey 5-Year Estimates

Year Housing Structure Built

Area	2020 or Later	2010 -2019	2000 -2009	1990 -1999	1980 -1989	1970 -1979	1960 -1969	1950 -1959	1940 -1949	Before 1940	Median Year
City	0.1	6.5	5.3	5.8	7.1	9.9	11.8	14.7	9.1	29.6	1958
MSA[1]	0.2	8.7	14.2	15.0	15.6	14.5	9.6	8.8	4.3	9.0	1982
U.S.	0.2	7.3	13.6	13.6	13.2	14.8	10.3	10.0	4.7	12.2	1979

Note: Figures are percentages except for Median Year; Note: (1) Figures cover the Richmond, VA Metropolitan Statistical Area
Source: U.S. Census Bureau, 2017-2021 American Community Survey 5-Year Estimates

Gross Monthly Rent

Area	Under $500	$500 -$999	$1,000 -$1,499	$1,500 -$1,999	$2,000 -$2,499	$2,500 -$2,999	$3,000 and up	Median ($)
City	11.2	26.1	41.7	16.2	3.6	0.6	0.7	1,132
MSA[1]	6.6	23.4	45.3	18.7	3.9	0.9	1.2	1,202
U.S.	8.1	30.5	30.8	16.8	7.3	3.1	3.5	1,163

Note: Figures are percentages except for median; Gross rent is the contract rent plus the estimated average monthly cost of utilities (electricity, gas, and water and sewer) and fuels (oil, coal, kerosene, wood, etc.) if these are paid by the renter (or paid for the renter by someone else); (1) Figures cover the Richmond, VA Metropolitan Statistical Area
Source: U.S. Census Bureau, 2017-2021 American Community Survey 5-Year Estimates

HEALTH

Health Risk Factors

Category	MSA[1] (%)	U.S. (%)
Adults aged 18–64 who have any kind of health care coverage	94.1	90.9
Adults who reported being in good or better health	85.1	85.2
Adults who have been told they have high blood cholesterol	40.4	35.7
Adults who have been told they have high blood pressure	35.8	32.4
Adults who are current smokers	14.4	14.4
Adults who currently use e-cigarettes	8.2	6.7
Adults who currently use chewing tobacco, snuff, or snus	3.6	3.5
Adults who are heavy drinkers[2]	7.6	6.3
Adults who are binge drinkers[3]	19.2	15.4
Adults who are overweight (BMI 25.0 - 29.9)	31.8	34.4
Adults who are obese (BMI 30.0 - 99.8)	35.8	33.9
Adults who participated in any physical activities in the past month	80.2	76.3

Note: (1) Figures cover the Richmond, VA Metropolitan Statistical Area; (2) Heavy drinkers are classified as adult men having more than 14 drinks per week and adult women having more than 7 drinks per week; (3) Binge drinkers are classified as males having five or more drinks on one occasion or females having four or more drinks on one occasion
Source: Centers for Disease Control and Prevention, Behaviorial Risk Factor Surveillance System, SMART: Selected Metropolitan Area Risk Trends, 2021

Acute and Chronic Health Conditions

Category	MSA[1] (%)	U.S. (%)
Adults who have ever been told they had a heart attack	4.1	4.0
Adults who have ever been told they have angina or coronary heart disease	3.8	3.8
Adults who have ever been told they had a stroke	4.2	3.0
Adults who have ever been told they have asthma	15.7	14.9
Adults who have ever been told they have arthritis	28.7	25.8
Adults who have ever been told they have diabetes[2]	12.7	10.9
Adults who have ever been told they had skin cancer	7.2	6.6
Adults who have ever been told they had any other types of cancer	8.4	7.5
Adults who have ever been told they have COPD	6.4	6.1
Adults who have ever been told they have kidney disease	2.8	3.0
Adults who have ever been told they have a form of depression	21.1	20.5

Note: (1) Figures cover the Richmond, VA Metropolitan Statistical Area; (2) Figures do not include pregnancy-related, borderline, or pre-diabetes
Source: Centers for Disease Control and Prevention, Behaviorial Risk Factor Surveillance System, SMART: Selected Metropolitan Area Risk Trends, 2021

Health Screening and Vaccination Rates

Category	MSA[1] (%)	U.S. (%)
Adults who have ever been tested for HIV	39.9	34.9
Adults who have had their blood cholesterol checked within the last five years	88.2	85.2
Adults aged 65+ who have had flu shot within the past year	71.1	68.6
Adults aged 65+ who have ever had a pneumonia vaccination	76.5	71.0

Note: (1) Figures cover the Richmond, VA Metropolitan Statistical Area.
Source: Centers for Disease Control and Prevention, Behaviorial Risk Factor Surveillance System, SMART: Selected Metropolitan Area Risk Trends, 2021

Disability Status

Category	MSA[1] (%)	U.S. (%)
Adults who reported being deaf	4.4	7.2
Are you blind or have serious difficulty seeing, even when wearing glasses?	4.3	4.8
Are you limited in any way in any of your usual activities due to arthritis?	11.9	11.1
Do you have difficulty doing errands alone?	7.4	7.0
Do you have difficulty dressing or bathing?	4.7	3.6
Do you have serious difficulty concentrating/remembering/making decisions?	11.5	12.1
Do you have serious difficulty walking or climbing stairs?	12.8	12.8

Note: (1) Figures cover the Richmond, VA Metropolitan Statistical Area.
Source: Centers for Disease Control and Prevention, Behaviorial Risk Factor Surveillance System, SMART: Selected Metropolitan Area Risk Trends, 2021

Richmond, Virginia

Mortality Rates for the Top 10 Causes of Death in the U.S.

ICD-10[a] Sub-Chapter	ICD-10[a] Code	Crude Mortality Rate[1] per 100,000 population	
		County[2]	U.S.
Malignant neoplasms	C00-C97	155.7	182.6
Ischaemic heart diseases	I20-I25	87.5	113.1
Other forms of heart disease	I30-I51	76.7	64.4
Other degenerative diseases of the nervous system	G30-G31	39.6	51.0
Cerebrovascular diseases	I60-I69	47.0	47.8
Other external causes of accidental injury	W00-X59	80.5	46.4
Chronic lower respiratory diseases	J40-J47	36.1	45.7
Organic, including symptomatic, mental disorders	F01-F09	34.8	35.9
Hypertensive diseases	I10-I15	30.0	35.0
Diabetes mellitus	E10-E14	32.2	29.6

Note: (a) ICD-10 = International Classification of Diseases 10th Revision; (1) Crude mortality rates are a three-year average covering 2019-2021; (2) Figures cover Richmond city.
Source: Centers for Disease Control and Prevention, National Center for Health Statistics. National Vital Statistics System, Mortality 2018-2021 on CDC WONDER Online Database

Mortality Rates for Selected Causes of Death

ICD-10[a] Sub-Chapter	ICD-10[a] Code	Crude Mortality Rate[1] per 100,000 population	
		County[2]	U.S.
Assault	X85-Y09	25.4	7.0
Diseases of the liver	K70-K76	13.5	19.8
Human immunodeficiency virus (HIV) disease	B20-B24	4.1	1.5
Influenza and pneumonia	J09-J18	10.4	14.7
Intentional self-harm	X60-X84	12.0	14.3
Malnutrition	E40-E46	Unreliable	4.3
Obesity and other hyperalimentation	E65-E68	3.2	3.0
Renal failure	N17-N19	21.6	15.7
Transport accidents	V01-V99	12.8	13.6
Viral hepatitis	B15-B19	Unreliable	1.2

Note: (a) ICD-10 = International Classification of Diseases 10th Revision; (1) Crude mortality rates are a three-year average covering 2019-2021; (2) Figures cover Richmond city; Data are suppressed when the data meet the criteria for confidentiality constraints; Crude mortality rates are flagged as unreliable when the rate would be calculated with a numerator of 20 or less.
Source: Centers for Disease Control and Prevention, National Center for Health Statistics. National Vital Statistics System, Mortality 2018-2021 on CDC WONDER Online Database

Health Insurance Coverage

Area	With Health Insurance	With Private Health Insurance	With Public Health Insurance	Without Health Insurance	Population Under Age 19 Without Health Insurance
City	89.3	63.7	35.5	10.7	6.9
MSA[1]	92.5	74.5	31.1	7.5	4.7
U.S.	91.2	67.8	35.4	8.8	5.3

Note: Figures are percentages that cover the civilian noninstitutionalized population; (1) Figures cover the Richmond, VA Metropolitan Statistical Area
Source: U.S. Census Bureau, 2017-2021 American Community Survey 5-Year Estimates

Number of Medical Professionals

Area	MDs[3]	DOs[3,4]	Dentists	Podiatrists	Chiropractors	Optometrists
Ind. City[1] (number)	1,763	63	341	27	17	38
Ind. City[1] (rate[2])	777.8	27.8	150.5	11.9	7.5	16.8
U.S. (rate[2])	289.3	23.5	72.5	6.2	28.7	17.4

Note: Data as of 2021 unless noted; (1) Data covers Richmond independent city; (2) Rate per 100,000 population; (3) Data as of 2020 and includes all active, non-federal physicians; (4) Doctor of Osteopathic Medicine
Source: U.S. Department of Health and Human Services, Health Resources and Services Administration, Bureau of Health Professions, Area Resource File (ARF) 2021-2022

Best Hospitals

According to *U.S. News,* the Richmond, VA metro area is home to one of the best hospitals in the U.S.: **VCU Medical Center** (1 adult specialty and 3 pediatric specialties). The hospital listed was nationally ranked in at least one of 15 adult or 10 pediatric specialties. The number of specialties shown cover the parent hospital. Only 164 U.S. hospitals performed well enough to be nationally ranked in one or more specialties. Twenty hospitals in the U.S. made the Honor Roll. The Best Hospitals Honor Roll takes both the national rankings and the procedure and condition ratings into account. Hospitals received points if they were nationally ranked in one of the 15 adult specialties—the higher they ranked, the more points they got—and how many ratings of "high performing" they earned in the 17 procedures and conditions. *U.S. News Online, "America's Best Hospitals 2022-23"*

According to *U.S. News,* the Richmond, VA metro area is home to one of the best children's hospitals in the U.S.: **Children's Hospital of Richmond at VCU** (3 pediatric specialties). The hospital listed was highly ranked in at least one of 10 pediatric specialties. Eighty-six children's hospitals in the U.S. were nationally ranked in at least one specialty. Hospitals received points for being ranked in a specialty, and the 10 hospitals with the most points across the 10 specialties make up the Honor Roll. *U.S. News Online, "America's Best Children's Hospitals 2022-23"*

EDUCATION

Public School District Statistics

District Name	Schls	Pupils	Pupil/ Teacher Ratio	Minority Pupils[1] (%)	LEP/ELL[2] (%)	IEP[3] (%)
Richmond City Public Schools	54	21,177	14.4	89.3	8.2	14.7

Note: Table includes school districts with 2,000 or more students; (1) Percentage of students that are not non-Hispanic white; (2) Percentage of students that are Limited English Proficient or English Language Learners (2018-19); (3) Percentage of students that have an Individualized Education Program (2019-20). Source: U.S. Department of Education, National Center for Education Statistics, Common Core of Data, Local Education Agency (School District) Universe Survey: School Year 2021-2022

Best High Schools

According to *U.S. News,* Richmond is home to two of the top 500 high schools in the U.S.: **Open High School** (#177); **Richmond Community High School** (#364). Nearly 18,000 public, magnet and charter schools were ranked based on their performance on state assessments and how well they prepare students for college. *U.S. News & World Report, "Best High Schools 2022"*

Highest Level of Education

Area	Less than H.S.	H.S. Diploma	Some College, No Deg.	Associate Degree	Bachelor's Degree	Master's Degree	Prof. School Degree	Doctorate Degree
City	12.3	20.4	19.2	5.0	25.1	12.1	3.7	2.2
MSA[1]	8.9	24.6	19.9	7.6	23.7	11.0	2.5	1.7
U.S.	11.1	26.5	20.0	8.7	20.6	9.3	2.2	1.5

Note: Figures cover persons age 25 and over; (1) Figures cover the Richmond, VA Metropolitan Statistical Area Source: U.S. Census Bureau, 2017-2021 American Community Survey 5-Year Estimates

Educational Attainment by Race

Area	High School Graduate or Higher (%)					Bachelor's Degree or Higher (%)				
	Total	White	Black	Asian	Hisp.[2]	Total	White	Black	Asian	Hisp.[2]
City	87.7	94.7	81.5	88.6	58.3	43.1	68.0	14.8	70.7	22.5
MSA[1]	91.1	94.0	87.4	89.9	68.9	38.9	45.5	22.8	65.6	22.8
U.S.	88.9	91.4	87.2	87.6	71.2	33.7	35.5	23.3	55.6	18.4

Note: Figures shown cover persons 25 years old and over; (1) Figures cover the Richmond, VA Metropolitan Statistical Area; (2) People of Hispanic origin can be of any race Source: U.S. Census Bureau, 2017-2021 American Community Survey 5-Year Estimates

School Enrollment by Grade and Control

Area	Preschool (%)		Kindergarten (%)		Grades 1 - 4 (%)		Grades 5 - 8 (%)		Grades 9 - 12 (%)	
	Public	Private	Public	Private	Public	Private	Public	Private	Public	Private
City	50.9	49.1	89.3	10.7	85.0	15.0	84.6	15.4	83.6	16.4
MSA[1]	44.8	55.2	87.7	12.3	88.8	11.2	89.4	10.6	90.2	9.8
U.S.	58.8	41.2	86.3	13.7	88.3	11.7	88.6	11.4	89.4	10.6

Note: Figures shown cover persons 3 years old and over; (1) Figures cover the Richmond, VA Metropolitan Statistical Area Source: U.S. Census Bureau, 2017-2021 American Community Survey 5-Year Estimates

Higher Education

Four-Year Colleges			Two-Year Colleges			Medical Schools[1]	Law Schools[2]	Voc/ Tech[3]
Public	Private Non-profit	Private For-profit	Public	Private Non-profit	Private For-profit			
2	5	2	3	2	3	1	1	5

Note: Figures cover institutions located within the Richmond, VA Metropolitan Statistical Area and include main campuses only; (1) includes schools accredited by the Liaison Committee on Medical Education and the American Osteopathic Association's Commission on Osteopathic College Accreditation; (2) includes ABA-accredited schools, schools with provisional ABA accreditation, and state accredited schools; (3) includes all schools with programs that are less than 2 years. Source: National Center for Education Statistics, Integrated Postsecondary Education System (IPEDS), 2021-22; Wikipedia, List of Medical Schools in the United States, accessed April 10, 2023; Wikipedia, List of Law Schools in the United States, accessed April 10, 2023

According to *U.S. News & World Report,* the Richmond, VA metro area is home to one of the top 200 national universities in the U.S.: **Virginia Commonwealth University** (#166 tie). The indicators used to capture academic quality fall into a number of categories: assessment by administrators at peer institutions; retention of students; faculty resources; student selectivity; financial resources; alumni giving; high school counselor ratings of colleges; and graduation rate. *U.S. News & World Report, "America's Best Colleges 2023"*

According to *U.S. News & World Report,* the Richmond, VA metro area is home to one of the top 100 liberal arts colleges in the U.S.: **University of Richmond** (#18 tie). The indicators used to capture academic quality fall into a number of categories: assessment by administrators at peer institutions; retention of students; faculty resources; student selectivity; financial resources; alumni giving; high school counselor ratings of colleges; and graduation rate. *U.S. News & World Report, "America's Best Colleges 2023"*

According to *U.S. News & World Report,* the Richmond, VA metro area is home to one of the top 100 law schools in the U.S.: **University of Richmond** (#52 tie). The rankings are based on a weighted average of 12 measures of quality: peer assessment score; assessment score by lawyers/judges; median LSAT scores; median undergrad GPA; acceptance rate; employment rates for graduates; placement success; bar passage rate; faculty resources; expenditures per student; student/faculty ratio; and library resources. *U.S. News & World Report, "America's Best Graduate Schools, Law, 2023"*

According to *U.S. News & World Report,* the Richmond, VA metro area is home to one of the top 75 medical schools for research in the U.S.: **Virginia Commonwealth University** (#62 tie). The rankings are based on a weighted average of 11 measures of quality: quality assessment; peer assessment score; assessment score by residency directors; research activity; total research activity; average research activity per faculty member; student selectivity; median MCAT total score; median undergraduate GPA; acceptance rate; and faculty resources. *U.S. News & World Report, "America's Best Graduate Schools, Medical, 2023"*

EMPLOYERS

Major Employers

Company Name	Industry
Altria Group	Cigarettes
Amazon.com	Retail
Anthem Blue Cross and Blue Shield	Insurance
Bank of America	Financial services
Bon Secours Richmond	Healthcare
Capital One Financial Corp.	Financial services
Dominion Resources	Power & energy
DuPont	Conglomerate
Federal Reserve Bank of Richmond	Financial services
Food Lion	Grocery stores
HCA	General medical & surgical hospitals
Markel Corporation	Specialty insurance products
SunTrust Banks	Financial services
The Kroger Co.	Grocery stores
United Parcel Service	Package delivery services
University of Richmond	Education
VCU Health System	Healthcare
Verizon Communications	Communications
Wal-Mart Stores	Retail
Wells Fargo	Financial services

Note: Companies shown are located within the Richmond, VA Metropolitan Statistical Area.
Source: Hoovers.com; Wikipedia

Best Companies to Work For

CarMax, headquartered in Richmond, is among "The 100 Best Companies to Work For." To pick the best companies, *Fortune* partnered with the Great Place to Work Institute. Two-thirds of a company's score is based on the results of the Institute's Trust Index survey, which is sent to a random sample of employees from each company. The questions related to attitudes about management's credibility, job satisfaction, and camaraderie. The other third of the scoring is based on the company's responses to the Institute's Culture Audit, which includes detailed questions about pay and benefit programs, and a series of open-ended questions about hiring practices, internal communication, training, recognition programs, and diversity efforts. Any company that is at least five years old with more than 1,000 U.S. employees is eligible. *Fortune, "The 100 Best Companies to Work For," 2023*

Richmond, Virginia 451

PUBLIC SAFETY

Crime Rate

Area	Total Crime	Violent Crime Rate				Property Crime Rate		
		Murder	Rape[3]	Robbery	Aggrav. Assault	Burglary	Larceny -Theft	Motor Vehicle Theft
City	3,269.8	28.3	8.6	117.4	194.6	330.4	2,328.7	261.8
Suburbs[1]	1,784.2	5.9	23.2	30.9	126.7	136.3	1,342.0	119.3
Metro[2]	2,050.3	9.9	20.6	46.4	138.8	171.1	1,518.7	144.8
U.S.	2,356.7	6.5	38.4	73.9	279.7	314.2	1,398.0	246.0

Note: Figures are crimes per 100,000 population; (1) All areas within the metro area that are located outside the city limits; (2) Figures cover the Richmond, VA Metropolitan Statistical Area; (3) All figures shown were reported using the revised Uniform Crime Reporting (UCR) definition of rape; Due to the transition to the National Incident-Based Reporting System (NIBRS), limited city and metro area data was released for 2021.
Source: FBI Uniform Crime Reports, 2020

Hate Crimes

Area	Number of Quarters Reported	Number of Incidents per Bias Motivation					
		Race/Ethnicity/ Ancestry	Religion	Sexual Orientation	Disability	Gender	Gender Identity
City	4	1	1	0	1	0	0
U.S.	4	5,227	1,244	1,110	130	75	266

Note: Due to the transition to the National Incident-Based Reporting System (NIBRS), limited crime data was released for 2021.
Source: Federal Bureau of Investigation, Hate Crime Statistics 2020

Identity Theft Consumer Reports

Area	Reports	Reports per 100,000 Population	Rank[2]
MSA[1]	4,932	385	35
U.S.	1,108,609	339	-

Note: (1) Figures cover the Richmond, VA Metropolitan Statistical Area; (2) Rank ranges from 1 to 391 where 1 indicates greatest number of identity theft reports per 100,000 population
Source: Federal Trade Commission, Consumer Sentinel Network Data Book 2022

Fraud and Other Consumer Reports

Area	Reports	Reports per 100,000 Population	Rank[2]
MSA[1]	16,413	1,280	35
U.S.	4,064,520	1,245	-

Note: (1) Figures cover the Richmond, VA Metropolitan Statistical Area; (2) Rank ranges from 1 to 391 where 1 indicates greatest number of fraud and other consumer reports per 100,000 population
Source: Federal Trade Commission, Consumer Sentinel Network Data Book 2022

POLITICS

2020 Presidential Election Results

Area	Biden	Trump	Jorgensen	Hawkins	Other
Richmond City	82.9	14.9	1.5	0.0	0.6
U.S.	51.3	46.8	1.2	0.3	0.5

Note: Results are percentages and may not add to 100% due to rounding
Source: Dave Leip's Atlas of U.S. Presidential Elections

SPORTS

Professional Sports Teams

Team Name	League	Year Established

No teams are located in the metro area
Source: Wikipedia, Major Professional Sports Teams of the United States and Canada, April 12, 2023

CLIMATE

Average and Extreme Temperatures

Temperature	Jan	Feb	Mar	Apr	May	Jun	Jul	Aug	Sep	Oct	Nov	Dec	Yr.
Extreme High (°F)	80	82	91	96	98	104	105	103	103	99	86	80	105
Average High (°F)	47	50	59	69	78	85	88	86	81	71	60	50	69
Average Temp. (°F)	38	40	48	58	66	75	78	77	71	60	50	41	58
Average Low (°F)	28	30	37	45	55	63	68	67	60	48	38	31	48
Extreme Low (°F)	-6	-8	11	19	31	40	51	47	35	21	14	1	-8

Note: Figures cover the years 1921-1990
Source: National Climatic Data Center, International Station Meteorological Climate Summary, 9/96

Average Precipitation/Snowfall/Humidity

Precip./Humidity	Jan	Feb	Mar	Apr	May	Jun	Jul	Aug	Sep	Oct	Nov	Dec	Yr.
Avg. Precip. (in.)	3.3	3.0	3.5	3.1	3.7	3.7	5.2	4.9	3.3	3.1	2.9	3.1	43.0
Avg. Snowfall (in.)	5	4	2	Tr	0	0	0	0	0	Tr	1	2	13
Avg. Rel. Hum. 7am (%)	79	79	78	76	81	82	85	89	90	89	84	80	83
Avg. Rel. Hum. 4pm (%)	54	51	46	43	51	53	56	58	57	53	51	55	52

Note: Figures cover the years 1921-1990; Tr = Trace amounts (<0.05 in. of rain; <0.5 in. of snow)
Source: National Climatic Data Center, International Station Meteorological Climate Summary, 9/96

Weather Conditions

Temperature			Daytime Sky			Precipitation		
10°F & below	32°F & below	90°F & above	Clear	Partly cloudy	Cloudy	0.01 inch or more precip.	0.1 inch or more snow/ice	Thunder-storms
3	79	41	90	147	128	115	7	43

Note: Figures are average number of days per year and cover the years 1921-1990
Source: National Climatic Data Center, International Station Meteorological Climate Summary, 9/96

HAZARDOUS WASTE

Superfund Sites

The Richmond, VA metro area is home to three sites on the EPA's Superfund National Priorities List: **Defense General Supply Center (DLA)** (final); **H & H Inc., Burn Pit** (final); **Rentokil, Inc. (Virginia Wood Preserving Division)** (final). There are a total of 1,165 Superfund sites with a status of proposed or final on the list in the U.S. *U.S. Environmental Protection Agency, National Priorities List, April 12, 2023*

AIR QUALITY

Air Quality Trends: Ozone

	1990	1995	2000	2005	2010	2015	2018	2019	2020	2021
MSA[1]	0.083	0.089	0.080	0.082	0.079	0.062	0.062	0.061	0.054	0.061
U.S.	0.087	0.089	0.081	0.080	0.072	0.067	0.069	0.065	0.065	0.067

Note: (1) Data covers the Richmond, VA Metropolitan Statistical Area. The values shown are the composite ozone concentration averages among trend sites based on the highest fourth daily maximum 8-hour concentration in parts per million. These trends are based on sites having an adequate record of monitoring data during the trend period. Data from exceptional events are included.
Source: U.S. Environmental Protection Agency, Air Quality Monitoring Information, "Air Quality Trends by City, 1990-2021"

Air Quality Index

Area	Percent of Days when Air Quality was...[2]					AQI Statistics[2]	
	Good	Moderate	Unhealthy for Sensitive Groups	Unhealthy	Very Unhealthy	Maximum	Median
MSA[1]	76.4	22.7	0.8	0.0	0.0	112	42

Note: (1) Data covers the Richmond, VA Metropolitan Statistical Area; (2) Based on 365 days with AQI data in 2021. Air Quality Index (AQI) is an index for reporting daily air quality. EPA calculates the AQI for five major air pollutants regulated by the Clean Air Act: ground-level ozone, particle pollution (aka particulate matter), carbon monoxide, sulfur dioxide, and nitrogen dioxide. The AQI runs from 0 to 500. The higher the AQI value, the greater the level of air pollution and the greater the health concern. There are six AQI categories: "Good" AQI is between 0 and 50. Air quality is considered satisfactory; "Moderate" AQI is between 51 and 100. Air quality is acceptable; "Unhealthy for Sensitive Groups" When AQI values are between 101 and 150, members of sensitive groups may experience health effects; "Unhealthy" When AQI values are between 151 and 200 everyone may begin to experience health effects; "Very Unhealthy" AQI values between 201 and 300 trigger a health alert; "Hazardous" AQI values over 300 trigger warnings of emergency conditions (not shown).
Source: U.S. Environmental Protection Agency, Air Quality Index Report, 2021

Air Quality Index Pollutants

Area	Percent of Days when AQI Pollutant was...[2]					
	Carbon Monoxide	Nitrogen Dioxide	Ozone	Sulfur Dioxide	Particulate Matter 2.5	Particulate Matter 10
MSA[1]	0.0	6.3	51.8	(3)	41.9	0.0

Note: (1) Data covers the Richmond, VA Metropolitan Statistical Area; (2) Based on 365 days with AQI data in 2021. The Air Quality Index (AQI) is an index for reporting daily air quality. EPA calculates the AQI for five major air pollutants regulated by the Clean Air Act: ground-level ozone, particle pollution (also known as particulate matter), carbon monoxide, sulfur dioxide, and nitrogen dioxide. The AQI runs from 0 to 500. The higher the AQI value, the greater the level of air pollution and the greater the health concern; (3) Sulfur dioxide is no longer included in this table (as of December 8, 2021) because SO_2 concentrations tend to be very localized and not necessarily representative of broad geographical areas like counties and CBSAs.
Source: U.S. Environmental Protection Agency, Air Quality Index Report, 2021

Maximum Air Pollutant Concentrations: Particulate Matter, Ozone, CO and Lead

	Particulate Matter 10 (ug/m^3)	Particulate Matter 2.5 Wtd AM (ug/m^3)	Particulate Matter 2.5 24-Hr (ug/m^3)	Ozone (ppm)	Carbon Monoxide (ppm)	Lead (ug/m^3)
MSA[1] Level	40	8.3	19	0.066	1	n/a
NAAQS[2]	150	15	35	0.075	9	0.15
Met NAAQS[2]	Yes	Yes	Yes	Yes	Yes	n/a

Note: (1) Data covers the Richmond, VA Metropolitan Statistical Area; Data from exceptional events are included; (2) National Ambient Air Quality Standards; ppm = parts per million; ug/m^3 = micrograms per cubic meter; n/a not available.
Concentrations: Particulate Matter 10 (coarse particulate)—highest second maximum 24-hour concentration; Particulate Matter 2.5 Wtd AM (fine particulate)—highest weighted annual mean concentration; Particulate Matter 2.5 24-Hour (fine particulate)—highest 98th percentile 24-hour concentration; Ozone—highest fourth daily maximum 8-hour concentration; Carbon Monoxide—highest second maximum non-overlapping 8-hour concentration; Lead—maximum running 3-month average
Source: U.S. Environmental Protection Agency, Air Quality Monitoring Information, "Air Quality Statistics by City, 2021"

Maximum Air Pollutant Concentrations: Nitrogen Dioxide and Sulfur Dioxide

	Nitrogen Dioxide AM (ppb)	Nitrogen Dioxide 1-Hr (ppb)	Sulfur Dioxide AM (ppb)	Sulfur Dioxide 1-Hr (ppb)	Sulfur Dioxide 24-Hr (ppb)
MSA[1] Level	13	48	n/a	3	n/a
NAAQS[2]	53	100	30	75	140
Met NAAQS[2]	Yes	Yes	n/a	Yes	n/a

Note: (1) Data covers the Richmond, VA Metropolitan Statistical Area; Data from exceptional events are included; (2) National Ambient Air Quality Standards; ppm = parts per million; ug/m^3 = micrograms per cubic meter; n/a not available.
Concentrations: Nitrogen Dioxide AM—highest arithmetic mean concentration; Nitrogen Dioxide 1-Hr—highest 98th percentile 1-hour daily maximum concentration; Sulfur Dioxide AM—highest annual mean concentration; Sulfur Dioxide 1-Hr—highest 99th percentile 1-hour daily maximum concentration; Sulfur Dioxide 24-Hr—highest second maximum 24-hour concentration
Source: U.S. Environmental Protection Agency, Air Quality Monitoring Information, "Air Quality Statistics by City, 2021"

Virginia Beach, Virginia

Background

Virginia Beach, on the shores of the Chesapeake Bay and the Atlantic Ocean, is a paradise for beach lovers, and one of the fastest-growing cities on the East Coast.

The history of Virginia Beach began in 1607 when English settlers led by Captain John Smith first reached Virginia's shore at Cape Henry aboard the *Susan Constant*, the *Godspeed*, and the *Discovery*. The 100 colonists, sent by the Virginia Company to investigate trade possibilities, shortly moved up the James River to found the first permanent English settlement in America at Jamestown. The first actual settlement within the Virginia Beach city limits was at Lynnhaven Bay in 1621. It was at Cape Henry that the French Admiral Comte de Grassein came to the aid of American patriots during the Revolutionary War by blockading the British fleet during the Battle of Yorktown. To this day, the area is home to strategically important military bases.

With the connection of a railway to Norfolk in the late nineteenth century, Virginia Beach became a popular shore resort. It was incorporated as a town in 1906, and a city in 1952. In 1963, all neighboring Princess Ann County merged with the city, and today's Virginia Beach covers a territory of 310 square miles with 38 miles of shoreline. It is the largest city in Virginia with tourism the economic mainstay. It hosts the East Coast Surfing Championship and the North American Sand Soccer Championship every year.

Virginia Beach is listed in the *Guinness Book of World Records* as having the longest pleasure beach in the world and is located at the southern end of the Chesapeake Bay Bridge Tunnel—which was the longest bridge-tunnel in the world until 2018, when it was surpassed by a tunnel in China.

The city naturally enjoys a lifestyle focused to the water, with 28 miles of public beaches and 79 miles of scenic waterways. The beaches are enjoyed most of the year, while sailing and fishing opportunities are plentiful. There are three state and regional parks and three national wildlife refuges in the city; with a total of 208 city parks it offers a unique mix of urban, natural, and ecotourist attractions.

Agribusiness also contributes to the vitality of the area, with more than 32,700 acres of land under cultivation, and the construction and real estate industries are robust. Convention and trade shows annually produce millions of dollars in revenues. The labor force is abundant, productive, and energetic, offering a rich range of professional, technical, blue-collar, and clerical skills. Local government receives high grades from residents and visitors alike, and the city received the American Society of Public Administration's first-ever Innovation Recognition Award for excellence in organizational development, strategic planning, quality initiatives, and process improvements.

Virginia Beach is located alongside the Port of Hampton Roads, one of the world's finest harbors. Rail service and nearby Norfolk International Airport serves major industrial centers and cities. Major companies headquartered in the city including Busch Vacuum Solutions, IMS Gear, Amerigroup, Christian Broadcasting Network, and Geico.

Virginia Beach and its environs are home to 11 colleges and universities, including the Virginia Beach Higher Education Center, College of William and Mary, Old Dominion University, Norfolk State University, Virginia Wesleyan College, Eastern Virginia Medical School, and Tidewater Community College.

There are hundreds of art and cultural organizations based in the city, including a symphony, opera, theater groups, and many museums. The Virginia Marine Science Museum hosts one of the most attended aquariums in the nation.

Virginia Beach enjoys a temperate maritime climate influenced by the Gulf Stream. Winters are mild, rarely freezing, and splendid beach weather characterizes the area from spring through fall.

Rankings

General Rankings

- For its "Best for Vets: Places to Live 2019" rankings, *Military Times* evaluated 599 cities (83 large, 234 medium, 282 small) and compared the locations across three broad categories: veteran and military culture/services; economic indicators; and livability factors such as health, crime, traffic, and school quality. Virginia Beach ranked #2 out of the top 25, in the large city category (population of more than 250,000). Data points more specific to veterans and the military weighed more heavily than others. *rebootcamp.militarytimes.com, "Military Times Best Places to Live 2019," September 10, 2018*

- *Insider* listed 23 places in the U.S. that travel industry trends reveal would be popular destinations in 2023. This year the list trends towards cultural and historical happenings, sports events, wellness experiences and invigorating outdoor escapes. According to the website insider.com Virginia Beach is a place to visit in 2023. *Insider, "23 of the Best Places You Should Travel to in the U.S. in 2023," December 17, 2022*

- In their ninth annual survey, Livability.com looked at data for more than 2,300 mid-sized U.S. cities to determine the rankings for Livability's "Top 100 Best Places to Live" in 2022. Virginia Beach ranked #43. Criteria: housing and economy; social and civic engagement; education; demographics; health care options; transportation & infrastructure; and community amenities. *Livability.com, "Top 100 Best Places to Live 2022" July 19, 2022*

Business/Finance Rankings

- The Brookings Institution ranked the nation's largest cities based on income inequality. Virginia Beach was ranked #96 (#1 = greatest inequality). Criteria: the "95/20 ratio," a figure representing the income at which a household earns more than 95 percent of all other households, divided by the income at which a household earns more than only 20 percent of all other households. *Brookings Institution, "Household Income Inequality, Largest Cities of 97 Large U.S. Metro Areas, 2014-2016," February 5, 2018*

- The Brookings Institution ranked the 100 largest metro areas in the U.S. based on income inequality. Virginia Beach was ranked #91 (#1 = greatest inequality). Criteria: the "95/20 ratio," a figure representing the income at which a household earns more than 95 percent of all other households, divided by the income at which a household earns more than only 20 percent of all other households. *Brookings Institution, "Household Income Inequality, 100 Largest U.S. Metro Areas, 2014-2016," February 5, 2018*

- Virginia Beach was identified as one of America's most frugal metro areas by *Coupons.com*. The city ranked #13 out of 25. Criteria: digital coupon usage. *Coupons.com, "America's Most Frugal Cities of 2017," March 22, 2018*

- The Virginia Beach metro area appeared on the Milken Institute "2022 Best Performing Cities" list. Rank: #140 out of 200 large metro areas (population over 250,000). Criteria: job growth; wage and salary growth; high-tech output growth; housing affordability; household broadband access. *Milken Institute, "Best-Performing Cities 2022," March 28, 2022*

- *Forbes* ranked the 200 most populous metro areas to determine the nation's "Best Places for Business and Careers." The Virginia Beach metro area was ranked #79. Criteria: costs (business and living); job growth (past and projected); income growth; quality of life; educational attainment (college and high school); projected economic growth; cultural and leisure opportunities; workplace tolerance laws; net migration patterns. *Forbes, "The Best Places for Business and Careers 2019: Seattle Still On Top," October 30, 2019*

Dating/Romance Rankings

- Virginia Beach was ranked #25 out of 25 cities that stood out for inspiring romance and attracting diners on the website OpenTable.com. Criteria: percentage of people who dined out on Valentine's Day in 2018; percentage of romantic restaurants as rated by OpenTable diner reviews; and percentage of tables seated for two. *OpenTable, "25 Most Romantic Cities in America for 2019," February 7, 2019*

Education Rankings

- Personal finance website *WalletHub* analyzed the 150 largest U.S. metropolitan statistical areas to determine where the most educated Americans are putting their degrees to work. Criteria: education levels; percentage of workers with degrees; education quality and attainment gap; public school quality rankings; quality and enrollment of each metro area's universities. Virginia Beach was ranked #42 (#1 = most educated city). *www.WalletHub.com, "Most & Least Educated Cities in America," July 18, 2022*

- Virginia Beach was selected as one of America's most literate cities. The city ranked #46 out of the 84 largest U.S. cities. Criteria: number of booksellers; library resources; Internet resources; educational attainment; periodical publishing resources; newspaper circulation. *Central Connecticut State University, "America's Most Literate Cities, 2018," February 2019*

Environmental Rankings

- Virginia Beach was highlighted as one of the cleanest metro areas for ozone air pollution in the U.S. during 2019 through 2021. The list represents cities with no monitored ozone air pollution in unhealthful ranges. *American Lung Association, "State of the Air 2023," April 19, 2023*

- Virginia Beach was highlighted as one of the top 59 cleanest metro areas for short-term particle pollution (24-hour PM 2.5) in the U.S. during 2019 through 2021. Monitors in these cities reported no days with unhealthful PM 2.5 levels. *American Lung Association, "State of the Air 2023," April 19, 2023*

Health/Fitness Rankings

- For each of the 100 largest cities in the United States, the American Fitness Index®, compiled in partnership between the American College of Sports Medicine and the Elevance Health Foundation, evaluated community infrastructure and 34 health behaviors including preventive health, levels of chronic disease conditions, food insecurity, sleep quality, pedestrian safety, air quality, and community/environment resources that support physical activity. Virginia Beach ranked #43 for "community fitness." *americanfitnessindex.org, "2022 ACSM American Fitness Index Summary Report," July 12, 2022*

- Virginia Beach was identified as a "2022 Spring Allergy Capital." The area ranked #56 out of 100. Three groups of factors were used to identify the most challenging cities for people with allergies during the spring season: annual spring pollen scores; over the counter allergy medicine use; number of board-certified allergy specialists. *Asthma and Allergy Foundation of America, "Spring Allergy Capitals 2022," March 2, 2022*

- Virginia Beach was identified as a "2022 Fall Allergy Capital." The area ranked #55 out of 100. Three groups of factors were used to identify the most challenging cities for people with allergies during the fall season: annual fall pollen scores; over the counter allergy medicine use; number of board-certified allergy specialists. *Asthma and Allergy Foundation of America, "Fall Allergy Capitals 2022," March 2, 2022*

- Virginia Beach was identified as a "2022 Asthma Capital." The area ranked #67 out of the nation's 100 largest metropolitan areas. Criteria: estimated asthma prevalence; asthma-related mortality; and ER visits due to asthma. Risk factors analyzed but not factored in the rankings: annual pollen score; annual air quality; public smoking laws; access to board-certified asthma specialists; rescue and controller medication use; uninsured rate; poverty rate. *Asthma and Allergy Foundation of America, "Asthma Capitals 2022: The Most Challenging Places to Live With Asthma," September 14, 2022*

Real Estate Rankings

- *WalletHub* compared the most populated U.S. cities to determine which had the best markets for real estate agents. Virginia Beach ranked #29 where demand was high and pay was the best. Criteria: sales per agent; annual median wage for real-estate agents; monthly average starting salary for real estate agents; real estate job density and competition; unemployment rate; home turnover rate; housing-market health index; and other relevant metrics. *www.WalletHub.com, "2021 Best Places to Be a Real Estate Agent," May 12, 2021*

- The Virginia Beach metro area was identified as one of the 10 worst condo markets in the U.S. in 2022. The area ranked #59 out of 63 markets. Criteria: year-over-year change of median sales price of existing apartment condo-coop homes between the 4th quarter of 2021 and the 4th quarter of 2022. *National Association of Realtors®, Median Sales Price of Existing Apartment Condo-Coops Homes for Metropolitan Areas, 4th Quarter 2022*

- Virginia Beach was ranked #66 out of 235 metro areas in terms of housing affordability in 2022 by the National Association of Home Builders (#1 = most affordable). Criteria: the share of homes sold in that area affordable to a family earning the local median income, based on standard mortgage underwriting criteria. *National Association of Home Builders®, NAHB-Wells Fargo Housing Opportunity Index, 4th Quarter 2022*

Safety Rankings

- Allstate ranked the 200 largest cities in America in terms of driver safety. Virginia Beach ranked #66. Criteria: internal property damage claims over a two-year period from January 2016 to December 2017. The report helps increase the importance of safety and awareness behind the wheel. *Allstate, "Allstate America's Best Drivers Report, 2019" June 24, 2019*

Seniors/Retirement Rankings

- Virginia Beach made *Southern Living's* list of southern places—by the beach, in the mountains, river or college town—to retire. From the incredible views and close knit communities, to the opportunities to put down new roots, and great places to eat and hike, these superb places are perfect for settling down. *Southern Living, "The Best Places to Retire in the South," March 7, 2022*

- From its Best Cities for Successful Aging indexes, the Milken Institute generated rankings for metropolitan areas, weighing data in nine categories—health care, wellness, living arrangements, transportation and convenience, financial characteristics, education, employment, community engagement, and overall livability. The Virginia Beach metro area was ranked #61 overall in the large metro area category. *Milken Institute, "Best Cities for Successful Aging, 2017" March 14, 2017*

- Virginia Beach made the 2022 *Forbes* list of "25 Best Places to Retire." Criteria, focused on overall affordability as well as quality of life indicators, include: housing/living costs compared to the national average and state taxes; air quality; crime rates; home price appreciation; risk associated with climate-change/natural hazards; availability of medical care; bikeability; walkability; healthy living. *Forbes.com, "The Best Places to Retire in 2022," May 13, 2022*

Women/Minorities Rankings

- *Women's Health*, together with the site Yelp, identified the 15 "Wellthiest" spots in the U.S. Virginia Beach appeared among the top for happiest, healthiest, outdoorsiest and Zen-iest. *Women's Health, "The 15 Wellthiest Cities in the U.S." July 5, 2017*

- Personal finance website *WalletHub* compared more than 180 U.S. cities across two key dimensions, "Hispanic Business-Friendliness" and "Hispanic Purchasing Power," to arrive at the most favorable conditions for Hispanic entrepreneurs. Virginia Beach was ranked #96 out of 182. Criteria includes: share of Hispanic-Owned Businesses; Hispanic entrepreneurship rate to median annual income of Hispanics; Small Business-Friendliness score; cost of living; and number of Hispanics with at least a bachelor's degree. *WalletHub.com, "2019's Best Cities for Hispanic Entrepreneurs," May 1, 2019*

Miscellaneous Rankings

- The financial planning site SmartAsset has compiled its annual study on the best places for Halloween in the U.S. for 2022. 146 cities were compared to determine that Virginia Beach ranked #15 out of 35 for still being able to enjoy the festivities despite COVID-19. Metrics included: safety, family-friendliness, percentage of children in the population, concentration of candy and costume shops, weather and COVID infection rates. *www.smartasset.com, "2022 Edition-Best Places to Celebrate Halloween," October 19, 2022*

- *WalletHub* compared the 150 most populated U.S. cities to determine their operating efficiency. A "Quality of Services" score was constructed for each city and then divided by the total budget per capita to reveal which were managed the best. Virginia Beach ranked #11. Criteria: financial stability; economy; education; safety; health; infrastructure and pollution. *www.WalletHub.com, "2022's Best- & Worst-Run Cities in America," June 21, 2022*

Business Environment

DEMOGRAPHICS

Population Growth

Area	1990 Census	2000 Census	2010 Census	2020 Census	Population Growth (%)	
					1990-2020	2010-2020
City	393,069	425,257	437,994	459,470	16.9	4.9
MSA[1]	1,449,389	1,576,370	1,671,683	1,799,674	24.2	7.7
U.S.	248,709,873	281,421,906	308,745,538	331,449,281	33.3	7.4

Note: (1) Figures cover the Virginia Beach-Norfolk-Newport News, VA-NC Metropolitan Statistical Area
Source: U.S. Census Bureau, 1990 Census, 2000 Census, 2010 Census, 2020 Census

Race

Area	White Alone[2] (%)	Black Alone[2] (%)	Asian Alone[2] (%)	AIAN[3] Alone[2] (%)	NHOPI[4] Alone[2] (%)	Other Race Alone[2] (%)	Two or More Races (%)
City	60.7	18.6	7.5	0.4	0.2	3.0	9.6
MSA[1]	54.0	30.3	4.1	0.4	0.2	2.9	8.1
U.S.	61.6	12.4	6.0	1.1	0.2	8.4	10.2

Note: (1) Figures cover the Virginia Beach-Norfolk-Newport News, VA-NC Metropolitan Statistical Area;
(2) Alone is defined as not being in combination with one or more other races; (3) American Indian and Alaska Native; (4) Native Hawaiian and Other Pacific Islander
Source: U.S. Census Bureau, 2020 Census

Hispanic or Latino Origin

Area	Total (%)	Mexican (%)	Puerto Rican (%)	Cuban (%)	Other (%)
City	8.6	2.7	2.2	0.3	3.4
MSA[1]	7.2	2.4	1.9	0.3	2.5
U.S.	18.4	11.2	1.8	0.7	4.7

Note: Persons of Hispanic or Latino origin can be of any race; (1) Figures cover the Virginia Beach-Norfolk-Newport News, VA-NC Metropolitan Statistical Area
Source: U.S. Census Bureau, 2017-2021 American Community Survey 5-Year Estimates

Age

Area	Percent of Population									Median Age
	Under Age 5	Age 5–19	Age 20–34	Age 35–44	Age 45–54	Age 55–64	Age 65–74	Age 75–84	Age 85+	
City	5.8	18.6	22.4	13.3	11.8	12.9	9.1	4.4	1.7	37.1
MSA[1]	5.8	18.8	22.2	12.5	11.5	13.4	9.5	4.6	1.7	37.3
U.S.	5.6	19.2	20.2	12.7	12.4	13.1	10.0	4.9	1.9	38.8

Note: (1) Figures cover the Virginia Beach-Norfolk-Newport News, VA-NC Metropolitan Statistical Area
Source: U.S. Census Bureau, 2020 Census

Disability by Age

Area	All Ages	Under 18 Years Old	18 to 64 Years Old	65 Years and Over
City	11.5	4.3	9.4	31.3
MSA[1]	13.3	5.3	11.3	33.7
U.S.	12.6	4.4	10.3	33.4

Note: Figures show percent of the civilian noninstitutionalized population that reported having a disability. Disability status is determined from six types of difficulty: vision, hearing, cognitive, ambulatory, self-care, and independent living. For children under 5 years old, hearing and vision difficulty are used to determine disability status. For children between the ages of 5 and 14, disability status is determined from hearing, vision, cognitive, ambulatory, and self-care difficulties. For people aged 15 years and older, they are considered to have a disability if they have difficulty with any one of the six difficulty types; Note: (1) Figures cover the Virginia Beach-Norfolk-Newport News, VA-NC Metropolitan Statistical Area
Source: U.S. Census Bureau, 2017-2021 American Community Survey 5-Year Estimates

Ancestry

Area	German	Irish	English	American	Italian	Polish	French[2]	Scottish	Dutch
City	11.3	10.7	10.1	7.8	5.6	2.1	2.2	2.2	0.8
MSA[1]	9.5	8.8	9.8	8.5	4.0	1.7	1.8	1.7	0.7
U.S.	12.8	9.6	8.1	5.7	5.0	2.7	2.2	1.6	1.1

Note: Figures are the percentage of the total population reporting a particular ancestry. The nine most commonly reported ancestries in the U.S. are shown. Figures include multiple ancestries (e.g. if a person reported being Irish and Italian, they were included in both columns); (1) Figures cover the Virginia Beach-Norfolk-Newport News, VA-NC Metropolitan Statistical Area; (2) Excludes Basque
Source: U.S. Census Bureau, 2017-2021 American Community Survey 5-Year Estimates

Foreign-born Population

Area	Any Foreign Country	Asia	Mexico	Europe	Caribbean	Central America[2]	South America	Africa	Canada
City	9.3	4.9	0.4	1.4	0.5	0.6	0.8	0.4	0.2
MSA[1]	6.6	2.8	0.4	1.1	0.6	0.7	0.4	0.4	0.1
U.S.	13.6	4.2	3.3	1.5	1.4	1.1	1.1	0.8	0.2

Note: (1) Figures cover the Virginia Beach-Norfolk-Newport News, VA-NC Metropolitan Statistical Area; (2) Excludes Mexico.
Source: U.S. Census Bureau, 2017-2021 American Community Survey 5-Year Estimates

Household Size

Area	One	Two	Three	Four	Five	Six	Seven or More	Average Household Size
City	24.5	35.6	17.6	13.8	6.0	1.8	0.7	2.50
MSA[1]	27.8	34.5	16.9	12.6	5.5	1.9	0.9	2.50
U.S.	28.1	33.8	15.5	12.9	6.0	2.3	1.4	2.60

Note: (1) Figures cover the Virginia Beach-Norfolk-Newport News, VA-NC Metropolitan Statistical Area
Source: U.S. Census Bureau, 2017-2021 American Community Survey 5-Year Estimates

Household Relationships

Area	House-holder	Opposite-sex Spouse	Same-sex Spouse	Opposite-sex Unmarried Partner	Same-sex Unmarried Partner	Child[2]	Grand-child	Other Relatives	Non-relatives
City	38.8	18.6	0.2	2.4	0.1	28.7	2.2	4.0	3.5
MSA[1]	39.0	17.4	0.2	2.3	0.1	27.7	2.5	4.0	3.3
U.S.	38.3	17.5	0.2	2.5	0.2	28.3	2.4	4.8	3.4

Note: Figures are percent of the total population; (1) Figures cover the Virginia Beach-Norfolk-Newport News, VA-NC Metropolitan Statistical Area; (2) Includes biological, adopted, and stepchildren of the householder
Source: U.S. Census Bureau, 2020 Census

Gender

Area	Males	Females	Males per 100 Females
City	224,059	235,411	95.2
MSA[1]	879,439	920,235	95.6
U.S.	162,685,811	168,763,470	96.4

Note: (1) Figures cover the Virginia Beach-Norfolk-Newport News, VA-NC Metropolitan Statistical Area
Source: U.S. Census Bureau, 2020 Census

Marital Status

Area	Never Married	Now Married[2]	Separated	Widowed	Divorced
City	30.9	50.8	2.1	5.1	11.2
MSA[1]	33.6	47.7	2.4	5.5	10.8
U.S.	33.8	48.0	1.8	5.6	10.8

Note: Figures are percentages and cover the population 15 years of age and older; (1) Figures cover the Virginia Beach-Norfolk-Newport News, VA-NC Metropolitan Statistical Area; (2) Excludes separated
Source: U.S. Census Bureau, 2017-2021 American Community Survey 5-Year Estimates

Religious Groups by Family

Area	Catholic	Baptist	Methodist	LDS[2]	Pentecostal	Lutheran	Islam	Adventist	Other
MSA[1]	8.3	9.5	4.8	0.7	2.0	0.5	1.0	0.9	16.1
U.S.	18.7	7.3	3.0	2.0	1.8	1.7	1.3	1.3	11.6

Note: Figures are the number of adherents as a percentage of the total population and cover the eight largest religious groups in the U.S; (1) Figures cover the Virginia Beach-Norfolk-Newport News, VA-NC Metropolitan Statistical Area; (2) Church of Jesus Christ of Latter-day Saints
Sources: 2020 U.S. Religion Census, Association of Statisticians of American Religious Bodies; The Association of Religion Data Archives (ARDA)

Religious Groups by Tradition

Area	Catholic	Evangelical Protestant	Mainline Protestant	Black Protestant	Islam	Judaism	Hinduism	Orthodox	Buddhism
MSA[1]	8.3	21.3	6.9	3.7	1.0	0.3	0.2	0.3	0.3
U.S.	18.7	16.5	5.2	2.3	1.3	0.6	0.4	0.4	0.3

Note: Figures are the number of adherents as a percentage of the total population; (1) Figures cover the Virginia Beach-Norfolk-Newport News, VA-NC Metropolitan Statistical Area
Sources: 2020 U.S. Religion Census, Association of Statisticians of American Religious Bodies; The Association of Religion Data Archives (ARDA)

Virginia Beach, Virginia   461

ECONOMY

Gross Metropolitan Product

Area	2020	2021	2022	2023	Rank[2]
MSA[1]	95.3	102.4	109.4	116.0	41

Note: Figures are in billions of dollars; (1) Figures cover the Virginia Beach-Norfolk-Newport News, VA-NC Metropolitan Statistical Area; (2) Rank is based on 2021 data and ranges from 1 to 381
Source: U.S. Conference of Mayors, U.S. Metro Economies: U.S. Metros Compared to Global and State Economies, June 2022

Economic Growth

Area	2018-20 (%)	2021 (%)	2022 (%)	2023 (%)	Rank[2]
MSA[1]	-1.4	3.5	1.1	2.5	247
U.S.	-0.6	5.7	3.1	2.9	–

Note: Figures are real gross metropolitan product (GMP) growth rates and represent average annual percent change; (1) Figures cover the Virginia Beach-Norfolk-Newport News, VA-NC Metropolitan Statistical Area; (2) Rank is based on 2020 2-year average annual percent change and ranges from 1 to 381
Source: U.S. Conference of Mayors, U.S. Metro Economies: U.S. Metros Compared to Global and State Economies, June 2022

Metropolitan Area Exports

Area	2016	2017	2018	2019	2020	2021	Rank[2]
MSA[1]	3,291.1	3,307.2	3,950.6	3,642.4	4,284.3	4,566.3	65

Note: Figures are in millions of dollars; (1) Figures cover the Virginia Beach-Norfolk-Newport News, VA-NC Metropolitan Statistical Area; (2) Rank is based on 2021 data and ranges from 1 to 388
Source: U.S. Department of Commerce, International Trade Administration, Office of Trade and Economic Analysis, Industry and Analysis, Exports by Metropolitan Area, data extracted March 16, 2023

Building Permits

Area	Single-Family			Multi-Family			Total		
	2021	2022	Pct. Chg.	2021	2022	Pct. Chg.	2021	2022	Pct. Chg.
City	335	231	-31.0	128	966	654.7	463	1,197	158.5
MSA[1]	4,712	3,680	-21.9	2,665	2,633	-1.2	7,377	6,313	-14.4
U.S.	1,115,400	975,600	-12.5	621,600	689,500	10.9	1,737,000	1,665,100	-4.1

Note: (1) Figures cover the Virginia Beach-Norfolk-Newport News, VA-NC Metropolitan Statistical Area; Figures represent new, privately-owned housing units authorized (unadjusted data); All permit data are based on estimates with imputation
Source: U.S. Census Bureau, Manufacturing, Mining, and Construction Statistics, Building Permits, 2021, 2022

Bankruptcy Filings

Area	Business Filings			Nonbusiness Filings		
	2021	2022	% Chg.	2021	2022	% Chg.
Virginia Beach city	11	15	36.4	788	711	-9.8
U.S.	14,347	13,481	-6.0	399,269	374,240	-6.3

Note: Business filings include Chapter 7, Chapter 9, Chapter 11, Chapter 12, Chapter 13, Chapter 15, and Section 304; Nonbusiness filings include Chapter 7, Chapter 11, and Chapter 13
Source: Administrative Office of the U.S. Courts, Business and Nonbusiness Bankruptcy, County Cases Commenced by Chapter of the Bankruptcy Code, During the 12-Month Period Ending December 31, 2021 and Business and Nonbusiness Bankruptcy, County Cases Commenced by Chapter of the Bankruptcy Code, During the 12-Month Period Ending December 31, 2022

Housing Vacancy Rates

Area	Gross Vacancy Rate[2] (%)			Year-Round Vacancy Rate[3] (%)			Rental Vacancy Rate[4] (%)			Homeowner Vacancy Rate[5] (%)		
	2020	2021	2022	2020	2021	2022	2020	2021	2022	2020	2021	2022
MSA[1]	7.9	7.7	8.1	7.0	6.9	7.3	5.5	5.5	6.3	0.6	0.6	1.0
U.S.	10.6	10.8	10.5	8.2	8.4	8.2	6.3	6.1	5.8	1.0	0.9	0.8

Note: (1) Figures cover the Virginia Beach-Norfolk-Newport News, VA-NC Metropolitan Statistical Area; (2) The percentage of the total housing inventory that is vacant; (3) The percentage of the housing inventory (excluding seasonal units) that is year-round vacant; (4) The percentage of rental inventory that is vacant for rent; (5) The percentage of homeowner inventory that is vacant for sale
Source: U.S. Census Bureau, Housing Vacancies and Homeownership Annual Statistics: 2020, 2021, 2022

INCOME

Income

Area	Per Capita ($)	Median Household ($)	Average Household ($)
City	41,803	81,810	105,521
MSA[1]	37,548	71,612	93,415
U.S.	37,638	69,021	97,196

Note: (1) Figures cover the Virginia Beach-Norfolk-Newport News, VA-NC Metropolitan Statistical Area
Source: U.S. Census Bureau, 2017-2021 American Community Survey 5-Year Estimates

Household Income Distribution

Area	Percent of Households Earning							
	Under $15,000	$15,000 -$24,999	$25,000 -$34,999	$35,000 -$49,999	$50,000 -$74,999	$75,000 -$99,999	$100,000 -$149,999	$150,000 and up
City	5.6	4.5	6.3	10.5	18.8	14.6	20.9	18.8
MSA[1]	8.0	7.0	7.6	11.3	18.3	13.9	18.4	15.5
U.S.	9.4	7.8	8.2	11.4	16.8	12.8	16.3	17.3

Note: (1) Figures cover the Virginia Beach-Norfolk-Newport News, VA-NC Metropolitan Statistical Area
Source: U.S. Census Bureau, 2017-2021 American Community Survey 5-Year Estimates

Poverty Rate

Area	All Ages	Under 18 Years Old	18 to 64 Years Old	65 Years and Over
City	7.8	10.5	7.6	4.8
MSA[1]	10.9	16.1	9.8	7.6
U.S.	12.6	17.0	11.8	9.6

Note: Figures are percentage of people whose income during the past 12 months was below the poverty level;
(1) Figures cover the Virginia Beach-Norfolk-Newport News, VA-NC Metropolitan Statistical Area
Source: U.S. Census Bureau, 2017-2021 American Community Survey 5-Year Estimates

EMPLOYMENT

Labor Force and Employment

Area	Civilian Labor Force			Workers Employed		
	Dec. 2021	Dec. 2022	% Chg.	Dec. 2021	Dec. 2022	% Chg.
City	222,270	227,788	2.5	216,500	221,941	2.5
MSA[1]	821,309	840,432	2.3	795,009	815,342	2.6
U.S.	161,696,000	164,224,000	1.6	155,732,000	158,872,000	2.0

Note: Data is not seasonally adjusted and covers workers 16 years of age and older; (1) Figures cover the Virginia Beach-Norfolk-Newport News, VA-NC Metropolitan Statistical Area
Source: Bureau of Labor Statistics, Local Area Unemployment Statistics

Unemployment Rate

Area	2022											
	Jan.	Feb.	Mar.	Apr.	May	Jun.	Jul.	Aug.	Sep.	Oct.	Nov.	Dec.
City	3.2	2.7	2.6	2.4	2.9	2.9	2.8	3.0	2.5	2.7	2.9	2.6
MSA[1]	3.9	3.4	3.1	3.0	3.4	3.4	3.3	3.6	3.0	3.2	3.4	3.0
U.S.	4.4	4.1	3.8	3.3	3.4	3.8	3.8	3.8	3.3	3.4	3.4	3.3

Note: Data is not seasonally adjusted and covers workers 16 years of age and older; (1) Figures cover the Virginia Beach-Norfolk-Newport News, VA-NC Metropolitan Statistical Area
Source: Bureau of Labor Statistics, Local Area Unemployment Statistics

Average Wages

Occupation	$/Hr.	Occupation	$/Hr.
Accountants and Auditors	36.48	Maintenance and Repair Workers	21.28
Automotive Mechanics	23.14	Marketing Managers	70.40
Bookkeepers	20.67	Network and Computer Systems Admin.	44.66
Carpenters	23.04	Nurses, Licensed Practical	24.37
Cashiers	12.50	Nurses, Registered	38.20
Computer Programmers	45.16	Nursing Assistants	15.13
Computer Systems Analysts	49.26	Office Clerks, General	18.11
Computer User Support Specialists	26.21	Physical Therapists	45.34
Construction Laborers	17.52	Physicians	n/a
Cooks, Restaurant	14.70	Plumbers, Pipefitters and Steamfitters	26.56
Customer Service Representatives	17.30	Police and Sheriff's Patrol Officers	27.70
Dentists	78.65	Postal Service Mail Carriers	26.24
Electricians	27.29	Real Estate Sales Agents	33.80
Engineers, Electrical	47.22	Retail Salespersons	15.11
Fast Food and Counter Workers	12.47	Sales Representatives, Technical/Scientific	45.63
Financial Managers	72.27	Secretaries, Exc. Legal/Medical/Executive	20.00
First-Line Supervisors of Office Workers	28.99	Security Guards	16.42
General and Operations Managers	54.70	Surgeons	n/a
Hairdressers/Cosmetologists	17.34	Teacher Assistants, Exc. Postsecondary*	16.04
Home Health and Personal Care Aides	12.57	Teachers, Secondary School, Exc. Sp. Ed.*	31.98
Janitors and Cleaners	14.20	Telemarketers	17.71
Landscaping/Groundskeeping Workers	16.35	Truck Drivers, Heavy/Tractor-Trailer	23.13
Lawyers	61.10	Truck Drivers, Light/Delivery Services	19.47
Maids and Housekeeping Cleaners	13.16	Waiters and Waitresses	15.39

Note: Wage data covers the Virginia Beach-Norfolk-Newport News, VA-NC Metropolitan Statistical Area;
(*) Hourly wages were calculated from annual wage data based on a 40 hour work week; n/a not available.
Source: Bureau of Labor Statistics, Metro Area Occupational Employment & Wage Estimates, May 2022

Employment by Industry

Sector	MSA[1]		U.S.
	Number of Employees	Percent of Total	Percent of Total
Construction, Mining, and Logging	41,500	5.2	5.4
Private Education and Health Services	117,500	14.8	16.1
Financial Activities	39,900	5.0	5.9
Government	156,500	19.7	14.5
Information	9,200	1.2	2.0
Leisure and Hospitality	88,100	11.1	10.3
Manufacturing	58,700	7.4	8.4
Other Services	33,500	4.2	3.7
Professional and Business Services	116,800	14.7	14.7
Retail Trade	82,900	10.4	10.2
Transportation, Warehousing, and Utilities	31,700	4.0	4.9
Wholesale Trade	19,200	2.4	3.9

Note: Figures are non-farm employment as of December 2022. Figures are not seasonally adjusted and include workers 16 years of age and older; (1) Figures cover the Virginia Beach-Norfolk-Newport News, VA-NC Metropolitan Statistical Area
Source: Bureau of Labor Statistics, Current Employment Statistics, Employment, Hours, and Earnings

Employment by Occupation

Occupation Classification	City (%)	MSA[1] (%)	U.S. (%)
Management, Business, Science, and Arts	44.0	40.7	40.3
Natural Resources, Construction, and Maintenance	7.9	9.0	8.7
Production, Transportation, and Material Moving	9.5	11.7	13.1
Sales and Office	21.7	21.0	20.9
Service	16.8	17.6	17.0

Note: Figures cover employed civilians 16 years of age and older; (1) Figures cover the Virginia Beach-Norfolk-Newport News, VA-NC Metropolitan Statistical Area
Source: U.S. Census Bureau, 2017-2021 American Community Survey 5-Year Estimates

Occupations with Greatest Projected Employment Growth: 2022 – 2024

Occupation[1]	2022 Employment	2024 Projected Employment	Numeric Employment Change	Percent Employment Change
Software Developers and Software Quality Assurance Analysts and Testers	86,590	90,990	4,400	5.1
Laborers and Freight, Stock, and Material Movers, Hand	65,350	68,080	2,730	4.2
Management Analysts	64,340	67,000	2,660	4.1
Stockers and Order Fillers	55,280	57,410	2,130	3.9
Cooks, Restaurant	29,990	31,930	1,940	6.5
Janitors and Cleaners, Except Maids and Housekeeping Cleaners	63,330	64,950	1,620	2.6
Retail Salespersons	101,360	102,940	1,580	1.6
Home Health and Personal Care Aides	54,320	55,870	1,550	2.9
General and Operations Managers	53,920	55,420	1,500	2.8
Accountants and Auditors	46,230	47,600	1,370	3.0

Note: Projections cover Virginia; (1) Sorted by numeric employment change
Source: www.projectionscentral.com, State Occupational Projections, 2022–2024 Short-Term Projections

Fastest-Growing Occupations: 2022 – 2024

Occupation[1]	2022 Employment	2024 Projected Employment	Numeric Employment Change	Percent Employment Change
Travel Agents	1,150	1,310	160	13.9
Nurse Practitioners	5,040	5,620	580	11.5
Ushers, Lobby Attendants, and Ticket Takers	1,740	1,920	180	10.3
Statisticians	1,360	1,480	120	8.8
Economists	1,430	1,550	120	8.4
Information Security Analysts (SOC 2018)	15,400	16,610	1,210	7.9
Medical Scientists, Except Epidemiologists	2,060	2,200	140	6.8
Physician Assistants	2,660	2,840	180	6.8
Fitness Trainers and Aerobics Instructors	14,290	15,250	960	6.7
Cooks, Restaurant	29,990	31,930	1,940	6.5

Note: Projections cover Virginia; (1) Sorted by percent employment change and excludes occupations with numeric employment change less than 50
Source: www.projectionscentral.com, State Occupational Projections, 2022–2024 Short-Term Projections

CITY FINANCES

City Government Finances

Component	2020 ($000)	2020 ($ per capita)
Total Revenues	2,102,090	4,672
Total Expenditures	2,168,639	4,819
Debt Outstanding	1,551,504	3,448
Cash and Securities[1]	1,141,637	2,537

Note: (1) Cash and security holdings of a government at the close of its fiscal year, including those of its dependent agencies, utilities, and liquor stores.
Source: U.S. Census Bureau, State & Local Government Finances 2020

City Government Revenue by Source

Source	2020 ($000)	2020 ($ per capita)	2020 (%)
General Revenue			
From Federal Government	114,270	254	5.4
From State Government	622,945	1,384	29.6
From Local Governments	22,849	51	1.1
Taxes			
Property	715,847	1,591	34.1
Sales and Gross Receipts	224,042	498	10.7
Personal Income	0	0	0.0
Corporate Income	0	0	0.0
Motor Vehicle License	10,015	22	0.5
Other Taxes	71,073	158	3.4
Current Charges	199,838	444	9.5
Liquor Store	0	0	0.0
Utility	90,081	200	4.3

Source: U.S. Census Bureau, State & Local Government Finances 2020

City Government Expenditures by Function

Function	2020 ($000)	2020 ($ per capita)	2020 (%)
General Direct Expenditures			
Air Transportation	0	0	0.0
Corrections	58,092	129	2.7
Education	910,188	2,022	42.0
Employment Security Administration	0	0	0.0
Financial Administration	21,844	48	1.0
Fire Protection	48,922	108	2.3
General Public Buildings	69,707	154	3.2
Governmental Administration, Other	43,796	97	2.0
Health	64,513	143	3.0
Highways	133,418	296	6.2
Hospitals	0	0	0.0
Housing and Community Development	36,066	80	1.7
Interest on General Debt	46,063	102	2.1
Judicial and Legal	20,486	45	0.9
Libraries	18,032	40	0.8
Parking	6,591	14	0.3
Parks and Recreation	156,661	348	7.2
Police Protection	87,195	193	4.0
Public Welfare	55,190	122	2.5
Sewerage	122,713	272	5.7
Solid Waste Management	34,322	76	1.6
Veterans' Services	0	0	0.0
Liquor Store	0	0	0.0
Utility	80,606	179	3.7

Source: U.S. Census Bureau, State & Local Government Finances 2020

TAXES

State Corporate Income Tax Rates

State	Tax Rate (%)	Income Brackets ($)	Num. of Brackets	Financial Institution Tax Rate (%)[a]	Federal Income Tax Ded.
Virginia	6.0	Flat rate	1	6.0	No

Note: Tax rates as of January 1, 2023; (a) Rates listed are the corporate income tax rate applied to financial institutions or excise taxes based on income. Some states have other taxes based upon the value of deposits or shares.
Source: Federation of Tax Administrators, State Corporate Income Tax Rates, January 1, 2023

State Individual Income Tax Rates

State	Tax Rate (%)	Income Brackets ($)	Personal Exemptions ($)			Standard Ded. ($)	
			Single	Married	Depend.	Single	Married
Virginia	2.0 - 5.75	3,000 - 17,001	930	1,860	930	7,500	15,000

Note: Tax rates as of January 1, 2023; Local- and county-level taxes are not included; Federal income tax is not deductible on state income tax returns
Source: Federation of Tax Administrators, State Individual Income Tax Rates, January 1, 2023

Various State Sales and Excise Tax Rates

State	State Sales Tax (%)	Gasoline[1] ($/gal.)	Cigarette[2] ($/pack)	Spirits[3] ($/gal.)	Wine[4] ($/gal.)	Beer[5] ($/gal.)	Recreational Marijuana (%)
Virginia	5.3	0.362	0.60	22.06	1.51	0.26	(s)

Note: All tax rates as of January 1, 2023; (1) The American Petroleum Institute has developed a methodology for determining the average tax rate on a gallon of fuel. Rates may include any of the following: excise taxes, environmental fees, storage tank fees, other fees or taxes, general sales tax, and local taxes; (2) The federal excise tax of $1.0066 per pack and local taxes are not included; (3) Rates are those applicable to off-premise sales of 40% alcohol by volume (a.b.v.) distilled spirits in 750ml containers. Local excise taxes are excluded; (4) Rates are those applicable to off-premise sales of 11% a.b.v. non-carbonated wine in 750ml containers; (5) Rates are those applicable to off-premise sales of 4.7% a.b.v. beer in 12 ounce containers; (s) 21% excise tax (retail price)
Source: Tax Foundation, 2023 Facts & Figures: How Does Your State Compare?

State Business Tax Climate Index Rankings

State	Overall Rank	Corporate Tax Rank	Individual Income Tax Rank	Sales Tax Rank	Property Tax Rank	Unemployment Insurance Tax Rank
Virginia	26	17	34	12	29	39

Note: The index is a measure of how each state's tax laws affect economic performance. The lower the rank, the more favorable a state's tax system is for business. States without a given tax are given a ranking of 1. The scores/rankings for the District of Columbia do not affect other states. The 2023 index represents the tax climate as of July 1, 2022.
Source: Tax Foundation, State Business Tax Climate Index 2023

TRANSPORTATION

Means of Transportation to Work

Area	Car/Truck/Van		Public Transportation			Bicycle	Walked	Other Means	Worked at Home
	Drove Alone	Car-pooled	Bus	Subway	Railroad				
City	79.1	7.6	0.7	0.0	0.0	0.4	2.1	1.6	8.4
MSA[1]	78.3	7.9	1.3	0.0	0.0	0.3	3.1	1.6	7.5
U.S.	73.2	8.6	2.0	1.6	0.5	0.5	2.5	1.5	9.7

Note: Figures are percentages and cover workers 16 years of age and older; (1) Figures cover the Virginia Beach-Norfolk-Newport News, VA-NC Metropolitan Statistical Area
Source: U.S. Census Bureau, 2017-2021 American Community Survey 5-Year Estimates

Travel Time to Work

Area	Less Than 10 Minutes	10 to 19 Minutes	20 to 29 Minutes	30 to 44 Minutes	45 to 59 Minutes	60 to 89 Minutes	90 Minutes or More
City	10.1	30.9	27.9	22.0	5.3	2.5	1.4
MSA[1]	11.1	31.1	23.5	21.4	7.1	4.0	1.7
U.S.	12.4	28.5	21.0	20.9	8.2	6.2	2.9

Note: Note: Figures are percentages and include workers 16 years old and over; (1) Figures cover the Virginia Beach-Norfolk-Newport News, VA-NC Metropolitan Statistical Area
Source: U.S. Census Bureau, 2017-2021 American Community Survey 5-Year Estimates

Key Congestion Measures

Measure	1990	2000	2010	2015	2020
Annual Hours of Delay, Total (000)	14,617	29,281	36,000	39,492	19,220
Annual Hours of Delay, Per Auto Commuter	24	39	38	44	22
Annual Congestion Cost, Per Auto Commuter ($)	524	788	771	781	399

Note: Covers the Virginia Beach VA urban area
Source: Texas A&M Transportation Institute, 2021 Urban Mobility Report

Freeway Travel Time Index

Measure	1985	1990	1995	2000	2005	2010	2015	2020
Urban Area Index[1]	1.08	1.10	1.14	1.17	1.18	1.17	1.17	1.06
Urban Area Rank[1,2]	40	47	41	36	41	41	46	75

Note: Freeway Travel Time Index—the ratio of travel time in the peak period to the travel time at free-flow conditions. For example, a value of 1.30 indicates a 20-minute free-flow trip takes 26 minutes in the peak (20 minutes x 1.30 = 26 minutes); (1) Covers the Virginia Beach VA urban area; (2) Rank is based on 101 larger urban areas (#1 = highest travel time index)
Source: Texas A&M Transportation Institute, 2021 Urban Mobility Report

Virginia Beach, Virginia

Public Transportation

Agency Name / Mode of Transportation	Vehicles Operated in Maximum Service[1]	Annual Unlinked Passenger Trips[2] (in thous.)	Annual Passenger Miles[3] (in thous.)
Hampton Roads Transit (HRT)			
Bus (directly operated)	240	5,490.7	25,767.6
Demand Response (purchased transportation)	65	238.9	2,403.6
Demand Response - Taxi	7	6.7	71.7
Demand Response - Transportation Network Company	10	17.4	162.8
Ferryboat (purchased transportation)	2	151.8	112.2
Light Rail (directly operated)	6	545.3	1,855.9
Vanpool (purchased transportation)	19	40.8	1,804.3

Note: (1) Number of revenue vehicles operated by the given mode and type of service to meet the annual maximum service requirement. This is the revenue vehicle count during the peak season of the year; on the week and day that maximum service is provided. Vehicles operated in maximum service (VOMS) exclude atypical days and one-time special events; (2) Number of passengers who boarded public transportation vehicles. Passengers are counted each time they board a vehicle no matter how many vehicles they use to travel from their origin to their destination. (3) Sum of the distances ridden by all passengers during the entire fiscal year.
Source: Federal Transit Administration, National Transit Database, 2021

Air Transportation

Airport Name and Code / Type of Service	Passenger Airlines[1]	Passenger Enplanements	Freight Carriers[2]	Freight (lbs)
Norfolk International (ORF)				
Domestic service (U.S. carriers - 2022)	31	2,064,741	9	24,081,810
International service (U.S. carriers - 2021)	1	148	0	0

Note: (1) Includes all U.S.-based major, minor and commuter airlines that carried at least one passenger during the year; (2) Includes all U.S.-based airlines and freight carriers that transported at least one pound of freight during the year.
Source: Bureau of Transportation Statistics, The Intermodal Transportation Database, Air Carriers: T-100 Domestic Market (U.S. Carriers), 2022; Bureau of Transportation Statistics, The Intermodal Transportation Database, Air Carriers: T-100 International Market (U.S. Carriers), 2021

BUSINESSES

Major Business Headquarters

Company Name	Industry	Rankings	
		Fortune[1]	Forbes[2]
No companies listed	-	-	-

Note: (1) Companies that produce a 10-K are ranked 1 to 500 based on 2021 revenue; (2) All private companies with at least $2 billion in annual revenue through the end of their most current fiscal year are ranked 1 to 246; companies listed are headquartered in the city; dashes indicate no ranking
Source: Fortune, "Fortune 500," 2022; Forbes, "America's Largest Private Companies," 2022

Fastest-Growing Businesses

According to *Inc.*, Virginia Beach is home to one of America's 500 fastest-growing private companies: **Kern Technology Group** (#261). Criteria: must be an independent, privately-held, for-profit, U.S. corporation, proprietorship or partnership as of December 31, 2021; revenues must be at least $100,000 in 2018 and $2 million in 2021; must have four-year operating/sales history. *Inc., "America's 500 Fastest-Growing Private Companies," 2022*

Living Environment

COST OF LIVING

Cost of Living Index

Composite Index	Groceries	Housing	Utilities	Trans-portation	Health Care	Misc. Goods/ Services
95.9	92.3	89.0	104.6	95.4	92.3	101.6

Note: The Cost of Living Index measures regional differences in the cost of consumer goods and services, excluding taxes and non-consumer expenditures, for professional and managerial households in the top income quintile. It is based on more than 50,000 prices covering almost 60 different items for which prices are collected three times a year by chambers of commerce, economic development organizations or university applied economic centers in each participating urban area. The numbers shown should be read as a percentage above or below the national average of 100. For example, a value of 115.4 in the groceries column indicates that grocery prices are 15.4% higher than the national average. Small differences in the index numbers should not be interpreted as significant; Figures cover the Hampton Roads-SE Virginia urban area.
Source: The Council for Community and Economic Research, Cost of Living Index, 2022

Grocery Prices

Area[1]	T-Bone Steak ($/pound)	Frying Chicken ($/pound)	Whole Milk ($/half gal.)	Eggs ($/dozen)	Orange Juice ($/64 oz.)	Coffee ($/11.5 oz.)
City[2]	12.02	1.45	2.24	1.64	3.95	3.93
Avg.	13.81	1.59	2.43	2.25	3.85	4.95
Min.	10.17	0.90	1.51	1.30	2.90	3.46
Max.	19.35	3.30	4.32	4.32	5.31	8.59

*Note: (1) Values for the local area are compared with the average, minimum and maximum values for all 286 areas in the Cost of Living Index; (2) Figures cover the Hampton Roads-SE Virginia urban area; **T-Bone Steak** (price per pound); **Frying Chicken** (price per pound, whole fryer); **Whole Milk** (half gallon carton); **Eggs** (price per dozen, Grade A, large); **Orange Juice** (64 oz. Tropicana or Florida Natural); **Coffee** (11.5 oz. can, vacuum-packed, Maxwell House, Hills Bros, or Folgers).*
Source: The Council for Community and Economic Research, Cost of Living Index, 2022

Housing and Utility Costs

Area[1]	New Home Price ($)	Apartment Rent ($/month)	All Electric ($/month)	Part Electric ($/month)	Other Energy ($/month)	Telephone ($/month)
City[2]	395,804	1,258	-	98.78	95.60	184.73
Avg.	450,913	1,371	176.41	99.93	76.96	190.22
Min.	229,283	546	100.84	31.56	27.15	174.27
Max.	2,434,977	4,569	356.86	249.59	272.24	208.31

*Note: (1) Values for the local area are compared with the average, minimum and maximum values for all 286 areas in the Cost of Living Index; (2) Figures cover the Hampton Roads-SE Virginia urban area; **New Home Price** (2,400 sf living area, 8,000 sf lot, in urban area with full utilities); **Apartment Rent** (950 sf 2 bedroom/1.5 or 2 bath, unfurnished, excluding all utilities except water); **All Electric** (average monthly cost for an all-electric home); **Part Electric** (average monthly cost for a part-electric home); **Other Energy** (average monthly cost for natural gas, fuel oil, coal, wood, and any other forms of energy except electricity); **Telephone** (price includes the base monthly rate plus taxes and fees for three lines of mobile phone service).*
Source: The Council for Community and Economic Research, Cost of Living Index, 2022

Health Care, Transportation, and Other Costs

Area[1]	Doctor ($/visit)	Dentist ($/visit)	Optometrist ($/visit)	Gasoline ($/gallon)	Beauty Salon ($/visit)	Men's Shirt ($)
City[2]	88.07	115.80	111.36	3.72	40.74	32.74
Avg.	124.91	107.77	117.66	3.86	43.31	34.21
Min.	36.61	58.25	51.79	2.90	22.18	13.05
Max.	250.21	162.58	371.96	5.54	85.61	63.54

*Note: (1) Values for the local area are compared with the average, minimum and maximum values for all 286 areas in the Cost of Living Index; (2) Figures cover the Hampton Roads-SE Virginia urban area; **Doctor** (general practitioners routine exam of an established patient); **Dentist** (adult teeth cleaning and periodic oral examination); **Optometrist** (full vision eye exam for established adult patient); **Gasoline** (one gallon regular unleaded, national brand, including all taxes, cash price at self-service pump if available); **Beauty Salon** (woman's shampoo, trim, and blow-dry); **Men's Shirt** (cotton/polyester dress shirt, pinpoint weave, long sleeves).*
Source: The Council for Community and Economic Research, Cost of Living Index, 2022

HOUSING

Homeownership Rate

Area	2015 (%)	2016 (%)	2017 (%)	2018 (%)	2019 (%)	2020 (%)	2021 (%)	2022 (%)
MSA[1]	59.4	59.6	65.3	62.8	63.0	65.8	64.4	61.4
U.S.	63.7	63.4	63.9	64.4	64.6	66.6	65.5	65.8

Note: (1) Figures cover the Virginia Beach-Norfolk-Newport News, VA-NC Metropolitan Statistical Area
Source: U.S. Census Bureau, Housing Vacancies and Homeownership Annual Statistics: 2015-2022

House Price Index (HPI)

Area	National Ranking[2]	Quarterly Change (%)	One-Year Change (%)	Five-Year Change (%)	Since 1991Q1 (%)
MSA[1]	131	0.74	11.17	43.79	243.78
U.S.[3]	—	0.34	8.41	58.44	289.08

Note: The HPI is a weighted repeat sales index. It measures average price changes in repeat sales or refinancings on the same properties. This information is obtained by reviewing repeat mortgage transactions on single-family properties whose mortgages have been purchased or securitized by Fannie Mae or Freddie Mac since January 1975; (1) Figures cover the Virginia Beach-Norfolk-Newport News, VA-NC Metropolitan Statistical Area; (2) Rankings are based on annual percentage change for all metro areas containing at least 15,000 transactions over the last 10 years and ranges from 1 to 257; (3) figures based on a weighted average of Census Division estimates using a seasonally adjusted, purchase-only index; all figures are for the period ending December 31, 2022
Source: Federal Housing Finance Agency, Change in FHFA Metropolitan Area House Price Indexes, 2022Q4

Median Single-Family Home Prices

Area	2020	2021	2022[p]	Percent Change 2021 to 2022
MSA[1]	275.0	285.0	323.9	13.6
U.S. Average	300.2	357.1	392.6	9.9

Note: Figures are median sales prices of existing single-family homes in thousands of dollars; (p) preliminary; (1) Figures cover the Virginia Beach-Norfolk-Newport News, VA-NC Metropolitan Statistical Area
Source: National Association of Realtors, Median Sales Price of Existing Single-Family Homes for Metropolitan Areas, 4th Quarter 2022

Qualifying Income Based on Median Sales Price of Existing Single-Family Homes

Area	With 5% Down ($)	With 10% Down ($)	With 20% Down ($)
MSA[1]	91,371	86,562	76,944
U.S. Average	112,234	106,237	94,513

Note: Figures are preliminary; Qualifying income is based on a mortgage rate of 6.77%. Monthly principal and interest payment is limited to 25% of income; (1) Figures cover the Virginia Beach-Norfolk-Newport News, VA-NC Metropolitan Statistical Area
Source: National Association of Realtors, Qualifying Income Based on Median Sales Price of Existing Single-Family Homes for Metropolitan Areas, 4th Quarter 2022

Home Value

Area	Under $100,000	$100,000 -$199,999	$200,000 -$299,999	$300,000 -$399,999	$400,000 -$499,999	$500,000 -$999,999	$1,000,000 or more	Median ($)
City	3.8	15.6	32.0	21.6	11.7	12.8	2.6	295,900
MSA[1]	6.5	23.8	31.1	18.5	9.8	9.0	1.3	261,800
U.S.	16.2	24.2	20.1	13.6	8.3	13.6	4.1	244,900

Note: Figures are percentages except for median and cover owner-occupied housing units; (1) Figures cover the Virginia Beach-Norfolk-Newport News, VA-NC Metropolitan Statistical Area
Source: U.S. Census Bureau, 2017-2021 American Community Survey 5-Year Estimates

Year Housing Structure Built

Area	2020 or Later	2010 -2019	2000 -2009	1990 -1999	1980 -1989	1970 -1979	1960 -1969	1950 -1959	1940 -1949	Before 1940	Median Year
City	0.1	6.4	11.1	14.1	27.1	20.4	12.4	6.1	1.2	1.1	1983
MSA[1]	0.2	8.0	12.6	14.8	18.4	15.2	11.6	9.3	4.2	5.7	1982
U.S.	0.2	7.3	13.6	13.6	13.2	14.8	10.3	10.0	4.7	12.2	1979

Note: Figures are percentages except for Median Year; Note: (1) Figures cover the Virginia Beach-Norfolk-Newport News, VA-NC Metropolitan Statistical Area
Source: U.S. Census Bureau, 2017-2021 American Community Survey 5-Year Estimates

Gross Monthly Rent

Area	Under $500	$500 -$999	$1,000 -$1,499	$1,500 -$1,999	$2,000 -$2,499	$2,500 -$2,999	$3,000 and up	Median ($)
City	2.3	9.1	45.2	30.5	8.6	2.5	1.8	1,433
MSA[1]	6.1	22.2	42.3	21.1	5.5	1.5	1.3	1,227
U.S.	8.1	30.5	30.8	16.8	7.3	3.1	3.5	1,163

Note: Figures are percentages except for median; Gross rent is the contract rent plus the estimated average monthly cost of utilities (electricity, gas, and water and sewer) and fuels (oil, coal, kerosene, wood, etc.) if these are paid by the renter (or paid for the renter by someone else); (1) Figures cover the Virginia Beach-Norfolk-Newport News, VA-NC Metropolitan Statistical Area
Source: U.S. Census Bureau, 2017-2021 American Community Survey 5-Year Estimates

HEALTH

Health Risk Factors

Category	MSA[1] (%)	U.S. (%)
Adults aged 18–64 who have any kind of health care coverage	92.7	90.9
Adults who reported being in good or better health	84.8	85.2
Adults who have been told they have high blood cholesterol	36.6	35.7
Adults who have been told they have high blood pressure	33.9	32.4
Adults who are current smokers	15.1	14.4
Adults who currently use e-cigarettes	8.3	6.7
Adults who currently use chewing tobacco, snuff, or snus	4.0	3.5
Adults who are heavy drinkers[2]	6.6	6.3
Adults who are binge drinkers[3]	16.1	15.4
Adults who are overweight (BMI 25.0 - 29.9)	33.7	34.4
Adults who are obese (BMI 30.0 - 99.8)	37.4	33.9
Adults who participated in any physical activities in the past month	78.6	76.3

Note: (1) Figures cover the Virginia Beach-Norfolk-Newport News, VA-NC Metropolitan Statistical Area;
(2) Heavy drinkers are classified as adult men having more than 14 drinks per week and adult women having
more than 7 drinks per week; (3) Binge drinkers are classified as males having five or more drinks on one
occasion or females having four or more drinks on one occasion
Source: Centers for Disease Control and Prevention, Behaviorial Risk Factor Surveillance System, SMART:
Selected Metropolitan Area Risk Trends, 2021

Acute and Chronic Health Conditions

Category	MSA[1] (%)	U.S. (%)
Adults who have ever been told they had a heart attack	4.0	4.0
Adults who have ever been told they have angina or coronary heart disease	3.3	3.8
Adults who have ever been told they had a stroke	4.3	3.0
Adults who have ever been told they have asthma	15.6	14.9
Adults who have ever been told they have arthritis	29.2	25.8
Adults who have ever been told they have diabetes[2]	11.6	10.9
Adults who have ever been told they had skin cancer	6.7	6.6
Adults who have ever been told they had any other types of cancer	6.0	7.5
Adults who have ever been told they have COPD	6.6	6.1
Adults who have ever been told they have kidney disease	2.8	3.0
Adults who have ever been told they have a form of depression	19.1	20.5

Note: (1) Figures cover the Virginia Beach-Norfolk-Newport News, VA-NC Metropolitan Statistical Area; (2)
Figures do not include pregnancy-related, borderline, or pre-diabetes
Source: Centers for Disease Control and Prevention, Behaviorial Risk Factor Surveillance System, SMART:
Selected Metropolitan Area Risk Trends, 2021

Health Screening and Vaccination Rates

Category	MSA[1] (%)	U.S. (%)
Adults who have ever been tested for HIV	48.7	34.9
Adults who have had their blood cholesterol checked within the last five years	88.0	85.2
Adults aged 65+ who have had flu shot within the past year	67.5	68.6
Adults aged 65+ who have ever had a pneumonia vaccination	74.4	71.0

Note: (1) Figures cover the Virginia Beach-Norfolk-Newport News, VA-NC Metropolitan Statistical Area.
Source: Centers for Disease Control and Prevention, Behaviorial Risk Factor Surveillance System, SMART:
Selected Metropolitan Area Risk Trends, 2021

Disability Status

Category	MSA[1] (%)	U.S. (%)
Adults who reported being deaf	6.1	7.2
Are you blind or have serious difficulty seeing, even when wearing glasses?	5.1	4.8
Are you limited in any way in any of your usual activities due to arthritis?	13.1	11.1
Do you have difficulty doing errands alone?	6.7	7.0
Do you have difficulty dressing or bathing?	3.8	3.6
Do you have serious difficulty concentrating/remembering/making decisions?	11.7	12.1
Do you have serious difficulty walking or climbing stairs?	13.4	12.8

Note: (1) Figures cover the Virginia Beach-Norfolk-Newport News, VA-NC Metropolitan Statistical Area.
Source: Centers for Disease Control and Prevention, Behaviorial Risk Factor Surveillance System, SMART:
Selected Metropolitan Area Risk Trends, 2021

Virginia Beach, Virginia

Mortality Rates for the Top 10 Causes of Death in the U.S.

ICD-10[a] Sub-Chapter	ICD-10[a] Code	Crude Mortality Rate[1] per 100,000 population	
		County[2]	U.S.
Malignant neoplasms	C00-C97	168.7	182.6
Ischaemic heart diseases	I20-I25	78.6	113.1
Other forms of heart disease	I30-I51	70.7	64.4
Other degenerative diseases of the nervous system	G30-G31	41.4	51.0
Cerebrovascular diseases	I60-I69	51.9	47.8
Other external causes of accidental injury	W00-X59	35.5	46.4
Chronic lower respiratory diseases	J40-J47	31.9	45.7
Organic, including symptomatic, mental disorders	F01-F09	38.9	35.9
Hypertensive diseases	I10-I15	13.1	35.0
Diabetes mellitus	E10-E14	21.5	29.6

Note: (a) ICD-10 = International Classification of Diseases 10th Revision; (1) Crude mortality rates are a three-year average covering 2019-2021; (2) Figures cover Virginia Beach city.
Source: Centers for Disease Control and Prevention, National Center for Health Statistics. National Vital Statistics System, Mortality 2018-2021 on CDC WONDER Online Database

Mortality Rates for Selected Causes of Death

ICD-10[a] Sub-Chapter	ICD-10[a] Code	Crude Mortality Rate[1] per 100,000 population	
		County[2]	U.S.
Assault	X85-Y09	5.7	7.0
Diseases of the liver	K70-K76	18.0	19.8
Human immunodeficiency virus (HIV) disease	B20-B24	Unreliable	1.5
Influenza and pneumonia	J09-J18	7.4	14.7
Intentional self-harm	X60-X84	14.6	14.3
Malnutrition	E40-E46	2.0	4.3
Obesity and other hyperalimentation	E65-E68	2.5	3.0
Renal failure	N17-N19	17.6	15.7
Transport accidents	V01-V99	7.1	13.6
Viral hepatitis	B15-B19	Suppressed	1.2

Note: (a) ICD-10 = International Classification of Diseases 10th Revision; (1) Crude mortality rates are a three-year average covering 2019-2021; (2) Figures cover Virginia Beach city; Data are suppressed when the data meet the criteria for confidentiality constraints; Crude mortality rates are flagged as unreliable when the rate would be calculated with a numerator of 20 or less.
Source: Centers for Disease Control and Prevention, National Center for Health Statistics. National Vital Statistics System, Mortality 2018-2021 on CDC WONDER Online Database

Health Insurance Coverage

Area	With Health Insurance	With Private Health Insurance	With Public Health Insurance	Without Health Insurance	Population Under Age 19 Without Health Insurance
City	92.9	79.8	27.6	7.1	4.3
MSA[1]	92.3	74.5	32.6	7.7	4.4
U.S.	91.2	67.8	35.4	8.8	5.3

Note: Figures are percentages that cover the civilian noninstitutionalized population; (1) Figures cover the Virginia Beach-Norfolk-Newport News, VA-NC Metropolitan Statistical Area
Source: U.S. Census Bureau, 2017-2021 American Community Survey 5-Year Estimates

Number of Medical Professionals

Area	MDs[3]	DOs[3,4]	Dentists	Podiatrists	Chiropractors	Optometrists
Ind. City[1] (number)	1,191	67	369	30	120	79
Ind. City[1] (rate[2])	259.3	14.6	80.6	6.6	26.2	17.3
U.S. (rate[2])	289.3	23.5	72.5	6.2	28.7	17.4

Note: Data as of 2021 unless noted; (1) Data covers Virginia Beach independent city; (2) Rate per 100,000 population; (3) Data as of 2020 and includes all active, non-federal physicians; (4) Doctor of Osteopathic Medicine
Source: U.S. Department of Health and Human Services, Health Resources and Services Administration, Bureau of Health Professions, Area Resource File (ARF) 2021-2022

EDUCATION

Public School District Statistics

District Name	Schls	Pupils	Pupil/Teacher Ratio	Minority Pupils[1] (%)	LEP/ELL[2] (%)	IEP[3] (%)
Virginia Beach City Pblc Schs	87	65,450	15.4	53.9	1.8	12.2

Note: Table includes school districts with 2,000 or more students; (1) Percentage of students that are not non-Hispanic white; (2) Percentage of students that are Limited English Proficient or English Language Learners (2018-19); (3) Percentage of students that have an Individualized Education Program (2019-20).
Source: U.S. Department of Education, National Center for Education Statistics, Common Core of Data, Local Education Agency (School District) Universe Survey: School Year 2021-2022

Highest Level of Education

Area	Less than H.S.	H.S. Diploma	Some College, No Deg.	Associate Degree	Bachelor's Degree	Master's Degree	Prof. School Degree	Doctorate Degree
City	5.5	20.8	24.1	11.0	24.3	10.7	2.3	1.4
MSA[1]	7.6	24.7	23.8	10.1	20.6	9.8	1.9	1.4
U.S.	11.1	26.5	20.0	8.7	20.6	9.3	2.2	1.5

Note: Figures cover persons age 25 and over; (1) Figures cover the Virginia Beach-Norfolk-Newport News, VA-NC Metropolitan Statistical Area
Source: U.S. Census Bureau, 2017-2021 American Community Survey 5-Year Estimates

Educational Attainment by Race

Area	High School Graduate or Higher (%)					Bachelor's Degree or Higher (%)				
	Total	White	Black	Asian	Hisp.[2]	Total	White	Black	Asian	Hisp.[2]
City	94.5	96.0	92.5	89.5	87.4	38.6	41.7	29.3	40.9	30.1
MSA[1]	92.4	94.9	88.7	88.4	84.8	33.8	38.2	23.8	44.2	28.3
U.S.	88.9	91.4	87.2	87.6	71.2	33.7	35.5	23.3	55.6	18.4

Note: Figures shown cover persons 25 years old and over; (1) Figures cover the Virginia Beach-Norfolk-Newport News, VA-NC Metropolitan Statistical Area; (2) People of Hispanic origin can be of any race
Source: U.S. Census Bureau, 2017-2021 American Community Survey 5-Year Estimates

School Enrollment by Grade and Control

Area	Preschool (%)		Kindergarten (%)		Grades 1 - 4 (%)		Grades 5 - 8 (%)		Grades 9 - 12 (%)	
	Public	Private	Public	Private	Public	Private	Public	Private	Public	Private
City	35.4	64.6	75.9	24.1	90.1	9.9	90.1	9.9	92.2	7.8
MSA[1]	50.5	49.5	79.9	20.1	88.8	11.2	90.0	10.0	90.1	9.9
U.S.	58.8	41.2	86.3	13.7	88.3	11.7	88.6	11.4	89.4	10.6

Note: Figures shown cover persons 3 years old and over; (1) Figures cover the Virginia Beach-Norfolk-Newport News, VA-NC Metropolitan Statistical Area
Source: U.S. Census Bureau, 2017-2021 American Community Survey 5-Year Estimates

Higher Education

Four-Year Colleges			Two-Year Colleges			Medical Schools[1]	Law Schools[2]	Voc/ Tech[3]
Public	Private Non-profit	Private For-profit	Public	Private Non-profit	Private For-profit			
5	7	6	4	1	5	1	2	12

Note: Figures cover institutions located within the Virginia Beach-Norfolk-Newport News, VA-NC Metropolitan Statistical Area and include main campuses only; (1) includes schools accredited by the Liaison Committee on Medical Education and the American Osteopathic Association's Commission on Osteopathic College Accreditation; (2) includes ABA-accredited schools, schools with provisional ABA accreditation, and state accredited schools; (3) includes all schools with programs that are less than 2 years.
Source: National Center for Education Statistics, Integrated Postsecondary Education System (IPEDS), 2021-22; Wikipedia, List of Medical Schools in the United States, accessed April 10, 2023; Wikipedia, List of Law Schools in the United States, accessed April 10, 2023

According to *U.S. News & World Report,* the Virginia Beach-Norfolk-Newport News, VA-NC metro area is home to one of the top 200 national universities in the U.S.: **William & Mary** (#41 tie). The indicators used to capture academic quality fall into a number of categories: assessment by administrators at peer institutions; retention of students; faculty resources; student selectivity; financial resources; alumni giving; high school counselor ratings of colleges; and graduation rate. *U.S. News & World Report, "America's Best Colleges 2023"*

According to *U.S. News & World Report,* the Virginia Beach-Norfolk-Newport News, VA-NC metro area is home to one of the top 100 law schools in the U.S.: **William & Mary Law School** (#30 tie). The rankings are based on a weighted average of 12 measures of quality: peer assessment score; assessment score by lawyers/judges; median LSAT scores; median undergrad GPA; acceptance rate; employment rates for graduates; placement success; bar passage rate; faculty resources; expenditures per student; student/faculty ratio; and library resources. *U.S. News & World Report, "America's Best Graduate Schools, Law, 2023"*

According to *U.S. News & World Report,* the Virginia Beach-Norfolk-Newport News, VA-NC metro area is home to one of the top 75 business schools in the U.S.: **William & Mary Mason** (#47 tie). The rankings are based on a weighted average of the following nine measures: quality assessment; peer assessment; recruiter assessment; placement success; mean starting salary and bonus; student selectivity; mean GMAT and GRE scores; mean undergraduate GPA; and acceptance rate. *U.S. News & World Report, "America's Best Graduate Schools, Business, 2023"*

EMPLOYERS

Major Employers

Company Name	Industry
Bank of America, National Association	National commerical banks
Chesapeake Hospital Authority	General medical & surgical hospitals
Children's Health System	Specialty hospitals, except psychiatric
City Line Apts.	Apartment building operators
City of Newport News	Municipal government
City of Virginia Beach	Municipal government
Cox Communications Hampton Roads	Cable & other pay television services
Ford Motor Company	Truck & tractor truck assembly
Gwaltney of Smithfield	Meat packing plants
Hampton Training School for Nurses	General medical & surgical hospitals
Northrop Grumman Systems Corporation	Systems integration services
Old Dominion University	University
Riverside Hospital	General medical & surgical hospitals
STIHL Incorporated	Power-driven handtools
The College of William & Mary	Colleges & universities
The Colonial Williamsburg Foundation	Management consulting services
The Smithfield Packing Company	Hams & picnics, from meat slaughtered on site
U.S. Navy	Offices & clinics of medical doctors
Williamsburg James City Co. Pub Schls	Schools & educational services, nec

Note: Companies shown are located within the Virginia Beach-Norfolk-Newport News, VA-NC Metropolitan Statistical Area.
Source: Hoovers.com; Wikipedia

PUBLIC SAFETY

Crime Rate

Area	Total Crime	Violent Crime Rate				Property Crime Rate		
		Murder	Rape[3]	Robbery	Aggrav. Assault	Burglary	Larceny -Theft	Motor Vehicle Theft
City	1,610.5	3.8	13.3	27.5	54.1	110.7	1,262.7	138.4
Suburbs[1]	2,536.3	12.5	30.6	67.3	327.6	197.9	1,701.5	198.8
Metro[2]	2,301.0	10.3	26.2	57.2	258.1	175.7	1,590.0	183.5
U.S.	2,356.7	6.5	38.4	73.9	279.7	314.2	1,398.0	246.0

Note: Figures are crimes per 100,000 population; (1) All areas within the metro area that are located outside the city limits; (2) Figures cover the Virginia Beach-Norfolk-Newport News, VA-NC Metropolitan Statistical Area; (3) All figures shown were reported using the revised Uniform Crime Reporting (UCR) definition of rape; Due to the transition to the National Incident-Based Reporting System (NIBRS), limited city and metro area data was released for 2021.
Source: FBI Uniform Crime Reports, 2020

Hate Crimes

Area	Number of Quarters Reported	Number of Incidents per Bias Motivation					
		Race/Ethnicity/ Ancestry	Religion	Sexual Orientation	Disability	Gender	Gender Identity
City	4	3	0	0	0	0	0
U.S.	4	5,227	1,244	1,110	130	75	266

Note: Due to the transition to the National Incident-Based Reporting System (NIBRS), limited crime data was released for 2021.
Source: Federal Bureau of Investigation, Hate Crime Statistics 2020

Identity Theft Consumer Reports

Area	Reports	Reports per 100,000 Population	Rank[2]
MSA[1]	5,623	318	58
U.S.	1,108,609	339	-

Note: (1) Figures cover the Virginia Beach-Norfolk-Newport News, VA-NC Metropolitan Statistical Area; (2) Rank ranges from 1 to 391 where 1 indicates greatest number of identity theft reports per 100,000 population
Source: Federal Trade Commission, Consumer Sentinel Network Data Book 2022

Fraud and Other Consumer Reports

Area	Reports	Reports per 100,000 Population	Rank[2]
MSA[1]	22,827	1,290	29
U.S.	4,064,520	1,245	-

Note: (1) Figures cover the Virginia Beach-Norfolk-Newport News, VA-NC Metropolitan Statistical Area; (2) Rank ranges from 1 to 391 where 1 indicates greatest number of fraud and other consumer reports per 100,000 population
Source: Federal Trade Commission, Consumer Sentinel Network Data Book 2022

Virginia Beach, Virginia   473

POLITICS

2020 Presidential Election Results

Area	Biden	Trump	Jorgensen	Hawkins	Other
Virginia Beach City	51.6	46.2	1.8	0.0	0.4
U.S.	51.3	46.8	1.2	0.3	0.5

Note: Results are percentages and may not add to 100% due to rounding
Source: Dave Leip's Atlas of U.S. Presidential Elections

SPORTS

Professional Sports Teams

Team Name	League	Year Established

No teams are located in the metro area
Source: Wikipedia, Major Professional Sports Teams of the United States and Canada, April 12, 2023

CLIMATE

Average and Extreme Temperatures

Temperature	Jan	Feb	Mar	Apr	May	Jun	Jul	Aug	Sep	Oct	Nov	Dec	Yr.
Extreme High (°F)	78	81	88	97	100	101	103	104	99	95	86	80	104
Average High (°F)	48	51	58	68	76	84	88	86	80	70	61	52	69
Average Temp. (°F)	41	42	49	58	67	75	79	78	72	62	53	44	60
Average Low (°F)	32	33	40	48	57	66	71	70	64	53	44	35	51
Extreme Low (°F)	-3	8	18	28	36	45	54	49	45	27	20	7	-3

Note: Figures cover the years 1948-1995
Source: National Climatic Data Center, International Station Meteorological Climate Summary, 9/96

Average Precipitation/Snowfall/Humidity

Precip./Humidity	Jan	Feb	Mar	Apr	May	Jun	Jul	Aug	Sep	Oct	Nov	Dec	Yr.
Avg. Precip. (in.)	3.6	3.3	3.8	3.0	3.7	3.5	5.2	5.3	3.9	3.3	3.0	3.1	44.8
Avg. Snowfall (in.)	3	3	1	Tr	0	0	0	0	0	0	Tr	1	8
Avg. Rel. Hum. 7am (%)	74	74	74	73	77	79	81	84	83	82	79	75	78
Avg. Rel. Hum. 4pm (%)	59	56	53	56	57	60	63	62	60	58	59	58

Note: Figures cover the years 1948-1995; Tr = Trace amounts (<0.05 in. of rain; <0.5 in. of snow)
Source: National Climatic Data Center, International Station Meteorological Climate Summary, 9/96

Weather Conditions

Temperature			Daytime Sky			Precipitation		
10°F & below	32°F & below	90°F & above	Clear	Partly cloudy	Cloudy	0.01 inch or more precip.	0.1 inch or more snow/ice	Thunder-storms
< 1	53	33	89	149	127	115	5	38

Note: Figures are average number of days per year and cover the years 1948-1995
Source: National Climatic Data Center, International Station Meteorological Climate Summary, 9/96

HAZARDOUS WASTE

Superfund Sites

The Virginia Beach-Norfolk-Newport News, VA-NC metro area is home to 13 sites on the EPA's Superfund National Priorities List: **Abex Corp.** (final); **Atlantic Wood Industries, Inc.** (final); **Chisman Creek** (final); **Former Nansemond Ordnance Depot** (final); **Fort Eustis (USARMY)** (final); **Langley Air Force Base/Nasa Langley Research Center** (final); **Naval Amphibious Base Little Creek** (final); **Naval Weapons Station - Yorktown** (final); **Norfolk Naval Base (Sewells Point Naval Complex)** (final); **Norfolk Naval Shipyard** (final); **NWS Yorktown - Cheatham Annex** (final); **Peck Iron and Metal** (final); **Saunders Supply Co.** (final). There are a total of 1,165 Superfund sites with a status of proposed or final on the list in the U.S. *U.S. Environmental Protection Agency, National Priorities List, April 12, 2023*

AIR QUALITY

Air Quality Trends: Ozone

	1990	1995	2000	2005	2010	2015	2018	2019	2020	2021
MSA[1]	0.085	0.084	0.083	0.078	0.074	0.061	0.061	0.059	0.053	0.057
U.S.	0.087	0.089	0.081	0.080	0.072	0.067	0.069	0.065	0.065	0.067

Note: (1) Data covers the Virginia Beach-Norfolk-Newport News, VA-NC Metropolitan Statistical Area. The values shown are the composite ozone concentration averages among trend sites based on the highest fourth daily maximum 8-hour concentration in parts per million. These trends are based on sites having an adequate record of monitoring data during the trend period. Data from exceptional events are included.
Source: U.S. Environmental Protection Agency, Air Quality Monitoring Information, "Air Quality Trends by City, 1990-2021"

Air Quality Index

Area	Percent of Days when Air Quality was...[2]					AQI Statistics[2]	
	Good	Moderate	Unhealthy for Sensitive Groups	Unhealthy	Very Unhealthy	Maximum	Median
MSA[1]	85.8	14.2	0.0	0.0	0.0	94	38

Note: (1) Data covers the Virginia Beach-Norfolk-Newport News, VA-NC Metropolitan Statistical Area; (2) Based on 365 days with AQI data in 2021. Air Quality Index (AQI) is an index for reporting daily air quality. EPA calculates the AQI for five major air pollutants regulated by the Clean Air Act: ground-level ozone, particle pollution (aka particulate matter), carbon monoxide, sulfur dioxide, and nitrogen dioxide. The AQI runs from 0 to 500. The higher the AQI value, the greater the level of air pollution and the greater the health concern. There are six AQI categories: "Good" AQI is between 0 and 50. Air quality is considered satisfactory; "Moderate" AQI is between 51 and 100. Air quality is acceptable; "Unhealthy for Sensitive Groups" When AQI values are between 101 and 150, members of sensitive groups may experience health effects; "Unhealthy" When AQI values are between 151 and 200 everyone may begin to experience health effects; "Very Unhealthy" AQI values between 201 and 300 trigger a health alert; "Hazardous" AQI values over 300 trigger warnings of emergency conditions (not shown).
Source: U.S. Environmental Protection Agency, Air Quality Index Report, 2021

Air Quality Index Pollutants

Area	Percent of Days when AQI Pollutant was...[2]					
	Carbon Monoxide	Nitrogen Dioxide	Ozone	Sulfur Dioxide	Particulate Matter 2.5	Particulate Matter 10
MSA[1]	0.0	6.8	49.6	(3)	43.6	0.0

Note: (1) Data covers the Virginia Beach-Norfolk-Newport News, VA-NC Metropolitan Statistical Area; (2) Based on 365 days with AQI data in 2021. The Air Quality Index (AQI) is an index for reporting daily air quality. EPA calculates the AQI for five major air pollutants regulated by the Clean Air Act: ground-level ozone, particle pollution (also known as particulate matter), carbon monoxide, sulfur dioxide, and nitrogen dioxide. The AQI runs from 0 to 500. The higher the AQI value, the greater the level of air pollution and the greater the health concern; (3) Sulfur dioxide is no longer included in this table (as of December 8, 2021) because SO_2 concentrations tend to be very localized and not necessarily representative of broad geographical areas like counties and CBSAs.
Source: U.S. Environmental Protection Agency, Air Quality Index Report, 2021

Maximum Air Pollutant Concentrations: Particulate Matter, Ozone, CO and Lead

	Particulate Matter 10 (ug/m³)	Particulate Matter 2.5 Wtd AM (ug/m³)	Particulate Matter 2.5 24-Hr (ug/m³)	Ozone (ppm)	Carbon Monoxide (ppm)	Lead (ug/m³)
MSA[1] Level	44	7.2	16	0.061	1	n/a
NAAQS[2]	150	15	35	0.075	9	0.15
Met NAAQS[2]	Yes	Yes	Yes	Yes	Yes	n/a

Note: (1) Data covers the Virginia Beach-Norfolk-Newport News, VA-NC Metropolitan Statistical Area; Data from exceptional events are included; (2) National Ambient Air Quality Standards; ppm = parts per million; ug/m³ = micrograms per cubic meter; n/a not available.
Concentrations: Particulate Matter 10 (coarse particulate)—highest second maximum 24-hour concentration; Particulate Matter 2.5 Wtd AM (fine particulate)—highest weighted annual mean concentration; Particulate Matter 2.5 24-Hour (fine particulate)—highest 98th percentile 24-hour concentration; Ozone—highest fourth daily maximum 8-hour concentration; Carbon Monoxide—highest second maximum non-overlapping 8-hour concentration; Lead—maximum running 3-month average
Source: U.S. Environmental Protection Agency, Air Quality Monitoring Information, "Air Quality Statistics by City, 2021"

Maximum Air Pollutant Concentrations: Nitrogen Dioxide and Sulfur Dioxide

	Nitrogen Dioxide AM (ppb)	Nitrogen Dioxide 1-Hr (ppb)	Sulfur Dioxide AM (ppb)	Sulfur Dioxide 1-Hr (ppb)	Sulfur Dioxide 24-Hr (ppb)
MSA[1] Level	7	40	n/a	3	n/a
NAAQS[2]	53	100	30	75	140
Met NAAQS[2]	Yes	Yes	n/a	Yes	n/a

Note: (1) Data covers the Virginia Beach-Norfolk-Newport News, VA-NC Metropolitan Statistical Area; Data from exceptional events are included; (2) National Ambient Air Quality Standards; ppm = parts per million; ug/m³ = micrograms per cubic meter; n/a not available.
Concentrations: Nitrogen Dioxide AM—highest arithmetic mean concentration; Nitrogen Dioxide 1-Hr—highest 98th percentile 1-hour daily maximum concentration; Sulfur Dioxide AM—highest annual mean concentration; Sulfur Dioxide 1-Hr—highest 99th percentile 1-hour daily maximum concentration; Sulfur Dioxide 24-Hr—highest second maximum 24-hour concentration
Source: U.S. Environmental Protection Agency, Air Quality Monitoring Information, "Air Quality Statistics by City, 2021"

Washington, District of Columbia

Background

The city and federal district of Washington, D.C., with its more than 150 foreign embassies, consulates, and ambassadors' residences, is cosmopolitan.

In 1793, the first cornerstone of the White House was laid. In 1800, the north wing was completed, a drifting Congress found its home, and President John Adams was the first president to reside at the White House. The building was burned down by the British in 1814 during the War of 1812, and its final reconstruction was completed in 1891.

The young capital, which grows more confident and worldly every year, is renowned for its brilliant annual springtime display of cherry blossoms, as well as a breathtaking collection of architectural styles, including Greek Revival, Federal, Victorian, and Baroque and six of the top ten buildings in the American Institute of Architects' 2007 ranking of America's Favorite Architecture are in D.C. Some of the city's monuments and well-known sites include the Washington Monument, Lincoln Memorial, the White House, Jefferson Memorial, Vietnam Veterans Memorial, and Arlington National Cemetery. In 2004, the National World War II Memorial was dedicated, as part of a four-day World War II Reunion, and the United States Air Force Memorial was completed in 2006.

As the political machine of the country, the main industry is government, with tourism enjoying the second spot. It is one of the most visited cities in the world. Other industries in D.C. include education, finance, public policy, and scientific research. In a recent survey, Washington was ranked as one of the most competitive financial centers in both the country and the world. Washington is also home to five major universities—American, Georgetown, George Washington, Howard, and Catholic University of America.

On September 11, 2001, the city suffered an attack orchestrated by Saudi terrorist Osama bin Laden as part of a wider assault on the U.S. that included the World Trade Center in New York on the same day. An airplane crashed through the Pentagon, killing several hundred people. The city suffered a domestic terrorist attack on January 6, 2021, when thousands stormed the Capitol building, seeking to overturn Donald Trump's defeat, believing that 2020 presidential winner Joe Biden stole the election. Several were killed, many were injured in a harrowing attempt at overthrowing the government. A massive investigation as to the role Trump and his advisors may have played in encouraging the attack continues more than two years later. Both these major incidents led to tightening of security in the district itself.

Despite such destruction, D.C. continues to be in an urban renaissance. Recent construction projects include the DC Streetcar system, a new Metro line, and Capital Bikeshare, one of the largest bicycle sharing systems in the country.

The Walter E. Washington Convention Center, open since 2004, hosts hundreds of events and welcomes over a million visitors annually. The convention center has sparked a new phase in the economic development of the city's northeast downtown area, which was devastated by the riots of 1968. In addition to the convention center, City Museum opened across the street at the old Carnegie Library. Just a few blocks south, restaurants fill the vicinity of the International Spy Museum and the Verizon Center, home to the NBA Wizards, WNBA Mystics, and the NHL Capitals. In 2005 the Montreal Expos baseball team became the Washington Nationals and the team moved to Washington D.C. Today they play at Nationals Park, a state-of-the-art, 41,000-seat facility, and the underdog team won the 2019 World Series.

As part of D.C.'s vibrant cultural scene, the John F. Kennedy Center for the Performing Arts was renovated in 2005, with improved access and visual improvements to its façade. More recent was the renovation of the Eisenhower Theater in the JFK Center.

The Smithsonian Institution's National Air and Space Museum has expanded into a second museum near the Washington Dulles International Airport in Virginia, which is called the Steven F. Udvar-Hazy Center. Other museums in the city include the National Gallery of Art, U.S. Holocaust Memorial Museum, Corcoran Gallery, Phillips Collection, Hirshhorn Museum and Sculpture Garden, and the many other Smithsonian museums. One of the city's newest museums, National Museum of the American Indian, is housed in a dramatic building on the National Mall, with a mission to explore and celebrate the histories and cultures of Native Americans from North, Central, and South America.

Washington, a global media center, has bureaus of all worldwide major news outlets and the country's largest concentrations of journalists. It is home to Black Entertainment Television, C-SPAN, National Public Radio, the Washington Post Company, and XM Satellite Radio.

Summertime in Washington is warm and humid, winters are cold and snowy, and the city is partly cloudy year-round. During the year, temperatures typically vary from a low of 29 degrees to a high of 88 degrees.

Rankings

General Rankings

- *US News & World Report* conducted a survey of more than 3,600 people and analyzed the 150 largest metropolitan areas to determine what matters most when selecting where to settle down. Washington ranked #19 out of the top 25 as having the best combination of desirable factors. Criteria: cost of living; quality of life and education; net migration; job market; desirability; and other factors. *money.usnews.com, "The 25 Best Places to Live in the U.S. in 2022-2023," May 17, 2022*

- The human resources consulting firm Mercer ranked 231 major cities worldwide in terms of overall quality of life. Washington ranked #53. Criteria: political, social, economic, and socio-cultural factors; medical and health considerations; schools and education; public services and transportation; recreation; consumer goods; housing; and natural environment. *Mercer, "Mercer 2019 Quality of Living Survey," March 13, 2019*

- For its 35th annual "Readers' Choice Awards" survey, *Condé Nast Traveler* ranked its readers' favorite cities in the U.S. Whether it be a longed-for visit or a first on the list, these are the places that inspired a return to travel. The list was broken into large cities and cities under 250,000. Washington ranked #9 in the big city category. *Condé Nast Traveler, Readers' Choice Awards 2022, "Best Big Cities in the U.S." October 4, 2022*

Business/Finance Rankings

- According to *Business Insider*, the Washington metro area is a prime place to run a startup or move an existing business to. The area ranked #3. More than 300 metro areas were analyzed for factors that were of top concern to new business owners. Data was based on the 2019 U.S. Census Bureau American Community Survey, statistics from the CDC, Bureau of Labor Statistics employment report, and University of Chicago analysis. Criteria: business formations; percentage of vaccinated population; percentage of households with internet subscriptions; median household income; and share of work that can be done from home. *www.businessinsider.com, "The 20 Best Cities for Starting a Business in 2022 Include Baltimore, Boulder, and Boston," January 5, 2022*

- Based on metro area social media reviews, the employment opinion group Glassdoor surveyed 50 of the most populous U.S. metro areas and equally weighed cost of living, hiring opportunity, and job satisfaction to compose a list of "25 Best Cities for Jobs." Median pay and home value, and number of active job openings were also factored in. The Washington metro area was ranked #17 in overall job satisfaction. *www.glassdoor.com, "Best Cities for Jobs," February 25, 2020*

- The Brookings Institution ranked the nation's largest cities based on income inequality. Washington was ranked #2 (#1 = greatest inequality). Criteria: the "95/20 ratio," a figure representing the income at which a household earns more than 95 percent of all other households, divided by the income at which a household earns more than only 20 percent of all other households. *Brookings Institution, "Household Income Inequality, Largest Cities of 97 Large U.S. Metro Areas, 2014-2016," February 5, 2018*

- The Brookings Institution ranked the 100 largest metro areas in the U.S. based on income inequality. Washington was ranked #70 (#1 = greatest inequality). Criteria: the "95/20 ratio," a figure representing the income at which a household earns more than 95 percent of all other households, divided by the income at which a household earns more than only 20 percent of all other households. *Brookings Institution, "Household Income Inequality, 100 Largest U.S. Metro Areas, 2014-2016," February 5, 2018*

- Payscale.com ranked the 32 largest metro areas in terms of wage growth. The Washington metro area ranked #27. Criteria: quarterly changes in private industry employee and education professional wage growth from the previous year. *PayScale, "Wage Trends by Metro Area-1st Quarter," April 20, 2023*

- The Washington metro area was identified as one of the most debt-ridden places in America by the finance site Credit.com. The metro area was ranked #1. Criteria: residents' average credit card debt as well as median income. *Credit.com, "25 Cities With the Most Credit Card Debt," February 28, 2018*

- For its annual survey of the "Most Expensive U.S. Cities to Live In," Kiplinger applied Cost of Living Index statistics developed by the Council for Community and Economic Research to U.S. Census Bureau population and median household income data for 265 urban areas. Washington ranked #5 among the most expensive in the country. *Kiplinger.com, "The 11 Most Expensive Cities to Live in the U.S.," April 15, 2023*

- Washington was identified as one of America's most frugal metro areas by *Coupons.com*. The city ranked #1 out of 25. Criteria: digital coupon usage. *Coupons.com, "America's Most Frugal Cities of 2017," March 22, 2018*

- Washington was cited as one of America's top metros for total corporate facility investment in 2022. The area ranked #10 in the large metro area category (population over 1 million). *Site Selection, "Top Metros of 2022," March 2023*

- The Washington metro area appeared on the Milken Institute "2022 Best Performing Cities" list. Rank: #67 out of 200 large metro areas (population over 250,000). Criteria: job growth; wage and salary growth; high-tech output growth; housing affordability; household broadband access. *Milken Institute, "Best-Performing Cities 2022," March 28, 2022*

- *Forbes* ranked the 200 most populous metro areas to determine the nation's "Best Places for Business and Careers." The Washington metro area was ranked #59. Criteria: costs (business and living); job growth (past and projected); income growth; quality of life; educational attainment (college and high school); projected economic growth; cultural and leisure opportunities; workplace tolerance laws; net migration patterns. *Forbes, "The Best Places for Business and Careers 2019: Seattle Still On Top," October 30, 2019*

- Mercer Human Resources Consulting ranked 227 cities worldwide in terms of cost-of-living. Washington ranked #29 (the lower the ranking, the higher the cost-of-living). The survey measured the comparative cost of over 200 items (such as housing, food, clothing, domestic supplies, transportation, and recreation/entertainment) in each location. *Mercer, "2022 Cost of Living City Ranking," June 29, 2022*

Dating/Romance Rankings

- *Apartment List* conducted its Annual Renter Satisfaction Survey and asked renters "how satisfied are you with opportunities for dating in your current city." The cities were ranked from highest to lowest based on their satisfaction scores. Washington ranked #7 out of 85 cities. *Apartment List, "Best Cities for Dating 2022 with Local Dating Insights from Bumble," February 7, 2022*

Education Rankings

- Personal finance website *WalletHub* analyzed the 150 largest U.S. metropolitan statistical areas to determine where the most educated Americans are putting their degrees to work. Criteria: education levels; percentage of workers with degrees; education quality and attainment gap; public school quality rankings; quality and enrollment of each metro area's universities. Washington was ranked #3 (#1 = most educated city). *www.WalletHub.com, "Most & Least Educated Cities in America," July 18, 2022*

- Washington was selected as one of the best cities for post grads by *Rent.com*. The city ranked among the top 10. Criteria: jobs per capita; unemployment rate; mean annual income; cost of living; rental inventory. *Rent.com, "Best Cities for College Grads," December 11, 2018*

- Washington was selected as one of America's most literate cities. The city ranked #2 out of the 84 largest U.S. cities. Criteria: number of booksellers; library resources; Internet resources; educational attainment; periodical publishing resources; newspaper circulation. *Central Connecticut State University, "America's Most Literate Cities, 2018," February 2019*

Environmental Rankings

- The U.S. Environmental Protection Agency (EPA) released its list of U.S. metropolitan areas with the most ENERGY STAR certified buildings in 2022. The Washington metro area was ranked #2 out of 25. *U.S. Environmental Protection Agency, "2023 Energy Star Top Cities," April 26, 2023*

- The U.S. Conference of Mayors and Walmart Stores sponsor the Mayors' Climate Protection Awards Program which recognize mayors for outstanding and innovative practices that address the climate crisis: increase energy efficiency in their cities, reduce carbon emissions and expand renewable energy. Washington received an Honorable Mention in the large city category. *U.S. Conference of Mayors, "2022 Mayors' Climate Protection Awards," June 3, 2022*

Food/Drink Rankings

- The U.S. Chamber of Commerce Foundation conducted an in-depth study on local food truck regulations, surveyed 288 food truck owners, and ranked 20 major American cities based on how friendly they are for operating a food truck. The compiled index assessed the following: procedures for obtaining permits and licenses; complying with restrictions; and financial obligations associated with operating a food truck. Washington ranked #19 overall (1 being the best). *www.foodtrucknation.us, "Food Truck Nation," March 20, 2018*

Health/Fitness Rankings

- For each of the 100 largest cities in the United States, the American Fitness Index®, compiled in partnership between the American College of Sports Medicine and the Elevance Health Foundation, evaluated community infrastructure and 34 health behaviors including preventive health, levels of chronic disease conditions, food insecurity, sleep quality, pedestrian safety, air quality, and community/environment resources that support physical activity. Washington ranked #4 for "community fitness." *americanfitnessindex.org, "2022 ACSM American Fitness Index Summary Report," July 12, 2022*

- Washington was identified as one of the 10 most walkable cities in the U.S. by Walk Score. The city ranked #7. Walk Score measures walkability by analyzing hundreds of walking routes to nearby amenities, and also measures pedestrian friendliness by analyzing population density and road metrics such as block length and intersection density. *WalkScore.com, April 13, 2021*

- The Washington metro area was identified as one of the worst cities for bed bugs in America by pest control company Orkin. The area ranked #9 out of 50 based on the number of bed bug treatments Orkin performed from December 2021 to November 2022. *Orkin, "The Windy City Can't Blow Bed Bugs Away: Chicago Ranks #1 For Third Consecutive Year On Orkin's Bed Bug Cities List," January 9, 2023*

- Washington was identified as a "2022 Spring Allergy Capital." The area ranked #85 out of 100. Three groups of factors were used to identify the most challenging cities for people with allergies during the spring season: annual spring pollen scores; over the counter allergy medicine use; number of board-certified allergy specialists. *Asthma and Allergy Foundation of America, "Spring Allergy Capitals 2022," March 2, 2022*

- Washington was identified as a "2022 Fall Allergy Capital." The area ranked #94 out of 100. Three groups of factors were used to identify the most challenging cities for people with allergies during the fall season: annual fall pollen scores; over the counter allergy medicine use; number of board-certified allergy specialists. *Asthma and Allergy Foundation of America, "Fall Allergy Capitals 2022," March 2, 2022*

- Washington was identified as a "2022 Asthma Capital." The area ranked #59 out of the nation's 100 largest metropolitan areas. Criteria: estimated asthma prevalence; asthma-related mortality; and ER visits due to asthma. Risk factors analyzed but not factored in the rankings: annual pollen score; annual air quality; public smoking laws; access to board-certified asthma specialists; rescue and controller medication use; uninsured rate; poverty rate. *Asthma and Allergy Foundation of America, "Asthma Capitals 2022: The Most Challenging Places to Live With Asthma," September 14, 2022*

- The Sharecare Community Well-Being Index evaluates 10 individual and social health factors in order to measure what matters to Americans in the communities in which they live. The Washington metro area ranked #3 in the top 10 across all 10 domains. Criteria: access to healthcare, food, and community resources; housng and transportation; economic security; feeling of purpose; physical, financial, social, and community well-being. *www.sharecare.com, "Community Well-Being Index: 2020 Metro Area & County Rankings Report," August 30, 2021*

Real Estate Rankings

- *WalletHub* compared the most populated U.S. cities to determine which had the best markets for real estate agents. Washington ranked #7 where demand was high and pay was the best. Criteria: sales per agent; annual median wage for real-estate agents; monthly average starting salary for real estate agents; real estate job density and competition; unemployment rate; home turnover rate; housing-market health index; and other relevant metrics. *www.WalletHub.com, "2021 Best Places to Be a Real Estate Agent," May 12, 2021*

- The Washington metro area was identified as one of the 10 worst condo markets in the U.S. in 2022. The area ranked #55 out of 63 markets. Criteria: year-over-year change of median sales price of existing apartment condo-coop homes between the 4th quarter of 2021 and the 4th quarter of 2022. *National Association of Realtors®, Median Sales Price of Existing Apartment Condo-Coops Homes for Metropolitan Areas, 4th Quarter 2022*

- The Washington metro area was identified as one of the 20 least affordable housing markets in the U.S. in 2022. The area ranked #167 out of 186 markets. Criteria: qualification for a mortgage loan with a 10 percent down payment on a typical home. *National Association of Realtors®, Qualifying Income Based on Sales Price of Existing Single-Family Homes for Metropolitan Areas, 2022*

- Washington was ranked #108 out of 235 metro areas in terms of housing affordability in 2022 by the National Association of Home Builders (#1 = most affordable). Criteria: the share of homes sold in that area affordable to a family earning the local median income, based on standard mortgage underwriting criteria. *National Association of Home Builders®, NAHB-Wells Fargo Housing Opportunity Index, 4th Quarter 2022*

Safety Rankings

- Allstate ranked the 200 largest cities in America in terms of driver safety. Washington ranked #199. Criteria: internal property damage claims over a two-year period from January 2016 to December 2017. The report helps increase the importance of safety and awareness behind the wheel. *Allstate, "Allstate America's Best Drivers Report, 2019" June 24, 2019*

- Washington was identified as one of the most dangerous cities in America by NeighborhoodScout. The city ranked #80 out of 100 (#1 = most dangerous). Criteria: number of violent crimes per 1,000 residents. The editors evaluated cities with 25,000 or more residents. *NeighborhoodScout.com, "2023 Top 100 Most Dangerous Cities in the U.S.," January 12, 2023*

Seniors/Retirement Rankings

- From its Best Cities for Successful Aging indexes, the Milken Institute generated rankings for metropolitan areas, weighing data in nine categories—health care, wellness, living arrangements, transportation and convenience, financial characteristics, education, employment, community engagement, and overall livability. The Washington metro area was ranked #48 overall in the large metro area category. *Milken Institute, "Best Cities for Successful Aging, 2017" March 14, 2017*

Sports/Recreation Rankings

- Washington was chosen as one of America's best cities for bicycling. The city ranked #11 out of 50. Criteria: cycling infrastructure that is safe and friendly for all ages; energy and bike culture. The editors evaluated cities with populations of 100,000 or more. *Bicycling, "The 50 Best Bike Cities in America," October 10, 2018*

Transportation Rankings

- Business Insider presented an AllTransit Performance Score ranking of public transportation in major U.S. cities and towns, with populations over 250,000, in which Washington earned the #4-ranked "Transit Score," awarded for frequency of service, access to jobs, quality and number of stops, and affordability. *www.businessinsider.com, "The 17 Major U.S. Cities with the Best Public Transportation," April 17, 2018*

- The business website *24/7 Wall St.* reviewed U.S. Census data to identify the 25 cities where the largest share of households do not own a vehicle. Washington held the #3 position. *247wallst.com, "Cities Where No One Wants to Drive," January 12, 2020*

- Washington was identified as one of the most congested metro areas in the U.S. The area ranked #2 out of 10. Criteria: yearly delay per auto commuter in hours. *Texas A&M Transportation Institute, "2021 Urban Mobility Report," June 2021*

- According to the INRIX "2022 Global Traffic Scorecard," Washington was identified as one of the most congested metro areas in the U.S. The area ranked #8 out of 25. Criteria: average annual time spent in traffic and average cost of congestion per motorist. *Inrix.com, "Return to Work, Higher Gas Prices & Inflation Drove Americans to Spend Hundreds More in Time and Money Commuting," January 10, 2023*

Women/Minorities Rankings

- Personal finance website *WalletHub* compared more than 180 U.S. cities across two key dimensions, "Hispanic Business-Friendliness" and "Hispanic Purchasing Power," to arrive at the most favorable conditions for Hispanic entrepreneurs. Washington was ranked #90 out of 182. Criteria includes: share of Hispanic-Owned Businesses; Hispanic entrepreneurship rate to median annual income of Hispanics; Small Business-Friendliness score; cost of living; and number of Hispanics with at least a bachelor's degree. *WalletHub.com, "2019's Best Cities for Hispanic Entrepreneurs," May 1, 2019*

Miscellaneous Rankings

- The watchdog site, Charity Navigator, conducted a study of charities in major markets both to analyze statistical differences in their financial, accountability, and transparency practices and to track year-to-year variations in individual philanthropic communities. The Washington metro area was ranked #24 among the 30 metro markets in the rating category of Overall Score. *www.charitynavigator.org, "2017 Metro Market Study," May 1, 2017*

- *WalletHub* compared the 150 most populated U.S. cities to determine their operating efficiency. A "Quality of Services" score was constructed for each city and then divided by the total budget per capita to reveal which were managed the best. Washington ranked #150. Criteria: financial stability; economy; education; safety; health; infrastructure and pollution. *www.WalletHub.com, "2022's Best- & Worst-Run Cities in America," June 21, 2022*

- The National Alliance to End Homelessness listed the 25 most populous metro areas with the highest rate of homelessness. The Washington metro area had a high rate of homelessness. Criteria: number of homeless people per 10,000 population in 2016. *National Alliance to End Homelessness, "Homelessness in the 25 Most Populous U.S. Metro Areas," September 1, 2017*

480 Washington, District of Columbia

Business Environment

DEMOGRAPHICS

Population Growth

Area	1990 Census	2000 Census	2010 Census	2020 Census	Population Growth (%)	
					1990-2020	2010-2020
City	606,900	572,059	601,723	689,545	13.6	14.6
MSA[1]	4,122,914	4,796,183	5,582,170	6,385,162	54.9	14.4
U.S.	248,709,873	281,421,906	308,745,538	331,449,281	33.3	7.4

Note: (1) Figures cover the Washington-Arlington-Alexandria, DC-VA-MD-WV Metropolitan Statistical Area
Source: U.S. Census Bureau, 1990 Census, 2000 Census, 2010 Census, 2020 Census

Race

Area	White Alone[2] (%)	Black Alone[2] (%)	Asian Alone[2] (%)	AIAN[3] Alone[2] (%)	NHOPI[4] Alone[2] (%)	Other Race Alone[2] (%)	Two or More Races (%)
City	39.6	41.4	4.9	0.5	0.1	5.4	8.1
MSA[1]	44.5	24.5	11.0	0.6	0.1	9.3	10.1
U.S.	61.6	12.4	6.0	1.1	0.2	8.4	10.2

Note: (1) Figures cover the Washington-Arlington-Alexandria, DC-VA-MD-WV Metropolitan Statistical Area;
(2) Alone is defined as not being in combination with one or more other races; (3) American Indian and Alaska Native; (4) Native Hawaiian and Other Pacific Islander
Source: U.S. Census Bureau, 2020 Census

Hispanic or Latino Origin

Area	Total (%)	Mexican (%)	Puerto Rican (%)	Cuban (%)	Other (%)
City	11.3	1.9	0.9	0.5	8.0
MSA[1]	16.2	2.3	1.2	0.3	12.4
U.S.	18.4	11.2	1.8	0.7	4.7

Note: Persons of Hispanic or Latino origin can be of any race; (1) Figures cover the Washington-Arlington-Alexandria, DC-VA-MD-WV Metropolitan Statistical Area
Source: U.S. Census Bureau, 2017-2021 American Community Survey 5-Year Estimates

Age

Area	Percent of Population									Median Age
	Under Age 5	Age 5–19	Age 20–34	Age 35–44	Age 45–54	Age 55–64	Age 65–74	Age 75–84	Age 85+	
City	5.4	13.9	32.9	15.2	10.0	9.9	7.4	3.6	1.5	33.9
MSA[1]	5.8	19.4	21.5	14.3	13.2	12.3	8.2	3.9	1.4	37.2
U.S.	5.6	19.2	20.2	12.7	12.4	13.1	10.0	4.9	1.9	38.8

Note: (1) Figures cover the Washington-Arlington-Alexandria, DC-VA-MD-WV Metropolitan Statistical Area
Source: U.S. Census Bureau, 2020 Census

Disability by Age

Area	All Ages	Under 18 Years Old	18 to 64 Years Old	65 Years and Over
City	11.2	4.4	9.2	33.7
MSA[1]	8.8	3.3	6.8	28.2
U.S.	12.6	4.4	10.3	33.4

Note: Figures show percent of the civilian noninstitutionalized population that reported having a disability. Disability status is determined from six types of difficulty: vision, hearing, cognitive, ambulatory, self-care, and independent living. For children under 5 years old, hearing and vision difficulty are used to determine disability status. For children between the ages of 5 and 14, disability status is determined from hearing, vision, cognitive, ambulatory, and self-care difficulties. For people aged 15 years and older, they are considered to have a disability if they have difficulty with any one of the six difficulty types; Note: (1) Figures cover the Washington-Arlington-Alexandria, DC-VA-MD-WV Metropolitan Statistical Area
Source: U.S. Census Bureau, 2017-2021 American Community Survey 5-Year Estimates

Ancestry

Area	German	Irish	English	American	Italian	Polish	French[2]	Scottish	Dutch
City	7.5	7.3	6.1	2.8	4.3	2.2	1.6	1.4	0.7
MSA[1]	9.0	8.4	7.5	4.0	4.2	2.1	1.5	1.5	0.7
U.S.	12.8	9.6	8.1	5.7	5.0	2.7	2.2	1.6	1.1

Note: Figures are the percentage of the total population reporting a particular ancestry. The nine most commonly reported ancestries in the U.S. are shown. Figures include multiple ancestries (e.g. if a person reported being Irish and Italian, they were included in both columns); (1) Figures cover the Washington-Arlington-Alexandria, DC-VA-MD-WV Metropolitan Statistical Area; (2) Excludes Basque
Source: U.S. Census Bureau, 2017-2021 American Community Survey 5-Year Estimates

Foreign-born Population

Area	Percent of Population Born in								
	Any Foreign Country	Asia	Mexico	Europe	Caribbean	Central America[2]	South America	Africa	Canada
City	13.5	3.0	0.6	2.4	1.2	2.4	1.5	2.1	0.3
MSA[1]	22.9	8.2	0.8	1.8	1.1	4.8	2.3	3.6	0.2
U.S.	13.6	4.2	3.3	1.5	1.4	1.1	1.1	0.8	0.2

Note: (1) Figures cover the Washington-Arlington-Alexandria, DC-VA-MD-WV Metropolitan Statistical Area; (2) Excludes Mexico.
Source: U.S. Census Bureau, 2017-2021 American Community Survey 5-Year Estimates

Household Size

Area	Persons in Household (%)							Average Household Size
	One	Two	Three	Four	Five	Six	Seven or More	
City	45.4	30.6	11.6	7.3	3.2	1.1	0.7	2.10
MSA[1]	27.8	30.7	16.1	14.6	6.6	2.6	1.6	2.70
U.S.	28.1	33.8	15.5	12.9	6.0	2.3	1.4	2.60

Note: (1) Figures cover the Washington-Arlington-Alexandria, DC-VA-MD-WV Metropolitan Statistical Area
Source: U.S. Census Bureau, 2017-2021 American Community Survey 5-Year Estimates

Household Relationships

Area	House-holder	Opposite-sex Spouse	Same-sex Spouse	Opposite-sex Unmarried Partner	Same-sex Unmarried Partner	Child[2]	Grand-child	Other Relatives	Non-relatives
City	45.3	10.3	0.6	3.1	0.5	20.4	2.4	4.2	7.1
MSA[1]	37.0	17.3	0.3	2.0	0.2	29.3	2.0	5.9	4.4
U.S.	38.3	17.5	0.2	2.5	0.2	28.3	2.4	4.8	3.4

Note: Figures are percent of the total population; (1) Figures cover the Washington-Arlington-Alexandria, DC-VA-MD-WV Metropolitan Statistical Area; (2) Includes biological, adopted, and stepchildren of the householder
Source: U.S. Census Bureau, 2020 Census

Gender

Area	Males	Females	Males per 100 Females
City	322,777	366,768	88.0
MSA[1]	3,091,711	3,293,451	93.9
U.S.	162,685,811	168,763,470	96.4

Note: (1) Figures cover the Washington-Arlington-Alexandria, DC-VA-MD-WV Metropolitan Statistical Area
Source: U.S. Census Bureau, 2020 Census

Marital Status

Area	Never Married	Now Married[2]	Separated	Widowed	Divorced
City	55.8	30.9	1.7	3.5	8.2
MSA[1]	36.2	49.2	1.7	4.2	8.7
U.S.	33.8	48.0	1.8	5.6	10.8

Note: Figures are percentages and cover the population 15 years of age and older; (1) Figures cover the Washington-Arlington-Alexandria, DC-VA-MD-WV Metropolitan Statistical Area; (2) Excludes separated
Source: U.S. Census Bureau, 2017-2021 American Community Survey 5-Year Estimates

Religious Groups by Family

Area	Catholic	Baptist	Methodist	LDS[2]	Pentecostal	Lutheran	Islam	Adventist	Other
MSA[1]	16.1	6.0	4.1	1.1	1.3	0.8	3.3	1.5	12.6
U.S.	18.7	7.3	3.0	2.0	1.8	1.7	1.3	1.3	11.6

Note: Figures are the number of adherents as a percentage of the total population and cover the eight largest religious groups in the U.S; (1) Figures cover the Washington-Arlington-Alexandria, DC-VA-MD-WV Metropolitan Statistical Area; (2) Church of Jesus Christ of Latter-day Saints
Sources: 2020 U.S. Religion Census, Association of Statisticians of American Religious Bodies; The Association of Religion Data Archives (ARDA)

Religious Groups by Tradition

Area	Catholic	Evangelical Protestant	Mainline Protestant	Black Protestant	Islam	Judaism	Hinduism	Orthodox	Buddhism
MSA[1]	16.1	12.3	6.5	3.3	3.3	1.0	0.9	0.9	0.5
U.S.	18.7	16.5	5.2	2.3	1.3	0.6	0.4	0.4	0.3

Note: Figures are the number of adherents as a percentage of the total population; (1) Figures cover the Washington-Arlington-Alexandria, DC-VA-MD-WV Metropolitan Statistical Area
Sources: 2020 U.S. Religion Census, Association of Statisticians of American Religious Bodies; The Association of Religion Data Archives (ARDA)

482 Washington, District of Columbia

ECONOMY

Gross Metropolitan Product

Area	2020	2021	2022	2023	Rank[2]
MSA[1]	560.7	600.8	647.6	688.6	6

Note: Figures are in billions of dollars; (1) Figures cover the Washington-Arlington-Alexandria, DC-VA-MD-WV Metropolitan Statistical Area; (2) Rank is based on 2021 data and ranges from 1 to 381
Source: U.S. Conference of Mayors, U.S. Metro Economies: U.S. Metros Compared to Global and State Economies, June 2022

Economic Growth

Area	2018-20 (%)	2021 (%)	2022 (%)	2023 (%)	Rank[2]
MSA[1]	-0.7	4.0	2.5	3.0	192
U.S.	-0.6	5.7	3.1	2.9	–

Note: Figures are real gross metropolitan product (GMP) growth rates and represent average annual percent change; (1) Figures cover the Washington-Arlington-Alexandria, DC-VA-MD-WV Metropolitan Statistical Area; (2) Rank is based on 2020 2-year average annual percent change and ranges from 1 to 381
Source: U.S. Conference of Mayors, U.S. Metro Economies: U.S. Metros Compared to Global and State Economies, June 2022

Metropolitan Area Exports

Area	2016	2017	2018	2019	2020	2021	Rank[2]
MSA[1]	13,582.4	12,736.1	13,602.7	14,563.8	13,537.3	12,210.8	31

Note: Figures are in millions of dollars; (1) Figures cover the Washington-Arlington-Alexandria, DC-VA-MD-WV Metropolitan Statistical Area; (2) Rank is based on 2021 data and ranges from 1 to 388
Source: U.S. Department of Commerce, International Trade Administration, Office of Trade and Economic Analysis, Industry and Analysis, Exports by Metropolitan Area, data extracted March 16, 2023

Building Permits

Area	Single-Family			Multi-Family			Total		
	2021	2022	Pct. Chg.	2021	2022	Pct. Chg.	2021	2022	Pct. Chg.
City	376	409	8.8	4,364	7,296	67.2	4,740	7,705	62.6
MSA[1]	13,729	11,657	-15.1	13,685	20,736	51.5	27,414	32,393	18.2
U.S.	1,115,400	975,600	-12.5	621,600	689,500	10.9	1,737,000	1,665,100	-4.1

Note: (1) Figures cover the Washington-Arlington-Alexandria, DC-VA-MD-WV Metropolitan Statistical Area; Figures represent new, privately-owned housing units authorized (unadjusted data); All permit data are based on estimates with imputation
Source: U.S. Census Bureau, Manufacturing, Mining, and Construction Statistics, Building Permits, 2021, 2022

Bankruptcy Filings

Area	Business Filings			Nonbusiness Filings		
	2021	2022	% Chg.	2021	2022	% Chg.
District of Columbia	36	36	0.0	264	200	-24.2
U.S.	14,347	13,481	-6.0	399,269	374,240	-6.3

Note: Business filings include Chapter 7, Chapter 9, Chapter 11, Chapter 12, Chapter 13, Chapter 15, and Section 304; Nonbusiness filings include Chapter 7, Chapter 11, and Chapter 13
Source: Administrative Office of the U.S. Courts, Business and Nonbusiness Bankruptcy, County Cases Commenced by Chapter of the Bankruptcy Code, During the 12-Month Period Ending December 31, 2021 and Business and Nonbusiness Bankruptcy, County Cases Commenced by Chapter of the Bankruptcy Code, During the 12-Month Period Ending December 31, 2022

Housing Vacancy Rates

Area	Gross Vacancy Rate[2] (%)			Year-Round Vacancy Rate[3] (%)			Rental Vacancy Rate[4] (%)			Homeowner Vacancy Rate[5] (%)		
	2020	2021	2022	2020	2021	2022	2020	2021	2022	2020	2021	2022
MSA[1]	6.5	5.5	5.2	6.2	5.3	5.0	5.5	5.9	5.3	0.7	0.5	0.6
U.S.	10.6	10.8	10.5	8.2	8.4	8.2	6.3	6.1	5.8	1.0	0.9	0.8

Note: (1) Figures cover the Washington-Arlington-Alexandria, DC-VA-MD-WV Metropolitan Statistical Area; (2) The percentage of the total housing inventory that is vacant; (3) The percentage of the housing inventory (excluding seasonal units) that is year-round vacant; (4) The percentage of rental inventory that is vacant for rent; (5) The percentage of homeowner inventory that is vacant for sale
Source: U.S. Census Bureau, Housing Vacancies and Homeownership Annual Statistics: 2020, 2021, 2022

INCOME

Income

Area	Per Capita ($)	Median Household ($)	Average Household ($)
City	63,793	93,547	138,421
MSA[1]	54,663	111,252	145,303
U.S.	37,638	69,021	97,196

Note: (1) Figures cover the Washington-Arlington-Alexandria, DC-VA-MD-WV Metropolitan Statistical Area
Source: U.S. Census Bureau, 2017-2021 American Community Survey 5-Year Estimates

Household Income Distribution

Area	Percent of Households Earning							
	Under $15,000	$15,000 -$24,999	$25,000 -$34,999	$35,000 -$49,999	$50,000 -$74,999	$75,000 -$99,999	$100,000 -$149,999	$150,000 and up
City	11.9	5.1	5.5	6.8	12.2	11.3	15.9	31.3
MSA[1]	5.7	3.7	4.4	6.8	12.6	12.0	19.6	35.4
U.S.	9.4	7.8	8.2	11.4	16.8	12.8	16.3	17.3

Note: (1) Figures cover the Washington-Arlington-Alexandria, DC-VA-MD-WV Metropolitan Statistical Area
Source: U.S. Census Bureau, 2017-2021 American Community Survey 5-Year Estimates

Poverty Rate

Area	All Ages	Under 18 Years Old	18 to 64 Years Old	65 Years and Over
City	15.4	22.8	13.7	13.9
MSA[1]	7.7	9.9	7.0	7.1
U.S.	12.6	17.0	11.8	9.6

Note: Figures are percentage of people whose income during the past 12 months was below the poverty level;
(1) Figures cover the Washington-Arlington-Alexandria, DC-VA-MD-WV Metropolitan Statistical Area
Source: U.S. Census Bureau, 2017-2021 American Community Survey 5-Year Estimates

EMPLOYMENT

Labor Force and Employment

Area	Civilian Labor Force			Workers Employed		
	Dec. 2021	Dec. 2022	% Chg.	Dec. 2021	Dec. 2022	% Chg.
City	378,144	386,520	2.2	358,132	370,787	3.5
MD[1]	2,676,340	2,681,074	0.2	2,582,644	2,604,564	0.8
U.S.	161,696,000	164,224,000	1.6	155,732,000	158,872,000	2.0

Note: Data is not seasonally adjusted and covers workers 16 years of age and older; (1) Figures cover the
Washington-Arlington-Alexandria, DC-VA-MD-WV Metropolitan Division
Source: Bureau of Labor Statistics, Local Area Unemployment Statistics

Unemployment Rate

Area	2022											
	Jan.	Feb.	Mar.	Apr.	May	Jun.	Jul.	Aug.	Sep.	Oct.	Nov.	Dec.
City	6.3	5.6	5.1	4.2	4.3	4.9	4.7	4.6	4.1	4.3	4.1	4.1
MD[1]	4.0	3.6	3.5	3.0	3.3	3.6	3.4	3.6	3.0	3.2	3.1	2.9
U.S.	4.4	4.1	3.8	3.3	3.4	3.8	3.8	3.8	3.3	3.4	3.4	3.3

Note: Data is not seasonally adjusted and covers workers 16 years of age and older; (1) Figures cover the
Washington-Arlington-Alexandria, DC-VA-MD-WV Metropolitan Division
Source: Bureau of Labor Statistics, Local Area Unemployment Statistics

Average Wages

Occupation	$/Hr.	Occupation	$/Hr.
Accountants and Auditors	48.98	Maintenance and Repair Workers	25.65
Automotive Mechanics	27.98	Marketing Managers	84.53
Bookkeepers	26.17	Network and Computer Systems Admin.	55.96
Carpenters	28.25	Nurses, Licensed Practical	29.10
Cashiers	15.21	Nurses, Registered	44.61
Computer Programmers	59.90	Nursing Assistants	18.33
Computer Systems Analysts	58.64	Office Clerks, General	22.52
Computer User Support Specialists	33.96	Physical Therapists	49.52
Construction Laborers	21.29	Physicians	101.91
Cooks, Restaurant	18.00	Plumbers, Pipefitters and Steamfitters	30.71
Customer Service Representatives	22.02	Police and Sheriff's Patrol Officers	37.25
Dentists	85.40	Postal Service Mail Carriers	27.72
Electricians	34.04	Real Estate Sales Agents	36.03
Engineers, Electrical	59.45	Retail Salespersons	17.61
Fast Food and Counter Workers	15.12	Sales Representatives, Technical/Scientific	62.98
Financial Managers	87.75	Secretaries, Exc. Legal/Medical/Executive	24.44
First-Line Supervisors of Office Workers	35.74	Security Guards	23.65
General and Operations Managers	72.97	Surgeons	186.07
Hairdressers/Cosmetologists	22.54	Teacher Assistants, Exc. Postsecondary*	19.39
Home Health and Personal Care Aides	15.70	Teachers, Secondary School, Exc. Sp. Ed.*	40.33
Janitors and Cleaners	17.34	Telemarketers	20.08
Landscaping/Groundskeeping Workers	19.67	Truck Drivers, Heavy/Tractor-Trailer	27.54
Lawyers	101.85	Truck Drivers, Light/Delivery Services	23.67
Maids and Housekeeping Cleaners	17.03	Waiters and Waitresses	19.91

Note: Wage data covers the Washington-Arlington-Alexandria, DC-VA-MD-WV Metropolitan Statistical Area;
(*) Hourly wages were calculated from annual wage data based on a 40 hour work week; n/a not available.
Source: Bureau of Labor Statistics, Metro Area Occupational Employment & Wage Estimates, May 2022

Employment by Industry

Sector	MD[1]		U.S.
	Number of Employees	Percent of Total	Percent of Total
Construction, Mining, and Logging	132,700	4.8	5.4
Private Education and Health Services	354,100	12.9	16.1
Financial Activities	120,900	4.4	5.9
Government	611,200	22.2	14.5
Information	67,900	2.5	2.0
Leisure and Hospitality	253,700	9.2	10.3
Manufacturing	38,100	1.4	8.4
Other Services	171,000	6.2	3.7
Professional and Business Services	668,900	24.3	14.7
Retail Trade	210,400	7.6	10.2
Transportation, Warehousing, and Utilities	73,400	2.7	4.9
Wholesale Trade	52,400	1.9	3.9

Note: Figures are non-farm employment as of December 2022. Figures are not seasonally adjusted and include workers 16 years of age and older; (1) Figures cover the Washington-Arlington-Alexandria, DC-VA-MD-WV Metropolitan Division
Source: Bureau of Labor Statistics, Current Employment Statistics, Employment, Hours, and Earnings

Employment by Occupation

Occupation Classification	City (%)	MSA[1] (%)	U.S. (%)
Management, Business, Science, and Arts	67.6	55.0	40.3
Natural Resources, Construction, and Maintenance	2.4	6.6	8.7
Production, Transportation, and Material Moving	3.5	6.6	13.1
Sales and Office	13.6	16.8	20.9
Service	13.0	15.0	17.0

Note: Figures cover employed civilians 16 years of age and older; (1) Figures cover the Washington-Arlington-Alexandria, DC-VA-MD-WV Metropolitan Statistical Area
Source: U.S. Census Bureau, 2017-2021 American Community Survey 5-Year Estimates

Occupations with Greatest Projected Employment Growth: 2022 – 2024

Occupation[1]	2022 Employment	2024 Projected Employment	Numeric Employment Change	Percent Employment Change
Management Analysts	25,050	25,970	920	3.7
Computer Occupations, All Other (SOC 2018)	21,750	22,320	570	2.6
Public Relations Specialists	18,580	19,130	550	3.0
General and Operations Managers	34,040	34,540	500	1.5
Project Management Specialists and Business Operations Specialists, All Other	55,590	56,050	460	0.8
Cooks, Restaurant	4,580	4,980	400	8.7
Security Guards	14,650	15,020	370	2.5
Software Developers and Software Quality Assurance Analysts and Testers	11,400	11,760	360	3.2
Home Health and Personal Care Aides	10,810	11,140	330	3.1
Waiters and Waitresses	9,130	9,460	330	3.6

Note: Projections cover District of Columbia; (1) Sorted by numeric employment change
Source: www.projectionscentral.com, State Occupational Projections, 2022–2024 Short-Term Projections

Fastest-Growing Occupations: 2022 – 2024

Occupation[1]	2022 Employment	2024 Projected Employment	Numeric Employment Change	Percent Employment Change
Photographers	520	570	50	9.6
Fitness Trainers and Aerobics Instructors	980	1,070	90	9.2
Cooks, Restaurant	4,580	4,980	400	8.7
Health Specialties Teachers, Postsecondary	940	1,000	60	6.4
Statisticians	1,590	1,680	90	5.7
Bartenders	3,740	3,950	210	5.6
Information Security Analysts (SOC 2018)	2,080	2,190	110	5.3
Data Scientists and Mathematical Science Occupations, All Other	1,570	1,650	80	5.1
Medical and Health Services Managers	1,800	1,890	90	5.0
Electricians	1,990	2,090	100	5.0

Note: Projections cover District of Columbia; (1) Sorted by percent employment change and excludes occupations with numeric employment change less than 50
Source: www.projectionscentral.com, State Occupational Projections, 2022–2024 Short-Term Projections

Washington, District of Columbia   485

CITY FINANCES

City Government Finances

Component	2020 ($000)	2020 ($ per capita)
Total Revenues	16,391,615	23,226
Total Expenditures	18,775,013	26,603
Debt Outstanding	17,903,738	25,368
Cash and Securities[1]	8,280,786	11,733

Note: (1) Cash and security holdings of a government at the close of its fiscal year, including those of its dependent agencies, utilities, and liquor stores.
Source: U.S. Census Bureau, State & Local Government Finances 2020

City Government Revenue by Source

Source	2020 ($000)	2020 ($ per capita)	2020 (%)
General Revenue			
From Federal Government	4,547,114	6,443	27.7
From State Government	248,789	353	1.5
From Local Governments	272,487	386	1.7
Taxes			
Property	2,927,157	4,148	17.9
Sales and Gross Receipts	1,611,088	2,283	9.8
Personal Income	2,377,236	3,368	14.5
Corporate Income	727,697	1,031	4.4
Motor Vehicle License	40,713	58	0.2
Other Taxes	650,558	922	4.0
Current Charges	805,879	1,142	4.9
Liquor Store	0	0	0.0
Utility	221,741	314	1.4

Source: U.S. Census Bureau, State & Local Government Finances 2020

City Government Expenditures by Function

Function	2020 ($000)	2020 ($ per capita)	2020 (%)
General Direct Expenditures			
Air Transportation	0	0	0.0
Corrections	262,352	371	1.4
Education	3,317,520	4,700	17.7
Employment Security Administration	38,555	54	0.2
Financial Administration	334,404	473	1.8
Fire Protection	327,858	464	1.7
General Public Buildings	282,966	400	1.5
Governmental Administration, Other	205,650	291	1.1
Health	664,785	942	3.5
Highways	660,965	936	3.5
Hospitals	282,451	400	1.5
Housing and Community Development	1,076,575	1,525	5.7
Interest on General Debt	631,094	894	3.4
Judicial and Legal	195,194	276	1.0
Libraries	138,018	195	0.7
Parking	28,478	40	0.2
Parks and Recreation	352,263	499	1.9
Police Protection	681,236	965	3.6
Public Welfare	4,393,854	6,225	23.4
Sewerage	385,734	546	2.1
Solid Waste Management	159,080	225	0.8
Veterans' Services	0	0	0.0
Liquor Store	0	0	0.0
Utility	555,115	786	3.0

Source: U.S. Census Bureau, State & Local Government Finances 2020

TAXES

State Corporate Income Tax Rates

State	Tax Rate (%)	Income Brackets ($)	Num. of Brackets	Financial Institution Tax Rate (%)[a]	Federal Income Tax Ded.
D.C.	8.25 (b)	Flat rate	1	8.25 (b)	No

Note: Tax rates as of January 1, 2023; (a) Rates listed are the corporate income tax rate applied to financial institutions or excise taxes based on income. Some states have other taxes based upon the value of deposits or shares; (b) Minimum tax is $800 in California, $250 in District of Columbia, $50 in Arizona and North Dakota (banks), $400 ($100 banks) in Rhode Island, $200 per location in South Dakota (banks), $100 in Utah, $300 in Vermont.
Source: Federation of Tax Administrators, State Corporate Income Tax Rates, January 1, 2023

State Individual Income Tax Rates

State	Tax Rate (%)	Income Brackets ($)	Personal Exemptions ($)			Standard Ded. ($)	
			Single	Married	Depend.	Single	Married
D.C.	4.0 - 10.75	10,000 - 1 million	(d)	(d)	(d)	13,850	27,700 (d)

Note: Tax rates as of January 1, 2023; Local- and county-level taxes are not included; Federal income tax is not deductible on state income tax returns; (d) These states use the personal exemption/standard deduction amounts provided in the federal Internal Revenue Code.
Source: Federation of Tax Administrators, State Individual Income Tax Rates, January 1, 2023

Various State Sales and Excise Tax Rates

State	State Sales Tax (%)	Gasoline[1] ($/gal.)	Cigarette[2] ($/pack)	Spirits[3] ($/gal.)	Wine[4] ($/gal.)	Beer[5] ($/gal.)	Recreational Marijuana (%)
D.C.	6	0.338	5.02	6.68	2.07	0.79	(u)

Note: All tax rates as of January 1, 2023; (1) The American Petroleum Institute has developed a methodology for determining the average tax rate on a gallon of fuel. Rates may include any of the following: excise taxes, environmental fees, storage tank fees, other fees or taxes, general sales tax, and local taxes; (2) The federal excise tax of $1.0066 per pack and local taxes are not included; (3) Rates are those applicable to off-premise sales of 40% alcohol by volume (a.b.v.) distilled spirits in 750ml containers. Local excise taxes are excluded; (4) Rates are those applicable to off-premise sales of 11% a.b.v. non-carbonated wine in 750ml containers; (5) Rates are those applicable to off-premise sales of 4.7% a.b.v. beer in 12 ounce containers; (u) District of Columbia voters approved legalization and purchase of marijuana in 2014 but federal law prohibits any action to implement it
Source: Tax Foundation, 2023 Facts & Figures: How Does Your State Compare?

State Business Tax Climate Index Rankings

State	Overall Rank	Corporate Tax Rank	Individual Income Tax Rank	Sales Tax Rank	Property Tax Rank	Unemployment Insurance Tax Rank
District of Columbia	48	29	48	39	49	38

Note: The index is a measure of how each state's tax laws affect economic performance. The lower the rank, the more favorable a state's tax system is for business. States without a given tax are given a ranking of 1. The scores/rankings for the District of Columbia do not affect other states. The 2023 index represents the tax climate as of July 1, 2022.
Source: Tax Foundation, State Business Tax Climate Index 2023

TRANSPORTATION

Means of Transportation to Work

Area	Car/Truck/Van		Public Transportation			Bicycle	Walked	Other Means	Worked at Home
	Drove Alone	Car-pooled	Bus	Subway	Railroad				
City	30.7	4.7	10.0	16.7	0.2	3.7	11.3	2.7	19.8
MSA[1]	60.7	8.5	3.6	5.8	0.6	0.7	2.9	1.7	15.4
U.S.	73.2	8.6	2.0	1.6	0.5	0.5	2.5	1.5	9.7

Note: Figures are percentages and cover workers 16 years of age and older; (1) Figures cover the Washington-Arlington-Alexandria, DC-VA-MD-WV Metropolitan Statistical Area
Source: U.S. Census Bureau, 2017-2021 American Community Survey 5-Year Estimates

Travel Time to Work

Area	Less Than 10 Minutes	10 to 19 Minutes	20 to 29 Minutes	30 to 44 Minutes	45 to 59 Minutes	60 to 89 Minutes	90 Minutes or More
City	5.3	19.0	22.3	33.1	11.6	6.6	2.1
MSA[1]	6.1	19.3	18.2	26.2	13.7	12.1	4.3
U.S.	12.4	28.5	21.0	20.9	8.2	6.2	2.9

Note: Note: Figures are percentages and include workers 16 years old and over; (1) Figures cover the Washington-Arlington-Alexandria, DC-VA-MD-WV Metropolitan Statistical Area
Source: U.S. Census Bureau, 2017-2021 American Community Survey 5-Year Estimates

Key Congestion Measures

Measure	1990	2000	2010	2015	2020
Annual Hours of Delay, Total (000)	84,125	137,652	211,442	234,531	101,775
Annual Hours of Delay, Per Auto Commuter	53	70	90	96	42
Annual Congestion Cost, Per Auto Commuter ($)	1,311	1,610	1,965	2,015	905

Note: Covers the Washington DC-VA-MD urban area
Source: Texas A&M Transportation Institute, 2021 Urban Mobility Report

Freeway Travel Time Index

Measure	1985	1990	1995	2000	2005	2010	2015	2020
Urban Area Index[1]	1.19	1.22	1.27	1.29	1.34	1.35	1.35	1.12
Urban Area Rank[1,2]	6	5	5	6	5	5	7	10

Note: Freeway Travel Time Index—the ratio of travel time in the peak period to the travel time at free-flow conditions. For example, a value of 1.30 indicates a 20-minute free-flow trip takes 26 minutes in the peak (20 minutes x 1.30 = 26 minutes); (1) Covers the Washington DC-VA-MD urban area; (2) Rank is based on 101 larger urban areas (#1 = highest travel time index)
Source: Texas A&M Transportation Institute, 2021 Urban Mobility Report

Public Transportation

Agency Name / Mode of Transportation	Vehicles Operated in Maximum Service[1]	Annual Unlinked Passenger Trips[2] (in thous.)	Annual Passenger Miles[3] (in thous.)
Washington Metropolitan Area Transit Authority (WMATA)			
Bus (directly operated)	963	51,179.1	156,237.2
Bus (purchased transportation)	47	1,146.5	6,546.5
Demand Response (purchased transportation)	644	1,058.8	8,720.6
Demand Response - Taxi	76	5.7	55.2
Heavy Rail (directly operated)	998	36,550.2	199,671.9

Note: (1) Number of revenue vehicles operated by the given mode and type of service to meet the annual maximum service requirement. This is the revenue vehicle count during the peak season of the year; on the week and day that maximum service is provided. Vehicles operated in maximum service (VOMS) exclude atypical days and one-time special events; (2) Number of passengers who boarded public transportation vehicles. Passengers are counted each time they board a vehicle no matter how many vehicles they use to travel from their origin to their destination. (3) Sum of the distances ridden by all passengers during the entire fiscal year.
Source: Federal Transit Administration, National Transit Database, 2021

Air Transportation

Airport Name and Code / Type of Service	Passenger Airlines[1]	Passenger Enplanements	Freight Carriers[2]	Freight (lbs)
Ronald Reagan Washington National (DCA)				
Domestic service (U.S. carriers - 2022)	17	11,418,170	7	1,350,157
International service (U.S. carriers - 2021)	3	11,983	0	0
Dulles International (IAD)				
Domestic service (U.S. carriers - 2022)	33	6,693,511	9	90,291,831
International service (U.S. carriers - 2021)	15	649,370	4	29,382,436

Note: (1) Includes all U.S.-based major, minor and commuter airlines that carried at least one passenger during the year; (2) Includes all U.S.-based airlines and freight carriers that transported at least one pound of freight during the year.
Source: Bureau of Transportation Statistics, The Intermodal Transportation Database, Air Carriers: T-100 Domestic Market (U.S. Carriers), 2022; Bureau of Transportation Statistics, The Intermodal Transportation Database, Air Carriers: T-100 International Market (U.S. Carriers), 2021

BUSINESSES

Major Business Headquarters

Company Name	Industry	Rankings	
		Fortune[1]	Forbes[2]
Carlyle Group	Private equity	398	-
Danaher	Scientific, photographic and control equipment	118	-
Fannie Mae	Diversified financials	33	-
Hogan Lovells	Services	-	211

Note: (1) Companies that produce a 10-K are ranked 1 to 500 based on 2021 revenue; (2) All private companies with at least $2 billion in annual revenue through the end of their most current fiscal year are ranked 1 to 246; companies listed are headquartered in the city; dashes indicate no ranking
Source: Fortune, "Fortune 500," 2022; Forbes, "America's Largest Private Companies," 2022

Fastest-Growing Businesses

According to *Inc.*, Washington is home to six of America's 500 fastest-growing private companies: **Pie Insurance** (#163); **Ordway** (#237); **Upside** (#308); **Gen3 Technology Consulting** (#318); **ThinkNimble** (#459); **Manuscripts** (#468). Criteria: must be an independent, privately-held, for-profit, U.S. corporation, proprietorship or partnership as of December 31, 2021; revenues must be at least $100,000 in 2018 and $2 million in 2021; must have four-year operating/sales history. *Inc., "America's 500 Fastest-Growing Private Companies," 2022*

According to *Initiative for a Competitive Inner City (ICIC)*, Washington is home to three of America's 100 fastest-growing "inner city" companies: **Hayat Brown** (#44); **TCG** (#73); **Star Enterprises** (#88). Criteria for inclusion: company must be headquartered in or have 51 percent or more of its physical operations in an economically distressed urban area; must be an independent, for-profit corporation, partnership or proprietorship; must have 10 or more employees and have a five-year sales history that includes sales of at least $200,000 in the base year and at least $1 million in the current year with no decrease in sales over the two most recent years. Companies were ranked overall by revenue growth over the five-year period between 2017 and 2021. *Initiative for a Competitive Inner City (ICIC), "Inner City 100 Companies," 2022*

According to Deloitte, Washington is home to six of North America's 500 fastest-growing high-technology companies: **Upside** (#88); **Fundrise** (#107); **Arcadia** (#177); **Morning Consult** (#362); **Clutch** (#425); **Sayari Labs** (#443). Companies are ranked by percentage growth in revenue over a four-year period. Criteria for inclusion: company must be headquartered within North America; must own proprietary intellectual property or technology that is sold to customers in products that contributes to a significant portion of the company's operating revenue; must have been in business for a minumum of four years with 2018 operating revenues of at least $50,000 USD/CD and 2021 operating revenues of at least $5 million USD/CD. *Deloitte, 2022 Technology Fast 500*[TM]

Living Environment

COST OF LIVING

Cost of Living Index

Composite Index	Groceries	Housing	Utilities	Transportation	Health Care	Misc. Goods/ Services
152.3	109.2	252.1	113.1	108.3	98.8	118.7

Note: The Cost of Living Index measures regional differences in the cost of consumer goods and services, excluding taxes and non-consumer expenditures, for professional and managerial households in the top income quintile. It is based on more than 50,000 prices covering almost 60 different items for which prices are collected three times a year by chambers of commerce, economic development organizations or university applied economic centers in each participating urban area. The numbers shown should be read as a percentage above or below the national average of 100. For example, a value of 115.4 in the groceries column indicates that grocery prices are 15.4% higher than the national average. Small differences in the index numbers should not be interpreted as significant; Figures cover the Washington DC urban area.
Source: The Council for Community and Economic Research, Cost of Living Index, 2022

Grocery Prices

Area[1]	T-Bone Steak ($/pound)	Frying Chicken ($/pound)	Whole Milk ($/half gal.)	Eggs ($/dozen)	Orange Juice ($/64 oz.)	Coffee ($/11.5 oz.)
City[2]	13.41	1.21	2.91	2.62	4.08	5.36
Avg.	13.81	1.59	2.43	2.25	3.85	4.95
Min.	10.17	0.90	1.51	1.30	2.90	3.46
Max.	19.35	3.30	4.32	4.32	5.31	8.59

*Note: (1) Values for the local area are compared with the average, minimum and maximum values for all 286 areas in the Cost of Living Index; (2) Figures cover the Washington DC urban area; **T-Bone Steak** (price per pound); **Frying Chicken** (price per pound, whole fryer); **Whole Milk** (half gallon carton); **Eggs** (price per dozen, Grade A, large); **Orange Juice** (64 oz. Tropicana or Florida Natural); **Coffee** (11.5 oz. can, vacuum-packed, Maxwell House, Hills Bros, or Folgers).*
Source: The Council for Community and Economic Research, Cost of Living Index, 2022

Housing and Utility Costs

Area[1]	New Home Price ($)	Apartment Rent ($/month)	All Electric ($/month)	Part Electric ($/month)	Other Energy ($/month)	Telephone ($/month)
City[2]	1,156,418	3,220	-	117.06	100.23	188.98
Avg.	450,913	1,371	176.41	99.93	76.96	190.22
Min.	229,283	546	100.84	31.56	27.15	174.27
Max.	2,434,977	4,569	356.86	249.59	272.24	208.31

*Note: (1) Values for the local area are compared with the average, minimum and maximum values for all 286 areas in the Cost of Living Index; (2) Figures cover the Washington DC urban area; **New Home Price** (2,400 sf living area, 8,000 sf lot, in urban area with full utilities); **Apartment Rent** (950 sf 2 bedroom/1.5 or 2 bath, unfurnished, excluding all utilities except water); **All Electric** (average monthly cost for an all-electric home); **Part Electric** (average monthly cost for a part-electric home); **Other Energy** (average monthly cost for natural gas, fuel oil, coal, wood, and any other forms of energy except electricity); **Telephone** (price includes the base monthly rate plus taxes and fees for three lines of mobile phone service).*
Source: The Council for Community and Economic Research, Cost of Living Index, 2022

Health Care, Transportation, and Other Costs

Area[1]	Doctor ($/visit)	Dentist ($/visit)	Optometrist ($/visit)	Gasoline ($/gallon)	Beauty Salon ($/visit)	Men's Shirt ($)
City[2]	129.71	105.20	75.00	3.98	81.00	37.83
Avg.	124.91	107.77	117.66	3.86	43.31	34.21
Min.	36.61	58.25	51.79	2.90	22.18	13.05
Max.	250.21	162.58	371.96	5.54	85.61	63.54

*Note: (1) Values for the local area are compared with the average, minimum and maximum values for all 286 areas in the Cost of Living Index; (2) Figures cover the Washington DC urban area; **Doctor** (general practitioners routine exam of an established patient); **Dentist** (adult teeth cleaning and periodic oral examination); **Optometrist** (full vision eye exam for established adult patient); **Gasoline** (one gallon regular unleaded, national brand, including all taxes, cash price at self-service pump if available); **Beauty Salon** (woman's shampoo, trim, and blow-dry); **Men's Shirt** (cotton/polyester dress shirt, pinpoint weave, long sleeves).*
Source: The Council for Community and Economic Research, Cost of Living Index, 2022

HOUSING

Homeownership Rate

Area	2015 (%)	2016 (%)	2017 (%)	2018 (%)	2019 (%)	2020 (%)	2021 (%)	2022 (%)
MSA[1]	64.6	63.1	63.3	62.9	64.7	67.9	65.8	66.2
U.S.	63.7	63.4	63.9	64.4	64.6	66.6	65.5	65.8

Note: (1) Figures cover the Washington-Arlington-Alexandria, DC-VA-MD-WV Metropolitan Statistical Area
Source: U.S. Census Bureau, Housing Vacancies and Homeownership Annual Statistics: 2015-2022

House Price Index (HPI)

Area	National Ranking[2]	Quarterly Change (%)	One-Year Change (%)	Five-Year Change (%)	Since 1991Q1 (%)
MD[1]	238	-1.35	6.16	35.79	253.98
U.S.[3]	—	0.34	8.41	58.44	289.08

Note: The HPI is a weighted repeat sales index. It measures average price changes in repeat sales or refinancings on the same properties. This information is obtained by reviewing repeat mortgage transactions on single-family properties whose mortgages have been purchased or securitized by Fannie Mae or Freddie Mac since January 1975; (1) Figures cover the Washington-Arlington-Alexandria, DC-VA-MD-WV Metropolitan Division; (2) Rankings are based on annual percentage change for all metro areas containing at least 15,000 transactions over the last 10 years and ranges from 1 to 257; (3) figures based on a weighted average of Census Division estimates using a seasonally adjusted, purchase-only index; all figures are for the period ending December 31, 2022
Source: Federal Housing Finance Agency, Change in FHFA Metropolitan Area House Price Indexes, 2022Q4

Median Single-Family Home Prices

Area	2020	2021	2022[p]	Percent Change 2021 to 2022
MSA[1]	475.4	544.3	585.0	7.5
U.S. Average	300.2	357.1	392.6	9.9

Note: Figures are median sales prices of existing single-family homes in thousands of dollars; (p) preliminary; (1) Figures cover the Washington-Arlington-Alexandria, DC-VA-MD-WV Metropolitan Statistical Area
Source: National Association of Realtors, Median Sales Price of Existing Single-Family Homes for Metropolitan Areas, 4th Quarter 2022

Qualifying Income Based on Median Sales Price of Existing Single-Family Homes

Area	With 5% Down ($)	With 10% Down ($)	With 20% Down ($)
MSA[1]	164,581	155,919	138,595
U.S. Average	112,234	106,237	94,513

Note: Figures are preliminary; Qualifying income is based on a mortgage rate of 6.77%. Monthly principal and interest payment is limited to 25% of income; (1) Figures cover the Washington-Arlington-Alexandria, DC-VA-MD-WV Metropolitan Statistical Area
Source: National Association of Realtors, Qualifying Income Based on Median Sales Price of Existing Single-Family Homes for Metropolitan Areas, 4th Quarter 2022

Home Value

Area	Under $100,000	$100,000 -$199,999	$200,000 -$299,999	$300,000 -$399,999	$400,000 -$499,999	$500,000 -$999,999	$1,000,000 or more	Median ($)
City	1.8	2.2	7.5	12.3	12.7	42.1	21.4	635,900
MSA[1]	2.4	4.9	14.2	19.7	16.6	34.4	7.8	453,100
U.S.	16.2	24.2	20.1	13.6	8.3	13.6	4.1	244,900

Note: Figures are percentages except for median and cover owner-occupied housing units; (1) Figures cover the Washington-Arlington-Alexandria, DC-VA-MD-WV Metropolitan Statistical Area
Source: U.S. Census Bureau, 2017-2021 American Community Survey 5-Year Estimates

Year Housing Structure Built

Area	2020 or Later	2010 -2019	2000 -2009	1990 -1999	1980 -1989	1970 -1979	1960 -1969	1950 -1959	1940 -1949	Before 1940	Median Year
City	0.2	10.3	7.9	3.1	4.7	6.8	11.1	12.1	10.8	32.9	1955
MSA[1]	0.2	9.0	14.0	14.0	15.4	13.5	11.8	8.9	4.9	8.3	1982
U.S.	0.2	7.3	13.6	13.6	13.2	14.8	10.3	10.0	4.7	12.2	1979

Note: Figures are percentages except for Median Year; Note: (1) Figures cover the Washington-Arlington-Alexandria, DC-VA-MD-WV Metropolitan Statistical Area
Source: U.S. Census Bureau, 2017-2021 American Community Survey 5-Year Estimates

Gross Monthly Rent

Area	Under $500	$500 -$999	$1,000 -$1,499	$1,500 -$1,999	$2,000 -$2,499	$2,500 -$2,999	$3,000 and up	Median ($)
City	9.2	10.4	22.3	22.4	15.2	9.2	11.3	1,681
MSA[1]	4.3	6.4	20.9	32.5	19.2	8.6	8.1	1,783
U.S.	8.1	30.5	30.8	16.8	7.3	3.1	3.5	1,163

Note: Figures are percentages except for median; Gross rent is the contract rent plus the estimated average monthly cost of utilities (electricity, gas, and water and sewer) and fuels (oil, coal, kerosene, wood, etc.) if these are paid by the renter (or paid for the renter by someone else); (1) Figures cover the Washington-Arlington-Alexandria, DC-VA-MD-WV Metropolitan Statistical Area
Source: U.S. Census Bureau, 2017-2021 American Community Survey 5-Year Estimates

HEALTH

Health Risk Factors

Category	MD[1] (%)	U.S. (%)
Adults aged 18–64 who have any kind of health care coverage	92.5	90.9
Adults who reported being in good or better health	87.8	85.2
Adults who have been told they have high blood cholesterol	36.0	35.7
Adults who have been told they have high blood pressure	31.2	32.4
Adults who are current smokers	7.5	14.4
Adults who currently use e-cigarettes	5.0	6.7
Adults who currently use chewing tobacco, snuff, or snus	1.5	3.5
Adults who are heavy drinkers[2]	5.6	6.3
Adults who are binge drinkers[3]	15.3	15.4
Adults who are overweight (BMI 25.0 - 29.9)	34.6	34.4
Adults who are obese (BMI 30.0 - 99.8)	31.0	33.9
Adults who participated in any physical activities in the past month	82.8	76.3

Note: (1) Figures cover the Washington-Arlington-Alexandria, DC-VA-MD-WV Metropolitan Division; (2) Heavy drinkers are classified as adult men having more than 14 drinks per week and adult women having more than 7 drinks per week; (3) Binge drinkers are classified as males having five or more drinks on one occasion or females having four or more drinks on one occasion
Source: Centers for Disease Control and Prevention, Behaviorial Risk Factor Surveillance System, SMART: Selected Metropolitan Area Risk Trends, 2021

Acute and Chronic Health Conditions

Category	MD[1] (%)	U.S. (%)
Adults who have ever been told they had a heart attack	2.5	4.0
Adults who have ever been told they have angina or coronary heart disease	2.6	3.8
Adults who have ever been told they had a stroke	2.5	3.0
Adults who have ever been told they have asthma	14.4	14.9
Adults who have ever been told they have arthritis	21.4	25.8
Adults who have ever been told they have diabetes[2]	9.5	10.9
Adults who have ever been told they had skin cancer	4.7	6.6
Adults who have ever been told they had any other types of cancer	6.0	7.5
Adults who have ever been told they have COPD	4.1	6.1
Adults who have ever been told they have kidney disease	2.4	3.0
Adults who have ever been told they have a form of depression	14.5	20.5

Note: (1) Figures cover the Washington-Arlington-Alexandria, DC-VA-MD-WV Metropolitan Division; (2) Figures do not include pregnancy-related, borderline, or pre-diabetes
Source: Centers for Disease Control and Prevention, Behaviorial Risk Factor Surveillance System, SMART: Selected Metropolitan Area Risk Trends, 2021

Health Screening and Vaccination Rates

Category	MD[1] (%)	U.S. (%)
Adults who have ever been tested for HIV	47.3	34.9
Adults who have had their blood cholesterol checked within the last five years	90.1	85.2
Adults aged 65+ who have had flu shot within the past year	71.6	68.6
Adults aged 65+ who have ever had a pneumonia vaccination	71.6	71.0

Note: (1) Figures cover the Washington-Arlington-Alexandria, DC-VA-MD-WV Metropolitan Division.
Source: Centers for Disease Control and Prevention, Behaviorial Risk Factor Surveillance System, SMART: Selected Metropolitan Area Risk Trends, 2021

Disability Status

Category	MD[1] (%)	U.S. (%)
Adults who reported being deaf	3.8	7.2
Are you blind or have serious difficulty seeing, even when wearing glasses?	3.6	4.8
Are you limited in any way in any of your usual activities due to arthritis?	7.7	11.1
Do you have difficulty doing errands alone?	4.9	7.0
Do you have difficulty dressing or bathing?	2.7	3.6
Do you have serious difficulty concentrating/remembering/making decisions?	8.7	12.1
Do you have serious difficulty walking or climbing stairs?	9.0	12.8

Note: (1) Figures cover the Washington-Arlington-Alexandria, DC-VA-MD-WV Metropolitan Division.
Source: Centers for Disease Control and Prevention, Behaviorial Risk Factor Surveillance System, SMART: Selected Metropolitan Area Risk Trends, 2021

Mortality Rates for the Top 10 Causes of Death in the U.S.

ICD-10[a] Sub-Chapter	ICD-10[a] Code	Crude Mortality Rate[1] per 100,000 population	
		County[2]	U.S.
Malignant neoplasms	C00-C97	143.3	182.6
Ischaemic heart diseases	I20-I25	102.9	113.1
Other forms of heart disease	I30-I51	36.4	64.4
Other degenerative diseases of the nervous system	G30-G31	21.3	51.0
Cerebrovascular diseases	I60-I69	39.7	47.8
Other external causes of accidental injury	W00-X59	70.6	46.4
Chronic lower respiratory diseases	J40-J47	18.9	45.7
Organic, including symptomatic, mental disorders	F01-F09	30.1	35.9
Hypertensive diseases	I10-I15	50.8	35.0
Diabetes mellitus	E10-E14	22.3	29.6

Note: (a) ICD-10 = International Classification of Diseases 10th Revision; (1) Crude mortality rates are a three-year average covering 2019-2021; (2) Figures cover District of Columbia.
Source: Centers for Disease Control and Prevention, National Center for Health Statistics. National Vital Statistics System, Mortality 2018-2021 on CDC WONDER Online Database

Mortality Rates for Selected Causes of Death

ICD-10[a] Sub-Chapter	ICD-10[a] Code	Crude Mortality Rate[1] per 100,000 population	
		County[2]	U.S.
Assault	X85-Y09	27.0	7.0
Diseases of the liver	K70-K76	10.9	19.8
Human immunodeficiency virus (HIV) disease	B20-B24	9.0	1.5
Influenza and pneumonia	J09-J18	11.1	14.7
Intentional self-harm	X60-X84	6.1	14.3
Malnutrition	E40-E46	1.1	4.3
Obesity and other hyperalimentation	E65-E68	2.9	3.0
Renal failure	N17-N19	6.8	15.7
Transport accidents	V01-V99	7.7	13.6
Viral hepatitis	B15-B19	2.7	1.2

Note: (a) ICD-10 = International Classification of Diseases 10th Revision; (1) Crude mortality rates are a three-year average covering 2019-2021; (2) Figures cover District of Columbia; Data are suppressed when the data meet the criteria for confidentiality constraints; Crude mortality rates are flagged as unreliable when the rate would be calculated with a numerator of 20 or less.
Source: Centers for Disease Control and Prevention, National Center for Health Statistics. National Vital Statistics System, Mortality 2018-2021 on CDC WONDER Online Database

Health Insurance Coverage

Area	With Health Insurance	With Private Health Insurance	With Public Health Insurance	Without Health Insurance	Population Under Age 19 Without Health Insurance
City	96.6	71.9	34.7	3.4	2.2
MSA[1]	92.7	77.8	26.4	7.3	4.5
U.S.	91.2	67.8	35.4	8.8	5.3

Note: Figures are percentages that cover the civilian noninstitutionalized population; (1) Figures cover the Washington-Arlington-Alexandria, DC-VA-MD-WV Metropolitan Statistical Area
Source: U.S. Census Bureau, 2017-2021 American Community Survey 5-Year Estimates

Number of Medical Professionals

Area	MDs[3]	DOs[3,4]	Dentists	Podiatrists	Chiropractors	Optometrists
DC[1] (number)	5,641	131	863	64	70	94
DC[1] (rate[2])	817.4	19.0	128.8	9.6	10.4	14.0
U.S. (rate[2])	289.3	23.5	72.5	6.2	28.7	17.4

Note: Data as of 2021 unless noted; (1) Data covers the District of Columbia; (2) Rate per 100,000 population; (3) Data as of 2020 and includes all active, non-federal physicians; (4) Doctor of Osteopathic Medicine
Source: U.S. Department of Health and Human Services, Health Resources and Services Administration, Bureau of Health Professions, Area Resource File (ARF) 2021-2022

Best Hospitals

According to *U.S. News,* the Washington-Arlington-Alexandria, DC-VA-MD-WV metro area is home to four of the best hospitals in the U.S.: **Inova Fairfax Hospital** (1 adult specialty and 1 pediatric specialty); **MedStar Georgetown University Hospital** (1 adult specialty); **MedStar Heart & Vascular Institute at MedStar Washington Hospital Center** (1 adult specialty); **MedStar National Rehabilitation Hospital** (1 adult specialty). The hospitals listed were nationally ranked in at least one of 15 adult or 10 pediatric specialties. The number of specialties shown cover the parent hospital. Only 164 U.S. hospitals performed well enough to be nationally ranked in one or more specialties. Twenty hospitals in the U.S. made the Honor Roll. The Best Hospitals Honor Roll takes both the national rankings and the procedure and condition ratings into account. Hospitals received points if they were nationally ranked in one of the 15 adult specialties—the higher they ranked, the more points they got—and how many ratings of "high performing" they earned in the 17 procedures and conditions. *U.S. News Online, "America's Best Hospitals 2022-23"*

According to *U.S. News,* the Washington-Arlington-Alexandria, DC-VA-MD-WV metro area is home to two of the best children's hospitals in the U.S.: **Children's National Hospital** (Honor Roll/10 pediatric specialties); **Inova L.J. Murphy Children's Hospital** (1 pediatric specialty). The hospitals listed were highly ranked in at least one of 10 pediatric specialties. Eighty-six children's hospitals in the U.S. were nationally ranked in at least one specialty. Hospitals received points for being ranked in a specialty, and the 10 hospitals with the most points across the 10 specialties make up the Honor Roll. *U.S. News Online, "America's Best Children's Hospitals 2022-23"*

EDUCATION

Public School District Statistics

District Name	Schls	Pupils	Pupil/ Teacher Ratio	Minority Pupils[1] (%)	LEP/ELL[2] (%)	IEP[3] (%)
District of Columbia Public Schls	116	48,635	11.8	83.0	12.6	16.4
Friendship PCS	15	4,854	12.0	99.5	1.4	15.4
Kipp DC PCS	20	7,000	10.7	99.8	0.7	16.1

Note: Table includes school districts with 2,000 or more students; (1) Percentage of students that are not non-Hispanic white; (2) Percentage of students that are Limited English Proficient or English Language Learners (2018-19); (3) Percentage of students that have an Individualized Education Program (2019-20). Source: U.S. Department of Education, National Center for Education Statistics, Common Core of Data, Local Education Agency (School District) Universe Survey: School Year 2021-2022

Best High Schools

According to *U.S. News,* Washington is home to three of the top 500 high schools in the U.S.: **Benjamin Banneker Academy High School** (#96); **School Without Walls High School** (#97); **BASIS DC** (#274). Nearly 18,000 public, magnet and charter schools were ranked based on their performance on state assessments and how well they prepare students for college. *U.S. News & World Report, "Best High Schools 2022"*

Highest Level of Education

Area	Less than H.S.	H.S. Diploma	Some College, No Deg.	Associate Degree	Bachelor's Degree	Master's Degree	Prof. School Degree	Doctorate Degree
City	7.8	15.5	12.4	3.0	25.5	21.9	9.7	4.3
MSA[1]	8.5	17.7	15.5	6.0	26.4	18.2	4.6	3.3
U.S.	11.1	26.5	20.0	8.7	20.6	9.3	2.2	1.5

Note: Figures cover persons age 25 and over; (1) Figures cover the Washington-Arlington-Alexandria, DC-VA-MD-WV Metropolitan Statistical Area Source: U.S. Census Bureau, 2017-2021 American Community Survey 5-Year Estimates

Educational Attainment by Race

Area	High School Graduate or Higher (%)					Bachelor's Degree or Higher (%)				
	Total	White	Black	Asian	Hisp.[2]	Total	White	Black	Asian	Hisp.[2]
City	92.2	98.6	88.0	94.4	78.6	61.4	90.8	31.1	82.4	52.8
MSA[1]	91.5	95.1	92.4	91.3	70.4	52.4	61.3	37.2	66.0	28.0
U.S.	88.9	91.4	87.2	87.6	71.2	33.7	35.5	23.3	55.6	18.4

Note: Figures shown cover persons 25 years old and over; (1) Figures cover the Washington-Arlington-Alexandria, DC-VA-MD-WV Metropolitan Statistical Area; (2) People of Hispanic origin can be of any race Source: U.S. Census Bureau, 2017-2021 American Community Survey 5-Year Estimates

School Enrollment by Grade and Control

Area	Preschool (%)		Kindergarten (%)		Grades 1 - 4 (%)		Grades 5 - 8 (%)		Grades 9 - 12 (%)	
	Public	Private	Public	Private	Public	Private	Public	Private	Public	Private
City	74.2	25.8	90.9	9.1	88.6	11.4	82.4	17.6	80.7	19.3
MSA[1]	45.8	54.2	84.0	16.0	87.7	12.3	87.4	12.6	88.2	11.8
U.S.	58.8	41.2	86.3	13.7	88.3	11.7	88.6	11.4	89.4	10.6

Note: Figures shown cover persons 3 years old and over; (1) Figures cover the Washington-Arlington-Alexandria, DC-VA-MD-WV Metropolitan Statistical Area Source: U.S. Census Bureau, 2017-2021 American Community Survey 5-Year Estimates

Higher Education

Four-Year Colleges			Two-Year Colleges			Medical Schools[1]	Law Schools[2]	Voc/ Tech[3]
Public	Private Non-profit	Private For-profit	Public	Private Non-profit	Private For-profit			
7	25	13	5	1	8	4	7	22

Note: Figures cover institutions located within the Washington-Arlington-Alexandria, DC-VA-MD-WV Metropolitan Statistical Area and include main campuses only; (1) includes schools accredited by the Liaison Committee on Medical Education and the American Osteopathic Association's Commission on Osteopathic College Accreditation; (2) includes ABA-accredited schools, schools with provisional ABA accreditation, and state accredited schools; (3) includes all schools with programs that are less than 2 years.
Source: National Center for Education Statistics, Integrated Postsecondary Education System (IPEDS), 2021-22; Wikipedia, List of Medical Schools in the United States, accessed April 10, 2023; Wikipedia, List of Law Schools in the United States, accessed April 10, 2023

According to *U.S. News & World Report,* the Washington-Arlington-Alexandria, DC-VA-MD-WV metro division is home to eight of the top 200 national universities in the U.S.: **Georgetown University** (#22 tie); **University of Maryland—College Park** (#55 tie); **George Washington University** (#62 tie); **American University** (#72 tie); **Howard University** (#89 tie); **Gallaudet University** (#127 tie); **George Mason University** (#137 tie); **The Catholic University of America** (#176 tie). The indicators used to capture academic quality fall into a number of categories: assessment by administrators at peer institutions; retention of students; faculty resources; student selectivity; financial resources; alumni giving; high school counselor ratings of colleges; and graduation rate. *U.S. News & World Report, "America's Best Colleges 2023"*

According to *U.S. News & World Report,* the Washington-Arlington-Alexandria, DC-VA-MD-WV metro division is home to six of the top 100 law schools in the U.S.: **Georgetown University** (#14); **George Washington University** (#25 tie); **George Mason University (Scalia)** (#30 tie); **American University (Washington)** (#73 tie); **The Catholic University of America** (#94 tie); **Howard University** (#98 tie). The rankings are based on a weighted average of 12 measures of quality: peer assessment score; assessment score by lawyers/judges; median LSAT scores; median undergrad GPA; acceptance rate; employment rates for graduates; placement success; bar passage rate; faculty resources; expenditures per student; student/faculty ratio; and library resources. *U.S. News & World Report, "America's Best Graduate Schools, Law, 2023"*

According to *U.S. News & World Report,* the Washington-Arlington-Alexandria, DC-VA-MD-WV metro division is home to two of the top 75 medical schools for research in the U.S.: **Georgetown University** (#56 tie); **George Washington University** (#61). The rankings are based on a weighted average of 11 measures of quality: quality assessment; peer assessment score; assessment score by residency directors; research activity; total research activity; average research activity per faculty member; student selectivity; median MCAT total score; median undergraduate GPA; acceptance rate; and faculty resources. *U.S. News & World Report, "America's Best Graduate Schools, Medical, 2023"*

According to *U.S. News & World Report,* the Washington-Arlington-Alexandria, DC-VA-MD-WV metro division is home to four of the top 75 business schools in the U.S.: **Georgetown University (McDonough)** (#22 tie); **University of Maryland—College Park (Smith)** (#45 tie); **George Washington University** (#55 tie); **Howard University** (#57 tie). The rankings are based on a weighted average of the following nine measures: quality assessment; peer assessment; recruiter assessment; placement success; mean starting salary and bonus; student selectivity; mean GMAT and GRE scores; mean undergraduate GPA; and acceptance rate. *U.S. News & World Report, "America's Best Graduate Schools, Business, 2023"*

EMPLOYERS

Major Employers

Company Name	Industry
Adventist HealthCare	General medical & surgical hospitals
Bechtel National	Engineering services
Computer Sciences Corporation	Computer related consulting services
Federal Aviation Administration	Air traffic control operations, government
Federal Bureau of Investigation	Police protection
Howard University	Colleges & universities
HR Solutions	Human resource consulting services
Internal Revenue Service	Finance, taxation, and monetary policy
Intl Bank for Recons. & Dev.	Foreign trade & international banks
Natl Inst of Standards & Technology	Administration of general economic programs
Office of the Secretary of Defense	National security
U.S. Department of Agriculture	Regulation of agricultural marketing
U.S. Department of Commerce	Regulation, miscellaneous commercial sectors
U.S. Department of Labor	Administration of social & manpower programs
U.S. Department of the Army	National security
U.S. Department of the Navy	National security
U.S. Department of Transportation	Regulation, administration of transportation
U.S. Environmental Protection Agency	Land, mineral, & wildlife conservation
U.S. Fish and Wildlife Service	Fish & wildlife conservation agency, government
Washington Hospital Center Corporation	General medical & surgical hospitals

Note: Companies shown are located within the Washington-Arlington-Alexandria, DC-VA-MD-WV Metropolitan Statistical Area.
Source: Hoovers.com; Wikipedia

Best Companies to Work For

Department of Veterans Affairs Office of Information and Technology; Fannie Mae; FINRA, headquartered in Washington, are among the "100 Best Places to Work in IT." To qualify, companies had to have a minimum of 100 total employees and five IT employees. The best places to work were selected based on DEI (diversity, equity, and inclusion) practices; IT turnover, promotions, and growth; IT retention and engagement programs; remote/hybrid working; benefits and perks (such as elder care and child care, flextime, and reimbursement for college tuition); and training and career development opportunities. *Computerworld, "Best Places to Work in IT," 2023*

PUBLIC SAFETY

Crime Rate

Area	Total Crime	Violent Crime Rate				Property Crime Rate		
		Murder	Rape[3]	Robbery	Aggrav. Assault	Burglary	Larceny -Theft	Motor Vehicle Theft
City	4,389.2	27.8	43.1	309.8	577.3	275.4	2,683.2	472.8
Suburbs[1]	n/a	n/a	n/a	n/a	n/a	n/a	n/a	n/a
Metro[2]	n/a	n/a	n/a	n/a	n/a	n/a	n/a	n/a
U.S.	2,356.7	6.5	38.4	73.9	279.7	314.2	1,398.0	246.0

Note: Figures are crimes per 100,000 population; (1) All areas within the metro area that are located outside the city limits; (2) Figures cover the Washington-Arlington-Alexandria, DC-VA-MD-WV Metropolitan Division; n/a not available; (3) All figures shown were reported using the revised Uniform Crime Reporting (UCR) definition of rape; Due to the transition to the National Incident-Based Reporting System (NIBRS), limited city and metro area data was released for 2021.
Source: FBI Uniform Crime Reports, 2020

Hate Crimes

Area	Number of Quarters Reported	Number of Incidents per Bias Motivation					
		Race/Ethnicity/ Ancestry	Religion	Sexual Orientation	Disability	Gender	Gender Identity
City	4	60	1	38	0	0	27
U.S.	4	5,227	1,244	1,110	130	75	266

Note: Due to the transition to the National Incident-Based Reporting System (NIBRS), limited crime data was released for 2021.
Source: Federal Bureau of Investigation, Hate Crime Statistics 2020

Identity Theft Consumer Reports

Area	Reports	Reports per 100,000 Population	Rank[2]
MSA[1]	20,376	326	54
U.S.	1,108,609	339	-

Note: (1) Figures cover the Washington-Arlington-Alexandria, DC-VA-MD-WV Metropolitan Statistical Area; (2) Rank ranges from 1 to 391 where 1 indicates greatest number of identity theft reports per 100,000 population
Source: Federal Trade Commission, Consumer Sentinel Network Data Book 2022

Washington, District of Columbia

Fraud and Other Consumer Reports

Area	Reports	Reports per 100,000 Population	Rank[2]
MSA[1]	84,395	1,350	18
U.S.	4,064,520	1,245	-

Note: (1) Figures cover the Washington-Arlington-Alexandria, DC-VA-MD-WV Metropolitan Statistical Area;
(2) Rank ranges from 1 to 391 where 1 indicates greatest number of fraud and other consumer reports per 100,000 population
Source: Federal Trade Commission, Consumer Sentinel Network Data Book 2022

POLITICS

2020 Presidential Election Results

Area	Biden	Trump	Jorgensen	Hawkins	Other
District of Columbia	92.1	5.4	0.6	0.5	1.4
U.S.	51.3	46.8	1.2	0.3	0.5

Note: Results are percentages and may not add to 100% due to rounding
Source: Dave Leip's Atlas of U.S. Presidential Elections

SPORTS

Professional Sports Teams

Team Name	League	Year Established
D.C. United	Major League Soccer (MLS)	1996
Washington Capitals	National Hockey League (NHL)	1974
Washington Nationals	Major League Baseball (MLB)	2005
Washington Redskins	National Football League (NFL)	1937
Washington Wizards	National Basketball Association (NBA)	1973

Note: Includes teams located in the Washington-Arlington-Alexandria, DC-VA-MD-WV Metropolitan Statistical Area.
Source: Wikipedia, Major Professional Sports Teams of the United States and Canada, April 12, 2023

CLIMATE

Average and Extreme Temperatures

Temperature	Jan	Feb	Mar	Apr	May	Jun	Jul	Aug	Sep	Oct	Nov	Dec	Yr.
Extreme High (°F)	79	82	89	95	97	101	104	103	101	94	86	75	104
Average High (°F)	43	46	55	67	76	84	88	86	80	69	58	47	67
Average Temp. (°F)	36	38	46	57	66	75	79	78	71	60	49	39	58
Average Low (°F)	28	30	37	46	56	65	70	69	62	50	40	31	49
Extreme Low (°F)	-5	4	14	24	34	47	54	49	39	29	16	3	-5

Note: Figures cover the years 1945-1990
Source: National Climatic Data Center, International Station Meteorological Climate Summary, 9/96

Average Precipitation/Snowfall/Humidity

Precip./Humidity	Jan	Feb	Mar	Apr	May	Jun	Jul	Aug	Sep	Oct	Nov	Dec	Yr.
Avg. Precip. (in.)	2.8	2.6	3.3	2.9	4.0	3.4	4.1	4.2	3.3	2.9	3.0	3.1	39.5
Avg. Snowfall (in.)	6	6	2	Tr	0	0	0	0	0	Tr	1	3	18
Avg. Rel. Hum. 7am (%)	71	70	70	70	74	75	77	80	82	80	76	72	75
Avg. Rel. Hum. 4pm (%)	54	50	46	45	51	52	53	54	54	53	53	55	52

Note: Figures cover the years 1945-1990; Tr = Trace amounts (<0.05 in. of rain; <0.5 in. of snow)
Source: National Climatic Data Center, International Station Meteorological Climate Summary, 9/96

Weather Conditions

Temperature			Daytime Sky			Precipitation		
10°F & below	32°F & below	90°F & above	Clear	Partly cloudy	Cloudy	0.01 inch or more precip.	0.1 inch or more snow/ice	Thunder-storms
2	71	34	84	143	138	112	9	30

Note: Figures are average number of days per year and cover the years 1945-1990
Source: National Climatic Data Center, International Station Meteorological Climate Summary, 9/96

HAZARDOUS WASTE

Superfund Sites

The Washington-Arlington-Alexandria, DC-VA-MD-WV metro division is home to nine sites on the EPA's Superfund National Priorities List: **Andrews Air Force Base** (final); **Avtex Fibers, Inc.** (final); **Beltsville Agricultural Research Center (USDA)** (final); **Brandywine Drmo** (final); **Culpeper Wood Preservers, Inc.** (final); **Hidden Lane Landfill** (final); **Indian Head Naval Surface Warfare Center** (final); **L.A. Clarke & Son** (final); **Marine Corps Combat Development Command** (final). There are a total of 1,165 Superfund sites with a status of proposed or final on the list in the U.S. *U.S. Environmental Protection Agency, National Priorities List, April 12, 2023*

Washington, District of Columbia 497

AIR QUALITY

Air Quality Trends: Ozone

	1990	1995	2000	2005	2010	2015	2018	2019	2020	2021
MSA[1]	0.075	0.083	0.073	0.069	0.069	0.067	0.068	0.064	0.057	0.066
U.S.	0.087	0.089	0.081	0.080	0.072	0.067	0.069	0.065	0.065	0.067

Note: (1) Data covers the Washington-Arlington-Alexandria, DC-VA-MD-WV Metropolitan Statistical Area. The values shown are the composite ozone concentration averages among trend sites based on the highest fourth daily maximum 8-hour concentration in parts per million. These trends are based on sites having an adequate record of monitoring data during the trend period. Data from exceptional events are included.
Source: U.S. Environmental Protection Agency, Air Quality Monitoring Information, "Air Quality Trends by City, 1990-2021"

Air Quality Index

Area	Percent of Days when Air Quality was...[2]					AQI Statistics[2]	
	Good	Moderate	Unhealthy for Sensitive Groups	Unhealthy	Very Unhealthy	Maximum	Median
MSA[1]	61.6	35.6	2.5	0.3	0.0	153	46

Note: (1) Data covers the Washington-Arlington-Alexandria, DC-VA-MD-WV Metropolitan Statistical Area; (2) Based on 365 days with AQI data in 2021. Air Quality Index (AQI) is an index for reporting daily air quality. EPA calculates the AQI for five major air pollutants regulated by the Clean Air Act: ground-level ozone, particle pollution (aka particulate matter), carbon monoxide, sulfur dioxide, and nitrogen dioxide. The AQI runs from 0 to 500. The higher the AQI value, the greater the level of air pollution and the greater the health concern. There are six AQI categories: "Good" AQI is between 0 and 50. Air quality is considered satisfactory; "Moderate" AQI is between 51 and 100. Air quality is acceptable; "Unhealthy for Sensitive Groups" When AQI values are between 101 and 150, members of sensitive groups may experience health effects; "Unhealthy" When AQI values are between 151 and 200 everyone may begin to experience health effects; "Very Unhealthy" AQI values between 201 and 300 trigger a health alert; "Hazardous" AQI values over 300 trigger warnings of emergency conditions (not shown).
Source: U.S. Environmental Protection Agency, Air Quality Index Report, 2021

Air Quality Index Pollutants

Area	Percent of Days when AQI Pollutant was...[2]					
	Carbon Monoxide	Nitrogen Dioxide	Ozone	Sulfur Dioxide	Particulate Matter 2.5	Particulate Matter 10
MSA[1]	0.0	8.5	52.1	(3)	39.5	0.0

Note: (1) Data covers the Washington-Arlington-Alexandria, DC-VA-MD-WV Metropolitan Statistical Area; (2) Based on 365 days with AQI data in 2021. The Air Quality Index (AQI) is an index for reporting daily air quality. EPA calculates the AQI for five major air pollutants regulated by the Clean Air Act: ground-level ozone, particle pollution (also known as particulate matter), carbon monoxide, sulfur dioxide, and nitrogen dioxide. The AQI runs from 0 to 500. The higher the AQI value, the greater the level of air pollution and the greater the health concern; (3) Sulfur dioxide is no longer included in this table (as of December 8, 2021) because SO_2 concentrations tend to be very localized and not necessarily representative of broad geographical areas like counties and CBSAs.
Source: U.S. Environmental Protection Agency, Air Quality Index Report, 2021

Maximum Air Pollutant Concentrations: Particulate Matter, Ozone, CO and Lead

	Particulate Matter 10 (ug/m^3)	Particulate Matter 2.5 Wtd AM (ug/m^3)	Particulate Matter 2.5 24-Hr (ug/m^3)	Ozone (ppm)	Carbon Monoxide (ppm)	Lead (ug/m^3)
MSA[1] Level	47	9.6	21	0.072	2	n/a
NAAQS[2]	150	15	35	0.075	9	0.15
Met NAAQS[2]	Yes	Yes	Yes	Yes	Yes	n/a

Note: (1) Data covers the Washington-Arlington-Alexandria, DC-VA-MD-WV Metropolitan Statistical Area; Data from exceptional events are included; (2) National Ambient Air Quality Standards; ppm = parts per million; ug/m^3 = micrograms per cubic meter; n/a not available.
Concentrations: Particulate Matter 10 (coarse particulate)—highest second maximum 24-hour concentration; Particulate Matter 2.5 Wtd AM (fine particulate)—highest weighted annual mean concentration; Particulate Matter 2.5 24-Hour (fine particulate)—highest 98th percentile 24-hour concentration; Ozone—highest fourth daily maximum 8-hour concentration; Carbon Monoxide—highest second maximum non-overlapping 8-hour concentration; Lead—maximum running 3-month average
Source: U.S. Environmental Protection Agency, Air Quality Monitoring Information, "Air Quality Statistics by City, 2021"

Maximum Air Pollutant Concentrations: Nitrogen Dioxide and Sulfur Dioxide

	Nitrogen Dioxide AM (ppb)	Nitrogen Dioxide 1-Hr (ppb)	Sulfur Dioxide AM (ppb)	Sulfur Dioxide 1-Hr (ppb)	Sulfur Dioxide 24-Hr (ppb)
MSA[1] Level	15	50	n/a	3	n/a
NAAQS[2]	53	100	30	75	140
Met NAAQS[2]	Yes	Yes	n/a	Yes	n/a

Note: (1) Data covers the Washington-Arlington-Alexandria, DC-VA-MD-WV Metropolitan Statistical Area; Data from exceptional events are included; (2) National Ambient Air Quality Standards; ppm = parts per million; ug/m^3 = micrograms per cubic meter; n/a not available.
Concentrations: Nitrogen Dioxide AM—highest arithmetic mean concentration; Nitrogen Dioxide 1-Hr—highest 98th percentile 1-hour daily maximum concentration; Sulfur Dioxide AM—highest annual mean concentration; Sulfur Dioxide 1-Hr—highest 99th percentile 1-hour daily maximum concentration; Sulfur Dioxide 24-Hr—highest second maximum 24-hour concentration
Source: U.S. Environmental Protection Agency, Air Quality Monitoring Information, "Air Quality Statistics by City, 2021"

Wilmington, North Carolina

Background

In pre-revolutionary times, Wilmington's importance as a port city was slow to take hold. While Wilmington played an important early role in the American Revoltiuon, lack of good roads amid its bogs and swamps were a hinderance. This boggy landscape would later be a boon to the city's growing economy, providing it with natural resources for shipbuilding (tar, pitch, rosin, and Turpentine) for the navy. The invention of better navigational tools for sailing, and of the steam-powered engine, helped Wilmington become North Carolina's largest city by 1840, and a major port for U.S. exports of peanuts, rice, flax, and cotton.

Wilmington was the site of one of the first rebellions in the United States' revolt against British rule. The Stamp Act required that colonists only use paper produced and stamped in London—a way for the British to earn the necessary revenue to "protect" the colonies. The Colonists objected, claiming it was an unfair tax, and they didn't need protection. In 1765, about 500 Wilmington citizens burned an effigy of their stamp collector, Lord Bute, and forced him to resign.

By the time of the Civil War, Wilmington had become a major port for the eastern seaboard, but wartime brought Wilmington's normal export industry to an abrupt end. The city turned its attention to importing supplies for the Confederate armies and was considered the "lifeline of the Confederacy." By late 1864, Wilmington was the only port not captured by Union forces.

Following the Civil War and the Emancipation Proclamation, Wilmington became home to large numbers of freed slaves, and free people of color, who sought employment in the city, where about two thirds of the population was black. A large middle-class grew and a significant number of black men were business professionals, holding important positions in the community, including police chief, deputy sheriff, and customs collector. Five out of the ten aldermen were black. Wilmington produced the first black attorney, George Mabson (admitted to the bar in 1871), and the nation's first black architect, Robert R. Taylor, who graduated from Massachusetts Institute of Technology.

Black citizens were achieving near political and social equality with white citizens—a situation that prompted white supremacists to overtake the legitimate, bi-racial government and institute the first Jim Crow laws in North Carolina. In one year, 1,400 black residents left Wilmington. Those who stayed were disenfranchised, precluded from voting when the new leadership adopted new literacy requirements.

In 1961, Wilmington became the permanent home of the USS *North Carolina*. Considered to be the greatest U. S. sea weapon in 1941, it is now a museum—and a major draw in Wilmington's vibrant tourism industry. Adding to its tourist appeal is the city's one-mile Riverwalk, and its location between beach and river, with several popular beach communities, including Ford Fisher, Wrightsville Beach, Carolina Beach, and Kure Beach.

Wilmington hosts many popular annual festivals, including the 3-day North Carolina Jazz Festival and the Azalea Festival.

In the late 70s, Wilmington began aggressive revitalization and restoration efforts, creating a revolving loan fund to draw in new small businesses. More recently, abandoned warehouses on the downtown's northern end have been demolished to make room for, among other things, headquarters of Pharmaceutical Product Development and mixed-use facilities. Project Grace is a redevelopment of Wilmington's downtown library and history museum.

An important, growing industry in Wilmington is film. The city is home to EUE Screen Gems Studios, the largest domestic television and movie production facility outside California. Its newest sound stage, Dream Stage 10, is the third largest in the country. Some of the most notable movies filmed in Wilmington include *The Color Purple*, *Dirty Dancing*, *Bull Durham*, and *Iron Man 3*. Television shows *Dawson's Creek* and *Sleepy Hollow* were also filmed here.

Wilimington boasts a large historic district. Twenty locations within the city are on the National Register of Historic Places, including Market Street Mansion District, Moores Creek National Battlefield, and USS *North Carolina* Historic National Landmark.

Winters in Wilmington are moderate, and spring is long. Given that Wilmington's climate is sub-tropical, summer can be very hot, and about once every seven years Wilmington finds itself in the path of a hurricane.

Rankings

General Rankings

- For its 35th annual "Readers' Choice Awards" survey, *Condé Nast Traveler* ranked its readers' favorite cities in the U.S. Whether it be a longed-for visit or a first on the list, these are the places that inspired a return to travel. The list was broken into large cities and cities under 250,000. Wilmington ranked #10 in the small city category. *Condé Nast Traveler, Readers' Choice Awards 2022, "Best Small Cities in the U.S." October 4, 2022*

Business/Finance Rankings

- Livability.com rated Wilmington as #8 of ten cities where new college grads' job prospects are brightest. Criteria included: number of 22- to 29-year olds; good job opportunities; affordable housing options; public transportation users; educational attainment; variety of fun things to do. *Livability.com, "2018 Top 10 Best Cities for Recent College Grads," April 26, 2018*

- The Wilmington metro area appeared on the Milken Institute "2022 Best Performing Cities" list. Rank: #21 out of 200 large metro areas (population over 250,000). Criteria: job growth; wage and salary growth; high-tech output growth; housing affordability; household broadband access. *Milken Institute, "Best-Performing Cities 2022," March 28, 2022*

- *Forbes* ranked the 200 most populous metro areas to determine the nation's "Best Places for Business and Careers." The Wilmington metro area was ranked #30. Criteria: costs (business and living); job growth (past and projected); income growth; quality of life; educational attainment (college and high school); projected economic growth; cultural and leisure opportunities; workplace tolerance laws; net migration patterns. *Forbes, "The Best Places for Business and Careers 2019: Seattle Still On Top," October 30, 2019*

Culture/Performing Arts Rankings

- Wilmington was selected as one of the ten best small North American cities and towns for moviemakers. Of cities with smaller populations, the area ranked #2. As with the 2023 list for bigger cities, the philosophy of freedom to pursue filmmaking dreams were highly factored in. Other criteria: film community and culture; access to equipment and facilities; affordability; tax incentives; and quality of life. *MovieMaker Magazine, "Best Places to Live and Work as a Moviemaker, 2023," January 18, 2023*

- Wilmington was selected as one of "America's Favorite Cities." The city ranked #8 in the "Architecture" category. Respondents to an online survey were asked to rate their favorite place (population over 100,000) in over 65 categories. *Travelandleisure.com, "America's Favorite Cities for Architecture 2016," March 2, 2017*

Dating/Romance Rankings

- Wilmington was selected as one of America's best cities for singles by the readers of *Travel + Leisure* in their annual "America's Favorite Cities" survey. Criteria included good-looking locals, cool shopping, an active bar scene and hipster-magnet coffee bars. *Travel + Leisure, "Best Cities in America for Singles," July 21, 2017*

Environmental Rankings

- Wilmington was highlighted as one of the cleanest metro areas for ozone air pollution in the U.S. during 2019 through 2021. The list represents cities with no monitored ozone air pollution in unhealthful ranges. *American Lung Association, "State of the Air 2023," April 19, 2023*

- Wilmington was highlighted as one of the top 25 cleanest metro areas for year-round particle pollution (Annual PM 2.5) in the U.S. during 2019 through 2021. The area ranked #3. *American Lung Association, "State of the Air 2023," April 19, 2023*

- Wilmington was highlighted as one of the top 59 cleanest metro areas for short-term particle pollution (24-hour PM 2.5) in the U.S. during 2019 through 2021. Monitors in these cities reported no days with unhealthful PM 2.5 levels. *American Lung Association, "State of the Air 2023," April 19, 2023*

Real Estate Rankings

- The Wilmington metro area was identified as one of the 20 best housing markets in the U.S. in 2022. The area ranked #19 out of 187 markets. Criteria: year-over-year change of median sales price of existing single-family homes between the 4th quarter of 2021 and the 4th quarter of 2022. *National Association of Realtors®, Median Sales Price of Existing Single-Family Homes for Metropolitan Areas, 4th Quarter 2022*

- The Wilmington metro area was identified as one of the 10 best condo markets in the U.S. in 2022. The area ranked #6 out of 63 markets. Criteria: year-over-year change of median sales price of existing apartment condo-coop homes between the 4th quarter of 2021 and the 4th quarter of 2022. *National Association of Realtors®, Median Sales Price of Existing Apartment Condo-Coops Homes for Metropolitan Areas, 4th Quarter 2022*

Safety Rankings

- The National Insurance Crime Bureau ranked 390 metro areas in the U.S. in terms of per capita rates of vehicle theft. The Wilmington metro area ranked #257 (#1 = highest rate). Criteria: number of vehicle theft offenses per 100,000 inhabitants in 2021. *National Insurance Crime Bureau, "Hot Spots 2021," September 1, 2022*

Seniors/Retirement Rankings

- From its Best Cities for Successful Aging indexes, the Milken Institute generated rankings for metropolitan areas, weighing data in nine categories—health care, wellness, living arrangements, transportation and convenience, financial characteristics, education, employment, community engagement, and overall livability. The Wilmington metro area was ranked #160 overall in the small metro area category. *Milken Institute, "Best Cities for Successful Aging, 2017" March 14, 2017*

Business Environment

DEMOGRAPHICS

Population Growth

Area	1990 Census	2000 Census	2010 Census	2020 Census	Population Growth (%)	
					1990-2020	2010-2020
City	64,609	75,838	106,476	115,451	78.7	8.4
MSA[1]	200,124	274,532	362,315	285,905	42.9	-21.1
U.S.	248,709,873	281,421,906	308,745,538	331,449,281	33.3	7.4

Note: (1) Figures cover the Wilmington, NC Metropolitan Statistical Area
Source: U.S. Census Bureau, 1990 Census, 2000 Census, 2010 Census, 2020 Census

Race

Area	White Alone[2] (%)	Black Alone[2] (%)	Asian Alone[2] (%)	AIAN[3] Alone[2] (%)	NHOPI[4] Alone[2] (%)	Other Race Alone[2] (%)	Two or More Races (%)
City	70.9	16.5	1.6	0.4	0.1	3.9	6.6
MSA[1]	75.6	12.2	1.3	0.5	0.1	3.8	6.4
U.S.	61.6	12.4	6.0	1.1	0.2	8.4	10.2

Note: (1) Figures cover the Wilmington, NC Metropolitan Statistical Area; (2) Alone is defined as not being in combination with one or more other races; (3) American Indian and Alaska Native; (4) Native Hawaiian and Other Pacific Islander
Source: U.S. Census Bureau, 2020 Census

Hispanic or Latino Origin

Area	Total (%)	Mexican (%)	Puerto Rican (%)	Cuban (%)	Other (%)
City	7.1	2.7	1.3	0.4	2.7
MSA[1]	6.2	2.5	1.0	0.3	2.4
U.S.	18.4	11.2	1.8	0.7	4.7

Note: Persons of Hispanic or Latino origin can be of any race; (1) Figures cover the Wilmington, NC Metropolitan Statistical Area
Source: U.S. Census Bureau, 2017-2021 American Community Survey 5-Year Estimates

Age

Area	Percent of Population									Median Age
	Under Age 5	Age 5–19	Age 20–34	Age 35–44	Age 45–54	Age 55–64	Age 65–74	Age 75–84	Age 85+	
City	4.3	15.1	27.2	11.8	11.0	12.1	10.8	5.7	2.3	37.8
MSA[1]	4.8	16.9	20.5	12.7	12.6	13.3	11.7	5.7	2.0	41.1
U.S.	5.6	19.2	20.2	12.7	12.4	13.1	10.0	4.9	1.9	38.8

Note: (1) Figures cover the Wilmington, NC Metropolitan Statistical Area
Source: U.S. Census Bureau, 2020 Census

Disability by Age

Area	All Ages	Under 18 Years Old	18 to 64 Years Old	65 Years and Over
City	13.0	5.1	10.0	32.0
MSA[1]	12.9	4.5	10.6	30.3
U.S.	12.6	4.4	10.3	33.4

Note: Figures show percent of the civilian noninstitutionalized population that reported having a disability. Disability status is determined from six types of difficulty: vision, hearing, cognitive, ambulatory, self-care, and independent living. For children under 5 years old, hearing and vision difficulty are used to determine disability status. For children between the ages of 5 and 14, disability status is determined from hearing, vision, cognitive, ambulatory, and self-care difficulties. For people aged 15 years and older, they are considered to have a disability if they have difficulty with any one of the six difficulty types; Note: (1) Figures cover the Wilmington, NC Metropolitan Statistical Area
Source: U.S. Census Bureau, 2017-2021 American Community Survey 5-Year Estimates

Ancestry

Area	German	Irish	English	American	Italian	Polish	French[2]	Scottish	Dutch
City	10.2	9.4	11.7	4.7	5.3	2.0	1.8	2.7	0.8
MSA[1]	11.3	10.8	12.1	5.8	5.6	2.3	1.8	3.0	0.8
U.S.	12.8	9.6	8.1	5.7	5.0	2.7	2.2	1.6	1.1

Note: Figures are the percentage of the total population reporting a particular ancestry. The nine most commonly reported ancestries in the U.S. are shown. Figures include multiple ancestries (e.g. if a person reported being Irish and Italian, they were included in both columns); (1) Figures cover the Wilmington, NC Metropolitan Statistical Area; (2) Excludes Basque
Source: U.S. Census Bureau, 2017-2021 American Community Survey 5-Year Estimates

Foreign-born Population

Area	Percent of Population Born in								
	Any Foreign Country	Asia	Mexico	Europe	Caribbean	Central America[2]	South America	Africa	Canada
City	4.7	1.2	1.1	1.0	0.2	0.4	0.4	0.1	0.2
MSA[1]	4.6	1.0	1.0	0.9	0.1	0.6	0.4	0.2	0.2
U.S.	13.6	4.2	3.3	1.5	1.4	1.1	1.1	0.8	0.2

Note: (1) Figures cover the Wilmington, NC Metropolitan Statistical Area; (2) Excludes Mexico.
Source: U.S. Census Bureau, 2017-2021 American Community Survey 5-Year Estimates

Household Size

Area	Persons in Household (%)							Average Household Size
	One	Two	Three	Four	Five	Six	Seven or More	
City	40.0	36.9	11.5	7.5	3.1	0.7	0.3	2.10
MSA[1]	33.6	36.5	14.5	10.1	3.6	1.3	0.4	2.30
U.S.	28.1	33.8	15.5	12.9	6.0	2.3	1.4	2.60

Note: (1) Figures cover the Wilmington, NC Metropolitan Statistical Area
Source: U.S. Census Bureau, 2017-2021 American Community Survey 5-Year Estimates

Household Relationships

Area	House-holder	Opposite-sex Spouse	Same-sex Spouse	Opposite-sex Unmarried Partner	Same-sex Unmarried Partner	Child[2]	Grand-child	Other Relatives	Non-relatives
City	45.7	14.9	0.3	3.4	0.3	21.2	1.5	3.0	5.9
MSA[1]	42.3	18.7	0.2	2.9	0.2	24.4	1.9	3.1	3.9
U.S.	38.3	17.5	0.2	2.5	0.2	28.3	2.4	4.8	3.4

Note: Figures are percent of the total population; (1) Figures cover the Wilmington, NC Metropolitan Statistical Area; (2) Includes biological, adopted, and stepchildren of the householder
Source: U.S. Census Bureau, 2020 Census

Gender

Area	Males	Females	Males per 100 Females
City	54,189	61,262	88.5
MSA[1]	137,791	148,114	93.0
U.S.	162,685,811	168,763,470	96.4

Note: (1) Figures cover the Wilmington, NC Metropolitan Statistical Area
Source: U.S. Census Bureau, 2020 Census

Marital Status

Area	Never Married	Now Married[2]	Separated	Widowed	Divorced
City	41.6	39.1	2.2	5.3	11.7
MSA[1]	33.0	48.2	2.2	5.7	11.0
U.S.	33.8	48.0	1.8	5.6	10.8

Note: Figures are percentages and cover the population 15 years of age and older; (1) Figures cover the Wilmington, NC Metropolitan Statistical Area; (2) Excludes separated
Source: U.S. Census Bureau, 2017-2021 American Community Survey 5-Year Estimates

Religious Groups by Family

Area	Catholic	Baptist	Methodist	LDS[2]	Pentecostal	Lutheran	Islam	Adventist	Other
MSA[1]	13.2	9.9	8.1	1.0	1.0	0.7	0.7	1.4	12.6
U.S.	18.7	7.3	3.0	2.0	1.8	1.7	1.3	1.3	11.6

Note: Figures are the number of adherents as a percentage of the total population and cover the eight largest religious groups in the U.S; (1) Figures cover the Wilmington, NC Metropolitan Statistical Area; (2) Church of Jesus Christ of Latter-day Saints
Sources: 2020 U.S. Religion Census, Association of Statisticians of American Religious Bodies; The Association of Religion Data Archives (ARDA)

Religious Groups by Tradition

Area	Catholic	Evangelical Protestant	Mainline Protestant	Black Protestant	Islam	Judaism	Hinduism	Orthodox	Buddhism
MSA[1]	13.2	17.9	9.3	4.6	0.7	0.3	0.1	0.3	n/a
U.S.	18.7	16.5	5.2	2.3	1.3	0.6	0.4	0.4	0.3

Note: Figures are the number of adherents as a percentage of the total population; (1) Figures cover the Wilmington, NC Metropolitan Statistical Area
Sources: 2020 U.S. Religion Census, Association of Statisticians of American Religious Bodies; The Association of Religion Data Archives (ARDA)

504 Wilmington, North Carolina

ECONOMY

Gross Metropolitan Product

Area	2020	2021	2022	2023	Rank[2]
MSA[1]	16.0	18.0	19.3	20.3	161

Note: Figures are in billions of dollars; (1) Figures cover the Wilmington, NC Metropolitan Statistical Area; (2) Rank is based on 2021 data and ranges from 1 to 381
Source: U.S. Conference of Mayors, U.S. Metro Economies: U.S. Metros Compared to Global and State Economies, June 2022

Economic Growth

Area	2018-20 (%)	2021 (%)	2022 (%)	2023 (%)	Rank[2]
MSA[1]	1.5	8.5	1.8	1.3	52
U.S.	-0.6	5.7	3.1	2.9	—

Note: Figures are real gross metropolitan product (GMP) growth rates and represent average annual percent change; (1) Figures cover the Wilmington, NC Metropolitan Statistical Area; (2) Rank is based on 2020 2-year average annual percent change and ranges from 1 to 381
Source: U.S. Conference of Mayors, U.S. Metro Economies: U.S. Metros Compared to Global and State Economies, June 2022

Metropolitan Area Exports

Area	2016	2017	2018	2019	2020	2021	Rank[2]
MSA[1]	598.7	759.8	634.4	526.4	553.6	497.8	218

Note: Figures are in millions of dollars; (1) Figures cover the Wilmington, NC Metropolitan Statistical Area; (2) Rank is based on 2021 data and ranges from 1 to 388
Source: U.S. Department of Commerce, International Trade Administration, Office of Trade and Economic Analysis, Industry and Analysis, Exports by Metropolitan Area, data extracted March 16, 2023

Building Permits

Area	Single-Family			Multi-Family			Total		
	2021	2022	Pct. Chg.	2021	2022	Pct. Chg.	2021	2022	Pct. Chg.
City	n/a	n/a	n/a	n/a	n/a	n/a	n/a	n/a	n/a
MSA[1]	2,671	2,489	-6.8	1,747	1,932	10.6	4,418	4,421	0.1
U.S.	1,115,400	975,600	-12.5	621,600	689,500	10.9	1,737,000	1,665,100	-4.1

Note: (1) Figures cover the Wilmington, NC Metropolitan Statistical Area; Figures represent new, privately-owned housing units authorized (unadjusted data); All permit data are based on estimates with imputation
Source: U.S. Census Bureau, Manufacturing, Mining, and Construction Statistics, Building Permits, 2021, 2022

Bankruptcy Filings

Area	Business Filings			Nonbusiness Filings		
	2021	2022	% Chg.	2021	2022	% Chg.
New Hanover County	12	6	-50.0	144	138	-4.2
U.S.	14,347	13,481	-6.0	399,269	374,240	-6.3

Note: Business filings include Chapter 7, Chapter 9, Chapter 11, Chapter 12, Chapter 13, Chapter 15, and Section 304; Nonbusiness filings include Chapter 7, Chapter 11, and Chapter 13
Source: Administrative Office of the U.S. Courts, Business and Nonbusiness Bankruptcy, County Cases Commenced by Chapter of the Bankruptcy Code, During the 12-Month Period Ending December 31, 2021 and Business and Nonbusiness Bankruptcy, County Cases Commenced by Chapter of the Bankruptcy Code, During the 12-Month Period Ending December 31, 2022

Housing Vacancy Rates

Area	Gross Vacancy Rate[2] (%)			Year-Round Vacancy Rate[3] (%)			Rental Vacancy Rate[4] (%)			Homeowner Vacancy Rate[5] (%)		
	2020	2021	2022	2020	2021	2022	2020	2021	2022	2020	2021	2022
MSA[1]	n/a	n/a	n/a	n/a	n/a	n/a	n/a	n/a	n/a	n/a	n/a	n/a
U.S.	10.6	10.8	10.5	8.2	8.4	8.2	6.3	6.1	5.8	1.0	0.9	0.8

Note: (1) Figures cover the Wilmington, NC Metropolitan Statistical Area; (2) The percentage of the total housing inventory that is vacant; (3) The percentage of the housing inventory (excluding seasonal units) that is year-round vacant; (4) The percentage of rental inventory that is vacant for rent; (5) The percentage of homeowner inventory that is vacant for sale; n/a not available
Source: U.S. Census Bureau, Housing Vacancies and Homeownership Annual Statistics: 2020, 2021, 2022

INCOME

Income

Area	Per Capita ($)	Median Household ($)	Average Household ($)
City	38,890	54,066	83,853
MSA[1]	38,607	63,036	89,355
U.S.	37,638	69,021	97,196

Note: (1) Figures cover the Wilmington, NC Metropolitan Statistical Area
Source: U.S. Census Bureau, 2017-2021 American Community Survey 5-Year Estimates

Household Income Distribution

Area	Percent of Households Earning							
	Under $15,000	$15,000 -$24,999	$25,000 -$34,999	$35,000 -$49,999	$50,000 -$74,999	$75,000 -$99,999	$100,000 -$149,999	$150,000 and up
City	14.8	9.7	8.2	13.5	18.5	10.4	12.5	12.5
MSA[1]	11.0	8.7	7.8	12.4	18.0	12.0	16.0	14.0
U.S.	9.4	7.8	8.2	11.4	16.8	12.8	16.3	17.3

Note: (1) Figures cover the Wilmington, NC Metropolitan Statistical Area
Source: U.S. Census Bureau, 2017-2021 American Community Survey 5-Year Estimates

Poverty Rate

Area	All Ages	Under 18 Years Old	18 to 64 Years Old	65 Years and Over
City	18.8	25.3	19.8	8.7
MSA[1]	13.4	16.6	14.2	7.0
U.S.	12.6	17.0	11.8	9.6

Note: Figures are percentage of people whose income during the past 12 months was below the poverty level; (1) Figures cover the Wilmington, NC Metropolitan Statistical Area
Source: U.S. Census Bureau, 2017-2021 American Community Survey 5-Year Estimates

EMPLOYMENT

Labor Force and Employment

Area	Civilian Labor Force			Workers Employed		
	Dec. 2021	Dec. 2022	% Chg.	Dec. 2021	Dec. 2022	% Chg.
City	65,317	66,641	2.0	63,471	64,589	1.8
MSA[1]	154,267	157,407	2.0	150,051	152,775	1.8
U.S.	161,696,000	164,224,000	1.6	155,732,000	158,872,000	2.0

Note: Data is not seasonally adjusted and covers workers 16 years of age and older; (1) Figures cover the Wilmington, NC Metropolitan Statistical Area
Source: Bureau of Labor Statistics, Local Area Unemployment Statistics

Unemployment Rate

Area	2022											
	Jan.	Feb.	Mar.	Apr.	May	Jun.	Jul.	Aug.	Sep.	Oct.	Nov.	Dec.
City	3.4	3.4	3.2	3.3	3.5	3.9	3.5	3.7	3.1	3.6	3.6	3.1
MSA[1]	3.3	3.2	3.1	3.0	3.3	3.7	3.3	3.5	3.0	3.6	3.4	2.9
U.S.	4.4	4.1	3.8	3.3	3.4	3.8	3.8	3.8	3.3	3.4	3.4	3.3

Note: Data is not seasonally adjusted and covers workers 16 years of age and older; (1) Figures cover the Wilmington, NC Metropolitan Statistical Area
Source: Bureau of Labor Statistics, Local Area Unemployment Statistics

Average Wages

Occupation	$/Hr.	Occupation	$/Hr.
Accountants and Auditors	37.58	Maintenance and Repair Workers	19.80
Automotive Mechanics	21.31	Marketing Managers	67.91
Bookkeepers	19.94	Network and Computer Systems Admin.	39.92
Carpenters	21.32	Nurses, Licensed Practical	25.28
Cashiers	11.98	Nurses, Registered	36.27
Computer Programmers	51.25	Nursing Assistants	14.86
Computer Systems Analysts	42.16	Office Clerks, General	17.25
Computer User Support Specialists	25.96	Physical Therapists	41.09
Construction Laborers	18.29	Physicians	112.33
Cooks, Restaurant	14.56	Plumbers, Pipefitters and Steamfitters	22.57
Customer Service Representatives	18.04	Police and Sheriff's Patrol Officers	23.49
Dentists	76.66	Postal Service Mail Carriers	26.03
Electricians	23.28	Real Estate Sales Agents	28.16
Engineers, Electrical	48.09	Retail Salespersons	15.41
Fast Food and Counter Workers	11.32	Sales Representatives, Technical/Scientific	60.83
Financial Managers	74.45	Secretaries, Exc. Legal/Medical/Executive	19.24
First-Line Supervisors of Office Workers	26.02	Security Guards	15.17
General and Operations Managers	53.42	Surgeons	n/a
Hairdressers/Cosmetologists	19.04	Teacher Assistants, Exc. Postsecondary*	12.82
Home Health and Personal Care Aides	12.45	Teachers, Secondary School, Exc. Sp. Ed.*	25.18
Janitors and Cleaners	13.87	Telemarketers	15.79
Landscaping/Groundskeeping Workers	16.23	Truck Drivers, Heavy/Tractor-Trailer	22.70
Lawyers	61.99	Truck Drivers, Light/Delivery Services	20.42
Maids and Housekeeping Cleaners	12.83	Waiters and Waitresses	13.33

Note: Wage data covers the Wilmington, NC Metropolitan Statistical Area; (*) Hourly wages were calculated from annual wage data based on a 40 hour work week; n/a not available.
Source: Bureau of Labor Statistics, Metro Area Occupational Employment & Wage Estimates, May 2022

Employment by Industry

Sector	MSA[1]		U.S.
	Number of Employees	Percent of Total	Percent of Total
Construction, Mining, and Logging	10,600	7.4	5.4
Private Education and Health Services	24,500	17.0	16.1
Financial Activities	7,400	5.1	5.9
Government	18,100	12.6	14.5
Information	2,900	2.0	2.0
Leisure and Hospitality	21,300	14.8	10.3
Manufacturing	6,100	4.2	8.4
Other Services	6,100	4.2	3.7
Professional and Business Services	18,800	13.1	14.7
Retail Trade	18,200	12.7	10.2
Transportation, Warehousing, and Utilities	4,700	3.3	4.9
Wholesale Trade	5,100	3.5	3.9

Note: Figures are non-farm employment as of December 2022. Figures are not seasonally adjusted and include workers 16 years of age and older; (1) Figures cover the Wilmington, NC Metropolitan Statistical Area
Source: Bureau of Labor Statistics, Current Employment Statistics, Employment, Hours, and Earnings

Employment by Occupation

Occupation Classification	City (%)	MSA[1] (%)	U.S. (%)
Management, Business, Science, and Arts	42.8	41.9	40.3
Natural Resources, Construction, and Maintenance	7.2	9.2	8.7
Production, Transportation, and Material Moving	8.5	9.1	13.1
Sales and Office	20.8	21.0	20.9
Service	20.6	18.8	17.0

Note: Figures cover employed civilians 16 years of age and older; (1) Figures cover the Wilmington, NC Metropolitan Statistical Area
Source: U.S. Census Bureau, 2017-2021 American Community Survey 5-Year Estimates

Occupations with Greatest Projected Employment Growth: 2022 – 2024

Occupation[1]	2022 Employment	2024 Projected Employment	Numeric Employment Change	Percent Employment Change
Cooks, Restaurant	45,830	53,440	7,610	16.6
Waiters and Waitresses	65,770	72,960	7,190	10.9
Software Developers	55,450	62,610	7,160	12.9
Cooks, Fast Food	82,470	88,860	6,390	7.7
Fast Food and Counter Workers	68,750	75,030	6,280	9.1
Laborers and Freight, Stock, and Material Movers, Hand	100,780	106,480	5,700	5.7
Retail Salespersons	125,490	130,210	4,720	3.8
General and Operations Managers	87,450	92,120	4,670	5.3
First-Line Supervisors of Food Preparation and Serving Workers	42,440	47,070	4,630	10.9
Stockers and Order Fillers	88,320	92,930	4,610	5.2

Note: Projections cover North Carolina; (1) Sorted by numeric employment change
Source: www.projectionscentral.com, State Occupational Projections, 2022–2024 Short-Term Projections

Fastest-Growing Occupations: 2022 – 2024

Occupation[1]	2022 Employment	2024 Projected Employment	Numeric Employment Change	Percent Employment Change
Cooks, Restaurant	45,830	53,440	7,610	16.6
Solar Photovoltaic Installers	390	450	60	15.4
Statisticians	1,710	1,960	250	14.6
Medical Scientists, Except Epidemiologists	3,630	4,160	530	14.6
Actuaries	950	1,080	130	13.7
Data Scientists	5,390	6,100	710	13.2
Soil and Plant Scientists	2,160	2,440	280	13.0
Software Developers	55,450	62,610	7,160	12.9
Software Quality Assurance Analysts and Testers	8,850	9,950	1,100	12.4
Bartenders	14,560	16,360	1,800	12.4

Note: Projections cover North Carolina; (1) Sorted by percent employment change and excludes occupations with numeric employment change less than 50
Source: www.projectionscentral.com, State Occupational Projections, 2022–2024 Short-Term Projections

CITY FINANCES

City Government Finances

Component	2020 ($000)	2020 ($ per capita)
Total Revenues	187,863	1,518
Total Expenditures	179,029	1,447
Debt Outstanding	241,860	1,955
Cash and Securities[1]	13,839	112

Note: (1) Cash and security holdings of a government at the close of its fiscal year, including those of its dependent agencies, utilities, and liquor stores.
Source: U.S. Census Bureau, State & Local Government Finances 2020

City Government Revenue by Source

Source	2020 ($000)	2020 ($ per capita)	2020 (%)
General Revenue			
From Federal Government	10,422	84	5.5
From State Government	23,194	187	12.3
From Local Governments	1,751	14	0.9
Taxes			
Property	77,907	630	41.5
Sales and Gross Receipts	34,087	275	18.1
Personal Income	0	0	0.0
Corporate Income	0	0	0.0
Motor Vehicle License	792	6	0.4
Other Taxes	482	4	0.3
Current Charges	34,349	278	18.3
Liquor Store	0	0	0.0
Utility	0	0	0.0

Source: U.S. Census Bureau, State & Local Government Finances 2020

City Government Expenditures by Function

Function	2020 ($000)	2020 ($ per capita)	2020 (%)
General Direct Expenditures			
Air Transportation	0	0	0.0
Corrections	0	0	0.0
Education	0	0	0.0
Employment Security Administration	0	0	0.0
Financial Administration	2,811	22	1.6
Fire Protection	18,173	146	10.2
General Public Buildings	5,153	41	2.9
Governmental Administration, Other	7,600	61	4.2
Health	0	0	0.0
Highways	3,187	25	1.8
Hospitals	0	0	0.0
Housing and Community Development	9,173	74	5.1
Interest on General Debt	8,557	69	4.8
Judicial and Legal	1,039	8	0.6
Libraries	0	0	0.0
Parking	9,037	73	5.0
Parks and Recreation	18,725	151	10.5
Police Protection	51,793	418	28.9
Public Welfare	645	5	0.4
Sewerage	13,590	109	7.6
Solid Waste Management	10,229	82	5.7
Veterans' Services	0	0	0.0
Liquor Store	0	0	0.0
Utility	3,051	24	1.7

Source: U.S. Census Bureau, State & Local Government Finances 2020

TAXES

State Corporate Income Tax Rates

State	Tax Rate (%)	Income Brackets ($)	Num. of Brackets	Financial Institution Tax Rate (%)[a]	Federal Income Tax Ded.
North Carolina	2.5	Flat rate	1	2.5	No

Note: Tax rates as of January 1, 2023; (a) Rates listed are the corporate income tax rate applied to financial institutions or excise taxes based on income. Some states have other taxes based upon the value of deposits or shares.
Source: Federation of Tax Administrators, State Corporate Income Tax Rates, January 1, 2023

State Individual Income Tax Rates

State	Tax Rate (%)	Income Brackets ($)	Personal Exemptions ($)			Standard Ded. ($)	
			Single	Married	Depend.	Single	Married
North Carolina	4.75	Flat rate	None	None	None	10,750	21,500

Note: Tax rates as of January 1, 2023; Local- and county-level taxes are not included; Federal income tax is not deductible on state income tax returns
Source: Federation of Tax Administrators, State Individual Income Tax Rates, January 1, 2023

Various State Sales and Excise Tax Rates

State	State Sales Tax (%)	Gasoline[1] ($/gal.)	Cigarette[2] ($/pack)	Spirits[3] ($/gal.)	Wine[4] ($/gal.)	Beer[5] ($/gal.)	Recreational Marijuana (%)
North Carolina	4.75	0.3875	0.45	16.40	1.00	0.62	Not legal

Note: All tax rates as of January 1, 2023; (1) The American Petroleum Institute has developed a methodology for determining the average tax rate on a gallon of fuel. Rates may include any of the following: excise taxes, environmental fees, storage tank fees, other fees or taxes, general sales tax, and local taxes; (2) The federal excise tax of $1.0066 per pack and local taxes are not included; (3) Rates are those applicable to off-premise sales of 40% alcohol by volume (a.b.v.) distilled spirits in 750ml containers. Local excise taxes are excluded; (4) Rates are those applicable to off-premise sales of 11% a.b.v. non-carbonated wine in 750ml containers; (5) Rates are those applicable to off-premise sales of 4.7% a.b.v. beer in 12 ounce containers.
Source: Tax Foundation, 2023 Facts & Figures: How Does Your State Compare?

State Business Tax Climate Index Rankings

State	Overall Rank	Corporate Tax Rank	Individual Income Tax Rank	Sales Tax Rank	Property Tax Rank	Unemployment Insurance Tax Rank
North Carolina	10	5	17	20	13	10

Note: The index is a measure of how each state's tax laws affect economic performance. The lower the rank, the more favorable a state's tax system is for business. States without a given tax are given a ranking of 1. The scores/rankings for the District of Columbia do not affect other states. The 2023 index represents the tax climate as of July 1, 2022.
Source: Tax Foundation, State Business Tax Climate Index 2023

TRANSPORTATION

Means of Transportation to Work

Area	Car/Truck/Van		Public Transportation			Bicycle	Walked	Other Means	Worked at Home
	Drove Alone	Car-pooled	Bus	Subway	Railroad				
City	75.4	7.5	0.7	0.0	0.0	0.6	2.5	0.8	12.6
MSA[1]	77.5	8.0	0.3	0.0	0.0	0.4	1.4	0.6	11.8
U.S.	73.2	8.6	2.0	1.6	0.5	0.5	2.5	1.5	9.7

Note: Figures are percentages and cover workers 16 years of age and older; (1) Figures cover the Wilmington, NC Metropolitan Statistical Area
Source: U.S. Census Bureau, 2017-2021 American Community Survey 5-Year Estimates

Travel Time to Work

Area	Less Than 10 Minutes	10 to 19 Minutes	20 to 29 Minutes	30 to 44 Minutes	45 to 59 Minutes	60 to 89 Minutes	90 Minutes or More
City	16.1	47.0	21.7	9.5	2.5	1.7	1.5
MSA[1]	12.7	38.0	22.6	16.0	5.7	2.8	2.1
U.S.	12.4	28.5	21.0	20.9	8.2	6.2	2.9

Note: Note: Figures are percentages and include workers 16 years old and over; (1) Figures cover the Wilmington, NC Metropolitan Statistical Area
Source: U.S. Census Bureau, 2017-2021 American Community Survey 5-Year Estimates

Key Congestion Measures

Measure	1990	2000	2010	2015	2020
Annual Hours of Delay, Total (000)	n/a	n/a	n/a	6,466	3,223
Annual Hours of Delay, Per Auto Commuter	n/a	n/a	n/a	27	13
Annual Congestion Cost, Per Auto Commuter ($)	n/a	n/a	n/a	539	271

Note: n/a not available
Source: Texas A&M Transportation Institute, 2021 Urban Mobility Report

Freeway Travel Time Index

Measure	1985	1990	1995	2000	2005	2010	2015	2020
Urban Area Index[1]	n/a	n/a	n/a	n/a	n/a	n/a	1.13	1.07
Urban Area Rank[1,2]	n/a	n/a	n/a	n/a	n/a	n/a	n/a	n/a

Note: Freeway Travel Time Index—the ratio of travel time in the peak period to the travel time at free-flow conditions. For example, a value of 1.30 indicates a 20-minute free-flow trip takes 26 minutes in the peak (20 minutes x 1.30 = 26 minutes); (1) Covers the Wilmington NC urban area; (2) Rank is based on 101 larger urban areas (#1 = highest travel time index); n/a not available
Source: Texas A&M Transportation Institute, 2021 Urban Mobility Report

Public Transportation

Agency Name / Mode of Transportation	Vehicles Operated in Maximum Service[1]	Annual Unlinked Passenger Trips[2] (in thous.)	Annual Passenger Miles[3] (in thous.)
Cape Fear Public Transportation Authority (Wave Transit)			
Bus (purchased transportation)	25	528.1	1,488.1
Demand Response (directly operated)	16	35.8	175.2
Vanpool (directly operated)	1	1.1	65.1

Note: (1) Number of revenue vehicles operated by the given mode and type of service to meet the annual maximum service requirement. This is the revenue vehicle count during the peak season of the year; on the week and day that maximum service is provided. Vehicles operated in maximum service (VOMS) exclude atypical days and one-time special events; (2) Number of passengers who boarded public transportation vehicles. Passengers are counted each time they board a vehicle no matter how many vehicles they use to travel from their origin to their destination. (3) Sum of the distances ridden by all passengers during the entire fiscal year.
Source: Federal Transit Administration, National Transit Database, 2021

Air Transportation

Airport Name and Code / Type of Service	Passenger Airlines[1]	Passenger Enplanements	Freight Carriers[2]	Freight (lbs)
Wilmington International Airport (ILM)				
Domestic service (U.S. carriers - 2022)	21	536,180	6	1,546,060
International service (U.S. carriers - 2021)	1	2	0	0

Note: (1) Includes all U.S.-based major, minor and commuter airlines that carried at least one passenger during the year; (2) Includes all U.S.-based airlines and freight carriers that transported at least one pound of freight during the year.
Source: Bureau of Transportation Statistics, The Intermodal Transportation Database, Air Carriers: T-100 Domestic Market (U.S. Carriers), 2022; Bureau of Transportation Statistics, The Intermodal Transportation Database, Air Carriers: T-100 International Market (U.S. Carriers), 2021

BUSINESSES

Major Business Headquarters

Company Name	Industry	Rankings	
		Fortune[1]	Forbes[2]
No companies listed	-	-	-

Note: (1) Companies that produce a 10-K are ranked 1 to 500 based on 2021 revenue; (2) All private companies with at least $2 billion in annual revenue through the end of their most current fiscal year are ranked 1 to 246; companies listed are headquartered in the city; dashes indicate no ranking
Source: Fortune, "Fortune 500," 2022; Forbes, "America's Largest Private Companies," 2022

Fastest-Growing Businesses

According to *Inc.*, Wilmington is home to two of America's 500 fastest-growing private companies: **LRB Group** (#277); **Summit Logistics Group** (#353). Criteria: must be an independent, privately-held, for-profit, U.S. corporation, proprietorship or partnership as of December 31, 2021; revenues must be at least $100,000 in 2018 and $2 million in 2021; must have four-year operating/sales history. *Inc., "America's 500 Fastest-Growing Private Companies," 2022*

Living Environment

510 Wilmington, North Carolina

COST OF LIVING

Cost of Living Index

Composite Index	Groceries	Housing	Utilities	Trans-portation	Health Care	Misc. Goods/ Services
n/a	n/a	n/a	n/a	n/a	n/a	n/a

Note: The Cost of Living Index measures regional differences in the cost of consumer goods and services, excluding taxes and non-consumer expenditures, for professional and managerial households in the top income quintile. It is based on more than 50,000 prices covering almost 60 different items for which prices are collected three times a year by chambers of commerce, economic development organizations or university applied economic centers in each participating urban area. The numbers shown should be read as a percentage above or below the national average of 100. For example, a value of 115.4 in the groceries column indicates that grocery prices are 15.4% higher than the national average. Small differences in the index numbers should not be interpreted as significant; n/a not available.
Source: The Council for Community and Economic Research, Cost of Living Index, 2022

Grocery Prices

Area[1]	T-Bone Steak ($/pound)	Frying Chicken ($/pound)	Whole Milk ($/half gal.)	Eggs ($/dozen)	Orange Juice ($/64 oz.)	Coffee ($/11.5 oz.)
City[2]	n/a	n/a	n/a	n/a	n/a	n/a
Avg.	13.81	1.59	2.43	2.25	3.85	4.95
Min.	10.17	0.90	1.51	1.30	2.90	3.46
Max.	19.35	3.30	4.32	4.32	5.31	8.59

*Note: (1) Values for the local area are compared with the average, minimum and maximum values for all 286 areas in the Cost of Living Index; (2) Figures cover the Wilmington NC urban area; n/a not available; **T-Bone Steak** (price per pound); **Frying Chicken** (price per pound, whole fryer); **Whole Milk** (half gallon carton); **Eggs** (price per dozen, Grade A, large); **Orange Juice** (64 oz. Tropicana or Florida Natural); **Coffee** (11.5 oz. can, vacuum-packed, Maxwell House, Hills Bros, or Folgers).*
Source: The Council for Community and Economic Research, Cost of Living Index, 2022

Housing and Utility Costs

Area[1]	New Home Price ($)	Apartment Rent ($/month)	All Electric ($/month)	Part Electric ($/month)	Other Energy ($/month)	Telephone ($/month)
City[2]	n/a	n/a	n/a	n/a	n/a	n/a
Avg.	450,913	1,371	176.41	99.93	76.96	190.22
Min.	229,283	546	100.84	31.56	27.15	174.27
Max.	2,434,977	4,569	356.86	249.59	272.24	208.31

*Note: (1) Values for the local area are compared with the average, minimum and maximum values for all 286 areas in the Cost of Living Index; (2) Figures cover the Wilmington NC urban area; n/a not available; **New Home Price** (2,400 sf living area, 8,000 sf lot, in urban area with full utilities); **Apartment Rent** (950 sf 2 bedroom/1.5 or 2 bath, unfurnished, excluding all utilities except water); **All Electric** (average monthly cost for an all-electric home); **Part Electric** (average monthly cost for a part-electric home); **Other Energy** (average monthly cost for natural gas, fuel oil, coal, wood, and any other forms of energy except electricity); **Telephone** (price includes the base monthly rate plus taxes and fees for three lines of mobile phone service).*
Source: The Council for Community and Economic Research, Cost of Living Index, 2022

Health Care, Transportation, and Other Costs

Area[1]	Doctor ($/visit)	Dentist ($/visit)	Optometrist ($/visit)	Gasoline ($/gallon)	Beauty Salon ($/visit)	Men's Shirt ($)
City[2]	n/a	n/a	n/a	n/a	n/a	n/a
Avg.	124.91	107.77	117.66	3.86	43.31	34.21
Min.	36.61	58.25	51.79	2.90	22.18	13.05
Max.	250.21	162.58	371.96	5.54	85.61	63.54

*Note: (1) Values for the local area are compared with the average, minimum and maximum values for all 286 areas in the Cost of Living Index; (2) Figures cover the Wilmington NC urban area; n/a not available; **Doctor** (general practitioners routine exam of an established patient); **Dentist** (adult teeth cleaning and periodic oral examination); **Optometrist** (full vision eye exam for established adult patient); **Gasoline** (one gallon regular unleaded, national brand, including all taxes, cash price at self-service pump if available); **Beauty Salon** (woman's shampoo, trim, and blow-dry); **Men's Shirt** (cotton/polyester dress shirt, pinpoint weave, long sleeves).*
Source: The Council for Community and Economic Research, Cost of Living Index, 2022

HOUSING

Homeownership Rate

Area	2015 (%)	2016 (%)	2017 (%)	2018 (%)	2019 (%)	2020 (%)	2021 (%)	2022 (%)
MSA[1]	n/a	n/a	n/a	n/a	n/a	n/a	n/a	n/a
U.S.	63.7	63.4	63.9	64.4	64.6	66.6	65.5	65.8

Note: (1) Figures cover the Wilmington, NC Metropolitan Statistical Area; n/a not available
Source: U.S. Census Bureau, Housing Vacancies and Homeownership Annual Statistics: 2015-2022

House Price Index (HPI)

Area	National Ranking[2]	Quarterly Change (%)	One-Year Change (%)	Five-Year Change (%)	Since 1991Q1 (%)
MSA[1]	18	-1.23	18.70	72.00	356.80
U.S.[3]	–	0.34	8.41	58.44	289.08

Note: The HPI is a weighted repeat sales index. It measures average price changes in repeat sales or refinancings on the same properties. This information is obtained by reviewing repeat mortgage transactions on single-family properties whose mortgages have been purchased or securitized by Fannie Mae or Freddie Mac since January 1975; (1) Figures cover the Wilmington, NC Metropolitan Statistical Area; (2) Rankings are based on annual percentage change for all metro areas containing at least 15,000 transactions over the last 10 years and ranges from 1 to 257; (3) figures based on a weighted average of Census Division estimates using a seasonally adjusted, purchase-only index; all figures are for the period ending December 31, 2022
Source: Federal Housing Finance Agency, Change in FHFA Metropolitan Area House Price Indexes, 2022Q4

Median Single-Family Home Prices

Area	2020	2021	2022p	Percent Change 2021 to 2022
MSA[1]	301.7	355.3	410.1	15.4
U.S. Average	300.2	357.1	392.6	9.9

Note: Figures are median sales prices of existing single-family homes in thousands of dollars; (p) preliminary; (1) Figures cover the Wilmington, NC Metropolitan Statistical Area
Source: National Association of Realtors, Median Sales Price of Existing Single-Family Homes for Metropolitan Areas, 4th Quarter 2022

Qualifying Income Based on Median Sales Price of Existing Single-Family Homes

Area	With 5% Down ($)	With 10% Down ($)	With 20% Down ($)
MSA[1]	124,101	117,570	104,506
U.S. Average	112,234	106,237	94,513

Note: Figures are preliminary; Qualifying income is based on a mortgage rate of 6.77%. Monthly principal and interest payment is limited to 25% of income; (1) Figures cover the Wilmington, NC Metropolitan Statistical Area
Source: National Association of Realtors, Qualifying Income Based on Median Sales Price of Existing Single-Family Homes for Metropolitan Areas, 4th Quarter 2022

Home Value

Area	Under $100,000	$100,000 -$199,999	$200,000 -$299,999	$300,000 -$399,999	$400,000 -$499,999	$500,000 -$999,999	$1,000,000 or more	Median ($)
City	5.9	23.6	25.8	19.2	8.2	13.7	3.7	279,900
MSA[1]	9.2	24.0	25.8	18.0	8.9	11.6	2.4	262,500
U.S.	16.2	24.2	20.1	13.6	8.3	13.6	4.1	244,900

Note: Figures are percentages except for median and cover owner-occupied housing units; (1) Figures cover the Wilmington, NC Metropolitan Statistical Area
Source: U.S. Census Bureau, 2017-2021 American Community Survey 5-Year Estimates

Year Housing Structure Built

Area	2020 or Later	2010 -2019	2000 -2009	1990 -1999	1980 -1989	1970 -1979	1960 -1969	1950 -1959	1940 -1949	Before 1940	Median Year
City	0.1	10.8	15.0	17.3	15.3	12.9	6.7	6.8	5.5	9.6	1986
MSA[1]	0.3	12.4	20.4	20.9	15.1	12.0	5.6	4.6	3.4	5.3	1992
U.S.	0.2	7.3	13.6	13.6	13.2	14.8	10.3	10.0	4.7	12.2	1979

Note: Figures are percentages except for Median Year; Note: (1) Figures cover the Wilmington, NC Metropolitan Statistical Area
Source: U.S. Census Bureau, 2017-2021 American Community Survey 5-Year Estimates

Gross Monthly Rent

Area	Under $500	$500 -$999	$1,000 -$1,499	$1,500 -$1,999	$2,000 -$2,499	$2,500 -$2,999	$3,000 and up	Median ($)
City	10.1	31.3	40.1	15.0	2.5	0.5	0.6	1,093
MSA[1]	8.0	29.7	41.7	15.1	3.2	1.5	0.8	1,118
U.S.	8.1	30.5	30.8	16.8	7.3	3.1	3.5	1,163

Note: Figures are percentages except for median; Gross rent is the contract rent plus the estimated average monthly cost of utilities (electricity, gas, and water and sewer) and fuels (oil, coal, kerosene, wood, etc.) if these are paid by the renter (or paid for the renter by someone else); (1) Figures cover the Wilmington, NC Metropolitan Statistical Area
Source: U.S. Census Bureau, 2017-2021 American Community Survey 5-Year Estimates

HEALTH

Health Risk Factors

Category	MSA[1] (%)	U.S. (%)
Adults aged 18–64 who have any kind of health care coverage	n/a	90.9
Adults who reported being in good or better health	n/a	85.2
Adults who have been told they have high blood cholesterol	n/a	35.7
Adults who have been told they have high blood pressure	n/a	32.4
Adults who are current smokers	n/a	14.4
Adults who currently use e-cigarettes	n/a	6.7
Adults who currently use chewing tobacco, snuff, or snus	n/a	3.5
Adults who are heavy drinkers[2]	n/a	6.3
Adults who are binge drinkers[3]	n/a	15.4
Adults who are overweight (BMI 25.0 - 29.9)	n/a	34.4
Adults who are obese (BMI 30.0 - 99.8)	n/a	33.9
Adults who participated in any physical activities in the past month	n/a	76.3

Note: (1) Figures for the Wilmington, NC Metropolitan Statistical Area were not available.
(2) Heavy drinkers are classified as adult men having more than 14 drinks per week and adult women having more than 7 drinks per week; (3) Binge drinkers are classified as males having five or more drinks on one occasion or females having four or more drinks on one occasion
Source: Centers for Disease Control and Prevention, Behaviorial Risk Factor Surveillance System, SMART: Selected Metropolitan Area Risk Trends, 2021

Acute and Chronic Health Conditions

Category	MSA[1] (%)	U.S. (%)
Adults who have ever been told they had a heart attack	n/a	4.0
Adults who have ever been told they have angina or coronary heart disease	n/a	3.8
Adults who have ever been told they had a stroke	n/a	3.0
Adults who have ever been told they have asthma	n/a	14.9
Adults who have ever been told they have arthritis	n/a	25.8
Adults who have ever been told they have diabetes[2]	n/a	10.9
Adults who have ever been told they had skin cancer	n/a	6.6
Adults who have ever been told they had any other types of cancer	n/a	7.5
Adults who have ever been told they have COPD	n/a	6.1
Adults who have ever been told they have kidney disease	n/a	3.0
Adults who have ever been told they have a form of depression	n/a	20.5

Note: (1) Figures for the Wilmington, NC Metropolitan Statistical Area were not available.
(2) Figures do not include pregnancy-related, borderline, or pre-diabetes
Source: Centers for Disease Control and Prevention, Behaviorial Risk Factor Surveillance System, SMART: Selected Metropolitan Area Risk Trends, 2021

Health Screening and Vaccination Rates

Category	MSA[1] (%)	U.S. (%)
Adults who have ever been tested for HIV	n/a	34.9
Adults who have had their blood cholesterol checked within the last five years	n/a	85.2
Adults aged 65+ who have had flu shot within the past year	n/a	68.6
Adults aged 65+ who have ever had a pneumonia vaccination	n/a	71.0

Note: (1) Figures for the Wilmington, NC Metropolitan Statistical Area were not available.
Source: Centers for Disease Control and Prevention, Behaviorial Risk Factor Surveillance System, SMART: Selected Metropolitan Area Risk Trends, 2021

Disability Status

Category	MSA[1] (%)	U.S. (%)
Adults who reported being deaf	n/a	7.2
Are you blind or have serious difficulty seeing, even when wearing glasses?	n/a	4.8
Are you limited in any way in any of your usual activities due to arthritis?	n/a	11.1
Do you have difficulty doing errands alone?	n/a	7.0
Do you have difficulty dressing or bathing?	n/a	3.6
Do you have serious difficulty concentrating/remembering/making decisions?	n/a	12.1
Do you have serious difficulty walking or climbing stairs?	n/a	12.8

Note: (1) Figures for the Wilmington, NC Metropolitan Statistical Area were not available.
Source: Centers for Disease Control and Prevention, Behaviorial Risk Factor Surveillance System, SMART: Selected Metropolitan Area Risk Trends, 2021

Mortality Rates for the Top 10 Causes of Death in the U.S.

ICD-10[a] Sub-Chapter	ICD-10[a] Code	Crude Mortality Rate[1] per 100,000 population	
		County[2]	U.S.
Malignant neoplasms	C00-C97	195.1	182.6
Ischaemic heart diseases	I20-I25	81.3	113.1
Other forms of heart disease	I30-I51	68.0	64.4
Other degenerative diseases of the nervous system	G30-G31	45.1	51.0
Cerebrovascular diseases	I60-I69	65.1	47.8
Other external causes of accidental injury	W00-X59	56.7	46.4
Chronic lower respiratory diseases	J40-J47	41.9	45.7
Organic, including symptomatic, mental disorders	F01-F09	63.8	35.9
Hypertensive diseases	I10-I15	18.7	35.0
Diabetes mellitus	E10-E14	21.4	29.6

Note: (a) ICD-10 = International Classification of Diseases 10th Revision; (1) Crude mortality rates are a three-year average covering 2019-2021; (2) Figures cover New Hanover County.
Source: Centers for Disease Control and Prevention, National Center for Health Statistics. National Vital Statistics System, Mortality 2018-2021 on CDC WONDER Online Database

Mortality Rates for Selected Causes of Death

ICD-10[a] Sub-Chapter	ICD-10[a] Code	Crude Mortality Rate[1] per 100,000 population	
		County[2]	U.S.
Assault	X85-Y09	7.1	7.0
Diseases of the liver	K70-K76	26.0	19.8
Human immunodeficiency virus (HIV) disease	B20-B24	Suppressed	1.5
Influenza and pneumonia	J09-J18	16.4	14.7
Intentional self-harm	X60-X84	16.0	14.3
Malnutrition	E40-E46	7.9	4.3
Obesity and other hyperalimentation	E65-E68	Unreliable	3.0
Renal failure	N17-N19	19.7	15.7
Transport accidents	V01-V99	14.0	13.6
Viral hepatitis	B15-B19	Suppressed	1.2

Note: (a) ICD-10 = International Classification of Diseases 10th Revision; (1) Crude mortality rates are a three-year average covering 2019-2021; (2) Figures cover New Hanover County; Data are suppressed when the data meet the criteria for confidentiality constraints; Crude mortality rates are flagged as unreliable when the rate would be calculated with a numerator of 20 or less.
Source: Centers for Disease Control and Prevention, National Center for Health Statistics. National Vital Statistics System, Mortality 2018-2021 on CDC WONDER Online Database

Health Insurance Coverage

Area	With Health Insurance	With Private Health Insurance	With Public Health Insurance	Without Health Insurance	Population Under Age 19 Without Health Insurance
City	88.9	70.3	32.6	11.1	6.5
MSA[1]	89.7	72.8	32.3	10.3	7.2
U.S.	91.2	67.8	35.4	8.8	5.3

Note: Figures are percentages that cover the civilian noninstitutionalized population; (1) Figures cover the Wilmington, NC Metropolitan Statistical Area
Source: U.S. Census Bureau, 2017-2021 American Community Survey 5-Year Estimates

Number of Medical Professionals

Area	MDs[3]	DOs[3,4]	Dentists	Podiatrists	Chiropractors	Optometrists
County[1] (number)	812	69	188	20	84	57
County[1] (rate[2])	359.2	30.5	82.1	8.7	36.7	24.9
U.S. (rate[2])	289.3	23.5	72.5	6.2	28.7	17.4

Note: Data as of 2021 unless noted; (1) Data covers New Hanover County; (2) Rate per 100,000 population; (3) Data as of 2020 and includes all active, non-federal physicians; (4) Doctor of Osteopathic Medicine
Source: U.S. Department of Health and Human Services, Health Resources and Services Administration, Bureau of Health Professions, Area Resource File (ARF) 2021-2022

EDUCATION

Public School District Statistics

District Name	Schls	Pupils	Pupil/ Teacher Ratio	Minority Pupils[1] (%)	LEP/ELL[2] (%)	IEP[3] (%)
New Hanover County Schools	43	24,933	14.1	41.2	5.2	12.9

Note: Table includes school districts with 2,000 or more students; (1) Percentage of students that are not non-Hispanic white; (2) Percentage of students that are Limited English Proficient or English Language Learners (2018-19); (3) Percentage of students that have an Individualized Education Program (2019-20).
Source: U.S. Department of Education, National Center for Education Statistics, Common Core of Data, Local Education Agency (School District) Universe Survey: School Year 2021-2022

Highest Level of Education

Area	Less than H.S.	H.S. Diploma	Some College, No Deg.	Associate Degree	Bachelor's Degree	Master's Degree	Prof. School Degree	Doctorate Degree
City	6.5	19.7	20.0	10.3	28.3	10.2	3.2	1.8
MSA[1]	7.2	20.8	21.3	10.9	26.2	9.4	2.8	1.5
U.S.	11.1	26.5	20.0	8.7	20.6	9.3	2.2	1.5

Note: Figures cover persons age 25 and over; (1) Figures cover the Wilmington, NC Metropolitan Statistical Area
Source: U.S. Census Bureau, 2017-2021 American Community Survey 5-Year Estimates

Educational Attainment by Race

Area	High School Graduate or Higher (%)					Bachelor's Degree or Higher (%)				
	Total	White	Black	Asian	Hisp.[2]	Total	White	Black	Asian	Hisp.[2]
City	93.5	95.6	87.4	84.0	78.0	43.6	49.0	20.9	60.7	32.3
MSA[1]	92.8	94.4	87.9	82.0	78.9	39.9	43.0	22.5	63.9	27.1
U.S.	88.9	91.4	87.2	87.6	71.2	33.7	35.5	23.3	55.6	18.4

Note: Figures shown cover persons 25 years old and over; (1) Figures cover the Wilmington, NC Metropolitan Statistical Area; (2) People of Hispanic origin can be of any race
Source: U.S. Census Bureau, 2017-2021 American Community Survey 5-Year Estimates

School Enrollment by Grade and Control

Area	Preschool (%)		Kindergarten (%)		Grades 1 - 4 (%)		Grades 5 - 8 (%)		Grades 9 - 12 (%)	
	Public	Private	Public	Private	Public	Private	Public	Private	Public	Private
City	62.4	37.6	84.8	15.2	75.5	24.5	74.3	25.7	88.8	11.2
MSA[1]	48.0	52.0	81.2	18.8	83.4	16.6	82.0	18.0	88.8	11.2
U.S.	58.8	41.2	86.3	13.7	88.3	11.7	88.6	11.4	89.4	10.6

Note: Figures shown cover persons 3 years old and over; (1) Figures cover the Wilmington, NC Metropolitan Statistical Area
Source: U.S. Census Bureau, 2017-2021 American Community Survey 5-Year Estimates

Higher Education

Four-Year Colleges			Two-Year Colleges			Medical Schools[1]	Law Schools[2]	Voc/ Tech[3]
Public	Private Non-profit	Private For-profit	Public	Private Non-profit	Private For-profit			
1	0	1	1	0	0	0	0	1

Note: Figures cover institutions located within the Wilmington, NC Metropolitan Statistical Area and include main campuses only; (1) includes schools accredited by the Liaison Committee on Medical Education and the American Osteopathic Association's Commission on Osteopathic College Accreditation; (2) includes ABA-accredited schools, schools with provisional ABA accreditation, and state accredited schools; (3) includes all schools with programs that are less than 2 years.
Source: National Center for Education Statistics, Integrated Postsecondary Education System (IPEDS), 2021-22; Wikipedia, List of Medical Schools in the United States, accessed April 10, 2023; Wikipedia, List of Law Schools in the United States, accessed April 10, 2023

EMPLOYERS

Major Employers

Company Name	Industry
Brunswick County Schools	Education
Cape Fear Community College	Education
City of Wilmington	Municipal government
Corning	Optical fiber
Duke Energy	Utility
GE Wilmington	Electronics & aviation
New Hanover County	Government
New Hanover County Schools	Education
New Hanover Reg Med Ctr/Cape Fear Hosp	Healthcare
Novant Medical/Brunswick Community Hosp	Healthcare
PPD	Discovery & development services to pharma/biotech
University of NC Wilmington	Education
Verizon Wireless	Communications
Wal-Mart Stores	Retail

Note: Companies shown are located within the Wilmington, NC Metropolitan Statistical Area.
Source: Hoovers.com; Wikipedia

Wilmington, North Carolina 515

PUBLIC SAFETY

Crime Rate

Area	Total Crime	Violent Crime Rate				Property Crime Rate		
		Murder	Rape[3]	Robbery	Aggrav. Assault	Burglary	Larceny -Theft	Motor Vehicle Theft
City	3,175.8	17.5	52.5	113.7	445.2	473.0	1,915.8	158.2
Suburbs[1]	1,803.5	2.3	27.7	24.3	135.2	300.9	1,220.4	92.7
Metro[2]	2,373.9	8.6	38.0	61.5	264.0	372.4	1,509.5	120.0
U.S.	2,356.7	6.5	38.4	73.9	279.7	314.2	1,398.0	246.0

Note: Figures are crimes per 100,000 population; (1) All areas within the metro area that are located outside the city limits; (2) Figures cover the Wilmington, NC Metropolitan Statistical Area; (3) All figures shown were reported using the revised Uniform Crime Reporting (UCR) definition of rape; Due to the transition to the National Incident-Based Reporting System (NIBRS), limited city and metro area data was released for 2021.
Source: FBI Uniform Crime Reports, 2020

Hate Crimes

Area	Number of Quarters Reported	Number of Incidents per Bias Motivation					
		Race/Ethnicity/ Ancestry	Religion	Sexual Orientation	Disability	Gender	Gender Identity
City	4	0	0	0	0	0	0
U.S.	4	5,227	1,244	1,110	130	75	266

Note: Due to the transition to the National Incident-Based Reporting System (NIBRS), limited crime data was released for 2021.
Source: Federal Bureau of Investigation, Hate Crime Statistics 2020

Identity Theft Consumer Reports

Area	Reports	Reports per 100,000 Population	Rank[2]
MSA[1]	494	168	208
U.S.	1,108,609	339	-

Note: (1) Figures cover the Wilmington, NC Metropolitan Statistical Area; (2) Rank ranges from 1 to 391 where 1 indicates greatest number of identity theft reports per 100,000 population
Source: Federal Trade Commission, Consumer Sentinel Network Data Book 2022

Fraud and Other Consumer Reports

Area	Reports	Reports per 100,000 Population	Rank[2]
MSA[1]	3,093	1,054	75
U.S.	4,064,520	1,245	-

Note: (1) Figures cover the Wilmington, NC Metropolitan Statistical Area; (2) Rank ranges from 1 to 391 where 1 indicates greatest number of fraud and other consumer reports per 100,000 population
Source: Federal Trade Commission, Consumer Sentinel Network Data Book 2022

POLITICS

2020 Presidential Election Results

Area	Biden	Trump	Jorgensen	Hawkins	Other
New Hanover County	50.2	48.0	1.2	0.3	0.4
U.S.	51.3	46.8	1.2	0.3	0.5

Note: Results are percentages and may not add to 100% due to rounding
Source: Dave Leip's Atlas of U.S. Presidential Elections

SPORTS

Professional Sports Teams

Team Name	League	Year Established

No teams are located in the metro area
Source: Wikipedia, Major Professional Sports Teams of the United States and Canada, April 12, 2023

CLIMATE

Average and Extreme Temperatures

Temperature	Jan	Feb	Mar	Apr	May	Jun	Jul	Aug	Sep	Oct	Nov	Dec	Yr.
Extreme High (°F)	82	85	89	95	98	104	102	102	98	95	87	81	104
Average High (°F)	56	59	65	74	81	86	90	88	84	75	67	59	74
Average Temp. (°F)	46	48	55	63	71	77	81	80	75	65	56	49	64
Average Low (°F)	36	37	43	51	60	67	72	71	65	54	45	37	53
Extreme Low (°F)	5	11	9	30	35	48	55	55	44	27	16	0	0

Note: Figures cover the years 1948-1995
Source: National Climatic Data Center, International Station Meteorological Climate Summary, 9/96

516 Wilmington, North Carolina

Average Precipitation/Snowfall/Humidity

Precip./Humidity	Jan	Feb	Mar	Apr	May	Jun	Jul	Aug	Sep	Oct	Nov	Dec	Yr.
Avg. Precip. (in.)	3.9	3.5	4.3	2.9	4.3	5.4	7.9	7.0	5.6	3.3	3.3	3.5	55.0
Avg. Snowfall (in.)	Tr	1	Tr	Tr	0	0	0	0	0	0	Tr	1	2
Avg. Rel. Hum. 7am (%)	82	80	82	81	84	85	87	90	90	89	86	82	85
Avg. Rel. Hum. 4pm (%)	58	55	54	51	58	62	66	67	66	60	58	58	59

Note: Figures cover the years 1948-1995; Tr = Trace amounts (<0.05 in. of rain; <0.5 in. of snow)
Source: National Climatic Data Center, International Station Meteorological Climate Summary, 9/96

Weather Conditions

Temperature			Daytime Sky			Precipitation		
10°F & below	32°F & below	90°F & above	Clear	Partly cloudy	Cloudy	0.01 inch or more precip.	0.1 inch or more snow/ice	Thunder-storms
< 1	42	46	96	150	119	115	1	47

Note: Figures are average number of days per year and cover the years 1948-1995
Source: National Climatic Data Center, International Station Meteorological Climate Summary, 9/96

HAZARDOUS WASTE

Superfund Sites

The Wilmington, NC metro area is home to one site on the EPA's Superfund National Priorities List: **Horton Iron and Metal** (final). There are a total of 1,165 Superfund sites with a status of proposed or final on the list in the U.S. *U.S. Environmental Protection Agency, National Priorities List, April 12, 2023*

AIR QUALITY

Air Quality Trends: Ozone

	1990	1995	2000	2005	2010	2015	2018	2019	2020	2021
MSA[1]	0.082	0.079	0.080	0.075	0.062	0.057	0.062	0.059	0.054	0.062
U.S.	0.087	0.089	0.081	0.080	0.072	0.067	0.069	0.065	0.065	0.067

Note: (1) Data covers the Wilmington, NC Metropolitan Statistical Area. The values shown are the composite ozone concentration averages among trend sites based on the highest fourth daily maximum 8-hour concentration in parts per million. These trends are based on sites having an adequate record of monitoring data during the trend period. Data from exceptional events are included.
Source: U.S. Environmental Protection Agency, Air Quality Monitoring Information, "Air Quality Trends by City, 1990-2021"

Air Quality Index

Area	Percent of Days when Air Quality was...[2]					AQI Statistics[2]	
	Good	Moderate	Unhealthy for Sensitive Groups	Unhealthy	Very Unhealthy	Maximum	Median
MSA[1]	89.4	10.6	0.0	0.0	0.0	93	34

Note: (1) Data covers the Wilmington, NC Metropolitan Statistical Area; (2) Based on 360 days with AQI data in 2021. Air Quality Index (AQI) is an index for reporting daily air quality. EPA calculates the AQI for five major air pollutants regulated by the Clean Air Act: ground-level ozone, particle pollution (aka particulate matter), carbon monoxide, sulfur dioxide, and nitrogen dioxide. The AQI runs from 0 to 500. The higher the AQI value, the greater the level of air pollution and the greater the health concern. There are six AQI categories: "Good" AQI is between 0 and 50. Air quality is considered satisfactory; "Moderate" AQI is between 51 and 100. Air quality is acceptable; "Unhealthy for Sensitive Groups" When AQI values are between 101 and 150, members of sensitive groups may experience health effects; "Unhealthy" When AQI values are between 151 and 200 everyone may begin to experience health effects; "Very Unhealthy" AQI values between 201 and 300 trigger a health alert; "Hazardous" AQI values over 300 trigger warnings of emergency conditions (not shown).
Source: U.S. Environmental Protection Agency, Air Quality Index Report, 2021

Air Quality Index Pollutants

Area	Percent of Days when AQI Pollutant was...[2]					
	Carbon Monoxide	Nitrogen Dioxide	Ozone	Sulfur Dioxide	Particulate Matter 2.5	Particulate Matter 10
MSA[1]	0.0	0.0	46.7	(3)	53.3	0.0

Note: (1) Data covers the Wilmington, NC Metropolitan Statistical Area; (2) Based on 360 days with AQI data in 2021. The Air Quality Index (AQI) is an index for reporting daily air quality. EPA calculates the AQI for five major air pollutants regulated by the Clean Air Act: ground-level ozone, particle pollution (also known as particulate matter), carbon monoxide, sulfur dioxide, and nitrogen dioxide. The AQI runs from 0 to 500. The higher the AQI value, the greater the level of air pollution and the greater the health concern; (3) Sulfur dioxide is no longer included in this table (as of December 8, 2021) because SO_2 concentrations tend to be very localized and not necessarily representative of broad geographical areas like counties and CBSAs.
Source: U.S. Environmental Protection Agency, Air Quality Index Report, 2021

Maximum Air Pollutant Concentrations: Particulate Matter, Ozone, CO and Lead

	Particulate Matter 10 (ug/m³)	Particulate Matter 2.5 Wtd AM (ug/m³)	Particulate Matter 2.5 24-Hr (ug/m³)	Ozone (ppm)	Carbon Monoxide (ppm)	Lead (ug/m³)
MSA[1] Level	41	4.8	13	0.062	n/a	n/a
NAAQS[2]	150	15	35	0.075	9	0.15
Met NAAQS[2]	Yes	Yes	Yes	Yes	n/a	n/a

Note: (1) Data covers the Wilmington, NC Metropolitan Statistical Area; Data from exceptional events are included; (2) National Ambient Air Quality Standards; ppm = parts per million; ug/m³ = micrograms per cubic meter; n/a not available.
Concentrations: Particulate Matter 10 (coarse particulate)—highest second maximum 24-hour concentration; Particulate Matter 2.5 Wtd AM (fine particulate)—highest weighted annual mean concentration; Particulate Matter 2.5 24-Hour (fine particulate)—highest 98th percentile 24-hour concentration; Ozone—highest fourth daily maximum 8-hour concentration; Carbon Monoxide—highest second maximum non-overlapping 8-hour concentration; Lead—maximum running 3-month average
Source: U.S. Environmental Protection Agency, Air Quality Monitoring Information, "Air Quality Statistics by City, 2021"

Maximum Air Pollutant Concentrations: Nitrogen Dioxide and Sulfur Dioxide

	Nitrogen Dioxide AM (ppb)	Nitrogen Dioxide 1-Hr (ppb)	Sulfur Dioxide AM (ppb)	Sulfur Dioxide 1-Hr (ppb)	Sulfur Dioxide 24-Hr (ppb)
MSA[1] Level	n/a	n/a	n/a	n/a	n/a
NAAQS[2]	53	100	30	75	140
Met NAAQS[2]	n/a	n/a	n/a	n/a	n/a

Note: (1) Data covers the Wilmington, NC Metropolitan Statistical Area; Data from exceptional events are included; (2) National Ambient Air Quality Standards; ppm = parts per million; ug/m³ = micrograms per cubic meter; n/a not available.
Concentrations: Nitrogen Dioxide AM—highest arithmetic mean concentration; Nitrogen Dioxide 1-Hr—highest 98th percentile 1-hour daily maximum concentration; Sulfur Dioxide AM—highest annual mean concentration; Sulfur Dioxide 1-Hr—highest 99th percentile 1-hour daily maximum concentration; Sulfur Dioxide 24-Hr—highest second maximum 24-hour concentration
Source: U.S. Environmental Protection Agency, Air Quality Monitoring Information, "Air Quality Statistics by City, 2021"

Winston-Salem, North Carolina

Background

The "Twin City" of Winston-Salem was formed by joining the towns of Winston and Salem, North Carolina. The combined name was created in 1899, due to a mistake by a postal office employee, and became official in 1913 and also became known as the "Twin City."

The town of Salem, North Carolina dates to January of 1753 when the Moravain Church purchased approximately 100,000 acres to form their first community in North Carolina. The eastern European based church settled in the Wachovia Tract. The settlement, originally known as Bethabara, was re-named Salem, from the Hebrew word for peace, in 1766. The community was established around a town square with all the property owned by the church; all the town's residents needed to be members of the church and only leased land to church members. The Moravains, known for their craftsmanship and artistry, as well arts and culture, soon established the town as an economic trade center. In 1856 the town of Salem was officially incorporated in what is now Forsyth County.

Winston, North Carolina was established in 1849 when Forsyth County purchased land from the Moravain congregation of Salem. Situated to the north of Salem, Winston was officially named in 1851 after local politician and Revolutionary War hero Mayor John Winston. At the end of the Civil War in 1865, Winston became a major industrial center. Soon Winston and Salem both began work to connect to the North Carolina Railroad to further strengthen their economies. In 1868, Winston's first tobacco factories were built by Thomas Jethro Brown and Pleasant Henderson Hanes. Richard Joshua Reynolds started his tobacco factory in 1875. Winston had nearly 40 tobacco factories by mid-1880. After two decades, Reynolds bought out Hanes, the last of the smaller companies, and began the reign of giant R.J. Reynolds Tobacco Company. Pleasant Henderson Hanes reinvested his proceeds and founded the P.H. Hanes Knitting Company manufacturing men's underwear.

The tobacco and textile industries fueled the economy of Winston-Salem. In 1917, 180 houses, known as Reynoldstown, were built by the Reynold's Company, and employees of R.J. Reynolds were able to purchase these houses at cost. The company built the 21-story Reynold's Building in 1929, one of the tallest buildings in the United States at the time, and the prototype to the Empire State Building.

The surging economy brought about the merger of Wachovia National Bank and Wachovia Loan and Trust (both established in 1879) to form the Wachovia Bank and Trust in 1911. In 2001 the bank be-came Wachovia and, in 2009, Wells Fargo. Today, Winston-Salem is headquarters to many thriving companies including Branch Banking and Trust Company (BB&T), Hanesbands, Beverage-Air, Novant Health, Primo Water, Krispy Kreme Doughnuts, and Reynolds Tobacco.

The city's downtown's Wake-Forest Innovation Quarter features businesses, education in biomedical research and engineering, information technology and digital media, as well as public gathering spaces and residences. Popular attractions include Reynolds Gardens, Wake Forest University Mu-seum of Anthropology, children's museums Kaleideum North and Kaleideum Downtown, and New Winston Museum.

Salem's Moravain Easter Sunrise Service has been an annual tradition since 1772 and the city is known as "Easter City." Salem boasts, like many towns, that George Washington slept there, at Sa-lem Tavern on May 31st and June 1st, while passing through North Carolina

Winston-Salem's climate is warm and temperate. Summers are hot and muggy, winters are cold and snowy, and it is partly cloudy year-round. Temperatures range from 32 degrees to 87 degrees and rainfall is significant.

Rankings

Business/Finance Rankings

- The Brookings Institution ranked the nation's largest cities based on income inequality. Winston-Salem was ranked #28 (#1 = greatest inequality). Criteria: the "95/20 ratio," a figure representing the income at which a household earns more than 95 percent of all other households, divided by the income at which a household earns more than only 20 percent of all other households. *Brookings Institution, "Household Income Inequality, Largest Cities of 97 Large U.S. Metro Areas, 2014-2016," February 5, 2018*

- The Brookings Institution ranked the 100 largest metro areas in the U.S. based on income inequality. Winston-Salem was ranked #52 (#1 = greatest inequality). Criteria: the "95/20 ratio," a figure representing the income at which a household earns more than 95 percent of all other households, divided by the income at which a household earns more than only 20 percent of all other households. *Brookings Institution, "Household Income Inequality, 100 Largest U.S. Metro Areas, 2014-2016," February 5, 2018*

- For its annual survey of the "Cheapest U.S. Cities to Live In," Kiplinger applied Cost of Living Index statistics developed by the Council for Community and Economic Research to U.S. Census Bureau population and median household income data for 265 urban areas. Only areas with at least 50,000 residents were considered. In the resulting ranking, Winston-Salem ranked #12. *Kiplinger.com, "The 25 Cheapest Places to Live: U.S. Cities Edition," April 3, 2023*

- The Winston-Salem metro area appeared on the Milken Institute "2022 Best Performing Cities" list. Rank: #96 out of 200 large metro areas (population over 250,000). Criteria: job growth; wage and salary growth; high-tech output growth; housing affordability; household broadband access. *Milken Institute, "Best-Performing Cities 2022," March 28, 2022*

- *Forbes* ranked the 200 most populous metro areas to determine the nation's "Best Places for Business and Careers." The Winston-Salem metro area was ranked #69. Criteria: costs (business and living); job growth (past and projected); income growth; quality of life; educational attainment (college and high school); projected economic growth; cultural and leisure opportunities; workplace tolerance laws; net migration patterns. *Forbes, "The Best Places for Business and Careers 2019: Seattle Still On Top," October 30, 2019*

Education Rankings

- Personal finance website *WalletHub* analyzed the 150 largest U.S. metropolitan statistical areas to determine where the most educated Americans are putting their degrees to work. Criteria: education levels; percentage of workers with degrees; education quality and attainment gap; public school quality rankings; quality and enrollment of each metro area's universities. Winston-Salem was ranked #111 (#1 = most educated city). *www.WalletHub.com, "Most & Least Educated Cities in America," July 18, 2022*

Environmental Rankings

- Winston-Salem was highlighted as one of the cleanest metro areas for ozone air pollution in the U.S. during 2019 through 2021. The list represents cities with no monitored ozone air pollution in unhealthful ranges. *American Lung Association, "State of the Air 2023," April 19, 2023*

Health/Fitness Rankings

- For each of the 100 largest cities in the United States, the American Fitness Index®, compiled in partnership between the American College of Sports Medicine and the Elevance Health Foundation, evaluated community infrastructure and 34 health behaviors including preventive health, levels of chronic disease conditions, food insecurity, sleep quality, pedestrian safety, air quality, and community/environment resources that support physical activity. Winston-Salem ranked #53 for "community fitness." *americanfitnessindex.org, "2022 ACSM American Fitness Index Summary Report," July 12, 2022*

- Winston-Salem was identified as a "2022 Spring Allergy Capital." The area ranked #55 out of 100. Three groups of factors were used to identify the most challenging cities for people with allergies during the spring season: annual spring pollen scores; over the counter allergy medicine use; number of board-certified allergy specialists. *Asthma and Allergy Foundation of America, "Spring Allergy Capitals 2022," March 2, 2022*

- Winston-Salem was identified as a "2022 Fall Allergy Capital." The area ranked #58 out of 100. Three groups of factors were used to identify the most challenging cities for people with allergies during the fall season: annual fall pollen scores; over the counter allergy medicine use; number of board-certified allergy specialists. *Asthma and Allergy Foundation of America, "Fall Allergy Capitals 2022," March 2, 2022*

- Winston-Salem was identified as a "2022 Asthma Capital." The area ranked #99 out of the nation's 100 largest metropolitan areas. Criteria: estimated asthma prevalence; asthma-related mortality; and ER visits due to asthma. Risk factors analyzed but not factored in the rankings: annual pollen score; annual air quality; public smoking laws; access to board-certified asthma specialists; rescue and controller medication use; uninsured rate; poverty rate. *Asthma and Allergy Foundation of America, "Asthma Capitals 2022: The Most Challenging Places to Live With Asthma," September 14, 2022*

Real Estate Rankings

- *WalletHub* compared the most populated U.S. cities to determine which had the best markets for real estate agents. Winston-Salem ranked #56 where demand was high and pay was the best. Criteria: sales per agent; annual median wage for real-estate agents; monthly average starting salary for real estate agents; real estate job density and competition; unemployment rate; home turnover rate; housing-market health index; and other relevant metrics. *www.WalletHub.com, "2021 Best Places to Be a Real Estate Agent," May 12, 2021*

- Winston-Salem was ranked #10 in the top 20 out of the 100 largest metro areas in terms of house price appreciation in 2022 (#1 = highest rate). *Federal Housing Finance Agency, House Price Index, 4th Quarter 2022*

- The Winston-Salem metro area was identified as one of the 20 best housing markets in the U.S. in 2022. The area ranked #7 out of 187 markets. Criteria: year-over-year change of median sales price of existing single-family homes between the 4th quarter of 2021 and the 4th quarter of 2022. *National Association of Realtors®, Median Sales Price of Existing Single-Family Homes for Metropolitan Areas, 4th Quarter 2022*

- Winston-Salem was ranked #88 out of 235 metro areas in terms of housing affordability in 2022 by the National Association of Home Builders (#1 = most affordable). Criteria: the share of homes sold in that area affordable to a family earning the local median income, based on standard mortgage underwriting criteria. *National Association of Home Builders®, NAHB-Wells Fargo Housing Opportunity Index, 4th Quarter 2022*

Safety Rankings

- Allstate ranked the 200 largest cities in America in terms of driver safety. Winston-Salem ranked #28. Criteria: internal property damage claims over a two-year period from January 2016 to December 2017. The report helps increase the importance of safety and awareness behind the wheel. *Allstate, "Allstate America's Best Drivers Report, 2019" June 24, 2019*

- Winston-Salem was identified as one of the most dangerous cities in America by NeighborhoodScout. The city ranked #58 out of 100 (#1 = most dangerous). Criteria: number of violent crimes per 1,000 residents. The editors evaluated cities with 25,000 or more residents. *NeighborhoodScout.com, "2023 Top 100 Most Dangerous Cities in the U.S.," January 12, 2023*

- The National Insurance Crime Bureau ranked 390 metro areas in the U.S. in terms of per capita rates of vehicle theft. The Winston-Salem metro area ranked #179 (#1 = highest rate). Criteria: number of vehicle theft offenses per 100,000 inhabitants in 2021. *National Insurance Crime Bureau, "Hot Spots 2021," September 1, 2022*

Seniors/Retirement Rankings

- From its Best Cities for Successful Aging indexes, the Milken Institute generated rankings for metropolitan areas, weighing data in nine categories—health care, wellness, living arrangements, transportation and convenience, financial characteristics, education, employment, community engagement, and overall livability. The Winston-Salem metro area was ranked #95 overall in the large metro area category. *Milken Institute, "Best Cities for Successful Aging, 2017" March 14, 2017*

- Winston-Salem made the 2022 *Forbes* list of "25 Best Places to Retire." Criteria, focused on overall affordability as well as quality of life indicators, include: housing/living costs compared to the national average and state taxes; air quality; crime rates; home price appreciation; risk associated with climate-change/natural hazards; availability of medical care; bikeability; walkability; healthy living. *Forbes.com, "The Best Places to Retire in 2022," May 13, 2022*

Business Environment

DEMOGRAPHICS

Population Growth

Area	1990 Census	2000 Census	2010 Census	2020 Census	Population Growth (%)	
					1990-2020	2010-2020
City	168,139	185,776	229,617	249,545	48.4	8.7
MSA[1]	361,091	421,961	477,717	675,966	87.2	41.5
U.S.	248,709,873	281,421,906	308,745,538	331,449,281	33.3	7.4

Note: (1) Figures cover the Winston-Salem, NC Metropolitan Statistical Area
Source: U.S. Census Bureau, 1990 Census, 2000 Census, 2010 Census, 2020 Census

Race

Area	White Alone[2] (%)	Black Alone[2] (%)	Asian Alone[2] (%)	AIAN[3] Alone[2] (%)	NHOPI[4] Alone[2] (%)	Other Race Alone[2] (%)	Two or More Races (%)
City	45.8	32.5	2.5	0.7	0.1	10.7	7.6
MSA[1]	67.0	17.2	1.8	0.6	0.1	6.7	6.5
U.S.	61.6	12.4	6.0	1.1	0.2	8.4	10.2

Note: (1) Figures cover the Winston-Salem, NC Metropolitan Statistical Area; (2) Alone is defined as not being in combination with one or more other races; (3) American Indian and Alaska Native; (4) Native Hawaiian and Other Pacific Islander
Source: U.S. Census Bureau, 2020 Census

Hispanic or Latino Origin

Area	Total (%)	Mexican (%)	Puerto Rican (%)	Cuban (%)	Other (%)
City	16.2	9.7	1.5	0.2	4.8
MSA[1]	10.8	6.7	1.1	0.2	2.8
U.S.	18.4	11.2	1.8	0.7	4.7

Note: Persons of Hispanic or Latino origin can be of any race; (1) Figures cover the Winston-Salem, NC Metropolitan Statistical Area
Source: U.S. Census Bureau, 2017-2021 American Community Survey 5-Year Estimates

Age

Area	Percent of Population									Median Age
	Under Age 5	Age 5–19	Age 20–34	Age 35–44	Age 45–54	Age 55–64	Age 65–74	Age 75–84	Age 85+	
City	5.8	20.5	22.0	12.2	11.6	12.1	9.1	4.5	2.0	36.2
MSA[1]	5.3	19.2	18.2	11.6	13.2	14.0	10.8	5.6	2.1	41.1
U.S.	5.6	19.2	20.2	12.7	12.4	13.1	10.0	4.9	1.9	38.8

Note: (1) Figures cover the Winston-Salem, NC Metropolitan Statistical Area
Source: U.S. Census Bureau, 2020 Census

Disability by Age

Area	All Ages	Under 18 Years Old	18 to 64 Years Old	65 Years and Over
City	11.3	3.5	9.9	30.6
MSA[1]	13.5	4.2	11.2	33.6
U.S.	12.6	4.4	10.3	33.4

Note: Figures show percent of the civilian noninstitutionalized population that reported having a disability. Disability status is determined from six types of difficulty: vision, hearing, cognitive, ambulatory, self-care, and independent living. For children under 5 years old, hearing and vision difficulty are used to determine disability status. For children between the ages of 5 and 14, disability status is determined from hearing, vision, cognitive, ambulatory, and self-care difficulties. For people aged 15 years and older, they are considered to have a disability if they have difficulty with any one of the six difficulty types; Note: (1) Figures cover the Winston-Salem, NC Metropolitan Statistical Area
Source: U.S. Census Bureau, 2017-2021 American Community Survey 5-Year Estimates

Ancestry

Area	German	Irish	English	American	Italian	Polish	French[2]	Scottish	Dutch
City	8.7	6.4	8.5	4.8	2.4	0.9	1.2	1.9	0.7
MSA[1]	11.3	8.1	11.0	8.5	2.3	1.1	1.2	2.2	0.8
U.S.	12.8	9.6	8.1	5.7	5.0	2.7	2.2	1.6	1.1

Note: Figures are the percentage of the total population reporting a particular ancestry. The nine most commonly reported ancestries in the U.S. are shown. Figures include multiple ancestries (e.g. if a person reported being Irish and Italian, they were included in both columns); (1) Figures cover the Winston-Salem, NC Metropolitan Statistical Area; (2) Excludes Basque
Source: U.S. Census Bureau, 2017-2021 American Community Survey 5-Year Estimates

Foreign-born Population

Area	Percent of Population Born in								
	Any Foreign Country	Asia	Mexico	Europe	Caribbean	Central America[2]	South America	Africa	Canada
City	10.2	2.2	4.1	0.6	0.5	1.5	0.7	0.7	0.1
MSA[1]	7.0	1.4	2.7	0.6	0.3	0.9	0.5	0.3	0.1
U.S.	13.6	4.2	3.3	1.5	1.4	1.1	1.1	0.8	0.2

Note: (1) Figures cover the Winston-Salem, NC Metropolitan Statistical Area; (2) Excludes Mexico.
Source: U.S. Census Bureau, 2017-2021 American Community Survey 5-Year Estimates

Household Size

Area	Persons in Household (%)							Average Household Size
	One	Two	Three	Four	Five	Six	Seven or More	
City	36.0	31.7	14.7	9.3	4.7	2.5	1.0	2.40
MSA[1]	30.2	35.7	15.7	10.8	4.7	2.0	0.9	2.50
U.S.	28.1	33.8	15.5	12.9	6.0	2.3	1.4	2.60

Note: (1) Figures cover the Winston-Salem, NC Metropolitan Statistical Area
Source: U.S. Census Bureau, 2017-2021 American Community Survey 5-Year Estimates

Household Relationships

Area	House-holder	Opposite-sex Spouse	Same-sex Spouse	Opposite-sex Unmarried Partner	Same-sex Unmarried Partner	Child[2]	Grand-child	Other Relatives	Non-relatives
City	40.9	14.6	0.2	2.5	0.2	28.1	2.4	4.3	2.7
MSA[1]	40.9	18.6	0.2	2.3	0.1	27.5	2.4	3.7	2.2
U.S.	38.3	17.5	0.2	2.5	0.2	28.3	2.4	4.8	3.4

Note: Figures are percent of the total population; (1) Figures cover the Winston-Salem, NC Metropolitan Statistical Area; (2) Includes biological, adopted, and stepchildren of the householder
Source: U.S. Census Bureau, 2020 Census

Gender

Area	Males	Females	Males per 100 Females
City	116,698	132,847	87.8
MSA[1]	324,467	351,499	92.3
U.S.	162,685,811	168,763,470	96.4

Note: (1) Figures cover the Winston-Salem, NC Metropolitan Statistical Area
Source: U.S. Census Bureau, 2020 Census

Marital Status

Area	Never Married	Now Married[2]	Separated	Widowed	Divorced
City	41.9	39.1	2.6	5.4	11.0
MSA[1]	31.0	48.9	2.4	6.4	11.3
U.S.	33.8	48.0	1.8	5.6	10.8

Note: Figures are percentages and cover the population 15 years of age and older; (1) Figures cover the Winston-Salem, NC Metropolitan Statistical Area; (2) Excludes separated
Source: U.S. Census Bureau, 2017-2021 American Community Survey 5-Year Estimates

Religious Groups by Family

Area	Catholic	Baptist	Methodist	LDS[2]	Pentecostal	Lutheran	Islam	Adventist	Other
MSA[1]	9.3	12.8	11.4	0.5	1.0	0.6	0.8	1.4	22.5
U.S.	18.7	7.3	3.0	2.0	1.8	1.7	1.3	1.3	11.6

Note: Figures are the number of adherents as a percentage of the total population and cover the eight largest religious groups in the U.S; (1) Figures cover the Winston-Salem, NC Metropolitan Statistical Area; (2) Church of Jesus Christ of Latter-day Saints
Sources: 2020 U.S. Religion Census, Association of Statisticians of American Religious Bodies; The Association of Religion Data Archives (ARDA)

Religious Groups by Tradition

Area	Catholic	Evangelical Protestant	Mainline Protestant	Black Protestant	Islam	Judaism	Hinduism	Orthodox	Buddhism
MSA[1]	9.3	31.4	13.6	3.4	0.8	n/a	<0.1	0.3	0.1
U.S.	18.7	16.5	5.2	2.3	1.3	0.6	0.4	0.4	0.3

Note: Figures are the number of adherents as a percentage of the total population; (1) Figures cover the Winston-Salem, NC Metropolitan Statistical Area
Sources: 2020 U.S. Religion Census, Association of Statisticians of American Religious Bodies; The Association of Religion Data Archives (ARDA)

524　Winston-Salem, North Carolina

ECONOMY

Gross Metropolitan Product

Area	2020	2021	2022	2023	Rank[2]
MSA[1]	34.0	37.6	40.9	43.7	88

Note: Figures are in billions of dollars; (1) Figures cover the Winston-Salem, NC Metropolitan Statistical Area; (2) Rank is based on 2021 data and ranges from 1 to 381
Source: U.S. Conference of Mayors, U.S. Metro Economies: U.S. Metros Compared to Global and State Economies, June 2022

Economic Growth

Area	2018-20 (%)	2021 (%)	2022 (%)	2023 (%)	Rank[2]
MSA[1]	-4.0	6.0	2.8	3.6	358
U.S.	-0.6	5.7	3.1	2.9	—

Note: Figures are real gross metropolitan product (GMP) growth rates and represent average annual percent change; (1) Figures cover the Winston-Salem, NC Metropolitan Statistical Area; (2) Rank is based on 2020 2-year average annual percent change and ranges from 1 to 381
Source: U.S. Conference of Mayors, U.S. Metro Economies: U.S. Metros Compared to Global and State Economies, June 2022

Metropolitan Area Exports

Area	2016	2017	2018	2019	2020	2021	Rank[2]
MSA[1]	1,234.6	1,131.7	1,107.5	1,209.1	913.1	918.2	164

Note: Figures are in millions of dollars; (1) Figures cover the Winston-Salem, NC Metropolitan Statistical Area; (2) Rank is based on 2021 data and ranges from 1 to 388
Source: U.S. Department of Commerce, International Trade Administration, Office of Trade and Economic Analysis, Industry and Analysis, Exports by Metropolitan Area, data extracted March 16, 2023

Building Permits

Area	Single-Family			Multi-Family			Total		
	2021	2022	Pct. Chg.	2021	2022	Pct. Chg.	2021	2022	Pct. Chg.
City	1,087	1,291	18.8	0	0	0.0	1,087	1,291	18.8
MSA[1]	3,887	3,983	2.5	319	67	-79.0	4,206	4,050	-3.7
U.S.	1,115,400	975,600	-12.5	621,600	689,500	10.9	1,737,000	1,665,100	-4.1

Note: (1) Figures cover the Winston-Salem, NC Metropolitan Statistical Area; Figures represent new, privately-owned housing units authorized (unadjusted data); All permit data are based on estimates with imputation
Source: U.S. Census Bureau, Manufacturing, Mining, and Construction Statistics, Building Permits, 2021, 2022

Bankruptcy Filings

Area	Business Filings			Nonbusiness Filings		
	2021	2022	% Chg.	2021	2022	% Chg.
Forsyth County	10	6	-40.0	240	240	0.0
U.S.	14,347	13,481	-6.0	399,269	374,240	-6.3

Note: Business filings include Chapter 7, Chapter 9, Chapter 11, Chapter 12, Chapter 13, Chapter 15, and Section 304; Nonbusiness filings include Chapter 7, Chapter 11, and Chapter 13
Source: Administrative Office of the U.S. Courts, Business and Nonbusiness Bankruptcy, County Cases Commenced by Chapter of the Bankruptcy Code, During the 12-Month Period Ending December 31, 2021 and Business and Nonbusiness Bankruptcy, County Cases Commenced by Chapter of the Bankruptcy Code, During the 12-Month Period Ending December 31, 2022

Housing Vacancy Rates

Area	Gross Vacancy Rate[2] (%)			Year-Round Vacancy Rate[3] (%)			Rental Vacancy Rate[4] (%)			Homeowner Vacancy Rate[5] (%)		
	2020	2021	2022	2020	2021	2022	2020	2021	2022	2020	2021	2022
MSA[1]	n/a	n/a	n/a	n/a	n/a	n/a	n/a	n/a	n/a	n/a	n/a	n/a
U.S.	10.6	10.8	10.5	8.2	8.4	8.2	6.3	6.1	5.8	1.0	0.9	0.8

Note: (1) Figures cover the Winston-Salem, NC Metropolitan Statistical Area; (2) The percentage of the total housing inventory that is vacant; (3) The percentage of the housing inventory (excluding seasonal units) that is year-round vacant; (4) The percentage of rental inventory that is vacant for rent; (5) The percentage of homeowner inventory that is vacant for sale; n/a not available
Source: U.S. Census Bureau, Housing Vacancies and Homeownership Annual Statistics: 2020, 2021, 2022

INCOME

Income

Area	Per Capita ($)	Median Household ($)	Average Household ($)
City	30,859	50,204	75,459
MSA[1]	31,238	55,454	76,451
U.S.	37,638	69,021	97,196

Note: (1) Figures cover the Winston-Salem, NC Metropolitan Statistical Area
Source: U.S. Census Bureau, 2017-2021 American Community Survey 5-Year Estimates

Household Income Distribution

				Percent of Households Earning				
Area	Under $15,000	$15,000 -$24,999	$25,000 -$34,999	$35,000 -$49,999	$50,000 -$74,999	$75,000 -$99,999	$100,000 -$149,999	$150,000 and up
City	13.8	10.6	11.2	14.2	16.4	12.3	11.7	9.8
MSA[1]	11.0	10.0	10.7	13.7	18.1	13.1	13.3	10.1
U.S.	9.4	7.8	8.2	11.4	16.8	12.8	16.3	17.3

Note: (1) Figures cover the Winston-Salem, NC Metropolitan Statistical Area
Source: U.S. Census Bureau, 2017-2021 American Community Survey 5-Year Estimates

Poverty Rate

Area	All Ages	Under 18 Years Old	18 to 64 Years Old	65 Years and Over
City	19.0	30.1	16.9	9.5
MSA[1]	15.1	23.7	13.6	9.0
U.S.	12.6	17.0	11.8	9.6

Note: Figures are percentage of people whose income during the past 12 months was below the poverty level;
(1) Figures cover the Winston-Salem, NC Metropolitan Statistical Area
Source: U.S. Census Bureau, 2017-2021 American Community Survey 5-Year Estimates

EMPLOYMENT

Labor Force and Employment

Area	Civilian Labor Force			Workers Employed		
	Dec. 2021	Dec. 2022	% Chg.	Dec. 2021	Dec. 2022	% Chg.
City	116,216	117,459	1.1	112,011	113,308	1.2
MSA[1]	322,524	326,477	1.2	312,552	316,261	1.2
U.S.	161,696,000	164,224,000	1.6	155,732,000	158,872,000	2.0

Note: Data is not seasonally adjusted and covers workers 16 years of age and older; (1) Figures cover the
Winston-Salem, NC Metropolitan Statistical Area
Source: Bureau of Labor Statistics, Local Area Unemployment Statistics

Unemployment Rate

Area	2022											
	Jan.	Feb.	Mar.	Apr.	May	Jun.	Jul.	Aug.	Sep.	Oct.	Nov.	Dec.
City	4.1	4.0	3.9	3.8	4.0	4.5	4.3	4.4	3.8	4.3	4.1	3.5
MSA[1]	3.6	3.5	3.4	3.3	3.6	4.0	3.6	3.8	3.3	3.8	3.7	3.1
U.S.	4.4	4.1	3.8	3.3	3.4	3.8	3.8	3.8	3.3	3.4	3.4	3.3

Note: Data is not seasonally adjusted and covers workers 16 years of age and older; (1) Figures cover the
Winston-Salem, NC Metropolitan Statistical Area
Source: Bureau of Labor Statistics, Local Area Unemployment Statistics

Average Wages

Occupation	$/Hr.	Occupation	$/Hr.
Accountants and Auditors	38.18	Maintenance and Repair Workers	21.32
Automotive Mechanics	21.78	Marketing Managers	72.60
Bookkeepers	20.62	Network and Computer Systems Admin.	42.13
Carpenters	20.32	Nurses, Licensed Practical	25.36
Cashiers	11.93	Nurses, Registered	38.57
Computer Programmers	48.29	Nursing Assistants	15.34
Computer Systems Analysts	46.37	Office Clerks, General	17.36
Computer User Support Specialists	26.98	Physical Therapists	47.28
Construction Laborers	17.33	Physicians	n/a
Cooks, Restaurant	14.50	Plumbers, Pipefitters and Steamfitters	22.79
Customer Service Representatives	18.08	Police and Sheriff's Patrol Officers	24.14
Dentists	91.37	Postal Service Mail Carriers	27.50
Electricians	23.79	Real Estate Sales Agents	33.61
Engineers, Electrical	49.50	Retail Salespersons	14.59
Fast Food and Counter Workers	12.15	Sales Representatives, Technical/Scientific	44.22
Financial Managers	74.71	Secretaries, Exc. Legal/Medical/Executive	19.35
First-Line Supervisors of Office Workers	27.78	Security Guards	16.60
General and Operations Managers	58.23	Surgeons	n/a
Hairdressers/Cosmetologists	18.87	Teacher Assistants, Exc. Postsecondary*	11.63
Home Health and Personal Care Aides	12.67	Teachers, Secondary School, Exc. Sp. Ed.*	25.01
Janitors and Cleaners	13.23	Telemarketers	n/a
Landscaping/Groundskeeping Workers	16.17	Truck Drivers, Heavy/Tractor-Trailer	24.69
Lawyers	81.73	Truck Drivers, Light/Delivery Services	18.96
Maids and Housekeeping Cleaners	13.42	Waiters and Waitresses	12.01

Note: Wage data covers the Winston-Salem, NC Metropolitan Statistical Area; (*) Hourly wages were
calculated from annual wage data based on a 40 hour work week; n/a not available.
Source: Bureau of Labor Statistics, Metro Area Occupational Employment & Wage Estimates, May 2022

Employment by Industry

Sector	MSA[1]		U.S.
	Number of Employees	Percent of Total	Percent of Total
Construction, Mining, and Logging	12,100	4.3	5.4
Private Education and Health Services	56,400	20.1	16.1
Financial Activities	13,900	5.0	5.9
Government	31,800	11.3	14.5
Information	1,900	0.7	2.0
Leisure and Hospitality	29,400	10.5	10.3
Manufacturing	35,200	12.6	8.4
Other Services	9,700	3.5	3.7
Professional and Business Services	36,200	12.9	14.7
Retail Trade	32,400	11.6	10.2
Transportation, Warehousing, and Utilities	12,500	4.5	4.9
Wholesale Trade	8,800	3.1	3.9

Note: Figures are non-farm employment as of December 2022. Figures are not seasonally adjusted and include workers 16 years of age and older; (1) Figures cover the Winston-Salem, NC Metropolitan Statistical Area
Source: Bureau of Labor Statistics, Current Employment Statistics, Employment, Hours, and Earnings

Employment by Occupation

Occupation Classification	City (%)	MSA[1] (%)	U.S. (%)
Management, Business, Science, and Arts	40.5	37.2	40.3
Natural Resources, Construction, and Maintenance	7.3	9.7	8.7
Production, Transportation, and Material Moving	13.8	16.3	13.1
Sales and Office	20.2	20.6	20.9
Service	18.2	16.2	17.0

Note: Figures cover employed civilians 16 years of age and older; (1) Figures cover the Winston-Salem, NC Metropolitan Statistical Area
Source: U.S. Census Bureau, 2017-2021 American Community Survey 5-Year Estimates

Occupations with Greatest Projected Employment Growth: 2022 – 2024

Occupation[1]	2022 Employment	2024 Projected Employment	Numeric Employment Change	Percent Employment Change
Cooks, Restaurant	45,830	53,440	7,610	16.6
Waiters and Waitresses	65,770	72,960	7,190	10.9
Software Developers	55,450	62,610	7,160	12.9
Cooks, Fast Food	82,470	88,860	6,390	7.7
Fast Food and Counter Workers	68,750	75,030	6,280	9.1
Laborers and Freight, Stock, and Material Movers, Hand	100,780	106,480	5,700	5.7
Retail Salespersons	125,490	130,210	4,720	3.8
General and Operations Managers	87,450	92,120	4,670	5.3
First-Line Supervisors of Food Preparation and Serving Workers	42,440	47,070	4,630	10.9
Stockers and Order Fillers	88,320	92,930	4,610	5.2

Note: Projections cover North Carolina; (1) Sorted by numeric employment change
Source: www.projectionscentral.com, State Occupational Projections, 2022–2024 Short-Term Projections

Fastest-Growing Occupations: 2022 – 2024

Occupation[1]	2022 Employment	2024 Projected Employment	Numeric Employment Change	Percent Employment Change
Cooks, Restaurant	45,830	53,440	7,610	16.6
Solar Photovoltaic Installers	390	450	60	15.4
Statisticians	1,710	1,960	250	14.6
Medical Scientists, Except Epidemiologists	3,630	4,160	530	14.6
Actuaries	950	1,080	130	13.7
Data Scientists	5,390	6,100	710	13.2
Soil and Plant Scientists	2,160	2,440	280	13.0
Software Developers	55,450	62,610	7,160	12.9
Software Quality Assurance Analysts and Testers	8,850	9,950	1,100	12.4
Bartenders	14,560	16,360	1,800	12.4

Note: Projections cover North Carolina; (1) Sorted by percent employment change and excludes occupations with numeric employment change less than 50
Source: www.projectionscentral.com, State Occupational Projections, 2022–2024 Short-Term Projections

Winston-Salem, North Carolina   527

CITY FINANCES

City Government Finances

Component	2020 ($000)	2020 ($ per capita)
Total Revenues	439,665	1,773
Total Expenditures	475,429	1,917
Debt Outstanding	772,987	3,118
Cash and Securities[1]	n/a	n/a

Note: (1) Cash and security holdings of a government at the close of its fiscal year, including those of its dependent agencies, utilities, and liquor stores; n/a not available.
Source: U.S. Census Bureau, State & Local Government Finances 2020

City Government Revenue by Source

Source	2020 ($000)	2020 ($ per capita)	2020 (%)
General Revenue			
From Federal Government	18,741	76	4.3
From State Government	30,987	125	7.0
From Local Governments	1,109	4	0.3
Taxes			
Property	145,805	588	33.2
Sales and Gross Receipts	51,984	210	11.8
Personal Income	0	0	0.0
Corporate Income	0	0	0.0
Motor Vehicle License	2,205	9	0.5
Other Taxes	1,620	7	0.4
Current Charges	93,793	378	21.3
Liquor Store	0	0	0.0
Utility	60,549	244	13.8

Source: U.S. Census Bureau, State & Local Government Finances 2020

City Government Expenditures by Function

Function	2020 ($000)	2020 ($ per capita)	2020 (%)
General Direct Expenditures			
Air Transportation	0	0	0.0
Corrections	0	0	0.0
Education	0	0	0.0
Employment Security Administration	0	0	0.0
Financial Administration	3,786	15	0.8
Fire Protection	36,433	146	7.7
General Public Buildings	3,877	15	0.8
Governmental Administration, Other	14,671	59	3.1
Health	0	0	0.0
Highways	23,829	96	5.0
Hospitals	0	0	0.0
Housing and Community Development	25,188	101	5.3
Interest on General Debt	47,654	192	10.0
Judicial and Legal	1,479	6	0.3
Libraries	0	0	0.0
Parking	1,446	5	0.3
Parks and Recreation	27,620	111	5.8
Police Protection	86,276	348	18.1
Public Welfare	0	0	0.0
Sewerage	65,602	264	13.8
Solid Waste Management	28,464	114	6.0
Veterans' Services	0	0	0.0
Liquor Store	0	0	0.0
Utility	94,858	382	20.0

Source: U.S. Census Bureau, State & Local Government Finances 2020

TAXES

State Corporate Income Tax Rates

State	Tax Rate (%)	Income Brackets ($)	Num. of Brackets	Financial Institution Tax Rate (%)[a]	Federal Income Tax Ded.
North Carolina	2.5	Flat rate	1	2.5	No

Note: Tax rates as of January 1, 2023; (a) Rates listed are the corporate income tax rate applied to financial institutions or excise taxes based on income. Some states have other taxes based upon the value of deposits or shares.
Source: Federation of Tax Administrators, State Corporate Income Tax Rates, January 1, 2023

State Individual Income Tax Rates

State	Tax Rate (%)	Income Brackets ($)	Personal Exemptions ($)			Standard Ded. ($)	
			Single	Married	Depend.	Single	Married
North Carolina	4.75	Flat rate	None	None	None	10,750	21,500

Note: Tax rates as of January 1, 2023; Local- and county-level taxes are not included; Federal income tax is not deductible on state income tax returns
Source: Federation of Tax Administrators, State Individual Income Tax Rates, January 1, 2023

Various State Sales and Excise Tax Rates

State	State Sales Tax (%)	Gasoline[1] ($/gal.)	Cigarette[2] ($/pack)	Spirits[3] ($/gal.)	Wine[4] ($/gal.)	Beer[5] ($/gal.)	Recreational Marijuana (%)
North Carolina	4.75	0.3875	0.45	16.40	1.00	0.62	Not legal

Note: All tax rates as of January 1, 2023; (1) The American Petroleum Institute has developed a methodology for determining the average tax rate on a gallon of fuel. Rates may include any of the following: excise taxes, environmental fees, storage tank fees, other fees or taxes, general sales tax, and local taxes; (2) The federal excise tax of $1.0066 per pack and local taxes are not included; (3) Rates are those applicable to off-premise sales of 40% alcohol by volume (a.b.v.) distilled spirits in 750ml containers. Local excise taxes are excluded; (4) Rates are those applicable to off-premise sales of 11% a.b.v. non-carbonated wine in 750ml containers; (5) Rates are those applicable to off-premise sales of 4.7% a.b.v. beer in 12 ounce containers.
Source: Tax Foundation, 2023 Facts & Figures: How Does Your State Compare?

State Business Tax Climate Index Rankings

State	Overall Rank	Corporate Tax Rank	Individual Income Tax Rank	Sales Tax Rank	Property Tax Rank	Unemployment Insurance Tax Rank
North Carolina	10	5	17	20	13	10

Note: The index is a measure of how each state's tax laws affect economic performance. The lower the rank, the more favorable a state's tax system is for business. States without a given tax are given a ranking of 1. The scores/rankings for the District of Columbia do not affect other states. The 2023 index represents the tax climate as of July 1, 2022.
Source: Tax Foundation, State Business Tax Climate Index 2023

TRANSPORTATION

Means of Transportation to Work

Area	Car/Truck/Van		Public Transportation			Bicycle	Walked	Other Means	Worked at Home
	Drove Alone	Car-pooled	Bus	Subway	Railroad				
City	77.7	8.9	1.3	0.0	0.0	0.3	2.1	1.2	8.5
MSA[1]	80.7	8.8	0.6	0.0	0.0	0.1	1.3	0.9	7.6
U.S.	73.2	8.6	2.0	1.6	0.5	0.5	2.5	1.5	9.7

Note: Figures are percentages and cover workers 16 years of age and older; (1) Figures cover the Winston-Salem, NC Metropolitan Statistical Area
Source: U.S. Census Bureau, 2017-2021 American Community Survey 5-Year Estimates

Travel Time to Work

Area	Less Than 10 Minutes	10 to 19 Minutes	20 to 29 Minutes	30 to 44 Minutes	45 to 59 Minutes	60 to 89 Minutes	90 Minutes or More
City	14.0	40.3	22.6	14.3	4.6	2.6	1.7
MSA[1]	12.5	32.5	24.3	19.3	6.1	3.2	2.2
U.S.	12.4	28.5	21.0	20.9	8.2	6.2	2.9

Note: Note: Figures are percentages and include workers 16 years old and over; (1) Figures cover the Winston-Salem, NC Metropolitan Statistical Area
Source: U.S. Census Bureau, 2017-2021 American Community Survey 5-Year Estimates

Key Congestion Measures

Measure	1990	2000	2010	2015	2020
Annual Hours of Delay, Total (000)	1,321	4,032	6,414	7,278	4,455
Annual Hours of Delay, Per Auto Commuter	9	17	20	24	15
Annual Congestion Cost, Per Auto Commuter ($)	154	357	449	474	303

Note: Covers the Winston-Salem NC urban area
Source: Texas A&M Transportation Institute, 2021 Urban Mobility Report

Freeway Travel Time Index

Measure	1985	1990	1995	2000	2005	2010	2015	2020
Urban Area Index[1]	1.05	1.05	1.06	1.10	1.12	1.12	1.11	1.04
Urban Area Rank[1,2]	64	89	93	85	86	89	96	101

Note: Freeway Travel Time Index—the ratio of travel time in the peak period to the travel time at free-flow conditions. For example, a value of 1.30 indicates a 20-minute free-flow trip takes 26 minutes in the peak (20 minutes x 1.30 = 26 minutes); (1) Covers the Winston-Salem NC urban area; (2) Rank is based on 101 larger urban areas (#1 = highest travel time index)
Source: Texas A&M Transportation Institute, 2021 Urban Mobility Report

Public Transportation

Agency Name / Mode of Transportation	Vehicles Operated in Maximum Service[1]	Annual Unlinked Passenger Trips[2] (in thous.)	Annual Passenger Miles[3] (in thous.)
Winston-Salem Transit Authority (WSTA)			
Bus (directly operated)	31	1,715.5	5,077.9
Demand Response (directly operated)	32	154.8	1,205.1

Note: (1) Number of revenue vehicles operated by the given mode and type of service to meet the annual maximum service requirement. This is the revenue vehicle count during the peak season of the year; on the week and day that maximum service is provided. Vehicles operated in maximum service (VOMS) exclude atypical days and one-time special events; (2) Number of passengers who boarded public transportation vehicles. Passengers are counted each time they board a vehicle no matter how many vehicles they use to travel from their origin to their destination. (3) Sum of the distances ridden by all passengers during the entire fiscal year.
Source: Federal Transit Administration, National Transit Database, 2021

Air Transportation

Airport Name and Code / Type of Service	Passenger Airlines[1]	Passenger Enplanements	Freight Carriers[2]	Freight (lbs)
Piedmont Triad International Airport (23 miles) (GSO)				
Domestic service (U.S. carriers - 2022)	20	792,106	13	157,492,875
International service (U.S. carriers - 2021)	0	0	2	99,193

Note: (1) Includes all U.S.-based major, minor and commuter airlines that carried at least one passenger during the year; (2) Includes all U.S.-based airlines and freight carriers that transported at least one pound of freight during the year.
Source: Bureau of Transportation Statistics, The Intermodal Transportation Database, Air Carriers: T-100 Domestic Market (U.S. Carriers), 2022; Bureau of Transportation Statistics, The Intermodal Transportation Database, Air Carriers: T-100 International Market (U.S. Carriers), 2021

BUSINESSES

Major Business Headquarters

Company Name	Industry	Rankings	
		Fortune[1]	Forbes[2]
Hanesbrands	Apparel	458	-

Note: (1) Companies that produce a 10-K are ranked 1 to 500 based on 2021 revenue; (2) All private companies with at least $2 billion in annual revenue through the end of their most current fiscal year are ranked 1 to 246; companies listed are headquartered in the city; dashes indicate no ranking
Source: Fortune, "Fortune 500," 2022; Forbes, "America's Largest Private Companies," 2022

Living Environment

COST OF LIVING

Cost of Living Index

Composite Index	Groceries	Housing	Utilities	Trans-portation	Health Care	Misc. Goods/ Services
95.7	98.9	79.3	91.6	95.4	116.7	106.0

Note: The Cost of Living Index measures regional differences in the cost of consumer goods and services, excluding taxes and non-consumer expenditures, for professional and managerial households in the top income quintile. It is based on more than 50,000 prices covering almost 60 different items for which prices are collected three times a year by chambers of commerce, economic development organizations or university applied economic centers in each participating urban area. The numbers shown should be read as a percentage above or below the national average of 100. For example, a value of 115.4 in the groceries column indicates that grocery prices are 15.4% higher than the national average. Small differences in the index numbers should not be interpreted as significant; Figures cover the Winston-Salem NC urban area.
Source: The Council for Community and Economic Research, Cost of Living Index, 2022

Grocery Prices

Area[1]	T-Bone Steak ($/pound)	Frying Chicken ($/pound)	Whole Milk ($/half gal.)	Eggs ($/dozen)	Orange Juice ($/64 oz.)	Coffee ($/11.5 oz.)
City[2]	13.05	1.11	2.31	2.28	3.98	4.30
Avg.	13.81	1.59	2.43	2.25	3.85	4.95
Min.	10.17	0.90	1.51	1.30	2.90	3.46
Max.	19.35	3.30	4.32	4.32	5.31	8.59

*Note: (1) Values for the local area are compared with the average, minimum and maximum values for all 286 areas in the Cost of Living Index; (2) Figures cover the Winston-Salem NC urban area; **T-Bone Steak** (price per pound); **Frying Chicken** (price per pound, whole fryer); **Whole Milk** (half gallon carton); **Eggs** (price per dozen, Grade A, large); **Orange Juice** (64 oz. Tropicana or Florida Natural); **Coffee** (11.5 oz. can, vacuum-packed, Maxwell House, Hills Bros, or Folgers).*
Source: The Council for Community and Economic Research, Cost of Living Index, 2022

Housing and Utility Costs

Area[1]	New Home Price ($)	Apartment Rent ($/month)	All Electric ($/month)	Part Electric ($/month)	Other Energy ($/month)	Telephone ($/month)
City[2]	319,961	1,290	157.68	-	-	180.76
Avg.	450,913	1,371	176.41	99.93	76.96	190.22
Min.	229,283	546	100.84	31.56	27.15	174.27
Max.	2,434,977	4,569	356.86	249.59	272.24	208.31

*Note: (1) Values for the local area are compared with the average, minimum and maximum values for all 286 areas in the Cost of Living Index; (2) Figures cover the Winston-Salem NC urban area; **New Home Price** (2,400 sf living area, 8,000 sf lot, in urban area with full utilities); **Apartment Rent** (950 sf 2 bedroom/1.5 or 2 bath, unfurnished, excluding all utilities except water); **All Electric** (average monthly cost for an all-electric home); **Part Electric** (average monthly cost for a part-electric home); **Other Energy** (average monthly cost for natural gas, fuel oil, coal, wood, and any other forms of energy except electricity); **Telephone** (price includes the base monthly rate plus taxes and fees for three lines of mobile phone service).*
Source: The Council for Community and Economic Research, Cost of Living Index, 2022

Health Care, Transportation, and Other Costs

Area[1]	Doctor ($/visit)	Dentist ($/visit)	Optometrist ($/visit)	Gasoline ($/gallon)	Beauty Salon ($/visit)	Men's Shirt ($)
City[2]	142.38	133.67	132.58	3.71	45.00	35.83
Avg.	124.91	107.77	117.66	3.86	43.31	34.21
Min.	36.61	58.25	51.79	2.90	22.18	13.05
Max.	250.21	162.58	371.96	5.54	85.61	63.54

*Note: (1) Values for the local area are compared with the average, minimum and maximum values for all 286 areas in the Cost of Living Index; (2) Figures cover the Winston-Salem NC urban area; **Doctor** (general practitioners routine exam of an established patient); **Dentist** (adult teeth cleaning and periodic oral examination); **Optometrist** (full vision eye exam for established adult patient); **Gasoline** (one gallon regular unleaded, national brand, including all taxes, cash price at self-service pump if available); **Beauty Salon** (woman's shampoo, trim, and blow-dry); **Men's Shirt** (cotton/polyester dress shirt, pinpoint weave, long sleeves).*
Source: The Council for Community and Economic Research, Cost of Living Index, 2022

HOUSING

Homeownership Rate

Area	2015 (%)	2016 (%)	2017 (%)	2018 (%)	2019 (%)	2020 (%)	2021 (%)	2022 (%)
MSA[1]	n/a	n/a	n/a	n/a	n/a	n/a	n/a	n/a
U.S.	63.7	63.4	63.9	64.4	64.6	66.6	65.5	65.8

Note: (1) Figures cover the Winston-Salem, NC Metropolitan Statistical Area; n/a not available
Source: U.S. Census Bureau, Housing Vacancies and Homeownership Annual Statistics: 2015-2022

House Price Index (HPI)

Area	National Ranking[2]	Quarterly Change (%)	One-Year Change (%)	Five-Year Change (%)	Since 1991Q1 (%)
MSA[1]	37	0.94	16.66	66.13	201.85
U.S.[3]	–	0.34	8.41	58.44	289.08

Note: The HPI is a weighted repeat sales index. It measures average price changes in repeat sales or refinancings on the same properties. This information is obtained by reviewing repeat mortgage transactions on single-family properties whose mortgages have been purchased or securitized by Fannie Mae or Freddie Mac since January 1975; (1) Figures cover the Winston-Salem, NC Metropolitan Statistical Area; (2) Rankings are based on annual percentage change for all metro areas containing at least 15,000 transactions over the last 10 years and ranges from 1 to 257; (3) figures based on a weighted average of Census Division estimates using a seasonally adjusted, purchase-only index; all figures are for the period ending December 31, 2022
Source: Federal Housing Finance Agency, Change in FHFA Metropolitan Area House Price Indexes, 2022Q4

Median Single-Family Home Prices

Area	2020	2021	2022[p]	Percent Change 2021 to 2022
MSA[1]	202.4	235.6	280.5	19.1
U.S. Average	300.2	357.1	392.6	9.9

Note: Figures are median sales prices of existing single-family homes in thousands of dollars; (p) preliminary; (1) Figures cover the Winston-Salem, NC Metropolitan Statistical Area
Source: National Association of Realtors, Median Sales Price of Existing Single-Family Homes for Metropolitan Areas, 4th Quarter 2022

Qualifying Income Based on Median Sales Price of Existing Single-Family Homes

Area	With 5% Down ($)	With 10% Down ($)	With 20% Down ($)
MSA[1]	85,327	80,836	71,855
U.S. Average	112,234	106,237	94,513

Note: Figures are preliminary; Qualifying income is based on a mortgage rate of 6.77%. Monthly principal and interest payment is limited to 25% of income; (1) Figures cover the Winston-Salem, NC Metropolitan Statistical Area
Source: National Association of Realtors, Qualifying Income Based on Median Sales Price of Existing Single-Family Homes for Metropolitan Areas, 4th Quarter 2022

Home Value

Area	Under $100,000	$100,000 -$199,999	$200,000 -$299,999	$300,000 -$399,999	$400,000 -$499,999	$500,000 -$999,999	$1,000,000 or more	Median ($)
City	22.4	44.2	16.7	7.0	3.5	5.6	0.6	158,600
MSA[1]	20.7	42.5	19.5	8.7	3.7	4.4	0.5	165,000
U.S.	16.2	24.2	20.1	13.6	8.3	13.6	4.1	244,900

Note: Figures are percentages except for median and cover owner-occupied housing units; (1) Figures cover the Winston-Salem, NC Metropolitan Statistical Area
Source: U.S. Census Bureau, 2017-2021 American Community Survey 5-Year Estimates

Year Housing Structure Built

Area	2020 or Later	2010 -2019	2000 -2009	1990 -1999	1980 -1989	1970 -1979	1960 -1969	1950 -1959	1940 -1949	Before 1940	Median Year
City	0.1	6.4	13.2	13.0	14.3	16.4	11.8	12.2	4.9	7.7	1978
MSA[1]	0.1	6.8	15.2	16.6	14.8	16.6	10.2	9.2	4.1	6.2	1982
U.S.	0.2	7.3	13.6	13.6	13.2	14.8	10.3	10.0	4.7	12.2	1979

Note: Figures are percentages except for Median Year; Note: (1) Figures cover the Winston-Salem, NC Metropolitan Statistical Area
Source: U.S. Census Bureau, 2017-2021 American Community Survey 5-Year Estimates

Gross Monthly Rent

Area	Under $500	$500 -$999	$1,000 -$1,499	$1,500 -$1,999	$2,000 -$2,499	$2,500 -$2,999	$3,000 and up	Median ($)
City	8.8	57.2	26.5	5.3	1.3	0.3	0.6	871
MSA[1]	11.0	59.4	23.7	4.3	1.0	0.2	0.4	834
U.S.	8.1	30.5	30.8	16.8	7.3	3.1	3.5	1,163

Note: Figures are percentages except for median; Gross rent is the contract rent plus the estimated average monthly cost of utilities (electricity, gas, and water and sewer) and fuels (oil, coal, kerosene, wood, etc.) if these are paid by the renter (or paid for the renter by someone else); (1) Figures cover the Winston-Salem, NC Metropolitan Statistical Area
Source: U.S. Census Bureau, 2017-2021 American Community Survey 5-Year Estimates

HEALTH

Health Risk Factors

Category	MSA[1] (%)	U.S. (%)
Adults aged 18–64 who have any kind of health care coverage	n/a	90.9
Adults who reported being in good or better health	n/a	85.2
Adults who have been told they have high blood cholesterol	n/a	35.7
Adults who have been told they have high blood pressure	n/a	32.4
Adults who are current smokers	n/a	14.4
Adults who currently use e-cigarettes	n/a	6.7
Adults who currently use chewing tobacco, snuff, or snus	n/a	3.5
Adults who are heavy drinkers[2]	n/a	6.3
Adults who are binge drinkers[3]	n/a	15.4
Adults who are overweight (BMI 25.0 - 29.9)	n/a	34.4
Adults who are obese (BMI 30.0 - 99.8)	n/a	33.9
Adults who participated in any physical activities in the past month	n/a	76.3

Note: (1) Figures for the Winston-Salem, NC Metropolitan Statistical Area were not available.
(2) Heavy drinkers are classified as adult men having more than 14 drinks per week and adult women having more than 7 drinks per week; (3) Binge drinkers are classified as males having five or more drinks on one occasion or females having four or more drinks on one occasion
Source: Centers for Disease Control and Prevention, Behaviorial Risk Factor Surveillance System, SMART: Selected Metropolitan Area Risk Trends, 2021

Acute and Chronic Health Conditions

Category	MSA[1] (%)	U.S. (%)
Adults who have ever been told they had a heart attack	n/a	4.0
Adults who have ever been told they have angina or coronary heart disease	n/a	3.8
Adults who have ever been told they had a stroke	n/a	3.0
Adults who have ever been told they have asthma	n/a	14.9
Adults who have ever been told they have arthritis	n/a	25.8
Adults who have ever been told they have diabetes[2]	n/a	10.9
Adults who have ever been told they had skin cancer	n/a	6.6
Adults who have ever been told they had any other types of cancer	n/a	7.5
Adults who have ever been told they have COPD	n/a	6.1
Adults who have ever been told they have kidney disease	n/a	3.0
Adults who have ever been told they have a form of depression	n/a	20.5

Note: (1) Figures for the Winston-Salem, NC Metropolitan Statistical Area were not available.
(2) Figures do not include pregnancy-related, borderline, or pre-diabetes
Source: Centers for Disease Control and Prevention, Behaviorial Risk Factor Surveillance System, SMART: Selected Metropolitan Area Risk Trends, 2021

Health Screening and Vaccination Rates

Category	MSA[1] (%)	U.S. (%)
Adults who have ever been tested for HIV	n/a	34.9
Adults who have had their blood cholesterol checked within the last five years	n/a	85.2
Adults aged 65+ who have had flu shot within the past year	n/a	68.6
Adults aged 65+ who have ever had a pneumonia vaccination	n/a	71.0

Note: (1) Figures for the Winston-Salem, NC Metropolitan Statistical Area were not available.
Source: Centers for Disease Control and Prevention, Behaviorial Risk Factor Surveillance System, SMART: Selected Metropolitan Area Risk Trends, 2021

Disability Status

Category	MSA[1] (%)	U.S. (%)
Adults who reported being deaf	n/a	7.2
Are you blind or have serious difficulty seeing, even when wearing glasses?	n/a	4.8
Are you limited in any way in any of your usual activities due to arthritis?	n/a	11.1
Do you have difficulty doing errands alone?	n/a	7.0
Do you have difficulty dressing or bathing?	n/a	3.6
Do you have serious difficulty concentrating/remembering/making decisions?	n/a	12.1
Do you have serious difficulty walking or climbing stairs?	n/a	12.8

Note: (1) Figures for the Winston-Salem, NC Metropolitan Statistical Area were not available.
Source: Centers for Disease Control and Prevention, Behaviorial Risk Factor Surveillance System, SMART: Selected Metropolitan Area Risk Trends, 2021

Mortality Rates for the Top 10 Causes of Death in the U.S.

ICD-10[a] Sub-Chapter	ICD-10[a] Code	Crude Mortality Rate[1] per 100,000 population	
		County[2]	U.S.
Malignant neoplasms	C00-C97	190.2	182.6
Ischaemic heart diseases	I20-I25	91.7	113.1
Other forms of heart disease	I30-I51	68.2	64.4
Other degenerative diseases of the nervous system	G30-G31	53.1	51.0
Cerebrovascular diseases	I60-I69	49.2	47.8
Other external causes of accidental injury	W00-X59	61.7	46.4
Chronic lower respiratory diseases	J40-J47	44.1	45.7
Organic, including symptomatic, mental disorders	F01-F09	55.4	35.9
Hypertensive diseases	I10-I15	23.2	35.0
Diabetes mellitus	E10-E14	33.3	29.6

Note: (a) ICD-10 = International Classification of Diseases 10th Revision; (1) Crude mortality rates are a three-year average covering 2019-2021; (2) Figures cover Forsyth County.
Source: Centers for Disease Control and Prevention, National Center for Health Statistics. National Vital Statistics System, Mortality 2018-2021 on CDC WONDER Online Database

Mortality Rates for Selected Causes of Death

ICD-10[a] Sub-Chapter	ICD-10[a] Code	Crude Mortality Rate[1] per 100,000 population	
		County[2]	U.S.
Assault	X85-Y09	9.9	7.0
Diseases of the liver	K70-K76	20.8	19.8
Human immunodeficiency virus (HIV) disease	B20-B24	2.3	1.5
Influenza and pneumonia	J09-J18	15.5	14.7
Intentional self-harm	X60-X84	12.6	14.3
Malnutrition	E40-E46	4.6	4.3
Obesity and other hyperalimentation	E65-E68	3.7	3.0
Renal failure	N17-N19	22.5	15.7
Transport accidents	V01-V99	13.6	13.6
Viral hepatitis	B15-B19	Unreliable	1.2

Note: (a) ICD-10 = International Classification of Diseases 10th Revision; (1) Crude mortality rates are a three-year average covering 2019-2021; (2) Figures cover Forsyth County; Data are suppressed when the data meet the criteria for confidentiality constraints; Crude mortality rates are flagged as unreliable when the rate would be calculated with a numerator of 20 or less.
Source: Centers for Disease Control and Prevention, National Center for Health Statistics. National Vital Statistics System, Mortality 2018-2021 on CDC WONDER Online Database

Health Insurance Coverage

Area	With Health Insurance	With Private Health Insurance	With Public Health Insurance	Without Health Insurance	Population Under Age 19 Without Health Insurance
City	87.7	62.3	36.6	12.3	4.5
MSA[1]	89.0	65.0	36.4	11.0	4.8
U.S.	91.2	67.8	35.4	8.8	5.3

Note: Figures are percentages that cover the civilian noninstitutionalized population; (1) Figures cover the Winston-Salem, NC Metropolitan Statistical Area
Source: U.S. Census Bureau, 2017-2021 American Community Survey 5-Year Estimates

Number of Medical Professionals

Area	MDs[3]	DOs[3,4]	Dentists	Podiatrists	Chiropractors	Optometrists
County[1] (number)	2,603	114	253	23	68	71
County[1] (rate[2])	680.1	29.8	65.6	6.0	17.6	18.4
U.S. (rate[2])	289.3	23.5	72.5	6.2	28.7	17.4

Note: Data as of 2021 unless noted; (1) Data covers Forsyth County; (2) Rate per 100,000 population; (3) Data as of 2020 and includes all active, non-federal physicians; (4) Doctor of Osteopathic Medicine
Source: U.S. Department of Health and Human Services, Health Resources and Services Administration, Bureau of Health Professions, Area Resource File (ARF) 2021-2022

EDUCATION

Public School District Statistics

District Name	Schls	Pupils	Pupil/ Teacher Ratio	Minority Pupils[1] (%)	LEP/ELL[2] (%)	IEP[3] (%)
Winston Salem/Forsyth Co. Schls	81	52,681	14.7	65.8	12.2	13.6

Note: Table includes school districts with 2,000 or more students; (1) Percentage of students that are not non-Hispanic white; (2) Percentage of students that are Limited English Proficient or English Language Learners (2018-19); (3) Percentage of students that have an Individualized Education Program (2019-20).
Source: U.S. Department of Education, National Center for Education Statistics, Common Core of Data, Local Education Agency (School District) Universe Survey: School Year 2021-2022

Highest Level of Education

Area	Less than H.S.	H.S. Diploma	Some College, No Deg.	Associate Degree	Bachelor's Degree	Master's Degree	Prof. School Degree	Doctorate Degree
City	12.0	24.9	20.7	7.7	20.3	9.2	2.8	2.2
MSA[1]	12.0	29.1	21.8	9.6	17.7	6.7	1.7	1.3
U.S.	11.1	26.5	20.0	8.7	20.6	9.3	2.2	1.5

Note: Figures cover persons age 25 and over; (1) Figures cover the Winston-Salem, NC Metropolitan Statistical Area
Source: U.S. Census Bureau, 2017-2021 American Community Survey 5-Year Estimates

Educational Attainment by Race

Area	High School Graduate or Higher (%)					Bachelor's Degree or Higher (%)				
	Total	White	Black	Asian	Hisp.[2]	Total	White	Black	Asian	Hisp.[2]
City	88.0	90.7	88.1	89.9	58.9	34.6	43.0	20.9	70.4	15.1
MSA[1]	88.0	89.3	87.7	88.3	60.1	27.4	28.9	21.0	54.6	13.5
U.S.	88.9	91.4	87.2	87.6	71.2	33.7	35.5	23.3	55.6	18.4

Note: Figures shown cover persons 25 years old and over; (1) Figures cover the Winston-Salem, NC Metropolitan Statistical Area; (2) People of Hispanic origin can be of any race
Source: U.S. Census Bureau, 2017-2021 American Community Survey 5-Year Estimates

School Enrollment by Grade and Control

Area	Preschool (%)		Kindergarten (%)		Grades 1 - 4 (%)		Grades 5 - 8 (%)		Grades 9 - 12 (%)	
	Public	Private	Public	Private	Public	Private	Public	Private	Public	Private
City	56.5	43.5	90.6	9.4	91.7	8.3	91.4	8.6	91.9	8.1
MSA[1]	52.2	47.8	88.5	11.5	90.0	10.0	89.8	10.2	88.4	11.6
U.S.	58.8	41.2	86.3	13.7	88.3	11.7	88.6	11.4	89.4	10.6

Note: Figures shown cover persons 3 years old and over; (1) Figures cover the Winston-Salem, NC Metropolitan Statistical Area
Source: U.S. Census Bureau, 2017-2021 American Community Survey 5-Year Estimates

Higher Education

Four-Year Colleges			Two-Year Colleges			Medical Schools[1]	Law Schools[2]	Voc/ Tech[3]
Public	Private Non-profit	Private For-profit	Public	Private Non-profit	Private For-profit			
2	4	0	2	0	0	1	1	2

Note: Figures cover institutions located within the Winston-Salem, NC Metropolitan Statistical Area and include main campuses only; (1) includes schools accredited by the Liaison Committee on Medical Education and the American Osteopathic Association's Commission on Osteopathic College Accreditation; (2) includes ABA-accredited schools, schools with provisional ABA accreditation, and state accredited schools; (3) includes all schools with programs that are less than 2 years.
Source: National Center for Education Statistics, Integrated Postsecondary Education System (IPEDS), 2021-22; Wikipedia, List of Medical Schools in the United States, accessed April 10, 2023; Wikipedia, List of Law Schools in the United States, accessed April 10, 2023

According to *U.S. News & World Report,* the Winston-Salem, NC metro area is home to one of the top 200 national universities in the U.S.: **Wake Forest University** (#29 tie). The indicators used to capture academic quality fall into a number of categories: assessment by administrators at peer institutions; retention of students; faculty resources; student selectivity; financial resources; alumni giving; high school counselor ratings of colleges; and graduation rate. *U.S. News & World Report, "America's Best Colleges 2023"*

According to *U.S. News & World Report,* the Winston-Salem, NC metro area is home to one of the top 100 law schools in the U.S.: **Wake Forest University** (#37 tie). The rankings are based on a weighted average of 12 measures of quality: peer assessment score; assessment score by lawyers/judges; median LSAT scores; median undergrad GPA; acceptance rate; employment rates for graduates; placement success; bar passage rate; faculty resources; expenditures per student; student/faculty ratio; and library resources. *U.S. News & World Report, "America's Best Graduate Schools, Law, 2023"*

According to *U.S. News & World Report,* the Winston-Salem, NC metro area is home to one of the top 75 medical schools for research in the U.S.: **Wake Forest University** (#47 tie). The rankings are based on a weighted average of 11 measures of quality: quality assessment; peer assessment score; assessment score by residency directors; research activity; total research activity; average research activity per faculty member; student selectivity; median MCAT total score; median undergraduate GPA; acceptance rate; and faculty resources. *U.S. News & World Report, "America's Best Graduate Schools, Medical, 2023"*

EMPLOYERS

Major Employers

Company Name	Industry
B/E Aerospace	Aerospace manufacturing
BB&T	Financial services headquarters
City of Winston-Salem	Municipal government
Deere-Hitachi	Machinery manufacturing
Forsyth Medical Center and Affiliates	Medical center & health services
Forsyth Technical Community College	Education
Hanesbrands	Apparel manufacturing
Lowes Food Stores	Retail grocery
Pepsi	Consumer goods operations
Reynolds American	Tobacco manufacturing
Wake Forest Baptist Medical Center	Academic medical center
Wake Forest University	Education
Wells Fargo	Financial services
Winston-Salem State University	Education
Winston-Salem/Forsyth County Schools	Educational system

Note: Companies shown are located within the Winston-Salem, NC Metropolitan Statistical Area.
Source: Hoovers.com; Wikipedia

PUBLIC SAFETY

Crime Rate

Area	Total Crime	Violent Crime Rate				Property Crime Rate		
		Murder	Rape[3]	Robbery	Aggrav. Assault	Burglary	Larceny -Theft	Motor Vehicle Theft
City	n/a	n/a	n/a	n/a	n/a	n/a	n/a	n/a
Suburbs[1]	n/a	n/a	n/a	n/a	n/a	n/a	n/a	n/a
Metro[2]	n/a	n/a	n/a	n/a	n/a	n/a	n/a	n/a
U.S.	2,356.7	6.5	38.4	73.9	279.7	314.2	1,398.0	246.0

Note: Figures are crimes per 100,000 population; (1) All areas within the metro area that are located outside the city limits; (2) Figures cover the Winston-Salem, NC Metropolitan Statistical Area; n/a not available; (3) All figures shown were reported using the revised Uniform Crime Reporting (UCR) definition of rape; Due to the transition to the National Incident-Based Reporting System (NIBRS), limited city and metro area data was released for 2021.
Source: FBI Uniform Crime Reports, 2020

Hate Crimes

Area	Number of Quarters Reported	Number of Incidents per Bias Motivation					
		Race/Ethnicity/ Ancestry	Religion	Sexual Orientation	Disability	Gender	Gender Identity
City	3	0	0	1	0	0	0
U.S.	4	5,227	1,244	1,110	130	75	266

Note: Due to the transition to the National Incident-Based Reporting System (NIBRS), limited crime data was released for 2021.
Source: Federal Bureau of Investigation, Hate Crime Statistics 2020

Identity Theft Consumer Reports

Area	Reports	Reports per 100,000 Population	Rank[2]
MSA[1]	1,573	234	124
U.S.	1,108,609	339	-

Note: (1) Figures cover the Winston-Salem, NC Metropolitan Statistical Area; (2) Rank ranges from 1 to 391 where 1 indicates greatest number of identity theft reports per 100,000 population
Source: Federal Trade Commission, Consumer Sentinel Network Data Book 2022

Fraud and Other Consumer Reports

Area	Reports	Reports per 100,000 Population	Rank[2]
MSA[1]	6,513	970	109
U.S.	4,064,520	1,245	-

Note: (1) Figures cover the Winston-Salem, NC Metropolitan Statistical Area; (2) Rank ranges from 1 to 391 where 1 indicates greatest number of fraud and other consumer reports per 100,000 population
Source: Federal Trade Commission, Consumer Sentinel Network Data Book 2022

POLITICS

2020 Presidential Election Results

Area	Biden	Trump	Jorgensen	Hawkins	Other
Forsyth County	56.2	42.3	0.9	0.2	0.4
U.S.	51.3	46.8	1.2	0.3	0.5

Note: Results are percentages and may not add to 100% due to rounding
Source: Dave Leip's Atlas of U.S. Presidential Elections

536 Winston-Salem, North Carolina

SPORTS

Professional Sports Teams

Team Name	League	Year Established
No teams are located in the metro area		

Source: Wikipedia, Major Professional Sports Teams of the United States and Canada, April 12, 2023

CLIMATE

Average and Extreme Temperatures

Temperature	Jan	Feb	Mar	Apr	May	Jun	Jul	Aug	Sep	Oct	Nov	Dec	Yr.
Extreme High (°F)	78	81	89	91	96	102	102	103	100	95	85	78	103
Average High (°F)	48	51	60	70	78	84	87	86	80	70	60	50	69
Average Temp. (°F)	38	41	49	58	67	74	78	76	70	59	49	40	58
Average Low (°F)	28	30	37	46	55	63	67	66	59	47	37	30	47
Extreme Low (°F)	-8	-1	5	23	32	42	49	45	37	20	10	0	-8

Note: Figures cover the years 1948-1990
Source: National Climatic Data Center, International Station Meteorological Climate Summary, 9/96

Average Precipitation/Snowfall/Humidity

Precip./Humidity	Jan	Feb	Mar	Apr	May	Jun	Jul	Aug	Sep	Oct	Nov	Dec	Yr.
Avg. Precip. (in.)	3.2	3.4	3.7	3.1	3.7	3.8	4.5	4.2	3.4	3.4	2.9	3.3	42.5
Avg. Snowfall (in.)	4	3	2	Tr	0	0	0	0	0	0	Tr	1	10
Avg. Rel. Hum. 7am (%)	80	78	78	77	82	84	87	90	90	88	83	80	83
Avg. Rel. Hum. 4pm (%)	53	50	47	44	51	54	57	58	56	51	51	54	52

Note: Figures cover the years 1948-1990; Tr = Trace amounts (<0.05 in. of rain; <0.5 in. of snow)
Source: National Climatic Data Center, International Station Meteorological Climate Summary, 9/96

Weather Conditions

Temperature			Daytime Sky			Precipitation		
10°F & below	32°F & below	90°F & above	Clear	Partly cloudy	Cloudy	0.01 inch or more precip.	0.1 inch or more snow/ice	Thunder-storms
3	85	32	94	143	128	113	5	43

Note: Figures are average number of days per year and cover the years 1948-1990
Source: National Climatic Data Center, International Station Meteorological Climate Summary, 9/96

HAZARDOUS WASTE

Superfund Sites

The Winston-Salem, NC metro area is home to one site on the EPA's Superfund National Priorities List: **Holcomb Creosote Co** (final). There are a total of 1,165 Superfund sites with a status of proposed or final on the list in the U.S. *U.S. Environmental Protection Agency, National Priorities List, April 12, 2023*

AIR QUALITY

Air Quality Trends: Ozone

	1990	1995	2000	2005	2010	2015	2018	2019	2020	2021
MSA[1]	0.084	0.086	0.089	0.080	0.078	0.065	0.064	0.062	0.058	0.062
U.S.	0.087	0.089	0.081	0.080	0.072	0.067	0.069	0.065	0.065	0.067

Note: (1) Data covers the Winston-Salem, NC Metropolitan Statistical Area. The values shown are the composite ozone concentration averages among trend sites based on the highest fourth daily maximum 8-hour concentration in parts per million. These trends are based on sites having an adequate record of monitoring data during the trend period. Data from exceptional events are included.
Source: U.S. Environmental Protection Agency, Air Quality Monitoring Information, "Air Quality Trends by City, 1990-2021"

Air Quality Index

Area	Percent of Days when Air Quality was...[2]					AQI Statistics[2]	
	Good	Moderate	Unhealthy for Sensitive Groups	Unhealthy	Very Unhealthy	Maximum	Median
MSA[1]	67.4	31.8	0.8	0.0	0.0	124	44

Note: (1) Data covers the Winston-Salem, NC Metropolitan Statistical Area; (2) Based on 365 days with AQI data in 2021. Air Quality Index (AQI) is an index for reporting daily air quality. EPA calculates the AQI for five major air pollutants regulated by the Clean Air Act: ground-level ozone, particle pollution (aka particulate matter), carbon monoxide, sulfur dioxide, and nitrogen dioxide. The AQI runs from 0 to 500. The higher the AQI value, the greater the level of air pollution and the greater the health concern. There are six AQI categories: "Good" AQI is between 0 and 50. Air quality is considered satisfactory; "Moderate" AQI is between 51 and 100. Air quality is acceptable; "Unhealthy for Sensitive Groups" When AQI values are between 101 and 150, members of sensitive groups may experience health effects; "Unhealthy" When AQI values are between 151 and 200 everyone may begin to experience health effects; "Very Unhealthy" AQI values between 201 and 300 trigger a health alert; "Hazardous" AQI values over 300 trigger warnings of emergency conditions (not shown).
Source: U.S. Environmental Protection Agency, Air Quality Index Report, 2021

Air Quality Index Pollutants

Area	Percent of Days when AQI Pollutant was...[2]					
	Carbon Monoxide	Nitrogen Dioxide	Ozone	Sulfur Dioxide	Particulate Matter 2.5	Particulate Matter 10
MSA[1]	0.0	1.6	46.6	(3)	51.8	0.0

Note: (1) Data covers the Winston-Salem, NC Metropolitan Statistical Area; (2) Based on 365 days with AQI data in 2021. The Air Quality Index (AQI) is an index for reporting daily air quality. EPA calculates the AQI for five major air pollutants regulated by the Clean Air Act: ground-level ozone, particle pollution (also known as particulate matter), carbon monoxide, sulfur dioxide, and nitrogen dioxide. The AQI runs from 0 to 500. The higher the AQI value, the greater the level of air pollution and the greater the health concern; (3) Sulfur dioxide is no longer included in this table (as of December 8, 2021) because SO_2 concentrations tend to be very localized and not necessarily representative of broad geographical areas like counties and CBSAs.
Source: U.S. Environmental Protection Agency, Air Quality Index Report, 2021

Maximum Air Pollutant Concentrations: Particulate Matter, Ozone, CO and Lead

	Particulate Matter 10 (ug/m^3)	Particulate Matter 2.5 Wtd AM (ug/m^3)	Particulate Matter 2.5 24-Hr (ug/m^3)	Ozone (ppm)	Carbon Monoxide (ppm)	Lead (ug/m^3)
MSA[1] Level	41	9.2	41	0.066	n/a	n/a
NAAQS[2]	150	15	35	0.075	9	0.15
Met NAAQS[2]	Yes	Yes	No	Yes	n/a	n/a

Note: (1) Data covers the Winston-Salem, NC Metropolitan Statistical Area; Data from exceptional events are included; (2) National Ambient Air Quality Standards; ppm = parts per million; ug/m^3 = micrograms per cubic meter; n/a not available.
Concentrations: Particulate Matter 10 (coarse particulate)—highest second maximum 24-hour concentration; Particulate Matter 2.5 Wtd AM (fine particulate)—highest weighted annual mean concentration; Particulate Matter 2.5 24-Hour (fine particulate)—highest 98th percentile 24-hour concentration; Ozone—highest fourth daily maximum 8-hour concentration; Carbon Monoxide—highest second maximum non-overlapping 8-hour concentration; Lead—maximum running 3-month average
Source: U.S. Environmental Protection Agency, Air Quality Monitoring Information, "Air Quality Statistics by City, 2021"

Maximum Air Pollutant Concentrations: Nitrogen Dioxide and Sulfur Dioxide

	Nitrogen Dioxide AM (ppb)	Nitrogen Dioxide 1-Hr (ppb)	Sulfur Dioxide AM (ppb)	Sulfur Dioxide 1-Hr (ppb)	Sulfur Dioxide 24-Hr (ppb)
MSA[1] Level	6	32	n/a	4	n/a
NAAQS[2]	53	100	30	75	140
Met NAAQS[2]	Yes	Yes	n/a	Yes	n/a

Note: (1) Data covers the Winston-Salem, NC Metropolitan Statistical Area; Data from exceptional events are included; (2) National Ambient Air Quality Standards; ppm = parts per million; ug/m^3 = micrograms per cubic meter; n/a not available.
Concentrations: Nitrogen Dioxide AM—highest arithmetic mean concentration; Nitrogen Dioxide 1-Hr—highest 98th percentile 1-hour daily maximum concentration; Sulfur Dioxide AM—highest annual mean concentration; Sulfur Dioxide 1-Hr—highest 99th percentile 1-hour daily maximum concentration; Sulfur Dioxide 24-Hr—highest second maximum 24-hour concentration
Source: U.S. Environmental Protection Agency, Air Quality Monitoring Information, "Air Quality Statistics by City, 2021"

Worcester, Massachusetts

Background

For the first one hundred years following European settlement in central Massachusetts, Worcester was the site of great conflict, making permanent settlement difficult. The Nimpuc Native Americans were Worcester's first inhabitants. In 1673, English settlers established a "praying town" where Christianized Native Americans could settle as a congregation. But the Indian Wars broke up any town cohesion as natives left the area to fight. It wasn't until 1713 that Worcester was permanently settled. By 1770, the town played a major role in the American Revolution. The radical Isaiah Thomas moved his *Massachusetts Spy* newspaper to Worcester from Boston, and read the newly penned Declaration of Independence from the step of Worcester's town hall—the declaration's first public reading in New England.

Thomas created the American Antiquarian Society (AAS) in 1812, in part, to protect precious historical documents from destruction in Boston during the War of 1812. AAS membership is by election, and has included 16 U. S. presidents, and 78 Pulitzer Prize winners. It houses the largest collection of pre-1812, American-printed materials in the world, and includes over 4 million documents, covering 25 miles worth of shelf space. Current membership includes such greats at Ken Burns, Doris Kearns Goodwin, David McCullough, and Henry Louis Gates.

Once Worcester established itself as a transportation hub—following the completion of the Blackstone Canal, and the opening of the Worcester and Boston Railroad—manufacturing took root. New industries brought teams of immigrants looking for work. In 1881, Ichabod Washburn established the Washburn & Moen Company that would become the largest wire manufacturer in the country. The Royal Worcester Corset Factory would become the nation's largest employer of women.

Besides the first public reading of the Declaration of Independence and formation of the AAS, Worcester hosted the first national women's rights convention in 1850. Worcester's Frances Perkins became the first woman to serve in a President's cabinet, under Franklin Roosevelt. The first ballpoint pen and the first typewriter were each manufactured in Worcester. And in 1963, Worcester native, Harvey Ball, created the ubiquitous, yellow "Smiley Face."

However, not all of the city's firsts were positive. In the early 20th century, the Ku Klux Klan had more members in Maine and Massachusettes than in any southern state (including Alabama and Mississippi). In 1924, Worcester hosted the largest gathering of the Ku Klux Klan in New England, resulting in townspeople rioting. Following the riots, klan membership in the area declined significantly.

In recent years, Worcester has donned the moniker "Wormtown," a term that has come to represent Worcester's independent, sometimes rebellious, spirit. In 1978, a local radio DJ named L. B. Worm coined the epithet to celebrate original thought in the burgeoning punk music scene. Since then, the underground movement hosts an annual music festival—the Wormtown Music Festival—and publishes the fanzine *Worm Town Punk Punk Press.* Some local businesses, such as the Wormtown Brewery, have adopted the name.

The city's larger employers include Hanover Insurance, Fallon Community Health Care, and Polar Beverages, the largest independent soft-drink bottler in the country.

Education and healthcare thrive in Worcester, which boasts 10 universities and over 100 biotech companies. The University of Massasachusetts Medical School is a leader in medical research. Dr. Craig Mello won the Nobel Prize in physiology while teaching at UMMS and conducting research at the Massachusetts Biotechnology Research Park. In 2000, the College of Pharmacy and Health Sciences (CPHS) built a new campus in the heart of downtown Worcester. Forty-four acres of unused, state-owned land on the former Worcester State Hospital campus is being developed into a biomanufacturing industrial part. Worcester Polytechnic Institute, UMMS, and CPHS have created a powerful consortium leading the charge in medical research. Clark University, founded in 1887, was the first university in the country to offer graduate degrees.

Like many progressive cities, Worcester has invested in urban renewal. In 2000, Union Station reopened after a $32 million renovation investment. Franklin Square Theater was revived as the Hanover Theatre for the Performing Arts. The Architectural Heritage Foundation spearheaded the renovation of the Worcester Memorial Auditorium into a multimedia and event center.

Worcester enjoys a temperate climate with warm summers and mild winters generally. However, the city can experience more extreme weather—the winters of 2009-10 and 2010-11 saw prolonged periods of sub-freezing temperatures and heavy snowfalls. In contrast, Worcester recorded 98.6 °F on 3 August 1990.

Rankings

General Rankings

- In their ninth annual survey, Livability.com looked at data for more than 2,300 mid-sized U.S. cities to determine the rankings for Livability's "Top 100 Best Places to Live" in 2022. Worcester ranked #75. Criteria: housing and economy; social and civic engagement; education; demographics; health care options; transportation & infrastructure; and community amenities. *Livability.com, "Top 100 Best Places to Live 2022" July 19, 2022*

Business/Finance Rankings

- The Brookings Institution ranked the nation's largest cities based on income inequality. Worcester was ranked #30 (#1 = greatest inequality). Criteria: the "95/20 ratio," a figure representing the income at which a household earns more than 95 percent of all other households, divided by the income at which a household earns more than only 20 percent of all other households. *Brookings Institution, "Household Income Inequality, Largest Cities of 97 Large U.S. Metro Areas, 2014-2016," February 5, 2018*

- The Brookings Institution ranked the 100 largest metro areas in the U.S. based on income inequality. Worcester was ranked #35 (#1 = greatest inequality). Criteria: the "95/20 ratio," a figure representing the income at which a household earns more than 95 percent of all other households, divided by the income at which a household earns more than only 20 percent of all other households. *Brookings Institution, "Household Income Inequality, 100 Largest U.S. Metro Areas, 2014-2016," February 5, 2018*

- The Worcester metro area appeared on the Milken Institute "2022 Best Performing Cities" list. Rank: #85 out of 200 large metro areas (population over 250,000). Criteria: job growth; wage and salary growth; high-tech output growth; housing affordability; household broadband access. *Milken Institute, "Best-Performing Cities 2022," March 28, 2022*

- *Forbes* ranked the 200 most populous metro areas to determine the nation's "Best Places for Business and Careers." The Worcester metro area was ranked #128. Criteria: costs (business and living); job growth (past and projected); income growth; quality of life; educational attainment (college and high school); projected economic growth; cultural and leisure opportunities; workplace tolerance laws; net migration patterns. *Forbes, "The Best Places for Business and Careers 2019: Seattle Still On Top," October 30, 2019*

Education Rankings

- Personal finance website *WalletHub* analyzed the 150 largest U.S. metropolitan statistical areas to determine where the most educated Americans are putting their degrees to work. Criteria: education levels; percentage of workers with degrees; education quality and attainment gap; public school quality rankings; quality and enrollment of each metro area's universities. Worcester was ranked #52 (#1 = most educated city). *www.WalletHub.com, "Most & Least Educated Cities in America," July 18, 2022*

Environmental Rankings

- Niche compiled a list of the nation's snowiest cities, based on the National Oceanic and Atmospheric Administration's 30-year average snowfall data. Among cities with a population of at least 50,000, Worcester ranked #12. *Niche.com, Top 25 Snowiest Cities in America, December 10, 2018*

Health/Fitness Rankings

- Worcester was identified as a "2022 Spring Allergy Capital." The area ranked #40 out of 100. Three groups of factors were used to identify the most challenging cities for people with allergies during the spring season: annual spring pollen scores; over the counter allergy medicine use; number of board-certified allergy specialists. *Asthma and Allergy Foundation of America, "Spring Allergy Capitals 2022," March 2, 2022*

- Worcester was identified as a "2022 Fall Allergy Capital." The area ranked #53 out of 100. Three groups of factors were used to identify the most challenging cities for people with allergies during the fall season: annual fall pollen scores; over the counter allergy medicine use; number of board-certified allergy specialists. *Asthma and Allergy Foundation of America, "Fall Allergy Capitals 2022," March 2, 2022*

- Worcester was identified as a "2022 Asthma Capital." The area ranked #63 out of the nation's 100 largest metropolitan areas. Criteria: estimated asthma prevalence; asthma-related mortality; and ER visits due to asthma. Risk factors analyzed but not factored in the rankings: annual pollen score; annual air quality; public smoking laws; access to board-certified asthma specialists; rescue and controller medication use; uninsured rate; poverty rate. *Asthma and Allergy Foundation of America, "Asthma Capitals 2022: The Most Challenging Places to Live With Asthma," September 14, 2022*

Real Estate Rankings

- *WalletHub* compared the most populated U.S. cities to determine which had the best markets for real estate agents. Worcester ranked #89 where demand was high and pay was the best. Criteria: sales per agent; annual median wage for real-estate agents; monthly average starting salary for real estate agents; real estate job density and competition; unemployment rate; home turnover rate; housing-market health index; and other relevant metrics. *www.WalletHub.com, "2021 Best Places to Be a Real Estate Agent," May 12, 2021*

- The Worcester metro area appeared on Realtor.com's list of hot housing markets to watch in 2023. The area ranked #4. Criteria: forecasted home price and sales growth; overall economy; population trends. *Realtor.com®, "Top 10 Housing Markets Positioned for Growth in 2023," December 7, 2022*

- The Worcester metro area was identified as one of the nations's 20 hottest housing markets in 2023. Criteria: listing views as an indicator of demand and number of days on the market as an indicator of pace. The area ranked #3. *Realtor.com, "January 2023 Top 20 Hottest Housing Markets," February 23, 2023*

- Worcester was ranked #104 out of 235 metro areas in terms of housing affordability in 2022 by the National Association of Home Builders (#1 = most affordable). Criteria: the share of homes sold in that area affordable to a family earning the local median income, based on standard mortgage underwriting criteria. *National Association of Home Builders®, NAHB-Wells Fargo Housing Opportunity Index, 4th Quarter 2022*

Safety Rankings

- Allstate ranked the 200 largest cities in America in terms of driver safety. Worcester ranked #197. Criteria: internal property damage claims over a two-year period from January 2016 to December 2017. The report helps increase the importance of safety and awareness behind the wheel. *Allstate, "Allstate America's Best Drivers Report, 2019" June 24, 2019*

- The National Insurance Crime Bureau ranked 390 metro areas in the U.S. in terms of per capita rates of vehicle theft. The Worcester metro area ranked #345 (#1 = highest rate). Criteria: number of vehicle theft offenses per 100,000 inhabitants in 2021. *National Insurance Crime Bureau, "Hot Spots 2021," September 1, 2022*

Seniors/Retirement Rankings

- From its Best Cities for Successful Aging indexes, the Milken Institute generated rankings for metropolitan areas, weighing data in nine categories—health care, wellness, living arrangements, transportation and convenience, financial characteristics, education, employment, community engagement, and overall livability. The Worcester metro area was ranked #68 overall in the large metro area category. *Milken Institute, "Best Cities for Successful Aging, 2017" March 14, 2017*

Women/Minorities Rankings

- Personal finance website *WalletHub* compared more than 180 U.S. cities across two key dimensions, "Hispanic Business-Friendliness" and "Hispanic Purchasing Power," to arrive at the most favorable conditions for Hispanic entrepreneurs. Worcester was ranked #175 out of 182. Criteria includes: share of Hispanic-Owned Businesses; Hispanic entrepreneurship rate to median annual income of Hispanics; Small Business-Friendliness score; cost of living; and number of Hispanics with at least a bachelor's degree. *WalletHub.com, "2019's Best Cities for Hispanic Entrepreneurs," May 1, 2019*

Miscellaneous Rankings

- *WalletHub* compared the 150 most populated U.S. cities to determine their operating efficiency. A "Quality of Services" score was constructed for each city and then divided by the total budget per capita to reveal which were managed the best. Worcester ranked #43. Criteria: financial stability; economy; education; safety; health; infrastructure and pollution. *www.WalletHub.com, "2022's Best-& Worst-Run Cities in America," June 21, 2022*

Business Environment

DEMOGRAPHICS

Population Growth

Area	1990 Census	2000 Census	2010 Census	2020 Census	Population Growth (%)	
					1990-2020	2010-2020
City	169,759	172,648	181,045	206,518	21.7	14.1
MSA[1]	709,728	750,963	798,552	978,529	37.9	22.5
U.S.	248,709,873	281,421,906	308,745,538	331,449,281	33.3	7.4

Note: (1) Figures cover the Worcester, MA-CT Metropolitan Statistical Area
Source: U.S. Census Bureau, 1990 Census, 2000 Census, 2010 Census, 2020 Census

Race

Area	White Alone[2] (%)	Black Alone[2] (%)	Asian Alone[2] (%)	AIAN[3] Alone[2] (%)	NHOPI[4] Alone[2] (%)	Other Race Alone[2] (%)	Two or More Races (%)
City	53.3	14.8	7.1	0.5	0.0	12.9	11.3
MSA[1]	74.5	5.2	4.9	0.4	0.0	6.3	8.6
U.S.	61.6	12.4	6.0	1.1	0.2	8.4	10.2

Note: (1) Figures cover the Worcester, MA-CT Metropolitan Statistical Area; (2) Alone is defined as not being in combination with one or more other races; (3) American Indian and Alaska Native; (4) Native Hawaiian and Other Pacific Islander
Source: U.S. Census Bureau, 2020 Census

Hispanic or Latino Origin

Area	Total (%)	Mexican (%)	Puerto Rican (%)	Cuban (%)	Other (%)
City	23.9	0.8	14.7	0.3	8.1
MSA[1]	12.3	0.9	7.2	0.2	4.0
U.S.	18.4	11.2	1.8	0.7	4.7

Note: Persons of Hispanic or Latino origin can be of any race; (1) Figures cover the Worcester, MA-CT Metropolitan Statistical Area
Source: U.S. Census Bureau, 2017-2021 American Community Survey 5-Year Estimates

Age

Area	Percent of Population									Median Age
	Under Age 5	Age 5–19	Age 20–34	Age 35–44	Age 45–54	Age 55–64	Age 65–74	Age 75–84	Age 85+	
City	5.4	18.9	26.8	12.1	11.5	11.9	7.9	3.7	1.9	34.3
MSA[1]	5.0	18.5	19.8	12.3	13.4	14.6	9.9	4.6	2.0	40.3
U.S.	5.6	19.2	20.2	12.7	12.4	13.1	10.0	4.9	1.9	38.8

Note: (1) Figures cover the Worcester, MA-CT Metropolitan Statistical Area
Source: U.S. Census Bureau, 2020 Census

Disability by Age

Area	All Ages	Under 18 Years Old	18 to 64 Years Old	65 Years and Over
City	14.3	4.7	12.9	37.3
MSA[1]	12.4	4.3	10.5	31.6
U.S.	12.6	4.4	10.3	33.4

Note: Figures show percent of the civilian noninstitutionalized population that reported having a disability. Disability status is determined from six types of difficulty: vision, hearing, cognitive, ambulatory, self-care, and independent living. For children under 5 years old, hearing and vision difficulty are used to determine disability status. For children between the ages of 5 and 14, disability status is determined from hearing, vision, cognitive, ambulatory, and self-care difficulties. For people aged 15 years and older, they are considered to have a disability if they have difficulty with any one of the six difficulty types; Note: (1) Figures cover the Worcester, MA-CT Metropolitan Statistical Area
Source: U.S. Census Bureau, 2017-2021 American Community Survey 5-Year Estimates

Ancestry

Area	German	Irish	English	American	Italian	Polish	French[2]	Scottish	Dutch
City	3.0	14.0	4.6	3.7	8.9	4.2	5.7	1.0	0.3
MSA[1]	5.5	17.6	9.3	5.5	11.8	5.6	9.5	2.0	0.5
U.S.	12.8	9.6	8.1	5.7	5.0	2.7	2.2	1.6	1.1

Note: Figures are the percentage of the total population reporting a particular ancestry. The nine most commonly reported ancestries in the U.S. are shown. Figures include multiple ancestries (e.g. if a person reported being Irish and Italian, they were included in both columns); (1) Figures cover the Worcester, MA-CT Metropolitan Statistical Area; (2) Excludes Basque
Source: U.S. Census Bureau, 2017-2021 American Community Survey 5-Year Estimates

Foreign-born Population

Area	Any Foreign Country	Asia	Mexico	Europe	Caribbean	Central America[2]	South America	Africa	Canada
City	21.9	6.1	0.3	3.6	3.0	1.3	2.5	4.9	0.1
MSA[1]	12.0	3.7	0.3	2.3	1.1	0.6	2.0	1.6	0.4
U.S.	13.6	4.2	3.3	1.5	1.4	1.1	1.1	0.8	0.2

Note: (1) Figures cover the Worcester, MA-CT Metropolitan Statistical Area; (2) Excludes Mexico.
Source: U.S. Census Bureau, 2017-2021 American Community Survey 5-Year Estimates

Household Size

Area	Persons in Household (%)							Average Household Size
	One	Two	Three	Four	Five	Six	Seven or More	
City	35.0	28.3	17.0	12.0	4.5	2.2	1.0	2.40
MSA[1]	27.0	33.0	17.5	14.6	5.4	1.7	0.9	2.50
U.S.	28.1	33.8	15.5	12.9	6.0	2.3	1.4	2.60

Note: (1) Figures cover the Worcester, MA-CT Metropolitan Statistical Area
Source: U.S. Census Bureau, 2017-2021 American Community Survey 5-Year Estimates

Household Relationships

Area	House-holder	Opposite-sex Spouse	Same-sex Spouse	Opposite-sex Unmarried Partner	Same-sex Unmarried Partner	Child[2]	Grand-child	Other Relatives	Non-relatives
City	38.3	12.2	0.3	2.8	0.2	26.3	1.7	5.7	5.3
MSA[1]	38.6	17.9	0.2	2.9	0.1	28.1	1.7	4.0	3.1
U.S.	38.3	17.5	0.2	2.5	0.2	28.3	2.4	4.8	3.4

Note: Figures are percent of the total population; (1) Figures cover the Worcester, MA-CT Metropolitan Statistical Area; (2) Includes biological, adopted, and stepchildren of the householder
Source: U.S. Census Bureau, 2020 Census

Gender

Area	Males	Females	Males per 100 Females
City	100,540	105,978	94.9
MSA[1]	482,355	496,174	97.2
U.S.	162,685,811	168,763,470	96.4

Note: (1) Figures cover the Worcester, MA-CT Metropolitan Statistical Area
Source: U.S. Census Bureau, 2020 Census

Marital Status

Area	Never Married	Now Married[2]	Separated	Widowed	Divorced
City	47.8	34.0	2.0	4.9	11.3
MSA[1]	34.4	47.7	1.5	5.4	11.0
U.S.	33.8	48.0	1.8	5.6	10.8

Note: Figures are percentages and cover the population 15 years of age and older; (1) Figures cover the Worcester, MA-CT Metropolitan Statistical Area; (2) Excludes separated
Source: U.S. Census Bureau, 2017-2021 American Community Survey 5-Year Estimates

Religious Groups by Family

Area	Catholic	Baptist	Methodist	LDS[2]	Pentecostal	Lutheran	Islam	Adventist	Other
MSA[1]	30.1	0.8	0.8	0.3	1.0	0.4	0.6	1.4	7.1
U.S.	18.7	7.3	3.0	2.0	1.8	1.7	1.3	1.3	11.6

Note: Figures are the number of adherents as a percentage of the total population and cover the eight largest religious groups in the U.S; (1) Figures cover the Worcester, MA-CT Metropolitan Statistical Area; (2) Church of Jesus Christ of Latter-day Saints
Sources: 2020 U.S. Religion Census, Association of Statisticians of American Religious Bodies; The Association of Religion Data Archives (ARDA)

Religious Groups by Tradition

Area	Catholic	Evangelical Protestant	Mainline Protestant	Black Protestant	Islam	Judaism	Hinduism	Orthodox	Buddhism
MSA[1]	30.1	4.9	3.6	0.2	0.6	0.4	0.3	1.0	0.4
U.S.	18.7	16.5	5.2	2.3	1.3	0.6	0.4	0.4	0.3

Note: Figures are the number of adherents as a percentage of the total population; (1) Figures cover the Worcester, MA-CT Metropolitan Statistical Area
Sources: 2020 U.S. Religion Census, Association of Statisticians of American Religious Bodies; The Association of Religion Data Archives (ARDA)

544 Worcester, Massachusetts

ECONOMY

Gross Metropolitan Product

Area	2020	2021	2022	2023	Rank[2]
MSA[1]	50.9	55.1	59.3	62.5	64

Note: Figures are in billions of dollars; (1) Figures cover the Worcester, MA-CT Metropolitan Statistical Area; (2) Rank is based on 2021 data and ranges from 1 to 381
Source: U.S. Conference of Mayors, U.S. Metro Economies: U.S. Metros Compared to Global and State Economies, June 2022

Economic Growth

Area	2018-20 (%)	2021 (%)	2022 (%)	2023 (%)	Rank[2]
MSA[1]	-0.9	5.3	2.5	2.4	204
U.S.	-0.6	5.7	3.1	2.9	—

Note: Figures are real gross metropolitan product (GMP) growth rates and represent average annual percent change; (1) Figures cover the Worcester, MA-CT Metropolitan Statistical Area; (2) Rank is based on 2020 2-year average annual percent change and ranges from 1 to 381
Source: U.S. Conference of Mayors, U.S. Metro Economies: U.S. Metros Compared to Global and State Economies, June 2022

Metropolitan Area Exports

Area	2016	2017	2018	2019	2020	2021	Rank[2]
MSA[1]	3,093.5	2,929.6	2,573.6	2,221.5	2,026.4	2,624.6	92

Note: Figures are in millions of dollars; (1) Figures cover the Worcester, MA-CT Metropolitan Statistical Area; (2) Rank is based on 2021 data and ranges from 1 to 388
Source: U.S. Department of Commerce, International Trade Administration, Office of Trade and Economic Analysis, Industry and Analysis, Exports by Metropolitan Area, data extracted March 16, 2023

Building Permits

Area	Single-Family			Multi-Family			Total		
	2021	2022	Pct. Chg.	2021	2022	Pct. Chg.	2021	2022	Pct. Chg.
City	66	94	42.4	112	718	541.1	178	812	356.2
MSA[1]	1,177	1,172	-0.4	876	1,080	23.3	2,053	2,252	9.7
U.S.	1,115,400	975,600	-12.5	621,600	689,500	10.9	1,737,000	1,665,100	-4.1

Note: (1) Figures cover the Worcester, MA-CT Metropolitan Statistical Area; Figures represent new, privately-owned housing units authorized (unadjusted data); All permit data are based on estimates with imputation
Source: U.S. Census Bureau, Manufacturing, Mining, and Construction Statistics, Building Permits, 2021, 2022

Bankruptcy Filings

Area	Business Filings			Nonbusiness Filings		
	2021	2022	% Chg.	2021	2022	% Chg.
Worcester County	24	26	8.3	569	550	-3.3
U.S.	14,347	13,481	-6.0	399,269	374,240	-6.3

Note: Business filings include Chapter 7, Chapter 9, Chapter 11, Chapter 12, Chapter 13, Chapter 15, and Section 304; Nonbusiness filings include Chapter 7, Chapter 11, and Chapter 13
Source: Administrative Office of the U.S. Courts, Business and Nonbusiness Bankruptcy, County Cases Commenced by Chapter of the Bankruptcy Code, During the 12-Month Period Ending December 31, 2021 and Business and Nonbusiness Bankruptcy, County Cases Commenced by Chapter of the Bankruptcy Code, During the 12-Month Period Ending December 31, 2022

Housing Vacancy Rates

Area	Gross Vacancy Rate[2] (%)			Year-Round Vacancy Rate[3] (%)			Rental Vacancy Rate[4] (%)			Homeowner Vacancy Rate[5] (%)		
	2020	2021	2022	2020	2021	2022	2020	2021	2022	2020	2021	2022
MSA[1]	4.8	5.5	4.5	4.6	4.9	4.0	1.3	2.2	1.6	0.4	0.7	0.4
U.S.	10.6	10.8	10.5	8.2	8.4	8.2	6.3	6.1	5.8	1.0	0.9	0.8

Note: (1) Figures cover the Worcester, MA-CT Metropolitan Statistical Area; (2) The percentage of the total housing inventory that is vacant; (3) The percentage of the housing inventory (excluding seasonal units) that is year-round vacant; (4) The percentage of rental inventory that is vacant for rent; (5) The percentage of homeowner inventory that is vacant for sale
Source: U.S. Census Bureau, Housing Vacancies and Homeownership Annual Statistics: 2020, 2021, 2022

INCOME

Income

Area	Per Capita ($)	Median Household ($)	Average Household ($)
City	30,855	56,746	76,859
MSA[1]	40,750	80,333	104,366
U.S.	37,638	69,021	97,196

Note: (1) Figures cover the Worcester, MA-CT Metropolitan Statistical Area
Source: U.S. Census Bureau, 2017-2021 American Community Survey 5-Year Estimates

Worcester, Massachusetts 545

Household Income Distribution

Area	Under $15,000	$15,000 -$24,999	$25,000 -$34,999	$35,000 -$49,999	$50,000 -$74,999	$75,000 -$99,999	$100,000 -$149,999	$150,000 and up
				Percent of Households Earning				
City	15.5	9.8	8.5	12.0	15.8	11.7	14.8	11.8
MSA[1]	8.6	6.8	7.0	9.6	15.3	12.5	18.5	21.8
U.S.	9.4	7.8	8.2	11.4	16.8	12.8	16.3	17.3

Note: (1) Figures cover the Worcester, MA-CT Metropolitan Statistical Area
Source: U.S. Census Bureau, 2017-2021 American Community Survey 5-Year Estimates

Poverty Rate

Area	All Ages	Under 18 Years Old	18 to 64 Years Old	65 Years and Over
City	19.3	24.8	18.1	16.6
MSA[1]	10.0	12.0	9.6	8.8
U.S.	12.6	17.0	11.8	9.6

Note: Figures are percentage of people whose income during the past 12 months was below the poverty level;
(1) Figures cover the Worcester, MA-CT Metropolitan Statistical Area
Source: U.S. Census Bureau, 2017-2021 American Community Survey 5-Year Estimates

EMPLOYMENT

Labor Force and Employment

Area	Civilian Labor Force			Workers Employed		
	Dec. 2021	Dec. 2022	% Chg.	Dec. 2021	Dec. 2022	% Chg.
City	93,362	90,627	-2.9	88,807	87,239	-1.8
NECTA[1]	358,980	351,150	-2.2	344,046	339,514	-1.3
U.S.	161,696,000	164,224,000	1.6	155,732,000	158,872,000	2.0

Note: Data is not seasonally adjusted and covers workers 16 years of age and older; (1) Figures cover the
Worcester, MA-CT New England City and Town Area
Source: Bureau of Labor Statistics, Local Area Unemployment Statistics

Unemployment Rate

Area	2022											
	Jan.	Feb.	Mar.	Apr.	May	Jun.	Jul.	Aug.	Sep.	Oct.	Nov.	Dec.
City	5.5	4.6	4.1	3.9	4.2	4.6	4.6	4.6	4.0	3.7	3.5	3.7
NECTA[1]	5.0	4.4	3.9	3.4	3.5	3.7	3.7	3.8	3.3	3.2	3.0	3.3
U.S.	4.4	4.1	3.8	3.3	3.4	3.8	3.8	3.8	3.3	3.4	3.4	3.3

Note: Data is not seasonally adjusted and covers workers 16 years of age and older; (1) Figures cover the
Worcester, MA-CT New England City and Town Area
Source: Bureau of Labor Statistics, Local Area Unemployment Statistics

Average Wages

Occupation	$/Hr.	Occupation	$/Hr.
Accountants and Auditors	42.78	Maintenance and Repair Workers	24.75
Automotive Mechanics	26.08	Marketing Managers	73.90
Bookkeepers	24.24	Network and Computer Systems Admin.	47.65
Carpenters	29.55	Nurses, Licensed Practical	30.85
Cashiers	15.32	Nurses, Registered	47.38
Computer Programmers	49.03	Nursing Assistants	18.71
Computer Systems Analysts	50.87	Office Clerks, General	21.03
Computer User Support Specialists	31.83	Physical Therapists	44.80
Construction Laborers	28.53	Physicians	108.84
Cooks, Restaurant	18.32	Plumbers, Pipefitters and Steamfitters	40.47
Customer Service Representatives	21.98	Police and Sheriff's Patrol Officers	30.41
Dentists	n/a	Postal Service Mail Carriers	27.11
Electricians	37.55	Real Estate Sales Agents	n/a
Engineers, Electrical	57.13	Retail Salespersons	17.84
Fast Food and Counter Workers	15.52	Sales Representatives, Technical/Scientific	55.25
Financial Managers	71.84	Secretaries, Exc. Legal/Medical/Executive	23.77
First-Line Supervisors of Office Workers	32.65	Security Guards	18.53
General and Operations Managers	61.97	Surgeons	n/a
Hairdressers/Cosmetologists	21.83	Teacher Assistants, Exc. Postsecondary*	19.32
Home Health and Personal Care Aides	16.77	Teachers, Secondary School, Exc. Sp. Ed.*	38.25
Janitors and Cleaners	18.83	Telemarketers	19.51
Landscaping/Groundskeeping Workers	20.03	Truck Drivers, Heavy/Tractor-Trailer	26.93
Lawyers	69.75	Truck Drivers, Light/Delivery Services	22.55
Maids and Housekeeping Cleaners	17.11	Waiters and Waitresses	18.31

Note: Wage data covers the Worcester, MA-CT New England City and Town Area; (*) Hourly wages were
calculated from annual wage data based on a 40 hour work week; n/a not available.
Source: Bureau of Labor Statistics, Metro Area Occupational Employment & Wage Estimates, May 2022

Employment by Industry

Sector	NECTA[1]		U.S.
	Number of Employees	Percent of Total	Percent of Total
Construction, Mining, and Logging	12,200	4.1	5.4
Private Education and Health Services	69,300	23.5	16.1
Financial Activities	14,300	4.8	5.9
Government	46,400	15.7	14.5
Information	2,700	0.9	2.0
Leisure and Hospitality	24,600	8.3	10.3
Manufacturing	27,200	9.2	8.4
Other Services	10,500	3.6	3.7
Professional and Business Services	32,900	11.1	14.7
Retail Trade	30,200	10.2	10.2
Transportation, Warehousing, and Utilities	15,600	5.3	4.9
Wholesale Trade	9,500	3.2	3.9

Note: Figures are non-farm employment as of December 2022. Figures are not seasonally adjusted and include workers 16 years of age and older; (1) Figures cover the Worcester, MA-CT New England City and Town Area
Source: Bureau of Labor Statistics, Current Employment Statistics, Employment, Hours, and Earnings

Employment by Occupation

Occupation Classification	City (%)	MSA[1] (%)	U.S. (%)
Management, Business, Science, and Arts	39.6	43.5	40.3
Natural Resources, Construction, and Maintenance	6.1	7.7	8.7
Production, Transportation, and Material Moving	14.1	12.2	13.1
Sales and Office	18.8	19.7	20.9
Service	21.4	17.0	17.0

Note: Figures cover employed civilians 16 years of age and older; (1) Figures cover the Worcester, MA-CT Metropolitan Statistical Area
Source: U.S. Census Bureau, 2017-2021 American Community Survey 5-Year Estimates

Occupations with Greatest Projected Employment Growth: 2022 – 2024

Occupation[1]	2022 Employment	2024 Projected Employment	Numeric Employment Change	Percent Employment Change
Home Health and Personal Care Aides	116,330	122,940	6,610	5.7
Fast Food and Counter Workers	92,850	95,950	3,100	3.3
Cooks, Restaurant	32,200	34,940	2,740	8.5
General and Operations Managers	117,860	119,220	1,360	1.2
Waiters and Waitresses	43,720	45,070	1,350	3.1
Management Analysts	35,540	36,880	1,340	3.8
Heavy and Tractor-Trailer Truck Drivers	29,700	30,790	1,090	3.7
Light Truck or Delivery Services Drivers	25,360	26,390	1,030	4.1
Medical and Health Services Managers	19,250	20,190	940	4.9
First-Line Supervisors of Food Preparation and Serving Workers	21,360	22,230	870	4.1

Note: Projections cover Massachusetts; (1) Sorted by numeric employment change
Source: www.projectionscentral.com, State Occupational Projections, 2022–2024 Short-Term Projections

Fastest-Growing Occupations: 2022 – 2024

Occupation[1]	2022 Employment	2024 Projected Employment	Numeric Employment Change	Percent Employment Change
Farmworkers and Laborers, Crop, Nursery, and Greenhouse	6,040	6,610	570	9.4
Farmers, Ranchers, and Other Agricultural Managers	8,170	8,930	760	9.3
Cooks, Restaurant	32,200	34,940	2,740	8.5
Actuaries	880	950	70	8.0
Statisticians	2,110	2,270	160	7.6
Nurse Practitioners	7,530	8,050	520	6.9
Information Security Analysts (SOC 2018)	3,850	4,080	230	6.0
Home Health and Personal Care Aides	116,330	122,940	6,610	5.7
Logisticians	3,470	3,660	190	5.5
Operations Research Analysts	3,440	3,630	190	5.5

Note: Projections cover Massachusetts; (1) Sorted by percent employment change and excludes occupations with numeric employment change less than 50
Source: www.projectionscentral.com, State Occupational Projections, 2022–2024 Short-Term Projections

Worcester, Massachusetts   **547**

CITY FINANCES

City Government Finances

Component	2020 ($000)	2020 ($ per capita)
Total Revenues	889,408	4,797
Total Expenditures	926,369	4,996
Debt Outstanding	844,397	4,554
Cash and Securities[1]	252,552	1,362

Note: (1) Cash and security holdings of a government at the close of its fiscal year, including those of its dependent agencies, utilities, and liquor stores.
Source: U.S. Census Bureau, State & Local Government Finances 2020

City Government Revenue by Source

Source	2020 ($000)	2020 ($ per capita)	2020 (%)
General Revenue			
From Federal Government	26,399	142	3.0
From State Government	397,317	2,143	44.7
From Local Governments	524	3	0.1
Taxes			
Property	326,574	1,761	36.7
Sales and Gross Receipts	5,053	27	0.6
Personal Income	0	0	0.0
Corporate Income	0	0	0.0
Motor Vehicle License	0	0	0.0
Other Taxes	7,443	40	0.8
Current Charges	66,817	360	7.5
Liquor Store	0	0	0.0
Utility	29,571	159	3.3

Source: U.S. Census Bureau, State & Local Government Finances 2020

City Government Expenditures by Function

Function	2020 ($000)	2020 ($ per capita)	2020 (%)
General Direct Expenditures			
Air Transportation	0	0	0.0
Corrections	0	0	0.0
Education	491,734	2,651	53.1
Employment Security Administration	0	0	0.0
Financial Administration	3,755	20	0.4
Fire Protection	41,593	224	4.5
General Public Buildings	15,998	86	1.7
Governmental Administration, Other	5,908	31	0.6
Health	3,668	19	0.4
Highways	24,889	134	2.7
Hospitals	0	0	0.0
Housing and Community Development	9,172	49	1.0
Interest on General Debt	28,752	155	3.1
Judicial and Legal	1,155	6	0.1
Libraries	6,534	35	0.7
Parking	2,765	14	0.3
Parks and Recreation	7,036	37	0.8
Police Protection	52,671	284	5.7
Public Welfare	1,851	10	0.2
Sewerage	50,110	270	5.4
Solid Waste Management	6,555	35	0.7
Veterans' Services	0	0	0.0
Liquor Store	0	0	0.0
Utility	29,777	160	3.2

Source: U.S. Census Bureau, State & Local Government Finances 2020

TAXES

State Corporate Income Tax Rates

State	Tax Rate (%)	Income Brackets ($)	Num. of Brackets	Financial Institution Tax Rate (%)[a]	Federal Income Tax Ded.
Massachusetts	8.0 (k)	Flat rate	1	9.0 (k)	No

Note: Tax rates as of January 1, 2023; (a) Rates listed are the corporate income tax rate applied to financial institutions or excise taxes based on income. Some states have other taxes based upon the value of deposits or shares; (k) Business and manufacturing corporations pay an additional tax of $2.60 per $1,000 on either taxable Massachusetts tangible property or taxable net worth allocable to the state (for intangible property corporations). The minimum tax for both corporations and financial institutions is $456.
Source: Federation of Tax Administrators, State Corporate Income Tax Rates, January 1, 2023

State Individual Income Tax Rates

State	Tax Rate (%)	Income Brackets ($)	Personal Exemptions ($)			Standard Ded. ($)	
			Single	Married	Depend.	Single	Married
Massachusetts	5.0 (m)	Flat rate	4,400	8,800	1,000	–	–

Note: Tax rates as of January 1, 2023; Local- and county-level taxes are not included; Federal income tax is not deductible on state income tax returns; (m) Short-term capital gains in Massachusetts istaxed at 12% rate. An additional tax of 4% on income of $1 million.
Source: Federation of Tax Administrators, State Individual Income Tax Rates, January 1, 2023

Various State Sales and Excise Tax Rates

State	State Sales Tax (%)	Gasoline[1] ($/gal.)	Cigarette[2] ($/pack)	Spirits[3] ($/gal.)	Wine[4] ($/gal.)	Beer[5] ($/gal.)	Recreational Marijuana (%)
Massachusetts	6.25	0.2654	3.51	4.05	0.55	0.11	(h)

Note: All tax rates as of January 1, 2023; (1) The American Petroleum Institute has developed a methodology for determining the average tax rate on a gallon of fuel. Rates may include any of the following: excise taxes, environmental fees, storage tank fees, other fees or taxes, general sales tax, and local taxes; (2) The federal excise tax of $1.0066 per pack and local taxes are not included; (3) Rates are those applicable to off-premise sales of 40% alcohol by volume (a.b.v.) distilled spirits in 750ml containers. Local excise taxes are excluded; (4) Rates are those applicable to off-premise sales of 11% a.b.v. non-carbonated wine in 750ml containers; (5) Rates are those applicable to off-premise sales of 4.7% a.b.v. beer in 12 ounce containers; (h) 10.75% excise tax (retail price)
Source: Tax Foundation, 2023 Facts & Figures: How Does Your State Compare?

State Business Tax Climate Index Rankings

State	Overall Rank	Corporate Tax Rank	Individual Income Tax Rank	Sales Tax Rank	Property Tax Rank	Unemployment Insurance Tax Rank
Massachusetts	34	36	11	13	46	50

Note: The index is a measure of how each state's tax laws affect economic performance. The lower the rank, the more favorable a state's tax system is for business. States without a given tax are given a ranking of 1. The scores/rankings for the District of Columbia do not affect other states. The 2023 index represents the tax climate as of July 1, 2022.
Source: Tax Foundation, State Business Tax Climate Index 2023

TRANSPORTATION

Means of Transportation to Work

Area	Car/Truck/Van		Public Transportation			Bicycle	Walked	Other Means	Worked at Home
	Drove Alone	Car-pooled	Bus	Subway	Railroad				
City	68.3	11.4	1.9	0.2	0.6	0.2	6.2	2.9	8.3
MSA[1]	76.2	7.6	0.7	0.2	0.7	0.2	2.6	1.7	10.2
U.S.	73.2	8.6	2.0	1.6	0.5	0.5	2.5	1.5	9.7

Note: Figures are percentages and cover workers 16 years of age and older; (1) Figures cover the Worcester, MA-CT Metropolitan Statistical Area
Source: U.S. Census Bureau, 2017-2021 American Community Survey 5-Year Estimates

Travel Time to Work

Area	Less Than 10 Minutes	10 to 19 Minutes	20 to 29 Minutes	30 to 44 Minutes	45 to 59 Minutes	60 to 89 Minutes	90 Minutes or More
City	13.4	34.6	19.5	17.8	5.9	6.3	2.5
MSA[1]	12.3	26.0	18.5	20.6	10.4	8.5	3.8
U.S.	12.4	28.5	21.0	20.9	8.2	6.2	2.9

Note: Note: Figures are percentages and include workers 16 years old and over; (1) Figures cover the Worcester, MA-CT Metropolitan Statistical Area
Source: U.S. Census Bureau, 2017-2021 American Community Survey 5-Year Estimates

Key Congestion Measures

Measure	1990	2000	2010	2015	2020
Annual Hours of Delay, Total (000)	3,809	7,552	10,514	12,228	8,922
Annual Hours of Delay, Per Auto Commuter	21	34	39	41	28
Annual Congestion Cost, Per Auto Commuter ($)	448	670	742	799	603

Note: Covers the Worcester MA-CT urban area
Source: Texas A&M Transportation Institute, 2021 Urban Mobility Report

Freeway Travel Time Index

Measure	1985	1990	1995	2000	2005	2010	2015	2020
Urban Area Index[1]	1.04	1.07	1.09	1.11	1.12	1.13	1.14	1.10
Urban Area Rank[1,2]	81	74	77	79	86	82	79	29

Note: Freeway Travel Time Index—the ratio of travel time in the peak period to the travel time at free-flow conditions. For example, a value of 1.30 indicates a 20-minute free-flow trip takes 26 minutes in the peak (20 minutes x 1.30 = 26 minutes); (1) Covers the Worcester MA-CT urban area; (2) Rank is based on 101 larger urban areas (#1 = highest travel time index)
Source: Texas A&M Transportation Institute, 2021 Urban Mobility Report

Public Transportation

Agency Name / Mode of Transportation	Vehicles Operated in Maximum Service[1]	Annual Unlinked Passenger Trips[2] (in thous.)	Annual Passenger Miles[3] (in thous.)
Worcester Regional Transit Authority			
Bus (directly operated)	42	2,196.1	9,368.2
Demand Response (directly operated)	10	25.6	117.1
Demand Response (purchased transportation)	32	47.8	292.8
Demand Response - Taxi	10	24.9	110.0

Note: (1) Number of revenue vehicles operated by the given mode and type of service to meet the annual maximum service requirement. This is the revenue vehicle count during the peak season of the year; on the week and day that maximum service is provided. Vehicles operated in maximum service (VOMS) exclude atypical days and one-time special events; (2) Number of passengers who boarded public transportation vehicles. Passengers are counted each time they board a vehicle no matter how many vehicles they use to travel from their origin to their destination. (3) Sum of the distances ridden by all passengers during the entire fiscal year. Source: Federal Transit Administration, National Transit Database, 2021

Air Transportation

Airport Name and Code / Type of Service	Passenger Airlines[1]	Passenger Enplanements	Freight Carriers[2]	Freight (lbs)
Worcester Regional Airport (ORH)				
Domestic service (U.S. carriers - 2022)	7	80,067	0	0
International service (U.S. carriers - 2021)	0	0	0	0
Boston Logan International Airport (50 miles) (BOS)				
Domestic service (U.S. carriers - 2022)	30	14,486,034	16	193,066,841
International service (U.S. carriers - 2021)	7	441,953	5	5,757,968

Note: (1) Includes all U.S.-based major, minor and commuter airlines that carried at least one passenger during the year; (2) Includes all U.S.-based airlines and freight carriers that transported at least one pound of freight during the year. Source: Bureau of Transportation Statistics, The Intermodal Transportation Database, Air Carriers: T-100 Domestic Market (U.S. Carriers), 2022; Bureau of Transportation Statistics, The Intermodal Transportation Database, Air Carriers: T-100 International Market (U.S. Carriers), 2021

BUSINESSES

Major Business Headquarters

Company Name	Industry	Rankings	
		Fortune[1]	Forbes[2]
No companies listed	-	-	-

Note: (1) Companies that produce a 10-K are ranked 1 to 500 based on 2021 revenue; (2) All private companies with at least $2 billion in annual revenue through the end of their most current fiscal year are ranked 1 to 246; companies listed are headquartered in the city; dashes indicate no ranking Source: Fortune, "Fortune 500," 2022; Forbes, "America's Largest Private Companies," 2022

Fastest-Growing Businesses

According to *Inc.*, Worcester is home to one of America's 500 fastest-growing private companies: **Solvus Global** (#293). Criteria: must be an independent, privately-held, for-profit, U.S. corporation, proprietorship or partnership as of December 31, 2021; revenues must be at least $100,000 in 2018 and $2 million in 2021; must have four-year operating/sales history. *Inc., "America's 500 Fastest-Growing Private Companies," 2022*

Living Environment

COST OF LIVING

Cost of Living Index

Composite Index	Groceries	Housing	Utilities	Trans-portation	Health Care	Misc. Goods/Services
n/a	n/a	n/a	n/a	n/a	n/a	n/a

Note: The Cost of Living Index measures regional differences in the cost of consumer goods and services, excluding taxes and non-consumer expenditures, for professional and managerial households in the top income quintile. It is based on more than 50,000 prices covering almost 60 different items for which prices are collected three times a year by chambers of commerce, economic development organizations or university applied economic centers in each participating urban area. The numbers shown should be read as a percentage above or below the national average of 100. For example, a value of 115.4 in the groceries column indicates that grocery prices are 15.4% higher than the national average. Small differences in the index numbers should not be interpreted as significant; n/a not available.
Source: The Council for Community and Economic Research, Cost of Living Index, 2022

Grocery Prices

Area[1]	T-Bone Steak ($/pound)	Frying Chicken ($/pound)	Whole Milk ($/half gal.)	Eggs ($/dozen)	Orange Juice ($/64 oz.)	Coffee ($/11.5 oz.)
City[2]	n/a	n/a	n/a	n/a	n/a	n/a
Avg.	13.81	1.59	2.43	2.25	3.85	4.95
Min.	10.17	0.90	1.51	1.30	2.90	3.46
Max.	19.35	3.30	4.32	4.32	5.31	8.59

*Note: (1) Values for the local area are compared with the average, minimum and maximum values for all 286 areas in the Cost of Living Index; (2) Figures cover the Worcester MA urban area; n/a not available; **T-Bone Steak** (price per pound); **Frying Chicken** (price per pound, whole fryer); **Whole Milk** (half gallon carton); **Eggs** (price per dozen, Grade A, large); **Orange Juice** (64 oz. Tropicana or Florida Natural); **Coffee** (11.5 oz. can, vacuum-packed, Maxwell House, Hills Bros, or Folgers).*
Source: The Council for Community and Economic Research, Cost of Living Index, 2022

Housing and Utility Costs

Area[1]	New Home Price ($)	Apartment Rent ($/month)	All Electric ($/month)	Part Electric ($/month)	Other Energy ($/month)	Telephone ($/month)
City[2]	n/a	n/a	n/a	n/a	n/a	n/a
Avg.	450,913	1,371	176.41	99.93	76.96	190.22
Min.	229,283	546	100.84	31.56	27.15	174.27
Max.	2,434,977	4,569	356.86	249.59	272.24	208.31

*Note: (1) Values for the local area are compared with the average, minimum and maximum values for all 286 areas in the Cost of Living Index; (2) Figures cover the Worcester MA urban area; n/a not available; **New Home Price** (2,400 sf living area, 8,000 sf lot, in urban area with full utilities); **Apartment Rent** (950 sf 2 bedroom/1.5 or 2 bath, unfurnished, excluding all utilities except water); **All Electric** (average monthly cost for an all-electric home); **Part Electric** (average monthly cost for a part-electric home); **Other Energy** (average monthly cost for natural gas, fuel oil, coal, wood, and any other forms of energy except electricity); **Telephone** (price includes the base monthly rate plus taxes and fees for three lines of mobile phone service).*
Source: The Council for Community and Economic Research, Cost of Living Index, 2022

Health Care, Transportation, and Other Costs

Area[1]	Doctor ($/visit)	Dentist ($/visit)	Optometrist ($/visit)	Gasoline ($/gallon)	Beauty Salon ($/visit)	Men's Shirt ($)
City[2]	n/a	n/a	n/a	n/a	n/a	n/a
Avg.	124.91	107.77	117.66	3.86	43.31	34.21
Min.	36.61	58.25	51.79	2.90	22.18	13.05
Max.	250.21	162.58	371.96	5.54	85.61	63.54

*Note: (1) Values for the local area are compared with the average, minimum and maximum values for all 286 areas in the Cost of Living Index; (2) Figures cover the Worcester MA urban area; n/a not available; **Doctor** (general practitioners routine exam of an established patient); **Dentist** (adult teeth cleaning and periodic oral examination); **Optometrist** (full vision eye exam for established adult patient); **Gasoline** (one gallon regular unleaded, national brand, including all taxes, cash price at self-service pump if available); **Beauty Salon** (woman's shampoo, trim, and blow-dry); **Men's Shirt** (cotton/polyester dress shirt, pinpoint weave, long sleeves).*
Source: The Council for Community and Economic Research, Cost of Living Index, 2022

HOUSING

Homeownership Rate

Area	2015 (%)	2016 (%)	2017 (%)	2018 (%)	2019 (%)	2020 (%)	2021 (%)	2022 (%)
MSA[1]	64.2	65.5	64.9	63.4	62.7	65.9	68.7	64.8
U.S.	63.7	63.4	63.9	64.4	64.6	66.6	65.5	65.8

Note: (1) Figures cover the Worcester, MA-CT Metropolitan Statistical Area
Source: U.S. Census Bureau, Housing Vacancies and Homeownership Annual Statistics: 2015-2022

House Price Index (HPI)

Area	National Ranking[2]	Quarterly Change (%)	One-Year Change (%)	Five-Year Change (%)	Since 1991Q1 (%)
MSA[1]	184	-1.36	9.48	52.36	218.67
U.S.[3]	–	0.34	8.41	58.44	289.08

Note: The HPI is a weighted repeat sales index. It measures average price changes in repeat sales or refinancings on the same properties. This information is obtained by reviewing repeat mortgage transactions on single-family properties whose mortgages have been purchased or securitized by Fannie Mae or Freddie Mac since January 1975; (1) Figures cover the Worcester, MA-CT Metropolitan Statistical Area; (2) Rankings are based on annual percentage change for all metro areas containing at least 15,000 transactions over the last 10 years and ranges from 1 to 257; (3) figures based on a weighted average of Census Division estimates using a seasonally adjusted, purchase-only index; all figures are for the period ending December 31, 2022
Source: Federal Housing Finance Agency, Change in FHFA Metropolitan Area House Price Indexes, 2022Q4

Median Single-Family Home Prices

Area	2020	2021	2022p	Percent Change 2021 to 2022
MSA[1]	325.2	371.7	409.1	10.1
U.S. Average	300.2	357.1	392.6	9.9

Note: Figures are median sales prices of existing single-family homes in thousands of dollars; (p) preliminary; (1) Figures cover the Worcester, MA-CT Metropolitan Statistical Area
Source: National Association of Realtors, Median Sales Price of Existing Single-Family Homes for Metropolitan Areas, 4th Quarter 2022

Qualifying Income Based on Median Sales Price of Existing Single-Family Homes

Area	With 5% Down ($)	With 10% Down ($)	With 20% Down ($)
MSA[1]	119,075	112,808	100,274
U.S. Average	112,234	106,237	94,513

Note: Figures are preliminary; Qualifying income is based on a mortgage rate of 6.77%. Monthly principal and interest payment is limited to 25% of income; (1) Figures cover the Worcester, MA-CT Metropolitan Statistical Area
Source: National Association of Realtors, Qualifying Income Based on Median Sales Price of Existing Single-Family Homes for Metropolitan Areas, 4th Quarter 2022

Home Value

Area	Under $100,000	$100,000 -$199,999	$200,000 -$299,999	$300,000 -$399,999	$400,000 -$499,999	$500,000 -$999,999	$1,000,000 or more	Median ($)
City	4.7	20.1	40.8	22.2	6.8	4.6	0.9	259,800
MSA[1]	3.6	16.4	30.3	22.9	12.3	13.1	1.3	298,900
U.S.	16.2	24.2	20.1	13.6	8.3	13.6	4.1	244,900

Note: Figures are percentages except for median and cover owner-occupied housing units; (1) Figures cover the Worcester, MA-CT Metropolitan Statistical Area
Source: U.S. Census Bureau, 2017-2021 American Community Survey 5-Year Estimates

Year Housing Structure Built

Area	2020 or Later	2010 -2019	2000 -2009	1990 -1999	1980 -1989	1970 -1979	1960 -1969	1950 -1959	1940 -1949	Before 1940	Median Year
City	0.0	2.1	4.6	5.2	10.1	7.9	7.8	11.6	7.5	43.3	1949
MSA[1]	0.1	3.8	8.7	9.5	12.4	11.3	8.9	11.0	5.6	28.9	1965
U.S.	0.2	7.3	13.6	13.6	13.2	14.8	10.3	10.0	4.7	12.2	1979

Note: Figures are percentages except for Median Year; Note: (1) Figures cover the Worcester, MA-CT Metropolitan Statistical Area
Source: U.S. Census Bureau, 2017-2021 American Community Survey 5-Year Estimates

Gross Monthly Rent

Area	Under $500	$500 -$999	$1,000 -$1,499	$1,500 -$1,999	$2,000 -$2,499	$2,500 -$2,999	$3,000 and up	Median ($)
City	13.8	21.1	41.4	18.7	3.6	0.7	0.7	1,179
MSA[1]	13.2	26.4	37.7	15.9	4.7	1.2	1.0	1,126
U.S.	8.1	30.5	30.8	16.8	7.3	3.1	3.5	1,163

Note: Figures are percentages except for median; Gross rent is the contract rent plus the estimated average monthly cost of utilities (electricity, gas, and water and sewer) and fuels (oil, coal, kerosene, wood, etc.) if these are paid by the renter (or paid for the renter by someone else); (1) Figures cover the Worcester, MA-CT Metropolitan Statistical Area
Source: U.S. Census Bureau, 2017-2021 American Community Survey 5-Year Estimates

552 Worcester, Massachusetts

HEALTH

Health Risk Factors

Category	MSA[1] (%)	U.S. (%)
Adults aged 18–64 who have any kind of health care coverage	96.0	90.9
Adults who reported being in good or better health	85.1	85.2
Adults who have been told they have high blood cholesterol	31.5	35.7
Adults who have been told they have high blood pressure	29.4	32.4
Adults who are current smokers	11.3	14.4
Adults who currently use e-cigarettes	4.8	6.7
Adults who currently use chewing tobacco, snuff, or snus	2.5	3.5
Adults who are heavy drinkers[2]	6.9	6.3
Adults who are binge drinkers[3]	15.2	15.4
Adults who are overweight (BMI 25.0 - 29.9)	33.5	34.4
Adults who are obese (BMI 30.0 - 99.8)	32.5	33.9
Adults who participated in any physical activities in the past month	79.5	76.3

Note: (1) Figures cover the Worcester, MA-CT Metropolitan Statistical Area; (2) Heavy drinkers are classified as adult men having more than 14 drinks per week and adult women having more than 7 drinks per week; (3) Binge drinkers are classified as males having five or more drinks on one occasion or females having four or more drinks on one occasion
Source: Centers for Disease Control and Prevention, Behaviorial Risk Factor Surveillance System, SMART: Selected Metropolitan Area Risk Trends, 2021

Acute and Chronic Health Conditions

Category	MSA[1] (%)	U.S. (%)
Adults who have ever been told they had a heart attack	3.8	4.0
Adults who have ever been told they have angina or coronary heart disease	2.2	3.8
Adults who have ever been told they had a stroke	2.3	3.0
Adults who have ever been told they have asthma	19.6	14.9
Adults who have ever been told they have arthritis	27.3	25.8
Adults who have ever been told they have diabetes[2]	10.7	10.9
Adults who have ever been told they had skin cancer	6.0	6.6
Adults who have ever been told they had any other types of cancer	8.5	7.5
Adults who have ever been told they have COPD	6.2	6.1
Adults who have ever been told they have kidney disease	3.1	3.0
Adults who have ever been told they have a form of depression	20.3	20.5

Note: (1) Figures cover the Worcester, MA-CT Metropolitan Statistical Area; (2) Figures do not include pregnancy-related, borderline, or pre-diabetes
Source: Centers for Disease Control and Prevention, Behaviorial Risk Factor Surveillance System, SMART: Selected Metropolitan Area Risk Trends, 2021

Health Screening and Vaccination Rates

Category	MSA[1] (%)	U.S. (%)
Adults who have ever been tested for HIV	36.1	34.9
Adults who have had their blood cholesterol checked within the last five years	89.1	85.2
Adults aged 65+ who have had flu shot within the past year	70.5	68.6
Adults aged 65+ who have ever had a pneumonia vaccination	70.7	71.0

Note: (1) Figures cover the Worcester, MA-CT Metropolitan Statistical Area.
Source: Centers for Disease Control and Prevention, Behaviorial Risk Factor Surveillance System, SMART: Selected Metropolitan Area Risk Trends, 2021

Disability Status

Category	MSA[1] (%)	U.S. (%)
Adults who reported being deaf	8.3	7.2
Are you blind or have serious difficulty seeing, even when wearing glasses?	2.8	4.8
Are you limited in any way in any of your usual activities due to arthritis?	10.5	11.1
Do you have difficulty doing errands alone?	7.2	7.0
Do you have difficulty dressing or bathing?	3.5	3.6
Do you have serious difficulty concentrating/remembering/making decisions?	13.0	12.1
Do you have serious difficulty walking or climbing stairs?	10.5	12.8

Note: (1) Figures cover the Worcester, MA-CT Metropolitan Statistical Area.
Source: Centers for Disease Control and Prevention, Behaviorial Risk Factor Surveillance System, SMART: Selected Metropolitan Area Risk Trends, 2021

Mortality Rates for the Top 10 Causes of Death in the U.S.

ICD-10[a] Sub-Chapter	ICD-10[a] Code	Crude Mortality Rate[1] per 100,000 population	
		County[2]	U.S.
Malignant neoplasms	C00-C97	179.4	182.6
Ischaemic heart diseases	I20-I25	85.0	113.1
Other forms of heart disease	I30-I51	70.5	64.4
Other degenerative diseases of the nervous system	G30-G31	26.6	51.0
Cerebrovascular diseases	I60-I69	34.1	47.8
Other external causes of accidental injury	W00-X59	58.6	46.4
Chronic lower respiratory diseases	J40-J47	43.5	45.7
Organic, including symptomatic, mental disorders	F01-F09	81.2	35.9
Hypertensive diseases	I10-I15	20.2	35.0
Diabetes mellitus	E10-E14	21.1	29.6

Note: (a) ICD-10 = International Classification of Diseases 10th Revision; (1) Crude mortality rates are a three-year average covering 2019-2021; (2) Figures cover Worcester County.
Source: Centers for Disease Control and Prevention, National Center for Health Statistics. National Vital Statistics System, Mortality 2018-2021 on CDC WONDER Online Database

Mortality Rates for Selected Causes of Death

ICD-10[a] Sub-Chapter	ICD-10[a] Code	Crude Mortality Rate[1] per 100,000 population	
		County[2]	U.S.
Assault	X85-Y09	1.8	7.0
Diseases of the liver	K70-K76	17.2	19.8
Human immunodeficiency virus (HIV) disease	B20-B24	Unreliable	1.5
Influenza and pneumonia	J09-J18	17.2	14.7
Intentional self-harm	X60-X84	9.5	14.3
Malnutrition	E40-E46	2.3	4.3
Obesity and other hyperalimentation	E65-E68	2.4	3.0
Renal failure	N17-N19	15.7	15.7
Transport accidents	V01-V99	6.2	13.6
Viral hepatitis	B15-B19	1.0	1.2

Note: (a) ICD-10 = International Classification of Diseases 10th Revision; (1) Crude mortality rates are a three-year average covering 2019-2021; (2) Figures cover Worcester County; Data are suppressed when the data meet the criteria for confidentiality constraints; Crude mortality rates are flagged as unreliable when the rate would be calculated with a numerator of 20 or less.
Source: Centers for Disease Control and Prevention, National Center for Health Statistics. National Vital Statistics System, Mortality 2018-2021 on CDC WONDER Online Database

Health Insurance Coverage

Area	With Health Insurance	With Private Health Insurance	With Public Health Insurance	Without Health Insurance	Population Under Age 19 Without Health Insurance
City	97.0	61.1	46.4	3.0	1.5
MSA[1]	97.4	73.0	37.5	2.6	1.3
U.S.	91.2	67.8	35.4	8.8	5.3

Note: Figures are percentages that cover the civilian noninstitutionalized population; (1) Figures cover the Worcester, MA-CT Metropolitan Statistical Area
Source: U.S. Census Bureau, 2017-2021 American Community Survey 5-Year Estimates

Number of Medical Professionals

Area	MDs[3]	DOs[3,4]	Dentists	Podiatrists	Chiropractors	Optometrists
County[1] (number)	3,106	164	650	57	171	163
County[1] (rate[2])	360.6	19.0	75.4	6.6	19.8	18.9
U.S. (rate[2])	289.3	23.5	72.5	6.2	28.7	17.4

Note: Data as of 2021 unless noted; (1) Data covers Worcester County; (2) Rate per 100,000 population; (3) Data as of 2020 and includes all active, non-federal physicians; (4) Doctor of Osteopathic Medicine
Source: U.S. Department of Health and Human Services, Health Resources and Services Administration, Bureau of Health Professions, Area Resource File (ARF) 2021-2022

EDUCATION

Public School District Statistics

District Name	Schls	Pupils	Pupil/ Teacher Ratio	Minority Pupils[1] (%)	LEP/ELL[2] (%)	IEP[3] (%)
WORCESTER	46	23,735	12.2	72.1	29.6	21.8

Note: Table includes school districts with 2,000 or more students; (1) Percentage of students that are not non-Hispanic white; (2) Percentage of students that are Limited English Proficient or English Language Learners (2018-19); (3) Percentage of students that have an Individualized Education Program (2019-20).
Source: U.S. Department of Education, National Center for Education Statistics, Common Core of Data, Local Education Agency (School District) Universe Survey: School Year 2021-2022

Highest Level of Education

Area	Less than H.S.	H.S. Diploma	Some College, No Deg.	Associate Degree	Bachelor's Degree	Master's Degree	Prof. School Degree	Doctorate Degree
City	14.2	28.3	17.1	8.2	19.2	8.8	2.0	2.3
MSA[1]	8.7	27.8	17.9	9.2	21.5	11.4	1.8	1.8
U.S.	11.1	26.5	20.0	8.7	20.6	9.3	2.2	1.5

Note: Figures cover persons age 25 and over; (1) Figures cover the Worcester, MA-CT Metropolitan Statistical Area
Source: U.S. Census Bureau, 2017-2021 American Community Survey 5-Year Estimates

Educational Attainment by Race

Area	High School Graduate or Higher (%)					Bachelor's Degree or Higher (%)				
	Total	White	Black	Asian	Hisp.[2]	Total	White	Black	Asian	Hisp.[2]
City	85.8	88.9	89.5	74.9	69.5	32.2	33.9	31.7	41.7	13.9
MSA[1]	91.3	92.9	89.3	85.0	73.7	36.4	36.4	34.4	59.8	16.6
U.S.	88.9	91.4	87.2	87.6	71.2	33.7	35.5	23.3	55.6	18.4

Note: Figures shown cover persons 25 years old and over; (1) Figures cover the Worcester, MA-CT Metropolitan Statistical Area; (2) People of Hispanic origin can be of any race
Source: U.S. Census Bureau, 2017-2021 American Community Survey 5-Year Estimates

School Enrollment by Grade and Control

Area	Preschool (%)		Kindergarten (%)		Grades 1 - 4 (%)		Grades 5 - 8 (%)		Grades 9 - 12 (%)	
	Public	Private	Public	Private	Public	Private	Public	Private	Public	Private
City	54.7	45.3	96.0	4.0	93.5	6.5	92.0	8.0	88.1	11.9
MSA[1]	59.0	41.0	91.1	8.9	92.2	7.8	90.6	9.4	90.5	9.5
U.S.	58.8	41.2	86.3	13.7	88.3	11.7	88.6	11.4	89.4	10.6

Note: Figures shown cover persons 3 years old and over; (1) Figures cover the Worcester, MA-CT Metropolitan Statistical Area
Source: U.S. Census Bureau, 2017-2021 American Community Survey 5-Year Estimates

Higher Education

Four-Year Colleges			Two-Year Colleges			Medical Schools[1]	Law Schools[2]	Voc/ Tech[3]
Public	Private Non-profit	Private For-profit	Public	Private Non-profit	Private For-profit			
4	6	0	3	0	0	1	0	8

Note: Figures cover institutions located within the Worcester, MA-CT Metropolitan Statistical Area and include main campuses only; (1) includes schools accredited by the Liaison Committee on Medical Education and the American Osteopathic Association's Commission on Osteopathic College Accreditation; (2) includes ABA-accredited schools, schools with provisional ABA accreditation, and state accredited schools; (3) includes all schools with programs that are less than 2 years.
Source: National Center for Education Statistics, Integrated Postsecondary Education System (IPEDS), 2021-22; Wikipedia, List of Medical Schools in the United States, accessed April 10, 2023; Wikipedia, List of Law Schools in the United States, accessed April 10, 2023

According to *U.S. News & World Report,* the Worcester, MA-CT metro area is home to two of the top 200 national universities in the U.S.: **Worcester Polytechnic Institute** (#67 tie); **Clark University** (#97 tie). The indicators used to capture academic quality fall into a number of categories: assessment by administrators at peer institutions; retention of students; faculty resources; student selectivity; financial resources; alumni giving; high school counselor ratings of colleges; and graduation rate. *U.S. News & World Report, "America's Best Colleges 2023"*

According to *U.S. News & World Report,* the Worcester, MA-CT metro area is home to one of the top 100 liberal arts colleges in the U.S.: **College of the Holy Cross** (#33 tie). The indicators used to capture academic quality fall into a number of categories: assessment by administrators at peer institutions; retention of students; faculty resources; student selectivity; financial resources; alumni giving; high school counselor ratings of colleges; and graduation rate. *U.S. News & World Report, "America's Best Colleges 2023"*

According to *U.S. News & World Report,* the Worcester, MA-CT metro area is home to one of the top 75 medical schools for research in the U.S.: **University of Massachusetts Chan Medical School** (#47 tie). The rankings are based on a weighted average of 11 measures of quality: quality assessment; peer assessment score; assessment score by residency directors; research activity; total research activity; average research activity per faculty member; student selectivity; median MCAT total score; median undergraduate GPA; acceptance rate; and faculty resources. *U.S. News & World Report, "America's Best Graduate Schools, Medical, 2023"*

EMPLOYERS

Major Employers

Company Name	Industry
3M Company	Manufacturer
Abb Vie Bioresearch Center	Pharmaceutical research & development
Abrasives Marketing Group	Marketing
Affiliated Podiatrists	Healthcare
Allegro Micro Systems Inc	Manufacturer
Amica Mutual Insurance Co	Insurance
Assumption College	Education
AstraZeneca Pharmaceuticals	Pharmaceutical research & development
Babcock Power Environmental	Utility
BJ's Wholesale Club	Retail
BNY Mellon Wealth Management	Financial services
College of the Holy Cross	Education
Commerce Insurance Co	Insurance
Community Healthlink	Healthcare
Hanover Insurance Co	Insurance
Hanover Insurance Group	Insurance
Integrated Genetics	Lab testing
Mapfre USA Corp	Insurance
Mt Wachusett Ski Area	Ski resort
PNC Global Investment Servicing	Financial services
Saint-Gobain Abrasives	Manufacturer
Saint-Gobain Ceramic Materials	Manufacturer
St. Vincent Hospital	Healthcare
VNA Care Network	Healthcare
Wachusett Mountain	Ski resort

Note: Companies shown are located within the Worcester, MA-CT Metropolitan Statistical Area.
Source: Hoovers.com; Wikipedia

PUBLIC SAFETY

Crime Rate

Area	Total Crime	Violent Crime Rate				Property Crime Rate		
		Murder	Rape[3]	Robbery	Aggrav. Assault	Burglary	Larceny -Theft	Motor Vehicle Theft
City	2,631.3	5.4	21.6	113.6	491.8	360.8	1,396.3	241.8
Suburbs[1]	922.7	0.4	32.3	16.3	166.2	115.4	522.3	69.7
Metro[2]	1,285.0	1.5	30.1	36.9	235.2	167.5	707.6	106.2
U.S.	2,356.7	6.5	38.4	73.9	279.7	314.2	1,398.0	246.0

Note: Figures are crimes per 100,000 population; (1) All areas within the metro area that are located outside the city limits; (2) Figures cover the Worcester, MA-CT Metropolitan Statistical Area; (3) All figures shown were reported using the revised Uniform Crime Reporting (UCR) definition of rape; Due to the transition to the National Incident-Based Reporting System (NIBRS), limited city and metro area data was released for 2021.
Source: FBI Uniform Crime Reports, 2020

Hate Crimes

Area	Number of Quarters Reported	Number of Incidents per Bias Motivation					
		Race/Ethnicity/ Ancestry	Religion	Sexual Orientation	Disability	Gender	Gender Identity
City	4	2	3	1	0	0	0
U.S.	4	5,227	1,244	1,110	130	75	266

Note: Due to the transition to the National Incident-Based Reporting System (NIBRS), limited crime data was released for 2021.
Source: Federal Bureau of Investigation, Hate Crime Statistics 2020

Identity Theft Consumer Reports

Area	Reports	Reports per 100,000 Population	Rank[2]
MSA[1]	1,559	165	216
U.S.	1,108,609	339	-

Note: (1) Figures cover the Worcester, MA-CT Metropolitan Statistical Area; (2) Rank ranges from 1 to 391 where 1 indicates greatest number of identity theft reports per 100,000 population
Source: Federal Trade Commission, Consumer Sentinel Network Data Book 2022

Fraud and Other Consumer Reports

Area	Reports	Reports per 100,000 Population	Rank[2]
MSA[1]	7,659	812	210
U.S.	4,064,520	1,245	-

Note: (1) Figures cover the Worcester, MA-CT Metropolitan Statistical Area; (2) Rank ranges from 1 to 391 where 1 indicates greatest number of fraud and other consumer reports per 100,000 population
Source: Federal Trade Commission, Consumer Sentinel Network Data Book 2022

556 Worcester, Massachusetts

POLITICS

2020 Presidential Election Results

Area	Biden	Trump	Jorgensen	Hawkins	Other
Worcester County	57.6	39.7	1.7	0.6	0.4
U.S.	51.3	46.8	1.2	0.3	0.5

Note: Results are percentages and may not add to 100% due to rounding
Source: Dave Leip's Atlas of U.S. Presidential Elections

SPORTS

Professional Sports Teams

Team Name	League	Year Established
No teams are located in the metro area		

Source: Wikipedia, Major Professional Sports Teams of the United States and Canada, April 12, 2023

CLIMATE

Average and Extreme Temperatures

Temperature	Jan	Feb	Mar	Apr	May	Jun	Jul	Aug	Sep	Oct	Nov	Dec	Yr.
Extreme High (°F)	67	67	81	91	92	98	96	97	99	85	79	70	99
Average High (°F)	32	34	42	55	66	75	79	77	69	59	47	35	56
Average Temp. (°F)	24	26	34	45	56	65	70	68	60	51	40	28	47
Average Low (°F)	16	18	25	35	46	55	61	59	51	41	32	21	38
Extreme Low (°F)	-13	-12	-6	11	28	36	43	38	30	20	6	-13	-13

Note: Figures cover the years 1949-1992
Source: National Climatic Data Center, International Station Meteorological Climate Summary, 9/96

Average Precipitation/Snowfall/Humidity

Precip./Humidity	Jan	Feb	Mar	Apr	May	Jun	Jul	Aug	Sep	Oct	Nov	Dec	Yr.
Avg. Precip. (in.)	3.6	3.4	4.1	4.0	4.3	3.7	3.7	4.1	4.0	4.1	4.5	4.1	47.6
Avg. Snowfall (in.)	16	16	11	3	Tr	0	0	0	Tr	1	4	13	62
Avg. Rel. Hum. 7am (%)	72	73	71	69	70	73	76	79	81	78	78	75	75
Avg. Rel. Hum. 4pm (%)	61	58	55	50	52	57	58	61	62	58	63	65	58

Note: Figures cover the years 1949-1992; Tr = Trace amounts (<0.05 in. of rain; <0.5 in. of snow)
Source: National Climatic Data Center, International Station Meteorological Climate Summary, 9/96

Weather Conditions

Temperature			Daytime Sky			Precipitation		
5°F & below	32°F & below	90°F & above	Clear	Partly cloudy	Cloudy	0.01 inch or more precip.	0.1 inch or more snow/ice	Thunder-storms
12	141	4	81	144	140	131	32	23

Note: Figures are average number of days per year and cover the years 1949-1992
Source: National Climatic Data Center, International Station Meteorological Climate Summary, 9/96

HAZARDOUS WASTE

Superfund Sites

The Worcester, MA-CT metro area is home to three sites on the EPA's Superfund National Priorities List: **Gallup's Quarry** (final); **Hocomonco Pond** (final); **Linemaster Switch Corp.** (final). There are a total of 1,165 Superfund sites with a status of proposed or final on the list in the U.S. *U.S. Environmental Protection Agency, National Priorities List, April 12, 2023*

AIR QUALITY

Air Quality Trends: Ozone

	1990	1995	2000	2005	2010	2015	2018	2019	2020	2021
MSA[1]	0.097	0.096	0.076	0.085	0.070	0.063	0.065	0.060	0.063	0.063
U.S.	0.087	0.089	0.081	0.080	0.072	0.067	0.069	0.065	0.065	0.067

Note: (1) Data covers the Worcester, MA-CT Metropolitan Statistical Area. The values shown are the composite ozone concentration averages among trend sites based on the highest fourth daily maximum 8-hour concentration in parts per million. These trends are based on sites having an adequate record of monitoring data during the trend period. Data from exceptional events are included.
Source: U.S. Environmental Protection Agency, Air Quality Monitoring Information, "Air Quality Trends by City, 1990-2021"

Air Quality Index

Area	Percent of Days when Air Quality was...[2]					AQI Statistics[2]	
	Good	Moderate	Unhealthy for Sensitive Groups	Unhealthy	Very Unhealthy	Maximum	Median
MSA[1]	81.6	17.5	0.8	0.0	0.0	140	39

Note: (1) Data covers the Worcester, MA-CT Metropolitan Statistical Area; (2) Based on 365 days with AQI data in 2021. Air Quality Index (AQI) is an index for reporting daily air quality. EPA calculates the AQI for five major air pollutants regulated by the Clean Air Act: ground-level ozone, particle pollution (aka particulate matter), carbon monoxide, sulfur dioxide, and nitrogen dioxide. The AQI runs from 0 to 500. The higher the AQI value, the greater the level of air pollution and the greater the health concern. There are six AQI categories: "Good" AQI is between 0 and 50. Air quality is considered satisfactory; "Moderate" AQI is between 51 and 100. Air quality is acceptable; "Unhealthy for Sensitive Groups" When AQI values are between 101 and 150, members of sensitive groups may experience health effects; "Unhealthy" When AQI values are between 151 and 200 everyone may begin to experience health effects; "Very Unhealthy" AQI values between 201 and 300 trigger a health alert; "Hazardous" AQI values over 300 trigger warnings of emergency conditions (not shown).
Source: U.S. Environmental Protection Agency, Air Quality Index Report, 2021

Air Quality Index Pollutants

Area	Percent of Days when AQI Pollutant was...[2]					
	Carbon Monoxide	Nitrogen Dioxide	Ozone	Sulfur Dioxide	Particulate Matter 2.5	Particulate Matter 10
MSA[1]	0.0	2.5	58.1	(3)	39.2	0.3

Note: (1) Data covers the Worcester, MA-CT Metropolitan Statistical Area; (2) Based on 365 days with AQI data in 2021. The Air Quality Index (AQI) is an index for reporting daily air quality. EPA calculates the AQI for five major air pollutants regulated by the Clean Air Act: ground-level ozone, particle pollution (also known as particulate matter), carbon monoxide, sulfur dioxide, and nitrogen dioxide. The AQI runs from 0 to 500. The higher the AQI value, the greater the level of air pollution and the greater the health concern; (3) Sulfur dioxide is no longer included in this table (as of December 8, 2021) because SO_2 concentrations tend to be very localized and not necessarily representative of broad geographical areas like counties and CBSAs.
Source: U.S. Environmental Protection Agency, Air Quality Index Report, 2021

Maximum Air Pollutant Concentrations: Particulate Matter, Ozone, CO and Lead

	Particulate Matter 10 (ug/m^3)	Particulate Matter 2.5 Wtd AM (ug/m^3)	Particulate Matter 2.5 24-Hr (ug/m^3)	Ozone (ppm)	Carbon Monoxide (ppm)	Lead (ug/m^3)
MSA[1] Level	31	9.1	19	0.068	1	n/a
NAAQS[2]	150	15	35	0.075	9	0.15
Met NAAQS[2]	Yes	Yes	Yes	Yes	Yes	n/a

Note: (1) Data covers the Worcester, MA-CT Metropolitan Statistical Area; Data from exceptional events are included; (2) National Ambient Air Quality Standards; ppm = parts per million; ug/m^3 = micrograms per cubic meter; n/a not available.
Concentrations: Particulate Matter 10 (coarse particulate)—highest second maximum 24-hour concentration; Particulate Matter 2.5 Wtd AM (fine particulate)—highest weighted annual mean concentration; Particulate Matter 2.5 24-Hour (fine particulate)—highest 98th percentile 24-hour concentration; Ozone—highest fourth daily maximum 8-hour concentration; Carbon Monoxide—highest second maximum non-overlapping 8-hour concentration; Lead—maximum running 3-month average
Source: U.S. Environmental Protection Agency, Air Quality Monitoring Information, "Air Quality Statistics by City, 2021"

Maximum Air Pollutant Concentrations: Nitrogen Dioxide and Sulfur Dioxide

	Nitrogen Dioxide AM (ppb)	Nitrogen Dioxide 1-Hr (ppb)	Sulfur Dioxide AM (ppb)	Sulfur Dioxide 1-Hr (ppb)	Sulfur Dioxide 24-Hr (ppb)
MSA[1] Level	9	44	n/a	2	n/a
NAAQS[2]	53	100	30	75	140
Met NAAQS[2]	Yes	Yes	n/a	Yes	n/a

Note: (1) Data covers the Worcester, MA-CT Metropolitan Statistical Area; Data from exceptional events are included; (2) National Ambient Air Quality Standards; ppm = parts per million; ug/m^3 = micrograms per cubic meter; n/a not available.
Concentrations: Nitrogen Dioxide AM—highest arithmetic mean concentration; Nitrogen Dioxide 1-Hr—highest 98th percentile 1-hour daily maximum concentration; Sulfur Dioxide AM—highest annual mean concentration; Sulfur Dioxide 1-Hr—highest 99th percentile 1-hour daily maximum concentration; Sulfur Dioxide 24-Hr—highest second maximum 24-hour concentration
Source: U.S. Environmental Protection Agency, Air Quality Monitoring Information, "Air Quality Statistics by City, 2021"

Appendixes

Appendix A: Comparative Statistics

Table of Contents

Demographics
Population Growth: City. A-4
Population Growth: Metro Area A-6
Male/Female Ratio: City A-8
Male/Female Ratio: Metro Area A-10
Race: City A-12
Race: Metro Area A-14
Hispanic Origin: City A-16
Hispanic Origin: Metro Area A-18
Household Size: City A-20
Household Size: Metro Area. A-22
Household Relationships: City A-24
Household Relationships: Metro Area A-26
Age: City A-28
Age: Metro Area A-30
Ancestry: City A-32
Ancestry: Metro Area. A-34
Foreign-born Population: City A-36
Foreign-born Population: Metro Area. A-38
Marital Status: City. A-40
Marital Status: Metro Area A-42
Disability by Age: City. A-44
Disability by Age: Metro Area A-46
Religious Groups by Family. A-48
Religious Groups by Tradition A-50

Economy
Gross Metropolitan Product A-52
Economic Growth A-54
Metropolitan Area Exports A-56
Building Permits: City A-58
Building Permits: Metro Area. A-60
Housing Vacancy Rates A-62
Bankruptcy Filings A-64

Income and Poverty
Income: City. A-66
Income: Metro Area A-68
Household Income Distribution: City A-70
Household Income Distribution: Metro Area A-72
Poverty Rate: City A-74
Poverty Rate: Metro Area. A-76

Employment and Earnings
Employment by Industry A-78
Labor Force, Employment and Job Growth: City A-80
Labor Force, Employment and Job Growth: Metro Area A-82
Unemployment Rate: City A-84
Unemployment Rate: Metro Area. A-86
Average Hourly Wages: Occupations A - C A-88
Average Hourly Wages: Occupations C - E A-90
Average Hourly Wages: Occupations F - J A-92
Average Hourly Wages: Occupations L - N A-94
Average Hourly Wages: Occupations N - P A-96
Average Hourly Wages: Occupations P - S. A-98

Average Hourly Wages: Occupations T - W. A-100
Means of Transportation to Work: City A-102
Means of Transportation to Work: Metro Area A-104
Travel Time to Work: City A-106
Travel Time to Work: Metro Area A-108

Election Results
2020 Presidential Election Results A-110

Housing
House Price Index (HPI). A-112
Home Value: City. A-114
Home Value: Metro Area A-116
Homeownership Rate A-118
Year Housing Structure Built: City. A-120
Year Housing Structure Built: Metro Area A-122
Gross Monthly Rent: City. A-124
Gross Monthly Rent: Metro Area A-126

Education
Highest Level of Education: City A-128
Highest Level of Education: Metro Area. A-130
School Enrollment by Grade and Control: City. A-132
School Enrollment by Grade and Control: Metro Area A-134
Educational Attainment by Race: City A-136
Educational Attainment by Race: Metro Area. A-138

Cost of Living
Cost of Living Index. A-140
Grocery Prices A-142
Housing and Utility Costs. A-144
Health Care, Transportation, and Other Costs. A-146

Health Care
Number of Medical Professionals. A-148
Health Insurance Coverage: City A-150
Health Insurance Coverage: Metro Area. A-152

Public Safety
Crime Rate: City. A-154
Crime Rate: Suburbs. A-156
Crime Rate: Metro Area. A-158

Climate
Temperature & Precipitation: Yearly Averages
  and Extremes A-160
Weather Conditions A-162

Air Quality
Air Quality Index A-164
Air Quality Index Pollutants A-166
Air Quality Trends: Ozone A-168
Maximum Air Pollutant Concentrations:
  Particulate Matter, Ozone, CO and Lead. A-170
Maximum Air Pollutant Concentrations:
  Nitrogen Dioxide and Sulfur Dioxide A-172

A-4   Appendix A: Comparative Statistics

Population Growth: City

Area	1990 Census	2000 Census	2010 Census	2020 Census	Population Growth (%)	
					1990-2020	2010-2020
Albuquerque, NM	388,375	448,607	545,852	564,559	45.4	3.4
Allentown, PA	105,066	106,632	118,032	125,845	19.8	6.6
Anchorage, AK	226,338	260,283	291,826	291,247	28.7	-0.2
Ann Arbor, MI	111,018	114,024	113,934	123,851	11.6	8.7
Athens, GA	86,561	100,266	115,452	127,315	47.1	10.3
Atlanta, GA	394,092	416,474	420,003	498,715	26.5	18.7
Austin, TX	499,053	656,562	790,390	961,855	92.7	21.7
Baltimore, MD	736,014	651,154	620,961	585,708	-20.4	-5.7
Boise City, ID	144,317	185,787	205,671	235,684	63.3	14.6
Boston, MA	574,283	589,141	617,594	675,647	17.7	9.4
Boulder, CO	87,737	94,673	97,385	108,250	23.4	11.2
Brownsville, TX	114,025	139,722	175,023	186,738	63.8	6.7
Cape Coral, FL	75,507	102,286	154,305	194,016	157.0	25.7
Cedar Rapids, IA	110,829	120,758	126,326	137,710	24.3	9.0
Charleston, SC	96,102	96,650	120,083	150,227	56.3	25.1
Charlotte, NC	428,283	540,828	731,424	874,579	104.2	19.6
Chicago, IL	2,783,726	2,896,016	2,695,598	2,746,388	-1.3	1.9
Cincinnati, OH	363,974	331,285	296,943	309,317	-15.0	4.2
Clarksville, TN	78,569	103,455	132,929	166,722	112.2	25.4
Cleveland, OH	505,333	478,403	396,815	372,624	-26.3	-6.1
College Station, TX	53,318	67,890	93,857	120,511	126.0	28.4
Colorado Springs, CO	283,798	360,890	416,427	478,961	68.8	15.0
Columbia, MO	71,069	84,531	108,500	126,254	77.6	16.4
Columbia, SC	115,475	116,278	129,272	136,632	18.3	5.7
Columbus, OH	648,656	711,470	787,033	905,748	39.6	15.1
Dallas, TX	1,006,971	1,188,580	1,197,816	1,304,379	29.5	8.9
Davenport, IA	95,705	98,359	99,685	101,724	6.3	2.0
Denver, CO	467,153	554,636	600,158	715,522	53.2	19.2
Des Moines, IA	193,569	198,682	203,433	214,133	10.6	5.3
Durham, NC	151,737	187,035	228,330	283,506	86.8	24.2
Edison, NJ	88,680	97,687	99,967	107,588	21.3	7.6
El Paso, TX	515,541	563,662	649,121	678,815	31.7	4.6
Fargo, ND	74,372	90,599	105,549	125,990	69.4	19.4
Fort Collins, CO	89,555	118,652	143,986	169,810	89.6	17.9
Fort Wayne, IN	205,671	205,727	253,691	263,886	28.3	4.0
Fort Worth, TX	448,311	534,694	741,206	918,915	105.0	24.0
Grand Rapids, MI	189,145	197,800	188,040	198,917	5.2	5.8
Greeley, CO	60,887	76,930	92,889	108,795	78.7	17.1
Green Bay, WI	96,466	102,313	104,057	107,395	11.3	3.2
Greensboro, NC	193,389	223,891	269,666	299,035	54.6	10.9
Honolulu, HI	376,465	371,657	337,256	350,964	-6.8	4.1
Houston, TX	1,697,610	1,953,631	2,099,451	2,304,580	35.8	9.8
Huntsville, AL	161,842	158,216	180,105	215,006	32.8	19.4
Indianapolis, IN	730,993	781,870	820,445	887,642	21.4	8.2
Jacksonville, FL	635,221	735,617	821,784	949,611	49.5	15.6
Kansas City, MO	434,967	441,545	459,787	508,090	16.8	10.5
Lafayette, LA	104,735	110,257	120,623	121,374	15.9	0.6
Las Cruces, NM	63,267	74,267	97,618	111,385	76.1	14.1
Las Vegas, NV	261,374	478,434	583,756	641,903	145.6	10.0
Lexington, KY	225,366	260,512	295,803	322,570	43.1	9.0
Lincoln, NE	193,629	225,581	258,379	291,082	50.3	12.7
Little Rock, AR	177,519	183,133	193,524	202,591	14.1	4.7
Los Angeles, CA	3,487,671	3,694,820	3,792,621	3,898,747	11.8	2.8
Louisville, KY	269,160	256,231	597,337	386,884	43.7	-35.2
Madison, WI	193,451	208,054	233,209	269,840	39.5	15.7

Table continued on following page.

Appendix A: Comparative Statistics   A-5

Area	1990 Census	2000 Census	2010 Census	2020 Census	Population Growth (%)	
					1990-2020	2010-2020
Manchester, NH	99,567	107,006	109,565	115,644	16.1	5.5
Miami, FL	358,843	362,470	399,457	442,241	23.2	10.7
Midland, TX	89,358	94,996	111,147	132,524	48.3	19.2
Milwaukee, WI	628,095	596,974	594,833	577,222	-8.1	-3.0
Minneapolis, MN	368,383	382,618	382,578	429,954	16.7	12.4
Nashville, TN	488,364	545,524	601,222	689,447	41.2	14.7
New Haven, CT	130,474	123,626	129,779	134,023	2.7	3.3
New Orleans, LA	496,938	484,674	343,829	383,997	-22.7	11.7
New York, NY	7,322,552	8,008,278	8,175,133	8,804,190	20.2	7.7
Oklahoma City, OK	445,065	506,132	579,999	681,054	53.0	17.4
Omaha, NE	371,972	390,007	408,958	486,051	30.7	18.9
Orlando, FL	161,172	185,951	238,300	307,573	90.8	29.1
Philadelphia, PA	1,585,577	1,517,550	1,526,006	1,603,797	1.1	5.1
Phoenix, AZ	989,873	1,321,045	1,445,632	1,608,139	62.5	11.2
Pittsburgh, PA	369,785	334,563	305,704	302,971	-18.1	-0.9
Portland, OR	485,833	529,121	583,776	652,503	34.3	11.8
Providence, RI	160,734	173,618	178,042	190,934	18.8	7.2
Provo, UT	87,148	105,166	112,488	115,162	32.1	2.4
Raleigh, NC	226,841	276,093	403,892	467,665	106.2	15.8
Reno, NV	139,950	180,480	225,221	264,165	88.8	17.3
Richmond, VA	202,783	197,790	204,214	226,610	11.7	11.0
Rochester, MN	74,151	85,806	106,769	121,395	63.7	13.7
Sacramento, CA	368,923	407,018	466,488	524,943	42.3	12.5
St. Louis, MO	396,685	348,189	319,294	301,578	-24.0	-5.5
Salem, OR	112,046	136,924	154,637	175,535	56.7	13.5
Salt Lake City, UT	159,796	181,743	186,440	199,723	25.0	7.1
San Antonio, TX	997,258	1,144,646	1,327,407	1,434,625	43.9	8.1
San Diego, CA	1,111,048	1,223,400	1,307,402	1,386,932	24.8	6.1
San Francisco, CA	723,959	776,733	805,235	873,965	20.7	8.5
San Jose, CA	784,324	894,943	945,942	1,013,240	29.2	7.1
Santa Rosa, CA	123,297	147,595	167,815	178,127	44.5	6.1
Savannah, GA	138,038	131,510	136,286	147,780	7.1	8.4
Seattle, WA	516,262	563,374	608,660	737,015	42.8	21.1
Sioux Falls, SD	102,262	123,975	153,888	192,517	88.3	25.1
Springfield, IL	108,997	111,454	116,250	114,394	5.0	-1.6
Tampa, FL	279,960	303,447	335,709	384,959	37.5	14.7
Tucson, AZ	417,942	486,699	520,116	542,629	29.8	4.3
Tulsa, OK	367,241	393,049	391,906	413,066	12.5	5.4
Tuscaloosa, AL	81,075	77,906	90,468	99,600	22.8	10.1
Virginia Beach, VA	393,069	425,257	437,994	459,470	16.9	4.9
Washington, DC	606,900	572,059	601,723	689,545	13.6	14.6
Wichita, KS	313,693	344,284	382,368	397,532	26.7	4.0
Wilmington, NC	64,609	75,838	106,476	115,451	78.7	8.4
Winston-Salem, NC	168,139	185,776	229,617	249,545	48.4	8.7
Worcester, MA	169,759	172,648	181,045	206,518	21.7	14.1
U.S.	248,709,873	281,421,906	308,745,538	331,449,281	33.3	7.4

Source: U.S. Census Bureau, 1990 Census,, 2000 Census,, 2010 Census,, 2020 Census

A-6   Appendix A: Comparative Statistics

Population Growth: Metro Area

Area	1990 Census	2000 Census	2010 Census	2020 Census	Population Growth (%)	
					1990-2020	2010-2020
Albuquerque, NM	599,416	729,649	887,077	916,528	52.9	3.3
Allentown, PA	686,666	740,395	821,173	861,889	25.5	5.0
Anchorage, AK	266,021	319,605	380,821	398,328	49.7	4.6
Ann Arbor, MI	282,937	322,895	344,791	372,258	31.6	8.0
Athens, GA	136,025	166,079	192,541	215,415	58.4	11.9
Atlanta, GA	3,069,411	4,247,981	5,268,860	6,089,815	98.4	15.6
Austin, TX	846,217	1,249,763	1,716,289	2,283,371	169.8	33.0
Baltimore, MD	2,382,172	2,552,994	2,710,489	2,844,510	19.4	4.9
Boise City, ID	319,596	464,840	616,561	764,718	139.3	24.0
Boston, MA	4,133,895	4,391,344	4,552,402	4,941,632	19.5	8.5
Boulder, CO	208,898	269,758	294,567	330,758	58.3	12.3
Brownsville, TX	260,120	335,227	406,220	421,017	61.9	3.6
Cape Coral, FL	335,113	440,888	618,754	760,822	127.0	23.0
Cedar Rapids, IA	210,640	237,230	257,940	276,520	31.3	7.2
Charleston, SC	506,875	549,033	664,607	799,636	57.8	20.3
Charlotte, NC	1,024,331	1,330,448	1,758,038	2,660,329	159.7	51.3
Chicago, IL	8,182,076	9,098,316	9,461,105	9,618,502	17.6	1.7
Cincinnati, OH	1,844,917	2,009,632	2,130,151	2,256,884	22.3	5.9
Clarksville, TN	189,277	232,000	273,949	320,535	69.3	17.0
Cleveland, OH	2,102,219	2,148,143	2,077,240	2,088,251	-0.7	0.5
College Station, TX	150,998	184,885	228,660	268,248	77.7	17.3
Colorado Springs, CO	409,482	537,484	645,613	755,105	84.4	17.0
Columbia, MO	122,010	145,666	172,786	210,864	72.8	22.0
Columbia, SC	548,325	647,158	767,598	829,470	51.3	8.1
Columbus, OH	1,405,176	1,612,694	1,836,536	2,138,926	52.2	16.5
Dallas, TX	3,989,294	5,161,544	6,371,773	7,637,387	91.4	19.9
Davenport, IA	368,151	376,019	379,690	384,324	4.4	1.2
Denver, CO	1,666,935	2,179,296	2,543,482	2,963,821	77.8	16.5
Des Moines, IA	416,346	481,394	569,633	709,466	70.4	24.5
Durham, NC	344,646	426,493	504,357	649,903	88.6	28.9
Edison, NJ	16,845,992	18,323,002	18,897,109	20,140,470	19.6	6.6
El Paso, TX	591,610	679,622	800,647	868,859	46.9	8.5
Fargo, ND	153,296	174,367	208,777	249,843	63.0	19.7
Fort Collins, CO	186,136	251,494	299,630	359,066	92.9	19.8
Fort Wayne, IN	354,435	390,156	416,257	419,601	18.4	0.8
Fort Worth, TX	3,989,294	5,161,544	6,371,773	7,637,387	91.4	19.9
Grand Rapids, MI	645,914	740,482	774,160	1,087,592	68.4	40.5
Greeley, CO	131,816	180,926	252,825	328,981	149.6	30.1
Green Bay, WI	243,698	282,599	306,241	328,268	34.7	7.2
Greensboro, NC	540,257	643,430	723,801	776,566	43.7	7.3
Honolulu, HI	836,231	876,156	953,207	1,016,508	21.6	6.6
Houston, TX	3,767,335	4,715,407	5,946,800	7,122,240	89.1	19.8
Huntsville, AL	293,047	342,376	417,593	491,723	67.8	17.8
Indianapolis, IN	1,294,217	1,525,104	1,756,241	2,111,040	63.1	20.2
Jacksonville, FL	925,213	1,122,750	1,345,596	1,605,848	73.6	19.3
Kansas City, MO	1,636,528	1,836,038	2,035,334	2,192,035	33.9	7.7
Lafayette, LA	208,740	239,086	273,738	478,384	129.2	74.8
Las Cruces, NM	135,510	174,682	209,233	219,561	62.0	4.9
Las Vegas, NV	741,459	1,375,765	1,951,269	2,265,461	205.5	16.1
Lexington, KY	348,428	408,326	472,099	516,811	48.3	9.5
Lincoln, NE	229,091	266,787	302,157	340,217	48.5	12.6
Little Rock, AR	535,034	610,518	699,757	748,031	39.8	6.9
Los Angeles, CA	11,273,720	12,365,627	12,828,837	13,200,998	17.1	2.9
Louisville, KY	1,055,973	1,161,975	1,283,566	1,285,439	21.7	0.1
Madison, WI	432,323	501,774	568,593	680,796	57.5	19.7

Table continued on following page.

Appendix A: Comparative Statistics   A-7

| Area | 1990 Census | 2000 Census | 2010 Census | 2020 Census | Population Growth (%) | |
					1990-2020	2010-2020
Manchester, NH	336,073	380,841	400,721	422,937	25.8	5.5
Miami, FL	4,056,100	5,007,564	5,564,635	6,138,333	51.3	10.3
Midland, TX	106,611	116,009	136,872	175,220	64.4	28.0
Milwaukee, WI	1,432,149	1,500,741	1,555,908	1,574,731	10.0	1.2
Minneapolis, MN	2,538,834	2,968,806	3,279,833	3,690,261	45.4	12.5
Nashville, TN	1,048,218	1,311,789	1,589,934	1,989,519	89.8	25.1
New Haven, CT	804,219	824,008	862,477	864,835	7.5	0.3
New Orleans, LA	1,264,391	1,316,510	1,167,764	1,271,845	0.6	8.9
New York, NY	16,845,992	18,323,002	18,897,109	20,140,470	19.6	6.6
Oklahoma City, OK	971,042	1,095,421	1,252,987	1,425,695	46.8	13.8
Omaha, NE	685,797	767,041	865,350	967,604	41.1	11.8
Orlando, FL	1,224,852	1,644,561	2,134,411	2,673,376	118.3	25.3
Philadelphia, PA	5,435,470	5,687,147	5,965,343	6,245,051	14.9	4.7
Phoenix, AZ	2,238,480	3,251,876	4,192,887	4,845,832	116.5	15.6
Pittsburgh, PA	2,468,289	2,431,087	2,356,285	2,370,930	-3.9	0.6
Portland, OR	1,523,741	1,927,881	2,226,009	2,512,859	64.9	12.9
Providence, RI	1,509,789	1,582,997	1,600,852	1,676,579	11.0	4.7
Provo, UT	269,407	376,774	526,810	671,185	149.1	27.4
Raleigh, NC	541,081	797,071	1,130,490	1,413,982	161.3	25.1
Reno, NV	257,193	342,885	425,417	490,596	90.8	15.3
Richmond, VA	949,244	1,096,957	1,258,251	1,314,434	38.5	4.5
Rochester, MN	141,945	163,618	186,011	226,329	59.4	21.7
Sacramento, CA	1,481,126	1,796,857	2,149,127	2,397,382	61.9	11.6
St. Louis, MO	2,580,897	2,698,687	2,812,896	2,820,253	9.3	0.3
Salem, OR	278,024	347,214	390,738	433,353	55.9	10.9
Salt Lake City, UT	768,075	968,858	1,124,197	1,257,936	63.8	11.9
San Antonio, TX	1,407,745	1,711,703	2,142,508	2,558,143	81.7	19.4
San Diego, CA	2,498,016	2,813,833	3,095,313	3,298,634	32.1	6.6
San Francisco, CA	3,686,592	4,123,740	4,335,391	4,749,008	28.8	9.5
San Jose, CA	1,534,280	1,735,819	1,836,911	2,000,468	30.4	8.9
Santa Rosa, CA	388,222	458,614	483,878	488,863	25.9	1.0
Savannah, GA	258,060	293,000	347,611	404,798	56.9	16.5
Seattle, WA	2,559,164	3,043,878	3,439,809	4,018,762	57.0	16.8
Sioux Falls, SD	153,500	187,093	228,261	276,730	80.3	21.2
Springfield, IL	189,550	201,437	210,170	208,640	10.1	-0.7
Tampa, FL	2,067,959	2,395,997	2,783,243	3,175,275	53.5	14.1
Tucson, AZ	666,880	843,746	980,263	1,043,433	56.5	6.4
Tulsa, OK	761,019	859,532	937,478	1,015,331	33.4	8.3
Tuscaloosa, AL	176,123	192,034	219,461	268,674	52.5	22.4
Virginia Beach, VA	1,449,389	1,576,370	1,671,683	1,799,674	24.2	7.7
Washington, DC	4,122,914	4,796,183	5,582,170	6,385,162	54.9	14.4
Wichita, KS	511,111	571,166	623,061	647,610	26.7	3.9
Wilmington, NC	200,124	274,532	362,315	285,905	42.9	-21.1
Winston-Salem, NC	361,091	421,961	477,717	675,966	87.2	41.5
Worcester, MA	709,728	750,963	798,552	978,529	37.9	22.5
U.S.	248,709,873	281,421,906	308,745,538	331,449,281	33.3	7.4

Note: Figures cover the Metropolitan Statistical Area (MSA)
Source: U.S. Census Bureau, 1990 Census,, 2000 Census,, 2010 Census,, 2020 Census

A-8   Appendix A: Comparative Statistics

Male/Female Ratio: City

City	Males	Females	Males per 100 Females
Albuquerque, NM	274,173	290,386	94.4
Allentown, PA	60,577	65,268	92.8
Anchorage, AK	147,894	143,353	103.2
Ann Arbor, MI	61,263	62,588	97.9
Athens, GA	59,963	67,352	89.0
Atlanta, GA	245,444	253,271	96.9
Austin, TX	485,739	476,116	102.0
Baltimore, MD	274,635	311,073	88.3
Boise City, ID	116,758	118,926	98.2
Boston, MA	319,326	356,321	89.6
Boulder, CO	55,982	52,268	107.1
Brownsville, TX	89,293	97,445	91.6
Cape Coral, FL	95,028	98,988	96.0
Cedar Rapids, IA	67,218	70,492	95.4
Charleston, SC	71,681	78,546	91.3
Charlotte, NC	421,316	453,263	93.0
Chicago, IL	1,332,725	1,413,663	94.3
Cincinnati, OH	149,736	159,581	93.8
Clarksville, TN	81,849	84,873	96.4
Cleveland, OH	180,991	191,633	94.4
College Station, TX	61,203	59,308	103.2
Colorado Springs, CO	236,731	242,230	97.7
Columbia, MO	60,766	65,488	92.8
Columbia, SC	67,155	69,477	96.7
Columbus, OH	441,869	463,879	95.3
Dallas, TX	647,963	656,416	98.7
Davenport, IA	49,751	51,973	95.7
Denver, CO	358,405	357,117	100.4
Des Moines, IA	105,618	108,515	97.3
Durham, NC	133,353	150,153	88.8
Edison, NJ	53,123	54,465	97.5
El Paso, TX	326,540	352,275	92.7
Fargo, ND	63,707	62,283	102.3
Fort Collins, CO	84,217	85,593	98.4
Fort Wayne, IN	128,678	135,208	95.2
Fort Worth, TX	449,923	468,992	95.9
Grand Rapids, MI	97,037	101,880	95.2
Greeley, CO	53,848	54,947	98.0
Green Bay, WI	53,407	53,988	98.9
Greensboro, NC	138,465	160,570	86.2
Honolulu, HI	172,783	178,181	97.0
Houston, TX	1,140,598	1,163,982	98.0
Huntsville, AL	104,200	110,806	94.0
Indianapolis, IN	430,358	457,284	94.1
Jacksonville, FL	459,204	490,407	93.6
Kansas City, MO	247,776	260,314	95.2
Lafayette, LA	58,213	63,161	92.2
Las Cruces, NM	53,571	57,814	92.7
Las Vegas, NV	317,700	324,203	98.0
Lexington, KY	155,876	166,694	93.5
Lincoln, NE	145,790	145,292	100.3
Little Rock, AR	96,018	106,573	90.1
Los Angeles, CA	1,925,675	1,973,072	97.6
Louisville, KY	186,813	200,071	93.4
Madison, WI	133,922	135,918	98.5

Table continued on following page.

Appendix A: Comparative Statistics   A-9

City	Males	Females	Males per 100 Females
Manchester, NH	57,668	57,976	99.5
Miami, FL	218,706	223,535	97.8
Midland, TX	66,552	65,972	100.9
Milwaukee, WI	278,386	298,836	93.2
Minneapolis, MN	216,381	213,573	101.3
Nashville, TN	332,568	356,879	93.2
New Haven, CT	64,141	69,882	91.8
New Orleans, LA	181,171	202,826	89.3
New York, NY	4,184,548	4,619,642	90.6
Oklahoma City, OK	335,613	345,441	97.2
Omaha, NE	239,675	246,376	97.3
Orlando, FL	148,481	159,092	93.3
Philadelphia, PA	760,383	843,414	90.2
Phoenix, AZ	799,456	808,683	98.9
Pittsburgh, PA	148,157	154,814	95.7
Portland, OR	322,690	329,813	97.8
Providence, RI	92,861	98,073	94.7
Provo, UT	56,944	58,218	97.8
Raleigh, NC	224,994	242,671	92.7
Reno, NV	134,002	130,163	102.9
Richmond, VA	107,678	118,932	90.5
Rochester, MN	58,643	62,752	93.5
Sacramento, CA	255,987	268,956	95.2
St. Louis, MO	147,340	154,238	95.5
Salem, OR	87,574	87,961	99.6
Salt Lake City, UT	102,530	97,193	105.5
San Antonio, TX	699,905	734,720	95.3
San Diego, CA	694,107	692,825	100.2
San Francisco, CA	446,144	427,821	104.3
San Jose, CA	509,260	503,980	101.0
Santa Rosa, CA	86,767	91,360	95.0
Savannah, GA	69,878	77,902	89.7
Seattle, WA	371,247	365,768	101.5
Sioux Falls, SD	95,676	96,841	98.8
Springfield, IL	54,215	60,179	90.1
Tampa, FL	187,761	197,198	95.2
Tucson, AZ	269,110	273,519	98.4
Tulsa, OK	201,814	211,252	95.5
Tuscaloosa, AL	47,020	52,580	89.4
Virginia Beach, VA	224,059	235,411	95.2
Washington, DC	322,777	366,768	88.0
Wichita, KS	196,575	200,957	97.8
Wilmington, NC	54,189	61,262	88.5
Winston-Salem, NC	116,698	132,847	87.8
Worcester, MA	100,540	105,978	94.9
U.S.	162,685,811	168,763,470	96.4

Source: U.S. Census Bureau, 2020 Census

A-10 Appendix A: Comparative Statistics

Male/Female Ratio: Metro Area

Metro Area	Males	Females	Males per 100 Females
Albuquerque, NM	449,092	467,436	96.1
Allentown, PA	419,780	442,109	94.9
Anchorage, AK	203,277	195,051	104.2
Ann Arbor, MI	182,825	189,433	96.5
Athens, GA	103,235	112,180	92.0
Atlanta, GA	2,933,974	3,155,841	93.0
Austin, TX	1,138,942	1,144,429	99.5
Baltimore, MD	1,365,439	1,479,071	92.3
Boise City, ID	380,892	383,826	99.2
Boston, MA	2,390,705	2,550,927	93.7
Boulder, CO	166,794	163,964	101.7
Brownsville, TX	203,223	217,794	93.3
Cape Coral, FL	371,444	389,378	95.4
Cedar Rapids, IA	136,845	139,675	98.0
Charleston, SC	389,850	409,786	95.1
Charlotte, NC	1,289,221	1,371,108	94.0
Chicago, IL	4,694,560	4,923,942	95.3
Cincinnati, OH	1,107,410	1,149,474	96.3
Clarksville, TN	159,552	160,983	99.1
Cleveland, OH	1,008,568	1,079,683	93.4
College Station, TX	134,329	133,919	100.3
Colorado Springs, CO	379,052	376,053	100.8
Columbia, MO	102,929	107,935	95.4
Columbia, SC	398,440	431,030	92.4
Columbus, OH	1,050,767	1,088,159	96.6
Dallas, TX	3,753,384	3,884,003	96.6
Davenport, IA	189,247	195,077	97.0
Denver, CO	1,481,349	1,482,472	99.9
Des Moines, IA	349,805	359,661	97.3
Durham, NC	312,256	337,647	92.5
Edison, NJ	9,693,702	10,446,768	92.8
El Paso, TX	422,688	446,171	94.7
Fargo, ND	125,674	124,169	101.2
Fort Collins, CO	177,804	181,262	98.1
Fort Wayne, IN	205,785	213,816	96.2
Fort Worth, TX	3,753,384	3,884,003	96.6
Grand Rapids, MI	540,561	547,031	98.8
Greeley, CO	164,843	164,138	100.4
Green Bay, WI	163,689	164,579	99.5
Greensboro, NC	370,483	406,083	91.2
Honolulu, HI	509,569	506,939	100.5
Houston, TX	3,505,374	3,616,866	96.9
Huntsville, AL	241,092	250,631	96.2
Indianapolis, IN	1,033,439	1,077,601	95.9
Jacksonville, FL	779,083	826,765	94.2
Kansas City, MO	1,076,104	1,115,931	96.4
Lafayette, LA	231,864	246,520	94.1
Las Cruces, NM	107,150	112,411	95.3
Las Vegas, NV	1,126,444	1,139,017	98.9
Lexington, KY	250,691	266,120	94.2
Lincoln, NE	170,718	169,499	100.7
Little Rock, AR	361,694	386,337	93.6
Los Angeles, CA	6,469,965	6,731,033	96.1
Louisville, KY	628,220	657,219	95.6
Madison, WI	338,757	342,039	99.0

Table continued on following page.

Appendix A: Comparative Statistics   A-11

Metro Area	Males	Females	Males per 100 Females
Manchester, NH	209,879	213,058	98.5
Miami, FL	2,954,448	3,183,885	92.8
Midland, TX	88,457	86,763	102.0
Milwaukee, WI	766,278	808,453	94.8
Minneapolis, MN	1,824,100	1,866,161	97.7
Nashville, TN	968,381	1,021,138	94.8
New Haven, CT	415,391	449,444	92.4
New Orleans, LA	610,653	661,192	92.4
New York, NY	9,693,702	10,446,768	92.8
Oklahoma City, OK	702,324	723,371	97.1
Omaha, NE	478,627	488,977	97.9
Orlando, FL	1,296,256	1,377,120	94.1
Philadelphia, PA	3,015,319	3,229,732	93.4
Phoenix, AZ	2,395,320	2,450,512	97.7
Pittsburgh, PA	1,157,964	1,212,966	95.5
Portland, OR	1,240,947	1,271,912	97.6
Providence, RI	812,496	864,083	94.0
Provo, UT	336,952	334,233	100.8
Raleigh, NC	687,440	726,542	94.6
Reno, NV	247,924	242,672	102.2
Richmond, VA	632,849	681,585	92.8
Rochester, MN	111,433	114,896	97.0
Sacramento, CA	1,170,850	1,226,532	95.5
St. Louis, MO	1,369,631	1,450,622	94.4
Salem, OR	214,703	218,650	98.2
Salt Lake City, UT	632,295	625,641	101.1
San Antonio, TX	1,254,014	1,304,129	96.2
San Diego, CA	1,642,796	1,655,838	99.2
San Francisco, CA	2,344,775	2,404,233	97.5
San Jose, CA	1,007,254	993,214	101.4
Santa Rosa, CA	238,535	250,328	95.3
Savannah, GA	194,814	209,984	92.8
Seattle, WA	2,007,150	2,011,612	99.8
Sioux Falls, SD	138,437	138,293	100.1
Springfield, IL	100,412	108,228	92.8
Tampa, FL	1,535,385	1,639,890	93.6
Tucson, AZ	512,753	530,680	96.6
Tulsa, OK	499,555	515,776	96.9
Tuscaloosa, AL	127,913	140,761	90.9
Virginia Beach, VA	879,439	920,235	95.6
Washington, DC	3,091,711	3,293,451	93.9
Wichita, KS	321,349	326,261	98.5
Wilmington, NC	137,791	148,114	93.0
Winston-Salem, NC	324,467	351,499	92.3
Worcester, MA	482,355	496,174	97.2
U.S.	162,685,811	168,763,470	96.4

Note: Figures cover the Metropolitan Statistical Area (MSA)
Source: U.S. Census Bureau, 2020 Census

A-12 Appendix A: Comparative Statistics

Race: City

City	White Alone[1] (%)	Black Alone[1] (%)	Asian Alone[1] (%)	AIAN[2] Alone[1] (%)	NHOPI[3] Alone[1] (%)	Other Race Alone[1] (%)	Two or More Races (%)
Albuquerque, NM	52.2	3.5	3.4	5.6	0.1	14.2	21.0
Allentown, PA	38.3	13.2	2.1	0.8	0.1	30.1	15.5
Anchorage, AK	56.5	5.0	9.5	8.1	3.4	3.5	14.0
Ann Arbor, MI	67.6	6.8	15.7	0.2	0.1	1.8	7.9
Athens, GA	58.1	24.7	3.9	0.5	0.1	6.1	6.7
Atlanta, GA	39.8	47.2	4.5	0.3	0.0	2.4	5.8
Austin, TX	54.7	7.3	9.0	1.0	0.1	11.9	16.1
Baltimore, MD	27.8	57.8	3.6	0.4	0.0	4.8	5.5
Boise City, ID	81.2	2.3	3.6	0.7	0.3	3.5	8.5
Boston, MA	47.1	20.6	11.3	0.4	0.1	10.1	10.5
Boulder, CO	78.8	1.3	6.4	0.6	0.1	4.7	8.1
Brownsville, TX	34.9	0.3	0.6	0.7	0.0	20.5	42.9
Cape Coral, FL	72.3	4.3	1.7	0.3	0.1	5.8	15.6
Cedar Rapids, IA	77.8	10.4	2.7	0.3	0.4	1.7	6.8
Charleston, SC	73.5	17.0	2.2	0.3	0.1	1.6	5.3
Charlotte, NC	41.7	33.1	7.1	0.6	0.1	9.6	7.9
Chicago, IL	35.9	29.2	7.0	1.3	0.0	15.8	10.8
Cincinnati, OH	47.7	40.6	2.5	0.3	0.1	3.0	5.8
Clarksville, TN	57.0	24.4	2.5	0.5	0.5	4.2	10.9
Cleveland, OH	34.5	48.4	2.8	0.4	0.0	6.3	7.6
College Station, TX	63.5	8.1	10.2	0.5	0.1	7.4	10.2
Colorado Springs, CO	70.3	5.9	3.4	1.1	0.3	6.2	12.8
Columbia, MO	72.5	11.9	5.6	0.3	0.1	2.2	7.4
Columbia, SC	50.7	38.5	3.1	0.3	0.1	2.3	5.1
Columbus, OH	53.2	28.6	6.2	0.4	0.0	4.3	7.2
Dallas, TX	36.1	23.3	3.7	1.2	0.1	19.5	16.2
Davenport, IA	74.1	12.0	2.2	0.4	0.0	2.6	8.7
Denver, CO	60.6	8.9	3.9	1.5	0.2	11.3	13.5
Des Moines, IA	64.5	11.7	6.8	0.7	0.1	6.6	9.6
Durham, NC	40.2	36.2	5.6	0.7	0.0	9.8	7.4
Edison, NJ	28.1	7.6	53.7	0.4	0.0	4.7	5.5
El Paso, TX	36.8	3.7	1.5	1.1	0.2	20.6	36.0
Fargo, ND	78.9	8.8	4.1	1.6	0.1	1.2	5.3
Fort Collins, CO	80.8	1.5	3.6	0.8	0.1	3.6	9.6
Fort Wayne, IN	65.0	15.3	5.8	0.5	0.0	5.6	7.8
Fort Worth, TX	44.9	19.6	5.2	0.9	0.1	14.2	15.1
Grand Rapids, MI	60.3	18.9	2.3	0.9	0.0	9.0	8.7
Greeley, CO	62.0	2.7	2.0	1.8	0.1	14.8	16.6
Green Bay, WI	66.6	5.5	4.4	4.4	0.1	8.4	10.6
Greensboro, NC	40.0	42.0	5.1	0.6	0.0	5.6	6.6
Honolulu, HI	16.4	1.7	52.9	0.2	9.2	1.3	18.2
Houston, TX	32.1	22.6	7.3	1.2	0.1	20.7	16.1
Huntsville, AL	56.6	29.3	2.5	0.7	0.1	3.4	7.3
Indianapolis, IN	52.0	27.9	4.3	0.5	0.0	7.7	7.5
Jacksonville, FL	50.1	30.6	5.1	0.4	0.1	4.6	9.1
Kansas City, MO	55.3	26.1	3.1	0.6	0.3	5.5	9.0
Lafayette, LA	58.1	30.7	2.6	0.4	0.0	2.3	5.8
Las Cruces, NM	51.9	2.7	1.9	2.3	0.1	16.6	24.5
Las Vegas, NV	46.0	12.9	7.2	1.1	0.7	17.0	15.0
Lexington, KY	68.3	14.9	4.2	0.3	0.0	5.2	7.1
Lincoln, NE	78.7	4.7	4.8	0.9	0.1	3.5	7.5
Little Rock, AR	43.5	40.6	3.5	0.6	0.0	6.0	5.7
Los Angeles, CA	34.9	8.6	11.9	1.7	0.2	29.5	13.3
Louisville, KY	66.3	17.5	3.5	0.3	0.1	4.2	8.0

Table continued on following page.

Appendix A: Comparative Statistics A-13

City	White Alone[1] (%)	Black Alone[1] (%)	Asian Alone[1] (%)	AIAN[2] Alone[1] (%)	NHOPI[3] Alone[1] (%)	Other Race Alone[1] (%)	Two or More Races (%)
Madison, WI	71.0	7.4	9.5	0.5	0.1	3.8	7.8
Manchester, NH	76.7	5.5	4.2	0.3	0.0	5.2	7.9
Miami, FL	30.2	12.9	1.4	0.4	0.0	14.3	40.7
Midland, TX	57.6	7.9	2.6	0.9	0.1	12.5	18.4
Milwaukee, WI	36.1	38.6	5.2	0.9	0.0	9.0	10.1
Minneapolis, MN	59.5	19.1	5.8	1.7	0.0	5.9	8.0
Nashville, TN	55.2	24.6	4.0	0.6	0.0	8.1	7.6
New Haven, CT	32.7	32.2	6.8	1.0	0.1	15.3	12.0
New Orleans, LA	32.9	54.2	2.8	0.3	0.0	3.2	6.4
New York, NY	34.1	22.1	15.7	1.0	0.1	17.0	10.1
Oklahoma City, OK	53.6	14.0	4.6	3.4	0.2	11.1	13.1
Omaha, NE	65.5	12.4	4.6	1.1	0.1	7.2	9.1
Orlando, FL	40.0	23.8	4.3	0.4	0.1	12.3	19.0
Philadelphia, PA	36.3	39.3	8.3	0.4	0.1	8.7	6.9
Phoenix, AZ	49.7	7.8	4.1	2.6	0.2	20.1	15.5
Pittsburgh, PA	62.7	22.8	6.5	0.2	0.0	1.8	5.9
Portland, OR	68.8	5.9	8.1	1.1	0.6	4.8	10.7
Providence, RI	37.7	13.5	6.1	1.5	0.1	26.9	14.2
Provo, UT	74.6	0.9	2.5	1.0	1.5	8.2	11.3
Raleigh, NC	53.3	26.3	5.0	0.6	0.1	7.5	7.4
Reno, NV	62.7	3.1	7.1	1.4	0.8	12.0	13.0
Richmond, VA	43.3	40.4	2.8	0.4	0.1	6.8	6.2
Rochester, MN	73.2	8.9	7.9	0.4	0.1	2.9	6.6
Sacramento, CA	34.8	13.2	19.9	1.4	1.6	15.3	13.8
St. Louis, MO	43.9	43.0	4.1	0.3	0.0	2.6	6.1
Salem, OR	69.1	1.7	3.2	1.7	1.4	10.9	12.1
Salt Lake City, UT	68.4	2.9	5.5	1.4	2.1	9.7	9.9
San Antonio, TX	44.3	7.2	3.3	1.2	0.1	16.7	27.1
San Diego, CA	46.4	5.9	17.9	0.9	0.4	14.1	14.4
San Francisco, CA	41.3	5.3	33.9	0.7	0.4	8.4	9.9
San Jose, CA	27.3	2.9	38.5	1.4	0.4	18.2	11.2
Santa Rosa, CA	55.7	2.3	6.1	2.3	0.6	19.1	13.9
Savannah, GA	37.9	49.1	3.8	0.3	0.2	3.1	5.5
Seattle, WA	61.3	7.0	17.1	0.7	0.3	3.2	10.5
Sioux Falls, SD	79.0	6.3	2.8	2.7	0.0	2.9	6.1
Springfield, IL	68.9	20.4	2.9	0.3	0.0	1.1	6.4
Tampa, FL	49.7	21.9	5.4	0.4	0.1	7.6	14.8
Tucson, AZ	54.5	5.6	3.2	2.9	0.3	15.2	18.3
Tulsa, OK	51.8	14.9	3.5	5.2	0.2	9.8	14.6
Tuscaloosa, AL	48.7	41.2	2.4	0.3	0.1	2.1	5.3
Virginia Beach, VA	60.7	18.6	7.5	0.4	0.2	3.0	9.6
Washington, DC	39.6	41.4	4.9	0.5	0.1	5.4	8.1
Wichita, KS	63.4	11.0	5.1	1.3	0.1	7.4	11.7
Wilmington, NC	70.9	16.5	1.6	0.4	0.1	3.9	6.6
Winston-Salem, NC	45.8	32.5	2.5	0.7	0.1	10.7	7.6
Worcester, MA	53.3	14.8	7.1	0.5	0.0	12.9	11.3
U.S.	61.6	12.4	6.0	1.1	0.2	8.4	10.2

Note: (1) Alone is defined as not being in combination with one or more other races; (2) American Indian and Alaska Native; (3) Native Hawaiian and Other Pacific Islander
Source: U.S. Census Bureau, 2020 Census

A-14   Appendix A: Comparative Statistics

Race: Metro Area

Metro Area	White Alone[1] (%)	Black Alone[1] (%)	Asian Alone[1] (%)	AIAN[2] Alone[1] (%)	NHOPI[3] Alone[1] (%)	Other Race Alone[1] (%)	Two or More Races (%)
Albuquerque, NM	52.8	2.8	2.5	6.6	0.1	14.5	20.6
Allentown, PA	72.9	6.3	3.2	0.3	0.0	8.5	8.8
Anchorage, AK	62.1	3.9	7.3	7.7	2.6	3.0	13.3
Ann Arbor, MI	69.2	11.5	9.0	0.3	0.1	2.0	7.9
Athens, GA	67.0	17.9	3.6	0.4	0.0	4.7	6.3
Atlanta, GA	45.5	33.6	6.6	0.5	0.0	6.0	7.7
Austin, TX	57.3	7.0	7.1	0.9	0.1	11.1	16.5
Baltimore, MD	53.9	28.5	6.3	0.4	0.0	4.0	6.8
Boise City, ID	80.0	1.3	2.1	0.9	0.3	5.9	9.6
Boston, MA	68.4	7.4	8.7	0.3	0.0	6.9	8.4
Boulder, CO	77.4	1.0	5.0	0.8	0.1	5.8	10.0
Brownsville, TX	38.6	0.5	0.7	0.7	0.0	19.0	40.4
Cape Coral, FL	69.7	7.7	1.7	0.5	0.0	7.5	12.8
Cedar Rapids, IA	84.7	6.1	2.0	0.2	0.2	1.2	5.6
Charleston, SC	64.0	23.0	2.0	0.5	0.1	3.9	6.5
Charlotte, NC	59.5	21.9	4.3	0.6	0.1	6.4	7.2
Chicago, IL	54.0	16.4	7.1	0.9	0.0	11.3	10.2
Cincinnati, OH	76.7	12.1	3.0	0.3	0.1	2.1	5.7
Clarksville, TN	65.8	19.1	2.0	0.5	0.4	3.2	9.0
Cleveland, OH	68.9	19.6	2.6	0.2	0.0	2.6	6.0
College Station, TX	60.7	11.0	5.6	0.7	0.1	9.8	12.1
Colorado Springs, CO	71.3	5.8	3.0	1.0	0.4	5.8	12.7
Columbia, MO	77.7	9.3	3.8	0.3	0.1	1.8	7.1
Columbia, SC	55.7	32.4	2.3	0.4	0.1	3.1	6.0
Columbus, OH	70.1	15.7	4.9	0.3	0.0	2.7	6.3
Dallas, TX	48.9	16.0	7.9	1.0	0.1	12.2	13.9
Davenport, IA	78.2	8.3	2.4	0.4	0.0	3.2	7.5
Denver, CO	66.7	5.6	4.6	1.2	0.2	8.8	12.8
Des Moines, IA	79.8	5.6	4.3	0.4	0.1	3.2	6.7
Durham, NC	54.3	25.0	4.9	0.7	0.0	7.9	7.2
Edison, NJ	46.5	16.1	12.5	0.8	0.1	14.1	10.0
El Paso, TX	36.3	3.3	1.4	1.2	0.2	21.7	35.8
Fargo, ND	82.8	6.5	2.7	1.5	0.0	1.1	5.3
Fort Collins, CO	82.4	1.1	2.4	0.8	0.1	3.8	9.4
Fort Wayne, IN	73.7	10.6	4.4	0.4	0.0	4.0	6.8
Fort Worth, TX	48.9	16.0	7.9	1.0	0.1	12.2	13.9
Grand Rapids, MI	78.0	6.9	2.8	0.6	0.0	4.7	7.0
Greeley, CO	70.5	1.4	1.8	1.3	0.1	11.2	13.8
Green Bay, WI	81.8	2.6	2.7	2.5	0.0	3.8	6.6
Greensboro, NC	56.7	26.7	4.1	0.6	0.0	5.5	6.4
Honolulu, HI	18.5	2.0	43.0	0.2	10.0	1.7	24.5
Houston, TX	41.4	17.4	8.4	1.0	0.1	16.0	15.7
Huntsville, AL	65.0	21.4	2.5	0.7	0.1	2.9	7.3
Indianapolis, IN	69.6	15.0	3.9	0.4	0.0	4.5	6.6
Jacksonville, FL	61.6	21.2	4.2	0.4	0.1	3.6	8.8
Kansas City, MO	70.9	12.0	3.1	0.6	0.2	4.2	9.0
Lafayette, LA	65.8	24.5	1.9	0.4	0.0	2.3	5.1
Las Cruces, NM	47.5	1.9	1.2	1.9	0.1	20.1	27.4
Las Vegas, NV	44.9	12.7	10.5	1.0	0.9	15.4	14.7
Lexington, KY	74.9	11.1	2.9	0.3	0.0	4.2	6.6
Lincoln, NE	80.8	4.1	4.2	0.8	0.1	3.1	6.9
Little Rock, AR	64.0	23.2	1.8	0.6	0.1	3.7	6.6
Los Angeles, CA	35.2	6.4	16.7	1.5	0.3	25.2	14.7
Louisville, KY	72.7	14.8	2.5	0.3	0.1	2.9	6.8

Table continued on following page.

Appendix A: Comparative Statistics   A-15

Metro Area	White Alone[1] (%)	Black Alone[1] (%)	Asian Alone[1] (%)	AIAN[2] Alone[1] (%)	NHOPI[3] Alone[1] (%)	Other Race Alone[1] (%)	Two or More Races (%)
Madison, WI	80.2	4.7	5.4	0.4	0.0	2.9	6.4
Manchester, NH	82.8	2.6	3.9	0.2	0.0	3.5	6.9
Miami, FL	39.6	19.5	2.7	0.4	0.0	9.7	28.1
Midland, TX	58.2	6.4	2.3	0.9	0.1	13.2	18.9
Milwaukee, WI	66.7	16.3	4.2	0.6	0.0	4.6	7.6
Minneapolis, MN	73.0	9.1	7.2	0.8	0.0	3.3	6.6
Nashville, TN	70.0	14.3	3.1	0.5	0.1	5.1	7.0
New Haven, CT	62.9	13.8	4.3	0.5	0.1	9.0	9.5
New Orleans, LA	50.3	33.3	2.9	0.5	0.0	4.8	8.1
New York, NY	46.5	16.1	12.5	0.8	0.1	14.1	10.0
Oklahoma City, OK	62.5	10.3	3.3	4.0	0.1	7.2	12.6
Omaha, NE	74.9	7.7	3.5	0.8	0.1	5.0	8.0
Orlando, FL	50.4	15.4	4.7	0.4	0.1	11.4	17.7
Philadelphia, PA	60.7	20.4	6.6	0.3	0.0	5.1	6.8
Phoenix, AZ	60.2	5.8	4.3	2.5	0.3	13.4	13.5
Pittsburgh, PA	82.7	8.4	2.9	0.1	0.0	0.9	4.9
Portland, OR	71.5	3.0	7.1	1.1	0.6	6.0	10.7
Providence, RI	73.9	5.2	3.1	0.6	0.0	8.0	9.1
Provo, UT	81.8	0.7	1.6	0.7	1.0	5.4	8.9
Raleigh, NC	60.1	18.3	7.0	0.6	0.0	6.4	7.6
Reno, NV	64.2	2.5	5.9	1.8	0.7	11.8	13.0
Richmond, VA	56.5	27.7	4.3	0.5	0.1	4.4	6.4
Rochester, MN	82.3	5.1	4.7	0.3	0.0	2.2	5.4
Sacramento, CA	52.5	7.0	14.9	1.1	0.9	10.4	13.2
St. Louis, MO	71.2	18.0	2.9	0.3	0.0	1.6	6.0
Salem, OR	69.6	1.1	2.1	2.0	1.0	12.2	12.0
Salt Lake City, UT	72.3	1.9	4.1	1.1	1.8	9.1	9.8
San Antonio, TX	50.3	7.1	2.9	1.1	0.2	14.0	24.4
San Diego, CA	49.5	4.7	12.5	1.2	0.5	15.8	15.8
San Francisco, CA	39.3	7.1	27.5	1.0	0.7	12.7	11.7
San Jose, CA	32.5	2.3	38.1	1.2	0.4	14.6	11.0
Santa Rosa, CA	62.7	1.6	4.7	1.8	0.4	15.3	13.5
Savannah, GA	55.6	30.8	3.1	0.4	0.1	3.4	6.6
Seattle, WA	60.1	6.1	15.4	1.1	1.1	5.3	11.0
Sioux Falls, SD	83.4	4.6	2.0	2.2	0.0	2.3	5.5
Springfield, IL	78.4	12.5	2.1	0.2	0.0	0.9	5.8
Tampa, FL	64.4	11.8	3.9	0.4	0.1	6.2	13.1
Tucson, AZ	60.7	3.8	3.0	3.3	0.2	12.2	16.7
Tulsa, OK	61.3	7.9	2.8	8.1	0.1	5.4	14.2
Tuscaloosa, AL	57.5	33.9	1.3	0.4	0.0	2.5	4.3
Virginia Beach, VA	54.0	30.3	4.1	0.4	0.2	2.9	8.1
Washington, DC	44.5	24.5	11.0	0.6	0.1	9.3	10.1
Wichita, KS	71.7	7.5	3.7	1.2	0.1	5.4	10.4
Wilmington, NC	75.6	12.2	1.3	0.5	0.1	3.8	6.4
Winston-Salem, NC	67.0	17.2	1.8	0.6	0.1	6.7	6.5
Worcester, MA	74.5	5.2	4.9	0.4	0.0	6.3	8.6
U.S.	61.6	12.4	6.0	1.1	0.2	8.4	10.2

Note: Figures cover the Metropolitan Statistical Area (MSA); (1) Alone is defined as not being in combination with one or more other races; (2) American Indian and Alaska Native; (3) Native Hawaiian & Other Pacific Islander
Source: U.S. Census Bureau, 2020 Census

A-16   Appendix A: Comparative Statistics

Hispanic Origin: City

City	Hispanic or Latino (%)	Mexican (%)	Puerto Rican (%)	Cuban (%)	Other Hispanic or Latino (%)
Albuquerque, NM	49.8	29.7	0.7	0.4	19.0
Allentown, PA	54.5	2.6	27.6	0.8	23.5
Anchorage, AK	9.5	4.6	1.5	0.4	3.0
Ann Arbor, MI	4.6	2.4	0.3	0.3	1.7
Athens, GA	11.0	5.9	0.4	0.6	4.0
Atlanta, GA	5.0	1.9	0.8	0.3	2.0
Austin, TX	33.1	25.6	1.0	0.7	5.8
Baltimore, MD	5.6	1.1	0.8	0.3	3.3
Boise City, ID	8.8	6.4	0.5	0.1	1.9
Boston, MA	19.8	1.1	5.2	0.4	13.1
Boulder, CO	10.6	6.3	0.4	0.4	3.6
Brownsville, TX	94.7	90.5	0.2	0.1	3.8
Cape Coral, FL	23.2	1.7	4.9	9.7	7.0
Cedar Rapids, IA	4.4	3.2	0.2	0.1	1.0
Charleston, SC	4.2	1.9	0.6	0.1	1.6
Charlotte, NC	14.9	5.3	1.1	0.6	7.9
Chicago, IL	28.7	21.2	3.5	0.3	3.8
Cincinnati, OH	4.4	1.4	0.6	0.2	2.2
Clarksville, TN	11.7	5.6	3.0	0.4	2.8
Cleveland, OH	12.2	1.6	8.6	0.2	1.8
College Station, TX	17.7	12.8	0.7	0.2	4.1
Colorado Springs, CO	18.4	12.1	1.2	0.3	4.9
Columbia, MO	3.7	2.1	0.3	0.0	1.2
Columbia, SC	5.6	2.4	1.1	0.3	1.8
Columbus, OH	6.5	3.1	1.0	0.1	2.3
Dallas, TX	42.0	34.7	0.6	0.3	6.4
Davenport, IA	8.9	8.2	0.3	0.1	0.3
Denver, CO	29.4	22.6	0.7	0.3	5.9
Des Moines, IA	14.6	11.6	0.3	0.2	2.4
Durham, NC	13.2	6.4	0.9	0.3	5.7
Edison, NJ	10.8	1.4	2.8	0.7	6.0
El Paso, TX	81.6	76.9	1.0	0.2	3.5
Fargo, ND	3.2	2.0	0.3	0.0	0.9
Fort Collins, CO	12.6	9.0	0.5	0.1	3.0
Fort Wayne, IN	9.5	7.2	0.6	0.1	1.6
Fort Worth, TX	35.3	29.8	1.2	0.4	3.9
Grand Rapids, MI	15.7	9.6	1.6	0.3	4.1
Greeley, CO	40.3	33.0	0.9	0.1	6.3
Green Bay, WI	16.6	13.0	1.9	0.0	1.8
Greensboro, NC	8.4	4.5	1.1	0.2	2.6
Honolulu, HI	7.2	2.2	2.0	0.1	2.8
Houston, TX	44.5	30.3	0.7	0.8	12.8
Huntsville, AL	6.4	3.6	1.1	0.2	1.6
Indianapolis, IN	10.8	7.3	0.7	0.2	2.6
Jacksonville, FL	10.9	2.0	3.4	1.6	3.9
Kansas City, MO	10.7	7.7	0.4	0.4	2.2
Lafayette, LA	4.6	1.4	0.1	0.2	2.9
Las Cruces, NM	61.8	51.1	0.6	0.2	9.9
Las Vegas, NV	34.1	24.9	1.2	1.4	6.5
Lexington, KY	7.4	4.7	0.6	0.2	1.9
Lincoln, NE	8.1	5.5	0.4	0.2	2.0
Little Rock, AR	7.8	4.7	0.2	0.3	2.5
Los Angeles, CA	48.4	31.5	0.5	0.4	16.1
Louisville, KY	6.5	2.3	0.4	2.3	1.4
Madison, WI	7.8	4.5	0.7	0.2	2.4

Table continued on following page.

Appendix A: Comparative Statistics   A-17

City	Hispanic or Latino (%)	Mexican (%)	Puerto Rican (%)	Cuban (%)	Other Hispanic or Latino (%)
Manchester, NH	11.0	1.6	3.9	0.1	5.4
Miami, FL	72.3	1.9	3.5	33.4	33.5
Midland, TX	46.5	42.5	0.5	1.0	2.5
Milwaukee, WI	19.9	13.4	4.9	0.2	1.4
Minneapolis, MN	9.8	5.3	0.5	0.2	3.8
Nashville, TN	10.6	5.9	0.6	0.4	3.8
New Haven, CT	30.3	5.3	16.5	0.4	8.1
New Orleans, LA	5.6	1.2	0.2	0.6	3.5
New York, NY	28.9	3.8	7.7	0.5	16.9
Oklahoma City, OK	19.9	16.1	0.4	0.1	3.3
Omaha, NE	14.5	10.9	0.5	0.2	2.9
Orlando, FL	34.2	1.8	15.8	3.0	13.6
Philadelphia, PA	15.4	1.3	8.7	0.3	5.1
Phoenix, AZ	42.7	37.9	0.7	0.4	3.8
Pittsburgh, PA	3.5	1.2	0.7	0.1	1.6
Portland, OR	10.3	7.0	0.5	0.4	2.3
Providence, RI	42.9	1.3	7.9	0.3	33.4
Provo, UT	17.8	11.3	0.7	0.2	5.6
Raleigh, NC	11.3	5.0	1.4	0.4	4.5
Reno, NV	23.3	17.8	0.7	0.3	4.6
Richmond, VA	7.3	1.3	0.8	0.3	4.9
Rochester, MN	5.8	3.7	0.6	0.1	1.4
Sacramento, CA	28.9	24.1	0.9	0.2	3.7
St. Louis, MO	4.2	2.5	0.2	0.2	1.3
Salem, OR	22.4	19.5	0.6	0.1	2.2
Salt Lake City, UT	19.9	14.2	0.4	0.3	5.0
San Antonio, TX	65.7	56.7	1.4	0.3	7.3
San Diego, CA	30.1	25.6	0.8	0.3	3.4
San Francisco, CA	15.4	7.8	0.7	0.3	6.7
San Jose, CA	31.0	26.0	0.5	0.2	4.3
Santa Rosa, CA	34.0	29.3	0.5	0.1	4.1
Savannah, GA	6.5	2.1	2.0	0.4	2.0
Seattle, WA	7.2	4.2	0.4	0.2	2.4
Sioux Falls, SD	5.5	2.6	0.3	0.1	2.6
Springfield, IL	2.9	1.5	0.6	0.1	0.7
Tampa, FL	26.2	3.1	6.9	8.0	8.3
Tucson, AZ	44.6	39.8	0.9	0.2	3.7
Tulsa, OK	17.1	13.4	0.6	0.1	3.0
Tuscaloosa, AL	4.4	2.5	0.6	0.3	0.9
Virginia Beach, VA	8.6	2.7	2.2	0.3	3.4
Washington, DC	11.3	1.9	0.9	0.5	8.0
Wichita, KS	17.6	15.1	0.5	0.1	1.9
Wilmington, NC	7.1	2.7	1.3	0.4	2.7
Winston-Salem, NC	16.2	9.7	1.5	0.2	4.8
Worcester, MA	23.9	0.8	14.7	0.3	8.1
U.S.	18.4	11.2	1.8	0.7	4.7

Note: Persons of Hispanic or Latino origin can be of any race
Source: U.S. Census Bureau, 2017-2021 American Community Survey 5-Year Estimates

A-18   Appendix A: Comparative Statistics

Hispanic Origin: Metro Area

Metro Area	Hispanic or Latino (%)	Mexican (%)	Puerto Rican (%)	Cuban (%)	Other Hispanic or Latino (%)
Albuquerque, NM	49.7	29.0	0.7	0.4	19.7
Allentown, PA	18.4	1.3	9.3	0.4	7.3
Anchorage, AK	8.4	4.1	1.3	0.4	2.6
Ann Arbor, MI	5.0	2.8	0.5	0.2	1.5
Athens, GA	8.9	4.7	0.8	0.4	2.9
Atlanta, GA	11.0	5.5	1.1	0.4	3.9
Austin, TX	32.7	26.3	1.0	0.5	5.0
Baltimore, MD	6.2	1.4	1.0	0.2	3.6
Boise City, ID	14.1	11.5	0.5	0.1	2.0
Boston, MA	11.6	0.7	2.8	0.3	7.8
Boulder, CO	14.0	9.9	0.5	0.3	3.3
Brownsville, TX	90.0	86.0	0.3	0.1	3.6
Cape Coral, FL	22.6	5.4	4.6	5.7	6.8
Cedar Rapids, IA	3.2	2.4	0.1	0.0	0.7
Charleston, SC	5.9	2.7	0.8	0.1	2.3
Charlotte, NC	10.6	4.6	1.1	0.4	4.6
Chicago, IL	22.5	17.5	2.2	0.3	2.6
Cincinnati, OH	3.5	1.6	0.4	0.1	1.4
Clarksville, TN	9.3	4.7	2.4	0.2	2.0
Cleveland, OH	6.2	1.4	3.5	0.1	1.1
College Station, TX	25.7	21.8	0.4	0.3	3.1
Colorado Springs, CO	17.5	10.9	1.4	0.4	4.9
Columbia, MO	3.4	2.1	0.2	0.1	1.0
Columbia, SC	5.8	2.8	1.1	0.2	1.7
Columbus, OH	4.5	2.1	0.8	0.1	1.6
Dallas, TX	29.3	23.6	0.8	0.3	4.5
Davenport, IA	9.1	8.0	0.3	0.1	0.7
Denver, CO	23.4	17.5	0.6	0.2	5.0
Des Moines, IA	7.4	5.5	0.3	0.1	1.5
Durham, NC	11.3	5.9	0.8	0.3	4.3
Edison, NJ	24.8	2.9	5.9	0.8	15.3
El Paso, TX	82.9	78.1	0.9	0.2	3.6
Fargo, ND	3.4	2.4	0.3	0.0	0.7
Fort Collins, CO	12.0	8.8	0.4	0.2	2.6
Fort Wayne, IN	7.4	5.6	0.4	0.1	1.3
Fort Worth, TX	29.3	23.6	0.8	0.3	4.5
Grand Rapids, MI	9.9	6.8	0.9	0.3	1.9
Greeley, CO	30.0	24.5	0.5	0.2	4.8
Green Bay, WI	8.1	6.1	0.9	0.1	1.0
Greensboro, NC	8.8	5.7	1.0	0.2	1.9
Honolulu, HI	10.2	3.2	3.5	0.1	3.5
Houston, TX	37.9	27.3	0.7	0.7	9.2
Huntsville, AL	5.4	3.2	0.8	0.1	1.3
Indianapolis, IN	7.1	4.6	0.6	0.1	1.8
Jacksonville, FL	9.6	1.9	3.0	1.3	3.5
Kansas City, MO	9.4	7.0	0.4	0.2	1.8
Lafayette, LA	4.1	1.8	0.2	0.1	2.0
Las Cruces, NM	68.9	60.8	0.4	0.1	7.6
Las Vegas, NV	31.8	23.3	1.1	1.5	5.9
Lexington, KY	6.3	4.2	0.5	0.1	1.5
Lincoln, NE	7.2	4.9	0.3	0.2	1.7
Little Rock, AR	5.5	3.7	0.2	0.1	1.5
Los Angeles, CA	45.2	34.5	0.5	0.4	9.8
Louisville, KY	5.3	2.4	0.4	1.3	1.1
Madison, WI	6.1	3.7	0.5	0.1	1.7

Table continued on following page.

Appendix A: Comparative Statistics   A-19

Metro Area	Hispanic or Latino (%)	Mexican (%)	Puerto Rican (%)	Cuban (%)	Other Hispanic or Latino (%)
Manchester, NH	7.4	1.1	2.5	0.2	3.5
Miami, FL	45.6	2.5	3.8	18.6	20.6
Midland, TX	46.3	42.7	0.4	0.9	2.3
Milwaukee, WI	11.3	7.5	2.6	0.2	1.1
Minneapolis, MN	6.1	3.8	0.4	0.1	1.8
Nashville, TN	7.7	4.3	0.6	0.3	2.5
New Haven, CT	19.2	2.2	10.6	0.4	6.0
New Orleans, LA	9.1	1.7	0.5	0.6	6.3
New York, NY	24.8	2.9	5.9	0.8	15.3
Oklahoma City, OK	13.9	10.9	0.4	0.1	2.5
Omaha, NE	11.0	8.2	0.5	0.1	2.1
Orlando, FL	31.8	2.8	15.0	2.5	11.5
Philadelphia, PA	9.9	1.9	4.6	0.3	3.2
Phoenix, AZ	31.5	27.1	0.7	0.3	3.4
Pittsburgh, PA	1.9	0.6	0.5	0.1	0.7
Portland, OR	12.5	9.4	0.4	0.3	2.4
Providence, RI	13.7	0.9	4.4	0.2	8.3
Provo, UT	12.1	7.5	0.3	0.1	4.1
Raleigh, NC	10.8	5.6	1.4	0.4	3.5
Reno, NV	25.1	19.3	0.7	0.4	4.6
Richmond, VA	6.7	1.6	1.0	0.2	3.8
Rochester, MN	4.7	2.9	0.4	0.1	1.3
Sacramento, CA	22.2	17.8	0.7	0.2	3.5
St. Louis, MO	3.2	2.0	0.3	0.1	0.9
Salem, OR	24.9	22.1	0.4	0.1	2.3
Salt Lake City, UT	18.5	13.1	0.5	0.2	4.7
San Antonio, TX	56.0	48.2	1.4	0.3	6.0
San Diego, CA	34.3	29.9	0.8	0.2	3.4
San Francisco, CA	22.0	14.1	0.7	0.2	7.0
San Jose, CA	26.2	21.5	0.5	0.2	4.1
Santa Rosa, CA	27.5	22.7	0.4	0.2	4.2
Savannah, GA	6.5	2.9	1.6	0.5	1.6
Seattle, WA	10.5	7.3	0.6	0.2	2.5
Sioux Falls, SD	4.6	2.3	0.2	0.1	2.1
Springfield, IL	2.4	1.4	0.4	0.1	0.5
Tampa, FL	20.5	3.7	6.3	4.3	6.3
Tucson, AZ	38.0	33.7	0.9	0.2	3.2
Tulsa, OK	10.5	8.1	0.4	0.1	1.9
Tuscaloosa, AL	3.8	2.4	0.3	0.2	0.9
Virginia Beach, VA	7.2	2.4	1.9	0.3	2.5
Washington, DC	16.2	2.3	1.2	0.3	12.4
Wichita, KS	13.6	11.5	0.4	0.1	1.6
Wilmington, NC	6.2	2.5	1.0	0.3	2.4
Winston-Salem, NC	10.8	6.7	1.1	0.2	2.8
Worcester, MA	12.3	0.9	7.2	0.2	4.0
U.S.	18.4	11.2	1.8	0.7	4.7

Note: Persons of Hispanic or Latino origin can be of any race; Figures cover the Metropolitan Statistical Area (MSA)
Source: U.S. Census Bureau, 2017-2021 American Community Survey 5-Year Estimates

A-20   Appendix A: Comparative Statistics

Household Size: City

City	Persons in Household (%)							Average Household Size
	One	Two	Three	Four	Five	Six	Seven or More	
Albuquerque, NM	36.4	32.9	13.6	10.1	4.7	1.2	0.7	2.36
Allentown, PA	29.4	29.5	14.0	14.3	7.3	3.0	2.1	2.65
Anchorage, AK	26.8	32.9	15.5	13.5	6.2	2.6	2.1	2.68
Ann Arbor, MI	33.6	37.5	13.0	10.6	2.8	1.6	0.5	2.21
Athens, GA	34.2	34.4	14.9	11.1	3.4	1.1	0.6	2.22
Atlanta, GA	45.8	31.9	10.9	6.7	2.5	1.1	0.7	2.06
Austin, TX	34.7	33.7	14.3	10.4	4.2	1.5	0.8	2.28
Baltimore, MD	41.4	29.8	13.8	8.1	3.7	1.6	1.1	2.32
Boise City, ID	31.6	36.5	14.9	9.9	4.9	1.3	0.5	2.37
Boston, MA	36.2	32.7	15.1	9.4	3.9	1.6	0.9	2.30
Boulder, CO	35.7	35.9	13.9	10.5	2.7	0.4	0.5	2.21
Brownsville, TX	19.2	23.6	17.0	19.2	12.4	4.6	3.5	3.31
Cape Coral, FL	26.0	42.6	13.7	10.6	5.0	1.1	0.7	2.59
Cedar Rapids, IA	33.7	34.3	14.6	10.3	4.4	1.4	0.9	2.31
Charleston, SC	35.0	38.5	13.2	9.6	2.7	0.6	0.1	2.23
Charlotte, NC	34.1	31.7	15.0	11.9	4.6	1.5	0.9	2.47
Chicago, IL	38.2	29.5	13.5	10.0	4.9	2.1	1.4	2.41
Cincinnati, OH	44.5	30.2	11.4	8.4	3.0	1.3	0.8	2.11
Clarksville, TN	24.5	32.7	17.0	15.9	6.0	2.3	1.4	2.69
Cleveland, OH	46.0	27.9	12.0	7.3	3.7	1.7	1.0	2.15
College Station, TX	32.4	31.1	14.8	14.9	3.5	2.4	0.5	2.51
Colorado Springs, CO	27.5	36.0	15.0	12.4	5.5	2.2	1.1	2.48
Columbia, MO	35.6	31.7	13.7	11.1	5.7	1.2	0.7	2.33
Columbia, SC	39.1	32.6	13.4	8.9	4.0	1.4	0.2	2.19
Columbus, OH	35.8	32.6	13.3	10.1	4.8	1.7	1.3	2.32
Dallas, TX	36.3	29.5	13.1	10.3	6.4	2.4	1.6	2.49
Davenport, IA	34.3	35.7	13.1	9.1	5.0	1.7	0.8	2.36
Denver, CO	38.5	33.5	11.7	9.4	3.8	1.5	1.2	2.21
Des Moines, IA	34.8	30.5	14.3	10.8	5.1	2.5	1.6	2.40
Durham, NC	35.5	33.9	14.1	9.6	4.3	1.6	0.7	2.27
Edison, NJ	17.7	28.6	20.6	22.7	6.3	2.2	1.7	2.90
El Paso, TX	25.4	28.5	17.5	15.6	8.2	3.0	1.4	2.83
Fargo, ND	38.0	33.9	13.2	9.0	4.1	1.1	0.4	2.15
Fort Collins, CO	25.2	37.4	17.6	14.0	4.0	1.1	0.4	2.36
Fort Wayne, IN	32.8	32.7	14.1	10.8	5.6	2.6	1.1	2.42
Fort Worth, TX	26.6	29.4	16.5	14.6	7.5	3.1	2.0	2.81
Grand Rapids, MI	33.2	30.9	15.1	10.2	6.0	2.2	2.1	2.47
Greeley, CO	25.4	32.8	16.1	13.5	7.3	3.0	1.6	2.73
Green Bay, WI	34.9	32.2	13.5	10.6	5.5	1.5	1.3	2.36
Greensboro, NC	35.1	31.9	15.5	10.3	4.5	1.4	0.9	2.36
Honolulu, HI	34.9	30.4	14.1	10.5	4.9	2.1	2.8	2.54
Houston, TX	32.7	29.1	15.6	11.9	6.2	2.5	1.5	2.57
Huntsville, AL	36.6	34.9	14.4	8.5	3.9	0.8	0.5	2.21
Indianapolis, IN	36.8	32.2	12.9	9.7	5.1	1.8	1.1	2.46
Jacksonville, FL	32.2	32.8	16.3	10.7	5.1	1.6	0.9	2.50
Kansas City, MO	36.7	32.0	12.7	10.8	4.4	1.9	1.1	2.31
Lafayette, LA	33.6	36.0	14.1	8.6	4.7	1.5	1.1	2.30
Las Cruces, NM	31.9	31.4	15.8	12.6	5.5	1.6	0.7	2.46
Las Vegas, NV	30.2	31.3	15.5	12.1	6.1	2.7	1.7	2.65
Lexington, KY	33.0	34.2	14.3	11.4	4.2	1.7	0.8	2.30
Lincoln, NE	31.6	33.7	13.7	11.8	5.4	2.4	0.9	2.37
Little Rock, AR	37.6	31.8	13.8	9.9	4.4	1.4	0.7	2.33
Los Angeles, CA	30.5	28.5	15.4	13.1	6.7	2.9	2.5	2.75
Louisville, KY	33.8	32.9	15.1	10.7	4.9	1.4	0.9	2.39

Table continued on following page.

Appendix A: Comparative Statistics   A-21

City	Persons in Household (%)							Average Household Size
	One	Two	Three	Four	Five	Six	Seven or More	
Madison, WI	37.7	35.2	12.4	9.4	3.4	1.0	0.5	2.16
Manchester, NH	33.9	33.2	15.8	10.3	3.5	1.9	1.0	2.32
Miami, FL	35.9	32.2	16.2	9.2	3.8	1.3	1.0	2.38
Midland, TX	26.8	28.2	17.2	15.2	8.2	2.8	1.3	2.57
Milwaukee, WI	37.7	28.8	13.7	10.0	5.7	2.3	1.5	2.45
Minneapolis, MN	40.4	31.6	11.5	9.5	3.4	1.7	1.5	2.24
Nashville, TN	35.2	33.3	14.5	9.6	4.6	1.4	1.1	2.34
New Haven, CT	36.7	29.1	16.1	9.0	5.3	2.0	1.4	2.48
New Orleans, LA	46.4	28.7	12.5	7.9	2.7	1.1	0.4	2.37
New York, NY	32.4	28.6	16.3	12.1	5.7	2.5	2.0	2.63
Oklahoma City, OK	31.3	31.8	15.1	11.6	6.4	2.5	1.0	2.49
Omaha, NE	33.6	31.6	13.6	10.7	6.1	2.5	1.6	2.44
Orlando, FL	32.8	33.5	16.0	10.8	4.3	1.3	1.0	2.53
Philadelphia, PA	37.1	29.4	14.9	10.2	4.8	1.8	1.3	2.40
Phoenix, AZ	27.9	30.0	15.2	13.0	7.4	3.6	2.7	2.71
Pittsburgh, PA	44.2	32.4	12.4	6.7	2.5	1.0	0.5	2.04
Portland, OR	34.9	35.2	13.7	10.3	3.5	1.2	0.8	2.26
Providence, RI	33.6	29.0	15.5	11.1	7.0	1.9	1.6	2.56
Provo, UT	15.1	34.8	17.3	14.9	7.2	6.9	3.4	3.10
Raleigh, NC	34.6	32.8	14.4	12.0	4.2	1.2	0.5	2.37
Reno, NV	31.9	34.0	14.6	11.2	5.3	1.4	1.2	2.37
Richmond, VA	42.4	33.0	12.0	7.6	2.8	1.3	0.5	2.19
Rochester, MN	31.0	34.7	13.0	12.2	5.5	1.9	1.4	2.40
Sacramento, CA	30.5	30.3	14.6	13.0	6.1	2.8	2.4	2.63
St. Louis, MO	46.2	30.2	10.8	7.3	3.2	0.9	1.0	2.08
Salem, OR	29.6	33.2	14.8	11.0	6.4	2.7	2.0	2.58
Salt Lake City, UT	38.2	32.7	11.9	9.3	4.1	1.9	1.7	2.32
San Antonio, TX	30.6	29.5	15.4	12.7	6.9	2.9	1.7	2.64
San Diego, CA	27.8	34.0	15.7	12.9	5.6	2.1	1.5	2.64
San Francisco, CA	36.5	32.9	13.9	10.1	3.6	1.4	1.3	2.34
San Jose, CA	19.7	28.9	18.8	17.9	8.0	3.2	3.2	3.08
Santa Rosa, CA	28.4	32.4	15.0	13.8	6.6	2.0	1.3	2.60
Savannah, GA	32.8	35.4	15.2	9.6	4.5	1.3	0.9	2.46
Seattle, WA	39.9	35.0	12.1	8.9	2.5	0.8	0.5	2.08
Sioux Falls, SD	32.2	33.4	14.0	11.2	6.1	1.8	1.0	2.37
Springfield, IL	39.3	32.5	12.3	9.5	3.8	1.2	1.0	2.18
Tampa, FL	35.9	31.1	15.6	10.7	4.2	1.5	0.6	2.41
Tucson, AZ	34.9	31.0	14.2	11.2	5.2	2.0	1.2	2.35
Tulsa, OK	35.5	32.2	13.2	10.4	5.0	2.2	1.1	2.41
Tuscaloosa, AL	37.2	32.9	14.0	9.9	3.8	1.3	0.6	2.45
Virginia Beach, VA	24.5	35.5	17.6	13.7	6.0	1.7	0.6	2.53
Washington, DC	45.4	30.6	11.6	7.3	3.1	1.0	0.6	2.08
Wichita, KS	32.8	32.4	13.0	11.2	6.2	2.5	1.7	2.51
Wilmington, NC	39.9	36.9	11.5	7.4	3.0	0.6	0.3	2.10
Winston-Salem, NC	36.0	31.7	14.7	9.3	4.6	2.4	1.0	2.43
Worcester, MA	34.9	28.3	17.0	11.9	4.4	2.1	1.0	2.40
U.S.	28.0	33.8	15.5	12.8	5.9	2.2	1.4	2.60

U.S. Census Bureau, 2017-2021 American Community Survey 5-Year Estimates

A-22   Appendix A: Comparative Statistics

Household Size: Metro Area

Metro Area	Persons in Household (%)							Average Household Size
	One	Two	Three	Four	Five	Six	Seven or More	
Albuquerque, NM	32.3	34.7	14.2	10.7	5.1	1.7	1.0	2.49
Allentown, PA	26.5	35.6	15.2	13.6	5.8	1.9	1.1	2.52
Anchorage, AK	25.7	33.3	15.5	13.4	6.7	2.8	2.3	2.70
Ann Arbor, MI	29.9	36.6	14.7	11.7	4.2	1.8	0.8	2.39
Athens, GA	28.7	34.5	16.6	13.2	4.5	1.3	0.9	2.46
Atlanta, GA	26.7	31.7	17.0	14.2	6.2	2.4	1.4	2.69
Austin, TX	27.2	33.7	15.9	13.5	5.9	2.2	1.2	2.54
Baltimore, MD	29.1	32.7	16.1	12.9	5.6	2.0	1.1	2.55
Boise City, ID	24.7	36.0	15.3	12.5	6.5	3.1	1.6	2.67
Boston, MA	27.5	33.0	16.6	14.4	5.5	1.7	0.9	2.50
Boulder, CO	29.4	36.3	14.8	13.1	4.2	1.5	0.4	2.41
Brownsville, TX	20.4	26.8	16.4	17.5	10.4	4.9	3.3	3.21
Cape Coral, FL	28.6	44.2	11.5	8.8	4.6	1.3	0.7	2.49
Cedar Rapids, IA	29.5	36.6	14.1	11.9	5.1	1.6	0.9	2.41
Charleston, SC	28.7	36.1	16.2	11.8	4.9	1.4	0.7	2.50
Charlotte, NC	27.4	34.0	16.1	13.8	5.6	1.8	0.9	2.59
Chicago, IL	29.2	31.1	15.6	13.6	6.5	2.3	1.4	2.61
Cincinnati, OH	29.2	33.9	15.0	12.8	5.5	2.1	1.1	2.49
Clarksville, TN	25.1	33.1	17.6	13.9	6.1	2.5	1.3	2.68
Cleveland, OH	34.8	33.5	13.9	10.5	4.5	1.5	0.8	2.32
College Station, TX	30.8	32.6	14.6	12.7	5.3	2.6	1.1	2.56
Colorado Springs, CO	24.5	35.7	15.9	13.2	6.6	2.3	1.5	2.60
Columbia, MO	31.5	35.1	13.7	11.9	5.3	1.4	0.8	2.41
Columbia, SC	30.4	34.2	15.4	11.8	5.1	1.9	0.9	2.46
Columbus, OH	28.8	33.9	15.2	12.8	5.8	2.0	1.2	2.49
Dallas, TX	25.1	30.7	16.7	14.9	7.7	2.9	1.7	2.77
Davenport, IA	31.2	36.3	13.2	11.4	5.0	1.8	0.8	2.39
Denver, CO	28.4	34.4	15.0	13.1	5.3	2.2	1.3	2.51
Des Moines, IA	28.5	34.1	14.2	13.7	6.2	2.0	1.0	2.48
Durham, NC	30.7	36.0	15.0	11.2	4.8	1.4	0.7	2.40
Edison, NJ	28.0	29.5	17.0	14.4	6.4	2.5	1.9	2.71
El Paso, TX	23.6	27.7	17.7	16.2	9.1	3.6	1.7	2.94
Fargo, ND	33.2	33.8	13.9	11.2	5.4	1.4	0.8	2.33
Fort Collins, CO	24.8	39.8	15.7	12.2	4.9	1.4	0.8	2.38
Fort Wayne, IN	29.0	34.3	14.1	12.1	6.1	2.6	1.4	2.51
Fort Worth, TX	25.1	30.7	16.7	14.9	7.7	2.9	1.7	2.77
Grand Rapids, MI	25.0	34.3	15.2	14.3	7.2	2.4	1.4	2.61
Greeley, CO	20.1	34.4	16.3	15.8	8.1	3.2	1.6	2.84
Green Bay, WI	28.3	37.5	14.0	11.7	5.5	1.7	0.9	2.41
Greensboro, NC	30.0	34.5	16.1	11.5	4.9	1.8	0.9	2.47
Honolulu, HI	24.5	30.4	16.5	13.4	7.1	3.7	4.0	2.96
Houston, TX	24.2	29.6	17.2	15.7	8.0	3.0	1.8	2.83
Huntsville, AL	29.3	36.0	15.3	11.9	5.0	1.5	0.6	2.42
Indianapolis, IN	29.2	34.1	14.7	12.9	5.8	1.8	1.1	2.54
Jacksonville, FL	28.0	34.8	16.4	12.1	5.7	1.8	1.0	2.57
Kansas City, MO	29.1	34.4	14.3	13.0	5.7	2.0	1.2	2.50
Lafayette, LA	27.5	33.6	16.7	13.1	5.7	2.0	1.1	2.56
Las Cruces, NM	27.3	33.2	15.7	13.5	6.4	2.0	1.5	2.66
Las Vegas, NV	28.0	32.7	15.5	12.2	6.7	2.7	1.8	2.71
Lexington, KY	29.8	35.1	15.5	12.1	4.5	1.8	0.8	2.39
Lincoln, NE	29.9	35.2	13.6	12.0	5.6	2.4	1.0	2.41
Little Rock, AR	30.3	34.4	15.8	11.7	5.1	1.7	0.7	2.47
Los Angeles, CA	24.6	28.6	17.0	15.4	7.9	3.3	2.8	2.95
Louisville, KY	30.3	34.4	15.5	11.7	5.2	1.7	0.9	2.47

Table continued on following page.

Appendix A: Comparative Statistics   A-23

| Metro Area | Persons in Household (%) | | | | | | | Average Household Size |
	One	Two	Three	Four	Five	Six	Seven or More	
Madison, WI	31.5	36.8	13.6	11.4	4.3	1.4	0.7	2.31
Manchester, NH	27.1	35.7	16.3	13.0	4.8	2.1	0.7	2.50
Miami, FL	28.0	32.4	17.0	13.3	5.9	2.0	1.1	2.68
Midland, TX	25.7	28.1	17.0	15.7	8.6	2.6	2.0	2.61
Milwaukee, WI	32.2	34.3	13.7	11.5	5.2	1.7	0.9	2.40
Minneapolis, MN	28.1	34.1	14.7	13.5	5.8	2.1	1.4	2.53
Nashville, TN	26.9	34.8	16.2	13.1	5.7	1.8	1.1	2.57
New Haven, CT	30.6	33.1	16.4	12.2	4.7	1.6	0.9	2.49
New Orleans, LA	34.1	32.0	15.3	11.2	4.6	1.6	0.9	2.52
New York, NY	28.0	29.5	17.0	14.4	6.4	2.5	1.9	2.71
Oklahoma City, OK	28.5	33.4	15.7	12.2	6.3	2.5	1.1	2.53
Omaha, NE	28.9	33.5	14.5	12.2	6.6	2.4	1.4	2.53
Orlando, FL	24.1	34.6	17.0	13.9	6.6	2.2	1.2	2.83
Philadelphia, PA	29.2	32.1	16.1	13.4	5.7	1.9	1.1	2.53
Phoenix, AZ	25.9	34.5	14.6	12.7	6.8	3.0	2.2	2.65
Pittsburgh, PA	33.7	35.3	14.1	10.7	4.1	1.2	0.5	2.27
Portland, OR	26.9	35.5	15.4	13.3	5.3	2.0	1.3	2.53
Providence, RI	29.6	33.1	16.7	12.7	5.1	1.6	0.8	2.46
Provo, UT	12.4	28.6	15.5	15.9	12.5	8.9	5.9	3.52
Raleigh, NC	25.4	34.1	16.6	14.8	5.9	1.9	0.9	2.61
Reno, NV	27.4	34.9	15.5	12.5	5.8	2.0	1.5	2.51
Richmond, VA	29.4	34.5	15.7	12.3	5.3	1.7	0.8	2.51
Rochester, MN	27.4	36.9	13.3	13.0	6.1	1.9	1.1	2.46
Sacramento, CA	24.6	32.9	15.9	14.7	6.9	2.7	1.9	2.73
St. Louis, MO	30.5	34.5	15.0	12.2	5.1	1.5	0.8	2.43
Salem, OR	25.3	34.1	15.2	12.4	7.4	3.3	2.0	2.74
Salt Lake City, UT	23.1	30.9	15.7	13.8	8.5	4.6	3.1	2.92
San Antonio, TX	26.2	30.9	16.2	14.0	7.5	3.0	1.8	2.74
San Diego, CA	24.0	32.8	16.8	14.6	6.8	2.7	1.9	2.81
San Francisco, CA	26.4	31.8	16.8	14.8	6.1	2.2	1.6	2.71
San Jose, CA	20.4	30.4	19.1	17.7	7.2	2.7	2.2	2.94
Santa Rosa, CA	26.9	35.1	14.8	13.7	6.1	1.9	1.1	2.56
Savannah, GA	27.9	36.7	15.8	12.1	4.8	1.5	0.9	2.56
Seattle, WA	27.2	33.9	16.0	13.9	5.4	1.9	1.3	2.53
Sioux Falls, SD	28.7	34.4	14.5	12.2	6.8	2.0	1.1	2.45
Springfield, IL	33.7	35.4	13.4	10.4	4.6	1.3	0.9	2.28
Tampa, FL	30.7	36.3	14.9	10.8	4.6	1.5	0.8	2.46
Tucson, AZ	30.7	35.4	13.4	11.3	5.2	2.3	1.3	2.41
Tulsa, OK	28.8	33.7	15.2	12.2	6.0	2.5	1.3	2.57
Tuscaloosa, AL	30.1	34.6	15.5	11.7	5.4	1.5	0.8	2.62
Virginia Beach, VA	27.8	34.4	16.9	12.5	5.5	1.8	0.8	2.49
Washington, DC	27.8	30.7	16.1	14.5	6.5	2.6	1.6	2.67
Wichita, KS	29.7	33.4	13.9	11.8	6.6	2.5	1.8	2.56
Wilmington, NC	33.6	36.4	14.4	10.1	3.6	1.2	0.4	2.30
Winston-Salem, NC	30.1	35.7	15.6	10.7	4.7	2.0	0.9	2.47
Worcester, MA	27.0	33.0	17.4	14.5	5.3	1.6	0.8	2.52
U.S.	28.0	33.8	15.5	12.8	5.9	2.2	1.4	2.60

Note: Figures cover the Metropolitan Statistical Area (MSA)
Source: U.S. Census Bureau, 2017-2021 American Community Survey 5-Year Estimates

A-24　Appendix A: Comparative Statistics

Household Relationships: City

City	House-holder	Opposite-sex Spouse	Same-sex Spouse	Opposite-sex Unmarried Partner	Same-sex Unmarried Partner	Child[1]	Grand-child	Other Relatives	Non-relatives
Albuquerque, NM	42.1	15.1	0.3	3.4	0.3	27.0	2.5	4.6	3.2
Allentown, PA	36.3	11.6	0.2	3.7	0.2	30.6	3.2	6.8	4.1
Anchorage, AK	37.5	17.0	0.2	3.0	0.2	28.3	1.9	4.6	4.2
Ann Arbor, MI	40.3	13.3	0.3	2.4	0.2	17.1	0.5	1.6	11.5
Athens, GA	40.1	11.6	0.2	2.7	0.2	20.8	2.0	3.7	10.7
Atlanta, GA	45.7	10.4	0.5	3.1	0.6	20.7	2.1	3.9	5.9
Austin, TX	42.7	14.5	0.4	3.6	0.4	23.2	1.5	4.1	6.4
Baltimore, MD	42.9	9.6	0.3	3.3	0.3	24.9	3.7	5.8	6.1
Boise City, ID	41.4	17.8	0.2	3.2	0.2	24.7	1.3	2.9	5.4
Boston, MA	41.4	10.4	0.5	3.1	0.4	20.6	1.7	5.3	9.7
Boulder, CO	40.2	13.0	0.3	3.1	0.2	16.4	0.3	1.6	12.3
Brownsville, TX	30.8	15.0	0.1	1.4	0.1	36.7	4.7	8.3	1.6
Cape Coral, FL	39.5	21.2	0.3	3.2	0.1	25.5	2.1	4.8	2.8
Cedar Rapids, IA	42.2	16.7	0.2	3.5	0.2	26.8	1.3	2.9	3.4
Charleston, SC	45.0	17.0	0.3	3.1	0.2	21.8	1.4	2.7	5.3
Charlotte, NC	40.6	15.2	0.2	2.8	0.2	28.0	2.1	4.9	4.2
Chicago, IL	41.6	12.2	0.3	3.0	0.3	26.6	3.0	6.4	4.8
Cincinnati, OH	45.1	10.2	0.3	3.4	0.3	24.6	2.2	3.4	5.3
Clarksville, TN	36.6	16.9	0.2	2.5	0.1	31.2	2.4	3.9	3.5
Cleveland, OH	45.0	8.5	0.2	3.5	0.3	27.0	3.3	5.0	3.8
College Station, TX	35.2	11.2	0.2	1.8	0.1	19.7	0.7	2.7	13.7
Colorado Springs, CO	39.7	18.3	0.3	2.6	0.2	27.5	1.9	3.6	4.3
Columbia, MO	40.5	14.1	0.2	2.8	0.2	22.4	1.0	2.5	7.8
Columbia, SC	39.2	10.5	0.2	2.1	0.2	19.5	1.6	2.8	5.8
Columbus, OH	42.2	12.9	0.3	3.6	0.3	26.2	2.1	4.4	5.2
Dallas, TX	40.1	13.4	0.4	2.6	0.3	28.6	3.2	6.2	4.0
Davenport, IA	41.9	15.9	0.2	3.7	0.2	27.0	2.0	3.0	3.2
Denver, CO	44.4	14.0	0.5	4.1	0.4	22.3	1.9	4.4	5.9
Des Moines, IA	41.1	14.2	0.3	3.5	0.2	27.9	2.0	4.4	3.9
Durham, NC	42.0	14.8	0.4	2.9	0.3	24.6	1.8	4.4	4.6
Edison, NJ	34.3	21.2	0.1	1.1	0.1	32.2	1.4	6.8	1.9
El Paso, TX	35.9	15.8	0.2	1.8	0.1	32.7	3.9	6.4	2.0
Fargo, ND	44.5	15.5	0.1	3.6	0.2	23.5	0.7	2.5	5.0
Fort Collins, CO	39.9	16.0	0.2	3.3	0.2	22.1	0.9	2.4	9.0
Fort Wayne, IN	40.7	15.6	0.2	3.1	0.2	29.7	2.0	3.4	3.0
Fort Worth, TX	35.2	15.8	0.2	2.1	0.1	33.0	3.1	5.6	3.0
Grand Rapids, MI	40.2	13.1	0.3	3.6	0.3	26.1	2.1	4.0	6.6
Greeley, CO	34.9	15.8	0.2	2.5	0.1	29.4	2.6	5.0	5.1
Green Bay, WI	40.7	15.2	0.2	4.0	0.2	28.6	1.6	3.4	3.0
Greensboro, NC	40.9	13.6	0.2	2.6	0.2	26.4	2.0	4.1	3.6
Honolulu, HI	39.1	15.0	0.3	2.4	0.2	22.2	3.1	9.1	5.6
Houston, TX	38.9	14.0	0.3	2.4	0.2	29.5	2.9	6.5	3.6
Huntsville, AL	42.8	16.5	0.2	2.2	0.2	25.1	2.1	3.5	3.1
Indianapolis, IN	40.7	14.0	0.3	3.4	0.3	28.6	2.5	4.5	3.9
Jacksonville, FL	39.9	15.6	0.2	2.8	0.2	27.7	2.8	4.9	3.6
Kansas City, MO	42.6	14.5	0.3	3.3	0.3	27.2	2.3	4.0	3.8
Lafayette, LA	43.0	15.3	0.2	2.8	0.2	27.0	2.3	3.5	3.8
Las Cruces, NM	41.1	14.9	0.2	3.4	0.3	28.5	2.5	4.5	3.6
Las Vegas, NV	37.5	15.2	0.3	2.9	0.2	29.3	2.7	6.7	4.3
Lexington, KY	41.7	16.0	0.3	2.9	0.3	25.3	1.6	3.4	4.4
Lincoln, NE	40.1	16.9	0.2	2.8	0.1	26.6	1.1	2.7	4.6
Little Rock, AR	43.5	14.5	0.3	2.4	0.3	27.1	2.3	3.9	3.1
Los Angeles, CA	36.2	13.1	0.3	2.8	0.3	26.5	2.8	9.0	6.3
Louisville, KY	40.0	18.0	0.2	2.9	0.2	28.8	2.6	4.2	2.7
Madison, WI	44.8	14.5	0.4	3.8	0.3	19.7	0.7	2.4	8.2

Table continued on following page.

Appendix A: Comparative Statistics   A-25

City	House-holder	Opposite-sex Spouse	Same-sex Spouse	Opposite-sex Unmarried Partner	Same-sex Unmarried Partner	Child[1]	Grand-child	Other Relatives	Non-relatives
Manchester, NH	42.5	14.9	0.3	4.3	0.2	24.3	1.6	4.3	4.7
Miami, FL	42.4	12.6	0.5	3.3	0.3	22.5	2.4	8.7	5.8
Midland, TX	36.4	18.5	0.1	2.1	0.1	31.9	3.0	4.2	2.5
Milwaukee, WI	40.8	10.2	0.2	3.6	0.2	30.2	2.7	4.9	4.4
Minneapolis, MN	43.7	12.0	0.6	3.9	0.5	22.1	1.1	3.5	8.0
Nashville, TN	42.1	14.3	0.3	3.0	0.3	24.0	1.9	4.7	5.7
New Haven, CT	39.0	9.4	0.3	2.9	0.2	27.0	2.5	5.0	5.7
New Orleans, LA	43.0	11.0	0.3	3.1	0.4	26.1	3.2	4.6	4.3
New York, NY	38.3	12.7	0.3	2.2	0.2	27.6	2.5	8.3	5.3
Oklahoma City, OK	39.4	16.6	0.2	2.6	0.2	29.4	2.3	4.3	3.1
Omaha, NE	39.8	16.0	0.2	2.8	0.2	29.6	1.8	3.7	3.6
Orlando, FL	41.7	13.7	0.5	3.5	0.4	26.1	2.0	5.9	5.0
Philadelphia, PA	41.0	10.9	0.3	3.1	0.3	26.8	3.6	5.9	5.2
Phoenix, AZ	36.3	14.4	0.3	3.1	0.3	30.2	2.9	6.6	4.2
Pittsburgh, PA	46.1	11.5	0.3	3.6	0.4	19.3	1.7	3.1	6.7
Portland, OR	43.2	14.9	0.7	4.4	0.6	21.2	1.1	3.7	7.2
Providence, RI	36.5	10.5	0.3	2.9	0.3	27.3	1.9	5.7	6.1
Provo, UT	29.6	15.9	0.1	0.6	0.0	25.7	1.6	4.0	12.7
Raleigh, NC	41.8	15.1	0.2	2.9	0.2	25.5	1.4	3.9	5.0
Reno, NV	41.1	15.2	0.3	3.8	0.2	24.8	1.7	4.7	5.7
Richmond, VA	45.2	10.4	0.4	4.0	0.4	20.8	2.1	4.3	7.4
Rochester, MN	41.1	18.5	0.2	2.8	0.1	27.8	0.9	2.8	3.3
Sacramento, CA	36.7	13.5	0.4	3.0	0.3	28.0	2.6	7.5	4.7
St. Louis, MO	48.0	10.3	0.4	3.7	0.4	22.5	2.6	4.0	4.3
Salem, OR	36.6	16.0	0.2	3.1	0.2	28.1	1.9	4.6	4.2
Salt Lake City, UT	42.3	13.9	0.5	3.4	0.4	22.1	1.7	4.2	7.6
San Antonio, TX	37.5	14.7	0.3	2.7	0.2	30.3	3.8	5.5	3.2
San Diego, CA	37.2	15.7	0.4	2.6	0.3	25.0	2.0	6.2	6.1
San Francisco, CA	42.6	13.6	0.8	3.3	0.6	17.6	1.3	6.8	10.3
San Jose, CA	32.4	17.1	0.2	1.9	0.1	28.6	2.3	9.8	6.1
Santa Rosa, CA	37.6	16.2	0.4	3.0	0.2	27.3	1.8	6.2	5.5
Savannah, GA	39.9	11.2	0.3	2.7	0.3	24.9	3.2	4.4	5.0
Seattle, WA	46.9	15.2	0.8	4.3	0.6	17.5	0.7	2.8	7.3
Sioux Falls, SD	40.7	18.0	0.1	3.2	0.1	28.4	1.1	2.7	3.1
Springfield, IL	44.8	15.5	0.2	3.2	0.2	25.7	1.9	2.8	2.8
Tampa, FL	40.9	13.8	0.3	3.2	0.3	25.8	2.3	4.9	4.5
Tucson, AZ	41.1	13.3	0.3	3.3	0.3	25.4	2.8	4.8	4.5
Tulsa, OK	41.6	14.8	0.2	2.9	0.2	27.8	2.3	4.3	3.4
Tuscaloosa, AL	41.0	10.6	0.1	2.1	0.1	21.3	2.4	3.5	8.7
Virginia Beach, VA	38.8	18.6	0.2	2.4	0.1	28.7	2.2	4.0	3.5
Washington, DC	45.3	10.3	0.6	3.1	0.5	20.4	2.4	4.2	7.1
Wichita, KS	40.0	16.4	0.2	2.7	0.2	29.1	2.2	3.7	3.1
Wilmington, NC	45.7	14.9	0.3	3.4	0.3	21.2	1.5	3.0	5.9
Winston-Salem, NC	40.9	14.6	0.2	2.5	0.2	28.1	2.4	4.3	2.7
Worcester, MA	38.3	12.2	0.3	2.8	0.2	26.3	1.7	5.7	5.3
U.S.	38.3	17.5	0.2	2.5	0.2	28.3	2.4	4.8	3.4

Note: Figures are percent of the total population; (1) Includes biological, adopted, and stepchildren of the householder
Source: U.S. Census Bureau, 2020 Census

A-26 Appendix A: Comparative Statistics

Household Relationships: Metro Area

Metro Area	House-holder	Opposite-sex Spouse	Same-sex Spouse	Opposite-sex Unmarried Partner	Same-sex Unmarried Partner	Child[1]	Grand-child	Other Relatives	Non-relatives
Albuquerque, NM	40.1	16.3	0.3	3.1	0.3	27.7	3.1	4.6	2.9
Allentown, PA	38.8	18.7	0.2	2.9	0.1	28.2	2.0	4.1	2.5
Anchorage, AK	37.1	17.6	0.2	2.9	0.1	29.1	1.9	4.2	4.0
Ann Arbor, MI	39.7	17.0	0.3	2.4	0.2	24.3	1.3	2.5	5.8
Athens, GA	38.6	15.6	0.2	2.3	0.2	25.1	2.3	3.7	7.3
Atlanta, GA	37.1	16.7	0.2	2.1	0.2	30.4	2.7	5.7	3.5
Austin, TX	38.6	17.3	0.3	2.7	0.3	27.8	1.9	4.4	4.6
Baltimore, MD	38.7	16.8	0.2	2.4	0.2	28.7	2.5	4.8	3.5
Boise City, ID	36.6	19.5	0.2	2.5	0.1	29.7	1.9	3.5	3.8
Boston, MA	38.7	17.4	0.3	2.5	0.2	27.1	1.6	4.5	4.4
Boulder, CO	40.1	18.0	0.3	2.8	0.2	23.8	1.0	2.6	6.8
Brownsville, TX	31.5	15.3	0.1	1.7	0.1	36.1	5.2	7.4	1.7
Cape Coral, FL	41.8	20.9	0.3	3.0	0.2	22.4	1.8	4.4	3.3
Cedar Rapids, IA	40.9	19.3	0.1	3.0	0.1	27.9	1.2	2.3	2.5
Charleston, SC	39.9	18.1	0.2	2.4	0.1	27.3	2.6	3.8	3.5
Charlotte, NC	38.9	18.3	0.2	2.4	0.2	29.2	2.4	4.2	2.8
Chicago, IL	38.2	17.1	0.2	2.3	0.1	30.3	2.4	5.1	2.8
Cincinnati, OH	39.5	18.1	0.2	2.7	0.1	28.9	2.3	3.2	2.9
Clarksville, TN	36.7	18.2	0.2	2.2	0.1	30.5	2.5	3.6	3.0
Cleveland, OH	42.5	17.1	0.1	2.7	0.1	27.7	2.1	3.3	2.3
College Station, TX	36.9	14.6	0.1	2.0	0.1	24.7	1.9	3.5	8.3
Colorado Springs, CO	37.5	19.3	0.2	2.2	0.1	28.5	2.0	3.6	3.8
Columbia, MO	39.8	16.5	0.2	2.8	0.2	24.9	1.4	2.5	5.7
Columbia, SC	39.9	17.0	0.2	2.1	0.2	27.5	2.7	3.8	3.0
Columbus, OH	39.4	17.4	0.2	2.9	0.2	28.5	2.0	3.5	3.3
Dallas, TX	36.2	17.6	0.2	2.0	0.2	31.7	2.7	5.5	2.9
Davenport, IA	41.4	18.8	0.2	2.9	0.1	27.9	1.8	2.5	2.2
Denver, CO	39.4	17.9	0.3	2.9	0.2	27.4	1.9	4.4	4.3
Des Moines, IA	39.6	19.2	0.2	2.7	0.1	29.6	1.3	2.8	2.6
Durham, NC	40.3	17.2	0.3	2.5	0.2	25.1	1.9	3.8	3.9
Edison, NJ	36.8	15.8	0.2	2.0	0.2	29.7	2.1	7.1	4.1
El Paso, TX	34.2	15.8	0.2	1.7	0.1	33.5	4.2	6.5	1.8
Fargo, ND	41.5	17.7	0.1	3.2	0.1	27.0	0.7	2.2	3.9
Fort Collins, CO	40.2	19.4	0.2	2.8	0.2	24.0	1.2	2.7	6.0
Fort Wayne, IN	39.5	18.0	0.2	2.7	0.1	30.5	1.9	2.9	2.5
Fort Worth, TX	36.2	17.6	0.2	2.0	0.2	31.7	2.7	5.5	2.9
Grand Rapids, MI	37.3	19.0	0.1	2.5	0.1	29.6	1.7	2.9	3.5
Greeley, CO	34.6	19.3	0.1	2.2	0.1	31.5	2.4	4.6	3.6
Green Bay, WI	40.5	19.8	0.1	3.3	0.1	28.1	1.2	2.2	2.2
Greensboro, NC	40.2	17.1	0.2	2.4	0.2	27.4	2.3	3.9	2.6
Honolulu, HI	33.1	16.3	0.2	1.9	0.1	26.2	4.5	9.2	4.9
Houston, TX	35.2	17.1	0.2	2.0	0.1	32.7	2.8	6.1	2.6
Huntsville, AL	40.1	19.3	0.1	1.9	0.1	27.8	2.3	3.4	2.3
Indianapolis, IN	39.2	17.9	0.2	2.8	0.2	29.6	2.1	3.5	2.8
Jacksonville, FL	39.1	17.9	0.2	2.6	0.2	28.0	2.6	4.3	3.2
Kansas City, MO	39.6	18.4	0.2	2.6	0.2	29.4	2.0	3.3	2.7
Lafayette, LA	39.5	17.1	0.2	2.7	0.2	30.4	2.9	3.5	2.5
Las Cruces, NM	37.5	15.9	0.2	2.7	0.2	30.0	3.6	5.1	2.7
Las Vegas, NV	37.3	15.5	0.3	3.0	0.2	28.7	2.6	7.0	4.4
Lexington, KY	40.5	17.4	0.2	2.8	0.2	26.5	2.0	3.4	3.7
Lincoln, NE	39.5	17.9	0.2	2.6	0.1	27.2	1.1	2.6	4.1
Little Rock, AR	40.8	17.7	0.2	2.3	0.2	27.9	2.6	3.6	2.7
Los Angeles, CA	34.0	15.2	0.2	2.3	0.2	29.0	3.0	9.1	5.1
Louisville, KY	40.5	17.7	0.2	2.8	0.2	27.6	2.5	3.6	2.9
Madison, WI	42.2	18.6	0.3	3.3	0.2	25.0	0.8	2.1	4.5

Table continued on following page.

Appendix A: Comparative Statistics A-27

Metro Area	House-holder	Opposite-sex Spouse	Same-sex Spouse	Opposite-sex Unmarried Partner	Same-sex Unmarried Partner	Child[1]	Grand-child	Other Relatives	Non-relatives
Manchester, NH	39.7	19.2	0.3	3.2	0.1	27.2	1.6	3.5	3.2
Miami, FL	38.0	16.0	0.3	2.6	0.2	27.6	2.5	7.8	3.7
Midland, TX	35.8	18.6	0.1	2.0	0.1	32.3	3.2	4.4	2.6
Milwaukee, WI	41.3	17.5	0.2	2.9	0.2	28.7	1.6	3.1	2.7
Minneapolis, MN	38.9	18.7	0.2	2.8	0.2	29.4	1.2	3.3	3.3
Nashville, TN	38.8	18.2	0.2	2.4	0.2	28.1	2.2	4.1	3.8
New Haven, CT	39.7	16.5	0.2	2.6	0.2	28.1	2.0	4.4	2.9
New Orleans, LA	40.3	15.3	0.2	2.7	0.2	28.8	3.1	4.6	2.9
New York, NY	36.8	15.8	0.2	2.0	0.2	29.7	2.1	7.1	4.1
Oklahoma City, OK	38.8	17.7	0.2	2.4	0.2	29.0	2.3	3.8	3.1
Omaha, NE	38.8	18.4	0.2	2.6	0.1	30.6	1.6	3.1	2.8
Orlando, FL	37.0	17.0	0.3	2.7	0.2	28.4	2.4	6.0	4.2
Philadelphia, PA	38.7	16.9	0.2	2.5	0.2	29.2	2.5	4.4	3.0
Phoenix, AZ	36.9	17.2	0.2	2.8	0.2	29.0	2.5	5.4	3.7
Pittsburgh, PA	43.2	19.0	0.2	2.8	0.2	25.6	1.6	2.6	2.4
Portland, OR	39.0	18.1	0.4	3.2	0.3	26.7	1.6	4.2	4.9
Providence, RI	40.0	16.9	0.2	3.0	0.2	27.2	1.9	4.1	3.0
Provo, UT	28.0	18.8	0.1	0.7	0.0	39.0	2.1	4.0	4.8
Raleigh, NC	38.4	19.2	0.2	2.2	0.2	30.0	1.5	3.7	3.0
Reno, NV	39.5	17.2	0.2	3.4	0.2	26.1	2.1	5.0	4.9
Richmond, VA	39.5	17.3	0.2	2.5	0.2	27.7	2.4	4.0	3.3
Rochester, MN	40.1	20.5	0.1	2.7	0.1	28.9	1.0	2.2	2.5
Sacramento, CA	36.2	17.1	0.3	2.4	0.2	29.4	2.2	6.0	4.2
St. Louis, MO	40.8	18.2	0.2	2.6	0.2	28.5	2.2	3.0	2.4
Salem, OR	35.7	17.6	0.2	2.7	0.1	29.3	2.3	5.0	4.1
Salt Lake City, UT	34.0	17.4	0.3	2.1	0.2	32.4	2.5	5.3	4.4
San Antonio, TX	36.2	16.9	0.2	2.3	0.2	31.0	3.5	5.1	2.8
San Diego, CA	35.1	16.9	0.3	2.3	0.2	27.8	2.3	6.6	5.1
San Francisco, CA	36.7	17.0	0.4	2.3	0.3	26.3	1.8	6.9	5.9
San Jose, CA	33.8	18.4	0.2	1.8	0.1	28.3	1.9	7.9	5.6
Santa Rosa, CA	38.4	17.6	0.4	2.9	0.2	26.1	1.9	5.2	5.5
Savannah, GA	38.7	16.6	0.2	2.4	0.2	28.0	2.8	4.1	3.4
Seattle, WA	38.9	18.3	0.3	2.9	0.2	26.7	1.5	4.6	4.7
Sioux Falls, SD	39.5	19.4	0.1	2.9	0.1	29.8	1.1	2.3	2.6
Springfield, IL	42.9	18.2	0.2	3.0	0.2	27.2	1.8	2.4	2.4
Tampa, FL	41.2	17.6	0.3	3.1	0.2	25.5	2.2	4.6	3.4
Tucson, AZ	40.9	17.2	0.3	2.9	0.2	25.5	2.6	4.4	3.4
Tulsa, OK	39.1	18.2	0.2	2.4	0.1	29.0	2.6	3.9	2.7
Tuscaloosa, AL	39.8	15.2	0.1	1.9	0.1	26.5	3.2	3.9	4.5
Virginia Beach, VA	39.0	17.4	0.2	2.3	0.1	27.7	2.5	4.0	3.3
Washington, DC	37.0	17.3	0.3	2.0	0.2	29.3	2.0	5.9	4.4
Wichita, KS	39.0	18.2	0.1	2.4	0.1	29.8	2.1	3.2	2.6
Wilmington, NC	42.3	18.7	0.2	2.9	0.2	24.4	1.9	3.1	3.9
Winston-Salem, NC	40.9	18.6	0.2	2.3	0.1	27.5	2.4	3.7	2.2
Worcester, MA	38.6	17.9	0.2	2.9	0.1	28.1	1.7	4.0	3.1
U.S.	38.3	17.5	0.2	2.5	0.2	28.3	2.4	4.8	3.4

Note: Figures are percent of the total population; Figures cover the Metropolitan Statistical Area; (1) Includes biological, adopted, and stepchildren of the householder
Source: U.S. Census Bureau, 2020 Census

A-28   Appendix A: Comparative Statistics

Age: City

City	Percent of Population									Median Age
	Under Age 5	Age 5–19	Age 20–34	Age 35–44	Age 45–54	Age 55–64	Age 65–74	Age 75–84	Age 85+	
Albuquerque, NM	5.1	18.6	21.8	13.2	11.7	12.7	10.2	4.9	1.9	38.2
Allentown, PA	6.8	21.0	23.3	12.4	11.4	11.6	7.8	3.9	1.7	34.2
Anchorage, AK	6.4	19.6	23.4	13.7	11.7	12.6	8.3	3.1	0.9	35.2
Ann Arbor, MI	3.9	15.5	42.4	9.6	7.8	8.1	7.3	3.6	1.7	27.9
Athens, GA	5.1	16.6	38.4	10.7	8.8	8.5	7.3	3.5	1.2	28.2
Atlanta, GA	4.9	15.5	33.3	14.3	11.2	9.5	6.8	3.3	1.3	33.1
Austin, TX	5.5	16.7	31.8	16.1	11.4	9.0	6.1	2.5	1.0	33.0
Baltimore, MD	5.5	16.6	27.0	13.1	10.7	12.6	8.9	4.0	1.6	35.5
Boise City, ID	5.1	18.4	23.4	13.6	11.7	12.0	9.5	4.5	1.8	37.1
Boston, MA	4.5	14.1	37.6	12.0	9.6	9.8	7.2	3.7	1.5	31.7
Boulder, CO	3.0	19.4	34.9	10.4	10.3	9.1	7.7	3.6	1.6	30.0
Brownsville, TX	6.6	25.8	20.0	12.3	12.0	10.1	7.9	3.8	1.5	32.9
Cape Coral, FL	4.5	16.6	14.9	11.3	13.4	16.0	14.5	6.8	2.1	47.2
Cedar Rapids, IA	6.3	19.1	22.5	13.0	11.2	12.0	8.9	4.6	2.4	36.4
Charleston, SC	5.6	14.6	28.5	13.9	10.3	11.2	9.7	4.4	1.8	35.7
Charlotte, NC	6.1	19.3	25.8	14.6	12.6	10.5	6.9	3.0	1.1	34.2
Chicago, IL	5.5	16.9	27.5	14.4	11.9	11.1	7.7	3.7	1.4	35.1
Cincinnati, OH	6.1	18.3	29.2	11.9	10.0	11.5	8.0	3.3	1.7	32.7
Clarksville, TN	8.3	21.9	28.4	13.0	9.9	9.2	5.8	2.5	0.8	29.9
Cleveland, OH	6.0	18.2	24.2	11.8	11.5	13.9	9.0	3.9	1.7	36.1
College Station, TX	5.4	24.3	43.8	8.4	6.3	5.2	3.8	2.1	0.6	22.5
Colorado Springs, CO	5.9	19.0	23.7	13.2	11.3	12.2	8.9	4.1	1.6	35.9
Columbia, MO	5.5	20.5	32.8	11.4	9.1	8.9	7.0	3.3	1.5	29.2
Columbia, SC	4.6	22.1	30.7	11.1	9.5	9.8	7.7	3.2	1.3	29.9
Columbus, OH	6.6	18.1	30.0	13.4	10.7	10.3	6.9	2.9	1.2	32.3
Dallas, TX	6.5	19.3	26.6	14.2	11.7	10.6	6.8	3.1	1.3	33.6
Davenport, IA	6.1	18.8	21.8	12.5	11.5	12.8	9.7	4.6	2.1	37.5
Denver, CO	5.4	15.5	31.0	15.8	11.1	9.4	7.4	3.2	1.3	34.1
Des Moines, IA	6.6	19.7	24.0	13.1	11.3	11.8	8.2	3.6	1.7	34.8
Durham, NC	6.0	17.6	28.2	13.9	11.1	10.4	8.1	3.4	1.3	33.9
Edison, NJ	5.3	19.7	18.1	16.5	13.3	12.2	8.9	4.2	1.9	39.0
El Paso, TX	5.9	21.7	21.9	11.9	11.9	11.9	8.6	4.3	1.9	35.4
Fargo, ND	6.2	17.8	30.1	13.0	9.7	10.3	7.7	3.5	1.8	32.5
Fort Collins, CO	4.4	19.4	31.1	12.7	10.2	9.5	7.7	3.4	1.6	31.7
Fort Wayne, IN	6.9	20.8	21.9	12.4	11.2	11.9	9.1	4.1	1.9	35.3
Fort Worth, TX	7.0	22.7	23.1	14.3	12.1	10.3	6.6	2.9	1.1	33.2
Grand Rapids, MI	6.4	18.1	31.1	12.2	9.3	10.1	7.3	3.4	2.1	31.7
Greeley, CO	6.9	22.5	25.0	12.3	10.2	9.8	7.9	3.9	1.6	31.9
Green Bay, WI	6.5	20.6	22.5	12.9	11.1	12.4	8.6	3.7	1.5	35.2
Greensboro, NC	5.5	20.0	24.9	12.1	11.5	11.3	8.7	4.2	1.8	34.7
Honolulu, HI	4.5	14.3	20.5	13.0	12.7	13.7	11.5	6.0	3.6	42.9
Houston, TX	6.6	19.7	25.1	14.3	11.6	10.7	7.3	3.4	1.3	34.2
Huntsville, AL	5.6	17.7	24.2	12.0	11.2	13.1	9.0	5.2	2.2	36.9
Indianapolis, IN	6.6	20.2	24.0	13.4	11.3	11.8	7.9	3.5	1.3	34.5
Jacksonville, FL	6.0	18.2	22.3	12.9	12.2	13.1	9.3	4.2	1.6	37.4
Kansas City, MO	6.2	18.5	25.0	13.6	11.4	11.9	8.2	3.7	1.5	35.1
Lafayette, LA	5.6	17.9	23.5	12.4	10.9	13.0	10.2	4.6	2.0	37.3
Las Cruces, NM	5.8	20.1	23.5	11.9	10.0	11.2	10.0	5.4	2.1	35.5
Las Vegas, NV	5.7	20.0	20.0	13.5	13.1	12.1	9.4	4.7	1.5	38.0
Lexington, KY	5.7	19.2	24.7	13.3	11.4	11.2	8.6	4.0	1.6	35.2
Lincoln, NE	6.0	20.5	24.9	12.9	10.4	10.8	8.8	3.9	1.7	34.0
Little Rock, AR	6.0	18.7	22.1	13.5	11.8	12.2	9.7	4.3	1.8	37.2
Los Angeles, CA	4.9	17.0	25.6	14.6	12.9	11.5	8.0	3.9	1.7	36.5
Louisville, KY	5.9	19.2	18.9	12.8	12.8	13.4	10.0	4.8	1.9	39.5

Table continued on following page.

Appendix A: Comparative Statistics   A-29

City	Percent of Population									Median Age
	Under Age 5	Age 5–19	Age 20–34	Age 35–44	Age 45–54	Age 55–64	Age 65–74	Age 75–84	Age 85+	
Madison, WI	5.0	16.4	33.7	12.6	9.4	9.6	8.1	3.5	1.6	32.0
Manchester, NH	5.3	15.7	26.0	12.6	12.1	13.4	9.0	3.9	2.0	37.0
Miami, FL	4.8	13.6	24.0	15.0	13.5	12.4	8.8	5.5	2.5	39.7
Midland, TX	7.9	21.7	23.5	14.4	10.3	11.0	6.7	3.0	1.5	33.3
Milwaukee, WI	6.8	21.9	25.6	12.6	10.8	10.8	7.3	2.9	1.3	32.1
Minneapolis, MN	5.6	16.1	32.8	14.7	10.3	9.7	7.1	2.6	1.0	32.6
Nashville, TN	6.1	16.6	29.5	14.1	10.7	10.8	7.5	3.3	1.3	33.8
New Haven, CT	5.6	20.8	30.4	12.8	10.0	9.4	6.6	3.1	1.2	31.0
New Orleans, LA	5.5	17.5	24.9	14.0	11.1	12.3	9.4	3.9	1.5	36.2
New York, NY	5.4	16.7	24.8	13.9	12.2	12.0	8.7	4.4	1.9	36.8
Oklahoma City, OK	6.7	20.7	22.7	13.9	11.2	11.4	8.3	3.8	1.5	34.9
Omaha, NE	6.6	20.7	23.1	13.0	11.0	11.7	8.4	3.8	1.6	34.7
Orlando, FL	5.7	17.6	27.2	15.6	12.4	10.1	6.8	3.2	1.3	34.7
Philadelphia, PA	5.5	17.6	27.2	12.9	10.9	11.6	8.5	4.0	1.7	34.8
Phoenix, AZ	6.3	21.6	22.9	13.7	12.4	11.3	7.5	3.2	1.1	34.5
Pittsburgh, PA	4.4	14.5	34.3	11.5	8.8	11.1	9.1	4.2	2.0	33.0
Portland, OR	4.5	14.6	25.8	17.2	13.1	10.8	8.9	3.7	1.4	37.6
Providence, RI	5.6	21.3	29.4	12.4	10.4	9.8	6.6	3.0	1.4	30.9
Provo, UT	7.1	21.4	44.5	8.3	6.1	5.4	3.8	2.2	1.1	23.8
Raleigh, NC	5.5	18.5	28.0	14.0	12.1	10.1	7.0	3.3	1.4	33.7
Reno, NV	5.5	18.0	24.5	12.7	11.3	11.9	9.9	4.6	1.5	36.3
Richmond, VA	5.5	15.8	33.4	12.0	9.3	10.8	8.2	3.4	1.5	32.4
Rochester, MN	6.5	18.6	23.3	13.4	10.5	11.9	8.5	5.0	2.3	36.0
Sacramento, CA	5.9	18.8	24.6	14.1	11.5	11.2	8.5	3.7	1.6	35.4
St. Louis, MO	5.3	15.1	28.8	13.6	10.9	12.8	8.7	3.4	1.4	35.4
Salem, OR	5.9	20.3	21.7	13.6	11.5	11.2	9.6	4.5	1.8	36.3
Salt Lake City, UT	5.1	16.7	33.3	14.1	10.3	9.2	7.0	2.9	1.3	32.1
San Antonio, TX	6.1	20.6	23.4	13.0	11.8	11.4	8.2	3.9	1.6	34.9
San Diego, CA	5.0	16.8	26.7	14.2	11.9	11.3	8.3	4.0	1.7	35.8
San Francisco, CA	4.0	10.5	29.3	15.8	12.5	11.4	9.2	4.6	2.4	38.2
San Jose, CA	5.3	18.5	22.2	14.7	13.9	12.2	7.7	4.0	1.6	37.6
Santa Rosa, CA	5.1	18.5	19.4	13.7	12.1	12.5	10.9	5.4	2.5	39.9
Savannah, GA	5.8	18.4	28.0	12.2	10.2	11.2	8.6	4.0	1.6	33.5
Seattle, WA	4.4	12.6	33.1	16.0	11.8	9.7	7.7	3.3	1.5	35.0
Sioux Falls, SD	7.0	19.8	22.7	13.8	10.7	11.4	8.7	4.0	1.8	35.3
Springfield, IL	5.8	17.6	19.4	12.2	11.6	14.1	11.5	5.5	2.4	40.7
Tampa, FL	5.4	18.7	24.6	13.6	12.4	11.9	8.0	3.8	1.5	35.8
Tucson, AZ	5.3	18.2	24.8	12.0	10.9	12.1	9.9	4.8	1.9	36.2
Tulsa, OK	6.5	19.8	22.5	12.9	11.1	11.8	9.0	4.3	2.0	35.8
Tuscaloosa, AL	5.1	20.8	34.3	10.0	8.8	9.0	7.2	3.3	1.5	27.1
Virginia Beach, VA	5.8	18.6	22.4	13.3	11.8	12.9	9.1	4.4	1.7	37.1
Washington, DC	5.4	13.9	32.9	15.2	10.0	9.9	7.4	3.6	1.5	33.9
Wichita, KS	6.3	21.0	21.7	12.4	11.1	12.4	9.1	4.1	1.8	35.7
Wilmington, NC	4.3	15.1	27.2	11.8	11.0	12.1	10.8	5.7	2.3	37.8
Winston-Salem, NC	5.8	20.5	22.0	12.2	11.6	12.1	9.1	4.5	2.0	36.2
Worcester, MA	5.4	18.9	26.8	12.1	11.5	11.9	7.9	3.7	1.9	34.3
U.S.	5.6	19.2	20.2	12.7	12.4	13.1	10.0	4.9	1.9	38.8

Source: U.S. Census Bureau, 2020 Census

A-30   Appendix A: Comparative Statistics

Age: Metro Area

Metro Area	Percent of Population									Median Age
	Under Age 5	Age 5–19	Age 20–34	Age 35–44	Age 45–54	Age 55–64	Age 65–74	Age 75–84	Age 85+	
Albuquerque, NM	5.1	19.2	19.8	12.6	11.7	13.4	11.0	5.2	1.8	39.4
Allentown, PA	5.0	18.5	18.2	11.8	12.9	14.6	11.0	5.6	2.5	41.9
Anchorage, AK	6.5	20.4	22.2	13.7	11.8	12.7	8.6	3.1	0.9	35.5
Ann Arbor, MI	4.7	17.5	28.4	11.6	11.3	11.6	9.1	4.1	1.6	34.5
Athens, GA	5.3	18.8	28.8	11.6	10.9	10.5	8.6	4.2	1.3	32.5
Atlanta, GA	5.7	20.6	20.9	13.7	13.8	12.1	8.3	3.7	1.2	36.9
Austin, TX	5.9	20.0	24.8	15.3	12.4	10.3	7.3	3.1	1.1	34.7
Baltimore, MD	5.6	18.8	20.5	13.0	12.4	13.6	9.6	4.7	1.9	38.6
Boise City, ID	5.9	21.8	19.7	13.4	11.9	11.7	9.5	4.6	1.6	36.9
Boston, MA	4.9	17.2	22.6	12.5	12.6	13.5	9.8	4.8	2.1	39.0
Boulder, CO	4.2	19.0	23.5	12.7	12.7	12.5	9.7	4.2	1.6	37.6
Brownsville, TX	6.5	25.3	19.3	12.0	11.9	10.6	8.6	4.3	1.6	34.0
Cape Coral, FL	4.3	15.4	15.4	10.1	11.0	14.7	16.4	9.7	3.0	49.7
Cedar Rapids, IA	5.9	19.9	19.1	12.8	11.9	13.2	9.7	5.1	2.2	38.8
Charleston, SC	5.8	18.6	21.4	13.5	11.8	12.6	10.0	4.6	1.5	37.8
Charlotte, NC	5.8	20.2	20.0	13.6	13.7	12.3	8.8	4.2	1.4	37.8
Chicago, IL	5.5	19.3	20.8	13.4	12.9	12.9	9.0	4.3	1.8	38.2
Cincinnati, OH	5.9	20.1	19.8	12.4	12.3	13.4	9.7	4.5	1.8	38.2
Clarksville, TN	7.9	21.3	25.4	12.4	10.7	10.6	7.3	3.3	1.1	31.8
Cleveland, OH	5.2	17.7	18.8	11.7	12.4	14.6	11.3	5.6	2.5	41.7
College Station, TX	5.9	22.0	32.3	10.5	8.8	9.1	6.8	3.3	1.3	27.5
Colorado Springs, CO	6.0	20.0	23.1	12.9	11.4	12.4	8.8	3.9	1.4	35.6
Columbia, MO	5.7	20.6	26.7	12.0	10.2	10.9	8.4	3.9	1.5	32.8
Columbia, SC	5.4	20.2	20.1	12.4	12.4	13.2	10.2	4.6	1.6	38.4
Columbus, OH	6.2	19.8	22.2	13.4	12.3	12.0	8.6	3.9	1.5	36.2
Dallas, TX	6.2	21.8	21.4	14.1	13.0	11.4	7.4	3.4	1.1	35.3
Davenport, IA	5.7	19.5	17.9	12.4	11.8	13.6	11.0	5.6	2.3	40.3
Denver, CO	5.5	18.8	23.0	14.7	12.6	11.7	8.5	3.7	1.4	36.6
Des Moines, IA	6.5	20.8	20.2	13.8	12.0	11.9	8.7	4.1	1.7	36.6
Durham, NC	5.2	18.4	23.1	12.7	12.1	12.3	9.9	4.6	1.6	37.4
Edison, NJ	5.4	18.0	21.5	13.3	12.8	13.0	9.2	4.7	2.1	38.7
El Paso, TX	6.1	22.6	22.4	12.1	11.8	11.5	8.0	3.9	1.7	34.2
Fargo, ND	6.7	19.9	25.7	13.7	10.4	10.7	7.7	3.5	1.7	33.5
Fort Collins, CO	4.6	18.5	23.6	12.9	11.0	12.4	10.5	4.8	1.8	37.4
Fort Wayne, IN	6.7	21.3	19.9	12.4	11.7	12.4	9.4	4.4	1.8	36.6
Fort Worth, TX	6.2	21.8	21.4	14.1	13.0	11.4	7.4	3.4	1.1	35.3
Grand Rapids, MI	6.1	20.6	21.8	12.5	11.5	12.5	8.9	4.3	1.8	36.2
Greeley, CO	6.9	22.6	21.3	13.9	11.6	11.1	8.0	3.4	1.2	34.5
Green Bay, WI	5.8	19.8	18.8	12.6	12.2	14.0	10.1	4.8	1.8	39.3
Greensboro, NC	5.3	19.6	19.9	11.7	12.9	13.2	10.2	5.1	1.9	39.4
Honolulu, HI	5.4	17.3	21.1	12.6	12.2	12.9	10.4	5.4	2.8	39.8
Houston, TX	6.5	22.1	21.0	14.3	12.7	11.4	7.7	3.3	1.1	35.3
Huntsville, AL	5.6	19.2	20.4	12.6	12.8	13.9	9.1	4.7	1.7	38.7
Indianapolis, IN	6.2	20.7	20.2	13.5	12.5	12.5	8.8	4.1	1.5	37.0
Jacksonville, FL	5.6	18.9	19.5	12.8	12.6	13.6	10.4	4.8	1.7	39.6
Kansas City, MO	6.1	20.2	19.9	13.4	12.1	12.8	9.3	4.4	1.7	37.7
Lafayette, LA	6.3	20.5	19.3	12.9	11.7	13.5	9.6	4.5	1.6	37.8
Las Cruces, NM	5.8	21.3	21.6	11.4	10.6	12.2	10.2	5.2	1.9	36.0
Las Vegas, NV	5.7	19.4	20.6	13.9	13.1	12.1	9.5	4.6	1.3	38.0
Lexington, KY	5.9	19.7	22.2	13.2	12.1	12.1	9.2	4.2	1.6	36.5
Lincoln, NE	6.0	20.9	23.4	12.9	10.6	11.4	9.1	4.1	1.7	34.8
Little Rock, AR	5.9	19.9	20.2	13.1	12.0	12.7	10.0	4.7	1.6	38.0
Los Angeles, CA	5.0	18.3	22.5	13.7	13.3	12.4	8.6	4.4	1.9	37.9
Louisville, KY	5.8	18.9	19.5	12.9	12.6	13.6	10.2	4.7	1.8	39.3

Table continued on following page.

Appendix A: Comparative Statistics　A-31

Metro Area	Percent of Population									Median Age
	Under Age 5	Age 5–19	Age 20–34	Age 35–44	Age 45–54	Age 55–64	Age 65–74	Age 75–84	Age 85+	
Madison, WI	5.3	18.3	23.6	13.3	11.5	12.3	9.6	4.2	1.8	36.9
Manchester, NH	5.0	17.5	20.0	12.3	13.5	15.2	10.0	4.7	1.9	40.9
Miami, FL	4.8	17.1	18.7	13.0	13.8	13.7	10.2	6.0	2.6	42.1
Midland, TX	7.8	22.3	22.9	14.3	10.7	11.2	6.7	2.9	1.3	33.3
Milwaukee, WI	5.8	19.6	19.9	12.6	12.0	13.5	9.7	4.6	2.1	38.5
Minneapolis, MN	6.1	19.8	20.5	13.7	12.3	13.0	8.9	4.1	1.7	37.5
Nashville, TN	6.0	19.6	22.1	13.9	12.5	12.1	8.6	3.9	1.3	36.4
New Haven, CT	4.9	18.1	20.3	11.9	12.6	14.1	10.4	5.3	2.5	40.4
New Orleans, LA	5.7	18.9	20.3	13.3	11.9	13.4	10.3	4.6	1.7	38.6
New York, NY	5.4	18.0	21.5	13.3	12.8	13.0	9.2	4.7	2.1	38.7
Oklahoma City, OK	6.2	21.0	21.6	13.4	11.3	12.0	8.9	4.2	1.6	35.8
Omaha, NE	6.6	21.5	20.4	13.4	11.5	12.2	8.8	4.0	1.6	36.0
Orlando, FL	5.2	19.5	21.2	13.5	12.9	12.2	9.2	4.6	1.7	37.9
Philadelphia, PA	5.3	18.7	20.7	12.6	12.4	13.7	9.8	4.8	2.1	39.1
Phoenix, AZ	5.7	20.5	20.5	12.8	12.1	11.9	9.8	5.1	1.7	37.5
Pittsburgh, PA	4.9	16.3	19.3	11.8	12.1	14.9	12.0	5.9	2.8	42.9
Portland, OR	5.2	18.3	21.0	14.8	12.8	12.0	9.8	4.4	1.6	38.6
Providence, RI	4.8	17.9	20.0	12.1	12.8	14.5	10.6	5.2	2.4	40.8
Provo, UT	8.9	27.9	26.5	12.8	8.9	6.9	4.9	2.5	0.9	25.9
Raleigh, NC	5.8	21.0	20.5	14.3	13.8	11.7	8.0	3.6	1.2	36.8
Reno, NV	5.4	18.5	21.4	12.3	11.8	13.1	10.9	5.0	1.5	38.5
Richmond, VA	5.5	18.9	20.8	12.7	12.3	13.3	10.1	4.6	1.8	38.6
Rochester, MN	6.2	19.8	19.3	13.2	11.2	13.4	9.4	5.3	2.3	38.4
Sacramento, CA	5.6	19.8	20.3	13.2	12.1	12.7	9.8	4.8	2.0	38.2
St. Louis, MO	5.6	18.9	19.4	12.6	12.1	14.1	10.3	5.0	2.1	39.7
Salem, OR	5.9	20.8	20.0	12.7	11.3	11.9	10.4	5.1	1.9	37.4
Salt Lake City, UT	6.7	22.8	23.7	14.7	11.1	9.7	7.0	3.1	1.1	32.8
San Antonio, TX	6.1	21.4	21.0	13.2	12.2	11.8	8.7	4.1	1.5	36.0
San Diego, CA	5.3	18.5	23.2	13.4	12.2	12.2	9.0	4.3	1.9	37.1
San Francisco, CA	5.0	16.8	21.7	14.7	13.3	12.4	9.3	4.7	2.0	39.1
San Jose, CA	5.3	18.4	22.4	14.6	13.6	12.0	7.7	4.2	1.9	37.5
Santa Rosa, CA	4.6	17.3	18.2	12.9	12.2	14.2	12.7	5.8	2.3	42.6
Savannah, GA	5.9	19.7	22.5	13.0	11.7	12.2	9.3	4.3	1.5	36.3
Seattle, WA	5.7	17.9	22.7	14.9	12.7	12.1	8.5	3.9	1.5	37.2
Sioux Falls, SD	7.0	20.9	20.5	13.8	11.1	11.9	8.8	4.0	1.7	36.0
Springfield, IL	5.6	18.9	17.6	12.5	12.1	14.5	11.4	5.3	2.1	41.2
Tampa, FL	4.8	17.1	18.3	12.3	12.8	14.2	11.8	6.2	2.3	42.7
Tucson, AZ	4.9	17.8	19.8	11.5	10.9	13.1	12.7	6.8	2.4	41.2
Tulsa, OK	6.2	20.6	19.6	12.8	11.8	12.7	9.7	4.9	1.8	37.6
Tuscaloosa, AL	5.8	20.1	24.7	11.9	11.1	11.8	9.0	4.1	1.5	34.5
Virginia Beach, VA	5.8	18.8	22.2	12.5	11.5	13.4	9.5	4.6	1.7	37.3
Washington, DC	5.8	19.4	21.5	14.3	13.2	12.3	8.2	3.9	1.4	37.2
Wichita, KS	6.2	21.6	19.9	12.5	11.2	12.9	9.5	4.4	1.9	36.7
Wilmington, NC	4.8	16.9	20.5	12.7	12.6	13.3	11.7	5.7	2.0	41.1
Winston-Salem, NC	5.3	19.2	18.2	11.6	13.2	14.0	10.8	5.6	2.1	41.1
Worcester, MA	5.0	18.5	19.8	12.3	13.4	14.6	9.9	4.6	2.0	40.3
U.S.	5.6	19.2	20.2	12.7	12.4	13.1	10.0	4.9	1.9	38.8

Note: Figures cover the Metropolitan Statistical Area (MSA)
Source: U.S. Census Bureau, 2020 Census

A-32   Appendix A: Comparative Statistics

Ancestry: City

City	German	Irish	English	American	Italian	Polish	French[1]	Scottish	Dutch
Albuquerque, NM	9.2	7.6	7.8	3.3	3.2	1.4	1.8	1.4	0.9
Allentown, PA	9.8	4.7	2.0	2.7	4.2	1.8	0.7	0.4	0.8
Anchorage, AK	13.8	9.4	8.5	3.6	3.2	2.0	2.3	1.9	1.3
Ann Arbor, MI	17.0	10.4	10.1	2.7	4.9	6.0	2.7	2.6	2.4
Athens, GA	8.4	8.2	9.8	3.5	3.4	1.5	2.0	2.8	0.8
Atlanta, GA	6.8	5.9	8.1	4.8	2.9	1.4	1.8	1.5	0.5
Austin, TX	10.9	8.3	8.7	2.9	3.0	1.8	2.4	2.1	0.7
Baltimore, MD	6.1	5.7	3.3	2.8	3.1	2.3	0.9	0.7	0.3
Boise City, ID	16.9	12.1	18.1	4.4	4.2	1.9	2.2	3.2	1.7
Boston, MA	4.8	13.1	4.9	2.2	7.2	2.1	1.8	1.1	0.4
Boulder, CO	16.2	11.5	11.4	2.4	6.0	3.6	2.4	3.3	1.3
Brownsville, TX	0.9	0.5	0.6	1.7	0.4	0.1	0.4	0.1	0.2
Cape Coral, FL	14.2	11.5	7.8	12.3	9.6	3.4	2.0	1.5	0.9
Cedar Rapids, IA	29.0	13.5	9.0	3.6	1.7	1.3	1.9	1.7	1.6
Charleston, SC	10.8	10.5	11.4	21.1	4.2	2.2	2.5	2.3	0.7
Charlotte, NC	8.0	6.9	7.0	4.8	3.4	1.5	1.3	1.7	0.5
Chicago, IL	7.3	7.3	2.8	2.1	3.9	5.2	0.9	0.7	0.5
Cincinnati, OH	17.3	9.4	6.2	3.5	3.8	1.6	1.4	1.1	0.9
Clarksville, TN	12.2	8.6	7.1	6.1	4.2	1.0	1.4	1.6	1.1
Cleveland, OH	9.5	8.5	3.2	2.2	4.6	3.9	0.9	0.6	0.5
College Station, TX	15.9	8.4	8.8	3.3	3.5	1.8	2.9	1.7	0.8
Colorado Springs, CO	17.7	10.6	11.4	4.2	4.7	2.2	2.7	2.7	1.4
Columbia, MO	24.6	12.0	11.0	4.4	3.6	2.2	1.9	2.3	1.2
Columbia, SC	9.6	6.9	7.7	5.5	3.3	1.1	1.9	1.9	0.6
Columbus, OH	15.2	10.2	6.9	4.0	4.9	2.1	1.3	1.6	0.8
Dallas, TX	5.1	4.2	5.1	4.2	1.7	0.8	1.2	1.1	0.4
Davenport, IA	27.7	15.3	7.5	3.4	2.2	2.0	1.5	1.6	1.6
Denver, CO	13.9	10.1	9.0	2.6	5.0	2.7	2.1	2.1	1.1
Des Moines, IA	19.1	11.9	8.2	3.1	3.6	1.2	1.5	1.2	2.3
Durham, NC	8.1	6.5	9.4	3.7	3.3	1.7	1.6	1.6	0.6
Edison, NJ	4.4	5.8	1.6	1.7	7.8	3.3	1.0	0.5	0.2
El Paso, TX	3.8	2.5	1.9	2.2	1.3	0.5	0.7	0.4	0.2
Fargo, ND	35.0	8.2	5.0	2.5	1.0	2.1	3.5	1.2	1.0
Fort Collins, CO	23.4	12.9	13.0	3.6	5.8	3.0	3.2	3.3	1.8
Fort Wayne, IN	23.1	9.4	7.8	5.5	2.3	2.2	2.7	1.6	1.1
Fort Worth, TX	7.2	6.1	6.5	4.2	1.8	1.0	1.3	1.5	0.7
Grand Rapids, MI	14.1	8.0	6.4	2.5	3.0	6.3	1.9	1.6	13.0
Greeley, CO	16.6	8.4	7.5	3.1	2.7	1.6	1.6	1.9	1.0
Green Bay, WI	28.7	8.5	4.3	4.1	2.1	8.0	3.6	1.0	2.6
Greensboro, NC	6.5	5.5	8.6	4.4	2.4	1.0	1.2	1.6	0.5
Honolulu, HI	4.4	3.1	3.2	1.4	1.7	0.8	0.8	0.6	0.2
Houston, TX	4.8	3.5	4.3	3.4	1.6	0.9	1.4	0.9	0.4
Huntsville, AL	9.4	8.9	10.6	10.2	2.3	1.2	1.8	1.9	0.9
Indianapolis, IN	12.8	8.2	7.0	4.9	2.0	1.5	1.6	1.5	0.9
Jacksonville, FL	7.5	7.6	6.5	5.7	3.7	1.4	1.3	1.5	0.6
Kansas City, MO	15.2	10.1	8.1	4.1	3.6	1.7	1.7	1.4	0.8
Lafayette, LA	8.0	5.4	5.9	5.9	3.6	0.3	16.2	1.0	0.4
Las Cruces, NM	7.0	5.8	6.4	2.6	1.9	1.0	1.2	1.1	0.8
Las Vegas, NV	8.5	7.3	6.2	3.2	5.2	1.8	1.6	1.3	0.7
Lexington, KY	13.1	11.0	12.1	8.2	3.1	1.6	1.6	2.6	1.1
Lincoln, NE	31.5	11.5	8.9	3.3	2.0	2.4	1.8	1.4	1.6
Little Rock, AR	7.3	6.2	8.8	5.2	1.4	0.9	1.5	1.6	0.4
Los Angeles, CA	3.8	3.6	3.1	3.9	2.7	1.4	1.1	0.7	0.4
Louisville, KY	15.2	11.5	9.3	6.5	2.6	1.1	1.7	1.6	0.9
Madison, WI	29.4	12.0	8.8	2.0	4.0	5.5	2.4	1.8	1.8
Manchester, NH	6.2	19.3	9.5	2.9	8.8	3.8	11.4	2.7	0.3

Table continued on following page.

Appendix A: Comparative Statistics   A-33

City	German	Irish	English	American	Italian	Polish	French[1]	Scottish	Dutch
Miami, FL	1.8	1.3	1.0	2.7	2.5	0.7	0.9	0.2	0.2
Midland, TX	5.8	5.2	6.0	4.7	1.0	0.5	1.5	1.4	0.3
Milwaukee, WI	15.1	5.6	2.1	1.3	2.5	5.9	1.2	0.4	0.6
Minneapolis, MN	20.9	10.5	6.5	1.9	2.6	3.9	2.7	1.4	1.3
Nashville, TN	8.4	7.8	8.7	6.8	2.6	1.4	1.6	1.9	0.7
New Haven, CT	3.9	6.2	3.2	2.0	8.2	2.0	1.2	0.5	0.5
New Orleans, LA	6.1	5.7	4.9	2.2	3.7	0.9	5.2	1.0	0.4
New York, NY	2.9	4.4	1.9	3.8	6.1	2.3	0.8	0.5	0.3
Oklahoma City, OK	10.0	7.8	7.7	5.7	1.8	0.7	1.3	1.6	0.9
Omaha, NE	24.7	13.0	7.8	3.0	4.0	3.5	1.9	1.6	1.4
Orlando, FL	6.2	5.7	5.7	5.6	4.7	1.6	1.5	1.0	0.6
Philadelphia, PA	6.7	9.9	2.8	2.5	6.9	3.1	0.8	0.6	0.3
Phoenix, AZ	9.8	7.4	6.3	2.8	3.8	1.8	1.6	1.2	0.8
Pittsburgh, PA	17.9	13.8	5.4	3.0	12.1	6.7	1.4	1.3	0.5
Portland, OR	15.3	11.2	11.9	4.5	4.5	2.3	2.8	2.9	1.7
Providence, RI	3.7	8.0	3.9	2.1	6.9	1.4	2.9	0.8	0.3
Provo, UT	9.9	5.2	25.3	2.6	1.8	0.7	1.4	4.1	1.7
Raleigh, NC	9.0	8.1	10.4	8.4	3.9	2.0	1.7	2.3	0.9
Reno, NV	12.0	10.6	10.5	4.2	5.7	1.9	2.4	2.0	1.2
Richmond, VA	7.3	7.0	8.9	4.5	3.5	1.4	1.5	1.9	0.5
Rochester, MN	28.7	10.2	6.7	3.1	1.5	2.9	1.8	1.3	1.6
Sacramento, CA	6.6	5.9	5.5	1.8	3.5	1.0	1.5	1.1	0.6
St. Louis, MO	15.7	9.7	5.4	4.4	4.0	1.7	2.3	1.2	0.8
Salem, OR	16.9	9.3	11.1	3.6	2.9	1.4	2.7	2.5	1.8
Salt Lake City, UT	10.9	6.9	17.7	3.2	4.1	1.4	2.1	3.5	1.8
San Antonio, TX	7.0	4.3	4.0	3.2	1.8	1.0	1.4	0.8	0.3
San Diego, CA	8.3	7.1	6.2	2.3	4.2	1.8	1.7	1.4	0.7
San Francisco, CA	6.9	7.6	5.5	2.5	4.6	1.8	2.1	1.3	0.7
San Jose, CA	4.6	4.0	3.8	1.8	3.3	0.8	1.1	0.8	0.5
Santa Rosa, CA	11.1	9.8	9.6	2.5	6.6	1.6	2.8	1.7	1.1
Savannah, GA	6.5	7.6	5.4	4.0	3.1	1.5	1.6	1.3	0.6
Seattle, WA	14.4	11.0	11.1	2.3	4.5	2.6	3.0	2.8	1.3
Sioux Falls, SD	33.6	10.9	6.5	4.2	1.6	1.5	1.8	0.9	6.1
Springfield, IL	18.9	11.4	9.6	4.1	4.5	2.0	1.9	1.8	1.1
Tampa, FL	8.7	7.5	6.7	6.5	6.2	2.0	1.8	1.4	0.7
Tucson, AZ	11.1	8.1	7.4	2.8	3.5	1.9	1.8	1.5	0.8
Tulsa, OK	10.8	8.7	9.3	5.4	2.0	0.9	1.9	2.0	0.8
Tuscaloosa, AL	5.2	6.1	6.4	5.7	1.9	0.7	1.3	2.1	0.5
Virginia Beach, VA	11.3	10.7	10.1	7.8	5.6	2.1	2.2	2.2	0.8
Washington, DC	7.5	7.3	6.1	2.8	4.3	2.2	1.6	1.4	0.7
Wichita, KS	19.0	9.6	9.7	4.8	1.6	0.9	2.0	1.6	1.2
Wilmington, NC	10.2	9.4	11.7	4.7	5.3	2.0	1.8	2.7	0.8
Winston-Salem, NC	8.7	6.4	8.5	4.8	2.4	0.9	1.2	1.9	0.7
Worcester, MA	3.0	14.0	4.6	3.7	8.9	4.2	5.7	1.0	0.3
U.S.	12.8	9.6	8.1	5.7	5.0	2.7	2.2	1.6	1.1

Note: Figures are the percentage of the total population reporting a particular ancestry. The nine most commonly reported ancestries in the U.S. are shown. Figures include multiple ancestries (e.g. if a person reported being Irish and Italian, they were included in both columns);
(1) Excludes Basque
Source: U.S. Census Bureau, 2017-2021 American Community Survey 5-Year Estimates

A-34　Appendix A: Comparative Statistics

Ancestry: Metro Area

Metro Area	German	Irish	English	American	Italian	Polish	French[1]	Scottish	Dutch
Albuquerque, NM	9.2	7.2	7.7	3.9	3.1	1.3	1.7	1.5	0.7
Allentown, PA	22.8	12.8	6.1	4.9	11.8	4.9	1.4	1.0	1.8
Anchorage, AK	14.7	9.9	8.8	4.0	3.0	2.0	2.4	2.0	1.4
Ann Arbor, MI	18.3	10.6	10.8	5.9	4.6	6.3	2.9	2.7	2.0
Athens, GA	8.4	10.1	11.7	6.7	2.9	1.1	1.8	2.6	1.0
Atlanta, GA	6.5	6.4	8.0	8.0	2.6	1.2	1.3	1.6	0.6
Austin, TX	12.3	8.1	9.1	3.7	2.8	1.6	2.3	2.1	0.8
Baltimore, MD	14.3	11.3	8.0	4.6	5.9	3.8	1.4	1.5	0.6
Boise City, ID	16.4	10.2	17.6	4.9	3.5	1.4	2.4	2.9	1.9
Boston, MA	5.8	20.3	9.7	3.3	12.4	3.1	4.2	2.1	0.5
Boulder, CO	18.4	11.9	13.4	3.0	5.4	3.2	2.7	3.0	1.7
Brownsville, TX	1.9	1.1	1.8	1.9	0.5	0.2	0.5	0.3	0.1
Cape Coral, FL	13.5	10.7	8.4	12.5	7.8	3.1	2.1	1.7	1.1
Cedar Rapids, IA	32.6	14.2	9.1	4.1	1.7	1.1	2.2	1.9	2.0
Charleston, SC	10.1	9.5	10.6	11.8	3.9	1.8	2.1	2.3	0.6
Charlotte, NC	10.7	8.5	8.9	8.8	3.9	1.8	1.5	2.1	0.8
Chicago, IL	13.7	10.5	4.5	2.5	6.4	8.3	1.3	0.9	1.1
Cincinnati, OH	26.1	13.2	10.0	6.2	4.0	1.6	1.8	1.8	1.0
Clarksville, TN	11.8	8.8	8.3	7.4	3.2	1.1	1.4	1.7	1.0
Cleveland, OH	18.7	13.4	7.7	4.2	9.4	7.4	1.5	1.4	0.8
College Station, TX	13.5	7.6	7.6	3.8	2.8	1.8	2.4	1.6	0.7
Colorado Springs, CO	17.8	10.6	10.9	4.4	4.5	2.3	2.6	2.6	1.4
Columbia, MO	25.0	11.7	11.6	6.2	2.9	1.7	2.1	2.1	1.3
Columbia, SC	9.5	7.1	8.3	7.5	2.3	1.3	1.4	1.8	0.6
Columbus, OH	20.7	12.7	9.6	5.7	5.2	2.3	1.7	2.1	1.1
Dallas, TX	8.2	6.5	7.6	5.9	2.1	1.0	1.5	1.5	0.6
Davenport, IA	25.9	13.5	8.2	4.0	2.3	2.1	1.7	1.4	1.8
Denver, CO	17.1	10.7	10.5	3.3	5.0	2.4	2.4	2.2	1.4
Des Moines, IA	26.2	13.0	10.1	4.0	3.1	1.4	1.7	1.5	3.6
Durham, NC	9.3	8.0	11.1	5.4	3.5	1.8	1.7	2.1	0.7
Edison, NJ	6.0	8.9	2.9	4.0	11.6	3.7	0.9	0.6	0.5
El Paso, TX	3.5	2.3	1.8	2.2	1.2	0.5	0.6	0.4	0.2
Fargo, ND	35.4	7.8	4.8	2.5	1.1	2.2	3.1	1.1	1.1
Fort Collins, CO	25.2	13.1	14.1	4.1	5.2	2.8	3.2	3.4	2.1
Fort Wayne, IN	26.4	9.5	8.3	6.4	2.5	2.1	3.1	1.6	1.1
Fort Worth, TX	8.2	6.5	7.6	5.9	2.1	1.0	1.5	1.5	0.6
Grand Rapids, MI	18.8	9.5	8.9	3.4	3.0	6.3	2.5	1.7	18.0
Greeley, CO	20.5	10.1	9.7	4.1	3.7	1.9	1.9	1.8	1.4
Green Bay, WI	35.4	9.6	4.8	3.8	2.1	9.5	3.9	0.8	4.1
Greensboro, NC	8.5	7.0	9.4	7.3	2.4	1.1	1.3	2.1	0.8
Honolulu, HI	5.2	3.9	3.7	1.3	1.9	0.8	1.1	0.8	0.4
Houston, TX	7.3	5.0	5.8	3.8	2.0	1.1	1.9	1.1	0.6
Huntsville, AL	8.9	9.5	11.1	11.7	2.2	1.3	1.6	1.9	0.8
Indianapolis, IN	16.6	9.6	9.5	8.1	2.5	1.7	1.7	1.7	1.2
Jacksonville, FL	9.3	9.4	8.9	7.9	4.3	1.8	1.7	2.0	0.7
Kansas City, MO	19.9	12.3	11.1	4.9	3.2	1.6	2.1	1.9	1.2
Lafayette, LA	6.3	4.3	4.2	6.4	2.6	0.4	16.5	0.6	0.3
Las Cruces, NM	6.5	4.7	5.3	2.5	1.6	0.7	1.1	1.1	0.7
Las Vegas, NV	8.2	6.9	6.3	3.0	4.9	1.8	1.5	1.2	0.6
Lexington, KY	12.7	11.3	12.6	11.4	2.8	1.4	1.6	2.5	1.1
Lincoln, NE	32.9	11.3	8.7	3.6	1.9	2.3	1.8	1.3	1.8
Little Rock, AR	8.9	8.8	9.6	7.1	1.5	0.8	1.5	1.8	0.7
Los Angeles, CA	5.1	4.3	4.1	3.5	2.9	1.2	1.2	0.8	0.5
Louisville, KY	17.3	12.5	10.8	8.1	2.5	1.2	1.9	1.9	1.0
Madison, WI	35.2	12.9	9.1	2.7	3.6	5.1	2.5	1.6	1.7
Manchester, NH	8.0	20.7	13.9	3.3	9.8	4.0	11.2	3.3	0.7

Table continued on following page.

Appendix A: Comparative Statistics A-35

Metro Area	German	Irish	English	American	Italian	Polish	French[1]	Scottish	Dutch
Miami, FL	4.3	4.2	2.9	5.9	4.9	1.8	1.2	0.6	0.4
Midland, TX	6.0	5.0	5.7	5.0	1.2	0.5	1.4	1.2	0.2
Milwaukee, WI	31.9	9.5	4.6	2.1	4.2	10.3	2.2	0.9	1.2
Minneapolis, MN	28.1	10.9	6.3	3.0	2.6	4.1	3.2	1.2	1.4
Nashville, TN	9.9	9.3	11.1	10.2	2.7	1.3	1.7	2.1	0.8
New Haven, CT	7.5	14.2	7.1	2.9	19.9	5.4	3.0	1.0	0.5
New Orleans, LA	9.6	7.9	5.5	4.8	7.3	0.7	11.0	1.0	0.4
New York, NY	6.0	8.9	2.9	4.0	11.6	3.7	0.9	0.6	0.5
Oklahoma City, OK	11.6	8.9	9.1	7.0	1.8	0.8	1.5	1.8	1.0
Omaha, NE	28.3	13.1	9.1	3.5	3.9	3.7	1.9	1.5	1.6
Orlando, FL	8.1	7.2	6.5	8.2	5.1	1.8	1.7	1.2	0.7
Philadelphia, PA	14.1	17.4	7.4	3.2	12.4	4.7	1.2	1.2	0.7
Phoenix, AZ	12.5	8.6	8.6	3.8	4.4	2.3	1.9	1.6	1.0
Pittsburgh, PA	25.1	17.0	8.6	3.3	15.2	8.1	1.6	1.9	1.0
Portland, OR	16.4	10.5	11.7	4.6	3.7	1.8	2.7	2.7	1.7
Providence, RI	4.5	17.2	10.7	3.2	13.1	3.4	8.6	1.5	0.4
Provo, UT	10.0	4.9	29.5	4.2	2.2	0.5	1.6	4.3	1.5
Raleigh, NC	9.9	9.1	11.6	8.2	4.6	2.1	1.8	2.4	0.8
Reno, NV	12.5	10.6	10.9	3.8	6.2	1.8	2.6	2.0	1.2
Richmond, VA	9.0	7.9	11.7	6.7	3.8	1.5	1.5	1.9	0.7
Rochester, MN	34.2	11.0	6.8	3.4	1.3	2.8	1.9	1.2	1.9
Sacramento, CA	10.1	7.9	8.7	2.6	4.7	1.2	1.9	1.6	0.9
St. Louis, MO	26.1	12.9	8.6	5.4	4.6	2.3	3.0	1.5	1.0
Salem, OR	16.9	9.0	10.6	3.7	2.8	1.2	2.6	2.3	1.8
Salt Lake City, UT	9.7	5.7	21.7	4.0	2.9	0.9	1.9	3.6	1.7
San Antonio, TX	10.0	5.7	5.8	3.6	2.1	1.4	1.7	1.2	0.4
San Diego, CA	8.9	7.4	6.7	2.7	4.1	1.7	1.8	1.4	0.8
San Francisco, CA	7.3	7.0	6.2	2.3	4.4	1.4	1.8	1.4	0.7
San Jose, CA	5.8	4.7	4.7	2.0	3.7	1.1	1.3	0.9	0.6
Santa Rosa, CA	12.8	12.2	10.9	2.5	8.3	1.7	3.1	2.5	1.2
Savannah, GA	9.1	9.9	8.7	7.4	3.5	1.4	1.7	1.7	0.6
Seattle, WA	13.8	9.4	10.1	3.0	3.5	1.8	2.6	2.5	1.3
Sioux Falls, SD	35.2	10.4	6.1	5.2	1.4	1.4	1.8	0.9	6.4
Springfield, IL	21.5	12.5	10.9	5.1	4.8	1.9	2.2	1.9	1.3
Tampa, FL	11.6	10.3	8.5	8.6	7.3	2.9	2.4	1.7	0.9
Tucson, AZ	13.1	8.9	9.1	3.3	3.9	2.3	2.1	1.9	1.0
Tulsa, OK	12.6	10.2	9.9	5.6	1.9	0.9	2.0	2.0	1.1
Tuscaloosa, AL	5.0	6.5	6.9	10.9	1.5	0.4	0.9	1.9	0.5
Virginia Beach, VA	9.5	8.8	9.8	8.5	4.0	1.7	1.8	1.7	0.7
Washington, DC	9.0	8.4	7.5	4.0	4.2	2.1	1.5	1.5	0.7
Wichita, KS	21.4	9.9	10.0	5.7	1.7	0.9	2.0	1.8	1.3
Wilmington, NC	11.3	10.8	12.1	5.8	5.6	2.3	1.8	3.0	0.8
Winston-Salem, NC	11.3	8.1	11.0	8.5	2.3	1.1	1.2	2.2	0.8
Worcester, MA	5.5	17.6	9.3	5.5	11.8	5.6	9.5	2.0	0.5
U.S.	12.8	9.6	8.1	5.7	5.0	2.7	2.2	1.6	1.1

Note: Figures are the percentage of the total population reporting a particular ancestry. The nine most commonly reported ancestries in the U.S. are shown. Figures include multiple ancestries (e.g. if a person reported being Irish and Italian, they were included in both columns); Figures cover the Metropolitan Statistical Area; (1) Excludes Basque
Source: U.S. Census Bureau, 2017-2021 American Community Survey 5-Year Estimates

A-36 Appendix A: Comparative Statistics

Foreign-born Population: City

City	Percent of Population Born in								
	Any Foreign Country	Asia	Mexico	Europe	Caribbean	Central America[1]	South America	Africa	Canada
Albuquerque, NM	10.2	2.5	5.1	0.9	0.4	0.1	0.4	0.5	0.1
Allentown, PA	20.4	3.1	1.0	0.8	11.5	0.8	2.0	1.3	0.1
Anchorage, AK	11.0	6.1	0.7	1.0	0.6	0.2	0.5	0.6	0.4
Ann Arbor, MI	18.6	12.3	0.5	2.9	0.1	0.1	0.7	1.2	0.8
Athens, GA	9.5	2.9	2.4	0.9	0.3	1.0	1.0	1.0	0.2
Atlanta, GA	8.3	3.4	0.7	1.4	0.8	0.2	0.8	0.8	0.3
Austin, TX	18.5	6.3	6.3	1.5	0.6	1.7	0.8	0.9	0.3
Baltimore, MD	8.1	2.2	0.3	0.9	1.3	1.0	0.4	1.9	0.1
Boise City, ID	6.5	2.8	1.1	1.2	0.1	0.0	0.3	0.5	0.5
Boston, MA	28.1	7.6	0.4	3.1	8.6	2.5	2.3	3.0	0.4
Boulder, CO	10.6	4.4	0.9	3.0	0.2	0.5	0.7	0.3	0.5
Brownsville, TX	27.1	0.5	25.5	0.2	0.0	0.7	0.1	0.0	0.1
Cape Coral, FL	17.4	1.5	0.6	2.4	8.3	0.9	3.2	0.1	0.5
Cedar Rapids, IA	6.8	2.6	0.7	0.5	0.1	0.2	0.2	2.3	0.1
Charleston, SC	5.0	1.5	0.6	1.3	0.4	0.1	0.6	0.3	0.1
Charlotte, NC	17.3	5.3	2.5	1.3	1.2	3.1	1.5	2.1	0.2
Chicago, IL	20.2	5.1	8.1	3.4	0.3	0.9	1.1	1.0	0.2
Cincinnati, OH	6.6	1.9	0.4	0.9	0.2	0.8	0.3	2.0	0.1
Clarksville, TN	6.3	2.0	1.3	0.8	0.5	0.7	0.4	0.4	0.2
Cleveland, OH	6.0	2.4	0.4	1.1	0.6	0.4	0.3	0.7	0.1
College Station, TX	12.3	7.3	1.5	0.9	0.2	0.3	1.1	0.8	0.2
Colorado Springs, CO	7.5	2.2	2.0	1.5	0.3	0.4	0.4	0.4	0.4
Columbia, MO	8.4	5.1	0.6	0.9	0.1	0.2	0.3	1.0	0.1
Columbia, SC	4.8	2.1	0.3	0.6	0.6	0.2	0.4	0.5	0.1
Columbus, OH	13.3	5.0	1.1	0.9	0.5	0.8	0.4	4.7	0.1
Dallas, TX	23.8	2.8	13.9	0.8	0.4	2.9	0.7	2.1	0.2
Davenport, IA	4.5	1.6	1.8	0.4	0.2	0.1	0.0	0.2	0.1
Denver, CO	14.2	2.8	6.6	1.4	0.3	0.6	0.7	1.4	0.3
Des Moines, IA	13.8	5.2	3.6	0.8	0.1	1.1	0.1	2.8	0.1
Durham, NC	14.6	4.4	2.8	1.4	0.6	2.7	0.7	1.5	0.3
Edison, NJ	46.1	37.1	0.5	2.2	1.8	0.6	1.8	1.8	0.3
El Paso, TX	22.8	1.0	20.2	0.5	0.2	0.3	0.2	0.3	0.0
Fargo, ND	9.9	3.7	0.1	0.5	0.1	0.1	0.2	4.8	0.5
Fort Collins, CO	7.3	2.9	1.4	1.4	0.1	0.3	0.6	0.3	0.2
Fort Wayne, IN	8.6	4.3	2.0	0.6	0.1	0.6	0.2	0.6	0.1
Fort Worth, TX	16.7	3.7	9.2	0.6	0.3	0.8	0.6	1.3	0.2
Grand Rapids, MI	10.8	2.4	3.2	1.0	0.7	1.4	0.2	1.7	0.2
Greeley, CO	12.2	0.8	8.3	0.5	0.1	1.1	0.2	1.2	0.1
Green Bay, WI	9.2	2.0	5.2	0.4	0.2	0.4	0.3	0.6	0.1
Greensboro, NC	12.1	4.1	1.8	1.2	0.7	0.5	0.7	2.9	0.2
Honolulu, HI	27.5	22.9	0.2	0.9	0.2	0.1	0.2	0.2	0.2
Houston, TX	28.9	5.9	10.6	1.1	1.0	6.5	1.6	2.0	0.2
Huntsville, AL	6.4	1.9	1.5	0.8	0.3	0.5	0.3	0.7	0.1
Indianapolis, IN	10.0	3.0	2.8	0.5	0.5	0.9	0.4	1.9	0.1
Jacksonville, FL	12.0	4.2	0.6	1.9	2.2	0.8	1.4	0.6	0.2
Kansas City, MO	8.0	2.3	2.2	0.5	0.6	0.6	0.3	1.3	0.1
Lafayette, LA	5.5	2.3	0.4	0.7	0.2	1.1	0.6	0.1	0.1
Las Cruces, NM	11.0	2.3	7.0	0.8	0.1	0.1	0.2	0.4	0.1
Las Vegas, NV	20.8	5.3	8.8	1.6	1.1	2.4	0.8	0.4	0.4
Lexington, KY	10.1	3.8	2.0	1.1	0.3	0.7	0.5	1.5	0.2
Lincoln, NE	9.1	4.9	1.3	1.0	0.4	0.5	0.3	0.8	0.1
Little Rock, AR	7.1	2.6	1.7	0.5	0.1	1.1	0.4	0.4	0.1
Los Angeles, CA	36.2	10.9	12.0	2.4	0.3	8.4	1.1	0.7	0.4
Louisville, KY	8.6	2.6	0.8	0.9	2.0	0.5	0.3	1.4	0.2

Table continued on following page.

Appendix A: Comparative Statistics   A-37

City	Percent of Population Born in								
	Any Foreign Country	Asia	Mexico	Europe	Caribbean	Central America[1]	South America	Africa	Canada
Madison, WI	12.0	6.2	1.4	1.6	0.2	0.3	1.0	1.0	0.3
Manchester, NH	14.6	4.3	0.5	2.7	1.7	1.4	1.0	2.1	1.0
Miami, FL	58.1	1.4	1.1	1.9	31.0	11.9	10.3	0.3	0.2
Midland, TX	15.1	2.1	9.0	0.2	1.0	0.5	0.5	1.3	0.5
Milwaukee, WI	10.1	2.8	4.9	0.7	0.4	0.3	0.2	0.8	0.1
Minneapolis, MN	14.8	3.7	1.8	1.2	0.3	0.4	1.5	5.8	0.3
Nashville, TN	13.7	4.0	2.8	0.9	0.3	2.0	0.3	3.0	0.3
New Haven, CT	17.4	4.2	2.7	2.4	2.6	1.3	2.3	1.5	0.3
New Orleans, LA	5.4	1.9	0.3	0.7	0.4	1.3	0.4	0.2	0.2
New York, NY	36.3	10.8	1.8	5.2	9.9	1.4	4.9	1.7	0.3
Oklahoma City, OK	11.6	3.2	5.3	0.5	0.2	1.2	0.4	0.6	0.2
Omaha, NE	10.8	3.3	3.4	0.7	0.1	1.2	0.4	1.5	0.2
Orlando, FL	22.8	2.8	0.6	2.0	6.7	1.1	8.8	0.5	0.3
Philadelphia, PA	14.3	5.5	0.5	2.1	2.9	0.7	0.9	1.6	0.1
Phoenix, AZ	19.2	3.2	11.7	1.4	0.4	0.9	0.4	0.8	0.4
Pittsburgh, PA	9.0	4.5	0.3	1.8	0.4	0.1	0.5	1.0	0.3
Portland, OR	13.1	6.0	1.9	2.5	0.2	0.4	0.3	0.9	0.5
Providence, RI	30.7	3.8	0.3	2.5	13.9	5.4	1.2	3.1	0.4
Provo, UT	11.3	1.9	4.3	0.4	0.4	0.9	2.4	0.4	0.4
Raleigh, NC	13.0	3.9	2.4	1.2	0.9	1.2	0.8	2.3	0.2
Reno, NV	15.6	5.4	5.1	1.4	0.2	1.7	0.4	0.6	0.4
Richmond, VA	7.5	1.6	0.6	0.8	0.6	2.7	0.4	0.7	0.1
Rochester, MN	13.6	5.4	1.0	1.7	0.1	0.2	0.5	4.5	0.2
Sacramento, CA	20.9	10.3	5.8	1.4	0.1	0.7	0.4	0.5	0.2
St. Louis, MO	6.8	2.8	0.7	1.2	0.2	0.3	0.2	1.3	0.1
Salem, OR	11.3	2.4	5.8	1.1	0.1	0.4	0.2	0.2	0.2
Salt Lake City, UT	15.3	4.1	4.9	1.9	0.2	0.7	1.3	1.0	0.4
San Antonio, TX	14.2	2.5	8.9	0.5	0.3	0.9	0.5	0.4	0.1
San Diego, CA	25.1	11.8	8.2	2.2	0.2	0.5	0.9	0.9	0.4
San Francisco, CA	34.1	22.0	2.4	4.5	0.2	2.4	1.1	0.5	0.6
San Jose, CA	40.7	26.4	8.6	2.3	0.1	1.2	0.7	0.8	0.3
Santa Rosa, CA	21.1	4.6	11.9	1.9	0.0	1.1	0.3	0.6	0.4
Savannah, GA	6.1	2.5	0.8	0.8	0.5	0.5	0.5	0.3	0.2
Seattle, WA	19.3	11.0	1.3	2.6	0.1	0.4	0.5	2.0	1.0
Sioux Falls, SD	8.7	2.1	0.5	1.1	0.1	1.1	0.1	3.4	0.1
Springfield, IL	4.4	2.3	0.5	0.5	0.1	0.1	0.2	0.6	0.0
Tampa, FL	18.1	3.8	1.1	1.8	7.1	1.2	2.3	0.5	0.3
Tucson, AZ	14.2	2.3	8.8	1.0	0.1	0.3	0.4	0.9	0.2
Tulsa, OK	11.0	2.6	5.2	0.6	0.2	1.0	0.5	0.6	0.1
Tuscaloosa, AL	4.5	2.3	1.0	0.4	0.1	0.3	0.1	0.2	0.1
Virginia Beach, VA	9.3	4.9	0.4	1.4	0.5	0.6	0.8	0.4	0.2
Washington, DC	13.5	3.0	0.6	2.4	1.2	2.4	1.5	2.1	0.3
Wichita, KS	9.9	3.7	4.2	0.5	0.1	0.5	0.3	0.5	0.1
Wilmington, NC	4.7	1.2	1.1	1.0	0.2	0.4	0.4	0.1	0.2
Winston-Salem, NC	10.2	2.2	4.1	0.6	0.5	1.5	0.7	0.7	0.1
Worcester, MA	21.9	6.1	0.3	3.6	3.0	1.3	2.5	4.9	0.1
U.S.	13.6	4.2	3.3	1.5	1.4	1.1	1.1	0.8	0.2

Note: (1) Excludes Mexico
Source: U.S. Census Bureau, 2017-2021 American Community Survey 5-Year Estimates

A-38 Appendix A: Comparative Statistics

Foreign-born Population: Metro Area

Metro Area	Any Foreign Country	Percent of Population Born in							
		Asia	Mexico	Europe	Caribbean	Central America[1]	South America	Africa	Canada
Albuquerque, NM	8.9	1.9	4.9	0.8	0.3	0.2	0.3	0.4	0.1
Allentown, PA	9.7	2.7	0.4	1.4	2.8	0.5	1.1	0.6	0.1
Anchorage, AK	9.0	4.8	0.6	1.1	0.4	0.2	0.4	0.4	0.4
Ann Arbor, MI	12.5	7.3	0.6	2.3	0.1	0.2	0.5	0.9	0.6
Athens, GA	7.4	2.5	1.7	0.7	0.2	0.8	0.7	0.6	0.2
Atlanta, GA	14.1	4.7	2.3	1.1	1.6	1.2	1.2	1.7	0.2
Austin, TX	15.2	4.8	5.8	1.2	0.4	1.2	0.7	0.7	0.3
Baltimore, MD	10.5	4.3	0.4	1.3	0.8	1.1	0.5	1.9	0.1
Boise City, ID	6.5	1.5	2.7	1.0	0.0	0.2	0.4	0.3	0.3
Boston, MA	19.3	6.3	0.2	3.2	3.6	1.6	2.2	1.7	0.4
Boulder, CO	9.9	3.4	2.3	2.3	0.1	0.3	0.6	0.3	0.5
Brownsville, TX	22.8	0.6	20.8	0.2	0.1	0.7	0.1	0.0	0.1
Cape Coral, FL	17.1	1.3	2.3	2.0	6.3	1.9	2.2	0.1	0.9
Cedar Rapids, IA	4.3	1.8	0.4	0.3	0.1	0.1	0.1	1.2	0.1
Charleston, SC	5.8	1.5	1.0	1.1	0.3	0.6	0.7	0.2	0.2
Charlotte, NC	10.5	3.1	2.0	1.1	0.7	1.5	1.0	1.0	0.2
Chicago, IL	17.7	5.3	6.3	3.7	0.2	0.5	0.7	0.7	0.2
Cincinnati, OH	5.1	2.2	0.5	0.7	0.1	0.4	0.2	0.8	0.1
Clarksville, TN	4.9	1.5	0.9	0.6	0.3	0.4	0.3	0.6	0.2
Cleveland, OH	6.0	2.2	0.4	2.2	0.2	0.2	0.2	0.4	0.2
College Station, TX	11.5	3.8	5.0	0.7	0.2	0.5	0.7	0.5	0.1
Colorado Springs, CO	6.7	1.9	1.6	1.5	0.4	0.3	0.4	0.3	0.3
Columbia, MO	5.7	3.3	0.5	0.7	0.1	0.2	0.2	0.7	0.1
Columbia, SC	5.3	1.8	1.0	0.7	0.4	0.6	0.3	0.3	0.1
Columbus, OH	8.8	3.7	0.7	0.8	0.3	0.4	0.3	2.4	0.1
Dallas, TX	18.7	5.7	7.8	0.8	0.3	1.6	0.7	1.6	0.2
Davenport, IA	5.3	1.7	1.7	0.5	0.1	0.1	0.1	0.9	0.1
Denver, CO	12.0	3.3	4.6	1.4	0.2	0.5	0.6	1.1	0.3
Des Moines, IA	8.1	3.2	1.5	1.0	0.1	0.5	0.2	1.5	0.1
Durham, NC	11.8	3.6	2.7	1.4	0.4	1.8	0.6	1.0	0.3
Edison, NJ	29.4	8.7	1.4	4.3	6.9	1.9	4.5	1.4	0.2
El Paso, TX	23.7	0.9	21.3	0.4	0.2	0.3	0.2	0.2	0.0
Fargo, ND	7.0	2.8	0.1	0.5	0.1	0.0	0.1	3.0	0.4
Fort Collins, CO	5.8	1.8	1.4	1.2	0.1	0.2	0.5	0.3	0.2
Fort Wayne, IN	6.7	3.3	1.5	0.6	0.1	0.4	0.2	0.4	0.1
Fort Worth, TX	18.7	5.7	7.8	0.8	0.3	1.6	0.7	1.6	0.2
Grand Rapids, MI	6.6	2.1	1.6	0.9	0.4	0.5	0.2	0.7	0.2
Greeley, CO	8.9	0.8	6.0	0.5	0.1	0.7	0.2	0.5	0.1
Green Bay, WI	4.9	1.6	2.1	0.4	0.1	0.3	0.1	0.2	0.1
Greensboro, NC	9.1	3.0	2.4	0.8	0.4	0.5	0.5	1.4	0.1
Honolulu, HI	19.5	15.7	0.2	0.7	0.2	0.1	0.2	0.2	0.2
Houston, TX	23.5	6.0	8.4	1.1	0.8	3.8	1.6	1.5	0.3
Huntsville, AL	5.2	1.9	1.0	0.7	0.2	0.4	0.3	0.4	0.1
Indianapolis, IN	7.3	2.7	1.6	0.6	0.2	0.5	0.4	1.2	0.1
Jacksonville, FL	9.8	3.3	0.5	1.8	1.6	0.7	1.2	0.4	0.2
Kansas City, MO	6.8	2.3	2.0	0.5	0.2	0.6	0.2	0.8	0.1
Lafayette, LA	3.3	1.3	0.5	0.3	0.2	0.7	0.2	0.1	0.1
Las Cruces, NM	16.0	1.4	13.3	0.6	0.1	0.1	0.1	0.2	0.1
Las Vegas, NV	22.0	7.3	7.8	1.5	1.2	2.0	0.9	0.8	0.4
Lexington, KY	7.6	2.6	1.7	1.0	0.2	0.5	0.3	1.1	0.2
Lincoln, NE	8.0	4.2	1.1	0.9	0.3	0.4	0.2	0.7	0.1
Little Rock, AR	4.2	1.4	1.2	0.4	0.1	0.6	0.2	0.2	0.1
Los Angeles, CA	32.5	12.7	11.5	1.7	0.3	4.3	1.0	0.6	0.3
Louisville, KY	6.4	2.0	0.9	0.7	1.1	0.4	0.2	0.9	0.1

Table continued on following page.

Appendix A: Comparative Statistics   A-39

Metro Area	Any Foreign Country	Percent of Population Born in							
		Asia	Mexico	Europe	Caribbean	Central America[1]	South America	Africa	Canada
Madison, WI	7.6	3.5	1.2	1.0	0.1	0.2	0.6	0.6	0.2
Manchester, NH	10.0	3.4	0.3	1.9	1.3	0.5	0.8	0.8	0.9
Miami, FL	41.2	2.2	1.2	2.3	20.9	4.2	9.5	0.4	0.6
Midland, TX	13.7	1.9	8.5	0.3	0.8	0.4	0.4	1.0	0.4
Milwaukee, WI	7.5	2.8	2.3	1.2	0.2	0.2	0.3	0.4	0.1
Minneapolis, MN	10.7	4.1	1.1	1.0	0.1	0.4	0.6	3.0	0.2
Nashville, TN	8.5	2.6	1.9	0.7	0.3	1.1	0.4	1.3	0.2
New Haven, CT	13.4	3.2	1.1	2.9	2.1	0.6	2.1	1.0	0.3
New Orleans, LA	7.6	2.1	0.5	0.5	0.9	2.7	0.4	0.3	0.1
New York, NY	29.4	8.7	1.4	4.3	6.9	1.9	4.5	1.4	0.2
Oklahoma City, OK	7.9	2.3	3.3	0.4	0.1	0.8	0.3	0.5	0.2
Omaha, NE	7.6	2.5	2.4	0.6	0.1	0.7	0.3	1.0	0.1
Orlando, FL	19.3	3.0	1.0	1.7	5.6	1.1	6.0	0.6	0.3
Philadelphia, PA	11.2	4.6	0.8	1.9	1.4	0.5	0.7	1.2	0.2
Phoenix, AZ	14.0	3.2	7.0	1.3	0.3	0.6	0.4	0.6	0.6
Pittsburgh, PA	4.1	2.0	0.1	0.9	0.2	0.1	0.2	0.3	0.1
Portland, OR	12.7	5.1	2.9	2.4	0.2	0.5	0.3	0.6	0.4
Providence, RI	13.9	2.3	0.3	4.1	2.6	1.6	1.2	1.6	0.2
Provo, UT	7.2	1.0	2.5	0.5	0.2	0.6	1.6	0.2	0.3
Raleigh, NC	12.2	4.7	2.4	1.3	0.6	0.9	0.6	1.2	0.3
Reno, NV	14.0	4.0	5.7	1.2	0.2	1.4	0.4	0.4	0.4
Richmond, VA	8.1	3.1	0.6	1.0	0.4	1.6	0.5	0.7	0.1
Rochester, MN	8.5	3.2	0.7	1.1	0.1	0.2	0.4	2.4	0.2
Sacramento, CA	18.6	9.1	4.3	2.7	0.1	0.7	0.4	0.4	0.3
St. Louis, MO	4.8	2.2	0.5	1.1	0.1	0.2	0.2	0.5	0.1
Salem, OR	11.5	1.5	7.2	1.1	0.1	0.5	0.3	0.1	0.2
Salt Lake City, UT	12.4	3.1	4.3	1.3	0.1	0.6	1.5	0.6	0.3
San Antonio, TX	11.7	2.1	7.1	0.6	0.3	0.7	0.4	0.3	0.1
San Diego, CA	22.7	8.8	9.6	1.8	0.2	0.6	0.7	0.6	0.4
San Francisco, CA	30.7	17.8	4.7	2.8	0.2	2.5	1.1	0.9	0.5
San Jose, CA	39.3	26.2	6.7	3.1	0.1	1.0	0.8	0.7	0.5
Santa Rosa, CA	16.3	3.1	8.9	1.9	0.1	0.9	0.4	0.3	0.4
Savannah, GA	6.0	1.9	1.2	1.0	0.6	0.3	0.4	0.3	0.2
Seattle, WA	19.5	10.4	2.3	2.8	0.2	0.6	0.6	1.6	0.7
Sioux Falls, SD	6.5	1.5	0.5	0.9	0.1	0.8	0.1	2.4	0.1
Springfield, IL	2.9	1.5	0.3	0.4	0.1	0.0	0.2	0.3	0.0
Tampa, FL	14.4	2.8	1.3	2.2	4.0	0.8	2.2	0.5	0.6
Tucson, AZ	12.2	2.2	7.0	1.2	0.2	0.3	0.3	0.6	0.3
Tulsa, OK	6.7	1.9	2.8	0.5	0.1	0.5	0.3	0.3	0.1
Tuscaloosa, AL	3.3	1.2	1.1	0.3	0.1	0.4	0.1	0.1	0.1
Virginia Beach, VA	6.6	2.8	0.4	1.1	0.6	0.7	0.4	0.4	0.1
Washington, DC	22.9	8.2	0.8	1.8	1.1	4.8	2.3	3.6	0.2
Wichita, KS	7.3	2.7	2.9	0.5	0.1	0.4	0.2	0.4	0.1
Wilmington, NC	4.6	1.0	1.0	0.9	0.1	0.6	0.4	0.2	0.2
Winston-Salem, NC	7.0	1.4	2.7	0.6	0.3	0.9	0.5	0.3	0.1
Worcester, MA	12.0	3.7	0.3	2.3	1.1	0.6	2.0	1.6	0.4
U.S.	13.6	4.2	3.3	1.5	1.4	1.1	1.1	0.8	0.2

Note: Figures cover the Metropolitan Statistical Area—see Appendix B for areas included; (1) Excludes Mexico
Source: U.S. Census Bureau, 2017-2021 American Community Survey 5-Year Estimates

A-40 Appendix A: Comparative Statistics

Marital Status: City

City	Never Married	Now Married[1]	Separated	Widowed	Divorced
Albuquerque, NM	38.2	40.1	1.4	5.5	14.8
Allentown, PA	46.7	34.6	3.9	5.0	9.8
Anchorage, AK	33.6	48.9	1.9	3.6	12.0
Ann Arbor, MI	56.5	34.4	0.4	2.4	6.3
Athens, GA	53.8	31.8	1.7	3.7	9.0
Atlanta, GA	55.1	29.0	1.8	4.0	10.1
Austin, TX	43.0	41.9	1.4	3.0	10.6
Baltimore, MD	52.3	27.2	3.1	6.0	11.4
Boise City, ID	34.8	47.0	1.0	4.4	12.9
Boston, MA	55.7	30.9	2.5	3.6	7.3
Boulder, CO	56.1	31.2	0.7	2.5	9.5
Brownsville, TX	34.2	47.6	4.3	6.2	7.8
Cape Coral, FL	24.4	53.3	1.2	7.3	13.8
Cedar Rapids, IA	35.5	45.7	1.0	5.6	12.2
Charleston, SC	40.3	43.3	1.6	5.1	9.8
Charlotte, NC	41.4	42.0	2.4	3.9	10.3
Chicago, IL	48.9	35.5	2.3	5.0	8.3
Cincinnati, OH	52.6	29.1	2.2	4.5	11.7
Clarksville, TN	30.2	50.3	2.1	3.9	13.6
Cleveland, OH	53.1	24.0	2.9	5.9	14.1
College Station, TX	59.4	31.9	0.8	2.4	5.5
Colorado Springs, CO	30.9	50.2	1.6	4.5	12.9
Columbia, MO	47.8	39.2	1.3	3.1	8.7
Columbia, SC	55.7	29.6	2.3	4.0	8.4
Columbus, OH	45.4	36.7	2.1	4.2	11.6
Dallas, TX	42.3	40.2	2.9	4.3	10.3
Davenport, IA	36.9	43.5	1.3	5.6	12.7
Denver, CO	43.4	39.6	1.6	3.5	11.8
Des Moines, IA	39.5	39.8	2.1	5.5	13.0
Durham, NC	43.1	40.7	2.2	4.1	9.9
Edison, NJ	26.3	61.4	0.8	5.3	6.1
El Paso, TX	34.9	44.8	3.6	5.7	11.1
Fargo, ND	43.0	43.4	1.0	3.9	8.6
Fort Collins, CO	46.6	40.9	0.7	3.3	8.5
Fort Wayne, IN	36.1	44.2	1.5	5.9	12.3
Fort Worth, TX	35.5	46.7	2.2	4.4	11.1
Grand Rapids, MI	45.3	38.1	1.2	4.9	10.5
Greeley, CO	35.4	46.5	1.9	4.8	11.4
Green Bay, WI	37.4	42.2	1.2	5.2	14.0
Greensboro, NC	43.8	36.8	2.6	5.9	11.0
Honolulu, HI	37.5	44.7	1.1	6.7	10.0
Houston, TX	41.1	41.2	3.0	4.5	10.2
Huntsville, AL	36.1	43.6	2.1	5.9	12.4
Indianapolis, IN	41.8	39.4	1.7	4.8	12.3
Jacksonville, FL	36.0	42.4	2.1	5.5	14.0
Kansas City, MO	39.3	40.6	2.0	4.8	13.3
Lafayette, LA	40.6	41.4	2.1	6.0	9.9
Las Cruces, NM	41.9	39.4	1.7	4.7	12.4
Las Vegas, NV	35.6	43.7	2.0	5.2	13.5
Lexington, KY	38.6	43.4	1.5	4.6	11.8
Lincoln, NE	39.7	45.3	0.9	4.0	10.1
Little Rock, AR	38.2	40.4	1.8	5.6	14.1
Los Angeles, CA	46.1	38.9	2.5	4.4	8.1
Louisville, KY	36.9	42.0	2.1	6.3	12.7
Madison, WI	50.3	37.2	0.7	3.3	8.5
Manchester, NH	39.2	39.2	1.8	5.4	14.3

Table continued on following page.

Appendix A: Comparative Statistics   A-41

City	Never Married	Now Married[1]	Separated	Widowed	Divorced
Miami, FL	39.7	37.3	3.5	6.0	13.6
Midland, TX	28.6	55.1	1.9	4.5	9.9
Milwaukee, WI	54.4	29.4	1.9	4.4	9.9
Minneapolis, MN	51.2	34.3	1.4	3.0	10.1
Nashville, TN	41.5	40.4	1.9	4.6	11.6
New Haven, CT	59.1	25.5	2.4	3.9	9.1
New Orleans, LA	49.7	29.4	2.6	5.5	12.8
New York, NY	43.8	39.9	2.9	5.3	8.1
Oklahoma City, OK	33.3	46.6	2.1	5.3	12.7
Omaha, NE	37.2	45.6	1.4	4.8	11.1
Orlando, FL	43.2	37.8	2.4	3.9	12.7
Philadelphia, PA	50.5	31.5	3.0	5.7	9.2
Phoenix, AZ	39.1	42.5	2.1	4.0	12.2
Pittsburgh, PA	53.1	30.4	1.9	5.4	9.2
Portland, OR	41.6	41.1	1.3	3.6	12.4
Providence, RI	53.6	31.9	2.0	4.2	8.4
Provo, UT	48.8	43.8	0.9	2.2	4.3
Raleigh, NC	43.2	40.0	2.1	3.8	11.0
Reno, NV	36.5	42.1	1.9	4.9	14.8
Richmond, VA	51.2	29.4	2.8	5.2	11.4
Rochester, MN	33.3	51.7	1.2	4.7	9.2
Sacramento, CA	40.5	41.1	2.6	4.8	11.2
St. Louis, MO	48.8	30.7	2.9	5.2	12.3
Salem, OR	34.6	45.1	1.6	5.2	13.4
Salt Lake City, UT	44.4	40.3	1.3	3.1	10.8
San Antonio, TX	38.3	41.7	2.8	5.1	12.0
San Diego, CA	40.1	44.8	1.6	4.0	9.5
San Francisco, CA	46.0	40.1	1.4	4.5	8.0
San Jose, CA	36.2	50.3	1.5	4.2	7.8
Santa Rosa, CA	33.8	46.4	2.0	5.4	12.3
Savannah, GA	47.5	32.1	2.6	5.6	12.2
Seattle, WA	45.5	40.3	1.2	3.0	10.0
Sioux Falls, SD	34.5	48.6	1.2	4.3	11.4
Springfield, IL	37.6	39.5	1.6	6.2	15.1
Tampa, FL	40.3	39.1	2.5	5.0	13.1
Tucson, AZ	42.0	36.7	2.2	5.2	13.9
Tulsa, OK	35.0	42.4	2.4	5.7	14.4
Tuscaloosa, AL	52.3	32.6	1.8	4.0	9.4
Virginia Beach, VA	30.9	50.8	2.1	5.1	11.2
Washington, DC	55.8	30.9	1.7	3.5	8.2
Wichita, KS	33.7	45.6	1.9	5.0	13.8
Wilmington, NC	41.6	39.1	2.2	5.3	11.7
Winston-Salem, NC	41.9	39.1	2.6	5.4	11.0
Worcester, MA	47.8	34.0	2.0	4.9	11.3
U.S.	33.8	48.0	1.8	5.6	10.8

Note: Figures are percentages and cover the population 15 years of age and older; (1) Excludes separated
Source: U.S. Census Bureau, 2017-2021 American Community Survey 5-Year Estimates

A-42 Appendix A: Comparative Statistics

Marital Status: Metro Area

Metro Area	Never Married	Now Married[1]	Separated	Widowed	Divorced
Albuquerque, NM	35.6	43.5	1.4	5.5	14.1
Allentown, PA	32.7	49.3	1.9	6.2	9.9
Anchorage, AK	32.2	50.5	1.8	3.8	11.8
Ann Arbor, MI	43.1	44.4	0.7	3.6	8.1
Athens, GA	43.0	41.5	1.6	4.4	9.5
Atlanta, GA	35.7	47.6	1.8	4.4	10.6
Austin, TX	35.5	49.4	1.4	3.5	10.3
Baltimore, MD	36.0	46.3	1.9	5.7	10.0
Boise City, ID	29.1	53.3	1.1	4.3	12.2
Boston, MA	37.3	47.6	1.6	4.9	8.7
Boulder, CO	38.5	45.5	0.9	3.7	11.4
Brownsville, TX	33.6	48.2	3.5	6.3	8.4
Cape Coral, FL	25.9	51.9	1.5	7.9	12.8
Cedar Rapids, IA	30.6	51.3	1.1	5.5	11.5
Charleston, SC	33.8	48.5	2.1	5.3	10.3
Charlotte, NC	33.1	49.3	2.3	5.0	10.3
Chicago, IL	37.2	47.0	1.6	5.2	8.9
Cincinnati, OH	32.8	48.7	1.5	5.6	11.4
Clarksville, TN	29.6	51.1	1.9	4.9	12.5
Cleveland, OH	35.8	44.4	1.5	6.3	11.9
College Station, TX	45.5	40.1	1.8	4.1	8.5
Colorado Springs, CO	29.5	53.3	1.4	4.0	11.7
Columbia, MO	40.0	44.8	1.3	4.0	9.8
Columbia, SC	36.3	45.0	2.6	5.6	10.6
Columbus, OH	34.8	47.6	1.7	4.8	11.1
Dallas, TX	32.8	50.8	1.9	4.2	10.3
Davenport, IA	30.5	49.9	1.4	6.2	12.0
Denver, CO	33.6	49.8	1.4	3.8	11.5
Des Moines, IA	30.9	51.7	1.2	4.9	11.2
Durham, NC	37.3	46.1	2.0	4.8	9.8
Edison, NJ	38.1	46.1	2.2	5.5	8.1
El Paso, TX	34.9	45.8	3.5	5.4	10.4
Fargo, ND	37.5	49.1	0.9	4.0	8.5
Fort Collins, CO	34.5	51.3	0.8	4.0	9.4
Fort Wayne, IN	31.5	50.0	1.3	5.6	11.6
Fort Worth, TX	32.8	50.8	1.9	4.2	10.3
Grand Rapids, MI	32.2	52.1	0.9	4.5	10.3
Greeley, CO	28.7	55.2	1.4	4.0	10.7
Green Bay, WI	30.6	52.2	0.7	5.1	11.4
Greensboro, NC	34.1	45.5	2.8	6.2	11.4
Honolulu, HI	34.4	49.7	1.2	6.0	8.7
Houston, TX	33.8	50.2	2.3	4.3	9.4
Huntsville, AL	29.9	51.5	1.6	5.5	11.4
Indianapolis, IN	33.0	49.2	1.3	4.9	11.5
Jacksonville, FL	31.7	47.7	1.8	5.6	13.2
Kansas City, MO	30.8	50.5	1.5	5.0	12.1
Lafayette, LA	33.8	47.9	2.1	5.6	10.6
Las Cruces, NM	38.8	43.7	2.0	4.9	10.7
Las Vegas, NV	35.2	44.3	2.1	5.0	13.4
Lexington, KY	34.1	47.0	1.5	5.1	12.3
Lincoln, NE	37.3	48.1	0.8	4.1	9.7
Little Rock, AR	30.6	48.1	1.9	5.8	13.6
Los Angeles, CA	40.3	44.5	2.0	4.7	8.4
Louisville, KY	31.9	47.5	1.8	6.0	12.9
Madison, WI	37.1	48.2	0.8	4.1	9.9
Manchester, NH	31.3	50.2	1.2	5.1	12.1

Table continued on following page.

Appendix A: Comparative Statistics　　A-43

Metro Area	Never Married	Now Married[1]	Separated	Widowed	Divorced
Miami, FL	34.1	44.4	2.5	6.2	12.9
Midland, TX	27.9	55.4	1.7	4.5	10.5
Milwaukee, WI	37.4	46.2	1.1	5.1	10.1
Minneapolis, MN	33.7	51.0	1.0	4.1	10.1
Nashville, TN	32.6	50.0	1.5	4.9	11.0
New Haven, CT	38.2	43.7	1.6	5.7	10.8
New Orleans, LA	37.8	41.7	2.3	6.0	12.1
New York, NY	38.1	46.1	2.2	5.5	8.1
Oklahoma City, OK	31.4	49.2	1.8	5.4	12.3
Omaha, NE	32.2	51.3	1.2	4.7	10.7
Orlando, FL	35.2	46.2	2.0	5.0	11.6
Philadelphia, PA	37.3	45.8	2.0	5.7	9.2
Phoenix, AZ	33.7	48.2	1.6	4.8	11.7
Pittsburgh, PA	32.6	48.7	1.7	6.9	10.1
Portland, OR	32.8	49.6	1.3	4.3	12.0
Providence, RI	36.5	45.0	1.5	5.9	11.1
Provo, UT	33.0	58.1	0.8	2.5	5.5
Raleigh, NC	32.2	51.9	2.0	4.2	9.7
Reno, NV	32.4	47.4	1.7	4.9	13.7
Richmond, VA	34.7	46.7	2.3	5.6	10.7
Rochester, MN	29.0	56.0	0.9	4.7	9.3
Sacramento, CA	33.9	48.6	2.0	4.9	10.6
St. Louis, MO	32.2	48.7	1.7	5.9	11.4
Salem, OR	31.8	48.7	1.7	5.3	12.6
Salt Lake City, UT	32.7	52.3	1.4	3.6	10.1
San Antonio, TX	34.0	47.6	2.4	4.9	11.1
San Diego, CA	36.2	47.9	1.6	4.4	9.8
San Francisco, CA	36.6	48.6	1.4	4.6	8.7
San Jose, CA	34.4	52.7	1.4	4.1	7.4
Santa Rosa, CA	32.3	48.7	1.5	5.1	12.5
Savannah, GA	35.7	45.2	2.3	5.3	11.7
Seattle, WA	33.2	50.7	1.3	4.0	10.8
Sioux Falls, SD	30.6	53.2	1.0	4.4	10.8
Springfield, IL	32.4	46.6	1.3	6.1	13.6
Tampa, FL	31.3	46.5	1.9	6.8	13.5
Tucson, AZ	34.3	45.5	1.7	5.6	12.9
Tulsa, OK	29.1	49.8	1.9	6.1	13.0
Tuscaloosa, AL	39.5	43.1	1.7	5.4	10.3
Virginia Beach, VA	33.6	47.7	2.4	5.5	10.8
Washington, DC	36.2	49.2	1.7	4.2	8.7
Wichita, KS	30.3	50.2	1.4	5.4	12.7
Wilmington, NC	33.0	48.2	2.2	5.7	11.0
Winston-Salem, NC	31.0	48.9	2.4	6.4	11.3
Worcester, MA	34.4	47.7	1.5	5.4	11.0
U.S.	33.8	48.0	1.8	5.6	10.8

Note: Figures are percentages and cover the population 15 years of age and older; Figures cover the Metropolitan Statistical Area;
(1) Excludes separated
Source: U.S. Census Bureau, 2017-2021 American Community Survey 5-Year Estimates

A-44 Appendix A: Comparative Statistics

Disability by Age: City

City	All Ages	Under 18 Years Old	18 to 64 Years Old	65 Years and Over
Albuquerque, NM	14.2	4.3	12.3	35.3
Allentown, PA	16.0	9.9	15.3	33.5
Anchorage, AK	11.1	3.8	10.0	33.3
Ann Arbor, MI	7.1	4.2	4.9	24.0
Athens, GA	11.8	6.1	9.6	35.6
Atlanta, GA	11.4	4.7	9.3	35.0
Austin, TX	8.7	4.1	7.4	28.5
Baltimore, MD	15.9	6.0	14.1	39.0
Boise City, ID	11.3	4.2	9.4	29.7
Boston, MA	11.8	6.3	8.7	38.3
Boulder, CO	6.6	2.9	4.7	23.1
Brownsville, TX	10.6	4.2	7.8	40.6
Cape Coral, FL	13.4	3.8	9.7	29.3
Cedar Rapids, IA	10.0	3.1	8.1	27.2
Charleston, SC	9.3	2.9	6.2	30.5
Charlotte, NC	7.8	2.6	6.5	27.9
Chicago, IL	10.9	3.3	8.8	34.8
Cincinnati, OH	12.8	5.2	11.8	32.0
Clarksville, TN	15.7	6.1	16.4	43.8
Cleveland, OH	19.5	8.4	18.5	41.9
College Station, TX	6.8	5.1	5.3	27.8
Colorado Springs, CO	13.1	5.2	12.1	30.9
Columbia, MO	11.4	4.6	9.8	33.9
Columbia, SC	12.8	5.1	10.7	38.5
Columbus, OH	11.6	5.2	10.3	34.5
Dallas, TX	10.5	4.5	9.0	34.3
Davenport, IA	13.1	5.2	11.3	31.6
Denver, CO	9.7	3.5	7.6	32.3
Des Moines, IA	13.7	5.3	12.8	35.6
Durham, NC	9.6	3.0	7.6	31.7
Edison, NJ	7.6	4.2	4.5	26.9
El Paso, TX	13.6	5.2	11.1	42.1
Fargo, ND	10.2	5.1	7.7	32.0
Fort Collins, CO	8.4	2.7	6.8	28.0
Fort Wayne, IN	13.9	5.5	12.8	34.2
Fort Worth, TX	9.7	3.4	8.6	34.4
Grand Rapids, MI	11.7	3.9	11.0	30.4
Greeley, CO	11.9	3.4	11.1	33.5
Green Bay, WI	13.8	6.7	12.2	34.9
Greensboro, NC	11.1	4.9	8.9	32.1
Honolulu, HI	11.5	3.1	6.9	32.4
Houston, TX	9.9	3.9	8.0	34.7
Huntsville, AL	13.5	4.4	11.3	33.7
Indianapolis, IN	13.5	5.3	12.4	35.5
Jacksonville, FL	13.1	4.8	11.3	35.3
Kansas City, MO	12.5	3.9	11.1	34.2
Lafayette, LA	12.1	2.8	9.7	34.5
Las Cruces, NM	15.9	7.9	13.6	38.0
Las Vegas, NV	12.5	4.0	10.4	34.8
Lexington, KY	12.5	4.9	10.8	33.2
Lincoln, NE	10.7	4.4	8.9	30.0
Little Rock, AR	13.2	4.7	11.6	34.5
Los Angeles, CA	10.3	3.1	7.5	36.6
Louisville, KY	14.3	4.5	12.8	35.6
Madison, WI	8.3	4.4	6.4	25.0

Table continued on following page.

Appendix A: Comparative Statistics — A-45

City	All Ages	Under 18 Years Old	18 to 64 Years Old	65 Years and Over
Manchester, NH	13.9	6.6	11.8	34.7
Miami, FL	11.9	4.5	7.6	37.2
Midland, TX	9.8	2.7	8.1	41.1
Milwaukee, WI	12.5	5.0	11.6	36.6
Minneapolis, MN	11.0	4.9	9.8	32.2
Nashville, TN	11.2	4.6	9.1	34.5
New Haven, CT	10.3	4.2	8.8	33.4
New Orleans, LA	13.7	4.7	11.8	34.0
New York, NY	10.9	3.6	8.0	33.9
Oklahoma City, OK	13.1	4.3	11.9	36.6
Omaha, NE	10.9	3.6	9.6	30.9
Orlando, FL	9.6	4.9	7.7	32.0
Philadelphia, PA	16.9	7.0	15.0	42.0
Phoenix, AZ	10.8	4.2	9.7	32.9
Pittsburgh, PA	14.3	7.7	11.3	35.4
Portland, OR	12.1	4.8	9.9	33.4
Providence, RI	13.6	5.9	12.4	36.4
Provo, UT	9.6	4.9	8.1	41.8
Raleigh, NC	9.0	4.2	7.2	30.1
Reno, NV	11.2	3.2	9.0	31.1
Richmond, VA	14.2	6.5	12.1	35.7
Rochester, MN	10.3	4.2	7.9	30.7
Sacramento, CA	11.8	3.3	9.6	36.7
St. Louis, MO	15.4	6.2	13.3	38.5
Salem, OR	15.2	6.3	13.9	35.5
Salt Lake City, UT	11.0	4.0	9.4	32.6
San Antonio, TX	15.0	6.3	13.2	41.6
San Diego, CA	9.2	3.3	6.5	31.3
San Francisco, CA	10.1	2.6	6.3	33.5
San Jose, CA	8.9	3.1	6.0	33.1
Santa Rosa, CA	11.7	3.2	9.5	29.7
Savannah, GA	15.7	6.4	13.1	42.3
Seattle, WA	9.3	2.5	7.2	30.6
Sioux Falls, SD	10.1	3.4	9.0	28.9
Springfield, IL	14.7	6.2	13.0	31.2
Tampa, FL	12.1	3.7	9.6	38.9
Tucson, AZ	15.0	5.8	12.8	37.5
Tulsa, OK	14.2	4.7	13.1	34.6
Tuscaloosa, AL	9.9	2.9	8.3	28.0
Virginia Beach, VA	11.5	4.3	9.4	31.3
Washington, DC	11.2	4.4	9.2	33.7
Wichita, KS	14.8	5.7	13.7	35.4
Wilmington, NC	13.0	5.1	10.0	32.0
Winston-Salem, NC	11.3	3.5	9.9	30.6
Worcester, MA	14.3	4.7	12.9	37.3
U.S.	12.6	4.4	10.3	33.4

Note: Figures show percent of the civilian noninstitutionalized population that reported having a disability. Disability status is determined from from six types of difficulty: vision, hearing, cognitive, ambulatory, self-care, and independent living. For children under 5 years old, hearing and vision difficulty are used to determine disability status. For children between the ages of 5 and 14, disability status is determined from hearing, vision, cognitive, ambulatory, and self-care difficulties. For people aged 15 years and older, they are considered to have a disability if they have difficulty with any one of the six difficulty types.
Source: U.S. Census Bureau, 2017-2021 American Community Survey 5-Year Estimates

A-46 Appendix A: Comparative Statistics

Disability by Age: Metro Area

Metro Area	All Ages	Under 18 Years Old	18 to 64 Years Old	65 Years and Over
Albuquerque, NM	15.1	4.2	13.2	36.3
Allentown, PA	12.7	5.5	10.2	30.3
Anchorage, AK	11.7	3.8	10.7	33.9
Ann Arbor, MI	9.7	3.8	7.7	27.2
Athens, GA	12.5	5.6	10.2	34.4
Atlanta, GA	10.3	4.0	8.6	31.5
Austin, TX	9.3	3.8	7.8	29.4
Baltimore, MD	11.8	4.6	9.7	30.8
Boise City, ID	12.1	4.4	10.6	31.6
Boston, MA	10.5	4.2	7.8	30.2
Boulder, CO	8.4	3.3	6.1	25.5
Brownsville, TX	12.2	5.6	9.5	39.0
Cape Coral, FL	13.6	3.9	9.8	26.9
Cedar Rapids, IA	10.3	4.1	8.1	27.2
Charleston, SC	11.6	3.9	9.2	32.1
Charlotte, NC	10.4	3.5	8.5	31.5
Chicago, IL	10.1	3.3	7.9	30.3
Cincinnati, OH	12.4	5.0	10.6	31.8
Clarksville, TN	16.7	7.1	16.3	42.9
Cleveland, OH	14.0	5.0	11.6	32.6
College Station, TX	9.9	5.5	7.6	33.3
Colorado Springs, CO	12.5	5.1	11.5	30.8
Columbia, MO	12.8	4.9	11.1	33.8
Columbia, SC	14.2	4.7	12.3	36.3
Columbus, OH	11.9	5.0	10.1	32.7
Dallas, TX	9.5	3.8	8.0	32.1
Davenport, IA	12.7	5.2	10.4	30.1
Denver, CO	9.7	3.5	7.8	29.8
Des Moines, IA	10.5	3.7	9.0	30.4
Durham, NC	11.0	3.4	8.6	30.7
Edison, NJ	10.1	3.3	7.3	30.5
El Paso, TX	13.3	5.4	10.9	43.0
Fargo, ND	9.8	4.0	7.8	31.7
Fort Collins, CO	10.0	2.7	7.7	28.8
Fort Wayne, IN	12.4	4.7	11.0	32.0
Fort Worth, TX	9.5	3.8	8.0	32.1
Grand Rapids, MI	10.9	3.8	9.4	29.8
Greeley, CO	10.7	3.6	9.1	34.7
Green Bay, WI	11.3	4.5	9.7	27.7
Greensboro, NC	13.1	4.9	10.9	32.7
Honolulu, HI	11.2	3.0	7.5	33.0
Houston, TX	9.6	3.8	7.9	32.6
Huntsville, AL	13.1	4.0	11.1	35.4
Indianapolis, IN	12.3	4.8	10.8	32.9
Jacksonville, FL	13.0	4.6	10.9	33.2
Kansas City, MO	11.7	4.0	9.9	32.2
Lafayette, LA	14.1	4.9	12.4	37.8
Las Cruces, NM	15.2	6.6	13.4	35.7
Las Vegas, NV	12.1	4.0	9.9	33.9
Lexington, KY	13.5	5.2	11.8	34.2
Lincoln, NE	10.7	4.1	8.8	30.4
Little Rock, AR	15.6	5.8	13.8	38.4
Los Angeles, CA	9.8	3.2	7.0	33.0
Louisville, KY	13.9	4.4	12.1	35.1
Madison, WI	8.9	4.2	6.9	24.6

Table continued on following page.

Appendix A: Comparative Statistics   A-47

Metro Area	All Ages	Under 18 Years Old	18 to 64 Years Old	65 Years and Over
Manchester, NH	11.6	4.7	9.5	29.8
Miami, FL	10.8	3.7	7.2	31.1
Midland, TX	9.9	2.6	8.2	41.3
Milwaukee, WI	11.0	3.9	8.9	29.8
Minneapolis, MN	10.0	3.9	8.2	28.5
Nashville, TN	11.6	4.0	9.7	33.6
New Haven, CT	11.6	3.7	9.2	29.9
New Orleans, LA	14.9	5.4	12.7	36.4
New York, NY	10.1	3.3	7.3	30.5
Oklahoma City, OK	14.0	4.5	12.4	38.4
Omaha, NE	11.0	3.6	9.5	31.4
Orlando, FL	12.3	5.7	9.6	33.8
Philadelphia, PA	12.7	5.1	10.5	32.2
Phoenix, AZ	11.8	4.3	9.7	31.4
Pittsburgh, PA	14.4	5.7	11.3	32.5
Portland, OR	12.1	4.1	10.0	32.3
Providence, RI	13.7	5.4	11.5	31.9
Provo, UT	8.3	3.6	8.0	31.9
Raleigh, NC	9.7	3.9	7.9	30.4
Reno, NV	11.7	4.0	9.2	30.9
Richmond, VA	12.8	5.3	10.5	32.1
Rochester, MN	10.0	3.8	7.6	28.6
Sacramento, CA	11.5	3.4	9.0	33.7
St. Louis, MO	13.0	4.7	10.8	32.4
Salem, OR	14.9	5.3	13.0	36.5
Salt Lake City, UT	9.5	3.9	8.4	30.0
San Antonio, TX	14.1	5.9	12.3	38.7
San Diego, CA	10.0	3.3	7.4	31.7
San Francisco, CA	9.6	3.1	6.7	30.0
San Jose, CA	8.3	2.7	5.5	30.7
Santa Rosa, CA	11.6	3.4	8.8	28.4
Savannah, GA	14.2	4.9	12.5	36.6
Seattle, WA	10.8	3.9	8.7	32.8
Sioux Falls, SD	9.9	3.2	8.7	28.5
Springfield, IL	13.7	6.2	11.6	30.4
Tampa, FL	14.1	5.0	10.8	33.6
Tucson, AZ	14.9	5.3	12.1	33.4
Tulsa, OK	14.7	4.8	13.1	37.4
Tuscaloosa, AL	14.3	4.5	12.5	37.4
Virginia Beach, VA	13.3	5.3	11.3	33.7
Washington, DC	8.8	3.3	6.8	28.2
Wichita, KS	14.5	5.8	12.9	35.7
Wilmington, NC	12.9	4.5	10.6	30.3
Winston-Salem, NC	13.5	4.2	11.2	33.6
Worcester, MA	12.4	4.3	10.5	31.6
U.S.	12.6	4.4	10.3	33.4

Note: Figures show percent of the civilian noninstitutionalized population that reported having a disability. Disability status is determined from from six types of difficulty: vision, hearing, cognitive, ambulatory, self-care, and independent living. For children under 5 years old, hearing and vision difficulty are used to determine disability status. For children between the ages of 5 and 14, disability status is determined from hearing, vision, cognitive, ambulatory, and self-care difficulties. For people aged 15 years and older, they are considered to have a disability if they have difficulty with any one of the six difficulty types; Figures cover the Metropolitan Statistical Area
Source: U.S. Census Bureau, 2017-2021 American Community Survey 5-Year Estimates

A-48 Appendix A: Comparative Statistics

Religious Groups by Family

Area[1]	Catholic	Baptist	Methodist	LDS[2]	Pentecostal	Lutheran	Islam	Adventist	Other
Albuquerque, NM	32.6	3.2	0.9	2.7	1.7	0.4	0.7	1.5	10.8
Allentown, PA	18.6	0.4	2.3	0.4	0.6	5.4	0.7	1.2	11.0
Anchorage, AK	4.9	3.4	1.0	5.1	1.7	1.5	0.1	1.7	16.3
Ann Arbor, MI	9.7	2.0	2.4	0.8	1.5	2.3	2.2	0.9	10.0
Athens, GA	6.4	12.8	5.7	1.0	2.4	0.3	0.2	1.3	7.9
Atlanta, GA	10.7	14.7	6.7	0.8	2.0	0.4	1.9	1.9	12.4
Austin, TX	18.8	6.5	2.2	1.3	0.7	1.1	1.0	1.0	9.9
Baltimore, MD	12.4	3.2	4.4	0.6	1.2	1.4	3.3	1.2	11.7
Boise City, ID	13.0	0.8	2.5	15.0	1.6	0.8	0.3	1.7	10.0
Boston, MA	37.0	1.0	0.7	0.5	0.7	0.2	2.2	0.9	7.1
Boulder, CO	16.0	0.3	0.7	0.7	0.5	1.7	0.4	0.9	15.2
Brownsville, TX	36.8	2.8	0.7	1.2	1.0	0.2	0.1	2.5	9.4
Cape Coral, FL	18.8	2.5	1.7	0.6	3.0	0.7	0.2	2.0	12.2
Cedar Rapids, IA	16.8	1.0	5.3	1.0	1.3	8.1	1.3	0.6	9.6
Charleston, SC	11.5	7.7	8.0	0.8	1.9	0.7	0.2	1.0	12.8
Charlotte, NC	12.1	13.9	7.0	0.7	2.2	1.1	1.7	1.4	15.9
Chicago, IL	28.6	3.4	1.4	0.3	1.5	2.1	4.7	1.1	9.2
Cincinnati, OH	17.0	5.7	2.3	0.6	1.5	0.8	1.1	0.7	21.8
Clarksville, TN	4.6	23.2	4.4	1.4	3.2	0.5	0.1	0.8	12.4
Cleveland, OH	26.1	4.3	2.3	0.4	1.5	1.8	1.1	1.3	16.8
College Station, TX	17.2	10.6	4.3	1.7	0.5	1.1	0.6	0.5	6.8
Colorado Springs, CO	16.4	2.6	1.3	3.0	1.0	1.2	0.1	1.0	16.2
Columbia, MO	7.1	9.0	3.5	1.7	1.1	1.6	1.4	1.2	12.4
Columbia, SC	6.6	15.1	8.5	1.2	3.8	2.3	0.3	1.3	15.4
Columbus, OH	11.7	3.4	3.0	0.8	1.9	1.7	2.1	0.9	17.5
Dallas, TX	14.2	14.3	4.7	1.4	2.2	0.5	1.8	1.3	13.8
Davenport, IA	13.2	3.2	3.6	0.8	1.5	6.6	0.7	0.8	6.7
Denver, CO	16.1	1.5	1.0	2.1	0.6	1.4	0.3	1.1	10.4
Des Moines, IA	12.1	1.8	4.0	0.9	2.5	6.6	1.6	0.8	8.7
Durham, NC	8.5	12.3	6.5	0.9	1.3	0.3	1.5	1.1	13.7
Edison, NJ	32.5	1.7	1.2	0.3	0.9	0.5	4.5	1.4	10.6
El Paso, TX	47.9	2.5	0.4	1.2	1.1	0.2	0.1	2.1	6.9
Fargo, ND	14.2	0.2	1.0	0.6	1.3	24.0	<0.1	0.6	8.1
Fort Collins, CO	9.9	1.2	1.3	4.0	2.7	2.5	<0.1	1.2	12.1
Fort Wayne, IN	13.1	8.1	3.9	0.4	1.1	7.1	1.0	0.9	17.6
Fort Worth, TX	14.2	14.3	4.7	1.4	2.2	0.5	1.8	1.3	13.8
Grand Rapids, MI	13.1	1.3	1.8	0.4	1.3	1.8	0.8	1.2	19.9
Greeley, CO	14.1	0.5	0.9	2.9	1.1	1.2	<0.1	1.1	6.1
Green Bay, WI	31.8	0.3	1.4	0.5	1.1	10.8	0.4	0.9	7.0
Greensboro, NC	7.9	10.0	8.0	0.7	2.8	0.4	1.5	1.4	17.8
Honolulu, HI	18.0	1.4	0.5	4.1	2.6	0.2	<0.1	1.9	9.8
Houston, TX	18.3	13.1	3.7	1.2	1.6	0.7	1.7	1.5	13.1
Huntsville, AL	7.5	23.6	6.6	1.4	1.2	0.4	0.8	2.7	17.5
Indianapolis, IN	11.5	6.2	3.3	0.7	1.3	1.1	1.1	1.0	17.4
Jacksonville, FL	13.0	14.5	3.0	1.0	1.4	0.4	0.6	1.3	20.5
Kansas City, MO	11.3	9.1	5.0	1.6	2.7	1.7	1.0	1.0	12.1
Lafayette, LA	44.3	9.3	2.0	0.4	1.8	0.1	0.1	0.8	7.0
Las Cruces, NM	19.3	4.1	1.6	2.5	2.5	0.4	0.6	2.2	4.2
Las Vegas, NV	26.2	1.9	0.3	5.8	1.5	0.6	0.3	1.3	5.5
Lexington, KY	5.8	14.9	5.5	1.2	1.6	0.3	0.5	1.2	16.6
Lincoln, NE	13.2	1.0	5.7	1.2	3.1	9.1	0.1	1.8	10.0
Little Rock, AR	4.9	23.5	6.2	0.8	3.7	0.4	0.4	1.0	13.6
Los Angeles, CA	31.1	2.6	0.8	1.5	2.4	0.4	1.4	1.5	9.1
Louisville, KY	11.9	14.5	3.2	0.8	0.9	0.5	1.0	1.0	12.4
Madison, WI	14.4	0.5	2.0	0.7	0.2	9.2	1.2	0.7	8.4
Manchester, NH	16.3	0.6	0.6	0.6	0.3	0.3	0.1	0.8	8.1

Table continued on following page.

Appendix A: Comparative Statistics   A-49

Area[1]	Catholic	Baptist	Methodist	LDS[2]	Pentecostal	Lutheran	Islam	Adventist	Other
Miami, FL	23.8	5.1	0.9	0.5	1.3	0.3	0.8	2.4	11.1
Midland, TX	15.4	25.5	2.5	2.0	1.2	0.3	0.4	1.3	16.5
Milwaukee, WI	24.5	3.0	1.0	0.4	2.8	9.1	2.8	0.9	10.7
Minneapolis, MN	19.8	0.8	1.4	0.5	2.5	10.7	2.9	0.7	7.4
Nashville, TN	6.2	16.4	4.8	0.9	1.6	0.4	0.8	1.3	19.4
New Haven, CT	29.9	1.4	1.2	0.4	1.2	0.4	0.9	1.2	9.9
New Orleans, LA	42.1	9.3	2.5	0.5	2.1	0.5	1.4	1.0	8.0
New York, NY	32.5	1.7	1.2	0.3	0.9	0.5	4.5	1.4	10.6
Oklahoma City, OK	10.0	16.6	6.2	1.3	3.9	0.6	0.6	0.9	21.4
Omaha, NE	19.9	2.8	2.8	1.6	1.0	6.1	0.2	1.0	9.0
Orlando, FL	17.6	5.7	2.1	0.9	2.7	0.6	1.3	2.8	14.6
Philadelphia, PA	26.8	3.3	2.4	0.3	1.0	1.2	2.6	1.0	10.5
Phoenix, AZ	22.9	1.7	0.6	6.2	1.5	1.0	1.9	1.5	9.3
Pittsburgh, PA	30.6	1.9	4.3	0.4	1.3	2.5	0.6	0.6	12.5
Portland, OR	11.8	0.8	0.6	3.3	1.4	1.1	0.2	2.0	14.4
Providence, RI	37.9	0.9	0.6	0.3	0.6	0.3	0.5	0.9	6.1
Provo, UT	4.9	0.1	<0.1	82.6	0.1	<0.1	0.3	0.3	0.4
Raleigh, NC	12.4	9.8	5.4	1.2	1.9	0.7	3.2	1.5	12.8
Reno, NV	24.4	1.4	0.5	4.0	0.9	0.5	0.3	1.4	5.3
Richmond, VA	12.3	14.2	4.8	0.9	3.2	0.5	2.1	1.2	14.8
Rochester, MN	15.6	0.4	2.8	1.5	1.9	19.3	1.0	0.7	10.1
Sacramento, CA	17.1	1.9	1.1	3.1	2.2	0.6	1.9	1.9	8.2
St. Louis, MO	21.2	8.6	2.9	0.7	1.4	3.2	1.3	0.8	11.1
Salem, OR	19.5	0.5	0.6	3.8	2.9	1.2	n/a	2.5	10.7
Salt Lake City, UT	9.0	0.6	0.2	52.0	0.7	0.2	1.6	0.7	2.6
San Antonio, TX	27.3	6.4	2.1	1.4	1.6	1.1	0.5	1.5	11.0
San Diego, CA	22.9	1.5	0.6	2.1	1.0	0.6	1.5	1.9	9.4
San Francisco, CA	21.5	2.2	0.9	1.5	1.4	0.4	2.0	1.0	7.7
San Jose, CA	27.2	1.2	0.6	1.4	0.9	0.4	2.0	1.3	11.4
Santa Rosa, CA	23.5	1.1	0.5	1.4	0.5	0.5	0.2	1.8	6.9
Savannah, GA	5.5	11.9	4.8	0.8	1.5	1.1	0.2	1.4	12.3
Seattle, WA	11.0	1.0	0.7	2.6	2.8	1.2	0.6	1.4	19.8
Sioux Falls, SD	13.1	0.7	2.9	0.7	1.7	16.4	0.1	0.6	20.3
Springfield, IL	15.2	4.7	4.3	0.5	1.5	4.7	0.5	0.8	14.6
Tampa, FL	23.1	6.3	2.9	0.5	1.9	0.6	0.7	1.8	12.1
Tucson, AZ	18.9	1.9	0.6	2.8	1.3	1.1	1.0	1.4	9.7
Tulsa, OK	5.6	15.5	7.7	1.2	2.5	0.5	0.5	1.2	22.2
Tuscaloosa, AL	2.6	25.1	6.2	0.6	1.5	0.1	0.3	0.7	13.3
Virginia Beach, VA	8.3	9.5	4.8	0.7	2.0	0.5	1.0	0.9	16.1
Washington, DC	16.1	6.0	4.1	1.1	1.3	0.8	3.3	1.5	12.6
Wichita, KS	12.7	23.5	4.5	1.5	1.4	1.3	0.1	1.1	15.0
Wilmington, NC	13.2	9.9	8.1	1.0	1.0	0.7	0.7	1.4	12.6
Winston-Salem, NC	9.3	12.8	11.4	0.5	1.0	0.6	0.8	1.4	22.5
Worcester, MA	30.1	0.8	0.8	0.3	1.0	0.4	0.6	1.4	7.1
U.S.	18.7	7.3	3.0	2.0	1.8	1.7	1.3	1.3	11.6

Note: Figures are the number of adherents as a percentage of the total population; (1) Figures cover the Metropolitan Statistical Area; (2) Church of Jesus Christ of Latter-day Saints
Source: 2020 U.S. Religion Census, Association of Statisticians of American Religious Bodies; The Association of Religion Data Archives (ARDA)

A-50   Appendix A: Comparative Statistics

Religious Groups by Tradition

Area	Catholic	Evangelical Protestant	Mainline Protestant	Black Protestant	Islam	Judaism	Hinduism	Orthodox	Buddhism
Albuquerque, NM	32.6	13.4	2.2	0.5	0.7	0.2	0.2	0.1	0.6
Allentown, PA	18.6	6.2	11.9	0.2	0.7	0.5	0.6	0.4	0.1
Anchorage, AK	4.9	19.2	2.4	0.9	0.1	0.1	0.1	0.5	1.3
Ann Arbor, MI	9.7	8.1	5.6	2.5	2.2	0.8	0.5	0.4	0.3
Athens, GA	6.4	19.1	7.2	2.6	0.2	0.2	0.2	0.1	<0.1
Atlanta, GA	10.7	22.3	7.4	5.3	1.9	0.5	0.7	0.3	0.2
Austin, TX	18.8	13.5	4.0	1.7	1.0	0.2	0.6	0.2	0.3
Baltimore, MD	12.4	10.6	5.9	3.3	3.3	1.7	0.1	0.5	0.1
Boise City, ID	13.0	11.9	3.9	<0.1	0.3	0.1	0.2	0.1	0.1
Boston, MA	37.0	3.4	3.2	0.3	2.2	1.1	0.3	0.9	0.4
Boulder, CO	16.0	12.7	3.4	n/a	0.4	0.7	0.5	0.2	1.0
Brownsville, TX	36.8	13.1	1.2	0.1	0.1	n/a	n/a	n/a	n/a
Cape Coral, FL	18.8	16.4	3.0	0.6	0.2	0.2	0.2	0.1	0.1
Cedar Rapids, IA	16.8	11.9	12.2	0.4	1.3	0.1	0.7	0.1	<0.1
Charleston, SC	11.5	17.1	6.8	6.6	0.2	0.4	<0.1	0.2	n/a
Charlotte, NC	12.1	26.4	9.5	3.4	1.7	0.2	0.2	0.4	0.1
Chicago, IL	28.6	8.2	3.7	3.6	4.7	0.7	0.4	0.7	0.4
Cincinnati, OH	17.0	24.9	4.1	2.0	1.1	0.4	0.3	0.3	0.1
Clarksville, TN	4.6	35.7	4.8	3.4	0.1	n/a	n/a	0.1	n/a
Cleveland, OH	26.1	15.1	5.6	3.5	1.1	1.3	0.3	0.8	0.2
College Station, TX	17.2	16.1	5.3	1.8	0.6	n/a	0.1	0.1	n/a
Colorado Springs, CO	16.4	18.3	2.9	0.9	0.1	<0.1	<0.1	0.1	0.3
Columbia, MO	7.1	19.4	6.3	1.9	1.4	0.2	0.1	0.1	<0.1
Columbia, SC	6.6	27.9	10.7	5.6	0.3	0.2	0.4	0.1	0.3
Columbus, OH	11.7	18.1	6.8	1.5	2.1	0.4	0.4	0.5	0.2
Dallas, TX	14.2	25.4	5.9	3.3	1.8	0.3	0.5	0.3	0.2
Davenport, IA	13.2	8.5	10.6	1.9	0.7	0.1	0.2	0.1	n/a
Denver, CO	16.1	9.6	2.8	0.6	0.3	0.4	0.5	0.4	0.5
Des Moines, IA	12.1	10.3	12.2	1.0	1.6	<0.1	0.2	0.1	0.1
Durham, NC	8.5	20.0	8.8	4.3	1.5	0.5	0.1	0.3	0.1
Edison, NJ	32.5	4.4	3.0	1.5	4.5	4.4	1.0	0.8	0.3
El Paso, TX	47.9	9.9	0.6	0.4	0.1	0.2	<0.1	<0.1	0.2
Fargo, ND	14.2	11.1	23.4	n/a	<0.1	<0.1	n/a	0.1	n/a
Fort Collins, CO	9.9	15.6	3.3	0.4	<0.1	n/a	0.1	0.1	0.1
Fort Wayne, IN	13.1	24.7	6.1	6.5	1.0	0.1	0.1	0.2	0.4
Fort Worth, TX	14.2	25.4	5.9	3.3	1.8	0.3	0.5	0.3	0.2
Grand Rapids, MI	13.1	17.6	7.4	1.0	0.8	0.1	0.2	0.2	<0.1
Greeley, CO	14.1	7.8	2.1	<0.1	<0.1	n/a	n/a	<0.1	0.2
Green Bay, WI	31.8	14.6	6.2	<0.1	0.4	n/a	n/a	<0.1	<0.1
Greensboro, NC	7.9	24.9	10.1	3.5	1.5	0.3	0.3	0.1	0.1
Honolulu, HI	18.0	8.1	2.3	0.2	<0.1	0.1	0.2	<0.1	4.0
Houston, TX	18.3	23.8	4.7	2.3	1.7	0.3	0.7	0.3	0.3
Huntsville, AL	7.5	34.8	8.2	7.2	0.8	0.1	0.9	0.1	0.1
Indianapolis, IN	11.5	16.8	7.6	4.2	1.1	0.4	0.2	0.3	0.1
Jacksonville, FL	13.0	29.8	3.5	5.6	0.6	0.3	0.3	0.3	0.2
Kansas City, MO	11.3	19.1	7.1	3.6	1.0	0.3	0.4	0.1	0.2
Lafayette, LA	44.3	12.6	2.4	5.0	0.1	n/a	<0.1	<0.1	0.1
Las Cruces, NM	19.3	9.8	2.4	0.2	0.6	0.1	0.2	<0.1	n/a
Las Vegas, NV	26.2	6.6	1.0	0.5	0.3	0.3	0.2	0.6	0.7
Lexington, KY	5.8	26.9	8.1	3.5	0.5	0.3	0.1	0.2	<0.1
Lincoln, NE	13.2	16.6	12.9	0.3	0.1	0.1	0.1	0.1	0.1
Little Rock, AR	4.9	32.1	6.6	8.5	0.4	0.1	<0.1	0.1	0.1
Los Angeles, CA	31.1	9.3	1.5	1.7	1.4	0.8	0.4	0.9	0.9
Louisville, KY	11.9	21.1	5.0	4.6	1.0	0.2	0.4	0.2	0.2
Madison, WI	14.4	8.0	10.6	0.2	1.2	0.4	0.1	0.1	0.9

Table continued on following page.

Appendix A: Comparative Statistics   A-51

Area	Catholic	Evangelical Protestant	Mainline Protestant	Black Protestant	Islam	Judaism	Hinduism	Orthodox	Buddhism
Manchester, NH	16.3	5.8	2.7	n/a	0.1	0.3	<0.1	0.9	n/a
Miami, FL	23.8	13.7	1.6	2.2	0.8	1.2	0.3	0.2	0.3
Midland, TX	15.4	35.5	3.0	7.6	0.4	n/a	0.2	n/a	n/a
Milwaukee, WI	24.5	16.3	5.4	3.3	2.8	0.4	0.4	0.5	0.4
Minneapolis, MN	19.8	10.6	10.3	0.5	2.9	0.6	0.2	0.3	0.3
Nashville, TN	6.2	30.1	6.0	5.2	0.8	0.2	0.4	1.1	0.2
New Haven, CT	29.9	6.4	4.4	1.4	0.9	1.0	0.3	0.5	0.4
New Orleans, LA	42.1	13.5	3.0	4.9	1.4	0.4	0.3	0.1	0.3
New York, NY	32.5	4.4	3.0	1.5	4.5	4.4	1.0	0.8	0.3
Oklahoma City, OK	10.0	38.7	7.1	2.2	0.6	0.1	0.4	0.1	0.4
Omaha, NE	19.9	10.8	7.9	1.5	0.2	0.3	1.0	0.2	0.2
Orlando, FL	17.6	20.6	2.5	2.7	1.3	0.2	0.5	0.3	0.3
Philadelphia, PA	26.8	7.3	6.6	2.2	2.6	1.1	0.6	0.4	0.4
Phoenix, AZ	22.9	11.0	1.6	0.3	1.9	0.3	0.5	0.4	0.2
Pittsburgh, PA	30.6	8.8	10.1	1.3	0.6	0.6	1.2	0.6	0.1
Portland, OR	11.8	14.6	2.3	0.4	0.2	0.3	0.7	0.3	0.4
Providence, RI	37.9	4.0	3.2	0.1	0.5	0.6	0.1	0.5	0.2
Provo, UT	4.9	0.4	<0.1	n/a	0.3	n/a	0.1	n/a	n/a
Raleigh, NC	12.4	19.3	7.4	2.8	3.2	0.2	0.4	0.3	0.4
Reno, NV	24.4	6.8	1.3	0.2	0.3	0.1	0.1	0.1	0.2
Richmond, VA	12.3	23.1	9.3	3.1	2.1	0.3	1.3	0.4	0.2
Rochester, MN	15.6	15.0	19.1	n/a	1.0	0.1	0.1	0.2	0.2
Sacramento, CA	17.1	10.4	1.4	1.1	1.9	0.2	0.4	0.3	0.5
St. Louis, MO	21.2	16.1	5.7	3.9	1.3	0.6	0.2	0.2	0.3
Salem, OR	19.5	14.4	2.0	0.2	n/a	0.1	<0.1	<0.1	<0.1
Salt Lake City, UT	9.0	2.4	0.7	0.1	1.6	0.1	0.3	0.4	0.3
San Antonio, TX	27.3	17.7	3.1	0.8	0.5	0.2	0.1	0.1	0.3
San Diego, CA	22.9	9.5	1.5	0.6	1.5	0.4	0.3	0.4	0.7
San Francisco, CA	21.5	5.2	2.2	1.8	2.0	0.7	1.1	0.7	1.1
San Jose, CA	27.2	8.4	1.4	0.3	2.0	0.6	2.4	0.6	1.2
Santa Rosa, CA	23.5	5.3	1.5	<0.1	0.2	0.4	0.3	0.4	1.7
Savannah, GA	5.5	19.0	5.7	5.9	0.2	0.7	0.5	0.1	n/a
Seattle, WA	11.0	19.5	2.7	0.6	0.6	0.4	0.4	0.6	1.6
Sioux Falls, SD	13.1	21.0	20.2	0.1	0.1	n/a	n/a	0.8	<0.1
Springfield, IL	15.2	19.0	7.7	2.4	0.5	0.2	0.3	0.1	<0.1
Tampa, FL	23.1	16.9	3.8	1.7	0.7	0.4	0.3	0.8	0.4
Tucson, AZ	18.9	10.4	2.4	0.6	1.0	0.4	0.4	0.2	0.3
Tulsa, OK	5.6	37.8	8.6	1.7	0.5	0.2	0.1	0.1	<0.1
Tuscaloosa, AL	2.6	34.3	4.6	7.3	0.3	0.1	n/a	n/a	n/a
Virginia Beach, VA	8.3	21.3	6.9	3.7	1.0	0.3	0.2	0.3	0.3
Washington, DC	16.1	12.3	6.5	3.3	3.3	1.0	0.9	0.9	0.5
Wichita, KS	12.7	19.4	23.2	2.6	0.1	<0.1	0.1	0.2	0.5
Wilmington, NC	13.2	17.9	9.3	4.6	0.7	0.3	0.1	0.3	n/a
Winston-Salem, NC	9.3	31.4	13.6	3.4	0.8	n/a	<0.1	0.3	0.1
Worcester, MA	30.1	4.9	3.6	0.2	0.6	0.4	0.3	1.0	0.4
U.S.	18.7	16.5	5.2	2.3	1.3	0.6	0.4	0.4	0.3

Note: Figures are the number of adherents as a percentage of the total population; (1) Figures cover the Metropolitan Statistical Area
Source: 2020 U.S. Religion Census, Association of Statisticians of American Religious Bodies; The Association of Religion Data Archives
(ARDA)

A-52   Appendix A: Comparative Statistics

Gross Metropolitan Product

MSA[1]	2020	2021	2022	2023	Rank[2]
Albuquerque, NM	45.1	50.3	56.1	58.2	70
Allentown, PA	46.7	51.6	56.6	59.9	67
Anchorage, AK	25.8	28.3	31.3	32.6	112
Ann Arbor, MI	25.8	28.1	30.4	32.1	113
Athens, GA	10.5	11.5	12.8	13.4	213
Atlanta, GA	425.4	465.1	507.9	540.7	11
Austin, TX	168.4	192.3	215.9	231.0	22
Baltimore, MD	205.8	219.9	238.6	255.0	19
Boise City, ID	37.9	42.9	46.9	50.4	80
Boston, MA	480.3	526.5	569.8	601.7	8
Boulder, CO	29.7	32.7	35.9	38.1	101
Brownsville, TX	11.9	13.1	14.8	15.6	195
Cape Coral, FL	34.5	38.8	42.7	45.6	85
Cedar Rapids, IA	18.5	20.7	21.9	23.3	147
Charleston, SC	45.6	50.4	55.3	59.2	69
Charlotte, NC	184.0	204.1	222.9	238.2	21
Chicago, IL	693.0	757.2	819.9	861.2	3
Cincinnati, OH	152.1	165.2	178.8	190.5	27
Clarksville, TN	12.3	13.7	14.8	15.6	191
Cleveland, OH	133.6	144.9	157.7	167.2	35
College Station, TX	13.6	14.9	16.6	17.4	185
Colorado Springs, CO	39.5	43.7	47.3	49.9	78
Columbia, MO	10.4	11.6	12.5	13.3	211
Columbia, SC	44.4	48.2	51.8	55.2	74
Columbus, OH	137.3	151.0	164.2	175.3	33
Dallas, TX	538.4	608.8	686.1	722.1	5
Davenport, IA	22.1	24.6	26.3	27.6	126
Denver, CO	223.1	246.9	271.0	286.2	18
Des Moines, IA	55.0	63.3	67.6	71.4	57
Durham, NC	51.6	57.3	61.8	65.6	60
Edison, NJ	1,844.7	1,993.2	2,157.6	2,278.7	1
El Paso, TX	34.1	37.5	40.5	42.6	89
Fargo, ND	15.7	18.0	19.9	20.6	160
Fort Collins, CO	21.6	23.7	25.7	27.3	130
Fort Wayne, IN	24.3	27.3	29.8	31.6	114
Fort Worth, TX	538.4	608.8	686.1	722.1	5
Grand Rapids, MI	61.4	67.8	73.0	78.0	55
Greeley, CO	16.7	17.9	20.0	22.3	162
Green Bay, WI	20.5	22.2	24.3	26.0	139
Greensboro, NC	42.0	46.1	49.5	51.7	75
Honolulu, HI	62.1	66.8	74.3	80.2	56
Houston, TX	488.1	543.0	619.8	654.0	7
Huntsville, AL	30.9	33.5	36.5	39.2	98
Indianapolis, IN	146.9	163.9	178.6	190.0	28
Jacksonville, FL	91.0	100.3	109.1	115.5	42
Kansas City, MO	142.5	154.3	165.9	176.9	32
Lafayette, LA	20.6	22.6	24.8	26.2	135
Las Cruces, NM	7.6	8.5	9.6	10.0	258
Las Vegas, NV	119.4	134.8	151.1	164.0	36
Lexington, KY	29.8	32.5	35.1	36.8	103
Lincoln, NE	21.2	23.8	25.4	26.9	129
Little Rock, AR	38.6	42.3	45.8	48.0	81
Los Angeles, CA	1,007.0	1,129.4	1,226.9	1,295.5	2
Louisville, KY	75.6	83.6	90.5	94.4	47
Madison, WI	51.5	56.1	60.8	64.9	63
Manchester, NH	28.8	32.2	34.1	35.6	104

Table continued on following page.

Appendix A: Comparative Statistics   A-53

MSA[1]	2020	2021	2022	2023	Rank[2]
Miami, FL	365.0	402.9	442.8	471.0	12
Midland, TX	21.8	25.3	30.1	33.9	121
Milwaukee, WI	102.4	110.1	119.2	126.3	38
Minneapolis, MN	270.7	298.9	324.7	344.9	15
Nashville, TN	136.6	157.4	173.7	184.5	31
New Haven, CT	53.0	57.1	61.7	64.7	61
New Orleans, LA	76.4	82.6	91.2	96.5	48
New York, NY	1,844.7	1,993.2	2,157.6	2,278.7	1
Oklahoma City, OK	74.4	81.6	92.9	98.2	49
Omaha, NE	69.1	77.9	83.2	88.2	50
Orlando, FL	144.1	160.5	180.2	194.2	30
Philadelphia, PA	439.1	478.2	521.7	553.7	9
Phoenix, AZ	281.0	310.1	336.3	358.7	14
Pittsburgh, PA	153.4	165.5	178.3	189.7	26
Portland, OR	168.4	184.1	201.8	214.4	25
Providence, RI	87.9	95.6	104.0	109.3	45
Provo, UT	31.9	36.5	40.2	43.1	91
Raleigh, NC	95.3	106.6	117.3	125.7	39
Reno, NV	31.8	35.9	39.3	41.9	92
Richmond, VA	91.2	97.3	104.5	110.5	44
Rochester, MN	14.2	15.8	17.1	18.1	178
Sacramento, CA	145.4	161.7	176.8	188.8	29
St. Louis, MO	171.5	187.7	201.8	212.8	23
Salem, OR	19.2	21.0	22.9	24.2	144
Salt Lake City, UT	103.9	114.9	124.5	132.3	37
San Antonio, TX	132.1	146.4	161.1	169.2	34
San Diego, CA	240.4	269.0	294.4	313.2	17
San Francisco, CA	588.3	652.7	713.1	748.9	4
San Jose, CA	360.5	400.1	431.2	450.9	13
Santa Rosa, CA	31.2	35.6	39.1	41.5	93
Savannah, GA	22.0	25.3	27.7	28.7	122
Seattle, WA	426.9	470.6	509.3	539.7	10
Sioux Falls, SD	23.4	26.6	28.7	30.6	118
Springfield, IL	11.7	13.1	13.8	14.6	196
Tampa, FL	169.3	187.4	205.4	217.8	24
Tucson, AZ	45.2	49.1	53.1	56.2	72
Tulsa, OK	53.7	58.3	65.1	68.5	59
Tuscaloosa, AL	11.4	12.2	13.2	13.9	205
Virginia Beach, VA	95.3	102.4	109.4	116.0	41
Washington, DC	560.7	600.8	647.6	688.6	6
Wichita, KS	36.7	40.2	44.0	47.1	83
Wilmington, NC	16.0	18.0	19.3	20.3	161
Winston-Salem, NC	34.0	37.6	40.9	43.7	88
Worcester, MA	50.9	55.1	59.3	62.5	64

Note: Figures are in billions of dollars; (1) Metropolitan Statistical Area; (2) Rank is based on 2021 data and ranges from 1 to 381.
Source: The U.S. Conference of Mayors, U.S. Metro Economies: U.S. Metros Compared to Global and State Economies,, June 2022

A-54   Appendix A: Comparative Statistics

Economic Growth

MSA[1]	2018-20 (%)	2021 (%)	2022 (%)	2023	Rank[2]
Albuquerque, NM	-0.4	5.6	4.6	3.6	167
Allentown, PA	-0.3	5.9	3.6	2.6	159
Anchorage, AK	-2.4	0.4	2.3	2.9	323
Ann Arbor, MI	-0.4	5.0	2.9	2.6	164
Athens, GA	-2.1	5.6	6.1	1.6	288
Atlanta, GA	-0.1	5.9	3.3	3.1	151
Austin, TX	3.2	10.1	5.9	3.8	13
Baltimore, MD	-2.0	3.2	2.7	3.5	284
Boise City, ID	2.0	7.4	3.2	4.2	35
Boston, MA	-0.1	6.7	3.2	2.4	146
Boulder, CO	1.5	5.6	3.5	3.8	49
Brownsville, TX	1.3	6.2	4.4	2.9	56
Cape Coral, FL	-0.4	8.7	5.0	2.9	165
Cedar Rapids, IA	-2.3	4.9	-0.2	3.5	310
Charleston, SC	0.4	6.3	3.8	3.8	106
Charlotte, NC	0.5	6.6	3.2	3.6	103
Chicago, IL	-2.4	5.5	2.6	1.8	324
Cincinnati, OH	0.0	4.2	2.4	3.3	145
Clarksville, TN	0.7	7.1	3.0	1.6	91
Cleveland, OH	-1.3	4.3	3.1	2.7	238
College Station, TX	1.1	5.1	4.2	2.8	61
Colorado Springs, CO	1.6	6.0	2.1	3.0	47
Columbia, MO	2.1	5.6	2.9	3.3	29
Columbia, SC	0.1	4.4	1.7	3.2	137
Columbus, OH	0.1	5.8	3.1	3.5	136
Dallas, TX	0.8	8.3	5.3	3.2	84
Davenport, IA	-0.6	5.6	1.2	1.8	184
Denver, CO	0.8	6.2	3.5	3.1	82
Des Moines, IA	1.7	8.2	0.9	2.7	46
Durham, NC	2.7	6.7	2.5	2.9	19
Edison, NJ	-1.5	5.6	3.3	2.4	250
El Paso, TX	2.0	5.5	2.3	1.9	36
Fargo, ND	-0.4	6.0	-0.2	1.2	170
Fort Collins, CO	2.2	5.3	2.6	4.0	27
Fort Wayne, IN	-2.0	8.3	3.1	2.7	285
Fort Worth, TX	0.8	8.3	5.3	3.2	84
Grand Rapids, MI	-2.1	6.3	1.8	3.7	294
Greeley, CO	-4.3	3.2	5.5	9.1	366
Green Bay, WI	-2.5	3.7	3.7	3.9	326
Greensboro, NC	-2.2	5.4	1.5	1.4	302
Honolulu, HI	-5.4	3.6	5.2	4.6	376
Houston, TX	-1.6	4.9	4.4	4.7	254
Huntsville, AL	1.8	4.9	3.4	3.9	42
Indianapolis, IN	-0.2	7.3	3.2	3.1	155
Jacksonville, FL	2.1	6.1	3.1	2.6	30
Kansas City, MO	0.0	4.0	1.7	3.5	140
Lafayette, LA	-3.7	4.2	2.6	3.3	356
Las Cruces, NM	-1.8	6.3	7.3	3.2	273
Las Vegas, NV	-3.4	7.7	5.7	5.1	349
Lexington, KY	-1.6	4.1	1.8	1.6	261
Lincoln, NE	0.1	5.0	0.9	2.8	131
Little Rock, AR	-0.6	5.2	2.2	1.9	182
Los Angeles, CA	-1.6	8.8	3.3	2.6	256
Louisville, KY	-0.4	5.8	2.2	1.2	169
Madison, WI	0.1	4.4	2.7	3.7	132
Manchester, NH	0.9	8.3	1.2	1.0	78

Table continued on following page.

Appendix A: Comparative Statistics   A-55

MSA[1]	2018-20 (%)	2021 (%)	2022 (%)	2023	Rank[2]
Miami, FL	-1.4	6.4	4.2	3.1	245
Midland, TX	3.5	15.8	10.1	12.3	12
Milwaukee, WI	-1.8	3.1	2.5	2.8	271
Minneapolis, MN	-1.9	5.9	2.8	3.0	276
Nashville, TN	-1.2	10.6	4.4	3.0	228
New Haven, CT	-0.9	4.6	2.8	1.7	206
New Orleans, LA	-2.2	2.6	1.8	3.3	304
New York, NY	-1.5	5.6	3.3	2.4	250
Oklahoma City, OK	-2.2	2.3	4.2	4.8	307
Omaha, NE	0.2	5.3	0.8	3.0	127
Orlando, FL	-1.2	7.5	6.4	4.4	229
Philadelphia, PA	-1.2	4.9	3.3	2.8	235
Phoenix, AZ	1.9	5.8	2.7	3.4	39
Pittsburgh, PA	-1.6	3.8	1.9	3.1	257
Portland, OR	-0.6	5.8	4.2	2.9	179
Providence, RI	-1.1	5.6	3.4	1.9	224
Provo, UT	5.1	10.9	6.1	4.3	3
Raleigh, NC	-0.1	7.7	4.4	4.0	148
Reno, NV	2.1	7.5	2.8	3.2	31
Richmond, VA	-0.3	3.0	1.7	2.3	160
Rochester, MN	-0.9	6.6	2.9	2.5	209
Sacramento, CA	0.0	7.4	3.6	3.6	142
St. Louis, MO	-1.2	5.3	1.6	2.0	232
Salem, OR	0.3	5.6	4.2	2.6	119
Salt Lake City, UT	1.9	6.1	2.7	3.1	38
San Antonio, TX	0.8	6.2	3.7	2.4	88
San Diego, CA	-0.5	8.2	3.9	3.3	174
San Francisco, CA	1.2	7.1	4.0	1.9	60
San Jose, CA	5.2	8.6	3.3	1.6	2
Santa Rosa, CA	-1.8	9.7	5.0	3.1	269
Savannah, GA	-1.6	10.3	4.8	0.1	262
Seattle, WA	2.2	7.2	3.3	2.6	26
Sioux Falls, SD	0.4	7.1	1.9	3.7	111
Springfield, IL	-3.3	9.4	0.6	2.6	346
Tampa, FL	1.0	7.2	4.1	2.8	72
Tucson, AZ	-1.3	4.0	2.1	2.5	240
Tulsa, OK	-1.7	1.1	3.1	3.5	266
Tuscaloosa, AL	0.9	3.1	3.9	2.4	80
Virginia Beach, VA	-1.4	3.5	1.1	2.5	247
Washington, DC	-0.7	4.0	2.5	3.0	192
Wichita, KS	-2.0	4.3	2.9	4.1	286
Wilmington, NC	1.5	8.5	1.8	1.3	52
Winston-Salem, NC	-4.0	6.0	2.8	3.6	358
Worcester, MA	-0.9	5.3	2.5	2.4	204
U.S.	-0.6	5.7	3.1	2.9	–

Note: Figures are real gross metropolitan product (GMP) growth rates and represent annual average percent change;
(1) Metropolitan Statistical Area; (2) Rank is based on 2020 2-year average annual percent change and ranges from 1 to 381
Source: The U.S. Conference of Mayors, U.S. Metro Economies: U.S. Metros Compared to Global and State Economies,, June 2022

A-56 Appendix A: Comparative Statistics

Metropolitan Area Exports

MSA[1]	2016	2017	2018	2019	2020	2021	Rank[2]
Albuquerque, NM	999.7	624.2	771.5	1,629.7	1,265.3	2,215.0	101
Allentown, PA	3,657.2	3,639.4	3,423.2	3,796.3	3,207.4	4,088.7	68
Anchorage, AK	1,215.4	1,675.9	1,510.8	1,348.0	990.9	n/a	n/a
Ann Arbor, MI	1,207.9	1,447.4	1,538.7	1,432.7	1,183.1	1,230.7	141
Athens, GA	332.1	297.7	378.1	442.1	338.7	448.1	223
Atlanta, GA	20,480.1	21,748.0	24,091.6	25,800.8	25,791.0	28,116.4	16
Austin, TX	10,682.7	12,451.5	12,929.9	12,509.0	13,041.5	15,621.9	25
Baltimore, MD	5,288.6	4,674.3	6,039.2	7,081.8	6,084.6	8,200.6	43
Boise City, ID	3,021.7	2,483.3	2,771.7	2,062.8	1,632.9	1,937.1	110
Boston, MA	21,168.0	23,116.2	24,450.1	23,505.8	23,233.8	32,084.2	12
Boulder, CO	956.3	1,012.0	1,044.1	1,014.9	1,110.4	1,078.0	152
Brownsville, TX	5,016.7	n/a	6,293.0	4,741.8	n/a	6,953.0	47
Cape Coral, FL	540.3	592.3	668.0	694.9	654.8	797.5	183
Cedar Rapids, IA	945.0	1,071.6	1,025.0	1,028.4	832.0	980.0	160
Charleston, SC	9,508.1	8,845.2	10,943.2	16,337.9	6,110.5	3,381.6	77
Charlotte, NC	11,944.1	13,122.5	14,083.2	13,892.4	8,225.6	10,554.3	33
Chicago, IL	43,932.7	46,140.2	47,287.8	42,438.8	41,279.4	54,498.1	4
Cincinnati, OH	26,326.2	28,581.8	27,396.3	28,778.3	21,002.2	23,198.7	19
Clarksville, TN	376.1	360.2	435.5	341.8	246.8	288.7	268
Cleveland, OH	8,752.9	8,944.9	9,382.9	8,829.9	7,415.8	8,560.4	41
College Station, TX	113.2	145.4	153.0	160.5	114.9	110.3	346
Colorado Springs, CO	786.9	819.7	850.6	864.2	979.2	866.9	175
Columbia, MO	213.7	224.0	238.6	291.4	256.2	335.4	255
Columbia, SC	2,007.7	2,123.9	2,083.8	2,184.6	2,058.8	2,100.2	104
Columbus, OH	5,675.4	5,962.2	7,529.5	7,296.6	6,304.8	6,557.9	51
Dallas, TX	27,187.8	30,269.1	36,260.9	39,474.0	35,642.0	43,189.0	6
Davenport, IA	4,497.6	5,442.7	6,761.9	6,066.3	5,097.5	6,341.0	52
Denver, CO	3,649.3	3,954.7	4,544.3	4,555.6	4,604.4	4,670.8	62
Des Moines, IA	1,052.2	1,141.2	1,293.7	1,437.8	1,414.0	1,706.6	118
Durham, NC	2,937.4	3,128.4	3,945.8	4,452.9	3,359.3	3,326.4	78
Edison, NJ	89,649.5	93,693.7	97,692.4	87,365.7	75,745.4	103,930.9	2
El Paso, TX	26,452.8	25,814.1	30,052.0	32,749.6	27,154.4	32,397.9	11
Fargo, ND	474.5	519.5	553.5	515.0	438.3	539.4	210
Fort Collins, CO	993.8	1,034.1	1,021.8	1,060.0	1,092.5	1,132.5	146
Fort Wayne, IN	1,322.2	1,422.8	1,593.3	1,438.5	1,144.6	1,592.7	123
Fort Worth, TX	27,187.8	30,269.1	36,260.9	39,474.0	35,642.0	43,189.0	6
Grand Rapids, MI	5,168.5	5,385.8	5,420.9	5,214.1	4,488.3	5,171.7	57
Greeley, CO	1,539.6	1,492.8	1,366.5	1,439.2	1,480.4	2,022.6	109
Green Bay, WI	1,044.0	1,054.8	1,044.3	928.2	736.4	765.6	185
Greensboro, NC	3,730.4	3,537.9	3,053.5	2,561.8	2,007.3	2,356.2	97
Honolulu, HI	330.3	393.6	438.9	308.6	169.0	164.3	319
Houston, TX	84,105.5	95,760.3	120,714.3	129,656.0	104,538.2	140,750.4	1
Huntsville, AL	1,827.3	1,889.2	1,608.7	1,534.2	1,263.0	1,579.5	124
Indianapolis, IN	9,655.4	10,544.2	11,069.9	11,148.7	11,100.4	12,740.4	30
Jacksonville, FL	2,159.0	2,141.7	2,406.7	2,975.5	2,473.3	2,683.7	90
Kansas City, MO	6,709.8	7,015.0	7,316.9	7,652.6	7,862.7	9,177.6	38
Lafayette, LA	1,335.2	954.8	1,001.7	1,086.2	946.2	895.7	167
Las Cruces, NM	1,568.6	1,390.2	1,467.5	n/a	2,149.5	2,408.2	95
Las Vegas, NV	2,312.3	2,710.6	2,240.6	2,430.8	1,705.9	1,866.2	115
Lexington, KY	2,069.6	2,119.8	2,148.0	2,093.8	1,586.3	1,880.0	113
Lincoln, NE	796.9	860.9	885.6	807.0	726.3	872.6	171
Little Rock, AR	1,871.0	2,146.1	1,607.4	1,642.5	n/a	1,370.6	132
Los Angeles, CA	61,245.7	63,752.9	64,814.6	61,041.1	50,185.4	58,588.4	3
Louisville, KY	7,793.3	8,925.9	8,987.0	9,105.5	8,360.3	10,262.8	35
Madison, WI	2,204.8	2,187.7	2,460.2	2,337.6	2,450.5	2,756.3	89
Manchester, NH	1,465.2	1,714.7	1,651.4	1,587.1	1,704.9	2,077.6	106

Table continued on following page.

Appendix A: Comparative Statistics   A-57

MSA[1]	2016	2017	2018	2019	2020	2021	Rank[2]
Miami, FL	32,734.5	34,780.5	35,650.2	35,498.9	29,112.1	36,011.3	7
Midland, TX	69.6	69.4	63.6	63.7	57.7	49.9	372
Milwaukee, WI	7,256.2	7,279.1	7,337.6	6,896.3	6,624.0	7,282.8	46
Minneapolis, MN	18,329.2	19,070.9	20,016.2	18,633.0	17,109.5	21,098.8	21
Nashville, TN	9,460.1	10,164.3	8,723.7	7,940.7	6,569.9	8,256.1	42
New Haven, CT	1,819.8	1,876.3	2,082.3	2,133.8	2,330.5	2,667.5	91
New Orleans, LA	29,518.8	31,648.5	36,570.4	34,109.6	31,088.4	35,773.5	8
New York, NY	89,649.5	93,693.7	97,692.4	87,365.7	75,745.4	103,930.9	2
Oklahoma City, OK	1,260.0	1,278.8	1,489.4	1,434.5	1,326.6	1,773.2	116
Omaha, NE	3,509.7	3,756.2	4,371.6	3,725.7	3,852.5	4,595.1	64
Orlando, FL	3,363.9	3,196.7	3,131.7	3,363.9	2,849.8	3,313.6	79
Philadelphia, PA	21,359.9	21,689.7	23,663.2	24,721.3	23,022.1	28,724.4	15
Phoenix, AZ	12,838.2	13,223.1	13,614.9	15,136.6	11,073.9	14,165.1	27
Pittsburgh, PA	7,971.0	9,322.7	9,824.2	9,672.9	7,545.1	9,469.6	36
Portland, OR	20,256.8	20,788.8	21,442.9	23,761.9	27,824.7	33,787.5	10
Providence, RI	6,595.7	7,125.4	6,236.6	7,424.8	6,685.2	6,708.2	49
Provo, UT	1,894.8	2,065.3	1,788.1	1,783.7	1,888.5	2,053.8	108
Raleigh, NC	2,620.4	2,865.8	3,193.2	3,546.8	3,372.0	3,962.7	71
Reno, NV	2,382.1	2,517.3	2,631.7	2,598.3	4,553.3	4,503.0	66
Richmond, VA	3,525.7	3,663.7	3,535.0	3,203.2	2,719.1	3,010.7	84
Rochester, MN	398.0	495.3	537.6	390.1	194.0	224.9	292
Sacramento, CA	7,032.1	6,552.6	6,222.8	5,449.2	4,980.9	5,682.3	54
St. Louis, MO	8,346.5	9,662.9	10,866.8	10,711.1	9,089.4	10,486.1	34
Salem, OR	358.2	339.0	410.2	405.7	350.5	372.0	244
Salt Lake City, UT	8,653.7	7,916.9	9,748.6	13,273.9	13,565.5	13,469.1	28
San Antonio, TX	5,621.2	9,184.1	11,678.1	11,668.0	10,987.9	13,086.4	29
San Diego, CA	18,086.6	18,637.1	20,156.8	19,774.1	18,999.7	23,687.8	18
San Francisco, CA	24,506.3	29,103.8	27,417.0	28,003.8	23,864.5	29,972.0	13
San Jose, CA	21,716.8	21,464.7	22,224.2	20,909.4	19,534.5	22,293.6	20
Santa Rosa, CA	1,194.3	1,168.2	1,231.7	1,234.5	1,131.4	1,301.8	137
Savannah, GA	4,263.4	4,472.0	5,407.8	4,925.5	4,557.0	5,520.5	55
Seattle, WA	61,881.0	59,007.0	59,742.9	41,249.0	23,851.0	28,866.7	14
Sioux Falls, SD	334.3	386.8	400.0	431.5	524.9	547.3	207
Springfield, IL	88.3	107.5	91.2	99.8	90.5	98.9	351
Tampa, FL	5,702.9	6,256.0	4,966.7	6,219.7	5,082.2	5,754.7	53
Tucson, AZ	2,563.9	2,683.9	2,824.8	2,943.7	2,640.7	2,846.1	87
Tulsa, OK	2,363.0	2,564.7	3,351.7	3,399.2	2,567.8	3,064.8	81
Tuscaloosa, AL	n/a	n/a	n/a	n/a	5,175.0	6,675.5	50
Virginia Beach, VA	3,291.1	3,307.2	3,950.6	3,642.4	4,284.3	4,566.3	65
Washington, DC	13,582.4	12,736.1	13,602.7	14,563.8	13,537.3	12,210.8	31
Wichita, KS	3,054.9	3,299.2	3,817.0	3,494.7	2,882.1	3,615.3	74
Wilmington, NC	598.7	759.8	634.4	526.4	553.6	497.8	218
Winston-Salem, NC	1,234.6	1,131.7	1,107.5	1,209.1	913.1	918.2	164
Worcester, MA	3,093.5	2,929.6	2,573.6	2,221.5	2,026.4	2,624.6	92

Note: Figures are in millions of dollars; (1) Metropolitan Statistical Area; (2) Rank is based on 2021 data and ranges from 1 to 388
Source: U.S. Department of Commerce, International Trade Administration, Office of Trade and Economic Analysis, Industry and Analysis, Exports by Metropolitan Area, extracted March 16, 2023

A-58　Appendix A: Comparative Statistics

Building Permits: City

City	Single-Family			Multi-Family			Total		
	2021	2022	Pct. Chg.	2021	2022	Pct. Chg.	2021	2022	Pct. Chg.
Albuquerque, NM	773	707	-8.5	894	902	0.9	1,667	1,609	-3.5
Allentown, PA	0	27	—	0	0	0.0	0	27	—
Anchorage, AK	840	124	-85.2	293	31	-89.4	1,133	155	-86.3
Ann Arbor, MI	175	135	-22.9	52	4	-92.3	227	139	-38.8
Athens, GA	180	227	26.1	986	1,548	57.0	1,166	1,775	52.2
Atlanta, GA	855	1,775	107.6	1,558	10,078	546.9	2,413	11,853	391.2
Austin, TX	4,180	3,344	-20.0	14,542	15,102	3.9	18,722	18,446	-1.5
Baltimore, MD	191	118	-38.2	1,366	1,539	12.7	1,557	1,657	6.4
Boise City, ID	856	392	-54.2	1,165	1,210	3.9	2,021	1,602	-20.7
Boston, MA	53	53	0.0	3,459	3,882	12.2	3,512	3,935	12.0
Boulder, CO	41	35	-14.6	253	269	6.3	294	304	3.4
Brownsville, TX	883	817	-7.5	246	353	43.5	1,129	1,170	3.6
Cape Coral, FL	4,279	3,813	-10.9	1,133	922	-18.6	5,412	4,735	-12.5
Cedar Rapids, IA	158	129	-18.4	280	225	-19.6	438	354	-19.2
Charleston, SC	1,091	942	-13.7	378	459	21.4	1,469	1,401	-4.6
Charlotte, NC	n/a	n/a	n/a	n/a	n/a	n/a	n/a	n/a	n/a
Chicago, IL	414	412	-0.5	4,927	6,712	36.2	5,341	7,124	33.4
Cincinnati, OH	206	104	-49.5	932	689	-26.1	1,138	793	-30.3
Clarksville, TN	1,452	973	-33.0	1,813	2,160	19.1	3,265	3,133	-4.0
Cleveland, OH	104	158	51.9	27	363	1,244.4	131	521	297.7
College Station, TX	674	592	-12.2	318	97	-69.5	992	689	-30.5
Colorado Springs, CO	n/a	n/a	n/a	n/a	n/a	n/a	n/a	n/a	n/a
Columbia, MO	487	303	-37.8	189	135	-28.6	676	438	-35.2
Columbia, SC	804	772	-4.0	896	1,359	51.7	1,700	2,131	25.4
Columbus, OH	913	642	-29.7	3,555	5,535	55.7	4,468	6,177	38.2
Dallas, TX	2,245	2,349	4.6	7,769	7,880	1.4	10,014	10,229	2.1
Davenport, IA	84	160	90.5	0	0	0.0	84	160	90.5
Denver, CO	1,550	1,323	-14.6	8,450	6,973	-17.5	10,000	8,296	-17.0
Des Moines, IA	248	256	3.2	380	284	-25.3	628	540	-14.0
Durham, NC	1,960	1,595	-18.6	1,361	2,771	103.6	3,321	4,366	31.5
Edison, NJ	105	104	-1.0	250	17	-93.2	355	121	-65.9
El Paso, TX	1,961	1,649	-15.9	272	319	17.3	2,233	1,968	-11.9
Fargo, ND	410	413	0.7	736	820	11.4	1,146	1,233	7.6
Fort Collins, CO	381	287	-24.7	458	515	12.4	839	802	-4.4
Fort Wayne, IN	n/a	n/a	n/a	n/a	n/a	n/a	n/a	n/a	n/a
Fort Worth, TX	7,236	7,421	2.6	4,338	4,557	5.0	11,574	11,978	3.5
Grand Rapids, MI	43	23	-46.5	243	211	-13.2	286	234	-18.2
Greeley, CO	315	345	9.5	600	1,725	187.5	915	2,070	126.2
Green Bay, WI	58	37	-36.2	2	0	-100.0	60	37	-38.3
Greensboro, NC	529	467	-11.7	1,363	676	-50.4	1,892	1,143	-39.6
Honolulu, HI	n/a	n/a	n/a	n/a	n/a	n/a	n/a	n/a	n/a
Houston, TX	7,146	6,800	-4.8	8,103	8,945	10.4	15,249	15,745	3.3
Huntsville, AL	1,483	1,083	-27.0	1,328	47	-96.5	2,811	1,130	-59.8
Indianapolis, IN	1,221	1,099	-10.0	968	1,011	4.4	2,189	2,110	-3.6
Jacksonville, FL	6,191	5,484	-11.4	3,778	5,862	55.2	9,969	11,346	13.8
Kansas City, MO	890	746	-16.2	1,448	1,241	-14.3	2,338	1,987	-15.0
Lafayette, LA	n/a	n/a	n/a	n/a	n/a	n/a	n/a	n/a	n/a
Las Cruces, NM	763	685	-10.2	99	26	-73.7	862	711	-17.5
Las Vegas, NV	2,700	3,001	11.1	1,048	1,024	-2.3	3,748	4,025	7.4
Lexington, KY	792	686	-13.4	863	1,045	21.1	1,655	1,731	4.6
Lincoln, NE	1,093	943	-13.7	1,227	2,179	77.6	2,320	3,122	34.6
Little Rock, AR	666	377	-43.4	460	644	40.0	1,126	1,021	-9.3
Los Angeles, CA	2,475	3,182	28.6	11,613	13,525	16.5	14,088	16,707	18.6
Louisville, KY	1,382	1,151	-16.7	466	1,637	251.3	1,848	2,788	50.9

Table continued on following page.

Appendix A: Comparative Statistics   A-59

City	Single-Family			Multi-Family			Total		
	2021	2022	Pct. Chg.	2021	2022	Pct. Chg.	2021	2022	Pct. Chg.
Madison, WI	327	314	-4.0	3,299	2,046	-38.0	3,626	2,360	-34.9
Manchester, NH	126	132	4.8	8	6	-25.0	134	138	3.0
Miami, FL	102	127	24.5	6,153	4,231	-31.2	6,255	4,358	-30.3
Midland, TX	858	593	-30.9	0	0	0.0	858	593	-30.9
Milwaukee, WI	28	42	50.0	176	134	-23.9	204	176	-13.7
Minneapolis, MN	63	55	-12.7	3,119	3,626	16.3	3,182	3,681	15.7
Nashville, TN	3,932	3,977	1.1	12,205	10,818	-11.4	16,137	14,795	-8.3
New Haven, CT	13	10	-23.1	286	491	71.7	299	501	67.6
New Orleans, LA	716	615	-14.1	860	1,007	17.1	1,576	1,622	2.9
New York, NY	151	61	-59.6	19,772	21,429	8.4	19,923	21,490	7.9
Oklahoma City, OK	4,127	3,298	-20.1	140	260	85.7	4,267	3,558	-16.6
Omaha, NE	1,620	1,217	-24.9	1,547	2,552	65.0	3,167	3,769	19.0
Orlando, FL	990	1,286	29.9	2,734	2,229	-18.5	3,724	3,515	-5.6
Philadelphia, PA	1,553	478	-69.2	23,704	2,745	-88.4	25,257	3,223	-87.2
Phoenix, AZ	4,922	3,982	-19.1	6,570	10,616	61.6	11,492	14,598	27.0
Pittsburgh, PA	198	115	-41.9	617	1,913	210.0	815	2,028	148.8
Portland, OR	474	489	3.2	2,554	1,708	-33.1	3,028	2,197	-27.4
Providence, RI	1	28	2,700.0	53	271	411.3	54	299	453.7
Provo, UT	98	134	36.7	617	327	-47.0	715	461	-35.5
Raleigh, NC	1,354	1,875	38.5	5,133	6,760	31.7	6,487	8,635	33.1
Reno, NV	1,414	1,158	-18.1	2,539	2,535	-0.2	3,953	3,693	-6.6
Richmond, VA	502	457	-9.0	565	2,192	288.0	1,067	2,649	148.3
Rochester, MN	251	234	-6.8	374	847	126.5	625	1,081	73.0
Sacramento, CA	1,004	905	-9.9	2,079	1,149	-44.7	3,083	2,054	-33.4
St. Louis, MO	146	122	-16.4	809	1,054	30.3	955	1,176	23.1
Salem, OR	447	318	-28.9	399	851	113.3	846	1,169	38.2
Salt Lake City, UT	172	144	-16.3	3,519	3,489	-0.9	3,691	3,633	-1.6
San Antonio, TX	6,567	4,686	-28.6	4,591	9,496	106.8	11,158	14,182	27.1
San Diego, CA	539	506	-6.1	4,249	3,916	-7.8	4,788	4,422	-7.6
San Francisco, CA	33	38	15.2	2,486	2,006	-19.3	2,519	2,044	-18.9
San Jose, CA	299	553	84.9	359	1,450	303.9	658	2,003	204.4
Santa Rosa, CA	420	286	-31.9	1,031	911	-11.6	1,451	1,197	-17.5
Savannah, GA	487	408	-16.2	5	24	380.0	492	432	-12.2
Seattle, WA	264	418	58.3	11,716	8,572	-26.8	11,980	8,990	-25.0
Sioux Falls, SD	1,313	1,036	-21.1	1,819	3,429	88.5	3,132	4,465	42.6
Springfield, IL	137	55	-59.9	87	10	-88.5	224	65	-71.0
Tampa, FL	1,312	1,058	-19.4	1,093	3,753	243.4	2,405	4,811	100.0
Tucson, AZ	1,134	918	-19.0	959	962	0.3	2,093	1,880	-10.2
Tulsa, OK	652	452	-30.7	165	369	123.6	817	821	0.5
Tuscaloosa, AL	401	299	-25.4	725	329	-54.6	1,126	628	-44.2
Virginia Beach, VA	335	231	-31.0	128	966	654.7	463	1,197	158.5
Washington, DC	376	409	8.8	4,364	7,296	67.2	4,740	7,705	62.6
Wichita, KS	760	787	3.6	368	276	-25.0	1,128	1,063	-5.8
Wilmington, NC	n/a	n/a	n/a	n/a	n/a	n/a	n/a	n/a	n/a
Winston-Salem, NC	1,087	1,291	18.8	0	0	0.0	1,087	1,291	18.8
Worcester, MA	66	94	42.4	112	718	541.1	178	812	356.2
U.S.	1,115,400	975,600	-12.5	621,600	689,500	10.9	1,737,000	1,665,100	-4.1

Note: Figures represent new, privately-owned housing units authorized (unadjusted data); All permit data are based on estimates with imputation
Source: U.S. Census Bureau, Manufacturing, Mining, and Construction Statistics, Building Permits, 2021, 2022

A-60 Appendix A: Comparative Statistics

Building Permits: Metro Area

Metro Area	Single-Family			Multi-Family			Total		
	2021	2022	Pct. Chg.	2021	2022	Pct. Chg.	2021	2022	Pct. Chg.
Albuquerque, NM	2,535	2,002	-21.0	1,486	1,055	-29.0	4,021	3,057	-24.0
Allentown, PA	1,716	1,586	-7.6	890	723	-18.8	2,606	2,309	-11.4
Anchorage, AK	877	166	-81.1	306	47	-84.6	1,183	213	-82.0
Ann Arbor, MI	795	580	-27.0	121	49	-59.5	916	629	-31.3
Athens, GA	856	771	-9.9	992	1,574	58.7	1,848	2,345	26.9
Atlanta, GA	31,560	26,623	-15.6	7,906	21,484	171.7	39,466	48,107	21.9
Austin, TX	24,486	19,717	-19.5	26,421	22,647	-14.3	50,907	42,364	-16.8
Baltimore, MD	4,783	2,832	-40.8	3,051	3,756	23.1	7,834	6,588	-15.9
Boise City, ID	8,342	5,925	-29.0	3,854	4,550	18.1	12,196	10,475	-14.1
Boston, MA	4,820	3,985	-17.3	11,782	10,469	-11.1	16,602	14,454	-12.9
Boulder, CO	343	661	92.7	894	981	9.7	1,237	1,642	32.7
Brownsville, TX	1,573	1,940	23.3	479	569	18.8	2,052	2,509	22.3
Cape Coral, FL	11,020	9,145	-17.0	2,374	4,476	88.5	13,394	13,621	1.7
Cedar Rapids, IA	546	453	-17.0	352	494	40.3	898	947	5.5
Charleston, SC	5,913	6,329	7.0	2,369	2,994	26.4	8,282	9,323	12.6
Charlotte, NC	20,830	19,029	-8.6	9,296	8,183	-12.0	30,126	27,212	-9.7
Chicago, IL	10,071	8,563	-15.0	8,440	9,073	7.5	18,511	17,636	-4.7
Cincinnati, OH	5,358	4,126	-23.0	3,071	2,084	-32.1	8,429	6,210	-26.3
Clarksville, TN	2,217	1,501	-32.3	1,895	2,592	36.8	4,112	4,093	-0.5
Cleveland, OH	2,949	2,915	-1.2	391	820	109.7	3,340	3,735	11.8
College Station, TX	1,765	1,545	-12.5	535	230	-57.0	2,300	1,775	-22.8
Colorado Springs, CO	5,074	3,646	-28.1	4,261	5,198	22.0	9,335	8,844	-5.3
Columbia, MO	838	628	-25.1	191	151	-20.9	1,029	779	-24.3
Columbia, SC	5,853	4,101	-29.9	1,028	1,703	65.7	6,881	5,804	-15.7
Columbus, OH	6,844	5,623	-17.8	5,218	6,472	24.0	12,062	12,095	0.3
Dallas, TX	51,996	43,645	-16.1	26,709	34,249	28.2	78,705	77,894	-1.0
Davenport, IA	436	416	-4.6	193	181	-6.2	629	597	-5.1
Denver, CO	13,113	10,108	-22.9	16,893	13,368	-20.9	30,006	23,476	-21.8
Des Moines, IA	4,888	3,646	-25.4	2,081	2,476	19.0	6,969	6,122	-12.2
Durham, NC	3,735	3,170	-15.1	2,165	3,222	48.8	5,900	6,392	8.3
Edison, NJ	12,947	12,089	-6.6	43,714	46,323	6.0	56,661	58,412	3.1
El Paso, TX	2,655	2,147	-19.1	334	319	-4.5	2,989	2,466	-17.5
Fargo, ND	1,229	1,123	-8.6	1,060	1,191	12.4	2,289	2,314	1.1
Fort Collins, CO	2,149	1,385	-35.6	1,072	1,187	10.7	3,221	2,572	-20.1
Fort Wayne, IN	1,799	1,453	-19.2	179	882	392.7	1,978	2,335	18.0
Fort Worth, TX	51,996	43,645	-16.1	26,709	34,249	28.2	78,705	77,894	-1.0
Grand Rapids, MI	2,811	2,488	-11.5	894	1,710	91.3	3,705	4,198	13.3
Greeley, CO	3,814	3,203	-16.0	1,454	2,940	102.2	5,268	6,143	16.6
Green Bay, WI	830	627	-24.5	578	622	7.6	1,408	1,249	-11.3
Greensboro, NC	2,593	2,161	-16.7	1,371	832	-39.3	3,964	2,993	-24.5
Honolulu, HI	938	652	-30.5	500	1,901	280.2	1,438	2,553	77.5
Houston, TX	52,719	47,701	-9.5	16,544	28,027	69.4	69,263	75,728	9.3
Huntsville, AL	4,230	3,617	-14.5	1,942	418	-78.5	6,172	4,035	-34.6
Indianapolis, IN	10,159	8,578	-15.6	3,292	4,915	49.3	13,451	13,493	0.3
Jacksonville, FL	16,536	14,410	-12.9	6,202	8,759	41.2	22,738	23,169	1.9
Kansas City, MO	7,051	5,204	-26.2	4,203	6,015	43.1	11,254	11,219	-0.3
Lafayette, LA	3,040	2,051	-32.5	4	20	400.0	3,044	2,071	-32.0
Las Cruces, NM	1,239	1,079	-12.9	99	26	-73.7	1,338	1,105	-17.4
Las Vegas, NV	12,156	9,199	-24.3	4,151	3,867	-6.8	16,307	13,066	-19.9
Lexington, KY	1,760	1,460	-17.0	1,183	1,249	5.6	2,943	2,709	-8.0
Lincoln, NE	1,378	1,132	-17.9	1,229	2,217	80.4	2,607	3,349	28.5
Little Rock, AR	2,505	1,863	-25.6	1,130	1,475	30.5	3,635	3,338	-8.2
Los Angeles, CA	11,090	11,184	0.8	20,061	21,326	6.3	31,151	32,510	4.4
Louisville, KY	4,136	3,345	-19.1	1,372	2,111	53.9	5,508	5,456	-0.9

Table continued on following page.

Appendix A: Comparative Statistics   A-61

Metro Area	Single-Family			Multi-Family			Total		
	2021	2022	Pct. Chg.	2021	2022	Pct. Chg.	2021	2022	Pct. Chg.
Madison, WI	1,737	1,530	-11.9	5,457	4,049	-25.8	7,194	5,579	-22.4
Manchester, NH	683	623	-8.8	659	224	-66.0	1,342	847	-36.9
Miami, FL	8,316	6,970	-16.2	16,997	13,051	-23.2	25,313	20,021	-20.9
Midland, TX	872	594	-31.9	0	0	0.0	872	594	-31.9
Milwaukee, WI	1,779	1,557	-12.5	1,150	1,609	39.9	2,929	3,166	8.1
Minneapolis, MN	11,734	9,114	-22.3	14,343	14,611	1.9	26,077	23,725	-9.0
Nashville, TN	17,422	15,388	-11.7	14,769	12,804	-13.3	32,191	28,192	-12.4
New Haven, CT	497	493	-0.8	486	770	58.4	983	1,263	28.5
New Orleans, LA	4,018	3,101	-22.8	1,264	1,065	-15.7	5,282	4,166	-21.1
New York, NY	12,947	12,089	-6.6	43,714	46,323	6.0	56,661	58,412	3.1
Oklahoma City, OK	7,637	5,971	-21.8	443	940	112.2	8,080	6,911	-14.5
Omaha, NE	3,677	2,651	-27.9	2,705	3,469	28.2	6,382	6,120	-4.1
Orlando, FL	17,795	16,213	-8.9	12,823	12,470	-2.8	30,618	28,683	-6.3
Philadelphia, PA	8,868	8,532	-3.8	27,439	5,881	-78.6	36,307	14,413	-60.3
Phoenix, AZ	34,347	26,857	-21.8	16,234	20,410	25.7	50,581	47,267	-6.6
Pittsburgh, PA	3,891	3,184	-18.2	1,332	2,481	86.3	5,223	5,665	8.5
Portland, OR	8,008	6,029	-24.7	7,015	6,949	-0.9	15,023	12,978	-13.6
Providence, RI	1,788	1,559	-12.8	470	563	19.8	2,258	2,122	-6.0
Provo, UT	7,562	5,153	-31.9	3,613	3,134	-13.3	11,175	8,287	-25.8
Raleigh, NC	14,227	12,488	-12.2	7,422	9,080	22.3	21,649	21,568	-0.4
Reno, NV	2,717	2,184	-19.6	2,620	3,628	38.5	5,337	5,812	8.9
Richmond, VA	5,946	4,503	-24.3	3,601	5,911	64.1	9,547	10,414	9.1
Rochester, MN	721	641	-11.1	414	1,080	160.9	1,135	1,721	51.6
Sacramento, CA	9,390	8,170	-13.0	3,044	2,630	-13.6	12,434	10,800	-13.1
St. Louis, MO	5,716	4,743	-17.0	2,610	4,388	68.1	8,326	9,131	9.7
Salem, OR	1,368	874	-36.1	786	1,943	147.2	2,154	2,817	30.8
Salt Lake City, UT	5,338	3,992	-25.2	6,304	6,110	-3.1	11,642	10,102	-13.2
San Antonio, TX	13,945	10,226	-26.7	8,319	14,113	69.6	22,264	24,339	9.3
San Diego, CA	3,227	3,517	9.0	6,821	5,829	-14.5	10,048	9,346	-7.0
San Francisco, CA	4,301	3,370	-21.6	9,305	7,834	-15.8	13,606	11,204	-17.7
San Jose, CA	2,400	3,899	62.5	2,129	4,308	102.3	4,529	8,207	81.2
Santa Rosa, CA	1,227	954	-22.2	1,391	1,310	-5.8	2,618	2,264	-13.5
Savannah, GA	2,752	2,228	-19.0	475	966	103.4	3,227	3,194	-1.0
Seattle, WA	8,828	7,029	-20.4	21,915	19,632	-10.4	30,743	26,661	-13.3
Sioux Falls, SD	1,893	1,626	-14.1	2,093	3,928	87.7	3,986	5,554	39.3
Springfield, IL	239	146	-38.9	93	64	-31.2	332	210	-36.7
Tampa, FL	19,305	15,678	-18.8	5,526	14,291	158.6	24,831	29,969	20.7
Tucson, AZ	5,116	3,735	-27.0	1,168	1,979	69.4	6,284	5,714	-9.1
Tulsa, OK	4,354	3,843	-11.7	566	1,280	126.1	4,920	5,123	4.1
Tuscaloosa, AL	771	714	-7.4	725	329	-54.6	1,496	1,043	-30.3
Virginia Beach, VA	4,712	3,680	-21.9	2,665	2,633	-1.2	7,377	6,313	-14.4
Washington, DC	13,729	11,657	-15.1	13,685	20,736	51.5	27,414	32,393	18.2
Wichita, KS	1,618	1,586	-2.0	766	1,264	65.0	2,384	2,850	19.5
Wilmington, NC	2,671	2,489	-6.8	1,747	1,932	10.6	4,418	4,421	0.1
Winston-Salem, NC	3,887	3,983	2.5	319	67	-79.0	4,206	4,050	-3.7
Worcester, MA	1,177	1,172	-0.4	876	1,080	23.3	2,053	2,252	9.7
U.S.	1,115,400	975,600	-12.5	621,600	689,500	10.9	1,737,000	1,665,100	-4.1

Note: Figures cover the Metropolitan Statistical Area; Figures represent new, privately-owned
housing units authorized (unadjusted data); All permit data are based on estimates with imputation
Source: U.S. Census Bureau, Manufacturing, Mining, and Construction Statistics, Building Permits, 2021, 2022

A-62 Appendix A: Comparative Statistics

Housing Vacancy Rates

MSA[1]	Gross Vacancy Rate[2] (%)			Year-Round Vacancy Rate[3] (%)			Rental Vacancy Rate[4] (%)			Homeowner Vacancy Rate[5] (%)		
	2020	2021	2022	2020	2021	2022	2020	2021	2022	2020	2021	2022
Albuquerque, NM	5.1	5.3	5.3	4.9	5.1	5.1	5.4	6.4	5.5	1.4	0.5	1.0
Allentown, PA	4.9	5.2	8.7	4.8	4.3	8.0	3.9	4.0	6.1	0.7	0.1	1.2
Anchorage, AK	n/a	n/a	n/a	n/a	n/a	n/a	n/a	n/a	n/a	n/a	n/a	n/a
Ann Arbor, MI	n/a	n/a	n/a	n/a	n/a	n/a	n/a	n/a	n/a	n/a	n/a	n/a
Athens, GA	n/a	n/a	n/a	n/a	n/a	n/a	n/a	n/a	n/a	n/a	n/a	n/a
Atlanta, GA	5.8	6.1	5.9	5.4	5.7	5.7	6.4	5.2	6.7	0.8	1.0	0.8
Austin, TX	7.0	6.5	5.5	6.8	6.2	4.9	6.6	8.5	5.6	2.0	1.3	0.6
Baltimore, MD	7.2	6.8	5.9	7.0	6.6	5.7	7.0	6.1	5.3	1.0	1.0	0.5
Boise City, ID	n/a	n/a	n/a	n/a	n/a	n/a	n/a	n/a	n/a	n/a	n/a	n/a
Boston, MA	6.8	7.4	6.2	5.6	6.2	5.4	4.7	4.5	2.5	0.4	0.5	0.7
Boulder, CO	n/a	n/a	n/a	n/a	n/a	n/a	n/a	n/a	n/a	n/a	n/a	n/a
Brownsville, TX	n/a	n/a	n/a	n/a	n/a	n/a	n/a	n/a	n/a	n/a	n/a	n/a
Cape Coral, FL	35.1	36.4	38.2	15.8	13.0	16.9	15.5	10.7	11.6	1.9	2.4	3.9
Cedar Rapids, IA	n/a	n/a	n/a	n/a	n/a	n/a	n/a	n/a	n/a	n/a	n/a	n/a
Charleston, SC	18.1	12.9	10.6	16.5	10.5	7.5	27.7	15.4	8.8	2.3	1.3	0.4
Charlotte, NC	6.6	7.7	7.4	6.3	7.4	7.0	5.6	6.8	5.9	1.0	1.3	0.7
Chicago, IL	7.4	8.7	7.3	7.2	8.6	7.1	7.4	8.0	6.1	1.2	1.3	1.1
Cincinnati, OH	6.6	7.9	6.8	6.2	7.3	6.3	7.9	7.2	6.3	0.7	0.5	0.3
Clarksville, TN	n/a	n/a	n/a	n/a	n/a	n/a	n/a	n/a	n/a	n/a	n/a	n/a
Cleveland, OH	9.3	7.7	7.0	8.8	7.5	6.8	5.5	3.6	3.2	0.7	0.4	1.0
College Station, TX	n/a	n/a	n/a	n/a	n/a	n/a	n/a	n/a	n/a	n/a	n/a	n/a
Colorado Springs, CO	n/a	n/a	n/a	n/a	n/a	n/a	n/a	n/a	n/a	n/a	n/a	n/a
Columbia, MO	n/a	n/a	n/a	n/a	n/a	n/a	n/a	n/a	n/a	n/a	n/a	n/a
Columbia, SC	7.2	7.6	12.0	7.1	7.6	12.0	4.5	4.7	6.1	0.7	1.1	0.6
Columbus, OH	4.7	6.8	5.6	4.5	6.6	5.4	5.9	6.5	3.8	0.3	0.8	0.8
Dallas, TX	6.4	6.6	6.6	6.4	6.5	6.3	7.2	7.0	6.8	0.7	0.7	0.7
Davenport, IA	n/a	n/a	n/a	n/a	n/a	n/a	n/a	n/a	n/a	n/a	n/a	n/a
Denver, CO	5.8	6.5	5.8	5.1	5.3	5.2	4.8	4.6	5.1	0.5	1.0	0.3
Des Moines, IA	n/a	n/a	n/a	n/a	n/a	n/a	n/a	n/a	n/a	n/a	n/a	n/a
Durham, NC	n/a	n/a	n/a	n/a	n/a	n/a	n/a	n/a	n/a	n/a	n/a	n/a
Edison, NJ	9.1	9.8	8.2	7.8	8.7	7.0	4.5	5.2	3.5	1.3	1.2	1.0
El Paso, TX	n/a	n/a	n/a	n/a	n/a	n/a	n/a	n/a	n/a	n/a	n/a	n/a
Fargo, ND	n/a	n/a	n/a	n/a	n/a	n/a	n/a	n/a	n/a	n/a	n/a	n/a
Fort Collins, CO	n/a	n/a	n/a	n/a	n/a	n/a	n/a	n/a	n/a	n/a	n/a	n/a
Fort Wayne, IN	n/a	n/a	n/a	n/a	n/a	n/a	n/a	n/a	n/a	n/a	n/a	n/a
Fort Worth, TX	6.4	6.6	6.6	6.4	6.5	6.3	7.2	7.0	6.8	0.7	0.7	0.7
Grand Rapids, MI	7.1	7.0	4.9	4.7	4.2	3.0	4.6	3.4	2.4	1.1	0.7	0.1
Greeley, CO	n/a	n/a	n/a	n/a	n/a	n/a	n/a	n/a	n/a	n/a	n/a	n/a
Green Bay, WI	n/a	n/a	n/a	n/a	n/a	n/a	n/a	n/a	n/a	n/a	n/a	n/a
Greensboro, NC	8.3	5.9	8.7	8.2	5.9	8.7	7.2	2.7	10.2	0.7	0.5	0.7
Honolulu, HI	10.0	10.6	10.6	9.6	10.1	10.0	5.5	5.1	5.7	1.0	0.6	0.6
Houston, TX	6.8	7.2	6.9	6.3	6.6	6.3	9.7	8.8	8.9	1.1	0.8	0.6
Huntsville, AL	n/a	n/a	n/a	n/a	n/a	n/a	n/a	n/a	n/a	n/a	n/a	n/a
Indianapolis, IN	7.3	6.2	7.7	7.0	6.1	7.2	10.4	8.2	11.0	0.8	0.7	1.0
Jacksonville, FL	9.5	8.3	8.9	9.3	7.6	7.7	7.5	5.6	6.2	1.5	0.4	1.7
Kansas City, MO	9.1	8.3	7.1	9.1	8.2	7.1	9.4	8.9	7.8	0.7	1.2	0.6
Lafayette, LA	n/a	n/a	n/a	n/a	n/a	n/a	n/a	n/a	n/a	n/a	n/a	n/a
Las Cruces, NM	n/a	n/a	n/a	n/a	n/a	n/a	n/a	n/a	n/a	n/a	n/a	n/a
Las Vegas, NV	7.8	7.7	9.2	7.1	7.1	8.3	5.0	3.7	5.7	1.1	0.9	0.9
Lexington, KY	n/a	n/a	n/a	n/a	n/a	n/a	n/a	n/a	n/a	n/a	n/a	n/a
Lincoln, NE	n/a	n/a	n/a	n/a	n/a	n/a	n/a	n/a	n/a	n/a	n/a	n/a
Little Rock, AR	9.4	11.4	9.4	9.1	11.2	9.2	9.1	10.0	11.4	1.3	1.2	0.7
Los Angeles, CA	5.5	6.4	5.9	4.8	5.9	5.5	3.6	4.6	4.1	0.6	0.7	0.5
Louisville, KY	6.9	8.3	5.7	6.9	8.3	5.7	6.4	8.5	5.3	1.4	0.7	0.5

Table continued on following page.

Appendix A: Comparative Statistics A-63

MSA[1]	Gross Vacancy Rate[2] (%)			Year-Round Vacancy Rate[3] (%)			Rental Vacancy Rate[4] (%)			Homeowner Vacancy Rate[5] (%)		
	2020	2021	2022	2020	2021	2022	2020	2021	2022	2020	2021	2022
Madison, WI	n/a	n/a	n/a	n/a	n/a	n/a	n/a	n/a	n/a	n/a	n/a	n/a
Manchester, NH	n/a	n/a	n/a	n/a	n/a	n/a	n/a	n/a	n/a	n/a	n/a	n/a
Miami, FL	12.6	12.2	12.6	6.8	6.8	7.5	5.4	5.5	6.3	1.4	1.0	1.1
Midland, TX	n/a	n/a	n/a	n/a	n/a	n/a	n/a	n/a	n/a	n/a	n/a	n/a
Milwaukee, WI	6.6	5.2	5.2	6.3	5.1	5.1	4.6	2.2	5.9	0.6	0.5	0.1
Minneapolis, MN	4.7	5.3	4.8	3.7	4.6	4.5	4.0	4.9	6.7	0.5	0.6	0.8
Nashville, TN	6.5	7.1	7.6	6.1	6.8	7.1	7.3	7.9	6.4	0.7	1.0	0.9
New Haven, CT	9.4	7.9	6.8	8.4	7.2	6.4	7.8	5.4	2.6	0.2	0.5	1.1
New Orleans, LA	10.7	12.6	13.4	9.8	11.1	11.5	6.1	7.2	6.6	1.3	1.0	1.6
New York, NY	9.1	9.8	8.2	7.8	8.7	7.0	4.5	5.2	3.5	1.3	1.2	1.0
Oklahoma City, OK	7.5	6.1	8.6	7.3	6.0	8.5	6.4	5.7	10.6	0.9	0.8	0.9
Omaha, NE	5.6	6.0	5.4	5.3	5.7	5.0	6.5	5.1	4.2	0.5	0.7	0.8
Orlando, FL	12.9	9.5	9.6	9.8	7.5	7.4	8.6	7.5	6.5	1.2	0.5	1.4
Philadelphia, PA	6.0	6.1	5.5	5.8	5.9	5.4	5.4	4.8	4.2	0.7	0.5	1.0
Phoenix, AZ	8.9	9.0	10.9	5.3	5.6	6.7	4.9	4.9	6.4	0.7	0.6	0.9
Pittsburgh, PA	11.5	11.4	11.5	11.3	10.8	11.0	9.3	9.4	8.3	1.0	0.4	0.7
Portland, OR	5.5	6.0	5.4	4.9	5.6	5.1	4.3	5.2	4.0	0.8	0.9	1.2
Providence, RI	8.7	7.9	9.5	6.6	5.8	7.6	3.5	2.7	4.5	0.8	0.7	0.4
Provo, UT	n/a	n/a	n/a	n/a	n/a	n/a	n/a	n/a	n/a	n/a	n/a	n/a
Raleigh, NC	4.6	6.3	7.4	4.5	6.3	7.3	2.3	2.9	7.1	0.4	1.1	0.5
Reno, NV	n/a	n/a	n/a	n/a	n/a	n/a	n/a	n/a	n/a	n/a	n/a	n/a
Richmond, VA	6.0	5.8	6.1	6.0	5.8	6.1	2.7	1.8	3.0	0.9	1.0	0.7
Rochester, MN	n/a	n/a	n/a	n/a	n/a	n/a	n/a	n/a	n/a	n/a	n/a	n/a
Sacramento, CA	6.1	6.7	6.3	5.8	6.5	6.1	4.2	3.6	2.3	1.0	0.7	0.6
St. Louis, MO	6.4	7.0	7.2	6.3	7.0	7.1	5.3	6.5	6.8	0.7	0.5	1.4
Salem, OR	n/a	n/a	n/a	n/a	n/a	n/a	n/a	n/a	n/a	n/a	n/a	n/a
Salt Lake City, UT	5.7	4.1	5.1	5.6	3.9	4.5	6.2	4.1	4.6	0.3	0.8	0.6
San Antonio, TX	7.4	7.6	7.5	6.7	6.9	7.1	7.2	8.4	8.1	1.0	1.1	0.9
San Diego, CA	6.0	6.9	6.9	5.6	6.7	6.6	3.9	3.1	3.6	0.8	0.7	0.6
San Francisco, CA	6.4	7.6	7.9	6.2	7.3	7.7	5.3	6.5	5.4	0.5	1.1	1.3
San Jose, CA	4.7	5.9	5.8	4.7	5.6	5.8	4.4	6.6	4.7	n/a	0.4	0.4
Santa Rosa, CA	n/a	n/a	n/a	n/a	n/a	n/a	n/a	n/a	n/a	n/a	n/a	n/a
Savannah, GA	n/a	n/a	n/a	n/a	n/a	n/a	n/a	n/a	n/a	n/a	n/a	n/a
Seattle, WA	4.7	6.2	5.7	4.5	5.5	5.2	3.6	5.3	4.9	0.6	0.7	0.7
Sioux Falls, SD	n/a	n/a	n/a	n/a	n/a	n/a	n/a	n/a	n/a	n/a	n/a	n/a
Springfield, IL	n/a	n/a	n/a	n/a	n/a	n/a	n/a	n/a	n/a	n/a	n/a	n/a
Tampa, FL	13.0	14.2	13.3	10.1	10.5	9.9	8.9	7.3	8.1	1.5	1.0	1.2
Tucson, AZ	12.1	10.0	13.5	7.7	6.9	10.3	8.6	5.0	8.0	0.5	0.6	1.4
Tulsa, OK	9.4	11.0	8.9	8.8	10.0	8.5	8.6	5.3	5.6	0.8	1.5	0.7
Tuscaloosa, AL	n/a	n/a	n/a	n/a	n/a	n/a	n/a	n/a	n/a	n/a	n/a	n/a
Virginia Beach, VA	7.9	7.7	8.1	7.0	6.9	7.3	5.5	5.5	6.3	0.6	0.6	1.0
Washington, DC	6.5	5.5	5.2	6.2	5.3	5.0	5.5	5.9	5.3	0.7	0.5	0.6
Wichita, KS	n/a	n/a	n/a	n/a	n/a	n/a	n/a	n/a	n/a	n/a	n/a	n/a
Wilmington, NC	n/a	n/a	n/a	n/a	n/a	n/a	n/a	n/a	n/a	n/a	n/a	n/a
Winston-Salem, NC	n/a	n/a	n/a	n/a	n/a	n/a	n/a	n/a	n/a	n/a	n/a	n/a
Worcester, MA	4.8	5.5	4.5	4.6	4.9	4.0	1.3	2.2	1.6	0.4	0.7	0.4
U.S.	10.6	10.8	10.5	8.2	8.4	8.2	6.3	6.1	5.8	1.0	0.9	0.8

Note: (1) Metropolitan Statistical Area; (2) The percentage of the total housing inventory that is vacant; (3) The percentage of the housing inventory (excluding seasonal units) that is year-round vacant; (4) The percentage of rental inventory that is vacant for rent; (5) The percentage of homeowner inventory that is vacant for sale; n/a not available
Source: U.S. Census Bureau, Housing Vacancies and Homeownership Annual Statistics: 2020, 2021, 2022

A-64   Appendix A: Comparative Statistics

Bankruptcy Filings

City	Area Covered	Business Filings			Nonbusiness Filings		
		2021	2022	% Chg.	2021	2022	% Chg.
Albuquerque, NM	Bernalillo County	21	15	-28.6	560	383	-31.6
Allentown, PA	Lehigh County	5	7	40.0	346	283	-18.2
Anchorage, AK	Anchorage Borough	12	4	-66.7	116	77	-33.6
Ann Arbor, MI	Washtenaw County	8	24	200.0	352	350	-0.6
Athens, GA	Clarke County	10	4	-60.0	162	212	30.9
Atlanta, GA	Fulton County	87	124	42.5	2,072	2,323	12.1
Austin, TX	Travis County	113	76	-32.7	443	372	-16.0
Baltimore, MD	Baltimore City	18	17	-5.6	1,323	1,167	-11.8
Boise City, ID	Ada County	13	16	23.1	393	326	-17.0
Boston, MA	Suffolk County	23	42	82.6	224	221	-1.3
Boulder, CO	Boulder County	13	27	107.7	216	160	-25.9
Brownsville, TX	Cameron County	0	4	n/a	171	195	14.0
Cape Coral, FL	Lee County	39	31	-20.5	928	711	-23.4
Cedar Rapids, IA	Linn County	6	10	66.7	193	166	-14.0
Charleston, SC	Charleston County	8	5	-37.5	176	228	29.5
Charlotte, NC	Mecklenburg County	56	21	-62.5	460	459	-0.2
Chicago, IL	Cook County	270	237	-12.2	10,430	10,849	4.0
Cincinnati, OH	Hamilton County	28	25	-10.7	1,500	1,164	-22.4
Clarksville, TN	Montgomery County	11	6	-45.5	333	352	5.7
Cleveland, OH	Cuyahoga County	48	53	10.4	3,240	2,994	-7.6
College Station, TX	Brazos County	8	4	-50.0	66	47	-28.8
Colorado Springs, CO	El Paso County	22	19	-13.6	728	609	-16.3
Columbia, MO	Boone County	1	5	400.0	193	171	-11.4
Columbia, SC	Richland County	8	13	62.5	348	424	21.8
Columbus, OH	Franklin County	128	38	-70.3	2,223	2,029	-8.7
Dallas, TX	Dallas County	186	237	27.4	1,797	1,984	10.4
Davenport, IA	Scott County	5	9	80.0	163	140	-14.1
Denver, CO	Denver County	72	37	-48.6	764	590	-22.8
Des Moines, IA	Polk County	22	17	-22.7	550	474	-13.8
Durham, NC	Durham County	10	5	-50.0	175	143	-18.3
Edison, NJ	Middlesex County	45	30	-33.3	843	746	-11.5
El Paso, TX	El Paso County	46	41	-10.9	961	1,092	13.6
Fargo, ND	Cass County	4	2	-50.0	131	100	-23.7
Fort Collins, CO	Larimer County	14	14	0.0	306	283	-7.5
Fort Wayne, IN	Allen County	6	13	116.7	872	767	-12.0
Fort Worth, TX	Tarrant County	151	200	32.5	2,277	2,447	7.5
Grand Rapids, MI	Kent County	8	10	25.0	469	439	-6.4
Greeley, CO	Weld County	9	16	77.8	447	400	-10.5
Green Bay, WI	Brown County	2	7	250.0	388	290	-25.3
Greensboro, NC	Guilford County	23	8	-65.2	369	336	-8.9
Honolulu, HI	Honolulu County	28	35	25.0	830	671	-19.2
Houston, TX	Harris County	269	213	-20.8	2,310	2,541	10.0
Huntsville, AL	Madison County	18	12	-33.3	894	806	-9.8
Indianapolis, IN	Marion County	45	37	-17.8	2,705	2,399	-11.3
Jacksonville, FL	Duval County	58	38	-34.5	1,336	1,226	-8.2
Kansas City, MO	Jackson County	22	16	-27.3	1,027	1,037	1.0
Lafayette, LA	Lafayette Parish	17	29	70.6	263	296	12.5
Las Cruces, NM	Dona Ana County	8	4	-50.0	187	178	-4.8
Las Vegas, NV	Clark County	181	163	-9.9	5,825	4,525	-22.3
Lexington, KY	Fayette County	8	7	-12.5	450	410	-8.9
Lincoln, NE	Lancaster County	6	14	133.3	430	304	-29.3
Little Rock, AR	Pulaski County	23	19	-17.4	1,157	1,352	16.9
Los Angeles, CA	Los Angeles County	672	626	-6.8	11,316	8,314	-26.5
Louisville, KY	Jefferson County	19	20	5.3	1,918	1,883	-1.8
Madison, WI	Dane County	26	10	-61.5	436	383	-12.2

Table continued on following page.

Appendix A: Comparative Statistics A-65

City	Area Covered	Business Filings			Nonbusiness Filings		
		2021	2022	% Chg.	2021	2022	% Chg.
Manchester, NH	Hillsborough County	19	11	-42.1	253	204	-19.4
Miami, FL	Miami-Dade County	201	224	11.4	6,432	5,081	-21.0
Midland, TX	Midland County	18	7	-61.1	64	73	14.1
Milwaukee, WI	Milwaukee County	20	20	0.0	3,237	2,957	-8.6
Minneapolis, MN	Hennepin County	52	55	5.8	1,240	1,200	-3.2
Nashville, TN	Davidson County	37	32	-13.5	959	989	3.1
New Haven, CT	New Haven County	14	12	-14.3	864	719	-16.8
New Orleans, LA	Orleans Parish	31	11	-64.5	263	287	9.1
New York, NY	Bronx County	23	27	17.4	1,219	862	-29.3
New York, NY	Kings County	108	212	96.3	1,238	1,062	-14.2
New York, NY	New York County	398	240	-39.7	721	595	-17.5
New York, NY	Queens County	82	126	53.7	1,447	1,478	2.1
New York, NY	Richmond County	24	25	4.2	310	352	13.5
Oklahoma City, OK	Oklahoma County	52	50	-3.8	1,424	1,199	-15.8
Omaha, NE	Douglas County	20	21	5.0	807	628	-22.2
Orlando, FL	Orange County	100	127	27.0	1,909	1,588	-16.8
Philadelphia, PA	Philadelphia County	31	28	-9.7	741	952	28.5
Phoenix, AZ	Maricopa County	223	172	-22.9	6,402	5,811	-9.2
Pittsburgh, PA	Allegheny County	79	72	-8.9	1,266	1,135	-10.3
Portland, OR	Multnomah County	33	17	-48.5	802	749	-6.6
Providence, RI	Providence County	16	21	31.3	638	507	-20.5
Provo, UT	Utah County	22	19	-13.6	814	790	-2.9
Raleigh, NC	Wake County	53	50	-5.7	614	536	-12.7
Reno, NV	Washoe County	25	26	4.0	592	467	-21.1
Richmond, VA	Richmond city	21	6	-71.4	590	511	-13.4
Rochester, MN	Olmsted County	0	1	n/a	90	119	32.2
Sacramento, CA	Sacramento County	80	61	-23.8	1,731	1,275	-26.3
St. Louis, MO	Saint Louis City	12	15	25.0	1,395	1,247	-10.6
Salem, OR	Marion County	7	4	-42.9	489	439	-10.2
Salt Lake City, UT	Salt Lake County	27	23	-14.8	2,389	2,147	-10.1
San Antonio, TX	Bexar County	143	84	-41.3	1,102	1,028	-6.7
San Diego, CA	San Diego County	194	158	-18.6	4,533	3,136	-30.8
San Francisco, CA	San Francisco County	65	55	-15.4	334	342	2.4
San Jose, CA	Santa Clara County	80	77	-3.8	868	655	-24.5
Santa Rosa, CA	Sonoma County	23	29	26.1	329	278	-15.5
Savannah, GA	Chatham County	9	7	-22.2	546	591	8.2
Seattle, WA	King County	56	55	-1.8	1,094	979	-10.5
Sioux Falls, SD	Minnehaha County	7	6	-14.3	221	201	-9.0
Springfield, IL	Sangamon County	6	5	-16.7	221	186	-15.8
Tampa, FL	Hillsborough County	87	94	8.0	2,061	1,686	-18.2
Tucson, AZ	Pima County	21	22	4.8	1,379	1,310	-5.0
Tulsa, OK	Tulsa County	30	51	70.0	874	758	-13.3
Tuscaloosa, AL	Tuscaloosa County	4	9	125.0	679	821	20.9
Virginia Beach, VA	Virginia Beach City	11	15	36.4	788	711	-9.8
Washington, DC	District of Columbia	36	36	0.0	264	200	-24.2
Wichita, KS	Sedgwick County	20	14	-30.0	760	658	-13.4
Wilmington, NC	New Hanover County	12	6	-50.0	144	138	-4.2
Winston-Salem, NC	Forsyth County	10	6	-40.0	240	240	0.0
Worcester, MA	Worcester County	24	26	8.3	569	550	-3.3
U.S.	U.S.	14,347	13,481	-6.0	399,269	374,240	-6.3

Note: Business filings include Chapter 7, Chapter 9, Chapter 11, Chapter 12, Chapter 13, Chapter 15, and Section 304; Nonbusiness filings include Chapter 7, Chapter 11, and Chapter 13
Source: Administrative Office of the U.S. Courts, Business and Nonbusiness Bankruptcy, County Cases Commenced by Chapter of the Bankruptcy Code, During the 12-Month Period Ending December 31, 2021 and Business and Nonbusiness Bankruptcy, County Cases Commenced by Chapter of the Bankruptcy Code, During the 12-Month Period Ending December 31, 2022

A-66   Appendix A: Comparative Statistics

Income: City

City	Per Capita ($)	Median Household ($)	Average Household ($)
Albuquerque, NM	33,494	56,366	76,833
Allentown, PA	22,976	47,703	61,780
Anchorage, AK	43,125	88,871	113,873
Ann Arbor, MI	47,883	73,276	107,368
Athens, GA	27,194	43,466	65,960
Atlanta, GA	54,466	69,164	118,074
Austin, TX	48,550	78,965	111,233
Baltimore, MD	34,378	54,124	79,399
Boise City, ID	40,056	68,373	93,693
Boston, MA	50,344	81,744	120,939
Boulder, CO	52,057	74,902	123,606
Brownsville, TX	18,207	43,174	58,147
Cape Coral, FL	34,586	65,282	84,169
Cedar Rapids, IA	35,566	63,170	82,815
Charleston, SC	50,240	76,556	111,903
Charlotte, NC	43,080	68,367	104,228
Chicago, IL	41,821	65,781	100,347
Cincinnati, OH	34,060	45,235	73,412
Clarksville, TN	27,437	58,838	71,824
Cleveland, OH	23,415	33,678	49,942
College Station, TX	28,705	50,089	76,307
Colorado Springs, CO	37,979	71,957	93,740
Columbia, MO	32,784	57,463	80,898
Columbia, SC	32,954	48,791	79,637
Columbus, OH	32,481	58,575	75,482
Dallas, TX	37,719	58,231	92,785
Davenport, IA	32,431	56,315	76,281
Denver, CO	50,642	78,177	111,981
Des Moines, IA	31,276	58,444	74,131
Durham, NC	39,496	66,623	91,960
Edison, NJ	47,410	110,896	136,606
El Paso, TX	25,165	51,325	69,692
Fargo, ND	37,522	60,243	82,974
Fort Collins, CO	38,949	72,932	96,301
Fort Wayne, IN	29,268	53,978	70,654
Fort Worth, TX	32,569	67,927	90,141
Grand Rapids, MI	29,060	55,385	72,017
Greeley, CO	28,480	60,601	78,033
Green Bay, WI	29,822	55,221	70,879
Greensboro, NC	31,812	51,667	76,282
Honolulu, HI	41,571	76,495	105,724
Houston, TX	35,578	56,019	90,511
Huntsville, AL	38,838	60,959	87,475
Indianapolis, IN	31,538	54,321	75,792
Jacksonville, FL	32,654	58,263	79,817
Kansas City, MO	35,352	60,042	81,577
Lafayette, LA	35,348	55,329	82,752
Las Cruces, NM	26,290	47,722	64,425
Las Vegas, NV	33,363	61,356	86,008
Lexington, KY	37,475	61,526	88,901
Lincoln, NE	33,955	62,566	83,225
Little Rock, AR	39,141	56,928	89,748
Los Angeles, CA	39,378	69,778	106,931
Louisville, KY	34,195	58,357	81,393
Madison, WI	42,693	70,466	94,746
Manchester, NH	36,440	66,929	83,913

Table continued on following page.

Appendix A: Comparative Statistics   A-67

City	Per Capita ($)	Median Household ($)	Average Household ($)
Miami, FL	34,295	47,860	79,886
Midland, TX	44,218	87,900	115,425
Milwaukee, WI	25,564	45,318	61,529
Minneapolis, MN	43,925	70,099	99,741
Nashville, TN	39,509	65,565	92,866
New Haven, CT	29,348	48,973	73,450
New Orleans, LA	34,036	45,594	76,715
New York, NY	43,952	70,663	113,315
Oklahoma City, OK	33,162	59,679	81,931
Omaha, NE	36,749	65,359	90,389
Orlando, FL	36,596	58,968	88,128
Philadelphia, PA	32,344	52,649	77,454
Phoenix, AZ	33,718	64,927	90,481
Pittsburgh, PA	37,655	54,306	80,248
Portland, OR	47,289	78,476	106,948
Providence, RI	31,757	55,787	83,046
Provo, UT	23,440	53,572	76,163
Raleigh, NC	42,632	72,996	102,100
Reno, NV	39,104	67,557	93,306
Richmond, VA	38,132	54,795	82,939
Rochester, MN	43,827	79,159	106,381
Sacramento, CA	35,793	71,074	93,320
St. Louis, MO	33,326	48,751	68,681
Salem, OR	31,610	62,185	82,450
Salt Lake City, UT	42,081	65,880	97,628
San Antonio, TX	28,579	55,084	74,154
San Diego, CA	46,460	89,457	121,230
San Francisco, CA	77,267	126,187	178,742
San Jose, CA	53,574	125,075	162,521
Santa Rosa, CA	41,880	84,823	108,164
Savannah, GA	27,952	49,832	69,653
Seattle, WA	68,836	105,391	144,955
Sioux Falls, SD	36,430	66,761	87,676
Springfield, IL	35,851	57,596	79,460
Tampa, FL	40,962	59,893	97,942
Tucson, AZ	26,373	48,058	63,665
Tulsa, OK	33,492	52,438	79,727
Tuscaloosa, AL	27,789	44,880	69,736
Virginia Beach, VA	41,803	81,810	105,521
Washington, DC	63,793	93,547	138,421
Wichita, KS	31,558	56,374	77,762
Wilmington, NC	38,890	54,066	83,853
Winston-Salem, NC	30,859	50,204	75,459
Worcester, MA	30,855	56,746	76,859
U.S.	37,638	69,021	97,196

Source: U.S. Census Bureau, 2017-2021 American Community Survey 5-Year Estimates

A-68　Appendix A: Comparative Statistics

Income: Metro Area

Metro Area	Per Capita ($)	Median Household ($)	Average Household ($)
Albuquerque, NM	32,622	58,335	78,771
Allentown, PA	37,945	73,091	96,205
Anchorage, AK	41,201	86,252	109,817
Ann Arbor, MI	45,500	79,198	110,102
Athens, GA	31,392	52,958	80,272
Atlanta, GA	39,267	75,267	104,478
Austin, TX	44,830	85,398	114,103
Baltimore, MD	45,226	87,513	115,291
Boise City, ID	35,114	69,801	92,742
Boston, MA	53,033	99,039	135,411
Boulder, CO	52,401	92,466	128,190
Brownsville, TX	19,371	43,057	60,107
Cape Coral, FL	37,550	63,235	89,228
Cedar Rapids, IA	37,291	70,210	90,560
Charleston, SC	39,923	70,275	98,682
Charlotte, NC	38,783	69,559	98,559
Chicago, IL	42,097	78,790	109,339
Cincinnati, OH	37,846	70,308	94,687
Clarksville, TN	28,243	57,963	74,308
Cleveland, OH	36,907	61,320	85,864
College Station, TX	30,182	53,541	78,104
Colorado Springs, CO	37,650	75,641	97,647
Columbia, MO	33,131	61,901	82,741
Columbia, SC	32,508	58,992	79,903
Columbus, OH	38,167	71,020	95,315
Dallas, TX	38,609	76,916	105,647
Davenport, IA	34,859	63,282	83,352
Denver, CO	47,026	88,512	117,250
Des Moines, IA	39,333	75,134	97,364
Durham, NC	40,502	68,913	99,164
Edison, NJ	47,591	86,445	127,555
El Paso, TX	23,934	50,849	68,522
Fargo, ND	38,367	68,560	91,642
Fort Collins, CO	42,596	80,664	104,442
Fort Wayne, IN	32,207	62,031	80,675
Fort Worth, TX	38,609	76,916	105,647
Grand Rapids, MI	34,581	70,347	91,126
Greeley, CO	35,707	80,843	99,568
Green Bay, WI	35,678	68,952	87,144
Greensboro, NC	31,655	55,544	77,839
Honolulu, HI	40,339	92,600	118,470
Houston, TX	36,821	72,551	103,497
Huntsville, AL	38,800	71,057	94,763
Indianapolis, IN	36,867	67,330	92,858
Jacksonville, FL	36,316	66,664	91,361
Kansas City, MO	39,175	73,299	96,817
Lafayette, LA	30,758	55,539	77,448
Las Cruces, NM	24,645	47,151	65,405
Las Vegas, NV	33,461	64,210	87,879
Lexington, KY	36,123	63,360	88,439
Lincoln, NE	35,055	65,508	87,123
Little Rock, AR	33,523	58,441	81,542
Los Angeles, CA	39,895	81,652	115,584
Louisville, KY	35,613	64,533	87,361
Madison, WI	43,359	77,519	100,891
Manchester, NH	45,238	86,930	111,733

Table continued on following page.

Appendix A: Comparative Statistics   A-69

Metro Area	Per Capita ($)	Median Household ($)	Average Household ($)
Miami, FL	36,174	62,870	94,059
Midland, TX	43,287	87,812	114,916
Milwaukee, WI	38,930	67,448	92,423
Minneapolis, MN	45,301	87,397	114,491
Nashville, TN	39,269	72,537	99,987
New Haven, CT	41,192	75,043	102,367
New Orleans, LA	33,792	57,656	83,052
New York, NY	47,591	86,445	127,555
Oklahoma City, OK	34,136	63,351	85,884
Omaha, NE	38,289	73,757	97,122
Orlando, FL	32,999	65,086	89,689
Philadelphia, PA	43,195	79,070	109,757
Phoenix, AZ	36,842	72,211	97,412
Pittsburgh, PA	39,416	65,894	90,001
Portland, OR	42,946	82,901	108,110
Providence, RI	39,267	74,422	97,540
Provo, UT	29,817	82,742	105,296
Raleigh, NC	42,554	83,581	110,195
Reno, NV	40,299	74,216	100,824
Richmond, VA	40,254	74,592	100,389
Rochester, MN	42,841	80,865	106,479
Sacramento, CA	39,510	81,264	107,069
St. Louis, MO	39,168	69,635	94,953
Salem, OR	31,447	65,881	85,642
Salt Lake City, UT	36,688	82,506	105,669
San Antonio, TX	32,580	65,355	88,127
San Diego, CA	42,696	88,240	118,474
San Francisco, CA	62,070	118,547	165,749
San Jose, CA	64,169	138,370	187,324
Santa Rosa, CA	47,580	91,607	121,206
Savannah, GA	34,908	64,703	89,172
Seattle, WA	51,872	97,675	130,964
Sioux Falls, SD	37,200	72,547	92,236
Springfield, IL	37,961	66,999	87,390
Tampa, FL	35,879	61,121	86,382
Tucson, AZ	33,016	59,215	80,772
Tulsa, OK	33,647	60,866	84,069
Tuscaloosa, AL	28,204	54,449	72,452
Virginia Beach, VA	37,548	71,612	93,415
Washington, DC	54,663	111,252	145,303
Wichita, KS	32,124	61,445	81,209
Wilmington, NC	38,607	63,036	89,355
Winston-Salem, NC	31,238	55,454	76,451
Worcester, MA	40,750	80,333	104,366
U.S.	37,638	69,021	97,196

Note: Figures cover the Metropolitan Statistical Area (MSA)
Source: U.S. Census Bureau, 2017-2021 American Community Survey 5-Year Estimates

A-70   Appendix A: Comparative Statistics

Household Income Distribution: City

City	Percent of Households Earning							
	Under $15,000	$15,000 -$24,999	$25,000 -$34,999	$35,000 -$49,999	$50,000 -$74,999	$75,000 -$99,999	$100,000 -$149,999	$150,000 and up
Albuquerque, NM	13.1	8.9	9.8	12.9	18.0	11.6	14.8	10.9
Allentown, PA	13.0	12.4	10.9	16.1	19.7	11.2	10.9	5.7
Anchorage, AK	5.5	5.1	5.5	9.0	17.1	14.1	20.2	23.6
Ann Arbor, MI	14.5	6.2	6.2	8.9	15.2	11.2	15.7	22.2
Athens, GA	17.8	12.2	12.4	12.8	15.4	9.2	11.3	8.8
Atlanta, GA	14.2	8.1	7.3	9.4	14.5	11.0	13.5	22.0
Austin, TX	8.3	5.5	6.7	10.4	16.8	12.6	17.7	22.1
Baltimore, MD	16.6	9.1	8.9	12.2	17.1	10.8	12.7	12.8
Boise City, ID	7.6	7.6	8.6	12.4	18.5	13.9	15.7	15.7
Boston, MA	14.9	7.2	5.5	7.7	11.9	10.5	16.1	26.2
Boulder, CO	13.1	7.8	6.7	8.9	13.6	9.5	13.8	26.6
Brownsville, TX	18.6	13.1	10.0	13.0	18.2	10.7	10.6	5.9
Cape Coral, FL	7.6	6.2	8.7	13.7	20.5	15.4	17.2	10.6
Cedar Rapids, IA	7.1	8.5	9.5	13.6	19.9	14.8	14.9	11.7
Charleston, SC	9.1	6.5	6.2	11.3	15.8	12.3	18.6	20.3
Charlotte, NC	7.8	6.7	8.5	12.7	18.3	12.5	15.8	17.7
Chicago, IL	13.1	8.7	8.2	10.2	14.9	11.7	14.7	18.6
Cincinnati, OH	18.0	11.9	10.5	12.6	15.3	10.1	10.6	11.0
Clarksville, TN	9.6	6.8	9.9	15.2	20.6	15.3	15.5	7.2
Cleveland, OH	25.4	13.8	12.4	13.8	14.7	8.7	7.0	4.4
College Station, TX	19.7	10.2	8.8	11.2	15.3	10.0	12.3	12.4
Colorado Springs, CO	7.8	6.6	7.6	12.0	18.0	14.2	17.3	16.4
Columbia, MO	12.8	9.6	9.8	12.6	17.3	11.5	13.2	13.2
Columbia, SC	18.9	10.2	9.7	12.6	14.8	10.5	11.2	12.1
Columbus, OH	10.8	8.4	9.5	13.6	19.5	13.5	15.3	9.5
Dallas, TX	11.3	8.6	9.6	13.7	18.4	11.3	12.1	14.8
Davenport, IA	10.9	9.1	9.0	13.6	20.8	12.8	14.6	9.2
Denver, CO	8.6	6.1	6.4	10.3	16.9	12.4	17.0	22.2
Des Moines, IA	10.0	8.9	9.4	14.7	20.2	14.3	13.6	8.9
Durham, NC	8.9	6.8	9.7	12.2	17.2	13.1	15.7	16.4
Edison, NJ	4.6	3.4	3.5	7.2	13.3	12.4	21.8	34.0
El Paso, TX	13.8	11.4	10.6	13.3	18.8	10.7	12.7	8.8
Fargo, ND	9.8	9.1	9.7	12.9	18.4	13.0	15.5	11.7
Fort Collins, CO	9.6	6.7	7.5	11.0	16.5	13.0	17.2	18.5
Fort Wayne, IN	10.4	10.4	10.8	14.8	19.8	13.2	13.1	7.5
Fort Worth, TX	8.7	7.0	8.7	11.6	18.6	13.5	17.2	14.6
Grand Rapids, MI	12.5	9.8	8.1	14.1	19.0	14.1	14.3	8.0
Greeley, CO	10.3	8.2	9.7	13.9	16.1	13.7	17.9	10.3
Green Bay, WI	10.1	9.4	10.0	15.0	21.7	13.0	13.6	7.3
Greensboro, NC	12.2	9.7	10.9	15.7	17.5	11.3	12.7	9.9
Honolulu, HI	9.1	6.3	6.1	11.0	16.5	13.2	17.1	20.6
Houston, TX	11.9	9.5	10.6	13.1	17.1	10.7	12.1	14.9
Huntsville, AL	11.5	9.2	10.1	12.3	15.2	11.4	14.4	15.9
Indianapolis, IN	12.1	9.6	9.9	14.5	18.8	11.9	12.9	10.4
Jacksonville, FL	10.9	8.4	9.6	13.8	18.9	13.2	14.3	10.9
Kansas City, MO	11.4	8.8	9.6	12.7	17.2	12.7	15.2	12.3
Lafayette, LA	16.0	8.5	9.7	11.5	15.4	11.4	13.3	14.2
Las Cruces, NM	17.5	12.3	10.4	12.2	17.4	9.8	13.1	7.4
Las Vegas, NV	11.6	8.1	8.7	12.9	17.3	13.1	15.2	13.0
Lexington, KY	10.6	8.9	9.5	12.1	17.6	12.3	14.9	14.1
Lincoln, NE	8.4	7.9	9.8	13.0	20.2	12.4	16.1	12.0
Little Rock, AR	11.5	10.1	10.4	13.4	16.2	11.5	12.3	14.4
Los Angeles, CA	11.6	7.8	7.8	10.4	15.1	11.7	15.4	20.1
Louisville, KY	11.2	8.8	9.5	13.3	18.5	12.3	14.3	11.9

Table continued on following page.

Appendix A: Comparative Statistics A-71

City	Percent of Households Earning							
	Under $15,000	$15,000 -$24,999	$25,000 -$34,999	$35,000 -$49,999	$50,000 -$74,999	$75,000 -$99,999	$100,000 -$149,999	$150,000 and up
Madison, WI	10.0	6.8	7.5	11.0	17.5	14.1	16.9	16.0
Manchester, NH	8.0	7.7	7.3	13.7	19.8	14.0	17.0	12.5
Miami, FL	17.7	11.8	10.1	11.8	16.1	9.4	11.1	12.0
Midland, TX	8.0	5.8	6.5	8.5	14.7	12.5	19.6	24.4
Milwaukee, WI	16.5	11.5	11.7	14.6	17.8	11.6	10.5	5.8
Minneapolis, MN	11.3	7.1	7.5	11.0	16.1	12.6	15.9	18.5
Nashville, TN	9.1	7.1	8.2	12.9	19.1	13.2	15.6	14.8
New Haven, CT	18.5	11.0	9.8	11.2	17.2	10.3	11.4	10.6
New Orleans, LA	21.3	11.3	9.5	10.4	15.0	9.4	10.8	12.3
New York, NY	13.2	8.0	7.3	9.6	14.0	11.0	15.0	21.9
Oklahoma City, OK	10.7	7.7	9.6	13.9	18.7	12.8	14.6	12.1
Omaha, NE	9.5	7.3	8.4	12.5	18.9	13.7	15.5	14.1
Orlando, FL	11.2	9.3	8.7	13.6	17.9	11.7	13.0	14.5
Philadelphia, PA	17.1	9.8	9.2	12.0	16.4	11.3	12.4	11.7
Phoenix, AZ	8.4	7.6	8.8	13.5	18.2	13.5	15.3	14.8
Pittsburgh, PA	16.3	9.8	9.6	11.2	16.1	11.7	12.6	12.8
Portland, OR	9.8	6.3	6.7	9.7	15.7	12.6	17.5	21.8
Providence, RI	15.7	10.6	8.8	11.3	17.4	11.9	12.0	12.4
Provo, UT	11.4	10.2	11.3	14.1	19.1	12.7	10.7	10.5
Raleigh, NC	7.5	6.5	8.7	12.1	16.7	12.9	17.0	18.8
Reno, NV	8.6	7.7	8.6	11.5	18.1	13.4	16.7	15.3
Richmond, VA	14.1	9.6	9.4	13.7	17.4	11.3	11.7	12.7
Rochester, MN	6.9	6.3	5.8	10.4	18.0	13.9	18.8	19.9
Sacramento, CA	10.5	6.9	7.2	10.4	17.3	13.8	17.2	16.7
St. Louis, MO	17.0	10.3	10.7	12.9	17.5	10.5	12.1	8.9
Salem, OR	9.9	8.3	8.7	12.8	19.4	13.0	16.6	11.3
Salt Lake City, UT	11.2	6.9	8.6	10.9	18.1	13.1	15.0	16.2
San Antonio, TX	12.2	9.5	10.3	13.6	19.1	12.0	13.3	10.0
San Diego, CA	7.3	5.4	5.9	8.6	15.2	12.6	19.0	26.0
San Francisco, CA	9.2	4.9	4.5	6.0	9.1	8.3	14.9	43.2
San Jose, CA	5.2	4.2	4.2	6.3	10.9	9.9	17.7	41.6
Santa Rosa, CA	7.3	4.9	6.0	10.1	15.6	13.8	20.2	22.1
Savannah, GA	14.7	11.5	10.4	13.6	18.3	11.2	11.7	8.6
Seattle, WA	7.8	4.5	4.7	7.5	12.8	10.6	17.9	34.1
Sioux Falls, SD	7.3	7.4	9.7	12.4	19.1	15.0	17.1	11.9
Springfield, IL	13.8	9.1	9.7	11.9	16.0	13.3	15.0	11.2
Tampa, FL	12.9	8.5	9.4	12.0	15.8	10.8	13.3	17.3
Tucson, AZ	13.9	11.4	11.3	15.2	18.1	12.0	11.7	6.4
Tulsa, OK	12.7	9.8	11.0	14.2	17.7	11.5	11.7	11.5
Tuscaloosa, AL	19.5	10.8	10.9	11.9	15.4	8.7	12.8	10.0
Virginia Beach, VA	5.6	4.5	6.3	10.5	18.8	14.6	20.9	18.8
Washington, DC	11.9	5.1	5.5	6.8	12.2	11.3	15.9	31.3
Wichita, KS	10.8	9.3	10.3	14.0	18.9	12.8	13.6	10.3
Wilmington, NC	14.8	9.7	8.2	13.5	18.5	10.4	12.5	12.5
Winston-Salem, NC	13.8	10.6	11.2	14.2	16.4	12.3	11.7	9.8
Worcester, MA	15.5	9.8	8.5	12.0	15.8	11.7	14.8	11.8
U.S.	9.4	7.8	8.2	11.4	16.8	12.8	16.3	17.3

Source: U.S. Census Bureau, 2017-2021 American Community Survey 5-Year Estimates

A-72 Appendix A: Comparative Statistics

Household Income Distribution: Metro Area

Metro Area	Percent of Households Earning							
	Under $15,000	$15,000 -$24,999	$25,000 -$34,999	$35,000 -$49,999	$50,000 -$74,999	$75,000 -$99,999	$100,000 -$149,999	$150,000 and up
Albuquerque, NM	12.0	8.9	9.3	13.0	18.0	12.3	15.0	11.5
Allentown, PA	7.3	7.6	7.6	11.8	17.0	13.7	17.9	17.2
Anchorage, AK	6.1	5.5	5.7	9.0	17.1	14.1	20.1	22.4
Ann Arbor, MI	9.7	6.0	6.9	9.7	15.5	12.5	17.4	22.3
Athens, GA	14.0	10.2	11.1	12.3	15.9	10.2	13.7	12.5
Atlanta, GA	7.6	6.5	7.5	11.1	17.2	13.3	17.3	19.5
Austin, TX	6.8	5.1	6.3	9.7	16.1	13.6	19.1	23.4
Baltimore, MD	8.0	5.5	5.9	9.3	14.8	12.5	18.8	25.1
Boise City, ID	7.0	7.1	7.6	12.0	20.4	14.6	17.3	14.2
Boston, MA	8.1	5.6	5.2	7.6	12.5	11.4	18.2	31.3
Boulder, CO	7.9	5.7	5.5	8.3	13.7	12.1	18.2	28.5
Brownsville, TX	16.8	13.4	11.5	12.9	17.9	10.7	10.6	6.3
Cape Coral, FL	9.1	7.9	9.2	13.2	19.0	13.8	14.9	12.8
Cedar Rapids, IA	6.6	7.4	8.5	12.1	19.2	14.9	17.0	14.4
Charleston, SC	8.4	7.7	7.8	11.6	17.3	13.4	17.1	16.7
Charlotte, NC	7.9	7.3	8.3	12.1	17.7	13.1	16.4	17.2
Chicago, IL	8.7	6.6	7.1	9.9	15.6	12.8	17.9	21.5
Cincinnati, OH	9.2	7.6	8.0	11.1	17.0	13.3	17.5	16.3
Clarksville, TN	10.8	7.6	10.3	14.0	19.6	14.5	14.8	8.5
Cleveland, OH	11.6	8.6	9.0	12.5	17.2	12.7	15.0	13.5
College Station, TX	16.0	9.6	8.9	12.5	17.0	11.2	13.1	11.7
Colorado Springs, CO	6.9	6.2	6.9	11.5	18.1	14.1	18.4	17.9
Columbia, MO	10.8	8.5	9.5	12.3	18.3	13.3	14.8	12.5
Columbia, SC	12.0	8.3	9.4	12.8	18.2	13.1	14.4	11.8
Columbus, OH	8.1	7.0	7.9	11.6	17.9	13.3	17.6	16.6
Dallas, TX	7.1	6.0	7.4	11.1	17.3	13.3	17.9	20.0
Davenport, IA	9.6	8.2	8.7	12.4	18.8	13.7	16.5	12.0
Denver, CO	6.2	4.8	5.7	9.5	16.3	13.2	19.9	24.5
Des Moines, IA	6.4	6.3	7.4	11.8	18.1	14.1	19.0	16.9
Durham, NC	9.2	7.1	9.1	11.5	16.4	12.4	15.6	18.8
Edison, NJ	9.7	6.6	6.3	8.6	13.3	11.2	16.7	27.5
El Paso, TX	13.8	11.2	10.7	13.5	19.0	10.9	12.5	8.3
Fargo, ND	8.7	7.9	7.9	11.8	17.3	13.8	17.9	14.7
Fort Collins, CO	7.9	6.2	6.6	10.0	16.0	14.2	18.8	20.3
Fort Wayne, IN	8.2	8.9	9.5	13.5	19.5	14.9	15.3	10.3
Fort Worth, TX	7.1	6.0	7.4	11.1	17.3	13.3	17.9	20.0
Grand Rapids, MI	7.1	7.4	7.5	12.3	19.2	14.8	17.9	13.9
Greeley, CO	6.6	5.7	7.3	10.2	16.7	14.3	22.2	16.9
Green Bay, WI	7.0	7.1	8.7	12.3	19.2	15.2	18.3	12.1
Greensboro, NC	11.3	9.5	10.3	14.5	17.9	12.1	13.8	10.5
Honolulu, HI	6.5	4.5	5.4	9.0	14.7	13.5	20.0	26.3
Houston, TX	8.4	7.1	8.2	11.0	16.6	12.3	16.5	19.8
Huntsville, AL	8.8	8.0	8.2	11.7	15.4	12.8	16.9	18.2
Indianapolis, IN	8.6	7.4	8.3	12.1	18.4	13.4	16.2	15.6
Jacksonville, FL	9.0	7.1	8.6	12.5	18.3	13.7	15.8	15.0
Kansas City, MO	7.5	6.9	8.1	11.4	17.1	13.9	18.1	17.0
Lafayette, LA	13.7	10.4	10.0	11.9	15.8	12.9	14.4	11.1
Las Cruces, NM	16.8	12.7	10.8	12.2	17.7	9.5	12.9	7.3
Las Vegas, NV	9.7	7.7	8.8	12.8	18.2	13.4	15.7	13.6
Lexington, KY	10.0	8.2	9.3	12.4	17.6	12.9	16.1	13.4
Lincoln, NE	7.8	7.5	9.4	12.6	19.7	12.8	17.1	13.1
Little Rock, AR	11.0	9.2	10.1	13.3	17.5	12.4	14.9	11.6
Los Angeles, CA	9.0	6.4	6.8	9.5	14.8	12.3	17.4	23.8
Louisville, KY	9.2	7.9	8.9	12.9	18.3	13.2	16.0	13.6

Table continued on following page.

Appendix A: Comparative Statistics   A-73

Metro Area	Percent of Households Earning							
	Under $15,000	$15,000 -$24,999	$25,000 -$34,999	$35,000 -$49,999	$50,000 -$74,999	$75,000 -$99,999	$100,000 -$149,999	$150,000 and up
Madison, WI	6.9	6.0	6.7	11.1	17.7	14.3	18.9	18.3
Manchester, NH	5.4	5.5	6.2	10.2	15.7	13.2	20.1	23.7
Miami, FL	10.8	8.5	9.0	12.2	17.2	12.2	14.6	15.5
Midland, TX	7.6	5.8	7.1	8.8	14.1	12.8	19.2	24.6
Milwaukee, WI	9.4	7.8	8.5	11.8	17.1	13.2	16.7	15.5
Minneapolis, MN	6.1	5.2	6.1	9.7	16.0	13.7	20.2	23.2
Nashville, TN	7.4	6.5	7.4	12.1	18.2	13.9	17.5	16.9
New Haven, CT	9.4	7.6	6.9	10.1	15.8	12.5	17.1	20.4
New Orleans, LA	14.1	9.6	9.1	11.5	16.5	11.7	14.0	13.5
New York, NY	9.7	6.6	6.3	8.6	13.3	11.2	16.7	27.5
Oklahoma City, OK	9.4	7.9	9.1	13.0	18.6	13.4	15.6	12.8
Omaha, NE	7.6	6.5	7.7	11.3	17.7	14.2	18.5	16.4
Orlando, FL	8.3	7.9	9.0	12.9	18.5	13.6	15.8	14.0
Philadelphia, PA	9.3	6.7	7.1	9.7	15.1	12.5	17.3	22.5
Phoenix, AZ	7.4	6.6	7.7	12.0	18.1	13.9	17.7	16.7
Pittsburgh, PA	9.7	8.4	8.7	11.8	17.0	12.9	16.5	14.9
Portland, OR	7.2	5.7	6.3	10.0	16.3	13.6	19.5	21.5
Providence, RI	9.7	7.9	7.3	10.1	15.2	13.2	18.2	18.3
Provo, UT	5.1	5.0	6.4	10.4	17.9	15.7	20.8	18.6
Raleigh, NC	6.3	6.0	7.0	10.4	15.8	12.8	19.5	22.3
Reno, NV	7.2	6.7	7.8	10.8	18.0	14.0	18.3	17.2
Richmond, VA	7.9	6.7	7.2	11.2	17.2	13.1	18.3	18.3
Rochester, MN	6.2	6.0	6.4	10.1	17.8	14.0	20.1	19.5
Sacramento, CA	8.3	6.1	6.7	9.5	15.9	13.2	18.3	22.1
St. Louis, MO	8.6	7.4	8.1	11.8	17.5	13.5	16.9	16.3
Salem, OR	8.5	7.8	8.7	12.3	18.9	13.8	17.5	12.3
Salt Lake City, UT	6.0	4.8	6.3	10.2	17.9	14.8	20.6	19.3
San Antonio, TX	9.6	7.9	8.9	12.0	18.2	13.0	16.1	14.4
San Diego, CA	6.9	5.7	6.3	9.1	15.0	12.6	18.9	25.5
San Francisco, CA	6.7	4.3	4.5	6.4	10.8	10.0	17.1	40.0
San Jose, CA	4.9	3.6	3.7	5.5	9.9	9.2	16.8	46.6
Santa Rosa, CA	6.5	5.0	5.9	9.0	14.3	13.4	19.6	26.3
Savannah, GA	9.4	7.9	8.6	12.0	18.6	14.1	15.9	13.5
Seattle, WA	5.9	4.6	5.1	8.2	14.7	12.5	19.8	29.2
Sioux Falls, SD	6.2	6.7	8.7	11.8	18.7	15.7	18.9	13.3
Springfield, IL	10.4	7.9	8.4	11.5	16.2	14.1	18.0	13.7
Tampa, FL	9.9	8.6	9.5	13.2	18.0	12.7	14.6	13.7
Tucson, AZ	10.8	9.2	9.6	13.4	17.3	13.1	14.9	11.7
Tulsa, OK	9.6	8.5	9.9	13.1	18.6	12.8	15.3	12.2
Tuscaloosa, AL	14.3	9.9	10.2	12.1	17.3	12.0	14.5	9.6
Virginia Beach, VA	8.0	7.0	7.6	11.3	18.3	13.9	18.4	15.5
Washington, DC	5.7	3.7	4.4	6.8	12.6	12.0	19.6	35.4
Wichita, KS	9.2	8.6	9.1	13.4	19.6	13.4	15.5	11.0
Wilmington, NC	11.0	8.7	7.8	12.4	18.0	12.0	16.0	14.0
Winston-Salem, NC	11.0	10.0	10.7	13.7	18.1	13.1	13.3	10.1
Worcester, MA	8.6	6.8	7.0	9.6	15.3	12.5	18.5	21.8
U.S.	9.4	7.8	8.2	11.4	16.8	12.8	16.3	17.3

Note: Figures cover the Metropolitan Statistical Area (MSA)
Source: Source: U.S. Census Bureau, 2017-2021 American Community Survey 5-Year Estimates

A-74 Appendix A: Comparative Statistics

Poverty Rate: City

City	All Ages	Under 18 Years Old	18 to 64 Years Old	65 Years and Over
Albuquerque, NM	16.2	21.0	15.7	11.7
Allentown, PA	23.3	34.9	19.6	16.6
Anchorage, AK	9.1	11.1	8.8	6.8
Ann Arbor, MI	22.5	10.8	27.7	6.3
Athens, GA	26.6	25.8	29.5	11.1
Atlanta, GA	18.5	27.1	16.5	16.9
Austin, TX	12.5	15.9	11.7	11.3
Baltimore, MD	20.3	27.9	18.2	18.6
Boise City, ID	11.6	13.8	11.6	8.6
Boston, MA	17.6	23.7	15.6	21.0
Boulder, CO	20.9	8.6	25.6	6.4
Brownsville, TX	26.5	36.4	21.2	28.2
Cape Coral, FL	9.9	15.4	8.7	8.8
Cedar Rapids, IA	11.2	15.5	10.9	6.4
Charleston, SC	12.0	14.6	12.6	6.4
Charlotte, NC	11.6	17.3	10.1	8.7
Chicago, IL	17.1	24.2	15.1	15.9
Cincinnati, OH	24.7	37.4	22.3	14.7
Clarksville, TN	13.2	16.9	12.4	7.2
Cleveland, OH	31.4	45.7	28.3	22.8
College Station, TX	28.2	13.2	34.3	5.9
Colorado Springs, CO	10.9	13.7	10.7	7.5
Columbia, MO	19.9	14.9	23.7	6.1
Columbia, SC	24.3	31.3	23.5	16.7
Columbus, OH	18.4	27.1	16.5	11.6
Dallas, TX	17.7	26.9	14.7	14.7
Davenport, IA	15.8	24.7	14.1	9.8
Denver, CO	11.6	16.0	10.4	11.3
Des Moines, IA	15.3	22.6	13.6	9.8
Durham, NC	13.5	19.6	12.5	8.9
Edison, NJ	5.8	7.1	5.1	6.6
El Paso, TX	18.3	25.3	15.1	19.1
Fargo, ND	12.9	14.1	14.1	4.8
Fort Collins, CO	15.7	8.9	18.7	7.3
Fort Wayne, IN	15.5	23.9	13.7	8.3
Fort Worth, TX	13.4	19.1	11.3	10.7
Grand Rapids, MI	18.6	25.6	17.1	13.9
Greeley, CO	15.3	20.5	14.5	9.1
Green Bay, WI	15.4	21.5	14.2	10.3
Greensboro, NC	17.4	24.3	15.9	13.0
Honolulu, HI	11.0	13.3	10.4	10.8
Houston, TX	19.5	29.7	16.3	15.1
Huntsville, AL	14.6	21.8	13.9	8.3
Indianapolis, IN	16.4	23.3	14.9	10.5
Jacksonville, FL	14.9	21.1	13.0	12.7
Kansas City, MO	15.0	22.2	13.4	10.1
Lafayette, LA	19.5	29.0	17.8	12.9
Las Cruces, NM	21.8	26.9	22.4	11.5
Las Vegas, NV	14.9	20.8	13.6	11.3
Lexington, KY	15.7	18.6	16.5	7.6
Lincoln, NE	13.0	13.5	14.4	6.1
Little Rock, AR	15.6	22.9	14.2	9.2
Los Angeles, CA	16.6	22.9	14.7	16.3
Louisville, KY	15.2	22.6	14.0	9.4
Madison, WI	16.6	13.0	19.2	7.1

Table continued on following page.

Appendix A: Comparative Statistics   A-75

City	All Ages	Under 18 Years Old	18 to 64 Years Old	65 Years and Over
Manchester, NH	12.5	22.1	10.7	8.6
Miami, FL	20.9	27.8	16.6	30.9
Midland, TX	10.6	13.5	9.1	11.8
Milwaukee, WI	24.1	33.4	21.6	15.9
Minneapolis, MN	17.0	21.2	16.3	13.6
Nashville, TN	14.5	22.7	12.7	10.4
New Haven, CT	24.6	31.4	23.3	17.4
New Orleans, LA	23.8	33.8	21.5	20.6
New York, NY	17.0	23.2	14.7	17.8
Oklahoma City, OK	14.9	21.5	13.6	8.4
Omaha, NE	12.1	15.7	11.4	8.4
Orlando, FL	15.5	21.5	13.7	14.5
Philadelphia, PA	22.8	31.9	20.6	18.9
Phoenix, AZ	15.4	22.7	13.3	10.5
Pittsburgh, PA	19.7	28.8	19.0	14.0
Portland, OR	12.6	13.5	12.7	10.6
Providence, RI	21.5	30.3	18.8	19.5
Provo, UT	24.6	17.7	28.2	10.0
Raleigh, NC	12.1	15.8	11.8	7.2
Reno, NV	12.6	13.6	12.4	11.8
Richmond, VA	19.8	30.2	18.3	13.5
Rochester, MN	8.7	9.6	8.9	6.4
Sacramento, CA	14.8	18.5	14.1	12.1
St. Louis, MO	19.6	27.3	18.3	15.4
Salem, OR	14.7	18.0	14.5	10.2
Salt Lake City, UT	14.7	15.4	15.2	10.3
San Antonio, TX	17.6	25.8	15.3	13.6
San Diego, CA	11.6	13.9	11.3	9.4
San Francisco, CA	10.3	10.1	9.4	14.4
San Jose, CA	7.7	8.2	7.1	9.5
Santa Rosa, CA	9.8	12.9	9.0	9.0
Savannah, GA	19.8	29.7	18.1	12.1
Seattle, WA	10.0	9.5	9.9	11.2
Sioux Falls, SD	9.5	10.6	9.6	6.8
Springfield, IL	18.5	28.2	17.6	9.2
Tampa, FL	17.2	23.7	14.6	19.3
Tucson, AZ	19.8	25.3	19.7	12.5
Tulsa, OK	18.0	26.8	16.7	8.8
Tuscaloosa, AL	22.6	21.7	24.5	14.8
Virginia Beach, VA	7.8	10.5	7.6	4.8
Washington, DC	15.4	22.8	13.7	13.9
Wichita, KS	15.2	20.8	14.5	8.5
Wilmington, NC	18.8	25.3	19.8	8.7
Winston-Salem, NC	19.0	30.1	16.9	9.5
Worcester, MA	19.3	24.8	18.1	16.6
U.S.	12.6	17.0	11.8	9.6

Note: Figures are percentage of people whose income during the past 12 months was below the poverty level;
Source: U.S. Census Bureau, 2017-2021 American Community Survey 5-Year Estimates

A-76 Appendix A: Comparative Statistics

Poverty Rate: Metro Area

Metro Area	All Ages	Under 18 Years Old	18 to 64 Years Old	65 Years and Over
Albuquerque, NM	15.3	19.5	14.9	11.3
Allentown, PA	10.4	15.9	9.4	7.3
Anchorage, AK	9.6	11.5	9.2	7.4
Ann Arbor, MI	13.4	11.1	15.8	5.8
Athens, GA	20.1	20.5	22.3	9.5
Atlanta, GA	11.1	15.5	9.9	8.5
Austin, TX	10.2	12.0	9.9	8.3
Baltimore, MD	9.8	12.7	9.0	8.8
Boise City, ID	9.9	11.2	9.9	7.6
Boston, MA	9.0	10.3	8.4	9.5
Boulder, CO	11.0	7.1	13.2	6.4
Brownsville, TX	26.3	37.9	21.2	21.8
Cape Coral, FL	12.0	18.7	11.5	9.0
Cedar Rapids, IA	9.5	12.0	9.4	6.5
Charleston, SC	12.1	18.2	10.9	8.1
Charlotte, NC	10.7	14.9	9.7	8.4
Chicago, IL	11.1	15.1	10.1	9.4
Cincinnati, OH	11.6	15.5	10.9	8.1
Clarksville, TN	13.5	17.0	12.6	9.2
Cleveland, OH	13.7	19.6	12.8	9.7
College Station, TX	22.3	20.5	25.3	8.6
Colorado Springs, CO	9.5	12.0	9.2	6.6
Columbia, MO	16.2	14.6	18.7	6.8
Columbia, SC	14.9	19.9	14.2	10.6
Columbus, OH	12.3	17.0	11.5	7.7
Dallas, TX	10.9	15.4	9.4	8.9
Davenport, IA	12.6	18.5	11.8	7.6
Denver, CO	8.1	10.2	7.6	7.1
Des Moines, IA	9.0	11.5	8.6	6.6
Durham, NC	13.2	17.8	12.9	8.2
Edison, NJ	12.3	16.6	10.8	12.1
El Paso, TX	19.3	26.5	15.9	20.0
Fargo, ND	11.3	12.1	12.2	5.5
Fort Collins, CO	11.1	8.8	13.0	6.6
Fort Wayne, IN	12.1	17.9	10.9	6.9
Fort Worth, TX	10.9	15.4	9.4	8.9
Grand Rapids, MI	9.8	11.7	9.5	7.8
Greeley, CO	9.7	12.1	9.0	7.7
Green Bay, WI	9.4	12.0	9.0	7.1
Greensboro, NC	15.1	21.5	14.0	10.3
Honolulu, HI	8.6	11.0	7.9	8.0
Houston, TX	13.3	18.9	11.5	10.5
Huntsville, AL	11.0	15.0	10.1	8.9
Indianapolis, IN	11.1	15.0	10.2	7.7
Jacksonville, FL	12.3	17.2	11.3	9.3
Kansas City, MO	9.8	13.5	9.0	7.0
Lafayette, LA	18.5	26.6	16.6	12.9
Las Cruces, NM	23.2	30.9	22.2	14.7
Las Vegas, NV	13.6	19.0	12.5	9.8
Lexington, KY	14.1	17.2	14.4	8.3
Lincoln, NE	11.8	11.9	13.1	5.9
Little Rock, AR	14.0	18.8	13.4	9.1
Los Angeles, CA	12.9	17.2	11.6	12.4
Louisville, KY	12.0	17.0	11.1	8.2
Madison, WI	10.1	9.0	11.5	5.8

Table continued on following page.

Appendix A: Comparative Statistics   A-77

Metro Area	All Ages	Under 18 Years Old	18 to 64 Years Old	65 Years and Over
Manchester, NH	7.2	9.8	6.5	6.2
Miami, FL	13.6	18.0	11.6	15.6
Midland, TX	11.2	15.9	8.9	11.2
Milwaukee, WI	12.6	17.7	11.6	9.0
Minneapolis, MN	8.1	10.1	7.7	6.8
Nashville, TN	10.9	14.6	10.2	8.3
New Haven, CT	11.5	15.8	11.1	7.9
New Orleans, LA	17.3	24.6	15.7	13.3
New York, NY	12.3	16.6	10.8	12.1
Oklahoma City, OK	13.6	18.6	12.9	7.8
Omaha, NE	9.3	11.2	9.0	7.1
Orlando, FL	12.6	17.1	11.7	9.9
Philadelphia, PA	11.7	16.0	10.9	9.2
Phoenix, AZ	12.0	16.9	11.0	8.3
Pittsburgh, PA	10.7	14.2	10.3	8.3
Portland, OR	9.9	11.3	9.8	8.2
Providence, RI	11.2	15.2	10.3	9.6
Provo, UT	9.3	7.9	10.7	5.2
Raleigh, NC	9.3	12.1	8.7	6.9
Reno, NV	11.0	12.8	10.6	9.9
Richmond, VA	10.2	14.1	9.4	7.7
Rochester, MN	7.4	8.6	7.4	6.0
Sacramento, CA	12.2	14.9	12.0	8.8
St. Louis, MO	10.5	14.4	9.9	7.7
Salem, OR	13.1	16.8	12.8	8.8
Salt Lake City, UT	8.2	9.2	8.0	6.5
San Antonio, TX	13.8	19.4	12.1	10.7
San Diego, CA	10.7	13.2	10.3	8.9
San Francisco, CA	8.4	9.1	8.1	9.1
San Jose, CA	6.7	6.8	6.3	8.2
Santa Rosa, CA	8.7	10.3	8.6	7.4
Savannah, GA	12.5	17.5	11.5	8.6
Seattle, WA	8.3	9.7	7.9	7.8
Sioux Falls, SD	7.9	8.5	8.0	6.3
Springfield, IL	13.6	20.0	13.2	7.3
Tampa, FL	12.9	17.4	12.1	10.9
Tucson, AZ	15.1	20.2	15.5	8.6
Tulsa, OK	13.4	19.0	12.6	7.6
Tuscaloosa, AL	17.5	22.8	17.0	11.8
Virginia Beach, VA	10.9	16.1	9.8	7.6
Washington, DC	7.7	9.9	7.0	7.1
Wichita, KS	12.6	16.7	12.0	7.6
Wilmington, NC	13.4	16.6	14.2	7.0
Winston-Salem, NC	15.1	23.7	13.6	9.0
Worcester, MA	10.0	12.0	9.6	8.8
U.S.	12.6	17.0	11.8	9.6

Note: Figures are percentage of people whose income during the past 12 months was below the poverty level;
Figures cover the Metropolitan Statistical Area
Source: U.S. Census Bureau, 2017-2021 American Community Survey 5-Year Estimates

A-78 Appendix A: Comparative Statistics

Employment by Industry

Metro Area[1]	(A)	(B)	(C)	(D)	(E)	(F)	(G)	(H)	(I)	(J)	(K)	(L)	(M)	(N)
Albuquerque, NM	6.2	n/a	16.6	5.0	19.4	1.4	10.6	4.2	n/a	2.9	16.6	10.5	3.7	2.8
Allentown, PA	3.4	n/a	20.9	3.3	10.0	1.3	8.6	10.5	n/a	3.7	13.2	10.4	11.0	3.7
Anchorage, AK	6.2	5.1	18.4	4.5	19.2	1.9	10.8	1.3	1.1	3.6	11.3	11.5	8.5	2.8
Ann Arbor, MI	2.0	n/a	13.1	3.1	38.2	2.6	7.0	5.5	n/a	2.6	13.6	7.2	2.2	3.0
Athens, GA	n/a	n/a	n/a	n/a	27.8	n/a	11.5	n/a	n/a	n/a	9.0	11.1	n/a	n/a
Atlanta, GA	4.7	4.6	13.1	6.7	11.3	3.8	9.8	5.9	0.1	3.5	19.4	10.1	6.5	5.3
Austin, TX	5.9	n/a	11.2	6.0	14.3	4.1	11.2	5.5	n/a	3.8	21.6	9.2	2.8	4.5
Baltimore, MD	6.0	n/a	19.1	5.5	16.0	1.1	8.6	4.2	n/a	3.4	17.7	9.0	5.8	3.7
Boise City, ID	8.4	n/a	14.8	5.8	13.2	1.2	10.1	7.6	n/a	3.4	15.4	10.6	4.4	5.0
Boston, MA[4]	3.9	n/a	22.9	8.3	10.3	3.6	9.0	4.0	n/a	3.4	21.9	7.2	2.5	3.0
Boulder, CO	2.9	n/a	12.7	3.5	19.4	4.0	9.5	10.8	n/a	4.0	20.6	8.0	1.1	3.6
Brownsville, TX	2.3	n/a	30.2	3.2	18.6	0.4	11.0	4.6	n/a	2.2	10.7	11.5	3.4	2.0
Cape Coral, FL	12.5	n/a	11.7	5.0	14.6	1.1	14.9	2.6	n/a	3.7	14.5	14.3	2.4	2.8
Cedar Rapids, IA	6.0	n/a	15.3	7.4	11.5	2.1	8.2	13.9	n/a	3.5	10.8	10.3	6.9	4.1
Charleston, SC	5.4	n/a	11.7	4.9	16.7	2.2	12.5	7.6	n/a	3.9	16.2	10.9	5.1	3.0
Charlotte, NC	5.6	n/a	10.4	9.1	12.2	2.0	10.6	8.3	n/a	3.7	16.9	10.5	6.0	4.8
Chicago, IL[2]	3.5	3.4	16.2	7.2	10.5	1.9	9.5	7.3	<0.1	4.1	19.2	8.9	6.6	5.0
Cincinnati, OH	4.5	n/a	14.7	6.8	11.2	1.2	10.4	10.4	n/a	3.5	16.2	9.4	6.4	5.1
Clarksville, TN	4.3	n/a	13.2	3.4	19.4	1.2	12.1	12.0	n/a	3.4	10.2	14.2	3.4	n/a
Cleveland, OH	3.7	n/a	19.4	7.0	12.3	1.5	9.0	11.4	n/a	3.6	14.4	9.1	3.6	5.0
College Station, TX	5.7	n/a	11.3	3.2	34.3	1.1	13.9	4.4	n/a	2.6	9.5	10.0	1.9	2.1
Colorado Springs, CO	5.9	n/a	13.8	5.8	17.7	1.6	12.1	3.7	n/a	6.8	17.0	10.3	3.3	2.0
Columbia, MO	n/a	n/a	n/a	n/a	28.2	n/a	n/a	n/a	n/a	n/a	n/a	10.5	n/a	n/a
Columbia, SC	4.0	n/a	12.8	8.6	19.9	1.2	9.2	7.6	n/a	4.1	13.7	10.8	4.2	3.8
Columbus, OH	4.2	n/a	14.1	7.3	16.0	1.6	9.1	6.4	n/a	3.8	16.5	9.0	8.5	3.6
Dallas, TX[2]	5.3	n/a	11.4	9.7	10.9	2.8	9.2	6.5	n/a	3.0	20.6	8.9	5.9	5.9
Davenport, IA	n/a	n/a	n/a	n/a	n/a	n/a	n/a	n/a	n/a	n/a	n/a	n/a	n/a	n/a
Denver, CO	6.9	n/a	12.2	7.3	12.7	3.3	10.6	4.5	n/a	4.1	19.6	8.9	5.0	4.9
Des Moines, IA	5.9	n/a	14.3	14.3	12.3	1.6	8.7	5.9	n/a	3.3	13.5	10.6	4.5	5.0
Durham, NC	2.9	n/a	21.9	4.8	18.9	1.8	7.7	8.5	n/a	3.4	17.5	7.1	2.5	2.8
Edison, NJ[2]	3.6	n/a	22.7	9.0	12.4	3.9	8.9	2.6	n/a	4.0	16.5	8.3	4.3	3.7
El Paso, TX	5.1	n/a	14.5	3.9	20.7	1.8	11.7	5.5	n/a	2.7	12.2	12.1	6.4	3.6
Fargo, ND	6.0	n/a	19.2	7.5	13.5	1.8	9.6	7.9	n/a	3.3	10.0	10.0	5.0	6.1
Fort Collins, CO	6.8	n/a	10.9	4.0	24.0	1.5	11.9	8.3	n/a	3.6	11.9	11.4	2.4	3.2
Fort Wayne, IN	5.2	n/a	18.4	5.5	9.4	0.8	9.0	16.4	n/a	5.0	9.7	10.7	5.1	4.8
Fort Worth, TX[2]	6.6	n/a	12.8	6.4	11.9	0.9	10.5	9.3	n/a	3.4	13.4	10.7	9.0	4.9
Grand Rapids, MI	4.7	n/a	16.5	4.8	8.6	1.2	8.2	20.0	n/a	3.9	13.8	8.7	3.5	6.0
Greeley, CO	15.1	n/a	9.9	4.1	16.5	0.5	9.3	12.3	n/a	3.2	10.5	10.6	4.2	4.0
Green Bay, WI	4.7	n/a	15.3	6.2	11.5	0.8	8.9	17.7	n/a	4.5	10.6	9.9	5.1	5.0
Greensboro, NC	4.8	n/a	14.6	4.6	11.9	1.1	9.9	13.8	n/a	3.4	12.6	11.2	6.3	5.8
Honolulu, HI	6.2	n/a	14.5	4.7	21.0	1.6	15.3	2.1	n/a	4.4	12.2	9.7	5.4	3.0
Houston, TX	8.8	6.7	13.2	5.5	13.4	1.0	10.3	6.9	2.0	3.5	16.6	9.8	5.9	5.2
Huntsville, AL	3.9	n/a	8.5	3.1	20.4	1.0	8.2	12.0	n/a	3.3	25.5	10.1	1.7	2.4
Indianapolis, IN	5.3	5.2	14.9	6.6	12.1	1.1	9.0	8.3	0.1	3.9	16.6	9.0	8.3	4.8
Jacksonville, FL	6.4	6.3	15.2	9.4	10.0	1.7	11.2	4.5	0.1	3.4	16.3	10.9	7.4	3.7
Kansas City, MO	5.1	n/a	14.5	7.0	12.9	1.5	9.7	7.6	n/a	4.0	17.1	9.8	6.3	4.6
Lafayette, LA	10.5	5.4	17.2	5.5	12.8	0.9	10.6	8.1	5.2	3.5	10.4	12.9	3.2	4.4
Las Cruces, NM	4.7	n/a	22.7	3.1	26.7	0.8	11.4	4.4	n/a	2.1	9.1	9.9	3.2	1.9
Las Vegas, NV	7.3	7.3	10.8	5.4	10.0	1.2	25.9	2.6	<0.1	2.9	14.8	10.4	6.4	2.4
Lexington, KY	4.8	n/a	13.0	4.0	19.0	1.0	11.1	10.8	n/a	4.4	13.2	10.2	4.5	3.8
Lincoln, NE	5.5	n/a	15.7	5.6	22.1	1.9	9.4	7.7	n/a	3.9	10.3	9.8	5.8	2.2
Little Rock, AR	4.9	n/a	16.2	6.4	17.9	1.5	8.6	5.1	n/a	6.6	12.3	10.2	5.8	4.6
Los Angeles, CA[2]	3.2	3.2	19.4	4.7	12.3	5.0	11.4	6.9	<0.1	3.4	14.9	9.2	5.1	4.4
Louisville, KY	4.3	n/a	14.7	6.8	10.5	1.3	9.3	12.4	n/a	3.7	12.9	9.4	10.2	4.6
Madison, WI	4.8	n/a	12.3	5.8	21.7	4.6	7.9	9.3	n/a	5.0	12.6	9.5	2.8	3.7
Manchester, NH[3]	5.0	n/a	22.7	6.5	10.3	2.2	8.4	6.9	n/a	4.1	16.2	10.8	3.0	3.9

Table continued on following page.

Appendix A: Comparative Statistics   A-79

Metro Area[1]	(A)	(B)	(C)	(D)	(E)	(F)	(G)	(H)	(I)	(J)	(K)	(L)	(M)	(N)
Miami, FL[2]	4.0	4.0	16.4	7.1	10.9	1.9	11.1	3.4	<0.1	3.7	16.4	11.6	7.5	6.0
Midland, TX	33.3	n/a	6.6	4.5	8.4	1.0	9.8	4.2	n/a	3.5	9.8	8.3	4.9	5.7
Milwaukee, WI	4.0	3.9	20.3	6.0	9.6	1.4	8.4	13.5	0.1	5.2	13.9	8.9	4.2	4.6
Minneapolis, MN	4.1	n/a	18.0	7.6	12.5	1.5	8.9	10.5	n/a	3.6	15.4	9.3	4.3	4.3
Nashville, TN	5.2	n/a	14.6	6.7	10.9	2.8	11.0	7.5	n/a	4.1	17.3	9.2	6.6	4.2
New Haven, CT[3]	3.7	n/a	29.2	3.9	11.9	1.3	8.7	7.8	n/a	3.5	10.4	9.0	6.7	3.9
New Orleans, LA	5.6	5.1	19.0	5.1	12.1	1.6	14.0	5.3	0.6	4.0	13.5	10.6	5.3	3.9
New York, NY[2]	3.6	n/a	22.7	9.0	12.4	3.9	8.9	2.6	n/a	4.0	16.5	8.3	4.3	3.7
Oklahoma City, OK	6.6	4.9	15.4	5.4	18.8	0.9	11.2	5.2	1.6	4.2	13.3	10.4	5.2	3.4
Omaha, NE	6.3	n/a	16.3	8.3	13.3	2.0	9.7	6.9	n/a	3.8	14.2	10.5	5.3	3.3
Orlando, FL	6.0	6.0	12.6	6.3	8.9	1.9	19.4	3.7	<0.1	3.1	19.3	10.8	4.5	3.6
Philadelphia, PA[2]	2.5	n/a	31.6	6.5	12.7	2.0	9.1	3.3	n/a	4.0	14.5	7.4	4.2	2.4
Phoenix, AZ	6.6	6.4	15.9	9.3	10.2	1.8	10.1	6.4	0.1	3.1	17.0	10.5	5.1	4.0
Pittsburgh, PA	5.4	4.7	21.2	6.5	9.7	1.9	9.6	7.2	0.7	4.0	16.6	10.1	4.4	3.6
Portland, OR	6.7	6.6	15.0	6.2	12.2	2.3	9.4	10.2	0.1	3.4	16.2	9.7	4.3	4.6
Providence, RI[3]	4.8	4.8	20.8	6.4	12.8	1.2	10.6	8.6	<0.1	4.4	12.7	10.9	3.4	3.4
Provo, UT	10.0	n/a	19.8	4.2	11.7	4.7	8.6	7.7	n/a	2.3	15.0	11.7	1.8	2.5
Raleigh, NC	6.6	n/a	13.0	5.7	13.8	3.6	10.4	4.7	n/a	4.0	20.4	10.2	3.5	4.1
Reno, NV	8.4	8.3	11.1	4.4	12.1	1.4	14.4	10.8	0.1	2.4	12.7	9.3	9.4	3.9
Richmond, VA	5.8	n/a	14.1	8.0	16.2	0.9	9.2	4.6	n/a	4.5	17.7	9.6	5.4	4.0
Rochester, MN	4.0	n/a	43.3	2.4	10.5	0.9	8.5	7.9	n/a	3.0	5.4	9.9	2.1	2.1
Sacramento, CA	6.8	6.8	16.9	4.9	22.7	1.0	10.3	3.7	<0.1	3.5	14.0	9.6	4.0	2.6
Salem, OR	7.6	7.3	17.8	3.8	24.5	0.9	8.8	6.7	0.3	3.0	9.5	11.0	4.1	2.3
Salt Lake City, UT	7.0	n/a	11.5	7.6	13.6	3.2	8.3	7.8	n/a	2.8	17.8	9.9	5.8	4.5
San Antonio, TX	5.9	5.3	14.9	8.9	15.6	1.7	12.2	5.1	0.6	3.5	14.0	10.9	4.1	3.3
San Diego, CA	5.7	5.6	15.0	4.8	15.9	1.4	12.8	7.6	<0.1	3.6	18.6	9.1	2.7	2.8
San Francisco, CA[2]	3.4	3.4	13.1	7.4	10.9	10.6	10.2	3.3	<0.1	3.2	26.3	5.7	4.1	1.9
San Jose, CA	4.8	4.7	16.3	3.3	8.3	9.1	8.5	15.4	<0.1	2.1	21.7	6.4	1.8	2.4
Santa Rosa, CA	7.9	7.8	17.3	4.0	12.7	1.3	12.4	11.5	0.1	3.6	12.2	11.4	2.3	3.5
Savannah, GA	4.7	n/a	14.1	3.5	11.8	0.8	13.7	9.8	n/a	4.0	12.6	12.0	9.5	3.5
Seattle, WA[2]	6.1	6.0	12.9	5.0	11.7	7.9	8.7	8.1	<0.1	3.3	20.0	8.1	4.2	4.1
Sioux Falls, SD	5.8	n/a	21.6	9.1	9.1	1.5	9.5	8.7	n/a	3.9	9.8	11.8	3.8	5.5
Springfield, IL	3.4	n/a	19.2	5.6	24.1	2.0	9.6	3.3	n/a	5.5	11.4	10.9	2.3	2.9
St. Louis, MO	5.0	n/a	18.6	6.9	10.9	2.0	10.0	8.3	n/a	3.8	15.5	9.6	4.7	4.8
Tampa, FL	6.2	6.2	15.2	9.1	10.2	1.9	10.8	4.9	<0.1	3.3	19.3	11.3	3.6	4.1
Tucson, AZ	5.4	4.9	16.8	4.8	19.3	1.3	11.2	7.2	0.5	3.5	12.8	10.6	5.2	2.0
Tulsa, OK	6.1	5.3	16.0	5.2	12.7	1.2	10.1	10.7	0.8	4.5	13.8	11.0	5.2	3.7
Tuscaloosa, AL	5.7	n/a	8.5	3.5	25.7	0.7	10.3	16.8	n/a	4.1	9.3	10.4	3.1	1.9
Virginia Beach, VA	5.2	n/a	14.8	5.0	19.7	1.2	11.1	7.4	n/a	4.2	14.7	10.4	4.0	2.4
Washington, DC[2]	4.8	n/a	12.9	4.4	22.2	2.5	9.2	1.4	n/a	6.2	24.3	7.6	2.7	1.9
Wichita, KS	5.7	n/a	14.9	3.9	14.3	1.2	10.8	16.8	n/a	3.7	11.3	10.3	4.0	3.1
Wilmington, NC	7.4	n/a	17.0	5.1	12.6	2.0	14.8	4.2	n/a	4.2	13.1	12.7	3.3	3.5
Winston-Salem, NC	4.3	n/a	20.1	5.0	11.3	0.7	10.5	12.6	n/a	3.5	12.9	11.6	4.5	3.1
Worcester, MA[3]	4.1	n/a	23.5	4.8	15.7	0.9	8.3	9.2	n/a	3.6	11.1	10.2	5.3	3.2
U.S.	5.4	5.0	16.1	5.9	14.5	2.0	10.3	8.4	0.4	3.7	14.7	10.2	4.9	3.9

Note: All figures are percentages covering non-farm employment as of December 2022 and are not seasonally adjusted;
(1) Figures cover the Metropolitan Statistical Area (MSA) except where noted. See Appendix B for areas included; (2) Metropolitan Division; (3) New England City and Town Area; (4) New England City and Town Area Division; (A) Construction, Mining, and Logging (some areas report Construction separate from Mining and Logging); (B) Construction; (C) Private Education and Health Services; (D) Financial Activities; (E) Government; (F) Information; (G) Leisure and Hospitality; (H) Manufacturing; (I) Mining and Logging; (J) Other Services; (K) Professional and Business Services; (L) Retail Trade; (M) Transportation and Utilities; (N) Wholesale Trade; n/a not available
Source: Bureau of Labor Statistics, Current Employment Statistics, Employment, Hours, and Earnings, December 2022

A-80 Appendix A: Comparative Statistics

Labor Force, Employment and Job Growth: City

City	Civilian Labor Force			Workers Employed		
	Dec. 2021	Dec. 2022	% Chg.	Dec. 2021	Dec. 2022	% Chg.
Albuquerque, NM	286,208	278,969	-2.5	272,867	270,719	-0.7
Allentown, PA	55,657	56,449	1.4	52,269	54,138	3.5
Anchorage, AK	154,601	155,471	0.5	148,017	150,605	1.7
Ann Arbor, MI	63,522	64,736	1.9	62,006	63,139	1.8
Athens, GA	60,379	61,240	1.4	58,643	59,627	1.6
Atlanta, GA	271,164	274,219	1.1	261,888	265,951	1.5
Austin, TX	626,475	642,058	2.4	609,403	625,541	2.6
Baltimore, MD	280,450	278,592	-0.6	262,676	266,256	1.3
Boise City, ID	135,152	140,433	3.9	132,075	137,857	4.3
Boston, MA	394,417	392,029	-0.6	379,015	380,790	0.4
Boulder, CO	66,246	67,538	1.9	64,727	66,197	2.2
Brownsville, TX	78,951	79,589	0.8	73,562	74,739	1.6
Cape Coral, FL	96,606	100,709	4.2	93,922	97,833	4.1
Cedar Rapids, IA	69,935	70,822	1.2	66,849	68,200	2.0
Charleston, SC	75,129	76,762	2.1	73,011	74,897	2.5
Charlotte, NC	498,644	513,354	2.9	481,757	496,911	3.1
Chicago, IL	1,370,152	1,365,082	-0.3	1,301,665	1,299,230	-0.1
Cincinnati, OH	147,147	145,962	-0.8	141,899	140,924	-0.6
Clarksville, TN	64,581	62,625	-3.0	62,259	60,449	-2.9
Cleveland, OH	154,230	153,656	-0.3	144,455	146,635	1.5
College Station, TX	63,443	64,403	1.5	61,598	62,625	1.6
Colorado Springs, CO	243,995	246,112	0.8	234,766	238,820	1.7
Columbia, MO	68,593	68,729	0.2	67,043	67,523	0.7
Columbia, SC	56,736	55,816	-1.6	54,797	54,043	-1.3
Columbus, OH	484,399	482,990	-0.2	469,341	467,547	-0.3
Dallas, TX	707,758	735,922	3.9	679,409	711,095	4.6
Davenport, IA	50,142	51,938	3.5	47,788	49,912	4.4
Denver, CO	428,646	439,359	2.5	411,447	426,400	3.6
Des Moines, IA	109,744	111,230	1.3	104,975	107,148	2.0
Durham, NC	155,641	159,589	2.5	151,405	155,264	2.5
Edison, NJ	55,370	56,778	2.5	53,727	55,594	3.4
El Paso, TX	302,469	303,815	0.4	288,907	292,314	1.1
Fargo, ND	72,514	72,188	-0.4	70,902	70,818	-0.1
Fort Collins, CO	100,891	102,741	1.8	98,235	100,394	2.2
Fort Wayne, IN	126,450	130,964	3.5	124,397	127,828	2.7
Fort Worth, TX	462,444	475,802	2.8	444,256	459,728	3.4
Grand Rapids, MI	101,134	105,118	3.9	96,771	100,836	4.2
Greeley, CO	51,681	51,829	0.2	49,366	50,105	1.5
Green Bay, WI	53,463	52,666	-1.4	52,235	51,500	-1.4
Greensboro, NC	143,008	144,251	0.8	137,220	138,826	1.1
Honolulu, HI	459,370	457,096	-0.5	440,467	441,407	0.2
Houston, TX	1,138,573	1,173,802	3.0	1,085,474	1,128,659	3.9
Huntsville, AL	102,295	104,297	1.9	100,086	102,254	2.1
Indianapolis, IN	450,127	464,032	3.0	441,617	452,513	2.4
Jacksonville, FL	470,543	493,413	4.8	456,509	481,988	5.5
Kansas City, MO	257,158	258,850	0.6	247,609	252,172	1.8
Lafayette, LA	59,534	60,606	1.8	57,818	58,830	1.7
Las Cruces, NM	48,477	48,211	-0.5	46,260	46,735	1.0
Las Vegas, NV	301,290	316,801	5.1	286,123	299,424	4.6
Lexington, KY	175,989	174,916	-0.6	170,668	170,430	-0.1
Lincoln, NE	161,763	164,641	1.7	159,144	161,093	1.2
Little Rock, AR	95,576	95,929	0.3	92,287	93,043	0.8
Los Angeles, CA	2,047,789	2,027,026	-1.0	1,931,445	1,935,875	0.2
Louisville, KY	400,329	398,800	-0.3	384,379	387,119	0.7
Madison, WI	162,642	161,298	-0.8	160,375	158,871	-0.9

Table continued on following page.

Appendix A: Comparative Statistics A-81

City	Civilian Labor Force			Workers Employed		
	Dec. 2021	Dec. 2022	% Chg.	Dec. 2021	Dec. 2022	% Chg.
Manchester, NH	63,249	66,044	4.4	61,619	64,357	4.4
Miami, FL	227,422	231,754	1.9	220,939	228,420	3.3
Midland, TX	83,370	84,916	1.8	80,102	82,715	3.2
Milwaukee, WI	272,797	266,036	-2.4	262,401	257,421	-1.9
Minneapolis, MN	241,913	246,063	1.7	235,948	240,094	1.7
Nashville, TN	413,734	407,521	-1.5	402,245	397,879	-1.0
New Haven, CT	65,615	66,515	1.3	62,503	64,310	2.8
New Orleans, LA	175,708	180,265	2.5	166,032	172,381	3.8
New York, NY	4,085,159	4,113,259	0.6	3,782,405	3,907,975	3.3
Oklahoma City, OK	327,538	333,291	1.7	320,689	324,655	1.2
Omaha, NE	250,414	253,695	1.3	244,895	246,725	0.7
Orlando, FL	168,524	173,274	2.8	162,788	169,122	3.8
Philadelphia, PA	712,569	723,233	1.5	667,785	690,464	3.4
Phoenix, AZ	865,943	889,029	2.6	842,267	864,868	2.6
Pittsburgh, PA	148,500	152,028	2.3	142,551	147,423	3.4
Portland, OR	387,410	393,179	1.4	373,537	376,724	0.8
Providence, RI	88,878	88,200	-0.7	85,136	85,603	0.5
Provo, UT	70,289	73,861	5.0	69,267	72,590	4.8
Raleigh, NC	255,398	264,381	3.5	247,896	256,967	3.6
Reno, NV	134,416	141,155	5.0	131,188	136,416	3.9
Richmond, VA	115,165	116,068	0.7	110,750	112,086	1.2
Rochester, MN	67,368	68,064	1.0	65,967	66,601	0.9
Sacramento, CA	237,842	239,915	0.8	226,017	231,146	2.2
Salem, OR	84,706	83,973	-0.8	81,711	80,171	-1.8
Salt Lake City, UT	121,702	125,773	3.3	119,545	123,299	3.1
San Antonio, TX	735,449	751,540	2.1	707,860	727,368	2.7
San Diego, CA	711,954	721,000	1.2	684,180	701,197	2.4
San Francisco, CA	560,450	578,421	3.2	543,659	566,695	4.2
San Jose, CA	546,462	558,687	2.2	529,424	546,728	3.2
Santa Rosa, CA	85,496	86,918	1.6	82,307	84,605	2.7
Savannah, GA	69,179	68,684	-0.7	66,698	66,661	0.0
Seattle, WA	483,713	490,565	1.4	471,546	477,991	1.3
Sioux Falls, SD	109,388	111,832	2.2	106,662	109,520	2.6
Springfield, IL	55,434	55,938	0.9	53,040	53,888	1.6
St. Louis, MO	150,418	149,690	-0.4	143,212	145,026	1.2
Tampa, FL	211,042	219,467	3.9	205,058	214,586	4.6
Tucson, AZ	257,903	262,655	1.8	249,443	254,180	1.9
Tulsa, OK	194,312	199,027	2.4	189,673	193,469	2.0
Tuscaloosa, AL	46,912	47,393	1.0	45,459	46,256	1.7
Virginia Beach, VA	222,270	227,788	2.4	216,500	221,941	2.5
Washington, DC	378,144	386,520	2.2	358,132	370,787	3.5
Wichita, KS	190,708	192,293	0.8	184,998	186,223	0.6
Wilmington, NC	65,317	66,641	2.0	63,471	64,589	1.7
Winston-Salem, NC	116,216	117,459	1.0	112,011	113,308	1.1
Worcester, MA	93,362	90,627	-2.9	88,807	87,239	-1.7
U.S.	161,696,000	164,224,000	1.6	155,732,000	158,872,000	2.0

Note: Data is not seasonally adjusted and covers workers 16 years of age and older
Source: Bureau of Labor Statistics, Local Area Unemployment Statistics

A-82   Appendix A: Comparative Statistics

Labor Force, Employment and Job Growth: Metro Area

Metro Area[1]	Civilian Labor Force			Workers Employed		
	Dec. 2021	Dec. 2022	% Chg.	Dec. 2021	Dec. 2022	% Chg.
Albuquerque, NM	445,726	434,352	-2.5	424,396	421,074	-0.7
Allentown, PA	447,351	458,516	2.5	428,287	443,287	3.5
Anchorage, AK	205,827	206,845	0.4	196,305	199,569	1.6
Ann Arbor, MI	192,598	196,315	1.9	187,000	190,417	1.8
Athens, GA	102,226	103,727	1.4	99,578	101,194	1.6
Atlanta, GA	3,175,581	3,216,104	1.2	3,085,734	3,133,430	1.5
Austin, TX	1,339,834	1,372,624	2.4	1,301,083	1,335,791	2.6
Baltimore, MD	1,501,247	1,502,740	0.1	1,434,164	1,455,751	1.5
Boise City, ID	400,832	416,686	3.9	390,861	407,819	4.3
Boston, MA[4]	1,673,210	1,666,434	-0.4	1,614,446	1,622,005	0.4
Boulder, CO	198,590	201,887	1.6	193,073	197,458	2.2
Brownsville, TX	175,175	176,374	0.6	163,657	166,276	1.6
Cape Coral, FL	362,039	377,849	4.3	352,239	366,908	4.1
Cedar Rapids, IA	140,768	142,727	1.3	135,170	137,743	1.9
Charleston, SC	400,171	408,735	2.1	388,529	398,569	2.5
Charlotte, NC	1,377,149	1,414,791	2.7	1,332,923	1,371,461	2.8
Chicago, IL[2]	3,826,621	3,838,545	0.3	3,671,983	3,676,358	0.1
Cincinnati, OH	1,123,242	1,116,215	-0.6	1,088,875	1,082,108	-0.6
Clarksville, TN	120,311	117,511	-2.3	115,795	113,311	-2.1
Cleveland, OH	1,006,515	1,010,141	0.3	963,990	975,650	1.2
College Station, TX	138,941	140,832	1.3	134,636	136,870	1.6
Colorado Springs, CO	364,630	367,853	0.8	350,819	356,889	1.7
Columbia, MO	100,630	100,708	0.0	98,278	98,981	0.7
Columbia, SC	399,511	392,721	-1.7	387,182	381,702	-1.4
Columbus, OH	1,121,138	1,118,600	-0.2	1,088,089	1,084,246	-0.3
Dallas, TX[2]	2,825,024	2,943,498	4.1	2,723,620	2,851,201	4.6
Davenport, IA	185,485	190,708	2.8	177,815	183,615	3.2
Denver, CO	1,691,446	1,735,541	2.6	1,629,015	1,687,640	3.6
Des Moines, IA	362,322	367,598	1.4	350,192	357,259	2.0
Durham, NC	311,304	319,367	2.5	303,354	310,936	2.5
Edison, NJ[2]	6,978,612	7,057,593	1.1	6,599,840	6,759,099	2.4
El Paso, TX	365,233	366,661	0.3	347,953	352,057	1.1
Fargo, ND	143,613	142,810	-0.5	140,498	140,046	-0.3
Fort Collins, CO	208,863	212,087	1.5	202,604	207,057	2.2
Fort Wayne, IN	213,153	220,727	3.5	210,157	215,921	2.7
Fort Worth, TX[2]	1,345,295	1,384,350	2.9	1,295,323	1,340,078	3.4
Grand Rapids, MI	563,869	586,790	4.0	545,813	568,603	4.1
Greeley, CO	167,574	168,716	0.6	161,228	163,640	1.5
Green Bay, WI	173,797	170,959	-1.6	170,171	167,408	-1.6
Greensboro, NC	360,317	364,357	1.1	347,114	351,304	1.2
Honolulu, HI	459,370	457,096	-0.5	440,467	441,407	0.2
Houston, TX	3,460,832	3,565,905	3.0	3,294,015	3,425,418	3.9
Huntsville, AL	239,285	244,014	1.9	234,543	239,596	2.1
Indianapolis, IN	1,076,300	1,110,642	3.1	1,060,871	1,086,712	2.4
Jacksonville, FL	806,862	847,564	5.0	785,663	829,550	5.5
Kansas City, MO	1,138,286	1,149,586	0.9	1,105,453	1,121,442	1.4
Lafayette, LA	211,602	215,089	1.6	204,894	208,467	1.7
Las Cruces, NM	99,600	99,107	-0.5	94,429	95,399	1.0
Las Vegas, NV	1,093,227	1,149,504	5.1	1,039,029	1,087,331	4.6
Lexington, KY	275,622	274,006	-0.5	267,238	266,822	-0.1
Lincoln, NE	188,166	191,439	1.7	185,143	187,374	1.2
Little Rock, AR	350,674	353,640	0.8	341,122	343,843	0.8
Los Angeles, CA[2]	5,001,852	4,965,511	-0.7	4,701,620	4,747,043	0.9
Louisville, KY	672,926	678,057	0.7	650,589	659,926	1.4
Madison, WI	400,355	395,887	-1.1	393,718	389,430	-1.0

Table continued on following page.

Appendix A: Comparative Statistics   A-83

Metro Area[1]	Civilian Labor Force			Workers Employed		
	Dec. 2021	Dec. 2022	% Chg.	Dec. 2021	Dec. 2022	% Chg.
Manchester, NH[3]	118,844	124,173	4.4	116,140	121,300	4.4
Miami, FL[2]	1,345,385	1,397,307	3.8	1,304,718	1,369,536	4.9
Midland, TX	103,649	105,497	1.7	99,519	102,761	3.2
Milwaukee, WI	817,582	799,375	-2.2	796,196	780,437	-1.9
Minneapolis, MN	1,991,752	2,028,489	1.8	1,943,478	1,975,295	1.6
Nashville, TN	1,124,910	1,111,047	-1.2	1,096,732	1,085,200	-1.0
New Haven, CT[3]	327,755	334,058	1.9	315,344	324,400	2.8
New Orleans, LA	582,640	600,820	3.1	558,375	579,744	3.8
New York, NY[2]	6,978,612	7,057,593	1.1	6,599,840	6,759,099	2.4
Oklahoma City, OK	699,178	711,592	1.7	685,472	694,168	1.2
Omaha, NE	502,000	508,654	1.3	490,956	495,693	0.9
Orlando, FL	1,366,646	1,407,116	2.9	1,323,163	1,374,399	3.8
Philadelphia, PA[2]	1,004,235	1,021,788	1.7	946,859	979,293	3.4
Phoenix, AZ	2,518,007	2,590,356	2.8	2,453,226	2,520,303	2.7
Pittsburgh, PA	1,147,805	1,177,164	2.5	1,096,709	1,134,155	3.4
Portland, OR	1,369,607	1,391,563	1.6	1,322,133	1,334,787	0.9
Providence, RI[3]	706,157	698,803	-1.0	679,845	680,282	0.0
Provo, UT	345,721	363,397	5.1	340,264	356,597	4.8
Raleigh, NC	737,649	764,883	3.6	718,092	744,560	3.6
Reno, NV	249,159	261,626	5.0	243,158	252,847	3.9
Richmond, VA	664,206	670,336	0.9	643,038	650,950	1.2
Rochester, MN	126,103	127,371	1.0	123,345	124,243	0.7
Sacramento, CA	1,102,380	1,115,511	1.1	1,055,002	1,078,900	2.2
Salem, OR	210,043	208,341	-0.8	202,733	198,916	-1.8
Salt Lake City, UT	699,196	722,471	3.3	686,309	707,898	3.1
San Antonio, TX	1,217,217	1,244,094	2.2	1,171,224	1,203,295	2.7
San Diego, CA	1,570,184	1,588,968	1.2	1,505,925	1,543,381	2.4
San Francisco, CA[2]	1,003,772	1,035,986	3.2	974,872	1,015,702	4.1
San Jose, CA	1,067,389	1,093,480	2.4	1,036,363	1,070,252	3.2
Santa Rosa, CA	243,938	248,408	1.8	235,525	242,101	2.7
Savannah, GA	199,752	198,853	-0.4	194,065	193,933	0.0
Seattle, WA[2]	1,724,262	1,779,111	3.1	1,675,402	1,725,495	2.9
Sioux Falls, SD	159,168	162,847	2.3	155,392	159,650	2.7
Springfield, IL	103,907	105,050	1.1	99,703	101,310	1.6
St. Louis, MO	1,460,514	1,459,027	-0.1	1,407,703	1,422,207	1.0
Tampa, FL	1,596,468	1,661,495	4.0	1,552,983	1,625,105	4.6
Tucson, AZ	482,383	492,280	2.0	468,330	477,224	1.9
Tulsa, OK	479,679	491,520	2.4	468,777	478,458	2.0
Tuscaloosa, AL	114,876	116,118	1.0	111,656	113,579	1.7
Virginia Beach, VA	821,309	840,432	2.3	795,009	815,342	2.5
Washington, DC[2]	2,676,340	2,681,074	0.1	2,582,644	2,604,564	0.8
Wichita, KS	317,498	320,744	1.0	309,104	311,289	0.7
Wilmington, NC	154,267	157,407	2.0	150,051	152,775	1.8
Winston-Salem, NC	322,524	326,477	1.2	312,552	316,261	1.1
Worcester, MA[3]	358,980	351,150	-2.1	344,046	339,514	-1.3
U.S.	161,696,000	164,224,000	1.6	155,732,000	158,872,000	2.0

Note: Data is not seasonally adjusted and covers workers 16 years of age and older; (1) Figures cover the Metropolitan Statistical Area (MSA) except where noted. See Appendix B for areas included; (2) Metropolitan Division; (3) New England City and Town Area; (4) New England City and Town Area Division
Source: Bureau of Labor Statistics, Local Area Unemployment Statistics

A-84 Appendix A: Comparative Statistics

Unemployment Rate: City

City	2022											
	Jan.	Feb.	Mar.	Apr.	May	Jun.	Jul.	Aug.	Sep.	Oct.	Nov.	Dec.
Albuquerque, NM	4.9	4.3	4.0	3.9	3.7	4.4	4.1	4.0	4.0	3.6	3.2	3.0
Allentown, PA	7.3	6.5	6.1	6.0	5.8	6.2	6.2	6.5	5.0	4.6	4.6	4.1
Anchorage, AK	4.8	4.4	4.0	3.9	3.7	3.8	3.6	2.9	2.9	3.1	3.3	3.1
Ann Arbor, MI	2.7	3.1	2.5	2.5	3.0	3.4	3.3	2.9	2.7	2.7	2.5	2.5
Athens, GA	3.2	3.2	3.2	2.3	2.7	3.5	2.9	3.2	2.5	3.1	2.7	2.6
Atlanta, GA	4.0	3.8	3.9	2.9	3.1	3.7	3.4	3.5	3.1	3.4	3.2	3.0
Austin, TX	3.2	3.2	2.6	2.4	2.6	2.9	2.9	2.9	2.7	2.7	2.6	2.6
Baltimore, MD	6.3	6.1	5.8	4.9	5.1	6.1	5.6	5.9	5.1	5.6	5.0	4.4
Boise City, ID	2.8	2.7	2.5	2.0	2.0	2.4	2.2	2.3	2.3	2.4	2.3	1.8
Boston, MA	4.4	3.5	3.2	3.0	3.2	3.5	3.6	3.5	3.0	2.9	2.7	2.9
Boulder, CO	2.6	2.7	2.3	2.1	2.2	2.8	3.0	2.4	2.3	2.6	2.7	2.0
Brownsville, TX	7.9	7.4	6.1	6.0	6.1	7.1	6.9	6.4	5.9	5.5	5.7	6.1
Cape Coral, FL	3.4	2.9	2.6	2.3	2.4	2.8	2.7	2.6	2.5	4.2	3.6	2.9
Cedar Rapids, IA	4.9	3.9	3.6	2.7	2.9	3.4	3.7	3.8	3.3	3.4	3.7	3.7
Charleston, SC	3.1	3.5	2.9	2.1	2.5	2.8	2.6	2.6	2.4	2.8	2.2	2.4
Charlotte, NC	4.0	3.8	3.7	3.5	3.5	3.9	3.6	3.9	3.3	3.8	3.7	3.2
Chicago, IL	5.8	5.5	5.0	4.7	4.9	5.7	5.8	5.9	5.6	5.2	5.3	4.8
Cincinnati, OH	4.6	4.2	3.8	3.5	3.5	4.6	4.8	4.8	3.9	4.2	3.3	3.5
Clarksville, TN	4.0	3.6	3.4	3.5	3.9	4.8	4.6	4.1	3.6	4.1	3.9	3.5
Cleveland, OH	7.7	8.0	8.2	7.5	7.2	7.7	6.5	6.0	5.9	6.4	5.8	4.6
College Station, TX	3.5	3.4	2.7	2.6	2.8	3.6	3.3	3.3	3.0	3.0	3.2	2.8
Colorado Springs, CO	4.1	4.2	3.6	3.2	3.1	3.4	3.8	3.6	3.5	3.7	3.5	3.0
Columbia, MO	3.0	2.2	2.4	1.7	2.4	1.9	2.4	2.5	1.5	1.9	1.9	1.8
Columbia, SC	3.7	4.3	3.5	2.9	3.9	4.0	3.9	3.7	3.4	4.2	3.3	3.2
Columbus, OH	3.9	3.8	3.4	3.1	3.1	3.9	3.8	4.0	3.4	3.7	2.9	3.2
Dallas, TX	4.5	4.4	3.6	3.4	3.5	4.0	4.0	3.9	3.6	3.6	3.5	3.4
Davenport, IA	5.5	4.4	4.1	3.1	3.2	4.0	4.0	3.9	3.3	3.4	3.8	3.9
Denver, CO	4.3	4.3	3.9	3.4	3.3	3.4	3.6	3.6	3.5	3.7	3.4	2.9
Des Moines, IA	5.7	4.7	4.3	3.0	2.8	3.0	3.2	3.3	2.8	2.9	3.2	3.7
Durham, NC	3.2	3.0	3.0	2.9	3.1	3.5	3.1	3.3	2.7	3.4	3.2	2.7
Edison, NJ	3.3	3.0	2.9	2.5	2.5	2.8	2.7	2.6	2.0	2.1	2.1	2.1
El Paso, TX	5.1	5.0	4.1	4.0	4.2	4.7	4.5	4.4	4.1	4.1	4.1	3.8
Fargo, ND	2.7	2.5	2.7	2.1	1.8	2.2	1.7	1.8	1.4	1.5	1.6	1.9
Fort Collins, CO	3.0	3.2	2.7	2.4	2.4	2.8	2.9	2.7	2.6	2.8	2.8	2.3
Fort Wayne, IN	2.5	2.7	2.8	2.5	2.6	3.3	3.6	3.1	2.3	2.9	2.9	2.4
Fort Worth, TX	4.5	4.4	3.6	3.4	3.6	4.2	4.2	4.0	3.7	3.6	3.5	3.4
Grand Rapids, MI	5.0	5.0	4.3	4.2	4.6	5.2	5.0	4.6	4.3	4.2	4.0	4.1
Greeley, CO	4.9	5.0	4.4	3.7	3.5	3.9	4.5	3.9	3.8	3.9	3.7	3.3
Green Bay, WI	3.1	3.1	3.1	2.9	2.8	3.4	3.2	3.4	3.3	2.9	2.5	2.2
Greensboro, NC	4.6	4.5	4.4	4.3	4.3	4.8	4.6	4.8	4.0	4.5	4.4	3.8
Honolulu, HI	3.7	3.5	3.2	3.3	3.4	3.9	3.5	3.4	3.3	3.4	3.8	3.4
Houston, TX	5.3	5.2	4.3	4.1	4.2	4.7	4.8	4.6	4.2	4.1	4.0	3.8
Huntsville, AL	2.8	2.6	2.1	1.7	2.1	3.0	2.8	2.6	2.3	2.3	2.1	2.0
Indianapolis, IN	2.7	3.0	3.0	2.5	2.8	3.5	3.8	3.4	2.4	2.9	3.0	2.5
Jacksonville, FL	3.6	3.2	2.7	2.5	2.6	3.3	3.2	3.1	2.7	2.8	2.7	2.3
Kansas City, MO	4.3	4.3	4.1	3.1	3.2	2.6	3.4	3.4	2.2	2.7	2.7	2.6
Lafayette, LA	3.6	3.1	3.1	2.9	3.1	3.9	3.8	3.2	3.0	2.7	2.6	2.9
Las Cruces, NM	4.8	3.9	3.6	3.5	3.4	4.9	4.7	4.6	4.5	3.8	3.4	3.1
Las Vegas, NV	5.9	5.4	5.2	5.2	5.4	5.8	5.7	5.8	5.4	5.8	5.7	5.5
Lexington, KY	3.3	3.0	3.1	2.8	2.9	3.5	3.3	3.0	2.8	3.3	3.1	2.6
Lincoln, NE	2.3	2.1	2.2	1.8	1.9	2.4	2.3	2.1	1.9	2.1	2.1	2.2
Little Rock, AR	4.3	4.2	3.7	3.8	3.6	4.1	4.6	3.9	3.9	3.3	3.2	3.0
Los Angeles, CA	6.3	5.5	5.0	4.9	4.6	5.3	5.2	5.1	4.6	4.6	4.6	4.5
Louisville, KY	4.7	3.9	4.7	3.1	4.1	3.8	4.1	3.4	3.0	3.5	3.3	2.9
Madison, WI	1.9	2.0	2.0	1.9	2.2	2.8	2.5	2.4	2.6	2.2	2.0	1.5

Table continued on following page.

Appendix A: Comparative Statistics A-85

City	2022											
	Jan.	Feb.	Mar.	Apr.	May	Jun.	Jul.	Aug.	Sep.	Oct.	Nov.	Dec.
Manchester, NH	3.6	2.6	2.5	2.3	1.9	2.0	2.0	2.4	2.4	2.7	2.7	2.6
Miami, FL	3.0	2.6	2.8	2.4	2.2	2.0	2.2	2.2	1.9	1.7	1.5	1.4
Midland, TX	4.3	4.3	3.4	3.2	3.2	3.6	3.5	3.3	3.0	3.0	2.8	2.6
Milwaukee, WI	4.8	5.1	5.0	5.0	4.9	5.4	5.5	5.5	4.8	4.6	4.1	3.2
Minneapolis, MN	3.0	2.2	2.4	1.5	1.7	2.4	2.2	2.3	2.0	1.9	2.0	2.4
Nashville, TN	3.3	2.9	2.7	2.7	2.9	3.5	3.2	2.9	2.5	2.8	2.7	2.4
New Haven, CT	5.5	5.4	4.4	4.1	4.8	5.0	5.6	5.4	4.7	4.7	4.0	3.3
New Orleans, LA	6.5	6.0	5.9	5.5	5.5	6.5	6.6	5.5	4.8	4.1	4.0	4.4
New York, NY	7.8	7.2	6.3	5.7	5.4	5.5	5.4	5.2	4.5	5.0	5.0	5.0
Oklahoma City, OK	2.9	3.0	2.9	2.7	2.8	3.4	3.0	3.3	3.2	3.4	2.9	2.6
Omaha, NE	2.9	2.8	2.7	2.3	2.3	2.9	3.1	2.7	2.4	2.6	2.5	2.7
Orlando, FL	3.9	3.6	3.1	2.9	2.9	3.3	3.1	3.1	2.7	2.8	2.7	2.4
Philadelphia, PA	7.7	6.8	6.3	6.0	5.7	6.2	6.2	6.4	4.9	4.7	4.8	4.5
Phoenix, AZ	3.4	3.3	2.5	2.8	3.0	3.4	3.4	3.5	3.6	3.5	3.0	2.7
Pittsburgh, PA	4.9	4.1	4.0	3.8	3.9	4.3	4.4	4.4	3.2	3.1	3.0	3.0
Portland, OR	4.5	3.9	3.9	3.4	3.0	3.5	3.7	4.1	3.8	3.8	4.1	4.2
Providence, RI	5.5	5.3	3.7	3.3	3.5	3.5	4.0	5.0	4.3	4.1	4.3	2.9
Provo, UT	1.8	1.5	1.6	1.7	2.0	2.4	1.8	1.8	1.6	1.8	1.8	1.7
Raleigh, NC	3.3	3.3	3.2	3.1	3.3	3.6	3.4	3.5	3.0	3.5	3.4	2.8
Reno, NV	3.1	2.8	2.5	2.7	2.9	3.3	3.2	3.5	3.1	3.6	3.5	3.4
Richmond, VA	4.6	4.1	3.7	3.5	3.9	3.8	3.7	4.1	3.4	3.5	3.9	3.4
Rochester, MN	2.6	2.0	2.1	1.2	1.3	1.9	1.7	1.8	1.6	1.5	1.6	2.1
Sacramento, CA	5.7	4.9	4.3	3.7	3.3	3.8	3.8	4.1	3.8	3.9	4.2	3.7
Salem, OR	4.4	4.0	4.0	3.7	3.1	3.8	4.2	4.5	4.1	4.2	4.3	4.5
Salt Lake City, UT	2.4	2.1	2.0	2.1	2.1	2.3	2.1	2.1	1.9	2.1	2.0	2.0
San Antonio, TX	4.3	4.2	3.5	3.3	3.5	4.0	3.9	3.8	3.5	3.5	3.4	3.2
San Diego, CA	4.5	3.9	3.3	2.9	2.6	3.0	2.9	3.2	2.9	3.0	3.2	2.7
San Francisco, CA	3.5	3.0	2.5	2.2	1.9	2.2	2.1	2.3	2.1	2.2	2.3	2.0
San Jose, CA	3.5	3.1	2.6	2.3	2.0	2.4	2.3	2.5	2.2	2.3	2.5	2.1
Santa Rosa, CA	4.3	3.8	3.3	2.7	2.4	2.8	2.7	2.9	2.7	2.8	3.1	2.7
Savannah, GA	4.2	4.0	4.1	3.1	3.2	3.8	3.3	3.5	3.0	3.4	3.1	2.9
Seattle, WA	3.0	2.5	2.1	1.6	1.9	2.4	2.6	2.8	2.6	2.6	2.7	2.6
Sioux Falls, SD	2.6	2.8	2.4	2.0	1.9	2.1	1.7	2.0	1.6	1.9	1.8	2.1
Springfield, IL	5.3	5.0	4.6	4.9	5.2	4.6	4.8	4.9	4.3	4.5	4.3	3.7
St. Louis, MO	5.4	5.0	4.9	3.6	3.8	3.3	4.1	4.1	2.5	3.0	3.2	3.1
Tampa, FL	3.5	3.0	2.6	2.3	2.4	2.9	2.8	2.8	2.6	2.7	2.6	2.2
Tucson, AZ	4.0	3.9	3.1	3.4	3.6	4.2	4.2	4.3	4.3	4.2	3.6	3.2
Tulsa, OK	3.2	3.3	3.2	3.0	3.1	3.7	3.4	3.7	3.6	3.7	3.2	2.8
Tuscaloosa, AL	3.6	3.4	2.6	2.4	2.9	4.1	4.0	3.4	2.9	3.1	2.7	2.4
Virginia Beach, VA	3.2	2.7	2.6	2.4	2.9	2.9	2.8	3.0	2.5	2.7	2.9	2.6
Washington, DC	6.3	5.6	5.1	4.2	4.3	4.9	4.7	4.6	4.1	4.3	4.1	4.1
Wichita, KS	3.7	3.6	3.6	2.8	3.2	3.5	4.1	3.8	3.1	3.2	3.1	3.2
Wilmington, NC	3.4	3.4	3.2	3.3	3.5	3.9	3.5	3.7	3.1	3.6	3.6	3.1
Winston-Salem, NC	4.1	4.0	3.9	3.8	4.0	4.5	4.3	4.4	3.8	4.3	4.1	3.5
Worcester, MA	5.5	4.6	4.1	3.9	4.2	4.6	4.6	4.6	4.0	3.7	3.5	3.7
U.S.	4.4	4.1	3.8	3.3	3.4	3.8	3.8	3.8	3.3	3.4	3.4	3.3

Note: Data is not seasonally adjusted and covers workers 16 years of age and older; All figures are percentages
Source: Bureau of Labor Statistics, Local Area Unemployment Statistics

A-86 Appendix A: Comparative Statistics

Unemployment Rate: Metro Area

Metro Area[1]	2022											
	Jan.	Feb.	Mar.	Apr.	May	Jun.	Jul.	Aug.	Sep.	Oct.	Nov.	Dec.
Albuquerque, NM	5.1	4.4	4.1	4.0	3.8	4.6	4.3	4.1	4.2	3.7	3.3	3.1
Allentown, PA	5.5	4.8	4.5	4.1	3.9	4.4	4.5	4.5	3.3	3.2	3.3	3.3
Anchorage, AK	5.3	4.9	4.5	4.3	4.0	4.2	3.9	3.2	3.2	3.3	3.6	3.5
Ann Arbor, MI	3.3	3.7	3.1	3.0	3.6	4.1	4.0	3.5	3.3	3.3	3.1	3.0
Athens, GA	2.9	2.9	2.9	2.1	2.5	3.1	2.6	2.9	2.3	2.9	2.5	2.4
Atlanta, GA	3.3	3.2	3.2	2.4	2.6	3.2	2.8	3.0	2.5	2.9	2.7	2.6
Austin, TX	3.3	3.3	2.7	2.5	2.7	3.1	3.1	3.0	2.8	2.8	2.8	2.7
Baltimore, MD	4.2	4.3	4.2	3.3	3.6	4.6	4.1	4.3	3.7	4.0	3.5	3.1
Boise City, ID	3.1	3.0	2.8	2.4	2.2	2.7	2.6	2.7	2.5	2.6	2.5	2.1
Boston, MA[4]	4.2	3.4	3.1	2.8	2.9	3.1	3.0	3.0	2.7	2.7	2.5	2.7
Boulder, CO	3.1	3.2	2.8	2.4	2.4	2.8	2.9	2.6	2.5	2.8	2.6	2.2
Brownsville, TX	7.6	7.3	6.1	5.9	6.0	6.9	6.8	6.4	5.8	5.6	5.7	5.7
Cape Coral, FL	3.4	2.9	2.5	2.2	2.4	2.9	2.8	2.7	2.6	4.0	3.6	2.9
Cedar Rapids, IA	4.9	4.0	3.7	2.6	2.6	3.0	3.2	3.4	2.9	3.0	3.3	3.5
Charleston, SC	3.2	3.6	2.9	2.3	2.8	3.0	2.7	2.8	2.7	3.1	2.2	2.5
Charlotte, NC	3.7	3.7	3.5	3.2	3.4	3.8	3.4	3.6	3.1	3.7	3.5	3.1
Chicago, IL[2]	5.2	5.0	4.4	4.3	4.5	5.3	5.1	5.2	4.6	4.5	4.4	4.2
Cincinnati, OH	3.9	3.8	3.5	3.0	3.0	3.9	3.9	3.8	3.3	3.6	3.0	3.1
Clarksville, TN	4.1	3.7	3.6	3.6	4.0	4.7	4.5	4.1	3.6	4.0	3.9	3.6
Cleveland, OH	5.6	6.0	5.6	4.8	4.9	5.3	4.9	4.5	4.1	3.9	3.6	3.4
College Station, TX	3.7	3.5	2.9	2.7	2.9	3.6	3.5	3.5	3.1	3.1	3.1	2.8
Colorado Springs, CO	4.1	4.2	3.8	3.3	3.3	3.5	3.9	3.6	3.5	3.8	3.6	3.0
Columbia, MO	3.0	2.3	2.6	1.7	2.3	1.8	2.3	2.4	1.4	1.9	1.8	1.7
Columbia, SC	3.5	3.8	3.1	2.5	3.0	3.3	3.1	3.1	2.9	3.4	2.6	2.8
Columbus, OH	3.8	3.7	3.3	2.9	2.9	3.8	3.7	3.8	3.3	3.5	2.7	3.1
Dallas, TX[2]	4.1	4.0	3.3	3.1	3.3	3.8	3.7	3.6	3.4	3.3	3.2	3.1
Davenport, IA	5.3	4.6	4.4	3.7	3.8	3.7	3.8	3.8	3.4	3.5	3.7	3.7
Denver, CO	4.0	4.0	3.6	3.2	3.1	3.3	3.5	3.3	3.2	3.5	3.3	2.8
Des Moines, IA	4.2	3.4	3.2	2.1	2.2	2.5	2.6	2.7	2.3	2.5	2.8	2.8
Durham, NC	3.0	2.9	2.8	2.8	3.0	3.4	3.1	3.2	2.7	3.3	3.2	2.6
Edison, NJ[2]	6.1	5.6	5.1	4.7	4.6	4.9	5.3	5.4	4.1	4.1	4.2	4.2
El Paso, TX	5.4	5.3	4.3	4.2	4.3	4.9	4.8	4.6	4.4	4.3	4.2	4.0
Fargo, ND	2.8	2.4	2.7	1.9	1.6	2.1	1.7	1.7	1.4	1.4	1.5	1.9
Fort Collins, CO	3.4	3.5	3.1	2.7	2.6	2.9	3.0	2.8	2.7	2.9	2.8	2.4
Fort Wayne, IN	2.2	2.4	2.6	2.2	2.3	3.0	3.2	2.8	2.0	2.7	2.6	2.2
Fort Worth, TX[2]	4.2	4.2	3.4	3.2	3.4	3.9	3.9	3.8	3.5	3.4	3.4	3.2
Grand Rapids, MI	3.7	3.8	3.3	3.1	3.4	3.9	3.8	3.4	3.2	3.1	3.0	3.1
Greeley, CO	4.2	4.3	3.9	3.4	3.3	3.6	3.8	3.6	3.4	3.7	3.5	3.0
Green Bay, WI	2.8	3.0	3.0	2.7	2.6	3.2	3.0	3.0	2.9	2.6	2.4	2.1
Greensboro, NC	4.2	4.1	4.0	3.8	4.0	4.5	4.2	4.4	3.7	4.3	4.1	3.6
Honolulu, HI	3.7	3.5	3.2	3.3	3.4	3.9	3.5	3.4	3.3	3.4	3.8	3.4
Houston, TX	5.5	5.3	4.4	4.1	4.3	4.8	4.8	4.6	4.2	4.1	4.0	3.9
Huntsville, AL	2.6	2.4	1.9	1.6	1.9	2.7	2.6	2.3	2.1	2.2	2.0	1.8
Indianapolis, IN	2.2	2.5	2.5	2.0	2.4	3.0	3.3	2.8	2.1	2.6	2.6	2.2
Jacksonville, FL	3.2	2.9	2.5	2.2	2.3	2.9	2.8	2.8	2.5	2.5	2.5	2.1
Kansas City, MO	3.4	3.7	3.3	2.4	2.7	2.6	3.2	3.1	2.2	2.6	2.5	2.4
Lafayette, LA	3.8	3.4	3.4	3.1	3.2	4.1	4.0	3.3	3.2	2.8	2.7	3.1
Las Cruces, NM	5.7	5.1	4.8	4.8	4.4	5.3	5.0	4.6	4.8	4.2	4.0	3.7
Las Vegas, NV	5.8	5.3	5.0	5.0	5.2	5.7	5.6	5.7	5.3	5.6	5.6	5.4
Lexington, KY	3.4	3.1	3.1	2.8	2.9	3.5	3.3	3.0	2.8	3.3	3.1	2.6
Lincoln, NE	2.3	2.1	2.1	1.8	1.9	2.4	2.3	2.1	1.9	2.0	2.1	2.1
Little Rock, AR	3.8	3.8	3.3	3.2	3.2	3.7	4.0	3.5	3.5	2.8	2.9	2.8
Los Angeles, CA[2]	6.5	5.8	5.2	4.8	4.5	4.9	4.9	4.7	4.3	4.5	4.5	4.4
Louisville, KY	4.1	3.5	4.3	2.8	3.7	3.5	3.8	3.1	2.7	3.3	3.1	2.7
Madison, WI	2.3	2.5	2.4	2.1	2.2	2.8	2.5	2.5	2.6	2.2	2.0	1.6

Table continued on following page.

Appendix A: Comparative Statistics   A-87

Metro Area[1]	2022											
	Jan.	Feb.	Mar.	Apr.	May	Jun.	Jul.	Aug.	Sep.	Oct.	Nov.	Dec.
Manchester, NH[3]	3.3	2.3	2.3	2.1	1.8	1.9	1.9	2.2	2.3	2.5	2.4	2.3
Miami, FL[2]	3.2	2.9	3.0	2.6	2.5	2.6	2.8	2.9	2.6	2.4	2.1	2.0
Midland, TX	4.4	4.3	3.5	3.2	3.3	3.6	3.5	3.3	3.0	2.9	2.8	2.6
Milwaukee, WI	3.4	3.7	3.6	3.5	3.4	4.0	4.0	3.9	3.6	3.3	3.0	2.4
Minneapolis, MN	3.0	2.4	2.6	1.5	1.6	2.2	2.0	2.2	1.9	1.7	1.9	2.6
Nashville, TN	2.9	2.7	2.4	2.5	2.8	3.4	3.1	2.7	2.4	2.7	2.6	2.3
New Haven, CT[3]	4.6	4.6	3.9	3.5	3.8	3.9	4.2	4.1	3.7	3.7	3.3	2.9
New Orleans, LA	4.9	4.5	4.4	4.1	4.1	5.1	5.0	4.1	3.8	3.3	3.1	3.5
New York, NY[2]	6.1	5.6	5.1	4.7	4.6	4.9	5.3	5.4	4.1	4.1	4.2	4.2
Oklahoma City, OK	2.8	2.9	2.7	2.6	2.7	3.2	2.9	3.1	3.1	3.3	2.8	2.4
Omaha, NE	2.9	2.7	2.6	2.1	2.1	2.7	2.7	2.5	2.2	2.4	2.4	2.5
Orlando, FL	3.8	3.4	2.9	2.6	2.7	3.2	3.0	2.9	2.7	2.8	2.7	2.3
Philadelphia, PA[2]	7.0	6.2	5.7	5.5	5.2	5.7	5.7	5.9	4.5	4.3	4.4	4.2
Phoenix, AZ	3.2	3.1	2.4	2.7	2.9	3.4	3.3	3.4	3.5	3.5	3.0	2.7
Pittsburgh, PA	5.8	5.1	4.6	4.2	4.0	4.6	4.7	4.8	3.4	3.3	3.5	3.7
Portland, OR	4.4	3.9	3.9	3.4	3.1	3.5	3.6	4.0	3.7	3.7	3.9	4.1
Providence, RI[3]	4.9	4.7	3.4	3.0	2.9	3.0	3.3	4.0	3.4	3.3	3.4	2.7
Provo, UT	2.0	1.8	1.8	1.8	2.0	2.3	1.8	1.9	1.7	1.9	1.9	1.9
Raleigh, NC	3.1	3.0	2.9	2.9	3.1	3.4	3.1	3.3	2.8	3.3	3.2	2.7
Reno, NV	3.2	2.8	2.6	2.7	2.9	3.3	3.2	3.5	3.1	3.5	3.5	3.4
Richmond, VA	3.7	3.2	2.9	2.8	3.2	3.2	3.1	3.4	2.8	3.0	3.2	2.9
Rochester, MN	3.0	2.3	2.4	1.3	1.3	1.9	1.7	1.8	1.5	1.4	1.6	2.5
Sacramento, CA	5.0	4.4	3.7	3.3	2.9	3.4	3.3	3.6	3.3	3.4	3.7	3.3
Salem, OR	4.5	3.9	3.9	3.6	3.1	3.7	4.0	4.4	4.0	4.2	4.3	4.5
Salt Lake City, UT	2.4	2.2	2.1	2.1	2.2	2.4	2.1	2.1	1.9	2.1	2.0	2.0
San Antonio, TX	4.3	4.2	3.5	3.3	3.5	4.0	4.0	3.8	3.5	3.5	3.4	3.3
San Diego, CA	4.7	4.0	3.4	3.0	2.7	3.2	3.1	3.4	3.1	3.2	3.3	2.9
San Francisco, CA[2]	3.3	2.9	2.4	2.1	1.8	2.1	2.1	2.3	2.1	2.1	2.3	2.0
San Jose, CA	3.4	3.0	2.5	2.2	1.9	2.3	2.2	2.4	2.2	2.2	2.4	2.1
Santa Rosa, CA	4.0	3.5	3.0	2.6	2.3	2.7	2.6	2.8	2.6	2.6	2.9	2.5
Savannah, GA	3.3	3.2	3.2	2.4	2.6	3.1	2.7	2.9	2.5	2.9	2.6	2.5
Seattle, WA[2]	3.3	2.8	2.6	2.3	2.6	3.0	3.3	3.3	3.3	3.4	2.9	3.0
Sioux Falls, SD	2.5	2.7	2.3	1.9	1.9	2.1	1.7	2.0	1.5	1.8	1.7	2.0
Springfield, IL	5.1	4.8	4.5	4.6	4.7	4.2	4.3	4.3	3.8	3.9	3.9	3.6
St. Louis, MO	4.3	3.7	3.7	2.9	3.2	2.8	3.2	3.3	2.3	2.7	2.7	2.5
Tampa, FL	3.3	2.9	2.5	2.3	2.4	2.9	2.7	2.7	2.5	2.6	2.6	2.2
Tucson, AZ	3.6	3.6	2.8	3.1	3.3	3.9	3.9	4.0	4.1	4.0	3.4	3.1
Tulsa, OK	3.1	3.3	3.1	2.9	3.0	3.6	3.3	3.4	3.4	3.5	3.0	2.7
Tuscaloosa, AL	3.5	3.2	2.5	2.1	2.5	3.6	3.4	3.0	2.6	2.7	2.4	2.2
Virginia Beach, VA	3.9	3.4	3.1	3.0	3.4	3.4	3.3	3.6	3.0	3.2	3.4	3.0
Washington, DC[2]	4.0	3.6	3.5	3.0	3.3	3.6	3.4	3.6	3.0	3.2	3.1	2.9
Wichita, KS	3.4	3.3	3.3	2.6	3.0	3.2	3.8	3.5	2.9	3.0	2.9	2.9
Wilmington, NC	3.3	3.2	3.1	3.0	3.3	3.7	3.3	3.5	3.0	3.6	3.4	2.9
Winston-Salem, NC	3.6	3.5	3.4	3.3	3.6	4.0	3.6	3.8	3.3	3.8	3.7	3.1
Worcester, MA[3]	5.0	4.4	3.9	3.4	3.5	3.7	3.7	3.8	3.3	3.2	3.0	3.3
U.S.	4.4	4.1	3.8	3.3	3.4	3.8	3.8	3.8	3.3	3.4	3.4	3.3

Note: Data is not seasonally adjusted and covers workers 16 years of age and older; All figures are percentages; (1) Figures cover the Metropolitan Statistical Area (MSA) except where noted. See Appendix B for areas included; (2) Metropolitan Division; (3) New England City and Town Area; (4) New England City and Town Area Division
Source: Bureau of Labor Statistics, Local Area Unemployment Statistics

A-88 Appendix A: Comparative Statistics

Average Hourly Wages: Occupations A – C

Metro Area[1]	Accountants/ Auditors	Automotive Mechanics	Book-keepers	Carpenters	Cashiers	Computer Program-mers	Computer Systems Analysts
Albuquerque, NM	35.62	21.48	20.91	23.25	13.53	39.45	44.30
Allentown, PA	38.74	23.90	21.73	26.50	12.78	48.46	45.52
Anchorage, AK	38.08	28.88	25.34	35.06	16.27	47.28	47.93
Ann Arbor, MI	41.17	24.91	22.53	27.04	13.30	46.31	50.46
Athens, GA	35.00	22.03	20.51	23.47	11.77	29.81	35.56
Atlanta, GA	42.89	23.34	23.13	24.77	12.29	47.05	50.28
Austin, TX	41.33	25.45	22.37	24.23	13.85	46.80	48.67
Baltimore, MD	42.20	24.80	24.11	26.91	14.41	50.01	51.61
Boise City, ID	34.92	22.86	21.24	21.41	13.64	37.89	44.85
Boston, MA[2]	46.85	25.85	27.28	34.31	16.21	55.26	57.55
Boulder, CO	46.88	27.50	24.94	27.55	16.30	71.67	61.71
Brownsville, TX	31.30	20.87	17.66	18.88	11.54	n/a	40.71
Cape Coral, FL	37.19	23.44	21.35	21.78	12.98	43.01	46.18
Cedar Rapids, IA	36.04	23.48	22.67	24.39	13.19	42.82	43.29
Charleston, SC	38.80	22.64	20.63	23.50	12.44	n/a	51.58
Charlotte, NC	45.21	24.42	22.12	22.36	12.80	54.86	52.23
Chicago, IL	42.15	25.15	25.13	35.45	14.91	43.54	49.11
Cincinnati, OH	38.18	21.73	22.50	26.23	12.78	44.15	50.79
Clarksville, TN	32.20	21.35	19.54	21.38	11.96	n/a	39.23
Cleveland, OH	39.26	22.70	22.17	27.47	12.94	40.92	48.16
College Station, TX	36.77	21.75	19.34	20.12	12.47	36.69	39.40
Colorado Springs, CO	36.34	25.04	21.56	25.51	14.94	56.28	53.00
Columbia, MO	32.30	21.77	20.39	25.95	12.91	37.12	38.74
Columbia, SC	31.51	22.42	19.63	22.23	11.56	46.56	41.41
Columbus, OH	38.54	23.63	22.84	26.80	12.98	44.12	48.82
Dallas, TX	43.06	24.09	22.81	23.70	13.14	46.27	54.07
Davenport, IA	34.44	23.03	21.58	25.54	13.39	41.58	42.03
Denver, CO	43.21	26.75	24.91	26.47	16.03	59.06	58.10
Des Moines, IA	36.71	23.68	23.50	25.01	13.40	44.45	45.98
Durham, NC	42.03	24.33	23.51	22.09	12.86	51.67	48.44
Edison, NJ	54.94	26.81	26.44	37.06	16.55	57.97	60.54
El Paso, TX	33.19	19.58	18.00	18.84	11.04	32.89	38.82
Fargo, ND	33.62	23.74	21.80	24.78	14.30	43.53	46.07
Fort Collins, CO	40.07	25.91	23.02	25.81	15.48	47.61	50.60
Fort Wayne, IN	35.91	21.07	20.51	24.46	12.43	41.88	40.51
Fort Worth, TX	43.06	24.09	22.81	23.70	13.14	46.27	54.07
Grand Rapids, MI	36.05	23.88	21.43	25.03	13.24	43.23	45.05
Greeley, CO	40.39	26.16	22.81	25.71	14.89	42.19	47.48
Green Bay, WI	35.84	24.15	21.27	27.33	13.29	48.63	44.13
Greensboro, NC	39.53	23.26	20.74	21.12	11.95	47.79	44.56
Honolulu, HI	35.01	25.53	23.01	40.03	15.19	40.35	44.09
Houston, TX	45.35	24.26	22.16	23.53	12.84	44.09	53.59
Huntsville, AL	38.65	23.32	19.18	21.60	12.06	48.90	59.97
Indianapolis, IN	38.48	24.17	21.02	26.70	12.72	55.30	46.41
Jacksonville, FL	37.78	21.66	22.39	21.96	12.81	45.61	47.46
Kansas City, MO	37.26	22.90	22.32	28.49	13.42	32.32	43.98
Lafayette, LA	33.20	21.50	19.60	21.95	10.71	46.32	40.06
Las Cruces, NM	31.08	19.52	19.12	19.82	12.79	32.88	40.51
Las Vegas, NV	32.32	23.93	22.52	31.29	12.95	46.77	45.39
Lexington, KY	34.78	19.88	21.74	24.79	12.65	41.29	41.63
Lincoln, NE	33.19	25.66	21.09	22.21	12.89	42.91	38.01
Little Rock, AR	34.54	21.76	20.43	20.73	12.61	39.86	36.35
Los Angeles, CA	44.41	27.03	25.38	32.48	16.40	52.39	56.78
Louisville, KY	37.30	20.62	21.86	24.50	12.91	39.53	43.77
Madison, WI	37.27	24.24	22.60	27.63	14.13	56.02	44.74

Table continued on following page.

Appendix A: Comparative Statistics A-89

Metro Area[1]	Accountants/ Auditors	Automotive Mechanics	Book-keepers	Carpenters	Cashiers	Computer Programmers	Computer Systems Analysts
Manchester, NH[2]	38.41	25.34	23.03	25.30	13.47	37.37	55.74
Miami, FL	40.21	23.98	22.09	23.23	13.04	57.52	49.49
Midland, TX	45.27	22.73	23.16	24.74	13.53	46.24	60.82
Milwaukee, WI	38.84	25.28	22.52	27.42	13.47	48.26	47.82
Minneapolis, MN	41.61	26.35	24.93	31.05	14.83	56.92	51.73
Nashville, TN	37.26	23.62	22.19	23.17	13.16	55.27	45.76
New Haven, CT[2]	40.18	25.11	25.93	29.63	14.82	46.28	50.48
New Orleans, LA	35.71	22.89	21.05	23.83	11.45	n/a	42.24
New York, NY	54.94	26.81	26.44	37.06	16.55	57.97	60.54
Oklahoma City, OK	37.21	22.78	20.87	21.48	12.66	43.42	43.52
Omaha, NE	36.79	24.01	22.22	22.88	13.40	45.89	44.58
Orlando, FL	39.04	22.82	21.76	22.25	13.41	44.68	49.23
Philadelphia, PA	41.83	25.23	23.94	30.34	13.39	48.86	51.32
Phoenix, AZ	40.79	24.61	23.11	24.95	14.93	42.27	50.03
Pittsburgh, PA	36.77	22.54	21.77	27.30	12.18	44.53	44.54
Portland, OR	40.08	26.62	24.24	30.98	16.34	54.65	56.22
Providence, RI[2]	44.90	22.35	24.22	29.76	14.61	43.32	51.67
Provo, UT	36.53	24.47	21.59	22.45	13.70	50.42	42.69
Raleigh, NC	40.68	23.79	21.92	22.09	12.55	51.36	48.99
Reno, NV	36.36	26.22	23.68	30.24	13.43	47.35	51.99
Richmond, VA	39.80	24.06	22.01	22.95	13.04	46.05	49.01
Rochester, MN	39.00	23.13	22.86	28.86	14.39	43.06	50.23
Sacramento, CA	41.27	28.35	25.70	32.41	16.67	54.48	52.53
Salem, OR	37.81	26.17	23.29	27.37	15.07	43.99	48.05
Salt Lake City, UT	38.26	24.06	23.32	24.89	13.79	48.36	47.68
San Antonio, TX	40.79	22.70	21.14	21.56	13.19	42.04	48.72
San Diego, CA	43.86	27.06	25.51	32.52	16.54	61.76	55.08
San Francisco, CA	54.83	31.95	30.30	38.33	18.96	64.89	70.44
San Jose, CA	55.92	37.42	29.94	37.76	19.15	70.63	79.75
Santa Rosa, CA	44.48	28.50	27.43	37.66	17.71	51.79	53.46
Savannah, GA	37.20	21.80	21.94	22.17	12.01	40.03	51.98
Seattle, WA	45.25	28.69	26.09	35.16	17.95	64.30	62.53
Sioux Falls, SD	36.65	24.92	19.54	20.96	13.46	31.23	41.70
Springfield, IL	37.41	23.85	22.33	28.27	13.91	43.32	48.50
St. Louis, MO	37.46	23.04	23.29	29.99	13.92	39.08	49.69
Tampa, FL	39.60	22.77	21.91	22.26	12.70	42.78	47.41
Tucson, AZ	34.99	23.11	21.61	21.37	14.27	39.03	51.23
Tulsa, OK	39.68	22.38	20.66	21.83	12.73	44.62	44.82
Tuscaloosa, AL	35.59	21.58	19.16	21.27	11.34	40.66	45.86
Virginia Beach, VA	36.48	23.14	20.67	23.04	12.50	45.16	49.26
Washington, DC	48.98	27.98	26.17	28.25	15.21	59.90	58.64
Wichita, KS	36.01	21.40	19.47	23.61	12.22	33.61	40.07
Wilmington, NC	37.58	21.31	19.94	21.32	11.98	51.25	42.16
Winston-Salem, NC	38.18	21.78	20.62	20.32	11.93	48.29	46.37
Worcester, MA[2]	42.78	26.08	24.24	29.55	15.32	49.03	50.87

Notes: (1) Figures cover the Metropolitan Statistical Area (MSA) except where noted. See Appendix B for areas included; (2) New England City and Town Area; n/a not available
Source: Bureau of Labor Statistics, May 2022 Metro Area Occupational Employment and Wage Estimates

A-90   Appendix A: Comparative Statistics

Average Hourly Wages: Occupations C – E

Metro Area	Comp. User Support Specialists	Construction Laborers	Cooks, Restaurant	Customer Service Reps.	Dentists	Electricians	Engineers, Electrical
Albuquerque, NM	25.04	17.98	15.25	17.46	92.90	27.76	63.45
Allentown, PA	29.17	23.73	15.53	19.08	76.30	35.65	52.01
Anchorage, AK	31.03	26.21	18.32	20.61	86.58	38.38	51.77
Ann Arbor, MI	26.14	23.76	16.10	19.39	76.15	34.45	48.28
Athens, GA	23.39	17.59	14.12	16.00	83.95	25.40	51.99
Atlanta, GA	30.05	19.06	14.12	19.35	n/a	27.76	56.29
Austin, TX	28.69	19.04	15.59	19.39	85.63	27.12	62.22
Baltimore, MD	28.42	20.10	16.72	20.48	78.23	31.44	56.06
Boise City, ID	26.11	19.73	15.37	18.74	71.88	26.06	55.65
Boston, MA[2]	35.38	31.95	19.78	24.00	89.08	39.81	61.23
Boulder, CO	37.04	20.81	18.99	21.92	77.69	28.91	61.37
Brownsville, TX	21.36	14.98	12.36	16.29	n/a	21.42	44.90
Cape Coral, FL	27.26	18.06	16.07	18.46	77.81	23.54	48.44
Cedar Rapids, IA	27.05	22.70	14.19	20.25	95.40	28.53	47.69
Charleston, SC	26.98	18.51	15.93	18.41	87.52	25.86	46.55
Charlotte, NC	30.39	18.19	15.26	19.72	98.68	25.03	49.35
Chicago, IL	29.52	32.85	17.06	21.26	67.54	42.79	50.03
Cincinnati, OH	25.81	24.39	15.01	19.74	86.77	28.47	48.44
Clarksville, TN	22.21	17.54	13.67	17.08	n/a	25.15	45.92
Cleveland, OH	26.60	26.17	15.16	20.42	78.04	29.88	46.94
College Station, TX	22.57	17.19	13.51	16.40	n/a	25.15	44.21
Colorado Springs, CO	31.65	20.22	17.67	19.52	88.61	27.65	54.86
Columbia, MO	26.05	25.63	14.43	17.49	80.29	27.19	40.87
Columbia, SC	26.44	18.07	14.25	17.29	76.98	25.73	41.58
Columbus, OH	26.03	26.04	15.34	20.25	69.07	29.48	53.22
Dallas, TX	28.45	18.68	15.57	19.64	76.46	26.46	50.66
Davenport, IA	27.11	23.89	14.54	19.17	75.24	30.25	46.40
Denver, CO	33.31	20.88	18.61	21.35	73.17	29.06	53.05
Des Moines, IA	27.24	22.43	14.73	21.45	80.98	30.12	48.91
Durham, NC	31.57	18.55	15.87	19.93	106.19	27.22	56.69
Edison, NJ	35.55	30.93	19.55	23.75	89.01	41.22	53.37
El Paso, TX	20.96	15.44	12.46	15.69	78.62	21.95	40.61
Fargo, ND	27.94	22.00	15.80	19.82	80.70	29.07	47.71
Fort Collins, CO	30.99	20.70	17.57	19.06	n/a	28.15	54.42
Fort Wayne, IN	25.05	22.43	14.31	19.63	81.34	29.66	48.26
Fort Worth, TX	28.45	18.68	15.57	19.64	76.46	26.46	50.66
Grand Rapids, MI	27.43	21.17	15.94	19.17	88.95	27.51	43.36
Greeley, CO	33.01	20.70	17.40	18.44	65.47	27.92	50.58
Green Bay, WI	29.31	22.68	15.04	20.32	81.73	30.20	43.80
Greensboro, NC	25.86	17.39	14.20	18.33	85.11	24.46	46.74
Honolulu, HI	29.83	32.93	19.44	20.16	n/a	43.15	50.24
Houston, TX	27.70	18.56	14.67	18.59	74.27	27.69	55.91
Huntsville, AL	24.38	16.49	14.48	17.51	87.97	25.26	53.71
Indianapolis, IN	25.93	23.51	14.76	20.25	98.07	31.79	46.72
Jacksonville, FL	27.33	18.20	15.75	19.12	82.64	24.62	48.04
Kansas City, MO	28.08	22.55	15.09	19.33	85.61	32.19	49.54
Lafayette, LA	26.07	17.53	12.87	16.84	63.45	25.23	43.20
Las Cruces, NM	22.91	17.03	14.13	15.26	76.28	25.44	44.62
Las Vegas, NV	25.53	21.97	17.17	18.68	n/a	33.87	42.86
Lexington, KY	25.84	20.07	14.54	17.87	n/a	25.25	44.15
Lincoln, NE	25.23	19.61	15.58	17.91	73.53	25.71	47.33
Little Rock, AR	22.91	17.13	14.00	18.06	85.98	21.91	46.55
Los Angeles, CA	33.66	25.96	18.92	22.21	n/a	37.09	65.13
Louisville, KY	26.08	21.24	14.55	19.09	87.22	28.92	45.08
Madison, WI	29.94	23.76	16.05	20.72	83.83	34.25	46.88

Table continued on following page.

Appendix A: Comparative Statistics   A-91

Metro Area	Comp. User Support Specialists	Construction Laborers	Cooks, Restaurant	Customer Service Reps.	Dentists	Electricians	Engineers, Electrical
Manchester, NH[2]	30.81	20.40	17.24	20.95	139.57	28.40	53.87
Miami, FL	27.62	18.58	16.91	19.16	80.27	25.35	47.59
Midland, TX	29.09	19.01	15.29	19.91	n/a	29.47	42.56
Milwaukee, WI	27.77	24.14	15.78	21.30	86.72	36.15	46.03
Minneapolis, MN	30.92	27.61	17.93	22.61	93.89	37.09	50.35
Nashville, TN	25.45	19.33	15.20	18.93	89.30	28.19	47.79
New Haven, CT[2]	31.79	25.19	17.29	21.99	95.87	33.24	50.00
New Orleans, LA	25.14	18.62	13.82	17.57	88.12	27.99	51.29
New York, NY	35.55	30.93	19.55	23.75	89.01	41.22	53.37
Oklahoma City, OK	26.61	19.08	14.94	18.11	84.37	27.58	47.89
Omaha, NE	26.48	20.49	15.05	18.92	78.54	27.41	47.76
Orlando, FL	26.77	17.79	17.07	18.69	91.27	24.05	50.65
Philadelphia, PA	31.04	26.48	16.51	21.24	93.37	38.35	53.63
Phoenix, AZ	29.29	21.22	18.08	19.49	87.37	25.61	49.97
Pittsburgh, PA	29.16	24.33	14.67	19.68	68.86	34.15	49.62
Portland, OR	30.08	25.00	18.56	21.22	91.21	41.15	51.53
Providence, RI[2]	29.79	26.46	17.00	21.03	97.31	30.94	54.51
Provo, UT	28.02	21.54	15.72	18.34	65.12	26.76	56.26
Raleigh, NC	31.64	18.40	15.45	19.52	107.63	24.71	52.39
Reno, NV	26.75	25.44	17.06	19.43	56.35	32.25	48.35
Richmond, VA	28.49	17.43	15.43	18.72	79.72	27.27	50.41
Rochester, MN	31.25	25.20	16.86	20.61	83.58	33.41	51.22
Sacramento, CA	44.86	26.69	18.68	22.15	81.12	35.93	59.48
Salem, OR	29.88	23.00	17.44	19.55	94.78	37.27	52.49
Salt Lake City, UT	30.53	20.17	16.82	20.02	64.38	28.08	58.74
San Antonio, TX	26.07	18.15	14.44	18.47	90.08	25.79	50.10
San Diego, CA	31.80	26.98	18.75	22.23	70.37	33.63	61.94
San Francisco, CA	40.10	31.48	20.39	25.95	98.09	46.31	77.67
San Jose, CA	39.13	30.35	21.53	26.29	103.12	47.71	n/a
Santa Rosa, CA	34.14	28.67	19.90	23.15	79.52	36.36	60.81
Savannah, GA	26.01	17.96	15.06	16.30	n/a	25.68	56.50
Seattle, WA	36.00	28.67	21.69	24.71	84.44	44.45	60.98
Sioux Falls, SD	21.59	18.01	15.46	18.54	69.39	26.54	46.30
Springfield, IL	26.48	30.22	16.03	19.00	72.48	35.32	47.34
St. Louis, MO	30.84	27.50	15.55	20.00	n/a	33.40	50.08
Tampa, FL	29.20	18.14	15.73	18.73	77.98	24.40	49.32
Tucson, AZ	27.18	19.78	16.51	17.76	87.60	24.71	56.86
Tulsa, OK	26.87	19.26	14.72	18.17	83.90	27.67	48.62
Tuscaloosa, AL	29.58	15.23	14.27	17.16	93.58	25.75	55.16
Virginia Beach, VA	26.21	17.52	14.70	17.30	78.65	27.29	47.22
Washington, DC	33.96	21.29	18.00	22.02	85.40	34.04	59.45
Wichita, KS	27.25	18.13	13.72	17.53	76.11	28.57	43.15
Wilmington, NC	25.96	18.29	14.56	18.04	76.66	23.28	48.09
Winston-Salem, NC	26.98	17.33	14.50	18.08	91.37	23.79	49.50
Worcester, MA[2]	31.83	28.53	18.32	21.98	n/a	37.55	57.13

Notes: (1) Figures cover the Metropolitan Statistical Area (MSA) except where noted. See Appendix B for areas included;
(2) New England City and Town Area; n/a not available
Source: Bureau of Labor Statistics, May 2022 Metro Area Occupational Employment and Wage Estimates

A-92 Appendix A: Comparative Statistics

Average Hourly Wages: Occupations F – J

Metro Area	Fast Food and Counter Workers	Financial Managers	First-Line Supervisors/ of Office Workers	General and Operations Managers	Hair-dressers/ Cosme-tologists	Home Health and Personal Care Aides	Janitors/ Cleaners
Albuquerque, NM	12.75	59.44	27.81	58.98	13.60	13.30	14.36
Allentown, PA	12.66	74.84	31.48	58.15	16.54	13.96	16.71
Anchorage, AK	14.73	72.72	32.44	54.98	15.13	17.28	16.95
Ann Arbor, MI	13.66	71.39	31.10	62.22	19.87	14.08	17.50
Athens, GA	11.00	67.23	27.18	47.82	17.24	12.56	14.99
Atlanta, GA	11.65	83.96	31.25	59.75	18.59	12.95	15.06
Austin, TX	12.48	81.29	32.79	56.28	16.04	12.07	14.63
Baltimore, MD	14.31	76.62	32.11	55.22	19.90	15.32	16.24
Boise City, ID	11.97	56.23	27.15	38.95	15.45	13.80	14.80
Boston, MA[2]	16.22	88.25	36.88	74.45	23.51	17.13	19.76
Boulder, CO	16.24	90.26	34.38	77.36	23.64	17.40	18.80
Brownsville, TX	10.12	59.69	25.20	41.63	12.81	10.33	12.36
Cape Coral, FL	12.56	69.72	30.29	51.54	18.15	15.99	14.30
Cedar Rapids, IA	12.59	60.69	29.72	45.54	15.24	16.20	15.98
Charleston, SC	11.69	65.85	29.33	52.71	16.62	13.41	13.93
Charlotte, NC	12.43	84.45	30.59	64.62	18.90	12.92	14.10
Chicago, IL	14.28	78.05	33.78	63.64	21.49	15.66	17.40
Cincinnati, OH	12.33	74.98	31.83	54.62	19.64	13.84	15.79
Clarksville, TN	11.02	59.25	27.42	46.82	16.59	12.82	13.88
Cleveland, OH	12.12	74.24	31.50	57.05	17.94	13.45	16.17
College Station, TX	10.89	65.41	26.24	47.87	13.68	11.46	13.57
Colorado Springs, CO	14.73	83.92	31.26	65.50	23.17	16.66	16.75
Columbia, MO	12.77	n/a	27.71	47.42	18.61	13.29	15.66
Columbia, SC	10.98	59.98	30.75	48.46	15.32	12.35	13.42
Columbus, OH	12.65	71.54	32.35	57.91	20.68	13.75	16.00
Dallas, TX	12.14	79.36	31.46	56.66	16.24	11.66	14.42
Davenport, IA	12.80	60.84	29.38	47.04	16.42	14.44	16.52
Denver, CO	15.81	94.94	34.80	75.18	21.59	16.85	17.70
Des Moines, IA	13.07	72.01	31.64	49.19	16.70	15.41	15.75
Durham, NC	13.08	84.49	31.92	70.01	22.31	13.24	16.43
Edison, NJ	16.08	110.67	38.32	83.82	20.85	17.10	20.14
El Paso, TX	10.10	62.87	24.90	40.58	13.11	9.83	12.05
Fargo, ND	13.47	68.39	30.87	48.98	16.61	16.62	16.77
Fort Collins, CO	14.91	86.90	31.88	63.72	26.75	16.84	17.15
Fort Wayne, IN	11.84	56.74	29.78	57.29	15.67	13.51	15.11
Fort Worth, TX	12.14	79.36	31.46	56.66	16.24	11.66	14.42
Grand Rapids, MI	13.09	65.10	29.78	55.04	18.45	14.38	15.34
Greeley, CO	14.57	83.73	32.68	64.82	19.24	16.62	17.37
Green Bay, WI	11.72	67.97	32.04	64.87	16.41	14.33	15.45
Greensboro, NC	11.81	73.43	28.58	57.79	18.33	12.20	13.36
Honolulu, HI	13.92	65.00	29.47	57.59	15.94	15.75	16.29
Houston, TX	11.74	84.66	31.01	56.99	13.81	11.18	13.63
Huntsville, AL	11.05	69.15	28.19	67.02	18.45	12.03	13.17
Indianapolis, IN	12.43	70.85	32.23	62.85	15.39	14.07	15.71
Jacksonville, FL	12.07	73.04	31.15	55.91	16.72	13.54	14.39
Kansas City, MO	13.01	74.13	31.26	52.71	19.13	13.99	16.10
Lafayette, LA	10.23	58.26	26.05	58.46	12.89	9.92	12.05
Las Cruces, NM	12.21	46.68	25.64	50.87	13.04	12.29	13.56
Las Vegas, NV	12.19	58.11	29.10	60.12	13.20	15.34	15.69
Lexington, KY	11.82	65.06	29.85	45.50	13.22	14.88	14.75
Lincoln, NE	12.48	61.87	26.83	47.07	17.83	14.17	14.69
Little Rock, AR	12.41	56.25	26.41	41.68	13.73	12.92	13.43
Los Angeles, CA	16.43	87.66	34.56	67.77	22.18	15.68	18.46
Louisville, KY	11.98	70.09	32.22	48.89	14.19	15.29	14.97

Table continued on following page.

Appendix A: Comparative Statistics   A-93

Metro Area	Fast Food and Counter Workers	Financial Managers	First-Line Supervisors/ of Office Workers	General and Operations Managers	Hair-dressers/ Cosme-tologists	Home Health and Personal Care Aides	Janitors/ Cleaners
Madison, WI	12.42	72.88	33.73	65.92	17.32	14.89	16.04
Manchester, NH[2]	13.09	72.83	33.58	67.22	16.38	15.63	17.06
Miami, FL	12.93	81.34	31.90	56.01	15.37	13.24	14.03
Midland, TX	12.27	94.45	32.60	59.45	14.46	12.12	14.35
Milwaukee, WI	12.08	74.52	33.87	68.48	18.97	13.83	15.71
Minneapolis, MN	14.79	76.74	34.96	56.37	20.87	15.64	17.94
Nashville, TN	12.17	72.46	32.48	67.20	19.75	13.96	15.14
New Haven, CT[2]	14.76	71.48	34.08	70.00	18.17	16.48	18.12
New Orleans, LA	12.70	67.00	26.71	61.48	14.26	11.09	12.91
New York, NY	16.08	110.67	38.32	83.82	20.85	17.10	20.14
Oklahoma City, OK	11.19	64.38	30.11	48.66	17.09	12.14	13.56
Omaha, NE	12.76	65.55	28.58	47.42	21.04	14.54	15.19
Orlando, FL	12.49	77.76	30.12	55.62	17.02	13.54	13.87
Philadelphia, PA	13.26	78.78	33.31	68.82	17.70	14.31	17.24
Phoenix, AZ	15.53	76.99	30.64	54.46	20.15	15.17	15.82
Pittsburgh, PA	11.65	73.72	29.71	55.74	16.69	13.88	16.22
Portland, OR	15.88	75.43	32.27	56.83	18.86	17.48	18.11
Providence, RI[2]	14.82	81.58	34.07	65.29	15.61	17.07	17.99
Provo, UT	12.33	68.82	29.37	47.51	18.44	15.63	13.80
Raleigh, NC	12.10	74.45	29.75	64.48	21.68	13.39	14.13
Reno, NV	12.62	59.63	29.96	61.79	16.20	17.81	15.57
Richmond, VA	12.47	80.46	31.31	59.05	18.60	13.05	14.79
Rochester, MN	14.09	65.15	31.71	51.56	19.51	15.54	18.28
Sacramento, CA	16.46	79.36	35.50	67.53	21.69	15.29	18.34
Salem, OR	14.60	64.50	30.14	46.82	18.25	17.28	17.05
Salt Lake City, UT	13.19	69.34	30.21	53.16	19.62	16.45	14.30
San Antonio, TX	11.50	73.39	30.02	50.98	14.16	10.89	14.02
San Diego, CA	16.37	83.73	33.77	n/a	21.87	16.23	18.06
San Francisco, CA	18.38	107.34	40.24	80.86	23.34	16.61	21.39
San Jose, CA	18.80	103.92	41.82	90.32	20.99	17.24	20.64
Santa Rosa, CA	17.13	81.95	34.88	64.13	21.59	16.52	22.75
Savannah, GA	11.64	71.42	27.26	51.37	16.53	12.70	14.18
Seattle, WA	17.49	87.94	37.50	72.41	23.93	18.81	20.41
Sioux Falls, SD	13.18	76.40	28.08	71.87	19.15	15.27	15.35
Springfield, IL	13.61	64.09	30.02	52.04	18.76	14.39	16.63
St. Louis, MO	13.40	72.89	31.51	54.93	18.85	13.32	16.09
Tampa, FL	12.44	76.40	30.65	53.47	17.46	13.80	13.88
Tucson, AZ	14.40	62.10	27.35	44.86	19.75	14.57	15.53
Tulsa, OK	11.21	72.14	29.35	51.65	16.50	12.65	14.02
Tuscaloosa, AL	11.34	62.63	28.60	55.95	17.32	11.32	14.40
Virginia Beach, VA	12.47	72.27	28.99	54.70	17.34	12.57	14.20
Washington, DC	15.12	87.75	35.74	72.97	22.54	15.70	17.34
Wichita, KS	11.16	70.00	28.52	46.78	16.45	12.10	14.45
Wilmington, NC	11.32	74.45	26.02	53.42	19.04	12.45	13.87
Winston-Salem, NC	12.15	74.71	27.78	58.23	18.87	12.67	13.23
Worcester, MA[2]	15.52	71.84	32.65	61.97	21.83	16.77	18.83

Notes: (1) Figures cover the Metropolitan Statistical Area (MSA) except where noted. See Appendix B for areas included; (2) New England City and Town Area; n/a not available
Source: Bureau of Labor Statistics, May 2022 Metro Area Occupational Employment and Wage Estimates

A-94   Appendix A: Comparative Statistics

Average Hourly Wages: Occupations L – N

Metro Area	Landscapers	Lawyers	Maids/ House- keepers	Main- tenance/ Repairers	Marketing Managers	Network Admin.	Nurses, Licensed Practical
Albuquerque, NM	16.24	54.41	13.69	20.91	61.49	44.73	28.50
Allentown, PA	17.57	64.68	14.89	24.13	66.34	41.40	26.64
Anchorage, AK	21.00	58.26	15.86	24.49	52.64	42.70	31.62
Ann Arbor, MI	17.82	60.75	15.15	22.11	66.72	43.40	28.93
Athens, GA	15.97	n/a	12.50	19.81	54.36	36.48	24.20
Atlanta, GA	17.07	84.73	13.58	21.53	73.79	50.54	26.03
Austin, TX	16.91	72.31	13.88	20.40	70.73	46.20	27.17
Baltimore, MD	18.68	77.46	14.74	23.34	69.41	52.41	28.83
Boise City, ID	17.90	48.56	15.14	20.73	51.10	39.68	27.38
Boston, MA[2]	21.78	97.55	19.01	27.11	80.96	52.37	33.67
Boulder, CO	21.69	n/a	17.31	27.19	85.56	48.32	29.85
Brownsville, TX	12.90	56.07	10.80	15.45	56.84	36.42	22.93
Cape Coral, FL	16.34	58.21	14.40	20.21	65.93	42.44	25.89
Cedar Rapids, IA	16.78	57.59	13.71	22.16	61.42	41.95	25.54
Charleston, SC	16.99	53.48	13.47	21.41	52.80	46.31	25.74
Charlotte, NC	17.24	78.03	13.43	22.36	71.03	44.85	26.52
Chicago, IL	18.93	78.47	17.07	26.11	70.74	44.98	30.01
Cincinnati, OH	16.69	64.18	13.58	23.48	69.92	46.45	25.99
Clarksville, TN	16.66	51.48	11.75	22.30	50.21	34.09	22.40
Cleveland, OH	17.23	64.28	14.02	23.06	69.27	45.69	26.09
College Station, TX	15.78	75.98	12.68	18.38	57.23	37.16	23.08
Colorado Springs, CO	n/a	53.62	16.06	22.51	79.04	47.29	27.54
Columbia, MO	15.24	58.60	13.42	20.64	52.19	38.68	23.50
Columbia, SC	15.84	53.72	12.62	20.68	59.00	43.75	25.20
Columbus, OH	17.46	65.26	13.91	23.16	69.18	47.97	26.41
Dallas, TX	16.86	87.42	13.78	21.23	67.66	45.36	26.59
Davenport, IA	16.43	56.57	13.68	22.09	60.27	40.41	25.09
Denver, CO	20.25	84.07	16.80	25.27	86.32	50.59	30.30
Des Moines, IA	17.60	59.08	14.22	22.01	64.50	44.01	25.09
Durham, NC	17.41	73.85	14.21	23.68	75.77	48.52	26.52
Edison, NJ	20.81	92.92	21.40	26.67	93.41	55.75	30.31
El Paso, TX	13.79	65.20	11.07	16.87	49.29	37.25	22.95
Fargo, ND	19.28	61.05	14.33	22.10	61.40	39.32	25.14
Fort Collins, CO	19.43	88.05	16.17	22.69	87.40	43.41	28.74
Fort Wayne, IN	16.18	62.54	13.34	23.13	56.84	37.68	25.80
Fort Worth, TX	16.86	87.42	13.78	21.23	67.66	45.36	26.59
Grand Rapids, MI	17.18	64.19	14.27	21.10	64.10	41.89	27.34
Greeley, CO	20.33	67.70	16.09	25.25	80.70	41.55	29.06
Green Bay, WI	17.41	72.57	14.43	22.47	75.00	42.60	23.59
Greensboro, NC	15.69	66.92	13.04	21.27	64.13	41.11	25.19
Honolulu, HI	19.21	50.95	23.06	25.25	59.72	44.72	27.07
Houston, TX	16.29	84.79	14.27	20.87	71.45	47.28	26.65
Huntsville, AL	15.92	69.72	11.97	20.71	68.35	45.60	22.75
Indianapolis, IN	17.19	74.02	14.20	23.30	65.78	42.49	27.80
Jacksonville, FL	16.00	62.74	13.79	20.57	72.46	43.58	24.97
Kansas City, MO	17.47	70.16	14.27	22.59	68.75	42.01	26.30
Lafayette, LA	14.42	53.24	10.93	18.12	47.53	41.24	21.48
Las Cruces, NM	15.38	53.03	12.60	18.02	n/a	41.48	27.19
Las Vegas, NV	17.85	82.94	17.87	23.05	51.14	49.43	30.50
Lexington, KY	15.64	51.22	12.88	22.07	55.36	38.28	24.21
Lincoln, NE	16.86	56.01	13.97	21.04	49.76	40.83	24.46
Little Rock, AR	15.21	50.96	12.84	18.37	51.80	38.74	23.12
Los Angeles, CA	19.81	93.69	18.69	24.86	81.73	49.56	32.95
Louisville, KY	16.00	52.07	13.67	23.69	68.37	40.49	25.32
Madison, WI	18.73	66.28	14.97	22.80	70.25	43.19	25.83

Table continued on following page.

Appendix A: Comparative Statistics   A-95

Metro Area	Landscapers	Lawyers	Maids/House-keepers	Main-tenance/Repairers	Marketing Managers	Network Admin.	Nurses, Licensed Practical
Manchester, NH[2]	19.05	69.50	15.17	23.02	70.51	42.70	31.39
Miami, FL	16.61	69.69	14.17	20.30	73.31	45.42	26.47
Midland, TX	16.75	87.92	13.55	20.19	76.35	46.75	26.25
Milwaukee, WI	17.75	80.34	14.73	22.70	68.47	46.07	26.39
Minneapolis, MN	19.96	83.25	17.58	25.64	78.99	46.85	27.70
Nashville, TN	17.05	73.05	13.44	21.40	76.32	44.89	23.71
New Haven, CT[2]	20.86	73.87	15.86	24.69	71.85	45.08	30.20
New Orleans, LA	14.72	68.27	12.41	20.69	61.89	39.84	24.25
New York, NY	20.81	92.92	21.40	26.67	93.41	55.75	30.31
Oklahoma City, OK	16.15	53.26	12.31	18.75	64.04	41.84	23.45
Omaha, NE	17.69	59.74	14.69	22.11	58.09	44.11	25.44
Orlando, FL	16.23	70.07	14.29	20.33	76.95	43.75	26.40
Philadelphia, PA	18.71	76.88	15.47	23.49	71.68	47.15	28.52
Phoenix, AZ	17.31	72.30	16.08	22.41	68.83	45.37	30.07
Pittsburgh, PA	16.84	66.28	14.29	22.49	60.70	45.38	25.74
Portland, OR	20.88	73.57	17.60	24.55	66.94	48.17	33.26
Providence, RI[2]	20.58	74.38	16.14	24.78	79.73	51.47	31.28
Provo, UT	18.30	72.07	14.71	21.46	62.12	43.16	25.28
Raleigh, NC	17.40	67.47	14.15	22.67	71.21	45.26	26.69
Reno, NV	18.37	72.00	16.74	23.76	64.64	55.57	32.19
Richmond, VA	16.43	80.05	13.35	22.55	72.33	48.67	25.75
Rochester, MN	18.74	57.71	15.90	23.54	62.16	48.04	25.78
Sacramento, CA	20.30	79.67	20.36	24.95	77.80	43.18	34.27
Salem, OR	19.59	67.46	16.44	22.28	52.32	46.22	30.83
Salt Lake City, UT	18.82	65.12	16.12	23.79	65.16	45.48	29.02
San Antonio, TX	15.69	68.81	13.15	19.50	60.00	41.81	25.93
San Diego, CA	19.61	89.63	18.37	24.59	84.68	49.31	32.57
San Francisco, CA	23.72	115.06	22.92	29.95	100.73	61.21	38.69
San Jose, CA	24.14	128.77	22.48	30.88	113.98	72.84	38.75
Santa Rosa, CA	21.42	88.92	20.35	26.12	75.37	46.00	36.88
Savannah, GA	15.94	n/a	11.85	20.32	68.95	44.17	24.10
Seattle, WA	23.52	83.85	18.50	27.19	82.15	53.30	35.34
Sioux Falls, SD	16.41	60.68	13.76	20.54	66.13	35.57	22.26
Springfield, IL	18.70	61.68	16.39	23.40	62.68	36.92	25.11
St. Louis, MO	17.58	68.34	14.77	24.01	64.07	45.06	26.06
Tampa, FL	15.63	66.40	13.55	19.72	72.41	44.44	25.31
Tucson, AZ	16.04	61.60	14.58	20.08	58.86	41.53	29.01
Tulsa, OK	15.90	60.61	12.45	19.66	69.45	41.63	24.26
Tuscaloosa, AL	15.89	55.63	11.48	18.71	54.09	37.32	21.53
Virginia Beach, VA	16.35	61.10	13.16	21.28	70.40	44.66	24.37
Washington, DC	19.67	101.85	17.03	25.65	84.53	55.96	29.10
Wichita, KS	15.78	54.07	12.87	19.99	63.35	40.60	23.92
Wilmington, NC	16.23	61.99	12.83	19.80	67.91	39.92	25.28
Winston-Salem, NC	16.17	81.73	13.42	21.32	72.60	42.13	25.36
Worcester, MA[2]	20.03	69.75	17.11	24.75	73.90	47.65	30.85

Notes: (1) Figures cover the Metropolitan Statistical Area (MSA) except where noted. See Appendix B for areas included; (2) New England City and Town Area; n/a not available
Source: Bureau of Labor Statistics, May 2022 Metro Area Occupational Employment and Wage Estimates

A-96   Appendix A: Comparative Statistics

Average Hourly Wages: Occupations N – P

Metro Area	Nurses, Registered	Nursing Assistants	Office Clerks	Physical Therapists	Physicians	Plumbers	Police Officers
Albuquerque, NM	41.94	16.74	16.26	44.66	129.51	25.36	27.99
Allentown, PA	39.14	17.79	20.19	48.05	n/a	32.16	36.38
Anchorage, AK	49.59	20.50	22.26	49.64	112.03	43.11	47.16
Ann Arbor, MI	41.54	18.36	19.11	46.21	120.10	33.25	34.05
Athens, GA	38.59	14.53	19.23	49.24	106.67	26.88	24.49
Atlanta, GA	43.40	17.12	19.42	46.86	123.80	28.56	26.02
Austin, TX	41.69	16.17	19.06	47.33	136.94	28.42	35.58
Baltimore, MD	43.03	17.71	19.28	45.91	120.21	28.83	34.65
Boise City, ID	39.06	17.88	17.66	43.44	148.73	28.88	30.67
Boston, MA[2]	51.44	20.42	23.38	46.36	106.88	39.70	36.32
Boulder, CO	44.57	19.72	25.81	48.20	142.09	32.34	40.88
Brownsville, TX	35.07	13.19	14.88	45.71	116.21	20.29	26.68
Cape Coral, FL	38.04	16.24	19.43	43.77	177.87	24.29	31.19
Cedar Rapids, IA	33.68	17.02	19.34	40.86	125.70	32.41	31.90
Charleston, SC	36.96	17.18	17.46	41.79	141.24	24.76	25.12
Charlotte, NC	38.24	15.93	18.96	46.12	133.48	25.11	28.24
Chicago, IL	40.99	18.37	21.22	48.81	100.40	43.17	41.59
Cincinnati, OH	38.82	16.53	19.80	45.46	108.34	31.67	33.83
Clarksville, TN	34.52	14.53	16.20	42.52	143.21	24.18	23.65
Cleveland, OH	38.95	17.21	20.05	47.43	79.22	31.97	34.02
College Station, TX	37.59	14.34	15.70	46.21	n/a	24.11	31.36
Colorado Springs, CO	39.78	18.31	23.24	45.18	n/a	28.01	37.67
Columbia, MO	34.00	15.71	18.99	41.76	132.62	28.50	24.89
Columbia, SC	35.37	15.81	16.30	41.97	142.61	22.81	24.96
Columbus, OH	38.80	16.67	20.13	48.56	102.84	31.99	37.43
Dallas, TX	42.24	16.34	18.59	50.76	118.86	26.94	35.82
Davenport, IA	32.77	16.26	18.58	41.53	n/a	32.66	32.09
Denver, CO	42.21	19.35	24.74	47.13	156.83	31.18	41.85
Des Moines, IA	34.16	17.50	19.96	41.72	105.11	31.79	34.32
Durham, NC	n/a	16.82	19.49	40.71	n/a	26.00	25.40
Edison, NJ	50.41	21.50	21.90	53.25	128.42	42.38	42.43
El Paso, TX	36.36	13.69	15.17	45.54	105.87	22.73	30.10
Fargo, ND	36.60	17.94	22.07	40.35	105.75	29.18	34.03
Fort Collins, CO	40.85	18.30	23.55	42.61	n/a	29.30	43.64
Fort Wayne, IN	35.21	15.77	18.98	44.25	n/a	33.18	31.73
Fort Worth, TX	42.24	16.34	18.59	50.76	118.86	26.94	35.82
Grand Rapids, MI	36.98	17.03	20.33	42.66	126.06	30.06	31.96
Greeley, CO	41.14	17.60	23.36	47.67	n/a	26.96	36.95
Green Bay, WI	37.41	17.41	19.40	44.40	177.48	33.56	34.37
Greensboro, NC	38.59	14.93	17.77	45.22	n/a	23.39	24.52
Honolulu, HI	55.38	19.29	20.72	49.00	132.28	37.07	43.41
Houston, TX	42.73	16.18	18.74	52.20	138.31	28.24	32.31
Huntsville, AL	31.99	14.59	13.92	46.53	139.48	24.93	25.54
Indianapolis, IN	38.68	16.97	20.15	45.55	161.40	33.28	32.70
Jacksonville, FL	37.74	15.99	19.42	44.49	132.91	23.81	27.88
Kansas City, MO	36.82	17.33	20.48	44.96	104.46	31.93	29.20
Lafayette, LA	35.91	12.92	13.92	44.44	140.81	25.47	22.67
Las Cruces, NM	37.30	14.84	15.58	40.75	135.79	22.92	27.37
Las Vegas, NV	46.96	19.90	19.84	51.20	126.98	31.07	36.94
Lexington, KY	37.36	16.43	17.56	40.93	146.74	29.90	24.95
Lincoln, NE	35.52	16.53	16.75	44.49	131.40	25.79	33.34
Little Rock, AR	34.48	15.09	17.64	44.50	90.44	22.44	23.08
Los Angeles, CA	60.26	20.49	21.66	52.02	113.43	34.45	50.13
Louisville, KY	39.08	16.62	18.11	43.91	144.45	29.23	25.96
Madison, WI	41.46	18.71	20.66	43.49	152.61	35.91	35.34

Table continued on following page.

Appendix A: Comparative Statistics   A-97

Metro Area	Nurses, Registered	Nursing Assistants	Office Clerks	Physical Therapists	Physicians	Plumbers	Police Officers
Manchester, NH[2]	39.38	18.40	22.10	43.45	n/a	28.32	30.78
Miami, FL	39.33	16.17	19.87	42.11	102.65	24.64	43.87
Midland, TX	39.34	16.60	20.43	50.09	124.58	26.81	34.27
Milwaukee, WI	39.44	17.93	19.83	45.40	104.93	35.62	35.72
Minneapolis, MN	44.32	22.36	22.34	43.60	145.35	39.07	39.69
Nashville, TN	37.13	16.08	17.70	44.33	131.73	26.77	26.07
New Haven, CT[2]	46.18	18.43	21.09	48.79	130.80	34.63	36.86
New Orleans, LA	38.18	14.49	14.52	46.62	151.73	27.73	23.68
New York, NY	50.41	21.50	21.90	53.25	128.42	42.38	42.43
Oklahoma City, OK	37.19	14.90	16.78	44.06	126.14	24.68	33.22
Omaha, NE	36.18	17.53	18.19	43.62	142.86	32.29	34.43
Orlando, FL	38.04	16.41	18.94	45.58	133.16	23.14	29.83
Philadelphia, PA	42.23	18.17	21.08	48.69	n/a	34.76	37.93
Phoenix, AZ	42.03	18.44	21.73	48.80	98.99	28.48	35.65
Pittsburgh, PA	36.65	17.51	19.95	45.42	59.50	34.72	36.66
Portland, OR	53.66	21.15	21.40	46.36	111.11	40.51	40.50
Providence, RI[2]	42.39	18.87	21.07	45.70	100.09	32.22	34.35
Provo, UT	34.96	15.59	18.82	43.16	82.30	25.73	28.90
Raleigh, NC	37.82	16.03	19.56	42.43	140.14	24.57	26.56
Reno, NV	44.85	19.69	21.19	49.42	142.69	32.67	35.21
Richmond, VA	39.75	15.79	18.79	46.28	79.68	25.66	29.03
Rochester, MN	43.30	19.09	21.24	41.61	143.61	37.05	34.21
Sacramento, CA	69.82	21.17	21.97	58.89	145.43	33.87	48.52
Salem, OR	46.17	21.59	20.38	45.54	158.13	34.34	37.37
Salt Lake City, UT	38.16	16.66	19.23	45.74	120.76	30.62	32.06
San Antonio, TX	39.92	15.47	18.02	45.42	145.35	24.88	31.55
San Diego, CA	56.65	20.39	21.38	52.92	125.61	34.09	47.51
San Francisco, CA	79.21	25.13	26.29	60.61	114.31	44.23	57.43
San Jose, CA	76.94	24.81	25.56	64.33	124.09	46.57	62.36
Santa Rosa, CA	72.67	20.99	22.86	60.31	112.97	36.74	49.57
Savannah, GA	40.41	14.89	18.02	45.44	100.61	28.19	25.28
Seattle, WA	50.74	21.40	24.29	50.43	120.27	41.46	48.78
Sioux Falls, SD	30.18	15.47	15.70	41.62	n/a	25.38	31.52
Springfield, IL	37.80	17.22	20.11	46.06	146.21	38.31	34.84
St. Louis, MO	36.14	16.41	20.76	44.14	142.81	35.55	29.89
Tampa, FL	38.42	16.72	19.64	46.29	132.49	23.00	33.26
Tucson, AZ	40.19	17.25	20.55	44.89	n/a	25.56	30.75
Tulsa, OK	38.32	15.05	17.16	43.95	78.82	26.43	26.48
Tuscaloosa, AL	30.81	14.13	13.87	48.68	105.13	23.92	27.48
Virginia Beach, VA	38.20	15.13	18.11	45.34	n/a	26.56	27.70
Washington, DC	44.61	18.33	22.52	49.52	101.91	30.71	37.25
Wichita, KS	33.08	15.61	14.16	43.47	100.53	27.23	25.83
Wilmington, NC	36.27	14.86	17.25	41.09	112.33	22.57	23.49
Winston-Salem, NC	38.57	15.34	17.36	47.28	n/a	22.79	24.14
Worcester, MA[2]	47.38	18.71	21.03	44.80	108.84	40.47	30.41

Notes: (1) Figures cover the Metropolitan Statistical Area (MSA) except where noted. See Appendix B for areas included; (2) New England City and Town Area; n/a not available
Source: Bureau of Labor Statistics, May 2022 Metro Area Occupational Employment and Wage Estimates

A-98 Appendix A: Comparative Statistics

Average Hourly Wages: Occupations P – S

Metro Area	Postal Mail Carriers	R.E. Sales Agents	Retail Sales-persons	Sales Reps., Technical/ Scientific	Secretaries, Exc. Leg./ Med./Exec.	Security Guards	Surgeons
Albuquerque, NM	26.30	22.73	15.08	37.39	20.16	15.37	n/a
Allentown, PA	27.45	27.37	16.75	51.14	20.39	17.28	n/a
Anchorage, AK	25.73	34.80	18.27	36.27	20.62	20.74	n/a
Ann Arbor, MI	27.10	33.57	16.77	128.93	22.52	18.34	n/a
Athens, GA	25.97	21.38	14.84	41.34	17.79	19.33	n/a
Atlanta, GA	26.65	28.00	15.55	52.79	19.44	16.02	212.04
Austin, TX	27.22	39.51	16.52	44.57	21.45	17.41	n/a
Baltimore, MD	27.22	32.50	15.99	50.13	21.48	20.09	162.71
Boise City, ID	27.00	21.80	16.72	41.57	18.67	16.67	n/a
Boston, MA[2]	28.27	38.33	18.39	54.97	25.44	19.80	148.22
Boulder, CO	28.10	49.41	18.86	n/a	22.19	21.46	n/a
Brownsville, TX	26.80	24.87	14.27	n/a	16.45	15.55	n/a
Cape Coral, FL	26.49	24.97	15.73	53.67	18.53	14.53	n/a
Cedar Rapids, IA	27.18	30.06	15.63	51.91	20.40	17.15	n/a
Charleston, SC	26.88	29.27	15.26	37.04	19.15	14.67	n/a
Charlotte, NC	27.50	27.29	15.72	54.96	20.17	14.89	276.15
Chicago, IL	27.84	21.56	17.49	56.01	23.34	17.98	136.81
Cincinnati, OH	28.15	27.69	16.23	51.86	20.51	17.09	184.17
Clarksville, TN	25.40	28.07	15.47	32.81	18.04	18.30	n/a
Cleveland, OH	27.79	20.71	16.56	52.20	20.38	17.47	n/a
College Station, TX	26.30	31.28	14.39	39.76	18.70	14.38	n/a
Colorado Springs, CO	26.35	34.84	17.44	46.25	19.90	17.50	n/a
Columbia, MO	26.18	20.94	14.99	n/a	18.33	16.33	n/a
Columbia, SC	25.68	28.52	14.63	40.39	18.64	13.48	n/a
Columbus, OH	27.37	21.29	16.00	58.13	20.96	17.83	n/a
Dallas, TX	27.30	38.08	16.19	43.31	20.33	16.99	142.82
Davenport, IA	26.31	33.24	15.72	50.09	19.78	18.10	n/a
Denver, CO	28.16	40.40	19.03	54.91	22.11	19.02	146.05
Des Moines, IA	27.78	34.49	15.88	54.80	21.22	17.63	n/a
Durham, NC	27.82	26.02	15.72	58.46	21.42	18.04	n/a
Edison, NJ	27.72	47.01	19.51	63.64	23.24	19.89	149.60
El Paso, TX	26.59	27.97	14.09	n/a	16.30	15.14	n/a
Fargo, ND	27.52	29.08	17.14	54.63	20.53	16.86	n/a
Fort Collins, CO	27.22	33.68	17.51	46.18	21.02	16.93	n/a
Fort Wayne, IN	26.91	27.25	14.91	51.06	18.31	17.67	n/a
Fort Worth, TX	27.30	38.08	16.19	43.31	20.33	16.99	142.82
Grand Rapids, MI	27.01	27.56	16.20	52.99	20.23	14.75	121.07
Greeley, CO	26.49	52.77	18.12	47.78	20.32	16.95	n/a
Green Bay, WI	27.20	29.62	16.28	34.34	20.34	16.22	n/a
Greensboro, NC	27.21	26.84	15.24	42.34	19.33	14.54	n/a
Honolulu, HI	26.72	26.75	17.85	54.70	23.30	17.09	205.79
Houston, TX	26.87	38.86	16.04	46.77	20.43	15.78	162.09
Huntsville, AL	26.36	41.38	14.54	38.34	20.21	15.35	n/a
Indianapolis, IN	27.71	32.61	15.60	52.85	20.15	16.75	185.56
Jacksonville, FL	27.22	29.37	15.49	46.55	19.30	15.13	n/a
Kansas City, MO	27.63	26.48	16.44	53.53	19.21	18.98	119.29
Lafayette, LA	26.29	17.52	13.84	40.17	17.91	13.48	n/a
Las Cruces, NM	25.66	22.91	13.98	n/a	18.37	15.27	n/a
Las Vegas, NV	26.97	38.35	16.82	41.45	21.22	15.06	n/a
Lexington, KY	27.17	27.67	15.76	45.14	20.09	14.57	n/a
Lincoln, NE	27.48	19.09	15.39	43.72	19.78	14.91	n/a
Little Rock, AR	26.80	n/a	14.90	44.97	18.48	15.34	n/a
Los Angeles, CA	28.35	35.65	18.93	52.61	24.22	18.19	n/a
Louisville, KY	27.28	22.31	15.89	49.19	19.91	16.60	194.02
Madison, WI	27.00	33.85	16.03	36.52	21.15	17.01	n/a

Table continued on following page.

Appendix A: Comparative Statistics   A-99

Metro Area	Postal Mail Carriers	R.E. Sales Agents	Retail Sales-persons	Sales Reps., Technical/ Scientific	Secretaries, Exc. Leg./ Med./Exec.	Security Guards	Surgeons
Manchester, NH[2]	27.77	30.34	16.93	41.73	20.73	18.41	n/a
Miami, FL	27.09	26.19	16.30	50.86	20.66	16.16	92.08
Midland, TX	25.08	48.44	16.59	48.08	20.58	17.08	n/a
Milwaukee, WI	27.42	24.00	16.36	39.18	20.72	16.44	n/a
Minneapolis, MN	27.77	n/a	17.68	47.57	23.29	18.79	176.40
Nashville, TN	27.31	19.02	16.18	40.84	20.51	15.94	135.32
New Haven, CT[2]	26.76	29.22	18.46	45.89	26.88	18.52	n/a
New Orleans, LA	26.86	24.99	14.66	40.90	18.95	15.17	n/a
New York, NY	27.72	47.01	19.51	63.64	23.24	19.89	149.60
Oklahoma City, OK	27.22	n/a	15.14	39.45	18.26	15.95	n/a
Omaha, NE	27.42	29.75	16.07	41.32	19.89	17.42	158.30
Orlando, FL	26.72	26.11	15.51	46.62	18.93	15.30	n/a
Philadelphia, PA	27.23	27.12	16.66	57.64	21.81	18.05	196.21
Phoenix, AZ	27.93	29.19	17.07	46.98	21.31	17.03	n/a
Pittsburgh, PA	26.80	30.60	15.60	50.53	19.68	16.59	n/a
Portland, OR	27.17	28.64	19.03	56.64	24.16	18.14	n/a
Providence, RI[2]	27.29	35.48	17.17	39.71	22.88	17.75	n/a
Provo, UT	27.30	27.88	16.90	43.62	19.25	15.75	n/a
Raleigh, NC	27.38	27.61	16.28	55.59	20.25	15.48	n/a
Reno, NV	27.69	24.89	17.26	42.94	22.47	16.07	n/a
Richmond, VA	26.92	35.50	15.56	47.20	19.90	17.63	n/a
Rochester, MN	27.15	n/a	16.90	35.30	21.71	17.79	156.35
Sacramento, CA	28.15	32.19	19.11	58.98	23.74	18.43	n/a
Salem, OR	26.44	29.11	17.64	53.51	22.97	18.21	n/a
Salt Lake City, UT	28.08	26.96	18.75	57.43	20.26	17.09	219.11
San Antonio, TX	26.74	32.87	15.92	41.27	19.44	15.80	n/a
San Diego, CA	27.48	41.65	18.69	57.24	23.50	18.37	n/a
San Francisco, CA	29.20	39.87	21.47	60.73	28.82	21.09	75.20
San Jose, CA	29.08	36.25	21.34	78.03	28.34	21.24	n/a
Santa Rosa, CA	27.31	39.25	19.94	53.84	25.29	19.11	n/a
Savannah, GA	26.97	23.15	14.40	40.36	18.89	15.54	n/a
Seattle, WA	28.57	34.93	19.75	74.86	26.09	20.72	97.57
Sioux Falls, SD	27.07	n/a	18.12	57.97	17.76	16.09	n/a
Springfield, IL	26.37	26.10	16.08	39.68	20.55	17.77	n/a
St. Louis, MO	27.22	23.21	17.00	48.57	19.80	17.68	n/a
Tampa, FL	26.91	27.94	16.01	45.68	18.84	15.00	191.11
Tucson, AZ	27.62	27.03	16.59	48.00	19.49	15.65	n/a
Tulsa, OK	27.22	40.04	15.59	38.20	18.07	15.18	n/a
Tuscaloosa, AL	27.01	29.05	14.09	n/a	19.12	15.31	n/a
Virginia Beach, VA	26.24	33.80	15.11	45.63	20.00	16.42	n/a
Washington, DC	27.72	36.03	17.61	62.98	24.44	23.65	186.07
Wichita, KS	26.65	27.02	15.34	51.87	17.74	15.50	n/a
Wilmington, NC	26.03	28.16	15.41	60.83	19.24	15.17	n/a
Winston-Salem, NC	27.50	33.61	14.59	44.22	19.35	16.60	n/a
Worcester, MA[2]	27.11	n/a	17.84	55.25	23.77	18.53	n/a

Notes: (1) Figures cover the Metropolitan Statistical Area (MSA) except where noted. See Appendix B for areas included; (2) New England City and Town Area; n/a not available
Source: Bureau of Labor Statistics, May 2022 Metro Area Occupational Employment and Wage Estimates

A-100   Appendix A: Comparative Statistics

Average Hourly Wages: Occupations T – W

Metro Area	Teacher Assistants[3]	Teachers, Secondary School[3]	Telemarketers	Truck Drivers, Heavy	Truck Drivers, Light	Waiters/ Waitresses
Albuquerque, NM	14.88	28.99	20.16	22.67	20.43	16.14
Allentown, PA	16.36	35.24	14.10	27.04	22.74	15.35
Anchorage, AK	17.44	36.14	n/a	27.93	26.04	13.47
Ann Arbor, MI	15.21	35.99	n/a	24.45	23.48	17.37
Athens, GA	11.12	31.25	n/a	26.85	22.03	13.09
Atlanta, GA	14.07	34.25	15.50	26.24	21.28	14.52
Austin, TX	15.16	30.16	16.31	23.73	22.03	13.42
Baltimore, MD	19.37	34.31	18.80	26.63	22.04	17.63
Boise City, ID	14.04	27.88	17.64	25.05	24.37	14.76
Boston, MA[2]	20.14	40.58	19.82	27.78	23.55	19.76
Boulder, CO	18.12	35.67	17.68	26.67	24.66	20.98
Brownsville, TX	13.50	26.50	n/a	22.21	18.91	10.94
Cape Coral, FL	14.90	33.25	16.95	22.84	20.22	15.70
Cedar Rapids, IA	14.26	28.59	n/a	25.17	19.97	13.27
Charleston, SC	12.32	27.85	n/a	25.58	19.54	11.64
Charlotte, NC	13.20	26.35	16.09	25.66	19.89	13.70
Chicago, IL	16.89	37.13	15.52	27.99	24.27	15.53
Cincinnati, OH	16.00	33.81	14.72	26.16	21.77	14.51
Clarksville, TN	14.59	26.06	n/a	22.96	19.13	11.97
Cleveland, OH	16.13	35.16	14.85	25.57	20.45	14.38
College Station, TX	13.43	25.97	n/a	22.43	22.97	12.47
Colorado Springs, CO	15.06	26.75	19.45	24.71	22.21	19.75
Columbia, MO	14.65	n/a	n/a	24.11	22.20	15.51
Columbia, SC	12.00	26.34	10.78	23.99	19.35	10.82
Columbus, OH	16.49	34.42	15.65	26.61	22.93	15.07
Dallas, TX	14.09	30.46	18.24	24.73	22.27	13.17
Davenport, IA	15.10	31.35	14.97	26.12	20.97	13.22
Denver, CO	17.40	32.50	20.16	27.32	23.68	18.48
Des Moines, IA	14.28	32.05	15.86	26.85	21.17	13.46
Durham, NC	13.63	26.62	15.07	24.94	19.89	14.16
Edison, NJ	18.07	45.24	20.35	29.43	23.63	23.01
El Paso, TX	12.23	27.72	14.74	20.95	18.70	11.05
Fargo, ND	16.83	28.97	n/a	27.94	23.00	14.71
Fort Collins, CO	16.36	28.98	18.28	25.19	22.91	19.93
Fort Wayne, IN	13.32	27.57	15.78	25.45	20.20	13.17
Fort Worth, TX	14.09	30.46	18.24	24.73	22.27	13.17
Grand Rapids, MI	15.09	31.35	15.93	24.69	20.89	17.53
Greeley, CO	16.03	27.26	n/a	26.14	23.11	18.76
Green Bay, WI	15.77	29.64	n/a	25.81	21.30	15.02
Greensboro, NC	12.50	24.32	18.68	24.84	18.97	12.88
Honolulu, HI	16.06	29.35	16.92	26.64	21.01	16.89
Houston, TX	13.73	30.64	17.46	24.72	22.19	13.02
Huntsville, AL	10.75	28.00	n/a	23.90	20.20	11.55
Indianapolis, IN	14.25	30.46	17.62	26.92	23.09	13.35
Jacksonville, FL	14.72	31.72	15.08	24.87	21.39	15.33
Kansas City, MO	15.24	28.68	20.21	26.24	22.59	15.86
Lafayette, LA	11.25	24.62	n/a	21.71	17.50	11.88
Las Cruces, NM	14.06	33.00	n/a	21.52	17.37	15.04
Las Vegas, NV	16.36	30.96	15.02	24.98	20.79	13.18
Lexington, KY	16.94	29.65	n/a	26.48	21.58	14.02
Lincoln, NE	12.27	28.33	13.08	35.10	21.50	14.17
Little Rock, AR	14.46	25.70	n/a	26.45	22.85	13.89
Los Angeles, CA	20.58	43.33	18.39	26.10	22.77	18.08
Louisville, KY	15.01	30.29	15.36	27.04	23.90	13.48
Madison, WI	16.63	29.79	n/a	25.52	20.60	15.98

Table continued on following page.

Appendix A: Comparative Statistics   A-101

Metro Area	Teacher Assistants[3]	Teachers, Secondary School[3]	Telemarketers	Truck Drivers, Heavy	Truck Drivers, Light	Waiters/ Waitresses
Manchester, NH[2]	16.19	33.56	15.33	25.70	20.52	16.61
Miami, FL	14.59	31.87	16.79	24.62	21.37	16.13
Midland, TX	13.37	30.50	n/a	25.69	20.91	12.89
Milwaukee, WI	16.86	33.03	16.38	26.40	21.54	15.68
Minneapolis, MN	18.50	31.91	22.98	28.77	23.50	13.34
Nashville, TN	13.61	26.44	n/a	26.23	21.56	11.99
New Haven, CT[2]	18.30	36.32	23.10	26.23	21.59	19.08
New Orleans, LA	14.50	27.00	n/a	24.66	19.53	12.15
New York, NY	18.07	45.24	20.35	29.43	23.63	23.01
Oklahoma City, OK	11.92	27.00	18.98	24.66	20.54	12.33
Omaha, NE	13.94	28.50	13.51	32.23	21.83	15.36
Orlando, FL	13.42	26.07	14.29	24.63	21.37	16.41
Philadelphia, PA	16.04	35.76	16.16	27.40	22.39	15.81
Phoenix, AZ	15.19	30.07	17.98	25.42	22.85	22.24
Pittsburgh, PA	15.05	39.73	16.91	25.67	20.10	14.85
Portland, OR	19.64	41.94	19.08	28.25	22.77	18.37
Providence, RI[2]	17.68	36.31	16.60	27.14	22.45	16.64
Provo, UT	13.34	31.61	17.82	25.28	20.06	17.18
Raleigh, NC	12.44	25.67	15.51	24.80	19.06	14.41
Reno, NV	18.08	36.23	n/a	26.51	21.26	13.12
Richmond, VA	14.32	37.47	n/a	24.27	20.61	16.35
Rochester, MN	17.00	31.98	n/a	26.90	21.79	12.51
Sacramento, CA	19.35	41.56	18.78	26.24	23.03	17.51
Salem, OR	19.13	39.59	16.13	26.69	21.33	16.15
Salt Lake City, UT	14.52	33.46	15.85	26.89	21.89	17.80
San Antonio, TX	14.17	29.61	17.04	22.61	20.69	13.14
San Diego, CA	19.50	47.51	17.68	25.83	22.99	17.49
San Francisco, CA	22.38	44.23	22.03	30.83	25.29	18.52
San Jose, CA	22.29	46.64	20.56	29.99	24.72	19.37
Santa Rosa, CA	20.52	43.10	n/a	27.66	24.22	18.13
Savannah, GA	15.18	29.79	n/a	24.85	20.20	13.87
Seattle, WA	22.89	44.03	20.78	30.34	24.18	23.47
Sioux Falls, SD	12.99	24.57	n/a	26.46	21.01	13.23
Springfield, IL	15.04	30.36	n/a	24.23	23.13	14.77
St. Louis, MO	15.52	29.12	18.25	26.27	22.92	16.19
Tampa, FL	14.33	32.73	14.35	23.41	20.06	15.84
Tucson, AZ	14.47	23.84	n/a	23.82	21.31	20.77
Tulsa, OK	12.67	28.15	18.01	24.99	19.91	11.71
Tuscaloosa, AL	10.07	26.64	n/a	24.19	20.50	10.78
Virginia Beach, VA	16.04	31.98	17.71	23.13	19.47	15.39
Washington, DC	19.39	40.33	20.08	27.54	23.67	19.91
Wichita, KS	14.41	28.44	n/a	23.66	20.17	14.48
Wilmington, NC	12.82	25.18	15.79	22.70	20.42	13.33
Winston-Salem, NC	11.63	25.01	n/a	24.69	18.96	12.01
Worcester, MA[2]	19.32	38.25	19.51	26.93	22.55	18.31

Notes: (1) Figures cover the Metropolitan Statistical Area (MSA) except where noted. See Appendix B for areas included;
(2) New England City and Town Area; (3) Hourly wages were calculated from annual wage data assuming a 40 hour work week;
n/a not available
Source: Bureau of Labor Statistics, May 2022 Metro Area Occupational Employment and Wage Estimates

A-102 Appendix A: Comparative Statistics

Means of Transportation to Work: City

City	Car/Truck/Van		Public Transportation			Bicycle	Walked	Other Means	Worked at Home
	Drove Alone	Car-pooled	Bus	Subway	Railroad				
Albuquerque, NM	76.6	8.9	1.3	0.0	0.1	0.8	1.9	1.1	9.4
Allentown, PA	67.4	15.5	3.7	0.0	0.0	0.1	4.4	1.9	6.9
Anchorage, AK	73.7	12.1	1.4	0.0	0.0	0.9	2.6	2.1	7.1
Ann Arbor, MI	48.5	4.9	7.9	0.2	0.0	3.1	15.5	0.6	19.1
Athens, GA	72.0	8.0	2.7	0.0	0.0	1.4	4.8	1.0	10.2
Atlanta, GA	59.8	4.8	4.8	3.6	0.2	1.0	4.4	2.8	18.6
Austin, TX	66.2	7.7	2.5	0.1	0.1	1.0	2.6	1.4	18.4
Baltimore, MD	58.2	7.8	11.8	1.2	1.1	0.8	5.9	2.7	10.8
Boise City, ID	73.8	6.9	0.5	0.0	0.0	2.5	2.9	1.6	11.7
Boston, MA	36.1	5.5	10.6	15.5	1.1	2.0	14.4	2.6	12.3
Boulder, CO	45.8	4.3	6.5	0.0	0.0	8.8	9.1	1.3	24.3
Brownsville, TX	80.7	10.2	0.7	0.0	0.0	0.1	1.3	1.2	5.7
Cape Coral, FL	79.3	7.8	0.1	0.0	0.0	0.2	0.9	1.9	9.8
Cedar Rapids, IA	80.2	7.6	0.4	0.0	0.0	0.5	2.0	1.0	8.5
Charleston, SC	74.5	6.2	0.8	0.0	0.0	1.8	3.8	1.3	11.6
Charlotte, NC	68.8	8.6	1.9	0.3	0.1	0.1	1.8	1.8	16.7
Chicago, IL	47.4	7.5	11.1	10.7	1.4	1.5	5.8	2.2	12.3
Cincinnati, OH	69.0	8.5	6.1	0.0	0.0	0.3	5.5	1.4	9.2
Clarksville, TN	84.5	7.7	0.7	0.0	0.0	0.0	1.2	1.4	4.5
Cleveland, OH	68.6	9.9	7.3	0.4	0.1	0.5	4.7	1.7	6.9
College Station, TX	74.7	8.8	2.1	0.0	0.0	1.8	2.6	0.9	9.0
Colorado Springs, CO	74.7	9.8	0.7	0.0	0.0	0.5	1.7	1.1	11.4
Columbia, MO	75.0	9.0	0.9	0.0	0.0	1.2	6.4	0.7	6.8
Columbia, SC	63.8	5.7	1.5	0.0	0.0	0.4	20.3	1.6	6.7
Columbus, OH	75.0	7.2	2.5	0.0	0.0	0.4	2.7	1.1	11.0
Dallas, TX	72.3	11.2	2.3	0.3	0.2	0.2	2.2	1.6	9.7
Davenport, IA	83.4	6.5	0.6	0.0	0.0	0.2	2.3	0.7	6.3
Denver, CO	62.7	6.8	3.5	0.6	0.4	2.0	4.4	2.3	17.2
Des Moines, IA	75.4	10.6	1.4	0.1	0.0	0.5	2.4	1.4	8.2
Durham, NC	70.7	8.0	2.6	0.0	0.0	0.5	2.2	1.3	14.6
Edison, NJ	64.0	8.1	0.7	0.5	9.9	0.1	1.1	1.3	14.1
El Paso, TX	79.1	10.2	1.4	0.0	0.0	0.1	1.1	2.4	5.7
Fargo, ND	79.5	7.8	1.2	0.0	0.0	0.5	3.5	1.9	5.5
Fort Collins, CO	66.7	6.3	1.8	0.0	0.0	4.4	4.3	1.1	15.5
Fort Wayne, IN	80.9	9.6	1.0	0.0	0.0	0.5	1.5	0.8	5.8
Fort Worth, TX	77.3	11.0	0.5	0.0	0.1	0.2	1.3	1.0	8.6
Grand Rapids, MI	71.5	10.0	3.3	0.0	0.0	0.9	4.4	1.0	8.8
Greeley, CO	76.0	12.4	0.5	0.0	0.0	0.5	3.1	0.7	6.8
Green Bay, WI	77.7	10.7	1.1	0.0	0.0	0.2	2.3	1.1	6.9
Greensboro, NC	78.2	7.7	2.3	0.0	0.0	0.2	2.3	1.0	8.3
Honolulu, HI	57.7	13.1	9.4	0.0	0.0	1.6	8.2	3.6	6.4
Houston, TX	73.7	9.8	3.4	0.1	0.0	0.4	1.9	2.4	8.3
Huntsville, AL	81.8	6.2	0.4	0.0	0.0	0.2	1.2	0.8	9.4
Indianapolis, IN	77.6	9.3	1.6	0.0	0.0	0.4	1.9	0.9	8.4
Jacksonville, FL	77.3	8.7	1.4	0.0	0.0	0.3	1.4	2.0	8.8
Kansas City, MO	77.2	7.4	2.2	0.0	0.0	0.2	1.7	1.5	9.8
Lafayette, LA	83.4	4.8	0.8	0.0	0.0	0.5	2.4	1.0	7.0
Las Cruces, NM	74.3	13.2	0.5	0.0	0.0	1.6	1.7	1.4	7.4
Las Vegas, NV	75.5	9.8	2.8	0.0	0.0	0.2	1.3	2.9	7.4
Lexington, KY	77.0	8.1	1.7	0.0	0.0	0.6	3.5	1.1	8.2
Lincoln, NE	78.2	9.1	1.0	0.0	0.0	0.8	3.3	0.7	7.0
Little Rock, AR	78.5	9.7	0.7	0.0	0.0	0.2	1.8	1.5	7.7
Los Angeles, CA	65.2	8.9	6.6	0.8	0.1	0.7	3.2	2.1	12.4
Louisville, KY	76.6	8.4	2.6	0.0	0.0	0.3	1.9	1.6	8.5

Table continued on following page.

Appendix A: Comparative Statistics   A-103

City	Car/Truck/Van		Public Transportation			Bicycle	Walked	Other Means	Worked at Home
	Drove Alone	Car-pooled	Bus	Subway	Railroad				
Madison, WI	60.5	6.6	7.0	0.0	0.1	3.6	8.9	1.3	12.1
Manchester, NH	77.8	8.9	0.5	0.0	0.0	0.2	2.6	1.2	8.8
Miami, FL	65.9	7.7	6.1	1.1	0.1	0.8	4.8	3.5	10.1
Midland, TX	82.4	10.4	0.2	0.0	0.0	0.3	0.6	0.7	5.5
Milwaukee, WI	71.2	9.5	5.8	0.0	0.0	0.6	4.1	1.0	7.7
Minneapolis, MN	56.4	6.3	8.6	0.6	0.2	2.9	6.6	2.6	15.8
Nashville, TN	72.8	9.1	1.6	0.0	0.1	0.2	2.2	1.3	12.7
New Haven, CT	58.6	8.0	7.5	0.1	1.1	2.1	11.6	1.9	9.1
New Orleans, LA	65.6	8.9	4.6	0.1	0.0	2.6	5.4	2.9	9.9
New York, NY	22.4	4.4	9.7	38.4	1.2	1.4	9.5	2.5	10.7
Oklahoma City, OK	80.0	9.7	0.4	0.0	0.0	0.2	1.6	1.4	6.8
Omaha, NE	77.2	8.9	1.3	0.0	0.0	0.2	2.1	1.0	9.3
Orlando, FL	75.2	8.1	2.3	0.0	0.0	0.6	1.4	2.7	9.7
Philadelphia, PA	48.3	7.8	13.5	5.2	2.2	2.0	7.6	2.7	10.8
Phoenix, AZ	70.8	11.5	2.1	0.0	0.0	0.5	1.5	1.9	11.5
Pittsburgh, PA	52.1	6.6	14.5	0.3	0.0	1.2	9.7	1.8	13.9
Portland, OR	53.8	7.4	7.2	0.5	0.2	4.7	5.1	3.2	18.0
Providence, RI	64.0	11.3	3.3	0.1	1.0	0.9	7.3	1.7	10.4
Provo, UT	59.2	11.2	3.2	0.1	0.9	2.0	11.8	1.0	10.5
Raleigh, NC	70.9	7.1	1.7	0.0	0.0	0.2	1.4	1.4	17.2
Reno, NV	71.1	12.0	2.7	0.0	0.0	0.7	2.8	2.5	8.3
Richmond, VA	67.8	8.5	4.2	0.1	0.0	1.8	4.5	1.6	11.5
Rochester, MN	67.8	11.9	5.4	0.0	0.0	0.8	4.2	1.2	8.8
Sacramento, CA	68.9	9.6	1.7	0.2	0.3	1.6	2.9	2.2	12.6
St. Louis, MO	69.9	6.6	5.8	0.4	0.1	0.9	4.4	1.4	10.5
Salem, OR	71.7	9.5	2.2	0.0	0.0	1.4	3.4	1.2	10.5
Salt Lake City, UT	63.1	8.8	3.8	0.3	0.6	2.1	4.8	3.2	13.2
San Antonio, TX	74.6	11.8	2.1	0.0	0.0	0.2	1.8	1.6	8.0
San Diego, CA	68.9	8.2	2.8	0.1	0.1	0.7	3.2	2.0	14.0
San Francisco, CA	29.4	6.5	17.8	7.0	1.3	3.3	11.0	5.6	18.0
San Jose, CA	69.2	10.5	2.0	0.3	0.9	0.6	1.9	1.8	13.0
Santa Rosa, CA	76.1	10.3	1.4	0.1	0.1	0.8	1.8	1.4	7.9
Savannah, GA	71.7	10.7	3.1	0.0	0.0	1.2	4.2	1.8	7.3
Seattle, WA	40.5	6.1	15.4	1.0	0.1	2.8	9.7	2.9	21.4
Sioux Falls, SD	81.7	7.8	0.6	0.0	0.0	0.3	2.1	0.7	6.8
Springfield, IL	79.6	6.4	1.6	0.1	0.0	0.5	1.6	1.7	8.7
Tampa, FL	71.9	8.2	1.9	0.0	0.0	0.8	2.1	1.9	13.2
Tucson, AZ	71.3	10.4	2.6	0.0	0.0	1.9	2.9	1.7	9.2
Tulsa, OK	78.4	9.9	0.6	0.0	0.0	0.2	1.8	1.9	7.2
Tuscaloosa, AL	80.0	9.7	1.4	0.0	0.0	0.5	1.8	1.0	5.6
Virginia Beach, VA	79.1	7.6	0.7	0.0	0.0	0.4	2.1	1.6	8.4
Washington, DC	30.7	4.7	10.0	16.7	0.2	3.7	11.3	2.7	19.8
Wichita, KS	81.4	9.8	0.6	0.0	0.0	0.4	1.2	1.4	5.1
Wilmington, NC	75.4	7.5	0.7	0.0	0.0	0.6	2.5	0.8	12.6
Winston-Salem, NC	77.7	8.9	1.3	0.0	0.0	0.3	2.1	1.2	8.5
Worcester, MA	68.3	11.4	1.9	0.2	0.6	0.2	6.2	2.9	8.3
U.S.	73.2	8.6	2.0	1.6	0.5	0.5	2.5	1.5	9.7

Note: Figures are percentages and cover workers 16 years of age and older
Source: U.S. Census Bureau, 2017-2021 American Community Survey 5-Year Estimates

A-104 Appendix A: Comparative Statistics

Means of Transportation to Work: Metro Area

Metro Area	Car/Truck/Van		Public Transportation			Bicycle	Walked	Other Means	Worked at Home
	Drove Alone	Car-pooled	Bus	Subway	Railroad				
Albuquerque, NM	76.8	9.4	1.0	0.0	0.1	0.6	1.7	1.1	9.4
Allentown, PA	78.4	7.9	1.2	0.1	0.1	0.1	2.3	1.2	8.7
Anchorage, AK	73.7	11.5	1.2	0.0	0.0	0.8	2.4	3.0	7.4
Ann Arbor, MI	66.1	6.5	4.1	0.1	0.0	1.3	6.9	0.8	14.2
Athens, GA	75.1	8.0	1.6	0.0	0.0	0.8	3.4	1.2	9.9
Atlanta, GA	72.7	8.7	1.5	0.7	0.1	0.2	1.2	1.7	13.2
Austin, TX	69.7	8.4	1.3	0.0	0.1	0.6	1.8	1.3	16.8
Baltimore, MD	72.5	7.4	3.4	0.7	0.7	0.2	2.3	1.5	11.2
Boise City, ID	76.4	7.9	0.2	0.0	0.0	1.1	1.9	1.3	11.0
Boston, MA	62.2	6.6	3.2	5.5	1.8	0.9	5.0	1.7	13.0
Boulder, CO	60.1	6.6	3.9	0.0	0.0	3.6	4.0	1.1	20.8
Brownsville, TX	81.3	9.1	0.4	0.0	0.0	0.1	1.6	1.2	6.3
Cape Coral, FL	76.3	9.6	0.5	0.0	0.0	0.7	1.0	2.3	9.6
Cedar Rapids, IA	80.3	7.0	0.3	0.0	0.0	0.3	1.8	0.8	9.4
Charleston, SC	79.1	7.6	0.6	0.0	0.0	0.6	1.8	1.2	9.1
Charlotte, NC	74.7	8.4	0.9	0.1	0.0	0.1	1.3	1.3	13.1
Chicago, IL	66.7	7.6	3.7	3.6	2.6	0.6	2.8	1.5	10.9
Cincinnati, OH	78.8	7.7	1.4	0.0	0.0	0.2	1.9	0.9	9.1
Clarksville, TN	82.2	8.6	0.5	0.0	0.0	0.2	2.9	1.3	4.3
Cleveland, OH	77.9	7.4	2.1	0.1	0.0	0.3	2.1	1.2	8.8
College Station, TX	78.2	9.5	1.1	0.0	0.0	1.1	1.7	1.2	7.2
Colorado Springs, CO	73.8	9.6	0.5	0.0	0.0	0.3	3.2	1.0	11.4
Columbia, MO	77.1	9.6	0.6	0.0	0.0	0.8	4.4	0.8	6.7
Columbia, SC	78.7	8.1	0.6	0.0	0.0	0.1	4.2	1.6	6.7
Columbus, OH	77.1	6.7	1.3	0.0	0.0	0.3	2.0	1.0	11.6
Dallas, TX	75.8	9.5	0.6	0.1	0.2	0.1	1.2	1.3	11.1
Davenport, IA	83.9	6.8	0.7	0.0	0.0	0.2	2.2	0.7	5.6
Denver, CO	69.8	7.5	2.2	0.3	0.2	0.8	2.1	1.7	15.4
Des Moines, IA	78.3	7.6	0.6	0.0	0.0	0.2	1.7	1.1	10.5
Durham, NC	70.8	7.7	2.6	0.0	0.0	0.6	2.3	1.3	14.5
Edison, NJ	47.4	6.1	6.7	17.4	3.1	0.7	5.5	2.3	10.6
El Paso, TX	78.6	10.6	1.1	0.0	0.0	0.1	1.4	2.3	5.8
Fargo, ND	79.8	8.0	0.9	0.0	0.0	0.4	2.6	1.4	6.9
Fort Collins, CO	70.7	6.4	1.1	0.1	0.0	2.4	2.8	1.1	15.4
Fort Wayne, IN	82.1	8.7	0.7	0.0	0.0	0.4	1.3	0.7	6.2
Fort Worth, TX	75.8	9.5	0.6	0.1	0.2	0.1	1.2	1.3	11.1
Grand Rapids, MI	79.0	8.5	1.2	0.0	0.0	0.4	2.2	0.7	7.9
Greeley, CO	76.7	10.4	0.4	0.0	0.0	0.2	1.9	0.8	9.5
Green Bay, WI	81.4	7.6	0.5	0.0	0.0	0.1	1.8	0.8	7.8
Greensboro, NC	79.8	8.8	1.1	0.0	0.0	0.2	1.5	1.1	7.5
Honolulu, HI	65.4	13.2	6.3	0.0	0.0	0.9	5.2	2.5	6.4
Houston, TX	77.1	9.3	1.7	0.0	0.0	0.3	1.2	1.6	8.7
Huntsville, AL	83.6	5.8	0.2	0.0	0.0	0.1	0.7	1.0	8.6
Indianapolis, IN	78.7	8.2	0.7	0.0	0.0	0.2	1.4	0.9	9.8
Jacksonville, FL	76.8	8.2	0.9	0.0	0.0	0.4	1.3	1.9	10.5
Kansas City, MO	79.0	7.3	0.7	0.0	0.0	0.1	1.1	1.0	10.6
Lafayette, LA	83.9	6.7	0.3	0.0	0.0	0.2	1.9	1.2	5.8
Las Cruces, NM	76.4	12.3	0.4	0.0	0.0	0.9	1.7	1.3	7.1
Las Vegas, NV	75.8	10.1	2.6	0.0	0.0	0.2	1.3	2.5	7.4
Lexington, KY	78.2	8.4	1.1	0.0	0.0	0.4	2.9	1.0	8.0
Lincoln, NE	78.5	8.9	0.8	0.0	0.0	0.8	3.2	0.7	7.2
Little Rock, AR	81.6	9.4	0.4	0.0	0.0	0.1	1.1	1.1	6.3
Los Angeles, CA	70.9	9.3	3.4	0.4	0.2	0.6	2.3	1.8	11.2
Louisville, KY	78.9	8.2	1.5	0.0	0.0	0.2	1.4	1.1	8.7

Table continued on following page.

Appendix A: Comparative Statistics   A-105

Metro Area	Car/Truck/Van		Public Transportation			Bicycle	Walked	Other Means	Worked at Home
	Drove Alone	Car-pooled	Bus	Subway	Railroad				
Madison, WI	71.0	6.5	3.3	0.0	0.0	1.8	4.9	1.0	11.5
Manchester, NH	77.6	7.2	0.6	0.1	0.1	0.2	1.8	0.9	11.5
Miami, FL	75.1	9.1	2.1	0.3	0.1	0.5	1.5	2.1	9.2
Midland, TX	82.7	9.9	0.1	0.0	0.0	0.2	1.2	0.7	5.1
Milwaukee, WI	77.4	7.1	2.4	0.0	0.0	0.4	2.3	0.8	9.5
Minneapolis, MN	72.1	7.4	3.2	0.1	0.1	0.6	2.1	1.3	13.1
Nashville, TN	76.7	8.6	0.7	0.0	0.1	0.1	1.2	1.1	11.6
New Haven, CT	74.9	8.1	2.3	0.1	0.7	0.4	3.4	1.3	8.7
New Orleans, LA	76.2	9.6	1.7	0.0	0.0	0.9	2.4	1.7	7.4
New York, NY	47.4	6.1	6.7	17.4	3.1	0.7	5.5	2.3	10.6
Oklahoma City, OK	80.6	9.1	0.3	0.0	0.0	0.3	1.6	1.2	7.0
Omaha, NE	79.5	8.0	0.7	0.0	0.0	0.1	1.7	1.0	9.0
Orlando, FL	75.8	9.4	1.1	0.0	0.1	0.4	1.1	1.9	10.2
Philadelphia, PA	68.2	7.1	4.2	1.7	1.7	0.6	3.2	1.5	11.7
Phoenix, AZ	71.6	10.3	1.3	0.0	0.0	0.6	1.4	1.8	13.0
Pittsburgh, PA	73.0	7.4	4.2	0.2	0.0	0.2	3.0	1.3	10.8
Portland, OR	66.2	8.4	3.6	0.4	0.2	1.7	3.1	2.0	14.4
Providence, RI	77.8	8.3	1.2	0.1	0.7	0.2	2.7	1.0	7.8
Provo, UT	70.1	10.3	1.0	0.1	0.7	0.7	3.3	1.0	12.8
Raleigh, NC	72.9	7.4	0.7	0.0	0.0	0.1	1.1	1.0	16.8
Reno, NV	73.1	12.0	2.0	0.0	0.0	0.5	2.0	2.0	8.3
Richmond, VA	76.2	7.7	1.2	0.0	0.1	0.4	1.4	1.1	11.9
Rochester, MN	71.2	11.0	3.4	0.0	0.0	0.5	3.5	1.0	9.4
Sacramento, CA	72.1	8.8	1.3	0.1	0.2	1.1	1.6	1.7	13.1
St. Louis, MO	79.2	6.7	1.4	0.2	0.1	0.2	1.6	1.0	9.8
Salem, OR	74.3	10.1	1.3	0.0	0.0	0.8	2.6	1.1	9.8
Salt Lake City, UT	71.0	10.3	1.5	0.2	0.4	0.6	1.9	1.7	12.5
San Antonio, TX	75.6	10.7	1.3	0.0	0.0	0.2	1.6	1.4	9.1
San Diego, CA	71.6	8.4	2.0	0.1	0.1	0.5	2.9	2.0	12.5
San Francisco, CA	53.4	8.6	6.1	5.7	1.2	1.6	4.3	2.8	16.3
San Jose, CA	67.1	9.4	1.8	0.3	1.0	1.4	2.1	1.6	15.3
Santa Rosa, CA	72.8	10.0	1.2	0.1	0.2	0.6	2.3	1.5	11.3
Savannah, GA	79.8	8.6	1.3	0.0	0.0	0.6	1.9	1.7	6.2
Seattle, WA	62.4	9.1	6.7	0.3	0.4	0.9	3.6	1.6	14.9
Sioux Falls, SD	81.7	7.6	0.5	0.0	0.0	0.3	1.9	0.6	7.4
Springfield, IL	81.6	6.4	0.9	0.1	0.0	0.4	1.4	1.3	8.0
Tampa, FL	74.8	8.2	1.0	0.0	0.0	0.5	1.3	1.6	12.4
Tucson, AZ	73.4	9.7	1.7	0.0	0.0	1.2	2.1	1.7	10.3
Tulsa, OK	80.7	9.1	0.3	0.0	0.0	0.1	1.3	1.3	7.1
Tuscaloosa, AL	82.3	10.3	0.8	0.0	0.0	0.2	0.9	0.6	5.0
Virginia Beach, VA	78.3	7.9	1.3	0.0	0.0	0.3	3.1	1.6	7.5
Washington, DC	60.7	8.5	3.6	5.8	0.6	0.7	2.9	1.7	15.4
Wichita, KS	82.2	8.7	0.4	0.0	0.0	0.3	1.5	1.3	5.6
Wilmington, NC	77.5	8.0	0.3	0.0	0.0	0.4	1.4	0.6	11.8
Winston-Salem, NC	80.7	8.8	0.6	0.0	0.0	0.1	1.3	0.9	7.6
Worcester, MA	76.2	7.6	0.7	0.2	0.7	0.2	2.6	1.7	10.2
U.S.	73.2	8.6	2.0	1.6	0.5	0.5	2.5	1.5	9.7

Note: Figures are percentages and cover workers 16 years of age and older; (1) Figures cover the Metropolitan Statistical Area
Source: U.S. Census Bureau, 2017-2021 American Community Survey 5-Year Estimates

A-106   Appendix A: Comparative Statistics

Travel Time to Work: City

City	Less Than 10 Minutes	10 to 19 Minutes	20 to 29 Minutes	30 to 44 Minutes	45 to 59 Minutes	60 to 89 Minutes	90 Minutes or More
Albuquerque, NM	11.0	35.9	27.8	18.1	3.1	2.5	1.6
Allentown, PA	10.6	33.2	30.0	15.2	4.3	4.6	2.1
Anchorage, AK	16.1	44.4	23.4	11.2	2.1	1.2	1.6
Ann Arbor, MI	13.9	45.7	18.6	14.0	5.0	2.4	0.5
Athens, GA	18.0	45.8	16.6	9.8	3.5	3.5	2.8
Atlanta, GA	6.9	29.5	25.6	21.8	7.3	5.4	3.5
Austin, TX	9.7	32.0	24.5	21.7	6.9	3.7	1.5
Baltimore, MD	6.7	23.6	23.3	25.6	8.7	7.4	4.7
Boise City, ID	13.6	44.5	26.2	11.4	1.6	1.5	1.2
Boston, MA	6.9	20.4	19.6	29.8	12.1	9.1	2.1
Boulder, CO	19.7	44.5	16.1	9.5	5.8	3.2	1.2
Brownsville, TX	8.7	42.9	28.9	14.3	2.5	1.7	1.0
Cape Coral, FL	8.0	25.3	22.2	27.4	9.4	5.4	2.3
Cedar Rapids, IA	20.0	48.9	17.0	9.2	1.9	1.5	1.5
Charleston, SC	11.4	30.7	26.6	20.6	7.6	1.6	1.4
Charlotte, NC	8.6	29.6	26.7	23.2	6.5	3.3	2.1
Chicago, IL	4.7	16.4	18.4	30.5	15.1	11.9	3.1
Cincinnati, OH	11.4	33.0	26.8	19.1	4.3	3.2	2.1
Clarksville, TN	10.3	33.0	25.3	14.1	6.8	8.5	2.2
Cleveland, OH	10.2	34.0	27.0	20.0	3.9	3.0	2.1
College Station, TX	17.6	55.5	17.1	6.2	0.5	2.0	1.1
Colorado Springs, CO	11.5	35.9	28.0	15.9	3.3	2.9	2.5
Columbia, MO	20.0	54.4	13.7	7.3	2.5	1.0	1.1
Columbia, SC	29.8	36.0	19.0	10.0	2.1	1.8	1.4
Columbus, OH	10.3	34.2	30.4	18.7	3.2	1.9	1.3
Dallas, TX	8.2	26.9	23.3	25.8	8.0	5.9	1.9
Davenport, IA	16.5	47.5	22.0	8.2	3.1	1.8	1.0
Denver, CO	7.9	29.0	24.7	26.0	7.2	3.7	1.4
Des Moines, IA	13.5	43.1	26.6	12.3	2.2	1.3	1.1
Durham, NC	9.2	38.4	25.5	17.9	4.8	2.7	1.4
Edison, NJ	7.6	22.0	18.1	17.8	12.2	12.6	9.6
El Paso, TX	9.5	33.5	28.5	19.7	4.7	2.2	1.8
Fargo, ND	20.6	56.3	15.2	3.6	1.4	1.9	0.9
Fort Collins, CO	15.4	43.8	20.6	10.0	5.4	3.3	1.5
Fort Wayne, IN	12.8	38.2	28.0	13.5	3.0	2.6	1.8
Fort Worth, TX	7.7	29.0	22.9	23.9	8.7	5.8	2.0
Grand Rapids, MI	14.5	44.0	23.5	11.6	3.7	2.0	0.8
Greeley, CO	15.9	37.3	15.3	14.4	5.9	9.2	1.9
Green Bay, WI	18.2	48.6	19.5	8.5	2.8	1.3	1.1
Greensboro, NC	12.5	40.0	23.6	15.9	3.2	3.0	2.0
Honolulu, HI	8.7	38.2	22.6	20.6	5.0	3.6	1.2
Houston, TX	7.2	25.5	23.0	27.7	8.9	5.9	1.8
Huntsville, AL	13.1	41.0	26.2	15.5	2.5	1.0	0.8
Indianapolis, IN	9.5	30.4	28.8	22.7	4.3	2.4	1.8
Jacksonville, FL	8.7	28.5	27.2	25.4	6.0	2.8	1.4
Kansas City, MO	11.6	33.4	27.9	20.3	4.0	1.7	1.2
Lafayette, LA	15.8	44.0	19.3	11.9	2.8	3.6	2.6
Las Cruces, NM	16.2	49.2	16.2	9.5	3.5	4.8	0.7
Las Vegas, NV	7.3	24.0	30.6	27.4	6.2	2.7	1.9
Lexington, KY	13.2	39.5	26.2	13.9	2.9	2.4	1.8
Lincoln, NE	16.7	44.7	22.8	9.9	2.6	2.1	1.2
Little Rock, AR	15.4	45.3	23.6	11.0	2.3	1.5	0.9
Los Angeles, CA	5.9	22.2	19.3	28.5	10.5	10.1	3.6
Louisville, KY	9.6	32.6	31.4	19.1	3.9	2.0	1.4
Madison, WI	14.9	39.6	24.8	15.1	3.0	1.8	0.8

Table continued on following page.

Appendix A: Comparative Statistics   A-107

City	Less Than 10 Minutes	10 to 19 Minutes	20 to 29 Minutes	30 to 44 Minutes	45 to 59 Minutes	60 to 89 Minutes	90 Minutes or More
Manchester, NH	12.6	35.5	23.4	14.6	6.4	5.1	2.4
Miami, FL	6.0	21.8	24.7	30.5	9.1	6.6	1.4
Midland, TX	14.2	47.3	18.9	12.0	2.9	2.4	2.4
Milwaukee, WI	10.4	36.6	26.1	19.1	3.5	2.7	1.7
Minneapolis, MN	7.9	32.6	30.2	20.9	4.5	2.7	1.1
Nashville, TN	9.1	29.0	26.6	23.2	7.0	3.6	1.5
New Haven, CT	13.2	40.4	21.6	13.6	4.5	4.2	2.5
New Orleans, LA	11.0	34.8	24.2	19.5	5.0	3.5	2.0
New York, NY	4.0	12.3	13.5	27.1	16.3	19.2	7.6
Oklahoma City, OK	10.5	36.0	29.0	18.2	3.5	1.4	1.4
Omaha, NE	14.5	41.2	26.7	12.4	2.5	1.9	0.9
Orlando, FL	7.2	25.4	27.6	26.6	7.2	3.9	2.2
Philadelphia, PA	6.1	19.2	20.2	28.1	12.9	9.5	4.0
Phoenix, AZ	8.6	26.6	26.6	24.5	7.4	4.5	1.8
Pittsburgh, PA	9.4	32.3	26.6	21.8	4.6	3.6	1.7
Portland, OR	8.3	28.2	26.8	24.0	7.1	4.1	1.5
Providence, RI	10.3	40.4	19.4	15.3	6.2	5.5	2.8
Provo, UT	21.4	44.2	16.8	9.8	3.5	3.1	1.2
Raleigh, NC	9.3	32.4	27.0	20.8	5.7	3.0	1.8
Reno, NV	15.6	40.3	22.8	12.5	4.7	2.7	1.4
Richmond, VA	11.4	37.4	27.3	16.8	2.9	2.7	1.5
Rochester, MN	17.7	55.5	14.1	6.5	2.8	2.2	1.2
Sacramento, CA	8.4	31.3	24.9	22.4	5.6	4.2	3.1
St. Louis, MO	9.2	35.2	26.5	19.7	4.3	2.9	2.1
Salem, OR	13.0	41.0	19.7	12.7	6.0	6.0	1.6
Salt Lake City, UT	14.1	45.1	21.4	12.6	3.5	2.2	1.2
San Antonio, TX	9.4	31.4	26.3	21.8	6.0	3.4	1.7
San Diego, CA	7.7	32.9	27.5	20.9	5.7	3.6	1.7
San Francisco, CA	4.5	19.3	21.4	29.5	11.6	10.1	3.7
San Jose, CA	5.6	24.6	23.2	26.1	10.1	7.5	3.0
Santa Rosa, CA	12.6	40.1	21.3	14.4	4.3	4.0	3.3
Savannah, GA	15.7	39.1	22.8	13.3	4.8	2.8	1.5
Seattle, WA	7.3	24.0	24.1	27.6	10.6	5.0	1.5
Sioux Falls, SD	16.7	51.6	22.0	5.8	1.7	1.2	1.0
Springfield, IL	17.4	53.1	17.9	6.3	1.8	2.3	1.3
Tampa, FL	11.1	30.2	22.5	23.4	6.8	4.3	1.8
Tucson, AZ	11.8	34.9	25.4	19.6	4.7	2.0	1.6
Tulsa, OK	14.2	44.9	26.3	10.1	1.9	1.4	1.2
Tuscaloosa, AL	16.8	46.6	21.7	7.6	3.1	3.1	1.1
Virginia Beach, VA	10.1	30.9	27.9	22.0	5.3	2.5	1.4
Washington, DC	5.3	19.0	22.3	33.1	11.6	6.6	2.1
Wichita, KS	14.3	44.9	26.7	9.9	1.6	1.4	1.2
Wilmington, NC	16.1	47.0	21.7	9.5	2.5	1.7	1.5
Winston-Salem, NC	14.0	40.3	22.6	14.3	4.6	2.6	1.7
Worcester, MA	13.4	34.6	19.5	17.8	5.9	6.3	2.5
U.S.	12.4	28.5	21.0	20.9	8.2	6.2	2.9

Note: Figures are percentages and include workers 16 years old and over
Source: U.S. Census Bureau, 2017-2021 American Community Survey 5-Year Estimates

A-108 Appendix A: Comparative Statistics

Travel Time to Work: Metro Area

Metro Area	Less Than 10 Minutes	10 to 19 Minutes	20 to 29 Minutes	30 to 44 Minutes	45 to 59 Minutes	60 to 89 Minutes	90 Minutes or More
Albuquerque, NM	10.7	31.5	26.0	20.7	5.7	3.5	1.8
Allentown, PA	12.6	27.7	23.5	18.5	7.3	6.6	3.8
Anchorage, AK	15.0	40.4	21.8	11.4	4.5	4.1	2.7
Ann Arbor, MI	11.5	32.6	24.5	19.1	7.3	3.8	1.1
Athens, GA	14.2	38.2	21.9	13.5	5.2	4.0	3.0
Atlanta, GA	6.9	22.5	19.9	25.2	12.2	9.6	3.5
Austin, TX	9.3	26.6	22.1	23.8	10.1	6.3	1.9
Baltimore, MD	8.0	23.3	21.0	24.7	11.0	8.3	3.7
Boise City, ID	12.8	33.4	25.0	19.7	5.5	2.2	1.4
Boston, MA	9.1	22.7	18.6	24.4	11.7	10.1	3.3
Boulder, CO	14.5	33.4	20.5	17.6	7.6	4.8	1.6
Brownsville, TX	12.8	40.5	25.7	15.0	3.4	1.6	1.0
Cape Coral, FL	8.6	25.3	22.8	26.0	9.8	5.2	2.3
Cedar Rapids, IA	18.8	40.1	20.6	12.8	4.3	2.0	1.5
Charleston, SC	8.8	26.0	24.1	25.1	9.5	4.8	1.7
Charlotte, NC	9.8	27.8	22.6	23.3	9.3	5.1	2.1
Chicago, IL	8.5	21.9	19.0	25.3	12.2	10.0	3.1
Cincinnati, OH	10.9	28.2	25.2	23.1	7.5	3.5	1.6
Clarksville, TN	14.8	31.0	22.4	16.1	6.5	6.5	2.7
Cleveland, OH	11.6	28.2	25.9	23.2	6.7	2.9	1.6
College Station, TX	16.1	49.4	18.4	10.4	2.3	2.1	1.4
Colorado Springs, CO	11.5	32.8	26.9	18.0	4.7	3.6	2.5
Columbia, MO	17.3	44.2	19.4	11.9	3.8	1.7	1.7
Columbia, SC	12.6	28.8	24.1	22.2	6.9	3.3	2.2
Columbus, OH	11.4	29.5	26.7	21.7	6.1	3.1	1.5
Dallas, TX	8.6	25.2	21.7	25.6	10.3	6.7	2.0
Davenport, IA	18.3	36.1	24.9	13.1	3.9	2.4	1.3
Denver, CO	8.4	25.1	23.0	26.5	9.6	5.5	1.9
Des Moines, IA	15.0	35.0	27.5	16.1	3.7	1.5	1.1
Durham, NC	9.8	31.4	24.8	21.0	7.3	4.2	1.5
Edison, NJ	7.0	18.5	16.3	24.0	12.7	14.7	6.8
El Paso, TX	10.3	31.9	27.4	21.0	5.2	2.3	1.9
Fargo, ND	17.8	52.1	18.3	6.0	2.4	1.9	1.4
Fort Collins, CO	13.5	35.4	21.8	15.9	6.3	4.9	2.2
Fort Wayne, IN	13.0	35.3	28.4	15.7	3.4	2.4	1.8
Fort Worth, TX	8.6	25.2	21.7	25.6	10.3	6.7	2.0
Grand Rapids, MI	14.8	35.3	24.7	16.1	5.0	2.6	1.5
Greeley, CO	11.6	26.7	18.8	22.8	9.8	8.1	2.3
Green Bay, WI	17.9	40.4	21.9	13.0	3.6	1.7	1.4
Greensboro, NC	12.8	34.6	24.4	18.6	4.8	3.0	1.9
Honolulu, HI	9.8	26.1	19.9	24.9	9.4	7.3	2.6
Houston, TX	7.6	23.2	20.4	26.7	11.6	8.2	2.3
Huntsville, AL	10.1	31.7	27.7	22.1	5.2	1.9	1.2
Indianapolis, IN	11.4	27.7	23.9	24.5	7.4	3.4	1.7
Jacksonville, FL	9.1	26.1	24.3	26.1	8.6	4.2	1.6
Kansas City, MO	12.3	30.6	25.5	21.6	6.3	2.5	1.3
Lafayette, LA	13.3	33.5	20.9	18.5	5.9	3.8	4.0
Las Cruces, NM	13.9	40.3	20.0	14.2	5.2	4.8	1.7
Las Vegas, NV	7.8	27.5	29.4	25.4	5.4	2.6	1.9
Lexington, KY	14.5	35.6	24.5	16.8	4.3	2.6	1.7
Lincoln, NE	16.9	41.6	23.5	11.6	3.0	2.2	1.3
Little Rock, AR	13.0	32.7	22.6	20.4	7.0	2.9	1.4
Los Angeles, CA	7.1	24.8	19.9	25.4	9.9	9.3	3.5
Louisville, KY	9.7	30.1	28.8	22.0	5.7	2.4	1.5
Madison, WI	15.9	32.2	24.8	18.2	5.3	2.5	1.1

Table continued on following page.

Appendix A: Comparative Statistics   A-109

Metro Area	Less Than 10 Minutes	10 to 19 Minutes	20 to 29 Minutes	30 to 44 Minutes	45 to 59 Minutes	60 to 89 Minutes	90 Minutes or More
Manchester, NH	10.9	29.7	21.2	19.5	8.7	6.7	3.4
Miami, FL	6.6	22.6	22.7	27.7	10.2	7.6	2.6
Midland, TX	14.7	42.7	21.0	13.5	3.3	2.5	2.2
Milwaukee, WI	12.1	32.1	25.7	21.2	5.0	2.5	1.4
Minneapolis, MN	10.6	28.0	25.2	23.2	7.7	4.0	1.4
Nashville, TN	9.4	26.2	21.5	23.5	10.9	6.5	2.0
New Haven, CT	11.7	31.6	23.1	19.7	6.3	4.6	3.0
New Orleans, LA	10.9	30.8	21.8	20.7	8.0	5.5	2.4
New York, NY	7.0	18.5	16.3	24.0	12.7	14.7	6.8
Oklahoma City, OK	11.9	32.3	25.4	20.6	5.7	2.5	1.6
Omaha, NE	14.1	36.1	27.3	16.0	3.6	1.9	1.1
Orlando, FL	7.2	22.9	22.3	28.1	11.2	6.0	2.4
Philadelphia, PA	9.6	23.9	20.6	24.0	11.1	7.8	3.1
Phoenix, AZ	9.9	26.1	24.0	23.6	8.9	5.6	1.9
Pittsburgh, PA	11.8	27.0	21.3	22.9	9.1	5.8	2.1
Portland, OR	10.8	27.5	23.0	22.7	8.9	5.1	2.0
Providence, RI	11.7	30.4	21.3	19.8	7.8	6.2	2.8
Provo, UT	17.1	34.7	20.2	16.5	6.2	3.9	1.5
Raleigh, NC	8.6	26.7	24.4	24.4	9.1	4.9	1.9
Reno, NV	13.0	35.6	24.5	17.2	5.2	2.9	1.6
Richmond, VA	9.3	28.8	26.7	23.5	6.6	3.1	2.1
Rochester, MN	18.1	41.7	18.6	12.6	4.3	2.9	1.9
Sacramento, CA	9.9	28.3	22.4	23.1	7.9	4.7	3.7
St. Louis, MO	11.0	27.3	24.4	24.0	7.9	3.8	1.7
Salem, OR	13.7	32.6	20.9	16.9	7.6	6.3	2.0
Salt Lake City, UT	10.8	33.5	26.9	19.2	5.5	3.0	1.2
San Antonio, TX	9.2	27.8	24.1	23.2	8.7	4.8	2.2
San Diego, CA	8.1	29.4	24.5	23.5	7.5	5.0	2.1
San Francisco, CA	7.0	22.9	17.8	23.6	11.9	12.0	4.9
San Jose, CA	7.0	26.5	23.0	24.3	9.1	7.0	3.1
Santa Rosa, CA	14.0	32.4	20.4	17.1	6.4	6.0	3.8
Savannah, GA	11.0	29.3	24.8	21.8	8.2	3.6	1.5
Seattle, WA	8.2	22.3	21.1	25.2	11.2	8.6	3.4
Sioux Falls, SD	16.8	43.8	24.1	10.0	2.6	1.4	1.2
Springfield, IL	15.0	43.3	23.5	11.8	2.5	2.1	1.8
Tampa, FL	9.6	26.9	21.0	23.7	10.2	6.3	2.3
Tucson, AZ	10.6	29.4	24.7	24.1	7.0	2.4	1.7
Tulsa, OK	13.3	33.7	26.9	18.0	4.6	2.1	1.4
Tuscaloosa, AL	11.1	33.8	23.3	17.4	6.7	5.7	2.0
Virginia Beach, VA	11.1	31.1	23.5	21.4	7.1	4.0	1.7
Washington, DC	6.1	19.3	18.2	26.2	13.7	12.1	4.3
Wichita, KS	16.1	37.2	26.2	15.1	2.7	1.5	1.3
Wilmington, NC	12.7	38.0	22.6	16.0	5.7	2.8	2.1
Winston-Salem, NC	12.5	32.5	24.3	19.3	6.1	3.2	2.2
Worcester, MA	12.3	26.0	18.5	20.6	10.4	8.5	3.8
U.S.	12.4	28.5	21.0	20.9	8.2	6.2	2.9

Note: Figures are percentages and include workers 16 years old and over; Figures cover the Metropolitan Statistical Area
Source: U.S. Census Bureau, 2017-2021 American Community Survey 5-Year Estimates

A-110   Appendix A: Comparative Statistics

2020 Presidential Election Results

City	Area Covered	Biden	Trump	Jorgensen	Hawkins	Other
Albuquerque, NM	Bernalillo County	61.0	36.6	1.5	0.5	0.4
Allentown, PA	Lehigh County	53.1	45.5	1.2	0.1	0.2
Anchorage, AK	State of Alaska	42.8	52.8	2.5	0.0	1.9
Ann Arbor, MI	Washtenaw County	72.4	25.9	0.9	0.3	0.4
Athens, GA	Clarke County	70.1	28.1	1.6	0.1	0.1
Atlanta, GA	Fulton County	72.6	26.2	1.2	0.0	0.0
Austin, TX	Travis County	71.4	26.4	1.5	0.3	0.4
Baltimore, MD	Baltimore City	87.3	10.7	0.7	0.6	0.7
Boise City, ID	Ada County	46.1	50.0	2.0	0.1	1.8
Boston, MA	Suffolk County	80.6	17.5	0.9	0.5	0.5
Boulder, CO	Boulder County	77.2	20.6	1.2	0.3	0.6
Brownsville, TX	Cameron County	56.0	42.9	0.6	0.3	0.1
Cape Coral, FL	Lee County	39.9	59.1	0.5	0.1	0.3
Cedar Rapids, IA	Linn County	55.6	41.9	1.6	0.3	0.7
Charleston, SC	Charleston County	55.5	42.6	1.5	0.3	0.1
Charlotte, NC	Mecklenburg County	66.7	31.6	1.0	0.3	0.5
Chicago, IL	Cook County	74.2	24.0	0.8	0.5	0.5
Cincinnati, OH	Hamilton County	57.1	41.3	1.2	0.3	0.0
Clarksville, TN	Montgomery County	42.3	55.0	1.9	0.2	0.7
Cleveland, OH	Cuyahoga County	66.4	32.3	0.7	0.3	0.3
College Station, TX	Brazos County	41.4	55.7	2.1	0.3	0.4
Colorado Springs, CO	El Paso County	42.7	53.5	2.4	0.3	1.0
Columbia, MO	Boone County	54.8	42.3	2.2	0.3	0.4
Columbia, SC	Richland County	68.4	30.1	1.0	0.4	0.1
Columbus, OH	Franklin County	64.7	33.4	1.2	0.3	0.4
Dallas, TX	Dallas County	64.9	33.3	1.0	0.4	0.4
Davenport, IA	Scott County	50.7	47.2	1.2	0.2	0.7
Denver, CO	Denver County	79.6	18.2	1.2	0.3	0.7
Des Moines, IA	Polk County	56.5	41.3	1.3	0.2	0.7
Durham, NC	Durham County	80.4	18.0	0.8	0.3	0.4
Edison, NJ	Middlesex County	60.2	38.2	0.7	0.3	0.6
El Paso, TX	El Paso County	66.7	31.6	1.0	0.5	0.2
Fargo, ND	Cass County	46.8	49.5	2.9	0.0	0.7
Fort Collins, CO	Larimer County	56.2	40.8	1.8	0.3	0.9
Fort Wayne, IN	Allen County	43.2	54.3	2.2	0.0	0.3
Fort Worth, TX	Tarrant County	49.3	49.1	1.2	0.3	0.0
Grand Rapids, MI	Kent County	51.9	45.8	1.5	0.3	0.5
Greeley, CO	Weld County	39.6	57.6	1.7	0.2	0.9
Green Bay, WI	Brown County	45.5	52.7	1.3	0.0	0.5
Greensboro, NC	Guilford County	60.8	37.7	0.8	0.2	0.4
Honolulu, HI	Honolulu County	62.5	35.7	0.9	0.6	0.4
Houston, TX	Harris County	55.9	42.7	1.0	0.3	0.0
Huntsville, AL	Madison County	44.8	52.8	1.9	0.0	0.5
Indianapolis, IN	Marion County	63.3	34.3	1.8	0.1	0.4
Jacksonville, FL	Duval County	51.1	47.3	1.0	0.2	0.5
Kansas City, MO	Jackson County	59.8	37.9	1.4	0.4	0.5
Lafayette, LA	Lafayette Parish	34.7	63.3	1.3	0.0	0.7
Las Cruces, NM	Dona Ana County	58.0	39.7	1.4	0.5	0.4
Las Vegas, NV	Clark County	53.7	44.3	0.9	0.0	1.1
Lexington, KY	Fayette County	59.2	38.5	1.6	0.1	0.6
Lincoln, NE	Lancaster County	52.3	44.6	2.4	0.0	0.7
Little Rock, AR	Pulaski County	60.0	37.5	1.0	0.3	1.3
Los Angeles, CA	Los Angeles County	71.0	26.9	0.8	0.5	0.8
Louisville, KY	Jefferson County	58.9	38.8	1.2	0.1	1.0
Madison, WI	Dane County	75.5	22.9	1.1	0.1	0.6
Manchester, NH	Hillsborough County	52.8	45.2	1.7	0.0	0.3

Table continued on following page.

Appendix A: Comparative Statistics   A-111

City	Area Covered	Biden	Trump	Jorgensen	Hawkins	Other
Miami, FL	Miami-Dade County	53.3	46.0	0.3	0.1	0.3
Midland, TX	Midland County	20.9	77.3	1.3	0.2	0.2
Milwaukee, WI	Milwaukee County	69.1	29.3	0.9	0.0	0.7
Minneapolis, MN	Hennepin County	70.5	27.2	1.0	0.3	1.0
Nashville, TN	Davidson County	64.5	32.4	1.1	0.2	1.8
New Haven, CT	New Haven County	58.0	40.6	0.9	0.4	0.0
New Orleans, LA	Orleans Parish	83.1	15.0	0.9	0.0	1.0
New York, NY	Bronx County	83.3	15.9	0.2	0.3	0.3
New York, NY	Kings County	76.8	22.1	0.3	0.4	0.4
New York, NY	New York County	86.4	12.2	0.5	0.4	0.5
New York, NY	Queens County	72.0	26.9	0.3	0.4	0.4
New York, NY	Richmond County	42.0	56.9	0.4	0.3	0.4
Oklahoma City, OK	Oklahoma County	48.1	49.2	1.8	0.0	0.9
Omaha, NE	Douglas County	54.4	43.1	2.0	0.0	0.6
Orlando, FL	Orange County	60.9	37.8	0.7	0.2	0.4
Philadelphia, PA	Philadelphia County	81.2	17.9	0.7	0.1	0.2
Phoenix, AZ	Maricopa County	50.1	48.0	1.5	0.0	0.3
Pittsburgh, PA	Allegheny County	59.4	39.0	1.2	0.0	0.4
Portland, OR	Multnomah County	79.2	17.9	1.2	0.6	1.0
Providence, RI	Providence County	60.5	37.6	0.8	0.0	1.0
Provo, UT	Utah County	26.3	66.7	3.6	0.3	3.1
Raleigh, NC	Wake County	62.3	35.8	1.2	0.3	0.5
Reno, NV	Washoe County	50.8	46.3	1.4	0.0	1.5
Richmond, VA	Richmond City	82.9	14.9	1.5	0.0	0.6
Rochester, MN	Olmsted County	54.2	43.4	1.2	0.3	0.9
Sacramento, CA	Sacramento County	61.4	36.1	1.4	0.5	0.7
St. Louis, MO	St. Louis City	81.9	16.0	1.1	0.4	0.5
Salem, OR	Marion County	48.9	47.7	2.0	0.5	0.9
Salt Lake City, UT	Salt Lake County	53.0	42.1	2.2	0.4	2.2
San Antonio, TX	Bexar County	58.2	40.1	1.1	0.4	0.2
San Diego, CA	San Diego County	60.2	37.5	1.3	0.5	0.5
San Francisco, CA	San Francisco County	85.3	12.7	0.7	0.6	0.7
San Jose, CA	Santa Clara County	72.6	25.2	1.1	0.5	0.6
Santa Rosa, CA	Sonoma County	74.5	23.0	1.3	0.6	0.6
Savannah, GA	Chatham County	58.6	39.9	1.4	0.0	0.0
Seattle, WA	King County	75.0	22.2	1.5	0.5	0.8
Sioux Falls, SD	Minnehaha County	43.8	53.3	2.8	0.0	0.0
Springfield, IL	Sangamon County	46.5	50.9	1.4	0.6	0.6
Tampa, FL	Hillsborough County	52.7	45.8	0.8	0.2	0.5
Tucson, AZ	Pima County	58.4	39.8	1.5	0.0	0.3
Tulsa, OK	Tulsa County	40.9	56.5	1.8	0.0	0.8
Tuscaloosa, AL	Tuscaloosa County	41.9	56.7	1.0	0.0	0.4
Virginia Beach, VA	Virginia Beach City	51.6	46.2	1.8	0.0	0.4
Washington, DC	District of Columbia	92.1	5.4	0.6	0.5	1.4
Wichita, KS	Sedgwick County	42.6	54.4	2.4	0.0	0.5
Wilmington, NC	New Hanover County	50.2	48.0	1.2	0.3	0.4
Winston-Salem, NC	Forsyth County	56.2	42.3	0.9	0.2	0.4
Worcester, MA	Worcester County	57.6	39.7	1.7	0.6	0.4
U.S.	U.S.	51.3	46.8	1.2	0.3	0.5

Note: Results are percentages and may not add to 100% due to rounding
Source: Dave Leip's Atlas of U.S. Presidential Elections

A-112 Appendix A: Comparative Statistics

House Price Index (HPI)

Metro Area[1]	National Ranking[3]	Quarterly Change (%)	One-Year Change (%)	Five-Year Change (%)	Since 1991Q1 (%)
Albuquerque, NM	67	0.95	14.03	58.76	256.02
Allentown, PA	104	-0.97	12.09	52.30	165.53
Anchorage, AK	215	-0.36	8.00	27.30	235.38
Ann Arbor, MI	210	-4.46	8.26	40.08	220.18
Athens, GA	33	0.64	16.98	76.16	301.70
Atlanta, GA	40	-0.35	16.14	73.42	274.52
Austin, TX	222	-5.35	7.56	75.92	618.91
Baltimore, MD	199	0.91	8.63	34.77	214.03
Boise City, ID	256	-6.44	1.06	96.45	501.63
Boston, MA[2]	195	-1.14	8.90	44.63	310.81
Boulder, CO	150	-1.96	10.66	47.80	588.29
Brownsville, TX	n/a	n/a	n/a	n/a	n/a
Cape Coral, FL	6	-0.47	20.91	83.64	358.39
Cedar Rapids, IA	243	-4.60	5.29	30.92	170.24
Charleston, SC	29	-0.34	17.51	66.55	441.52
Charlotte, NC	19	0.48	18.66	78.79	310.41
Chicago, IL[2]	205	-1.86	8.51	31.58	168.46
Cincinnati, OH	96	-0.52	12.38	55.37	199.65
Clarksville, TN	n/a	n/a	n/a	n/a	n/a
Cleveland, OH	189	-1.76	9.23	49.32	153.83
College Station, TX	n/a	n/a	n/a	n/a	n/a
Colorado Springs, CO	231	-3.83	6.63	67.59	425.90
Columbia, MO	148	1.10	10.69	48.19	225.68
Columbia, SC	23	1.44	18.32	59.58	209.37
Columbus, OH	94	-1.27	12.41	59.08	243.03
Dallas, TX[2]	43	-1.44	15.77	61.60	325.13
Davenport, IA	220	0.26	7.72	30.21	202.26
Denver, CO	216	-2.41	7.96	52.15	548.72
Des Moines, IA	108	0.29	12.00	40.34	223.17
Durham, NC	45	-3.85	15.68	66.89	294.13
Edison, NJ[2]	212	-0.09	8.22	34.61	258.57
El Paso, TX	21	2.05	18.42	54.29	201.64
Fargo, ND	133	0.78	11.14	32.39	270.20
Fort Collins, CO	141	-2.34	10.88	51.04	508.13
Fort Wayne, IN	68	1.56	14.01	67.52	186.04
Fort Worth, TX[2]	53	-1.47	15.09	66.00	306.95
Grand Rapids, MI	116	n/a	11.72	62.74	262.62
Greeley, CO	207	-3.14	8.35	53.74	462.73
Green Bay, WI	25	3.83	17.89	59.68	250.27
Greensboro, NC	26	0.70	17.71	64.64	188.62
Honolulu, HI	122	-5.39	11.51	33.52	222.93
Houston, TX	81	0.53	13.01	46.44	300.24
Huntsville, AL	109	-1.12	11.99	73.58	211.74
Indianapolis, IN	99	-1.53	12.29	62.22	209.62
Jacksonville, FL	35	-1.80	16.79	76.35	371.41
Kansas City, MO	102	-0.14	12.17	58.36	257.00
Lafayette, LA	179	-0.60	9.73	25.29	232.27
Las Cruces, NM	n/a	n/a	n/a	n/a	n/a
Las Vegas, NV	157	-3.37	10.38	70.87	260.78
Lexington, KY	72	0.70	13.70	53.19	235.38
Lincoln, NE	107	0.03	12.01	49.08	257.46
Little Rock, AR	119	0.21	11.59	41.21	196.34
Los Angeles, CA[2]	200	-1.90	8.62	46.01	298.97
Louisville, KY	147	1.02	10.70	47.57	251.74
Madison, WI	121	-1.67	11.52	45.50	303.94

Table continued on following page.

Appendix A: Comparative Statistics   A-113

Metro Area[1]	National Ranking[3]	Quarterly Change (%)	One-Year Change (%)	Five-Year Change (%)	Since 1991Q1 (%)
Manchester, NH	126	-0.32	11.34	59.79	253.04
Miami, FL[2]	4	2.23	21.62	75.85	539.14
Midland, TX	n/a	n/a	n/a	n/a	n/a
Milwaukee, WI	134	-1.54	11.11	45.94	239.44
Minneapolis, MN	239	-1.83	6.08	41.05	273.41
Nashville, TN	34	-1.19	16.94	75.36	429.41
New Haven, CT	113	0.91	11.80	48.13	135.81
New Orleans, LA	202	0.06	8.58	36.52	291.68
New York, NY[2]	212	-0.09	8.22	34.61	258.57
Oklahoma City, OK	97	0.36	12.37	49.27	260.86
Omaha, NE	161	-0.79	10.26	51.61	252.12
Orlando, FL	13	0.53	19.76	74.99	330.12
Philadelphia, PA[2]	187	1.72	9.32	47.35	257.72
Phoenix, AZ	144	-4.25	10.82	83.46	453.06
Pittsburgh, PA	224	-1.54	7.43	42.48	223.87
Portland, OR	247	-2.87	4.63	43.13	493.76
Providence, RI	153	-0.93	10.48	54.47	232.15
Provo, UT	206	-3.27	8.39	75.92	514.28
Raleigh, NC	57	-2.71	14.97	69.49	298.33
Reno, NV	244	-1.71	5.01	60.21	333.43
Richmond, VA	79	-0.25	13.11	53.64	254.70
Rochester, MN	234	-3.55	6.25	42.75	234.69
Sacramento, CA	253	-3.63	3.17	45.83	234.41
St. Louis, MO	190	-0.80	9.10	40.60	193.95
Salem, OR	204	-1.19	8.51	62.82	461.52
Salt Lake City, UT	197	-2.92	8.70	74.37	596.70
San Antonio, TX	50	0.79	15.27	62.24	345.76
San Diego, CA	181	-2.11	9.62	51.34	344.82
San Francisco, CA[2]	177	3.28	9.77	19.08	360.06
San Jose, CA	101	1.47	12.23	31.21	389.33
Santa Rosa, CA	250	-4.80	3.50	26.56	276.48
Savannah, GA	12	1.20	19.86	70.81	361.13
Seattle, WA[2]	236	-3.59	6.21	48.84	436.06
Sioux Falls, SD	92	-1.20	12.49	55.67	315.04
Springfield, IL	158	-0.16	10.38	29.11	125.30
Tampa, FL	10	-0.71	19.98	91.22	438.13
Tucson, AZ	73	-1.74	13.68	74.77	329.80
Tulsa, OK	58	0.72	14.67	52.24	236.95
Tuscaloosa, AL	n/a	n/a	n/a	n/a	n/a
Virginia Beach, VA	131	0.74	11.17	43.79	243.78
Washington, DC[2]	238	-1.35	6.16	35.79	253.98
Wichita, KS	151	-1.84	10.63	47.99	197.78
Wilmington, NC	18	-1.23	18.70	72.00	356.80
Winston-Salem, NC	37	0.94	16.66	66.13	201.85
Worcester, MA	184	-1.36	9.48	52.36	218.67
U.S.[4]	–	0.34	8.41	58.44	289.08

Note: The HPI is a weighted repeat sales index. It measures average price changes in repeat sales or refinancings on the same properties. This information is obtained by reviewing repeat mortgage transactions on single-family properties whose mortgages have been purchased or securitized by Fannie Mae or Freddie Mac since January 1975; all figures are for the period ended December 31, 2022; (1) figures cover the Metropolitan Statistical Area (MSA) unless noted otherwise; (2) Metropolitan Division; (3) Rankings are based on annual percentage change, for all MSAs containing at least 15,000 transactions over the last 10 years and ranges from 1 to 257; (4) figures based on a weighted division average; (a) Not ranked because of increased index variability due to smaller sample size; n/a not available
Source: Federal Housing Finance Agency, Change in FHFA Metropolitan Area House Price Indexes, 2022Q4

A-114   Appendix A: Comparative Statistics

Home Value: City

City	Under $100,000	$100,000 -$199,999	$200,000 -$299,999	$300,000 -$399,999	$400,000 -$499,999	$500,000 -$999,999	$1,000,000 or more	Median ($)
Albuquerque, NM	8.2	36.2	31.9	13.0	5.9	4.2	0.6	214,600
Allentown, PA	19.9	58.7	14.0	3.6	1.8	1.4	0.5	145,700
Anchorage, AK	6.7	10.2	25.3	28.2	13.9	14.3	1.4	327,500
Ann Arbor, MI	2.4	10.8	20.5	24.6	18.8	19.9	3.0	366,600
Athens, GA	16.0	34.3	25.3	10.4	5.8	6.9	1.2	199,300
Atlanta, GA	8.9	17.3	17.4	13.6	10.3	23.2	9.3	346,600
Austin, TX	3.6	8.4	20.6	21.5	15.3	24.7	6.0	381,400
Baltimore, MD	21.5	35.5	21.4	10.3	4.3	5.9	1.0	175,300
Boise City, ID	5.2	12.8	27.2	22.0	13.5	17.2	2.3	322,300
Boston, MA	2.6	1.0	5.5	11.1	15.0	48.4	16.5	610,400
Boulder, CO	5.2	3.5	3.6	5.3	6.9	44.1	31.4	790,100
Brownsville, TX	53.5	34.4	9.1	1.4	0.6	0.8	0.1	95,700
Cape Coral, FL	3.4	25.6	35.3	19.8	6.7	8.1	1.2	255,700
Cedar Rapids, IA	18.6	53.5	19.0	5.4	1.7	1.5	0.3	149,000
Charleston, SC	3.1	7.6	23.0	23.5	11.5	23.2	8.1	369,500
Charlotte, NC	7.8	27.5	23.8	14.8	8.8	13.3	4.0	258,000
Chicago, IL	8.5	22.4	24.5	16.5	9.6	14.2	4.3	277,600
Cincinnati, OH	24.5	35.2	17.3	9.2	4.7	7.2	1.8	162,300
Clarksville, TN	13.0	51.0	25.3	6.3	1.6	2.6	0.3	172,700
Cleveland, OH	67.7	23.2	4.6	2.2	0.7	1.3	0.2	74,700
College Station, TX	2.2	18.2	39.2	25.7	7.6	6.3	0.7	269,100
Colorado Springs, CO	4.6	11.0	28.1	26.0	14.7	14.1	1.4	324,100
Columbia, MO	8.9	35.8	29.2	14.1	6.5	5.1	0.5	215,300
Columbia, SC	17.9	34.1	18.9	9.7	5.5	11.7	2.2	193,100
Columbus, OH	19.2	40.1	25.2	9.3	2.9	2.8	0.5	174,400
Dallas, TX	17.6	27.3	15.3	11.0	8.6	14.8	5.5	230,000
Davenport, IA	28.0	44.6	17.1	7.5	1.1	1.4	0.3	138,000
Denver, CO	2.3	4.6	12.8	20.0	17.5	34.9	7.9	459,100
Des Moines, IA	20.9	53.8	17.0	4.6	1.5	1.9	0.3	149,700
Durham, NC	5.0	24.8	31.4	20.4	8.2	9.0	1.1	264,100
Edison, NJ	3.9	3.9	14.5	26.0	20.3	29.1	2.3	408,100
El Paso, TX	25.7	52.3	14.1	4.5	1.7	1.4	0.3	137,600
Fargo, ND	7.4	30.1	36.2	16.5	4.6	4.4	0.7	232,900
Fort Collins, CO	4.0	2.8	10.0	24.0	29.5	27.3	2.4	431,300
Fort Wayne, IN	32.7	46.5	14.2	4.0	1.2	1.1	0.2	130,700
Fort Worth, TX	15.9	29.7	31.6	12.1	4.7	4.8	1.2	212,300
Grand Rapids, MI	16.4	49.8	24.0	6.0	2.0	1.4	0.3	168,700
Greeley, CO	9.3	8.9	33.0	31.0	10.6	6.8	0.3	296,300
Green Bay, WI	17.2	57.2	16.1	5.1	2.4	1.8	0.2	151,000
Greensboro, NC	19.7	40.5	20.3	9.3	4.4	4.8	1.0	169,100
Honolulu, HI	1.6	1.6	5.5	11.7	10.7	41.2	27.6	726,000
Houston, TX	19.1	30.8	17.1	11.0	6.7	11.3	4.0	200,700
Huntsville, AL	21.0	30.5	21.8	12.5	6.6	6.4	1.1	194,500
Indianapolis, IN	23.7	43.7	17.7	7.2	3.1	3.9	0.7	156,300
Jacksonville, FL	17.0	32.0	28.0	12.0	4.8	4.9	1.4	203,400
Kansas City, MO	23.0	34.6	21.2	11.4	4.1	4.8	0.8	175,400
Lafayette, LA	13.7	33.6	25.7	11.7	7.0	6.7	1.6	209,100
Las Cruces, NM	17.4	49.1	21.5	7.7	1.5	2.5	0.3	167,800
Las Vegas, NV	4.3	14.0	31.2	23.5	11.7	13.1	2.2	302,100
Lexington, KY	9.0	36.1	25.2	14.5	6.4	7.6	1.2	216,800
Lincoln, NE	9.6	42.9	27.9	11.1	4.5	3.2	0.7	193,800
Little Rock, AR	22.0	33.4	17.9	11.1	5.5	8.4	1.6	179,500
Los Angeles, CA	2.2	1.3	2.4	6.2	11.3	50.1	26.6	705,900
Louisville, KY	17.5	40.5	20.3	10.8	5.0	5.1	0.9	174,400
Madison, WI	3.4	18.6	35.0	22.5	10.9	8.3	1.3	277,800

Table continued on following page.

Appendix A: Comparative Statistics   A-115

City	Under $100,000	$100,000 -$199,999	$200,000 -$299,999	$300,000 -$399,999	$400,000 -$499,999	$500,000 -$999,999	$1,000,000 or more	Median ($)
Manchester, NH	4.7	21.9	39.9	23.6	6.6	3.1	0.1	258,100
Miami, FL	4.5	9.8	20.4	22.1	14.7	20.0	8.4	369,100
Midland, TX	11.2	22.4	32.5	17.2	6.3	8.8	1.5	250,300
Milwaukee, WI	30.6	48.6	14.1	3.3	1.2	1.8	0.5	135,600
Minneapolis, MN	4.2	19.5	31.1	20.3	9.7	12.6	2.5	284,400
Nashville, TN	4.4	18.9	29.1	21.3	9.6	13.3	3.3	291,400
New Haven, CT	11.0	36.4	29.4	10.5	5.4	5.7	1.6	207,600
New Orleans, LA	9.7	28.7	20.4	13.4	8.3	15.2	4.2	255,500
New York, NY	4.3	3.6	5.5	8.2	10.8	44.7	22.9	660,700
Oklahoma City, OK	23.1	38.5	21.4	8.2	3.8	3.8	1.2	168,900
Omaha, NE	15.7	42.7	23.3	9.7	4.0	3.9	0.7	177,700
Orlando, FL	7.5	23.3	22.9	20.6	10.8	12.3	2.6	283,700
Philadelphia, PA	21.6	33.0	22.8	10.0	4.6	6.6	1.4	184,100
Phoenix, AZ	7.3	19.8	28.5	18.6	9.6	13.8	2.4	277,700
Pittsburgh, PA	33.7	31.4	13.9	7.9	4.8	7.2	1.1	147,600
Portland, OR	2.6	2.8	9.9	21.8	20.5	38.3	4.1	462,800
Providence, RI	4.9	27.5	34.7	14.0	4.1	11.6	3.2	248,900
Provo, UT	5.3	9.2	27.9	26.4	12.3	16.1	2.7	328,500
Raleigh, NC	4.0	21.6	28.3	18.3	11.0	14.2	2.7	285,400
Reno, NV	5.9	5.9	14.6	25.8	20.2	24.1	3.5	391,500
Richmond, VA	9.5	26.4	21.0	16.5	8.6	14.2	3.8	263,000
Rochester, MN	5.8	30.7	30.8	16.9	8.6	6.8	0.5	236,400
Sacramento, CA	4.0	5.0	19.4	25.1	19.3	24.0	3.0	385,500
St. Louis, MO	29.9	36.3	17.8	8.4	3.4	3.4	0.9	153,200
Salem, OR	7.5	13.6	32.7	26.7	11.1	7.9	0.5	289,500
Salt Lake City, UT	3.8	10.8	19.8	19.3	14.6	26.2	5.3	380,200
San Antonio, TX	24.0	38.4	21.9	8.7	3.3	3.1	0.6	167,700
San Diego, CA	2.6	1.4	3.1	8.1	13.7	51.4	19.8	664,000
San Francisco, CA	1.5	0.8	1.0	1.9	1.6	26.1	67.1	1,194,500
San Jose, CA	2.3	2.5	2.0	1.6	2.6	40.3	48.6	986,700
Santa Rosa, CA	4.1	2.6	4.0	7.3	13.6	60.0	8.4	598,700
Savannah, GA	19.1	41.2	21.4	6.7	4.4	5.9	1.3	170,500
Seattle, WA	1.1	0.6	2.7	6.3	8.6	55.3	25.4	767,500
Sioux Falls, SD	10.1	32.4	31.9	12.6	6.1	5.6	1.3	218,600
Springfield, IL	34.4	38.8	15.9	6.3	2.4	1.9	0.4	132,900
Tampa, FL	9.0	22.7	22.8	14.6	9.9	14.9	6.1	277,700
Tucson, AZ	17.8	41.3	26.3	8.4	3.0	2.4	0.7	177,800
Tulsa, OK	28.0	36.9	15.4	8.2	4.4	5.5	1.5	151,500
Tuscaloosa, AL	14.2	37.7	19.5	11.1	6.0	10.0	1.6	194,500
Virginia Beach, VA	3.8	15.6	32.0	21.6	11.7	12.8	2.6	295,900
Washington, DC	1.8	2.2	7.5	12.3	12.7	42.1	21.4	635,900
Wichita, KS	31.2	39.6	17.3	6.7	2.2	2.7	0.3	145,300
Wilmington, NC	5.9	23.6	25.8	19.2	8.2	13.7	3.7	279,900
Winston-Salem, NC	22.4	44.2	16.7	7.0	3.5	5.6	0.6	158,600
Worcester, MA	4.7	20.1	40.8	22.2	6.8	4.6	0.9	259,800
U.S.	16.2	24.2	20.1	13.6	8.3	13.6	4.1	244,900

Note: Figures are percentages except for median and cover owner-occupied housing units.
Source: U.S. Census Bureau, 2017-2021 American Community Survey 5-Year Estimates

A-116　Appendix A: Comparative Statistics

Home Value: Metro Area

MSA[1]	Under $100,000	$100,000 -$199,999	$200,000 -$299,999	$300,000 -$399,999	$400,000 -$499,999	$500,000 -$999,999	$1,000,000 or more	Median ($)
Albuquerque, NM	11.7	34.6	28.4	12.3	5.9	5.9	1.1	210,700
Allentown, PA	9.9	31.5	28.8	17.1	7.2	5.1	0.6	227,900
Anchorage, AK	6.7	12.7	28.8	26.2	12.5	12.0	1.1	306,700
Ann Arbor, MI	9.2	18.2	24.0	19.4	12.7	14.5	1.9	293,800
Athens, GA	16.8	30.0	23.5	12.5	7.6	8.0	1.7	211,500
Atlanta, GA	8.9	26.9	25.0	16.1	9.3	11.7	2.0	252,100
Austin, TX	6.2	12.5	25.9	20.6	12.6	18.1	4.1	326,400
Baltimore, MD	6.7	15.8	23.5	20.6	12.8	18.2	2.4	319,500
Boise City, ID	6.9	15.9	25.8	21.3	13.1	14.9	2.1	306,300
Boston, MA	2.5	3.6	10.6	18.0	17.3	38.5	9.4	487,600
Boulder, CO	4.1	2.1	5.7	13.1	16.3	44.3	14.5	575,700
Brownsville, TX	53.6	31.8	8.9	2.9	1.1	1.4	0.2	94,200
Cape Coral, FL	12.0	23.6	27.5	16.4	7.3	10.5	2.8	248,300
Cedar Rapids, IA	17.2	44.7	22.6	8.4	3.7	3.0	0.5	165,500
Charleston, SC	10.8	21.0	24.9	16.5	8.1	14.0	4.6	270,700
Charlotte, NC	13.0	27.8	23.7	15.3	8.0	10.0	2.3	237,300
Chicago, IL	8.6	25.3	26.7	17.5	8.5	10.9	2.5	258,500
Cincinnati, OH	16.4	37.7	23.2	11.6	4.9	5.4	0.9	187,000
Clarksville, TN	19.0	41.2	23.4	9.2	2.9	3.7	0.7	174,300
Cleveland, OH	23.8	37.8	20.5	9.2	4.1	3.9	0.6	164,400
College Station, TX	20.3	25.9	24.8	14.8	5.2	7.7	1.3	213,600
Colorado Springs, CO	4.6	10.9	26.6	25.1	14.8	16.3	1.6	331,300
Columbia, MO	14.6	36.8	24.4	12.8	5.2	5.2	1.0	195,600
Columbia, SC	22.5	38.6	19.7	9.2	4.2	4.9	1.0	167,800
Columbus, OH	14.2	32.0	25.3	14.2	6.8	6.6	0.9	213,600
Dallas, TX	10.9	24.1	26.2	17.0	9.3	10.2	2.4	255,600
Davenport, IA	27.9	41.0	17.1	8.3	2.8	2.6	0.4	145,200
Denver, CO	3.2	3.4	11.5	22.5	21.7	32.8	4.9	443,400
Des Moines, IA	12.8	35.7	26.8	13.6	5.6	5.0	0.6	205,200
Durham, NC	10.6	23.8	24.0	17.7	9.2	12.7	1.9	264,400
Edison, NJ	3.5	5.2	11.1	16.7	16.1	36.2	11.2	483,500
El Paso, TX	29.8	49.6	13.5	4.1	1.4	1.2	0.3	131,200
Fargo, ND	8.0	29.3	32.7	16.9	6.0	6.3	0.8	235,600
Fort Collins, CO	4.9	3.0	11.4	25.9	23.2	28.1	3.4	420,200
Fort Wayne, IN	26.2	42.9	18.0	6.8	2.7	2.8	0.5	150,600
Fort Worth, TX	10.9	24.1	26.2	17.0	9.3	10.2	2.4	255,600
Grand Rapids, MI	14.0	34.9	27.4	12.2	5.7	4.7	1.1	203,500
Greeley, CO	7.1	7.0	21.1	28.5	17.5	17.3	1.5	352,000
Green Bay, WI	12.8	41.4	26.0	10.9	4.6	3.6	0.7	188,800
Greensboro, NC	22.8	39.9	19.0	9.0	4.4	4.2	0.7	162,700
Honolulu, HI	1.6	1.6	3.6	8.3	9.7	53.8	21.5	726,800
Houston, TX	13.5	30.4	25.4	13.7	6.5	8.0	2.5	221,400
Huntsville, AL	17.1	33.2	24.5	12.5	6.2	5.8	0.7	199,000
Indianapolis, IN	17.1	37.2	22.1	11.7	5.5	5.6	0.9	186,700
Jacksonville, FL	13.2	26.5	26.7	15.0	7.8	8.5	2.2	235,300
Kansas City, MO	15.2	31.5	24.6	14.0	6.8	6.8	1.1	211,900
Lafayette, LA	28.0	34.1	21.1	9.0	3.7	3.3	0.7	167,400
Las Cruces, NM	26.6	38.7	19.7	7.3	3.9	3.4	0.4	162,200
Las Vegas, NV	5.6	12.8	29.4	25.2	12.4	12.3	2.3	308,800
Lexington, KY	10.9	37.5	24.2	13.2	6.0	7.1	1.2	206,000
Lincoln, NE	9.4	39.9	27.0	12.5	5.5	4.7	0.9	202,300
Little Rock, AR	23.2	39.9	20.4	8.5	3.2	4.0	0.8	164,200
Los Angeles, CA	3.2	1.7	3.2	7.0	11.9	52.3	20.7	671,700
Louisville, KY	15.4	37.8	23.3	12.0	5.0	5.4	0.9	189,900
Madison, WI	5.1	20.5	30.8	21.7	10.9	9.4	1.6	277,400

Table continued on following page.

Appendix A: Comparative Statistics   A-117

MSA[1]	Under $100,000	$100,000 -$199,999	$200,000 -$299,999	$300,000 -$399,999	$400,000 -$499,999	$500,000 -$999,999	$1,000,000 or more	Median ($)
Manchester, NH	4.2	13.5	30.7	27.5	12.9	10.7	0.5	306,000
Miami, FL	8.7	15.9	21.8	20.7	12.8	15.2	4.9	317,800
Midland, TX	16.5	20.8	29.5	16.1	6.9	8.7	1.4	243,400
Milwaukee, WI	10.6	29.0	27.8	16.4	7.5	7.4	1.2	235,100
Minneapolis, MN	4.6	17.1	32.2	21.8	11.2	11.4	1.7	287,600
Nashville, TN	6.6	19.5	27.4	19.2	9.9	14.1	3.2	286,800
New Haven, CT	6.4	25.9	29.4	18.7	10.0	8.3	1.2	259,400
New Orleans, LA	11.5	34.6	25.7	13.3	5.8	7.5	1.7	214,300
New York, NY	3.5	5.2	11.1	16.7	16.1	36.2	11.2	483,500
Oklahoma City, OK	21.7	39.2	20.6	9.0	4.1	4.1	1.2	169,300
Omaha, NE	13.4	38.4	24.8	12.5	5.4	4.7	0.8	195,000
Orlando, FL	10.4	20.5	30.9	19.9	8.1	8.3	1.9	260,800
Philadelphia, PA	9.6	21.9	25.7	18.4	10.4	12.1	1.8	270,400
Phoenix, AZ	8.3	15.9	27.3	20.3	11.4	13.9	2.9	294,700
Pittsburgh, PA	25.5	34.6	19.9	9.9	4.5	4.9	0.7	167,500
Portland, OR	4.2	3.7	12.4	25.2	21.3	29.7	3.5	421,300
Providence, RI	3.5	12.7	31.4	24.1	12.7	13.5	2.1	309,600
Provo, UT	3.1	6.2	22.3	28.1	17.5	20.2	2.6	365,500
Raleigh, NC	7.0	20.0	25.5	20.2	12.4	13.2	1.7	289,700
Reno, NV	5.5	6.4	16.4	25.0	18.1	22.9	5.9	387,400
Richmond, VA	6.4	24.3	29.8	18.4	9.3	10.4	1.5	262,900
Rochester, MN	9.2	29.8	26.8	16.1	8.6	8.3	1.2	234,700
Sacramento, CA	4.1	3.6	11.7	22.0	20.6	33.7	4.4	441,800
St. Louis, MO	20.0	33.1	22.7	12.1	5.2	5.7	1.2	189,600
Salem, OR	8.1	12.8	29.6	24.3	12.1	12.1	1.0	298,400
Salt Lake City, UT	3.8	8.2	22.9	24.5	16.6	21.1	2.9	361,600
San Antonio, TX	18.7	31.5	24.5	12.0	5.8	6.2	1.3	199,200
San Diego, CA	4.2	2.2	3.5	7.9	14.3	52.3	15.7	627,200
San Francisco, CA	2.0	1.4	1.7	3.8	5.9	40.7	44.4	933,300
San Jose, CA	2.1	2.0	1.7	1.6	2.3	32.2	58.0	1,113,700
Santa Rosa, CA	3.9	2.9	2.9	5.1	9.9	58.1	17.2	665,800
Savannah, GA	14.2	32.9	25.4	11.2	5.1	9.1	2.1	210,400
Seattle, WA	3.3	3.2	9.5	16.3	15.8	39.3	12.5	518,000
Sioux Falls, SD	11.0	31.1	29.9	14.0	6.4	6.5	1.2	221,500
Springfield, IL	29.8	38.6	19.5	7.3	2.4	2.0	0.4	148,000
Tampa, FL	16.4	25.3	26.4	14.8	6.9	8.1	2.0	229,400
Tucson, AZ	15.0	29.7	26.3	13.5	6.8	7.4	1.3	217,700
Tulsa, OK	24.2	39.1	19.5	8.6	3.5	4.1	0.9	163,100
Tuscaloosa, AL	24.9	35.9	20.8	9.4	3.6	4.6	0.8	171,100
Virginia Beach, VA	6.5	23.8	31.1	18.5	9.8	9.0	1.3	261,800
Washington, DC	2.4	4.9	14.2	19.7	16.6	34.4	7.8	453,100
Wichita, KS	28.6	40.0	18.4	7.4	2.6	2.6	0.4	151,900
Wilmington, NC	9.2	24.0	25.8	18.0	8.9	11.6	2.4	262,500
Winston-Salem, NC	20.7	42.5	19.5	8.7	3.7	4.4	0.5	165,000
Worcester, MA	3.6	16.4	30.3	22.9	12.3	13.1	1.3	298,900
U.S.	16.2	24.2	20.1	13.6	8.3	13.6	4.1	244,900

Note: (1) Figures cover the Metropolitan Statistical Area (MSA); Figures are percentages except for median and cover owner-occupied housing units.
Source: U.S. Census Bureau, 2017-2021 American Community Survey 5-Year Estimates

A-118   Appendix A: Comparative Statistics

Homeownership Rate

Metro Area	2015	2016	2017	2018	2019	2020	2021	2022
Albuquerque, NM	64.3	66.9	67.0	67.9	70.0	69.5	66.5	67.3
Allentown, PA	69.2	68.9	73.1	72.1	67.8	68.8	70.4	73.1
Anchorage, AK	n/a	n/a	n/a	n/a	n/a	n/a	n/a	n/a
Ann Arbor, MI	n/a	n/a	n/a	n/a	n/a	n/a	n/a	n/a
Athens, GA	n/a	n/a	n/a	n/a	n/a	n/a	n/a	n/a
Atlanta, GA	61.7	61.5	62.4	64.0	64.2	66.4	64.2	64.4
Austin, TX	57.5	56.5	55.6	56.1	59.0	65.4	62.2	62.4
Baltimore, MD	65.3	68.5	67.5	63.5	66.5	70.7	67.5	70.4
Boise City, ID	n/a	n/a	n/a	n/a	n/a	n/a	n/a	n/a
Boston, MA	59.3	58.9	58.8	61.0	60.9	61.2	60.7	59.4
Boulder, CO	n/a	n/a	n/a	n/a	n/a	n/a	n/a	n/a
Brownsville, TX	n/a	n/a	n/a	n/a	n/a	n/a	n/a	n/a
Cape Coral, FL	62.9	66.5	65.5	75.1	72.0	77.4	76.1	70.8
Cedar Rapids, IA	n/a	n/a	n/a	n/a	n/a	n/a	n/a	n/a
Charleston, SC	65.8	62.1	67.7	68.8	70.7	75.5	73.2	71.9
Charlotte, NC	62.3	66.2	64.6	67.9	72.3	73.3	70.0	68.7
Chicago, IL	64.3	64.5	64.1	64.6	63.4	66.0	67.5	66.8
Cincinnati, OH	65.9	64.9	65.7	67.3	67.4	71.1	72.1	67.1
Clarksville, TN	n/a	n/a	n/a	n/a	n/a	n/a	n/a	n/a
Cleveland, OH	68.4	64.8	66.6	66.7	64.4	66.3	64.7	63.0
College Station, TX	n/a	n/a	n/a	n/a	n/a	n/a	n/a	n/a
Colorado Springs, CO	n/a	n/a	n/a	n/a	n/a	n/a	n/a	n/a
Columbia, MO	n/a	n/a	n/a	n/a	n/a	n/a	n/a	n/a
Columbia, SC	66.1	63.9	70.7	69.3	65.9	69.7	69.4	70.9
Columbus, OH	59.0	57.5	57.9	64.8	65.7	65.6	64.6	61.5
Dallas, TX	57.8	59.7	61.8	62.0	60.6	64.7	61.8	60.4
Davenport, IA	n/a	n/a	n/a	n/a	n/a	n/a	n/a	n/a
Denver, CO	61.6	61.6	59.3	60.1	63.5	62.9	62.8	64.6
Des Moines, IA	n/a	n/a	n/a	n/a	n/a	n/a	n/a	n/a
Durham, NC	n/a	n/a	n/a	n/a	n/a	n/a	n/a	n/a
Edison, NJ	49.9	50.4	49.9	49.7	50.4	50.9	50.7	50.5
El Paso, TX	n/a	n/a	n/a	n/a	n/a	n/a	n/a	n/a
Fargo, ND	n/a	n/a	n/a	n/a	n/a	n/a	n/a	n/a
Fort Collins, CO	n/a	n/a	n/a	n/a	n/a	n/a	n/a	n/a
Fort Wayne, IN	n/a	n/a	n/a	n/a	n/a	n/a	n/a	n/a
Fort Worth, TX	57.8	59.7	61.8	62.0	60.6	64.7	61.8	60.4
Grand Rapids, MI	75.8	76.2	71.7	73.0	75.2	71.8	65.0	68.1
Greeley, CO	n/a	n/a	n/a	n/a	n/a	n/a	n/a	n/a
Green Bay, WI	n/a	n/a	n/a	n/a	n/a	n/a	n/a	n/a
Greensboro, NC	65.4	62.9	61.9	63.2	61.7	65.8	61.9	70.0
Honolulu, HI	59.6	57.9	53.8	57.7	59.0	56.9	55.9	57.7
Houston, TX	60.3	59.0	58.9	60.1	61.3	65.3	64.1	63.7
Huntsville, AL	n/a	n/a	n/a	n/a	n/a	n/a	n/a	n/a
Indianapolis, IN	64.6	63.9	63.9	64.3	66.2	70.0	70.1	68.8
Jacksonville, FL	62.5	61.8	65.2	61.4	63.1	64.8	68.1	70.6
Kansas City, MO	65.0	62.4	62.4	64.3	65.0	66.7	63.8	63.8
Lafayette, LA	n/a	n/a	n/a	n/a	n/a	n/a	n/a	n/a
Las Cruces, NM	n/a	n/a	n/a	n/a	n/a	n/a	n/a	n/a
Las Vegas, NV	52.1	51.3	54.4	58.1	56.0	57.3	57.7	58.7
Lexington, KY	n/a	n/a	n/a	n/a	n/a	n/a	n/a	n/a
Lincoln, NE	n/a	n/a	n/a	n/a	n/a	n/a	n/a	n/a
Little Rock, AR	65.8	64.9	61.0	62.2	65.0	67.7	64.6	64.4
Los Angeles, CA	49.1	47.1	49.1	49.5	48.2	48.5	47.9	48.3
Louisville, KY	67.7	67.6	71.7	67.9	64.9	69.3	71.4	71.7
Madison, WI	n/a	n/a	n/a	n/a	n/a	n/a	n/a	n/a
Manchester, NH	n/a	n/a	n/a	n/a	n/a	n/a	n/a	n/a

Table continued on following page.

Appendix A: Comparative Statistics   A-119

Metro Area	2015	2016	2017	2018	2019	2020	2021	2022
Miami, FL	58.6	58.4	57.9	59.9	60.4	60.6	59.4	58.3
Midland, TX	n/a	n/a	n/a	n/a	n/a	n/a	n/a	n/a
Milwaukee, WI	57.0	60.4	63.9	62.3	56.9	58.5	56.8	57.3
Minneapolis, MN	67.9	69.1	70.1	67.8	70.2	73.0	75.0	73.0
Nashville, TN	67.4	65.0	69.4	68.3	69.8	69.8	65.7	70.4
New Haven, CT	64.6	59.4	58.7	65.0	65.1	63.4	61.0	63.3
New Orleans, LA	62.8	59.3	61.7	62.6	61.1	66.3	66.2	66.3
New York, NY	49.9	50.4	49.9	49.7	50.4	50.9	50.7	50.5
Oklahoma City, OK	61.4	63.1	64.7	64.6	64.3	68.3	61.9	64.8
Omaha, NE	69.6	69.2	65.5	67.8	66.9	68.6	68.6	67.9
Orlando, FL	58.4	58.5	59.5	58.5	56.1	64.2	63.0	62.1
Philadelphia, PA	67.0	64.7	65.6	67.4	67.4	69.2	69.8	68.2
Phoenix, AZ	61.0	62.6	64.0	65.3	65.9	67.9	65.2	68.0
Pittsburgh, PA	71.0	72.2	72.7	71.7	71.5	69.8	69.1	72.7
Portland, OR	58.9	61.8	61.1	59.2	60.0	62.5	64.1	65.2
Providence, RI	60.0	57.5	58.6	61.3	63.5	64.8	64.1	66.3
Provo, UT	n/a	n/a	n/a	n/a	n/a	n/a	n/a	n/a
Raleigh, NC	67.4	65.9	68.2	64.9	63.0	68.2	62.7	65.1
Reno, NV	n/a	n/a	n/a	n/a	n/a	n/a	n/a	n/a
Richmond, VA	67.4	61.7	63.1	62.9	66.4	66.5	64.9	66.3
Rochester, MN	n/a	n/a	n/a	n/a	n/a	n/a	n/a	n/a
Sacramento, CA	60.8	60.5	60.1	64.1	61.6	63.4	63.2	63.5
St. Louis, MO	68.7	66.4	65.6	65.8	68.1	71.1	73.8	69.9
Salem, OR	n/a	n/a	n/a	n/a	n/a	n/a	n/a	n/a
Salt Lake City, UT	69.1	69.2	68.1	69.5	69.2	68.0	64.1	66.6
San Antonio, TX	66.0	61.6	62.5	64.4	62.6	64.2	62.7	62.9
San Diego, CA	51.8	53.3	56.0	56.1	56.7	57.8	52.6	51.6
San Francisco, CA	56.3	55.8	55.7	55.6	52.8	53.0	54.7	56.4
San Jose, CA	50.7	49.9	50.4	50.4	52.4	52.6	48.4	53.1
Santa Rosa, CA	n/a	n/a	n/a	n/a	n/a	n/a	n/a	n/a
Savannah, GA	n/a	n/a	n/a	n/a	n/a	n/a	n/a	n/a
Seattle, WA	59.5	57.7	59.5	62.5	61.5	59.4	58.0	62.7
Sioux Falls, SD	n/a	n/a	n/a	n/a	n/a	n/a	n/a	n/a
Springfield, IL	n/a	n/a	n/a	n/a	n/a	n/a	n/a	n/a
Tampa, FL	64.9	62.9	60.4	64.9	68.0	72.2	68.3	68.4
Tucson, AZ	61.4	56.0	60.1	63.8	60.1	67.1	63.5	71.6
Tulsa, OK	65.2	65.4	66.8	68.3	70.5	70.1	63.8	63.7
Tuscaloosa, AL	n/a	n/a	n/a	n/a	n/a	n/a	n/a	n/a
Virginia Beach, VA	59.4	59.6	65.3	62.8	63.0	65.8	64.4	61.4
Washington, DC	64.6	63.1	63.3	62.9	64.7	67.9	65.8	66.2
Wichita, KS	n/a	n/a	n/a	n/a	n/a	n/a	n/a	n/a
Wilmington, NC	n/a	n/a	n/a	n/a	n/a	n/a	n/a	n/a
Winston-Salem, NC	n/a	n/a	n/a	n/a	n/a	n/a	n/a	n/a
Worcester, MA	64.2	65.5	64.9	63.4	62.7	65.9	68.7	64.8
U.S.	63.7	63.4	63.9	64.4	64.6	66.6	65.5	65.8

Note: Figures are percentages and cover the Metropolitan Statistical Area; n/a not available
Source: U.S. Census Bureau, Housing Vacancies and Homeownership Annual Statistics: 2015-2022

A-120 Appendix A: Comparative Statistics

Year Housing Structure Built: City

City	2020 or Later	2010 -2019	2000 -2009	1990 -1999	1980 -1989	1970 -1979	1960 -1969	1950 -1959	1940 -1949	Before 1940	Median Year
Albuquerque, NM	0.2	5.7	16.1	14.9	15.1	19.1	9.8	11.8	4.3	3.1	1981
Allentown, PA	0.1	2.3	4.6	3.4	5.3	10.8	11.5	15.0	7.2	39.7	1952
Anchorage, AK	<0.1	4.7	11.9	11.9	25.8	28.0	10.2	5.8	1.2	0.5	1982
Ann Arbor, MI	0.2	5.0	5.8	11.7	11.3	16.9	18.0	11.1	5.0	15.0	1971
Athens, GA	0.1	5.7	17.6	18.6	15.8	15.8	12.5	6.6	2.2	5.1	1985
Atlanta, GA	0.4	12.7	22.0	10.2	7.6	7.7	11.0	10.6	5.7	12.1	1984
Austin, TX	0.2	17.5	17.1	14.7	18.6	15.0	7.7	4.5	2.1	2.6	1990
Baltimore, MD	<0.1	3.4	3.6	3.9	4.3	5.7	8.6	15.8	11.9	42.8	1946
Boise City, ID	0.1	9.0	11.0	22.5	15.8	17.1	7.8	6.8	3.9	6.2	1985
Boston, MA	0.2	7.2	6.6	4.4	5.6	7.5	7.6	7.3	5.4	48.2	1943
Boulder, CO	0.1	7.9	7.7	12.0	16.7	19.6	17.7	9.0	1.7	7.7	1977
Brownsville, TX	0.2	12.9	22.9	18.0	14.8	15.5	6.2	4.4	2.8	2.3	1992
Cape Coral, FL	0.1	8.4	34.8	17.6	21.6	11.7	4.6	0.8	0.2	0.1	1996
Cedar Rapids, IA	0.1	7.7	11.5	10.5	7.1	14.6	14.8	12.8	4.1	16.8	1971
Charleston, SC	0.3	18.9	20.0	10.6	12.0	8.8	8.5	5.5	3.4	11.9	1990
Charlotte, NC	0.2	13.2	21.5	19.3	14.4	11.2	8.7	6.3	2.5	2.7	1992
Chicago, IL	<0.1	3.8	8.0	5.1	4.8	7.7	9.6	11.8	8.8	40.3	1951
Cincinnati, OH	0.1	3.3	3.7	4.2	6.0	9.4	12.2	11.5	8.4	41.4	1950
Clarksville, TN	0.2	15.6	22.2	20.2	12.9	12.0	7.2	4.8	2.8	2.1	1994
Cleveland, OH	0.1	2.9	3.5	3.4	2.8	5.5	7.8	12.7	11.2	50.0	<1940
College Station, TX	0.6	20.8	20.7	20.0	16.6	14.8	3.5	2.0	0.4	0.6	1996
Colorado Springs, CO	0.3	9.5	14.7	15.4	18.9	17.2	9.4	7.0	2.0	5.5	1985
Columbia, MO	0.1	15.5	20.0	18.1	11.8	12.1	10.5	4.4	2.3	5.3	1992
Columbia, SC	0.2	9.3	15.2	11.3	10.2	10.2	10.2	13.9	10.1	9.5	1976
Columbus, OH	0.1	8.0	11.7	15.1	12.9	14.3	11.5	10.4	4.3	11.8	1978
Dallas, TX	0.2	9.8	10.5	10.8	16.4	16.5	12.5	13.2	4.9	5.2	1979
Davenport, IA	<0.1	3.9	8.5	8.7	6.8	15.2	12.5	10.9	5.6	27.8	1965
Denver, CO	0.3	12.8	11.1	6.7	7.6	12.7	10.6	14.2	5.8	18.2	1971
Des Moines, IA	0.1	5.5	6.7	7.0	6.4	13.6	10.0	14.9	7.8	28.0	1960
Durham, NC	0.4	17.0	17.9	16.6	14.6	10.4	8.1	5.7	3.3	5.9	1991
Edison, NJ	0.1	2.5	5.7	9.8	24.2	11.6	18.6	17.8	4.0	5.5	1973
El Paso, TX	0.1	12.1	14.1	12.9	14.4	16.3	10.5	11.1	3.7	4.8	1982
Fargo, ND	0.3	18.3	14.2	15.1	13.1	14.2	6.1	8.0	2.3	8.3	1988
Fort Collins, CO	0.3	13.1	18.0	21.0	15.0	16.8	6.7	3.0	1.5	4.6	1991
Fort Wayne, IN	0.1	2.2	6.7	13.6	11.5	17.5	14.9	12.8	6.5	14.2	1971
Fort Worth, TX	0.3	14.8	21.3	12.3	13.5	9.4	7.7	10.2	4.9	5.7	1989
Grand Rapids, MI	<0.1	3.8	4.9	6.3	6.6	8.5	9.0	14.9	8.9	37.1	1953
Greeley, CO	0.1	9.4	17.2	16.7	10.2	21.2	9.4	6.4	2.2	7.2	1984
Green Bay, WI	0.1	2.3	7.0	10.4	12.0	18.6	12.9	15.6	6.5	14.7	1970
Greensboro, NC	0.1	8.0	15.0	16.8	16.5	13.3	11.3	10.2	3.7	5.1	1984
Honolulu, HI	0.1	6.0	6.8	8.2	9.8	26.1	21.0	11.9	5.2	5.0	1973
Houston, TX	0.2	11.8	12.7	9.8	14.6	19.6	13.0	10.0	4.2	4.2	1980
Huntsville, AL	0.2	13.6	12.4	11.0	15.8	12.8	20.6	8.6	2.4	2.6	1982
Indianapolis, IN	0.1	5.0	9.2	12.5	11.5	12.9	13.6	12.8	6.2	16.3	1971
Jacksonville, FL	0.6	8.4	18.1	14.7	15.6	12.4	9.9	10.8	4.5	5.0	1985
Kansas City, MO	0.2	6.9	9.8	9.2	8.9	11.8	12.5	13.4	5.9	21.3	1968
Lafayette, LA	<0.1	10.1	10.7	10.1	19.5	22.0	12.8	9.0	3.2	2.5	1980
Las Cruces, NM	0.3	10.7	19.9	15.0	16.9	15.5	8.1	8.9	2.1	2.6	1988
Las Vegas, NV	0.2	7.1	21.8	31.0	16.3	10.1	7.6	4.2	1.1	0.5	1993
Lexington, KY	0.2	8.4	14.2	16.5	13.2	15.2	13.5	8.9	2.9	7.1	1982
Lincoln, NE	0.1	10.3	13.1	14.2	10.4	15.4	9.4	10.7	3.4	13.0	1979
Little Rock, AR	0.0	8.0	11.4	12.3	13.7	18.5	13.8	9.4	5.1	7.8	1978
Los Angeles, CA	0.1	4.8	5.5	6.0	10.6	13.4	13.6	16.8	9.3	19.7	1963
Louisville, KY	0.2	6.6	11.0	11.1	6.9	12.4	13.6	14.6	7.2	16.5	1969
Madison, WI	0.1	10.1	13.5	12.8	9.8	13.7	11.8	9.4	4.5	14.2	1977

Table continued on following page.

Appendix A: Comparative Statistics   A-121

City	2020 or Later	2010 -2019	2000 -2009	1990 -1999	1980 -1989	1970 -1979	1960 -1969	1950 -1959	1940 -1949	Before 1940	Median Year
Manchester, NH	0.3	2.5	6.2	8.3	16.3	11.9	8.1	10.1	7.2	29.1	1965
Miami, FL	0.2	11.5	18.0	6.6	7.5	12.8	10.0	14.4	9.9	9.1	1975
Midland, TX	0.2	18.2	8.1	13.4	18.0	11.7	8.9	17.8	2.6	1.2	1984
Milwaukee, WI	0.1	2.6	3.5	3.3	4.1	8.7	11.4	19.5	10.4	36.5	1952
Minneapolis, MN	<0.1	7.3	6.3	4.0	6.8	8.2	7.5	9.0	6.9	43.9	1949
Nashville, TN	0.8	13.4	13.8	12.3	14.5	13.5	11.6	9.7	4.0	6.4	1983
New Haven, CT	0.0	3.8	4.6	3.1	6.8	9.5	11.2	10.3	7.4	43.2	1949
New Orleans, LA	0.1	4.4	6.9	3.3	7.6	13.9	10.9	12.1	7.3	33.4	1958
New York, NY	<0.1	4.1	5.4	3.8	4.9	7.0	12.5	12.9	9.5	39.9	1950
Oklahoma City, OK	0.3	12.0	13.4	9.9	14.2	15.9	11.5	10.0	5.0	7.9	1980
Omaha, NE	0.1	5.1	8.3	12.4	10.9	15.1	14.4	10.9	4.6	18.3	1971
Orlando, FL	0.2	13.7	20.3	14.7	15.6	14.5	7.2	8.3	2.8	2.8	1989
Philadelphia, PA	0.1	3.6	3.0	3.2	4.0	7.4	11.1	15.7	11.2	40.7	1948
Phoenix, AZ	0.2	6.4	16.3	15.4	17.5	19.4	11.0	9.6	2.4	1.9	1983
Pittsburgh, PA	0.1	3.9	3.0	3.6	4.4	6.6	8.3	13.2	8.3	48.8	1941
Portland, OR	0.2	8.9	9.9	7.9	6.8	10.8	8.6	11.4	7.8	27.7	1964
Providence, RI	0.1	1.2	4.6	4.6	5.7	7.9	5.4	7.1	5.7	57.7	<1940
Provo, UT	0.4	6.9	10.7	18.8	14.4	18.5	9.9	7.8	5.0	7.6	1981
Raleigh, NC	0.3	14.6	23.4	18.5	16.8	9.9	7.6	4.2	1.6	3.1	1994
Reno, NV	1.0	9.8	19.0	17.3	13.8	18.0	8.8	6.1	3.1	3.1	1988
Richmond, VA	0.1	6.5	5.3	5.8	7.1	9.9	11.8	14.7	9.1	29.6	1958
Rochester, MN	0.4	12.3	18.0	14.4	12.0	12.5	10.0	8.8	3.4	8.1	1986
Sacramento, CA	0.1	4.6	14.5	8.7	15.6	14.2	11.4	12.3	7.3	11.3	1975
St. Louis, MO	<0.1	2.4	4.0	3.0	3.2	4.4	6.5	10.2	8.1	58.2	<1940
Salem, OR	0.2	6.9	12.5	16.8	9.7	19.9	9.5	10.6	4.9	9.0	1978
Salt Lake City, UT	0.2	8.1	6.8	6.4	7.6	11.3	9.8	12.8	9.2	27.8	1960
San Antonio, TX	0.2	10.2	14.9	12.9	16.2	14.4	10.3	9.9	5.5	5.4	1983
San Diego, CA	0.2	5.7	10.2	11.0	17.5	20.7	12.5	11.5	4.1	6.7	1977
San Francisco, CA	0.1	5.4	6.3	4.2	5.4	7.2	7.9	8.6	8.8	46.2	1944
San Jose, CA	0.2	6.4	9.2	10.1	12.5	24.3	18.0	11.1	2.8	5.3	1975
Santa Rosa, CA	0.5	4.6	12.5	13.2	17.9	21.1	12.0	8.1	4.7	5.5	1979
Savannah, GA	0.1	9.6	9.7	6.5	10.9	11.5	12.2	14.5	8.0	17.0	1969
Seattle, WA	0.1	14.7	11.9	8.3	7.6	7.7	8.3	9.1	8.0	24.2	1971
Sioux Falls, SD	0.3	17.8	17.9	14.7	9.7	12.1	7.0	8.3	3.1	9.1	1990
Springfield, IL	<0.1	3.0	8.6	13.0	8.8	17.4	12.6	10.8	6.0	19.7	1971
Tampa, FL	0.3	10.8	17.3	12.5	11.9	11.3	9.3	13.0	5.1	8.6	1982
Tucson, AZ	0.1	3.4	12.6	13.3	17.2	20.5	11.0	13.9	4.6	3.4	1978
Tulsa, OK	0.1	4.6	6.2	9.2	13.4	20.6	14.4	16.5	6.4	8.7	1972
Tuscaloosa, AL	0.1	16.7	16.7	14.4	11.6	14.9	9.8	8.3	3.9	3.6	1988
Virginia Beach, VA	0.1	6.4	11.1	14.1	27.1	20.4	12.4	6.1	1.2	1.1	1983
Washington, DC	0.2	10.3	7.9	3.1	4.7	6.8	11.1	12.1	10.8	32.9	1955
Wichita, KS	0.1	5.9	9.9	12.2	12.3	13.1	9.8	18.6	8.0	10.2	1973
Wilmington, NC	0.1	10.8	15.0	17.3	15.3	12.9	6.7	6.8	5.5	9.6	1986
Winston-Salem, NC	0.1	6.4	13.2	13.0	14.3	16.4	11.8	12.2	4.9	7.7	1978
Worcester, MA	0.0	2.1	4.6	5.2	10.1	7.9	7.8	11.6	7.5	43.3	1949
U.S.	0.2	7.3	13.6	13.6	13.2	14.8	10.3	10.0	4.7	12.2	1979

Note: Figures are percentages except for median year
Source: U.S. Census Bureau, 2017-2021 American Community Survey 5-Year Estimates

A-122 Appendix A: Comparative Statistics

Year Housing Structure Built: Metro Area

Metro Area	2020 or Later	2010 -2019	2000 -2009	1990 -1999	1980 -1989	1970 -1979	1960 -1969	1950 -1959	1940 -1949	Before 1940	Median Year
Albuquerque, NM	0.2	5.9	17.2	17.3	16.8	17.8	8.7	9.3	3.6	3.2	1984
Allentown, PA	0.1	4.0	11.4	10.3	11.0	12.0	9.5	10.9	5.2	25.7	1969
Anchorage, AK	0.1	6.4	17.2	13.3	25.0	23.5	8.3	4.7	1.0	0.5	1985
Ann Arbor, MI	0.2	4.8	12.8	17.0	11.2	16.0	12.4	9.7	4.5	11.5	1977
Athens, GA	0.2	7.5	17.8	20.4	16.4	15.2	10.0	5.3	1.9	5.2	1988
Atlanta, GA	0.3	9.4	23.6	20.8	17.1	12.4	7.3	4.5	1.7	2.8	1992
Austin, TX	0.6	22.4	22.8	16.7	15.5	10.6	4.9	3.0	1.5	2.1	1997
Baltimore, MD	0.1	6.0	9.4	13.4	13.4	12.9	10.4	12.8	6.2	15.4	1974
Boise City, ID	0.5	14.3	23.2	20.7	9.8	14.1	5.2	4.3	2.8	5.2	1994
Boston, MA	0.1	5.8	7.5	7.4	10.4	10.8	10.1	10.7	5.0	32.2	1962
Boulder, CO	0.2	9.4	11.7	19.4	16.4	19.7	10.6	4.8	1.3	6.3	1984
Brownsville, TX	0.2	11.0	22.2	17.0	17.9	16.0	5.7	5.3	2.6	2.1	1990
Cape Coral, FL	0.2	8.9	29.7	17.4	21.0	14.4	5.2	2.2	0.4	0.6	1994
Cedar Rapids, IA	0.1	8.3	13.7	12.7	7.2	13.8	12.3	10.4	3.5	18.0	1974
Charleston, SC	0.3	16.4	20.8	15.5	15.4	13.0	7.7	4.8	2.4	3.7	1992
Charlotte, NC	0.2	13.6	22.6	18.9	12.9	10.8	7.7	6.3	2.9	4.1	1993
Chicago, IL	0.1	3.6	11.4	11.2	9.1	14.1	11.5	12.7	5.9	20.5	1969
Cincinnati, OH	0.1	5.3	12.0	13.8	10.7	13.8	10.5	11.6	4.8	17.3	1974
Clarksville, TN	0.4	13.8	19.7	20.2	12.2	13.9	7.9	6.0	2.9	3.0	1992
Cleveland, OH	0.1	3.4	6.8	8.9	6.9	12.4	13.6	17.7	7.6	22.5	1962
College Station, TX	0.6	17.0	18.8	18.0	16.6	14.4	6.0	4.3	2.1	2.3	1992
Colorado Springs, CO	0.3	10.7	17.8	16.4	17.6	16.2	8.1	6.2	1.6	5.1	1987
Columbia, MO	<0.1	12.1	18.1	17.6	13.2	14.8	9.6	4.7	2.6	7.2	1988
Columbia, SC	0.3	11.3	18.6	18.3	13.7	14.9	9.2	6.7	3.2	3.7	1989
Columbus, OH	0.2	8.0	14.2	15.9	11.6	13.8	10.7	9.8	3.7	12.2	1980
Dallas, TX	0.4	14.0	19.1	15.6	17.3	13.3	8.3	7.1	2.4	2.6	1989
Davenport, IA	0.1	4.6	7.9	8.5	6.8	15.9	12.8	12.1	7.2	24.2	1965
Denver, CO	0.3	10.7	16.0	14.8	13.8	17.2	9.0	9.0	2.6	6.5	1984
Des Moines, IA	0.3	14.1	15.7	12.5	8.0	13.3	7.9	8.8	3.9	15.4	1981
Durham, NC	0.5	13.4	17.9	18.2	15.3	12.0	8.4	6.1	2.9	5.3	1990
Edison, NJ	0.1	4.1	6.5	6.2	7.8	9.7	13.5	15.6	8.5	28.1	1959
El Paso, TX	0.2	14.0	15.8	14.1	14.5	15.2	9.2	9.4	3.3	4.3	1986
Fargo, ND	0.4	17.5	17.3	13.6	10.2	15.0	6.8	7.8	2.5	8.9	1989
Fort Collins, CO	0.4	14.9	18.1	19.1	12.4	17.9	6.6	3.3	1.8	5.6	1991
Fort Wayne, IN	0.2	5.9	11.5	14.3	10.4	15.3	12.4	11.0	5.4	13.7	1975
Fort Worth, TX	0.4	14.0	19.1	15.6	17.3	13.3	8.3	7.1	2.4	2.6	1989
Grand Rapids, MI	0.2	6.9	12.6	15.8	11.3	13.6	9.3	10.0	5.1	15.2	1978
Greeley, CO	0.7	16.2	26.7	15.4	7.2	14.6	5.6	3.9	1.9	7.7	1996
Green Bay, WI	<0.1	7.5	13.4	16.3	11.6	15.4	9.8	9.5	4.3	12.3	1979
Greensboro, NC	0.1	7.3	15.8	17.9	14.5	14.4	10.4	9.5	4.1	6.0	1984
Honolulu, HI	0.1	6.7	9.7	11.8	12.4	24.3	17.9	10.1	3.8	3.1	1976
Houston, TX	0.4	15.6	20.3	13.9	15.3	15.8	8.1	5.9	2.4	2.4	1990
Huntsville, AL	0.2	14.6	18.9	16.7	16.1	10.6	13.0	5.9	1.9	2.1	1990
Indianapolis, IN	0.2	8.8	14.9	16.3	10.3	12.1	10.6	10.1	4.5	12.3	1980
Jacksonville, FL	0.7	11.2	21.2	15.9	16.4	12.0	7.7	7.7	3.2	4.0	1989
Kansas City, MO	0.2	7.1	13.3	14.1	12.0	14.7	11.7	11.0	4.3	11.7	1978
Lafayette, LA	0.2	12.8	14.8	12.9	15.8	15.9	10.3	9.0	3.7	4.5	1984
Las Cruces, NM	0.2	11.0	17.9	19.3	18.3	15.3	7.0	6.3	1.9	2.7	1989
Las Vegas, NV	0.3	10.0	29.1	27.6	14.2	10.6	4.9	2.1	0.7	0.4	1996
Lexington, KY	0.2	8.7	16.1	17.4	13.4	14.8	11.1	7.7	3.0	7.6	1984
Lincoln, NE	0.1	10.1	13.5	14.2	10.1	15.6	9.6	9.8	3.3	13.7	1979
Little Rock, AR	0.3	12.0	17.4	16.6	14.0	15.9	10.0	6.8	3.2	3.8	1987
Los Angeles, CA	0.1	4.2	6.1	7.7	12.4	16.1	15.5	18.2	8.0	11.7	1968
Louisville, KY	0.2	6.7	12.8	13.8	9.2	14.8	12.1	12.2	5.9	12.3	1975
Madison, WI	0.2	9.4	15.4	15.5	10.7	14.3	9.5	7.6	3.5	13.9	1981

Table continued on following page.

Appendix A: Comparative Statistics   A-123

Metro Area	2020 or Later	2010 -2019	2000 -2009	1990 -1999	1980 -1989	1970 -1979	1960 -1969	1950 -1959	1940 -1949	Before 1940	Median Year
Manchester, NH	0.1	4.2	9.7	10.9	20.4	15.6	9.5	7.0	3.8	18.8	1977
Miami, FL	0.2	6.0	12.7	14.6	19.2	21.0	11.9	9.8	2.7	2.1	1981
Midland, TX	0.2	19.5	11.0	14.2	17.8	10.9	7.8	14.6	2.6	1.4	1987
Milwaukee, WI	0.1	4.2	8.2	10.9	7.8	12.9	11.5	15.7	6.9	21.8	1965
Minneapolis, MN	0.2	7.0	13.5	13.9	14.2	14.3	9.8	9.5	3.7	13.8	1979
Nashville, TN	0.6	15.4	18.5	16.8	13.5	12.5	8.8	6.4	2.8	4.5	1991
New Haven, CT	<0.1	2.5	5.8	7.4	12.6	13.6	12.2	14.8	7.1	23.9	1963
New Orleans, LA	0.2	5.1	12.1	10.0	13.3	19.0	12.9	9.7	4.6	13.0	1975
New York, NY	0.1	4.1	6.5	6.2	7.8	9.7	13.5	15.6	8.5	28.1	1959
Oklahoma City, OK	0.3	11.8	14.7	11.0	14.3	16.8	11.4	9.2	4.6	5.9	1981
Omaha, NE	0.3	9.0	14.4	12.5	9.8	14.1	11.7	8.4	3.5	16.3	1977
Orlando, FL	0.3	12.7	22.2	19.4	19.4	12.6	5.8	5.1	1.2	1.5	1992
Philadelphia, PA	0.1	4.3	7.9	9.4	9.8	12.0	12.0	15.3	7.2	22.0	1965
Phoenix, AZ	0.3	9.8	24.5	19.4	16.8	15.4	6.9	4.8	1.2	0.9	1992
Pittsburgh, PA	0.1	4.0	6.2	7.6	7.7	12.0	11.4	16.5	8.6	25.9	1959
Portland, OR	0.3	9.2	14.0	17.3	11.3	16.7	8.2	6.9	4.5	11.7	1982
Providence, RI	0.1	2.7	6.1	8.1	11.2	12.1	10.7	11.5	6.0	31.4	1961
Provo, UT	0.4	19.6	24.2	17.6	8.9	12.7	4.7	5.0	2.7	4.2	1997
Raleigh, NC	0.5	17.9	23.9	21.6	14.6	8.6	5.4	3.4	1.4	2.7	1996
Reno, NV	0.7	8.8	20.1	18.8	14.8	18.9	8.6	4.7	2.3	2.3	1989
Richmond, VA	0.2	8.7	14.2	15.0	15.6	14.5	9.6	8.8	4.3	9.0	1982
Rochester, MN	0.3	9.6	17.9	14.4	10.8	13.2	9.0	7.6	3.4	13.8	1983
Sacramento, CA	0.2	5.3	16.9	14.9	16.7	18.0	10.6	9.7	3.4	4.2	1982
St. Louis, MO	0.2	5.3	11.4	12.1	11.1	13.0	12.6	12.6	5.5	16.2	1972
Salem, OR	0.2	6.5	13.4	17.3	9.7	22.3	10.3	8.0	4.0	8.4	1979
Salt Lake City, UT	0.2	12.6	14.8	15.1	11.9	17.4	8.6	8.3	3.5	7.5	1984
San Antonio, TX	0.5	16.2	19.2	13.9	14.5	12.4	8.0	7.2	3.8	4.3	1990
San Diego, CA	0.2	5.1	11.8	12.2	18.6	22.2	11.9	10.5	3.4	4.2	1979
San Francisco, CA	0.1	4.6	7.6	8.1	10.9	14.7	13.1	13.6	7.7	19.7	1967
San Jose, CA	0.2	7.5	8.9	10.0	12.1	21.3	17.6	13.9	3.5	5.0	1975
Santa Rosa, CA	0.3	4.0	10.3	13.7	18.2	20.6	11.6	8.9	4.4	8.0	1978
Savannah, GA	0.3	13.3	19.8	14.7	13.2	11.2	7.6	7.8	4.2	8.0	1989
Seattle, WA	0.2	10.6	14.7	15.2	14.1	13.4	10.8	7.1	4.2	9.7	1983
Sioux Falls, SD	0.2	16.0	18.0	14.9	8.7	12.7	6.7	7.4	3.2	12.2	1989
Springfield, IL	<0.1	4.3	10.0	13.2	8.7	17.3	11.7	11.0	6.0	17.8	1972
Tampa, FL	0.3	8.2	15.8	14.0	19.9	19.9	9.1	8.3	2.0	2.6	1984
Tucson, AZ	0.2	6.2	18.1	17.3	17.7	19.1	8.4	8.2	2.8	2.0	1985
Tulsa, OK	0.3	9.1	13.7	12.1	14.1	18.8	10.5	10.5	4.3	6.7	1980
Tuscaloosa, AL	0.1	12.4	18.5	18.3	13.5	14.7	9.0	6.6	3.2	3.6	1989
Virginia Beach, VA	0.2	8.0	12.6	14.8	18.4	15.2	11.6	9.3	4.2	5.7	1982
Washington, DC	0.2	9.0	14.0	14.0	15.4	13.5	11.8	8.9	4.9	8.3	1982
Wichita, KS	0.1	6.7	11.8	13.5	12.4	13.1	8.8	16.4	6.5	10.7	1976
Wilmington, NC	0.3	12.4	20.4	20.9	15.1	12.0	5.6	4.6	3.4	5.3	1992
Winston-Salem, NC	0.1	6.8	15.2	16.6	14.8	16.6	10.2	9.2	4.1	6.2	1982
Worcester, MA	0.1	3.8	8.7	9.5	12.4	11.3	8.9	11.0	5.6	28.9	1965
U.S.	0.2	7.3	13.6	13.6	13.2	14.8	10.3	10.0	4.7	12.2	1979

Note: Figures are percentages except for median year; Figures cover the Metropolitan Statistical Area
Source: U.S. Census Bureau, 2017-2021 American Community Survey 5-Year Estimates

A-124　Appendix A: Comparative Statistics

Gross Monthly Rent: City

City	Under $500	$500 -$999	$1,000 -$1,499	$1,500 -$1,999	$2,000 -$2,499	$2,500 -$2,999	$3,000 and up	Median ($)
Albuquerque, NM	7.3	49.4	31.5	9.8	1.1	0.5	0.5	932
Allentown, PA	7.6	31.1	44.6	14.9	1.3	0.3	0.3	1,100
Anchorage, AK	4.8	20.1	34.7	23.1	11.6	4.0	1.8	1,350
Ann Arbor, MI	3.9	17.0	37.0	24.4	9.7	3.5	4.4	1,382
Athens, GA	5.4	52.2	29.1	9.4	2.2	0.8	0.8	939
Atlanta, GA	11.0	18.0	31.3	25.2	9.2	2.9	2.4	1,342
Austin, TX	2.8	10.6	43.9	26.9	10.3	3.0	2.6	1,415
Baltimore, MD	14.9	22.2	37.2	17.6	5.5	1.5	1.1	1,146
Boise City, ID	4.2	34.8	42.3	15.3	1.9	0.7	0.8	1,103
Boston, MA	14.1	10.7	13.3	20.9	17.7	9.6	13.6	1,783
Boulder, CO	3.1	6.2	29.1	27.4	16.5	6.4	11.3	1,711
Brownsville, TX	20.5	54.9	19.9	3.9	0.7	0.2	0.0	794
Cape Coral, FL	1.2	11.9	40.8	37.8	5.8	0.9	1.5	1,456
Cedar Rapids, IA	12.8	56.9	24.8	3.1	0.6	0.2	1.7	836
Charleston, SC	5.1	13.9	39.7	27.1	8.4	2.8	3.0	1,400
Charlotte, NC	3.4	19.6	48.2	21.7	4.5	1.5	1.2	1,260
Chicago, IL	8.6	25.4	32.7	17.7	8.6	3.9	3.2	1,209
Cincinnati, OH	15.9	52.7	21.5	6.4	2.1	0.7	0.7	814
Clarksville, TN	4.2	44.4	38.0	10.4	2.6	0.3	0.1	1,016
Cleveland, OH	20.3	53.7	19.1	4.7	1.3	0.6	0.4	774
College Station, TX	2.2	44.2	33.0	14.9	3.9	1.4	0.5	1,042
Colorado Springs, CO	3.3	21.7	39.4	25.1	6.5	2.8	1.2	1,300
Columbia, MO	5.7	52.3	30.3	6.6	4.2	0.8	0.1	935
Columbia, SC	10.3	38.9	37.0	11.2	2.0	0.3	0.3	1,007
Columbus, OH	5.2	37.8	43.6	10.1	2.3	0.4	0.6	1,061
Dallas, TX	3.5	28.7	42.6	16.5	5.2	1.7	1.8	1,178
Davenport, IA	9.4	61.7	21.9	4.3	0.7	0.5	1.5	815
Denver, CO	7.1	10.5	32.7	27.6	14.0	5.1	3.0	1,495
Des Moines, IA	7.8	52.1	31.7	6.4	1.7	0.2	0.2	916
Durham, NC	6.7	26.5	44.8	17.4	3.1	0.4	1.1	1,157
Edison, NJ	3.2	3.3	26.6	39.0	22.8	4.0	1.1	1,716
El Paso, TX	12.3	48.4	31.0	6.7	1.2	0.3	0.2	910
Fargo, ND	5.7	65.4	21.2	5.3	1.9	0.3	0.2	841
Fort Collins, CO	2.0	17.4	34.7	28.6	13.4	2.2	1.7	1,443
Fort Wayne, IN	9.5	63.9	22.8	3.0	0.4	0.2	0.2	823
Fort Worth, TX	3.7	28.4	40.5	19.2	5.9	1.4	0.9	1,187
Grand Rapids, MI	10.7	38.1	37.4	9.2	3.4	0.8	0.4	1,013
Greeley, CO	9.1	29.7	37.4	16.2	6.0	1.1	0.5	1,134
Green Bay, WI	9.1	66.5	22.1	1.8	0.2	0.0	0.2	805
Greensboro, NC	5.7	53.2	33.2	5.9	1.2	0.3	0.6	944
Honolulu, HI	6.7	10.1	27.5	24.0	13.2	7.9	10.7	1,620
Houston, TX	3.4	34.1	38.9	15.8	4.4	1.5	1.8	1,136
Huntsville, AL	7.5	52.1	31.9	6.8	0.7	0.5	0.5	912
Indianapolis, IN	6.0	49.3	34.3	7.9	1.7	0.4	0.4	962
Jacksonville, FL	5.4	29.0	43.7	17.5	3.6	0.5	0.4	1,146
Kansas City, MO	7.2	39.0	38.6	11.6	2.4	0.7	0.5	1,040
Lafayette, LA	6.9	50.5	32.1	8.7	1.0	0.2	0.6	948
Las Cruces, NM	13.0	56.6	25.0	4.0	1.0	0.1	0.4	824
Las Vegas, NV	4.0	25.7	42.9	20.6	4.9	1.0	0.9	1,219
Lexington, KY	6.4	47.7	34.5	8.1	2.3	0.5	0.4	967
Lincoln, NE	6.2	53.4	30.1	7.6	1.4	0.3	1.1	920
Little Rock, AR	7.8	49.3	33.3	6.7	1.4	0.7	0.8	940
Los Angeles, CA	4.9	11.1	27.1	24.6	15.1	8.1	9.2	1,641
Louisville, KY	11.4	47.2	32.6	6.8	1.2	0.2	0.6	931
Madison, WI	4.2	25.0	44.1	17.9	5.5	1.6	1.7	1,212

Table continued on following page.

Appendix A: Comparative Statistics   A-125

City	Under $500	$500 -$999	$1,000 -$1,499	$1,500 -$1,999	$2,000 -$2,499	$2,500 -$2,999	$3,000 and up	Median ($)
Manchester, NH	7.0	21.3	43.4	20.8	5.4	1.4	0.8	1,220
Miami, FL	9.1	17.6	31.5	20.1	11.7	5.0	4.9	1,361
Midland, TX	2.8	19.5	44.3	19.5	9.2	3.6	1.1	1,273
Milwaukee, WI	7.7	55.0	28.4	6.3	1.6	0.6	0.4	910
Minneapolis, MN	10.9	27.0	33.1	17.8	7.4	2.0	1.9	1,159
Nashville, TN	7.4	20.6	41.1	20.6	6.9	1.9	1.5	1,250
New Haven, CT	13.5	14.2	40.8	20.6	7.4	2.4	1.1	1,267
New Orleans, LA	10.9	31.7	36.8	13.8	4.6	1.2	0.8	1,079
New York, NY	9.5	12.4	24.4	23.3	13.3	6.6	10.5	1,579
Oklahoma City, OK	6.5	51.2	32.1	7.8	1.6	0.4	0.4	933
Omaha, NE	5.4	44.7	36.8	10.2	1.6	0.4	0.9	999
Orlando, FL	3.4	15.1	45.7	26.9	6.3	1.6	1.1	1,346
Philadelphia, PA	9.3	27.7	38.4	15.3	5.5	2.0	1.8	1,149
Phoenix, AZ	3.8	28.5	43.3	18.5	4.2	0.9	0.8	1,175
Pittsburgh, PA	13.0	33.7	31.0	13.9	5.5	2.0	0.9	1,043
Portland, OR	5.6	14.2	37.6	25.6	10.8	3.9	2.3	1,406
Providence, RI	19.3	21.5	38.2	14.8	3.7	1.3	1.2	1,098
Provo, UT	9.1	44.7	29.6	11.4	4.1	0.5	0.6	973
Raleigh, NC	3.2	19.5	52.4	19.0	4.3	0.9	0.9	1,237
Reno, NV	5.7	27.4	37.5	21.1	6.4	1.0	1.0	1,213
Richmond, VA	11.2	26.1	41.7	16.2	3.6	0.6	0.7	1,132
Rochester, MN	7.8	34.8	32.6	17.7	3.4	1.3	2.4	1,120
Sacramento, CA	5.5	16.1	33.0	30.1	11.3	2.5	1.6	1,434
St. Louis, MO	10.6	54.3	26.8	6.1	1.7	0.3	0.2	873
Salem, OR	6.3	30.7	43.7	15.2	2.8	0.6	0.7	1,125
Salt Lake City, UT	8.0	30.3	36.6	17.7	5.4	1.2	0.8	1,141
San Antonio, TX	6.2	34.8	41.6	13.5	2.6	0.7	0.6	1,090
San Diego, CA	2.7	6.1	19.8	27.8	21.3	11.6	10.7	1,885
San Francisco, CA	8.6	10.0	13.7	14.1	13.3	11.6	28.5	2,130
San Jose, CA	3.7	5.6	9.3	17.0	19.6	18.0	26.7	2,366
Santa Rosa, CA	4.9	5.3	21.2	27.5	21.2	11.7	8.1	1,837
Savannah, GA	8.6	29.0	45.1	13.3	2.8	0.5	0.7	1,116
Seattle, WA	5.4	6.3	21.6	27.9	19.6	9.7	9.6	1,801
Sioux Falls, SD	6.2	58.7	27.7	5.7	0.6	0.4	0.8	892
Springfield, IL	10.6	58.7	23.8	4.8	0.9	0.8	0.4	852
Tampa, FL	7.4	21.2	39.2	19.4	8.2	2.4	2.1	1,249
Tucson, AZ	6.0	53.6	30.2	8.0	1.2	0.5	0.6	907
Tulsa, OK	8.9	54.8	28.8	4.8	1.3	0.5	0.9	882
Tuscaloosa, AL	11.0	51.3	28.3	5.9	2.0	0.6	0.9	907
Virginia Beach, VA	2.3	9.1	45.2	30.5	8.6	2.5	1.8	1,433
Washington, DC	9.2	10.4	22.3	22.4	15.2	9.2	11.3	1,681
Wichita, KS	8.1	60.2	26.3	3.9	0.8	0.2	0.5	856
Wilmington, NC	10.1	31.3	40.1	15.0	2.5	0.5	0.6	1,093
Winston-Salem, NC	8.8	57.2	26.5	5.3	1.3	0.3	0.6	871
Worcester, MA	13.8	21.1	41.4	18.7	3.6	0.7	0.7	1,179
U.S.	8.1	30.5	30.8	16.8	7.3	3.1	3.5	1,163

Note: Figures are percentages except for Median; Gross rent is the contract rent plus the estimated average monthly cost of utilities (electricity, gas, and water and sewer) and fuels (oil, coal, kerosene, wood, etc.) if these are paid by the renter (or paid for the renter by someone else).
Source: U.S. Census Bureau, 2017-2021 American Community Survey 5-Year Estimates

A-126 Appendix A: Comparative Statistics

Gross Monthly Rent: Metro Area

MSA[1]	Under $500	$500 -$999	$1,000 -$1,499	$1,500 -$1,999	$2,000 -$2,499	$2,500 -2,999	$3,000 and up	Median ($)
Albuquerque, NM	7.2	47.4	32.9	10.2	1.3	0.4	0.5	952
Allentown, PA	8.9	28.4	39.4	17.7	3.9	0.9	0.9	1,141
Anchorage, AK	5.1	21.7	34.9	22.4	10.8	3.5	1.5	1,314
Ann Arbor, MI	5.1	24.0	40.6	18.9	6.1	2.2	3.1	1,218
Athens, GA	5.6	51.9	28.9	9.1	2.7	0.9	0.8	939
Atlanta, GA	4.3	19.1	43.9	23.8	6.2	1.5	1.2	1,294
Austin, TX	2.6	12.4	43.5	26.5	9.9	2.7	2.4	1,398
Baltimore, MD	8.2	14.4	35.1	26.4	11.0	3.0	2.0	1,387
Boise City, ID	6.5	32.7	40.5	16.2	2.6	0.8	0.7	1,107
Boston, MA	10.9	10.8	20.5	24.5	16.4	8.4	8.6	1,659
Boulder, CO	3.5	7.0	27.3	31.3	15.9	6.9	8.0	1,694
Brownsville, TX	18.4	59.0	18.3	3.2	0.7	0.2	0.2	785
Cape Coral, FL	3.6	19.1	45.6	21.7	5.9	1.8	2.4	1,307
Cedar Rapids, IA	13.4	57.1	23.0	4.2	0.8	0.1	1.4	806
Charleston, SC	4.6	20.9	43.3	20.1	6.9	2.0	2.1	1,274
Charlotte, NC	4.8	31.3	41.3	16.7	3.6	1.2	1.0	1,147
Chicago, IL	6.9	25.3	36.0	18.6	7.6	2.9	2.5	1,209
Cincinnati, OH	10.6	49.6	28.4	7.8	2.1	0.7	0.8	906
Clarksville, TN	7.7	45.9	35.8	8.3	1.9	0.2	0.1	967
Cleveland, OH	11.5	52.2	27.1	6.5	1.4	0.5	0.8	880
College Station, TX	5.0	44.7	32.9	12.3	3.1	1.2	0.7	1,003
Colorado Springs, CO	3.3	20.8	36.2	28.6	7.6	2.6	1.1	1,349
Columbia, MO	7.4	52.9	29.9	5.6	3.5	0.6	0.2	917
Columbia, SC	7.1	43.7	35.6	9.8	2.7	0.5	0.5	993
Columbus, OH	6.0	38.6	41.3	10.3	2.4	0.7	0.6	1,049
Dallas, TX	2.6	22.1	43.0	21.2	7.7	1.9	1.5	1,264
Davenport, IA	12.9	58.7	21.1	4.7	1.2	0.4	1.1	808
Denver, CO	4.5	9.6	32.5	31.5	14.2	5.0	2.7	1,554
Des Moines, IA	6.8	46.8	34.7	8.9	2.0	0.3	0.6	972
Durham, NC	6.6	30.7	41.7	15.5	3.6	0.7	1.3	1,127
Edison, NJ	8.4	11.4	26.5	24.9	13.4	6.3	9.1	1,573
El Paso, TX	12.0	48.6	30.8	7.0	1.2	0.2	0.2	908
Fargo, ND	6.6	60.9	22.5	7.6	1.6	0.4	0.3	855
Fort Collins, CO	2.8	17.7	34.1	28.7	12.2	2.9	1.7	1,433
Fort Wayne, IN	8.9	62.4	23.7	4.1	0.6	0.2	0.2	839
Fort Worth, TX	2.6	22.1	43.0	21.2	7.7	1.9	1.5	1,264
Grand Rapids, MI	8.4	45.1	34.9	7.7	2.5	0.9	0.6	973
Greeley, CO	7.1	26.4	33.6	21.2	7.5	2.6	1.6	1,234
Green Bay, WI	6.8	64.8	24.4	2.9	0.3	0.3	0.4	851
Greensboro, NC	9.0	55.6	28.9	4.6	1.1	0.3	0.6	900
Honolulu, HI	5.4	8.4	20.9	20.8	15.0	12.0	17.6	1,870
Houston, TX	3.3	29.1	39.7	19.2	5.7	1.5	1.6	1,189
Huntsville, AL	8.0	51.8	30.9	7.1	1.1	0.6	0.5	912
Indianapolis, IN	5.7	46.0	35.5	9.7	2.0	0.5	0.6	987
Jacksonville, FL	4.9	27.9	41.7	18.9	4.6	1.0	1.0	1,175
Kansas City, MO	6.5	38.5	38.5	11.8	3.0	0.8	0.9	1,052
Lafayette, LA	13.8	54.5	25.3	4.8	1.1	0.1	0.4	853
Las Cruces, NM	16.4	55.8	22.5	3.8	1.2	0.1	0.3	785
Las Vegas, NV	2.3	24.0	42.7	23.4	5.6	1.2	0.8	1,257
Lexington, KY	7.5	50.4	32.5	7.0	1.8	0.4	0.3	934
Lincoln, NE	6.5	53.2	30.0	7.4	1.5	0.3	1.1	918
Little Rock, AR	8.1	55.9	29.1	5.3	0.9	0.4	0.4	893
Los Angeles, CA	3.8	8.7	24.8	26.8	17.5	8.9	9.5	1,737
Louisville, KY	11.0	47.2	33.5	6.2	1.3	0.2	0.6	934
Madison, WI	4.5	31.5	41.8	15.7	4.3	1.1	1.2	1,143

Table continued on following page.

Appendix A: Comparative Statistics   A-127

MSA[1]	Under $500	$500 -$999	$1,000 -$1,499	$1,500 -$1,999	$2,000 -$2,499	$2,500 -2,999	$3,000 and up	Median ($)
Manchester, NH	6.7	18.6	40.2	24.7	6.8	1.9	1.1	1,305
Miami, FL	4.5	11.5	34.6	28.5	12.9	4.5	3.6	1,492
Midland, TX	4.2	19.9	43.6	19.0	9.0	3.3	1.0	1,271
Milwaukee, WI	6.9	48.0	32.3	9.1	2.4	0.7	0.5	963
Minneapolis, MN	8.1	24.0	37.9	20.4	6.3	1.7	1.6	1,207
Nashville, TN	6.7	25.1	39.7	20.0	5.7	1.6	1.2	1,211
New Haven, CT	10.6	19.5	41.4	19.9	5.6	1.6	1.4	1,223
New Orleans, LA	8.0	35.7	39.3	12.2	3.5	0.7	0.6	1,064
New York, NY	8.4	11.4	26.5	24.9	13.4	6.3	9.1	1,573
Oklahoma City, OK	6.8	50.2	32.3	8.0	1.6	0.5	0.6	937
Omaha, NE	6.4	43.7	36.5	10.2	1.7	0.5	1.2	1,000
Orlando, FL	2.7	16.2	43.2	27.2	7.5	1.9	1.2	1,363
Philadelphia, PA	7.2	22.3	40.2	19.2	6.7	2.3	2.0	1,230
Phoenix, AZ	3.0	23.1	41.3	22.9	6.3	1.7	1.7	1,268
Pittsburgh, PA	14.0	47.0	26.4	7.9	2.9	0.9	0.9	892
Portland, OR	4.1	12.6	38.8	28.4	10.8	3.2	2.0	1,434
Providence, RI	14.9	29.3	35.5	14.2	4.1	1.0	0.9	1,066
Provo, UT	4.6	31.0	36.2	20.0	6.2	1.0	1.1	1,193
Raleigh, NC	4.4	22.5	46.4	19.1	5.2	1.2	1.2	1,230
Reno, NV	4.8	26.6	36.7	22.2	6.7	1.5	1.5	1,250
Richmond, VA	6.6	23.4	45.3	18.7	3.9	0.9	1.2	1,202
Rochester, MN	10.2	39.0	30.7	14.7	2.8	1.0	1.8	1,013
Sacramento, CA	4.3	14.1	34.2	27.8	13.3	3.9	2.5	1,465
St. Louis, MO	7.9	47.8	33.0	7.6	2.1	0.6	1.1	952
Salem, OR	5.9	30.4	45.3	14.0	2.9	1.0	0.5	1,128
Salt Lake City, UT	4.6	21.7	43.4	22.2	6.0	1.1	0.9	1,253
San Antonio, TX	5.6	32.5	41.5	15.3	3.5	0.9	0.7	1,122
San Diego, CA	2.9	5.9	21.1	29.4	19.7	10.6	10.4	1,842
San Francisco, CA	5.6	7.0	13.2	18.3	19.2	14.0	22.8	2,155
San Jose, CA	3.0	4.7	7.8	14.7	19.4	18.5	31.9	2,511
Santa Rosa, CA	4.8	7.8	19.2	25.6	21.0	11.3	10.3	1,856
Savannah, GA	5.5	26.3	47.1	16.1	3.7	0.6	0.6	1,161
Seattle, WA	4.3	8.4	25.0	30.5	17.7	7.5	6.6	1,701
Sioux Falls, SD	7.0	57.8	27.5	5.8	0.8	0.3	0.7	889
Springfield, IL	10.4	57.4	25.5	4.8	0.8	0.6	0.5	857
Tampa, FL	4.1	24.2	42.4	19.8	6.2	1.8	1.5	1,230
Tucson, AZ	5.5	46.8	33.6	10.3	1.9	0.8	1.1	976
Tulsa, OK	8.7	51.9	30.3	6.3	1.6	0.4	0.8	909
Tuscaloosa, AL	14.9	50.5	27.1	4.8	1.5	0.6	0.5	879
Virginia Beach, VA	6.1	22.2	42.3	21.1	5.5	1.5	1.3	1,227
Washington, DC	4.3	6.4	20.9	32.5	19.2	8.6	8.1	1,783
Wichita, KS	8.8	57.8	26.3	5.4	0.9	0.4	0.5	868
Wilmington, NC	8.0	29.7	41.7	15.1	3.2	1.5	0.8	1,118
Winston-Salem, NC	11.0	59.4	23.7	4.3	1.0	0.2	0.4	834
Worcester, MA	13.2	26.4	37.7	15.9	4.7	1.2	1.0	1,126
U.S.	8.1	30.5	30.8	16.8	7.3	3.1	3.5	1,163

Note: (1) Figures cover the Metropolitan Statistical Area (MSA); Figures are percentages except for Median; Gross rent is the contract rent plus the estimated average monthly cost of utilities (electricity, gas, and water and sewer) and fuels (oil, coal, kerosene, wood, etc.) if these are paid by the renter (or paid for the renter by someone else).
Source: U.S. Census Bureau, 2017-2021 American Community Survey 5-Year Estimates

A-128 Appendix A: Comparative Statistics

Highest Level of Education: City

City	Less than H.S.	H.S. Diploma	Some College, No Deg.	Associate Degree	Bachelors Degree	Masters Degree	Profess. School Degree	Doctorate Degree
Albuquerque, NM	9.1	21.8	22.7	9.1	20.4	11.5	2.9	2.6
Allentown, PA	19.4	36.5	19.3	7.5	11.5	3.8	1.1	0.8
Anchorage, AK	5.8	23.7	25.0	8.6	22.8	9.8	2.8	1.3
Ann Arbor, MI	2.2	7.6	8.9	4.0	30.5	26.8	8.3	11.6
Athens, GA	10.3	19.2	17.0	6.4	23.4	14.8	2.7	6.1
Atlanta, GA	7.9	17.5	13.6	5.4	31.6	15.8	5.6	2.7
Austin, TX	9.4	14.4	15.7	5.4	34.2	14.9	3.5	2.6
Baltimore, MD	13.7	28.1	18.8	5.2	17.2	11.3	3.2	2.5
Boise City, ID	4.8	20.4	22.8	8.3	28.0	10.8	2.8	2.0
Boston, MA	11.8	18.5	12.9	4.7	27.8	15.7	5.1	3.6
Boulder, CO	3.1	5.9	10.6	3.6	37.1	25.0	5.7	9.0
Brownsville, TX	32.0	24.2	16.0	7.3	14.6	4.7	0.9	0.3
Cape Coral, FL	7.1	37.1	23.0	9.2	15.6	5.3	1.5	1.3
Cedar Rapids, IA	6.2	25.7	22.8	12.5	22.7	7.2	2.0	0.8
Charleston, SC	4.2	16.8	16.1	7.3	34.5	13.6	4.8	2.9
Charlotte, NC	10.3	16.9	19.2	7.9	29.5	12.2	2.9	1.2
Chicago, IL	13.7	21.9	17.0	5.7	24.1	12.2	3.6	1.8
Cincinnati, OH	11.4	24.0	17.6	7.4	23.0	11.0	3.4	2.2
Clarksville, TN	6.4	26.9	26.3	11.6	18.7	8.2	0.8	1.1
Cleveland, OH	17.4	33.3	22.8	7.4	11.4	5.2	1.7	0.8
College Station, TX	5.2	13.1	17.0	6.7	30.3	15.4	2.1	10.3
Colorado Springs, CO	6.1	19.1	24.0	10.7	24.3	12.0	2.3	1.7
Columbia, MO	4.5	17.5	17.6	6.6	28.4	15.5	4.6	5.3
Columbia, SC	9.5	19.3	18.8	7.7	25.1	11.7	4.5	3.3
Columbus, OH	9.7	24.8	20.3	7.4	24.3	10.0	2.1	1.6
Dallas, TX	20.4	21.8	17.4	4.8	22.1	9.0	3.2	1.3
Davenport, IA	7.9	31.4	22.0	11.7	17.9	6.6	1.6	0.9
Denver, CO	10.0	16.0	16.0	5.6	32.0	13.9	4.5	2.1
Des Moines, IA	12.9	29.6	20.2	9.2	19.3	6.2	1.8	0.8
Durham, NC	9.4	16.2	14.7	6.9	27.7	15.8	4.3	5.0
Edison, NJ	7.9	18.1	11.9	5.8	30.1	21.4	2.6	2.3
El Paso, TX	18.6	23.1	22.7	8.8	17.7	6.6	1.4	1.0
Fargo, ND	5.2	19.3	20.3	13.6	28.1	9.9	1.8	2.0
Fort Collins, CO	3.0	14.4	17.3	8.6	32.8	17.5	2.5	3.8
Fort Wayne, IN	11.1	28.9	21.9	10.1	19.0	7.1	1.1	0.8
Fort Worth, TX	16.5	24.5	20.8	7.2	20.6	7.8	1.6	1.1
Grand Rapids, MI	11.3	22.2	20.1	7.6	25.6	9.7	2.2	1.4
Greeley, CO	16.4	26.0	22.8	8.8	15.9	7.7	1.4	1.2
Green Bay, WI	12.2	31.3	19.7	11.7	18.3	5.0	0.9	0.8
Greensboro, NC	9.8	21.3	20.4	9.0	24.5	10.7	2.4	1.9
Honolulu, HI	9.6	23.1	18.1	10.8	24.0	9.1	3.1	2.1
Houston, TX	20.5	21.6	17.2	6.0	20.9	9.1	3.0	1.8
Huntsville, AL	8.9	17.6	20.9	7.9	26.7	13.7	1.9	2.5
Indianapolis, IN	13.3	27.3	18.8	7.6	21.1	8.2	2.3	1.2
Jacksonville, FL	9.7	28.7	21.5	9.9	20.3	7.2	1.6	1.0
Kansas City, MO	9.0	24.9	22.2	7.4	23.0	9.8	2.6	1.2
Lafayette, LA	9.7	26.2	19.5	5.2	24.9	8.7	3.9	1.9
Las Cruces, NM	12.5	19.8	22.0	9.3	20.5	11.7	2.2	2.0
Las Vegas, NV	14.6	27.4	24.0	8.0	16.7	6.4	1.9	0.9
Lexington, KY	7.6	18.9	20.0	7.9	25.9	12.2	4.2	3.4
Lincoln, NE	7.1	20.7	20.9	11.2	25.3	9.8	2.2	2.8
Little Rock, AR	8.1	21.7	19.8	6.4	25.3	11.8	4.3	2.8
Los Angeles, CA	21.6	18.8	17.2	6.3	23.7	8.1	3.0	1.5
Louisville, KY	9.8	28.2	22.1	8.3	18.9	9.0	2.1	1.5
Madison, WI	4.4	14.2	15.4	7.5	32.5	15.9	4.2	5.9

Table continued on following page.

Appendix A: Comparative Statistics   A-129

City	Less than H.S.	H.S. Diploma	Some College, No Deg.	Associate Degree	Bachelors Degree	Masters Degree	Profess. School Degree	Doctorate Degree
Manchester, NH	11.4	28.8	18.8	9.1	21.5	8.0	1.5	1.0
Miami, FL	20.8	25.8	12.6	7.8	19.8	8.2	3.9	1.1
Midland, TX	15.5	23.4	22.1	8.1	22.5	6.4	1.4	0.6
Milwaukee, WI	15.1	30.9	21.1	7.4	16.3	6.7	1.4	1.0
Minneapolis, MN	9.3	14.2	16.4	7.4	31.7	14.5	3.9	2.5
Nashville, TN	10.0	21.5	18.4	6.2	27.5	10.7	3.2	2.6
New Haven, CT	14.6	30.2	14.2	4.6	16.3	11.9	4.0	4.3
New Orleans, LA	11.8	22.4	21.6	5.0	21.9	10.4	4.5	2.2
New York, NY	16.8	23.6	13.5	6.5	22.9	11.8	3.3	1.6
Oklahoma City, OK	12.5	24.6	22.5	8.1	20.5	8.0	2.6	1.2
Omaha, NE	9.7	21.7	22.0	7.8	24.9	9.1	3.1	1.6
Orlando, FL	8.4	23.2	16.8	11.5	25.0	10.3	3.1	1.7
Philadelphia, PA	13.4	31.4	16.7	6.0	18.4	9.3	3.0	1.8
Phoenix, AZ	16.5	22.9	22.1	8.0	19.1	8.2	2.1	1.2
Pittsburgh, PA	6.5	24.7	14.9	8.2	23.5	13.7	4.6	3.9
Portland, OR	6.7	15.1	19.4	6.9	31.2	13.9	4.3	2.4
Providence, RI	16.5	30.6	14.6	5.1	17.4	9.5	3.5	2.9
Provo, UT	7.3	14.4	25.3	8.6	31.6	8.7	1.6	2.4
Raleigh, NC	7.7	15.7	16.9	7.3	32.7	13.7	3.5	2.5
Reno, NV	10.2	22.7	23.3	8.3	21.6	9.2	2.5	2.3
Richmond, VA	12.3	20.4	19.2	5.0	25.1	12.1	3.7	2.2
Rochester, MN	5.6	18.6	15.8	11.3	26.6	13.1	5.2	3.6
Sacramento, CA	13.6	20.3	22.6	8.4	22.2	8.4	3.2	1.4
St. Louis, MO	10.8	24.4	20.3	6.5	21.3	11.3	3.2	2.2
Salem, OR	11.6	23.2	25.8	9.4	18.4	8.4	1.8	1.4
Salt Lake City, UT	8.9	16.6	17.9	6.7	28.3	13.4	4.6	3.5
San Antonio, TX	16.7	25.5	22.5	8.0	16.9	7.2	2.0	1.2
San Diego, CA	10.7	15.4	18.6	7.7	27.9	12.8	3.6	3.4
San Francisco, CA	11.2	11.4	12.7	5.2	35.4	16.0	5.1	3.0
San Jose, CA	14.5	16.3	16.2	7.6	26.0	14.5	2.2	2.8
Santa Rosa, CA	14.5	18.0	23.2	10.0	21.3	8.7	3.0	1.3
Savannah, GA	11.2	26.9	24.6	6.8	19.3	7.9	2.1	1.2
Seattle, WA	4.5	9.7	13.9	6.0	37.3	19.4	5.3	3.9
Sioux Falls, SD	6.7	24.6	20.5	12.2	24.3	8.3	2.4	1.0
Springfield, IL	8.7	26.6	22.1	8.2	20.2	9.6	3.5	1.2
Tampa, FL	11.6	23.4	15.3	7.9	24.8	10.6	4.4	2.0
Tucson, AZ	13.7	22.8	25.7	8.9	17.5	8.2	1.4	1.8
Tulsa, OK	12.1	25.3	22.1	8.0	20.7	7.7	2.7	1.3
Tuscaloosa, AL	9.9	27.1	18.6	6.8	20.5	11.0	2.1	4.0
Virginia Beach, VA	5.5	20.8	24.1	11.0	24.3	10.7	2.3	1.4
Washington, DC	7.8	15.5	12.4	3.0	25.5	21.9	9.7	4.3
Wichita, KS	11.8	26.2	23.4	8.1	19.3	8.4	1.7	1.1
Wilmington, NC	6.5	19.7	20.0	10.3	28.3	10.2	3.2	1.8
Winston-Salem, NC	12.0	24.9	20.7	7.7	20.3	9.2	2.8	2.2
Worcester, MA	14.2	28.3	17.1	8.2	19.2	8.8	2.0	2.3
U.S.	11.1	26.5	20.0	8.7	20.6	9.3	2.2	1.5

Note: Figures cover persons age 25 and over
Source: U.S. Census Bureau, 2017-2021 American Community Survey 5-Year Estimates

A-130 Appendix A: Comparative Statistics

Highest Level of Education: Metro Area

Metro Area	Less than H.S.	H.S. Diploma	Some College, No Deg.	Associate Degree	Bachelors Degree	Masters Degree	Profess. School Degree	Doctorate Degree
Albuquerque, NM	10.0	23.8	23.2	9.2	18.6	10.5	2.4	2.2
Allentown, PA	9.1	33.6	16.6	9.4	19.5	8.7	1.6	1.4
Anchorage, AK	6.0	26.2	25.5	9.1	20.9	8.8	2.4	1.2
Ann Arbor, MI	4.3	14.6	17.0	6.9	26.9	19.0	5.0	6.2
Athens, GA	10.6	22.7	17.6	7.4	20.8	13.0	3.2	4.7
Atlanta, GA	9.5	23.3	18.9	7.8	24.9	11.1	2.6	1.6
Austin, TX	9.0	18.2	18.9	6.5	30.1	12.7	2.6	2.0
Baltimore, MD	8.4	24.1	18.9	6.9	22.7	13.7	3.0	2.3
Boise City, ID	7.9	24.1	24.9	9.2	22.6	8.1	1.9	1.3
Boston, MA	7.9	21.2	14.1	7.1	26.9	15.8	3.6	3.5
Boulder, CO	4.5	11.1	15.0	6.6	34.5	19.1	3.9	5.3
Brownsville, TX	30.5	26.1	17.1	7.4	13.2	4.4	0.9	0.5
Cape Coral, FL	10.2	30.8	20.5	9.4	17.8	7.5	2.3	1.4
Cedar Rapids, IA	5.2	28.0	21.3	13.4	22.1	7.4	1.7	0.9
Charleston, SC	8.5	24.3	19.7	9.5	24.0	10.0	2.6	1.4
Charlotte, NC	10.1	22.9	20.5	9.4	24.5	9.7	2.0	0.9
Chicago, IL	10.5	23.4	19.0	7.3	23.8	11.6	2.8	1.5
Cincinnati, OH	8.2	29.3	18.7	8.4	21.9	9.8	2.1	1.5
Clarksville, TN	8.6	28.9	25.1	11.0	17.0	7.4	1.2	0.9
Cleveland, OH	8.6	28.5	21.3	8.8	19.8	9.2	2.5	1.3
College Station, TX	12.1	23.4	19.3	6.7	21.6	9.8	2.0	5.1
Colorado Springs, CO	5.4	19.8	24.4	10.9	23.9	12.0	1.9	1.6
Columbia, MO	5.9	23.1	18.3	7.5	25.4	12.6	3.3	3.8
Columbia, SC	9.4	26.0	21.5	9.5	20.5	9.2	2.1	1.8
Columbus, OH	7.9	26.7	19.4	7.6	24.0	10.4	2.5	1.5
Dallas, TX	13.4	22.0	20.6	7.3	23.8	9.8	1.9	1.2
Davenport, IA	8.2	29.9	22.9	11.1	17.8	7.7	1.5	0.9
Denver, CO	8.1	19.2	18.9	7.6	29.1	12.5	2.8	1.8
Des Moines, IA	6.6	25.6	19.5	10.7	25.8	8.4	2.1	1.3
Durham, NC	9.9	19.0	15.8	7.9	24.4	14.1	4.1	4.8
Edison, NJ	12.7	24.0	14.4	6.8	24.2	12.7	3.4	1.7
El Paso, TX	20.4	23.8	22.3	9.0	16.5	6.0	1.3	0.8
Fargo, ND	4.8	19.7	21.1	14.1	27.8	8.9	1.8	1.7
Fort Collins, CO	3.7	17.4	20.4	9.1	29.5	14.4	2.4	3.1
Fort Wayne, IN	9.8	29.0	21.0	11.0	19.8	7.1	1.5	1.0
Fort Worth, TX	13.4	22.0	20.6	7.3	23.8	9.8	1.9	1.2
Grand Rapids, MI	7.7	26.7	21.6	9.5	22.5	9.1	1.8	1.2
Greeley, CO	11.9	25.4	23.8	9.5	19.3	7.8	1.3	1.1
Green Bay, WI	7.5	31.5	19.1	12.8	20.5	6.3	1.4	0.8
Greensboro, NC	11.8	26.7	21.4	9.7	19.8	7.9	1.5	1.3
Honolulu, HI	7.3	25.6	19.8	11.1	23.2	8.9	2.5	1.6
Houston, TX	15.6	22.7	20.2	7.4	21.6	8.8	2.2	1.5
Huntsville, AL	9.2	20.9	21.0	8.0	25.2	12.4	1.5	1.8
Indianapolis, IN	9.4	27.3	18.9	8.0	23.2	9.4	2.3	1.3
Jacksonville, FL	8.6	27.5	21.0	9.9	21.6	8.4	2.0	1.1
Kansas City, MO	7.3	25.1	21.6	8.0	23.8	10.6	2.4	1.3
Lafayette, LA	14.0	36.5	18.4	6.5	17.0	5.1	1.7	0.8
Las Cruces, NM	19.3	21.5	20.9	8.3	17.5	9.2	1.7	1.7
Las Vegas, NV	13.6	28.0	24.3	8.3	17.1	6.2	1.7	0.9
Lexington, KY	8.3	23.8	20.5	8.3	22.4	10.8	3.4	2.5
Lincoln, NE	6.6	21.4	20.7	11.7	25.1	9.8	2.1	2.6
Little Rock, AR	8.4	29.1	22.2	8.3	19.9	8.6	2.2	1.4
Los Angeles, CA	18.4	19.6	18.8	7.2	23.2	8.6	2.7	1.5
Louisville, KY	9.1	29.3	21.7	8.7	18.9	8.8	2.1	1.4
Madison, WI	4.3	20.6	17.5	9.8	28.8	12.3	3.1	3.5

Table continued on following page.

Appendix A: Comparative Statistics   A-131

Metro Area	Less than H.S.	H.S. Diploma	Some College, No Deg.	Associate Degree	Bachelors Degree	Masters Degree	Profess. School Degree	Doctorate Degree
Manchester, NH	7.1	25.6	17.7	9.9	25.0	11.4	1.7	1.6
Miami, FL	13.5	25.8	16.9	9.6	21.1	8.6	3.2	1.3
Midland, TX	15.6	24.5	23.1	8.2	20.0	6.8	1.2	0.5
Milwaukee, WI	7.9	26.1	19.7	8.9	24.3	9.4	2.3	1.5
Minneapolis, MN	6.0	20.5	19.4	10.6	28.3	10.9	2.6	1.7
Nashville, TN	9.0	25.7	19.6	7.3	24.9	9.4	2.3	1.8
New Haven, CT	9.7	29.6	16.7	7.3	19.4	11.9	3.2	2.2
New Orleans, LA	11.9	26.9	22.4	6.5	20.0	8.0	2.9	1.3
New York, NY	12.7	24.0	14.4	6.8	24.2	12.7	3.4	1.7
Oklahoma City, OK	10.2	26.4	22.9	8.1	20.7	8.1	2.2	1.4
Omaha, NE	7.7	23.1	22.0	9.4	24.3	9.6	2.4	1.4
Orlando, FL	9.9	25.4	19.4	11.6	21.9	8.6	2.0	1.1
Philadelphia, PA	8.4	27.9	16.5	7.3	23.3	11.5	2.9	2.0
Phoenix, AZ	11.3	22.8	23.8	9.0	20.9	9.0	2.0	1.3
Pittsburgh, PA	5.5	31.4	16.0	10.5	22.2	10.3	2.3	1.7
Portland, OR	7.2	20.1	22.9	8.9	25.5	10.8	2.7	2.0
Providence, RI	12.0	28.7	17.5	8.6	20.2	9.4	2.0	1.6
Provo, UT	4.9	17.2	25.6	10.4	29.0	9.4	1.7	1.7
Raleigh, NC	7.4	17.3	17.7	9.0	30.1	13.6	2.6	2.3
Reno, NV	11.4	23.8	23.9	8.6	19.8	8.5	2.2	1.8
Richmond, VA	8.9	24.6	19.9	7.6	23.7	11.0	2.5	1.7
Rochester, MN	5.3	23.2	17.8	12.6	23.9	10.6	4.1	2.4
Sacramento, CA	10.2	20.8	24.1	9.9	22.3	8.3	2.8	1.5
St. Louis, MO	7.2	25.7	21.7	9.2	21.5	10.9	2.2	1.6
Salem, OR	13.2	25.1	26.3	9.7	16.7	6.8	1.3	1.0
Salt Lake City, UT	8.2	22.8	23.5	9.2	23.4	9.3	2.2	1.5
San Antonio, TX	13.6	25.2	22.7	8.2	19.0	8.2	1.9	1.2
San Diego, CA	11.7	18.2	21.5	8.4	24.5	10.5	2.9	2.3
San Francisco, CA	10.3	15.1	16.5	6.7	29.9	14.5	3.9	3.1
San Jose, CA	11.0	14.1	14.7	6.9	27.5	18.7	2.8	4.4
Santa Rosa, CA	10.8	18.3	24.2	9.5	23.2	9.2	3.3	1.5
Savannah, GA	9.3	26.5	22.9	7.8	20.7	9.0	2.4	1.5
Seattle, WA	6.8	19.1	20.3	9.4	27.1	12.5	2.7	2.0
Sioux Falls, SD	6.3	25.7	20.2	13.0	24.1	7.8	2.0	1.0
Springfield, IL	7.1	28.0	22.7	8.8	20.3	9.4	2.6	1.1
Tampa, FL	9.6	28.1	20.0	9.8	20.8	8.2	2.2	1.2
Tucson, AZ	10.6	21.4	24.6	9.0	19.7	10.2	2.2	2.2
Tulsa, OK	10.0	28.8	23.3	9.2	19.2	6.7	1.8	1.0
Tuscaloosa, AL	11.5	31.7	20.2	8.8	16.6	7.6	1.2	2.4
Virginia Beach, VA	7.6	24.7	23.8	10.1	20.6	9.8	1.9	1.4
Washington, DC	8.5	17.7	15.5	6.0	26.4	18.2	4.6	3.3
Wichita, KS	9.8	26.5	23.8	8.8	20.1	8.5	1.5	1.0
Wilmington, NC	7.2	20.8	21.3	10.9	26.2	9.4	2.8	1.5
Winston-Salem, NC	12.0	29.1	21.8	9.6	17.7	6.7	1.7	1.3
Worcester, MA	8.7	27.8	17.9	9.2	21.5	11.4	1.8	1.8
U.S.	11.1	26.5	20.0	8.7	20.6	9.3	2.2	1.5

Note: Figures cover persons age 25 and over; Figures cover the Metropolitan Statistical Area
Source: U.S. Census Bureau, 2017-2021 American Community Survey 5-Year Estimates

A-132 Appendix A: Comparative Statistics

School Enrollment by Grade and Control: City

City	Preschool (%)		Kindergarten (%)		Grades 1 - 4 (%)		Grades 5 - 8 (%)		Grades 9 - 12 (%)	
	Public	Private	Public	Private	Public	Private	Public	Private	Public	Private
Albuquerque, NM	57.2	42.8	86.7	13.3	86.7	13.3	90.7	9.3	91.7	8.3
Allentown, PA	80.2	19.8	86.2	13.8	87.7	12.3	90.5	9.5	89.0	11.0
Anchorage, AK	50.1	49.9	91.5	8.5	87.5	12.5	89.0	11.0	92.0	8.0
Ann Arbor, MI	34.0	66.0	86.6	13.4	88.7	11.3	87.6	12.4	94.0	6.0
Athens, GA	61.1	38.9	96.2	3.8	91.8	8.2	88.7	11.3	91.8	8.2
Atlanta, GA	50.7	49.3	75.7	24.3	85.9	14.1	78.5	21.5	79.9	20.1
Austin, TX	52.0	48.0	87.1	12.9	88.8	11.2	87.9	12.1	90.9	9.1
Baltimore, MD	69.2	30.8	83.5	16.5	84.0	16.0	85.0	15.0	85.3	14.7
Boise City, ID	32.0	68.0	77.1	22.9	89.8	10.2	91.7	8.3	88.4	11.6
Boston, MA	51.0	49.0	87.0	13.0	84.7	15.3	86.1	13.9	88.8	11.2
Boulder, CO	50.4	49.6	88.4	11.6	88.7	11.3	90.1	9.9	89.7	10.3
Brownsville, TX	95.8	4.2	92.3	7.7	95.6	4.4	94.7	5.3	97.5	2.5
Cape Coral, FL	73.5	26.5	96.9	3.1	88.6	11.4	94.2	5.8	90.2	9.8
Cedar Rapids, IA	69.1	30.9	85.6	14.4	88.0	12.0	91.4	8.6	87.2	12.8
Charleston, SC	42.4	57.6	81.0	19.0	83.5	16.5	83.8	16.2	76.6	23.4
Charlotte, NC	48.9	51.1	86.9	13.1	89.2	10.8	85.8	14.2	89.3	10.7
Chicago, IL	54.2	45.8	80.2	19.8	82.7	17.3	84.1	15.9	86.0	14.0
Cincinnati, OH	64.4	35.6	70.7	29.3	76.8	23.2	78.9	21.1	80.3	19.7
Clarksville, TN	61.1	38.9	85.7	14.3	93.4	6.6	92.1	7.9	87.1	12.9
Cleveland, OH	71.3	28.7	80.0	20.0	81.4	18.6	78.8	21.2	78.0	22.0
College Station, TX	51.4	48.6	86.9	13.1	91.0	9.0	93.9	6.1	88.3	11.7
Colorado Springs, CO	56.0	44.0	89.3	10.7	88.6	11.4	89.0	11.0	91.0	9.0
Columbia, MO	42.1	57.9	84.4	15.6	86.5	13.5	85.4	14.6	91.4	8.6
Columbia, SC	50.6	49.4	75.0	25.0	88.4	11.6	86.6	13.4	91.7	8.3
Columbus, OH	63.4	36.6	78.5	21.5	84.4	15.6	84.8	15.2	86.2	13.8
Dallas, TX	71.3	28.7	91.0	9.0	91.3	8.7	91.4	8.6	90.6	9.4
Davenport, IA	59.7	40.3	83.7	16.3	85.5	14.5	86.6	13.4	94.0	6.0
Denver, CO	57.4	42.6	85.2	14.8	90.6	9.4	89.6	10.4	91.8	8.2
Des Moines, IA	73.4	26.6	90.8	9.2	89.8	10.2	89.4	10.6	92.0	8.0
Durham, NC	53.6	46.4	84.7	15.3	89.3	10.7	84.4	15.6	88.5	11.5
Edison, NJ	18.4	81.6	71.4	28.6	88.2	11.8	89.7	10.3	91.9	8.1
El Paso, TX	88.6	11.4	92.5	7.5	94.3	5.7	94.0	6.0	95.8	4.2
Fargo, ND	43.0	57.0	92.4	7.6	92.6	7.4	90.6	9.4	94.5	5.5
Fort Collins, CO	44.8	55.2	89.3	10.7	93.6	6.4	93.0	7.0	93.8	6.2
Fort Wayne, IN	50.8	49.2	76.9	23.1	79.4	20.6	82.2	17.8	79.9	20.1
Fort Worth, TX	62.1	37.9	83.6	16.4	90.6	9.4	90.1	9.9	92.2	7.8
Grand Rapids, MI	66.8	33.2	74.2	25.8	78.3	21.7	82.3	17.7	82.3	17.7
Greeley, CO	72.4	27.6	92.8	7.2	94.1	5.9	92.8	7.2	94.4	5.6
Green Bay, WI	70.8	29.2	87.5	12.5	87.8	12.2	84.9	15.1	91.3	8.7
Greensboro, NC	55.5	44.5	90.0	10.0	93.3	6.7	91.0	9.0	89.1	10.9
Honolulu, HI	40.2	59.8	73.5	26.5	79.4	20.6	75.4	24.6	71.9	28.1
Houston, TX	64.5	35.5	89.1	10.9	93.1	6.9	92.0	8.0	92.5	7.5
Huntsville, AL	58.2	41.8	85.2	14.8	81.8	18.2	78.4	21.6	82.1	17.9
Indianapolis, IN	58.5	41.5	86.4	13.6	83.9	16.1	84.2	15.8	87.5	12.5
Jacksonville, FL	54.4	45.6	85.0	15.0	83.7	16.3	80.4	19.6	84.8	15.2
Kansas City, MO	55.9	44.1	86.9	13.1	87.6	12.4	88.5	11.5	83.8	16.2
Lafayette, LA	63.6	36.4	67.4	32.6	70.2	29.8	72.4	27.6	79.5	20.5
Las Cruces, NM	84.8	15.2	91.5	8.5	92.9	7.1	96.6	3.4	96.2	3.8
Las Vegas, NV	63.4	36.6	88.2	11.8	90.3	9.7	91.1	8.9	92.5	7.5
Lexington, KY	37.3	62.7	84.6	15.4	83.2	16.8	83.9	16.1	85.4	14.6
Lincoln, NE	50.3	49.7	73.0	27.0	83.5	16.5	83.1	16.9	87.0	13.0
Little Rock, AR	67.9	32.1	88.9	11.1	78.3	21.7	79.1	20.9	76.2	23.8
Los Angeles, CA	57.1	42.9	85.7	14.3	88.0	12.0	87.6	12.4	89.1	10.9
Louisville, KY	51.6	48.4	80.2	19.8	82.9	17.1	82.3	17.7	78.3	21.7
Madison, WI	51.2	48.8	87.9	12.1	88.7	11.3	88.1	11.9	90.6	9.4

Table continued on following page.

Appendix A: Comparative Statistics   A-133

City	Preschool (%)		Kindergarten (%)		Grades 1 - 4 (%)		Grades 5 - 8 (%)		Grades 9 - 12 (%)	
	Public	Private	Public	Private	Public	Private	Public	Private	Public	Private
Manchester, NH	58.7	41.3	86.5	13.5	89.0	11.0	93.0	7.0	92.0	8.0
Miami, FL	58.9	41.1	85.5	14.5	85.8	14.2	84.2	15.8	90.8	9.2
Midland, TX	70.6	29.4	83.7	16.3	83.1	16.9	77.6	22.4	83.9	16.1
Milwaukee, WI	74.3	25.7	77.9	22.1	75.8	24.2	74.5	25.5	81.4	18.6
Minneapolis, MN	55.0	45.0	85.0	15.0	87.3	12.7	88.9	11.1	90.7	9.3
Nashville, TN	48.4	51.6	84.0	16.0	84.6	15.4	80.0	20.0	81.9	18.1
New Haven, CT	80.4	19.6	89.7	10.3	95.2	4.8	93.4	6.6	92.5	7.5
New Orleans, LA	49.2	50.8	78.4	21.6	81.5	18.5	81.9	18.1	80.2	19.8
New York, NY	63.8	36.2	79.0	21.0	81.8	18.2	80.9	19.1	80.3	19.7
Oklahoma City, OK	70.9	29.1	87.6	12.4	89.5	10.5	88.2	11.8	88.1	11.9
Omaha, NE	52.7	47.3	81.2	18.8	82.9	17.1	83.3	16.7	83.2	16.8
Orlando, FL	62.9	37.1	84.3	15.7	88.0	12.0	87.0	13.0	86.7	13.3
Philadelphia, PA	54.6	45.4	78.1	21.9	79.2	20.8	80.8	19.2	79.4	20.6
Phoenix, AZ	61.2	38.8	86.5	13.5	90.6	9.4	91.6	8.4	93.1	6.9
Pittsburgh, PA	50.4	49.6	76.4	23.6	76.9	23.1	76.5	23.5	79.5	20.5
Portland, OR	37.9	62.1	84.9	15.1	87.2	12.8	88.2	11.8	87.1	12.9
Providence, RI	56.9	43.1	80.9	19.1	88.4	11.6	84.5	15.5	89.6	10.4
Provo, UT	63.9	36.1	91.4	8.6	92.1	7.9	95.5	4.5	90.2	9.8
Raleigh, NC	37.3	62.7	87.2	12.8	85.6	14.4	87.7	12.3	87.7	12.3
Reno, NV	59.8	40.2	92.4	7.6	94.3	5.7	92.0	8.0	93.1	6.9
Richmond, VA	50.9	49.1	89.3	10.7	85.0	15.0	84.6	15.4	83.6	16.4
Rochester, MN	52.1	47.9	90.2	9.8	90.8	9.2	88.0	12.0	89.3	10.7
Sacramento, CA	65.0	35.0	91.0	9.0	93.1	6.9	91.5	8.5	90.9	9.1
St. Louis, MO	56.8	43.2	73.9	26.1	82.9	17.1	78.8	21.2	80.6	19.4
Salem, OR	61.3	38.7	87.8	12.2	90.0	10.0	93.3	6.7	96.5	3.5
Salt Lake City, UT	42.5	57.5	86.4	13.6	88.6	11.4	91.0	9.0	94.8	5.2
San Antonio, TX	74.0	26.0	89.7	10.3	92.1	7.9	92.3	7.7	91.5	8.5
San Diego, CA	46.8	53.2	89.4	10.6	90.4	9.6	91.7	8.3	91.2	8.8
San Francisco, CA	34.0	66.0	67.4	32.6	71.0	29.0	66.6	33.4	75.5	24.5
San Jose, CA	43.4	56.6	81.8	18.2	87.0	13.0	87.6	12.4	85.9	14.1
Santa Rosa, CA	53.7	46.3	86.2	13.8	92.9	7.1	89.1	10.9	93.8	6.2
Savannah, GA	77.0	23.0	89.0	11.0	91.9	8.1	91.5	8.5	88.5	11.5
Seattle, WA	36.3	63.7	79.0	21.0	79.2	20.8	73.5	26.5	77.3	22.7
Sioux Falls, SD	53.8	46.2	92.3	7.7	86.4	13.6	88.8	11.2	84.6	15.4
Springfield, IL	53.6	46.4	80.8	19.2	80.5	19.5	86.1	13.9	86.8	13.2
Tampa, FL	51.4	48.6	81.9	18.1	87.9	12.1	83.5	16.5	82.2	17.8
Tucson, AZ	70.3	29.7	84.3	15.7	86.8	13.2	88.9	11.1	93.6	6.4
Tulsa, OK	63.6	36.4	82.4	17.6	85.0	15.0	83.0	17.0	81.8	18.2
Tuscaloosa, AL	78.7	21.3	94.7	5.3	84.3	15.7	96.4	3.6	94.9	5.1
Virginia Beach, VA	35.4	64.6	75.9	24.1	90.1	9.9	90.1	9.9	92.2	7.8
Washington, DC	74.2	25.8	90.9	9.1	88.6	11.4	82.4	17.6	80.7	19.3
Wichita, KS	62.8	37.2	84.4	15.6	86.4	13.6	83.7	16.3	84.5	15.5
Wilmington, NC	62.4	37.6	84.8	15.2	75.5	24.5	74.3	25.7	88.8	11.2
Winston-Salem, NC	56.5	43.5	90.6	9.4	91.7	8.3	91.4	8.6	91.9	8.1
Worcester, MA	54.7	45.3	96.0	4.0	93.5	6.5	92.0	8.0	88.1	11.9
U.S.	58.8	41.2	86.3	13.7	88.3	11.7	88.6	11.4	89.4	10.6

Note: Figures shown cover persons 3 years old and over
Source: U.S. Census Bureau, 2017-2021 American Community Survey 5-Year Estimates

A-134 Appendix A: Comparative Statistics

School Enrollment by Grade and Control: Metro Area

Metro Area	Preschool (%)		Kindergarten (%)		Grades 1 - 4 (%)		Grades 5 - 8 (%)		Grades 9 - 12 (%)	
	Public	Private	Public	Private	Public	Private	Public	Private	Public	Private
Albuquerque, NM	57.8	42.2	84.8	15.2	86.4	13.6	89.8	10.2	90.8	9.2
Allentown, PA	52.6	47.4	86.9	13.1	89.7	10.3	91.2	8.8	91.3	8.7
Anchorage, AK	51.6	48.4	90.9	9.1	87.2	12.8	88.1	11.9	90.9	9.1
Ann Arbor, MI	49.9	50.1	89.4	10.6	87.1	12.9	88.1	11.9	93.0	7.0
Athens, GA	64.9	35.1	93.2	6.8	89.6	10.4	87.0	13.0	88.4	11.6
Atlanta, GA	54.8	45.2	85.7	14.3	89.8	10.2	88.2	11.8	89.0	11.0
Austin, TX	49.5	50.5	89.5	10.5	90.6	9.4	89.8	10.2	91.7	8.3
Baltimore, MD	47.8	52.2	82.9	17.1	85.3	14.7	84.6	15.4	83.2	16.8
Boise City, ID	35.5	64.5	84.5	15.5	87.8	12.2	90.3	9.7	89.0	11.0
Boston, MA	45.1	54.9	88.5	11.5	91.0	9.0	89.6	10.4	86.5	13.5
Boulder, CO	50.1	49.9	84.8	15.2	90.1	9.9	90.4	9.6	94.6	5.4
Brownsville, TX	95.5	4.5	95.8	4.2	97.0	3.0	96.5	3.5	96.7	3.3
Cape Coral, FL	60.7	39.3	89.9	10.1	90.4	9.6	90.7	9.3	90.5	9.5
Cedar Rapids, IA	69.0	31.0	86.7	13.3	89.3	10.7	90.5	9.5	91.0	9.0
Charleston, SC	46.6	53.4	83.0	17.0	86.2	13.8	88.5	11.5	88.5	11.5
Charlotte, NC	50.3	49.7	87.4	12.6	89.5	10.5	87.5	12.5	89.9	10.1
Chicago, IL	56.6	43.4	84.4	15.6	88.3	11.7	88.6	11.4	90.3	9.7
Cincinnati, OH	53.2	46.8	79.7	20.3	82.8	17.2	83.5	16.5	82.3	17.7
Clarksville, TN	62.6	37.4	88.2	11.8	86.8	13.2	88.6	11.4	87.0	13.0
Cleveland, OH	52.8	47.2	79.0	21.0	81.1	18.9	82.0	18.0	82.4	17.6
College Station, TX	59.9	40.1	86.3	13.7	91.4	8.6	92.1	7.9	92.3	7.7
Colorado Springs, CO	58.9	41.1	87.2	12.8	88.7	11.3	90.1	9.9	90.8	9.2
Columbia, MO	52.3	47.7	87.6	12.4	85.9	14.1	87.6	12.4	91.3	8.7
Columbia, SC	58.5	41.5	90.7	9.3	92.0	8.0	92.7	7.3	92.9	7.1
Columbus, OH	57.3	42.7	82.1	17.9	87.4	12.6	87.9	12.1	88.7	11.3
Dallas, TX	59.0	41.0	88.8	11.2	91.3	8.7	91.6	8.4	91.9	8.1
Davenport, IA	68.6	31.4	88.3	11.7	91.0	9.0	92.0	8.0	92.1	7.9
Denver, CO	58.0	42.0	88.1	11.9	90.8	9.2	90.9	9.1	91.5	8.5
Des Moines, IA	67.2	32.8	90.4	9.6	91.9	8.1	90.5	9.5	92.2	7.8
Durham, NC	47.9	52.1	81.8	18.2	88.9	11.1	86.0	14.0	90.4	9.6
Edison, NJ	56.6	43.4	81.6	18.4	84.6	15.4	84.8	15.2	84.1	15.9
El Paso, TX	88.3	11.7	93.1	6.9	94.3	5.7	94.7	5.3	96.3	3.7
Fargo, ND	59.7	40.3	91.9	8.1	91.0	9.0	91.1	8.9	91.6	8.4
Fort Collins, CO	45.2	54.8	88.9	11.1	88.9	11.1	86.8	13.2	88.3	11.7
Fort Wayne, IN	46.6	53.4	75.5	24.5	76.6	23.4	77.4	22.6	80.7	19.3
Fort Worth, TX	59.0	41.0	88.8	11.2	91.3	8.7	91.6	8.4	91.9	8.1
Grand Rapids, MI	61.5	38.5	81.4	18.6	82.3	17.7	85.8	14.2	85.3	14.7
Greeley, CO	71.5	28.5	91.2	8.8	92.1	7.9	91.7	8.3	94.2	5.8
Green Bay, WI	67.1	32.9	86.7	13.3	88.4	11.6	86.7	13.3	91.8	8.2
Greensboro, NC	55.7	44.3	86.7	13.3	88.5	11.5	88.1	11.9	88.2	11.8
Honolulu, HI	38.4	61.6	78.3	21.7	82.6	17.4	79.3	20.7	75.9	24.1
Houston, TX	56.6	43.4	88.9	11.1	92.0	8.0	92.4	7.6	92.5	7.5
Huntsville, AL	57.2	42.8	80.7	19.3	82.7	17.3	81.5	18.5	81.8	18.2
Indianapolis, IN	52.2	47.8	87.2	12.8	86.8	13.2	87.0	13.0	88.4	11.6
Jacksonville, FL	54.8	45.2	86.3	13.7	84.9	15.1	83.2	16.8	87.2	12.8
Kansas City, MO	59.2	40.8	88.2	11.8	88.3	11.7	89.5	10.5	88.8	11.2
Lafayette, LA	66.3	33.7	78.7	21.3	80.8	19.2	78.8	21.2	78.7	21.3
Las Cruces, NM	83.3	16.7	92.7	7.3	90.3	9.7	96.5	3.5	94.7	5.3
Las Vegas, NV	60.9	39.1	88.6	11.4	91.5	8.5	92.4	7.6	92.7	7.3
Lexington, KY	44.3	55.7	82.5	17.5	85.0	15.0	84.0	16.0	86.6	13.4
Lincoln, NE	49.5	50.5	74.6	25.4	81.6	18.4	83.9	16.1	87.2	12.8
Little Rock, AR	70.5	29.5	90.1	9.9	87.0	13.0	86.6	13.4	86.4	13.6
Los Angeles, CA	55.8	44.2	86.9	13.1	90.0	10.0	90.1	9.9	91.1	8.9
Louisville, KY	52.4	47.6	81.8	18.2	82.3	17.7	82.4	17.6	80.7	19.3
Madison, WI	67.4	32.6	88.0	12.0	89.6	10.4	90.2	9.8	94.3	5.7

Table continued on following page.

Appendix A: Comparative Statistics   A-135

Metro Area	Preschool (%)		Kindergarten (%)		Grades 1 - 4 (%)		Grades 5 - 8 (%)		Grades 9 - 12 (%)	
	Public	Private	Public	Private	Public	Private	Public	Private	Public	Private
Manchester, NH	49.7	50.3	81.7	18.3	87.4	12.6	87.8	12.2	88.9	11.1
Miami, FL	51.1	48.9	82.4	17.6	85.2	14.8	85.6	14.4	86.1	13.9
Midland, TX	75.7	24.3	79.8	20.2	83.8	16.2	82.0	18.0	85.2	14.8
Milwaukee, WI	58.0	42.0	78.8	21.2	79.9	20.1	79.6	20.4	85.4	14.6
Minneapolis, MN	61.4	38.6	87.3	12.7	89.0	11.0	89.6	10.4	91.6	8.4
Nashville, TN	50.2	49.8	85.0	15.0	85.7	14.3	84.7	15.3	83.3	16.7
New Haven, CT	65.6	34.4	93.4	6.6	92.1	7.9	90.4	9.6	88.9	11.1
New Orleans, LA	54.1	45.9	76.7	23.3	77.8	22.2	77.5	22.5	74.9	25.1
New York, NY	56.6	43.4	81.6	18.4	84.6	15.4	84.8	15.2	84.1	15.9
Oklahoma City, OK	71.5	28.5	87.9	12.1	89.2	10.8	88.8	11.2	89.1	10.9
Omaha, NE	57.9	42.1	83.0	17.0	85.1	14.9	85.4	14.6	85.4	14.6
Orlando, FL	50.4	49.6	81.5	18.5	84.1	15.9	85.5	14.5	87.5	12.5
Philadelphia, PA	46.2	53.8	81.2	18.8	84.8	15.2	84.6	15.4	83.3	16.7
Phoenix, AZ	61.7	38.3	86.0	14.0	89.6	10.4	91.1	8.9	92.7	7.3
Pittsburgh, PA	50.8	49.2	82.7	17.3	88.7	11.3	89.0	11.0	89.6	10.4
Portland, OR	41.3	58.7	85.1	14.9	87.5	12.5	89.1	10.9	90.2	9.8
Providence, RI	56.5	43.5	88.3	11.7	90.4	9.6	89.4	10.6	88.4	11.6
Provo, UT	54.2	45.8	89.1	10.9	91.5	8.5	93.7	6.3	94.4	5.6
Raleigh, NC	33.6	66.4	84.1	15.9	86.7	13.3	86.5	13.5	88.1	11.9
Reno, NV	54.1	45.9	89.2	10.8	93.0	7.0	92.3	7.7	92.1	7.9
Richmond, VA	44.8	55.2	87.7	12.3	88.8	11.2	89.4	10.6	90.2	9.8
Rochester, MN	63.8	36.2	91.4	8.6	90.6	9.4	89.8	10.2	91.2	8.8
Sacramento, CA	59.9	40.1	90.0	10.0	91.7	8.3	91.9	8.1	91.7	8.3
St. Louis, MO	53.6	46.4	80.8	19.2	83.8	16.2	82.7	17.3	85.1	14.9
Salem, OR	59.7	40.3	86.9	13.1	89.6	10.4	91.7	8.3	93.9	6.1
Salt Lake City, UT	55.1	44.9	86.9	13.1	90.6	9.4	93.7	6.3	93.7	6.3
San Antonio, TX	67.2	32.8	89.3	10.7	91.6	8.4	91.2	8.8	91.1	8.9
San Diego, CA	49.0	51.0	89.7	10.3	90.8	9.2	91.8	8.2	92.3	7.7
San Francisco, CA	40.5	59.5	83.1	16.9	85.1	14.9	84.7	15.3	86.2	13.8
San Jose, CA	36.0	64.0	78.9	21.1	85.4	14.6	86.0	14.0	85.9	14.1
Santa Rosa, CA	48.2	51.8	87.3	12.7	92.4	7.6	89.8	10.2	92.0	8.0
Savannah, GA	53.9	46.1	81.7	18.3	85.0	15.0	88.0	12.0	85.4	14.6
Seattle, WA	42.0	58.0	82.0	18.0	86.4	13.6	86.9	13.1	90.2	9.8
Sioux Falls, SD	56.2	43.8	91.6	8.4	87.3	12.7	90.0	10.0	87.1	12.9
Springfield, IL	58.6	41.4	85.1	14.9	85.1	14.9	89.7	10.3	90.4	9.6
Tampa, FL	54.7	45.3	82.3	17.7	84.8	15.2	85.9	14.1	87.4	12.6
Tucson, AZ	67.5	32.5	85.8	14.2	87.9	12.1	88.9	11.1	91.0	9.0
Tulsa, OK	66.3	33.7	85.2	14.8	86.1	13.9	86.5	13.5	85.9	14.1
Tuscaloosa, AL	71.4	28.6	87.3	12.7	86.8	13.2	89.9	10.1	88.1	11.9
Virginia Beach, VA	50.5	49.5	79.9	20.1	88.8	11.2	90.0	10.0	90.1	9.9
Washington, DC	45.8	54.2	84.0	16.0	87.7	12.3	87.4	12.6	88.2	11.8
Wichita, KS	64.9	35.1	83.7	16.3	86.6	13.4	86.2	13.8	87.4	12.6
Wilmington, NC	48.0	52.0	81.2	18.8	83.4	16.6	82.0	18.0	88.8	11.2
Winston-Salem, NC	52.2	47.8	88.5	11.5	90.0	10.0	89.8	10.2	88.4	11.6
Worcester, MA	59.0	41.0	91.1	8.9	92.2	7.8	90.6	9.4	90.5	9.5
U.S.	58.8	41.2	86.3	13.7	88.3	11.7	88.6	11.4	89.4	10.6

Note: Figures shown cover persons 3 years old and over; Figures cover the Metropolitan Statistical Area
Source: U.S. Census Bureau, 2017-2021 American Community Survey 5-Year Estimates

A-136   Appendix A: Comparative Statistics

Educational Attainment by Race: City

City	High School Graduate or Higher (%)					Bachelor's Degree or Higher (%)				
	Total	White	Black	Asian	Hisp.[1]	Total	White	Black	Asian	Hisp.[1]
Albuquerque, NM	90.9	93.0	94.3	87.7	84.8	37.4	41.1	36.2	54.1	24.3
Allentown, PA	80.6	84.7	83.6	80.4	70.5	17.3	21.5	11.2	42.3	7.7
Anchorage, AK	94.2	96.4	93.2	88.4	85.6	36.8	44.0	21.6	26.4	24.5
Ann Arbor, MI	97.8	98.5	93.2	98.0	92.7	77.2	79.5	36.4	85.6	69.9
Athens, GA	89.7	94.3	83.2	92.5	67.4	47.1	59.0	23.3	72.4	27.0
Atlanta, GA	92.1	98.3	86.3	96.7	84.0	55.6	79.9	29.9	86.1	48.0
Austin, TX	90.6	93.2	89.5	92.7	76.2	55.1	59.5	31.6	76.5	30.9
Baltimore, MD	86.3	91.5	84.1	90.2	72.2	34.2	59.7	18.7	71.6	32.9
Boise City, ID	95.2	96.2	78.5	90.0	82.7	43.7	43.9	31.0	57.7	26.7
Boston, MA	88.2	94.7	85.2	80.6	72.7	52.1	68.7	25.0	57.1	25.7
Boulder, CO	96.9	98.2	89.2	95.5	81.4	76.8	78.0	34.2	84.3	51.2
Brownsville, TX	68.0	67.8	78.7	92.7	66.5	20.5	20.4	37.3	61.2	19.3
Cape Coral, FL	92.9	94.0	84.8	87.3	88.5	23.6	23.9	22.7	44.4	16.4
Cedar Rapids, IA	93.8	95.3	83.0	86.2	82.8	32.8	33.6	17.8	51.5	22.4
Charleston, SC	95.8	97.8	89.2	98.6	86.5	55.7	63.7	24.3	66.2	41.3
Charlotte, NC	89.7	94.7	91.2	84.3	60.8	45.7	59.2	30.8	61.5	19.1
Chicago, IL	86.3	90.8	86.4	87.6	70.9	41.7	55.5	23.5	64.1	18.5
Cincinnati, OH	88.6	92.9	83.1	94.7	76.9	39.6	54.9	16.8	80.3	33.3
Clarksville, TN	93.6	94.2	94.0	87.4	87.1	28.7	30.6	25.3	37.3	17.2
Cleveland, OH	82.6	85.7	81.1	75.3	71.4	19.2	27.6	11.2	46.9	9.2
College Station, TX	94.8	95.9	91.0	94.2	87.1	58.0	58.7	31.9	78.7	41.2
Colorado Springs, CO	93.9	95.5	93.8	85.8	82.6	40.2	43.4	28.1	42.7	20.4
Columbia, MO	95.5	96.6	92.6	94.7	89.1	53.8	56.5	29.4	68.9	47.1
Columbia, SC	90.5	96.2	83.5	95.7	87.6	44.7	63.4	21.6	76.0	35.4
Columbus, OH	90.3	93.0	87.0	86.5	73.5	37.9	44.5	20.1	60.7	24.1
Dallas, TX	79.6	80.5	88.4	87.4	55.4	35.6	44.3	22.3	66.0	13.5
Davenport, IA	92.1	93.9	87.7	71.8	78.3	27.1	29.1	13.6	35.3	15.4
Denver, CO	90.0	93.6	89.8	85.6	69.6	52.5	60.7	27.7	56.5	19.4
Des Moines, IA	87.1	91.9	82.1	58.6	60.2	28.1	31.1	16.4	21.8	10.1
Durham, NC	90.6	93.8	90.0	93.0	54.7	52.8	65.7	35.4	77.8	19.8
Edison, NJ	92.1	94.0	95.0	92.0	86.3	56.4	38.6	43.0	76.2	25.0
El Paso, TX	81.4	84.1	96.1	88.5	77.8	26.7	28.7	32.3	56.8	22.7
Fargo, ND	94.8	96.7	79.3	82.7	91.6	41.8	43.5	19.0	57.2	16.4
Fort Collins, CO	97.0	97.6	91.7	93.4	87.4	56.6	58.0	36.7	73.4	33.1
Fort Wayne, IN	88.9	93.5	85.4	47.6	63.7	28.0	31.6	15.3	21.6	11.6
Fort Worth, TX	83.5	88.1	89.1	80.9	63.5	31.0	37.5	22.7	44.5	14.4
Grand Rapids, MI	88.7	92.6	86.4	80.6	57.7	38.8	46.0	20.4	44.7	13.3
Greeley, CO	83.6	86.1	69.8	81.6	64.7	26.1	28.3	21.9	50.3	9.1
Green Bay, WI	87.8	90.7	76.5	75.1	57.7	25.1	27.0	16.9	26.0	9.3
Greensboro, NC	90.2	93.9	89.3	77.0	68.0	39.5	50.5	26.7	47.0	19.3
Honolulu, HI	90.4	97.9	94.5	87.4	93.9	38.4	54.2	31.3	37.9	31.6
Houston, TX	79.5	82.2	89.1	87.1	59.6	34.7	42.7	25.0	62.3	15.5
Huntsville, AL	91.1	93.8	86.8	88.8	72.3	44.8	51.8	29.4	56.2	29.2
Indianapolis, IN	86.7	89.7	85.3	70.5	60.6	32.9	38.4	20.9	44.3	15.8
Jacksonville, FL	90.3	92.0	88.2	87.8	83.9	30.2	33.0	21.3	49.4	27.0
Kansas City, MO	91.0	93.9	88.6	86.1	71.3	36.5	45.2	16.9	48.4	19.0
Lafayette, LA	90.3	95.1	80.3	92.2	72.5	39.4	49.1	15.2	63.9	33.0
Las Cruces, NM	87.5	90.4	83.9	85.3	83.2	36.4	38.7	47.4	63.0	24.8
Las Vegas, NV	85.4	89.5	88.3	91.9	66.0	25.9	29.4	18.8	43.3	11.6
Lexington, KY	92.4	94.8	88.9	89.4	64.1	45.6	49.7	23.7	69.0	25.3
Lincoln, NE	92.9	95.0	87.1	79.8	69.0	40.1	41.7	26.6	43.7	19.9
Little Rock, AR	91.9	94.1	90.0	87.5	67.6	44.1	57.8	25.7	61.9	13.0
Los Angeles, CA	78.4	84.6	89.3	90.9	58.3	36.2	44.9	29.3	56.8	14.0
Louisville, KY	90.2	91.8	88.2	80.0	77.1	31.6	35.2	18.8	50.7	24.4
Madison, WI	95.6	97.2	88.8	92.4	79.2	58.5	60.9	24.7	70.9	40.0

Table continued on following page.

Appendix A: Comparative Statistics   A-137

City	High School Graduate or Higher (%)					Bachelor's Degree or Higher (%)				
	Total	White	Black	Asian	Hisp.[1]	Total	White	Black	Asian	Hisp.[1]
Manchester, NH	88.6	90.4	78.2	81.0	67.1	31.9	32.9	17.6	40.8	13.0
Miami, FL	79.2	80.7	75.7	96.5	76.5	33.1	37.3	15.6	68.9	29.6
Midland, TX	84.5	88.0	88.2	72.1	71.2	30.9	35.0	16.2	45.8	15.5
Milwaukee, WI	84.9	90.5	84.9	74.8	64.4	25.5	37.6	13.5	32.7	10.8
Minneapolis, MN	90.7	96.7	74.7	84.7	66.1	52.6	63.7	17.2	57.3	25.6
Nashville, TN	90.0	92.2	89.3	80.3	59.3	43.9	50.7	28.8	52.3	17.2
New Haven, CT	85.4	87.2	87.3	94.8	71.6	36.5	49.2	22.5	78.5	14.5
New Orleans, LA	88.2	96.4	83.7	76.7	80.9	39.1	65.3	21.0	47.9	40.4
New York, NY	83.2	90.5	84.7	76.8	70.8	39.6	54.6	25.3	44.0	20.1
Oklahoma City, OK	87.5	89.5	91.2	80.6	57.6	32.3	35.4	24.3	42.3	10.4
Omaha, NE	90.3	93.1	87.9	72.2	60.3	38.7	42.8	17.7	49.8	13.8
Orlando, FL	91.6	94.7	84.5	92.5	90.2	40.1	48.5	20.6	54.5	32.2
Philadelphia, PA	86.6	91.8	86.9	73.2	71.9	32.5	46.4	19.3	41.4	18.1
Phoenix, AZ	83.5	87.0	89.8	86.8	65.5	30.6	33.8	25.9	60.2	12.0
Pittsburgh, PA	93.5	95.0	89.1	92.5	87.3	45.7	51.2	19.8	77.7	49.3
Portland, OR	93.3	95.7	89.2	79.9	79.1	51.9	56.1	26.6	43.6	34.5
Providence, RI	83.5	88.8	85.7	84.1	73.3	33.3	41.9	27.0	50.4	12.3
Provo, UT	92.7	94.5	95.3	84.4	73.5	44.3	46.4	17.0	47.4	19.3
Raleigh, NC	92.3	96.3	91.6	89.4	62.6	52.4	64.4	32.6	61.7	23.0
Reno, NV	89.8	93.9	90.8	92.4	66.3	35.5	38.3	31.1	49.5	13.5
Richmond, VA	87.7	94.7	81.5	88.6	58.3	43.1	68.0	14.8	70.7	22.5
Rochester, MN	94.4	96.8	70.6	88.5	76.7	48.7	49.9	19.9	61.8	33.6
Sacramento, CA	86.4	91.5	91.3	81.6	75.4	35.1	42.6	24.8	39.3	21.6
St. Louis, MO	89.2	94.4	83.1	87.1	79.1	38.0	53.9	16.6	57.9	36.7
Salem, OR	88.4	92.3	95.0	84.5	61.8	30.0	32.6	27.1	44.4	11.1
Salt Lake City, UT	91.1	95.3	84.5	83.1	69.3	49.8	54.8	32.1	57.8	21.2
San Antonio, TX	83.3	84.8	91.5	86.1	76.7	27.3	28.9	25.7	55.7	18.0
San Diego, CA	89.3	91.8	91.2	89.2	73.4	47.6	52.0	28.3	55.1	22.6
San Francisco, CA	88.8	97.3	87.3	80.4	79.2	59.5	75.4	31.5	48.9	38.1
San Jose, CA	85.5	90.9	91.4	87.6	69.6	45.4	48.2	38.3	57.5	16.6
Santa Rosa, CA	85.5	92.6	83.5	86.8	62.4	34.3	40.0	27.4	48.4	14.4
Savannah, GA	88.8	94.8	84.1	78.6	84.0	30.5	45.4	16.3	50.7	31.9
Seattle, WA	95.5	98.2	89.8	90.1	85.7	65.9	70.7	32.9	66.9	46.5
Sioux Falls, SD	93.3	95.3	83.9	74.3	73.5	36.0	37.9	20.0	44.2	17.9
Springfield, IL	91.3	93.6	80.0	94.0	86.8	34.4	37.2	14.3	69.9	43.3
Tampa, FL	88.4	91.9	84.1	87.7	78.2	41.8	49.8	18.7	65.4	26.7
Tucson, AZ	86.3	89.9	84.2	87.3	75.0	28.9	32.7	20.8	51.6	15.5
Tulsa, OK	87.9	90.8	89.6	74.0	59.8	32.4	37.6	17.8	37.0	11.5
Tuscaloosa, AL	90.1	95.5	85.9	91.4	66.5	37.6	57.4	15.7	67.5	20.2
Virginia Beach, VA	94.5	96.0	92.5	89.5	87.4	38.6	41.7	29.3	40.9	30.1
Washington, DC	92.2	98.6	88.0	94.4	78.6	61.4	90.8	31.1	82.4	52.8
Wichita, KS	88.2	91.6	87.8	73.7	63.9	30.5	33.6	17.7	35.1	13.3
Wilmington, NC	93.5	95.6	87.4	84.0	78.0	43.6	49.0	20.9	60.7	32.3
Winston-Salem, NC	88.0	90.7	88.1	89.9	58.9	34.6	43.0	20.9	70.4	15.1
Worcester, MA	85.8	88.9	89.5	74.9	69.5	32.2	33.9	31.7	41.7	13.9
U.S.	88.9	91.4	87.2	87.6	71.2	33.7	35.5	23.3	55.6	18.4

Note: Figures shown cover persons 25 years old and over; (1) People of Hispanic origin can be of any race
Source: U.S. Census Bureau, 2017-2021 American Community Survey 5-Year Estimates

A-138 Appendix A: Comparative Statistics

Educational Attainment by Race: Metro Area

Metro Area	High School Graduate or Higher (%)					Bachelor's Degree or Higher (%)				
	Total	White	Black	Asian	Hisp.[1]	Total	White	Black	Asian	Hisp.[1]
Albuquerque, NM	90.0	92.1	92.0	89.6	83.8	33.7	37.5	34.4	54.4	21.7
Allentown, PA	90.9	92.5	87.6	89.0	77.5	31.2	32.2	21.7	61.7	15.7
Anchorage, AK	94.0	95.8	92.9	88.2	86.4	33.3	38.1	21.8	26.1	24.3
Ann Arbor, MI	95.7	96.8	90.8	95.7	87.2	57.2	58.9	29.1	82.1	46.1
Athens, GA	89.4	92.3	82.2	89.7	69.1	41.7	46.6	21.7	67.5	30.6
Atlanta, GA	90.5	92.5	91.5	87.7	67.2	40.4	44.6	32.6	59.7	22.9
Austin, TX	91.0	93.4	92.3	92.8	77.1	47.4	50.3	33.1	73.7	26.1
Baltimore, MD	91.6	93.9	89.0	89.1	76.2	41.8	46.4	28.4	63.1	32.4
Boise City, ID	92.1	94.1	80.8	88.2	70.7	33.9	35.1	25.3	52.0	16.6
Boston, MA	92.1	95.1	86.2	86.6	73.7	49.7	52.5	29.6	64.1	24.9
Boulder, CO	95.5	97.0	86.9	92.5	75.8	62.9	64.6	30.4	70.8	31.3
Brownsville, TX	69.5	70.7	82.1	89.3	66.1	19.0	18.7	26.6	59.8	16.2
Cape Coral, FL	89.8	92.0	81.0	91.5	74.4	29.0	30.9	16.7	50.0	14.7
Cedar Rapids, IA	94.8	95.7	83.9	87.6	79.9	32.1	32.5	18.5	49.3	23.6
Charleston, SC	91.5	94.6	85.7	89.7	70.2	38.0	45.2	18.5	50.8	23.0
Charlotte, NC	89.9	92.2	89.9	86.7	65.7	37.1	40.0	28.1	60.8	20.5
Chicago, IL	89.5	92.9	88.7	91.1	70.5	39.7	44.4	24.5	66.5	16.8
Cincinnati, OH	91.8	92.7	87.3	89.4	77.4	35.4	36.4	21.6	65.9	29.4
Clarksville, TN	91.4	91.9	90.6	87.5	85.7	26.5	27.3	23.3	42.7	18.7
Cleveland, OH	91.4	93.3	86.1	86.8	77.9	32.7	36.2	16.8	63.5	17.6
College Station, TX	87.9	89.3	87.7	94.5	67.8	38.6	40.7	18.3	76.8	17.3
Colorado Springs, CO	94.6	95.8	95.1	87.2	84.7	39.4	41.9	29.6	42.2	21.4
Columbia, MO	94.1	94.7	91.6	94.2	88.0	45.1	46.2	25.5	67.1	38.5
Columbia, SC	90.6	92.8	88.1	92.3	70.0	33.6	37.9	24.7	62.2	23.1
Columbus, OH	92.1	93.6	87.6	88.4	76.8	38.4	40.3	22.7	64.1	27.4
Dallas, TX	86.6	88.9	91.8	88.8	63.9	36.8	38.9	30.0	62.8	16.2
Davenport, IA	91.8	93.9	80.3	78.7	75.3	27.9	29.0	11.8	51.7	16.9
Denver, CO	91.9	94.5	90.4	84.9	74.1	46.2	50.1	29.2	53.1	19.6
Des Moines, IA	93.4	95.6	84.8	71.0	68.2	37.6	39.0	20.7	37.1	15.8
Durham, NC	90.1	93.0	87.9	92.8	56.5	47.4	54.2	30.3	77.1	21.3
Edison, NJ	87.3	92.2	86.3	84.1	73.1	42.0	49.1	26.8	56.0	21.3
El Paso, TX	79.6	82.4	96.1	89.2	76.0	24.6	26.5	32.2	54.0	20.8
Fargo, ND	95.2	96.5	78.9	85.9	86.7	40.3	41.5	20.4	55.6	21.7
Fort Collins, CO	96.3	96.9	94.2	93.2	84.3	49.4	50.0	33.0	66.7	28.5
Fort Wayne, IN	90.2	93.3	86.0	55.8	66.3	29.3	31.4	16.4	30.4	12.5
Fort Worth, TX	86.6	88.9	91.8	88.8	63.9	36.8	38.9	30.0	62.8	16.2
Grand Rapids, MI	92.3	94.3	87.7	75.5	69.4	34.5	36.4	20.6	40.5	16.2
Greeley, CO	88.1	90.1	79.6	89.1	67.8	29.5	31.3	31.0	41.1	10.1
Green Bay, WI	92.5	94.3	76.4	83.4	61.7	29.1	29.8	19.0	47.3	13.4
Greensboro, NC	88.2	90.3	87.8	78.5	61.1	30.5	32.9	24.1	47.0	14.3
Honolulu, HI	92.7	97.6	97.1	90.3	95.1	36.2	50.0	33.8	37.4	28.7
Houston, TX	84.4	86.6	91.8	87.3	66.4	34.2	36.5	30.0	56.9	16.7
Huntsville, AL	90.8	92.5	87.5	89.5	74.7	40.9	43.4	32.1	60.6	27.7
Indianapolis, IN	90.6	92.5	86.5	81.0	67.3	36.3	38.5	22.9	55.5	21.3
Jacksonville, FL	91.4	92.5	88.4	89.4	85.5	33.1	35.6	22.0	49.9	27.9
Kansas City, MO	92.7	94.3	89.8	88.2	72.4	38.0	40.9	20.4	56.2	19.1
Lafayette, LA	86.0	88.8	79.2	76.0	70.7	24.6	27.7	13.2	38.0	19.1
Las Cruces, NM	80.7	83.8	84.8	88.6	73.5	30.0	32.5	44.9	60.3	19.8
Las Vegas, NV	86.4	90.0	89.9	90.6	68.4	25.8	28.3	19.8	41.0	11.9
Lexington, KY	91.7	93.3	89.0	89.2	63.6	39.0	40.9	22.8	65.5	22.1
Lincoln, NE	93.4	95.2	87.1	79.5	69.3	39.6	40.9	26.6	43.4	20.1
Little Rock, AR	91.6	92.8	90.2	87.1	70.1	32.1	34.4	24.8	51.1	15.5
Los Angeles, CA	81.6	86.5	90.5	88.8	64.5	36.0	40.8	29.5	54.5	15.1
Louisville, KY	90.9	91.9	88.1	85.5	73.8	31.1	32.7	19.7	57.5	21.6
Madison, WI	95.7	96.8	90.1	90.5	77.2	47.7	48.1	25.2	68.5	30.6

Table continued on following page.

Appendix A: Comparative Statistics   A-139

Metro Area	High School Graduate or Higher (%)					Bachelor's Degree or Higher (%)				
	Total	White	Black	Asian	Hisp.[1]	Total	White	Black	Asian	Hisp.[1]
Manchester, NH	92.9	93.8	82.8	89.8	73.6	39.6	39.8	20.5	62.1	19.0
Miami, FL	86.5	88.7	83.6	87.9	81.2	34.1	38.5	21.2	54.3	29.8
Midland, TX	84.4	87.4	89.1	75.0	71.5	28.5	31.3	16.7	51.6	14.1
Milwaukee, WI	92.1	95.2	85.9	86.1	71.0	37.4	42.3	15.1	53.3	16.6
Minneapolis, MN	94.0	96.6	82.8	82.7	73.9	43.5	46.1	23.6	46.0	24.1
Nashville, TN	91.0	92.2	90.0	86.0	64.9	38.4	39.9	30.0	55.3	19.4
New Haven, CT	90.3	92.7	88.2	89.7	74.5	36.6	39.8	23.0	64.1	15.6
New Orleans, LA	88.1	91.7	84.1	80.3	74.7	32.2	39.2	19.9	43.4	22.4
New York, NY	87.3	92.2	86.3	84.1	73.1	42.0	49.1	26.8	56.0	21.3
Oklahoma City, OK	89.8	91.3	91.6	83.3	62.2	32.4	34.4	24.0	47.2	13.2
Omaha, NE	92.3	94.2	88.8	75.9	66.1	37.7	39.7	20.5	49.0	17.3
Orlando, FL	90.1	92.1	85.6	89.2	85.5	33.7	36.3	23.3	52.0	25.7
Philadelphia, PA	91.6	94.4	89.0	84.5	73.0	39.8	44.5	23.0	58.3	20.7
Phoenix, AZ	88.7	91.3	91.7	89.3	71.8	33.1	35.2	28.2	59.7	14.9
Pittsburgh, PA	94.5	95.1	90.8	87.5	88.5	36.6	37.0	21.6	69.2	37.5
Portland, OR	92.8	94.6	90.8	87.6	73.2	41.0	41.6	31.3	54.0	22.1
Providence, RI	88.0	89.8	84.7	86.4	73.3	33.2	34.9	25.8	53.2	15.5
Provo, UT	95.1	95.8	95.1	93.1	79.7	41.9	42.6	34.1	54.0	24.9
Raleigh, NC	92.6	95.1	91.1	92.7	65.6	48.6	52.8	32.3	75.7	21.1
Reno, NV	88.6	92.8	90.7	92.0	64.2	32.3	34.9	28.0	47.1	13.2
Richmond, VA	91.1	94.0	87.4	89.9	68.9	38.9	45.5	22.8	65.6	22.8
Rochester, MN	94.7	96.1	71.8	88.1	77.4	41.0	41.1	19.5	59.6	31.3
Sacramento, CA	89.8	93.2	91.2	84.7	76.7	35.0	36.8	25.5	44.8	20.1
St. Louis, MO	92.8	94.2	87.5	90.8	82.3	36.2	38.6	20.4	68.0	31.3
Salem, OR	86.8	90.9	92.8	81.5	60.7	25.7	28.0	25.2	37.3	10.0
Salt Lake City, UT	91.8	94.9	84.6	86.6	73.5	36.4	38.9	25.4	49.1	17.1
San Antonio, TX	86.4	88.1	92.7	87.8	78.4	30.3	32.0	31.4	53.9	19.4
San Diego, CA	88.3	90.8	91.6	90.0	73.1	40.3	43.2	27.4	53.0	19.6
San Francisco, CA	89.7	95.0	91.3	88.1	73.1	51.4	58.7	31.6	57.6	23.9
San Jose, CA	89.0	92.7	92.4	91.4	71.9	53.4	53.4	41.7	67.5	19.0
Santa Rosa, CA	89.2	94.2	87.2	88.3	66.1	37.1	41.5	32.1	48.5	15.9
Savannah, GA	90.7	93.4	87.0	83.3	84.4	33.6	39.7	21.0	51.4	25.1
Seattle, WA	93.2	95.5	90.8	90.0	75.9	44.3	44.9	27.5	58.3	25.0
Sioux Falls, SD	93.7	95.1	84.5	75.7	73.0	34.8	36.1	19.6	44.4	18.6
Springfield, IL	92.9	94.4	80.8	90.9	89.3	33.4	34.8	15.5	68.2	42.6
Tampa, FL	90.4	91.9	88.7	85.1	81.4	32.4	33.1	25.0	51.8	24.6
Tucson, AZ	89.4	92.5	87.6	87.7	77.9	34.4	38.1	27.6	55.7	18.5
Tulsa, OK	90.0	91.7	90.1	76.7	65.8	28.7	31.1	19.6	34.9	14.0
Tuscaloosa, AL	88.5	91.2	84.9	86.9	64.6	27.8	34.2	15.3	61.0	17.4
Virginia Beach, VA	92.4	94.9	88.7	88.4	84.8	33.8	38.2	23.8	44.2	28.3
Washington, DC	91.5	95.1	92.4	91.3	70.4	52.4	61.3	37.2	66.0	28.0
Wichita, KS	90.2	92.8	87.6	74.2	66.9	31.1	33.0	19.0	35.5	16.4
Wilmington, NC	92.8	94.4	87.9	82.0	78.9	39.9	43.0	22.5	63.9	27.1
Winston-Salem, NC	88.0	89.3	87.7	88.3	60.1	27.4	28.9	21.0	54.6	13.5
Worcester, MA	91.3	92.9	89.3	85.0	73.7	36.4	36.4	34.4	59.8	16.6
U.S.	88.9	91.4	87.2	87.6	71.2	33.7	35.5	23.3	55.6	18.4

Note: Figures shown cover persons 25 years old and over; Figures cover the Metropolitan Statistical Area; (1) People of Hispanic origin can be of any race
Source: U.S. Census Bureau, 2017-2021 American Community Survey 5-Year Estimates

A-140 Appendix A: Comparative Statistics

Cost of Living Index

Urban Area	Composite	Groceries	Housing	Utilities	Transp.	Health	Misc.
Albuquerque, NM	93.8	104.8	84.5	87.7	97.2	99.8	96.6
Allentown, PA	104.4	98.4	114.0	103.4	104.8	94.6	100.6
Anchorage, AK	124.5	132.6	140.0	124.0	114.8	144.2	109.7
Ann Arbor, MI	n/a	n/a	n/a	n/a	n/a	n/a	n/a
Athens, GA	n/a	n/a	n/a	n/a	n/a	n/a	n/a
Atlanta, GA	102.8	103.4	103.5	85.1	103.6	107.1	106.0
Austin, TX	99.7	91.2	105.5	95.2	90.7	105.8	101.4
Baltimore, MD	n/a	n/a	n/a	n/a	n/a	n/a	n/a
Boise City, ID	98.7	94.5	97.5	81.9	108.5	103.0	102.8
Boston, MA	151.0	109.3	228.6	120.5	112.0	118.3	129.3
Boulder, CO	n/a	n/a	n/a	n/a	n/a	n/a	n/a
Brownsville, TX	76.6	80.2	58.0	108.2	88.1	80.3	79.6
Cape Coral, FL	100.6	107.8	89.6	98.8	98.7	108.5	106.3
Cedar Rapids, IA	96.2	94.8	83.0	102.1	96.6	107.0	103.9
Charleston, SC	97.2	99.7	93.2	120.4	86.6	97.5	95.9
Charlotte, NC	98.2	101.7	88.8	95.6	90.7	105.1	106.0
Chicago, IL	120.6	101.9	155.7	92.4	125.9	100.0	109.4
Cincinnati, OH	99.7	91.2	105.5	95.2	90.7	105.8	101.4
Clarksville, TN	n/a	n/a	n/a	n/a	n/a	n/a	n/a
Cleveland, OH	96.9	106.0	83.3	96.1	99.4	104.4	102.6
College Station, TX	n/a	n/a	n/a	n/a	n/a	n/a	n/a
Colorado Springs, CO	101.1	95.9	101.3	97.2	97.7	108.6	104.1
Columbia, MO	91.8	95.5	75.0	100.0	92.0	102.6	99.8
Columbia, SC	93.5	103.1	72.7	126.2	87.1	79.9	100.5
Columbus, OH	92.6	98.6	81.2	89.1	95.5	88.5	99.7
Dallas, TX	108.2	100.2	118.8	106.8	96.7	105.4	106.7
Davenport, IA	92.0	99.7	76.9	98.9	105.8	105.3	93.7
Denver, CO	111.3	98.3	139.3	80.5	100.9	103.6	106.6
Des Moines, IA	89.9	95.2	80.2	90.1	99.1	95.4	92.3
Durham, NC[1]	n/a	n/a	n/a	n/a	n/a	n/a	n/a
Edison, NJ[2]	120.6	108.7	149.3	105.8	107.8	102.5	112.4
El Paso, TX	87.7	102.3	73.7	85.7	99.0	99.3	89.0
Fargo, ND	98.6	111.5	77.6	90.5	100.4	120.1	108.9
Fort Collins, CO	n/a	n/a	n/a	n/a	n/a	n/a	n/a
Fort Wayne, IN	86.9	86.7	62.3	95.7	99.5	101.5	98.6
Fort Worth, TX	94.9	92.4	88.4	107.2	96.9	101.5	96.2
Grand Rapids, MI	94.1	92.8	87.4	98.5	104.1	92.3	96.3
Greeley, CO	n/a	n/a	n/a	n/a	n/a	n/a	n/a
Green Bay, WI	91.1	91.0	77.9	97.4	97.7	101.8	96.6
Greensboro, NC	n/a	n/a	n/a	n/a	n/a	n/a	n/a
Honolulu, HI	192.9	165.0	332.6	172.3	138.2	118.8	124.2
Houston, TX	95.8	88.4	91.2	105.8	95.2	92.0	100.3
Huntsville, AL	91.3	95.1	66.6	99.0	97.3	96.4	104.7
Indianapolis, IN	92.4	94.1	78.4	105.4	97.9	90.6	98.0
Jacksonville, FL	91.7	98.4	88.0	97.7	86.0	83.7	92.7
Kansas City, MO	95.8	102.4	82.6	100.6	92.6	105.9	101.7
Lafayette, LA	88.9	101.8	72.0	88.0	104.7	88.0	93.3
Las Cruces, NM	n/a	n/a	n/a	n/a	n/a	n/a	n/a
Las Vegas, NV	103.6	95.8	118.3	98.6	114.0	100.2	94.2
Lexington, KY	92.7	89.9	83.7	95.6	96.7	78.9	100.7
Lincoln, NE	93.0	95.6	78.7	90.2	93.4	105.8	102.2
Little Rock, AR	96.0	95.1	88.1	97.4	94.7	89.6	103.2
Los Angeles, CA	146.7	116.3	230.6	106.2	134.8	110.8	112.0
Louisville, KY	94.1	91.8	79.8	94.6	98.1	105.2	103.7
Madison, WI	107.0	107.6	108.6	99.8	104.4	124.0	106.0
Manchester, NH	108.9	102.2	109.6	117.9	104.1	116.0	108.9

Table continued on following page.

Appendix A: Comparative Statistics   A-141

Urban Area	Composite	Groceries	Housing	Utilities	Transp.	Health	Misc.
Miami, FL	115.0	110.5	144.3	102.0	101.5	100.6	102.7
Midland, TX	102.1	93.6	91.5	106.6	104.1	96.5	112.6
Milwaukee, WI	96.7	93.4	100.5	94.8	99.8	115.9	92.4
Minneapolis, MN	106.6	103.6	102.9	97.5	104.4	105.6	113.9
Nashville, TN	98.9	99.5	98.5	97.0	97.9	92.4	100.4
New Haven, CT	122.3	111.0	128.5	136.7	110.6	115.8	121.9
New Orleans, LA	105.0	102.6	125.5	81.5	101.3	115.1	96.1
New York, NY[3]	181.6	128.4	339.0	121.4	113.7	107.1	123.1
Oklahoma City, OK	86.0	93.3	69.6	95.3	86.2	95.0	92.1
Omaha, NE	92.3	96.8	83.6	99.4	98.3	96.4	93.3
Orlando, FL	92.1	100.7	85.1	97.2	89.3	88.3	94.1
Philadelphia, PA	110.9	118.7	116.5	105.6	116.1	101.8	104.8
Phoenix, AZ	99.3	99.7	103.8	109.5	107.2	90.1	91.9
Pittsburgh, PA	103.1	111.9	105.7	116.1	114.0	93.1	92.6
Portland, OR	134.7	112.4	186.4	87.1	131.0	115.6	119.4
Providence, RI	119.2	106.7	132.8	126.4	112.1	109.3	114.6
Provo, UT	98.2	93.0	96.1	84.7	100.7	94.5	105.4
Raleigh, NC	95.4	92.7	89.0	98.3	90.9	103.8	100.9
Reno, NV	114.1	118.7	125.8	85.9	126.3	113.9	107.6
Richmond, VA	94.2	89.0	86.0	97.6	86.9	106.7	102.1
Rochester, MN	n/a	n/a	n/a	n/a	n/a	n/a	n/a
Sacramento, CA	118.4	120.2	134.2	102.9	139.0	113.6	104.8
Saint Louis, MO	n/a	n/a	n/a	n/a	n/a	n/a	n/a
Salem, OR	n/a	n/a	n/a	n/a	n/a	n/a	n/a
Salt Lake City, UT	103.6	108.0	106.7	87.8	103.6	105.7	103.6
San Antonio, TX	89.5	88.0	82.2	87.6	89.1	87.2	96.5
San Diego, CA	142.1	116.1	216.3	123.2	129.2	107.3	107.3
San Francisco, CA	197.9	131.3	368.9	123.0	145.3	129.6	133.4
San Jose, CA	n/a	n/a	n/a	n/a	n/a	n/a	n/a
Santa Rosa, CA	n/a	n/a	n/a	n/a	n/a	n/a	n/a
Savannah, GA	89.5	95.7	66.2	96.0	94.9	106.1	100.0
Seattle, WA	157.5	129.1	227.6	108.0	137.8	128.6	136.2
Sioux Falls, SD	92.5	96.3	86.3	84.7	91.9	107.7	96.3
Springfield, IL	n/a	n/a	n/a	n/a	n/a	n/a	n/a
Tampa, FL	91.2	104.8	79.2	85.9	99.4	98.3	93.7
Tucson, AZ	97.5	100.5	87.9	99.9	101.1	98.7	102.0
Tulsa, OK	86.0	96.2	62.7	99.5	84.4	91.6	96.1
Tuscaloosa, AL	n/a	n/a	n/a	n/a	n/a	n/a	n/a
Virginia Beach, VA[4]	94.1	92.7	89.1	97.4	92.2	90.4	98.7
Washington, DC	159.9	116.0	277.1	117.9	110.6	95.8	118.1
Wichita, KS	91.1	94.3	69.6	99.3	95.3	96.1	102.5
Wilmington, NC	n/a	n/a	n/a	n/a	n/a	n/a	n/a
Winston-Salem, NC	90.8	101.4	66.7	94.6	92.0	119.5	100.5
Worcester, MA	n/a	n/a	n/a	n/a	n/a	n/a	n/a
U.S.	100.0	100.0	100.0	100.0	100.0	100.0	100.0

Note: The Cost of Living Index measures regional differences in the cost of consumer goods and services, excluding taxes and non-consumer expenditures, for professional and managerial households in the top income quintile. It is based on more than 50,000 prices covering almost 60 different items for which prices are collected three times a year by chambers of commerce, economic development organizations or university applied economic centers in each participating urban area. The numbers shown should be read as a percentage above or below the national average of 100. For example, a value of 115.4 in the groceries column indicates that grocery prices are 15.4% higher than the national average. Small differences in the index numbers should not be interpreted as significant. In cases where data is not available for the city, data for the metro area or for a neighboring city has been provided and noted as follows: (1) Chapel Hill NC; (2) Middlesex-Monmouth NJ; (3) Brooklyn, NY; (4) Hampton Roads-SE Virginia
Source: The Council for Community and Economic Research, Cost of Living Index, 2022

A-142 Appendix A: Comparative Statistics

Grocery Prices

Urban Area	T-Bone Steak ($/pound)	Frying Chicken ($/pound)	Whole Milk ($/half gal.)	Eggs ($/dozen)	Orange Juice ($/64 oz.)	Coffee ($/11.5 oz.)
Albuquerque, NM	11.88	1.01	2.29	2.30	3.89	5.52
Allentown, PA	15.80	1.61	2.56	2.11	3.74	3.90
Anchorage, AK	16.43	2.25	2.85	2.16	4.61	6.29
Ann Arbor, MI	n/a	n/a	n/a	n/a	n/a	n/a
Athens, GA	n/a	n/a	n/a	n/a	n/a	n/a
Atlanta, GA	12.23	1.21	1.94	1.87	3.63	4.51
Austin, TX	11.44	1.08	2.14	2.18	3.36	4.26
Baltimore, MD	15.04	1.96	2.45	2.54	4.38	5.31
Boise City, ID	13.59	1.60	2.21	1.69	3.58	5.27
Boston, MA	n/a	n/a	n/a	n/a	n/a	n/a
Boulder, CO	n/a	n/a	n/a	n/a	n/a	n/a
Brownsville, TX	10.74	1.02	2.10	2.06	3.34	3.77
Cape Coral, FL	14.43	2.34	2.55	1.83	4.28	4.04
Cedar Rapids, IA	14.03	1.66	2.19	2.32	3.68	5.08
Charleston, SC	12.23	1.63	2.11	2.00	4.07	4.90
Charlotte, NC	13.63	1.23	2.11	2.12	3.68	5.31
Chicago, IL	n/a	n/a	n/a	n/a	n/a	n/a
Cincinnati, OH	13.66	2.66	2.15	1.68	3.92	6.05
Clarksville, TN	n/a	n/a	n/a	n/a	n/a	n/a
Cleveland, OH	16.00	2.16	1.86	2.08	3.91	4.91
College Station, TX	n/a	n/a	n/a	n/a	n/a	n/a
Colorado Springs, CO	14.09	1.35	2.17	2.04	3.53	5.14
Columbia, MO	12.00	1.39	3.08	2.51	3.99	5.68
Columbia, SC	12.03	1.56	2.36	2.02	3.66	4.95
Columbus, OH	14.20	1.44	1.93	1.99	4.00	5.76
Dallas, TX	12.76	1.26	2.34	2.12	3.60	4.62
Davenport, IA	13.66	2.17	2.57	2.18	3.81	5.91
Denver, CO	13.30	1.65	2.07	2.07	3.66	4.97
Des Moines, IA	11.66	2.33	2.79	2.40	3.41	5.05
Durham, NC[1]	13.15	1.77	1.97	2.14	4.23	5.04
Edison, NJ[2]	n/a	n/a	n/a	n/a	n/a	n/a
El Paso, TX	14.35	2.08	2.19	2.14	3.96	5.58
Fargo, ND	n/a	n/a	n/a	n/a	n/a	n/a
Fort Collins, CO	n/a	n/a	n/a	n/a	n/a	n/a
Fort Wayne, IN	12.91	1.22	2.46	1.84	3.53	4.98
Fort Worth, TX	13.46	1.51	2.16	2.25	3.40	4.73
Grand Rapids, MI	15.24	1.48	1.92	2.07	3.33	3.68
Greeley, CO	n/a	n/a	n/a	n/a	n/a	n/a
Green Bay, WI	15.09	1.55	2.25	1.74	3.86	4.01
Greensboro, NC	n/a	n/a	n/a	n/a	n/a	n/a
Honolulu, HI	18.12	2.74	4.32	4.32	5.31	8.59
Houston, TX	11.65	1.42	2.10	2.00	3.76	4.58
Huntsville, AL	14.42	1.54	2.22	2.04	3.86	5.03
Indianapolis, IN	14.69	1.70	2.12	1.99	3.50	4.75
Jacksonville, FL	13.82	1.79	2.26	2.53	3.59	4.86
Kansas City, MO	13.21	1.90	2.42	2.03	3.44	4.53
Lafayette, LA	12.53	1.49	2.57	3.19	3.66	5.04
Las Cruces, NM	13.28	1.47	2.51	2.47	3.97	5.37
Las Vegas, NV	14.35	1.87	2.51	2.43	4.05	5.47
Lexington, KY	13.65	1.26	2.02	1.80	3.65	4.54
Lincoln, NE	13.05	1.58	2.23	1.79	3.20	4.97
Little Rock, AR	12.30	1.41	2.12	2.08	3.74	3.90
Los Angeles, CA	14.79	1.77	2.76	3.66	4.20	6.21
Louisville, KY	14.49	1.35	1.51	1.48	3.61	4.28
Madison, WI	16.50	1.80	2.27	1.88	3.60	5.26

Table continued on following page.

Appendix A: Comparative Statistics   A-143

Urban Area	T-Bone Steak ($/pound)	Frying Chicken ($/pound)	Whole Milk ($/half gal.)	Eggs ($/dozen)	Orange Juice ($/64 oz.)	Coffee ($/11.5 oz.)
Manchester, NH	16.69	1.85	2.66	2.57	4.36	5.25
Miami, FL	11.37	1.69	3.62	2.72	4.62	5.14
Midland, TX	12.66	1.09	2.11	2.23	3.77	4.78
Milwaukee, WI	15.29	1.57	2.52	2.18	3.77	4.12
Minneapolis, MN	14.32	1.95	2.28	1.83	3.78	4.69
Nashville, TN	14.63	1.68	2.33	1.83	3.95	4.92
New Haven, CT	13.03	1.44	2.84	2.53	3.81	4.79
New Orleans, LA	15.23	1.37	2.57	2.32	3.68	4.26
New York, NY[3]	16.18	1.70	2.88	2.77	4.42	4.89
Oklahoma City, OK	12.72	1.51	2.34	2.04	3.32	4.72
Omaha, NE	15.11	1.71	2.00	1.72	3.59	5.20
Orlando, FL	13.49	1.37	2.67	2.44	3.89	3.89
Philadelphia, PA	16.43	1.91	2.57	2.47	4.19	5.67
Phoenix, AZ	14.66	1.65	2.06	2.51	4.00	5.82
Pittsburgh, PA	16.67	2.16	2.50	1.93	3.90	5.33
Portland, OR	12.15	1.28	2.88	2.75	4.10	6.48
Providence, RI	15.73	1.68	2.42	2.52	3.90	3.94
Provo, UT	14.23	1.44	2.04	2.18	4.02	5.39
Raleigh, NC	11.98	1.14	1.99	1.71	4.00	3.54
Reno, NV	13.35	1.68	2.82	2.46	3.75	5.69
Richmond, VA	12.49	1.38	2.09	1.44	3.87	4.49
Rochester, MN	n/a	n/a	n/a	n/a	n/a	n/a
Sacramento, CA	12.12	1.51	3.08	3.34	4.02	5.25
Saint Louis, MO	17.61	1.85	1.97	2.17	3.66	4.65
Salem, OR	n/a	n/a	n/a	n/a	n/a	n/a
Salt Lake City, UT	13.19	1.85	2.28	2.25	4.46	5.46
San Antonio, TX	11.06	1.05	2.20	1.86	3.41	4.07
San Diego, CA	14.80	1.85	2.70	3.71	4.32	5.91
San Francisco, CA	18.36	1.95	3.38	3.83	4.48	7.00
San Jose, CA	n/a	n/a	n/a	n/a	n/a	n/a
Santa Rosa, CA	n/a	n/a	n/a	n/a	n/a	n/a
Savannah, GA	13.73	1.29	2.24	1.99	3.42	4.55
Seattle, WA	17.83	2.43	2.97	2.23	4.41	6.55
Sioux Falls, SD	12.85	1.47	2.61	2.26	3.63	5.53
Springfield, IL	14.11	2.05	1.85	1.54	3.88	4.88
Tampa, FL	12.92	1.93	2.78	2.83	4.18	4.31
Tucson, AZ	12.19	1.47	2.37	2.22	4.03	5.97
Tulsa, OK	13.52	1.46	2.57	1.97	3.57	4.66
Tuscaloosa, AL	n/a	n/a	n/a	n/a	n/a	n/a
Virginia Beach, VA[4]	12.02	1.45	2.24	1.64	3.95	3.93
Washington, DC	13.41	1.21	2.91	2.62	4.08	5.36
Wichita, KS	13.71	1.63	2.05	1.95	4.15	4.95
Wilmington, NC	n/a	n/a	n/a	n/a	n/a	n/a
Winston-Salem, NC	13.05	1.11	2.31	2.28	3.98	4.30
Worcester, MA	n/a	n/a	n/a	n/a	n/a	n/a
Average*	13.81	1.59	2.43	2.25	3.85	4.95
Minimum*	10.17	0.90	1.51	1.30	2.90	3.46
Maximum*	19.35	3.30	4.32	4.32	5.31	8.59

*Note: **T-Bone Steak** (price per pound); **Frying Chicken** (price per pound, whole fryer); **Whole Milk** (half gallon carton); **Eggs** (price per dozen, Grade A, large); **Orange Juice** (64 oz. Tropicana or Florida Natural); **Coffee** (11.5 oz. can, vacuum-packed, Maxwell House, Hills Bros, or Folgers); (*) Average, minimum, and maximum values for all 286 areas in the Cost of Living Index report; n/a not available; In cases where data is not available for the city, data for the metro area or for a neighboring city has been provided and noted as follows: (1) Chapel Hill NC; (2) Middlesex-Monmouth NJ; (3) Brooklyn, NY; (4) Hampton Roads-SE Virginia*
Source: The Council for Community and Economic Research, Cost of Living Index, 2022

A-144 Appendix A: Comparative Statistics

Housing and Utility Costs

Urban Area	New Home Price ($)	Apartment Rent ($/month)	All Electric ($/month)	Part Electric ($/month)	Other Energy ($/month)	Telephone ($/month)
Albuquerque, NM	383,227	1,215	-	107.21	43.71	191.37
Allentown, PA	485,339	1,679	-	99.25	82.35	193.11
Anchorage, AK	656,122	1,516	-	102.07	130.31	188.62
Ann Arbor, MI	n/a	n/a	n/a	n/a	n/a	n/a
Athens, GA	n/a	n/a	n/a	n/a	n/a	n/a
Atlanta, GA	489,573	1,551	-	90.61	44.15	188.95
Austin, TX	484,044	1,807	-	101.22	51.85	196.79
Baltimore, MD	440,295	1,868	-	92.51	93.60	196.85
Boise City, ID	576,971	1,640	-	63.81	63.35	174.27
Boston, MA	n/a	n/a	n/a	n/a	n/a	n/a
Boulder, CO	n/a	n/a	n/a	n/a	n/a	n/a
Brownsville, TX	274,631	757	-	139.72	54.99	196.56
Cape Coral, FL	495,794	1,824	182.94	-	-	195.37
Cedar Rapids, IA	339,825	846	-	106.96	45.22	189.46
Charleston, SC	423,780	1,572	224.48	-	-	195.28
Charlotte, NC	377,295	1,498	155.34	-	-	184.19
Chicago, IL	n/a	n/a	n/a	n/a	n/a	n/a
Cincinnati, OH	368,833	1,083	-	76.34	81.75	184.60
Clarksville, TN	n/a	n/a	n/a	n/a	n/a	n/a
Cleveland, OH	347,809	1,302	-	89.55	82.10	188.12
College Station, TX	n/a	n/a	n/a	n/a	n/a	n/a
Colorado Springs, CO	497,622	1,512	-	104.56	85.71	186.39
Columbia, MO	442,644	861	-	96.49	65.29	194.74
Columbia, SC	322,903	1,107	-	112.85	167.25	190.68
Columbus, OH	366,506	1,200	-	88.37	72.63	184.15
Dallas, TX	439,403	1,563	-	136.69	79.10	196.79
Davenport, IA	285,682	1,014	-	88.01	57.06	198.79
Denver, CO	639,886	1,841	-	58.60	78.48	190.08
Des Moines, IA	337,128	741	-	79.63	53.25	188.32
Durham, NC[1]	582,565	1,411	-	85.31	62.68	176.30
Edison, NJ[2]	n/a	n/a	n/a	n/a	n/a	n/a
El Paso, TX	292,519	1,130	-	93.81	47.74	200.02
Fargo, ND	n/a	n/a	n/a	n/a	n/a	n/a
Fort Collins, CO	n/a	n/a	n/a	n/a	n/a	n/a
Fort Wayne, IN	296,241	1,083	-	105.04	65.35	191.60
Fort Worth, TX	372,205	1,327	-	137.89	75.49	199.27
Grand Rapids, MI	384,672	1,273	-	105.38	79.74	190.37
Greeley, CO	n/a	n/a	n/a	n/a	n/a	n/a
Green Bay, WI	382,340	881	-	83.06	80.95	186.93
Greensboro, NC	n/a	n/a	n/a	n/a	n/a	n/a
Honolulu, HI	1,605,915	3,589	309.47	-	-	182.54
Houston, TX	378,106	1,292	-	123.18	45.33	195.79
Huntsville, AL	350,811	1,023	173.74	-	-	186.08
Indianapolis, IN	340,588	1,325	-	111.24	89.87	188.71
Jacksonville, FL	385,800	1,507	187.84	-	-	196.12
Kansas City, MO	439,207	1,471	-	98.92	78.39	198.58
Lafayette, LA	284,856	1,063	-	89.62	58.12	186.23
Las Cruces, NM	364,513	926	-	95.18	40.12	192.31
Las Vegas, NV	491,447	1,600	-	121.78	57.89	196.21
Lexington, KY	351,975	982	-	90.87	109.72	189.80
Lincoln, NE	359,724	1,066	-	63.75	64.03	199.14
Little Rock, AR	395,450	946	-	81.77	91.69	204.44
Los Angeles, CA	1,098,874	3,182	-	123.99	84.34	192.21
Louisville, KY	338,400	1,315	-	90.92	105.78	184.63
Madison, WI	475,954	1,205	-	114.02	94.46	183.66

Table continued on following page.

Appendix A: Comparative Statistics   A-145

Urban Area	New Home Price ($)	Apartment Rent ($/month)	All Electric ($/month)	Part Electric ($/month)	Other Energy ($/month)	Telephone ($/month)
Manchester, NH	441,922	2,064	-	107.51	118.35	184.25
Miami, FL	584,754	2,690	192.68	-	-	195.67
Midland, TX	366,614	927	-	121.06	40.30	195.66
Milwaukee, WI	432,791	1,481	-	104.40	98.25	186.18
Minneapolis, MN	404,076	1,318	-	102.55	74.40	188.30
Nashville, TN	483,320	1,465	-	90.92	51.95	190.02
New Haven, CT	434,014	2,127	-	166.18	115.11	186.44
New Orleans, LA	654,349	1,851	-	71.40	46.62	187.68
New York, NY[3]	1,349,755	3,727	-	106.15	87.34	195.04
Oklahoma City, OK	333,325	860	-	90.04	66.60	195.02
Omaha, NE	350,853	1,290	-	92.74	60.25	198.80
Orlando, FL	448,493	1,766	154.33	-	-	192.14
Philadelphia, PA	430,067	1,542	-	105.62	103.27	196.34
Phoenix, AZ	497,561	2,083	187.70	-	-	185.99
Pittsburgh, PA	418,872	1,281	-	118.68	149.99	194.84
Portland, OR	661,664	2,636	-	80.74	76.64	181.33
Providence, RI	462,061	2,085	-	132.22	119.10	193.25
Provo, UT	532,268	1,449	-	67.96	72.66	194.35
Raleigh, NC	400,445	1,614	-	112.40	74.47	184.19
Reno, NV	576,610	1,515	-	97.93	44.46	185.65
Richmond, VA	383,637	1,334	-	95.49	99.23	182.67
Rochester, MN	n/a	n/a	n/a	n/a	n/a	n/a
Sacramento, CA	582,334	2,402	-	152.89	43.30	189.21
Saint Louis, MO	339,758	981	-	80.89	68.47	201.40
Salem, OR	n/a	n/a	n/a	n/a	n/a	n/a
Salt Lake City, UT	575,689	1,609	-	77.74	74.42	194.94
San Antonio, TX	327,632	1,388	-	99.94	37.03	198.89
San Diego, CA	1,001,748	3,057	-	145.75	74.47	183.97
San Francisco, CA	1,502,557	3,585	-	172.31	95.33	201.38
San Jose, CA	n/a	n/a	n/a	n/a	n/a	n/a
Santa Rosa, CA	n/a	n/a	n/a	n/a	n/a	n/a
Savannah, GA	297,041	1,176	158.44	-	-	186.50
Seattle, WA	940,665	3,031	188.83	-	-	198.78
Sioux Falls, SD	450,933	1,111	-	84.19	47.87	182.72
Springfield, IL	408,667	1,152	-	91.51	94.77	185.67
Tampa, FL	414,223	1,528	167.09	-	-	192.89
Tucson, AZ	481,931	1,410	-	103.78	69.05	186.26
Tulsa, OK	313,413	852	-	90.90	68.43	190.79
Tuscaloosa, AL	n/a	n/a	n/a	n/a	n/a	n/a
Virginia Beach, VA[4]	395,804	1,258	-	98.78	95.60	184.73
Washington, DC	1,156,418	3,220	-	117.06	100.23	188.98
Wichita, KS	314,516	978	-	93.16	71.97	198.70
Wilmington, NC	n/a	n/a	n/a	n/a	n/a	n/a
Winston-Salem, NC	319,961	1,290	157.68	-	-	180.76
Worcester, MA	n/a	n/a	n/a	n/a	n/a	n/a
Average*	450,913	1,371	176.41	99.93	76.96	190.22
Minimum*	229,283	546	100.84	31.56	27.15	174.27
Maximum*	2,434,977	4,569	356.86	249.59	272.24	208.31

Note: **New Home Price** *(2,400 sf living area, 8,000 sf lot, in urban area with full utilities);* **Apartment Rent** *(950 sf 2 bedroom/1.5 or 2 bath, unfurnished, excluding all utilities except water);* **All Electric** *(average monthly cost for an all-electric home);* **Part Electric** *(average monthly cost for a part-electric home);* **Other Energy** *(average monthly cost for natural gas, fuel oil, coal, wood, and any other forms of energy except electricity);* **Telephone** *(price includes the base monthly rate plus taxes and fees for three lines of mobile phone service); (*) Average, minimum, and maximum values for all 286 areas in the Cost of Living Index report; n/a not available; In cases where data is not available for the city, data for the metro area or for a neighboring city has been provided and noted as follows: (1) Chapel Hill NC; (2) Middlesex-Monmouth NJ; (3) Brooklyn, NY; (4) Hampton Roads-SE Virginia*
Source: The Council for Community and Economic Research, Cost of Living Index, 2022

A-146 Appendix A: Comparative Statistics

Health Care, Transportation, and Other Costs

Urban Area	Doctor ($/visit)	Dentist ($/visit)	Optometrist ($/visit)	Gasoline ($/gallon)	Beauty Salon ($/visit)	Men's Shirt ($)
Albuquerque, NM	114.36	105.38	123.65	3.81	45.00	29.72
Allentown, PA	107.20	115.92	108.43	4.12	53.07	35.54
Anchorage, AK	228.37	152.08	252.89	4.49	55.00	34.08
Ann Arbor, MI	n/a	n/a	n/a	n/a	n/a	n/a
Athens, GA	n/a	n/a	n/a	n/a	n/a	n/a
Atlanta, GA	115.86	132.58	128.60	3.87	51.09	40.24
Austin, TX	122.17	119.14	118.78	3.47	52.91	34.72
Baltimore, MD	80.00	115.58	87.78	3.67	56.91	27.22
Boise City, ID	140.88	86.46	138.00	4.43	39.00	43.44
Boston, MA	n/a	n/a	n/a	n/a	n/a	n/a
Boulder, CO	n/a	n/a	n/a	n/a	n/a	n/a
Brownsville, TX	90.00	91.61	73.32	3.46	23.67	13.19
Cape Coral, FL	127.67	112.88	96.64	3.86	50.60	29.74
Cedar Rapids, IA	139.68	101.88	94.68	3.84	34.39	26.11
Charleston, SC	146.94	92.17	71.32	3.61	59.17	37.27
Charlotte, NC	140.33	135.13	125.78	3.68	31.70	49.35
Chicago, IL	n/a	n/a	n/a	n/a	n/a	n/a
Cincinnati, OH	142.44	100.47	107.60	4.01	43.10	45.33
Clarksville, TN	n/a	n/a	n/a	n/a	n/a	n/a
Cleveland, OH	113.00	109.47	94.21	3.86	35.71	41.99
College Station, TX	n/a	n/a	n/a	n/a	n/a	n/a
Colorado Springs, CO	134.96	108.29	123.36	3.96	47.60	44.38
Columbia, MO	125.84	92.11	110.19	3.84	43.33	29.87
Columbia, SC	124.17	82.50	53.00	3.26	42.36	37.12
Columbus, OH	118.38	87.19	61.70	3.77	42.53	38.24
Dallas, TX	141.13	129.77	139.62	3.39	64.32	38.33
Davenport, IA	136.67	84.83	102.07	3.46	34.89	37.75
Denver, CO	106.00	118.21	115.00	3.72	47.09	35.52
Des Moines, IA	131.59	90.21	119.28	3.34	39.44	39.61
Durham, NC[1]	143.27	113.91	132.86	3.70	53.11	22.22
Edison, NJ[2]	n/a	n/a	n/a	n/a	n/a	n/a
El Paso, TX	146.74	84.59	98.23	3.61	28.33	30.52
Fargo, ND	n/a	n/a	n/a	n/a	n/a	n/a
Fort Collins, CO	n/a	n/a	n/a	n/a	n/a	n/a
Fort Wayne, IN	140.00	105.42	88.55	3.70	34.67	39.66
Fort Worth, TX	92.61	96.41	111.17	3.58	55.08	32.87
Grand Rapids, MI	104.35	109.29	109.72	4.13	36.00	26.03
Greeley, CO	n/a	n/a	n/a	n/a	n/a	n/a
Green Bay, WI	152.75	98.67	75.78	3.45	27.46	26.90
Greensboro, NC	n/a	n/a	n/a	n/a	n/a	n/a
Honolulu, HI	168.32	97.93	209.95	5.03	75.67	53.63
Houston, TX	99.00	115.42	103.21	3.53	64.48	26.78
Huntsville, AL	124.50	99.17	88.78	3.55	49.33	33.22
Indianapolis, IN	97.22	99.33	68.63	3.65	39.23	42.46
Jacksonville, FL	90.43	93.90	72.66	3.68	63.00	25.84
Kansas City, MO	90.64	101.00	89.60	3.40	33.07	36.41
Lafayette, LA	109.56	100.77	100.99	3.43	43.28	30.76
Las Cruces, NM	114.46	118.68	146.98	3.89	41.11	36.87
Las Vegas, NV	108.58	98.81	101.71	4.55	46.52	20.35
Lexington, KY	97.28	98.17	80.03	3.78	58.71	52.93
Lincoln, NE	157.42	104.71	103.26	3.64	38.48	50.37
Little Rock, AR	116.78	58.25	94.06	3.52	52.55	37.55
Los Angeles, CA	130.00	128.20	132.27	5.54	82.67	36.49
Louisville, KY	82.50	87.22	61.89	4.13	84.44	45.50
Madison, WI	207.78	115.45	65.67	3.59	54.45	43.08

Table continued on following page.

Appendix A: Comparative Statistics A-147

Urban Area	Doctor ($/visit)	Dentist ($/visit)	Optometrist ($/visit)	Gasoline ($/gallon)	Beauty Salon ($/visit)	Men's Shirt ($)
Manchester, NH	175.70	152.18	115.00	4.03	59.17	41.12
Miami, FL	109.83	94.65	100.82	3.81	80.15	24.94
Midland, TX	118.20	107.50	108.50	3.51	45.00	25.17
Milwaukee, WI	181.86	123.58	75.00	3.66	37.70	33.64
Minneapolis, MN	161.06	88.15	100.90	3.94	37.88	35.74
Nashville, TN	106.23	100.08	86.77	3.57	41.35	27.39
New Haven, CT	146.79	125.96	131.33	4.04	46.14	28.74
New Orleans, LA	168.89	125.56	105.55	3.92	42.78	39.00
New York, NY[3]	124.61	125.08	113.20	4.34	68.52	42.89
Oklahoma City, OK	111.16	120.92	115.53	3.36	43.00	21.10
Omaha, NE	140.67	89.91	120.78	3.75	30.74	28.27
Orlando, FL	98.00	108.72	79.50	3.83	60.44	45.42
Philadelphia, PA	136.17	96.17	118.67	4.19	63.11	34.67
Phoenix, AZ	99.00	99.00	117.08	4.30	50.83	19.04
Pittsburgh, PA	98.25	112.80	96.58	3.99	37.03	20.62
Portland, OR	142.04	113.83	122.48	4.72	56.61	32.88
Providence, RI	143.54	117.33	120.06	3.98	51.00	34.08
Provo, UT	105.44	95.74	116.76	4.24	40.94	46.89
Raleigh, NC	121.09	115.41	113.39	3.86	50.42	26.62
Reno, NV	124.83	110.67	109.50	4.63	36.67	21.59
Richmond, VA	145.32	104.74	115.73	3.61	49.08	29.41
Rochester, MN	n/a	n/a	n/a	n/a	n/a	n/a
Sacramento, CA	176.26	109.67	149.00	5.48	57.08	33.30
Saint Louis, MO	86.89	101.96	85.05	3.81	39.83	21.57
Salem, OR	n/a	n/a	n/a	n/a	n/a	n/a
Salt Lake City, UT	114.47	93.33	109.59	4.14	39.28	46.00
San Antonio, TX	123.35	111.47	125.52	3.43	58.84	35.83
San Diego, CA	116.25	118.33	126.18	5.50	66.33	36.49
San Francisco, CA	174.07	148.07	154.96	5.42	85.61	50.77
San Jose, CA	n/a	n/a	n/a	n/a	n/a	n/a
Santa Rosa, CA	n/a	n/a	n/a	n/a	n/a	n/a
Savannah, GA	119.64	141.34	89.22	3.40	37.92	35.96
Seattle, WA	176.92	144.83	170.85	4.95	65.43	43.45
Sioux Falls, SD	164.33	103.08	126.50	3.57	33.33	24.13
Springfield, IL	120.00	103.33	123.00	3.95	28.33	17.09
Tampa, FL	100.17	104.90	106.73	3.80	31.35	28.97
Tucson, AZ	140.00	101.33	108.10	4.09	39.50	37.99
Tulsa, OK	126.65	101.50	105.72	3.23	43.68	29.27
Tuscaloosa, AL	n/a	n/a	n/a	n/a	n/a	n/a
Virginia Beach, VA[4]	88.07	115.80	111.36	3.72	40.74	32.74
Washington, DC	129.71	105.20	75.00	3.98	81.00	37.83
Wichita, KS	106.36	92.39	162.06	3.75	41.30	51.01
Wilmington, NC	n/a	n/a	n/a	n/a	n/a	n/a
Winston-Salem, NC	142.38	133.67	132.58	3.71	45.00	35.83
Worcester, MA	n/a	n/a	n/a	n/a	n/a	n/a
Average*	124.91	107.77	117.66	3.86	43.31	34.21
Minimum*	36.61	58.25	51.79	2.90	22.18	13.05
Maximum*	250.21	162.58	371.96	5.54	85.61	63.54

Note: **Doctor** *(general practitioners routine exam of an established patient);* **Dentist** *(adult teeth cleaning and periodic oral examination);* **Optometrist** *(full vision eye exam for established adult patient);* **Gasoline** *(one gallon regular unleaded, national brand, including all taxes, cash price at self-service pump if available);* **Beauty Salon** *(woman's shampoo, trim, and blow-dry);* **Men's Shirt** *(cotton/polyester dress shirt, pinpoint weave, long sleeves); (*) Average, minimum, and maximum values for all 286 areas in the Cost of Living Index report; n/a not available; In cases where data is not available for the city, data for the metro area or for a neighboring city has been provided and noted as follows: (1) Chapel Hill NC; (2) Middlesex-Monmouth NJ; (3) Brooklyn, NY; (4) Hampton Roads-SE Virginia*
Source: The Council for Community and Economic Research, Cost of Living Index, 2022

A-148　　Appendix A: Comparative Statistics

Number of Medical Professionals

City	Area Covered	MDs[1]	DOs[1,2]	Dentists	Podiatrists	Chiropractors	Optometrists
Albuquerque, NM	Bernalillo County	472.2	22.0	87.6	8.9	25.1	16.3
Allentown, PA	Lehigh County	359.4	84.6	88.1	12.5	28.8	20.8
Anchorage, AK	Anchorage Borough	383.0	45.1	130.5	5.6	64.2	31.2
Ann Arbor, MI	Washtenaw County	1,319.8	42.2	198.4	7.9	26.8	18.4
Athens, GA	Clarke County	326.1	16.3	52.1	4.7	22.5	15.5
Atlanta, GA	Fulton County	536.7	14.7	74.5	5.3	58.4	19.8
Austin, TX	Travis County	327.2	18.8	74.5	4.5	35.0	17.9
Baltimore, MD	Baltimore City	1,113.1	23.8	82.9	8.3	14.9	16.0
Boise City, ID	Ada County	283.7	33.7	81.1	3.9	53.3	20.7
Boston, MA	Suffolk County	1,576.4	17.2	235.9	9.9	15.7	36.8
Boulder, CO	Boulder County	361.2	31.7	107.7	6.1	82.8	27.9
Brownsville, TX	Cameron County	140.1	7.1	31.4	3.1	7.8	6.6
Cape Coral, FL	Lee County	203.1	31.1	53.7	8.1	27.9	13.2
Cedar Rapids, IA	Linn County	182.0	23.5	74.3	7.9	58.5	17.5
Charleston, SC	Charleston County	831.9	31.3	113.3	5.8	52.1	24.5
Charlotte, NC	Mecklenburg County	343.0	16.9	72.0	3.7	35.2	14.5
Chicago, IL	Cook County	434.1	22.5	95.4	12.6	29.2	21.1
Cincinnati, OH	Hamilton County	614.9	25.9	76.1	10.2	20.5	22.8
Clarksville, TN	Montgomery County	97.7	16.3	43.0	2.2	12.3	11.8
Cleveland, OH	Cuyahoga County	715.5	51.1	110.1	18.9	19.1	17.3
College Station, TX	Brazos County	270.8	16.2	55.3	3.4	17.7	16.5
Colorado Springs, CO	El Paso County	207.1	31.6	104.2	5.3	45.4	25.1
Columbia, MO	Boone County	808.6	57.6	71.6	5.4	38.2	28.5
Columbia, SC	Richland County	357.2	15.4	93.7	7.2	22.5	19.8
Columbus, OH	Franklin County	442.5	62.5	93.6	7.6	25.4	28.6
Dallas, TX	Dallas County	357.1	21.3	93.4	4.3	37.6	14.7
Davenport, IA	Scott County	240.7	53.3	81.0	4.6	184.3	17.2
Denver, CO	Denver County	611.2	31.8	81.0	6.5	39.4	16.9
Des Moines, IA	Polk County	215.9	99.2	77.3	11.3	59.4	21.7
Durham, NC	Durham County	1,130.5	16.3	75.4	4.3	19.9	14.1
Edison, NJ	Middlesex County	377.3	20.2	88.4	9.9	24.9	20.0
El Paso, TX	El Paso County	204.1	13.3	47.4	3.9	9.1	10.4
Fargo, ND	Cass County	404.1	21.1	82.5	4.3	75.6	32.7
Fort Collins, CO	Larimer County	251.3	31.4	83.6	6.1	56.8	21.2
Fort Wayne, IN	Allen County	263.0	29.3	66.9	5.9	23.4	26.0
Fort Worth, TX	Tarrant County	190.1	33.9	62.9	4.5	29.2	16.6
Grand Rapids, MI	Kent County	358.3	69.8	76.9	5.0	39.2	25.4
Greeley, CO	Weld County	126.4	18.1	46.2	2.1	23.2	12.9
Green Bay, WI	Brown County	253.8	27.9	80.9	3.0	49.7	18.5
Greensboro, NC	Guilford County	257.0	14.8	60.5	4.8	14.4	10.3
Honolulu, HI	Honolulu County	351.4	16.2	97.1	3.6	20.4	24.8
Houston, TX	Harris County	348.8	12.3	73.7	4.9	23.1	21.2
Huntsville, AL	Madison County	274.6	13.3	51.6	3.3	23.5	19.0
Indianapolis, IN	Marion County	451.2	21.7	92.0	6.4	16.8	20.9
Jacksonville, FL	Duval County	341.1	22.8	79.5	7.1	25.9	15.9
Kansas City, MO	Jackson County	314.4	59.1	91.9	6.4	47.6	20.2
Lafayette, LA	Lafayette Parish	377.7	11.6	71.7	3.7	32.8	14.3
Las Cruces, NM	Dona Ana County	166.0	13.6	59.1	6.3	18.5	8.6
Las Vegas, NV	Clark County	182.9	36.0	65.4	4.5	20.5	14.1
Lexington, KY	Fayette County	764.3	38.2	146.7	7.8	24.5	26.4
Lincoln, NE	Lancaster County	223.6	13.0	102.6	5.5	47.1	21.3
Little Rock, AR	Pulaski County	743.0	15.3	77.7	4.8	22.1	21.9
Los Angeles, CA	Los Angeles County	315.0	14.6	94.2	6.5	30.7	19.7
Louisville, KY	Jefferson County	480.0	18.7	104.9	8.1	27.8	16.6
Madison, WI	Dane County	615.0	20.6	73.4	4.8	45.0	20.9
Manchester, NH	Hillsborough County	240.8	24.4	82.8	5.7	26.2	21.9

Table continued on following page.

Appendix A: Comparative Statistics   A-149

City	Area Covered	MDs[1]	DOs[1,2]	Dentists	Podiatrists	Chiropractors	Optometrists
Miami, FL	Miami-Dade County	375.0	18.6	75.2	10.2	19.4	15.6
Midland, TX	Midland County	157.4	7.6	63.7	2.4	13.1	12.5
Milwaukee, WI	Milwaukee County	388.3	22.2	88.0	7.1	21.1	11.5
Minneapolis, MN	Hennepin County	532.0	24.0	103.5	5.2	77.1	21.6
Nashville, TN	Davidson County	647.1	14.1	81.0	5.3	26.8	17.5
New Haven, CT	New Haven County	577.3	10.3	77.7	9.6	27.2	16.6
New Orleans, LA	Orleans Parish	887.3	24.0	81.2	4.2	10.1	8.2
New York, NY	New York City	471.8	16.8	87.4	13.4	16.3	18.2
Oklahoma City, OK	Oklahoma County	423.1	43.0	109.1	5.3	28.9	20.5
Omaha, NE	Douglas County	547.3	26.0	101.4	5.0	42.2	21.7
Orlando, FL	Orange County	323.9	23.6	51.7	3.8	28.7	13.2
Philadelphia, PA	Philadelphia County	587.8	43.6	81.6	16.8	15.4	19.0
Phoenix, AZ	Maricopa County	255.3	33.2	71.1	7.0	33.9	16.7
Pittsburgh, PA	Allegheny County	640.1	44.3	97.1	9.2	44.0	20.7
Portland, OR	Multnomah County	646.7	32.2	101.6	5.1	76.3	24.8
Providence, RI	Providence County	489.8	17.1	58.3	9.7	21.1	21.6
Provo, UT	Utah County	119.4	20.8	59.3	4.7	26.4	11.7
Raleigh, NC	Wake County	289.4	12.4	72.7	3.7	28.3	16.8
Reno, NV	Washoe County	298.1	20.5	69.5	3.9	29.0	23.9
Richmond, VA	Richmond City	777.8	27.8	150.5	11.9	7.5	16.8
Rochester, MN	Olmsted County	2,470.7	46.0	125.4	6.7	44.1	22.6
Sacramento, CA	Sacramento County	329.3	16.6	80.7	4.6	21.8	18.4
St. Louis, MO	St. Louis City	1,222.5	35.3	63.1	4.8	21.1	19.4
Salem, OR	Marion County	182.0	15.0	84.4	5.8	34.0	16.4
Salt Lake City, UT	Salt Lake County	387.4	18.7	79.5	6.4	28.2	14.1
San Antonio, TX	Bexar County	329.0	18.9	94.2	5.4	17.2	18.9
San Diego, CA	San Diego County	346.3	19.7	96.3	4.7	35.5	20.4
San Francisco, CA	San Francisco County	834.7	13.1	171.0	11.8	43.1	31.8
San Jose, CA	Santa Clara County	445.9	12.0	124.2	6.9	45.0	28.8
Santa Rosa, CA	Sonoma County	284.4	19.0	96.7	7.4	43.0	18.3
Savannah, GA	Chatham County	352.3	19.0	68.5	6.7	20.2	13.8
Seattle, WA	King County	502.8	16.6	113.5	6.3	47.7	22.8
Sioux Falls, SD	Minnehaha County	369.1	23.8	56.1	5.5	58.1	19.0
Springfield, IL	Sangamon County	644.3	24.0	86.3	5.6	39.0	21.6
Tampa, FL	Hillsborough County	366.3	31.8	61.6	6.0	27.7	15.0
Tucson, AZ	Pima County	372.3	24.5	67.2	5.9	19.2	17.0
Tulsa, OK	Tulsa County	264.3	111.5	70.3	4.3	38.8	23.6
Tuscaloosa, AL	Tuscaloosa County	223.2	9.2	44.9	4.0	18.9	15.9
Virginia Beach, VA	Virginia Beach City	259.3	14.6	80.6	6.6	26.2	17.3
Washington, DC	District of Columbia	817.4	19.0	128.8	9.6	10.4	14.0
Wichita, KS	Sedgwick County	252.9	34.0	69.1	1.9	43.3	29.0
Wilmington, NC	New Hanover County	359.2	30.5	82.1	8.7	36.7	24.9
Winston-Salem, NC	Forsyth County	680.1	29.8	65.6	6.0	17.6	18.4
Worcester, MA	Worcester County	360.6	19.0	75.4	6.6	19.8	18.9
U.S.	U.S.	289.3	23.5	72.5	6.2	28.7	17.4

Note: All figures are rates per 100,000 population; Data as of 2021 unless noted; (1) Data as of 2020 and includes all active, non-federal physicians; (2) Doctor of Osteopathic Medicine
Source: U.S. Department of Health and Human Services, Health Resources and Services Administration, Bureau of Health Professions, Area Resource File (ARF) 2021-2022

A-150   Appendix A: Comparative Statistics

Health Insurance Coverage: City

City	With Health Insurance	With Private Health Insurance	With Public Health Insurance	Without Health Insurance	Population Under Age 19 Without Health Insurance
Albuquerque, NM	92.1	60.6	44.2	7.9	4.3
Allentown, PA	88.6	46.4	50.2	11.4	4.7
Anchorage, AK	89.5	69.7	32.7	10.5	7.6
Ann Arbor, MI	97.4	87.5	20.3	2.6	1.3
Athens, GA	87.5	70.8	25.1	12.5	9.1
Atlanta, GA	89.4	70.1	27.0	10.6	6.2
Austin, TX	87.2	74.3	20.3	12.8	7.9
Baltimore, MD	94.1	59.3	45.9	5.9	3.4
Boise City, ID	92.1	75.5	28.2	7.9	4.2
Boston, MA	96.6	68.6	35.9	3.4	1.7
Boulder, CO	96.0	83.6	21.0	4.0	1.1
Brownsville, TX	69.2	37.3	35.7	30.8	18.5
Cape Coral, FL	87.2	64.4	38.6	12.8	10.1
Cedar Rapids, IA	95.2	73.2	34.4	4.8	2.2
Charleston, SC	93.2	79.8	25.0	6.8	2.4
Charlotte, NC	87.2	68.2	26.4	12.8	7.7
Chicago, IL	90.2	61.6	35.5	9.8	3.6
Cincinnati, OH	92.7	60.4	40.5	7.3	5.2
Clarksville, TN	91.5	71.6	34.9	8.5	3.5
Cleveland, OH	92.5	44.5	56.6	7.5	3.3
College Station, TX	91.3	84.1	14.3	8.7	5.6
Colorado Springs, CO	92.1	69.2	36.4	7.9	4.6
Columbia, MO	92.5	80.0	22.1	7.5	3.8
Columbia, SC	91.4	70.7	30.7	8.6	3.4
Columbus, OH	90.7	63.4	34.7	9.3	5.6
Dallas, TX	76.5	53.3	29.3	23.5	16.0
Davenport, IA	93.3	66.2	39.9	6.7	4.9
Denver, CO	90.4	66.9	31.3	9.6	5.5
Des Moines, IA	93.7	63.7	42.0	6.3	2.2
Durham, NC	88.1	69.6	27.9	11.9	7.7
Edison, NJ	95.2	80.5	23.8	4.8	1.9
El Paso, TX	80.0	54.6	33.9	20.0	10.2
Fargo, ND	93.8	79.9	25.1	6.2	3.8
Fort Collins, CO	93.9	78.5	23.9	6.1	5.1
Fort Wayne, IN	90.8	64.6	37.0	9.2	6.2
Fort Worth, TX	81.2	61.1	26.9	18.8	12.5
Grand Rapids, MI	91.6	63.6	37.7	8.4	4.9
Greeley, CO	90.2	60.8	40.2	9.8	5.1
Green Bay, WI	91.7	64.2	36.7	8.3	5.5
Greensboro, NC	90.3	66.3	34.1	9.7	4.1
Honolulu, HI	96.0	76.9	36.2	4.0	1.9
Houston, TX	76.2	51.7	30.5	23.8	14.5
Huntsville, AL	90.1	72.6	33.3	9.9	3.9
Indianapolis, IN	90.2	62.4	37.4	9.8	6.3
Jacksonville, FL	87.9	64.4	34.2	12.1	6.9
Kansas City, MO	88.2	68.9	28.9	11.8	6.9
Lafayette, LA	91.5	64.4	38.6	8.5	4.0
Las Cruces, NM	92.0	54.9	50.8	8.0	2.2
Las Vegas, NV	87.1	60.7	36.0	12.9	8.6
Lexington, KY	93.2	70.9	33.1	6.8	3.1
Lincoln, NE	92.6	77.1	26.4	7.4	4.9
Little Rock, AR	91.3	63.9	38.7	8.7	4.4
Los Angeles, CA	89.3	55.1	40.8	10.7	3.8
Louisville, KY	94.4	66.2	41.2	5.6	3.4
Madison, WI	96.0	82.9	23.3	4.0	2.4

Table continued on following page.

Appendix A: Comparative Statistics   A-151

City	With Health Insurance	With Private Health Insurance	With Public Health Insurance	Without Health Insurance	Population Under Age 19 Without Health Insurance
Manchester, NH	90.9	65.9	35.1	9.1	3.8
Miami, FL	81.0	49.9	34.5	19.0	8.1
Midland, TX	83.5	69.9	20.7	16.5	14.2
Milwaukee, WI	90.6	54.1	44.8	9.4	3.5
Minneapolis, MN	93.9	68.8	33.0	6.1	3.1
Nashville, TN	87.6	68.7	29.3	12.4	8.2
New Haven, CT	92.2	51.9	46.3	7.8	3.1
New Orleans, LA	91.2	54.1	45.3	8.8	5.0
New York, NY	93.1	58.8	43.6	6.9	2.4
Oklahoma City, OK	85.6	64.7	32.3	14.4	7.5
Omaha, NE	89.7	70.8	28.7	10.3	7.0
Orlando, FL	84.9	64.3	27.5	15.1	8.9
Philadelphia, PA	92.6	57.7	45.8	7.4	4.1
Phoenix, AZ	85.5	57.9	35.0	14.5	10.0
Pittsburgh, PA	94.5	73.0	33.7	5.5	3.9
Portland, OR	93.9	72.1	31.8	6.1	2.3
Providence, RI	93.2	55.8	45.4	6.8	3.9
Provo, UT	89.3	78.1	17.5	10.7	10.8
Raleigh, NC	89.6	74.3	24.5	10.4	6.1
Reno, NV	90.0	69.1	30.5	10.0	8.4
Richmond, VA	89.3	63.7	35.5	10.7	6.9
Rochester, MN	96.2	79.1	30.9	3.8	2.0
Sacramento, CA	94.3	64.2	40.8	5.7	2.4
St. Louis, MO	89.5	62.6	35.2	10.5	4.3
Salem, OR	92.9	64.7	41.5	7.1	2.1
Salt Lake City, UT	88.9	74.0	22.7	11.1	9.9
San Antonio, TX	82.8	58.9	33.4	17.2	9.2
San Diego, CA	92.8	71.1	31.1	7.2	3.7
San Francisco, CA	96.4	76.2	29.5	3.6	1.9
San Jose, CA	94.9	72.9	29.9	5.1	2.1
Santa Rosa, CA	92.4	68.5	36.9	7.6	5.5
Savannah, GA	84.3	58.4	35.4	15.7	7.7
Seattle, WA	95.6	80.7	23.5	4.4	1.5
Sioux Falls, SD	92.0	77.5	26.1	8.0	5.2
Springfield, IL	95.7	69.7	41.8	4.3	1.4
Tampa, FL	88.9	63.5	33.0	11.1	5.1
Tucson, AZ	88.7	57.2	42.3	11.3	7.6
Tulsa, OK	83.3	58.7	35.8	16.7	8.7
Tuscaloosa, AL	92.1	70.9	32.9	7.9	2.3
Virginia Beach, VA	92.9	79.8	27.6	7.1	4.3
Washington, DC	96.6	71.9	34.7	3.4	2.2
Wichita, KS	87.8	65.8	33.6	12.2	5.8
Wilmington, NC	88.9	70.3	32.6	11.1	6.5
Winston-Salem, NC	87.7	62.3	36.6	12.3	4.5
Worcester, MA	97.0	61.1	46.4	3.0	1.5
U.S.	91.2	67.8	35.4	8.8	5.3

Note: Figures are percentages that cover the civilian noninstitutionalized population
Source: U.S. Census Bureau, 2017-2021 American Community Survey 5-Year Estimates

A-152 Appendix A: Comparative Statistics

Health Insurance Coverage: Metro Area

Metro Area	With Health Insurance	With Private Health Insurance	With Public Health Insurance	Without Health Insurance	Population Under Age 19 Without Health Insurance
Albuquerque, NM	92.0	60.1	45.5	8.0	4.7
Allentown, PA	94.6	72.8	35.7	5.4	2.9
Anchorage, AK	88.6	68.1	33.5	11.4	9.0
Ann Arbor, MI	96.6	82.5	27.2	3.4	1.8
Athens, GA	88.1	70.2	27.8	11.9	7.0
Atlanta, GA	87.4	69.4	27.2	12.6	7.9
Austin, TX	87.7	75.1	21.7	12.3	8.1
Baltimore, MD	95.2	75.1	33.7	4.8	3.2
Boise City, ID	90.5	72.3	30.7	9.5	5.4
Boston, MA	97.0	76.8	32.6	3.0	1.6
Boulder, CO	95.4	79.9	26.0	4.6	2.3
Brownsville, TX	71.5	38.4	38.3	28.5	17.1
Cape Coral, FL	86.9	61.9	43.5	13.1	9.8
Cedar Rapids, IA	96.2	75.9	33.5	3.8	1.8
Charleston, SC	89.7	71.5	31.4	10.3	6.7
Charlotte, NC	89.7	70.1	29.6	10.3	5.5
Chicago, IL	92.4	70.5	31.6	7.6	3.3
Cincinnati, OH	94.6	72.7	33.0	5.4	3.5
Clarksville, TN	91.6	69.8	36.8	8.4	5.6
Cleveland, OH	94.6	68.7	38.7	5.4	3.4
College Station, TX	87.5	73.3	23.8	12.5	8.4
Colorado Springs, CO	92.7	71.3	35.4	7.3	4.7
Columbia, MO	92.4	78.6	25.0	7.6	4.7
Columbia, SC	90.4	69.8	34.4	9.6	4.5
Columbus, OH	93.0	71.1	31.8	7.0	4.5
Dallas, TX	83.4	66.4	24.5	16.6	11.7
Davenport, IA	94.5	71.5	37.8	5.5	3.5
Denver, CO	92.2	72.6	29.1	7.8	4.7
Des Moines, IA	95.7	76.3	31.8	4.3	2.2
Durham, NC	90.0	71.8	30.0	10.0	5.7
Edison, NJ	93.2	67.3	36.5	6.8	3.0
El Paso, TX	78.7	52.8	33.7	21.3	10.9
Fargo, ND	94.5	80.8	25.2	5.5	4.4
Fort Collins, CO	94.0	76.6	28.9	6.0	4.4
Fort Wayne, IN	91.9	69.8	33.3	8.1	6.1
Fort Worth, TX	83.4	66.4	24.5	16.6	11.7
Grand Rapids, MI	95.0	76.1	31.3	5.0	3.0
Greeley, CO	91.2	68.7	32.3	8.8	4.7
Green Bay, WI	94.9	74.8	31.6	5.1	3.7
Greensboro, NC	89.9	64.9	36.0	10.1	4.5
Honolulu, HI	96.5	79.2	34.3	3.5	2.3
Houston, TX	81.3	61.6	26.6	18.7	12.3
Huntsville, AL	91.9	77.2	29.5	8.1	3.1
Indianapolis, IN	92.4	71.4	31.8	7.6	5.2
Jacksonville, FL	89.3	68.7	33.1	10.7	6.7
Kansas City, MO	90.9	74.8	27.2	9.1	5.6
Lafayette, LA	91.9	61.3	41.3	8.1	3.5
Las Cruces, NM	89.4	48.3	52.6	10.6	4.8
Las Vegas, NV	88.1	63.3	34.7	11.9	8.0
Lexington, KY	93.9	71.2	34.6	6.1	3.4
Lincoln, NE	93.1	78.1	26.2	6.9	4.7
Little Rock, AR	92.3	66.2	39.1	7.7	4.3
Los Angeles, CA	91.4	61.2	37.6	8.6	3.6
Louisville, KY	94.6	70.7	37.3	5.4	3.5
Madison, WI	96.1	83.0	25.6	3.9	2.4

Table continued on following page.

Appendix A: Comparative Statistics   A-153

Metro Area	With Health Insurance	With Private Health Insurance	With Public Health Insurance	Without Health Insurance	Population Under Age 19 Without Health Insurance
Manchester, NH	93.8	77.2	28.7	6.2	3.4
Miami, FL	85.3	59.9	33.0	14.7	8.3
Midland, TX	84.0	69.8	21.3	16.0	13.0
Milwaukee, WI	94.3	71.8	34.1	5.7	2.8
Minneapolis, MN	95.7	77.9	29.9	4.3	2.8
Nashville, TN	90.5	72.7	28.4	9.5	5.7
New Haven, CT	94.9	66.9	39.6	5.1	2.5
New Orleans, LA	91.2	58.8	42.8	8.8	4.5
New York, NY	93.2	67.3	36.5	6.8	3.0
Oklahoma City, OK	87.4	68.4	31.5	12.6	6.9
Omaha, NE	92.3	75.4	27.6	7.7	5.0
Orlando, FL	87.8	65.8	31.3	12.2	6.8
Philadelphia, PA	94.7	73.0	34.8	5.3	3.2
Phoenix, AZ	89.2	65.8	34.2	10.8	8.6
Pittsburgh, PA	96.3	76.2	36.5	3.7	1.9
Portland, OR	93.9	73.0	32.9	6.1	3.1
Providence, RI	96.0	70.2	39.4	4.0	2.2
Provo, UT	92.2	82.4	17.0	7.8	6.2
Raleigh, NC	90.9	75.9	25.2	9.1	5.2
Reno, NV	90.2	69.8	31.2	9.8	7.8
Richmond, VA	92.5	74.5	31.1	7.5	4.7
Rochester, MN	95.7	79.6	30.8	4.3	3.3
Sacramento, CA	95.1	70.1	38.0	4.9	2.6
St. Louis, MO	93.7	74.5	30.5	6.3	3.4
Salem, OR	92.2	63.8	41.9	7.8	3.1
Salt Lake City, UT	90.2	77.7	20.2	9.8	8.2
San Antonio, TX	85.0	64.7	31.2	15.0	8.9
San Diego, CA	92.5	69.4	33.6	7.5	3.9
San Francisco, CA	95.9	76.0	30.5	4.1	2.3
San Jose, CA	95.8	77.5	26.7	4.2	1.9
Santa Rosa, CA	94.1	72.5	36.2	5.9	3.5
Savannah, GA	87.2	68.1	30.9	12.8	6.3
Seattle, WA	94.3	75.8	29.2	5.7	2.6
Sioux Falls, SD	92.8	79.1	25.2	7.2	4.7
Springfield, IL	96.2	74.4	37.3	3.8	1.4
Tampa, FL	88.3	63.7	36.4	11.7	6.2
Tucson, AZ	91.1	62.9	42.4	8.9	6.9
Tulsa, OK	86.3	65.3	33.3	13.7	7.7
Tuscaloosa, AL	92.6	70.5	34.5	7.4	2.6
Virginia Beach, VA	92.3	74.5	32.6	7.7	4.4
Washington, DC	92.7	77.8	26.4	7.3	4.5
Wichita, KS	89.8	70.6	31.6	10.2	5.2
Wilmington, NC	89.7	72.8	32.3	10.3	7.2
Winston-Salem, NC	89.0	65.0	36.4	11.0	4.8
Worcester, MA	97.4	73.0	37.5	2.6	1.3
U.S.	91.2	67.8	35.4	8.8	5.3

Note: Figures are percentages that cover the civilian noninstitutionalized population; Figures cover the Metropolitan Statistical Area (MSA)—see Appendix B for areas included
Source: U.S. Census Bureau, 2017-2021 American Community Survey 5-Year Estimates

A-154 Appendix A: Comparative Statistics

Crime Rate: City

City	Total Crime	Violent Crime Rate				Property Crime Rate		
		Murder	Rape	Robbery	Aggrav. Assault	Burglary	Larceny -Theft	Motor Vehicle Theft
Albuquerque, NM	6,355.7	14.2	78.5	256.0	994.9	902.9	3,225.8	883.3
Allentown, PA[1]	2,669.6	5.7	52.5	139.5	188.7	427.6	1,656.1	199.4
Anchorage, AK	4,659.4	6.3	194.8	194.8	816.4	504.2	2,541.7	401.2
Ann Arbor, MI	1,563.2	0.8	40.6	31.5	170.7	126.8	1,125.6	67.1
Athens, GA	3,463.9	3.1	81.9	79.6	345.7	465.9	2,213.8	273.9
Atlanta, GA[2]	5,423.2	17.7	49.4	221.5	480.1	621.2	3,366.4	666.8
Austin, TX	4,098.2	4.4	47.8	110.1	304.7	477.3	2,747.3	406.6
Baltimore, MD[1]	6,169.9	58.3	54.2	813.1	933.1	906.5	2,745.1	659.5
Boise City, ID	1,933.2	1.7	73.5	23.8	193.8	207.2	1,312.6	120.7
Boston, MA	2,490.8	8.3	26.4	131.8	457.9	243.5	1,439.4	183.6
Boulder, CO	4,092.0	1.9	29.1	67.5	223.3	613.5	2,808.7	348.0
Brownsville, TX	2,250.2	3.8	45.2	83.3	269.6	219.5	1,563.0	65.9
Cape Coral, FL	1,195.5	0.5	9.0	10.0	108.3	152.9	848.1	66.7
Cedar Rapids, IA	3,488.4	8.2	11.9	75.9	225.6	619.4	2,132.8	414.7
Charleston, SC	2,771.1	12.2	38.7	71.6	343.2	233.6	1,747.4	324.5
Charlotte, NC	4,076.6	12.4	25.6	184.0	614.4	449.9	2,478.9	311.4
Chicago, IL	n/a	28.6	50.0	292.1	616.2	320.9	n/a	373.2
Cincinnati, OH	4,576.3	30.2	70.6	246.1	546.1	762.0	2,427.1	494.2
Clarksville, TN	2,852.9	9.3	52.1	48.4	500.1	273.6	1,715.6	253.8
Cleveland, OH	5,727.5	42.2	103.7	420.2	1,090.7	973.8	2,321.2	775.7
College Station, TX	2,082.2	1.7	45.5	22.3	110.1	265.7	1,463.2	173.8
Colorado Springs, CO	3,976.6	7.4	82.5	77.5	429.6	533.5	2,344.8	501.4
Columbia, MO	3,106.6	10.4	71.3	46.5	314.0	323.6	1,985.1	355.7
Columbia, SC	5,227.8	14.4	65.3	156.3	516.0	552.4	3,442.2	481.1
Columbus, OH	3,686.0	19.1	89.5	197.1	249.9	609.1	2,180.6	340.7
Dallas, TX	4,291.0	17.3	41.7	241.5	544.2	727.6	1,955.6	763.1
Davenport, IA	4,661.8	9.8	65.8	133.6	527.5	895.8	2,568.6	460.7
Denver, CO	5,506.6	13.1	90.8	165.1	588.9	708.0	2,800.8	1,139.9
Des Moines, IA	4,606.3	15.3	55.3	114.3	519.8	894.1	2,347.1	660.5
Durham, NC	4,596.6	12.6	43.9	219.7	582.6	668.9	2,730.2	338.7
Edison, NJ	1,242.2	1.0	9.0	31.1	62.3	131.5	889.7	117.5
El Paso, TX	1,557.6	4.1	38.1	42.2	231.9	123.6	1,057.2	60.6
Fargo, ND	3,929.0	5.5	84.3	48.1	322.2	800.5	2,302.1	366.4
Fort Collins, CO[1]	2,389.9	0.6	24.0	21.1	171.5	204.8	1,834.5	133.4
Fort Wayne, IN	2,659.5	14.3	35.6	90.0	272.9	240.6	1,818.8	187.3
Fort Worth, TX	3,274.2	11.8	48.0	93.3	387.9	366.9	1,988.9	377.4
Grand Rapids, MI	2,666.0	13.8	59.7	94.8	544.2	228.6	1,437.9	286.9
Greeley, CO	2,888.6	8.1	48.0	70.6	298.6	333.9	1,774.6	354.7
Green Bay, WI	2,056.4	5.7	67.8	43.0	410.9	196.8	1,222.2	109.9
Greensboro, NC	4,513.0	19.7	31.7	193.7	656.6	737.6	2,501.9	371.8
Honolulu, HI	n/a	n/a	n/a	n/a	n/a	n/a	n/a	n/a
Houston, TX	5,435.1	17.0	48.5	373.2	817.5	672.9	2,875.9	630.0
Huntsville, AL	n/a	n/a	n/a	n/a	n/a	n/a	n/a	n/a
Indianapolis, IN	4,440.6	24.3	64.3	243.2	538.9	580.6	2,376.9	612.5
Jacksonville, FL	3,569.3	15.2	49.5	100.8	532.3	419.3	2,129.5	322.6
Kansas City, MO	5,705.4	35.2	76.5	257.3	1,216.8	615.2	2,595.1	909.2
Lafayette, LA	5,081.3	11.1	13.4	116.0	421.5	843.9	3,352.6	322.9
Las Cruces, NM[1]	4,077.5	9.7	61.8	55.1	370.0	631.8	2,652.6	296.6
Las Vegas, NV	2,738.2	5.7	63.1	100.8	358.1	416.8	1,390.7	403.0
Lexington, KY	3,191.6	8.6	54.6	102.8	154.1	445.0	2,108.3	318.2
Lincoln, NE[1]	3,133.7	1.7	110.9	57.0	213.3	339.4	2,255.4	155.9
Little Rock, AR	6,707.0	24.8	99.1	190.2	1,535.8	772.4	3,572.3	512.4
Los Angeles, CA	2,869.9	8.8	49.6	200.3	463.3	344.3	1,274.6	529.1
Louisville, KY[1]	4,578.4	13.9	29.8	149.2	494.0	638.9	2,670.2	582.4

Table continued on following page.

Appendix A: Comparative Statistics   A-155

City	Total Crime	Violent Crime Rate				Property Crime Rate		
		Murder	Rape	Robbery	Aggrav. Assault	Burglary	Larceny -Theft	Motor Vehicle Theft
Madison, WI	3,099.3	3.8	28.2	62.8	225.7	497.5	2,034.7	246.6
Manchester, NH	2,858.0	4.4	64.6	97.3	426.5	253.9	1,854.6	156.6
Miami, FL	3,305.4	12.8	19.7	128.1	394.9	305.2	2,104.0	340.7
Midland, TX	2,436.7	6.6	53.8	33.2	271.0	268.4	1,494.1	309.6
Milwaukee, WI	4,325.4	32.4	73.2	326.8	1,164.5	578.5	1,388.2	761.8
Minneapolis, MN	5,713.0	18.2	83.0	409.5	644.2	899.8	2,747.1	911.3
Nashville, TN	5,228.7	16.4	56.0	253.2	830.1	544.3	3,086.9	441.9
New Haven, CT	4,218.8	16.1	22.3	257.9	411.4	419.8	2,507.3	584.0
New Orleans, LA	5,863.9	51.0	180.8	280.9	811.6	506.4	3,138.3	894.9
New York, NY	2,136.3	5.6	27.1	158.8	386.2	167.5	1,279.4	111.5
Oklahoma City, OK	4,621.5	9.5	84.2	123.1	509.1	881.3	2,444.3	569.9
Omaha, NE	3,805.8	7.7	73.1	96.6	453.9	316.7	2,227.2	630.7
Orlando, FL	4,663.8	10.6	57.6	172.8	619.4	408.4	3,003.8	391.3
Philadelphia, PA[2]	4,005.6	22.1	69.0	331.6	486.0	409.4	2,329.5	357.9
Phoenix, AZ	3,788.0	10.9	62.5	191.8	533.2	433.4	2,121.4	434.7
Pittsburgh, PA[2]	3,594.8	18.8	40.0	230.0	289.9	443.2	2,331.9	241.0
Portland, OR	5,261.6	8.0	39.5	121.7	353.4	567.0	3,211.0	960.9
Providence, RI	2,900.8	9.5	36.7	101.9	338.0	335.2	1,776.7	302.9
Provo, UT[1]	1,623.0	0.9	37.5	11.1	65.7	139.1	1,259.5	109.2
Raleigh, NC	2,412.8	4.4	34.2	97.0	256.5	270.0	1,468.3	282.4
Reno, NV	2,710.2	6.6	108.4	110.4	338.0	426.4	1,345.1	375.4
Richmond, VA	3,269.8	28.3	8.6	117.4	194.6	330.4	2,328.7	261.8
Rochester, MN	2,172.3	4.2	61.5	36.6	147.1	275.9	1,519.1	128.0
Sacramento, CA	3,428.4	8.1	24.1	169.3	481.8	546.0	1,715.2	483.8
Saint Louis, MO	7,846.6	88.1	78.4	416.2	1,433.5	855.2	3,895.8	1,079.3
Salem, OR	4,187.2	1.1	15.9	83.8	294.4	383.8	2,780.4	627.9
Salt Lake City, UT	8,274.5	8.4	137.0	240.9	536.1	764.1	5,503.8	1,084.1
San Antonio, TX	4,362.2	8.3	75.5	137.5	514.2	503.4	2,679.8	443.7
San Diego, CA	2,060.6	3.9	33.7	84.0	247.3	231.2	1,116.0	344.5
San Francisco, CA	4,938.4	5.4	22.5	270.9	245.3	845.4	2,872.2	676.8
San Jose, CA	2,741.2	3.9	55.0	115.1	251.0	392.9	1,237.2	686.2
Santa Rosa, CA	2,120.0	2.3	62.2	76.3	375.3	306.3	1,059.7	237.9
Savannah, GA[2]	2,865.5	11.6	35.1	110.2	248.5	364.9	1,824.4	270.8
Seattle, WA	5,498.9	6.7	39.0	190.7	389.9	1,351.5	2,884.6	636.5
Sioux Falls, SD	3,729.0	6.9	51.8	54.4	484.6	365.1	2,273.0	493.1
Springfield, IL	n/a	9.7	88.7	171.2	676.8	822.6	n/a	223.0
Tampa, FL	1,885.4	10.1	24.8	79.8	405.5	227.1	980.2	157.8
Tucson, AZ	4,319.0	11.1	84.1	177.7	425.3	381.0	2,898.7	341.2
Tulsa, OK	6,244.2	17.9	94.0	184.3	836.5	1,095.8	3,045.0	970.7
Tuscaloosa, AL[2]	4,843.6	4.9	46.2	137.6	316.4	739.9	3,289.0	309.5
Virginia Beach, VA	1,610.5	3.8	13.3	27.5	54.1	110.7	1,262.7	138.4
Washington, DC	4,389.2	27.8	43.1	309.8	577.3	275.4	2,683.2	472.8
Wichita, KS[1]	6,462.8	9.0	94.1	118.2	919.8	686.3	4,044.6	590.9
Wilmington, NC	3,175.8	17.5	52.5	113.7	445.2	473.0	1,915.8	158.2
Winston-Salem, NC	n/a	n/a	n/a	n/a	n/a	n/a	n/a	n/a
Worcester, MA	2,631.3	5.4	21.6	113.6	491.8	360.8	1,396.3	241.8
U.S.	2,356.7	6.5	38.4	73.9	279.7	314.2	1,398.0	246.0

Note: Figures are crimes per 100,000 population in 2020 except where noted; n/a not available; (1) 2019 data; (2) 2018 data; Due to the transition to the National Incident-Based Reporting System (NIBRS), limited city and metro area data was released for 2021
Source: FBI Uniform Crime Reports, 2018, 2019, 2020

A-156   Appendix A: Comparative Statistics

Crime Rate: Suburbs

Suburbs[1]	Total Crime	Violent Crime Rate				Property Crime Rate		
		Murder	Rape	Robbery	Aggrav. Assault	Burglary	Larceny -Theft	Motor Vehicle Theft
Albuquerque, NM	2,025.9	1.9	34.6	40.4	405.3	354.2	870.1	319.4
Allentown, PA	n/a	n/a	n/a	n/a	n/a	n/a	n/a	n/a
Anchorage, AK	3,312.3	0.0	63.6	42.4	445.2	233.2	2,247.1	280.9
Ann Arbor, MI	1,734.3	3.2	74.1	38.7	378.3	167.6	942.7	129.7
Athens, GA	1,270.6	2.3	20.5	11.4	171.1	219.0	735.7	110.6
Atlanta, GA[3]	2,666.3	4.6	24.0	82.5	168.8	373.2	1,770.4	242.7
Austin, TX	1,578.6	2.3	40.3	25.2	129.8	227.0	1,028.7	125.3
Baltimore, MD[2]	2,213.3	3.9	31.8	88.1	260.3	217.8	1,485.2	126.1
Boise City, ID	1,206.5	1.9	52.0	6.9	189.1	178.4	674.0	104.3
Boston, MA	1,043.0	1.2	21.0	22.6	147.3	96.5	677.6	76.8
Boulder, CO	2,552.6	0.9	66.0	30.7	181.8	304.8	1,686.2	282.2
Brownsville, TX	2,358.5	2.5	38.8	39.2	248.9	317.7	1,598.9	112.6
Cape Coral, FL	1,333.2	5.3	37.6	48.3	222.8	148.9	761.7	108.6
Cedar Rapids, IA	1,291.6	0.7	39.3	10.0	135.0	318.6	660.1	127.9
Charleston, SC	2,958.7	11.2	35.6	81.5	313.9	324.5	1,914.7	277.3
Charlotte, NC	n/a	n/a	n/a	n/a	n/a	n/a	n/a	n/a
Chicago, IL	n/a	n/a	n/a	n/a	n/a	n/a	n/a	n/a
Cincinnati, OH	1,469.5	1.9	27.0	24.3	78.3	177.6	1,049.2	111.1
Clarksville, TN	1,659.2	4.0	32.5	25.9	161.9	300.0	988.2	146.7
Cleveland, OH	1,328.9	3.0	20.9	35.0	104.7	154.4	907.3	103.7
College Station, TX	2,209.2	5.4	86.2	41.4	262.1	349.1	1,310.7	154.2
Colorado Springs, CO	1,620.4	4.1	66.6	24.3	191.2	193.8	966.8	173.6
Columbia, MO	1,789.7	2.3	52.8	19.9	179.4	218.1	1,128.2	188.8
Columbia, SC	3,572.6	8.2	37.6	61.2	415.2	504.0	2,183.1	363.3
Columbus, OH	1,664.0	1.5	28.2	27.2	77.2	205.1	1,223.7	101.1
Dallas, TX	n/a	n/a	n/a	n/a	n/a	n/a	n/a	n/a
Davenport, IA	n/a	5.8	57.2	48.2	268.5	345.6	n/a	174.3
Denver, CO	3,233.8	3.8	57.7	70.7	238.2	357.6	1,904.0	601.8
Des Moines, IA	1,384.2	2.2	25.9	9.9	141.1	218.8	859.4	126.9
Durham, NC	1,768.6	4.6	17.6	32.3	169.1	319.6	1,113.7	111.7
Edison, NJ	n/a	n/a	n/a	n/a	n/a	n/a	n/a	n/a
El Paso, TX	1,026.7	3.1	36.2	20.0	217.8	121.7	554.9	73.0
Fargo, ND	2,397.0	5.8	53.5	17.3	159.7	489.9	1,455.9	214.9
Fort Collins, CO[2]	1,855.9	1.1	44.9	14.6	189.3	184.4	1,296.7	124.9
Fort Wayne, IN	988.4	1.4	22.3	16.7	146.5	136.7	579.0	85.8
Fort Worth, TX	n/a	n/a	n/a	n/a	n/a	n/a	n/a	n/a
Grand Rapids, MI	1,390.3	2.5	70.8	21.3	172.1	149.8	837.9	135.8
Greeley, CO	2,286.0	3.2	56.2	25.4	188.9	212.4	1,410.9	389.1
Green Bay, WI	816.1	0.9	22.7	3.2	54.1	122.4	580.0	32.8
Greensboro, NC	2,458.1	7.5	28.3	53.6	282.3	415.1	1,477.5	193.7
Honolulu, HI	n/a	n/a	n/a	n/a	n/a	n/a	n/a	n/a
Houston, TX	2,188.3	5.4	42.8	68.3	212.3	270.6	1,338.7	250.2
Huntsville, AL	n/a	n/a	n/a	n/a	n/a	n/a	n/a	n/a
Indianapolis, IN	n/a	n/a	n/a	n/a	n/a	n/a	n/a	n/a
Jacksonville, FL	1,375.4	2.4	28.0	23.8	169.5	172.0	880.2	99.5
Kansas City, MO	n/a	n/a	n/a	n/a	n/a	n/a	n/a	n/a
Lafayette, LA	2,189.8	7.4	23.9	35.5	344.1	400.2	1,210.2	168.4
Las Cruces, NM[2]	1,781.8	1.7	52.3	10.5	546.8	362.8	699.5	108.1
Las Vegas, NV	1,944.4	5.0	31.6	99.0	209.5	261.9	1,057.0	280.4
Lexington, KY	2,178.6	1.5	29.6	28.6	75.6	317.7	1,508.9	216.6
Lincoln, NE[2]	1,017.1	0.0	77.9	0.0	41.1	119.0	705.4	73.6
Little Rock, AR	3,185.5	8.9	56.1	52.4	493.6	457.2	1,830.0	287.2
Los Angeles, CA	2,435.2	4.2	28.0	102.7	228.4	355.9	1,303.4	412.7
Louisville, KY[2]	1,847.8	1.9	21.7	30.8	98.0	230.7	1,263.0	201.7

Table continued on following page.

Appendix A: Comparative Statistics   A-157

Suburbs[1]	Total Crime	Violent Crime Rate				Property Crime Rate		
		Murder	Rape	Robbery	Aggrav. Assault	Burglary	Larceny -Theft	Motor Vehicle Theft
Madison, WI	1,304.6	1.7	21.3	17.4	85.0	157.7	930.9	90.6
Manchester, NH	801.4	0.0	34.0	8.8	36.6	64.3	609.1	48.6
Miami, FL	2,551.6	7.0	31.8	85.7	280.9	220.2	1,689.2	236.7
Midland, TX	2,973.5	8.2	30.0	13.6	360.1	349.2	1,606.8	605.6
Milwaukee, WI	1,624.3	1.5	20.3	29.8	78.2	114.7	1,274.1	105.6
Minneapolis, MN	n/a	n/a	n/a	n/a	n/a	n/a	n/a	n/a
Nashville, TN	1,755.3	3.0	29.0	27.7	266.9	199.9	1,090.1	138.6
New Haven, CT	2,076.3	4.2	20.2	61.1	82.9	193.7	1,413.6	300.7
New Orleans, LA	2,268.4	8.6	24.1	45.2	233.6	244.1	1,581.0	131.9
New York, NY	n/a	n/a	n/a	n/a	n/a	n/a	n/a	n/a
Oklahoma City, OK	2,313.8	6.3	37.1	28.2	177.5	392.7	1,432.3	239.8
Omaha, NE	1,602.2	1.5	37.1	23.2	163.9	191.7	977.7	207.1
Orlando, FL	1,994.4	5.4	40.1	59.7	267.8	251.1	1,217.2	153.1
Philadelphia, PA[3]	1,935.5	7.6	16.3	96.8	235.8	202.8	1,235.3	140.9
Phoenix, AZ	2,118.2	3.8	35.2	43.8	211.2	276.5	1,380.4	167.3
Pittsburgh, PA[3]	1,402.7	3.5	23.7	33.2	168.7	159.1	958.5	55.9
Portland, OR	n/a	n/a	41.7	37.9	150.0	262.3	1,381.0	296.2
Providence, RI	1,264.5	1.7	40.2	29.7	189.1	149.7	749.5	104.7
Provo, UT[2]	1,312.0	1.1	30.2	7.2	46.1	131.5	1,018.1	77.8
Raleigh, NC	1,376.5	2.8	12.2	21.8	100.3	201.3	956.0	82.2
Reno, NV	1,808.3	4.5	59.7	39.2	243.4	304.1	959.0	198.4
Richmond, VA	1,784.2	5.9	23.2	30.9	126.7	136.3	1,342.0	119.3
Rochester, MN	824.5	1.0	36.1	2.9	75.1	191.3	456.7	61.5
Sacramento, CA	2,102.6	3.8	27.9	64.5	196.3	323.1	1,274.4	212.6
Saint Louis, MO	n/a	5.6	29.6	39.0	241.8	262.7	n/a	283.8
Salem, OR	2,400.4	1.9	29.2	29.6	123.4	258.0	1,578.0	380.3
Salt Lake City, UT	3,411.8	4.1	53.4	45.4	176.7	364.6	2,327.6	439.9
San Antonio, TX	1,759.0	3.9	36.2	22.5	151.5	297.8	1,074.4	172.6
San Diego, CA	1,655.8	3.1	25.4	69.7	229.9	210.0	887.9	229.9
San Francisco, CA	3,106.9	5.3	33.9	157.3	219.7	345.9	1,757.2	587.6
San Jose, CA	2,331.9	1.7	27.1	56.1	116.6	343.6	1,474.4	312.3
Santa Rosa, CA	1,554.3	1.9	41.1	41.8	329.5	232.8	807.9	99.2
Savannah, GA[3]	3,497.3	5.3	37.2	67.1	245.2	497.1	2,366.1	279.1
Seattle, WA	3,022.6	4.0	29.2	70.5	168.3	442.6	1,893.4	414.8
Sioux Falls, SD	1,410.7	2.3	31.5	8.2	172.8	462.4	597.9	135.5
Springfield, IL	n/a	1.1	36.1	21.9	259.1	349.8	n/a	122.4
Tampa, FL	1,648.1	3.1	34.5	42.4	204.3	176.5	1,068.6	118.6
Tucson, AZ	2,196.1	4.9	16.1	37.5	172.4	257.0	1,582.6	125.6
Tulsa, OK	2,005.9	3.6	31.0	21.9	174.2	380.7	1,150.1	244.3
Tuscaloosa, AL[3]	2,503.0	3.3	28.5	41.7	249.6	518.3	1,449.1	212.5
Virginia Beach, VA	2,536.3	12.5	30.6	67.3	327.6	197.9	1,701.5	198.8
Washington, DC	n/a	n/a	n/a	n/a	n/a	n/a	n/a	n/a
Wichita, KS[2]	n/a	1.6	42.3	14.5	156.8	271.8	n/a	129.8
Wilmington, NC	1,803.5	2.3	27.7	24.3	135.2	300.9	1,220.4	92.7
Winston-Salem, NC	n/a	n/a	n/a	n/a	n/a	n/a	n/a	n/a
Worcester, MA	922.7	0.4	32.3	16.3	166.2	115.4	522.3	69.7
U.S.	2,356.7	6.5	38.4	73.9	279.7	314.2	1,398.0	246.0

Note: Figures are crimes per 100,000 population in 2020 except where noted; n/a not available; (1) All areas within the metro area that are located outside the city limits; (2) 2019 data; (3) 2018 data; Due to the transition to the National Incident-Based Reporting System (NIBRS), limited city and metro area data was released for 2021
Source: FBI Uniform Crime Reports, 2018, 2019, 2020

A-158   Appendix A: Comparative Statistics

Crime Rate: Metro Area

Metro Area[1]	Total Crime	Violent Crime Rate				Property Crime Rate		
		Murder	Rape	Robbery	Aggrav. Assault	Burglary	Larceny -Theft	Motor Vehicle Theft
Albuquerque, NM	4,660.5	9.4	61.3	171.6	764.1	688.1	2,303.5	662.5
Allentown, PA[3]	n/a	n/a	n/a	n/a	n/a	n/a	n/a	n/a
Anchorage, AK	4,576.1	5.9	186.7	185.4	793.4	487.5	2,523.4	393.8
Ann Arbor, MI	1,678.4	2.4	63.2	36.3	310.4	154.3	1,002.5	109.3
Athens, GA	2,572.9	2.8	57.0	51.9	274.8	365.6	1,613.3	207.6
Atlanta, GA[4]	2,895.7	5.7	26.1	94.1	194.7	393.9	1,903.2	278.0
Austin, TX	2,682.2	3.2	43.6	62.4	206.4	336.6	1,781.5	248.5
Baltimore, MD[3]	3,057.2	15.5	36.6	242.7	403.8	364.7	1,753.9	239.9
Boise City, ID	1,424.4	1.8	58.5	11.9	190.5	187.0	865.5	109.2
Boston, MA[2]	1,249.7	2.2	21.8	38.2	191.6	117.5	786.3	92.1
Boulder, CO	3,053.3	1.2	54.0	42.7	195.3	405.2	2,051.3	303.6
Brownsville, TX	2,311.6	3.1	41.6	58.3	257.9	275.1	1,583.3	92.3
Cape Coral, FL	1,298.3	4.1	30.4	38.6	193.8	149.9	783.6	98.0
Cedar Rapids, IA	2,367.4	4.4	25.9	42.3	179.4	465.9	1,381.3	268.3
Charleston, SC	2,926.8	11.3	36.1	79.8	318.9	309.0	1,886.2	285.4
Charlotte, NC	n/a	n/a	n/a	n/a	n/a	n/a	n/a	n/a
Chicago, IL[2]	n/a	n/a	n/a	n/a	n/a	n/a	n/a	n/a
Cincinnati, OH	1,894.4	5.7	33.0	54.6	142.3	257.5	1,237.7	163.5
Clarksville, TN	2,276.1	6.7	42.6	37.5	336.7	286.4	1,364.1	202.0
Cleveland, OH	2,145.2	10.3	36.2	106.5	287.7	306.5	1,169.7	228.4
College Station, TX	2,152.0	3.7	67.9	32.8	193.6	311.5	1,379.4	163.0
Colorado Springs, CO	3,139.6	6.2	76.8	58.6	344.9	412.8	1,855.2	384.9
Columbia, MO	2,572.2	7.1	63.8	35.7	259.4	280.8	1,637.3	288.0
Columbia, SC	3,830.0	9.2	41.9	76.0	430.9	511.5	2,378.9	381.6
Columbus, OH	2,523.0	9.0	54.3	99.3	150.6	376.7	1,630.2	202.9
Dallas, TX[2]	n/a	n/a	n/a	n/a	n/a	n/a	n/a	n/a
Davenport, IA	n/a	6.9	59.6	71.2	338.3	493.9	n/a	251.4
Denver, CO	3,793.1	6.1	65.8	93.9	324.5	443.9	2,124.7	734.2
Des Moines, IA	2,362.1	6.2	34.8	41.6	256.0	423.8	1,310.9	288.8
Durham, NC	3,000.9	8.1	29.1	113.9	349.3	471.8	1,818.1	210.6
Edison, NJ[2]	n/a	n/a	n/a	n/a	n/a	n/a	n/a	n/a
El Paso, TX	1,457.0	3.9	37.7	38.0	229.2	123.2	962.0	62.9
Fargo, ND	3,180.0	5.6	69.3	33.0	242.8	648.6	1,888.3	292.3
Fort Collins, CO[3]	2,112.3	0.8	34.8	17.7	180.7	194.2	1,555.0	129.0
Fort Wayne, IN	2,083.1	9.9	31.0	64.7	229.3	204.7	1,391.1	152.3
Fort Worth, TX[2]	n/a	n/a	n/a	n/a	n/a	n/a	n/a	n/a
Grand Rapids, MI	1,628.8	4.6	68.8	35.1	241.6	164.6	950.1	164.0
Greeley, CO	2,487.0	4.8	53.4	40.4	225.5	253.0	1,532.2	377.6
Green Bay, WI	1,216.1	2.5	37.3	16.0	169.2	146.4	787.1	57.6
Greensboro, NC	3,250.8	12.2	29.6	107.7	426.7	539.5	1,872.7	262.4
Honolulu, HI[3]	n/a	n/a	n/a	n/a	n/a	n/a	n/a	n/a
Houston, TX	3,249.2	9.2	44.7	167.9	410.0	402.1	1,841.0	374.3
Huntsville, AL	n/a	n/a	n/a	n/a	n/a	n/a	n/a	n/a
Indianapolis, IN	n/a	n/a	n/a	n/a	n/a	n/a	n/a	n/a
Jacksonville, FL	2,653.0	9.9	40.5	68.6	380.8	316.0	1,607.7	229.4
Kansas City, MO	n/a	n/a	n/a	n/a	n/a	n/a	n/a	n/a
Lafayette, LA	2,937.4	8.4	21.2	56.3	364.1	514.9	1,764.1	208.4
Las Cruces, NM[3]	2,871.0	5.5	56.8	31.6	462.9	490.4	1,626.2	197.5
Las Vegas, NV	2,525.2	5.5	54.6	100.3	318.2	375.2	1,301.2	370.1
Lexington, KY	2,811.4	5.9	45.2	75.0	124.6	397.2	1,883.4	280.1
Lincoln, NE[3]	2,843.7	1.5	106.4	49.2	189.7	309.2	2,043.0	144.7
Little Rock, AR	4,117.3	13.1	67.5	88.9	769.4	540.6	2,291.0	346.8
Los Angeles, CA[2]	2,567.7	5.6	34.6	132.5	300.0	352.3	1,294.6	448.2
Louisville, KY[3]	3,300.8	8.3	26.0	93.8	308.7	447.9	2,011.8	404.3

Table continued on following page.

Appendix A: Comparative Statistics   A-159

Metro Area[1]	Total Crime	Violent Crime Rate				Property Crime Rate		
		Murder	Rape	Robbery	Aggrav. Assault	Burglary	Larceny -Theft	Motor Vehicle Theft
Madison, WI	2,007.2	2.5	24.0	35.2	140.1	290.7	1,363.0	151.7
Manchester, NH	1,355.7	1.2	42.2	32.7	141.6	115.4	944.8	77.7
Miami, FL[2]	2,609.4	7.5	30.9	88.9	289.6	226.7	1,721.0	244.7
Midland, TX	2,541.9	6.9	49.1	29.4	288.5	284.2	1,516.1	367.5
Milwaukee, WI	2,634.0	13.1	40.0	140.8	484.3	288.1	1,316.8	350.9
Minneapolis, MN	n/a	n/a	n/a	n/a	n/a	n/a	n/a	n/a
Nashville, TN	2,968.8	7.7	38.4	106.5	463.7	320.3	1,787.7	244.5
New Haven, CT	2,425.5	6.1	20.5	93.2	136.5	230.5	1,591.8	346.9
New Orleans, LA	3,378.9	21.7	72.5	118.0	412.2	325.1	2,061.9	367.5
New York, NY[2]	n/a	n/a	n/a	n/a	n/a	n/a	n/a	n/a
Oklahoma City, OK	3,387.0	7.8	59.0	72.3	331.7	619.9	1,902.9	393.3
Omaha, NE	2,710.6	4.6	55.2	60.1	309.8	254.6	1,606.2	420.2
Orlando, FL	2,288.9	5.9	42.0	72.2	306.6	268.4	1,414.3	179.4
Philadelphia, PA[2,4]	3,462.1	18.3	55.2	270.0	420.3	355.2	2,042.3	300.9
Phoenix, AZ	2,681.7	6.2	44.4	93.8	319.9	329.5	1,630.4	257.5
Pittsburgh, PA[4]	1,687.7	5.5	25.8	58.8	184.5	196.1	1,137.0	80.0
Portland, OR	n/a	n/a	41.1	60.0	203.7	342.7	1,864.0	471.6
Providence, RI	1,445.8	2.5	39.8	37.7	205.6	170.2	863.3	126.6
Provo, UT[3]	1,368.4	1.1	31.6	7.9	49.6	132.9	1,061.8	83.5
Raleigh, NC	1,727.9	3.3	19.7	47.3	153.3	224.6	1,129.7	150.1
Reno, NV	2,291.8	5.6	85.8	77.4	294.1	369.6	1,165.9	293.3
Richmond, VA	2,050.3	9.9	20.6	46.4	138.8	171.1	1,518.7	144.8
Rochester, MN	1,552.4	2.7	49.8	21.1	114.0	237.0	1,030.4	97.4
Sacramento, CA	2,393.6	4.8	27.0	87.5	259.0	372.0	1,371.2	272.1
Saint Louis, MO	n/a	14.3	34.8	79.2	368.7	325.8	n/a	368.6
Salem, OR	3,123.1	1.6	23.8	51.5	192.6	308.9	2,064.3	480.4
Salt Lake City, UT	4,200.7	4.8	67.0	77.1	235.0	429.5	2,842.9	544.4
San Antonio, TX	3,339.5	6.6	60.1	92.3	371.7	422.6	2,049.1	337.2
San Diego, CA	1,830.5	3.4	29.0	75.8	237.4	219.1	986.3	279.3
San Francisco, CA[2]	3,448.3	5.3	31.8	178.5	224.5	439.0	1,965.0	604.2
San Jose, CA	2,543.9	2.8	41.6	86.7	186.2	369.1	1,351.5	506.0
Santa Rosa, CA	1,758.4	2.0	48.7	54.2	346.0	259.4	898.8	149.2
Savannah, GA[4]	3,107.5	9.2	35.9	93.7	247.2	415.6	2,032.0	274.0
Seattle, WA[2]	3,496.7	4.5	31.1	93.5	210.7	616.6	2,083.1	457.2
Sioux Falls, SD	3,001.8	5.5	45.4	39.9	386.8	395.6	1,747.6	381.0
Springfield, IL	n/a	5.8	65.2	104.7	490.8	612.0	n/a	178.2
Tampa, FL	1,678.0	4.0	33.3	47.1	229.7	182.8	1,057.5	123.6
Tucson, AZ	3,298.3	8.1	51.4	110.3	303.7	321.4	2,265.9	237.5
Tulsa, OK	3,701.1	9.3	56.2	86.8	439.1	666.7	1,908.0	534.9
Tuscaloosa, AL[4]	3,445.1	4.0	35.6	80.3	276.5	607.5	2,189.7	251.6
Virginia Beach, VA	2,301.0	10.3	26.2	57.2	258.1	175.7	1,590.0	183.5
Washington, DC[2]	n/a	n/a	n/a	n/a	n/a	n/a	n/a	n/a
Wichita, KS[3]	n/a	6.1	74.0	77.9	623.3	525.2	n/a	411.7
Wilmington, NC	2,373.9	8.6	38.0	61.5	264.0	372.4	1,509.5	120.0
Winston-Salem, NC	n/a	n/a	n/a	n/a	n/a	n/a	n/a	n/a
Worcester, MA	1,285.0	1.5	30.1	36.9	235.2	167.5	707.6	106.2
U.S.	2,356.7	6.5	38.4	73.9	279.7	314.2	1,398.0	246.0

Note: Figures are crimes per 100,000 population in 2020 except where noted; n/a not available; (1) Figures cover the Metropolitan Statistical Area except where noted; (2) Metropolitan Division (MD); (3) 2019 data; (4) 2018 data; Due to the transition to the National Incident-Based Reporting System (NIBRS), limited city and metro area data was released for 2021
Source: FBI Uniform Crime Reports, 2018, 2019, 2020

A-160   Appendix A: Comparative Statistics

Temperature & Precipitation: Yearly Averages and Extremes

City	Extreme Low (°F)	Average Low (°F)	Average Temp. (°F)	Average High (°F)	Extreme High (°F)	Average Precip. (in.)	Average Snow (in.)
Albuquerque, NM	-17	43	57	70	105	8.5	11
Allentown, PA	-12	42	52	61	105	44.2	32
Anchorage, AK	-34	29	36	43	85	15.7	71
Ann Arbor, MI	-21	39	49	58	104	32.4	41
Athens, GA	-8	52	62	72	105	49.8	2
Atlanta, GA	-8	52	62	72	105	49.8	2
Austin, TX	-2	58	69	79	109	31.1	1
Baltimore, MD	-7	45	56	65	105	41.2	21
Boise City, ID	-25	39	51	63	111	11.8	22
Boston, MA	-12	44	52	59	102	42.9	41
Boulder, CO	-25	37	51	64	103	15.5	63
Brownsville, TX	16	65	74	83	106	25.8	Trace
Cape Coral, FL	26	65	75	84	103	53.9	0
Cedar Rapids, IA	-34	36	47	57	105	34.4	33
Charleston, SC	6	55	66	76	104	52.1	1
Charlotte, NC	-5	50	61	71	104	42.8	6
Chicago, IL	-27	40	49	59	104	35.4	39
Cincinnati, OH	-25	44	54	64	103	40.9	23
Clarksville, TN	-17	49	60	70	107	47.4	11
Cleveland, OH	-19	41	50	59	104	37.1	55
College Station, TX	-2	58	69	79	109	31.1	1
Colorado Springs, CO	-24	36	49	62	99	17.0	48
Columbia, MO	-20	44	54	64	111	40.6	25
Columbia, SC	-1	51	64	75	107	48.3	2
Columbus, OH	-19	42	52	62	104	37.9	28
Dallas, TX	-2	56	67	77	112	33.9	3
Davenport, IA	-24	40	50	60	108	31.8	33
Denver, CO	-25	37	51	64	103	15.5	63
Des Moines, IA	-24	40	50	60	108	31.8	33
Durham, NC	-9	48	60	71	105	42.0	8
Edison, NJ	-8	46	55	63	105	43.5	27
El Paso, TX	-8	50	64	78	114	8.6	6
Fargo, ND	-36	31	41	52	106	19.6	40
Fort Collins, CO	-25	37	51	64	103	15.5	63
Fort Wayne, IN	-22	40	50	60	106	35.9	33
Fort Worth, TX	-1	55	66	76	113	32.3	3
Grand Rapids, MI	-22	38	48	57	102	34.7	73
Greeley, CO	-25	37	51	64	103	15.5	63
Green Bay, WI	-31	34	44	54	99	28.3	46
Greensboro, NC	-8	47	58	69	103	42.5	10
Honolulu, HI	52	70	77	84	94	22.4	0
Houston, TX	7	58	69	79	107	46.9	Trace
Huntsville, AL	-11	50	61	71	104	56.8	4
Indianapolis, IN	-23	42	53	62	104	40.2	25
Jacksonville, FL	7	58	69	79	103	52.0	0
Kansas City, MO	-23	44	54	64	109	38.1	21
Lafayette, LA	8	57	68	78	103	58.5	Trace
Las Cruces, NM	-8	50	64	78	114	8.6	6
Las Vegas, NV	8	53	67	80	116	4.0	1
Lexington, KY	-21	45	55	65	103	45.1	17
Lincoln, NE	-33	39	51	62	108	29.1	27
Little Rock, AR	-5	51	62	73	112	50.7	5
Los Angeles, CA	27	55	63	70	110	11.3	Trace
Louisville, KY	-20	46	57	67	105	43.9	17
Madison, WI	-37	35	46	57	104	31.1	42

Table continued on following page.

Appendix A: Comparative Statistics   A-161

City	Extreme Low (°F)	Average Low (°F)	Average Temp. (°F)	Average High (°F)	Extreme High (°F)	Average Precip. (in.)	Average Snow (in.)
Manchester, NH	-33	34	46	57	102	36.9	63
Miami, FL	30	69	76	83	98	57.1	0
Midland, TX	-11	50	64	77	116	14.6	4
Milwaukee, WI	-26	38	47	55	103	32.0	49
Minneapolis, MN	-34	35	45	54	105	27.1	52
Nashville, TN	-17	49	60	70	107	47.4	11
New Haven, CT	-7	44	52	60	103	41.4	25
New Orleans, LA	11	59	69	78	102	60.6	Trace
New York, NY	-2	47	55	62	104	47.0	23
Oklahoma City, OK	-8	49	60	71	110	32.8	10
Omaha, NE	-23	40	51	62	110	30.1	29
Orlando, FL	19	62	72	82	100	47.7	Trace
Philadelphia, PA	-7	45	55	64	104	41.4	22
Phoenix, AZ	17	59	72	86	122	7.3	Trace
Pittsburgh, PA	-18	41	51	60	103	37.1	43
Portland, OR	-3	45	54	62	107	37.5	7
Providence, RI	-13	42	51	60	104	45.3	35
Provo, UT	-22	40	52	64	107	15.6	63
Raleigh, NC	-9	48	60	71	105	42.0	8
Reno, NV	-16	33	50	67	105	7.2	24
Richmond, VA	-8	48	58	69	105	43.0	13
Rochester, MN	-40	34	44	54	102	29.4	47
Sacramento, CA	18	48	61	73	115	17.3	Trace
Saint Louis, MO	-18	46	56	66	115	36.8	20
Salem, OR	-12	41	52	63	108	40.2	7
Salt Lake City, UT	-22	40	52	64	107	15.6	63
San Antonio, TX	0	58	69	80	108	29.6	1
San Diego, CA	29	57	64	71	111	9.5	Trace
San Francisco, CA	24	49	57	65	106	19.3	Trace
San Jose, CA	21	50	59	68	105	13.5	Trace
Santa Rosa, CA	23	42	57	71	109	29.0	n/a
Savannah, GA	3	56	67	77	105	50.3	Trace
Seattle, WA	0	44	52	59	99	38.4	13
Sioux Falls, SD	-36	35	46	57	110	24.6	38
Springfield, IL	-24	44	54	63	112	34.9	21
Tampa, FL	18	63	73	82	99	46.7	Trace
Tucson, AZ	16	55	69	82	117	11.6	2
Tulsa, OK	-8	50	61	71	112	38.9	10
Tuscaloosa, AL	-6	51	63	74	106	53.5	2
Virginia Beach, VA	-3	51	60	69	104	44.8	8
Washington, DC	-5	49	58	67	104	39.5	18
Wichita, KS	-21	45	57	68	113	29.3	17
Wilmington, NC	0	53	64	74	104	55.0	2
Winston-Salem, NC	-8	47	58	69	103	42.5	10
Worcester, MA	-13	38	47	56	99	47.6	62

Source: National Climatic Data Center, International Station Meteorological Climate Summary, 9/96; NOAA

A-162   Appendix A: Comparative Statistics

Weather Conditions

City	Temperature			Daytime Sky			Precipitation		
	10°F & below	32°F & below	90°F & above	Clear	Partly cloudy	Cloudy	0.01 inch or more precip.	1.0 inch or more snow/ice	Thunder-storms
Albuquerque, NM	4	114	65	140	161	64	60	9	38
Allentown, PA	n/a	123	15	77	148	140	123	20	31
Anchorage, AK	n/a	194	n/a	50	115	200	113	49	2
Ann Arbor, MI	n/a	136	12	74	134	157	135	38	32
Athens, GA	1	49	38	98	147	120	116	3	48
Atlanta, GA	1	49	38	98	147	120	116	3	48
Austin, TX	< 1	20	111	105	148	112	83	1	41
Baltimore, MD	6	97	31	91	143	131	113	13	27
Boise City, ID	n/a	124	45	106	133	126	91	22	14
Boston, MA	n/a	97	12	88	127	150	253	48	18
Boulder, CO	24	155	33	99	177	89	90	38	39
Brownsville, TX	n/a	n/a	116	86	180	99	72	0	27
Cape Coral, FL	n/a	n/a	115	93	220	52	110	0	92
Cedar Rapids, IA	n/a	156	16	89	132	144	109	28	42
Charleston, SC	< 1	33	53	89	162	114	114	1	59
Charlotte, NC	1	65	44	98	142	125	113	3	41
Chicago, IL	n/a	132	17	83	136	146	125	31	38
Cincinnati, OH	14	107	23	80	126	159	127	25	39
Clarksville, TN	5	76	51	98	135	132	119	8	54
Cleveland, OH	n/a	123	12	63	127	175	157	48	34
College Station, TX	< 1	20	111	105	148	112	83	1	41
Colorado Springs, CO	21	161	18	108	157	100	98	33	49
Columbia, MO	17	108	36	99	127	139	110	17	52
Columbia, SC	< 1	58	77	97	149	119	110	1	53
Columbus, OH	n/a	118	19	72	137	156	136	29	40
Dallas, TX	1	34	102	108	160	97	78	2	49
Davenport, IA	n/a	137	26	99	129	137	106	25	46
Denver, CO	24	155	33	99	177	89	90	38	39
Des Moines, IA	n/a	137	26	99	129	137	106	25	46
Durham, NC	n/a	n/a	39	98	143	124	110	3	42
Edison, NJ	n/a	90	24	80	146	139	122	16	46
El Paso, TX	1	59	106	147	164	54	49	3	35
Fargo, ND	n/a	180	15	81	145	139	100	38	31
Fort Collins, CO	24	155	33	99	177	89	90	38	39
Fort Wayne, IN	n/a	131	16	75	140	150	131	31	39
Fort Worth, TX	1	40	100	123	136	106	79	3	47
Grand Rapids, MI	n/a	146	11	67	119	179	142	57	34
Greeley, CO	24	155	33	99	177	89	90	38	39
Green Bay, WI	n/a	163	7	86	125	154	120	40	33
Greensboro, NC	3	85	32	94	143	128	113	5	43
Honolulu, HI	n/a	n/a	23	25	286	54	98	0	7
Houston, TX	n/a	n/a	96	83	168	114	101	1	62
Huntsville, AL	2	66	49	70	118	177	116	2	54
Indianapolis, IN	19	119	19	83	128	154	127	24	43
Jacksonville, FL	< 1	16	83	86	181	98	114	1	65
Kansas City, MO	22	110	39	112	134	119	103	17	51
Lafayette, LA	< 1	21	86	99	150	116	113	< 1	73
Las Cruces, NM	1	59	106	147	164	54	49	3	35
Las Vegas, NV	< 1	37	134	185	132	48	27	2	13
Lexington, KY	11	96	22	86	136	143	129	17	44
Lincoln, NE	n/a	145	40	108	135	122	94	19	46
Little Rock, AR	1	57	73	110	142	113	104	4	57
Los Angeles, CA	0	< 1	5	131	125	109	34	0	1
Louisville, KY	8	90	35	82	143	140	125	15	45

Table continued on following page.

Appendix A: Comparative Statistics   A-163

City	Temperature			Daytime Sky			Precipitation		
	10°F & below	32°F & below	90°F & above	Clear	Partly cloudy	Cloudy	0.01 inch or more precip.	1.0 inch or more snow/ice	Thunder-storms
Madison, WI	n/a	161	14	88	119	158	118	38	40
Manchester, NH	n/a	171	12	87	131	147	125	32	19
Miami, FL	n/a	n/a	55	48	263	54	128	0	74
Midland, TX	1	62	102	144	138	83	52	3	38
Milwaukee, WI	n/a	141	10	90	118	157	126	38	35
Minneapolis, MN	n/a	156	16	93	125	147	113	41	37
Nashville, TN	5	76	51	98	135	132	119	8	54
New Haven, CT	n/a	n/a	7	80	146	139	118	17	22
New Orleans, LA	0	13	70	90	169	106	114	1	69
New York, NY	n/a	n/a	18	85	166	114	120	11	20
Oklahoma City, OK	5	79	70	124	131	110	80	8	50
Omaha, NE	n/a	139	35	100	142	123	97	20	46
Orlando, FL	n/a	n/a	90	76	208	81	115	0	80
Philadelphia, PA	5	94	23	81	146	138	117	14	27
Phoenix, AZ	0	10	167	186	125	54	37	< 1	23
Pittsburgh, PA	n/a	121	8	62	137	166	154	42	35
Portland, OR	n/a	37	11	67	116	182	152	4	7
Providence, RI	n/a	117	9	85	134	146	123	21	21
Provo, UT	n/a	128	56	94	152	119	92	38	38
Raleigh, NC	n/a	n/a	39	98	143	124	110	3	42
Reno, NV	14	178	50	143	139	83	50	17	14
Richmond, VA	3	79	41	90	147	128	115	7	43
Rochester, MN	n/a	165	9	87	126	152	114	40	41
Sacramento, CA	0	21	73	175	111	79	58	< 1	2
Saint Louis, MO	13	100	43	97	138	130	109	14	46
Salem, OR	n/a	66	16	78	118	169	146	6	5
Salt Lake City, UT	n/a	128	56	94	152	119	92	38	38
San Antonio, TX	n/a	n/a	112	97	153	115	81	1	36
San Diego, CA	0	< 1	4	115	126	124	40	0	5
San Francisco, CA	0	6	4	136	130	99	63	< 1	5
San Jose, CA	0	5	5	106	180	79	57	< 1	6
Santa Rosa, CA	n/a	43	30	n/a	365	n/a	n/a	n/a	2
Savannah, GA	< 1	29	70	97	155	113	111	< 1	63
Seattle, WA	n/a	38	3	57	121	187	157	8	8
Sioux Falls, SD	n/a	n/a	n/a	95	136	134	n/a	n/a	n/a
Springfield, IL	19	111	34	96	126	143	111	18	49
Tampa, FL	n/a	n/a	85	81	204	80	107	< 1	87
Tucson, AZ	0	18	140	177	119	69	54	2	42
Tulsa, OK	6	78	74	117	141	107	88	8	50
Tuscaloosa, AL	1	57	59	91	161	113	119	1	57
Virginia Beach, VA	< 1	53	33	89	149	127	115	5	38
Washington, DC	2	71	34	84	144	137	112	9	30
Wichita, KS	13	110	63	117	132	116	87	13	54
Wilmington, NC	< 1	42	46	96	150	119	115	1	47
Winston-Salem, NC	3	85	32	94	143	128	113	5	43
Worcester, MA	n/a	141	4	81	144	140	131	32	23

Note: Figures are average number of days per year
Source: National Climatic Data Center, International Station Meteorological Climate Summary, 9/96; NOAA

A-164   Appendix A: Comparative Statistics

Air Quality Index

MSA[1] (Days[2])	Percent of Days when Air Quality was...					AQI Statistics	
	Good	Moderate	Unhealthy for Sensitive Groups	Unhealthy	Very Unhealthy	Maximum	Median
Albuquerque, NM (365)	23.6	70.7	5.2	0.5	0.0	166	62
Allentown, PA (365)	69.9	29.0	0.8	0.3	0.0	153	43
Anchorage, AK (365)	80.3	18.6	0.8	0.3	0.0	160	25
Ann Arbor, MI (365)	76.2	23.8	0.0	0.0	0.0	100	40
Athens, GA (365)	71.8	27.9	0.3	0.0	0.0	107	41
Atlanta, GA (365)	57.3	40.5	2.2	0.0	0.0	150	47
Austin, TX (365)	68.2	31.5	0.3	0.0	0.0	101	43
Baltimore, MD (365)	68.8	27.1	4.1	0.0	0.0	140	45
Boise City, ID (365)	55.1	39.5	4.4	1.1	0.0	168	49
Boston, MA (365)	77.0	21.6	1.1	0.3	0.0	153	40
Boulder, CO (365)	55.9	34.5	8.8	0.8	0.0	159	48
Brownsville, TX (365)	64.4	35.6	0.0	0.0	0.0	99	43
Cape Coral, FL (365)	91.0	9.0	0.0	0.0	0.0	97	36
Cedar Rapids, IA (365)	64.4	34.5	1.1	0.0	0.0	123	44
Charleston, SC (365)	79.5	20.5	0.0	0.0	0.0	93	40
Charlotte, NC (365)	64.4	34.8	0.8	0.0	0.0	128	46
Chicago, IL (365)	34.2	58.1	7.1	0.5	0.0	169	58
Cincinnati, OH (365)	45.8	52.1	2.2	0.0	0.0	140	52
Clarksville, TN (365)	70.4	29.3	0.3	0.0	0.0	138	43
Cleveland, OH (365)	47.4	50.4	2.2	0.0	0.0	122	52
College Station, TX (356)	87.6	12.4	0.0	0.0	0.0	84	30
Colorado Springs, CO (365)	64.7	27.7	7.7	0.0	0.0	140	47
Columbia, MO (245)	95.1	4.9	0.0	0.0	0.0	77	37
Columbia, SC (365)	74.0	25.5	0.5	0.0	0.0	102	41
Columbus, OH (365)	71.2	28.8	0.0	0.0	0.0	100	43
Dallas, TX (365)	54.0	37.5	7.4	0.8	0.3	209	49
Davenport, IA (365)	56.2	43.0	0.8	0.0	0.0	112	49
Denver, CO (365)	30.1	51.5	13.7	4.7	0.0	177	61
Des Moines, IA (365)	77.8	21.9	0.3	0.0	0.0	110	40
Durham, NC (365)	81.6	18.4	0.0	0.0	0.0	90	40
Edison, NJ (365)	54.8	39.5	4.9	0.8	0.0	154	49
El Paso, TX (365)	38.6	56.2	5.2	0.0	0.0	150	54
Fargo, ND (363)	76.6	18.7	2.2	2.5	0.0	192	37
Fort Collins, CO (365)	54.0	36.4	8.8	0.8	0.0	156	50
Fort Wayne, IN (365)	70.7	29.3	0.0	0.0	0.0	100	41
Fort Worth, TX (365)	54.0	37.5	7.4	0.8	0.3	209	49
Grand Rapids, MI (365)	62.2	36.4	1.4	0.0	0.0	143	44
Greeley, CO (365)	54.5	36.2	9.0	0.3	0.0	154	49
Green Bay, WI (365)	73.4	25.2	1.4	0.0	0.0	125	40
Greensboro, NC (365)	75.9	24.1	0.0	0.0	0.0	100	42
Honolulu, HI (365)	99.7	0.3	0.0	0.0	0.0	52	26
Houston, TX (365)	38.6	53.2	5.8	2.5	0.0	179	54
Huntsville, AL (357)	75.4	24.1	0.6	0.0	0.0	105	41
Indianapolis, IN (365)	42.2	55.9	1.9	0.0	0.0	114	53
Jacksonville, FL (365)	73.4	26.6	0.0	0.0	0.0	93	43
Kansas City, MO (365)	52.9	43.6	3.6	0.0	0.0	147	50
Lafayette, LA (365)	81.6	18.4	0.0	0.0	0.0	87	38
Las Cruces, NM (365)	38.4	53.2	5.5	2.2	0.3	665	55
Las Vegas, NV (365)	32.6	58.1	8.5	0.8	0.0	174	59
Lexington, KY (363)	77.4	22.0	0.6	0.0	0.0	108	40
Lincoln, NE (276)	93.1	6.9	0.0	0.0	0.0	84	35
Little Rock, AR (365)	58.4	41.1	0.5	0.0	0.0	112	47
Los Angeles, CA (365)	10.7	62.5	19.5	7.1	0.3	281	77
Louisville, KY (365)	60.8	37.3	1.9	0.0	0.0	143	46

Table continued on following page.

Appendix A: Comparative Statistics   A-165

MSA[1] (Days[2])	Percent of Days when Air Quality was...					AQI Statistics	
	Good	Moderate	Unhealthy for Sensitive Groups	Unhealthy	Very Unhealthy	Maximum	Median
Madison, WI (365)	67.1	32.6	0.3	0.0	0.0	101	42
Manchester, NH (365)	91.8	7.7	0.5	0.0	0.0	144	36
Miami, FL (365)	70.4	28.8	0.8	0.0	0.0	135	44
Midland, TX (n/a)	n/a	n/a	n/a	n/a	n/a	n/a	n/a
Milwaukee, WI (365)	57.3	39.5	3.3	0.0	0.0	129	47
Minneapolis, MN (365)	63.0	34.8	1.4	0.8	0.0	182	44
Nashville, TN (365)	60.5	38.1	1.4	0.0	0.0	133	46
New Haven, CT (365)	77.0	19.2	3.3	0.5	0.0	159	40
New Orleans, LA (365)	76.4	22.7	0.8	0.0	0.0	108	42
New York, NY (365)	54.8	39.5	4.9	0.8	0.0	154	49
Oklahoma City, OK (365)	48.2	49.0	2.7	0.0	0.0	140	51
Omaha, NE (365)	72.9	25.8	1.4	0.0	0.0	150	42
Orlando, FL (365)	82.7	17.3	0.0	0.0	0.0	97	39
Philadelphia, PA (365)	49.9	46.0	3.6	0.5	0.0	152	51
Phoenix, AZ (365)	3.0	32.1	28.2	16.7	20.0	272	123
Pittsburgh, PA (365)	44.9	52.6	2.2	0.3	0.0	153	53
Portland, OR (365)	79.7	20.0	0.0	0.3	0.0	161	37
Providence, RI (365)	76.2	22.7	1.1	0.0	0.0	147	41
Provo, UT (365)	60.0	35.3	4.7	0.0	0.0	144	46
Raleigh, NC (365)	71.0	29.0	0.0	0.0	0.0	97	43
Reno, NV (365)	54.2	36.2	4.4	4.4	0.8	291	49
Richmond, VA (365)	76.4	22.7	0.8	0.0	0.0	112	42
Rochester, MN (361)	83.4	16.1	0.6	0.0	0.0	125	36
Sacramento, CA (365)	37.8	46.3	10.4	3.3	1.4	448	62
St. Louis, MO (365)	38.1	57.8	3.6	0.5	0.0	187	55
Salem, OR (363)	87.1	12.9	0.0	0.0	0.0	93	33
Salt Lake City, UT (365)	47.4	39.5	10.7	2.5	0.0	177	52
San Antonio, TX (365)	54.5	42.2	3.3	0.0	0.0	147	48
San Diego, CA (365)	26.8	68.8	4.4	0.0	0.0	133	64
San Francisco, CA (365)	58.1	39.2	2.5	0.3	0.0	151	46
San Jose, CA (365)	60.5	37.5	1.9	0.0	0.0	147	46
Santa Rosa, CA (365)	87.9	12.1	0.0	0.0	0.0	88	33
Savannah, GA (363)	75.8	24.0	0.3	0.0	0.0	103	41
Seattle, WA (365)	72.1	26.0	1.4	0.5	0.0	177	43
Sioux Falls, SD (349)	81.7	16.9	0.9	0.6	0.0	182	36
Springfield, IL (362)	80.7	19.3	0.0	0.0	0.0	97	38
Tampa, FL (365)	72.9	26.8	0.3	0.0	0.0	129	44
Tucson, AZ (365)	39.2	57.0	3.6	0.0	0.0	315	53
Tulsa, OK (365)	60.3	37.0	2.2	0.5	0.0	163	47
Tuscaloosa, AL (281)	94.3	5.7	0.0	0.0	0.0	90	31
Virginia Beach, VA (365)	85.8	14.2	0.0	0.0	0.0	94	38
Washington, DC (365)	61.6	35.6	2.5	0.3	0.0	153	46
Wichita, KS (365)	59.7	38.9	1.4	0.0	0.0	147	47
Wilmington, NC (360)	89.4	10.6	0.0	0.0	0.0	93	34
Winston-Salem, NC (365)	67.4	31.8	0.8	0.0	0.0	124	44
Worcester, MA (365)	81.6	17.5	0.8	0.0	0.0	140	39

Note: The Air Quality Index (AQI) is an index for reporting daily air quality. EPA calculates the AQI for five major air pollutants regulated by the Clean Air Act: ground-level ozone, particle pollution (also known as particulate matter), carbon monoxide, sulfur dioxide, and nitrogen dioxide. The AQI runs from 0 to 500. The higher the AQI value, the greater the level of air pollution and the greater the health concern. There are six AQI categories: "Good" The AQI is between 0 and 50. Air quality is considered satisfactory; "Moderate" The AQI is between 51 and 100. Air quality is acceptable; "Unhealthy for Sensitive Groups" When AQI values are between 101 and 150, members of sensitive groups may experience health effects; "Unhealthy" When AQI values are between 151 and 200 everyone may begin to experience health effects; "Very Unhealthy" AQI values between 201 and 300 trigger a health alert; "Hazardous" AQI values over 300 trigger health warnings of emergency conditions; (1) Data covers the Metropolitan Statistical Area; (2) Number of days with AQI data in 2021
Source: U.S. Environmental Protection Agency, Air Quality Index Report, 2021

A-166   Appendix A: Comparative Statistics

Air Quality Index Pollutants

MSA[1] (Days[2])	Percent of Days when AQI Pollutant was...					
	Carbon Monoxide	Nitrogen Dioxide	Ozone	Sulfur Dioxide	Particulate Matter 2.5	Particulate Matter 10
Albuquerque, NM (365)	0.0	0.0	49.6	(3)	16.7	33.7
Allentown, PA (365)	0.0	1.6	48.8	(3)	49.6	0.0
Anchorage, AK (365)	0.0	0.0	0.0	(3)	68.5	31.5
Ann Arbor, MI (365)	0.0	0.0	62.5	(3)	37.5	0.0
Athens, GA (365)	0.0	0.0	32.9	(3)	67.1	0.0
Atlanta, GA (365)	0.0	3.6	40.8	(3)	55.6	0.0
Austin, TX (365)	0.0	1.6	50.7	(3)	46.6	1.1
Baltimore, MD (365)	0.0	7.4	60.5	(3)	32.1	0.0
Boise City, ID (365)	0.0	0.8	44.9	(3)	51.2	3.0
Boston, MA (365)	0.0	3.3	53.4	(3)	43.0	0.3
Boulder, CO (365)	0.0	0.0	74.8	(3)	24.7	0.5
Brownsville, TX (365)	0.0	0.0	31.2	(3)	68.8	0.0
Cape Coral, FL (365)	0.0	0.0	66.0	(3)	32.9	1.1
Cedar Rapids, IA (365)	0.0	0.0	35.1	(3)	64.7	0.3
Charleston, SC (365)	0.0	0.0	41.4	(3)	58.6	0.0
Charlotte, NC (365)	0.0	0.3	59.2	(3)	40.5	0.0
Chicago, IL (365)	0.0	4.9	34.2	(3)	51.0	9.9
Cincinnati, OH (365)	0.0	3.0	28.8	(3)	64.1	4.1
Clarksville, TN (365)	0.0	0.0	47.4	(3)	52.6	0.0
Cleveland, OH (365)	0.0	1.4	35.9	(3)	60.8	1.9
College Station, TX (356)	0.0	0.0	0.0	(3)	100.0	0.0
Colorado Springs, CO (365)	0.0	0.0	95.1	(3)	4.9	0.0
Columbia, MO (245)	0.0	0.0	100.0	(3)	0.0	0.0
Columbia, SC (365)	0.0	0.0	51.8	(3)	48.2	0.0
Columbus, OH (365)	0.0	2.7	44.7	(3)	52.6	0.0
Dallas, TX (365)	0.0	3.3	61.4	(3)	35.3	0.0
Davenport, IA (365)	0.0	0.0	33.4	(3)	46.8	19.7
Denver, CO (365)	0.0	18.6	63.6	(3)	11.2	6.6
Des Moines, IA (365)	0.0	3.6	43.3	(3)	51.8	1.4
Durham, NC (365)	0.0	0.0	51.8	(3)	48.2	0.0
Edison, NJ (365)	0.0	12.3	41.4	(3)	46.3	0.0
El Paso, TX (365)	0.0	5.8	53.2	(3)	35.9	5.2
Fargo, ND (363)	0.0	1.4	54.5	(3)	44.1	0.0
Fort Collins, CO (365)	0.0	0.0	91.0	(3)	9.0	0.0
Fort Wayne, IN (365)	0.0	0.0	51.0	(3)	49.0	0.0
Fort Worth, TX (365)	0.0	3.3	61.4	(3)	35.3	0.0
Grand Rapids, MI (365)	0.0	1.9	50.1	(3)	47.9	0.0
Greeley, CO (365)	0.0	0.3	78.6	(3)	21.1	0.0
Green Bay, WI (365)	0.0	0.0	48.8	(3)	51.2	0.0
Greensboro, NC (365)	0.0	0.0	52.9	(3)	46.3	0.8
Honolulu, HI (365)	0.3	0.8	83.8	(3)	11.5	3.6
Houston, TX (365)	0.0	0.8	38.9	(3)	55.3	4.9
Huntsville, AL (357)	0.0	0.0	33.3	(3)	63.0	3.6
Indianapolis, IN (365)	0.0	2.2	25.5	(3)	72.3	0.0
Jacksonville, FL (365)	0.0	0.0	36.4	(3)	63.6	0.0
Kansas City, MO (365)	0.0	0.3	38.6	(3)	50.1	11.0
Lafayette, LA (365)	0.0	0.0	61.9	(3)	38.1	0.0
Las Cruces, NM (365)	0.0	2.5	58.1	(3)	6.3	33.2
Las Vegas, NV (365)	0.0	1.6	66.6	(3)	24.9	6.8
Lexington, KY (363)	0.0	5.5	38.3	(3)	55.9	0.3
Lincoln, NE (276)	0.0	0.0	78.6	(3)	21.4	0.0
Little Rock, AR (365)	0.0	1.6	27.9	(3)	70.4	0.0
Los Angeles, CA (365)	0.0	6.6	46.0	(3)	45.2	2.2
Louisville, KY (365)	0.0	2.2	39.5	(3)	58.4	0.0

Table continued on following page.

Appendix A: Comparative Statistics   A-167

MSA[1] (Days[2])	Percent of Days when AQI Pollutant was...					
	Carbon Monoxide	Nitrogen Dioxide	Ozone	Sulfur Dioxide	Particulate Matter 2.5	Particulate Matter 10
Madison, WI (365)	0.0	0.0	39.2	(3)	60.8	0.0
Manchester, NH (365)	0.0	0.0	92.1	(3)	7.9	0.0
Miami, FL (365)	0.0	6.8	33.7	(3)	59.5	0.0
Midland, TX (n/a)	n/a	n/a	n/a	(3)	n/a	n/a
Milwaukee, WI (365)	0.0	1.4	52.3	(3)	43.6	2.7
Minneapolis, MN (365)	0.0	3.3	47.7	(3)	41.1	7.9
Nashville, TN (365)	0.0	5.2	33.4	(3)	61.4	0.0
New Haven, CT (365)	0.0	5.2	55.9	(3)	37.5	1.4
New Orleans, LA (365)	0.0	0.0	48.2	(3)	51.5	0.3
New York, NY (365)	0.0	12.3	41.4	(3)	46.3	0.0
Oklahoma City, OK (365)	0.0	3.0	41.6	(3)	54.8	0.5
Omaha, NE (365)	0.0	0.0	53.4	(3)	38.4	8.2
Orlando, FL (365)	0.0	0.0	66.0	(3)	33.2	0.8
Philadelphia, PA (365)	0.0	6.0	39.7	(3)	54.0	0.3
Phoenix, AZ (365)	0.0	0.0	75.3	(3)	6.3	18.4
Pittsburgh, PA (365)	0.0	0.3	32.6	(3)	67.1	0.0
Portland, OR (365)	0.0	0.5	61.1	(3)	38.4	0.0
Providence, RI (365)	0.0	2.2	63.0	(3)	34.8	0.0
Provo, UT (365)	0.0	3.3	78.9	(3)	16.4	1.4
Raleigh, NC (365)	0.0	0.5	53.7	(3)	45.8	0.0
Reno, NV (365)	0.0	1.4	72.6	(3)	24.9	1.1
Richmond, VA (365)	0.0	6.3	51.8	(3)	41.9	0.0
Rochester, MN (361)	0.0	0.0	61.5	(3)	38.5	0.0
Sacramento, CA (365)	0.0	0.0	66.0	(3)	33.4	0.5
St. Louis, MO (365)	0.0	0.5	25.8	(3)	70.1	3.6
Salem, OR (363)	0.0	0.0	39.7	(3)	60.3	0.0
Salt Lake City, UT (365)	0.0	7.9	64.4	(3)	24.1	3.6
San Antonio, TX (365)	0.0	0.3	44.9	(3)	54.2	0.5
San Diego, CA (365)	0.0	1.1	59.5	(3)	38.6	0.8
San Francisco, CA (365)	0.0	1.1	47.9	(3)	51.0	0.0
San Jose, CA (365)	0.0	0.0	54.8	(3)	44.1	1.1
Santa Rosa, CA (365)	0.0	0.0	59.5	(3)	37.5	3.0
Savannah, GA (363)	0.0	0.0	24.5	(3)	75.5	0.0
Seattle, WA (365)	0.0	2.2	62.2	(3)	35.6	0.0
Sioux Falls, SD (349)	0.0	4.6	65.9	(3)	22.3	7.2
Springfield, IL (362)	0.0	0.0	43.1	(3)	56.9	0.0
Tampa, FL (365)	0.0	0.0	51.2	(3)	48.2	0.5
Tucson, AZ (365)	0.0	0.0	54.8	(3)	15.9	29.3
Tulsa, OK (365)	0.0	0.0	52.9	(3)	46.3	0.8
Tuscaloosa, AL (281)	0.0	0.0	72.6	(3)	27.4	0.0
Virginia Beach, VA (365)	0.0	6.8	49.6	(3)	43.6	0.0
Washington, DC (365)	0.0	8.5	52.1	(3)	39.5	0.0
Wichita, KS (365)	0.0	0.5	42.7	(3)	48.8	7.9
Wilmington, NC (360)	0.0	0.0	46.7	(3)	53.3	0.0
Winston-Salem, NC (365)	0.0	1.6	46.6	(3)	51.8	0.0
Worcester, MA (365)	0.0	2.5	58.1	(3)	39.2	0.3

Note: The Air Quality Index (AQI) is an index for reporting daily air quality. EPA calculates the AQI for five major air pollutants regulated by the Clean Air Act: ground-level ozone, particle pollution (also known as particulate matter), carbon monoxide, sulfur dioxide, and nitrogen dioxide. The AQI runs from 0 to 500. The higher the AQI value, the greater the level of air pollution and the greater the health concern; (1) Data covers the Metropolitan Statistical Area—see Appendix B for areas included; (2) Number of days with AQI data in 2021; (3) Sulfur dioxide is no longer included in this table (as of December 8, 2021) because SO_2 concentrations tend to be very localized and not necessarily representative of broad geographical areas like counties and CBSAs.
Source: U.S. Environmental Protection Agency, Air Quality Index Report, 2021

A-168 Appendix A: Comparative Statistics

Air Quality Trends: Ozone

MSA[1]	1990	1995	2000	2005	2010	2015	2018	2019	2020	2021
Albuquerque, NM	0.072	0.070	0.072	0.073	0.066	0.066	0.074	0.067	0.071	0.071
Allentown, PA	0.093	0.091	0.091	0.086	0.080	0.070	0.067	0.064	0.063	0.063
Anchorage, AK	n/a	n/a	n/a	n/a	n/a	n/a	n/a	n/a	n/a	n/a
Ann Arbor, MI	0.025	0.034	0.035	0.023	0.034	0.064	0.072	0.058	0.067	0.063
Athens, GA	n/a	n/a	n/a	n/a	n/a	n/a	n/a	n/a	n/a	n/a
Atlanta, GA	0.088	0.089	0.089	0.077	0.067	0.069	0.068	0.070	0.059	0.064
Austin, TX	0.088	0.089	0.088	0.082	0.074	0.073	0.072	0.065	0.066	0.066
Baltimore, MD	0.100	0.103	0.088	0.089	0.084	0.073	0.071	0.070	0.064	0.071
Boise City, ID	n/a	n/a	n/a	n/a	n/a	n/a	n/a	n/a	n/a	n/a
Boston, MA	0.078	0.085	0.067	0.075	0.066	0.065	0.061	0.052	0.053	0.059
Boulder, CO	n/a	n/a	n/a	n/a	n/a	n/a	n/a	n/a	n/a	n/a
Brownsville, TX	n/a	n/a	n/a	n/a	n/a	n/a	n/a	n/a	n/a	n/a
Cape Coral, FL	0.069	0.066	0.073	0.071	0.065	0.058	0.065	0.062	0.061	0.055
Cedar Rapids, IA	n/a	n/a	n/a	n/a	n/a	n/a	n/a	n/a	n/a	n/a
Charleston, SC	0.068	0.071	0.078	0.073	0.067	0.054	0.058	0.064	0.059	0.062
Charlotte, NC	0.094	0.091	0.099	0.089	0.082	0.071	0.070	0.073	0.060	0.067
Chicago, IL	0.074	0.094	0.073	0.084	0.070	0.066	0.073	0.069	0.076	0.071
Cincinnati, OH	0.083	0.082	0.074	0.075	0.069	0.069	0.073	0.067	0.067	0.065
Clarksville, TN	n/a	n/a	n/a	n/a	n/a	n/a	n/a	n/a	n/a	n/a
Cleveland, OH	0.084	0.090	0.079	0.084	0.074	0.069	0.072	0.067	0.069	0.066
College Station, TX	n/a	n/a	n/a	n/a	n/a	n/a	n/a	n/a	n/a	n/a
Colorado Springs, CO	n/a	n/a	n/a	n/a	n/a	n/a	n/a	n/a	n/a	n/a
Columbia, MO	n/a	n/a	n/a	n/a	n/a	n/a	n/a	n/a	n/a	n/a
Columbia, SC	0.091	0.079	0.089	0.082	0.069	0.058	0.059	0.063	0.053	0.061
Columbus, OH	0.090	0.091	0.085	0.084	0.073	0.066	0.062	0.060	0.062	0.061
Dallas, TX	0.094	0.103	0.096	0.096	0.079	0.078	0.079	0.070	0.070	0.076
Davenport, IA	0.065	0.072	0.064	0.065	0.057	0.060	0.067	0.066	0.063	0.066
Denver, CO	0.077	0.070	0.069	0.072	0.070	0.073	0.071	0.068	0.079	0.080
Des Moines, IA	n/a	n/a	n/a	n/a	n/a	n/a	n/a	n/a	n/a	n/a
Durham, NC	0.078	0.080	0.082	0.079	0.074	0.061	0.063	0.063	0.051	0.063
Edison, NJ	0.101	0.105	0.089	0.090	0.080	0.074	0.073	0.067	0.064	0.069
El Paso, TX	0.080	0.078	0.082	0.074	0.072	0.071	0.077	0.074	0.076	0.071
Fargo, ND	n/a	n/a	n/a	n/a	n/a	n/a	n/a	n/a	n/a	n/a
Fort Collins, CO	0.066	0.072	0.074	0.075	0.072	0.070	0.073	0.065	0.070	0.077
Fort Wayne, IN	0.086	0.094	0.086	0.081	0.067	0.061	0.071	0.063	0.064	0.062
Fort Worth, TX	0.094	0.103	0.096	0.096	0.079	0.078	0.079	0.070	0.070	0.076
Grand Rapids, MI	0.098	0.092	0.073	0.084	0.069	0.066	0.070	0.063	0.074	0.067
Greeley, CO	0.076	0.072	0.069	0.078	0.073	0.073	0.073	0.065	0.072	0.076
Green Bay, WI	n/a	n/a	n/a	n/a	n/a	n/a	n/a	n/a	n/a	n/a
Greensboro, NC	0.097	0.089	0.089	0.082	0.076	0.064	0.067	0.064	0.057	0.066
Honolulu, HI	0.034	0.049	0.044	0.042	0.046	0.048	0.046	0.053	0.044	0.045
Houston, TX	0.119	0.114	0.102	0.087	0.079	0.083	0.073	0.074	0.067	0.072
Huntsville, AL	0.079	0.080	0.088	0.075	0.071	0.063	0.065	0.063	0.057	0.061
Indianapolis, IN	0.085	0.095	0.081	0.081	0.070	0.065	0.076	0.066	0.065	0.067
Jacksonville, FL	0.080	0.068	0.072	0.076	0.068	0.060	0.060	0.062	0.057	0.061
Kansas City, MO	0.075	0.095	0.087	0.082	0.067	0.063	0.072	0.061	0.064	0.067
Lafayette, LA	n/a	n/a	n/a	n/a	n/a	n/a	n/a	n/a	n/a	n/a
Las Cruces, NM	0.073	0.075	0.075	0.070	0.060	0.070	0.072	0.068	0.071	0.079
Las Vegas, NV	n/a	n/a	n/a	n/a	n/a	n/a	n/a	n/a	n/a	n/a
Lexington, KY	0.078	0.088	0.077	0.078	0.070	0.069	0.063	0.059	0.060	0.064
Lincoln, NE	0.057	0.060	0.057	0.056	0.050	0.061	0.062	0.056	0.054	0.059
Little Rock, AR	0.080	0.086	0.090	0.083	0.072	0.063	0.066	0.059	0.062	0.066
Los Angeles, CA	0.128	0.109	0.090	0.086	0.074	0.082	0.082	0.080	0.096	0.076
Louisville, KY	0.082	0.091	0.087	0.083	0.076	0.071	0.069	0.064	0.063	0.064
Madison, WI	0.077	0.084	0.072	0.079	0.062	0.064	0.066	0.059	0.070	0.066
Manchester, NH	0.085	0.088	0.070	0.082	0.067	0.061	0.066	0.054	0.055	0.061

Table continued on following page.

Appendix A: Comparative Statistics   A-169

MSA[1]	1990	1995	2000	2005	2010	2015	2018	2019	2020	2021
Miami, FL	0.068	0.072	0.075	0.065	0.064	0.061	0.064	0.058	0.058	0.057
Midland, TX	n/a	n/a	n/a	n/a	n/a	n/a	n/a	n/a	n/a	n/a
Milwaukee, WI	0.095	0.106	0.082	0.092	0.079	0.069	0.073	0.066	0.074	0.072
Minneapolis, MN	0.068	0.084	0.065	0.074	0.066	0.061	0.065	0.059	0.060	0.067
Nashville, TN	0.089	0.092	0.084	0.078	0.073	0.065	0.068	0.064	0.061	0.064
New Haven, CT	0.121	0.117	0.087	0.092	0.079	0.081	0.077	0.084	0.080	0.083
New Orleans, LA	0.082	0.088	0.091	0.079	0.074	0.067	0.065	0.062	0.061	0.060
New York, NY	0.101	0.105	0.089	0.090	0.080	0.074	0.073	0.067	0.064	0.069
Oklahoma City, OK	0.080	0.087	0.083	0.077	0.071	0.067	0.072	0.065	0.066	0.068
Omaha, NE	0.054	0.075	0.063	0.069	0.058	0.055	0.063	0.050	0.055	0.055
Orlando, FL	0.081	0.075	0.080	0.083	0.069	0.060	0.062	0.062	0.059	0.061
Philadelphia, PA	0.102	0.109	0.099	0.091	0.083	0.074	0.075	0.067	0.065	0.068
Phoenix, AZ	0.080	0.086	0.082	0.077	0.075	0.072	0.073	0.071	0.079	0.079
Pittsburgh, PA	0.080	0.100	0.084	0.083	0.077	0.070	0.070	0.062	0.066	0.066
Portland, OR	0.081	0.065	0.059	0.059	0.056	0.064	0.062	0.058	0.058	0.058
Providence, RI	0.106	0.107	0.087	0.090	0.072	0.070	0.074	0.064	0.065	0.067
Provo, UT	n/a	n/a	n/a	n/a	n/a	n/a	n/a	n/a	n/a	n/a
Raleigh, NC	0.093	0.081	0.087	0.082	0.071	0.065	0.063	0.064	0.054	0.062
Reno, NV	0.074	0.069	0.067	0.069	0.068	0.071	0.077	0.063	0.073	0.078
Richmond, VA	0.083	0.089	0.080	0.082	0.079	0.062	0.062	0.061	0.054	0.061
Rochester, MN	n/a	n/a	n/a	n/a	n/a	n/a	n/a	n/a	n/a	n/a
Sacramento, CA	0.087	0.092	0.085	0.084	0.072	0.073	0.074	0.067	0.072	0.073
St. Louis, MO	0.077	0.084	0.074	0.078	0.069	0.067	0.072	0.066	0.066	0.067
Salem, OR	n/a	n/a	n/a	n/a	n/a	n/a	n/a	n/a	n/a	n/a
Salt Lake City, UT	n/a	n/a	n/a	n/a	n/a	n/a	n/a	n/a	n/a	n/a
San Antonio, TX	0.090	0.095	0.078	0.084	0.072	0.079	0.072	0.075	0.069	0.070
San Diego, CA	0.110	0.085	0.079	0.074	0.073	0.068	0.069	0.069	0.078	0.068
San Francisco, CA	0.062	0.077	0.060	0.060	0.063	0.064	0.056	0.062	0.062	0.064
San Jose, CA	0.078	0.084	0.065	0.063	0.072	0.067	0.059	0.061	0.066	0.067
Santa Rosa, CA	0.063	0.071	0.061	0.050	0.053	0.059	0.055	0.052	0.052	0.052
Savannah, GA	n/a	n/a	n/a	n/a	n/a	n/a	n/a	n/a	n/a	n/a
Seattle, WA	0.082	0.062	0.056	0.053	0.053	0.059	0.067	0.052	0.052	0.052
Sioux Falls, SD	n/a	n/a	n/a	n/a	n/a	n/a	n/a	n/a	n/a	n/a
Springfield, IL	n/a	n/a	n/a	n/a	n/a	n/a	n/a	n/a	n/a	n/a
Tampa, FL	0.080	0.075	0.081	0.075	0.067	0.062	0.065	0.065	0.063	0.060
Tucson, AZ	0.073	0.078	0.074	0.075	0.068	0.065	0.069	0.065	0.070	0.068
Tulsa, OK	0.086	0.091	0.081	0.072	0.069	0.061	0.067	0.062	0.061	0.063
Tuscaloosa, AL	n/a	n/a	n/a	n/a	n/a	n/a	n/a	n/a	n/a	n/a
Virginia Beach, VA	0.085	0.084	0.083	0.078	0.074	0.061	0.061	0.059	0.053	0.057
Washington, DC	0.075	0.083	0.073	0.069	0.069	0.067	0.068	0.064	0.057	0.066
Wichita, KS	0.077	0.069	0.080	0.074	0.075	0.064	0.064	0.062	0.059	0.061
Wilmington, NC	0.082	0.079	0.080	0.075	0.062	0.057	0.062	0.059	0.054	0.062
Winston-Salem, NC	0.084	0.086	0.089	0.080	0.078	0.065	0.064	0.062	0.058	0.062
Worcester, MA	0.097	0.096	0.076	0.085	0.070	0.063	0.065	0.060	0.063	0.063
U.S.	0.087	0.089	0.081	0.080	0.072	0.067	0.069	0.065	0.065	0.067

Note: (1) Data covers the Metropolitan Statistical Area; n/a not available. The values shown are the composite ozone concentration averages among trend sites based on the highest fourth daily maximum 8-hour concentration in parts per million. These trends are based on sites having an adequate record of monitoring data during the trend period. Data from exceptional events are included.
Source: U.S. Environmental Protection Agency, Air Quality Monitoring Information, "Air Quality Trends by City, 1990-2021"

A-170 Appendix A: Comparative Statistics

Maximum Air Pollutant Concentrations: Particulate Matter, Ozone, CO and Lead

Metro Aea	PM 10 (ug/m^3)	PM 2.5 Wtd AM (ug/m^3)	PM 2.5 24-Hr (ug/m^3)	Ozone (ppm)	Carbon Monoxide (ppm)	Lead (ug/m^3)
Albuquerque, NM	221	11.3	28	0.076	1	n/a
Allentown, PA	44	9.9	27	0.069	n/a	0.06
Anchorage, AK	97	6	21	n/a	2	n/a
Ann Arbor, MI	n/a	8.8	18	0.066	n/a	n/a
Athens, GA	n/a	10.1	25	0.06	n/a	n/a
Atlanta, GA	44	9.7	22	0.07	2	n/a
Austin, TX	91	9.4	21	0.066	1	n/a
Baltimore, MD	27	8.9	21	0.075	1	n/a
Boise City, ID	113	9.2	37	0.075	1	n/a
Boston, MA	50	8.3	18	0.067	1	n/a
Boulder, CO	51	10	54	0.082	n/a	n/a
Brownsville, TX	n/a	9.2	24	0.056	n/a	n/a
Cape Coral, FL	54	7.3	17	0.055	n/a	n/a
Cedar Rapids, IA	57	8.8	24	0.064	n/a	n/a
Charleston, SC	40	9.5	20	0.059	n/a	n/a
Charlotte, NC	39	9.3	21	0.067	1	n/a
Chicago, IL	166	10.8	27	0.079	1	0.03
Cincinnati, OH	178	12.1	27	0.07	2	n/a
Clarksville, TN	n/a	10.4	27	0.06	n/a	n/a
Cleveland, OH	89	12.6	29	0.072	2	0.01
College Station, TX	n/a	8	21	n/a	n/a	n/a
Colorado Springs, CO	39	6	21	0.078	1	n/a
Columbia, MO	n/a	n/a	n/a	0.058	n/a	n/a
Columbia, SC	42	9	22	0.064	1	n/a
Columbus, OH	32	9.9	24	0.064	1	n/a
Dallas, TX	56	9.6	23	0.085	1	0.02
Davenport, IA	137	9.4	26	0.066	1	n/a
Denver, CO	96	10.3	41	0.089	2	n/a
Des Moines, IA	54	8.3	23	0.061	n/a	n/a
Durham, NC	40	8	18	0.063	n/a	n/a
Edison, NJ	40	9.8	26	0.079	2	n/a
El Paso, TX	153	9.2	37	0.073	3	n/a
Fargo, ND	n/a	11	60	0.063	n/a	n/a
Fort Collins, CO	n/a	8.5	29	0.085	1	n/a
Fort Wayne, IN	n/a	9	21	0.065	n/a	n/a
Fort Worth, TX	56	9.6	23	0.085	1	0.02
Grand Rapids, MI	42	10.1	26	0.069	1	n/a
Greeley, CO	n/a	9.8	31	0.083	1	n/a
Green Bay, WI	n/a	8.7	26	0.068	n/a	n/a
Greensboro, NC	35	7.7	18	0.066	n/a	n/a
Honolulu, HI	34	3.3	6	0.047	2	n/a
Houston, TX	103	11.4	24	0.083	2	n/a
Huntsville, AL	36	7.5	17	0.061	n/a	n/a
Indianapolis, IN	55	12.6	32	0.067	2	n/a
Jacksonville, FL	54	8.8	18	0.061	1	n/a
Kansas City, MO	103	11.2	31	0.071	1	n/a
Lafayette, LA	56	7.6	16	0.063	n/a	n/a
Las Cruces, NM	439	9.3	26	0.086	n/a	n/a
Las Vegas, NV	176	9.9	33	0.076	2	n/a
Lexington, KY	27	9.6	23	0.064	n/a	n/a
Lincoln, NE	n/a	7.1	21	0.059	n/a	n/a
Little Rock, AR	32	9.7	25	0.067	1	n/a
Los Angeles, CA	113	13.4	48	0.097	3	0.06
Louisville, KY	46	11.2	28	0.073	1	n/a
Madison, WI	49	9.5	27	0.066	n/a	n/a

Table continued on following page.

Appendix A: Comparative Statistics   A-171

Metro Aea	PM 10 (ug/m³)	PM 2.5 Wtd AM (ug/m³)	PM 2.5 24-Hr (ug/m³)	Ozone (ppm)	Carbon Monoxide (ppm)	Lead (ug/m³)
Manchester, NH	n/a	4.5	13	0.062	1	n/a
Miami, FL	73	9.5	26	0.058	1	n/a
Midland, TX	n/a	n/a	n/a	n/a	n/a	n/a
Milwaukee, WI	70	10.2	27	0.073	1	n/a
Minneapolis, MN	115	8.8	30	0.07	2	0.08
Nashville, TN	50	9.4	24	0.066	2	n/a
New Haven, CT	68	8.8	22	0.083	1	n/a
New Orleans, LA	45	7.6	17	0.063	1	0.05
New York, NY	40	9.8	26	0.079	2	n/a
Oklahoma City, OK	64	11.2	28	0.07	1	n/a
Omaha, NE	70	8.9	26	0.066	1	0.09
Orlando, FL	51	7.6	15	0.062	1	n/a
Philadelphia, PA	60	10.1	25	0.077	1	0
Phoenix, AZ	225	12.7	36	0.083	3	n/a
Pittsburgh, PA	81	11.8	30	0.068	4	0
Portland, OR	29	6.4	16	0.062	1	n/a
Providence, RI	29	9.3	21	0.069	1	n/a
Provo, UT	100	7.7	31	0.077	1	n/a
Raleigh, NC	56	9.2	22	0.066	1	n/a
Reno, NV	284	12.4	105	0.08	2	n/a
Richmond, VA	40	8.3	19	0.066	1	n/a
Rochester, MN	n/a	n/a	n/a	0.067	n/a	n/a
Sacramento, CA	406	11.3	57	0.085	1	n/a
St. Louis, MO	161	10	23	0.073	1	0.06
Salem, OR	n/a	n/a	n/a	0.063	n/a	n/a
Salt Lake City, UT	103	10.3	43	0.087	1	n/a
San Antonio, TX	87	8.9	22	0.078	1	n/a
San Diego, CA	119	11.2	24	0.078	1	0.02
San Francisco, CA	35	9.1	23	0.074	2	n/a
San Jose, CA	76	10.9	25	0.074	1	n/a
Santa Rosa, CA	53	n/a	n/a	0.055	1	n/a
Savannah, GA	n/a	10.1	22	0.058	n/a	n/a
Seattle, WA	22	7.1	22	0.078	1	n/a
Sioux Falls, SD	110	n/a	n/a	0.065	1	n/a
Springfield, IL	n/a	8.7	22	0.057	n/a	n/a
Tampa, FL	61	8.5	18	0.063	1	0.08
Tucson, AZ	249	6.6	14	0.068	1	n/a
Tulsa, OK	99	10.1	29	0.068	1	n/a
Tuscaloosa, AL	n/a	7.8	20	0.053	n/a	n/a
Virginia Beach, VA	44	7.2	16	0.061	1	n/a
Washington, DC	47	9.6	21	0.072	2	n/a
Wichita, KS	89	11.3	31	0.067	n/a	n/a
Wilmington, NC	41	4.8	13	0.062	n/a	n/a
Winston-Salem, NC	41	9.2	41	0.066	n/a	n/a
Worcester, MA	31	9.1	19	0.068	1	n/a
NAAQS[1]	150	15.0	35	0.075	9	0.15

Note: Data from exceptional events are included; Data covers the Metropolitan Statistical Area; (1) National Ambient Air Quality Standards; ppm = parts per million; ug/m³ = micrograms per cubic meter; n/a not available
Concentrations: Particulate Matter 10 (coarse particulate)—highest second maximum 24-hour concentration; Particulate Matter 2.5 Wtd AM (fine particulate)—highest weighted annual mean concentration; Particulate Matter 2.5 24-Hour (fine particulate)—highest 98th percentile 24-hour concentration; Ozone—highest fourth daily maximum 8-hour concentration; Carbon Monoxide—highest second maximum non-overlapping 8-hour concentration; Lead—maximum running 3-month average
Source: U.S. Environmental Protection Agency, Air Quality Monitoring Information, "Air Quality Statistics by City, 2021"

A-172 Appendix A: Comparative Statistics

Maximum Air Pollutant Concentrations: Nitrogen Dioxide and Sulfur Dioxide

Metro Area	Nitrogen Dioxide AM (ppb)	Nitrogen Dioxide 1-Hr (ppb)	Sulfur Dioxide AM (ppb)	Sulfur Dioxide 1-Hr (ppb)	Sulfur Dioxide 24-Hr (ppb)
Albuquerque, NM	8	44	n/a	3	n/a
Allentown, PA	10	42	n/a	6	n/a
Anchorage, AK	n/a	n/a	n/a	n/a	n/a
Ann Arbor, MI	n/a	n/a	n/a	n/a	n/a
Athens, GA	n/a	n/a	n/a	n/a	n/a
Atlanta, GA	17	50	n/a	4	n/a
Austin, TX	13	44	n/a	3	n/a
Baltimore, MD	16	51	n/a	16	n/a
Boise City, ID	10	45	n/a	2	n/a
Boston, MA	12	45	n/a	9	n/a
Boulder, CO	n/a	n/a	n/a	n/a	n/a
Brownsville, TX	n/a	n/a	n/a	n/a	n/a
Cape Coral, FL	n/a	n/a	n/a	n/a	n/a
Cedar Rapids, IA	n/a	n/a	n/a	40	n/a
Charleston, SC	n/a	n/a	n/a	9	n/a
Charlotte, NC	7	37	n/a	2	n/a
Chicago, IL	17	54	n/a	73	n/a
Cincinnati, OH	16	49	n/a	28	n/a
Clarksville, TN	n/a	n/a	n/a	n/a	n/a
Cleveland, OH	9	38	n/a	39	n/a
College Station, TX	n/a	n/a	n/a	11	n/a
Colorado Springs, CO	n/a	n/a	n/a	10	n/a
Columbia, MO	n/a	n/a	n/a	n/a	n/a
Columbia, SC	n/a	n/a	n/a	1	n/a
Columbus, OH	10	47	n/a	2	n/a
Dallas, TX	13	48	n/a	8	n/a
Davenport, IA	n/a	n/a	n/a	4	n/a
Denver, CO	26	71	n/a	7	n/a
Des Moines, IA	6	34	n/a	n/a	n/a
Durham, NC	n/a	n/a	n/a	1	n/a
Edison, NJ	19	65	n/a	17	n/a
El Paso, TX	14	57	n/a	n/a	n/a
Fargo, ND	4	31	n/a	n/a	n/a
Fort Collins, CO	n/a	n/a	n/a	n/a	n/a
Fort Wayne, IN	n/a	n/a	n/a	n/a	n/a
Fort Worth, TX	13	48	n/a	8	n/a
Grand Rapids, MI	8	39	n/a	4	n/a
Greeley, CO	6	42	n/a	n/a	n/a
Green Bay, WI	n/a	n/a	n/a	5	n/a
Greensboro, NC	n/a	n/a	n/a	n/a	n/a
Honolulu, HI	3	22	n/a	44	n/a
Houston, TX	12	49	n/a	16	n/a
Huntsville, AL	n/a	n/a	n/a	n/a	n/a
Indianapolis, IN	12	40	n/a	3	n/a
Jacksonville, FL	11	41	n/a	39	n/a
Kansas City, MO	10	44	n/a	9	n/a
Lafayette, LA	n/a	n/a	n/a	n/a	n/a
Las Cruces, NM	8	48	n/a	n/a	n/a
Las Vegas, NV	22	53	n/a	3	n/a
Lexington, KY	6	n/a	n/a	5	n/a
Lincoln, NE	n/a	n/a	n/a	n/a	n/a
Little Rock, AR	7	38	n/a	6	n/a
Los Angeles, CA	25	76	n/a	4	n/a
Louisville, KY	15	50	n/a	13	n/a
Madison, WI	n/a	n/a	n/a	2	n/a

Table continued on following page.

Appendix A: Comparative Statistics   A-173

Metro Area	Nitrogen Dioxide AM (ppb)	Nitrogen Dioxide 1-Hr (ppb)	Sulfur Dioxide AM (ppb)	Sulfur Dioxide 1-Hr (ppb)	Sulfur Dioxide 24-Hr (ppb)
Manchester, NH	n/a	n/a	n/a	1	n/a
Miami, FL	13	49	n/a	2	n/a
Midland, TX	n/a	n/a	n/a	n/a	n/a
Milwaukee, WI	13	42	n/a	n/a	n/a
Minneapolis, MN	8	38	n/a	14	n/a
Nashville, TN	13	52	n/a	4	n/a
New Haven, CT	12	48	n/a	3	n/a
New Orleans, LA	9	37	n/a	56	n/a
New York, NY	19	65	n/a	17	n/a
Oklahoma City, OK	13	47	n/a	1	n/a
Omaha, NE	n/a	n/a	n/a	48	n/a
Orlando, FL	n/a	n/a	n/a	n/a	n/a
Philadelphia, PA	14	54	n/a	6	n/a
Phoenix, AZ	26	59	n/a	7	n/a
Pittsburgh, PA	10	36	n/a	54	n/a
Portland, OR	9	31	n/a	3	n/a
Providence, RI	16	36	n/a	3	n/a
Provo, UT	9	42	n/a	n/a	n/a
Raleigh, NC	8	31	n/a	2	n/a
Reno, NV	12	47	n/a	3	n/a
Richmond, VA	13	48	n/a	3	n/a
Rochester, MN	n/a	n/a	n/a	n/a	n/a
Sacramento, CA	7	41	n/a	n/a	n/a
St. Louis, MO	10	46	n/a	34	n/a
Salem, OR	n/a	n/a	n/a	n/a	n/a
Salt Lake City, UT	16	51	n/a	7	n/a
San Antonio, TX	7	32	n/a	3	n/a
San Diego, CA	13	54	n/a	1	n/a
San Francisco, CA	12	40	n/a	11	n/a
San Jose, CA	12	39	n/a	2	n/a
Santa Rosa, CA	3	20	n/a	n/a	n/a
Savannah, GA	n/a	n/a	n/a	50	n/a
Seattle, WA	16	49	n/a	3	n/a
Sioux Falls, SD	n/a	n/a	n/a	n/a	n/a
Springfield, IL	n/a	n/a	n/a	n/a	n/a
Tampa, FL	9	37	n/a	29	n/a
Tucson, AZ	8	38	n/a	1	n/a
Tulsa, OK	7	38	n/a	5	n/a
Tuscaloosa, AL	n/a	n/a	n/a	n/a	n/a
Virginia Beach, VA	7	40	n/a	3	n/a
Washington, DC	15	50	n/a	3	n/a
Wichita, KS	7	39	n/a	4	n/a
Wilmington, NC	n/a	n/a	n/a	n/a	n/a
Winston-Salem, NC	6	32	n/a	4	n/a
Worcester, MA	9	44	n/a	2	n/a
NAAQS[1]	53	100	30	75	140

Note: Data from exceptional events are included; Data covers the Metropolitan Statistical Area; (1) National Ambient Air Quality Standards; ppb = parts per billion; n/a not available
Concentrations: Nitrogen Dioxide AM—highest arithmetic mean concentration; Nitrogen Dioxide 1-Hr—highest 98th percentile 1-hour daily maximum concentration; Sulfur Dioxide AM—highest annual mean concentration; Sulfur Dioxide 1-Hr—highest 99th percentile 1-hour daily maximum concentration; Sulfur Dioxide 24-Hr—highest second maximum 24-hour concentration
Source: U.S. Environmental Protection Agency, Air Quality Monitoring Information, "Air Quality Statistics by City, 2021"

Appendix B: Metropolitan Area Definitions

Metropolitan Statistical Areas (MSA), Metropolitan Divisions (MD), New England City and Town Areas (NECTA), and New England City and Town Area Divisions (NECTAD)

Note: In March 2020, the Office of Management and Budget (OMB) announced changes to metropolitan and micropolitan statistical area definitions. Both current and historical definitions (December 2009) are shown below. If the change only affected the name of the metro area, the counties included were not repeated.

Albuquerque, NM MSA
Bernalillo, Sandoval, Torrance, and Valencia Counties

Allentown-Bethlehem-Easton, PA-NJ MSA
Carbon, Lehigh, and Northampton Counties, PA; Warren County, NJ

Anchorage, AK MSA
Anchorage Municipality and Matanuska-Susitna Borough

Ann Arbor, MI MSA
Washtenaw County

Athens-Clarke County, GA MSA
Clarke, Madison, Oconee, and Oglethorpe Counties

Atlanta-Sandy Springs-Roswell, GA MSA
Barrow, Bartow, Butts, Carroll, Cherokee, Clayton, Cobb, Coweta, Dawson, DeKalb, Douglas, Fayette, Forsyth, Fulton, Gwinnett, Haralson, Heard, Henry, Jasper, Lamar, Meriwether, Morgan, Newton, Paulding, Pickens, Pike, Rockdale, Spalding, and Walton Counties
Previously Atlanta-Sandy Springs-Marietta, GA MSA
Barrow, Bartow, Butts, Carroll, Cherokee, Clayton, Cobb, Coweta, Dawson, DeKalb, Douglas, Fayette, Forsyth, Fulton, Gwinnett, Haralson, Heard, Henry, Jasper, Lamar, Meriwether, Newton, Paulding, Pickens, Pike, Rockdale, Spalding, and Walton Counties

Austin-Round Rock, TX MSA
Previously Austin-Round Rock-San Marcos, TX MSA
Bastrop, Caldwell, Hays, Travis, and Williamson Counties

Baltimore-Columbia-Towson, MD MSA
Previously Baltimore-Towson, MD MSA
Baltimore city; Anne Arundel, Baltimore, Carroll, Harford, Howard, and Queen Anne's Counties

Boise City, ID MSA
Previously Boise City-Nampa, ID MSA
Ada, Boise, Canyon, Gem, and Owyhee Counties

Boston, MA

Boston-Cambridge-Newton, MA-NH MSA
Previously Boston-Cambridge-Quincy, MA-NH MSA
Essex, Middlesex, Norfolk, Plymouth, and Suffolk Counties, MA; Rockingham and Strafford Counties, NH

Boston, MA MD
Previously Boston-Quincy, MA MD
Norfolk, Plymouth, and Suffolk Counties

Boston-Cambridge-Nashua, MA-NH NECTA
Includes 157 cities and towns in Massachusetts and 34 cities and towns in New Hampshire
Previously Boston-Cambridge-Quincy, MA-NH NECTA
Includes 155 cities and towns in Massachusetts and 38 cities and towns in New Hampshire

Boston-Cambridge-Newton, MA NECTA Division
Includes 92 cities and towns in Massachusetts
Previously Boston-Cambridge-Quincy, MA NECTA Division
Includes 97 cities and towns in Massachusetts

Boulder, CO MSA
Boulder County

Brownsville-Harlingen, TX MSA
Cameron County

Cape Coral-Fort Myers, FL MSA
Lee County

Cedar Rapids, IA, MSA
Benton, Jones, and Linn Counties

Charleston-North Charleston, SC MSA
Previously Charleston-North Charleston-Summerville, SC MSA
Berkeley, Charleston, and Dorchester Counties

Charlotte-Concord-Gastonia, NC-SC MSA
Cabarrus, Gaston, Iredell, Lincoln, Mecklenburg, Rowan, and Union Counties, NC; Chester, Lancaster, and York Counties, SC
Previously Charlotte-Gastonia-Rock Hill, NC-SC MSA
Anson, Cabarrus, Gaston, Mecklenburg, and Union Counties, NC; York County, SC

Chicago, IL

Chicago-Naperville-Elgin, IL-IN-WI MSA
Previous name: Chicago-Joliet-Naperville, IL-IN-WI MSA
Cook, DeKalb, DuPage, Grundy, Kane, Kendall, Lake, McHenry, and Will Counties, IL; Jasper, Lake, Newton, and Porter Counties, IN; Kenosha County, WI

Chicago-Naperville-Arlington Heights, IL MD
Cook, DuPage, Grundy, Kendall, McHenry, and Will Counties
Previous name: Chicago-Joliet-Naperville, IL MD
Cook, DeKalb, DuPage, Grundy, Kane, Kendall, McHenry, and Will Counties

Elgin, IL MD
DeKalb and Kane Counties
Previously part of the Chicago-Joliet-Naperville, IL MD

Gary, IN MD
Jasper, Lake, Newton, and Porter Counties

Lake County-Kenosha County, IL-WI MD
Lake County, IL; Kenosha County, WI

Cincinnati, OH-KY-IN MSA
Brown, Butler, Clermont, Hamilton, and Warren Counties, OH; Boone, Bracken, Campbell, Gallatin, Grant, Kenton, and Pendleton County, KY; Dearborn, Franklin, Ohio, and Union Counties, IN
Previously Cincinnati-Middletown, OH-KY-IN MSA
Brown, Butler, Clermont, Hamilton, and Warren Counties, OH; Boone, Bracken, Campbell, Gallatin, Grant, Kenton, and Pendleton County, KY; Dearborn, Franklin, and Ohio Counties, IN

Clarksville, TN-KY MSA
Montgomery and Stewart Counties, TN; Christian and Trigg Counties, KY

Cleveland-Elyria-Mentor, OH MSA
Cuyahoga, Geauga, Lake, Lorain, and Medina Counties

A-176   Appendix B: Metropolitan Area Definitions

College Station-Bryan, TX MSA
Brazos, Burleson and Robertson Counties

Colorado Springs, CO MSA
El Paso and Teller Counties

Columbia, MO MSA
Boone and Howard Counties

Columbia, SC MSA
Calhoun, Fairfield, Kershaw, Lexington, Richland and Saluda Counties

Columbus, OH MSA
Delaware, Fairfield, Franklin, Licking, Madison, Morrow, Pickaway, and Union Counties

Dallas, TX

Dallas-Fort Worth-Arlington, TX MSA
Collin, Dallas, Denton, Ellis, Hunt, Johnson, Kaufman, Parker, Rockwall, Tarrant, and Wise Counties

Dallas-Plano-Irving, TX MD
Collin, Dallas, Denton, Ellis, Hunt, Kaufman, and Rockwall Counties

Davenport-Moline-Rock Island, IA-IL MSA
Henry, Mercer, and Rock Island Counties, IA; Scott County

Denver-Aurora-Lakewood, CO MSA
Previously Denver-Aurora-Broomfield, CO MSA
Adams, Arapahoe, Broomfield, Clear Creek, Denver, Douglas, Elbert, Gilpin, Jefferson, and Park Counties

Des Moines-West Des Moines, IA MSA
Dallas, Guthrie, Madison, Polk, and Warren Counties

Durham-Chapel Hill, NC MSA
Chatham, Durham, Orange, and Person Counties

Edison, NJ
See New York, NY (New York-Jersey City-White Plains, NY-NJ MD)

El Paso, TX MSA
El Paso County

Fargo, ND-MN MSA
Cass County, ND; Clay County, MN

Fort Collins, CO MSA
Previously Fort Collins-Loveland, CO MSA
Larimer County

Fort Wayne, IN MSA
Allen, Wells, and Whitley Counties

Fort Worth, TX

Dallas-Fort Worth-Arlington, TX MSA
Collin, Dallas, Denton, Ellis, Hunt, Johnson, Kaufman, Parker, Rockwall, Tarrant, and Wise Counties

Fort Worth-Arlington, TX MD
Hood, Johnson, Parker, Somervell, Tarrant, and Wise Counties

Grand Rapids-Wyoming, MI MSA
Barry, Kent, Montcalm, and Ottawa Counties
Previously Grand Rapids-Wyoming, MI MSA
Barry, Ionia, Kent, and Newaygo Counties

Greeley, CO MSA
Weld County

Green Bay, WI MSA
Brown, Kewaunee, and Oconto Counties

Greensboro-High Point, NC MSA
Guilford, Randolph, and Rockingham Counties

Honolulu, HI MSA
Honolulu County

Houston-The Woodlands-Sugar Land-Baytown, TX MSA
Austin, Brazoria, Chambers, Fort Bend, Galveston, Harris, Liberty, Montgomery, and Waller Counties
Previously Houston-Sugar Land-Baytown, TX MSA
Austin, Brazoria, Chambers, Fort Bend, Galveston, Harris, Liberty, Montgomery, San Jacinto, and Waller Counties

Huntsville, AL MSA
Limestone and Madison Counties

Indianapolis-Carmel, IN MSA
Boone, Brown, Hamilton, Hancock, Hendricks, Johnson, Marion, Morgan, Putnam, and Shelby Counties

Jacksonville, FL MSA
Baker, Clay, Duval, Nassau, and St. Johns Counties

Kansas City, MO-KS MSA
Franklin, Johnson, Leavenworth, Linn, Miami, and Wyandotte Counties, KS; Bates, Caldwell, Cass, Clay, Clinton, Jackson, Lafayette, Platte, and Ray Counties, MO

Lafayette, LA MSA
Acadia, Iberia, Lafayette, St. Martin, and Vermilion Parishes

Las Cruces, NM MSA
Doña Ana County
Previously Las Cruces, NM MSA
Doña Ana and San Miguel Counties

Las Vegas-Henderson-Paradise, NV MSA
Previously Las Vegas-Paradise, NV MSA
Clark County

Lexington-Fayette, KY MSA
Bourbon, Clark, Fayette, Jessamine, Scott, and Woodford Counties

Lincoln, NE MSA
Lancaster and Seward Counties

Little Rock-North Little Rock-Conway, AR MSA
Faulkner, Grant, Lonoke, Perry, Pulaski, and Saline Counties

Los Angeles, CA

Los Angeles-Long Beach-Anaheim, CA MSA
Previously Los Angeles-Long Beach-Santa Ana, CA MSA
Los Angeles and Orange Counties

Los Angeles-Long Beach-Glendale, CA MD
Los Angeles County

Anaheim-Santa Ana-Irvine, CA MD
Previously Santa Ana-Anaheim-Irvine, CA MD
Orange County

Louisville/Jefferson, KY-IN MSA
Clark, Floyd, Harrison, Scott, and Washington Counties, IN; Bullitt, Henry, Jefferson, Oldham, Shelby, Spencer, and Trimble Counties, KY

Madison, WI MSA
Columbia, Dane, and Iowa Counties

Manchester, NH

Manchester-Nashua, NH MSA
Hillsborough County

Appendix B: Metropolitan Area Definitions   A-177

Manchester, NH NECTA
Includes 11 cities and towns in New Hampshire
Previously Manchester, NH NECTA
Includes 9 cities and towns in New Hampshire

Miami, FL

Miami-Fort Lauderdale-West Palm Beach, FL MSA
Previously Miami-Fort Lauderdale-Pompano Beach, FL MSA
Broward, Miami-Dade, and Palm Beach Counties

Miami-Miami Beach-Kendall, FL MD
Miami-Dade County

Midland, TX MSA
Martin, and Midland Counties

Milwaukee-Waukesha-West Allis, WI MSA
Milwaukee, Ozaukee, Washington, and Waukesha Counties

Minneapolis-St. Paul-Bloomington, MN-WI MSA
Anoka, Carver, Chisago, Dakota, Hennepin, Isanti, Le Sueur, Mille Lacs, Ramsey, Scott, Sherburne, Sibley, Washington, and Wright Counties, MN; Pierce and St. Croix Counties, WI

Nashville-Davidson-Murfreesboro-Franklin, TN MSA
Cannon, Cheatham, Davidson, Dickson, Hickman, Macon, Robertson, Rutherford, Smith, Sumner, Trousdale, Williamson, and Wilson Counties

New Haven-Milford, CT MSA
New Haven County

New Orleans-Metarie-Kenner, LA MSA
Jefferson, Orleans, Plaquemines, St. Bernard, St. Charles, St. James, St. John the Baptist, and St. Tammany Parish
Previously New Orleans-Metarie-Kenner, LA MSA
Jefferson, Orleans, Plaquemines, St. Bernard, St. Charles, St. John the Baptist, and St. Tammany Parish

New York, NY

New York-Newark-Jersey City, NY-NJ-PA MSA
Bergen, Essex, Hudson, Hunterdon, Middlesex, Monmouth, Morris, Ocean, Passaic, Somerset, Sussex, and Union Counties, NJ; Bronx, Dutchess, Kings, Nassau, New York, Orange, Putnam, Queens, Richmond, Rockland, Suffolk, and Westchester Counties, NY; Pike County, PA
Previous name: New York-Northern New Jersey-Long Island, NY-NJ-PA MSA
Bergen, Essex, Hudson, Hunterdon, Middlesex, Monmouth, Morris, Ocean, Passaic, Somerset, Sussex, and Union Counties, NJ; Bronx, Kings, Nassau, New York, Putnam, Queens, Richmond, Rockland, Suffolk, and Westchester Counties, NY; Pike County, PA

Dutchess County-Putnam County, NY MD
Dutchess and Putnam Counties
Dutchess County was previously part of the Poughkeepsie-Newburgh-Middletown, NY MSA. Putnam County was previously part of the New York-Wayne-White Plains, NY-NJ MD

Nassau-Suffolk, NY MD
Nassau and Suffolk Counties

New York-Jersey City-White Plains, NY-NJ MD
Bergen, Hudson, Middlesex, Monmouth, Ocean, and Passaic Counties, NJ; Bronx, Kings, New York, Orange, Queens, Richmond, Rockland, and Westchester Counties, NY
Previous name: New York-Wayne-White Plains, NY-NJ MD
Bergen, Hudson, and Passaic Counties, NJ; Bronx, Kings, New York, Putnam, Queens, Richmond, Rockland, and Westchester Counties, NY

Newark, NJ-PA MD
Essex, Hunterdon, Morris, Somerset, Sussex, and Union Counties, NJ; Pike County, PA
Previous name: Newark-Union, NJ-PA MD
Essex, Hunterdon, Morris, Sussex, and Union Counties, NJ; Pike County, PA

Oklahoma City, OK MSA
Canadian, Cleveland, Grady, Lincoln, Logan, McClain, and Oklahoma Counties

Omaha-Council Bluffs, NE-IA MSA
Harrison, Mills, and Pottawattamie Counties, IA; Cass, Douglas, Sarpy, Saunders, and Washington Counties, NE

Orlando-Kissimmee-Sanford, FL MSA
Lake, Orange, Osceola, and Seminole Counties

Philadelphia, PA

Philadelphia-Camden-Wilmington, PA-NJ-DE-MD MSA
New Castle County, DE; Cecil County, MD; Burlington, Camden, Gloucester, and Salem Counties, NJ; Bucks, Chester, Delaware, Montgomery, and Philadelphia Counties, PA

Camden, NJ MD
Burlington, Camden, and Gloucester Counties

Montgomery County-Bucks County-Chester County, PA MD
Bucks, Chester, and Montgomery Counties
Previously part of the Philadelphia, PA MD

Philadelphia, PA MD
Delaware and Philadelphia Counties
Previous name: Philadelphia, PA MD
Bucks, Chester, Delaware, Montgomery, and Philadelphia Counties

Wilmington, DE-MD-NJ MD
New Castle County, DE; Cecil County, MD; Salem County, NJ

Phoenix-Mesa-Scottsdale, AZ MSA
Previously Phoenix-Mesa-Glendale, AZ MSA
Maricopa and Pinal Counties

Pittsburgh, PA MSA
Allegheny, Armstrong, Beaver, Butler, Fayette, Washington, and Westmoreland Counties

Portland-Vancouver-Hillsboro, OR-WA MSA
Clackamas, Columbia, Multnomah, Washington, and Yamhill Counties, OR; Clark and Skamania Counties, WA

Providence, RI

Providence-New Bedford-Fall River, RI-MA MSA
Previously Providence-New Bedford-Fall River, RI-MA MSA
Bristol County, MA; Bristol, Kent, Newport, Providence, and Washington Counties, RI

Providence-Warwick, RI-MA NECTA
Includes 12 cities and towns in Massachusetts and 36 cities and towns in Rhode Island
Previously Providence-Fall River-Warwick, RI-MA NECTA
Includes 12 cities and towns in Massachusetts and 37 cities and towns in Rhode Island

Provo-Orem, UT MSA
Juab and Utah Counties

Raleigh, NC MSA
Previously Raleigh-Cary, NC MSA
Franklin, Johnston, and Wake Counties

A-178   Appendix B: Metropolitan Area Definitions

Reno, NV MSA
Previously Reno-Sparks, NV MSA
Storey and Washoe Counties

Richmond, VA MSA
Amelia, Caroline, Charles City, Chesterfield, Dinwiddie, Goochland, Hanover, Henrico, King William, New Kent, Powhatan, Prince George, and Sussex Counties; Colonial Heights, Hopewell, Petersburg, and Richmond Cities

Rochester, MN MSA
Dodge, Fillmore, Olmsted, and Wabasha Counties

Sacramento—Roseville—Arden-Arcade, CA MSA
El Dorado, Placer, Sacramento, and Yolo Counties

Saint Louis, MO-IL MSA
Bond, Calhoun, Clinton, Jersey, Macoupin, Madison, Monroe, and St. Clair Counties, IL; St. Louis city; Franklin, Jefferson, Lincoln, St. Charles, St. Louis, and Warren Counties, MO
Previously Saint Louis, MO-IL MSA
Bond, Calhoun, Clinton, Jersey, Macoupin, Madison, Monroe, and St. Clair Counties, IL; St. Louis city; Crawford (part), Franklin, Jefferson, Lincoln, St. Charles, St. Louis, Warren, and Washington Counties, MO

Salem, OR MSA
Marion and Polk Counties

Salt Lake City, UT MSA
Salt Lake and Tooele Counties

San Antonio-New Braunfels, TX MSA
Atascosa, Bandera, Bexar, Comal, Guadalupe, Kendall, Medina, and Wilson Counties

San Diego-Carlsbad, CA MSA
Previously San Diego-Carlsbad-San Marcos, CA MSA
San Diego County

San Francisco, CA

San Francisco-Oakland-Hayward, CA MSA
Previously San Francisco-Oakland- Fremont, CA MSA
Alameda, Contra Costa, Marin, San Francisco, and San Mateo Counties

San Francisco-Redwood City-South San Francisco, CA MD
San Francisco and San Mateo Counties

Previously San Francisco-San Mateo-Redwood City, CA MD
Marin, San Francisco, and San Mateo Counties

San Jose-Sunnyvale-Santa Clara, CA MSA
San Benito and Santa Clara Counties

Santa Rosa, CA MSA
Previously Santa Rosa-Petaluma, CA MSA
Sonoma County

Savannah, GA MSA
Bryan, Chatham, and Effingham Counties

Seattle, WA

Seattle-Tacoma-Bellevue, WA MSA
King, Pierce, and Snohomish Counties

Seattle-Bellevue-Everett, WA MD
King and Snohomish Counties

Sioux Falls, SD MSA
Lincoln, McCook, Minnehaha, and Turner Counties

Springfield, IL MSA
Menard and Sangamon Counties

Tampa-St. Petersburg-Clearwater, FL MSA
Hernando, Hillsborough, Pasco, and Pinellas Counties

Tucson, AZ MSA
Pima County

Tulsa, OK MSA
Creek, Okmulgee, Osage, Pawnee, Rogers, Tulsa, and Wagoner Counties

Tuscaloosa, AL MSA
Hale, Pickens, and Tuscaloosa Counties

Virginia Beach-Norfolk-Newport News, VA-NC MSA
Currituck County, NC; Chesapeake, Hampton, Newport News, Norfolk, Poquoson, Portsmouth, Suffolk, Virginia Beach and Williamsburg cities, VA; Gloucester, Isle of Wight, James City, Mathews, Surry, and York Counties, VA

Washington, DC

Washington-Arlington-Alexandria, DC-VA-MD-WV MSA
District of Columbia; Calvert, Charles, Frederick, Montgomery, and Prince George's Counties, MD; Alexandria, Fairfax, Falls Church, Fredericksburg, Manassas Park, and Manassas cities, VA; Arlington, Clarke, Culpepper, Fairfax, Fauquier, Loudoun, Prince William, Rappahannock, Spotsylvania, Stafford, and Warren Counties, VA; Jefferson County, WV
Previously Washington-Arlington-Alexandria, DC-VA-MD-WV MSA
District of Columbia; Calvert, Charles, Frederick, Montgomery, and Prince George's Counties, MD; Alexandria, Fairfax, Falls Church, Fredericksburg, Manassas Park, and Manassas cities, VA; Arlington, Clarke, Fairfax, Fauquier, Loudoun, Prince William, Spotsylvania, Stafford, and Warren Counties, VA; Jefferson County, WV

Washington-Arlington-Alexandria, DC-VA-MD-WV MD
District of Columbia; Calvert, Charles, and Prince George's Counties, MD; Alexandria, Fairfax, Falls Church, Fredericksburg, Manassas Park, and Manassas cities, VA; Arlington, Clarke, Culpepper, Fairfax, Fauquier, Loudoun, Prince William, Rappahannock, Spotsylvania, Stafford, and Warren Counties, VA; Jefferson County, WV
Previously Washington-Arlington-Alexandria, DC-VA-MD-WV MD
District of Columbia; Calvert, Charles, and Prince George's Counties, MD; Alexandria, Fairfax, Falls Church, Fredericksburg, Manassas Park, and Manassas cities, VA; Arlington, Clarke, Fairfax, Fauquier, Loudoun, Prince William, Spotsylvania, Stafford, and Warren Counties, VA; Jefferson County, WV

Wichita, KS MSA
Butler, Harvey, Kingman, Sedgwick, and Sumner Counties

Wilmington, NC MSA
New Hanover and Pender Counties
Previously Wilmington, NC MSA
Brunswick, New Hanover and Pender Counties

Winston-Salem, NC MSA
Davidson, Davie, Forsyth, Stokes, and Yadkin Counties

Worcester, MA

Worcester, MA-CT MSA
Windham County, CT; Worcester County, MA
Previously Worcester, MA MSA
Worcester County

Worcester, MA-CT NECTA
Includes 40 cities and towns in Massachusetts and 8 cities and towns in Connecticut
Previously Worcester, MA-CT NECTA
Includes 37 cities and towns in Massachusetts and 3 cities and towns in Connecticut

Appendix C: Government Type and Primary County

This appendix includes the government structure of each place included in this book. It also includes the county or county equivalent in which each place is located. If a place spans more than one county, the county in which the majority of the population resides is shown.

Albuquerque, NM
Government Type: City
County: Bernalillo

Allentown, PA
Government Type: City
County: Lehigh

Anchorage, AK
Government Type: Municipality
Borough: Anchorage

Ann Arbor, MI
Government Type: City
County: Washtenaw

Athens, GA
Government Type: Consolidated
  city-county
County: Clarke

Atlanta, GA
Government Type: City
County: Fulton

Austin, TX
Government Type: City
County: Travis

Baltimore, MD
Government Type: Independent city

Baton Rouge, LA
Government Type: Consolidated city-parish
Parish: East Baton Rouge

Boise City, ID
Government Type: City
County: Ada

Boston, MA
Government Type: City
County: Suffolk

Boulder, CO
Government Type: City
County: Boulder

Brownsville, TX
Government Type: City
County: Cameron

Cape Coral, FL
Government Type: City
County: Lee

Cedar Rapids, IA
Government Type: City
County: Linn

Charleston, SC
Government Type: City
County: Charleston

Charlotte, NC
Government Type: City
County: Mecklenburg

Chicago, IL
Government Type: City
County: Cook

Cincinnati, OH
Government Type: City
County: Hamilton

Clarksville, TN
Government Type: City
County: Montgomery

Cleveland, OH
Government Type: City
County: Cuyahoga

College Station, TX
Government Type: City
County: Brazos

Colorado Springs, CO
Government Type: City
County: El Paso

Columbia, MO
Government Type: City
County: Boone

Columbia, SC
Government Type: City
County: Richland

Columbus, OH
Government Type: City
County: Franklin

Dallas, TX
Government Type: City
County: Dallas

Davenport, IA
Government Type: City
County: Scott

Denver, CO
Government Type: City
County: Denver

Des Moines, IA
Government Type: City
County: Polk

Durham, NC
Government Type: City
County: Durham

Edison, NJ
Government Type: Township
County: Middlesex

El Paso, TX
Government Type: City
County: El Paso

Fargo, ND
Government Type: City
County: Cass

Fort Collins, CO
Government Type: City
County: Larimer

Fort Wayne, IN
Government Type: City
County: Allen

Fort Worth, TX
Government Type: City
County: Tarrant

Grand Rapids, MI
Government Type: City
County: Kent

Greeley, CO
Government Type: City
County: Weld

Green Bay, WI
Government Type: City
County: Brown

Greensboro, NC
Government Type: City
County: Guilford

Honolulu, HI
Government Type: Census Designated Place (CDP)
County: Honolulu

Houston, TX
Government Type: City
County: Harris

Huntsville, AL
Government Type: City
County: Madison

Indianapolis, IN
Government Type: City
County: Marion

Jacksonville, FL
Government Type: City
County: Duval

Kansas City, MO
Government Type: City
County: Jackson

Lafayette, LA
Government Type: City
Parish: Lafayette

A-180 Appendix C: Government Type and Primary County

Las Cruces, NM
Government Type: City
County: Doña Ana

Las Vegas, NV
Government Type: City
County: Clark

Lexington, KY
Government Type: Consolidated city-county
County: Fayette

Lincoln, NE
Government Type: City
County: Lancaster

Little Rock, AR
Government Type: City
County: Pulaski

Los Angeles, CA
Government Type: City
County: Los Angeles

Louisville, KY
Government Type: Consolidated city-county
County: Jefferson

Madison, WI
Government Type: City
County: Dane

Manchester, NH
Government Type: City
County: Hillsborough

Memphis, TN
Government Type: City
County: Shelby

Miami, FL
Government Type: City
County: Miami-Dade

Midland, TX
Government Type: City
County: Midland

Milwaukee, WI
Government Type: City
County: Milwaukee

Minneapolis, MN
Government Type: City
County: Hennepin

Nashville, TN
Government Type: Consolidated city-county
County: Davidson

New Haven, CT
Government Type: City
County: New Haven

New Orleans, LA
Government Type: City
Parish: Orleans

New York, NY
Government Type: City
Counties: Bronx; Kings; New York; Queens; Staten Island

Oklahoma City, OK
Government Type: City
County: Oklahoma

Omaha, NE
Government Type: City
County: Douglas

Orlando, FL
Government Type: City
County: Orange

Philadelphia, PA
Government Type: City
County: Philadelphia

Phoenix, AZ
Government Type: City
County: Maricopa

Pittsburgh, PA
Government Type: City
County: Allegheny

Portland, OR
Government Type: City
County: Multnomah

Providence, RI
Government Type: City
County: Providence

Provo, UT
Government Type: City
County: Utah

Raleigh, NC
Government Type: City
County: Wake

Reno, NV
Government Type: City
County: Washoe

Richmond, VA
Government Type: Independent city

Riverside, CA
Government Type: City
County: Riverside

Rochester, MN
Government Type: City
County: Olmsted

Rochester, NY
Government Type: City
County: Monroe

Sacramento, CA
Government Type: City
County: Sacramento

Saint Louis, MO
Government Type: Independent city

Salem, OR
Government Type: City
County: Marion

Salt Lake City, UT
Government Type: City
County: Salt Lake

San Antonio, TX
Government Type: City
County: Bexar

San Diego, CA
Government Type: City
County: San Diego

San Francisco, CA
Government Type: City
County: San Francisco

San Jose, CA
Government Type: City
County: Santa Clara

Santa Rosa, CA
Government Type: City
County: Sonoma

Savannah, GA
Government Type: City
County: Chatham

Seattle, WA
Government Type: City
County: King

Sioux Falls, SD
Government Type: City
County: Minnehaha

Springfield, IL
Government Type: City
County: Sangamon

Tampa, FL
Government Type: City
County: Hillsborough

Tucson, AZ
Government Type: City
County: Pima

Tulsa, OK
Government Type: City
County: Tulsa

Tuscaloosa, AL
Government Type: City
County: Tuscaloosa

Virginia Beach, VA
Government Type: Independent city

Washington, DC
Government Type: City
County: District of Columbia

Wichita, KS
Government Type: City
County: Sedgwick

Wilmington, NC
Government Type: City
County: New Hanover

Winston-Salem, NC
Government Type: City
County: Forsyth

Worcester, MA
Government Type: City
County: Worcester

Appendix D: Chambers of Commerce

Albuquerque, NM
Albuquerque Chamber of Commerce
P.O. Box 25100
Albuquerque, NM 87125
Phone: (505) 764-3700
Fax: (505) 764-3714
www.abqchamber.com

Albuquerque Economic Development Dept
851 University Blvd SE, Suite 203
Albuquerque, NM 87106
Phone: (505) 246-6200
Fax: (505) 246-6219
www.cabq.gov/econdev

Allentown, PA
Greater Lehigh Valley Chamber of
Commerce
Allentown Office
840 Hamilton Street, Suite 205
Allentown, PA 18101
Phone: (610) 751-4929
Fax: (610) 437-4907
www.lehighvalleychamber.org

Anchorage, AK
Anchorage Chamber of Commerce
1016 W Sixth Avenue
Suite 303
Anchorage, AK 99501
Phone: (907) 272-2401
Fax: (907) 272-4117
www.anchoragechamber.org

Anchorage Economic Development
Department
900 W 5th Avenue
Suite 300
Anchorage, AK 99501
Phone: (907) 258-3700
Fax: (907) 258-6646
aedcweb.com

Ann Arbor, MI
Ann Arbor Area Chamber of Commerce
115 West Huron
3rd Floor
Ann Arbor, MI 48104
Phone: (734) 665-4433
Fax: (734) 665-4191
www.annarborchamber.org

Ann Arbor Economic Development
Department
201 S Division
Suite 430
Ann Arbor, MI 48104
Phone: (734) 761-9317
www.annarborspark.org

Athens, GA
Athens Area Chamber of Commerce
246 W Hancock Avenue
Athens, GA 30601
Phone: (706) 549-6800
Fax: (706) 549-5636
www.aacoc.org

Athens-Clarke County Economic
Development Department
246 W. Hancock Avenue
Athens, GA 30601
Phone: (706) 613-3233
Fax: (706) 613-3812
www.athensbusiness.org

Atlanta, GA
Metro Atlanta Chamber of Commerce
235 Andrew Young International Blvd NW
Atlanta, GA 30303
Phone: (404) 880-9000
Fax: (404) 586-8464
www.metroatlantachamber.com

Austin, TX
Greater Austin Chamber of Commerce
210 Barton Springs Road
Suite 400
Austin, TX 78704
Phone: (512) 478-9383
Fax: (512) 478-6389
www.austin-chamber.org

Baltimore, MD
Baltimore City Chamber of Commerce
P.O. Box 43121
Baltimore, MD 21236
443-860-2020
baltimorecitychamber.org

Baltimore County Chamber of Commerce
102 W. Pennsylvania Avenue
Suite 305
Towson, MD, 21204
Phone: (410) 825-6200
Fax: (410) 821-9901
www.baltcountychamber.com

Boise City, ID
Boise Metro Chamber of Commerce
250 S 5th Street
Suite 800
Boise City, ID 83701
Phone: (208) 472-5200
Fax: (208) 472-5201
www.boisechamber.org

Boston, MA
Greater Boston Chamber of Commerce
265 Franklin Street
12th Floor
Boston, MA 02110
Phone: (617) 227-4500
Fax: (617) 227-7505
www.bostonchamber.com

Boulder, CO
Boulder Chamber of Commerce
2440 Pearl Street
Boulder, CO 80302
Phone: (303) 442-1044
Fax: (303) 938-8837
www.boulderchamber.com

City of Boulder Economic Vitality Program
P.O. Box 791
Boulder, CO 80306
Phone: (303) 441-3090
www.bouldercolorado.gov

Brownsville, TX
Brownsville Chamber of Commerce
1600 University Blvd.
Brownsville, TX 78520
Phone: (956) 542-4341
brownsvillechamber.com

Cape Coral, FL
Chamber of Commerce of Cape Coral
2051 Cape Coral Parkway East
Cape Coral, FL 33904
Phone: (239) 549-6900
Fax: (239) 549-9609
www.capecoralchamber.com

Cedar Rapids, IA
Cedar Rapids Chamber of Commerce
424 First Avenue NE
Cedar Rapids, IA 52401
Phone: (319) 398-5317
Fax: (319) 398-5228
www.cedarrapids.org

Cedar Rapids Economic Development
50 Second Avenue Bridge, Sixth Floor
Cedar Rapids, IA 52401-1256
Phone: (319) 286-5041
Fax: (319) 286-5141
www.cedar-rapids.org

Charleston, SC
Charleston Metro Chamber of Commerce
P.O. Box 975
Charleston, SC 29402
Phone: (843) 577-2510
www.charlestonchamber.net

Charlotte, NC
Charlotte Chamber of Commerce
330 S Tryon Street
P.O. Box 32785
Charlotte, NC 28232
Phone: (704) 378-1300
Fax: (704) 374-1903
www.charlottechamber.com

Charlotte Regional Partnership
1001 Morehead Square Drive, Suite 200
Charlotte, NC 28203
Phone: (704) 347-8942
Fax: (704) 347-8981
www.charlotteusa.com

Chicago, IL
Chicagoland Chamber of Commerce
200 E Randolph Street
Suite 2200
Chicago, IL 60601-6436
Phone: (312) 494-6700
Fax: (312) 861-0660
www.chicagolandchamber.org

A-182 Appendix D: Chambers of Commerce

City of Chicago Department of Planning
and Development
City Hall, Room 1000
121 North La Salle Street
Chicago, IL 60602
Phone: (312) 744-4190
Fax: (312) 744-2271
www.cityofchicago.org/city/en/depts/dcd.html

Cincinnati, OH
Cincinnati USA Regional Chamber
3 East 4th Street, Suite 200
Cincinnati, Ohio 45202
Phone: (513) 579-3111
www.cincinnatichamber.com

Clarksville, TN
Clarksville Area Chamber of Commerce
25 Jefferson Street, Suite 300
Clarksville, TN 37040
Phone: (931) 647-2331
www.clarksvillechamber.com

Cleveland, OH
Greater Cleveland Partnership
1240 Huron Rd. E, Suite 300
Cleveland, OH 44115
Phone: (216) 621-3300
www.gcpartnership.com

College Station, TX
Bryan-College Station Chamber of
Commerce
4001 East 29th St, Suite 175
Bryan, TX 77802
Phone: (979) 260-5200
www.bcschamber.org

Colorado Springs, CO
Colorado Springs Chamber and EDC
102 South Tejon Street
Suite 430
Colorado Springs, CO 80903
Phone: (719) 471-8183
coloradospringschamberedc.com

Columbia, MO
Columbia Chamber of Commerce
300 South Providence Rd.
P.O. Box 1016
Columbia, MO 65205-1016
Phone: (573) 874-1132
Fax: (573) 443-3986
www.columbiamochamber.com

Columbia, SC
The Columbia Chamber
930 Richland Street
Columbia, SC 29201
Phone: (803) 733-1110
Fax: (803) 733-1113
www.columbiachamber.com

Columbus, OH
Greater Columbus Chamber
37 North High Street
Columbus, OH 43215
Phone: (614) 221-1321
Fax: (614) 221-1408
www.columbus.org

Dallas, TX
City of Dallas Economic Development
Department
1500 Marilla Street
5C South
Dallas, TX 75201
Phone: (214) 670-1685
Fax: (214) 670-0158
www.dallas-edd.org

Greater Dallas Chamber of Commerce
700 North Pearl Street
Suite1200
Dallas, TX 75201
Phone: (214) 746-6600
Fax: (214) 746-6799
www.dallaschamber.org

Davenport, IA
Quad Cities Chamber
331 W. 3rd Street
Suite 100
Davenport, IA 52801
Phone: (563) 322-1706
quadcitieschamber.com

Denver, CO
Denver Metro Chamber of Commerce
1445 Market Street
Denver, CO 80202
Phone: (303) 534-8500
Fax: (303) 534-3200
www.denverchamber.org

Downtown Denver Partnership
511 16th Street
Suite 200
Denver, CO 80202
Phone: (303) 534-6161
Fax: (303) 534-2803
www.downtowndenver.com

Des Moines, IA
Des Moines Downtown Chamber
301 Grand Ave
Des Moines, IA 50309
Phone: (515) 309-3229
desmoinesdowntownchamber.com

Greater Des Moines Partnership
700 Locust Street
Suite 100
Des Moines, IA 50309
Phone: (515) 286-4950
Fax: (515) 286-4974
www.desmoinesmetro.com

Durham, NC
Durham Chamber of Commerce
P.O. Box 3829
Durham, NC 27702
Phone: (919) 682-2133
Fax: (919) 688-8351
www.durhamchamber.org

North Carolina Institute of Minority
Economic Development
114 W Parish Street
Durham, NC 27701
Phone: (919) 956-8889
Fax: (919) 688-7668
www.ncimed.com

Edison, NJ
Edison Chamber of Commerce
939 Amboy Avenue
Edison, NJ 08837
Phone: (732) 738-9482
www.edisonchamber.com

El Paso, TX
City of El Paso Department of Economic
Development
2 Civic Center Plaza
El Paso, TX 79901
Phone: (915) 541-4000
Fax: (915) 541-1316
www.elpasotexas.gov

Greater El Paso Chamber of Commerce
10 Civic Center Plaza
El Paso, TX 79901
Phone: (915) 534-0500
Fax: (915) 534-0510
www.elpaso.org

Fargo, ND
Chamber of Commerce of Fargo Moorhead
202 First Avenue North
Fargo, ND 56560
Phone: (218) 233-1100
Fax: (218) 233-1200
www.fmchamber.com

Greater Fargo-Moorhead Economic
Development Corporation
51 Broadway, Suite 500
Fargo, ND 58102
Phone: (701) 364-1900
Fax: (701) 293-7819
www.gfmedc.com

Fort Collins, CO
Fort Collins Chamber of Commerce
225 South Meldrum
Fort Collins, CO 80521
Phone: (970) 482-3746
Fax: (970) 482-3774
fortcollinschamber.com

Fort Wayne, IN
City of Fort Wayne Economic Development
1 Main St
1 Main Street
Fort Wayne, IN 46802
Phone: (260) 427-1111
Fax: (260) 427-1375
www.cityoffortwayne.org

Greater Fort Wayne Chamber of Commerce
826 Ewing Street
Fort Wayne, IN 46802
Phone: (260) 424-1435
Fax: (260) 426-7232
www.fwchamber.org

Fort Worth, TX
City of Fort Worth Economic Development
City Hall
900 Monroe Street
Suite 301
Fort Worth, TX 76102
Phone: (817) 392-6103
Fax: (817) 392-2431
www.fortworthgov.org

Appendix D: Chambers of Commerce   A-183

Fort Worth Chamber of Commerce
777 Taylor Street, Suite 900
Fort Worth, TX 76102-4997
Phone: (817) 336-2491
Fax: (817) 877-4034
www.fortworthchamber.com

Grand Rapids, MI
Grands Rapids Area Chamber of Commerce
111 Pearl Street N.W.
Grand Rapids, MI 49503
Phone: (616) 771-0300
Fax: (616) 771-0318
www.grandrapids.org

Greeley, CO
Greeley Area Chamber of Commerce
902 7th Avenue
Greeley, CO 80631
Phone: (970) 352-3566
www.greeleychamber.com

Green Bay, WI
Economic Development
100 N Jefferson Street
Room 202
Green Bay, WI 54301
Phone: (920) 448-3397
Fax: (920) 448-3063
www.ci.green-bay.wi.us

Green Bay Area Chamber of Commerce
300 N. Broadway
Suite 3A
Green Bay, WI 54305-1660
Phone: (920) 437-8704
Fax: (920) 593-3468
www.titletown.org

Greensboro, NC
Greensboro Chamber of Commerce
111 W. February One Place
Greensboro, NC 27401
Phone: (336) 387-8301
greensboro.org

Honolulu, HI
The Chamber of Commerce of Hawaii
1132 Bishop Street
Suite 402
Honolulu, HI 96813
Phone: (808) 545-4300
Fax: (808) 545-4369
www.cochawaii.com

Houston, TX
Greater Houston Partnership
1200 Smith Street, Suite 700
Houston, TX 77002-4400
Phone: (713) 844-3600
Fax: (713) 844-0200
www.houston.org

Huntsville, AL
Chamber of Commerce of
Huntsville/Madison County
225 Church Street
Huntsville, AL 35801
Phone: (256) 535-2000
Fax: (256) 535-2015
www.huntsvillealabamausa.com

Indianapolis, IN
Greater Indianapolis Chamber of Commerce
111 Monument Circle, Suite 1950
Indianapolis, IN 46204
Phone: (317) 464-2222
Fax: (317) 464-2217
www.indychamber.com

The Indy Partnership
111 Monument Circle, Suite 1800
Indianapolis, IN 46204
Phone: (317) 236-6262
Fax: (317) 236-6275
indypartnership.com

Jacksonville, FL
Jacksonville Chamber of Commerce
3 Independent Drive
Jacksonville, FL 32202
Phone: (904) 366-6600
Fax: (904) 632-0617
www.myjaxchamber.com

Kansas City, MO
Greater Kansas City Chamber of Commerce
2600 Commerce Tower
911 Main Street
Kansas City, MO 64105
Phone: (816) 221-2424
Fax: (816) 221-7440
www.kcchamber.com

Kansas City Area Development Council
2600 Commerce Tower
911 Main Street
Kansas City, MO 64105
Phone: (816) 221-2121
Fax: (816) 842-2865
www.thinkkc.com

Lafayette, LA
Greater Lafayette Chamber of Commerce
804 East Saint Mary Blvd.
Lafayette, LA 70503
Phone: (337) 233-2705
Fax: (337) 234-8671
www.lafchamber.org

Las Cruces, NM
Greater Las Cruces Chamber of Commerce
505 S Main Street, Suite 134
Las Cruces, NM 88001
Phone: (575) 524-1968
Fax: (575) 527-5546
www.lascruces.org

Las Vegas, NV
Las Vegas Chamber of Commerce
6671 Las Vegas Blvd South
Suite 300
Las Vegas, NV 89119
Phone: (702) 735-1616
Fax: (702) 735-0406
www.lvchamber.org

Las Vegas Office of Business Development
400 Stewart Avenue
City Hall
Las Vegas, NV 89101
Phone: (702) 229-6011
Fax: (702) 385-3128
www.lasvegasnevada.gov

Lexington, KY
Greater Lexington Chamber of Commerce
330 East Main Street
Suite 100
Lexington, KY 40507
Phone: (859) 254-4447
Fax: (859) 233-3304
www.commercelexington.com

Lexington Downtown Development
Authority
101 East Vine Street
Suite 500
Lexington, KY 40507
Phone: (859) 425-2296
Fax: (859) 425-2292
www.lexingtondda.com

Lincoln, NE
Lincoln Chamber of Commerce
1135 M Street
Suite 200
Lincoln, NE 68508
Phone: (402) 436-2350
Fax: (402) 436-2360
www.lcoc.com

Little Rock, AR
Little Rock Regional Chamber
One Chamber Plaza
Little Rock, AR 72201
Phone: (501) 374-2001
Fax: (501) 374-6018
www.littlerockchamber.com

Los Angeles, CA
Los Angeles Area Chamber of Commerce
350 South Bixel Street
Los Angeles, CA 90017
Phone: (213) 580-7500
Fax: (213) 580-7511
www.lachamber.org

Los Angeles County Economic
Development Corporation
444 South Flower Street
34th Floor
Los Angeles, CA 90071
Phone: (213) 622-4300
Fax: (213) 622-7100
www.laedc.org

Louisville, KY
The Greater Louisville Chamber of
Commerce
614 West Main Street
Suite 6000
Louisville, KY 40202
Phone: (502) 625-0000
Fax: (502) 625-0010
www.greaterlouisville.com

Madison, WI
Greater Madison Chamber of Commerce
615 East Washington Avenue
P.O. Box 71
Madison, WI 53701-0071
Phone: (608) 256-8348
Fax: (608) 256-0333
www.greatermadisonchamber.com

A-184   Appendix D: Chambers of Commerce

Manchester, NH
Greater Manchester Chamber of Commerce
889 Elm Street
Manchester, NH 03101
Phone: (603) 666-6600
Fax: (603) 626-0910
www.manchester-chamber.org

Manchester Economic Development Office
One City Hall Plaza
Manchester, NH 03101
Phone: (603) 624-6505
Fax: (603) 624-6308
www.yourmanchesternh.com

Miami, FL
Greater Miami Chamber of Commerce
1601 Biscayne Boulevard
Miami, FL 33132-1260
Phone: (305) 350-7700
Fax: (305) 374-6902
www.miamichamber.com

The Beacon Council
80 Southwest 8th Street, Suite 2400
Miami, FL 33130
Phone: (305) 579-1300
Fax: (305) 375-0271
www.beaconcouncil.com

Midland, TX
Midland Chamber of Commerce
109 N. Main
Midland, TX 79701
Phone: (432) 683-3381
Fax: (432) 686-3556
www.midlandtxchamber.com

Milwaukee, WI
Greater Milwaukee Chamber of Commerce
6815 W. Capitol Drive
Suite 300
Milwaukee, WI 53216
Phone: (414) 465-2422
www.gmcofc.org

Metropolitan Milwaukee Association of
Commerce
756 N. Milwaukee Street
Suite 400
Milwaukee, WI 53202
Phone: (414) 287-4100
Fax: (414) 271-7753
www.mmac.org

Minneapolis, MN
Minneapolis Regional Chamber
81 South Ninth Street, Suite 200
Minneapolis, MN 55402
Phone: (612) 370-9100
Fax: (612) 370-9195
www.minneapolischamber.org

Minneapolis Community Development
Agency
Crown Roller Mill
105 5th Avenue South
Suite 200
Minneapolis, MN 55401
Phone: (612) 673-5095
Fax: (612) 673-5100
www.ci.minneapolis.mn.us

Nashville, TN
Nashville Area Chamber of Commerce
211 Commerce Street, Suite 100
Nashville, TN 37201
Phone: (615) 743-3000
Fax: (615) 256-3074
www.nashvillechamber.com

Tennessee Valley Authority Economic
Development
400 West Summit Hill Drive
Knoxville TN 37902
Phone: (865) 632-2101
www.tvaed.com

New Haven, CT
Greater New Haven Chamber of Commerce
900 Chapel Street, 10th Floor
New Haven, CT 06510
Phone: (203) 787-6735
www.gnhcc.com

New Orleans, LA
New Orleans Chamber of Commerce
1515 Poydras Street
Suite 1010
New Orleans, LA 70112
Phone: (504) 799-4260
Fax: (504) 799-4259
www.neworleanschamber.org

New York, NY
New York City Economic Development
Corporation
110 William Street
New York, NY 10038
Phone: (212) 619-5000
www.nycedc.com

The Partnership for New York City
One Battery Park Plaza
5th Floor
New York, NY 10004
Phone: (212) 493-7400
Fax: (212) 344-3344
www.pfnyc.org

Oklahoma City, OK
Greater Oklahoma City Chamber of
Commerce
123 Park Avenue
Oklahoma City, OK 73102
Phone: (405) 297-8900
Fax: (405) 297-8916
www.okcchamber.com

Omaha, NE
Omaha Chamber of Commerce
1301 Harney Street
Omaha, NE 68102
Phone: (402) 346-5000
Fax: (402) 346-7050
www.omahachamber.org

Orlando, FL
Metro Orlando Economic Development
Commission of Mid-Florida
301 East Pine Street, Suite 900
Orlando, FL 32801
Phone: (407) 422-7159
Fax: (407) 425.6428
www.orlandoedc.com

Orlando Regional Chamber of Commerce
75 South Ivanhoe Boulevard
P.O. Box 1234
Orlando, FL 32802
Phone: (407) 425-1234
Fax: (407) 839-5020
www.orlando.org

Philadelphia, PA
Greater Philadelphia Chamber of
Commerce
200 South Broad Street
Suite 700
Philadelphia, PA 19102
Phone: (215) 545-1234
Fax: (215) 790-3600
www.greaterphilachamber.com

Phoenix, AZ
Greater Phoenix Chamber of Commerce
201 North Central Avenue
27th Floor
Phoenix, AZ 85073
Phone: (602) 495-2195
Fax: (602) 495-8913
www.phoenixchamber.com

Greater Phoenix Economic Council
2 North Central Avenue
Suite 2500
Phoenix, AZ 85004
Phone: (602) 256-7700
Fax: (602) 256-7744
www.gpec.org

Pittsburgh, PA
Allegheny County Industrial Development
Authority
425 6th Avenue
Suite 800
Pittsburgh, PA 15219
Phone: (412) 350-1067
Fax: (412) 642-2217
www.alleghenycounty.us

Greater Pittsburgh Chamber of Commerce
425 6th Avenue
12th Floor
Pittsburgh, PA 15219
Phone: (412) 392-4500
Fax: (412) 392-4520
www.alleghenyconference.org

Portland, OR
Portland Business Alliance
200 SW Market Street
Suite 1770
Portland, OR 97201
Phone: (503) 224-8684
Fax: (503) 323-9186
www.portlandalliance.com

Providence, RI
Greater Providence Chamber of Commerce
30 Exchange Terrace
Fourth Floor
Providence, RI 02903
Phone: (401) 521-5000
Fax: (401) 351-2090
www.provchamber.com

Appendix D: Chambers of Commerce   A-185

Rhode Island Economic Development
Corporation
Providence City Hall
25 Dorrance Street
Providence, RI 02903
Phone: (401) 421-7740
Fax: (401) 751-0203
www.providenceri.com

Provo, UT
Provo-Orem Chamber of Commerce
51 South University Avenue, Suite 215
Provo, UT 84601
Phone: (801) 851-2555
Fax: (801) 851-2557
www.thechamber.org

Raleigh, NC
Greater Raleigh Chamber of Commerce
800 South Salisbury Street
Raleigh, NC 27601-2978
Phone: (919) 664-7000
Fax: (919) 664-7099
www.raleighchamber.org

Reno, NV
Greater Reno-Sparks Chamber of Commerce
1 East First Street, 16th Floor
Reno, NV 89505
Phone: (775) 337-3030
Fax: (775) 337-3038
www.reno-sparkschamber.org

The Chamber Reno-Sparks-Northern Nevada
449 S. Virginia Street, 2nd Floor
Reno, NV 89501
Phone: (775) 636-9550
www.thechambernv.org

Richmond, VA
Greater Richmond Chamber
600 East Main Street
Suite 700
Richmond, VA 23219
Phone: (804) 648-1234
www.grcc.com

Greater Richmond Partnership
901 East Byrd Street
Suite 801
Richmond, VA 23219-4070
Phone: (804) 643-3227
Fax: (804) 343-7167
www.grpva.com

Rochester, MN
Rochester Area Chamber of Commerce
220 South Broadway
Suite 100
Rochester, MN 55904
Phone: (507) 288-1122
Fax: (507) 282-8960
www.rochestermnchamber.com

Sacramento, CA
Sacramento Metro Chamber
One Capitol Mall
Suite 700
Sacramento, CA 95814
Phone: (916) 552-6800
metrochamber.org

Saint Louis, MO
St. Louis Regional Chamber
One Metropolitan Square, Suite 1300
St. Louis, MO 63102
Phone: (314) 231-5555
www.stlregionalchamber.com

Salem, OR
Salem Chamber
1110 Commercial Street NE
Salem, OR 97301
Phone: (503) 581-1466
salemchamber.org

Salt Lake City, UT
Salt Lake Chamber
175 E. University Blvd. (400 S), Suite 600
Salt Lake City, UT 84111
Phone: (801) 364-3631
www.slchamber.com

San Antonio, TX
The Greater San Antonio Chamber of
Commerce
602 E. Commerce Street
San Antonio, TX 78205
Phone: (210) 229-2100
Fax: (210) 229-1600
www.sachamber.org

San Antonio Economic Development
Department
P.O. Box 839966
San Antonio, TX 78283-3966
Phone: (210) 207-8080
Fax: (210) 207-8151
www.sanantonio.gov/edd

San Diego, CA
San Diego Economic Development Corp.
401 B Street
Suite 1100
San Diego, CA 92101
Phone: (619) 234-8484
Fax: (619) 234-1935
www.sandiegobusiness.org

San Diego Regional Chamber of Commerce
402 West Broadway
Suite 1000
San Diego, CA 92101-3585
Phone: (619) 544-1300
Fax: (619) 744-7481
www.sdchamber.org

San Francisco, CA
San Francisco Chamber of Commerce
235 Montgomery Street
12th Floor
San Francisco, CA 94104
Phone: (415) 392-4520
Fax: (415) 392-0485
www.sfchamber.com

San Jose, CA
Office of Economic Development
60 South Market Street
Suite 470
San Jose, CA 95113
Phone: (408) 277-5880
Fax: (408) 277-3615
www.sba.gov

The Silicon Valley Organization
101 W Santa Clara Street
San Jose, CA 95113
Phone: (408) 291-5250
www.thesvo.com

Santa Rosa, CA
Santa Rosa Chamber of Commerce
1260 North Dutton Avenue
Suite 272
Santa Rosa, CA 95401
Phone: (707) 545-1414
www.santarosachamber.com

Savannah, GA
Economic Development Authority
131 Hutchinson Island Road
4th Floor
Savannah, GA 31421
Phone: (912) 447-8450
Fax: (912) 447-8455
www.seda.org

Savannah Chamber of Commerce
101 E. Bay Street
Savannah, GA 31402
Phone: (912) 644-6400
Fax: (912) 644-6499
www.savannahchamber.com

Seattle, WA
Greater Seattle Chamber of Commerce
1301 Fifth Avenue
Suite 2500
Seattle, WA 98101
Phone: (206) 389-7200
Fax: (206) 389-7288
www.seattlechamber.com

Sioux Falls, SD
Sioux Falls Area Chamber of Commerce
200 N. Phillips Avenue
Suite 102
Sioux Falls, SD 57104
Phone: (605) 336-1620
Fax: (605) 336-6499
www.siouxfallschamber.com

Springfield, IL
The Greater Springfield Chamber of
Commerce
1011 S. Second Street
Springfield, IL 62704
Phone: (217) 525-1173
Fax: (217) 525-8768
www.gscc.org

Tampa, FL
Greater Tampa Chamber of Commerce
P.O. Box 420
Tampa, FL 33601-0420
Phone: (813) 276-9401
Fax: (813) 229-7855
www.tampachamber.com

Tucson, AZ
Tucson Metro Chamber
212 E. Broadway Blvd
Tucson, AZ 85701
Phone: (520) 792-1212
tucsonchamber.org

Appendix D: Chambers of Commerce

Tulsa, OK
Tulsa Regional Chamber
One West Third Street
Suite 100
Tulsa, OK 74103
Phone: (918) 585-1201
www.tulsachamber.com

Tuscaloosa, AL
The Chamber of Commerce of West
Alabama
2201 Jack Warner Parkway
Building C
Tuscaloosa, AL 35401
Phone: (205) 758-7588
tuscaloosachamber.com

Virginia Beach, VA
Hampton Roads Chamber of Commerce
500 East Main Street, Suite 700
Virginia Beach, VA 23510
Phone: (757) 664-2531
www.hamptonroadschamber.com

Washington, DC
District of Columbia Chamber of Commerce
1213 K Street NW
Washington, DC 20005
Phone: (202) 347-7201
Fax: (202) 638-6762
www.dcchamber.org

District of Columbia Office of Planning and
Economic Development
J.A. Wilson Building
1350 Pennsylvania Ave NW, Suite 317
Washington, DC 20004
Phone: (202) 727-6365
Fax: (202) 727-6703
www.dcbiz.dc.gov

Wichita, KS
Wichita Regional Chamber of Commerce
350 W Douglas Avennue
Wichita, KS 67202
Phone: (316) 265-7771
www.wichitachamber.org

Wilmington, NC
Wilmington Chamber of Commerce
One Estell Lee Place
Wilmington, NC 28401
Phone: (910) 762-2611
www.wilmingtonchamber.org

Winston-Salem, NC
Winston-Salem Chamber of Commerce
411 West Fourth Street
Suite 211
Winston-Salem, NC 27101
Phone: (336) 728-9200
www.winstonsalem.com

Worcester, MA
Worcester Regional Chamber of Commerce
311 Main Street, Suite 200
Worcester, MA 01608
Phone: (508) 753-2924
worcesterchamber.org

Appendix E: State Departments of Labor

Alabama
Alabama Department of Labor
P.O. Box 303500
Montgomery, AL 36130-3500
Phone: (334) 242-3072
www.labor.alabama.gov

Alaska
Dept of Labor and Workforce Devel.
P.O. Box 11149
Juneau, AK 99822-2249
Phone: (907) 465-2700
www.labor.state.ak.us

Arizona
Industrial Commission or Arizona
800 West Washington Street
Phoenix, AZ 85007
Phone: (602) 542-4411
www.azica.gov

Arkansas
Department of Labor
10421 West Markham
Little Rock, AR 72205
Phone: (501) 682-4500
www.labor.ar.gov

California
Labor and Workforce Development
445 Golden Gate Ave., 10th Floor
San Francisco, CA 94102
Phone: (916) 263-1811
www.labor.ca.gov

Colorado
Dept of Labor and Employment
633 17th St., 2nd Floor
Denver, CO 80202-3660
Phone: (888) 390-7936
cdle.colorado.gov

Connecticut
Department of Labor
200 Folly Brook Blvd.
Wethersfield, CT 06109-1114
Phone: (860) 263-6000
www.ctdol.state.ct.us

Delaware
Department of Labor
4425 N. Market St., 4th Floor
Wilmington, DE 19802
Phone: (302) 451-3423
dol.delaware.gov

District of Columbia
Department of Employment Services
614 New York Ave., NE, Suite 300
Washington, DC 20002
Phone: (202) 671-1900
does.dc.gov

Florida
Florida Department of Economic Opportunity
The Caldwell Building
107 East Madison St. Suite 100
Tallahassee, FL 32399-4120
Phone: (800) 342-3450
www.floridajobs.org

Georgia
Department of Labor
Sussex Place, Room 600
148 Andrew Young Intl Blvd., NE
Atlanta, GA 30303
Phone: (404) 656-3011
dol.georgia.gov

Hawaii
Dept of Labor & Industrial Relations
830 Punchbowl Street
Honolulu, HI 96813
Phone: (808) 586-8842
labor.hawaii.gov

Idaho
Department of Labor
317 W. Main St.
Boise, ID 83735-0001
Phone: (208) 332-3579
www.labor.idaho.gov

Illinois
Department of Labor
160 N. LaSalle Street, 13th Floor
Suite C-1300
Chicago, IL 60601
Phone: (312) 793-2800
www.illinois.gov/idol

Indiana
Indiana Department of Labor
402 West Washington Street, Room W195
Indianapolis, IN 46204
Phone: (317) 232-2655
www.in.gov/dol

Iowa
Iowa Workforce Development
1000 East Grand Avenue
Des Moines, IA 50319-0209
Phone: (515) 242-5870
www.iowadivisionoflabor.gov

Kansas
Department of Labor
401 S.W. Topeka Blvd.
Topeka, KS 66603-3182
Phone: (785) 296-5000
www.dol.ks.gov

Kentucky
Department of Labor
1047 U.S. Hwy 127 South, Suite 4
Frankfort, KY 40601-4381
Phone: (502) 564-3070
www.labor.ky.gov

Louisiana
Louisiana Workforce Commission
1001 N. 23rd Street
Baton Rouge, LA 70804-9094
Phone: (225) 342-3111
www.laworks.net

Maine
Department of Labor
45 Commerce Street
Augusta, ME 04330
Phone: (207) 623-7900
www.state.me.us/labor

Maryland
Department of Labor, Licensing & Regulation
500 N. Calvert Street
Suite 401
Baltimore, MD 21202
Phone: (410) 767-2357
www.dllr.state.md.us

Massachusetts
Dept of Labor & Workforce Development
One Ashburton Place
Room 2112
Boston, MA 02108
Phone: (617) 626-7100
www.mass.gov/lwd

Michigan
Department of Licensing and Regulatory
Affairs
611 W. Ottawa
P.O. Box 30004
Lansing, MI 48909
Phone: (517) 373-1820
www.michigan.gov/lara

Minnesota
Dept of Labor and Industry
443 Lafayette Road North
Saint Paul, MN 55155
Phone: (651) 284-5070
www.doli.state.mn.us

Mississippi
Dept of Employment Security
P.O. Box 1699
Jackson, MS 39215-1699
Phone: (601) 321-6000
www.mdes.ms.gov

Missouri
Labor and Industrial Relations
P.O. Box 599
3315 W. Truman Boulevard
Jefferson City, MO 65102-0599
Phone: (573) 751-7500
labor.mo.gov

Montana
Dept of Labor and Industry
P.O. Box 1728
Helena, MT 59624-1728
Phone: (406) 444-9091
www.dli.mt.gov

A-188   Appendix E: State Departments of Labor

Nebraska
Department of Labor
550 S 16th Street
Lincoln, NE 68508
Phone: (402) 471-9000
dol.nebraska.gov

Nevada
Dept of Business and Industry
3300 W. Sahara Ave, Suite 425
Las Vegas, NV 89102
Phone: (702) 486-2750
business.nv.gov

New Hampshire
Department of Labor
State Office Park South
95 Pleasant Street
Concord, NH 03301
Phone: (603) 271-3176
www.nh.gov/labor

New Jersey
Department of Labor & Workforce Devel.
John Fitch Plaza, 13th Floor, Suite D
Trenton, NJ 08625-0110
Phone: (609) 777-3200
lwd.dol.state.nj.us/labor

New Mexico
Department of Workforce Solutions
401 Broadway, NE
Albuquerque, NM 87103-1928
Phone: (505) 841-8450
www.dws.state.nm.us

New York
Department of Labor
State Office Bldg. # 12
W.A. Harriman Campus
Albany, NY 12240
Phone: (518) 457-9000
www.labor.ny.gov

North Carolina
Department of Labor
4 West Edenton Street
Raleigh, NC 27601-1092
Phone: (919) 733-7166
www.labor.nc.gov

North Dakota
North Dakota Department of Labor and
Human Rights
State Capitol Building
600 East Boulevard, Dept 406
Bismark, ND 58505-0340
Phone: (701) 328-2660
www.nd.gov/labor

Ohio
Department of Commerce
77 South High Street, 22nd Floor
Columbus, OH 43215
Phone: (614) 644-2239
www.com.state.oh.us

Oklahoma
Department of Labor
4001 N. Lincoln Blvd.
Oklahoma City, OK 73105-5212
Phone: (405) 528-1500
www.ok.gov/odol

Oregon
Bureau of Labor and Industries
800 NE Oregon St., #32
Portland, OR 97232
Phone: (971) 673-0761
www.oregon.gov/boli

Pennsylvania
Dept of Labor and Industry
1700 Labor and Industry Bldg
7th and Forster Streets
Harrisburg, PA 17120
Phone: (717) 787-5279
www.dli.pa.gov

Rhode Island
Department of Labor and Training
1511 Pontiac Avenue
Cranston, RI 02920
Phone: (401) 462-8000
www.dlt.state.ri.us

South Carolina
Dept of Labor, Licensing & Regulations
P.O. Box 11329
Columbia, SC 29211-1329
Phone: (803) 896-4300
www.llr.state.sc.us

South Dakota
Department of Labor & Regulation
700 Governors Drive
Pierre, SD 57501-2291
Phone: (605) 773-3682
dlr.sd.gov

Tennessee
Dept of Labor & Workforce Development
Andrew Johnson Tower
710 James Robertson Pkwy
Nashville, TN 37243-0655
Phone: (615) 741-6642
www.tn.gov/workforce

Texas
Texas Workforce Commission
101 East 15th St.
Austin, TX 78778
Phone: (512) 475-2670
www.twc.state.tx.us

Utah
Utah Labor Commission
160 East 300 South, 3rd Floor
Salt Lake City, UT 84114-6600
Phone: (801) 530-6800
laborcommission.utah.gov

Vermont
Department of Labor
5 Green Mountain Drive
P.O. Box 488
Montpelier, VT 05601-0488
Phone: (802) 828-4000
labor.vermont.gov

Virginia
Dept of Labor and Industry
Powers-Taylor Building
13 S. 13th Street
Richmond, VA 23219
Phone: (804) 371-2327
www.doli.virginia.gov

Washington
Dept of Labor and Industries
P.O. Box 44001
Olympia, WA 98504-4001
Phone: (360) 902-4200
www.lni.wa.gov

West Virginia
Division of Labor
749 B Building 6
Capitol Complex
Charleston, WV 25305
Phone: (304) 558-7890
labor.wv.gov

Wisconsin
Dept of Workforce Development
201 E. Washington Ave., #A400
P.O. Box 7946
Madison, WI 53707-7946
Phone: (608) 266-6861
dwd.wisconsin.gov

Wyoming
Department of Workforce Services
1510 East Pershing Blvd.
Cheyenne, WY 82002
Phone: (307) 777-7261
www.wyomingworkforce.org

Titles from Grey House

Visit www.GreyHouse.com for Product Information, Table of Contents, and Sample Pages.

Opinions Throughout History
Opinions Throughout History: Church & State
Opinions Throughout History: Conspiracy Theories
Opinions Throughout History: The Death Penalty
Opinions Throughout History: Diseases & Epidemics
Opinions Throughout History: Drug Use & Abuse
Opinions Throughout History: The Environment
Opinions Throughout History: Free Speech & Censorship
Opinions Throughout History: Gender: Roles & Rights
Opinions Throughout History: Globalization
Opinions Throughout History: Guns in America
Opinions Throughout History: Immigration
Opinions Throughout History: Law Enforcement in America
Opinions Throughout History: Mental Health
Opinions Throughout History: Nat'l Security vs. Civil & Privacy Rights
Opinions Throughout History: Presidential Authority
Opinions Throughout History: Robotics & Artificial Intelligence
Opinions Throughout History: Social Media Issues
Opinions Throughout History: The Supreme Court
Opinions Throughout History: Voters' Rights
Opinions Throughout History: War & the Military
Opinions Throughout History: Workers Rights & Wages

This is Who We Were
This is Who We Were: Colonial America (1492-1775)
This is Who We Were: 1880-1899
This is Who We Were: In the 1900s
This is Who We Were: In the 1910s
This is Who We Were: In the 1920s
This is Who We Were: A Companion to the 1940 Census
This is Who We Were: In the 1940s (1940-1949)
This is Who We Were: In the 1950s
This is Who We Were: In the 1960s
This is Who We Were: In the 1970s
This is Who We Were: In the 1980s
This is Who We Were: In the 1990s
This is Who We Were: In the 2000s
This is Who We Were: In the 2010s

Working Americans
Working Americans—Vol. 1: The Working Class
Working Americans—Vol. 2: The Middle Class
Working Americans—Vol. 3: The Upper Class
Working Americans—Vol. 4: Children
Working Americans—Vol. 5: At War
Working Americans—Vol. 6: Working Women
Working Americans—Vol. 7: Social Movements
Working Americans—Vol. 8: Immigrants
Working Americans—Vol. 9: Revolutionary War to the Civil War
Working Americans—Vol. 10: Sports & Recreation
Working Americans—Vol. 11: Inventors & Entrepreneurs
Working Americans—Vol. 12: Our History through Music
Working Americans—Vol. 13: Education & Educators
Working Americans—Vol. 14: African Americans
Working Americans—Vol. 15: Politics & Politicians
Working Americans—Vol. 16: Farming & Ranching
Working Americans—Vol. 17: Teens in America
Working Americans—Vol. 18: Health Care Workers
Working Americans—Vol. 19: The Performing Arts

Grey House Health & Wellness Guides
Addiction Handbook & Resource Guide
The Autism Spectrum Handbook & Resource Guide
Autoimmune Disorders Handbook & Resource Guide
Cardiovascular Disease Handbook & Resource Guide
Dementia Handbook & Resource Guide
Depression Handbook & Resource Guide
Diabetes Handbook & Resource Guide
Nutrition, Obesity & Eating Disorders Handbook & Resource Guide

Consumer Health
Complete Mental Health Resource Guide
Complete Resource Guide for Pediatric Disorders
Complete Resource Guide for People with Chronic Illness
Complete Resource Guide for People with Disabilities
Older Americans Information Resource
Parenting: Styles & Strategies
Teens: Growing Up, Skills & Strategies

General Reference
American Environmental Leaders
Constitutional Amendments
Encyclopedia of African-American Writing
Encyclopedia of Invasions & Conquests
Encyclopedia of Prisoners of War & Internment
Encyclopedia of the Continental Congresses
Encyclopedia of the United States Cabinet
Encyclopedia of War Journalism
The Environmental Debate
Financial Literacy Starter Kit
From Suffrage to the Senate
The Gun Debate: Gun Rights & Gun Control in the U.S.
Historical Warrior Peoples & Modern Fighting Groups
Human Rights and the United States
Political Corruption in America
Privacy Rights in the Digital Age
The Religious Right and American Politics
Speakers of the House of Representatives, 1789-2021
US Land & Natural Resources Policy
The Value of a Dollar 1600-1865 Colonial to Civil War
The Value of a Dollar 1860-2019

Business Information
Business Information Resources
Complete Broadcasting Industry Guide: TV, Radio, Cable & Streaming
Directory of Mail Order Catalogs
Environmental Resource Handbook
Food & Beverage Market Place
The Grey House Guide to Homeland Security Resources
The Grey House Performing Arts Industry Guide
Guide to Healthcare Group Purchasing Organizations
Guide to U.S. HMOs and PPOs
Guide to Venture Capital & Private Equity Firms
Hudson's Washington News Media Contacts Guide
New York State Directory
Sports Market Place

Grey House Publishing | Salem Press | H.W. Wilson | 4919 Route 22, PO Box 56, Amenia, NY 12501-0056

Grey House Imprints

Visit www.GreyHouse.com for Product Information, Table of Contents, and Sample Pages.

Grey House Titles, continued

Education
Complete Learning Disabilities Resource Guide
Digital Literacy: Skills & Strategies
Educators Resource Guide
The Comparative Guide to Elem. & Secondary Schools
Special Education: Policy & Curriculum Development

Statistics & Demographics
America's Top-Rated Cities
America's Top-Rated Smaller Cities
The Comparative Guide to American Suburbs
Profiles of America
Profiles of California
Profiles of Florida
Profiles of Illinois
Profiles of Indiana
Profiles of Massachusetts
Profiles of Michigan
Profiles of New Jersey
Profiles of New York
Profiles of North Carolina & South Carolina
Profiles of Ohio
Profiles of Pennsylvania
Profiles of Texas
Profiles of Virginia
Profiles of Wisconsin

Canadian Resources
Associations Canada
Canadian Almanac & Directory
Canadian Environmental Resource Guide
Canadian Parliamentary Guide
Canadian Venture Capital & Private Equity Firms
Canadian Who's Who
Cannabis Canada
Careers & Employment Canada
Financial Post: Directory of Directors
Financial Services Canada
FP Bonds: Corporate
FP Bonds: Government
FP Equities: Preferreds & Derivatives
FP Survey: Industrials
FP Survey: Mines & Energy
FP Survey: Predecessor & Defunct
Health Guide Canada
Libraries Canada

Weiss Financial Ratings
Financial Literacy Basics
Financial Literacy: How to Become an Investor
Financial Literacy: Planning for the Future
Weiss Ratings Consumer Guides
Weiss Ratings Guide to Banks
Weiss Ratings Guide to Credit Unions
Weiss Ratings Guide to Health Insurers
Weiss Ratings Guide to Life & Annuity Insurers
Weiss Ratings Guide to Property & Casualty Insurers
Weiss Ratings Investment Research Guide to Bond & Money Market
  Mutual Funds
Weiss Ratings Investment Research Guide to Exchange-Traded Funds
Weiss Ratings Investment Research Guide to Stock Mutual Funds
Weiss Ratings Investment Research Guide to Stocks

Books in Print Series
American Book Publishing Record® Annual
American Book Publishing Record® Monthly
Books In Print®
Books In Print® Supplement
Books Out Loud™
Bowker's Complete Video Directory™
Children's Books In Print®
El-Hi Textbooks & Serials In Print®
Forthcoming Books®
Law Books & Serials In Print™
Medical & Health Care Books In Print™
Publishers, Distributors & Wholesalers of the US™
Subject Guide to Books In Print®
Subject Guide to Children's Books In Print®

Grey House Publishing | Salem Press | H.W. Wilson | 4919 Route, 22 PO Box 56, Amenia NY 12501-0056

Titles from Salem Press

SALEM PRESS

Visit www.SalemPress.com for Product Information, Table of Contents, and Sample Pages.

LITERATURE

Critical Insights: Authors

Louisa May Alcott
Sherman Alexie
Isabel Allende
Maya Angelou
Isaac Asimov
Margaret Atwood
Jane Austen
James Baldwin
Saul Bellow
Roberto Bolano
Ray Bradbury
The Brontë Sisters
Gwendolyn Brooks
Albert Camus
Raymond Carver
Willa Cather
Geoffrey Chaucer
John Cheever
Joseph Conrad
Charles Dickens
Emily Dickinson
Frederick Douglass
T. S. Eliot
George Eliot
Harlan Ellison
Ralph Waldo Emerson
Louise Erdrich
William Faulkner
F. Scott Fitzgerald
Gustave Flaubert
Horton Foote
Benjamin Franklin
Robert Frost
Neil Gaiman
Gabriel Garcia Marquez
Thomas Hardy
Nathaniel Hawthorne
Robert A. Heinlein
Lillian Hellman
Ernest Hemingway
Langston Hughes
Zora Neale Hurston
Henry James
Thomas Jefferson
James Joyce
Jamaica Kincaid
Stephen King
Martin Luther King, Jr.
Barbara Kingsolver
Abraham Lincoln
C.S. Lewis
Mario Vargas Llosa
Jack London
James McBride
Cormac McCarthy
Herman Melville
Arthur Miller
Toni Morrison
Alice Munro
Tim O'Brien
Flannery O'Connor
Eugene O'Neill
George Orwell
Sylvia Plath
Edgar Allan Poe
Philip Roth
Salman Rushdie
J.D. Salinger
Mary Shelley
John Steinbeck
Amy Tan
Leo Tolstoy
Mark Twain
John Updike
Kurt Vonnegut
Alice Walker
David Foster Wallace
Edith Wharton
Walt Whitman
Oscar Wilde
Tennessee Williams
Virginia Woolf
Richard Wright
Malcolm X

Critical Insights: Works

Absalom, Absalom!
Adventures of Huckleberry Finn
The Adventures of Tom Sawyer
Aeneid
All Quiet on the Western Front
All the Pretty Horses
Animal Farm
Anna Karenina
The Awakening
The Bell Jar
Beloved
Billy Budd, Sailor
The Book Thief
Brave New World
The Canterbury Tales
Catch-22
The Catcher in the Rye
The Color Purple
The Crucible
Death of a Salesman
The Diary of a Young Girl
Dracula
Fahrenheit 451
The Grapes of Wrath
Great Expectations
The Great Gatsby
Hamlet
The Handmaid's Tale
Harry Potter Series
Heart of Darkness
The Hobbit
The House on Mango Street
How the Garcia Girls Lost Their Accents
The Hunger Games Trilogy
I Know Why the Caged Bird Sings
In Cold Blood
The Inferno
Invisible Man
Jane Eyre
The Joy Luck Club
Julius Caesar
King Lear
The Kite Runner
Life of Pi
Little Women
Lolita
Lord of the Flies
The Lord of the Rings
Macbeth
The Merchant of Venice
The Metamorphosis
Midnight's Children
A Midsummer Night's Dream
Moby-Dick
Mrs. Dalloway
Nineteen Eighty-Four
The Odyssey
Of Mice and Men
The Old Man and the Sea
On the Road
One Flew Over the Cuckoo's Nest
One Hundred Years of Solitude
Othello
The Outsiders
Paradise Lost
The Pearl
The Plague
The Poetry of Baudelaire
The Poetry of Edgar Allan Poe
A Portrait of the Artist as a Young Man
Pride and Prejudice
A Raisin in the Sun
The Red Badge of Courage
Romeo and Juliet
The Scarlet Letter
Sense and Sensibility
Short Fiction of Flannery O'Connor
Slaughterhouse-Five
The Sound and the Fury
A Streetcar Named Desire
The Sun Also Rises
A Tale of Two Cities
The Tales of Edgar Allan Poe
Their Eyes Were Watching God
Things Fall Apart
To Kill a Mockingbird
War and Peace
The Woman Warrior

Critical Insights: Themes

The American Comic Book
American Creative Non-Fiction
The American Dream
American Multicultural Identity
American Road Literature
American Short Story
American Sports Fiction
The American Thriller
American Writers in Exile
Censored & Banned Literature
Civil Rights Literature, Past & Present
Coming of Age
Conspiracies
Contemporary Canadian Fiction
Contemporary Immigrant Short Fiction
Contemporary Latin American Fiction
Contemporary Speculative Fiction

Grey House Publishing | Salem Press | H.W. Wilson | 4919 Route, 22 PO Box 56, Amenia NY 12501-0056

Titles from Salem Press

Visit www.SalemPress.com for Product Information, Table of Contents, and Sample Pages.

Crime and Detective Fiction
Crisis of Faith
Cultural Encounters
Dystopia
Family
The Fantastic
Feminism Flash Fiction
Gender, Sex and Sexuality
Good & Evil
The Graphic Novel
Greed
Harlem Renaissance
The Hero's Quest
Historical Fiction
Holocaust Literature
The Immigrant Experience
Inequality
LGBTQ Literature
Literature in Times of Crisis
Literature of Protest
Love
Magical Realism
Midwestern Literature
Modern Japanese Literature
Nature & the Environment
Paranoia, Fear & Alienation
Patriotism
Political Fiction
Postcolonial Literature
Power & Corruption
Pulp Fiction of the '20s and '30s
Rebellion
Russia's Golden Age
Satire
The Slave Narrative
Social Justice and American Literature
Southern Gothic Literature
Southwestern Literature
Survival
Technology & Humanity
Truth & Lies
Violence in Literature
Virginia Woolf & 20th Century Women Writers
War

Critical Insights: Film
Bonnie & Clyde
Casablanca
Alfred Hitchcock
Stanley Kubrick

Critical Approaches to Literature
Critical Approaches to Literature: Feminist
Critical Approaches to Literature: Moral
Critical Approaches to Literature: Multicultural
Critical Approaches to Literature: Psychological

Literary Classics
Recommended Reading: 600 Classics Reviewed

Novels into Film
Novels into Film: Adaptations & Interpretation
Novels into Film: Adaptations & Interpretation, Volume 2

Critical Surveys of Literature
Critical Survey of American Literature
Critical Survey of Drama
Critical Survey of Long Fiction
Critical Survey of Mystery and Detective Fiction
Critical Survey of Poetry
Critical Survey of Poetry: Contemporary Poets
Critical Survey of Science Fiction & Fantasy Literature
Critical Survey of Shakespeare's Plays
Critical Survey of Shakespeare's Sonnets
Critical Survey of Short Fiction
Critical Survey of World Literature
Critical Survey of Young Adult Literature

Critical Surveys of Graphic Novels
Heroes & Superheroes
History, Theme, and Technique
Independents & Underground Classics
Manga

Critical Surveys of Mythology & Folklore
Creation Myths
Deadly Battles & Warring Enemies
Gods & Goddesses
Heroes and Heroines
Love, Sexuality, and Desire
World Mythology

Cyclopedia of Literary Characters & Places
Cyclopedia of Literary Characters
Cyclopedia of Literary Places

Introduction to Literary Context
American Poetry of the 20th Century
American Post-Modernist Novels
American Short Fiction
English Literature
Plays
World Literature

Magill's Literary Annual
Magill's Literary Annual, 2023
Magill's Literary Annual, 2022
Magill's Literary Annual, 2021
Magill's Literary Annual (Backlist Issues 2020-1977)

Masterplots
Masterplots, Fourth Edition
Masterplots, 2010-2018 Supplement

Notable Writers
Notable African American Writers
Notable American Women Writers
Notable Mystery & Detective Fiction Writers
Notable Writers of the American West & the Native American Experience
Notable Writers of LGBTQ+ Literature

Grey House Publishing | Salem Press | H.W. Wilson | 4919 Route, 22 PO Box 56, Amenia NY 12501-0056

Titles from Salem Press

Visit www.SalemPress.com for Product Information, Table of Contents, and Sample Pages.

HISTORY
The Decades
The 1910s in America
The Twenties in America
The Thirties in America
The Forties in America
The Fifties in America
The Sixties in America
The Seventies in America
The Eighties in America
The Nineties in America
The 2000s in America
The 2010s in America

Defining Documents in American History
Defining Documents: The 1900s
Defining Documents: The 1910s
Defining Documents: The 1920s
Defining Documents: The 1930s
Defining Documents: The 1950s
Defining Documents: The 1960s
Defining Documents: The 1970s
Defining Documents: The 1980s
Defining Documents: American Citizenship
Defining Documents: The American Economy
Defining Documents: The American Revolution
Defining Documents: The American West
Defining Documents: Business Ethics
Defining Documents: Capital Punishment
Defining Documents: Civil Rights
Defining Documents: Civil War
Defining Documents: The Constitution
Defining Documents: The Cold War
Defining Documents: Dissent & Protest
Defining Documents: Domestic Terrorism & Extremism
Defining Documents: Drug Policy
Defining Documents: The Emergence of Modern America
Defining Documents: Environment & Conservation
Defining Documents: Espionage & Intrigue
Defining Documents: Exploration and Colonial America
Defining Documents: The First Amendment
Defining Documents: The Free Press
Defining Documents: The Great Depression
Defining Documents: The Great Migration
Defining Documents: The Gun Debate
Defining Documents: Immigration & Immigrant Communities
Defining Documents: The Legacy of 9/11
Defining Documents: LGBTQ+
Defining Documents: Manifest Destiny and the New Nation
Defining Documents: Native Americans
Defining Documents: Political Campaigns, Candidates & Discourse
Defining Documents: Postwar 1940s
Defining Documents: Prison Reform
Defining Documents: Secrets, Leaks & Scandals
Defining Documents: Slavery
Defining Documents: Supreme Court Decisions
Defining Documents: Reconstruction Era
Defining Documents: The Vietnam War
Defining Documents: U.S. Involvement in the Middle East
Defining Documents: Workers' Rights
Defining Documents: World War I
Defining Documents: World War II

Defining Documents in World History
Defining Documents: The 17th Century
Defining Documents: The 18th Century
Defining Documents: The 19th Century
Defining Documents: The 20th Century (1900-1950)
Defining Documents: The Ancient World
Defining Documents: Asia
Defining Documents: Genocide & the Holocaust
Defining Documents: Human Rights
Defining Documents: The Middle Ages
Defining Documents: The Middle East
Defining Documents: Nationalism & Populism
Defining Documents: The Nuclear Age
Defining Documents: Pandemics, Plagues & Public Health
Defining Documents: Renaissance & Early Modern Era
Defining Documents: Revolutions
Defining Documents: Women's Rights

Great Events from History
Great Events from History: American History, Exploration to the Colonial Era, 1492-1775
Great Events from History: The Ancient World
Great Events from History: The Middle Ages
Great Events from History: The Renaissance & Early Modern Era
Great Events from History: The 17th Century
Great Events from History: The 18th Century
Great Events from History: The 19th Century
Great Events from History: The 20th Century, 1901-1940
Great Events from History: The 20th Century, 1941-1970
Great Events from History: The 20th Century, 1971-2000
Great Events from History: Modern Scandals
Great Events from History: African American History
Great Events from History: The 21st Century, 2000-2016
Great Events from History: LGBTQ Events
Great Events from History: Human Rights
Great Events from History: Women's History

Great Lives from History
Great Athletes
Great Athletes of the Twenty-First Century
Great Lives from History: The 17th Century
Great Lives from History: The 18th Century
Great Lives from History: The 19th Century
Great Lives from History: The 20th Century
Great Lives from History: The 21st Century, 2000-2017
Great Lives from History: African Americans
Great Lives from History: The Ancient World
Great Lives from History: American Heroes
Great Lives from History: American Women
Great Lives from History: Asian and Pacific Islander Americans
Great Lives from History: Autocrats & Dictators
Great Lives from History: The Incredibly Wealthy
Great Lives from History: Inventors & Inventions
Great Lives from History: Jewish Americans
Great Lives from History: Latinos
Great Lives from History: The Middle Ages
Great Lives from History: The Renaissance & Early Modern Era
Great Lives from History: Scientists and Science

Grey House Publishing | Salem Press | H.W. Wilson | 4919 Route, 22 PO Box 56, Amenia NY 12501-0056

Titles from Salem Press

Visit www.SalemPress.com for Product Information, Table of Contents, and Sample Pages.

History & Government
American First Ladies
American Presidents
The 50 States
The Ancient World: Extraordinary People in Extraordinary Societies
The Bill of Rights
The Criminal Justice System
The U.S. Supreme Court

Innovators
Computer Technology Innovators
Fashion Innovators
Human Rights Innovators
Internet Innovators
Music Innovators
Musicians and Composers of the 20th Century
World Political Innovators

SOCIAL SCIENCES
Civil Rights Movements: Past & Present
Countries, Peoples and Cultures
Countries: Their Wars & Conflicts: A World Survey
Education Today: Issues, Policies & Practices
Encyclopedia of American Immigration
Ethics: Questions & Morality of Human Actions
Issues in U.S. Immigration
Principles of Sociology: Group Relationships & Behavior
Principles of Sociology: Personal Relationships & Behavior
Principles of Sociology: Societal Issues & Behavior
Racial & Ethnic Relations in America
Weapons, Warfare & Military Technology
World Geography

HEALTH
Addictions, Substance Abuse & Alcoholism
Adolescent Health & Wellness
Aging
Cancer
Community & Family Health Issues
Integrative, Alternative & Complementary Medicine
Genetics and Inherited Conditions
Infectious Diseases and Conditions
Magill's Medical Guide
Nutrition
Parenting: Styles & Strategies
Psychology & Behavioral Health
Teens: Growing Up, Skills & Strategies
Women's Health

Principles of Health
Principles of Health: Allergies & Immune Disorders
Principles of Health: Anxiety & Stress
Principles of Health: Depression
Principles of Health: Diabetes
Principles of Health: Nursing
Principles of Health: Obesity
Principles of Health: Occupational Therapy & Physical Therapy
Principles of Health: Pain Management
Principles of Health: Prescription Drug Abuse

SCIENCE
Ancient Creatures
Applied Science
Applied Science: Engineering & Mathematics
Applied Science: Science & Medicine
Applied Science: Technology
Biomes and Ecosystems
Digital Literacy: Skills & Strategies
Earth Science: Earth Materials and Resources
Earth Science: Earth's Surface and History
Earth Science: Earth's Weather, Water and Atmosphere
Earth Science: Physics and Chemistry of the Earth
Encyclopedia of Climate Change
Encyclopedia of Energy
Encyclopedia of Environmental Issues
Encyclopedia of Global Resources
Encyclopedia of Mathematics and Society
Forensic Science
Notable Natural Disasters
The Solar System
USA in Space

Principles of Science
Principles of Aeronautics
Principles of Anatomy
Principles of Astronomy
Principles of Behavioral Science
Principles of Biology
Principles of Biotechnology
Principles of Botany
Principles of Chemistry
Principles of Climatology
Principles of Computer-aided Design
Principles of Computer Science
Principles of Digital Arts & Multimedia
Principles of Ecology
Principles of Energy
Principles of Fire Science
Principles of Forestry & Conservation
Principles of Geology
Principles of Information Technology
Principles of Marine Science
Principles of Mathematics
Principles of Mechanics
Principles of Microbiology
Principles of Modern Agriculture
Principles of Pharmacology
Principles of Physical Science
Principles of Physics
Principles of Programming & Coding
Principles of Robotics & Artificial Intelligence
Principles of Scientific Research
Principles of Sports Medicine & Exercise Science
Principles of Sustainability
Principles of Zoology

Grey House Publishing | Salem Press | H.W. Wilson | 4919 Route, 22 PO Box 56, Amenia NY 12501-0056

Titles from Salem Press

Visit www.SalemPress.com for Product Information, Table of Contents, and Sample Pages.

CAREERS

Careers: Paths to Entrepreneurship
Careers in Archaeology & Museum Services
Careers in Artificial Intelligence
Careers in the Arts: Fine, Performing & Visual
Careers in the Automotive Industry
Careers in Biology
Careers in Biotechnology
Careers in Building Construction
Careers in Business
Careers in Chemistry
Careers in Communications & Media
Careers in Cybersecurity
Careers in Education & Training
Careers in Engineering
Careers in Environment & Conservation
Careers in Financial Services
Careers in Fish & Wildlife
Careers in Forensic Science
Careers in Gaming
Careers in Green Energy
Careers in Healthcare
Careers in Hospitality & Tourism
Careers in Human Services
Careers in Information Technology
Careers in Law, Criminal Justice & Emergency Services
Careers in the Music Industry
Careers in Manufacturing & Production
Careers in Nursing
Careers in Physics
Careers in Protective Services
Careers in Psychology & Behavioral Health
Careers in Public Administration
Careers in Sales, Insurance & Real Estate
Careers in Science & Engineering
Careers in Social Media
Careers in Sports & Fitness
Careers in Sports Medicine & Training
Careers in Technical Services & Equipment Repair
Careers in Transportation
Careers in Writing & Editing
Careers Outdoors
Careers Overseas
Careers Working with Infants & Children
Careers Working with Animals

BUSINESS

Principles of Business: Accounting
Principles of Business: Economics
Principles of Business: Entrepreneurship
Principles of Business: Finance
Principles of Business: Globalization
Principles of Business: Leadership
Principles of Business: Management
Principles of Business: Marketing

Grey House Publishing | Salem Press | H.W. Wilson | 4919 Route, 22 PO Box 56, Amenia NY 12501-0056

Titles from H.W. Wilson

Visit www.HWWilsonInPrint.com for Product Information, Table of Contents, and Sample Pages.

The Reference Shelf
Affordable Housing
Aging in America
Alternative Facts, Post-Truth and the Information War
The American Dream
Artificial Intelligence
The Business of Food
Campaign Trends & Election Law
College Sports
Democracy Evolving
The Digital Age
Embracing New Paradigms in Education
Food Insecurity & Hunger in the United States
Future of U.S. Economic Relations: Mexico, Cuba, & Venezuela
Gene Editing & Genetic Engineering
Global Climate Change
Guns in America
Hacktivism
Hate Crimes
Immigration
Income Inequality
Internet Abuses & Privacy Rights
Internet Law
LGBTQ in the 21st Century
Marijuana Reform
Mental Health Awareness
Money in Politics
National Debate Topic 2014/2015: The Ocean
National Debate Topic 2015/2016: Surveillance
National Debate Topic 2016/2017: US/China Relations
National Debate Topic 2017/2018: Education Reform
National Debate Topic 2018/2019: Immigration
National Debate Topic 2019/2021: Arms Sales
National Debate Topic 2020/2021: Criminal Justice Reform
National Debate Topic 2021/2022: Water Resources
National Debate Topic 2022/2023: Emerging Technologies & International Security
National Debate Topic 2023/2024: Economic Inequality
New Frontiers in Space
Policing in 2020
Pollution
Prescription Drug Abuse
Propaganda and Misinformation
Racial Tension in a Postracial Age
Reality Television
Renewable Energy
Representative American Speeches, Annual Editions
Rethinking Work
Revisiting Gender
The South China Sea Conflict
Sports in America
The Supreme Court
The Transformation of American Cities
The Two Koreas
UFOs
Vaccinations
Voting Rights
Whistleblowers

Core Collections
Children's Core Collection
Fiction Core Collection
Graphic Novels Core Collection
Middle & Junior High School Core
Public Library Core Collection: Nonfiction
Senior High Core Collection
Young Adult Fiction Core Collection

Current Biography
Current Biography Cumulative Index 1946-2021
Current Biography Monthly Magazine
Current Biography Yearbook

Readers' Guide to Periodical Literature
Abridged Readers' Guide to Periodical Literature
Readers' Guide to Periodical Literature

Indexes
Index to Legal Periodicals & Books
Short Story Index
Book Review Digest

Sears List
Sears List of Subject Headings
Sears List of Subject Headings, Online Database
Sears: Lista de Encabezamientos de Materia

History
American Game Changers: Invention, Innovation & Transformation
American Reformers
Speeches of the American Presidents

Facts About Series
Facts About the 20th Century
Facts About American Immigration
Facts About China
Facts About the Presidents
Facts About the World's Languages

Nobel Prize Winners
Nobel Prize Winners: 1901-1986
Nobel Prize Winners: 1987-1991
Nobel Prize Winners: 1992-1996
Nobel Prize Winners: 1997-2001
Nobel Prize Winners: 2002-2018

Famous First Facts
Famous First Facts
Famous First Facts About American Politics
Famous First Facts About Sports
Famous First Facts About the Environment
Famous First Facts: International Edition

American Book of Days
The American Book of Days
The International Book of Days

Grey House Publishing | Salem Press | H.W. Wilson | 4919 Route, 22 PO Box 56, Amenia NY 12501-0056